Napoleon and the Struggle for Germany

VOLUME II

The first comprehensive history of the decisive Fall Campaign of 1813, which determined control of Central Europe following Napoleon's catastrophic defeat in Russia the previous year. Using German, French, British, Russian, Austrian, and Swedish sources, Michael V. Leggiere provides a panoramic history that covers the full sweep of the struggle in Germany. He shows how Prussia, the weakest of the great powers, led the struggle against Napoleon and his empire. By reconstructing the principal campaigns and operations in Germany, the book reveals how the defeat of Napoleon in Germany was made possible by Prussian victories. In particular, it features detailed analysis of the strategy, military operations, and battles in Germany that culminated with the epic four-day Battle of Nations at Leipzig and Napoleon's retreat to France. This study not only highlights the breakdown of Napoleon's strategy in 1813, but also constitutes a fascinating study in coalition warfare, international relations, and civil–military relations.

Michael V. Leggiere is Professor of History and Deputy Director of the Military History Center at the University of North Texas.

CAMBRIDGE MILITARY HISTORIES

Edited by

HEW STRACHAN   Chichele Professor of the History of War, University of
Oxford and Fellow of All Souls College, Oxford

GEOFFREY WAWRO   Professor of Military History and Director of the
Military History Center, University of North Texas

The aim of this series is to publish outstanding works of research on warfare
throughout the ages and throughout the world. Books in the series take a
broad approach to military history, examining war in all its military,
strategic, political, and economic aspects. The series complements Studies
in the Social and Cultural History of Modern Warfare by focusing on the
"hard" military history of armies, tactics, strategy, and warfare. Books in the
series consist mainly of single-author works – academically rigorous and
groundbreaking – which are accessible to both academics and the interested
general reader.

A full list of titles in the series can be found at: www.cambridge.org/
militaryhistories

Napoleon and the Struggle for Germany: The Franco-Prussian War of 1813

Volume II

The Defeat of Napoleon

MICHAEL V. LEGGIERE

University of North Texas

CAMBRIDGE
UNIVERSITY PRESS

University Printing House, Cambridge CB2 8BS, United Kingdom

One Liberty Plaza, 20th Floor, New York, NY 10006, USA

477 Williamstown Road, Port Melbourne, VIC 3207, Australia

4843/24, 2nd Floor, Ansari Road, Daryaganj, Delhi - 110002, India

79 Anson Road, #06-04/06, Singapore 079906

Cambridge University Press is part of the University of Cambridge.

It furthers the University's mission by disseminating knowledge in the pursuit of education, learning and research at the highest international levels of excellence.

www.cambridge.org
Information on this title: www.cambridge.org/9781107080546

© Michael V. Leggiere 2015

First published 2015

A catalogue record for this publication is available from the British Library

Library of Congress Cataloging in Publication data
Leggiere, Michael V., 1969–
Napoleon and the struggle for Germany : The Franco-Prussian War of 1813 ;
The War of Liberation, Spring 1813 / Michael V. Leggiere, University of North Texas.
page cm. – (Cambridge military histories)
ISBN 978-1-107-08054-6 (Hardback) – ISBN 978-1-107-43975-7 (Paperback)
1. Napoleonic Wars, 1800-1815–Campaigns–Germany.
2. Wars of Liberation, 1813-1814–Campaigns–Germany. 3. Napoleon I, Emperor of the French, 1769-1821–Military leadership. 4. France. Armée. Grande Armée–History. 5. France–History, Military–1789-1815. I. Title.
DC236.L443 2015
940.2'740943–dc23 2014022386

ISBN 978-1-107-08054-6 Hardback
ISBN 978-1-107-43975-7 Paperback

For my little man,
Nicholas Thomas Leggiere

Contents

Contents

Figures

All illustrations reproduced courtesy of Anne S. K. Brown
Military Collection, Brown University Library

Maps

Preface

This seven-year project has been greatly assisted by many dear friends and colleagues who gave limitless support, shared their research, and focused early drafts. Alexander Mikaberidze is a friend like no other: for years he has not merely graciously provided me with Russian sources, but he also translates them; I am deeply indebted to Alex. His help in canvassing Russia's archival collection as well as his insight have greatly improved this work. Other dear friends such as Rick Schneid, Huw Davies, Jack Gill, Dennis Showalter, Jeremy Black, Chuck White, and Peter Hofschröer have provided endless support, inspiration, and assistance. I must also convey my deepest appreciation to Peter Harrington of the Anne S. K. Brown Military Collection at Brown University for providing all the artwork that accompanies the text on the shortest notice. At Cambridge University Press, I wish to thank Hew Strachan for his support, Michael Watson for his patience and understanding, and especially for granting me the opportunity to present the 1813 campaign in two volumes, Rosalyn Scott and Rachel Cox for seeing the manuscript through production, and Karen Anderson Howes for being the superb copy-editor for both volumes on 1813. At the University of North Texas, I am indebted to the Department of History, the Military History Center, and the College of Arts and Sciences for their generous financial support. Behind all three is my chairman, colleague, and friend, Rick McCaslin, who has been a steady source of support and encouragement. I am fortunate to work with two of the foremost military historians in the world: Geoff Wawro and Rob Citino. Both set the standard extremely high but their steadfast advice and encouragement are boundless. I especially want to thank Geoff for his friendship, confidence, and support. Last but not least, I thank my graduate students for their patience when they found the door to my office closed: Jon Abel, Chad Tomaselli, Jordan Hayworth, Nate Jarrett, Casey Baker, and Eric Smith.

I must thank the Sixth Count Bülow von Dennewitz, Hasso, for providing a constant stream of documents and information. I offer special thanks to
Bertrand Fonck as well as the staff of the Service historique de l'armée de
terre at Vincennes for patiently handling my requests to exceed the daily
limit of cartons. I also express my gratitude to the helpful staff of Berlin's
Geheimes Staatsarchiv Preußischer Kulturbesitz for producing repositoria
from the former German General Staff archive previously thought to have
been lost during the Second World War. I express my sincere gratitude to my
mentor, Donald D. Horward, for seeing the potential in me, releasing it, and
stopping me from making the mistake of attending law school. My wife of
sixteen years and companion of more than twenty, Michele, has always been
my source of strength. Our beautiful children, Jordyn and Nicholas, have
likewise endured countless hours of having to entertain themselves while
I was writing. Finally, I wish to thank my mother, Rosalie, who is always a
source of solid support. Many others have contributed in many ways. To
them: thanks and an apology for any omission. Whatever merits this work
has are due in part to their contributions; whatever faults may lie here are
those of the author.

In the text, I employ native, modern spellings of villages, towns, smaller
cities, and geographic features as much as possible. Larger cities, capitals,
and rivers are Anglicized. I also provide at first mention the modern Polish,
Russian, Lithuanian, and Czech names of population centers and geographic
features in regions that once belonged to Prussia or Austria. Names of
persons are likewise native, except for monarchs, whose names are Anglicized. To avoid confusion, all general officers are referred to simply as
"general." Lastly, I use "imperials" to refer to the French and their allies
after 1804.

Introduction

After losing 500,000 soldiers in Russia between June and December 1812, Napoleon started rebuilding his army in early 1813 to stop the Russians in Germany. At the end of 1812, Tsar Alexander I of Russia made the momentous decision to continue his war with Napoleon and drive the French from Central Europe. The destruction of the Grande Armée of 1812 provided Alexander with an opportunity to build a Russian-dominated coalition to liberate Europe. Russian pressure forced the French to fall back from the Vistula (Wisła) River and then across the Oder (Odra) River to Berlin by mid February 1813. Hoping to stop the pursuing Russians before they could step foot onto German soil, Napoleon looked to his ally, King Frederick William III of Prussia, for assistance. As Eugène de Beauharnais, the viceroy of Italy and commander of imperial forces on the eastern front, surrendered land for time, direct negotiations between the Russians and Prussians commenced.

With two-thirds of Prussia occupied by Napoleon's forces, Frederick William made the bold decision to break the French alliance and join the Russians to form the Sixth Coalition. Negotiations culminated on 28 February 1813 with the signing of the Treaty of Kalisch: the much-anticipated Russo-Prussian military alliance. The Prussians agreed to field an army of 80,000 men to assist a Russian contingent of 150,000; both states pledged not to make a separate peace with Napoleon. The British did their part to bolster the new coalition by promptly dispatching arms and ammunition to the Baltic for use by the Russians and Prussians. Alexander also hoped for an Austrian alliance in early 1813 but Austria's foreign minister, the adroit Klemens von Metternich, feared Russian success would be accompanied by Russian territorial expansion. With Alexander's armies approaching Central Europe, the Austrians declared neutrality.

For Napoleon, 1813 brought a fresh series of challenges. As French forces in the east steadily retreated, his political-military situation likewise deteriorated. Failure in Russia not only resulted in the loss of the Grand Duchy of Warsaw, but also threatened French control of Germany, which Napoleon had organized into the Confederation of the Rhine in 1806. As Napoleon's prestige plummeted, German nationalists called for a *Befreiungskrieg*, a war of liberation, against French hegemony. Prussia's declaration of war only added to the complex set of problems that confronted Napoleon. Austria stood as an armed neutral, endeavoring to mediate between Napoleon and his enemies. Despite the dynastic ties between France and Austria due to the marriage between Napoleon and Marie Louise, the daughter of Kaiser Francis I, the Austrians could not be trusted.

The burden of waging war in Central Europe fell on Tsar Alexander in the early stage of the contest. Russia's frontline army, likewise devastated by the winter campaign in 1812, consisted of 51,745 tired soldiers, 12,283 Cossacks, and 439 guns when it crossed the Prussian frontier. Reinforcements, not expected to reach the front until the beginning of April, amounted to 12,674 men, 2,307 Cossacks, and 48 guns. Russian second-line troops – 56,776 men, 9,989 Cossacks, and 319 guns – besieged French-controlled fortresses on the Oder and the Vistula Rivers. A reserve of 48,100 men had yet to depart from Russia. As for the Russian High Command, it had been divided for some time. While Tsar Alexander fashioned himself as the liberator of Germany, Russian commander in chief General Mikhail Kutuzov opposed carrying the war into Central Europe to emancipate the same countries that had supported Napoleon's bid to conquer Russia. Other Russian commanders expressed concerns over their tenuous lines of communication. This boded well for the French, for crushing the Russian army in battle amid so much disagreement would certainly put the Russians to flight, similar to the 1805 campaign.

Of the 600,000 men and 1,300 guns of the Grande Armée of 1812, only 93,000 men and 250 pieces returned. Of the 93,000, more than half were Austrians and Prussians. Undaunted by such catastrophic and unprecedented losses, Napoleon planned to have 656,000 men mobilized by June of 1813. For leadership, the emperor transferred experienced noncommissioned officers from his armies in Spain to the new units. In a little more than four months, Napoleon's unrivaled organizational skills produced the 140,000-strong Army of the Main. Together with Eugene's Army of the Elbe, imperial forces amounted to almost 200,000 men by the end of April. With the French having lost 180,000 horses in Russia, critical deficiencies remained in the cavalry; this robbed the army not only of its shock tactics, but also of its eyes and ears. Napoleon adequately replaced the losses sustained in Russia, but draft horses remained in short supply. Reflective of the army itself, the French officer corps in 1813 contained strengths and weaknesses. In the senior ranks, the Russian campaign had taken its toll on the aging marshalate. However, one asset remained: the army's field-grade officers, most of whom were battle-hardened veterans. Nevertheless, the Grande Armée of 1813 lacked many of the tactical attributes of previous French armies, which in turn placed strategic and operational limitations on Napoleon.

Several factors hampered Prussian mobilization in January and February 1813. French troops still occupied half of the country and held all of Prussia's significant fortresses. Tedious negotiations with the Russians also slowed the process. Concentration of the field army, scheduled to begin on 12 February, had to be postponed until the formation of the Coalition. After creating the alliance at Kalisch, the mobilization continued at an accelerated pace and culminated with the 17 March 1813 decrees creating a national Landwehr (militia). Aside from a few battalions, the militia would not be ready for field service until August. At the beginning of the war, the Prussian regular army consisted of 127,394 men and 269 guns. Of this figure, only 65,675 men had received sufficient training to be utilized in the field; only half of Prussia's armed forces were trained regulars or reservists.

During initial operations, the Allies liberated Berlin with their northern army of 30,000 Prussians and 18,000 Russians commanded by Russian general Ludwig Adolph zu Wittgenstein, while Prussian general Gebhard Leberecht von Blücher's 26,000 Prussians and 10,500 Russians took the Saxon capital of Dresden with the Coalition's smaller southern army. Behind these two armies followed the Allied commander in chief, Kutuzov, with the Russian main army and reserve. After clearing Berlin, Wittgenstein drove southwest through a detachment of the French Army of the Elbe at Möckern near Magdeburg on 5 April, allowing for his union with Blücher east of the Saale River in the vicinity of Leipzig. Following Kutuzov's death on 28 April 1813, Tsar Alexander named Wittgenstein Allied commander in chief.

The appearance of Allied forces in Saxony in late March prompted Napoleon to concentrate his forces on the left bank of the Saale River throughout April. The emperor began his counteroffensive on 30 April by leading 120,000 men across the Saale to confront the Allied army near Leipzig. Reports of French movements indicated that the emperor would converge on Leipzig in two columns: Eugene's Army of the Elbe marching southeast from Magdeburg and Napoleon's Army of the Main due east from Weißenfels. The Allies resolved to attack.

Approximately 88,000 Russians and Prussians with 552 guns prepared to engage Napoleon's army of 145,000 men and 372 guns. Although Napoleon possessed fewer total guns, he had more heavy batteries than the Allies, which granted the French artillery an advantage in range and effectiveness. Early on 2 May 1813, the Allied army advanced southeast to northwest in the hope of smashing through the imperial armies as they moved east. Wittgenstein opened the battle of Lützen by having the Prussian II Corps attack a supposed French rearguard holding the quadrilateral of villages immediately north of the Allied army: Großgörschen, Kleingörschen, Rahna, and Kaja. This French force turned out to be Napoleon's massive III Corps. Although surprised by the Allies, Napoleon quickly recovered and ordered a double-envelopment. After eight hours of brutal fighting, his enveloping forces reached their positions. With both flanks threatened, Wittgenstein ordered a retreat.

The 2 May 1813 battle of Lützen proved extremely bloody. Prussia's new army shouldered the weight of the engagement and paid dearly in its debut, losing 8,400 men. In addition, Gerhard von Scharnhorst received the wound that took his life on 28 June. Russian losses are not known, but can be estimated at 3,000 casualties. Imperial forces lost some 22,000 combatants and 5 guns. Operationally, the battle of Lützen again demonstrated Napoleon's supremacy. His ability to move units to the battlefield where and when they were needed to deliver maximum combat power remained unrivaled. Indeed, on 2 May, the Sixth Coalition came within hours of being destroyed by a double-envelopment that would have been so crushing it would have ended the war.

Following Lützen, the shortage of cavalry prevented Napoleon from unleashing a deadly pursuit to annihilate the Allies and make his victory decisive. Therefore, he hoped an operation in North Germany would create strategic opportunities that had thus far eluded him in Saxony. On 4 May, Napoleon directed Marshal Michel Ney to the Elbe fortress of Torgau, which, along with Wittenberg, provided the gateway to Berlin and North Germany. Ney's army eventually numbered 84,300 men, while Napoleon commanded 119,000. Napoleon knew that Ney's march to Torgau would signal to the Allies the start of a French offensive against Berlin. He hoped this would prompt the Prussians to separate from the Russians and march north to save their capital. Similar to his First Italian Campaign, he would then execute a *manoeuvre sur position centrale* to destroy the Prussians and Russians in succession.

Meanwhile, Wittgenstein retreated to the Spree River, where he placed the Allied army in a commanding position just east of the river and the town of Bautzen. The imperials followed slowly and cautiously, engaging in almost daily combat with Wittgenstein's rearguard. Instead of effecting a split among the Allies, Napoleon found his adversaries in a fortified position around Bautzen and along the Spree River. Although the emperor intended to engage the Allies at Bautzen and still move against Berlin with a portion of Ney's army, the marshal mistakenly brought his entire army south to join the battle.

Napoleon issued orders to attack the Allied left wing and center at Bautzen on 20 May. While his Guard, IV, VI, XI, and XII Corps fixed the Allies, Ney's III, V, VII, and II Corps would swing southeast to envelop the

Allied right. By nightfall on the 21st, he planned to have 144,000 combatants on the battlefield facing 96,000 Coalition soldiers. To facilitate Ney's operation against the Allied right flank, Napoleon sought to deceive the Allies into thinking he intended to turn their left. Napoleon spent the morning of 20 May 1813 moving his pieces around the board to increase Allied concern over the left wing. Although Wittgenstein did not fall for the ruse, Alexander did. Ignoring Wittgenstein's objections, Alexander transferred his few reserves to the left wing. Having had enough of being ignored, Wittgenstein napped under a tree. Around noon, French artillery blasted the Allied positions while IV, VI, XI, and XII Corps advanced east across the Spree. Combat lasted until 8:30 that night. Altogether the Allies lost some 1,400 Russians and 500 Prussians; French losses are not known. The engagement on the 20th won Napoleon the keys to Wittgenstein's forward position: the city of Bautzen and the crossings over the Spree north and south of the town. By pinning the Allies and deceiving them over the point of his attack, the emperor attained basic objectives through the simplest of means.

Napoleon resumed the offensive by attacking the Allied left at dawn on 21 May. Around 11:00 A.M., he directed his VI Corps to move against the Allied center. Around 2:00 P.M., two divisions of IV Corps crossed the river and prepared to assault the Allied right on the Kreckwitz heights from the west. One hour later, Ney mistakenly turned southwest to storm the Kreckwitz heights from the east instead of proceeding southeast to sever Wittgenstein's only line of retreat. As imperial forces closed on the right of the Allied position from the west, north, and east, Tsar Alexander reluctantly agreed to break off the battle.

Allied losses on the second day of Bautzen are estimated to be 10,850 men. By comparison, French losses reached 22,500 men including 3,700 missing. Napoleon could not interpret the battle of Bautzen as anything but a disappointment. Fortunately for the Allies, the compulsive Ney could not turn away from the Kreckwitz heights. Had Ney followed orders, the war quite conceivably could have ended with both Alexander and Frederick William being taken prisoner. Ney's blunder could not have been more fortuitous for the Allies and therefore disappointing for Napoleon.

Retreating to Silesia in the aftermath of Bautzen, the Coalition experienced a crisis just when it appeared that Austria would join the alliance against Napoleon. Prior to Bautzen, an Austrian envoy, the anti-French former foreign minister Johann Philipp von Stadion, met with Prussian chancellor Karl von Hardenberg and the de facto Russian foreign minister, Karl Robert Nesselrode, to discuss the Coalition's peace terms. More importantly for the Allies, he announced that Kaiser Francis would decide for either war or neutrality by 1 June. Consequently, Stadion came prepared to engage the Allies in serious military planning in the event his master chose war against Napoleon. He shared a memo drafted in Vienna on 10 May by

General Jan Josef Václav Radetzky von Radetz, the chief of staff of the Austrian army assembling in Bohemia. The memo presupposed that Austria would join the Sixth Coalition and wage war against the French Empire. Regardless of the whereabouts of the main Allied army, Radetzky declared that Napoleon would fall on the Austrian army with his main force as soon as Francis declared war on him.[1]

Acknowledging Radetzky's views, the Russians and Prussians drafted the Wurschen Plan for future combined operations. The blueprint strongly emphasized unprecedented communication, cooperation, and understanding between the Austrian and Russo-Prussian armies. Both would take a position facing one of Napoleon's flanks. Whichever Allied army he did not target would immediately take the offensive against him. When drafting his memo, Radetzky had envisioned the theater of war being somewhere between the Saale and the Elbe Rivers. However, by the time Stadion delivered the memo, the Allies had already abandoned the Elbe and had prepared to accept a second battle with Napoleon on the Spree. If the Russo-Prussian army were forced to retreat across the Oder, the Wurschen Plan called for it to remain close to the Austrians by hugging the Bohemian frontier and leaning on the Riesengebirge (Karkonosze), part of the Sudetes Mountain system. If pressed by Napoleon, the Allied army could maintain contact with Austria by moving into one of the entrenched positions in Silesia such as Schweidnitz (Świdnica). Thus, the Wurschen Plan signaled the Coalition's recognition that unreserved, close collaboration with Austria would be the primary objective of future operations.[2]

After being named Allied commander in chief on 26 May 1813, Russian general Michael Andreas Barclay de Tolly rejected the Wurschen Plan out of concern over the condition of the Russian army. Instead of placing the Allied army in a position to immediately cooperate with the Austrians, Barclay advocated a retreat across the Oder and into Poland for a six-week hiatus for rest and reorganization. The Prussians could either follow or face Napoleon on their own. However, Tsar Alexander imposed his will on Barclay, ordering the retreat to turn southeast toward Schweidnitz in south-central Silesia. Not only did Alexander spare Frederick William from having to make a very difficult decision, but the Russian monarch also maintained the Wurschen Plan's implied commitment to cooperate with Austria. Thanks to Alexander, the signing of the armistice on 4 June found the Russo-Prussian army still west of the Oder, a crucial factor for a partnership with the Austrians. Alexander's devotion to the Wurschen Plan along with Napoleon's inability to drive the Allies across the Oder opened the door for unprecedented collaboration with the Austrians.

As for Napoleon, despite defeating the Allies at Lützen and Bautzen, decisive victory eluded him mainly because he lacked cavalry to exploit his success. After pursuing the Allied army into Silesia, Napoleon failed to maneuver it into a third battle. By late May 1813, marauding and straggling in the Grande Armée had increased to epic proportions. With 90,000 men on the sick list, the emperor realized he had pushed his army beyond exhaustion. Although not the ultimate factor in Napoleon's decision to accept an Austrian proposal for an armistice, these ugly indicators as well as the realization that he simply could not substitute infantry for cavalry and expect to win a decisive victory led him to open negotiations with the Prussians and Russians. An Austrian proposal to prolong a temporary armistice to 20 July was signed at Pläswitz in Silesia on 4 June and eventually extended to 17 August.

The Armistice of Pläswitz saw the failure of Austria's attempts to mediate a peace between Napoleon and the Allies. After Austria declared in favor of the Coalition, the Allies finalized their plans to field three multinational armies. The 42-year-old Austrian general Karl Philipp zu Schwarzenberg received command of all Allied forces, including the main army – the Army of Bohemia – which consisted of 220,000 Austrians, Prussians, and Russians. Blücher commanded the Army of Silesia – 105,000 Russians and Prussians – while the former French marshal, Jean-Baptiste Bernadotte, took command of the Army of North Germany – 140,000 Prussians, Russians, Swedes, and North Germans. A fourth Allied army, General Levin August von Bennigsen's Army of Poland, was expected to reach Silesia in September. The Allies created these multinational armies both to prevent Napoleon from defeating them piecemeal, and to limit politically motivated acts of national self-interest.

For operations, the Russians and Prussians accepted the Austrian-authored Reichenbach Plan as the Coalition's operational doctrine. According to it, the three Allied armies would form a wide arc around French forces in Saxony and Silesia and engage only detached enemy corps: pitched battles with Napoleon would be avoided. Should the emperor concentrate against any one army, it would retreat, while the other two attacked his flanks and communications. As Napoleon could personally command only one army at a time and thus could directly challenge only one Allied army at a time, the other two Allied armies would attack his flanks and lines of communication, while the threatened army refused battle but induced the emperor to pursue, thus extending and exposing his line of operation. The plan aimed to split and exhaust French forces. Although Napoleon had the advantage of interior lines, he would be forced to fight against armies advancing simultaneously against his center, flanks, and communications.

To cover his base of operations at Dresden, maintain his mastery of the Elbe River, and capitalize on the enemy's mistakes, Napoleon assembled his forces in three groups. In the center, the Grande Armée (I, IV, and V Cavalry Corps, Guard, and I, II, VI, and XIV Corps) stood between Bautzen and

Görlitz. On his left in Silesia, he posted III, V, and XI Corps and II Cavalry Corps under Ney's command. After the expiration of the armistice, he wanted his center to march west to Silesia and unite with his left. This would enable him to concentrate his left and center – almost 270,000 infantry and 30,000 cavalry – to oppose what he believed to be the Coalition's main army of 200,000 Russians and Prussians in Silesia. Based on the actions of the Allies in May, Napoleon counted on them accepting battle in Silesia, where he planned to decisively defeat them before the Austrians could launch a serious operation against Dresden. Meanwhile, on his right wing, the IV, VII, and XII Corps and III Cavalry Corps of Marshal Nicolas Oudinot's Army of Berlin supported by Marshal Nicolas Davout's XIII Corps coming from Hamburg would conduct an offensive against the Prussian capital. After defeating the Coalition's Army of North Germany, Napoleon planned for the Army of Berlin to liberate the besieged imperial garrisons along the Oder River and advance to the Vistula, wheeling behind the Allied army in Silesia, which itself would be retreating eastward after being defeated by the emperor. Should Bernadotte somehow check the Army of Berlin, Napoleon could easily shift forces from the Silesian theater to Brandenburg to complete the work.

After learning that the Allies had actually assembled their main army in Bohemia, Napoleon still planned to destroy Blücher's Army of Silesia, thus removing its threat to the rear of both his Grande Armée in Saxony and Oudinot's Army of Berlin. Although he did not know where Schwarzenberg would lead the Army of Bohemia, Napoleon decided to march against Blücher, defeat him, and then rush back to Dresden. As for Blücher, from 15 to 20 August 1813 he chased Ney's forces westward from the banks of the Katzbach River to Bunzlau on the Bober River. Napoleon likewise reached the Bober on the 20th, attacking Blücher on the 21st. Complying with the Reichenbach Plan, Blücher retreated eastward for the next four days. Meanwhile, Schwarzenberg led the Bohemian Army across the Saxon frontier on 22 August en route to Dresden. With Blücher running, Napoleon's attention immediately switched to Saxony. On the night of 22/23 August, he issued orders for the Guard, VI Corps, and I Cavalry Corps to return to Dresden. With the forces that remained in Silesia (III, V, and XI Corps and II Cavalry Corps – 100,000 men, according to Napoleon's calculations), he formed the Army of the Bober commanded by Marshal Étienne Jacques Macdonald.

Always seeking a decisive victory, Napoleon welcomed Schwarzenberg's advance on Dresden as an opportunity rather than a setback. He planned to concentrate 200,000 men at Dresden to confront the Army of Bohemia. Little did Napoleon know that, as he made these plans, Bernadotte's Army of North Germany was holding its ground eleven miles south of Berlin at the battle of Großbeeren on 23 August 1813. Again shouldering the brunt of the combat, the Prussians suffered losses amounting to more than

1,000 killed, wounded, and missing. Imperial casualties numbered more than 3,000 men and 14 guns. Despite the low body count, Oudinot ordered a headlong retreat that did not stop until his army reached the safety of Wittenberg on the Elbe. The Coalition's victory at Großbeeren saved Berlin and provided much-needed confidence for the Prussians.

Back in Silesia, Macdonald eagerly prepared to move against Blücher's suspected position east of the Katzbach River on 26 August. Meanwhile, Blücher, assuming Napoleon had departed for Dresden, likewise ordered his army to resume the offensive. On that day, the Army of the Bober collided with the Army of the Silesia along the banks of the Katzbach River. In a heavy downpour, the Allies repulsed the imperials, losing fewer than 1,000 men. Macdonald's losses on the 26th are not known, but his army suffered acute attrition during the ensuing retreat west to Saxony. By 1 September 1813, the Army of the Bober had lost 30,000 men and 103 guns.

Meanwhile, the Bohemian Army moved across the Saxon frontier on 22 August and stormed the imperial camp at Pirna on the 23rd. As the Silesian Army engaged the Army of the Bober on the 26th, Schwarzenberg assailed Dresden. In the midst of the engagement, Napoleon unexpectedly arrived with the Guard to repel Schwarzenberg's assault. During the night, II and VI Corps came up, increasing Napoleon's combatants to 135,000 men against 215,000 Allied soldiers. Continuing the battle on the 27th, Napoleon enveloped Schwarzenberg's left, crushing two Austrian corps. With the French also steadily working around his right, Schwarzenberg ordered a retreat. The Army of Bohemia withdrew after losing 38,000 killed, wounded, and captured along with 40 guns. Although the imperials sustained far fewer casualties (10,000), decisive victory again eluded Napoleon. Despite his having adequate cavalry, illness forced the emperor to leave the field rather than personally direct the pursuit.

In the aftermath of Dresden, General Dominique Vandamme's I Corps followed by XIV and VI Corps led the pursuit. On the 29th, Vandamme caught one of Schwarzenberg's Russian corps at Kulm, thirty-five miles south of Dresden and just inside the Bohemian frontier. Neither side gained an advantage despite savage fighting. With the battle continuing on the 30th, Schwarzenberg's Prussian II Corps attacked Vandamme's rear as the Russians pushed against his front and an Austrian corps enveloped his left. With XIV and VI Corps too distant to support, Vandamme attempted but failed to drive through the Prussians. Imperial losses on 29 and 30 August amounted to 25,000 killed, wounded, and captured along with 82 guns; Allied casualties numbered 11,000 men.

Following the defeats at Großbeeren, the Katzbach, and Kulm, Napoleon considered either an offensive against Prague or another march on Berlin for his next step. Both projects sacrificed the principle of annihilating the main enemy army, which would have provided the most direct means of achieving total victory. Rather than a decisive battle with one of the three Allied armies, geographic objectives dominated the emperor's planning. Rejecting the Prague offensive, Napoleon returned to the capture of Berlin. A victory over the Army of North Germany and the timid Bernadotte appeared certain. Therefore, the emperor decided to allow the Army of Bohemia to recover after its drubbing at Dresden while he personally commanded the march on Berlin. He planned to lead 30,000 men from Dresden, unite with the Army of Berlin, and resume the operation against the Prussian capital.

Thanks to Blücher, Napoleon never executed the Berlin offensive as planned. Due to events in southeast Saxony, he neither marched north nor provided reinforcements for the Army of Berlin. Blücher's pressure on Macdonald's beleaguered Army of the Bober required Napoleon's personal intervention. Ney, who replaced Oudinot as commander of the Army of Berlin on 3 September, never received word of the emperor's change of plans. Therefore, when he began his operation on the 4th, he ordered the Army of Berlin to march eastward to unite with Napoleon, who, according to Ney's information, would reach Luckau on 6 September. Instead of his emperor, Ney found the Prussian III and IV Corps of the Army of North Germany at Dennewitz on the 6th. Ney's losses amounted to 21,500 dead, wounded, and captured along with 53 guns. Prussian casualties numbered 9,700 killed and wounded. After this victory, the Army of North Germany pursued the wreck of the Army of Berlin to Wittenberg and Torgau on the Elbe.

Unlike the victories he had enjoyed during the Spring Campaign, Napoleon's situation became critical after less than one month of campaigning. The success of the Reichenbach Plan depleted the ranks of the Grande Armée: since the expiration of the armistice, the imperials had lost 150,000 men and 300 guns – an additional 50,000 names filled the sick rolls. While French commanders suffered defeats at Großbeeren, the Katzbach, Kulm, and Dennewitz, the emperor raced back and forth between the Elbe and the Bober Rivers in futile attempts to achieve a decisive victory. Under normal conditions, the constant marches and countermarches would have exhausted his conscripts both mentally and physically. Yet the conditions remained far from normal. Heavy rains had washed out the roads and Cossacks menaced the lines of communication. Although the poor conditions forced Napoleon to grant his men plenty of rest, the slow starvation of the army could not be ignored. Supply shortages and the exhaustion of the Saxon countryside prompted Napoleon to write: "The army is no longer fed; to view it in any other way would be mere self-deception."[3]

The battle of Dennewitz provided a crucial turning point in the Fall Campaign. In its aftermath, both sides changed strategy. Blücher led his Army of Silesia down the Elbe to Wartenburg, where it crossed the river on

3 October and defeated the French IV Corps. Based on an agreement with Blücher, Bernadotte also ordered his Army of North Germany to cross the Elbe and move into the Saxon theater. Blücher's decisions in early October and the efficient work of the Prussian General Staff throughout the campaign made the battle of Leipzig possible. For his part, Napoleon made one final attempt to catch Blücher and Bernadotte south of Wittenberg. On 9 October, Napoleon and 150,000 imperial soldiers stood ready to destroy the two Allied armies in the region of Bad Düben and Dessau. Yet, both Blücher and Bernadotte escaped by retreating west across the Saale River, thus exposing Berlin and their own communications. At this juncture, Napoleon decided to draw the Allies to Leipzig for an epic struggle: the Battle of Nations. Knowing that Schwarzenberg was slowly advancing on this city, the emperor accepted the fact that he would soon be surrounded. After months of chasing an elusive enemy who had smashed his lieutenants, Napoleon welcomed the prospect of a showdown.

After the monumental Allied victory at Leipzig in mid October, the Bohemian and Silesian Armies pursued Napoleon to Mainz but the Army of North Germany split. Two of its corps insured the collapse of the Confederation of the Rhine by marching through the heart of Germany while Bernadotte led the rest of his forces north to contend with Marshal Davout's XIII Corps at Hamburg. Reaching the Rhine the second week of November, the Allies convened a council of war at Frankfurt to plan the invasion of France. Deliberations lasted for the better part of the next six weeks. In the midst of the military planning, the Allies offered Napoleon a conditional peace. Although Napoleon would have remained ruler of a France that included the natural frontiers of the Rhine, Alps, and Pyrenees, he rejected the offer. During a council of war on 7 December 1813, the Allies agreed to invade France across a front that stretched from the North Sea to Switzerland.

Similar to Volume I, *The War of Liberation*, which focuses on Prussia's role in 1813, the current volume, *The Fall Campaign*, describes how Prussia played a pivotal role in the multinational coalition that formed during the armistice and wrested Germany from Napoleon's control by the first week of November. It continues to expand Gordon Craig's assertion that the war against Napoleon was not a political struggle but an ideological "fight against evil, a struggle against the anti-Christ and his minions." More so than the Russians and later the Austrians, the Prussians fought a holy war against Napoleon. Enthusiasm and popular support did vary greatly, yet Prusso-German patriotism permeated the public mind. Although Russians made up two-thirds of the Army of Silesia, it was still viewed by the Coalition as *the* Prussian army by virtue of its all-Prussian leadership at the army level. This work is the first unofficial history of the 1813 Fall Campaign that reconstructs the principal campaigns and operations of the

Army of Silesia to focus on how the Prussians attempted to wage a Franco-Prussian war within the framework of a multinational war effort. Like Napoleon, they believed decisive battles should settle the war. Similar to Paul von Hindenburg's relationship to Eric von Ludendorff during the First World War, Blücher relied on his chief of staff, August Wilhelm von Gneisenau, to provide the brains while he provided dauntless, unwavering leadership. By consistently thwarting Napoleon's plans and carrying the war to the French, the Prussians channeled their impetuosity through the Silesian Army to change the course of history in 1813. By reconstructing Blücher's principal campaigns, this book will reveal the magnitude of Blücher's operations and how they led to the Coalition's complete victory over Napoleon in Germany.

My 2002 book, *Napoleon and Berlin: The Franco-Prussian War in North Germany, 1813*, builds on Gordon Craig's assertion that the Prussian military establishment wanted to wage an almost fanatical holy war against the French for emancipation and freedom.[4] While *Napoleon and Berlin* focuses on the Prussian defense of their capital, the two volumes of *Napoleon and the Struggle for Germany*, which constitute my penultimate work on 1813, continue to develop Craig's thesis by exploring the role played by the Prussians in the main theater of war and particularly their relations with the Russians.[5] Prussia's foremost commanders at the start of the war, Blücher, Scharnhorst, and Gneisenau, labored to fight a different kind of war – a war guided by "mystical nationalism," according to Craig – than their Russian allies, many of whom believed Russia should play only an auxiliary role following the great exertions of 1812. After six years of French occupation, the leaders of the Prussian military establishment labored to restore both national and international honor to their profession, their army, and, most of all, their state. Prussian generals took the initiative to precipitate a rupture with France, and personal feelings translated into political action. Frederick William allowed himself to embrace the nationalistic fervor that it aroused and summon his people to arms. More so than the Russians and Austrians, the Prussians turned their war against Napoleon into a total war between two peoples: a Franco-Prussian War.[6]

The weakest of Napoleon's adversaries, the Prussians managed to field an army of 250,000 men in August 1813. Although dispersed among the three principal Allied armies and besieging French garrisons in Prussia, the Prussians truly fought a war of liberation to drive the French from Germany. Although languishing under Russian leadership during the Spring Campaign of 1813, the Prussians willingly shouldered the weight of the conflict and demanded the opportunity to take the war to Napoleon. This volume explains how Prussian impetuosity not only led to Allied victories in August and September, but also created the conditions that led to the colossal four-day battle at Leipzig in mid October.

The hundred years from 1813 to 1913 witnessed the publication of numerous Prusso-German, French, and Russian official General Staff histories of 1813 as well as a plethora of works written by military officers and contemporaries of the period. Each borrowed from the others freely but the Prusso-German General Staff histories were viewed as authoritative. In some cases, whole sections of the Prusso-German histories were reproduced verbatim in the studies of the war by French and Russian historians. While the Prussian archives at the Geheimes Staatsarchiv in Berlin contain tomes of documents on the 1813–1815 period that did survive the Second World War, the principal papers – mainly the inter-army correspondence – of the Silesian Army 1813–1814 (as well as the Prussian Army of the Lower Rhine that fought in 1815) are not among them. Whether these papers were actually destroyed or carried off by the Russians remains to be seen. Be that as it may, Gneisenau's Nachlaß has been extremely helpful, particularly the huge Paket Nr. 18 titled "Various Papers from the 1813 and 1814 Campaigns," but it too has gaps in the documentary record. Blücher's Nachlaß is one of the greatest disappointments I have encountered in archival research: it consists only of fourteen letters (including five to his wife), all of which have been published, and Blücher's service record. Fortunately, the Prussian General Staff's official history of the Silesian Army, written by Eduard von Höpfner and published in the 1843–1847 editions of the *Militär-Wochenblatt*, contains a treasure trove of the Silesian Army's inter-army correspondence reproduced in full. Unlike the *Geschichte der Befreiungskriege 1813–1815* written by the Great German General Staff during the first decade of the twentieth century, Höpfner's account is much less of a teaching tool and instead presents the documents to the readers, allowing them to form their own judgments.[7] It would have been impossible to reconstruct Blücher's campaigns without the primary documents contained in Höpfner's account.

I have been able to make good use of copies of correspondence between the Silesian Army's leadership and other Allied commanders contained in other archival collections. The British Manuscript Collection contains copies of most of the following correspondence: Blücher to/from Bernadotte; Blücher to/from Schwarzenberg; and Blücher's daily orders or "dispositions" to his corps commanders. The French military archives (SHAT) at Paris contain a pristine copy of all of Bernadotte's orders to his corps commanders, no doubt a "gift" from the former marshal of France. Although many of the *delos* of the Russian state archive's RGVIA (Rossiiskii Gosudarstvennyi Voenno-Istoricheskii Arkhiv) that cover Russia's wars with Napoleon 1805–1815 have been microfilmed, the *delos* concerning the Silesian Army in the Fall Campaign of 1813 have not. I attempted unsuccessfully to work with the Russians for three years to provide me with documents pertaining to the Silesian Army.

Since 1913, few historians have attempted to piece together an operational history of 1813. The damage to the Prusso-German General Staff archives during the Second World War makes the task daunting. Moreover, in their exhaustive studies the historians of first the Prussian and then the German General Staff published much of the official correspondence coming from the headquarters of Blücher and Gneisenau during this period. In addition, thanks to the historiographic war between the German General Staff and Hans Delbrück, this prolific historian likewise published vast quantities of the official correspondence in his massive five-volume biography of Gneisenau. Thus, we have much in terms of primary sources.

Based on Prussian, French, Russian, British, Austrian, Swedish, and private archival documents, this book, written from the Coalition's perspective, describes how Napoleon confronted the armed might of the other great powers united for the first time ever in a war against him. After miraculously assembling a new army of 200,000 men in April 1813 for a campaign in Germany, Napoleon drove the Russo-Prussian army from the banks of the Saale to the banks of the Oder. On reaching the Oder, the Russo-Prussian alliance came perilously close to imploding only to be saved by an eleventh-hour armistice. The Armistice of Pläswitz provides a clear line dividing the one-dimensional conflict between the French Empire and the Russo-Prussian alliance that ensued during the spring of 1813, and the multidimensional war of a multinational coalition against a French Empire dwindling in resources in the autumn of 1813. During the Spring Campaign, Napoleon essentially faced a single Russo-Prussian army that numbered barely 100,000 men. To end French hegemony east of the Rhine, some Russians and Prussians hoped to ignite Germany and fan the flames of a people's war based on the Spanish model. Aside from the Russo-Prussian alliance, mutual suspicion and traditional rivalries resulted in nothing more than a series of nonbinding bilateral agreements between the Prussians, Russians, Swedes, and British. Yet the military and political situation completely changed after the armistice. As this volume will describe, Napoleon faced not one enemy army but three (Army of Silesia, Army of Bohemia, and Army of North Germany), which he opposed with three of his own. Allied forces in Central Europe numbered more than 500,000 men while Napoleon's exceeded 400,000. Austria and Sweden joined the Sixth Coalition. Although a grand treaty of alliance would not be signed until March 1814, the Sixth Coalition was bound by subsidy agreements with Great Britain to continue the war against Napoleon. Metternich was now the prime minister of the coalition and his tool, Prince Karl zu Schwarzenberg, was named Allied commander in chief. The nature of the conflict changed. Talk of a people's war on a par with that in Spain ended, and Metternich did everything he could to separate British interests from the Russo-Prussian war aims, which he likewise sought to undermine.

Notes

1 Radetzky to Schwarzenberg, "Memoire über den Zweck der Operationen und deren muthmaßlichen Gang, so wie die anzuwendenden Mittel," Vienna, 10 May 1813, reproduced in full in Radetzky, *Denkschriften*, 101–04. The key paragraphs are located on pages 103–04.
2 The plan is reproduced in Oncken, *Österreich und Preußen*, II:321–22 in German and 658–59 in French.
3 *Correspondance de Napoléon Ier* (hereafter cited as *CN*), No. 20619, XXVI:236–38.
4 Craig, "Problems of Coalition Warfare," 42. To avoid repetition, the two volumes of *Napoleon and the Struggle for Germany* will focus on the military and diplomatic history of 1813. See *Napoleon and Berlin* for discussions concerning the myths, fabrications, and realities about the origins of Prussian-German nationalism during the war of 1813.
5 My final work on 1813 will focus on Austria's role in 1813 and detail the battles of Dresden, Leipzig, and Hanau.
6 Nipperdey, *Germany from Napoleon to Bismarck*, 68–69. In the book, *Leyer und Schwert*, 37, Theodore Körner, a Saxon who served in a Prussian volunteer unit – the Lützow Rifles – reflected the mood of the educated and the young when he wrote: "It is not a war of the kind the kings know about, it is a crusade, 'tis a holy war."
7 In 1821, Major August Wagner of the Prussian General Staff published three volumes titled *Plane der Schlachten und Treffen welche von der preussischen Armee in den Feldzügen der Jahre 1813, 14, und 15 geliefert worden*. Four years later, he published the fourth volume of the series. In 1831, he published *Die Tage von Dresden und Kulm in dem Feldzuge 1813* as an appendix to the earlier work; it has a slight modification of the title in this fifth volume: *Plane der Schlachten und Treffen, welche der preussischen Armee und ihren Verbüdteten in den Feldzügen der Jahre 1813, 14, und 15 geliefert worden*. In all five studies, Wagner not only utilized the papers of the Prussian General Staff, primarily after-action reports, but he also received much material and support from French officers and General Staff historians such as Marmont, Pelet, Haxo, Kellermann, Reille, and Koch. He also utilized archival material from the Russian General Staff, provided by Diebitsch, as well as the archives of Bavaria, Württemberg, Hanover, Baden, and Hesse-Darmstadt. As the title indicates, Wagner's study is an analysis of the major battles fought during the period with details of the operations leading up to the battles. Moreover, the work does not follow the chronology of the campaigns. The first volume examines Lützen, Großbeeren, Hagelberg, and Dennewitz; volume II: the Katzbach, Wartenburg, and Möckern; volume III: Bautzen and Laon; volume IV: Ligny, Waterloo, and Wavre. Unlike the study of the Silesian Army in the 1813 Campaign published by the Prussian General Staff in the *Militär-Wochenblatt* in the mid 1840s, and certainly very different from the German General Staff's *Geschichte der Befreiungskriege 1813–1815* published by Rudolf Friederich in the first decade of the twentieth century, Wagner's work does not provide critical analysis but is an excellent source for studying the course of the battles noted above.

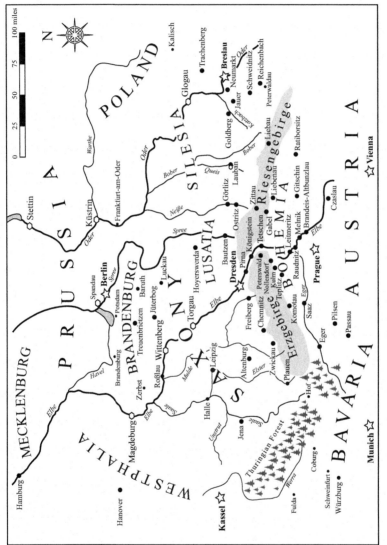

1. The theater of war, 1813

16

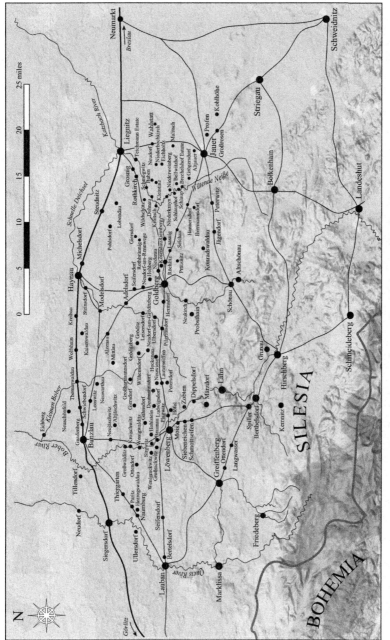

2. Region between the Queis and the Katzbach Rivers

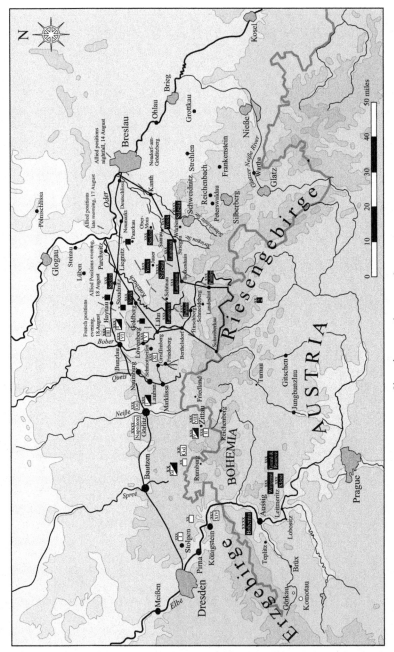

N

Kosel

Brieg

Ohlau

Breslau

Grottkau

Neudorf-am-Gröditzberg

Allied positions nightfall, 14 August

Polnischlissa

Oder

Allied positions late morning, 17 August

Schweidnitz Strehlen

Reichenbach

Petersdau

Frankenstein

Nieße

Glatzer Neiße River

Wartha

Glatz

Silberberg

Schweidnitzer Str.

Striegau Wa.

Glogau

Steinau

Lüben

Parchwitz

Allied positions evening, 18 August

Neumarkt Panzkau Ober-Mois Deutschlissa Kunth

Liegnitz

Jauer Saarau

Schönau

Bürkenhain

Landeshut

Riesengebirge

French positions evening, 18 August

Haynau

Steudnitz

Goldberg

Lähn

Kaugbach

Schmiedeberg

Hirschberg

Schreiberhau

Bober

Löwenberg Greiffenberg Friedeberg

Bunzlau Schmottseifen

Berthelsdorf

AUSTRIA

Quets

Naumburg

Lauban

Marklissa

Friedland

Turnau

Gitschen

Neiße

Görlitz

Napoleon

Reichenberg

Jungbunzlau

Zittau

Bautzen

Rumburg

BOHEMIA

Guard & Reserves

Prague

Spree

Stolpen

Königstein Pirna

Aussig

Wittgenst Leitmeritz Klein

Böhmin

Lobositz

Teplitz

Görkau Komotau

Brüx

Meißen

Elbe

Dresden

Erzgebirge

3. Situation, 19 August 1813

4. Region between the Spree and the Elbe Rivers

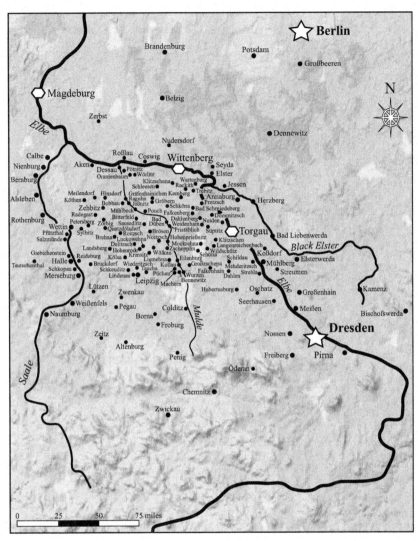

5. Region between the Black Elster and the Saale Rivers

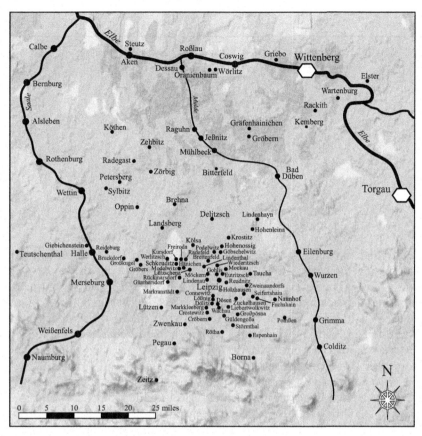

6. Region between the Mulde and the Saale Rivers

I

Trachenberg and Reichenbach

Like Napoleon, the Russians and Prussians entered the armistice committed to continuing the war on 20 July 1813. Yet what hope did they have for victory? During the Spring Campaign, the French emperor had driven their army more than 200 miles from the Saale to the Oder in one month's time. Two major battles had been fought and lost. Who among the Russians and Prussians could challenge Napoleon? Although they had ejected the French from their motherland in 1812, the Russians did not achieve a decisive victory over Napoleon himself during that entire campaign. Forsaking the Prussians and returning home remained an option after the failures of the Spring Campaign, yet leaving Central Europe under Napoleon's control offered Russia little long-term security. As for the Prussians, zeal and hatred on their own failed to liberate their state in the first six months of 1813. By breaking his alliance with Napoleon, Frederick William jeopardized his very crown. To avoid the same fate that had befallen the previous five coalitions that had waged war against France, the military and political leaders of both states understood that they needed more than the unprecedented cooperation that had characterized their operations during the Spring Campaign. With the stakes so high, they realized that only an unconventional strategic plan would allow them to again challenge French dominance in Central Europe.

Moreover, Napoleon's success in the Spring Campaign merely impressed upon the Russians and Prussians how much they needed the Austrian army to successfully oppose the legions of the French Empire. In fact, both sides sought Austria as a partner to continue the war. While Napoleon refused to believe that his father-in-law, Kaiser Francis, would declare war against him, the Russians and Prussians as well as their allies, the Swedes and British, had less reason to be optimistic. In addition to the general suspicion of Austria shared by all who opposed Napoleon, the Swedes and British looked askance at the Russians and Prussians as the latter negotiated with the Austrians in secret. The British paymaster in London desperately sought to meld a system of bilateral arrangements into a grand alliance but Austria stood in the way. Consequently, Allied monarchs, diplomats, and generals labored during the armistice to achieve two goals. First, they wanted to draft an incomparable plan of campaign that offered the promise of defeating Napoleon. Second, they sought to bring Austria into the Sixth Coalition. The two objectives became intertwined as the Allies had to plan on fighting Napoleon either with or without the Austrians.

Shortly after establishing his headquarters at Reichenbach (Dzierżoniów) in Silesia, the commander in chief of Coalition forces, Barclay de Tolly, received a request from the Austrian commander in chief, Schwarzenberg, for information concerning the Allied campaign plan should the war against Napoleon resume. This proved problematic for two reasons. First, as Austria still had not joined the Sixth Coalition, Barclay could not divulge any plans. Second, the Allies had no plans to divulge. However, the industrious Russian general, Karl Wilhelm von Toll, had been tinkering with the Wurschen Plan. Refining the plan's concepts, Toll presented a new draft to Alexander on 9 June. Before we examine the plan's details, it is important to bear in mind two points. First, the Allies expected the armistice to expire on 20 July. Following an eight-day suspension of hostilities, the war would resume on the 28th. Second, neither the Russians nor the Prussians could estimate the number of troops they would have under arms when hostilities resumed. Written in French so that it could be immediately communicated to the Prussians, Toll's "Mémoire" actually offered two plans: one in the event Austria remained neutral, and a second that included Austria in the Coalition. As the former never came to pass, we will examine only the latter.

Toll advocated a premature rupture of the armistice by the Allies if they should detect French forces withdrawing west from Silesia to the left bank of the Elbe. Should the armistice run its course, he calculated the total strength of the Allied army in Silesia to be 150,000 men by 20 July, with the Austrians fielding an additional 120,000 combatants. Underestimating Napoleon's organizational abilities, he allotted the emperor only 160,000 soldiers. Toll's "Mémoire" called for the Russo-Prussian main army to be united at Schweidnitz in Silesia no later than 26 July. On that same day, the Austrians would commence their march to Upper Lusatia (Lausitz, Łużyee) in two columns: the first through Gabel (Jablonné) and Ostritz to Görlitz, the second through Liebau (Lubawka) to Reichenbach. Likewise on the 26th, General Friedrich Wilhelm von Bülow would lead his corps of 25,000 Prussians from Berlin south to Görlitz and unite with the Austrians in Lusatia. Any enemy forces that Bülow encountered during the march would be attacked unless they outgunned his own.

1 Field-Marshal Prince Karl Philipp zu Schwarzenberg, 1771–1820

Toll assumed that, as soon as the armistice expired, Napoleon would seize the offensive and turn against either the main Russo-Prussian army at Schweidnitz or the Austrians advancing on Görlitz. From his central position, Napoleon could attack one of these armies before the other could pressure his rear and flank. However, because both Allied armies would have sufficient strength to face Napoleon's main force and oppose it for a few days, Toll did not consider this danger to be significant. Moreover, Allied *Streifkorps* would maintain constant contact with French forces to provide accurate information on their movements and thus enable the Allied armies to be in position at the right time.

If Napoleon decided to operate against the Russo-Prussian army at Schweidnitz, Toll maintained that the Allies should accept battle while the Austrians and Bülow's Prussian corps closed on the rear of the French army. Should the main Russo-Prussian army be defeated at Schweidnitz and forced to retreat, then the 145,000 Austrians and Prussians threatening Napoleon's rear would prevent him from exploiting the victory. With the emperor's troops already exhausted and weakened from fighting the Russo-Prussian army, Toll believed that the threat posed by the Austro-Prussian army in Lusatia would force Napoleon to immediately turn around and fight a second battle against these fresh Allied forces. In the meantime, the Russo-Prussian army would also turn around and advance against his rear. Should Napoleon seek to attack the Austro-Prussian army in Lusatia, the two armies would simply exchange roles and the execution of the plan would remain the same. In both cases, Allied forces on the lower Elbe – mainly Russians under Mikhail Vorontsov and Aleksandr Chernishev – would advance against the enemy's rearward communications at Leipzig, Dresden, and Altenburg while at the same time observing the French forces at Hamburg and Magdeburg.

In a third scenario, Toll envisioned Napoleon evacuating all territory east of the Elbe and concentrating his forces at Dresden. Should this occur, Toll recommended that, as soon as the armistice expired, Blücher's Prussian corps and General Fabian Gottlieb von der Osten-Sacken's Russian corps – both part of the main Russo-Prussian army in Silesia – pursue the French to Dresden. From Berlin, Bülow would also drive on the Saxon capital to unite with Blücher and Sacken to form an army of 70,000 men. Meanwhile, approximately 100,000 Russians from the main Russo-Prussian army in Silesia would march to Bohemia and unite with the Austrians on the Eger (Ohře) River to form an army of 220,000 men. This army would then advance toward the upper Saale River to threaten Napoleon's rear. Toll predicted that this movement would prompt Napoleon to cover his communication with France by immediately evacuating the left or western bank of the Elbe. However, should Napoleon remain at Dresden and defend the Elbe against Blücher's Russo-Prussian army, then the Austro-Russian army in Bohemia would cross the Elbe at Leitmeritz (Litoměřice) and advance through Teplitz (Teplice) into Saxony and threaten Napoleon's rear and flank.

Toll's belief that strategic maneuvering against Napoleon's line of communication would force him to abandon the Elbe suggests a certain ignorance of the emperor's mastery of operations on interior lines. Moreover, hoping to fix Napoleon at Dresden with 70,000 Russians and Prussians under Blücher long enough for the Austro-Russian army to reach the upper Saale does not strongly recommend Toll. In addition, his inaccurate estimate of French forces burdened his plan with one inherent flaw. The whole situation would change significantly if Napoleon were to add a mere 50,000 combatants to the 160,000 men estimated by Toll. With more than 200,000 effectives at his disposal, Napoleon would be able to mask one of the Allied armies while he led the bulk of his forces against the other. In addition, Toll makes no mention of the active participation of Swedish forces – an understandable oversight based on Bernadotte's total inactivity during the Spring Campaign.

Yet beyond the basic errors concerning numbers, Toll's plan offered much. First and foremost, he recommended that the Allied armies seize the initiative and seek battle in either Silesia or Lusatia. The principle of one army holding its ground against the emperor's main force until the other

Allied army could make its presence felt to his rear as well as having Bülow force-march to Lusatia or Silesia suggests a boldness of action that the Allies lacked during the Spring Campaign. Toll's concepts generated much discussion at Barclay's headquarters and ultimately provided the foundation for all future drafts of the Allied campaign plan. As a result of their discussions, the Russians modified some of Toll's essential points. Few details have survived regarding the participants and the date the changes were made, but evidence suggests that Barclay authored the modifications. A Corfu native in Russian diplomatic service, Count Ioannis Antonios Kapodistrias, drafted the new plan, Barclay signed it, and Toll personally delivered it to Austrian headquarters at Gitschin (Jičín).[1] Placing faith in the Austrians, he also provided a detailed report on the strength and dislocation of Russian and Prussian forces.[2]

Following an introduction that partly blamed the Allied retreat from the Saale to the Oder on Austria's refusal to enter the war during the Spring Campaign, Barclay's plan provides three scenarios. The first, and in Barclay's opinion the most likely, would be a French offensive against Austria. Although Radetzky first expressed this concern in his memo of 10 May, Toll completely ignored this possibility. According to Barclay, Napoleon would leave some forces on the right bank of the Elbe facing the Russo-Prussian army in Silesia but unite his main mass on the left bank of the Elbe and turn against the Austrian army. In this case, the Austrians would have to contend with a much larger enemy force. To reinforce the Austrians, Barclay suggested sending the 25,000 men of Wittgenstein's Russian army corps from Silesia to Bohemia to unite with the Austrian army at Leitmeritz. With these reinforcements, the Austrian army would be strong enough to either stand against Napoleon's attack or take the offensive against him. Should the Austrians seize the offensive, the Russo-Prussian army in Silesia would support their operations through an energetic advance on Dresden.

In his second scenario, Barclay speculated that Napoleon would concentrate his forces between the Elbe and the Oder. In this case, the main Russo-Prussian army in Silesia would advance west while the Austrian army simultaneously drove north from Bohemia. Barclay's third scenario, and the one he considered the least likely – although Toll thought it to be the most likely – found Napoleon massing his forces in Silesia to confront the Russo-Prussian army that he had pursued to the Oder during the Spring Campaign. Should this occur, all Allied forces would take the offensive: the Russo-Prussian army in Silesia would advance west, the Austrian army northeast through Zittau against Napoleon's right flank, and Bülow southeast against his left. As for the troops under the crown prince of Sweden, which included Russian corps commanded by Vorontsov and General Ludwig Georg von Wallmoden, they would observe Hamburg and Magdeburg and remain on the defensive until a decisive battle on the upper Elbe decided the fate of Germany. As soon as the Allied armies achieved this victory, the crown prince would cross the Elbe and move west across the Weser River toward the lower Rhine.

Barclay omitted or changed some aspects of Toll's plan in part to make the whole more palatable to the Austrians, in part to maintain control over his own troops. Unable to gauge the Austrian reaction, he disregarded Toll's recommendation to prematurely terminate the armistice should Napoleon withdraw his forces to left bank of the Elbe. Moreover, Barclay assigned tasks to the troops commanded by the crown prince of Sweden. Regarding Toll's third scenario, which required 100,000 Russians to reinforce the Austrians in Bohemia, Barclay lowered the number to 25,000 men. As Barclay still served as Allied commander in chief, this change is certainly understandable: few generals in such a position would voluntarily turn over three-quarters of their men for use by an ally. Moreover, even with 100,000 Russians, the majority of the troops would still be Austrian, meaning command of this Austro-Russian army would go to an Austrian general.[3]

Meanwhile, per a request from Schwarzenberg, Radetzky drafted another memo known as the Prague Memorandum. Written on 10 June at Prague, it addressed troop strengths, strategy, and operations. According to Radetzky, Napoleon would resume the struggle with 230,000–250,000 men. Should Austria enter the war, he assumed Napoleon would leave some 50,000 to 60,000 men in Silesia to mask the Russo-Prussian army while he directed his main force of 150,000 to 180,000 men against the Austrians. Radetzky stressed the need for the Austrians to seize the offensive and defeat Napoleon's main force. For the Austrians to be successful, the army in Bohemia needed to number 150,000 combatants, based on Radetzky's calculations. To achieve this number solely with Austrian troops, he recommended the mobilization of the third battalion of each regiment posted in Galicia. To oppose the French forces assembling in Italy and Bavaria, Radetzky proposed the use of Landwehr and small detachments of line units posted in well-chosen and strongly entrenched positions, where they would remain on the defensive until the main army achieved success. After the first decisive victory, all Austrian forces would conduct a double offensive in Italy and Germany.[4]

Radetzky's memo stated nothing about Allied operations in Silesia or Germany. By assuming Napoleon would leave 50,000 to 60,000 men in Silesia facing triple the number of Russo-Prussian soldiers, either he accepted as obvious that Allied forces there would smash this masking force and reach the rear of the main French army advancing against Austria, or he deferred mention of combined operations with the Allies. Regardless, his statements about seizing the offensive, defeating the main French army, and

2 Johann Josef Wenzel Anton Franz Karl Count Radetzky von Radetz, 1766–1858

maintaining the defensive in all secondary theaters marked significant progress in the mindset of the Austrian General Staff after the splitting of forces between the Italian and German theaters had contributed to Austria's defeats in 1805 and 1809. However, beyond these theoretical statements, Radetzky's Prague Memorandum lacked initiative and failed to explain how the Austrians would defeat Napoleon.[5]

After receiving the tsar's approval, Toll again traveled to Gitschin, where he delivered Barclay's plan to Schwarzenberg and Radetzky on 14 June. In particular, Barclay tasked him with explaining the movements the Allies planned to make at the commencement of hostilities. Despite the inherent differences in the Allied plan and Radetzky's Prague Memorandum, Toll found common ground with the Austrians during a meeting on the 15th. Purportedly, they attained total agreement after just a few hours.[6] Although Barclay omitted Toll's original suggestion to prematurely rupture the armistice, the staff officer mentioned the idea to Radetzky, who agreed. Radetzky also accepted Barclay's proposal to dispatch Wittgenstein's 25,000 Russians to unite with the Austrian army. As for operations, the Austro-Russian army in Bohemia would cross the Elbe at Leitmeritz and fall on the enemy's right flank while the Russo-Prussian army in Silesia crossed the Elbe between Torgau and Dresden. Bülow's corps would observe Wittenberg and Torgau as Vorontsov's monitored Magdeburg. Should Napoleon maintain his forces in Silesia facing the Russo-Prussian army, the latter would assemble at Schweidnitz and advance through Jauer (Jawor) and Goldberg (Złotoryja) directly against the French while the Austro-Russian army debouched through Zittau and proceeded north to Görlitz. At Görlitz, it would unite with Bülow and the Russian corps of General Ferdinand von Wintzingerode, turn east, and threaten Napoleon's rear. Toll assumed Napoleon would attack the Austro-Russian army first, but felt confident that within two days the Russo-Prussian army would reach the rear of his army.

A 17 June letter from Toll to Scharnhorst provides the only evidence available regarding the former's meeting with the Austrian generals and the resulting Gitschen Agreement.[7] Aside from commending "the good spirit of the commanders of the Austrian army, especially its quartermaster-general, Radetzky, for the good cause," Toll explained the basis of the plan of operations that emerged after just a few hours of discussion:

> (1) The six-week armistice will give the enemy the means to move up reinforcements of all arms and because he has much to fear from Austria it is very probable that he will leave a chain of posts along the Katzbach [Kaczawa River] facing us and he will gradually withdraw all of his forces to the left bank of the Elbe to be closer to his reinforcements and magazines ...
>
> Should it occur that the enemy makes these movements, we will immediately break the armistice by following the enemy with the combined Russo-Prussian army; Wintzingerode will also start his march, but Bülow will go to Roßlau and cross the Elbe there. The Austrian army, which will be joined by Wittgenstein's corps of 25,000 men, will go to Leitmeritz, where it will cross the Elbe in order to fall on the enemy's right flank while the combined Russo-Prussian army crosses this river between Torgau and Dresden. Bülow's corps will observe Wittenberg and Torgau; Vorontsov's will observe Magdeburg. Both generals will send their partisans as far as possible against the enemy's communications.
>
> (2) The second supposition is that the enemy will remain at the Katzbach. Should this be the case, the Russo-Prussian army will assemble at Schweidnitz, the Austrian army will debouch through Zittau upon Görlitz, to which Bülow and a portion of Wintzingerode's corps will also take their direction to establish communication with the Austrian army as quickly as possible and together threaten the rear of the enemy. The combined Russo-Prussian army will march through Jauer and Goldberg straight at the enemy; the Austrians will proceed from Görlitz to Lauban [Lubań] in the enemy's right flank ...
>
> Based on all of these combinations, the enemy probably will attack the first army with all his forces. We will therefore assume that the Austrian army will be attacked by superior enemy forces. After a two-day battle, the Russo-Prussian army will be completely to the enemy's rear so that if the Austrian army is forced to yield, the enemy will have to face a new and numerous army or must flee.
>
> However, to execute this with precision and advantage, the commanding general, Barclay de Tolly, has ordered that as soon as the reserve – which is due in twenty days – arrives, the armistice will be broken and the strongest

offensive seized; the Austrian commander in chief will be informed of this in a timely manner.[8]

At this point, the Allies reached an encouraging agreement with the Austrians. Both sides viewed a French invasion of Bohemia as Napoleon's first step in a renewed conflict and both believed that the Austrian army needed to be increased to 150,000 men. Radetzky initially sought to reach this number by mobilizing additional Austrian troops but accepted Barclay's offer of 25,000 Russians for operations in Bohemia. Moreover, the Austrians concurred with Toll's idea of breaking the armistice to commence a general offensive before Napoleon could launch his own. Although Schwarzenberg and Radetzky apparently agreed with Toll and Barclay, no definitive plan of operations could be established until Austria officially joined the Coalition. Consequently, military talks between the Allies and the Austrians ceased for the next few weeks, yet both sides continued planning at a furious pace.[9]

As for forming a grand alliance against Napoleon, the chances of achieving a diplomatic consensus appeared bleak, due to British and Swedish suspicion of Russia, Prussia, and Austria. The British goodwill that the Russians and Prussians had earned by way of the 16 May Wurschen Convention fizzled with the cessation of hostilities.[10] Neither the Russians nor the Prussians had informed the British and Swedes of their negotiations with the Austrians that had led to the armistice. Much of the diplomatic impasse lay in Russia's hostility toward Great Britain. Although the tsar desperately needed British aid to continue the war, he did not want to share leadership of the Coalition with London. While the British viewed Russia as a natural ally, the tsar's government still considered Great Britain a rival for trade and influence from the New World to the Near East. The alliance created by the Kalisch–Breslau accords established the war aims of a Russo-Prussian coalition and largely omitted British interests. In addition, London viewed Russia's offer to mediate between Great Britain and the United States to end the War of 1812 as "an attempt to save the American fleet as a counterweight to British maritime supremacy and as a way of forcing Britain to end its maritime despotism."[11] Thus, as Charles Webster notes in his mammoth study of the foreign policy of Robert Stewart, Viscount Castlereagh, "the Coalition was, indeed, undergoing a severe strain and at moments seemed as if it would suffer the same fate as its predecessors. By their treaties, it is true, Russia and Prussia had promised not to make peace without Britain. But already, after two defeats, they had accepted an armistice without consulting her. The opportunity of Austria had, at last, arrived."[12]

As for the Austrians, Nesselrode met with Francis, Metternich, and Schwarzenberg between 3 and 7 June. He returned convinced that the kaiser would not join the coalition "until Napoleon had been offered and rejected very moderate and minimal terms of peace." Nesselrode also delivered to

Tsar Alexander a memorandum drafted by Metternich outlining these conditions. Although the Austrian minister agreed in principle with the provisions of the Wurschen Convention, he feared Napoleon would reject its harsh demands. He felt that the Allies would have to propose a minimum set of conditions just to attract the French emperor to the peace table. Thus, Metternich formulated the "four points" to offer Napoleon as the price for a peace conference: the partition of the Grand Duchy of Warsaw among Russia, Prussia, and Austria; the complete evacuation of all imperial forces from Prussia and the Grand Duchy of Warsaw as well as the return of Danzig (Gdańsk) to Prussia; the return of the Adriatic coast (Illyria) to Austria; and the independence of Hamburg and Lübeck in North Germany. Debate then ensued at Reichenbach over whether Russia and Prussia could accept these terms.

As the Spring Campaign demonstrated, the Allies desperately needed the Austrian army. Russia and Prussia, even supported by Great Britain and Sweden, could not achieve victory in Central Europe over Napoleon and the resources of the French Empire. Although the four points fell far short of the Wurschen Convention, particularly in regard to the Third Germany, few options remained open for the Russians and Prussians given the mindset of the Austrian kaiser. Regardless, Nesselrode attempted to explain the Russian view to Metternich: any peace concluded on the basis of the four points would only be a truce. As soon as Napoleon rebuilt his forces, he would seek to reestablish French hegemony over the continent. The Russians maintained that Austria and Prussia had to be sufficiently strengthened to balance France and prevent Napoleon from challenging any peace settlement. Should a peace fail to achieve this point, history eventually would repeat itself. Just as in 1805 and 1806, Napoleon would crush the Austrians and Prussians before Russia's distant legions could arrive. Nesselrode urged Metternich to avoid this mistake by taking advantage of the present circumstances. For the first time in the French Wars, the armies of the three Eastern powers stood within 150 miles of each other and could be quickly concentrated in the same theater. Despite the logic of these arguments, the Austrians stood firm. Thus, the Russians and Prussians decided that they would negotiate with the French based on the four points but would not approve a peace settlement that left the Third Germany in Napoleon's hands. As the end of June approached, they could do little but hope Napoleon would reject Metternich's offer.[13]

Metternich himself feared a separate peace between France and Russia that would divide Europe between them. Alexander's victory in 1812 led Metternich to dread Russian preponderance almost as much as that of the French. He desired not only to break French power east of the Rhine, but also to limit Russian influence west of the Vistula River. To take the wind out of Alexander's sails, Metternich targeted the stipulations of the

Kalisch–Breslau accords that called for Frederick William to cede Prussian Poland to Alexander in return for Saxony. Such an exchange would run counter to Austria's policy of limiting Prussia's influence in Germany and restraining Russia's expansion in Central Europe. Metternich also sought to outmaneuver the growing Anglo-Russian-Prussian consensus. It appeared that these three powers would soon establish the Coalition's general goals: Russian domination of Poland, Prussian compensation in Germany, and a free hand for Great Britain in Iberia, the Low Countries, Sicily, and the colonies, and on the high seas. Metternich recognized that a settlement for Central Europe would never be reached with Napoleon as long as the Russians and Prussians championed British interests. To achieve peace in Central Europe, he decided to isolate Great Britain and completely ignore British objectives. Metternich not only excluded the British from the negotiations that produced the armistice but also insisted that neither Britain nor Sweden be informed of them.[14]

Napoleon's victory at Bautzen considerably strengthened Metternich's hand by making Austrian cooperation much more urgent for the Russians and Prussians. Over the next month, he worked diligently to convince the Allies to offer Napoleon the four points as the basis for a peace conference. His envoy at Napoleon's headquarters, General Ferdinand von Bubna, assured the French emperor that due to London's hostile attitude no hope existed for a general peace that would cover the issues of maritime rights. Instead, the British would have to be forced into negotiations by a peace that ended the war in Central Europe.[15] Such a peace would leave Great Britain isolated and exposed to the full weight of Napoleon's military machine. Conversely, Metternich explained to his representative at Allied headquarters, Johann Philipp von Stadion, that a general peace could be established only if the British made maritime concessions: British domination of the seas had proved equal to French domination of the continent. Should London refuse, then Austria would seek a settlement for Central Europe only.[16]

Metternich's machinations caused great trepidation among the British envoys at Allied Headquarters. Not only did the goal of creating a grand alliance seem out of reach, but the survival of the Coalition itself appeared to be at stake. Months of careful negotiations with the Russians and Prussians unraveled as the British found themselves next to the Swedes on the outside looking in. Much progress had been made by the British since London had committed an army to Iberia in 1808. Portugal had been liberated from French control and Joseph Bonaparte's kingdom of Spain teetered on collapse thanks to the campaigns of General Sir Arthur Wellesley, the marquess of Wellington. Yet the British knew that, despite all their great efforts in Iberia, the fate of Europe would be decided on the plains of Saxony. Should the Allies be defeated or come to terms with Napoleon, the master then would be free to send his masses to Spain. All that the British had accomplished in Iberia after five long years of war would be for naught. How helpless the British envoys to Russia, Prussia, and Sweden must have felt as the redcoats of Wellington's army waged war on the other side of Europe. Without boots on the ground, the only leverage they had was the promise of subsidies and diplomatic support. As long as London steadfastly refused to put the issue of maritime rights on the agenda of a general peace conference, the term "Perfidious Albion" echoed in the ears of its allies.

From Reichenbach, General Charles Stewart, the British ambassador and military commissioner to Prussia, wrote a sour note on 6 June to his half-brother, Castlereagh, Britain's foreign secretary.[17] "The news we send home is not the best, and, from what I see, I fear political treachery and the machinations that are in the wind more than any evils from Bonaparte's myrmidons. We must keep a sharp look-out, especially since our refusal of Austrian mediation. The accounts from Hamburg and Stralsund are bad. I fear the Swedes will go [home], and Bonaparte gets 20,000 Danes in the North. The disorder in the Russian army is great." He continued by warning Castlereagh that Tsar Alexander had mismanaged Bernadotte to such an extent that the former needed to be wary of the latter seizing Finland. Stewart also hoped Wellington could provide a victory to offset the anticipated negative reaction by the British public to the news of the armistice.[18] "I cannot help thinking that the great personages of the drama here will meet, and Metternich will attempt some *family* alliances to aid the object of peace. If things turn to a Congress, and if you acquiesce in sending a negotiator, pray select a very able man. Depend upon it, he will be required. I have seen enough in a little time of the windings and turnings of diplomatic chicane to fear." In a subsequent letter, Stewart lamented the failure to finalize firm treaties of alliance during the preceding months. "I hope you will get us through our Treaties," he exhorted his brother; "it is best to show something, even under doubtful circumstances. Had we finished as we ought, and as I would easily have accomplished a month since, we should have been able throughout to play a higher game, and an armistice might have been more combated."[19]

On the positive side of the ledger, Stewart lauded the Prussians, calling them "infinitely better" than the Russians. "They have everywhere greatly distinguished themselves, and will do much more in a little time. You cannot send them too much ammunition and arms. Russia rides the bear over them, but they are obedient and patient, and I will pledge my faith for theirs; although the Germans will not burn *their Moscow*, and lay waste to their country, still they will be true; and Prussia will not be the first power that will withdraw from [the] English alliance."[20]

Stewart's letter conveying news of the armistice reached Castlereagh on 22 June. With his confidence shaken, Castlereagh responded: "we are in great anxiety to hear from you upon the armistice. Its extension to 20 July puzzles and alarms us for the temper of Austria."[21] Despite this, Castlereagh initially played into Metternich's hands by declining the Austrian mediation and by refusing to send a negotiator or even "precise orders as to the negotiations that may possibly arise, pending the armistice. Our *general views* and *existing engagements* are sufficiently understood . . . to have their due influence in any decision to be taken."[22] He instructed the British ambassador and military commissioner to Russia, General William Cathcart, "to guard against a Continental peace being made to our exclusion."[23]

Castlereagh also urged both Stewart and Cathcart to do all they could to heal the rift between Alexander and Bernadotte. In early 1813, before Frederick William broke his alliance with Napoleon, Castlereagh resigned himself to granting very generous terms to Bernadotte "to raise the north of Germany, where Prussia still lay apparently supine." Pressed to decide between Denmark and Russian-backed Sweden, Castlereagh chose the latter and so threw British support behind Bernadotte's plan to annex Norway. According to the initial plan, Bernadotte's Swedes, reinforced by North Germans who rallied for liberation from the French yoke, would form a large force to strike Napoleon's flank while the Russians attacked his front. After making his deal with the devil, Castlereagh endeavored "to get as much value as possible out of Bernadotte for the common cause." Despite giving money and the promise of Norway, the British found a troublesome bedfellow in the former French marshal. Negotiations between the Russians and Danes had left him feeling double-crossed by Alexander, particularly after the tsar did not provide the Russian auxiliary corps stipulated in their treaty arrangements. The failure of North Germany to rise and rally to the Allied cause soured all parties involved.[24]

"We have done everything to prevail upon the Prince Royal to manage matters with *your parties*," Castlereagh wrote to Stewart, "and I trust all may be arranged before the resumption of hostilities." The foreign secretary insisted that "nothing would have half so good an effect as a *personal* interview" between Alexander and Bernadotte. "I have written officially to recommend it; and I do hope Lord Cathcart and you will labor to bring it about." Castlereagh also pressed Cathcart to arrange a meeting between Alexander and Bernadotte: "I am sorry to observe asperities still existing between the Tsar and Prince Royal. As the Prince Royal has expressed his wish that they should meet and settle all matters in the true spirit of a common cause, I hope you will be enabled to bring this about. I am sure three hours would do more, so employed, than volumes of dispatches and autographical letters."[25] To lay the groundwork for such a meeting, the Swedish diplomat Anders Fredrik Skjöldebrand made his way to Reichenbach in mid June. At the end of the month, Bernadotte received a letter from Alexander inviting the crown prince to meet with him at the Silesian town of Trachenberg (Żmigród).[26]

Despite the suspicion caused by the armistice, Stewart and Cathcart continued to negotiate with the Prussians and Russians respectively over £2,000,000 in subsidies that London had offered to divide between the two. A strong push by Hardenberg to secure Hanover for Prussia momentarily damaged relations until the British firmly declared Hanover to be off limits. With this matter settled, Stewart and Hardenberg concluded a subsidy agreement on 14 June that granted the Prussians £666,666 in monthly payments to maintain a field army of 80,000 men. Although the Prussians eventually fielded double this number, they still received only one-third of the £2,000,000. Cathcart and Nesselrode concluded a similar Anglo-Russian treaty on 15 June 1813 after the British accepted Alexander's claim that the armistice and subsequent negotiations were necessary to bind Austria to the coalition. Per the treaty signed at the tsar's headquarters in Peterwaldau (Pieszyce) near Reichenbach, the British pledged to pay the Russians £1,133,334 in monthly installments ending on 1 January 1814 for the maintenance of a field army of 160,000 men. In addition, the Russians would receive £500,000 for the support of their fleet. As for Austria, Castlereagh instructed Stewart "to bring Austria to a point, and, if she takes the field, to give her half a million to help her on."[27]

In addition to the subsidy treaties, the British accepted a Russian request for a special issue of paper money called "federative paper" to enable the Russians and Prussians to pay their military expenses. The British proposed limiting the issue to £5,000,000 redeemable at 5 percent interest six months after the peace or on 1 July 1815, whichever came first. All federative paper could be used only to cover the cost of military expenditure. Moreover, Great Britain would assume responsibility for half the capital and interest, Russia one-third, and Prussia one-sixth. Finally, London would never be asked to assume responsibility for more than one-half the total issue. Although the British accepted this last point, the Allies then insisted that London assume the capital and interest for the full amount.[28]

Castlereagh "fully approved" of the conduct of his two envoys "in concluding the treaties at the period they were signed."[29] Regardless, the foreign secretary balked at the Russo-Prussian request for London to assume the capital and interest for the full £5,000,000 of federative paper. He explained to Stewart in a letter of 22 June that:

> We did not hesitate to agree to bear our share, if the system could be reduced to practice; but it is too much to expect that we should take the whole, with all its possible abuses, upon ourselves.[30] There would be nearly equal difficulty in introducing a British paper into circulation in Germany, under the present circumstances, with one jointly issued by the combined powers. If it should be found that the credits of the three powers cannot be advantageously combined in the same paper, we might undertake to be answerable for an issue not

exceeding 750,000 Thalers per month in paper, for the reimbursement of which Great Britain should be separately liable, till the whole sum of £2,500,000 was issued, which would be in about twenty months – but our responsibility cannot be pushed beyond the original limits, nor should we bear more than our share of the progressive monthly expenditure of the armies.[31]

Castlereagh also reminded Stewart to urge the Allies to give "full scope to British commerce, in order that they might draw their subsidy at a more favorable rate of exchange. It is too unrealistic, first to cramp our commerce by prohibitions and high duties, and then expect us to incur the loss of exchange produced by their own injudicious policy." In general, the foreign secretary explained to his brother that "the whole question of money has become a very difficult one, since Hamburg has been reoccupied, and the Allies have fallen back. I trust, however, Austria will take her part and the sources of remittance may again be extended." Until the subsidy treaties with the Russians and Prussians could be ratified, Castlereagh authorized Stewart and Cathcart to "draw to the extent of the monthly installments, which, upon the £2,000,000 sterling, ought not, with a view to the exchange, exceed £200,000 in any one month."[32] Negotiations continued until 11 August, when the British government accepted an Allied proposal that reduced the issue of federative paper to £2,500,000 with London accepting responsibility for the full amount.[33] In return for this financial assistance, no separate peace with Napoleon would be signed and Hanover would be restored to Great Britain. Another stipulation allowed British officers to accompany the operations of each Allied army. Cathcart signed an additional agreement with the Russians for London to cover the costs of 10,000 men of the German Legion.[34]

As for Sweden, on 21 June the British minister-plenipotentiary to Stockholm, Edward Thornton, relayed to Castlereagh the details of a discussion he had had with Bernadotte about "the measures to be taken by Great Britain and by Sweden in concert, in case the present armistice should be terminated by a pacification between Russia and France, to the exclusion of the two former powers." Although Thornton guaranteed Castlereagh that he had received assurances from numerous officials as well as from Bernadotte himself that nothing in particular had moved the Swedish crown prince to raise the subject, the memory of Tilsit and Franco-Russian rapprochement still lingered. Thornton forwarded Bernadotte's suggestion that the size of the Anglo-Swedish force in North Germany be increased to 50,000 men with a view "to cooperate with Russia and Prussia at the close of the armistice, but also with that of being able to act independently of those powers, in case they should make a separate peace." The crown prince assured Thornton that, should Russia conclude a separate peace with France, an Anglo-Swedish force of 50,000 men could reembark, take the island of Zealand, and there "carry on a successful war, in this or the succeeding campaign, even on the Continent, or at any rate present a point of union for any future struggles which might be made on the Continent for the liberties of Europe." According to Thornton, Bernadotte then proceeded to the heart of the matter, stating that "while Sweden should obtain by this measure the kingdom of Norway (without which it was impossible, he said, that he or the Swedish army could return to Sweden) Great Britain might keep the island of Zealand as a means for the restitution of Hanover at a future peace; and if that was not obtained, might possess it, with the neighboring islands in perpetuity." Although he remained silent on this subject during the conversation with Bernadotte, Thornton expressed to Castlereagh his personal support of the proposal, citing "the importance of Zealand to the security of Sweden and of the Baltic for England." Admitting the sensitivity of the subject, the British envoy nevertheless encouraged Castlereagh to consider the proposal. "It was, in fact," he wrote, "the first time that the Prince Royal spoke of it to me or before me with so much detail, sensible perhaps of the repugnance which I felt at entertaining such propositions at this particular moment, of which even the discussion is calculated to alienate and to embitter, though they cannot, in common political and military prudence, be too soon maturely considered and determined upon, at least in secret."[35]

In a second dispatch written on 21 June, Thornton alerted Castlereagh to a 7 June letter from Tsar Alexander to Bernadotte that explained the former's reasons for accepting the armistice. On Bernadotte's orders, the Swedish statesman Baron Gustaf af Wetterstedt shared the contents of the letter with Thornton.[36] With a hint of relief, he informed Castlereagh that, "from the views taken in that letter of the motives of the armistice, and of the determination of the courts of Prussia and Russia to take the first opportunity of declaring it broken, it is not to be thought that there exists any intention of coming to a congress for the purpose of a general, and still less of a separate pacification; and the gentleman who showed me this letter ... was earnest to impress this opinion on me, for the sake of its being imparted to his Majesty's Government." Although the French took "for granted" the meeting of a congress for further negotiations, Thornton assured Castlereagh that "nothing in the Russian correspondence quite warrants them to draw this conclusion." Nevertheless, he did not rule out the possibility of a peace congress. Moreover, he warned that Bernadotte harbored "a very great distrust and jealousy" of the tsar that would not be "easy entirely to eradicate." Thornton hoped to "soften it as not to let it interfere with the most cordial cooperation (if cooperation is intended), which is as much as can be done at present."

As noted, Bernadotte requested a meeting with Alexander but at the time Thornton penned his report no answer had arrived. Should the Russian monarch decline, Thornton feared "the distrust w[ould] be almost irremovable; and all the movements, even on a renewal of hostilities, w[ould] be calculated on a latent idea of the possibility of being abandoned." He explained that the failure of both the Russian and the Prussian courts to give "the very earliest intimation of the first proposition by the French of an armistice is another ground of mistrust, which has really been of great injury to the cause." As proof that the negotiations for an armistice had been underway for some time, Bernadotte explained to Thornton his belief that all French operations had been based on the certainty of an armistice being concluded on a specific date. According to Thornton's report on this conversation, "Hamburg was pressed with that sole view: and the Prince declared that Oudinot (the Duke of Reggio) had orders to get possession of Berlin, even at the expense of half his corps, because an armistice, dating its dispositions from 8 June, at midnight, would have left this capital, as well as Hamburg, in possession of the French." Thanks to Bülow's victory over Oudinot at Luckau on 6 June, the French had failed to reach Berlin. Yet Bernadotte assured Thornton that the important city of Hamburg likewise would have remained in Allied hands during the armistice "if the Prince Royal, by being apprised of an intended armistice, could have seized Hamburg by the sudden advance of a considerable force."[37]

Castlereagh reacted to Bernadotte's concerns by upping Great Britain's ante in North Germany and dispatching all spare regiments to Stralsund. Including artillery and cavalry, he estimated these reinforcements to number 5,000 men. Moreover, he authorized Thornton to expand the German Legion from 10,000 to 15,000 combatants. An arms depot with 20,000 to 30,000 stands would be established at Stralsund which the Russians and Prussians could also draw from as soon as they exhausted the 70,000 stands shipped to Kolberg.[38] Nevertheless, Great Britain could not provide an endless supply of war materiel. "As our supplies are becoming scarce," Castlereagh informed Cathcart, "we must not let them lie idle in the magazines of our Allies – they must now be spared only upon an actual need that is proven to exist, and in their distribution, relative claims must be weighed upon principles of military efficiency."[39]

Stewart also finalized the subsidy treaty first negotiated with the Swedes on 3 March to insure that Bernadotte would not seek a friend in Napoleon. Although the Swedish contribution during the Spring Campaign was negligible, the British accepted Bernadotte's claim of logistical and financial hardship. They agreed to a £1,000,000 subsidy for 30,000 Swedes to fight on the continent, naval support in Sweden's war against Denmark for Norway, and the acquisition of the island of Guadeloupe. Moreover, Russia and Prussia pledged to support the 30,000 Swedes with 35,000 Russians and 27,000 Prussians – no strings attached. Such a commitment to Bernadotte's army excited Castlereagh: "It has occurred to me that, in the event of hostilities recommencing, and the Prince Royal advancing, the Northern operation may become a great feature, and essentially interesting to Prussia." At the same time, concern that Bernadotte would remain idle just as he had done in the Spring Campaign prompted Castlereagh to suggest that Stewart join the crown prince's headquarters after hostilities resumed; Cathcart would remain with Allied Headquarters. Castlereagh mentioned to Stewart that General Alexander Hope believed that the crown prince "would be glad to have you with him, and to lean on your advice and support. Of course this could only be done with perfect concurrence of the King of Prussia; but it occurs to me that, as his Majesty cannot well in person superintend the Prince Royal's operations, the King of Prussia might find a particular advantage in having you with him to animate his exertions, and to direct them as far as possible in the spirit of his policy and interests." This set the stage for Charles Stewart to be assigned to Bernadotte's headquarters during the Fall Campaign.[40] Despite his presence, Allied military operations in North Germany would be held hostage by the Swedish prince royal.[41]

Meanwhile, the Allies continued their councils of war after Toll returned to Reichenbach with the Gitschin Agreement. Comprehensive plans flowed in from many sources, including three from Bernadotte, all of which concerned a neutral Austria. Bernadotte's desire to be placed at the head of the strongest Russo-Prussian army provided the common thread in all three of his proposals. If Austria entered the war on the side of the Allies, the Austrian army would act as an "auxiliary corps" in Bohemia and proceed accordingly.[42] Moreover, he did not advise seizing the offensive against Napoleon himself but instead advocated conducting the war against his rearward communication with France, liberating Hamburg and Lübeck, conquering Holstein and Westphalia, invading Denmark, and sparking revolt in Holland and Belgium. Thus, his plans sought to avoid an encounter with his former master by operating on the lower Elbe, the lower Weser, and the lower Rhine. His proposals attracted little interest at Reichenbach.[43]

Despite Bernadotte's bloviating, a pessimistic 20 June memorandum by Frederick William's adjutant-general, Colonel Karl Friedrich von dem Knesebeck, influenced Allied Headquarters by introducing the concept of a third Allied army and proposing an Austria-first strategy. One of the best-educated officers in the Prussian army, Knesebeck served as Frederick William's "strategist," and Alexander also held his military opinions "in high esteem."[44] Major Rudolf Friederich, whose three-volume study of the Fall Campaign led to his appointment as chief of Military Historical Section II of Germany's Great General Staff in 1908, describes Knesebeck thus:

> He belonged to a school of strategy that based its ideas of warfare on the latter stages of the Seven Years War, particularly the warfare waged by Prince Henry's army in which strategy was reduced to a scientific formula based in part on geography and in part on mathematics. He had studied the wars of

CAROLUS XIV IOANNES.
Rex Suecia; Norvegie.

3 Jean-Baptiste Bernadotte, Charles XIV John of Sweden, 1763–1844

the French Revolution with care and also followed Napoleon's feats of arms with thoroughness, without ever being completely clear on the real causes of the successes of this man. By nature tending to be extremely cautious, pessimistic, and pusillanimous, he sought the decisive moment by avoiding battle against Napoleon; ambiguous ideas on the influence of geographic conditions and strategic lines, which mastered so many of the excellent officers of that time, determined his view of the situation, and he believed that the same fundamental beliefs were also accepted by Napoleon, and so it was that he ascribed plans to the enemy that were the farthest from the minds of French commanders.[45]

With a captive audience, Knesebeck's memo began with an overview of available field forces for both sides: 390,000 men for the Allies and a total of 270,000 for Napoleon with 150,000 spread east from Dresden to the neutral zone in Silesia and the remaining 120,000 at Würzburg. As for theaters, Knesebeck urged the Allies to consider the Danube valley: "A look at the map shows that the extended line of the Danube falls right in the middle of the French forces; pursue a war on this river and France will fall much easier than pursuing a war on the Elbe and the Oder. Indeed, one can add that a war on these latter rivers would be possible only through a shift in French forces, where a war on the Danube itself moves them back to their natural tracks. Austria's entry into the Coalition again brings France back to its natural theater of war." He speculated that, as soon as Austria declared against him, Napoleon would transfer the theater of war either to Bohemia or to the Danube valley, therefore directing his main blow against Austria. To invade Bohemia, his main force could follow the course of the Elbe while the secondary army advanced from Würzburg through Eger (Cheb) or Pilsen (Plzeň). Conversely, Napoleon could shift forces so that his main army marched from Würzburg through München and Passau to reach the Danube's right bank and then head straight to Vienna. The troops north of Bohemia would support this movement by inundating Austrian territory from Dresden and Zittau.

"In both cases," continued Knesebeck, "he will attack the Austrian army with superior forces. A mere auxiliary corps in Bohemia will not suffice, one must see in the course of the armistice 130,000 to 140,000 men (i.e. the entire army standing in Silesia) march to Bohemia. Czaslau [Čáslav] or Prague, each according to time and situation, might be chosen as the point of union." Knesebeck then called for a third Allied army – "the Combined Army of the North" – to immediately advance from Berlin to Dresden or Leipzig "while in Silesia the Landwehr battalions and the strongly occupied fortresses must suffice." In his opinion, the best case for the Allies but the least likely to unfold would be if Napoleon turned against the Russians and Prussians in Silesia with his main army and against the Austrians with his secondary army. This would require the Allies "to advance from Brandenburg, Silesia, and Bohemia against the enemy's main army, which would be on the Elbe or in Lusatia or in Silesia." If the Allies quickly executed these movements so that their armies could cooperate within a few days, Knesebeck predicted that "victory [would be] very probable. However, it should not be assumed that Napoleon will place himself in this position, nor is he likely to proceed against Berlin."

Knesebeck concluded by suggesting that, as soon as Austria declared war, the main Russo-Prussian army in Silesia "rush" to Bohemia and unite with the Austrians. He assigned the Combined Army of the North the task of advancing toward Dresden to operate against Napoleon's left flank and communications. Referencing Bernadotte's plans, Knesebeck cautioned against an eccentric operation in North Germany by the Combined Army. Instead, it should always seek to move as close as possible to the main Allied army in Bohemia:

> If all powers devote strength, unity, decisiveness, goodwill, and resolve to such an operation, the outcome of the campaign could be successful for the Allies. In the opposite case, one can expect no favorable results, even if Austria participates in the war. The mere addition of this power means more forces, but does not secure success. Only the march to Bohemia, executed in a

timely fashion during the course of the armistice, makes it possible to start operations with a successful offensive; its objective is the French army that stands on the Elbe; against Würzburg the defensive can be maintained. Indeed, even if it does not again come to war, such a union of the Allies would have the greatest influence on the peace negotiations. It would militarily and politically impress Napoleon. In any case this operation is so necessary that one can say that the fate of Europe depends on it; only this can save Austria.[46]

Although he granted the Allies a numerical superiority of 120,000 men, Knesebeck viewed Austria as seriously threatened; in his opinion, saving Austria had to be the Coalition's primary responsibility. Rather than Barclay's proposal of 25,000 men, he advocated sending the entire Russo-Prussian army to Bohemia. He accepted that this step would grant Austria both military and political leadership of the Allied war effort and in return Russia and Prussia should show "goodwill and determination." While his plan contained offensive elements, it surrendered the initiative to Napoleon, allowing the emperor to concentrate his troops at any point and direct them anywhere. An unexpected positive result did emerge from Knesebeck's plan and subsequent lobbying: making "the fate of Europe" solely dependent on the salvation of Austria increased the willingness of Kaiser Francis and the Austrian General Staff to join the Coalition.[47]

The idea of a third Allied army resonated in two separate plans submitted to Frederick William by Prussian officers – Karl Leopold von Borstell, and Bülow along with Hermann von Boyen of the General Staff. Both plans discount Austria's participation, meaning that Napoleon would direct his main offensive against Berlin and North Germany. Similar to Napoleon's own "master plan," they envision an offensive through Berlin to Stettin (Szczecin) with 150,000 men. Up to this point, the protection of Brandenburg and Berlin had not figured in Allied war planning. Toll did not consider a French offensive to the north because he understood Napoleonic warfare: Napoleon would force a decisive battle in Silesia or Saxony. In his narrow, Austria-first view, Knesebeck likewise did not give thought to Brandenburg or the Baltic coast. Nevertheless, to protect North Germany and thwart an operation to reach the Oder, the Borstell and Bülow/Boyen plans suggested that all Allied forces found between the lower Elbe and the lower Vistula should be concentrated. They wanted this army placed in the hands of a field commander vested with unlimited authority, "who lives large and exalted only in the promotion of the general cause, subordinating everything to the success of the war and the understanding to act independently." Although they would come to regret it, the Prussians proposed Bernadotte as their man.

Neither plan carried enough clout to impact Allied High Command at Reichenbach, yet they did influence Frederick William.[48] The Prussians knew that, according to the 1812 Convention of Åbo, the tsar had agreed to provide a Russian auxiliary corps to support the Swedes in North Germany. They also knew that the Russians fell far short of providing the numbers Alexander had promised. As a result, Bernadotte did not take part in the Spring Campaign. Instead of viewing his idleness as grounds for suspicion, Frederick William believed that the Allies could count on Bernadotte's active participation if they placed him at the head of significant forces. Both Toll's plan and the Gitschin Agreement envisioned Bülow's corps operating as a completely independent unit. "Anxiously conscientious and devoted to agreements," the king wanted to place Bülow as well as the small Russian units already in North Germany under Bernadotte's command. In this way, Bernadotte would have no reason to be discontented. Based on Frederick William's arguments, the Russians revisited the idea of dividing all Allied forces. Both monarchs rejected the earlier idea found in Toll's plan as well as the Gitschin Agreement of dividing Allied forces between Silesia and Bohemia, whereby Berlin would be guarded only by weak detachments. Instead, they accepted Knesebeck's proposal that all Allied forces be divided between Bohemia and Brandenburg with two-thirds posted in the former and one-third in the latter.

Political considerations snapped the Prussians back to reality. It mattered little whether the Allies posted their main army in Bohemia, Silesia, or Brandenburg because Napoleon could not ignore it; he eventually would confront it with his main force. However, if the Allies assembled two-thirds of all their forces in Bohemia, the position of commander in chief would be placed in the hands of an Austrian general. Posted in Brandenburg, the remaining third would be commanded by the crown prince of Sweden in part, ironically, due to Prussian insistence. This meant that Prussia, the state fighting for its very existence, would have little influence on the conduct of the war. Instead, Austria and Sweden – two states that had thus far provided little proof that they deserved such responsibility – would direct the war. Although Alexander would be an omniscient force at Allied Headquarters, the Prussians realized that they could not place their fate in the hands of Metternich and Bernadotte. Consequently, the Allies drew up a compromise between Toll's plan and the various proposals submitted by Knesebeck, Borstell, and Bülow. A strong army under Bernadotte would be posted in Brandenburg while the Austrian army in Bohemia would be increased by two-thirds of the Russo-Prussian forces posted in Silesia. They calculated that enough forces would remain in Silesia to form a third army of some 55,000 men. This army would be placed under the command of a Prussian general, so that Prussia at least would have some influence on the course of operations. It is not clear who made these proposals but it is clear that they came from the Prussians. Likewise, it is certain that Alexander and his generals assessed and endorsed this plan, especially because an Allied army in Silesia could better cover Russian communications with Poland than the Landwehr battalions Knesebeck suggested. Little did the Allies know how crucial this decision would be for their war effort.

Sensing a drift toward war before all diplomatic efforts were exhausted, Kaiser Francis reeled in his generals and urged caution. On 26 June, the Prussian envoy to the Austrian camps at Prague and Brandeis, Colonel Karl Wilhelm von Grolman, reported to his king that Francis did not agree with a premature rupture of the armistice. Grolman did not receive an explanation and found that Austria's mobilization had progressed far enough to risk such a step. Moreover, the Austrians expressed concern that Napoleon would mask the Russo-Prussian army in Silesia and use the armistice to concentrate the bulk of his army on the left bank of the Elbe. In this way, he could immediately launch an offensive against Austria as soon as the armistice expired. Austria would then be forced to endure the entire weight of his attack until the Allies marched 155 miles from eastern Silesia to Dresden. Therefore, the Austrian generals requested that Wittgenstein's corps be assembled at Liebau (Lubawka) on the Austro-Prussian frontier to commence the march to Bohemia as soon as the armistice expired on 20 July. Lastly, the Austrians suggested that a powerful French offensive against Austria would require the union of *all* Allied armies in Bohemia. In such a scenario, the Allies could utilize three bridges over the Elbe at Leitmeritz, Raudnitz (Roudnice nad Labem), and Melnik (Mělník).[49]

Meanwhile, Austria's diplomatic maneuvering resulted in Metternich's meeting with the Russians and Prussians at Reichenbach to determine a minimum set of demands to present Napoleon as the price for a peace conference. By the time he left for Dresden on 24 June at Napoleon's invitation, Metternich had achieved a victory at the exclusion of the British and Swedes. The resulting Convention of Reichenbach authorized Metternich to present Napoleon the four points as the price for convening a preliminary peace conference. Should Napoleon refuse these conditions, Austria would join the Sixth Coalition with at least 150,000 men and fight for the harsher Allied peace terms as formulated by Hardenberg and Nesselrode in the Wurschen Convention of 16 May, mainly the dissolution of the Confederation of the Rhine and the restoration of Prussia to its full 1806 status. Moreover, if the war resumed, Russia and Prussia could demand further conditions for peace; again, the British and Swedes were not informed of the existence of the Reichenbach Convention.[50]

Metternich departed for Dresden believing he had fair terms to offer for the basis of a peace between the continental powers. Should Napoleon refuse, he could threaten him with a coalition consisting of all four powers. The famous nine-hour meeting between Napoleon and Metternich on 26 June fell far short of the Austrian minister's expectations. Metternich offered to end the war through negotiation, claiming that a peace settlement would preserve Napoleon's crown. In return, the Austrians demanded an independent and neutral Central Europe. After the French had driven the Allies from the Saale to the Oder in less than one month, Metternich's veiled threat enraged Napoleon. Calling Metternich a liar, he demanded that the Austrian reveal his government's true objective.[51] "So you want war? Well, you shall have it," screamed Napoleon. "I annihilated the Prussian army at Lützen; I smashed the Russians at Bautzen; now you want to have your turn. Very well – we shall meet at Vienna."[52]

Metternich's negotiations with Napoleon, which continued on 27, 28, and 29 June, revealed the futility of making any demands on the French emperor as a price for commencing peace negotiations. After four days of wrangling, Metternich completely dropped the four points of his minimum program. In this way, he managed to convince Napoleon to accept the Convention of Dresden on 30 June. Thus, Napoleon consented to an Austrian-led preliminary peace conference to convene at Prague on 5 July. Should this conference establish a preliminary settlement, a general congress would convene to establish continental peace. Not only did the Convention of Dresden ignore the stipulations of the Reichenbach Convention, but it also extended the armistice from 20 July to 10 August with a further six-day suspension of hostilities. In the hot seat, Stadion explained to the Allies that the extension was serving as a ploy to gain time for the Austrian army to complete its mobilization.[53] The peace conference began at Prague on 5 July with Baron Johann von Anstedt representing Russia and Wilhelm von Humboldt Prussia, but the chief French representative, Armand de Caulaincourt, did not arrive until the 28th, thus revealing Napoleon's ultimate indifference to the meeting's success. As Cathcart wrote, "He was too aware that for him, personally, the end of war could not be peace. The demon he had unchained and let lose upon the world, if deprived of its prey, would have turned inevitably in vengeance on the hand which should attempt to curb it."[54]

From the Austrian viewpoint, Metternich's failure to impose the four points on Napoleon signaled the improbability of a negotiated peace. Consequently, Vienna moved closer to the Russians and Prussians, who reluctantly accepted Stadion's explanations. Joining the Coalition and fighting France in a fifth war since 1792 seemed likely for Austria.[55] Yet as of 3 July, "the prospects of gaining Austria" as an ally appeared bleak to the British and Swedes. Thornton reported that, despite the tsar's upcoming visit with Francis at Gitschin, "the Emperor of Austria is not to be gained to a hostile declaration against France by any inducements that Russia and Prussia can at present offer to him." After the details of Metternich's minimum peace plan became known, the situation only worsened. Thornton described the four points as containing "the most unpalatable conditions of peace." Although he predicted that Napoleon would ultimately reject them, Thornton still faulted Metternich: "instead of acting upon them, [he] retrenches, modifies, and retouches them, in order to render them more palatable to Bonaparte. This is the conduct of a power seeking reconciliation, rather than justifiable grounds for a declaration of hostilities." Thornton hoped that Bernadotte, who planned to meet with Alexander and Frederick William at Trachenberg, "might have influence enough to encourage the two Allied courts to continue the war, and to draw Austria into it by an application to her fears, since every other motive is ineffectual." According to his Russian opposite at Bernadotte's headquarters, Carl Andreas Pozzo di Borgo, Alexander would have to threaten to make a separate peace with Napoleon to force Francis into the war. "It is evident that Austria dreads as much a peace between the Allied courts and France, to which she is not a party, as a hostile declaration against the latter."[56]

Regarding Sweden, Bernadotte could hardly contain himself after learning that the tsar had accepted Metternich's four points, which said nothing of Sweden receiving Norway. Nesselrode attempted to explain that the subject could not be broached "without giving France a right of interfering in a business already decided." Thornton claimed that, despite the "force and justice" of Nesselrode's reasoning, the neglect of Sweden's interests "has once more mortified the Prince Royal, and he has expressed himself to me upon it, and upon the want of attention to the interests of Great Britain, with a great deal of warmth." To calm him, Thornton observed that, in declining the Austrian mediation, Great Britain could not expect Metternich to champion the interests of George III. In the case of Sweden, he asserted that reminding Napoleon of Denmark's interests "by having the claims of Sweden put forward" might not be the best way for Bernadotte to attain his prize.[57] At the least, Bernadotte could take comfort in the fact that he would meet with Alexander at Trachenberg.

Metternich's twists and turns along with troubling reports from the British envoys in Central Europe caused much trepidation at London. On 30 June, Castlereagh instructed Cathcart "to endeavor to bring the court of Vienna to a private explanation of its views. It is not for Great Britain to goad other powers into exertions which they deem inconsistent with their own safety; but ... we should know on what we have to reckon. The rapid progress of the British arms in Spain will, I trust, prove that we are not disposed to be inactive."[58] On 6 July, he described the renewal of hostilities, with Austria fighting against France, "as the safest policy for Europe in the long run." Yet Castlereagh feared that "impracticability on our part" could lead to a Franco-Austrian rapprochement which in turn would produce a general peace that ignored British interests "notwithstanding our treaties." He insisted that Cathcart avow London's "readiness to treat with our Allies ... [so] that they have no reproach to make against us. The great practical question is a renewal of hostilities or a prolongation of armistice.

If the accomplishment of a reasonably solid peace, through negotiation, is not clear, *hesitation* in recurring to hostilities will damp and disunite the confederacy, and the resources of the Allies will be wasted in inactivity; better in that case try the fate of war for the remainder of the campaign, and let future policy be governed by the result."

Coming when British interests seemed so neglected by the Eastern powers, Wellington's 21 June victory over Joseph Bonaparte at Vitoria appeared to provide London with much-needed leverage.[59] "The recent successes in Spain have put us on strong ground," Castlereagh explained to Cathcart on 6 July. "We can now with honor evince a disposition to concur with our Continental Allies in negotiations; having done so, we shall act on our own part with more effect, if fortune and friends should forsake us. Lord Wellington's successes may now give us the title to treat for our Allies, the Spaniards, with the possession of the Peninsula on our side; to hazard such an advantage by showing a reluctance to negotiate, while Russia and Prussia are negotiating under the Austrian mediation, could not be borne out as a line of separate policy." Despite Metternich's efforts to ignore the British, Castlereagh recognized the importance of maintaining at least the semblance of a united coalition against Napoleon. "The risk of treating with France is great, but the risk of losing our Continental Allies and the confidence of our own nation is greater. We must preserve our own faith inviolate to Spain, Portugal, Sicily, and Sweden."[60] Still, Castlereagh believed a coalition consisting of Great Britain, Russia, Prussia, and Sweden could defeat Napoleon in Central Europe. As for Austria, on 28 July[61] he expressed his hope to Cathcart that "Lord Wellington's progress and victory will have animated the councils at Trachenberg, and induced Austria to take a more decisive tone. Of all the Powers, Austria will be the first sacrifice of an inadequate arrangement; and if, with the present means assembled against France, she cannot erect an adequate barrier for her own preservation, she ought never to have emerged from her servile relations to Buonaparte."[62]

Alexander's upcoming meeting with Bernadotte provided an opportunity to finalize a plan of operations. Thus, the Allied monarchs called a conference at the estate near Trachenberg belonging to Prussian general Franz Ludwig von Hatzfeldt. The Russian and Prussian monarchs arrived around noon on 9 July; the crown prince of Sweden and his entourage shortly after midnight. Talks on the 10th focused on diplomacy. Bernadotte came to Trachenberg convinced that Austria would not join the Coalition. Instead, he believed Francis would remain neutral while the other powers cannibalized themselves in a bloody struggle. He predicted that the Austrians would enter the war at the last moment to play the main role at the peace table. Backed by his fresh legions, Francis would win the lion's share of the spoils. Alexander and Frederick William sought to reconcile the prince royal, assuring him that they at least intended to renew the war with

Napoleon. Although pleased by these statements, Bernadotte received no satisfactory answer regarding their thoughts on Austria. Hoping the Allies had received a written pledge from Francis to join the Sixth Coalition, he learned to his dismay that they had not. Instead, Alexander shared a letter from Francis promising war should Napoleon reject any of the four points contained in the Convention of Reichenbach, which the Convention of Dresden had already rendered worthless. Moreover, neither monarch thought it prudent to reveal the terms of the Reichenbach Convention to Bernadotte. Instead, they made a poor attempt to portray Metternich's verbal duel with Napoleon as proof of Austria's goodwill. Despite "winning the favor of both monarchs in the shortest time," neither Frederick William nor Alexander could change Bernadotte's opinion.[63]

Ultimately, two meetings with Stadion that lasted for several hours on 11 July managed to allay the crown prince's deep mistrust of the Habsburgs. Initially reserved, he became more relaxed as the Austrian envoy explained his state's certain path to war with Napoleon. Bernadotte then turned the conversation to Norway, stating that he came not to save Central Europe as Gustavus Adolphus had in the seventeenth century, but only to gain Norway for Sweden; he demanded to know where Austria stood on the matter. Informed by the tsar of Bernadotte's displeasure with Metternich for omitting the issue of Norway in his discussions with Napoleon, Stadion strummed the right chords. He explained that Metternich had not mentioned the issue because Austria considered the affair to be between Great Britain and the Scandinavian states. At a general European peace congress rather than the preliminary conference convening at Prague, Sweden's interests would be ranked alongside those of the other powers. Should the Prague conference fail to bring about conditions for a general peace congress, Austria would join the Sixth Coalition. Stadion pledged that Vienna would abide by the agreements Stockholm made with Russia and Prussia to support Sweden's claim to Norway. Although Stadion had no authority to make such guarantees, Bernadotte appeared very satisfied.

Later on the 11th, Toll, Knesebeck, the Dutch-born Russian general and diplomat Jan Pieter van Suchtelen, and the chief of staff of the Russian Army General Pyotr Volkonsky represented the Allies in a council of war with Bernadotte and Swedish general Curt Stedingk. Due to Stadion's success, Bernadotte agreed that Napoleon would direct his first attack against Austria. In this case, he vowed to conduct an energetic advance from North Germany to cross the Elbe and reach Dresden as soon as possible. If the Allied army in Silesia advanced through Lusatia "or on the most direct road toward the enemy," he held Napoleon to be as good as lost. Bernadotte urged the Allies "to advance with energy, without being delayed by maneuvers, calculations, and those fallacies of military science that through wavering reservations so often confound the surest and best-laid plans."[64]

Toll also presented his plan along with the ideas contained in the Gitschin Agreement. Bernadotte purportedly responded with shouts of *"très bien! C'est très vrai."* To allow for the freedom of discussion, neither Alexander nor Frederick William participated in the talks on the 11th. Stadion did not attend any of the general meetings, which indicates that the Trachenberg conference sought to establish agreement between the Russians, Prussians, British, and Swedes rather than draft a final plan of operations.[65] In particular, the Russians and Prussians wanted to assign the crown prince a specific task and place at his disposal the necessary forces to accomplish it. Müffling provides insight into the tsar's interest in cultivating Bernadotte as a means to smooth relations between Sweden and Russia after the latter had not fulfilled the promises made at Åbo: "The tsar required his cooperation in settling relations between Russia and Sweden; and this was sufficient reason for us to endeavor to satisfy the crown prince to the extent that the tsar would have confidence in him and thus be able to employ his forces outside the Russian Empire and against Napoleon to the advantage of his allies, and be able to advance to the Rhine without apprehension for his own states. From our proceedings, the crown prince discovered that the fortunate moment had placed him in a position to make large demands."[66]

The stars seemed to align for the crown prince of Sweden on 11 July. That night, the tsar promised Bernadotte that he would break diplomatic relations with Denmark. Conversely, the crown prince accepted advice from Alexander and Frederick William to demonstrate good faith toward Austria by approving the continuation of the armistice. Bernadotte likewise declined an indirect invitation to participate in the Prague conference on the grounds that the agenda did not include Norway and that he did not want to offend the British, who had not sent an envoy to Prague. In military matters, Bernadotte learned that evening that, should the war resume, his "army" would receive one Russian corps numbering 22,000 men and more than 40,000 Prussians. Combined with his 30,000 Swedes and the 20,000 men of German and Hanseatic Legions, Bernadotte would command well over 100,000 men. This news more than satisfied his vanity.[67] "There is no denying that the crown prince is an engaging and intelligent gentleman," said Frederick William to his adjutant, Wilhelm Ludwig Viktor Henckel von Donnersmarck, shortly before breakfast on the 12th.[68]

Before noon on 12 June, Stadion delivered a response from Kaiser Francis to a letter penned by Bernadotte on 23 May. Although filled with phrases to flatter the prince royal, Francis assured him that, "animated by an equal spirit of benevolence," both Austria and Sweden would fight for the "common rights of all states." He explained that these views "dictate the efforts I am making through negotiations and, if they should fail, then through arms to achieve a state of peace, which is Europe's primary need.

The latest information I have received from the headquarters of Their Majesties the Tsar of Russia and the King of Prussia brought me the greatest pleasure by giving me the hope that the obstacles that seemed opposed to the cooperation of the forces under Your Royal Majesty's command have been removed. I regard this cooperation as one of the strongest supports for the cause of the powers, which may again have to be defended by a war that does not stand a chance of success unless supported by the greatest means and especially the greatest unity."[69]

Stadion also related the latest intelligence from Dresden courtesy of the snooping Bubna: news of Wellington's victory at Vitoria and the headlong flight of Joseph's army caused chaos at the French emperor's headquarters. A very reliable source confided to Bubna that the retreat of Joseph's army to the mountains of Pamplona could be compared to Napoleon's retreat from Moscow. For damage control, Napoleon immediately dispatched Marshal Jean-de-Dieu Soult to Spain to take command. Napoleon's figurehead foreign minister, Hugues-Bernard Maret, confided to Bubna that the Allies should soon expect to learn "of the evacuation of Madrid" and "of great concentrations" of French forces in the Biscay region of northeastern Spain. Thornton maintained that the news of Wellington's victory would influence the Austrians to take heed of Anglo-Swedish interests: "this is visible" he concluded, "in the answer of the Kaiser to the Crown Prince, which came today from Austrian headquarters." Euphoric at this news, the Swedish crown prince told Thornton that Wellington's victory probably would induce Napoleon to withdraw his forces from Silesia and move his army closer to the Rhine.[70] Bernadotte went as far as to say:

> If the results, which can be easily foreseen, soon arise, it cannot be doubted that they will provide Napoleon with even more reason to withdraw the majority of his troops behind the Elbe, perhaps to the upper Main to Würzburg and Bamberg and to attack us in Bohemia; this would be a decision of desperation, which for the emperor of the French inevitably must be disastrous, especially if he ventures too far and reaches the vicinity of Vienna. In this case, the Allies need only to march on him from the various directions where they are located. Some 60,000 to 80,000 Russians united with the Bohemian army would suffice to stop the French or even defeat them and secure the fruits of their victory. With 80,000 to 100,000 men, he [Bernadotte] himself would then march against the rear of the enemy as the troops in Silesia marched against his flank ... Thus, the French would find themselves in a desperate situation, and the center of the Austrian monarchy would be the grave of the great Napoleon and his boundless power outside the borders of France.[71]

Although Bernadotte could not have been happier, the kaiser's letter still managed to earn Thornton's suspicion.[72] He informed Castlereagh that, according to Bubna, Napoleon had accepted the extension of the armistice from 20 July to 10 August only so he could better assess the situation in Spain after Vitoria. Because Bubna learned that the reinforcements Napoleon expected from Spain would reach him before 20 July, Thornton speculated that gaining "time to divide the Allies, to accede to the modified bases of pacification proposed by Austria," represented Napoleon's true motive for extending the armistice. Thornton believed that the Russians and Prussians ultimately would reject Metternich's four points rather than base a general European peace on them, but "such an acceptance on the part of Bonaparte is calculated to put the cooperation of Austria to some hazard, unless she be fully determined to have recourse to arms. It is from that point, more than from any other, that danger is now to be apprehended."[73]

Later in the day, the council of war reconvened in the presence of Alexander and Frederick William. Seated between the two monarchs, Bernadotte took the lead role, making statements similar to those he had made to Stadion and presenting specific proposals. After his adjutant-general, Karl Löwenhjelm, read a written memorandum, he summarized his proposals verbally:

(1) Three armies, the Grand or Bohemian Army, the Silesian, and the Northern, should maneuver so that the enemy was not in a position to attack one of them with all his forces.
(2) Therefore, these armies should operate at a distance from each other that allowed them to support each other so that the enemy was not in a position to attack one of them with his main force.
(3) If Napoleon's main force attacks, the target must withdraw while the other two armies attack the enemy's line of communication so that he will always be threatened in his flank and rear.
(4) The main force of the Allied armies should threaten the flanks and interrupt the enemy's line of operation.
(5) All should avoid decisive battles and instead maneuver to exhaust the enemy. But if the enemy is divided, he should be attacked.[74]

As in June, Bernadotte's military proposals again failed to attract the interest of the Russians and Prussians. With all his experience as a marshal of France, it is surprising how little the crown prince's five points reflected Napoleon's art of war. Instead, true fear of his former master mastered his thoughts. Insuring that under no circumstance would he have to face Napoleon alone remained Bernadotte's ultimate objective. Although far from the principles that the Allies had formally accepted at Trachenberg, the crown prince's ideas closely resembled the campaign plans being prepared in Bohemia by Radetzky.

Following this final discussion, Knesebeck, Volkonsky, and Swedish general Löwenhjelm signed the Trachenberg Protocol for their respective states. Russian general Hans Karl von Diebitsch immediately departed to deliver a copy to Kaiser Francis at Brandeis-Altbunzlau (Brandýs nad Labem-Stará Boleslav). The Allies took great pains to keep the Protocol secret but unconfirmed rumors later spread that a copy had been smuggled to Napoleon. Knesebeck claimed credit for designing the decisive plan and for prevailing over the crown prince after vigorous debate. Toll did as well, but for a long time public opinion regarded the crown prince of Sweden as the sole author. Basically, the issue is moot. The Trachenberg Protocol included ideas from earlier drafts made by Toll, Barclay, Radetzky, Knesebeck, Boyen, and Bernadotte so that the whole was a compromise of the views of these men and the interests of the three countries and armies they represented.

According to the Protocol, the Allies would open the campaign with three field armies. This decision arose more from the Coalition's political concerns than from strategic planning. Austria's position remained vital: only with the Austrians could the Allies achieve numerical superiority over the French and their allies. Therefore, the Coalition needed to protect the Austrian heartland, particularly Bohemia. A French offensive into the Austrian interior that led to a separate peace between Kaiser Francis and Napoleon would be devastating for the Russians and Prussians. Based on this consideration, a large Allied army capable of both defending Bohemia as well as executing offensive operations would be organized in Bohemia. Meanwhile, the alliance with Great Britain and Sweden as well as with the North German states such as Mecklenburg necessitated the posting of another considerable Allied force in Brandenburg and along the lower Elbe to maintain communication with Stralsund and Kolberg and to protect North Germany from imperial forces at Lübeck and Hamburg. Finally, the Allies deemed they needed a third army to cover Silesia and secure communications with Russia. Consequently, the Coalition formed the Bohemian, North German, and Silesian Armies. A fourth army – the 50,000 men assembling on the lower Vistula to form General Levin August von Bennigsen's Russian Reserve Army, later dubbed the Army of Poland – would either reinforce the Army of Silesia if Napoleon conducted his main offensive in that province or secure Poland should it be invaded.[75]

For the Allied army in Bohemia to be strong enough to both protect the province and conduct offensive operations, a portion of the Russo-Prussian army in Silesia, "90,000 to 100,000 men," would march a few days before the expiration of the armistice through Landeshut (Kamienna Góra) and Glatz (Kłodzko) to unite with 120,000 Austrians at Jungbunzlau (Mladá Boleslav) and Brandeis-Altbunzlau northeast of Prague to form the Army of Bohemia.[76] Also referred to as the Hauptarmee (main army) or Grand Army, this force of 200,000 to 220,000 soldiers[77] would serve as the Coalition's version of Napoleon's Grande Armée by virtue of the presence of the three Allied monarchs and their accompanying Guard formations. Bernadotte received command of the second Allied army: the Army of North Germany. While a corps of 15,000–20,000 soldiers took a position on the lower Elbe to observe the Franco-Danish forces at Lübeck and Hamburg, approximately 70,000 men would assemble south of Berlin around Treuenbrietzen. According to the Protocol, Bernadotte would "cross the Elbe between Torgau and Magdeburg, and then march on Leipzig without delay."

The third Allied force, the new Army of Silesia, would consist of the 50,000 Russo-Prussian troops that remained in the province after the departure of the "90,000 to 100,000 men" to Bohemia. Moreover, it would consist of both Russians and Prussians as opposed to the army assigned to Blücher in late May, which contained only Prussian units. The 12 July meeting ended before the Allies named a commander for the Army of Silesia. Müffling maintains that, in addition to his own Army of North Germany, Bernadotte actually requested command of the Silesian Army. Moreover, he wanted General Bogislav Friedrich von Tauentzien's Prussian IV Corps assigned to the Army of North Germany. "These demands were too great," recalled Müffling, "and could not be conceded by the sovereigns. The extension of the armistice from 20 July to 10 August with an ensuing six-day suspension of hostilities minimized the immediate need to name a commander for the Silesian Army. Nevertheless, Alexander and Frederick William wanted Bernadotte to leave Trachenberg satisfied, and so admitted that circumstances might occur that rendered it necessary for him to assume command of Tauentzien's corps as well as the Silesian Army." By the end of the armistice, Bernadotte had achieved his goal in regards to Tauentzien's corps, and he would not forget the promise made to him concerning the Silesian Army.[78]

As for operations, the Bohemian Army either would invade Bavaria through Eger and Hof, or move north into Saxony or northeast to Silesia, or debouch south toward the Danube depending on the circumstances. Should Napoleon invade Bohemia, Bernadotte would drive "as fast as possible in forced marches" against his rear. If Napoleon turned against the crown prince, the Bohemian Army would operate against his communications to force him to deliver a battle. As for the "Allied army in Silesia," the plan stipulated that it would pursue the imperial forces in Silesia to the Elbe, avoiding a general battle unless under extremely favorable conditions. It would cross the Elbe between Torgau and Dresden, and unite with the Army of North Germany to provide a total of 120,000 men for Bernadotte's operations. Although not directly stated in the Protocol, such a union would place the Silesian Army under his command. However, should the Bohemian Army require reinforcements before the Army of Silesia joined the North German Army, the Silesian

Army would march "without delay" to Bohemia. These stipulations would also not be forgotten.

In general, the Trachenberg Protocol called for the three Allied armies to form a wide arc around the imperial forces in Saxony and Silesia. Yet nothing is stated in the Protocol about retreating ahead of Napoleon's onslaught. Nor does the document contain any statements about attacking detached French corps while avoiding the emperor's main force. In fact, the Protocol states exactly the opposite:

> It has been agreed to adopt as the general principle that all Allied forces will always go where the largest enemy forces are found. They will proceed in the following manner:
>
> (1) The corps that operate against the flanks and rear of the enemy must always choose the line that leads most directly to the enemy's line of operations.
> (2) The largest Allied force must choose a position that places it in a position to face the enemy wherever he wants to turn. The salient bastion of Bohemia seems advantageous for this.

In its essence, the Trachenberg Protocol established four basic yet crucial tenets. First, all Allied forces would target the enemy's main force. Second, any Allied corps maneuvering against the enemy's rear and flanks should always seek the most direct route to strike the enemy's main line of operations. Third, the Allies should always position their main force to be able to make front in any direction taken by the enemy – the Protocol suggests Bohemia. Finally, "all Allied armies will seize the offensive, and the enemy camp shall be their rendezvous." Thus, the core principles of the Trachenberg Protocol reflect the main lessons of modern war taught by Napoleon: taking the initiative and targeting the enemy's main force.[79]

Following Russian, Prussian, and Swedish acceptance of the Trachenberg Protocol, the fate of the plan depended on Austrian approval. Yet the Austrians had ideas of their own. In a second memo drafted in June, Radetzky provided various offensive options for Napoleon and explained the best Austro-Allied responses. Napoleon's ability to allocate 180,000 to 200,000 men for use against the Austrians while still possessing enough manpower to mask Allied forces in Brandenburg and Silesia concerned Radetzky. To reinforce the Austrians, he sought 70,000 Russian reinforcements from the Russo-Prussian army in Silesia, yet lowered the size of the Austrian contingent to 80,000 men so that this combined Austro-Russian army would total only 150,000 soldiers. If Napoleon invaded Bohemia by way of the right bank of the Elbe, Radetzky suggested that the Austro-Russian army fight a defensive battle at the Polzen (Ploučnice) River near its confluence with the Elbe at Tetschen (Děčín). Radetzky predicted success as long as Bernadotte led his army from Brandenburg across the Elbe and south through Saxony toward Bohemia. Should Napoleon advance up the left bank of the Elbe – the operation Radetzky viewed as most likely – the Austro-Russian army would meet him at Saaz (Žatec) on the Eger River. Only in his third scenario – Napoleon's offensive against Berlin – did Radetzky approve an offensive for the Austro-Russian army down the left bank of the Elbe with the main effort directed at Chemnitz. Should Bernadotte survive the blow from his former master, Radetzky planned for the Austro-Russian army to continue its operations "by severing the enemy's communications." On the other hand, should Bernadotte's forces be destroyed, the Austro-Russian army would retreat across the Erzgebirge and behind the Eger. Radetzky's fourth option, which he considered least likely, pictured Napoleon remaining on the defensive astride both banks of the Elbe. Radetzky called for the Austro-Russian army to advance but predicted Napoleon would seek battle in the region of Marienberg to drive the Allied army's right away from the Erzgebirge.[80] Because of their proposal to base Allied operations on these principles of eighteenth-century warfare, it is difficult to defend the Austrians against the accusation that in the Napoleonic wars they neither learned anything nor forgot anything.

Yet a few days before the Allies met at Trachenberg, Radetzky drafted another plan of operations for Austro-Allied forces. Simply titled "Operationsentwurf" (Operations Outline), he submitted the plan to Schwarzenberg on 7 July, who forwarded it to Kaiser Francis on 12 July. Radetzky estimated the total strength of Coalition forces to number 405,000 men while Napoleon would field a total of 450,000 combatants. He maintained that Napoleon intended to concentrate his main force of 190,000 men on the Elbe. Radetzky understood that the French emperor would seek to deliver a massive first blow that would dissolve the Sixth Coalition just as his 1805 victory at Austerlitz had caused the end of the War of the Third Coalition. For Napoleon to achieve success, he needed to direct his first offensive against the Austrian army in Bohemia. Consequently, Radetzky believed that he would invade Bohemia with his main army of 190,000 men while the remainder of his forces conducted demonstrations against the Allied armies in Brandenburg and Silesia. Therefore, to reduce the number of men Napoleon could bring to bear on the Austrians, Radetzky called for immediate offensive operations by the Allied armies operating outside Bohemia. As for the Austrian army, Radetzky advised a "well-calculated defensive" until the other two Allied armies could "effect a separation of French forces."[81] This made perfect sense because at the time he drafted the "Operationsentwurf," Radetzky expected that only Wittgenstein's 25,000 Russians would reinforce the Austrian army in Bohemia. According to the Austrian staff chief, the fate of the Coalition depended on the Allied armies in Brandenburg and Silesia launching and conducting bold offensive operations as soon as the war resumed. Only by sustaining such operations could they force Napoleon to lessen his pressure on the

Austrians. In turn, the Austrians would be able to take the offensive and possibly unite with the other Allied armies to deliver a decisive battle against French forces, who would be exhausted from constant engagements. Radetzky viewed this strategy as the best chance for the Allies to gain the advantage over Napoleon.

Should Napoleon decide against invading Austria, Radetzky cited three possible courses that the French emperor could pursue. The first envisioned Napoleon leading his main force north against Bernadotte's army in Brandenburg. In this case, the crown prince would avoid the main blow until the other two Allied armies could unite and advance against the enemy. The second scenario called for Napoleon to seize the offensive against the Russo-Prussian army in Silesia. As in the first case, the threatened Allied army would avoid a decisive battle while Bernadotte's army and the Austrian army united and advanced. Third, Radetzky speculated that Napoleon could maintain a general defensive posture. In this case, both the Russo-Prussian army in Silesia and Bernadotte's army would seize the offensive while the Austrian army remained on the defensive. As soon as the Russo-Prussian army and Bernadotte's came within supporting distance, all three Allied armies would unite for a decisive battle.[82]

Thus, delivering a decisive blow with numerical superiority became the main objective of Radetzky's combined operations. To avoid compromising this main objective, he advised that no single Allied army accept battle with a force superior in number. To defeat Napoleon, the Austrian staff chief recommended a gradual escalation of minor engagements. Instead of an immediate offensive by all three Allied armies to seek a decisive battle, he suggested operations that would divide and incessantly harass French forces; the Allies should take the offensive only against points where the enemy appeared weak. Providing the quintessential Prusso-German analysis of the "Operationsentwurf," Friederich explains that "only when the French army was contained by the three Allied armies in a semicircle on both banks of the Elbe, fatigued by incessant back-and-forth marches, demoralized by the lack of physical and moral upkeep, when through defeats, hardships, and hunger it would be reduced in size so that it was no longer numerically superior to the Allies, only when that moment arrived according to Radetzky's view should all forces unite for a major blow." Conversely, Alan Sked argues that Radetzky's plan "deprived Napoleon of all his traditional advantages, [threw] him from the offensive to the defensive, and forced him into a number of choices, none of which was ideal. The strategy was to force Napoleon onto the defensive, leaving him to decide whether to move in strength and leave his communication lines open to attack or whether to divide his forces and march back and forth against one Allied army after another and exhaust his troops. Eventually, after encircling and wearing down Napoleon and pushing him back the three armies would come together with superior force and defeat him in a decisive encounter – exactly what happened at Leipzig."[83]

Few similarities can be found between Radetzky's "Operationsentwurf," which is better known as the Reichenbach Plan, and the Trachenberg Protocol. No mention is made in the Austrian plan of the Allies seizing the initiative through a general offensive.[84] Instead, Napoleon was free to operate as he pleased. Should he attack any Allied army and not just the army in Silesia, it should retreat and conduct a defensive until the two other armies could operate against his rear and flanks. The only point of convergence is the supposition that Napoleon would attack the Austrians first. While the Trachenberg Protocol embraced the main concept of Napoleonic warfare: the *Niederwerfungsstrategie* (strategy of annihilation), the Reichenbach Plan paid homage to the *Ermattungsstrategie* (strategy of attrition) of the eighteenth century. Where the Trachenberg Protocol required the Allies to take the initiative and target the enemy's main force, the Reichenbach Plan rejected the principle of bringing about a decision through a rapid, decisive blow with all forces. With respect to operations, the general principle of the Trachenberg Protocol was a vigorous offensive by all Allied armies, which would always advance against the enemy's main body; his camp would be their rendezvous. The idea was not to avoid battle, but to accept it with the confidence of receiving assistance from the other Allied armies. In contrast, the Reichenbach Plan sought to defeat the master of the operational art through slow-paced warfare with small means by threatening his lines of communication, operating against his rear and flanks, attacking his individual corps, and cutting off his supplies. This bias toward the strategy of attrition of the previous century dominated the Reichenbach Plan while the Trachenberg Protocol's strategy of annihilation – uniting all forces to deliver a decisive blow – was ignored.

On 16 July 1813, the Trachenberg Protocol arrived at Austrian headquarters. Although the Protocol called for the Austrian army to be reinforced by 90,000 to 100,000 Russians and Prussians, Radetzky made only minor changes to his "Operationsentwurf." After receiving the approval of both Schwarzenberg and Kaiser Francis, he sent it to Allied Headquarters at Reichenbach three days later. The bearer, Colonel Theodor Franz von Baillet de Latour, received the following instructions:

> The colonel is tasked with delivering the operations plan of the Austrian army in Bohemia to His Majesty the Tsar of All the Russias and to engage with him in its detail to which you will be instructed by His Majesty. Because this operations plan summarizes all suspected chances, only engage in the details of the following:

(1) The march of Wittgenstein's corps to this army.
(2) The operations. In respect of the same, in addition to the information contained in the Operations Plan, the following is still noted in particular:

If the enemy takes the offensive against the Austrian army along either the right or the left bank of the Elbe, the Russian and Prussian army will likewise take the offensive with all forces in the direction of Dresden; the same offensive will occur if the French army advances against the crown prince of Sweden.

If the emperor of the French takes the offensive with all his forces against the Imperial Russian and Royal Prussian Armies [in Silesia], this combined Allied army will remain on the defensive and the Austrian [army] will begin an offensive through Zittau.

If at the commencement of operations the Austrian army is weaker than the enemy's combatants and if all French forces advance against it, then the Austrians will sacrifice territory and remain on the defensive until either the enemy weakens his forces or the Russians and Prussians link with the Austrians.[85]

By the time Baillet de Latour reached Allied Headquarters at Reichenbach on 22 July, all influential parties unanimously agreed that Napoleon would aim his first blow at Austria.[86] For this reason as well as their increasing dependency on Austria, the Russians and Prussians insisted on sending "90,000 to 100,000 men" to Bohemia as further proof of their commitment to the Austrian monarchy. In return, they hoped such a display of goodwill would convince Kaiser Francis to declare war against his son-in-law. Admittedly, the Austrians initially expressed concerns about the ability to supply the huge Russo-Prussian contingent coming from Silesia. "As much as we recognized the accuracy of this principle," recalled Baillet de Latour, "we were not prepared to accept such a large army. We explained that we would not be able to supply more than 70,000 Allied soldiers." Moreover, the issue of command and control concerned the Austrians as it did not seem likely that either Alexander or Frederick William would surrender control of their elite formations. Also, the presence of the two monarchs at Austrian headquarters did not seem appealing to Schwarzenberg. "But as the Russian tsar placed a great value on following Wittgenstein's 70,000 men with his entire reserve," concludes Baillet de Latour, "we finally accepted the proposal."[87]

Aside from insisting on the point of sending such a large force to Bohemia, Allied leaders at Reichenbach accepted Radetzky's "Operationsentwurf."[88] As a result, they retracted the statements in the Trachenberg Protocol regarding a general Allied offensive to produce the final Allied blueprint for operations: the Reichenbach Plan. The Russians and Prussians recognized that, if Austria joined the Coalition, circumstances would determine where the Army of Bohemia would advance: west to Bavaria, north to Saxony, or northeast to Silesia. They deemed that a position in northern Bohemia west of the Elbe would best serve the purpose of facilitating its march in any of these directions. Moreover, Knesebeck, Toll, and Volkonsky assumed that Napoleon's operations would be governed by three inter-related factors: Austria's entry into the war, Bohemia's geographic position, and concern about an Austrian envelopment of Dresden from the west. In particular, they thought that the Army of Bohemia's proximity to Dresden would induce Napoleon to withdraw all the forces he had posted east of the Elbe and ultimately evacuate that river's right bank. They speculated that he would then unite his main army and turn against either the Austrians in Bohemia or Bernadotte in Brandenburg, with the former viewed as the more likely target. In either case, the leaders at Reichenbach expected the Bohe-mian Army to cross the Erzgebirge and seek battle with Napoleon, despite the statements in Radetzky's plan. Enabling the Army of Bohemia to con-duct offensive operations in part justified the sending of 110,000 Russians and Prussians to join the Austrians. Only the Army of Bohemia possessed sufficient strength to challenge Napoleon head on, and thus the Allied leaders at Reichenbach expected it to commence offensive operations at the resumption of hostilities.

At first glance, this insistence on the Bohemian Army's seeking battle with Napoleon appears to violate Radetzky's principle of retreating before the emperor's onslaught and conducting a defensive until the operations of the two other armies against his rear and flanks could be felt. Although this is a grey area in Allied planning, Radetzky's "Operationsentwurf" stated that, if Napoleon's main army "remained on the defensive *à cheval* the Elbe, the Austrian army would undertake an offensive along the left bank of the Elbe at the moment when the Allied army approached the Elbe [from Silesia]. If the enemy's superiority on the left bank is too great, it [the Austrian army] would act as noted above," meaning it would conduct a defensive until the operations of the main Russo-Prussian army coming from Silesia could impact Napoleon.[89] Moreover, the Allies at Reichenbach understood that Radetzky based his plans for the Austrian army in Bohemia on the idea that it would be reinforced by only 25,000 Russians rather than 100,000 Russo-Prussian troops.

Should Napoleon's main army operate against Allied forces in Silesia or Brandenburg, the Russians and Prussians presumed that the Army of Bohe-mia would take advantage of the French emperor's absence by overwhelm-ing any masking force and then conducting an offensive either to take Dresden or to threaten his communication with France, presumably by marching on Leipzig. Despite these offensive components, the change of strategy from the Trachenberg Protocol to the Reichenbach Plan meant that the Allies had ceded the initiative to Napoleon: his actions would determine their response. Thus, the Army of Bohemia could do nothing until Allied High Command determined Napoleon's intentions. How many times in the past had such an approach led to disaster for the enemies of France?

As for the two other Allied forces, the Russians and Prussians agreed to assign secondary roles to the Silesian and North German Armies. These two armies would secure territory too valuable to abandon to the enemy. Yet in doing so, they should not under any circumstances engage Napoleon in a general battle where his superior numbers and operational talent would provide him with a decisive advantage. Therefore, the architects of the Reichenbach Plan agreed that the Silesian and North German Armies should never accept battle with the emperor himself but should always retire before his onslaught – especially the Silesian Army, which did not have a national capital to protect. These two armies should seek to distance themselves from Napoleon's line of operation, exhaust his troops by compelling them to make forced marches, and always keep the French emperor in their sights. The instant Napoleon quit the pursuit of one Allied army to move against another, the former should immediately resume the offensive against the masking force left behind by Napoleon. As Allied planners at Reichenbach expected Napoleon would withdraw his forces from Silesia for a general concentration as the prelude for an invasion of either Bohemia or Branden-burg, the Silesian Army should follow imperial forces during their with-drawal from Silesia, delay these forces, and continuously harass them with light troops but still avoid battle against superior forces. At the same time, this army would protect Silesia and guard Russian communications in unison with Bennigsen's Army of Poland.

Very little is known about this last period of planning. In fact, no written revision of the Trachenberg Protocol has been found in the German or Austrian archives, suggesting that the final plan of operations was concluded verbally. Moreover, no written or spoken reports emerged regarding a change in the Trachenberg Protocol. Regardless, referring to the Allied plan of campaign as the "Trachenberg Plan" is a misnomer, as the Trachenberg Protocol proved to be very different from the Reichenbach Plan that emerged after the Russians and Prussians accepted Radetzky's "Operationsentwurf." Despite the silence, Allied leaders recognized the differences between the plans. Over time, the variances between the two blurred, leading to the Coalition's final plan of operations simply being called the Trachenberg Plan because of the celebrated meeting that took place there in July 1813. Consequently, the Trachenberg Protocol should be regarded as only a step in the development of the Reichenbach Plan. Moreover, the identity of individuals deserving credit for the Reichenbach Plan becomes moot. Radetzky and the Austrian General Staff provided the theoretical frame-work that ultimately trumped the offensive aspects of the Trachenberg Protocol.[90]

Returning to diplomacy, Castlereagh may have hoped for too much from the impact of Vitoria but the foreign secretary remained sober in his expectations. He recognized that, at the least, Vitoria would raise British prestige and influence on the continent.[91] Based on this consideration, Castlereagh reversed his position concerning the Prague conference. In a letter dated 14 July, he authorized Cathcart "to accept the Austrian mediation, if the state of affairs should continue." Castlereagh also accredited Cathcart full authority to begin the preliminary negotiations for "a general pacification." However, he emphasized that Cathcart could not sign any treaty, but instead would learn "the basis on which the Continental Powers are prepared to negotiate." After the foreign secretary received this information, a "Minister" would be sent from London with instructions "to act for us." Castlereagh advised Cathcart of "the importance of ascertaining clearly the Continental basis before we can say a word as to particular cessions; beyond the mere admission of the principle, we cannot advance till this is known." Although he hoped the contrary, Castlereagh supposed it possible "that the basis agreed to by the Continental Powers under the Austrian mediation might be so defective as to afford no temptation to Great Britain to make a sacrifice of any of her conquests for the purpose of giving effect to such an arrangement." Thus, the British government needed to "know the nature of the object aimed at" before judging "what it becomes us to do." Lastly, he stressed the need for Cathcart to "make the Tsar feel that we cannot advance money for armistices, and that it is, therefore, of more importance to bring matters to a short notice."[92] In a second dispatch written on the 14th, Castlereagh addressed another pointed letter to Cathcart explaining "the importance of awakening the Tsar's mind to the necessity, for his own interests as well as ours, of peremptorily excluding from the general negotiations every maritime question. If he does not, he will risk a misunderstanding between those powers on whose union the safety of Europe now rests. Great Britain may be driven out of a Congress, but not out of her own maritime rights, and, if the Continental Powers know their own interests, they will not hazard this."[93]

Overestimating the impact of Vitoria, Castlereagh assumed that Metternich would soon add some British demands to his conditions for peace. He predicted that, by doing so, the "preliminary" basis of peace would be so expanded that it would "materially diminish the chance of Buonaparte yielding." He doubted Napoleon "could stoop so low" as to accept Metternich's conditions. Moreover, Castlereagh expected the Allies to demand some immediate physical proof of Napoleon's goodwill should the French emperor agree to Metternich's conditions. As security, Castlereagh considered the evacuation of all Prussian fortresses and the retreat of the Grande Armée. He predicted that any demands for "substantial securities" beyond "a mere paper engagement" would present "a new stumbling block." Ultimately,

Castlereagh could "hardly conceive it possible that the Conferences at Prague can, under present circumstances, end in peace, if the Allies are true to themselves and to each other. Buonaparte has had a severe lesson; but, whilst he has such a force under arms, he will not submit to any arrangement which even Count Metternich could have the face to sign his name to, as providing on the solid principles for the repose of Europe." Again he urged Cathcart to emphasize Wellington's contribution to the overall war effort:

> Before Lord W. forms his future plans, he must know what is to happen in Germany; his whole policy must be governed upon that of the Allies. He writes in great spirits, and the Continental Powers may rely on his doing his best for them. Fatal would it be for them, and for the world, if they could for a moment think of seeking their safety in what is called a Continental peace. We have done wonders in the Peninsula ... We *may* sink before the undivided power of France: and if we do, Germany, and even Russia, will soon resume their fetters. We have now the bull close pinioned between us, and if either of us let go our hold till we render him harmless, we shall deserve to suffer for it.

Castlereagh appeared satisfied by the positive diplomatic outcome of the Trachenberg conference, despite Thornton's pessimistic view. Not having received Cathcart's report on the proceedings at Trachenberg until 7 August, the foreign secretary responded that the letter from Francis to Bernadotte "renders the whole of that proceeding a most important and, I trust, auspicious incident in the Continental drama. The *dénouement* of the plot is yet a matter of anxiety. I trust, however, the impulse which has been given will not yield to nominal concessions. I should hope, if the Austrian terms were not opened by Metternich at Dresden, that the Kaiser is yet free to insist upon an arrangement more consonant to the general interests." Again Castlereagh pointed to Wellington's success, insisting that the "events in Spain not only justify, but require his Imperial Majesty, as a mediator, to alter his terms. He must see how fatal it would be to all were he to separate his cause from that of the other Powers. Neutrality must exhaust his resources as much as war; and, if Buonaparte should triumph over the others, his own fate is sealed." Castlereagh urged Cathcart "to bring our claims forward." He could not see the Russians and Prussians rejecting London's demands, which he termed to be "so just and moderate in themselves." Likewise, he could not see how Austria could ignore British national security objectives yet mediate "a general peace."[94]

As much as the British wanted to believe that Wellington provided the deciding factor in the fate of Europe, initial news from Prague indicated the likelihood of a settlement. Metternich's gag order closed the normal sources of information the British envoys relied on to provide Castlereagh with news. Despondency soon seized the British Cabinet and Castlereagh's anxiety soared. "I wish you to ascertain clearly," he wrote to Cathcart, "whether any and what basis of alliance between the three great powers has been laid out at Prague. I have the greatest confidence in the Tsar; but I do not like his concealing anything ... of which there has been a striking instance recently. Engagements of secrecy against us are of bad precedence and must not be."[95] Inevitably the darkness cleared as 10 August approached and the Prague peace conference dissolved in failure despite Napoleon's eleventh-hour concessions. On 9 August, he offered to restore Prussia to its 1806 material extent and surrender the Grand Duchy of Warsaw as well as Illyria but insisted on retaining Danzig, Trieste, and Istria. Rejecting Napoleon's offer, Kaiser Francis declared war on his son-in-law three days later. The British pound would bring Austria and Great Britain together in early October. Regardless, the British could not derail Metternich directly, nor could they prevent him from making separate deals with the Russians and Prussians.[96]

To insure that the effort of a multinational coalition served Austria's needs, Metternich sought to control the three principal Allied armies. For this reason, Kaiser Francis insisted on the post of Allied commander in chief being filled by an Austrian; he selected the 42-year-old Schwarzenberg to be "*l'homme de la coalition,*" as Tsar Alexander aptly observed. That Francis – the ally sought after by both sides – wanted an Austrian general at the post of commander in chief is understandable. With the memory of Austerlitz having yet to fade, Francis could not simply hand his army to the tsar. According to the German General Staff historian August von Janson, while Schwarzenberg's appointment satisfied Alexander, it greatly displeased Frederick William, who would have been satisfied with the tsar serving as commander in chief; the Prussian monarch purportedly acquiesced with reluctance to the selection of Schwarzenberg. He expressed his reservations over a dinner with Francis on 18 August, greatly upsetting the Austrian emperor, especially because after the Spring Campaign the king had no reason to hold the leadership of the Russian army in high esteem. His preference for Alexander to be Allied commander in chief appears to have been based on their personal friendship and the king's ability to negotiate personally with the tsar. With a foreign general who was not a sovereign, it would be much more difficult for him, and Kaiser Francis showed no inclination to engage in direct discussions about the war. By nature cold and calculating, Francis showed little interest in the day-to-day operations of the war and often remained isolated from the other two monarchs; only rarely did he appear on the battlefield. Thus, personal contact between him and Frederick William seldom occurred. Moreover, from the beginning, Frederick William "appeared to harbor a personal dislike for Schwarzenberg, which, as a rule in such cases and to the detriment of the cause, soon became mutual. Schwarzenberg was hurt by his own regular and uniform nature of sharply opposing the short and often biting nature of the king, who always attributed bad motives to Schwarzenberg and judged him unfairly."[97]

Keeping the Austrian army united and not distributing its corps to the Silesian or North German Armies can also be viewed as a step toward controlling the Coalition. Schwarzenberg's ability to direct the operations of the other two Allied armies quickly foundered after the war resumed, and the tsar eventually eclipsed him as Allied generalissimo. Nevertheless, the sheer size of Schwarzenberg's army meant that the Coalition could only go as far and as fast as Schwarzenberg wanted. Although by no means a great *Feldherr* (field commander), the Austrian possessed the extraordinary ability to manage people and to balance divergent opinions.[98] Schwarzenberg's erudite chief of staff, Radetzky, has received credit for formulating the Reichenbach plan of operations adopted by the Allies. Yet, in the end, credit for Allied success in 1813 belongs to the operations of the Silesian Army. The following chapters will tell its story.

Notes

1 To be closer to Allied Headquarters, Kaiser Francis and Metternich also established their quarters at Gitschin, less than eighty miles southwest of Reichenbach. Several meetings were held between the Austrians and the Russians and Prussians at Gitschin as well as thirty-five miles to the east at the château of Ratiborsitz (Ratibořice). See Lieven, *Russia Against Napoleon*, 357.

2 Toll's "Mémoire sur les opérations militaires, présenté à Sa Majesté L'Empereur Alexandre à Reichenbach le 28 Mai/9 Juin 1813" is reproduced in full in Bernhardi, *Toll*, II:481–84; Barclay's instructions to Toll, his cover letter to Schwarzenberg, and "General-Dislocation der verbundenen Kaiserliche Russischen und Königlich Preußischen Truppen mit der Anzeige der wirklichen Stärke dieser Armee" are all reproduced *ibid.*, II:484–87. See also Friederich, *Herbstfeldzug 1813*, I:72.

3 Mikhailovsky-Danilevsky, *Denkwürdigkeiten*, 123–24.

4 Aside from the 150,000 men in Bohemia, the Austrians sought to post some 30,000 men along the Danube and 40,000 in Inner Austria. See Baillet de Latour, *Erinnerungen*, 114.

5 "Über den Waffenstillstand zwischen Frankreich einerseits dann Rußland und Preußen andererseits und was derselbe für Folgen haben wird" is reproduced in full in Radetzky, *Denkschriften*, 105–11. See the commentary in Oncken, *Österreich und Preußen*, II:342–44.

6 See Schwarzenberg to Barclay de Tolly, Gitschin, 16 June 1813, reproduced in full in Bernhardi, *Toll*, II:488–89.

7 See Oncken, *Österreich und Preußen*, II:346.

8 Toll to Scharnhorst, Opotschna, 17 June 1813, reproduced in full in Friederich, *Herbstfeldzug 1813*, I:80–81.

9 Bernhardi, *Toll*, II:36–37; Mikhailovsky-Danilevsky, *Denkwürdigkeiten*, 123–24.

10 "Wurschen Plan" is used to reference the plans for military operations while "Wurschen Convention" is used to denote the revised Allied war aims. On 16 May, the Russians and Prussians expanded the war aims established by the Kalisch–Breslau accords to include British interests. According to the Wurschen Convention, the Allies demanded the complete dissolution of Napoleon's Confederation of the Rhine and the complete independence of all German states. In addition, they pledged to fight for the liberation of Spain, Holland, and Italy. The seven articles of the Wurschen Convention can be found in Oncken, *Österreich und Preußen*, II:318.

11 Schroeder, *European Politics*, 457.

12 Webster, *The Foreign Policy of Castlereagh*, I:134.

13 According to Lieven, "Nesselrode trusted and saw eye-to-eye with Metternich, whom he had known for many years." Both statesmen satisfactorily concluded these meetings with an understanding and appreciation of their "two countries' interests and positions." He also notes that Alexander and Nesselrode focused exclusively on the German question as the means of achieving a stable peace that would guarantee Russian security. He maintains that both believed Napoleon's control of the Third Germany would have to be broken in order to establish a true European balance of power as well as security for Russia, Prussia, and Austria. They tied Russia's security to Prussia's standing in Germany. While the Wurschen Convention called for the abolition of Napoleon's Confederation of the Rhine, Metternich's fourth point demanded only the independence of Hamburg and Lübeck. This would leave the Confederation and its centerpiece, Jerome Bonaparte's kingdom of Westphalia, under Napoleon's control, giving the French emperor control of the Elbe and its fortresses from the North Sea to Bohemia. Lieven cites Alexander's thoughts on such a scenario: "any hope for the independence of any part of Germany would be lost for good. Prussia would constantly be exposed to attacks which could come at any moment and against which it could only offer a feeble defense, and the emperor Napoleon could almost at will make himself master of the Baltic coastline, so that any hope of the security of trade would be merely illusory." The Russians also thought the four points did not satisfy Austria's security needs. In their opinion, regaining only Illyria would leave Austria vulnerable. According to Lieven, the Russians believed that Austria at a minimum needed to get back Tyrol, the fortress of Mantua, and a defensible frontier along the Mincio River in northern Italy. As Prussia had no choice but to follow Russia's lead, a discussion of Prussian views of the four points is superfluous. See Lieven, *Russia Against Napoleon*, 357–59.

14 In *European Politics*, 475–76, Schroeder points out that "Austria had plenty to object to in British ideas and attitudes. Britain renewed its old tactics of raising European insurrections against France regardless of their consequences for other powers." He states incorrectly that the British expected Austria to enter the war before London provided any subsidies; Castlereagh's correspondence states otherwise. Schroeder also claims that the British ignored "vital Austrian concerns in Central Europe," a difficult accusation to substantiate because Castlereagh did not receive an opportunity to negotiate with Metternich until his arrival on the continent in the winter of 1813. According to Webster in *The Foreign Policy of Castlereagh*, I:140–41, because London had refused to allow Metternich to raise

maritime and colonial issues, he punished Britain by excluding it "from all influence on the continental basis which was to be offered to Napoleon. She would thus be forced to use her colonial conquests to obtain those points in which she was especially interested." See also Nicolson, *The Congress of Vienna*, 53; For Metternich's attempts to undermine Russia and Prussia, see Leggiere, *Napoleon and Berlin*, 122–27.

15 The phrase employed at the time was "continental peace" but, as Metternich had little interest in Iberia, the Low Countries, and Sicily, it is misleading and so I refer to a settlement for Central Europe.

16 Nipperdey, *Germany from Napoleon to Bismarck*, 70; Nicolson, *The Congress of Vienna*, 42–43; Ross, *European Diplomatic History*, 332; Kissinger, *A World Restored*, 73; Kraehe, *Metternich's German Policy*, I:174; Webster, *The Foreign Policy of Castlereagh*, I:135–36.

17 That same day, 6 June, Colonel Hudson Lowe wrote General Sir Henry Bunbury, Britain's under-secretary of state for war and the colonies, a long and carefully considered exposé of the situation. Lowe speculated that the six-week duration of the armistice appeared to be designed to prevent the British from participating in the negotiations with Napoleon that would occur during that period. He also explained that Kaiser Francis "has arrived at Gitschin (the castle of Wallenstein) within twelve German miles of this place." According to the rumors Lowe had heard, the Habsburg monarch had already submitted to Napoleon his price for Austria's continued neutrality: the return of the Austrian littoral, Dalmatia, Trieste, and Fiume as well as seven regiments of Croats currently in French service. See Lowe to Bunbury, Reichenbach, 6 June 1813, British Library Additional Manuscripts (hereafter cited as Add MSS), 20111, 31–35.

18 Although unconcerned about British public opinion, the British minister-plenipotentiary to Sweden, Edward Thornton, likewise suggested an acceleration of British military operations by suggesting "the vast importance of military demonstrations, during the armistice, on the coast of England opposite Holland and East Friesland, and the North of Germany between it and the Elbe, in order to prevent as much as possible the withdrawing from thence of troops to reinforce the French army in Silesia. The most vigorous prosecution possible of the campaign in Spain would have the same effect, but no man is more sensible than Lord Wellington of the importance of such a measure; and Bonaparte, in making a six weeks' armistice, certainly calculated on drawing reinforcements from Spain." See Thornton to Castlereagh, Stralsund, 14 June 1813, *Correspondence of Viscount Castlereagh* (hereafter cited as *CVC*), VIII:399.

19 Stewart to Castlereagh, Reichenbach, 6 June 1813, *CVC*, IX:22; Stewart to Castlereagh, Reichenbach, 19 June 1813, *ibid.*, IX:29.

20 Stewart to Castlereagh, Reichenbach, 6 June 1813, *CVC*, IX:22–23.

21 Castlereagh to Stewart, Foreign Office, 22 June 1813, *CVC*, VIII:408.

22 Castlereagh to Cathcart, Foreign Office, 30 June 1813, *CVC*, VIII:411.

23 Castlereagh to Cathcart, Foreign Office, 6 July 1813, *CVC*, IX:30.

24 Webster, *The Foreign Policy of Castlereagh*, I:119–20, 133; Schroeder, *European Politics*, 457.

25 Castlereagh to Stewart, Foreign Office, 22 June 1813, *CVC*, VIII:408–09; Castlereagh to Cathcart, Foreign Office, 22 June 1813, *ibid.*, VIII:404–05.

26 Scott, *Bernadotte*, 83.

27 Castlereagh to Stewart, Foreign Office, 30 June 1813, *CVC*, VIII:409; Webster, *The Foreign Policy of Castlereagh*, I:128–30, 139. Stewart, the junior partner, remained highly critical of Cathcart's negotiations with the Russians. On 28 June, Stewart complained to Castlereagh that "Lord C. is desirous of being as agreeable as possible to the Emperor of Russia. This, in the long run, will be seen": Stewart to Castlereagh, Berlin, 28 June 1813, *CVC*, IX:29. Others noticed the rivalry: "Lord Cathcart is not much pleased with his Dispatch of the Battle of Bautzen not having been published while that of Sir Charles Stewart has appeared in the *Gazette*." See Lowe to Bunbury, Reichenbach, 28 June 1813, Add MSS, 20111, 44.

28 A copy of the Russian proposal submitted to Cathcart by Nesselrode is in Stewart to Castlereagh, Wurschen, 17 May 1813, *CVC*, VIII:391–97; Castlereagh to Stewart, Foreign Office, 22 June 1813, *ibid.*, VIII:409.

29 Castlereagh to Cathcart, Foreign Office, 6 July 1813, *CVC*, IX:30.

30 In a second letter written on the 22nd, Castlereagh explained that "the House of Commons, after the Austrian loans, will never hear of lending again to a foreign power; and we do not feel that we could possibly propose such an amount in any shape to Parliament": Castlereagh to Stewart, Foreign Office, 22 June 1813, *CVC*, VIII:409.

31 Moreover, Castlereagh insisted that "the mode of realizing the subsidy on the Continent ... was expressly stated from the first that the credit was to be in London." He instructed Stewart to impress on the Russians and Prussians the need to follow the Swedish example of redeeming British credit: "What you represented in reference to Sweden was perfectly correct. Having a credit to a certain extent on the British Treasury, the Swedish Government draws bills on London, or [Gotthard Mauritz von] Rehausen [Swedish minister plenipotentiary in London] orders a banking house here to remit to Sweden or Stralsund, arranging with the Treasury the payment of such bills to the extent of the monthly installment receivable on account of subsidy. Russia and Prussia must, when you have settled the installments, authorize their ministers here to act in the same manner, or the Russian and Prussian Governments may draw on London, as above described, to the extent of the monthly payments. The funds will be ready for them, subject to a proportional deduction in each month for stores, etc., sent": Castlereagh to Stewart, Foreign Office, 22 June 1813, *CVC*, VIII:406–08.

32 Castlereagh to Stewart, Foreign Office, 22 June 1813, *CVC*, VIII:406–08.

33 Castlereagh to Stewart, Foreign Office, 14 July 1813, *CVC*, IX:33, and Stewart to D'Ivernois, Reichenbach, 12 August 1813, *ibid.*, IX:42. Muir claims that the official treaty was signed on 30 September "but it was followed by further delays and in the end no securities were actually issued, Britain discharging her obligation by paying Russia and Prussia directly, and in full, in 1814 and 1815": Muir, *Britain and the Defeat of Napoleon*, 253–54.

34 Cathcart to Castlereagh, Reichenbach, 28 June 1813, Add MSS, 20111, 46–50; Cathcart, *Commentaries*, 185–86.

35 "The publicity with which these conversations are held, and the vanity of persons with whom they are discussed, are injurious circumstances; but they are in the character of the Prince Royal, though they are not always the effect of a voluntary

effusion, but I believe are the result of deliberate reflection": Thornton to Castlereagh, Stralsund, 21 June 1813, *CVC*, VIII:400–02.

36 Although Count Lars von Engeström (1751–1826) served as First Prime Minister for Foreign Affairs from 1809 to 1824, Wetterstedt can be regarded as Sweden's *de facto* minister of foreign affairs beginning in 1812. Wetterstedt had been appointed secretary of state in 1809. Named court chancellor the same year, he accompanied Bernadotte to the meeting with Tsar Alexander at Turku in 1812 and remained by his side during the campaigns in Germany, Holstein, and Norway from 1813 to 1814.

37 Thornton to Castlereagh, Stralsund, 21 June 1813, *CVC*, VIII:402–04.

38 Castlereagh to Stewart, Foreign Office, 30 June 1813, *CVC*, VIII:409–10.

39 Castlereagh to Cathcart, Foreign Office, 30 June 1813, *CVC*, VIII:411–12.

40 Castlereagh to Stewart, Foreign Office, 30 June 1813, *CVC*, VIII:410.

41 For Bernadotte's standing in the Coalition at this point, see Oncken, *Österreich und Preußen*, II:410–16; Woynar, *Österrikes förhållande*, 88–101.

42 Boyen, *Erinnerungen*, ed. Schmidt, II:602.

43 For a comprehensive summary of Bernadotte's plans, see Pertz and Delbrück, *Gneisenau*, III:109–11.

44 Müffling, *Aus meinem Leben*, 52.

45 Friederich, *Herbstfeldzug 1813*, I:81–82. One French source describes him as "militarily erudite, but systematic and the enemy of great resolutions": Anon., *Précis militaire de la campagne de 1813 en Allemagne*, 82.

46 Knesebeck's memorandum, titled "Betrachtungen über die nächste Kriegsoperationen," is reproduced in full in Friederich, *Herbstfeldzug 1813*, I:83–84. See also Pertz and Delbrück, *Gneisenau*, III:108–09.

47 Friederich, *Herbstfeldzug 1813*, I:84–85. In *Russia Against Napoleon*, 389, Lieven notes: "Potentially, Austria remained the weak link in the Coalition. If the main army was destroyed or seriously weakened and Bohemia was invaded, then there was a real chance that Austria would renew negotiations with Napoleon or even drop out of the war."

48 Boyen's cover letter to Frederick William and his plan of operations containing Bülow's comments in the margin is reproduced in full in Boyen, *Errinerungen*, ed. Nippold, II:449–53.

49 Friederich, *Herbstfeldzug 1813*, I:85–88.

50 Stadion actually signed the Convention of Reichenbach on 27 June so Metternich could tell Napoleon that no formal agreements bound Austria to the Allies.

51 Webster, *The Foreign Policy of Castlereagh*, I:141; Schroeder, *European Politics*, 467–71; Krahe, *Metternich's German Policy*, I:177; Scott, *Bernadotte*, 83.

52 Quoted in Oncken, *Österreich und Preußen*, II:389.

53 According to Baillet de Latour, "the mobilization and reorganization of the militia progressed only slowly in terms of outfitting because despite all efforts the lack of available uniforms could not be easily remedied. There was so little seriousness in the peace negotiations that 20 July had almost passed without one even agreeing on the basics. As our mobilization still had not been completed, the truce was extended to 10 August with an ensuing six-day cessation of hostilities": Baillet de Latour, *Erinnerungen*, 114. See also Oncken, *Österreich und Preußen*,

II:384–95; Kraehe, *Metternich's German Policy*, I:180–81; Nicolson, *The Congress of Vienna*, 41.

54 Cathcart, *Commentaries*, 180.

55 Webster, *The Foreign Policy of Castlereagh*, I:142.

56 Thornton to Castlereagh, Greifswald, 3 July 1813, *CVC*, VIII:414. Webster notes that "Thornton, who had been putting forward some very wild ideas, was not very competent": Webster, *The Foreign Policy of Castlereagh*, I:119.

57 Thornton to Castlereagh, Greifswald, 3 July 1813, *CVC*, VIII:414.

58 Castlereagh to Cathcart, Foreign Office, 30 June 1813, *CVC*, VIII:411.

59 On 3 July Castlereagh wrote to Cathcart: "I consider it of so much importance that your lordship be informed of the state of affairs in Spain ... that may give so new and important a character to the relative situation of all the belligerent powers." See Castlereagh to Cathcart, Foreign Office, 3 July 1813, *CVC*, VIII:412; Webster, *Foreign Policy of Castlereagh*, I:143.

60 Castlereagh to Cathcart, Foreign Office, 6 July 1813, *CVC*, IX:30–32.

61 When he wrote this letter on 28 July, Castlereagh was responding to the arrival of dispatches written by Cathcart prior to 8 July. The Trachenberg conference that the foreign secretary alludes to took place from 9 to 12 July.

62 Castlereagh to Cathcart, Foreign Office, 28 July 1813, *CVC*, IX:37.

63 Woynar, *Österrikes förhållande*, 88–93; Scott, *Bernadotte*, 84; Henckel von Donnersmarck, *Erinnerungen*, 202.

64 Oncken, *Österreich und Preußen*, II:422.

65 Janson, *Friedrich Wilhelm*, 183.

66 Müffling, *Aus meinem Leben*, 55–56.

67 Stadion to Metternich, 14 July 1813, reproduced in Woynar, *Österrikes förhållande*, 163–65; Scott, *Bernadotte*, 85–87. However, requests from Wetterstedt to Nesselrode and Hardenberg for assurances that in the case of peace both courts would demand Napoleon's approval of the cessation of Norway to Sweden were refused on the familiar grounds that it would be best to keep Napoleon out of this affair. Sweden would have to act before receiving further pledges of support.

68 Henckel von Donnersmarck, *Erinnerungen*, 203.

69 A copy of this letter is in *CVC*, VIII:416–17.

70 Thornton to Castlereagh, Trachenberg, noon, 12 July 1813, *CVC*, VIII:420.

71 Quoted in Oncken, *Österreich und Preußen*, II:423.

72 "This answer of the Kaiser contains a more formal avowal than appears to have been given in the writing of his determination to enforce by arms the general security and independence, if negotiation should fail": Thornton to Castlereagh, Trachenberg, 12 July 1813, *CVC*, VIII:415. Scott, in *Bernadotte*, 87, states: "Bernadotte himself was personally pleased to receive ... a flattering note from the Emperor Francis; it promised nothing, but implied Austrian cooperation; hence Bernadotte and Stadion expressed anew the mutual regard and need of Austria and Sweden."

73 Thornton to Castlereagh, Trachenberg, 12 July 1813, *CVC*, VIII:415–16.

74 Quoted in Friederich, *Herbstfeldzug 1813*, I:90–91.

75 Höpfner, "Darstellung," 1843:25–26.

76 Various versions of the Protocol state Budin (Budyně) rather than Brandeis-Altbunzlau.

77 Various versions of the Protocol state 200,000 to 250,000 men.

78 Müffling, *Aus meinen Leben*, 56–57.

79 Copies of the Trachenberg Protocol can be found in Beilage I of the second volume of Plotho's *Der Krieg in Deutschland und Frankreich*, as well as Nr. 160 in Pflugk-Harttung's collection of primary documents assembled from the holdings of the Prussian Geheimen Staatsarchiv (Secret State Archives): *Das Befreiungsjahr 1813*, 229–30; and Mikhailovsky-Danilevsky, *Denkwürdigkeiten*, 124–27. See also Bernhardi, *Toll*, II:49–52; Janson, *Friedrich Wilhelm*, 183; Friederich, *Herbstfeldzug 1813*, I:94; Bogdanovich, *Geschichte des Krieges im Jahre 1813*, Ib:262–64. For an accurate and concise French account of the Coalition's war planning, see Anon., *Précis militaire de la campagne de 1813 en Allemagne*, 71–73. Accusations by Maude that the plan demonstrated that the Allies "had neither learned anything nor forgotten anything" are off the mark: Maude, *Leipzig Campaign*, 161.

80 "Was ist nötig um die Offensiv-Unternehmungen berechnen zu können" is reproduced in full in Radetzky, *Denkschriften*, 121–27.

81 "Operationsentwurf," Lieben, 7 July 1813, is reproduced in full in Hellwald and Schönhals, *Radetzky*, 160.

82 Hellwald and Schönhals, *Radetzky*, 156–67.

83 Friederich, *Herbstfeldzug 1813*, I:96; Sked, *Radetzky*, 41.

84 The authors of the 1858 biography of Radetzky, one of whom was the Austrian General Staff officer and veteran of the War of the Sixth Coalition, Feldmarschall-leutnant Friedrich Jakob Heller von Hellwald, admits that the "Operationsentwurf" was "not based on offensive action but instead took the greatest care to secure the Austrian monarchy by keeping the theater of war as far as possible from Austria": Hellwald and Schönhals, *Radetzky*, 156.

85 Quoted in Friederich, *Herbstfeldzug 1813*, I:96–97.

86 Janson, *Friedrich Wilhelm*, 184.

87 Lieven follows Baillet de Latour's remark about being "surprised" when he learned at Reichenbach that the Allies planned to send 110,000 men instead of 25,000 to Bohemia. Yet Radetzky already knew per the Trachenberg Protocol that he had received before Baillet de Latour's departure for Reichenbach that the Allies planned to send "90,000 to 100,000 men." According to Baillet, he left for Reichenbach with the understanding that "an operational plan had been drafted according to which the Austrian army, reinforced by 25,000 Russians under Wittgenstein, should act according to circumstances": Baillet de Latour, *Erinnerungen*, 115–16; Lieven, *Russia Against Napoleon*, 389.

88 Hellwald and Schönhals maintain that the Allies never really agreed with Radetzky's plan: "It is understandable that Prussia and Russia could not accept it because both were animated by the same desire for their own territories. Russia's main concern was to remove the war as far as possible from the area of the Grand Duchy of Warsaw." See Hellwald and Schönhals, *Radetzky*, 156.

89 Hellwald and Schönhals, *Radetzky*, 166.

90 Sked, *Radetzky*, 41; Freytag-Loringhoven, *Aufklärung und Armeeführung*, 3; Langeron, *Mémoires*, 207; Friederich, *Herbstfeldzug 1813*, I:97–98, 154–55.

91 Webster, *The Foreign Policy of Castlereagh*, I:143.

92 Castlereagh to Cathcart, Foreign Office, 14 July 1813, *CVC*, IX:36.

93 In particular, Castlereagh notes that Alexander, "if he knows anything of England, must be convinced that no Government dare surrender the right of search for enemy's property, or British subjects." Any interference on this subject by a third party "would probably decide the nation against it." See Castlereagh to Cathcart, St. James Square, 14 July 1813, *CVC*, IX:34–35.

94 Castlereagh to Cathcart, Cray Farm, 7 August 1813, *CVC*, IX:39–41.

95 Castlereagh to Cathcart, Foreign Office, 1 September 1813, *CVC*, IX:46.

96 Signed on 3 October 1813, the Anglo-Austrian subsidy treaty was modeled on the agreements made with Russia and Prussia in June. The Austrians would receive a subsidy in the amount of £1,000,000. Half had already been advanced to the Austrians and the remaining half was payable at £100,000 per month until 1 April. See Webster, *The Foreign Policy of Castlereagh*, I:157–58; Ross, *European Diplomatic History*, 333; Kissinger, *A World Restored*, 82.

97 Janson used Hardenberg's journal to support this argument. For example, despite the Allied victory at Kulm on 30 August 1813, Hardenberg noted on 2 September that "the king is displeased with Schwarzenberg" and again on 6 September: "Have been with Schwarzenberg. The king will not award him the Black Eagle!" See Janson, *Friedrich Wilhelm*, 184–86, 210.

98 As Lieven points out, "under no circumstances was Schwarzenberg a commander who would seize the initiative and impose his will on Napoleon": Lieven, *Russia Against Napoleon*, 389.

The Silesian Army

Prior to the armistice, several Allied *Streifkorps* conducted operations in the rear of the French army ranging from raids and surprise attacks to severing imperial communications. Pressing deep into Thuringia, a portion of Lützow's *Streifkorps* outdistanced Allied communications and for a while remained uninformed of the armistice. After learning of the cessation of hostilities, the small unit attempted to reach Allied lines. Yet on 17 June a superior French and Württemberger force attacked and routed the Prussians at Kitzen near Leipzig, purportedly on Napoleon's order. Those who surrendered spent the next nine months aboard France's notorious prison hulks. Emphatic Allied protests fell on deaf ears. Blücher, Gneisenau, Bülow, and several other high-ranking Prussian officers loudly claimed that this French treachery rendered the armistice void. They particularly urged the termination of Article Five, which stipulated that the besieged imperial garrisons at Danzig, Zamosc (Zamość), Modlin (Nowy Dwór Mazowiecki), Stettin, and Küstrin (Kostrzyn) each receive fresh supplies every five days. Frederick William and Alexander agreed, forcing the imperials to tighten their belts. The early surrender of these fortresses can be attributed to the threat of starvation caused by this measure.[1]

During June and July, the Coalition's uncertain future forced the Prussians in Silesia to plan for the worst. Should the Sixth Coalition collapse and the Russians withdraw to Poland, Gneisenau planned to position the Prussian army in the mountains of Upper Silesia. Supported by the fortresses of Neiße (Nysa), Glatz, and Silberberg (Srebrna Górna), he envisioned the army fighting to the last man.[2] Frederick William named him military governor of Silesia, tasking the staff officer with the defense of the province and the mobilization of the Silesian Landwehr. "Return to me when the feud resumes," Blücher begged Gneisenau. "In every regard it is necessary that we are together."

4 Field-Marshal Gebhard Leberecht von Blücher, 1742–1819

News about Scharnhorst challenged Blücher's usual optimism. For some time, reports had indicated an unfavorable turn in his health. While traveling to Vienna, Scharnhorst neglected to properly care for the wound he received at the 2 May battle of Lützen even after the onset of gangrene. "It does not go well with our brave Scharnhorst," Blücher informed Gneisenau on 29 June. "I'd rather lose a battle than lose Scharnhorst!"[3] But the 57-year-old Scharnhorst was already dead, having passed away at Prague on 28 June.

A 12 July order from Frederick William established three army corps under General Hans David von Yorck, General Friedrich Heinrich von Kleist, and Bülow, as well as a fourth commanded by Tauentzien consisting primarily of Landwehr. Frederick William also formed his Royal Guard, which had been divided between I and II Corps, into a special brigade separate from the army corps.[4] Like Scharnhorst, Gneisenau believed that only Blücher possessed the ability to command this Prussian army. Due to Hardenberg's confidence in Gneisenau's judgment, the chancellor championed Blücher's interests. In addition, Stein diligently lobbied Alexander to have faith in Blücher. Despite this strong support, neither Blücher nor Gneisenau had been invited to attend the councils of war at Trachenberg, Reichenbach, and Gitschin. Ultimately, the Allied decision to distribute the various Prussian and Russian army corps among multinational armies eliminated the need to name a commander in chief of the Prussian army.

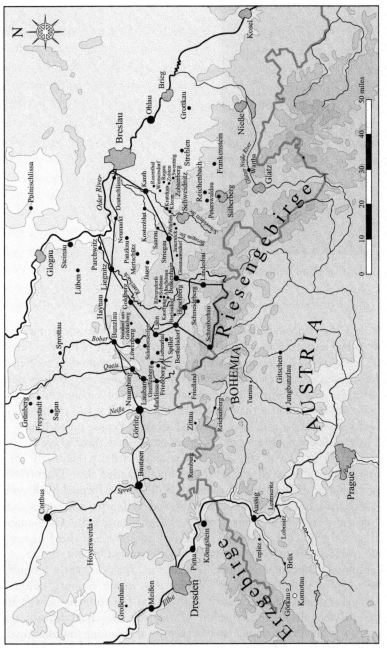

7 Neutral zone in Silesia

5 General August Wilhelm Antonius Neidhardt von Gneisenau, 1760–1831

As for Gneisenau, he formally succeeded Scharnhorst as Chief of the General Staff of the Prussian Army at the end of July. This post jeopardized his position as Blücher's staff chief because of its exacting duties, particularly in view of the army's rapid expansion, as well as its requirement of remaining close to the king and state chancellor. Official acknowledgment that he had succeeded his friend did little to assuage Gneisenau's fierce temper, which had been stoked by Frederick William's total reliance on Knesebeck. His 3 August complaint to the king perfectly captures his frustration: "If I remain uninformed of the war plans, inevitably I will not be able to execute useful projects." Gneisenau requested command of a brigade, suggesting that the king name Knesebeck Chief of the General Staff. Blücher refused to remain silent on this issue and resolutely protested to Hardenberg through Hippel: "Unfortunately our good Scharnhorst is now dead. Believe me this is worse for us than a lost battle. Gneisenau now remains; where he goes, I will follow dead or alive because I do not agree with Herr Knesebeck's ideas, and even less with Herr [General Friedrich Wilhelm von] Krusemarck's," whose name had also surfaced as a potential candidate for the position of Prussian staff chief. Citing the latter's 1811 stint as ambassador to France, Blücher chided that Krusemarck had "sucked up too much Parisian air."[5]

Although he took Scharnhorst's death very badly, Blücher's impatience with the armistice eclipsed his grief. He and Gneisenau had opposed the ceasefire from the start, fearing that a dishonorable peace would be the result. Stewart noted the concerns that most Allied commanders harbored: "Bonaparte, it was stated, could make greater efforts during the period of the truce than the Allies; and the general conduct of Austria led to a supposition that she was more anxious to dictate a peace than to incur all the dangers that might result from a protracted war in the center of her own empire. On the other hand, the object of Great Britain was to preserve the Allies from again entering into those separate treaties with Revolutionary France that had always proved so fallacious in themselves, and injurious to the common cause of Europe."[6] Heinrich Steffens, a professor attached to Blücher's staff to serve as a propaganda specialist, provides insight of the prevailing view at Blücher's headquarters at this time:

> The two battles [Lützen and Bautzen] that had been fought raised rather than depressed the hope of future victories; and it was loudly proclaimed that the war must be continued in the spirit that gave rise to it, and that it would remain a deep national disgrace if it were abandoned without a signal triumph that would cripple Napoleon's power forever. I was too much behind the scenes not to be aware of the doubtful and dangerous point on which our deepest interests turned. We were reduced at last to rest our hopes on one man, and that was Napoleon himself: our chief reliance was on his obstinacy, which might exhaust the patience of the negotiating princes. The truce was declared on 5 June, but the war was apparently suspended only to be secretly pursued by our enemy by means of different but more dangerous tactics; and the better informed among us knew that the secret weapons of the foe were now being used in our very midst. Two months passed on with the daily anxious inquiry: "Will Napoleon win Austria, or will Austria be true to us?" The news of Scharnhorst's death, which occurred at Prague, was an inauspicious omen, and increased the painful doubts of that most anxious period.[7]

The proximity of four imperial army corps forced the Prussians in Silesia to maintain a constant state of readiness.[8] German historians claim that the daily cost of supplying just the headquarters of each imperial corps averaged 200 thaler.[9] Of course their soldiers sustained themselves only through the pitiless extraction of Silesia's resources, yet such was the discrepancy between supply and demand that malnutrition soon ushered in his deadlier brothers: illness and starvation. Discipline continued to be a challenge, with persistent desertion thinning imperial ranks. According to Allied intelligence, Marshal Ney's III Corps had dwindled from 45,000 men on 1 May to a mere 3,700 by 6 June. According to a 16 July report from a spy at Liegnitz, fewer than half of 1,700 recently arrived Westphalians still mustered. Desertion among the French troops had likewise increased. "The rumor of the extension of the armistice has dashed all fortitude," notes the report. "One foresees only death by starvation."[10]

As supplies became scarce, imperial requisitions increased exponentially, before collapsing into chaotic arbitrariness. Similar to East Prussia in 1812, the length of French-held Silesia suffered the oppressive consequences of foreign occupation. Plundering became so general that French officers privately advised their distraught hosts to send all livestock and valuables to the neutral zone.[11] Decreeing that only one male beast should be left in each commune, the imperials assembled legions of cattle and horses. They conscripted men and collected money in the disputed Cottbus District, and extorted 600,000 thaler from the Sagan (Żagań) District and 300,000 thaler from the Grünberg (Zielona Góra) District.[12] The Goldberg and Löwenberg Districts scraped together requisitions worth 400,000 thaler; Löwenberg alone provided yards of cloth estimated to be worth 80,000 thaler. "All cattle are gone from every estate in the Bunzlau District," continued the spy report of 16 July. "They now take the sheep herds. Cattle and sheep for the most part have been taken to Saxony probably to replenish this region. Several estates have been abandoned and are completely deserted. The misery increases with each day and really is beyond all description."[13] Near the end of the armistice, the French administration ordered all cattle, corn, bread, hay, and cloth transferred to Saxony. For this task, each district had to provide fifty wagons. Even the new crop, which had yet to be harvested, was targeted for removal. Imperial raiding parties frequently violated the neutral zone partly to forage, partly to threaten the villagers with fire and death to prevent the delivery of supplies to the Allies.

Despite the problems caused by inadequate supply, numerous reinforcements flowed into the imperial camps located in eastern Saxony, Lower Lusatia, and Lower Silesia from France, Italy, and Germany. War-ravaged Saxony alone provided an additional 24,000 soldiers for the emperor. By his decree of 12 March 1813, Napoleon had established a new Grande Armée. Although the campaign opened before all thirteen army corps reached combat-ready status, tens of thousands of recruits from the levée of 1813 as well as hundreds of apprehended *réfractaires* (deserters) had left their depots well before Napoleon concluded the armistice. Thus, sufficient manpower arrived not only to fill the gaps in the corps that had fought during the Spring Campaign (III, IV, V, VI, VII, XI, and XII), but also to complete the mobilization of four additional corps (I, II, XIII, and XIV). Moreover, the total number of troopers and mounts enabled Napoleon to field five cavalry corps of varying size.[14] By mid July, the imperial army in Silesia alone had increased to approximately 142,000 men including almost 9,000 cavalry. At the expiration of the armistice in mid August, the Prussians assessed the total strength of Napoleon's mobile forces to be 373,500 men.[15]

As noted, Frederick William and Alexander agreed to augment the Austrian army with approximately 115,000 men, namely: Kleist's II Corps, the Prussian Guard Brigade, Wittgenstein's corps, and the massive Russian

Guard and Reserve commanded by the tsar's brother, Grand Duke Constantine. Barclay received nominal command of these units as well as the title of Commander in Chief of All Russian Troops; he remained at Reichenbach until the eve of the commencement of hostilities. In addition, Alexander assigned Wintzingerode's corps to Bernadotte's Army of North Germany while those commanded by Sacken and the French émigré, Louis Alexandre de Langeron, joined the Silesian Army. Dispensing with protocol, the tsar instructed his commanders to employ the generals under their orders according to ability rather than seniority. "As embarrassing as this order was to execute," commented Langeron, "I nevertheless used the rights it gave me on several occasions. At the beginning of the campaign, [Aleksandr] Rudzevich was only a major-general, and he often had 12,000–15,000 men under his command, and during the passage of the Mulde [October 1813], I gave him 18,000 infantry and the better part of my cavalry, and I left fourteen generals in the rear (of which three were lieutenant-generals) with six squadrons."[16]

All of this happened very quickly, catching Gneisenau by surprise. Using his privilege as Chief of the Prussian General Staff to communicate directly with the king, he strongly protested against the parceling of Prussia's four army corps among the three Allied armies. That Gneisenau did not participate in this decision-making process and that he learned of it through hearsay illustrate just how far removed he was from genuinely filling Scharnhorst's boots. "On my last trip to Schweidnitz," continued Gneisenau in his letter of 3 August, "I learned that the Allied armies would be divided among the theaters of war. With distress I also learned that Your Majesty's Silesian Army will be divided so that half will go to Bohemia and the other half will operate in Silesia. I can foresee nothing but disadvantages of such a division of Your Majesty's army. It will suffer reproach for any defeat of the other troops while the Prussian name will never be cited in victory. This will only serve to aggrieve or weaken national honor." More importantly, he expressed concern that the distribution of Prussian corps would leave only a small force to defend Silesia against a reportedly huge imperial army. Gneisenau also criticized the decision to place Kleist under Barclay's command, who in turn would take orders from Schwarzenberg. He complained that this relegated Kleist to being "the subordinate of a subordinate. Furthermore, Barclay's character leaves me very fearful of the outcome. Of course he will obey the direct orders of his monarch ... but otherwise, when it can, intrigue will cause a destructive effect because his secret ambition will not abide the indignity of being subordinated to the general of a foreign power."

Gneisenau concluded his letter to the king by posing four questions: "First, who will occupy Breslau [Wrocław] immediately on the 11th; second, what assignment has been given to the Russian troops in Poland; third, how strong will be the corps that assumes the defense of Silesia and how many

Russian troops will join the [Prussian] I Corps; and fourth, what shall its task be in general: must it go on the defensive or can it take the offensive?"[17] Unbeknownst to Gneisenau, the answer to his second question had already been decided: Bennigsen's Army of Poland would link with the Army of Silesia as soon as the Russians completed its mobilization. Gneisenau withdrew his ridiculous request to lead a brigade after receiving assurances that he could serve as Blücher's chief of staff and that Blücher would command an independent army. As for distributing the various corps of the Prussian army, his petition to the king achieved nothing. Bülow's III Corps and Tauentzien's IV were assigned to Bernadotte's Army of North Germany while Kleist's II Corps and the Guard Brigade were attached to Schwarzenberg's Army of Bohemia. Only Yorck's I Corps and the Silesian Landwehr would remain in Silesia.

By the end of the armistice, Coalition field forces in the German theater amounted to 512,113 men divided into 556.5 battalions and 572 squadrons with 1,380 guns and 68 Cossack regiments. In round figures, 350,000 second-line troops could also be made available. Regarding the field armies, the 254,404 men of Schwarzenberg's Army of Bohemia included 127,345 Austrians, 82,062 Russians, and 44,907 Prussians. Bernadotte's Army of North Germany consisted of 73,648 Prussians, 29,357 Russians, and 23,449 Swedes. In addition, Bernadotte held nominal command over Wallmoden's 28,000-man corps that consisted of various contingents (the German Legion, Mecklenburgers, Swedes, Hanoverians, Hanseatic Germans, and Prussians). This corps guarded Mecklenburg, observing Davout at Hamburg and the Danes in Holstein.

On 9 August, the 124,000 men and 402 guns of Kleist's II Corps, Wittgenstein's corps, and the Russo-Prussian Guard and Reserve moved into the district of Landeshut and the County of Glatz along the Bohemian frontier. The Army of Silesia received the Prussian and Russian forces that remained in the province – 104,974 soldiers and 339 guns – a force much larger than the 50,000 men first anticipated by the Allies. A further 47,650 men, mainly Landwehr, assembled under the command of Lieutenant-Colonel Johann Wilhelm von Krauseneck for the defense of Silesia and the siege of Glogau (Głogów). In the long run, the creation of multinational armies helped overcome the problems experienced by previous coalitions and paid dividends in solidifying unity of effort, at least during the war in Germany.[18]

Although the monarchs had made the decision five days earlier, Alexander and Frederick William officially appointed Blücher commander of the Silesian Army on 8 August. Gneisenau also received orders to assume his post as Chief of the General Staff of the Prussian Army at Blücher's headquarters, where he would likewise serve as chief of staff of the Silesian Army. Both Alexander and Frederick William insisted that a Prussian command this army. In the tsar's mind, Blücher's bold attack at Haynau (Chojnów) helped erase the stigma associated with his name following Bautzen. Blücher's nomination received strong support from both Hardenberg and Stein, who believed he possessed the charisma to both motivate the soldiers and electrify the nation. Yet the decision to place Blücher at the head of the new Army of Silesia rankled many Russian and Prussian officers. Critics felt that Blücher's age (seventy-one), uncertain health, and vices such as gambling and excessive alcohol consumption made him a poor choice for this massive responsibility. Others questioned his experience, claiming that Blücher knew only of the cavalry. Some pointed to the fact that, prior to the Spring Campaign, he had never commanded more than 20,000 men. Despite their monarch's role in the decision-making process, the Russians noted that foreigners commanded all three principal Allied armies. "From the choice of the commanders in chief of the three armies," noted Langeron, "one can see that there was no Russian army properly speaking. Tsar Alexander wished to appear a mere auxiliary to the great struggle that was destined to liberate Germany, for which he was then fighting, but this auxiliary greatly resembled the Supreme Chief and one can say without undue flattery that he was the Agamemnon of the Allies."[19]

The efficient staff officer and member of Scharnhorst's inner circle, Karl Wilhelm von Grolman, received the task of accompanying Barclay de Tolly, ostensibly to keep an eye on the Russian commander. News that the monarchs had officially announced Blücher's appointment as commander in chief of the Silesian Army came in the form of a pessimistic report from Grolman at Barclay's headquarters in Reichenbach:

> The situation here has been resolved: the tsar, Barclay, and all will go to Bohemia, Blücher will retain the command here [in Silesia] ... Great disputes over the command in Bohemia will occur. The Austrians believe that everything will be placed under Schwarzenberg; here one says that the commanders [Barclay and Schwarzenberg] will be equal; it appears to me that some gentlemen have the idea of solving everything through sit-down councils; thus all the previous madness and problems will occur again. Unfortunately, I am attached to Barclay and cannot get free. Everything remains wretched for the internal condition of the army; Boyen comes not, but instead remains with Bülow as chief of staff. Knesebeck will direct the entire internal business of the army but without having received the appropriate authority for this. Hardenberg is in mortal terror because the troops that are to go to Bohemia need money, and he has none. The English refuse to unload the £100,000 sterling and the military supplies that arrived at Kolberg until hostilities resume; one keeps all negotiations secret from them.

Despite this negative view of the situation, Grolman offered one tantalizing nugget. Referring to the situation in Silesia, he assured Gneisenau: "You will find here the best fate because all the wretches go to Bohemia, and so you will be your own master."[20]

The advantages this independence offered depended on how well Blücher worked with his staff, especially Gneisenau. Since 1807, Blücher's rapport with Gneisenau had blossomed into an intimate friendship. During the Spring Campaign, they proved that the stress caused by their increasing responsibilities did not affect their working relationship but had instead brought them closer. Friederich best defines their relationship: "Bound closely together by supreme leadership skills, identical military and political convictions, a burning love and respect for king and Fatherland, and a burning hatred of all things French, similar to each other in desires, insight, energy, and stamina, Blücher and Gneisenau belonged together; one cannot think of one without the other." Blücher explains the nature of their working relationship: "My very reliable chief of staff, Gneisenau, reports to me over the proposed maneuvers to be executed. Once convinced he is right, I drive my troops through hell toward the goal and I never stop until the desired goal has been accomplished – indeed, although the officers trained in the old school pout and complain and all but mutiny."[21]

Aside from a cordial relationship with the field commander, the chief of staff needed to possess the knowledge, abilities, and skills that the former lacked in order for the military marriage to work. If Blücher represented the Frederician period, Gneisenau belonged to the new age. Born near Torgau in 1760 to an impoverished Saxon lieutenant and his wife, he studied at the University of Erfurt for only two years before enlisting in the Austrian army. Enticed by an officer's commission, Gneisenau transferred to the margrave of Ansbach-Bayreuth's army and served in a regiment hired by the British to fight in the American Revolutionary War. After returning from that conflict, Gneisenau applied for Prussian service, being commissioned by Frederick II as a first lieutenant in the infantry. Like Napoleon, he possessed a voracious appetite for reading and learning. Ironically, the early career of General Bonaparte captured Gneisenau's attention. He zealously followed Napoleon's life and campaigns, seeking to uncover the secret of his success. "Thus the great Corsican was actually his master in the art of war," continues Friederich. "In his subsequent positions, he [Gneisenau] learned how the army was a living organism as well as the nature of its various branches; travels in foreign lands sharpened and expanded his view so that he belonged to the educated officers of his time but without being able to make any special claim of erudition."

An engaging outward appearance that exuded self-confidence characterized the 52-year-old. Irrepressible liveliness complemented an amiable, witty nature. Like Blücher, he combined fiery optimism with selfless patriotism. The confidant of Hardenberg, and politically connected in Austria, Russia, Sweden, and Great Britain, Gneisenau could project Blücher's voice both nationally and internationally. Always ready to recognize another's merit, Gneisenau, like Blücher, never shirked his responsibility or sought a scapegoat to blame for his own mistakes. "Through a perceptive and confident view," concludes Friederich, "through bravery and the love of taking risks, through freshness of spirit and an untiring body, he was certainly the man to place at the side of a commander like Blücher, assuming the second place with self-denial, when he probably deserved the first."[22] According to Gerhard Ritter,

> The classic human ideal Clausewitz envisaged, was, as we have seen, the universal man of culture, not yet spoiled by mechanization and specialization. It was from this living tradition that he constructed his ideal image of the general in whose mind military and political leadership were to fuse into a higher unity. If there ever was a Prussian general who met these criteria, it was his much-admired friend Neithard von Gneisenau, beyond doubt the most inspired personality among all generals who ever pitted themselves against Napoleon in combat. A quartermaster-general without proper expert training, as he himself knew and frankly admitted, he possessed the qualities of character and the intellectual faculties of the born military leader. The sweep and grandeur of his mind exert their effect even on posterity, by the impact of his eloquence, the creative imagery of his style. He was a soldier who remained sensitive to the great political ideas of his time, apprehending foreign and domestic affairs with equal enthusiasm, ever pursuing the supreme goals of national policy far beyond petty day-to-day affairs.[23]

Lieutenant-Colonel Friedrich Karl von Müffling received the quartermaster-general's position due to recommendations from his friends, Knesebeck, and the Prussian war minister, General Karl Georg von Hake. Gneisenau wanted Colonel Carl von Clausewitz, his personal friend and Scharnhorst's prodigy, and frankly told Müffling, who likewise had been trained in General Staff work by Scharnhorst. Gneisenau bemoaned the departure of Clausewitz and Grolman: Clausewitz, technically still in Russian service, went to Wallmoden's corps while Grolman soon exchanged Barclay's headquarters for that of Kleist, where he served as chief of staff of II Corps. This left Müffling, who had a history with Blücher that fell far short of amicable. In 1805, he had served on Blücher's staff and accompanied him during the retreat to Lübeck following the disaster of Jena–Auerstedt in 1806. After the French captured Scharnhorst, Müffling served as acting staff chief, persuading Blücher to surrender at Ratkau. Blücher never forgave Müffling for this and forever harbored a grudge against him. Despite being friends and comrades-in-arms with Müffling's father, Blücher despised "the lurking observer in Müffling, who possessed a great satirical talent and the gift to imitate to an exceptional degree, but concealed both and only seldom with great caution allowed them to show; instead, he aspired to have a serious, educated demeanor, a diplomatic reserve, which he succeeded at all too well. Blücher knew that Müffling frequently made jokes about him, mimicked his speech and gestures, and in general exposed his infirmities, and it irked him all the more the way he would conceal all of this." Indeed, although Blücher never said a word about the mocking, he could not tolerate "the Philosopher of Weimar," a relatively sanitary nickname he had for Müffling compared to other, less flattering monikers. Until the end of the armistice, Blücher referred to him as the "commandant of the headquarters."[24]

Apparently, Müffling did not resent Blücher for the ill-feelings the old hussar harbored toward him and even believed that the general liked him. Müffling maintains that "Blücher was friendly to me; and since the conflict at Haynau, which I had proposed, and for which I had drafted the plan . . . I rose in his favor, because in it he thought I understood the cavalry service. This was an advantage I did not underrate; yet I was not placed immediately under him, but under Gneisenau; and with the great difference of our views, the idea that I could gain his entire confidence would have been hopeless." According to Hans Delbrück, "Müffling was very different from Gneisenau and Blücher; he relied more on the watch and the compass, without confidence in spiritual greatness ... almost pedantically observing the minutes." Although Gneisenau initially valued Müffling's sober, reflective nature, the relationship soon soured. Müffling intimates that he and Gneisenau possessed opposing views of warfare, but that the latter "declared that the difference lay rather in my [Müffling's] being softer and less self-confident than he, and that this inclined me to listen to considerations he disregarded."[25]

Despite their differences, Müffling always obeyed Gneisenau's instructions. A future Chief of the General Staff of the Prussian Army, he faithfully and indefatigably drafted orders based on Gneisenau's directives. Like Napoleon's renowned chief of staff, Marshal Alexandre Berthier, Müffling possessed the great ability to process numerous commands and quickly present them accurately and concisely. Gneisenau discussed operations with him, listened to his opinion, yet made the final decision. In important matters, Gneisenau followed his own conviction based on the similar beliefs he shared with Blücher. If Müffling initially opposed an idea, Gneisenau attempted to understand his arguments and to correct and educate him. Based on this open dialogue, Gneisenau confidently allowed Müffling to compose the instructions for the army based on his directives: a responsibility that Müffling executed with great utility during the campaigns of 1813 and 1814. Müffling's ability to speak French made him valuable to Gneisenau, who never mastered the language. In the hope of winning Gneisenau's "esteem," Müffling felt it necessary to distance himself from Blücher, lest he come between field commander and staff chief.[26]

For decades, Müffling had concealed his jealousy of Blücher, Gneisenau, Grolman, and Clausewitz. After they died and the truth appeared to be buried in the past, Müffling went to work on his memoirs, actually noting in them that "now, when the heat and passion of the time have died away, and many questions important to military history still remain, accounts may be supplied of many verbal transactions known to few persons still living. False conclusions may thus be corrected, and false accusations that have received acceptance for a period of thirty years will be refuted." The 75-year-old Müffling died on 16 January 1851; that same year saw the publication of his *Aus meinem Leben,* or *Passages from My Life.* Filled with unjustified innuendo and outright defamation, his memoirs paint an objectionable picture of his colleagues, accusing them of being members of a secret society, the Tugendbund, who pursued their own political agendas. For example, in describing their difference of opinion over the armistice, Müffling wrote that it had been "censured, especially by the members of the Tugendbund (a so-called alliance of students), as unnecessary and as a mistake; nay, it was regarded as a misfortune for the state. I had many heated disputes with General Gneisenau who, in his excitement, had sent a letter to the king bitterly censuring the armistice. The general wanted to convince me. I opposed him very calmly, but was determined not to yield, because he spoke as the head of a party, which had its seat in the army."[27] Yet not all who had lived during the Napoleonic Wars were dead. On 29 April 1854, General Ferdinand Theodor von Stosch, Gneisenau's adjutant in 1813, explained to Hans Delbrück: "I have had only three opportunities to look at Müffling's attack on Gneisenau in his posthumous memoir. The book itself is a stigma of Müffling's vanity."[28]

During the course of the war, Gneisenau used Müffling's friendship with Knesebeck for the good of the Silesian Army and the war effort itself.[29] "Remaining on good terms with Knesebeck was an exercise in cleverness," wrote one of Blücher's biographers, General Wolfgang von Unger, "which Scharnhorst had also practiced. Now it was even more important since Hardenberg did not always find himself with the king's entourage and was not always familiar with the military situation." Knesebeck likewise saw it as beneficial to maintain a close relationship with Gneisenau. Thus, both Blücher and Gneisenau managed to have an outwardly cordial relationship with Knesebeck, who in his position as the king's adjutant-general received all incoming correspondence over the course of events even though this task did not pertain to his actual sphere of jurisdiction. For the sake of the war effort, Gneisenau wisely established direct communication with Knesebeck. Neither infrequently nor insignificantly did their views of strategy differ over the course of the campaign. Fortunately for Blücher and Gneisenau, their relationship with Stein and Tsar Alexander offset Knesebeck's conservative influence on Frederick William. Blücher, Gneisenau, Stein, and Alexander firmly resolved that the war could end only with Napoleon's downfall and the restoration of an independent Germany. Early in the war, Stein provided the link between Blücher/Gneisenau and the tsar by sharing with Alexander every memo that Gneisenau wrote to the former Prussian minister. Through this support, Stein helped facilitate the excellent relationship that developed between Blücher and Alexander. Long after Stein faded from the military scene, the beneficial understanding between Blücher and Alexander proved decisive.[30]

On 9 August, Blücher received an invitation from Barclay, now the ranking Allied general in Silesia, to meet with him at Reichenbach on the 10th to discuss "various important circumstances." That same day, the 9th, a comprehensive letter arrived in which Barclay officially informed Blücher that he would command the Army of Silesia. "Because a considerable portion of the army stationed in Silesia until now will march to Bohemia and ... I will follow this army, our two monarchs have decided to place all Allied troops that remain behind in Silesia under your tried and tested command." Barclay explained that he would provide Blücher an overview "of the entire course of operations decided upon by our two monarchs in agreement with the emperor of Austria and the crown prince of Sweden and in this way provide guidance for your future operations which, because of your military experience, will certainly add new laurels to the glory of the Allies."

Choosing not to reveal the details of the new Reichenbach Plan, Barclay simply stated that "the guiding principle of all our operations is the Protocol agreed upon by our two monarchs and the crown prince of Sweden at Trachenberg, of which I enclose a copy." He then explained that as the "main idea for the general plan of military operations in Silesia," Blücher would seek to do the greatest possible damage to any enemy forces that turned against the Army of Bohemia or the Army of North Germany. "Nevertheless," continued the Russian commander, "at the same time you must seek to avoid a battle against superior forces. In this regard, it is absolutely necessary for the army left behind in Silesia to constantly seek to harass the enemy with its advance guard and all of its light troops so that he is never lost from sight and cannot win a march toward Saxony; yet the main body can never engage in a battle with a superior enemy."

Barclay advised that, if Napoleon committed his main force against the Silesian Army, Blücher should slow the enemy's march as much as possible, withdraw east-southeast toward the Glatzer Neiße River, and avoid a battle against superior forces.[31] Blücher's right wing – Sacken's Russian army corps – would withdraw up the Oder, posting some of its light cavalry on the right bank to maintain communication with Bennigsen's Army of Poland. Blücher's left, General Guillaume-Guignard St.-Priest's Russian army corps, would withdraw to Glatz on the Glatzer Neiße, hugging the Riesengebirge (Krkonoše, Karkonosze) to secure communication with the Bohemian Army and Allied Headquarters. Meanwhile, the main body of the Silesian Army would take its direction toward the fortress of Neiße on the Glatzer Neiße, "finding a new strongpoint in this fortress and its entrenched camp, which must be placed in readiness while the Army of Bohemia and that of the crown prince of Sweden will operate against the enemy's rear." He advised Blücher to insure that all Silesian fortresses received their assigned garrisons sooner rather than later.

"On the other hand, should Napoleon direct his main force to Saxony or the Mark [Brandenburg], it will be necessary for the army in Silesia to likewise take the offensive."[32] Barclay instructed Blücher to move his left wing – St.-Priest's corps – from Landeshut along the Riesengebirge "*durch schnelles Vordingen* [through rapid advances]" to Marklissa (Leśna) on the left bank of the Queis (Kwisa) River, bypassing the considerable entrench-ments the imperials had purportedly erected along the Bober (Bóbr) River. In the meantime, Blücher would lead his main body toward Goldberg. As for Sacken and Blücher's right wing, if the imperials did not force a union with the main body by making a stand on either the Bober or the Queis, Sacken would move further northwest, "advancing in forced marches between Bunzlau and Sagan toward Großenhain and seeking to open com-munication with the crown prince of Sweden through a strong cavalry detachment." If Napoleon directly targeted the Army of North Germany, Blücher would proceed according to these same instructions, but continue all the way to the Elbe. Thus, in the case of a French offensive against the Army of North Germany, Barclay explained that "we [the Bohemian Army] must then concentrate our main force on the Elbe and immediately march against the enemy's rear, with the main force on the left bank of the Elbe and the Silesian Army on the right bank." Sacken's corps and especially all of its cavalry would march "more in the direction of Berlin and operate with the greatest force against the enemy's rear."

Barclay recognized that, for Blücher to react in time to these possible movements by the enemy, he needed a constant flow of accurate news. Because the Silesian Army lacked large numbers of light cavalry, the Russian commander strongly urged Blücher to form *Streifkorps*. "General [Sergey] Lanskoy with his cavalry detachment can provide good service; also Colonels [Vasily] Rakhmanov and [Aleksandr] Figner of Sacken's corps and General [Paisi] Kaysarov on the left wing ... can be advantageously employed for this task." He also expressed concern that the imperial forces in Silesia would occupy the neutral zone before Blücher's forces. Calling the prevention of this "desirable," Barclay suggested that Blücher enter the neutral zone before 16 August if he detected that the enemy had crossed the line of demarcation. If not, he advised Blücher to enter the neutral zone shortly after 12:00 A.M. on 17 August. Barclay believed that Sacken's vanguard should march to Neu-markt (Środa Śląska) while his main body occupied Breslau. Yorck and Langeron should concentrate their corps at Striegau (Strzegom), pushing their vanguards to Jauer. Barclay recommended that, on Blücher's left,

St.-Priest's corps should forward its vanguard from Landeshut to Hirschberg (Jelenia Góra). Concluding, Barclay stated: "These are the main ideas drafted for the plan of operations for the army in Silesia according to the views of our sovereigns. Based on your well-known military experience and insight, you will adapt them to the circumstances and modify them according to the enemy's operations. In the case that you do so, it is desired that you establish direct and rapid communication with the main army in Bohemia and the Polish Army ... Likewise it would be good to open a rapid form of communication with the crown prince of Sweden."[33]

In a second letter dated 10 August, the Russian commander reminded Blücher that, although the armistice formally expired that very day, a six-day suspension of hostilities would ensue. Thus, the neutral zone could not be entered until 17 August. However, in a postscript he added: "Nevertheless, if the enemy undertakes hostilities, this prohibition should be disregarded." Between 8 and 10 August, reports reached Blücher's headquarters about extensive French movements toward the neutral zone: the march of imperial troops to Glogau, the concentration of considerable forces at Liegnitz, and the advance of elements from the enemy's right wing into the Riesengebirge as well as toward Spiller (Pasiecznik) on the road to Hirschberg. At the same time, rumors reached Barclay that the French did not intend to honor the six-day suspension of hostilities. This led to the belief that the imperials would enter the neutral zone at the earliest possible moment, thus prompting a third letter from Barclay on 10 August: "From the enclosed reports, you will see that we believe the enemy will enter the neutral zone before the expiration of the six-day suspension of hostilities, thus making it necessary to double all security measures." Barclay instructed Blücher to act according to the disposition contained in his first letter of 10 August "as soon as one squad of enemy troops crosses the line of demarcation."[34]

During their meeting on 10 August, Barclay reiterated the main points of his letters, adding that the Silesian Army (1) would advance toward the enemy; (2) could never lose contact with the enemy; and (3) could never engage a superior enemy force. Should Napoleon advance into Silesia, Blücher would retreat and draw imperial forces into the interior. Yet, as soon as the imperials broke off the chase and turned around to confront another Allied army, Blücher would pursue them. If Napoleon allocated his main force to operations in Saxony or Brandenburg, Blücher would advance toward the imperial forces that remained in Silesia or pursue them wherever they went. If Napoleon directed his main strength against the Army of North Germany, which was rumored to be likely, the Bohemian Army would pursue along the left bank of the Elbe while the Silesian Army moved down its right bank. Only Schwarzenberg's army received authorization to take the offensive by advancing from Bohemia to Saxony by way of Teplitz. As his main goal, Blücher would avoid being defeated, but remain close enough to the imperial forces in Silesia to follow them and arrive in time to participate in a general battle in the vicinity of the Elbe.

As Barclay lectured, Blücher listened quietly, shaking his head in doubt. After the Russian commander finished, Blücher rejected the assignment. He offered his resignation, claiming he could not operate so tightly bound to the defensive. Barclay and his quartermaster-general, Diebitsch, maintained that Blücher had misinterpreted the instructions, that they were not to be taken literally, and that the Prussian could take the offensive under favorable circumstances: "An officer in command of an army of 100,000 men can never be tied down absolutely to the defensive; thus, if a good opportunity arose, he could attack and defeat his enemy." Blücher demanded approval in writing from the monarchs. If they did not agree with this condition, then they could find another assignment for him. Barclay did not dare amend instructions he had received from the monarchs but Blücher insisted that he would accept command of the Silesian Army only on the condition that the instructions be modified. Moreover, he asked Barclay to notify Alexander and Frederick William of this condition. Müffling believed that Barclay had informed the sovereigns but that nothing ever resulted either verbally or in writing. Receiving no other assignment from the sovereigns, Blücher assumed the monarchs had approved his demand and thus considered his assignment to be modified. In his mind, Blücher unfettered himself from a Fabian strategy and protected himself against any reproach of having disobeyed orders should he suffer a setback. He informed Bernadotte that "the Trachenberg Convention forms the basis of my instructions."[35]

Totaling 104,974 men, the Army of Silesia numbered approximately 74,000 infantry, 24,000 cavalry, and 339 guns. Russian troops provided the majority of Blücher's forces, some 66,490 men grouped in three army corps led by Langeron (34,551 men), Sacken (18,353 men), and St.-Priest (13,586 men); General Pyotr Pahlen, known as Pahlen III, temporarily commanded until St.-Priest arrived from Vienna. Blücher's Prussian troops consisted of the 39,243 men of Yorck's I Army Corps.[36] Behind the field army, the mainly Landwehr Prussian auxiliary forces, numbering 47,650 men, garrisoned the fortresses and depots of Upper Silesia. Of these, one Landwehr detachment of 12,990 men in 8 battalions and 12 squadrons supported by 4 guns received the assignment of blockading Glogau after hostilities resumed.[37]

Prussian and Russian army organization differed considerably. While the Prussians utilized regiments, brigades, and army corps, the Russians formed regiments, brigades, divisions, infantry/cavalry corps, and army corps. The Prussians integrated infantry, cavalry, and artillery on the brigade level while the Russians did so at the army corps level. Each Russian infantry corps consisted of two infantry divisions and foot artillery but no cavalry. Russian cavalry corps *usually* contained at least one regular cavalry division, one Cossack division, and horse artillery. To create army corps, which the

Russians did not numerically designate, they combined their infantry and cavalry corps.[38] For the Silesian Army, the Russians allocated five infantry corps and two ad hoc cavalry corps. The XI Infantry Corps and 1 pioneer company along with a cavalry corps consisting of 2nd Hussar Division, 1 brigade from 3rd Dragoon Division, and 12 Cossack regiments (4,700 men) formed Sacken's army corps. St.-Priest's VIII Infantry Corps technically belonged to Wittgenstein's army corps but the Russians created an independent army corps by combining St.-Priest's infantry with another ad hoc cavalry corps formed by 1st Dragoon Division, 2 regiments from 4th Dragoon Division, and 3 Cossack regiments (1,000 men).[39] The VI, IX, and X Infantry Corps combined with I Cavalry Corps, which included 4,800 Cossacks, to form Langeron's army corps. Conversely, Yorck's corps contained four combined-arms brigades composed of ten to twelve battalions, four squadrons, and one battery of eight six-pound guns. His Reserve Cavalry consisted of three brigades and horse batteries, with Landwehr accounting for four of its seven regiments. Fifty-six guns including two batteries of twelve-pound pieces, two batteries of six, two batteries of horse, and one battery of three-pound pieces constituted the Reserve Artillery. Neither the Silesian nor the North German Armies contained reserves or elite forces at the army level.

Forming the right wing of the Silesian Army, Sacken's corps camped just east of Breslau on the right bank of the Oder. Nine Cossack Regiments (3,743 men) formed a cordon along the right bank of the Oder between Steinau and Breslau while two regiments each of Hussars and Cossacks (2,213 men) under Lanskoy pushed north on the right flank to Polnischlissa (Leszno), thirty miles east of Glogau. Between Breslau and Schweidnitz, Yorck's corps formed the center.[40] As the left wing, Langeron's army corps camped north of Schweidnitz at Jauernick (Stary Jaworów). Langeron's thirteen Cossack regiments extended northeast along the line of demarcation formed by the Striegau stream (Strzegomka) from the mountains to Kanth. On the extreme left wing, Pahlen III's corps took post in the mountains by Landeshut, establishing communication with the 6,000 men of Schwarzenberg's Austrian 2nd Light Division, commanded by Bubna, on the opposite side of the Riesengebirge.

To feed the troops, the Prussian leadership of the Silesian Army sought to improve on hard lessons recently learned. During the armistice, the Russians and Prussians utilized magazines to supply their men. Although the provincial and municipal authorities of Silesia did their utmost to provide for the magazines, problems inevitably surfaced. First and foremost, the vast number of Allied soldiers – some 200,000 – automatically strained the supply system. Second, the region's shortage of wagons – many of which had been confiscated by the opposing armies – hindered the transport of food to the magazines. Dependent on Polish grain imports, both Upper and Lower

Silesia quickly suffered from resource exhaustion. Obtaining adequate amounts of forage for the horses also proved problematic. As the truncated eastern portion of Lower Silesia allotted to the Allies by the armistice did not produce enough oats, they supplemented the feed with corn and barley. Horses in the Prussian service found their diets reduced to peacetime rations. The Allies completely exhausted the territory they occupied, which prompted some Russians to pillage. A late June protest to the Prussians lodged by Barclay on multiple accounts offers insight into the growing dilemma over resources. Gneisenau forwarded the letter to Hardenberg, adding: "you much more than I can better judge this complaint – mainly that the Russian army suffers a shortage of all necessities while ours is provided with everything. If these shortages in the Russian army are due to negligence of our officials they will not go unpunished by you. For this reason, I asked the general [Barclay] to inform you."[41]

Although the Allies suffered from supply shortages, the French fared worse because their problems had started in May. By early August, Blücher's spies reported a complete lack of food in the imperial camps. Deserters confirmed that the daily ration for soldiers amounted to one-half to one-quarter pound of meat and little salt while bread rations consisted of one and one-half pounds every other day. Thus, from the pure standpoint of feeding the troops, the neutral zone offered pristine supplies of food and forage. As it had been untouched for more than two months, both armies desired to be the first to take possession of this oasis. The Prussians became increasingly concerned that the imperials would forage as much as they could as soon as the armistice expired. "But what if the French army attempted this foraging during the armistice?" asked Müffling. "Complaints over the violation of international law would not return what was lost. For this reason, it was Blücher's burning desire to find cause to occupy the neutral zone . . . before the expiration of the armistice."[42]

The march to Bohemia of more than 100,000 Russians and Prussians did little to ease supply problems. After two months, Silesia reached the point of exhaustion. Regardless, Friedrich Wilhelm Ribbentrop, Blücher's longtime friend and commissar of the Silesian Army, sought to prepare the troops for the advance into the French occupation zone, which he believed would be stripped bare by the time the Allies arrived. Overambitious to a fault, Ribbentrop planned to provide each soldier with various victuals in the following daily supply amounts: biscuit (three days), bread (one day), rice (six days), and salt (seven days). He wanted each brigade supplied with four days of meat and brandy, and the chuck wagons loaded with a three-day supply of biscuit and a four-day supply of rice, salt, meat, and flour for baking bread. Reserve magazines would contain a four-day supply of biscuit and an eight-day supply of liquor. For the horses, the troops would be supplied grain fodder for two days.[43]

To achieve these goals, the district government of Frankenstein (Ząbkowice Śląskie) gathered a four-month supply of victuals to feed 120,000 men and 40,000 horses. On 17 August, Blücher's army received one month's worth of these stores, while Ribbentrop equally divided the supplies for the remaining three months among the fortresses of Schweidnitz, Glatz, Neiße, and Kosel (Koźle). After the war resumed, the Liegnitz District government received orders to provide the same amount of supplies to satisfy three months. For each corps of the Silesian Army, the Prussians established three supply depots and two field bakeries.[44] Each depot contained a park of 120 four-team farm wagons under a foreman to oversee the care of the horses and vehicles as well as a government commissar to coordinate deliveries. Each depot contained an emergency supply of six days of food for its corps. Blücher's staff allocated three-eighths of the total amount of supplies to Yorck and Langeron each; Sacken received the rest. For provisions, Yorck's corps alone possessed 180 wagons divided into 3 trains of 50 each and 1 reserve train of 30. A military commissar administered each. Despite Ribbentrop's efforts, tremendous difficulties arose following the resumption of hostilities due to the Silesian Army's unique assignment as well as the rainy season's corrosive impact on the roads. The fact that the Russians lacked field bakeries had apparently escaped Ribbentrop's attention. Moreover, his allies refused to build earthen ovens, which the Russians had first utilized in 1812 at the fortified camp of Drissa, as long as the prospect remained of receiving "better and cleaner" – according to Prussian General Staff historian Colonel Eduard Friedrich von Höpfner – Prussian bread. Although the Prussians assigned commissary officers to the Russian corps, they could not completely eliminate all the difficulties "that are always raised by foreign troops with foreign supply requirements."[45]

As for troops, the Prussians moved heaven and earth to replace the losses of the Spring Campaign, expand the regular army, and complete the mobilization of more than 100,000 Landwehr. From a population of some 5,000,000, the Prussians fielded approximately 275,000 men for the Fall Campaign.[46] A 12 July order decreed that each Prussian brigade would include one Line regiment, one Reserve regiment consisting of *Krümpern*, thus soldiers who had received military training, and four Landwehr battalions. Frederick William later decided to organize the militia into regiments, thus changing this formula slightly so that each brigade consisted of one regiment each of Line, Reserve, and Landwehr. The order of battle for Kleist's II and Bülow's III Corps reflected this ratio, yet the War Department instructed Yorck to transfer three of his four Reserve regiments to Tauentzien's IV Corps and replace them with Landwehr regiments. Of Yorck's forty-five battalions, the Landwehr accounted for twenty-four while Kleist's ratio was sixteen of forty-one, and Bülow's twelve of forty-one. The final organization gave the impression that Yorck's corps would serve an auxiliary role only.[47]

Not only did the Prussians expand their combat power, but they also continuously sought improvement. In particular, Frederick William emphasized the need for flexibility, mobility, and speed. In a cabinet order issued from Neiße on 29 July, he prohibited the use of an entire Prussian brigade as the vanguard for an army corps. Instead, when a vanguard needed to be formed, the king's instructions specifically called for Fusilier and Reserve Infantry Battalions only, which would be drawn from all four brigades of a Prussian army corps. For every Fusilier Battalion employed in the van, one Reserve Infantry Battalion would likewise be assigned to it. However, each regiment would be required to provide only one battalion until the Landwehr received sufficient field experience to likewise serve in the vanguard. As for cavalry, the king stipulated that only hussars and uhlans drawn from the brigade cavalry be utilized for advance guard duty. Should a vanguard require more sabers, the squadrons from the Reserve Cavalry should be used, but not cuirassiers.[48]

In Silesia, Gneisenau labored to make the Silesian Landwehr combat-ready in accordance with the king's announcement that militia regiments would be amalgamated with their Line and Reserve counterparts at the brigade level. Auxiliaries no longer, Frederick William expected the Landwehr to fight alongside the army. As noted, Gneisenau took control of the Military Government of Silesia for the duration of the armistice to direct both the mobilization of the province's Landwehr as well as the measures to defend the province; Bülow assumed the same post in Brandenburg. Gneisenau utilized his boundless energy to oversee the equipping and training of the Landwehr. He immediately recognized the militia's value for defensive purposes, but transforming the Landwehr into a field army in nine weeks proved extremely challenging. Hardenberg did all he could to remedy the persistent shortage of cash, which did much to hinder the mobilization. Slowly but steadily, Gneisenau received shipments of shoes, muskets, uniforms, and cooking gear so that the number of men who were marching barefoot armed only with pikes gradually decreased. For the defense of Silesia, Gneisenau's assistants inspected the fortresses of Schweidnitz, Glatz, Kosel, and Silberberg. As much as funds allowed, he ordered their fortifications improved and warehouses stocked; any surpluses went straight to the troops.[49]

Blücher praised Gneisenau's work with the militia. *"Landwehren Sie man immer druff!* [Really let those militiamen have it!]," he exclaimed in a 29 June response to Gneisenau's request for his opinion of the first Silesian militia battalions (four in total) deemed combat-ready. Three weeks later he again wrote Gneisenau: "Yesterday I inspected twenty battalions and four squadrons of the Landwehr organized by you. I must confess that I am very satisfied with their condition, the grand duke [Constantine] joined me during the inspection; he mounted a horse that I gave him and the troops marched past him: he admitted his amazement about their fine condition. Another sixteen battalions of all strengths that will join the two corps arrived today. Tomorrow I will inspect Kleist's corps; I have already inspected Yorck's. The troops are in fine condition."[50] Eventually, the Silesian Landwehr provided ten infantry regiments (forty battalions) and seven cavalry regiments (twenty-eight squadrons) for the Prussian I and II Corps.[51] Compared to Prussia's other provinces, Gneisenau's success in Silesia remained unparalleled. However, recruited mainly from the impoverished regions of Silesia, from the weaving and factory districts, the men – although willing and quick to learn – were far inferior in physical strength to the young men drafted from the agricultural provinces. Thus, in terms of endurance, the Silesian Landwehr proved to be the worst militia of the entire state.[52]

As a matter of principle, the Landwehr received only the equipment that the regular army did not need. Consequently, the militia's shortages of uniforms and equipment grossly overshadowed the Line's deficiencies. One soaking from the summer rains rendered the ill-prepared tunics and blue jackets far too tight while the linen trousers shrank to the point of discomfort; the shoes proved so poor that many preferred to go barefoot. The caps that covered their heads offered little protection against rain drops or saber cuts. Overcoats could not be provided, cooking gear remained sparse, and the men received linen bags rather than rucksacks. "The spirit and goodwill of the Prussian troops were beyond all description," judged Müffling. "Yet at this time they were far behind the Russians in arms and equipment. The Silesian Landwehr was particularly ill supplied with uniforms; they were even lacking shoes at the beginning of the campaign. Cloth had been obtained wherever it could be found. There had been no time to take the usual precautions in preparing it, and after the first rain the jackets shrank so much that they barely covered body and arms. The sick lists of the first four weeks of the campaign proved how much the health of the men was affected by insufficient clothing."[53]

Limited supplies of muskets meant one-third of the Silesian Landwehr marched with pikes until captured enemy firearms could replace them. This meant that target practice remained a luxury that few Prussian recruits enjoyed. Despite the hard work that went into the mobilization of the Landwehr, many battalions still lacked the necessary gear for campaigning. Training fell short of satisfactory for the Landwehr mainly due to the limited number of experienced men to lead the drills. Nevertheless, exercises progressed far enough by the time the militia battalions joined Yorck's corps that they could maneuver on par with the relatively inexperienced Line units. Discipline remained a concern as even the best intentions could not create unit cohesion instantaneously, especially when some of the officers possessed no more military knowledge or education than their men. Among four militia companies that reported to Yorck's corps at the same time, not a single sergeant could write. "In order to increase my difficulties, they have assigned to me four of the worst Landwehr battalions," complained Yorck. "On account of some personages, the poor state must be bled and afflicted; you can easily imagine, my friend, the kind of mood this places me in."[54] In general, more officers with military training could be found among the Landwehr cavalry than the infantry but the lack of experienced leaders remained the militia's greatest obstacle.

For any army, the creation of cavalry within a short timeframe posed almost insurmountable challenges. Yorck's corps contained three forms of cavalry: Line, Landwehr, and National. Voluntary enlistment and contributions from the provinces formed the last category: the East Prussian National Cavalry and the Mecklenburg-Strelitz Hussars, both of which served in Yorck's corps. Pride as well as wallets deep enough to keep a son at home with minimal public shame insured that both regiments received quality equipment and sufficient arms. Each Mecklenburg-Strelitzer Hussar carried two pistols and one rifled carbine while the depot of the East Prussian National Cavalry Regiment supplied each soldier with a lance, but only a portion of the men received pistols. Both units benefited from the large number of unemployed veteran officers from the pre-Jena army but few experienced troopers served in the ranks. Moreover, while the quality of mounts for both regiments exceeded those of the Line cavalry in quality, age, and strength, the average soldier's equestrian skill and knowledge of horse care remained poor, resulting in the premature exhausting of many mounts. The East Prussian National Regiment possessed one Jäger squadron; the Mecklenburgers one detachment of forty Jäger.[55]

Numerous experienced veterans from the pre-Jena army filled the gaps in Yorck's Line cavalry regiments, meaning that very few raw recruits needed to be trained but horses remained in short supply. The Lithuanian Dragoons, 2nd Leib Hussars, and Brandenburg Hussars each contained one volunteer Jäger squadron as their fifth field squadron. Many of these volunteer troopers had already gained combat experience in the Spring Campaign, making them extremely valuable, particularly as dispatch riders and orderlies. The Jäger of the Brandenburg Hussars benefited from a full complement of carbines. Although the least valuable of the three, the Silesian Landwehr cavalry not only possessed good mounts, but because former officers of the pre-Jena army conducted their exercises they also progressed much further than the Silesian Landwehr infantry. On the whole, the troopers of the Silesian Landwehr cavalry appeared zealous and hardy compared to their poorer counterparts on foot.

Morale remained positive among officers and soldiers in all three categories of cavalry but goodwill did not suffice to overcome the inherent difficulties that arose with the army's rapid expansion. The contrast between Yorck's twenty Landwehr squadrons and twenty-eight Line squadrons remained glaring, although the former eventually became adept at using the lance. On the average, Yorck's cavalry regiments fell short of their full complement by 30 men and between 50 and 100 mounts; only the Brandenburg and Mecklenburg-Strelitz Hussars as well as the Landwehr regiments approached full capacity. While the quality of horses and overall training varied, Prussia's empty arsenals and depleted pastures affected both Line and Landwehr. Prior to the Russian campaign, the imperials requisitioned every horse they could find. Foreign horses, which the state purchased mainly from Russia for use by the Line, took time to arrive. As a result, numerous unbroken horses, coach horses, and older horses needed to be employed, producing a multifarious composition. Horses for the Landwehr's cavalry remained in even shorter supply, resulting in the employment of many poor and unserviceable beasts that should have been enjoying the quiet of the pasture. Regarding arms, the Prussians attempted to provide each soldier with a saber and pistol. Line regiments had to surrender their second pistols to the Landwehr. In total, only 25 percent of the Prussian cavalry carried carbines. As uhlans, the East Prussian National Cavalry Regiment and all Landwehr troopers bore lances. The volunteer Jäger squadrons formed the best armed of their respective regiments.

In general, uniforms and equipment for both man and horse likewise varied in terms of quality. Yorck's two national cavalry regiments generally possessed satisfactory equipment and uniforms while those of the Line bordered on worn and poor; the equipment and uniforms of the Landwehr cavalry ranged from extremely poor to incomplete or even nonexistent. Yorck's Line units stood far behind the Russians as well as the Prussians of Kleist's corps in terms of equipment and arms. The Landwehr – 13,370 men of his 30,000 infantry and 1,320 troopers of his 6,000 cavalry – looked the least impressive. After an inspection, he explained to the king the needs of his men, especially footgear. Frederick William lamely responded: "This is very displeasing to me, but the war has needs and everything has started."[56]

As for the Prussian artillery, inadequate funds coupled with equipment shortages caused dire problems. Among the thirteen batteries assigned to I Corps and commanded by Lieutenant-Colonel Johann Heinrich Otto von Schmidt, the majority struck Yorck as being pitiful. "Regarding the uniforms of the gunners," stated an inspection report from Yorck's corps dated 21 July, "everything is very poor; the gunners assigned to the horse batteries are almost naked. With each horse battery there are more than thirty men who have no overalls but instead perform their duties in tattered and coarse cotton trousers. Also, the overcoats and the linen sacks as well as the caparisons are extremely poor." Regarding the guns and carriages, the report noted that, "due to the shortage of funds, only the most pressing repairs were made and much still remains to be done. Harnesses and stall equipment and everything belonging to the guns are in a very pitiful condition by every battery."[57]

Yorck's Line infantry contained several companies that had never experienced combat and had not completed their training before the armistice expired. In general, replacements for the Line and Reserve had been under arms for three months when they reported to their units during the armistice.[58] Approximately one-third of the eight battalions designated as "veteran" consisted of conscripts. "The I Army Corps has had great changes," he wrote on 4 July. "It now consists solely of recruits: I do not have 1,000 veteran soldiers."[59] On the other hand, I Corps received four of the Army's six Grenadier Battalions: the 1st East Prussian, Leib, West Prussian, and Silesian. Led by proven commanders, these elite units combined with two companies of East Prussian Jäger to form a special ad hoc Grenadier Brigade commanded by Major August von Hiller; they would soon demonstrate the meaning of being the "*Zange und Hammer* [hammer and tongs]" of Yorck's corps. The Grenadiers along with the 5th and 13th Silesian Landwehr Infantry Regiments (four battalions each), the 2nd Leib Hussar Regiment, known as the Black Hussars and bearing the death's head on their shakos, and one battery of eight-pound foot artillery formed Yorck's 1st Brigade commanded by Colonel Karl Friedrich Franciscus von Steinmetz. Apart from only one Landwehr infantry regiment – the 6th Silesian – Yorck's 2nd Brigade consisted of the veteran 1st and 2nd East Prussian Infantry Regiments (three battalions each). Lieutenant-Colonel Karl Friedrich von Lobenthal, who had already distinguished himself, commanded the former while Colonel Ludwig Friedrich von Sjöholm "the Silent," as Yorck once called him, led the later. The imposingly equipped troopers and excellent steeds of the Mecklenburg-Strelitz Hussar Regiment served as the brigade cavalry. Suspecting these units to be hand-picked, Yorck soon discovered the reason. Because General Friedrich Heinrich von Hünerbein still had not recovered from the wound he received at Lützen, Duke Karl of Mecklenburg-Strelitz (Frederick William's brother-in-law), received command of his brigade. "I'd rather have the devil instead of another prince," exclaimed Yorck after receiving the news of Karl's appointment. He viewed this as the beginning of an attempt to relieve him of command as retribution for Tauroggen. Embittered, Yorck felt that his detractors could have at least openly launched their attack. While he could not be cashiered or brushed aside altogether, they should have awarded Karl command of the corps and placed a brigade in Yorck's hands "so that all would report to the right source" in his opinion.[60]

To further increase Yorck's angst, Karl did not have a favorable reputation in the army after he had furloughed himself following the battle of

Auerstedt and returned to Mecklenburg-Strelitz. His reinstatement in the army – probably in 1810 – caused much indignation. Despite his relationship to the king and the Black Eagle he wore on his breast, Yorck received the army's youngest brigade commander with the cold aristocratic politeness that his entourage feared more than his wrath. Before the resumption of hostilities, Yorck traveled to Klein Öls to inspect 2nd Brigade. Dismounting, he walked through the ranks of the 1st and 2nd East Prussian Infantry Regiments, minutely inspecting everything but finding no cause to complain. Every so often he tested a musket: all were flawless. He finally found one whose firing mechanism was not in the proper order. He turned to the entourage that followed him: "The gentleman," he said, staring at the prince, "should nevertheless always remember that soldiers are for war and are not toys; such neglect of a weapon is inexcusable, one loses battles because of such disorder and negligence, and the fate of the monarchy possibly hangs on one lost battle." Although Karl remained silent as Yorck's very offensive tirade continued, his face grew pale and then red with rage. At the conclusion of the review, Karl extended Yorck an invitation to breakfast with him, which the corps commander accepted. A kinder and friendlier Yorck broke bread with his subordinates, allowing them to see a side that few ever did: the accomplished man of the world. After a cheerful hour he took his leave. As the prince accompanied him to his carriage, Yorck wished him "a favorable reunion on the battlefield." Driving away, Yorck turned to one of the adjutants accompanying him: "There, I have given the gracious gentleman his lesson; he will immediately write to the king over everything and that is just what I want."[61]

Like 1st Brigade, General Heinrich Wilhelm von Horn's 7th Brigade contained two Landwehr infantry regiments – the 4th and 15th Silesian – but only one Line regiment, the Leib. In addition, two companies of Guard Jäger were attached to the brigade as well as the Thuringian Battalion from Weimar. Still uniformed in the French style and still adhering to French regulations, the battalion had mobilized in the spring to join Napoleon's army as it marched to the Saale. The soldiers had purportedly waited for the opportunity to allow themselves to be surrounded by Prussian Hussars at Ruhla. During the Spring Campaign, the battalion had joined the Allied forces blockading Glogau. Possessing scores of marksmen, the Prussians decided to attach this unit to 7th Brigade as an auxiliary fusilier battalion. Yorck joked with the officers that they would take revenge on him for his poaching of rabbits in their homeland during the 1806 Campaign. As brigade cavalry, Horn received two squadrons of the 3rd Silesian Landwehr Cavalry Regiment – which mainly operated as raiding parties under Major Friedrich von Falkenhausen – as well as three squadrons of Brandenburg Hussars.

With his arm still in a sling, Hünerbein arrived in time to take command of Yorck's 8th Brigade, which received several newly formed battalions. Yet the 1st and 2nd Reserve Battalions of the Leib Regiment and the 3rd Battalion of the 1st West Prussian Regiment had already received their baptism of fire at Bautzen. In particular, the 1st Reserve Battalion had participated in the terrifying bayonet struggle around the village of Kreckwitz, which had led to the capture of 300 Württembergers. During the armistice, the War Department formed these three battalions into the Brandenburg Infantry Regiment commanded by Lieutenant-Colonel Karl August Ferdinand von Borcke, the recipient of the first Iron Cross (second class) to be awarded, which he received for his actions at Lüneburg on 21 April 1813. To form his second infantry regiment – the 12th Reserve – Hünerbein received three Reserve battalions, only one of which actually saw action during the Spring Campaign. One Landwehr Regiment completed 8th Brigade's infantry contingent. For the brigade's cavalry, the two other squadrons of the Brandenburg Hussar Regiment were joined with the two remaining squadrons of the 3rd Silesian Landwehr Cavalry Regiment. The former had participated in the 1812 Campaign, marching on Moscow with Napoleon's main host. As most of the troopers had not come back, the squadrons needed to be rebuilt, a process completed during the armistice.

With his wound from the engagement at Haynau still not completely healed, Colonel Georg Ludwig von Jürgaß assumed command of Yorck's Reserve Cavalry, consisting of three brigades. The Lithuanian and West Prussian Dragoon Regiments received the king's wing adjutant, Count Henckel von Donnersmarck, as their brigade commander. Henckel had served under Yorck during the Russian campaign but had hardly earned his respect. He recalled how the corps commander greeted him during the armistice: "I found him by the troops riding around the camp when I arrived and reported to him. His first words were: 'I know nothing of you, Herr Count!' which was just not very encouraging. I pulled out my cabinet order to present it to him. He shouted: 'That means nothing to me.' After he had ridden around a full mile, he called me over to him and said: 'You can assume your command for the present.'"[62]

Colonel Friedrich von Katzler enjoyed a better greeting, although Yorck considered him to be one of Blücher's pets. Droysen describes Katzler as a "natural-born advance guard commander, cunning, light-hearted, adventurous, [and] always as harsh as possible toward the enemy. As long as he still saw enemy posts in front of him, he would not rest until he overwhelmed them all. If comfortable accommodations, especially any Schloß with a good cellar, remained within reach of the enemy's outpost, he spared nothing to drive it off for the sake of inserting himself and refreshing himself and his comrades … taking care that they could feast and booze in peace. How Yorck often raged about him … For the present, as brigade commander, this sly and amusing Katzler received the Brandenburg Uhlans and the East Prussian National Cavalry Regiment." Insinuating that Blücher had engineered Katzler's appointment to brigade commander, Droysen concludes: "We know the reason for this." The third and final Reserve Cavalry brigade consisted of three Landwehr regiments: two from Silesia and one from Neumark. As with the entire Silesian Army, Yorck's corps did not contain any elite cavalry units such as cuirassiers because all were assigned to Kleist's II Corps.[63]

Equipment shortages combined with the raw manpower produced by the general mobilization to shape Yorck's view of how the war should be conducted and how much could be demanded of the soldiers. According to Langeron, Yorck possessed "a hard, uncompromising personality; he is violent, hateful, and crude, and it is difficult to have him as a comrade or subordinate."[64] Yorck's attitude and character had monumental repercussions on his relations with Blücher. "Yorck," Maude poignantly remarks, "who undoubtedly had higher claims in the army itself, and who was intellectually and morally immensely Blücher's superior, was his exact antithesis. His conduct at Tauroggen should have made him the idol of the nation, but somehow it failed to do so, and though the men immediately under his command loved him for his care of them and devotion to their interests, it was precisely this attitude of fatherly solicitude for their welfare that would have rendered him useless in the supreme command; he lacked the stern resolution requisite for great emergencies."[65] It would seem that Yorck's very actions at Tauroggen proved him capable of confronting great emergencies. While Maude's assessment is unfair, he correctly hints that Yorck's concern for his men put him at odds with Blücher and Gneisenau. As one historian states:

> Yorck, the commander of the Prussians, was an incommodious subordinate, who saw himself more as Blücher's equal than his subordinate. With a self-confidence based on a thorough knowledge of the service and unshakeable courage, he scrutinized every order he received and often couched his divergent views in biting words. With particular bitterness he expressed himself against Gneisenau, in whom he correctly recognized the leading personality, but also poured forth his ridicule against his assistant, Müffling. He believed it was his duty to protect the troops from the extraordinary exertions demanded by headquarters and in this way to keep his corps fresh.[66]

Droysen best captures the reaction of the man of Tauroggen to being assigned to the Army of Silesia:

> Before long it emerged that not Kleist, not Bülow, but instead he would be in the army commanded by Blücher, therefore he actually would remain directly under Gneisenau's leadership. When Yorck labeled this arrangement a misfortune, it was not merely the typical ill-temper with which he usually greeted any change. From Gneisenau he saw nothing but impractical things,

overexcitement, and his personality: abundantly offensive and deliberately insulting. Any contact with him gave new fuel to the increasing bitterness of his mood. Müffling's wise cautiousness and urbane skillfulness appeared too inadequate to completely ensnare old Blücher, who was the only choice for the supreme command because he alone would allow another to command in his name; through this, the *"Kraftgenies* [dynamic geniuses]," whose influence now counted for everything, were indeed handed the command.

Droysen admits that Yorck "judged the people and the circumstances in his harsh and acrimonious way. It took him a while to gruffly come to terms with this."[67] "The armistice approaches its end," wrote Yorck, "the French reinforced themselves considerably. I am convinced not only that the struggle will resume with new fury but that our side will be led with the same indecisiveness and ignorance. With complete justification we must shudder for the future."[68] According to Droysen, Yorck's personality contained too many "fetters and forces" to prevent the inevitable polarization of the two Prussian camps. Yorck drew "his entourage, which increasingly adopted his view, firmly and solidly around him. Soon a complete antithesis between Yorck's and Blücher's headquarters formed, a contrast that the different methods of conducting business only made all the more striking. If Blücher, free of envy and full of great, thoughtful confidence, granted Gneisenau, as well as Müffling, complete freedom, and allowed the junior staff officers to operate in competing independence, at Yorck's [headquarters] every staff member adhered to the strictest regulations, the most precise order. 'Yorck commanded, ordered, [and] led everything himself,' wrote one of his adjutants, 'he demanded from his subordinates only rapport and obedience; none, from the first to the last, exercised the slightest influence on him.'" Comparing the two headquarters, Droysen echoes Yorck's derisive views to conclude that Blücher's was the domain of the "strategists," and the "geniuses and enthusiasts," while Yorck's was the sanctuary of the tacticians, who "all the more turned to the practical." Adding to the differences, Yorck's chief of staff, Karl Heinrich von Zielinsky, "did everything in his power to see that the poor relations with Blücher's headquarters persisted in their entirety."[69]

Turning to the Russians, although the armistice proved to be less productive in filling the gaps in their regiments because of the great distance from their depots, it was still a watershed. The Russians indeed faced several obstacles, conscripting more than 650,000 men, largely between August 1812 and August 1813.[70] "The Russian army received a great quantity of convalescents and recruits," noted Langeron, "so well-armed, equipped, and trained that we could consider them veteran and excellent soldiers. These preparatory advantages were due to the excellent organization of the Russian army."[71] By the end of the armistice, a total of 184,123 Russians with

639 guns stood ready in Silesia, Brandenburg, and Mecklenburg to continue the war against Napoleon. Behind them in second line, 30,000 regulars and militia besieged Danzig with 59 guns; Bennigsen's Army of Poland, which eventually numbered 70,000 men and 200 guns, was forming in the Grand Duchy of Warsaw, which itself was occupied by Prince Dmitry Lobanov-Rostovsky's 50,000-man Reserve Army.

In general, the quality of Russian equipment as well as the quantity of supply varies according to the source, yet most agree with the claim made by the nineteenth-century Russian general and military historian Modest Bog-danovich[72] that arms and uniforms left little to be desired.[73] "At the recommencement of the war," continued Langeron, "munitions were in abundance, the soldiers were rested, dressed and equipped, the weapons were repaired, and the soldiers were in a good state, which equaled that at the very beginning of the war."[74] Nevertheless, many Russian regiments still consisted of only one battalion, which seldom numbered more than 500 men. Despite Langeron's glowing review, most of the replacements consisted of raw recruits. Fortunately for Blücher, Sacken's corps contained "formidable divisions, packed with more veterans than any other corps apart from the Guard: Dmitry Neverovsky's excellent 27th Division."[75] "This corps was the remnant of an army that had been employed against the Turks," noted Müffling, "and had not been recruited for a long time. It was composed of old and seasoned soldiers."[76]

Instead of seven or eight squadrons, Russian cavalry regiments consisted of only three or four, some of only two. Although not at full strength, the Russian cavalry remained impressive. The regiments possessed very good mounts, the artillery excellent teams, and the equipment was in good condition. In addition to sabers, Russian dragoons and mounted Jäger carried muskets, the hussars lances. The Cossacks carried sabers and lances, and many had muskets. Several Cossack commanders were cavalry officers from the regular army, and regulars actually formed the three regiments of the Ukrainianskii Cossack Division. Created in 1812, it consisted for the most part of Polish and Ukrainian farmers, people generally known to be good riders. Their officers lacked military experience and the division itself had yet to see combat but Russian commanders later commended its bravery and utility. Among the other Cossack regiments, that from the Black Sea distinguished itself for its military bearing. In addition to the Cossacks, thousands of Bashkirs and Kalmyks, unfit for pitched combat and barely suitable for gathering intelligence, could swarm the front, flanks, and rear of the enemy to disrupt communication, terrorize stragglers, and screen the movement of friendly forces.[77]

On 6 August, Barclay ordered Langeron to assemble his army corps in the entrenched camp at Schweidnitz. There, he learned a few days later that the monarchs awarded command of the Silesian Army to Blücher. Langeron, a finely cultured French émigré, could not have been more incompatible with the hoary Prussian in terms of personality and mannerisms. Naturally, Blücher's lack of a formal military education and unrefined exterior offended the Old Regime aristocrat, who derisively referred to the Prussian as the "*bon sabreur* [good swordsman]." Born in Paris in 1763, Langeron had served with French forces in the American Revolutionary War, attaining the rank of colonel in 1788. After emigrating during the French Revolution, he received a lateral commission in the Russian army in 1790. Distinguished service during the Russo-Turkish War of 1787–1792 helped launch his Russian career, earning him the rank of lieutenant-general by 1798. Although disgraced for his poor performance at Austerlitz, Langeron had redeemed his reputation in the Russo-Turkish War of 1806–1812, during which he attained the rank of general of infantry and held an independent command. In the 1812 campaign, he led a corps in the Army of the Danube, seeing action at the Berezina. Aside from his haughty disposition, Langeron enjoyed the reputation of being a solid officer much respected by his men. His chief of staff, General Rudzevich, ranked among the very best of Russia's general officers. Although trained in staff work, Rudzevich had gained tough combat experience during numerous years of service in the rugged Caucasus. Langeron wisely took advantage of his subordinate's extensive skills, employing him as his advance guard commander and having the quartermaster-general of the corps, Colonel Paul von Neydhardt, fill the role of staff chief.[78]

Not seeing the magnanimity of their master's decision to distribute his forces among the three Allied armies, the Russian generals felt slighted by their posting to the Silesian Army. Wishing to fight in the tsar's presence, they believed their assignment to Blücher's army drastically if not fatally diminished their opportunity to earn glory. That a Russian had not been selected to command one of the Allied armies likewise galled them. Some still opposed Alexander's decision to continue the war into Central Europe. As the senior Russian officer in the Silesian Army, Langeron felt obligated to do his best to maintain the harmony between his adopted countrymen and the Prussians. Unfortunately, he did little to hide his dissatisfaction over being superseded by Blücher. An extensive and successful military career made it difficult for Langeron to subordinate himself to Blücher, a feeling that quickly spread among the thirty-five generals in his corps, causing a "veiled hostility" to persist throughout the war. Blücher's personality and notorious vices probably pleased their soldiers, but could not satisfy the Russian generals, who in the spirit of the time looked for commanders equipped with high intelligence, knowledge, and an education rooted in military science. Langeron himself "would have hated serving under any foreign officer, but might have submitted with better grace to a man of acknowledged military education and more courtier-like manners that those of rough old Blücher."[79] Disdainful of everything German and unable to speak the language, he could not communicate directly with Blücher, but instead had to have Müffling translate his French. Gneisenau held a low opinion of him, and Langeron returned the favor.[80]

Langeron's disgruntlement and complaints induced Barclay to provide some sign that the French émigré still enjoyed the tsar's trust and confidence. To appease him, Barclay informed Langeron of the secret instructions conveyed to Blücher, but failed to mention the concessions he had granted the Prussian. Consequently, Langeron came to believe that his posting to the Silesian Army had political overtones that superseded military protocol. Viewing himself as Blücher's appointed overseer, the native Frenchman believed that Tsar Alexander expected him to hold Blücher true to Barclay's cautious directives.[81] Thus, the Prussian liaison assigned to Langeron's headquarters, Lieutenant-Colonel Friedrich Albrecht von Ende, experienced numerous difficulties impressing Blücher's views on the senior Russian corps commander. "He saw in every energetic move of Blücher's an overstepping of the bounds of his authority," wrote one historian, "and felt justified in quietly placing what difficulties he could in the way of obeying commands that he felt sure his own imperial master would disapprove; and Blücher had not the least inkling of what was the cause of this passive resistance. The worst of it was that Langeron had much influence with the officers under him and had their moral support even when committing acts that verged on open insubordination."[82] Langeron, judged Müffling, "no doubt with the best intentions, predetermined Blücher's conduct based on these instructions, which he also made the guide of his own actions. When, in consequence of this, the situation went contrary to Blücher's orders, Langeron believed himself to be on the right course while Blücher pursued the wrong one. His generals shared this opinion, and misunderstandings accumulated." It did not help that Langeron proceeded with excessive caution and feared the recklessness of the Prussian veteran and his staff.[83]

As we will see, Langeron made mistakes, but to his credit he recognized them. In his reports to Blücher, both written and verbally, Langeron admitted his errors so openly that the Prussian actually became sympathetic and rejected any notion of malice on the part of his subordinate. Nevertheless, Blücher felt that Langeron easily lost his head under pressure and lacked sound military judgment. Johann Nepomuk von Nostitz, one of Blücher's adjutants and confidants, wrote in his journal: "Langeron absolutely was not a man who Blücher could speak to; a Frenchman by birth, he had the characteristics of his nation and held on to the mannerisms of his early experiences. He loved to discuss his previous campaigns: describe them, tell what he did, and what he would now do, but when it came to action he vacillated and was indecisive. His intentions and actions lacked the energy and endurance that Blücher considered to be the foremost requirement of a good general, prompting Blücher to say of him: 'Langeron is not one of the people I need or like.'"[84]

Langeron's exact thoughts regarding the Prussians who received command of the Silesian Army are not known but his memoirs tell us how he felt when they parted ways after the war. Although the extract is lengthy, it is beneficial to allow Langeron to speak:

General Blücher, to whom the Army of Silesia was confided, was more than seventy years old but his spirit and body had lost none of their vigor. He was an old hussar in the clearest sense of the word: a drinker and debaucher; he had all the faults that one is at pains to excuse in a young man. But he redeemed them by many qualities: an intrepid soldier, an ardent patriot, frank, loyal, possessing a martial figure in the style of a grenadier; he knew how to inspire the most complete confidence in his troops and win the love of his soldiers: he was soon adored by the Russian soldiers just as much as he was by the Prussians.[85]

His activity was prodigious, he was always on horseback; on the battle-field, he had the experience and routine of an old soldier; his *coup d'oeil* was excellent; his heroic bravery carried the troops but his talent as a general was limited to these qualities. It was a great deal but would not have been enough had he not been seconded; he had little strategic ability, could not find himself on a map, and was incapable of making a campaign plan or disposition. He left all military and political details to the three people that were given and attached direct to him; these three people had his entire confidence and merited much praise.

General Gneisenau, chief of Blücher's staff, was well trained, a brave soldier, and a distinguished general; his studies and experience of the wars of the French Revolution had taught him to reject old ideas about a tight and faint-hearted tactical system which still inspired, not long ago, a servile respect, and which had caused, for twenty-two years, every reverse suffered by the enemies of France, especially Austria's defeats. He realized that, to defeat Napoleon, it was necessary to adopt his style of war and surprise him with grand operations, just as Napoleon himself had surprised Europe by the audacity of his maneuvers.

But, in rendering justice to General Gneisenau's talents, I cannot give the same praise for his character: his pride and *amour-propre* did not allow him to suffer the least contradiction. Egotistical, stiff, fiery, crass, and brutal, even to a fellow German, he handled no one with tact; he was generally detested and deservedly so. Moreover, his liberal principles, his attachment to the disastrous opinions of German propagandists and professors, his hatred of his king, all rendered him equally dangerous to his sovereign and his country . . .

Colonel Müffling, the army's quartermaster-general, rivaled the spirit and talents of General Gneisenau but his character was greatly different: Müffling was soft, ingratiating, full of affability, and through his amiable manner brought back those who Gneisenau distanced or scared away. He became quartermaster-general of the Prussian Army and was well suited to fill that post.

These two officers knew Silesia and Saxony perfectly and all the different regions in which the events of the campaign of 1813 occurred. This was an immense advantage for our army: in France, they did not possess the same knowledge of the country and this was reflected in our operations.

Colonel Count Goltz, in charge of political relations, showed as much talent in this sphere as did Gneisenau and Müffling in military affairs. Count Goltz had often served in war and was a very distinguished officer.

The other soldiers who surrounded Blücher and composed his staff, and especially the quartermaster officers, were commendable for their talent and bravery. During the entire war, every individual in the Prussian army – princes, generals, officers, soldiers, and militiamen – covered themselves in glory; one could not carry military honor further than them; but they left to be desired a greater degree of modesty: their boasting was truly insupportable. They remembered too much of the Seven Years War, too little of the war of 1806. Our officers were required to display a highly meritorious prudence and self-abnegation, dictated by the circumstances and the orders of our sovereign. I myself had more need than others of these two qualities; Blücher, Gneisenau, Müffling, etc., saw me arrive in their army with a marked and unique repugnance because I was French; they did not know me personally, and some knowledge of my successes against the Turks could have weakened their prejudices against me; but I was French, and their hatred, their rage (if it is permissible to express it thus), against those who had so humiliated them on the battlefield and in the cabinets of the capitals was such that it was impossible for them to make a single exception among the French nation.

Moreover, I had a great fault amongst these men: I did not know a single word of German, which was a great inconvenience when serving with a Prussian army. Almost all of the Prussian officers spoke French but General Blücher did not even understand it.[86]

Ten years younger than Blücher, the other Russian corps commander, Sacken, was the scion of German nobles from Courland. "Prince Fabian von der Osten-Sacken," states one Russian source, "was of medium height, pleasant appearance, sharp, intelligent glance; mocking smile; and refined mind. He combined his military talents with extraordinary gallantry and experience; was enterprising, firm, just, considerate with subordinates and at the same time strict and demanding. In society, he was known for his cheery disposition, courteousness, and quick wit, often making biting remarks in conversation. Impregnable firmness of character was a distinctive trait of his personality."[87]

A veteran of the Russo-Turkish Wars on 1769–1770 and 1787–1792, Sacken received his promotion to general officer in October 1797. During the War of the Second Coalition (1798–1801), he fought in Switzerland, commanding the Russian rearguard at Zurich. He next saw action in East Prussia during the War of the Fourth Coalition but ran afoul of Bennigsen, who accused him of insubordination. Court-martialed and found guilty, Sacken was relieved of his command on 10 June 1807. Reinstated in 1812, he commanded a corps in the III Reserve Army of Observation. Now, in 1813, he found himself subordinated to Blücher. Knowing little of his Prussian commander, Sacken harbored no ill-will toward Blücher and could at least communicate with him in German. Although purported to be "an active soldier and an able man," he came with the reputation of being a difficult subordinate. Historian Dominic Lieven describes him as "a sharp-tongued and short-tempered man," yet compared to Yorck he was "an angel." According to Müffling, all that the Prussians knew of him was the rumor that the court-martial had soured Sacken, rendering the general "so irritable that his superiors found it difficult to deal with him." Energetic and brave, he soon developed a close relationship with Blücher, who described him as "reliable in the highest degree, bold and decisive in battle, intelligent and careful in the assessment of his enemy."[88]

As for Blücher, the decision made by Frederick William and Alexander to create multinational armies did not sit well with him either. Through Hippel, he harangued Hardenberg to convince the king to reverse his decision. "Can't it be arranged," he queried, "so that our troops play their own part and the Russians play theirs? If so, I will comfortably wager my head on good success; but together it will not go well. Our allies demand too much from us; we have done the most possible but the Russian Guard and their heavy cavalry are conserved like ammunition chests while all else is spent."[89] Regardless, Blücher took a very pragmatic approach in his relations with the Russians. Müffling claimed that simply avoiding discord was not Blücher's ultimate goal. Instead, he sought to "establish brotherly harmony" so that the Russians would execute the war "if not with pleasure, at least without reluctance." Blücher rejected the opinion shared by many Prussians that the Russians should adopt German customs while in Germany. Instead, he believed that the Prussians should conform to the Russians. As standard operating procedure, Blücher maintained that the Prussian army should "earn and preserve the respect of their allies through great actions." Thus, in his opinion, the Prussians should receive the most difficult tasks, march on the worst roads, lead every attack, and claim the least credit for success.[90] Yorck eventually protested, yet Müffling insists that this belief formed "the fundamental condition" of Blücher's command. "Without the assistance of the Russians, we were unable to crush the colossus that threatened us with degradation and eternal slavery; but to desire more than assistance, when our own strength did not suffice, would be unfair." No fan of Blücher, Müffling concluded: "Russia had freed itself in 1812; our turn now came, and General Blücher had too exalted a notion of national honor to balance it against a policy that might teach us cunningly to shift on others the heavy labors from which we hoped to reap the advantages."[91] In the end Blücher could not remove all of the discontent, yet the Army of Silesia managed to play the most decisive role in the War of the Sixth Coalition.

In mid August, the Allies fielded approximately 512,000 soldiers, with reserves and besieging forces providing an additional 143,000 men. Napoleon's field army exceeded 400,000 men; the armistice had served his needs by allowing him to replace the losses from the grueling Spring Campaign.[92] His field forces amounted to 372,236 infantry and 40,764 cavalry and some 29,810 gunners, engineers, and support personnel for a total of 442,810 men with 1,284 guns and 101,301 horses.[93] An additional 26,068 men garrisoned the fortresses on the Elbe: Hamburg (12,000); Bremen (1,500); Magdeburg (3,250); Wittenberg (2,318); Torgau (2,000); and Dresden (5,000). Second-line troops, including 10,000 men who would eventually be part of IX Corps as well as 25,000 Bavarians, amounted to 42,900 men. A further 51,000 exhausted and sick imperial soldiers, many being survivors of the Russian campaign, held fortresses on the Oder and in Poland.[94] In round figures, a conservative estimate of Napoleon's available forces in the German theater amounts to almost 575,000 combatants. By comparison, the imperial troops who took the field in August held a qualitative edge over those who had marched to the Saale in April, although the conscripts were serving at a younger age than those called up in the wake of the Russian disaster. The rigors of the Spring Campaign and the hardships of the armistice combined to purge the weak and deficient from the ranks. While the cavalry still suffered mainly from want of adequate mounts, the artillery remained far superior to that of the Allies. By far, Napoleon's unchallenged mastery of operations provided the imperials with their greatest advantage over the Coalition.

The length of the Elbe between Hamburg and Königstein on the Bohemian frontier – an extent of 290 miles – provided Napoleon's front line. He stood at the center of the Allied armies that formed a semi-circle around him, and although inferior in numbers he possessed strategic advantages by virtue of his central position that granted him the initiative to move rapidly and by the shortest line against any one of the three armies opposing him. Although this line extended north to the mouth of the Elbe, the emperor's communications continued to run west through southern Germany, indicating that he would not venture too far from the line he had taken in June. While a *coup de théâtre* remained an option throughout the campaign, he did little to prepare his communications to run through northern Germany to France. In hindsight, exchanging Saxony for Brandenburg in October would have been a better option than challenging the Allies to a showdown at Leipzig. In addition, the emperor should have built more roads during the armistice to facilitate his internal communications.

Be that as it may, Dresden served as Napoleon's main supply base with secondary depots throughout Germany. To guard its southern approaches, he ordered the construction of an entrenched camp twelve miles to the south at Pirna. Six miles south of Pirna, imperial forces occupied and fortified

Königstein. Bridges at Dresden, Pirna, and Königstein provided three immediate crossing points over the Elbe. Further afield, the bridgeheads at Magdeburg, Wittenberg, and Torgau provided intermediate bases from where
imperial forces could move north or east. Before Austria joined the Coalition, Napoleon planned to resume the war by continuing operations through
Silesia to Poland. As he had reached the Oder in early June and imperial
forces held the river's great fortresses of Stettin, Küstrin, and Glogau, this
appeared to be the most logical plan. Thus, the emperor considered delivering a decisive battle as close as possible to Liegnitz on the Katzbach River in
Silesia: the terminal point of his communication. This made sense considering he expected the entire Russo-Prussian main army (including Wittgenstein, Kleist, and the Russian Guard and Reserve) to remain in Silesia.[95]

Napoleon echeloned the 300,000 men of the Grande Armée in the
triangle formed by the Katzbach, the Elbe, and the northern border of
Bohemia. In eastern Saxony he spread the Guard, I, IV, and V Cavalry
Corps, and II, VIII, and XIV Corps between the Elbe and the Neiße
Rivers while III, V, VI, and XI Corps along with II Cavalry Corps camped
in Silesia between the Neiße and the Katzbach. Although necessitated weeks
earlier by the demands of supply, this distribution of forces would allow
Napoleon to quickly concentrate overwhelming mass on one of three river
lines: the Bober, the Neiße, or the Elbe itself. After hostilities with the
Russians and Prussians recommenced, he planned to shift the troops in
Saxony east toward Bunzlau on the Bober while his forces in Silesia withdrew west likewise to the Bober. In this way, the emperor could concentrate
almost 270,000 infantry and 30,000 cavalry to oppose the 200,000 Russians
and Prussians he expected to confront in Silesia. Based on the spirit they
displayed in May and early June, Napoleon counted on Alexander and
Frederick William accepting battle in Silesia.

While his larger right wing attacked the main Russo-Prussian army in
Silesia, he entrusted Marshal Oudinot with his left wing. In compliance with
Napoleon's "master plan," Oudinot would conduct an offensive against
Berlin with IV, VII, and XII Infantry and III Cavalry Corps – altogether
70,000 men – supported by Davout's XIII Corps (30,000 men) at Hamburg
and one division of 10,000 men coming from Magdeburg. After defeating the
Army of North Germany, Oudinot's "Army of Berlin" would liberate the
Oder garrisons and advance to the Vistula, swooping behind the main Russo-
Prussian army, which would be reeling eastward after being defeated in Silesia
by the emperor. Oudinot's arrival at the Vistula would, in Napoleon's opinion, force the Russians to withdraw through Poland. Should Bernadotte
somehow check the Army of Berlin, Napoleon could easily dispatch forces
from the Silesian theater to Brandenburg to finish the job.

After receiving Austria's declaration of war, Napoleon scrapped the
Silesian offensive on 12 August. In view of protecting his main base against

the Austrians, the 115 miles that separated Dresden from Liegnitz rendered impractical a concentration at the latter. To better cover Dresden, Napoleon decided to assemble the 300,000 men of the Grande Armée between Bautzen and Görlitz. Moreover, he uncharacteristically surrendered the initiative to the Allies. As he explained to Marshals Ney and Auguste Frédéric de Marmont: "So that these 300,000 men cannot be cut off from the Elbe, I will take a position between Görlitz and Bautzen that will make me master of the course of this river, allow me to supply myself through Dresden, and enable me to wait and see what the Russians and Austrians will do and then take advantage of the circumstances." He still believed he would decisively defeat the Russo-Prussian army before the Austrians launched a serious operation against Dresden. Even if he ran afoul of his timetable, Napoleon did not think the Austrians could assemble more than 100,000 to 120,000 men in Bohemia after sending an estimated 50,000 men to Italy and posting another 30,000 along the Austro-Bavarian border. As for Oudinot's army, the emperor made no changes to the allocation of 110,000 men for the implementation of the master plan. In his mind, Austria's declaration of war increased the importance of Oudinot's operation. By reaching the Vistula, the Army of Berlin undoubtedly would force the Russians "to detach themselves from the Austrians."[96]

For the purpose of supply, the troops in Silesia did not commence the retrograde movement west until the armistice had expired. After slight modifications, the situation by mid August found Napoleon's forces organized in three main groups. In Silesia, the 130,000 men of III, V, VI, and XI Corps and II Cavalry Corps provided a strong vanguard to oppose the Russo-Prussian army there. West of this army group stood Napoleon's main body: 150,000 men of the Guard, I, II, and VIII Corps and I, IV, and V Cavalry Corps between Bautzen, Görlitz, and Zittau. South of Dresden, the 26,000 men of XIV Corps guarded the Elbe from Königstein to the Saxon capital. In Lower Lusatia the majority of Oudinot's 70,000-man Army of Berlin assembled at Luckau to advance against the Prussian capital in unison with Davout's 30,000 men as well as 15,000 men from the garrisons of Wittenberg and Magdeburg. As we will see, the Coalition's decision to form its main army in Bohemia as opposed to Silesia caught Napoleon by surprise.

French forces in Silesia outnumbered Blücher's field forces by 25,000 men. The foremost imperial troops held the western edge of the neutral zone from Liegnitz to Goldberg along the Katzbach. Based at Löwenberg (Lwówek Śląski), Macdonald's XI Corps – 24,410 French, Italian, Neapolitan, Westphalian, and Würzburger troops – formed the right wing. From Goldberg to Haynau on the Katzbach, General Jacques Alexandre Lauriston's V Corps – 27,905 predominantly French troops – provided the center of the French line. The left wing consisted of the 40,006 mostly

French troops of Ney's III Corps, which camped between the Bober and the lower Katzbach. At the end of the armistice, General Horace-François Sébastiani's II Cavalry Corps linked with III Corps in the region of Liegnitz. In second line, the 27,754 men of Marmont's mainly French VI Corps quartered in and around Bunzlau.[97]

On 11 August, Blücher and Gneisenau reviewed Yorck's corps at Rogau (Rogów Sobócki) near the foot of the expansive Zobtenberg (Przedgórze Sudeckie), a mountain in the foothills of the Riesengebirge. After having inspected the Russo-Prussian troops assigned to the Bohemian Army and then Langeron's corps, they found Yorck's not as pleasing to the eye as the Russian troops or even Kleist's corps, yet no time remained for improvement. That night, bonfires illuminated the skies from Prague to Reichenbach, signaling the end of the peace negotiations. In Silesia, Barclay notified the enemy's forward posts that the Allies had acknowledged the end of the armistice. Metternich submitted Austria's declaration of war on 12 August. On that day, more than 100,000 Russian and Prussian troops commenced the march from Silesia to Bohemia. That evening, Hardenberg gave Blücher and Gneisenau a farewell dinner at neutral Breslau. After the two rejoined army headquarters at Zobten, Blücher dispatched Professor Steffens to Landeshut with the task of reconnoitering imperial forces on the upper Bober with Pahlen III's vanguard. Steffens claims that Blücher believed the right wing of the French army would advance east from the Bober to Schmiedeberg (Kowary), only thirty-five miles from Schweidnitz.[98]

Although the armistice had expired, the ensuing six-day suspension of hostilities took effect. With each passing day, both sides eyed the twenty-mile-wide neutral zone in Silesia with hungry eyes. "The country from Upper Silesia to the Elbe," noted Müffling in 1827, "where the armies of both sides had stood during the armistice, was exhausted; only the neutral zone between them, including Breslau, could maintain an army until the harvest." While the neutral zone offered Blücher a solution to the problem of feeding man and horse, it also presented a quandary. Strategically, the neutral zone prevented Blücher from establishing and maintaining contact with the imperial army in Silesia. Should Napoleon summon them to Saxony for an offensive against the Bohemian Army, Blücher would not know until his light troops crossed the neutral zone – a move he could not make until 17 August when hostilities officially resumed – and sought contact with the French. Crossing the neutral zone itself would take the army two days, thus providing the French with an advantageous headstart.[99]

Echeloned from the Katzbach across the Bober to the Queis, the various French corps did not escape the prying eyes of Blücher's agents. Deserters, spies, locals, and volunteer Jäger disguised as peasants provided enough intelligence for Blücher's staff to form a general picture of imperial forces in Silesia. On the left wing of the enemy's first line, 9th and 10th Divisions of

III Corps stood at Liegnitz, 8th Division to the northeast at Parchwitz (Prochowice), 39th Division at Lüben (Lubin), and 11th Division at Steinau on the Oder. Far to the north on the extreme left wing, Sébastiani's II Cavalry Corps quartered in the region of Freystadt (Kożuchów). Macdonald's XI Corps formed the right wing with one division each at Lähn (Wleń), Löwenberg–Greiffenberg (Gryfów Śląski), and Friedeberg (Mirsk). In second line, Lauriston's V Corps distributed one division each to Goldberg, Neudorf-am-Gröditzberg (Nowa Wieś Grodziska), and Haynau. Marmont's VI Corps, in and around Bunzlau, formed the third line. The infantry camped in barracks while the cavalry and artillery received billets. Discord purportedly reigned in the imperial camps, prompting numerous desertions, especially by Italian troops. Throughout the armistice, the imperials purportedly constructed extensive fortifications at Liegnitz. Moreover, the Prussians knew that additional imperial forces occupied Upper Lusatia, just west of the troops on the Katzbach and Bober. From what they could gather, Marshal Claude Victor's II Corps held Görlitz, the Imperial Guard camped between Görlitz and Bautzen, and I Cavalry Corps quartered at Bautzen. General Józef Antoni Poniatowski's VIII Corps along with IV Cavalry Corps occupied Zittau, due south of Görlitz and not far from the Bohemian frontier. These 112,000 men could be readily utilized either in Bohemia or Silesia.[100]

Knowing the positions of the imperial army facing him added to Blücher's anxiety over his assignment.[101] Like other Allied commanders, he assumed Napoleon would attack the Austrians in Bohemia first. Blücher feared the emperor would use the six-day cessation of hostilities to concentrate all his forces. Without violating an international agreement, Napoleon could move the majority of his troops from Silesia to Saxony by 16 August and be in position to crush Schwarzenberg before the other Allied armies could threaten his rear and flanks. Even if Blücher's spies informed him of a French march to Saxony, he could not enter the neutral zone before the 17th. While the withdrawal of imperial forces from Silesia to Saxony remained likely, the Prussians actually knew little regarding French intentions. Intelligence gleaned from deserters did not clarify the situation. As Ney appeared to be the ranking officer, the Prussians assumed he commanded this army. From 10 August onward, Allied spies reported much back-and-forth movement between the imperial camps but offered no indication of purpose. Only Macdonald's corps began assembling between Löwenberg, Liebenthal (Lubomierz), and Lähn. His cavalry stood on the road that led to Hirschberg and occupied Spiller, a few miles west of the French line of demarcation. According to rumors circulating in the French camps, the army would march east to Breslau or northeast toward Glogau to make a diversion in Poland, or west to Saxony. Transports of livestock steadily rumbled west, giving credence to the rumors that the French would march west when the war resumed. According to Professor Steffens: "The occupation of Lähn strongly influenced Blücher to break the unexpired armistice ... which proved so important for the success of the campaign."[102]

Blücher and Gneisenau recognized the difficulties of reaching the Elbe at the same time as Ney to prevent Napoleon from achieving overwhelming mass against Schwarzenberg. The seriousness with which Blücher executed his responsibility of maintaining constant contact with imperial forces in Silesia became the hallmark of his operations in August and September. In a 12 August note to Sacken, he emphasized the importance of the Cossacks following hard on the heels of the enemy: "I assume that if no other means for the crossing are available, they will swim across the Oder."[103]

On the 13th, Blücher tasked Gneisenau with drafting instructions for the army to cross the neutral zone around midnight on 17 August unless the enemy entered it before the six-day suspension of hostilities expired. His orders specifically expressed the importance of gaining possession of this rich tract of land. As of the 13th, the imperials still maintained their forward positions along the Katzbach. However, the French commissioner who along with his Russian and Prussian counterparts oversaw the maintenance of the neutral zone planned to leave their headquarters at Neumarkt the next day. "Because the enemy cannot be trusted to honor the armistice until the morning of the 17th," wrote Blücher, "I will take all precautions to be ready to receive him." To counter a French advance into the neutral zone on the 14th, Blücher instructed Sacken to prepare his corps to cross the Oder, occupy Breslau, and push light cavalry to Neumarkt. Yorck received orders to form a vanguard consisting of six battalions, eight squadrons, and one battery each of foot and horse and move it east to Saarau (Żarów) on the Striegau stream – the line of demarcation for the Allies in this sector of Silesia – on the morning of the 14th. Blücher wanted the vanguard to bivouac but remain ready to enter the neutral zone while the main body of I Corps bivouacked between Kratz-kau (Krasków) and Klettendorf (Klecin) on the Schweidnitz stream. Blücher planned to transfer his headquarters to Schweidnitz on the 14th.[104]

While still drafting these orders to Yorck on the evening of 13 August, Blücher received Langeron's summary of the intelligence collected by his corps during the course of the morning and early afternoon. Langeron's vanguard commander, Rudzevich, reported the presence of a French patrol in the neutral zone between Liegnitz and Neumarkt. In addition, Rudzevich learned from the *Landrat* (district magistrate) of Striegau that the imperials had received orders to move out but he did not know where they would march. From Pahlen III came news of an imperial foraging party consisting of twenty troopers east of the Katzbach operating in the highlands between Goldberg and Hirschberg. Pahlen reported that this party had raided the villages of Ober and Nieder Röversdorf (Sędziszowa Górna and Dolna) and Schönau (Świerzawa), all at least ten miles inside the neutral zone. Moreover, the French had purportedly made large requisitions and collected all remaining livestock throughout the border regions just inside the neutral zone along a line extending from Liegnitz through Goldberg to Hirschberg. Langeron also included a letter from the Russian spy Borzucki written at 3:30 on the afternoon of the 12th at Berbisdorf (Dziwiszów), itself deep inside the southern portion of the neutral zone. "The enemy is in full advance," wrote the agent, "and has pushed as far as Altschönau [Stara Kraśnica]. The town of Schönau must immediately deliver 300 pounds of bread and 16 kegs of brandy as well as hay and other supplies. It is highly probable that the enemy will go to Jauer." This confirmed Pahlen III's report, as Altschönau stood in the same area as the villages named in his report. According to Borzucki, 200 cavalry and 150 infantry representing the vanguard of a larger French formation occupied Altschönau around 11:00 A.M. Pledging his head on the accuracy of his statements, he speculated that enemy forces already must have reached Kauffung (Wojcieszów), three miles south of Altschönau.[105]

Blücher hoped that a French violation of the neutral zone would provide a pretext for his troops to cross the line of demarcation. The starving imperials appeared to have fulfilled his wishes. After confirmation of Langeron's report arrived from various sources, Blücher felt absolved of having to respect any international agreement. "The French violated the armistice by advancing into the neutral zone," he later explained to Hardenberg, "carrying off supplies and cattle; I have stolen a march on them and have saved the entire neutral zone from being plundered; we found everything [we need] in the neutral zone." To Bernadotte he wrote: "After the enemy sent reconnaissance parties into the neutral territory, I did not hesitate for one moment to likewise cross our line of demarcation." Gneisenau reiterated: "A detachment that the enemy sent into the neutral zone to make requisitions has provided justification for Blücher's army to advance." According to the official history of the Silesian Army written in the 1840s by the Prussian General Staff, "the enemy did not throw down the gauntlet in a challenge but instead simply let it fall to the ground. Blücher picked it up, but not to hold it temporarily or return it, but to immediately take the proper distance between himself and the duelist facing him, which in his situation was the most appropriate action."[106]

After reading Langeron's summary, Blücher added a postscript to the orders drafted for Yorck: "Because I just now received news that the enemy has violated his line of demarcation, you will disregard my above instructions for you to respect ours. The vanguard can send patrols into the neutral zone to obtain news of the enemy's movements." At 7:00 that same evening, the 13th, Blücher dictated a general order to Langeron, Yorck, and Sacken: "The enemy has crossed into the neutral zone. Enclosed you will find the disposition for the march. If you encounter the enemy in the neutral zone you are to attack him." However, if the French remained behind their line of demarcation, Blücher instructed his subordinates not to cross it. A new disposition issued by Silesian Army Headquarters covered both 14 and 15 August. For the 14th, the vanguards of each corps would push deep into the neutral zone while their main bodies concentrated along the Coalition's line of demarcation. As march objectives for the 14th, Gneisenau instructed Sacken to occupy Breslau, move his corps west to Deutschlissa (Leśnica), and push his vanguard to the halfway point between Deutschlissa and Neumarkt, with its light cavalry reaching the latter. Sacken would also seek to establish communication with the left wing of Bernadotte's army. In the center, Yorck's corps would march at 2:00 A.M. on the 14th in three columns to a position at Saarau on the Striegau stream. In front of the corps, his vanguard would proceed sixteen miles northwest of Saarau to Mertschütz (Mierczyce), with patrols reconnoitering further northwest toward Liegnitz. On Blücher's left wing, Rudzevich would lead Langeron's vanguard ten miles northwest to Jauer, dispatching strong patrols toward Goldberg. Langeron's main body received orders to march at 7:00 A.M. on the 14th to a position just east of Striegau. On the extreme left wing, Pahlen III would move his main body ten miles west from Landeshut to Schmiedeberg, pushing his vanguard northwest to Hirschberg and dispatching strong cavalry patrols toward Lähn and Berthelsdorf (Barcinek). For security, Blücher ordered the formation of a Cossack chain extending from Kanth through Striegau to the Bohemian frontier.[107]

The disposition for the 15th instructed all vanguards to patrol toward the French line of demarcation at daybreak. Should the imperials concentrate and take the offensive against the reconnoitering forces with superior numbers, Blücher explained that they – the patrols – should fall back on their respective vanguards, which in turn would fall back on their respective corps. If the enemy withdrew or started to withdraw in the face of the reconnoitering forces, Blücher gave permission for the patrols to cross the Katzbach and do as much damage to the enemy as possible. "This must be reported immediately so that the corps can follow." Early on the 14th, Gneisenau wrote his wife from Schwentnig (Świątniki): "The movements of the army begin today. The enemy is concentrating his forces. Most reports claim that he is in the process of evacuating Silesia. At present we must seize the opportunity. In any case, we will provide him with an escort."[108] At dawn on 14 August, the Silesian Army entered the neutral zone.

Notes

1 Vaudoncourt, *Histoire de la guerre*, I:282; Pertz and Delbrück, *Gneisenau*, III:8–12. Geheimes Staatsarchiv Preußischer Kulturbesitz (hereafter cited as GStA PK), VI HA Rep. 92 Nl. Albrecht, Nr. 52, is dedicated to the Lützow affair. For

the French side of the story, see Weil, *Campagne de 1813*, 78–79; Pertz and Delbrück, *Gneisenau*, III:8–12.

2 As a defensive position for an army, Gneisenau later suggested the ridges northeast of Glatz between Frankenstein (Ząbkowice Śląskie) and Wartha (Bardo) on the Glatzer Neiße (Nysa Kłodzka) forty miles south of Breslau (Wrocław). If Prussian forces alone were to defend Silesia, he advocated a narrower position extending from Wartha to Silberberg. Both positions required entrenchments. See Gneisenau to Frederick William, Glatz, 3 August 1813, in Pertz and Delbrück, *Gneisenau*, III:82.

3 Blücher to Gneisenau, Strehlen (Strzelin), 29 June 1813, GStA PK, VI HA Rep. 92 Nl. Gneisenau, Nr. 23.

4 GStA PK, VI HA Rep. 92 Nl. Gneisenau, Nr. 16.

5 Blücher to Hippel, July 1813, *Blüchers Briefe*, ed. Unger, 169–70; Gneisenau to Frederick William, Glatz, 3 August 1813, reproduced in Pertz and Delbrück, *Gneisenau*, III:81.

6 Stewart, *Narrative*, 57.

7 Steffens, *Adventures*, 108.

8 Napoleon's III, VI, XI, and V Corps camped at Liegnitz (Legnica), Lüben (Lubin), Steinau (Ścinawa), Goldberg, Polkwitz (Polkowice), Glogau, Haynau (Chojnów), Bunzlau (Bolesławiec), and Löwenberg (Lwówek Śląski).

9 In 1900, the thaler corresponded to three marks, and the mark at that time was worth 1,500% more than the German mark in 1996. Thus, 200 thaler in 1900 was equal to 9,000 marks in 1996. Therefore, approximately 200 years ago, 200 thaler was worth around 18,000 marks in 1996 and 12,000 US dollars. As of 2012, 200 thaler was equal to $17,560.

10 Quoted in Pertz and Delbrück, *Gneisenau*, III:12.

11 Awarding western Germany as far as the mouth of the Elbe, all of Saxony, and the majority of Lower Silesia to the imperials, the armistice created a neutral zone ranging from fourteen to twenty-eight miles in length to separate the opposing armies in Silesia. On the French side, the line of demarcation extended north from the Bohemian frontier through Schreiberhau to the Bober just east of Berthelsdorf and along this river to Lähn. From there it followed the Katzbach to the Oder. Imperial forces could occupy the towns of Lähn, Goldberg, Liegnitz, and Parchwitz. Hungry imperial soldiers eventually exhausted the territory on their side of the neutral zone in addition to Saxony and Lusatia. On the Allied side, the demarcation line likewise started at the Bohemian frontier, running northeast through Landeshut, Bolkenhain, and Striegau, then along the Striegau stream to Kanth, and from there along the Schweidnitz stream to the Oder slightly downstream of Breslau. Allied troops could occupy these towns but neither side could enter Breslau or the neutral zone. North of the neutral zone, Allied forces retained possession of Mecklenburg, Brandenburg, and Pomerania.

12 As of 2012, 200,000 thaler in 1813 was equal to $17,560,000 and 600,000 thaler was equivalent to $52,680,000.

13 GStA PK, VI HA Rep. 92 Nl. Gneisenau, Nr. 18.

14 Maude, *Leipzig Campaign*, 147–49. I Cavalry Corps numbered 16,537 men (78 squadrons and 36 guns); II Cavalry Corps: 10,304 men (52 squadrons and 18 guns); III Cavalry Corps: 6,000 men (27 squadrons and 24 guns); IV Cavalry Corps: 3,923 men (24 squadrons and 12 guns); V Cavalry Corps: 4,000 men (20 squadrons and 6 guns).

15 GStA PK, VI HA Rep. 92 Nl. Gneisenau, Nr. 18.

16 Langeron, *Mémoires*, 223.

17 Gneisenau to Frederick William, Glatz, 3 August 1813, reproduced in Pertz and Delbrück, *Gneisenau*, III:81–83.

18 Höpfner, "Darstellung," 1843:26–28; Bogdanovich, *Geschichte des Krieges*, Ib:275; Friederich, *Herbstfeldzug 1813*, I:567–74, 85–90.

19 Langeron, *Mémoires*, 204; GStA PK, VI HA Rep. 92 Nl. Gneisenau, Nr. 18; Höpfner, "Darstellung," 1843:26; Maude, *Leipzig Campaign*, 159.

20 Grolman to Gneisenau, Reichenbach, 8 August 1813, GStA PK, VI HA Rep. 92 Nl. Gneisenau, Nr. 23.

21 Quoted in Henderson, *Blücher*, 116.

22 Friederich, *Herbstfeldzug 1813*, I:229–230; Unger, *Blücher*, II:64.

23 Ritter, *The Sword and the Scepter*, I:71.

24 Pertz and Delbrück, *Gneisenau*, III:148.

25 Müffling, *Aus meinem Leben*, 50, 57–58; Pertz and Delbrück, *Gneisenau*, III:148–49.

26 Unger, *Blücher*, II:60.

27 Müffling, *Aus meinem Leben*, 54–55, 59.

28 Quoted in Pertz and Delbrück, *Gneisenau*, III:150.

29 Müffling, in *Aus meinem Leben*, 52, describes Knesebeck as "a friend of my youth."

30 Unger, *Blücher*, II:61; Pertz and Delbrück, *Gneisenau*, III:152. Prince William of Prussia, the king's younger brother by thirteen years, was also assigned to Blücher's headquarters but it does not appear that he used his voice to influence Frederick William: Schneidawind, *Prinz Wilhelm*, 79.

31 The Glatzer Neiße (Nysa Kłodzka) or Eastern Neisse is a river in southwestern Poland, a left tributary of the Oder. It should not be confused with the Lusatian Neiße (German: Lausitzer Neiße; Polish: Nysa Łużycka), a left-bank tributary of the Oder that formed the border between Silesia and Saxony in 1813 and today forms the Polish–German border from its junction with the Oder. Being the longest and most notable of the three rivers named Neiße (the third being the Wütende Neiße), the Lusatian Neiße is simply referred to as the Neiße or Nysa.

32 Here, Barclay refers to the province of Brandenburg as a geographic objective, differentiating between a French offensive into Brandenburg and one against the Army of North Germany.

33 Barclay to Blücher, Reichenbach, 10 August 1813, reproduced in Höpfner, "Darstellung," 1843:29–30.

34 Quoted in Höpfner, "Darstellung," 1843:35.

35 Blücher to Bernadotte, Schwentnig, 12 August 1813, Riksarkivet (National Archives of Sweden, Stockholm) Krigsarkivet (Military Archives) (hereafter cited as

RA KrA), 25; Höpfner, "Darstellung," 1843:30; Müffling, *Die Feldzüge*, 2–3; Bogdanovich, *Geschichte des Krieges*, IIa:17–19.

36 Yorck's corps contained 31,000 infantry, 6,000 cavalry, and 1,660 gunners servicing 104 pieces; Langeron's: 25,000 infantry, 7,000 cavalry, and 2,500 gunners servicing 139 pieces; Sacken's: 9,000 infantry, 8,500 cavalry, and 1,000 gunners servicing 60 pieces; and St.-Priest's: 9,000 infantry, 4,000 cavalry, and 535 gunners servicing 36 pieces. As for the crucial horse artillery, Yorck possessed four batteries of eight guns each; Langeron: two batteries of twelve guns each; and Sacken: one battery of twelve guns; St.-Priest's corps possessed none.

37 GStA PK, VI HA Rep. 92 Nl. Gneisenau, Nr. 108; Bogdanovich, *Geschichte des Krieges*, IIa:22; Freytag-Loringhoven, *Aufklärung und Armeeführung*, 4–5; Höpfner, "Darstellung," 1843:26–29. The remaining 34,660 Prussians in Silesia were distributed as follows: at Schweidnitz under Krauseneck's personal supervision stood 8 Landwehr and 3 garrison battalions as well as 4 Landwehr cavalry squadrons totaling 10,050 effectives and 450 cavalry. At Glatz assembled 5 Landwehr battalions, 2.5 garrison battalions, and the replacement squadron of the 1st West Prussian Dragoon Regiment for a total of 6,110 effectives and 150 cavalry. Four Landwehr and 2 garrison battalions as well as 2 replacement squadrons for the Neumark Dragoon Regiment and the 2nd Silesian Hussars totaling 5,100 effectives and 300 cavalry held the fortress of Neiße. A garrison of 1 each Landwehr and garrison battalion totaling 1,600 men guarded Silberberg while Kosel (Koźle) was held by 1 Landwehr and 3 garrison battalions as well as the replacement squadron for the 1st Silesian Hussars totaling 2,250 effectives and 150 cavalry. Three Landwehr battalions and 8 Landwehr cavalry squadrons totaling 3,300 infantry and 900 cavalry quartered in and around Frankenstein. The Royal Guard Reserve Battalion, 4 replacement battalions, and the replacement squadron for the Silesian Cuirassiers totaling 4,150 infantry and 150 cavalry billeted in and around Grottkau (Grodków). As soon as the Silesian Army advanced through Schweidnitz, the troops at Frankenstein would unite with Krauseneck's men at Schweidnitz, form a reserve of eight battalions and twelve squadrons, and follow Blücher's army. If the enemy evacuated Silesia, this reserve would join the siege troops at Glogau. If the French commenced an offensive in Silesia, the reserve would reinforce the garrison at either Glatz or Neiße. Meanwhile, the troops at Grottkau would occupy Breslau as soon as Blücher's army crossed the neutral zone. If the Silesian Army suffered a reverse, they would reinforce the garrison at either Neiße or Kosel.

38 Lieven notes that the Russians went to war in 1812 with the army organized in corps, divisions, and brigades, but that during the armistice of 1813 the command structure had to be reorganized because of the glut of recently promoted major- and lieutenant-generals. Although Russian lieutenant-generals saw it as beneath them to command mere divisions, not enough army corps existed for each to have his own command. As a result, an intermediary level between army corps and division was created: the infantry and cavalry corps, themselves barely larger than a pre-1812 Russian division. A Russian infantry corps was approximately the same size as a Prussian brigade in terms of numbers but lacked attached cavalry, making them analogous to French divisions. A Prussian brigade and a Russian infantry

corps each contained 7,000–9,000 infantry but the Prussian brigade contained about 600 cavalry. What the Russians lacked in cavalry, they made up for by possessing much more artillery than the Prussians: where the Prussian brigade had only eight guns attached, the Russian infantry corps usually possessed two batteries of twelve guns each: one heavy and one light. Lieven acknowledges that the creation of infantry and cavalry corps made "the Russian command structure top-heavy and complicated relations with the Prussians." Although the Prussian brigade and the Russian infantry corps were approximately the same size, colonels could command Prussian brigades while lieutenant-generals commanded Russian infantry corps. This increased the likelihood of friction emerging over seniority and status whenever the troops became mixed. Five Russian army corps commenced the Fall Campaign: two (Langeron and Sacken) were attached to the Silesian Army; two (Wittgenstein and Grand Duke Constantine) joined the Army of Bohemia; and one (Wintzingerode) served in the Army of North Germany. After the failed experiment with the Napoleonic corps system in 1809, the Austrians divided their field army for the 1813 Campaign into the combined-arms 1st and 2nd Light Divisions, both numbering fewer than 5,000 combatants, and three combined-arms "Armee-Abteilung" that lacked cavalry or artillery reserves. Corresponding to left and right wings and a reserve, the Abteilung numbered 27,983 men, 52,736 men, and 46,626 men respectively. The left wing Abteilung consisted of two infantry and two cavalry divisions subdivided into three infantry and two cavalry brigades respectively. Unlike Prussian brigades, Austrian divisions did not contain organic cavalry. Three batteries of six-pound guns were assigned to each infantry division, but each battery consisted of six guns rather than the eight of the Prussian battery or twelve of the Russian. The huge right wing Abteilung contained two infantry divisions, three reserve infantry divisions, and two cavalry divisions while the Reserve Abteilung was assigned the combined-arms 3rd Light Division and two divisions of infantry and one of cavalry. By the end of September, reorganization had doubled the size of 2nd Light Division, established five Abteilungen (I, II, III, IV, and Reserve) as well as an Army Artillery Reserve, and created a handful of combined-arms divisions. For example, I Abteilung (20,735 men and 50 guns) contained 3 divisions of which the 1st Division received all 3 arms; II (12,129 men and 50 guns) and III (18,689 men) each were made up of 2 divisions with the 1st of each likewise being a combined-arms unit; IV Abteilung (24,354 men) included 3 divisions with 1st and 3rd having combined-arms. The four regular Abteilungen contained artillery reserves. The Austrian Reserve Abteilung (19,771 men and 40 guns) consisted of 1 cavalry and 2 infantry divisions. The Army Artillery Reserve fielded 112 guns including 8 twelve-pound batteries and 2 eighteen-pound batteries. For simplicity, "corps" will be used throughout this work rather than "Abteilung." See Lieven, *Russia Against Napoleon*, 390.

39 St.-Priest maintained his independent command until the Leipzig campaign in October when he operated with the Silesian Army and so was subordinated to Langeron, who outranked him. St.-Priest remained in command of VIII Infantry Corps but it as well as his cavalry were absorbed into Langeron's army corps. "Until the arrival of St.-Priest (then at Vienna)," explained Langeron, "Pahlen ... was placed under my orders, even though this corps belonged to Wittgenstein's

army corps. It was destined to maintain communication between the Army of Silesia's left and the Army of Bohemia's right, and to join whomsoever had the most need of it; it was tied to my army corps until the end of the war": Langeron, *Mémoires*, 224.

40 Yorck's main body cantoned at Zobten (Sobótka), Wernersdorf (Wojnarowice), and Rosenthal (Mirosławice). He placed his outposts – two Fusilier battalions, the Mecklenburg-Strelitz Hussar Regiment, and 8th Brigade's four squadrons – on the line of the Schweidnitz stream from Kanth to Breslau.

41 Höpfner, "Darstellung," 1843:32. At least one clash between the Russians and native Silesians occurred during the armistice. Regarding "the incident at Giesmannsdorf [Gostków] between a Russian detachment and the peasants of that village," wrote Gneisenau, "I have already ordered an investigation and politely requested that the general [Barclay] appoint a Russian officer to be present at the inquiry and bear witness that strict impartiality was practiced": Gneisenau to Hardenberg, Ober-Peilau (Piława Górna), 30 June 1813, *Briefe des Generals Neidhardt von Gneisenau*, ed. Pflugk-Harttung, Nr. 94, 126. For an excellent discussion of the issue of Russian supply, see Bogdanovich, *Geschichte des Krieges*, Ib:248–49 and IIa:1–16.

42 Müffling, *Die Feldzüge*, 9.

43 Höpfner, "Darstellung," 1843:32, 35.

44 Depots for Sacken's corps were established at Parchwitz (Prochowice), Neumarkt, and Breslau; Yorck's corps at Jauer, Schweidnitz, and Ohlau (Oława); and Langeron's and St.-Priest's corps at Falkenhain (Sokołówka, but cannot be located on modern maps), Reichenbach, and Brieg (Brzeg).

45 Pertz and Delbrück, *Gneisenau*, III:92–93; Friederich, *Herbstfeldzug 1813*, II:260; Höpfner, "Darstellung," 1843:32. Kankrin, *Über die Militairökonomie*, II:56. Located at the confluence of the Drysa River and the Daugava River, Verkhnyadzvinsk (Belarusian) or Verkhnedvinsk (Russian), a city in Belarus in the northwest of the Vitebsk Region, was named Drysa (in Russian transliteration, Drissa) until 1962.

46 Varying figures for the Prussian army at the beginning of August can be found. According to Plotho's calculations for 10 August, the army numbered 277,900 men organized into 249 battalions, 224 squadrons, and 47.5 batteries. By comparison, the Austrians fielded a total of 262,000 men for all theaters, the Russians 249,000, and the Swedes 24,000. According to one official estimate cited by Delbrück, the Prussian army contained 231,838 infantry and cavalry, 15,000 artillerists, and 3,000 volunteer Jäger, altogether 249,838 men, of which 144,500 were for offensive operations and 87,334 for siege and garrison duty. Another estimate he found in the papers of the War Ministry cites an infantry total of 224,241 comprising 90 battalions of the field army numbering 72,130 noncommissioned officers, musicians, and enlisted men; 39 battalions and 5 companies of garrison and replacement troops numbering 31,838 men; 8 battalions and 35 companies of volunteer Jäger and Freikorps numbering 11,153 men; 151 battalions of Landwehr numbering 109,120 men. As for cavalry, a total of 30,780 men with 30,663 horses, comprising 89 squadrons of the field army numbering 13,375 men with 13,375 horses; 22 squadrons of replacement cavalry numbering 3,389 men

and 3,389 horses; 23 squadrons of volunteer Jäger and Freikorps numbering 3,064 men with 2,947 horses; 113 squadrons of Landwehr numbering 10,952 men and 10,952 horses. Artillery was calculated at 50.5 batteries, 36 companies numbering 15,315 men, and 9,112 horses; pioneers consisted of 14 companies numbering 1,305 men. These figures amount to 271,641 men with 39,775 horses excluding 4,000 officers and train personnel. See Plotho, *Der Krieg*, VI, appendix 2; Pertz and Delbrück, *Gneisenau*, II:80–81.

47 This also reflected the original plan of having the Prussian Landwehr defend Silesia. Frederick William probably wanted to make a good impression on his allies and thus made sure that his strongest corps in terms of Line units served under Schwarzenberg and Bernadotte. See Droysen, *Yorck*, II:107–11; Friederich, *Herbstfeldzug 1813*, I:223–24.

48 GStA PK, VI HA Rep. 92 Nl. Gneisenau, Nr. 16.

49 Blasendorff, *Blücher*, 199.

50 Blücher to Gneisenau, Strehlen, 29 June and 24 July 1813, GStA PK, VI HA Rep. 92 Nl. Gneisenau, Nr. 23.

51 The 4th, 5th, 6th, 13th, 14th, and 15th Silesian Landwehr Infantry Regiments and the 3rd, 5th, and 10th, Silesian Landwehr Cavalry Regiments were assigned to the brigades of I Corps. Two of I Corps's four brigades, the 1st and 7th, were "supersized" with heavy infantry and did not conform to the model of one regiment each of Line, Reserve, and Landwehr. Instead, the order of battle lists the 1st Brigade as containing the 1st East Prussian Grenadier Battalion, Leib Grenadier Battalion, West Prussian Grenadier Battalion, Silesian Grenadier Battalion, two companies of the East Prussian Jäger Battalion, and an unnumbered, ad hoc "Landwehr Infantry Brigade" composed of the 5th and 13th Silesian Landwehr Regiments each of four battalions. Including cavalry and gunners, the 1st Brigade of I Corps totaled 9,353 men – almost 2,000 more effectives than the brigades that followed the model of one regiment each of Line, Reserve, and, Landwehr. For example, Yorck's 2nd and 8th Brigades mustered 7,847 men and 7,638 men respectively. Kleist's II Corps received the 7th, 8th, 9th, and 10th Silesian Landwehr Infantry Regiments as well as the 1st, 2nd, 7th, and 8th Silesian Landwehr Cavalry Regiments. See Friederich, *Herbstfeldzug 1813*, I:569–70, 576–77.

52 Droysen, *Yorck*, II:108.

53 Müffling, *Die Feldzüge*, 5.

54 Yorck to Rohr, 4 July 1813, quoted in Droysen, *Yorck*, II:108.

55 Freytag-Loringhoven, *Aufklärung und Armeeführung*, 6–8.

56 Quoted in Droysen, *Yorck*, II:117.

57 Quoted in Droysen, *Yorck*, II:115.

58 Maude, *Leipzig Campaign*, 151.

59 Quoted in Droysen, *Yorck*, II:108.

60 Droysen, *Yorck*, II:109–11.

61 Quoted in Droysen, *Yorck*, II:109–10.

62 Quoted in Droysen, *Yorck*, II:113–14.

63 Droysen, *Yorck*, II:114–15.

64 Langeron, *Mémoires*, 223.

65 Maude, *Leipzig Campaign*, 159–60.

66 Blasendorff, *Blücher*, 202.

67 Droysen, *Yorck*, II:106.

68 Quoted in Droysen, *Yorck*, II:117.

69 Droysen, *Yorck*, II:107, 109.

70 Lieven, *Russia Against Napoleon*, 340.

71 Langeron, *Mémoires*, 200–01.

72 Bogdanovich (1805–1882) was a Russian lieutenant-general and military historian. A nephew of the poet Ippolit Bogdanovich, he received his commission in 1823 and served in the war against the Poles. In 1839 he became a professor of military history and strategy at the St. Petersburg Military Academy.

73 Bogdanovich, *Geschichte des Krieges*, Ib:247–48. See also Mikhailovsky-Danilevsky, *Denkwürdigkeiten*, 117–18. Lieven, in *Russia Against Napoleon*, 329, states that "the Russian army was transformed" during the armistice. Müffling, in *Die Feldzüge*, 4, describes Langeron's troops as being "in excellent condition."

74 Langeron, *Mémoires*, 201.

75 Lieven, *Russia Against Napoleon*, 324, 364–66.

76 Müffling, *Die Feldzüge*, 4.

77 Friederich, *Herbstfeldzug 1813*, I:223; According to Freytag-Loringhoven in *Aufklärung und Armeeführung*, 8–9, the corps assigned to the Silesian Army had to reorganize the Dragoon and Mounted Jäger Regiments from five to two squadrons, and the Hussar Regiments from eight to between five and seven squadrons.

78 Mikaberidze, *The Russian Officer Corps*, 218–20; Langeron, *Mémoires*, 211, 220. Langeron describes Rudzevich as "A Tartar from the Crimea (he was baptized at twelve years old); he brought together every military quality: instruction, bravery, activity, *sang-froid*, prudence; he was an excellent advance guard commander, and I believe he is very much of a quality to someday be commander in chief; however, in his character, he was a bit of a braggart and sometimes partial, thereby rendering himself less agreeable to his commanders and subordinates than he was useful (in 1813 he was only thirty-six-years-old)." In *Russia Against Napoleon*, 376, Lieven explains that Langeron employed Rudzevich "as his troubleshooter wherever the going was toughest."

79 Maude, *Leipzig Campaign*, 160.

80 Höpfner, "Darstellung," 1843:31; Lieven, *Russia Against Napoleon*, 374–75.

81 In *Russia Against Napoleon*, 377, Lieven notes that the tsar "remained very nervous about where Blücher's aggressive nature would lead."

82 Henderson, *Blücher*, 124–25.

83 Müffling, *Die Feldzüge*, 7–8; Bogdanovich, *Geschichte des Krieges*, IIa:19; Höpfner, "Darstellung," 1843:31.

84 Nostitz, *Tagebuch*, 56; Unger, *Blücher*, II:59; Blasendorff, *Blücher*, 203. Lieven, *Russia Against Napoleon*, 374, counters that, on the battlefield, Langeron "was calm and imposing and had a good eye for terrain."

85 In Anon., *Précis militaire de la campagne de 1813 en Allemagne*, 82, Blücher is described as having "all the resilience of youth, despite his seventy years, and [being]

distinguished by the energy and straightforwardness of his character, a natural good sense and firmness in reverses – all qualities that are always demanded first in a commander in chief and remind us of what Napoleon wrote to General Henri Gatien Bertrand: 'War is made with the strength of decision and a constant desire.'"

86 Langeron, *Mémoires*, 209–11.

87 Bantysh-Kamenskii, *Slovar dostopamyatnykh lyudei russkoi zemli*, II:553.

88 Quoted in Unger, *Blücher*, II:59–60; Lieven, *Russia Against Napoleon*, 375; Müffling, *Die Feldzüge*, 5; Mikaberidze, *The Russian Officer Corps*, 285–86; Blasendorff, *Blücher*, 203.

89 Blücher to Hippel, Strehlen, July 1813, *Blüchers Briefe*, ed. Unger, 168–69.

90 Steffens noted that "the account of the battle of Möckern [16 October 1813] as given by [Blücher's] headquarters was singularly short; it was contained in a few lines, and the heroism displayed, and the important consequences that promised to result from it, were scarcely noted. On the second day, between that and the great battle of Leipzig, an attack of cavalry took place under General [Illarion] Vasilchikov, which was duly praised. It was plainly intended to pass slightly over the Prussian exploits and to bring forward those of the allied Russians as much as possible": Steffens, *Adventures*, 120.

91 Müffling, *Die Feldzüge*, 6–7.

92 According to Friederich, *Herbstfeldzug 1813*, I:62, Napoleon's forces amounted to the following: Imperial Guard: 58,191 men and 218 guns; I Corps: 33,298 men and 76 guns; II Corps: 25,158 men and 76 guns; III Corps: 40,006 men and 122 guns; IV Corps: 23,633 men and 72 guns; V Corps: 27,905 men and 74 guns; VI Corps: 27,754 men and 84 guns; VII Corps: 21,283 men and 68 guns; VIII Corps: 7,573 men and 44 guns; XI Corps: 24,418 men and 90 guns; XII Corps: 19,324 men and 58 guns; XIII Corps: 37,514 men and 76 guns; XIV Corps: 26,411 men and 92 guns; I Cavalry Corps: 16,537 men and 36 guns; II Cavalry Corps: 10,304 men and 18 guns; III Cavalry Corps: 6,000 men and 24 guns; IV Cavalry Corps: 3,923 men and 12 guns; V Cavalry Corps: 4,000 men and 6 guns; mobile troops at Magdeburg and Wittenberg: 15,000 men and 28 guns; Corps of Observation at Leipzig: 7,800 men and 10 guns; and Artillery, Engineers, and Reserve Park: 8,010 men. These numbers correspond to Pelet's with the following exceptions: IV Corps: 21,217 men; XII Corps: 18,986; XIV Corps: 36,149 men; III Cavalry Corps: 10,801 men; and IV Cavalry Corps: 4,831 men. Pelet does not provide a figure for V Cavalry Corps; the mobile troops at Magdeburg and Wittenberg; the Corps of Observation at Leipzig; or the Artillery, Engineers, and Reserve Park. See Pelet, *Des principales opérations de la campagne de 1813*, 164.

93 Friederich, *Herbstfeldzug 1813*, I:62. Pelet reduces this total to 312,306 infantry, 69,707 cavalry, 32,528 gunners, 4,087 engineers, and 3,333 support personnel for a total of 421,961: Pelet, *Des principales opérations de la campagne de 1813*, 165. Anon., *Précis militaire de la campagne de 1813 en Allemagne*, 79–80, provides a round figure of 400,000 effectives as of 6 August.

94 Friederich, *Herbstfeldzug 1813*, I:62. Danzig (25,000 men); Zamość (4,000); Modlin (3,000); Stettin (8,500); Küstrin (4,000); and Glogau (5,500).

95 Napoleon's initial plans can best be seen in his supply requisitions, see *CN*, Nos. 20142 and 20173, XXV:393–97, 420–22; Pelet, *Des principales opérations de la campagne de 1813*, 160–63; Maude, *Leipzig Campaign*, 162–63.

96 *CN*, Nos. 20306, 20336, 20339, 20360, and 20364, XXVI:8–9, 13–18, 34–41; Pelet, *Des principales opérations de la campagne de 1813*, 172; Anon., *Précis militaire de la campagne de 1813 en Allemagne*, 65–66; Maude, *Leipzig Campaign*, 165.

97 Specifically, XI Corps consisted of three infantry divisions and one light cavalry brigade, amounting to thirty-eight battalions, seven squadrons, and ninety guns. Macdonald's forces camped in the following areas: 36th Division at Friedeberg, 35th at Lähn, and 31st at Löwenberg with forward elements at Schmottseifen (Pławna) and Greiffenberg; Macdonald quartered at Löwenberg. Lauriston's V Corps likewise consisted of three infantry divisions and one light cavalry brigade, totaling thirty-seven battalions, seven squadrons, and seventy-four guns. Lauriston's divisions camped in the following locales: 16th in and around Goldberg, 17th at Neudorf on the Gröditzberg, 19th at Haynau, headquarters at Goldberg. Ney's III Corps consisted of 5 infantry divisions and 1 light cavalry brigade, totaling 62 battalions, 11 squadrons, and 122 guns. His 9th and 10th Divisions camped in and around Liegnitz while 8th Division quartered to the northeast at Parchwitz, 11th Division at Steinau on the left bank of the Oder, and 39th Division, which consisted of Badeners and Hessians, at Lüben, halfway between Liegnitz and Glogau; Ney quartered at Liegnitz. Only two-thirds of Sébastiani's fifty-two squadrons – totaling 10,304 men and 18 guns on paper – were available when hostilities resumed. The cavalry corps consisted of two light divisions and one of cuirassiers. Marmont's VI Corps likewise consisted of three infantry divisions and one light cavalry brigade, totaling forty-eight battalions, eight squadrons, and eighty-four guns. Its troops were mainly French units, with one battalion of Spaniards and a Württemberger light cavalry brigade. Sailors composed seventeen of Marmont's forty-eight battalions. See Friederich, *Herbstfeldzug 1813*, I:581–84.

98 Nostitz, *Tagebuch*, 53; Steffens, *Adventures*, 108; Pertz, *Stein*, III:403; For a copy of Austria's declaration, see Stewart, *Narrative*, 374–76.

99 Müffling, *Die Feldzüge*, 9.

100 Höpfner, "Darstellung," 1843:39–40; Freytag-Loringhoven, *Aufklärung und Armeeführung*, 9–10.

101 As of 14 August, Blücher knew the location and troop strengths of the French forces that faced him: 4,000 infantry, 150 cavalry, and 26 guns at Friedeberg; 6,000 infantry, 500 cavalry, and 25 guns at Liebenthal; 3,000 infantry and 1,000 cavalry at Lähn; 6,000 infantry, 1,500 cavalry, and 30 guns at Goldberg; 5,000 infantry, 500 cavalry, and 24 guns at Löwenberg; 25,000 infantry, 1,500 cavalry, and 100 guns at Liegnitz; 5,200 infantry, 1,000 cavalry, and 30 guns at Haynau; and 24,000 infantry, 1,500 cavalry, and 65 guns at Bunzlau. Reports on the size of the imperial forces at Parchwitz, Steinau, and Lüben fluctuated wildly and failed to provide a clear picture. See GStA PK, VI HA Rep. 92 Nl. Gneisenau, Nr. 109.

102 Höpfner, "Darstellung," 1843:35, 39–40; Bogdanovich, *Geschichte des Krieges*, IIa:21; Freytag-Loringhoven, *Aufklärung und Armeeführung*, 9–10; Steffens, *Adventures*, 108–09.

103 Quoted in Freytag-Loringhoven, *Aufklärung und Armeeführung*, 42.

104 Yorck would remain in this position on the 15th, but on the 16th have his advance posts unite at Kanth by noon. At midnight, after the suspension of hostilities officially ended, these forward units would advance east almost twenty miles through Kostenblut (Kostomłoty) to Panzkau (Pęczków). Likewise on the 17th, Sacken's light cavalry would reach Neumarkt, seven miles northeast of Kanth. For the 17th, Yorck's corps would march in two columns at 1:00 A.M. to a bivouac at Saarau. As for Langeron, Blücher instructed him to lead his corps in two columns from Jauernich to Striegau. From Landeshut, Pahlen III's corps would take a position at Schmiedeberg. On the 17th, all corps would advance west. "Disposition in the Event That the Enemy Respects the Neutral Zone Until Early on the 17th," in Höpfner, "Darstellung," 1843:36–37.

105 Langeron to Blücher, 13 August 1813, in Höpfner, "Darstellung," 1843:37; Langeron to Barclay, Report on Langeron's operations from 7 August to 2 September, 2 September 1813, GStA PK, VI HA Rep. 92 Nl. Gneisenau, Nr. 18; Bogdanovich, *Geschichte des Krieges*, IIa:22; Nostitz, *Tagebuch*, 53.

106 Blücher to Hardenberg, Striegau, 16 August 1813, *Blüchers Briefe*, ed. Unger, 173; Blücher to Bernadotte, Würben (Wierzbna), 15 August 1813, RA KrA, volym 25, and Add MSS, 20112, 39; Gneisenau to Eichhorn, Jauer, 16 August 1813, *Gneisenau*, ed. Griewank, Nr. 133, 241; Höpfner, "Darstellung," 1843:39; Maude, *Leipzig Campaign*, 175. According to Freytag-Loringhoven in *Aufklärung und Armeeführung*, 16, French commanders neither authorized nor knew of violations of the neutral zone for the purpose of requisitions.

107 Blücher to Yorck, Schwentnig, 13 August 1813, in Höpfner, "Darstellung," 1843:37; Blücher to Bernadotte, Schwentnig, 12 August 1813, RA KrA, volym 25. A pristine copy of Blücher's disposition can be found in Add MSS, 20112, 117.

108 Blücher to Bernadotte, Wurben, 15 August 1813, RA KrA, volym 25, and Add MSS, 20112, 39; Blücher to Langeron, Yorck, and Sacken, Schwentnig, 7:00 P.M., 13 August 1813, in Höpfner, "Darstellung," 1843:37–38; Gneisenau to Caroline, Schwentnig, 14 August 1813, GStA PK, VI HA Rep. 92 Nl. Gneisenau, Nr. 21.

3

"The infamous conduct of the Prussians"

Yorck's van – a combined-arms detachment commanded by Lobenthal – spearheaded the drive into the neutral zone.[1] Departing from Lorzendorf (Wawrzeńczyce), the Prussians marched almost twenty miles northwest to secure Mertschütz, itself halfway to Liegnitz. From Panzkau (Pęczków), one cavalry detachment under Major Schenk consisting of two squadrons each from the 2nd Leib Hussars and the Brandenburg Hussars established communication with Sacken's corps. Yorck's main body trooped to Saarau and Konradswaldau (Mrowiny) in three columns. For added security, the Prussian corps commander kept the cavalry of each of his four brigades close to the infantry. To the left of the Prussians, Langeron's vanguard reached Jauer; the main body halted ten miles to its southeast at Striegau, itself four miles west of Yorck's main body.[2] Two hundred Cossacks maintained communication between Yorck's and Langeron's vanguards. On Blücher's right, Sacken's corps marched into Breslau but did not achieve its objectives of Neumarkt and Deutschlissa. After occupying the provincial capital, the Russian corps commander continued only to Breslau's western suburbs instead of the Schweidnitz stream. He pushed six Cossack regiments to Deutschlissa rather than Neumarkt. Purportedly, Sacken admitted to purposefully deviating from the disposition. On Blücher's extreme left wing, Kaysarov led Pahlen III's van of four Jäger battalions and three Cossack regiments only to Schmiedeberg, likewise falling short of his objective of reaching Hirschberg. Blücher's headquarters moved to Würben, four miles north of Schweidnitz (see Map 2).[3]

At noon on the 14th, the Allies received their first break in the new campaign. Ney's chief of staff, the Swiss-born General Antoine-Henri Jomini, defected. Already an accomplished military writer with an international reputation, he had attracted Napoleon's attention in Spain during the 1808 campaign. No doubt Jomini had rendered valuable service as Ney's staff chief, yet Berthier – possibly out of jealousy – had blamed him for the marshal's mistakes earlier in the year at Bautzen. Subsequently, he made sure that Jomini did not receive a promotion in August.[4] According to Langeron:

> My advanced post at Striegau sent me a letter from General Jomini, the famous author of *Traité des grandes opérations militaires*, at that time Marshal Ney's chief of staff; he asked to speak with me. I knew that our enemies, especially at the beginning of campaigns, were in the habit of sending such emissaries in attempts to uncover or learn something that was highly disadvantageous for us to let them know; I refused to see Monsieur Jomini. A second letter arrived and I gave the same response. Finally, he wrote me that he was coming to join our army and remain with it; at the same moment, Lieutenant-Colonel [Pavel] Brozin, adjutant to the tsar, arrived at my camp and was looking for him [Jomini], and they left together for the headquarters of the sovereigns. This long-plotted desertion caused great commotion, produced little honor for Monsieur Jomini (although he is not French, but Swiss), and resulted in little profit for the Allied armies. On the spot, Jomini lost the reputation he had acquired, justly so, by means of his excellent works. He soon became a general and the tsar's adjutant.[5]

Jomini revealed that French forces in Silesia had received orders to proceed defensively and mask the Silesian Army while the emperor turned with his main force against Berlin and the Army of North Germany.[6] Blücher immediately forwarded this information to Bernadotte: "He [Jomini] told the Russian general Count Langeron, whom he met for a moment, that the emperor Napoleon would attack the army under your command to take the city of Berlin." Blücher promised to inform the crown prince as soon as he could verify this news. If Napoleon "moved with the majority of his forces" against the Army of North Germany, Blücher pledged "not to fail to follow closely and assist in the most active way the operations of Your Royal Highness." Despite Blücher's assurances, this news placed Bernadotte in panic mode for the remainder of the campaign.[7]

Although Blücher's troops did not encounter the enemy on the 14th, the general did have some explaining to do. First, he had to answer to the three armistice commissioners at Neumarkt. Just a few days earlier, Blücher had promised the Prussian representative, General Krusemarck, that he would not enter the neutral zone before 16 August. Pleased, Krusemarck shared this news with the French commissioner, who in turn pledged that imperial forces likewise would not enter the neutral zone until the 17th. Blücher felt obligated to inform Krusemarck of his change of mind. Krusemarck received the news with dismay, refusing to believe Blücher's claim that the imperials had violated the neutral zone first. It did not help Blücher's case that all the reports that Krusemarck had thus far received indicated that the French intended to withdraw west when the campaign resumed. The fact that the imperials had already begun transporting their sick and their supplies – as well as all the cattle that they had recently requisitioned – to Saxony served to reinforce Krusemarck's conviction. He demanded that Blücher refrain from any premature action. Blücher refused, writing to Krusemarck that "the diplomatic buffoonery and letter-writing must end. I will beat time without notes." A few days later, after completing his assignment at Neumarkt, Krusemarck passed through Silesian Army Headquarters en route to his next post with the Army of North Germany. He rebuked Blücher for violating the terms of the armistice and for compromising him as the king's commissioner. "Regardless," noted Nostitz, "this had no result other than the general dismissing this accusation with the remark that he was responsible for his actions only to the king and no one else, least of all the French, and that, on the contrary, it made him extremely happy if this act annoyed Krusemarck."[8]

Second, the Russians disagreed with Blücher's high-handed actions. "The entry into the neutral zone," explained Müffling, "caused a multitude of remarks in the Russian corps, which were loud enough to spread in the army: 'this was against intentions and instructions; General Barclay, *who actually commanded the army*, would oppose this, and had to return to the Silesian Army and lead it; the Russian corps could not be placed under General Blücher, etc.' General Blücher learned of these statements but, as unpleasant as they must have been to him, he paid no attention and did not change his demeanor toward the Russian troops." Be that as it may, Blücher issued an order of the day to the troops, perhaps with an eye to his Russian generals: "Hereby, the army will be informed that during the night of 10/11 August, Austria declared war on France and at the same time His Imperial Highness the Tsar of Russia and His Royal Highness the King of Prussia terminated the armistice. Therefore, hostilities can resume on the expiration of the 16th of this month unless the enemy breaks the truce sooner." After having time to reflect on the circumstances, Langeron noted in his memoirs that "this movement, somewhat precipitate, was nevertheless imposed by necessity and by the approach of French troops, who appeared to want to advance on Breslau and exhaust the country which we needed to furnish our subsistence."[9]

By nightfall on the 14th, the main bodies of Blücher's three principal corps held a forty-mile line extending from Striegau through Saarau to Breslau while the vanguards extended across a front of thirty-six miles from Jauer to Mertschütz to Deutschlissa. The reports that arrived did little to clarify the situation. From Deutschlissa, Sacken's Cossacks patrolled northwest to the Oder and due west to Neumarkt without encountering French forces. From Mertschütz, Lobenthal reported that his patrols likewise had not detected any imperials in the neutral zone west of Yorck's front. Locals informed his men that, up to that point, the enemy had not crossed his line

of demarcation but Colonel Steinmetz learned of an imperial patrol at
Malitsch (Małuszów), four miles north of Jauer. Langeron's patrols observed
only weak detachments east of the Katzbach. It appeared that the French
intended to evacuate the line of the Katzbach on the 15th and withdraw to
Upper Lusatia. On the other hand, work on the fortifications at Liegnitz
accelerated, signaling a desire to hold that town. To clarify the situation as well
as mask the movement of his army, Blücher wanted a large cavalry screen to
reconnoiter at dawn on the 15th. Specifically, the vanguard of each corps
would patrol toward the line of the Katzbach. Gneisenau instructed each
corps commander to dispatch large cavalry detachments with horse artillery
toward the opposite line of demarcation but not across it (see Map 3).[10]

At daybreak on the 15th, strong detachments of cavalry and horse
artillery from the vanguards of Blücher's army moved toward the French
line of demarcation but the army remained idle. They rode west with
instructions to attack any imperial forces found inside the neutral zone but
to refrain from hostilities on the French side of the line. From Sacken's
corps, General Vasilchikov led one infantry, three cavalry, and six Cossack
regiments supported by twelve horse guns west through Neumarkt. His
cavalry reached Parchwitz without encountering the French. After posting
General Akim Karpov there with four Cossack regiments, Vasilchikov
returned to Neumarkt. In the center, Lobenthal rode northwest from
Mertschütz toward Liegnitz on the Katzbach with all the cavalry of Yorck's
vanguard. Some eight miles southeast of Liegnitz, the Prussians found ten
starving imperial soldiers searching for food. Lobenthal's troopers passed
through several villages where they encountered only individual soldiers
scavenging for food. The staff officer accompanying Lobenthal's lead elem-
ent reported that, despite the existence of French camps north of Liegnitz at
Pfaffendorf (Piątnicka) and on the Pfaffendorf hills, he had observed only a
small enemy post at the Katzbach monitoring the road to Pfaffendorf. As the
staff officer continued toward Liegnitz, he received reports of large enemy
columns marching west from the town. This led to the assumption that the
French would evacuate their two camps and limit themselves to holding
Liegnitz.

French security measures and vigilance improved considerably after
Blücher's surprise attack at Haynau on 25 May. Several times between
10 and 13 August, French patrols reported Allied violations of the neutral
zone. As the Prussians approached Liegnitz on the 15th, they encountered a
French post on the right bank of the Katzbach guarding the bridge.
Although the post was technically in the neutral zone, the Prussians did
not attack, purportedly because the staff officer "gave strict orders that in no
case could they be the first to open fire." On seeing the Prussians, the French
fell back but fired their muskets, mortally wounding Lieutenant Albrecht of
the Brandenburg Uhlans. Thus fell the first shots of the Fall Campaign.

Incensed by the loss of their officer, the uhlans attacked, wounding a few imperials and bringing back one prisoner. The withdrawal of the post allowed the staff officer to move closer and view Liegnitz's much-heralded fortifications, which he found to consist of only a few earthworks and palisades. He deemed Liegnitz to be weak enough to take with cavalry alone. This report arrived at Yorck's headquarters with a copy of a message written by a credible spy stating that on the previous day the imperials had evacuated from the area around Liegnitz all the wagons and animals that could be harnessed. After transporting the sick to Glogau, all imperial forces withdrew from Liegnitz, leaving behind one battalion each of French and Spanish troops – the latter looked to desert at the first opportunity. Although Ney's headquarters remained there, the French generally believed they would soon march west.[11]

In the meantime, Lobenthal's patrol reached Liegnitz and received fire from the left bank of the Katzbach. He could not ascertain the size of the enemy force holding the town. Moreover, another staff officer, Lieutenant Röder, reported the existence of a French camp eight miles west of Liegnitz. According to deserters, Liegnitz itself would be evacuated during the night, with part of its garrison going west to Haynau, the other part heading southwest to Goldberg. Throughout the night, bivouac fires could be seen on the opposite bank of the Katzbach; drums beating the march could be clearly heard.

On Blücher's left, Langeron's quartermaster and acting chief of staff, Colonel Neydhardt, led the cavalry of the Russian van northwest from Jauer toward Goldberg, likewise on the Katzbach. En route, his troopers saw nothing of the enemy and found Goldberg's defenses insignificant; an estimated 1,500 men garrisoned the town. Although the entrenchments built to guard the camp on the left bank of the Katzbach still stood, the imperials were gone. Locals claimed that some of them had marched west toward Löwenberg, others northwest toward Bunzlau. Russian patrols that approached the Katzbach received fire from posts on the opposite bank.[12]

During the course of the 15th, Gneisenau, Müffling, and several staff officers rushed to Jauer to obtain the results of the reconnaissance and to direct the vanguards accordingly. Yet Silesian Army Headquarters did not move to Jauer with the chief of staff and quartermaster-general, leading to an excess of problems and headaches for the commander in chief. Nevertheless, the intelligence Gneisenau received in the afternoon indicated that an enemy offensive in Silesia seemed unlikely. Instead, French forces *appeared* to be marching west. However, as the enemy's position immediately west of the Katzbach did not change, Gneisenau felt that the French had yet to decide whether they would abandon the Katzbach without a fight. For this reason, the staff chief informed Blücher that he and Müffling would pass the night at Jauer. He also provided a disposition for the army to continue its general advance on the 16th with Sacken's corps marching southwest on the Neumarkt–Jauer road to Eisendorf (Jarostów) and Ober-Mois (Ujazd Górny), fifteen miles east of Jauer. Yorck would direct his vanguard to Jauer while his main body marched eleven miles west from Konradswaldau to Fehebeutel (Wieśnica). Gneisenau wanted Langeron to advance west to Bolkenhain, pushing his vanguard to Schönau. Pahlen III would move to Hirschberg and forward his van toward Lähn. After dispatching the disposition to Blücher at Würben, Gneisenau wrote a somber letter to his wife: "Yesterday, I joined the vanguard. The first shots have already fallen. We have a gravely wounded officer here. Please open the accompanying letter upon my death. Many signs lead us to conclude that the enemy has started his retreat. Our army is still rearward and today reached only Striegau."[13]

During the night of 15/16 August, Blücher waited in vain for the return of his staff chief and quartermaster-general. To pass the time, he penned his thoughts to Hardenberg: "Reports indicate that the enemy is marching with his main force through Torgau on Magdeburg and have pulled back units from Liegnitz. Today, I will move the army to the Katzbach; I will not loaf if the enemy retreats tomorrow. Since I am now my own master, the king will see that I will not twiddle my thumbs. All the same, I will not act rashly."[14] After neither Gneisenau nor Müffling had returned by dawn on the 16th, Blücher notified his corps commanders that the army would march that day according to a disposition that would be delivered in a few hours. For reasons unknown, Gneisenau's letter and disposition did not reach Blücher until 10:00 on the morning of 16 August. The noon hour had already passed by the time Blücher's staff issued Gneisenau's instructions.

Meanwhile, Lobenthal remained active throughout the night of 15/16 August. His patrols provided Gneisenau with three key reports. The first, sent at 9:00 P.M. on the 15th, confirmed that four French infantry regiments remained at a camp near Parchwitz. The second, submitted at 4:30 A.M. on the 16th, stated that twelve fully armed Spaniards who had defected to the Prussians insisted that the French would evacuate Liegnitz on the 16th and withdraw west through Bunzlau and Goldberg. Their statements confirmed a report received from an agent at Liegnitz who informed the Prussians that the imperials had sent their equipment and baggage rolling west on the 15th and that the two French divisions (9th and 10th of III Corps) stationed there had received orders to depart for Saxony at 7:00 P.M. on the 16th. According to the spy, all enemy troops had received orders to fall back to Torgau on the Elbe. Napoleon still quartered at Dresden but planned to move east with cavalry on the 16th or 17th to cover the withdrawal of his forces from Silesia. The reason cited for this withdrawal was that the imperial army in Silesia stood too far from Napoleon's main forces. The third and final report provided by Lobenthal, dated 7:30 A.M. on 16 August, stated that the patrol he had sent toward Liegnitz during the previous night had found the bridge over the Katzbach down and encountered only one small post consisting of eight enemy troopers. This patrol also learned that the imperials had evacuated Liegnitz during the night but had kept their watch fires burning to deceive the Allies. Lobenthal expressed his opinion that the French had already withdrawn their forces from the left bank of the Katzbach.[15]

With the army already marching, Blücher received a second letter from Gneisenau at 12:30 informing him of this latest intelligence. Because all signs indicated that the imperials intended to evacuate Liegnitz, Gneisenau suggested that Yorck press further west by having his vanguard reach Goldberg and his main body Jauer. Blücher concurred, ordering Yorck to cover an additional eight miles to Jauer. With his crops marching from Konradswaldau in two columns, Yorck received Blücher's revised orders between 2:00 and 3:00 in the afternoon. The crotchety corps commander was already in a foul mood because of the late start, but the day only became worse for him. His first column – 2nd and 7th Brigades and the Reserve Cavalry – managed to reach the bivouac at Jauer around 11:00 P.M. on the 16th without mishap. However, his second column – 1st and 8th Brigades and the Reserve Artillery – collided with units of Langeron's corps en route to Bolkenhain. After untangling the columns had claimed several hours, the Prussians marched through the night to reach Jauer, where they arrived after dawn on the 17th. Heavy summer downpours and the resulting mud rendered the march doubly unpleasant. Yorck's Landwehr particularly suffered; many men fell out because their boots remained stuck in the unyielding mud and continuing through the muck barefooted did not seem appealing.[16]

The factors that led to the night march on 16/17 August can be attributed to Gneisenau's absence from headquarters, which one military observer accurately labels "an interruption of the mechanism of command" and another attributes to "the want of experience in the Prussian staff."[17] Although the separation from Blücher led to "friction" on the army level, Gneisenau's presence at Jauer represents an understandable desire to obtain information through visual inspection rather than depending on reports generated by inexperienced junior officers and the conflicting statements of local inhabitants. More importantly, this night march marked the beginning of a campaign that would be grueling and costly from the very start because of what Yorck viewed as Blücher's excessive and contradictory demands. Yorck, Langeron, and Sacken viewed the orders coming from Army Headquarters with extreme skepticism. In this case, judgment comes down squarely on their side: Gneisenau and Blücher should not have separated. Gneisenau's messenger wasted precious hours delivering the staff chief's report to Blücher. Moreover, the orders issued at noon and then expanded led to collisions and night marches, neither of which made a favorable impression. Thus, 16 August ultimately proved to be the opening round of Blücher's struggle with his corps commanders.

Two miles west of Jauer, Yorck's van reached only Peterwitz (Piotrowice) on the evening of the 16th, pushing patrols toward Goldberg. Yorck dispatched an additional five squadrons from his 7th Brigade north from Jauer toward Liegnitz to secure his right flank. One patrol encountered imperial forces just south of Liegnitz. Blücher himself rushed to Jauer but the rest of the army could not keep up. Already behind, Sacken did not receive the disposition for 16 August until 4:00 that afternoon. Consequently, his men also needed the entire night to march twenty miles before halting between Eisendorf and Ober-Mois around 9:00 on the morning of the 17th. Vasilchikov led Sacken's vanguard on a night march to Panzkau. Sacken's units furthest to the west, Karpov's Cossacks, rode northwest on the afternoon of the 16th to verify reports that the imperials had evacuated their camps at Parchwitz and Lüben. Passing through the former en route to the latter, Karpov confirmed the French withdrawal. He then turned south, taking a position at Großtinz (Tyniec Legnicki) some eleven miles east of Liegnitz. On the left wing, Langeron's troops reached Bolkenhain between 12:00 and 1:00 A.M. on the 17th. Rudzevich with Langeron's vanguard halted around 6:00 A.M. on the hills east of Schönau (see Map 2).[18]

In the meantime, Kaysarov dispatched three strong patrols from Pahlen III's vanguard to reconnoiter Kemnitz (Stara Kamienica), Berthelsdorf, and Lähn on the morning of 16 August. Some ten miles west of Hirschberg, the Russians found enemy detachments of 500 infantry each at Kemnitz and Berthelsdorf. The Russians attacked, prompting the imperials to withdraw to Spiller, where they offered stubborn resistance in the village cemetery before continuing their retreat. Meanwhile, the third detachment, which Steffens accompanied, encountered a French post east of Lähn. It too received the Russians with sustained small-arms fire before several flank attacks prompted the imperials to retreat to Lähn. The day's fighting cost the Russians six killed, seventeen wounded, and three missing. Sent from Schmiedeberg on the evening of the 16th, Pahlen's report on these events reached Langeron's headquarters at Bolkenhain on the afternoon of the 17th. From there, Langeron forwarded the communiqué to Jauer, where it reached Blücher at 8:00 P.M. – more than twenty-four hours later.[19]

By late morning on the 17th, the Silesian Army reached the following positions along a 45-mile front: Pahlen III at Hirschberg, Langeron at Bolkenhain, Yorck and Army Headquarters at Jauer, and Sacken at Ober-Mois. Granting Sacken's men no rest, Gneisenau instructed the Russian general to push his vanguard to Liegnitz but move his main body closer to Yorck's by marching to the hills of Wahlstatt (Legnickie Pole), eight miles north-northeast of Jauer. Based on Barclay's suggestion one week earlier, he authorized Sacken to form *Streifkorps* commanded by Rakhmanov and

Figner. Gneisenau tasked them with leading their units through Parchwitz to harass the enemy's left flank.[20] Finally, news arrived that the lead elements of Bennigsen's Army of Poland had reached Polnischlissa (Leszno), some seventy miles north-northeast of Jauer. Blücher requested that Bennigsen immediately return the cavalry brigade from Sacken's corps stationed there: two regiments each of hussars and Cossacks commanded by Lanskoy (see Map 3).[21]

According to the reports, the French appeared to be marching from the northeast to the southwest along the thirty-mile line of Liegnitz–Goldberg–Löwenberg. As Blücher noted in his letter to Hardenberg, they seemed content to completely evacuate the Katzbach. Gneisenau expressed this same conviction to Sacken at 7:00 on the morning of the 17th. With hostilities officially resuming on the 17th, the Prussians no longer felt constrained in their pursuit of news of the enemy. For extensive reconnoitering, Yorck's Reserve Cavalry received orders to leave the main body and join the vanguard. Before the additional troopers could arrive, Gneisenau and Müffling decided to personally conduct reconnaissance late on the morning of the 17th to confirm that the French had evacuated the Katzbach. Seven miles northeast of Jauer at the village of Seichau (Sichów), Gneisenau and Müffling separated: each led a column northwest toward the Katzbach. Escorted by a detachment of Lobenthal's vanguard, Gneisenau struck the highway that ran through Laasnig (Łaźniki) and Röchlitz (Rokitnica).[22] A few miles south of Gneisenau, Lobenthal's remaining troopers accompanied Müffling through Prausnitz (Prusice) on the road to Goldberg. An imperial post at Prausnitz retreated without offering any resistance, thus opening the road to Goldberg. From Prausnitz, Müffling covered three miles to reach the hills on the right bank of the Katzbach close to Goldberg. In this position, he observed a large imperial camp extending from Goldberg to Röchlitz; troops could be seen forming as the alarm sounded. Smoke rising from the hills west and north of Goldberg indicated French camps in those areas. After completing the mission, Müffling's column withdrew through Seichau to the hills of Hennersdorf (Chroślice) on the Goldberg–Jauer road.

Meanwhile, Gneisenau's column found a French post two miles northwest of Seichau at Laasnig. Pursued by the Prussians, the French withdrew to Röchlitz on the right bank of the Katzbach. A sharp skirmish ensued when the Prussian fusiliers of Yorck's van moved up to take possession of the village. This prompted the Prussians to envelop the enemy position. Led by two platoons of skirmishers, three companies assaulted the entrance to Röchlitz. The remaining company turned the left (south) of the village while two platoons of skirmishers moved around its right (north). This maneuver succeeded: the imperials abandoned the enceinte but one detachment withdrew into the village's church and cemetery. Situated on a hill and surrounded by a wall, the position could not be taken. Although the

Prussians moved up two pieces of horse artillery, a firing position could not be located, forcing the gunners to withdraw with some loss. Resolved to take the cemetery, the Prussians committed one platoon of skirmishers and half a company to eject the French while the remaining companies completed the envelopment of Röchlitz. Before the attack could unfold, Gneisenau rescinded the orders after observing numerous imperial squadrons on the opposite bank of the Katzbach. Soon, French infantry reached Röchlitz, forcing Gneisenau to retreat through Seichau to Hennersdorf, where he reunited with Müffling. With a loss of eight dead as well as two officers and twenty-eight soldiers wounded, Gneisenau's reconnaissance mission had found the enemy.

Elsewhere on the 17th, Sacken's patrols noted the continued presence of French forces at Liegnitz, despite the reports of the enemy's withdrawal. His main body marched northwest from Ober-Mois and Eisendorf to Wahlstatt, seven miles southeast of Liegnitz. It arrived on the evening of the 17th, completely exhausted from the strenuous efforts needed to make up for the short march on the 14th. Langeron's corps maintained its position at Bolkenhain with the vanguard east of Schönau. His forward troops established communication with the Prussians of Yorck's corps to the north and Pahlen III's Russians to the south. That evening, Rudzevich reported that his patrols had encountered French outposts east of Goldberg; peasants claimed that Lauriston's entire V Corps was bivouacking on the hills at Goldberg. One patrol that proceeded through Lähn learned from the village mayor that 20,000 French troops were camping east of the Bober and south of Löwenberg at Schmottseifen, Liebenthal, and Friedeberg.

On the extreme left of Blücher's front, Kaysarov led Pahlen III's vanguard north along the Bober, crossing the river at Lähn. From there, he dispatched Cossack patrols west and north. At Märzdorf (Marczów), seven miles south of Löwenberg, the Russians found 200 French infantry. Kaysarov ordered an attack by two companies of the 33rd Jäger Regiment that resulted in the capture of two prisoners and the deaths of nineteen imperial soldiers. While pursuing the French, Kaysarov observed a column of approximately 1,000 infantry supported by cavalry emerge from the village of Mois (Mojesz) less than two miles south of Löwenberg to take in their beleaguered comrades. Kaysarov withdrew to Märzdorf, posting his pickets two miles west of this village on the road to Löwenberg. His patrols confirmed the reports of large and, according to locals, entrenched camps at Löwenberg and Schmottseifen, identifying the 20,000 men as belonging to Macdonald's XI Corps. Peasants informed the Russians that enemy camps also existed at Liebenthal and Ottendorf (Radoniów). Apparently, the imperials had remained in their camps awaiting an Allied attack; Kaysarov directed his Cossacks and spies to confirm these reports. Around 4:00 that afternoon, the French probed Märzdorf as part of a reconnaissance mission.

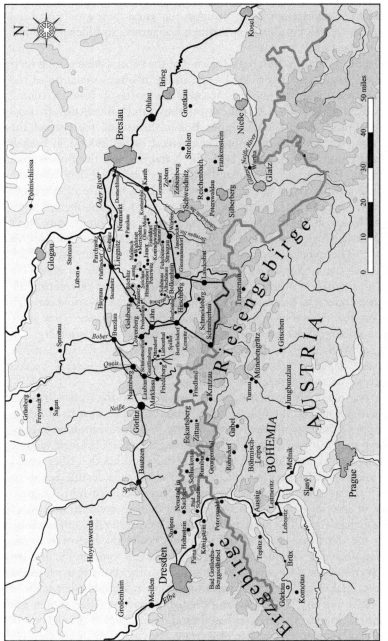

8 Crossing the neutral zone

Fearing this would result in an attack by larger imperial forces the next day, Kaysarov withdrew his infantry that same day to Lähn, leaving only posts at Märzdorf and Schmottseifen. His 17 August report on these events made its way from Pahlen III's headquarters through Langeron's to Blücher's by late morning on the 18th.[23]

Turning to the French, Blücher's crossing of the neutral zone earned their ire. "Without regard for sworn oaths and in an infamous violation of the armistice treaty, today the enemy attacked the posts of 36th Division," reported Macdonald from Löwenberg on the 17th.[24] Blücher's offensive against the French right on the upper Bober threatened the rear of the imperial army. In turn, this prompted the retreat of the individual French corps and divisions posted along both the Katzbach and the Bober. Like Napoleon, the French corps commanders in Silesia believed they faced the main Allied army, having not yet learned of the departure of Barclay's 100,000 men for Bohemia. "Instead of being wary of his opponent," notes one French historian, "and concentrating the various corps of his army on 11 August, Marshal Ney found himself surprised and forced to abandon his positions."[25] The initial movements of the French army occurred haphazardly because the emperor had yet to name a commander in chief. He remedied this situation on the 15th by appointing Ney and instructing the marshal to withdraw to Bunzlau if the enemy's main force advanced through Liegnitz on the east–west highway. Should Blücher advance from Jauer through Goldberg, Napoleon directed him to retreat to Löwenberg. On the 16th and 17th, Ney concentrated III Corps and II Cavalry Corps at Liegnitz. All departed west for Haynau as part of the general French movement across the Katzbach on 17 August.[26]

As for Napoleon, the emperor initially assumed that the Russo-Prussian army he had pursued to the Oder in May would advance west from Silesia toward Upper Lusatia while the Austrian army in Bohemia invaded Saxony either along the right bank of the Elbe or through Zittau. He knew vaguely of the arrangements made at Trachenberg, but did not think the Allies would dare leave Silesia only weakly guarded by sending considerable forces to Bohemia.[27] Despite its length, Napoleon's position offered him the great advantage of interior lines, which would allow him to concentrate a force much larger than any Allied army threatening his center or one of his wings. Although the defensive character of his plans ceded the initiative to the Allies, Napoleon felt confident as long as his forces could hold Dresden for at least one week. Moreover, the extensive fortifications that protected the Saxon capital made an Allied operation against it along the left bank of the Elbe seem unlikely. He hoped and predicted that the Allies would not break their tradition of waging war based on the principles of the eighteenth century. By adhering to this system of warfare, the Coalition would view his communications with France as their main objective and thus target Leipzig.

That the Trachenberg Protocol called for the Allies to advance on Leipzig demonstrates how well the emperor knew his opponents.

At Dresden on his birthday, 15 August, the emperor of the French climbed into his carriage followed by his brother-in-law, Joachim Murat, the king of Naples by the grace of Napoleon, and proceeded south. He inspected the fortifications and bridges at Pirna at 9:00 P.M., followed by the pontoon bridge at Königstein around midnight before turning northeast toward Bautzen.[28] General Marie Victor de Latour-Maubourg's I Cavalry Corps and the Old Guard followed. After his aide-de-camp took a wrong turn, costing the emperor thirty minutes and greatly fouling his mood, Napoleon reached Bautzen at 2:00 A.M. on the 16th. Later that morning, he received intelligence from spies that Barclay and Wittgenstein had led the Russian army from Silesia to Bohemia. There, it would join Schwarzenberg's army, which had already moved to the left bank of the Elbe. In addition, Blücher's army – a mere 50,000 men according to the emperor's estimate – started driving west from Breslau. Blücher's violation of the six-day suspension of hostilities irked the emperor, who referred to it as "the infamous conduct of the Prussians." The support of the Russian and Prussian commissioners at Neumarkt did little to assuage him.[29]

Although Napoleon wanted confirmation that the Russians had left Silesia, the spy reports concerning the movements of Barclay and Wittgenstein from Silesia to Bohemia allowed him to tighten his plans. To threaten Prague and distract Schwarzenberg, Napoleon planned to push 100,000 men south to the Bohemian frontier with II and VIII Corps actually moving onto Austrian soil. To the east, Macdonald's 50,000 men (XI and V Corps) would defend the Bober crossing at Löwenberg while Ney did the same with 70,000 men (III and VI Corps) at Bunzlau. West of them at Lauban on the Queis stood Marshal Adolph Édouard Mortier's three Young Guard divisions. Napoleon himself would lead the Old Guard, I Corps, and I Cavalry Corps to Silesia to commence the campaign by destroying Blücher's *small* army, thus removing the threat it posed to the rear of both his Grande Armée in Saxony as well as Oudinot's Army of Berlin. Two conditions had to be met for him to march against Blücher. First, the Prussian would have to advance on Bunzlau and, second, Barclay's Russians would have to be in Bohemia, marching north toward Dresden or Zwickau. Napoleon assured Macdonald that, as soon as he received this confirmation, "I will march to destroy Blücher."[30]

With the official resumption of hostilities on the 17th, Napoleon ordered a general reconnaissance. One Guard cavalry division followed by one Young Guard infantry division crossed the Bohemian frontier at Rumburg (Rumburk) while thirteen miles to their left (east) the Poles of IV Cavalry Corps and VIII Corps filed across the border at Zittau. Napoleon himself left Bautzen on the evening of the 17th en route to Görlitz on the east–west highway. According to Odeleben, during the ride, Napoleon's "active concern for the plan of campaign began; he labored incessantly; couriers and officers were dispatched to all points. The rupture with Austria became certain. Although the war that was about to break out with Austria was hardly mentioned at headquarters, it was known that the combined Russian and Prussian army had left Silesia, taking the direction of Bohemia, and that it was already in the region of Münchengrätz [Mnichovo Hradiště], thus signaling the Allied intention to cross the Bohemian mountains either through the Lusatian mountain passes to their north [near Zittau] or the Saxon passes [near Pirna] further west."[31]

On 17 August, news reached Imperial Headquarters at Bautzen that some 40,000 Russians had entered Bohemia by way of Glatz on 13 August. Although it would appear that this information confirmed the spy reports that Napoleon had received on the 16th, he viewed the intelligence with skepticism. Yet, if true, and should these troops make for Prague, the emperor figured they could not reach the Bohemian capital until the 25th or 26th, which would give him plenty of time to crush Blücher. Thus, Napoleon remained determined to move his headquarters to Görlitz, where he would unite I, III, V, VI, and XI Corps while I and II Cavalry Corps held a forward position at Bunzlau. According to his numbers, this would produce an army of 130,000 to 140,000 men, which combined with the five divisions of his Guard, would total 180,000.[32] Napoleon confidently informed St.-Cyr that the Austrians would not cross the upper Elbe, march northeast, and attempt to enter Lusatia by way of Zittau. However, should the Austrians and Russians combine in an attempt to punch through Zittau, VIII and II Corps and IV Cavalry Corps held a strong position. "I have occupied the position from Eckartsberg to Zittau with 40,000 men, making it impossible to debouch through this gorge." If need be, I Corps could reach Zittau in thirty-six hours to increase imperial forces to 70,000 men while Napoleon could arrive with another 50,000 in one march to reach 120,000 men.

With Zittau thus covered, the emperor arranged for the protection of Dresden. He suspected the Austrians would follow the banks of the Elbe to the Saxon capital. The responsibility for blocking these approaches fell mainly to the 26,000 men and 92 guns of St.-Cyr's XIV Corps, which Napoleon directed to occupy Pirna and Bad Gottleuba-Berggießhübel on the left bank of the Elbe, and Stolpen, Hohnstein, and Bad Schandau on the right bank. St.-Cyr's 42nd Division would relieve two divisions of I Corps guarding the defiles further east at Neustadt in Sachsen, Schluckenau (Šluknov), and Rumburg. If all Austro-Russian forces moved on Dresden by way of the left bank of the Elbe, Napoleon assured St.-Cyr that General Dominique-Joseph Vandamme's I Corps would "march to Dresden; two of his divisions can arrive within twenty-four hours, the third within thirty-six hours: you will thus be able to unite 60,000 men around Dresden on both banks of the river. Moreover an Allied movement down the Elbe would allow the 40,000 men at Zittau to reach Dresden within four days to total 100,000 defenders." If circumstances allowed, Napoleon claimed that he himself could be there within four days with "the 50,000 men of my Guard."

It is this letter to St.-Cyr that contains the oft-quoted passage stating that, if the Austro-Russian army moved due west from Prague to invade Bavaria through Bayreuth, Napoleon would wish it *bon voyage* knowing the Allies would return faster than they had gone. Hardly concerned about his communication with France, the master nevertheless instinctively recognized the importance of Dresden and the Elbe. Thus, the other famous quote from this letter: "It is clear that one cannot turn 400,000 men based on a system of fortresses, on a river like the Elbe, and able to debouch at will through Dresden, Torgau, Wittenberg, and Magdeburg." With the 180,000 men at the Görlitz–Bunzlau position, the emperor planned to "debouch on Blücher, Sacken ... who, it appears, are marching on my troops today and after I have destroyed or routed these corps the balance will be restored." After smashing the enemy army in Silesia, Napoleon planned to either march to Berlin depending on Oudinot's situation or drive through Bohemia to reach the rear of the Austro-Russian army if it invaded Bavaria.[33]

On 18 August, Marmont's VI Corps concluded its march east by reaching Bunzlau on the Bober. In the center, Lauriston's V Corps fell back west to Löwenberg, likewise on the Bober. On the right wing, Macdonald assembled his 35th and 36th Divisions at Schmottseifen, leaving the 31st Division further west at Greiffenberg to secure the right flank. Fearing an envelopment of his right, Macdonald ordered 35th Division to eject the enemy posts reported to be along the Bober at Lähn and Berthelsdorf. Napoleon reached Görlitz that evening, where he received "confusing" news over the enemy's movements. He learned that the Austrians had crossed the Elbe en route to an unknown destination. "One report claims that 60,000 Russians and Prussians have entered Bohemia, and that Tsar Alexander reached Prague on the 15th," he informed his minister of war, Henri Clarke. Regardless, he remained confident that his subordinates could hold either Zittau or Pirna long enough for him to arrive should the Allied army in Bohemia follow one of these invasion routes. Vandamme, whose I Corps lagged far behind Napoleon's main body, received orders to lead his 1st Division from Stolpen to Rumburg rather than Bautzen. At Rumburg, he would unite with St.-Cyr's 42nd Division and 3,000 sabers of 1st Guard Cavalry Division as well as 3rd Infantry Division of the Young Guard. Should the Allies go west from Prague to Bavaria, "then they would allow me to conduct an offensive in all of Bohemia. If, however, the news of the arrival of the Russian army in Bohemia is false, or if it is only a small corps, then in two days I will unite

200,000 men against the enemy army in Silesia. As you can see, this war is based on a large scale."[34]

To slow the retreat of Ney's army, Berthier started issuing directives from Görlitz at 6:00 A.M. on 19 August based on the emperor's instructions. Reacting to Macdonald's belief that he had cut off an Allied corps advancing west from Greiffenberg, Berthier ordered the infantry of the Guard as well as I Cavalry Corps to support the marshal in destroying this enemy force. One hour later, he conveyed the emperor's instructions for Macdonald to drive the Cossacks across the Bober and hold the river line instead of falling back to the Queis. Latour-Maubourg's I Cavalry Corps received a second order calling for it to take a position that day, the 19th, at Lauban and to dispatch patrols along the Queis to prevent the Cossacks from crossing. At 7:00 on the morning of the 19th, Napoleon dispatched a letter to Ney explaining that "according to all available news, the Russian army has entered Bohemia; it is certain that Barclay de Tolly himself arrived there on the 15th and every indication is that Wittgenstein, with a corps of 40,000 men, was at Böhmisch-Leipa [Česká Lípa] on the 17th. We know that Wintzingerode and Mikhail Miloradovich went in another direction. All of this suggests that, while there are few Russians in Silesia, there is the Prussian army, which seems to maneuver in the direction along the mountains, intending to win Zittau to establish communication with the Austrian army through this great pass."[35]

While these conditions met Napoleon's requirements to commence the offensive against Blücher, he still did not have a clear picture of Schwarzenberg's intentions. Regardless, the master of war enjoyed an uncanny ability to make his opponent do exactly what he wanted. Needing to know where Schwarzenberg would lead his massive army before he departed for Silesia, Napoleon believed he could dictate the Allied commander in chief's first move. Moreover, he wanted to see for himself if an operation from Lusatia could have success against the flank of the Russian columns purportedly marching west through Bohemia to join Schwarzenberg on the left bank of the Elbe. If time allowed, he could fall on Barclay with superior forces and considerably frustrate the Coalition's plans. To answer these questions, Napoleon returned to Zittau on the 19th. Forty-five miles southwest of Löwenberg, twenty-two miles south of Görlitz, fifty-three miles east of Dresden, and seventy miles north of Prague, Zittau provided Napoleon with the ultimate central position between Schwarzenberg and Blücher. After reviewing elements of Poniatowski's VIII Corps, including the newly formed Polish Cossacks, the emperor followed a large reconnaissance force consisting of 4,000–5,000 men eleven miles south to the Bohemian town of Gabel (Jablonné v Podještědí). Meeting little resistance, the French advanced beyond Gabel, obtaining "such information concerning the Allied armies as the common inhabitants and ignorant peasants could afford." Another large reconnaissance force from Poniatowski's VIII Corps reached Kratzau (Chrastava), southeast of Zittau, while west of Zittau a third did not venture beyond Rumburg.[36]

Napoleon returned to Zittau around midnight with a clear understanding of the situation. First, he could not reach Barclay's army group. To give Napoleon a wide berth, the Russians moved across the northeastern frontier of Bohemia from Upper Silesia and struck a road that ran southwest from Trautenau (Trutnov) to Jungbunzlau, forty miles south of Zittau. From there, they continued west to Melnik on the right bank of the upper Elbe seventy miles south of Dresden. Kleist's II Corps and the Prussian Guard took a road that ran even further south. On 17, 18, and 19 August, the Russian and Prussian columns marched through the vineyards and orchards of Leitmeritz to cross the Elbe, forty-eight miles southwest of Zittau and forty-seven miles southeast of Dresden. Thus, the French only found the troops of the Austrian 2nd Light Division in northeastern Bohemia, maintaining communication between Allied Headquarters and Blücher through the Landeshut–Trautenau pass. Napoleon received confirmation that the three Allied sovereigns had met either at Prague or Schlan (Slaný) on the previous day, the 18th, and that a Prussian corps had likewise marched with the Russians to Bohemia.[37]

As noted, Napoleon suspected Schwarzenberg would march to the left bank of the upper Elbe – a movement that prisoners now confirmed. Apparently, the Allies intended to employ their main strength against his line of communication by marching on Leipzig or Dresden or some other point. At the same time, he received Ney's report on the determined advance of the Silesian Army. This caused Napoleon to return to the idea that Schwarzenberg would make for Zittau. He did not know exactly where Schwarzenberg would lead the Army of Bohemia but that no longer mattered. Napoleon predicted that, as soon as the Allied commander in chief learned that he had been at Gabel, the Austrian would direct his army to Zittau. By the time the Allies arrived there, the emperor would be in Silesia crushing Blücher. Thus, Napoleon decided to continue his plan to march against Blücher, defeat him, and then rush back to Dresden. To increase the number of bayonets in the Zittau sector, 1st Division arrived at Rumburg, while Vandamme's 2rd and 3rd Divisions echeloned between there and Dresden, but St.-Cyr's 42nd Division returned to the Pirna sector.[38]

Not having the numbers to simultaneously crush Blücher and stop Schwarzenberg's advance through Zittau, Napoleon based his plans on a very tight timetable. In turn, his timing depended on the notoriously slow and methodical movements of the Austrians as well as the difficulties inherent in the operations of a multinational army. He calculated that the 65,000 soldiers of I, II, and VIII Corps and IV Cavalry Corps as well as 1st Guard Cavalry Division and elements of V Cavalry Corps would have at least four or five days to entrench positions in the passes and on the roads between Upper Lusatia and Bohemia. The passes would be secured by I Corps at Rumburg and II Corps at Zittau. With VIII Corps and IV Cavalry Corps, Prince Poniatowski would move south to Gabel and remain on Bohemian soil. On the 20th, 1st Division of I Corps would cross the Bohemian frontier at Rumburg and push south to St. Georgenthal (Jiřetín pod Jedlovou) and Rohrsdorf (Svor), the latter being nine miles west of Gabel. Expecting the troops to tenaciously defend their well-fortified mountain positions, Berthier instructed Vandamme that "the emperor intends for you to fight to the last man." In this way, Napoleon believed he would have time to destroy Blücher in Silesia and return to Upper Lusatia before Schwarzenberg could push across the mountains. The French drive through Rumburg and Zittau sufficed to send the Austrian 2nd Light Division running thirty-three miles south of Zittau to Turnau (Turnov), but the question remained: would Schwarzenberg take the bait and march on Zittau?[39]

Despite the optimism that permeated Blücher's headquarters on 16 August, all intelligence collected on the 17th indicated that strong French forces still held both the Katzbach and the upper Bober. Thoughts that the imperials would withdraw to Lusatia or Saxony now appeared premature at best. Piecing together the numerous reports, Gneisenau figured that Ney held a forty-mile front running northeast to southwest, with his left at Liegnitz, center at Goldberg, and right between Löwenberg and Greiffenberg. At least two of his corps stood at the Katzbach between Goldberg and Liegnitz while a third camped at Löwenberg on the Bober. Blücher informed Langeron that the day's reconnaissance had not only detected imperial forces at Liegnitz and Goldberg, but had also signaled their intent to hold those positions. To be certain, Blücher issued orders on the evening of the 17th for more reconnaissance to be conducted on the army's flanks early on 18 August. He instructed Sacken to have an officer of his general staff at Army Headquarters by noon on the 18th with the result of this reconnaissance. At the least, the majority of Sacken's men would be able to rest their weary legs on the 18th. As for Langeron, Blücher ordered him to push his main body to Schönau on the 18th, with the vanguard moving across the Katzbach to Probsthain (Proboszczów). He instructed Langeron to have an officer of his staff at Army Headquarters by 2:00 P.M. on the 18th to receive the disposition for the 19th. Frustrated by his inability to attack sooner, Blücher hoped to assemble the army at Jauer and Schönau to smash through the French center at Goldberg on the 19th.[40]

As Sacken and Langeron executed these orders, news reached Army Headquarters midmorning on 18 August that completely changed the situation. From Wahlstatt at 6:30 A.M., Sacken reported that the French had evacuated Liegnitz during the night. Elements of Vasilchikov's vanguard occupied the town while other units pursued the imperials west on the highway to Haynau. Reports from Yorck's patrols confirmed the French departure: the Prussian troopers had observed the campfires go out at Liegnitz around midnight. Moreover, Jürgaß reported that the French also withdrew from Goldberg. To determine the direction they took, he dispatched Katzler with the Brandenburg Uhlans. For support, the Lithuanian Dragoon Regiment thundered along the two roads that ran from Seichau to Prausnitz and Röchlitz. Further south at Schönau, Rudzevich also confirmed the French withdrawal from Goldberg. Reporting at 8:00 A.M., the Russian general added that the imperials were marching north-northwest toward Haynau. Finally, Kaysarov's report from 17 August arrived explaining that the French apparently intended to remain in and around Löwenberg on the Bober.[41]

Despite Macdonald's presence at Löwenberg, the fact that the French had evacuated the line of the Katzbach mattered most to Blücher. He and his staff incorrectly attributed this retrograde movement to the Bohemian Army's advance on Dresden, which presumably caused Napoleon to summon Ney's forces from Silesia for a general concentration on the left bank of the Elbe. Craving to win the first laurels of the new campaign, Blücher and Gneisenau intended to drive to the Neiße in four columns spread across a 25-mile front. Displaying a flair for maneuver reminiscent of Napoleon, the Prussians planned to reach Görlitz on the Saxon frontier before Ney. Issued at noon on the 18th, "The First Disposition for the Continued Pursuit of the Enemy" called for the Silesian Army to reach a 25-mile line extending south from Steuditz (Studnica) through Goldberg to Altschönau during the course of the 18th. Blücher's cover letter to his corps commanders opened by stating: "The enemy has evacuated his position on the Katzbach; it is therefore probable that he will also withdraw from his positions in the highlands." Gneisenau directed Blücher's right – Sacken's corps – through Liegnitz and Haynau to Bunzlau while in the center Yorck's corps would proceed west through Goldberg to Löwenberg and from there turn northwest toward Naumburg. On the left wing, Langeron's corps would march west through Löwenberg to Lauban on the Bober and then move northwest to Görlitz to block the east–west highway that led to Dresden. South of Langeron, Pahlen III would advance twenty-five miles west from Hirschberg toward Marklissa, due south of Lauban. Langeron and Yorck received instructions to form *Streifkorps* and send them toward Dresden to disrupt French communication along the east–west highway.[42] "I have sent all the corps instructions to dispatch *Streifkorps* that can turn both the enemy's flanks and explode into the middle of his columns," Blücher informed Bernadotte. "I hope for good results from this measure because the parties I have already detached have advanced as far as Parchwitz and Lüben but found few enemy forces there. The retreat of the enemy army has principally been directed toward Saxony and on Dresden."[43]

Blücher regarded the movement as a pursuit but cautioned his corps commanders. The French army numbered around 90,000 men. Should any corps encounter a superior enemy force, it would "fix him in the front until the other columns envelop him on the left and on the right and attack him in the rear." For speed, his orders called for the army to be marching in several columns by 5:00 A.M. on the 19th. All but the vanguards would halt between 10:00 and 11:00 to allow the men to cook and feed the horses. The advance would continue from 3:00 P.M. to 7:00 or 8:00 P.M. As for the vanguard, Blücher insisted that it maintain constant contact with the enemy and halt only in the evening to eat. Escorted by Yorck's corps, Blücher planned to transfer his headquarters to Löwenberg on the 19th.[44]

Gneisenau and Müffling typically drafted the orders and Blücher approved them. Very similar to Wittgenstein's first efforts prior to Lützen, these instructions included rookie mistakes and have received their due criticism. First, the Prussians placed too much stock in the reports of the evacuation of Liegnitz and Goldberg. They based their planning on the *supposition* that the French would evacuate Silesia and withdraw as far as the Elbe. Yet no evidence supported this belief other than the retreat from the Katzbach, which certainly did not provide compelling proof that the imperials would recede all the way to Dresden. To the Prussians, Kaysarov's report, which confirmed the presence of Macdonald's XI Corps south of Löwenberg, appeared to be a logical French precaution: Ney's right wing would hold the upper Bober while his left wing fell back from the Katzbach to come on line with the right. Army Headquarters did take into account the possibility that the French could stop and thus instructed the nearest column to fix the enemy in the front for as long as possible until the neighboring corps could envelop his flanks. Regardless, the Prussians appeared to ignore the fact that each corps could encounter a large enemy force before one of the neighboring corps could provide assistance.

Advancing in several columns along a front twenty-five miles wide entailed a considerable amount of risk. Considering that the disposition provided no march objectives or stages for the corps commanders, Blücher's headquarters significantly increased the chances that friction could wreak havoc on the internal cohesion of the army. Driving against an unshaken opponent and wanting to orchestrate the symmetrical advance of three corps by regulating their time of departure instead of assigning their daily march goals "surrendered the tight, uniform management of the whole." From a practical viewpoint, the late arrival of the reports from the corps commanders led to the issuing of the disposition late in the day. This in turn led to another night march. While Blücher could not prevent it if he wanted to remain in close contact with the imperials, another night march did not sit well with the troops or their commanders.[45]

Blücher's desire for the imperials to leave Silesia probably fathered the thought. As the Silesian Army proceeded west on the 18th, the French demonstrated their intent to defend the Bober. "It appeared that the Bober was the fixed point for the enemy for the final concentration of their troops and the end of their retreats," explained Langeron. On Blücher's right wing, Sacken's vanguard under Vasilchikov crossed the Katzbach at Liegnitz and continued west toward Haynau. At Steudnitz, the Russians caught the French rearguard and drove it to Haynau, capturing 6 officers and 200 men. Vasilchikov halted east of Haynau while Sacken's main body bivouacked at Steudnitz after a march of only eleven miles. With Lanskoy's cavalry brigade still detached at Polnischlissa, Sacken's shortage of cavalry prevented any exploitation of this success.[46] Intelligence indicated that the withdrawing troops – as well as the divisions moving southwest from Parchwitz, Steinau, and Lüben – belonged to Ney's III Corps. Although reports identified several divisions, the Allies calculated the strength of III Corps to be only 25,000 men and Lauriston's V Corps to number around 18,000 men.

In Blücher's center, Jürgaß led Yorck's vanguard west on the morning of the 18th to confirm that the enemy had evacuated Goldberg. Katzler joined his Brandenburg Uhlan Regiment, which served as Jürgaß's lead unit. On his own initiative, Katzler proceeded toward Goldberg accompanied only by his adjutant, the future Chief of the General Staff of the Prussian Army (1849–1857) Karl Friedrich Wilhelm von Reyher, and one orderly. Reaching Röchlitz, he found the town clear of the enemy and continued to the outskirts of Goldberg, where he united with two of his Brandenburg Uhlan squadrons returning from a patrol. Two horse guns and the six remaining squadrons of his brigade soon caught up. Katzler then led these eight squadrons through Goldberg along the highway to Löwenberg. On the hills between Pilgramsdorf (Pielgrzymka) and Hermsdorf (Jerzmanice-Zdrój) he found Lauriston's rearguard: an estimated 2,000–3,000 men escorting a large herd of cattle. Katzler reported his position to Jürgaß and requested reinforcements.

West of Pilgramsdorf, the extensive Hainwald (Hain Forest) provided the French infantry with protection from Katzler's cavalry. Knowing that the Prussians would gain the advantage on the open ground west of the wood, the French resolved to make a stand. After emerging on the opposite side of the forest, one French battalion supported by cavalry turned to face the Prussians and buy time for the main body to escape to Lauterseiffen (Bielanka) with its priceless booty. As the Prussians deployed from the wood, five French squadrons charged them. Although the French broke Katzler's lead squadron, the others managed to repulse the imperials. Katzler waited in vain for Jürgaß to arrive with the vanguard's main body. During this time, French skirmishers utilized the undulating terrain on both sides of the road to maneuver against the flanks of the Prussian cavalry. Refusing to needlessly expose his lancers to enemy musketry, Katzler ordered a retreat east through the Hainwald to Pilgramsdorf after netting three officers and fifty soldiers as prisoners.

In the Hainwald, the Prussians encountered Langeron's vanguard cavalry, which informed them that Rudzevich had mistakenly led Langeron's vanguard to Goldberg, where it had collided with Jürgaß's main body. Thus, the time needed to clear the roads accounted for Jürgaß's inability to support Katzler. Due to the bottleneck at Goldberg, Jürgaß had led the main body of Yorck's vanguard north from Goldberg on the highway to Haynau, patrolling the many roads that intersected this area. He sought to confirm rumors of the existence of imperial camps along the left bank of the Schnelle Deichsel (Skora River) at Steinsdorf (Osetnica) and Modelsdorf (Modlikowice), three and six miles southwest of Haynau respectively. After nightfall, Katzler's uhlans rejoined Jürgaß at Adelsdorf (Zagrodno), some nine miles south of Haynau on the right bank of the Schnelle Deichsel.

As the headquarters of both the army and I Corps passed the night of 17/18 August at Jauer, Yorck instantly received the "First Disposition for the Pursuit of the Enemy" that Blücher had issued at noon. These orders directed Yorck's main body west through Goldberg that day. Shortly after noon, I Corps commenced the fourteen-mile march from Jauer to Goldberg in two columns. Yorck's right column (2nd and 1st Brigades) utilized a side road to troop northwest across the plateau on which it would fight the battle of the Katzbach eight days later and then crossed the Katzbach at Röchlitz. Yorck's left column (8th and 7th Brigades and Reserve Artillery) struck the main Jauer–Goldberg highway. After ten miles of marching, the brigades took a dilapidated detour at Prausnitz to continue west to Goldberg while the Reserve Artillery remained on the highway. At Röchlitz, the artillery joined the right column and crossed the Katzbach in the evening. This column bivouacked along the left bank of the Katzbach not long after dusk. However, the poor state of the detour so delayed the march of the left column that the troops did not trudge through Goldberg until midnight. Utterly exhausted, they continued to their bivouac on the hills east of the town. Again, Yorck raged over the incompetence of Army Headquarters.

As noted, Rudzevich had incorrectly led Langeron's vanguard due north to Goldberg, becoming entangled with Yorck's vanguard. He eventually continued west toward Löwenberg, stopping for the night between Pilgramsdorf and Hermsdorf. Ahead of Rudzevich, General Pyotr Grekov VIII's Cossack regiment took 180 prisoners and advanced as far as Lauterseiffen, five miles east of Löwenberg, before returning to Pilgramsdorf for the night. Unlike Yorck, Langeron received Blücher's "First Disposition for the Pursuit of the Enemy" late on the afternoon of the 18th while leading his main body to the crossroads at Altschönau.[47]

Further south on Blücher's extreme left, the Russians suffered their first setback of the new campaign. Pahlen III's main body passed the night of 17/18 August at Hirschberg. Thirteen miles north of Hirschberg, Pahlen's vanguard under Kaysarov held Lähn on the Bober with posts near Märzdorf and Schmottseifen. At 3:00 A.M. on the 18th, strong Neapolitan columns from General Carlo Zucchi's 2nd Brigade of Macdonald's 35th Division marched from Schmottseifen, scattering the Cossack posts in their path. Seven hours later, additional combined-arms columns debouched from Schmottseifen, Mois, and Siebeneichen (Dębowy Gaj) to assail Lähn.

With the 33rd Jäger Regiment and the sole battalion of the Yeletskii Infantry Regiment, General Adam Bistrom prepared to defend the portion of Lähn that stood on the left bank of the Bober. Without firing a shot, the imperials burst into the town to gain a foothold. Bistrom's soldiers counterattacked with the bayonet but could not drive them from Lähn. Hoping to at least hold their ground, the Jäger sought cover in the houses and various structures. Halted by withering fire from the concealed Russians, the imperials moved up artillery to lambast the streets with canister. After sustaining considerable losses, the Russians retreated across the Bober bridge. Kaysarov directed Bistrom's men to occupy the houses on the right bank and those nearest to the bridge. Covered by two companies of the 1st Jäger Regiment, the Russians quickly moved into these positions. By maintaining an impressive volume of fire, they prevented some 8,000 imperial soldiers from crossing the Bober.

Riding north from Hirschberg, Pahlen III reached Lähn around 1:00 P.M. when Kaysarov appeared to have control of the situation. After ordering him to hold his ground for as long as possible before retreating to Hirschberg, Pahlen departed. For another five hours, Kaysarov's soldiers defended the bridge over the Bober at Lähn, until he received disturbing news at 6:00 P.M. that strong imperial forces coming from Greiffenberg had attacked the Russian post at Berthelsdorf, eleven miles southwest of Lähn and seven miles west-northwest of Hirschberg. After ejecting the Russians, the imperials continued their advance toward Hirschberg. To slow their progress, Pahlen dispatched four battalions from his main body toward Berthelsdorf. He ordered Kaysarov to evacuate Lähn and withdraw halfway to Hirschberg. Leaving Cossack posts all along the Bober, the Russians retreated almost ten miles south to Grunau (Jeżów Sudecki), itself only three miles north of Hirschberg. The day's fighting cost Kaysarov 2 officers and 48 soldiers killed, and 6 officers and 192 men wounded. French losses are not known and they did not cross the Bober to pursue Kaysarov.

Breaching protocol, Kaysarov reported directly to Langeron over the "lengthy, intense, and bloody engagement at Lähn, of the march of enemy troops from Greiffenberg through Berthelsdorf toward Hirschberg, and of the necessity of his retreat to Hirschberg." Based on a report from Steffens,

Pahlen informed Langeron that Macdonald's 30,000 men and 100 guns stood between their respective corps. In addition, Steffens reported to Pahlen that an imperial corps of 60,000 men and one cavalry corps of 16,000 sabers stood between Bunzlau and Liegnitz. Additional French forces had left Görlitz and were marching *east* toward Bunzlau while Polish and Saxon troops from Upper Lusatia moved east to replace them. In particular, Steffens's report of a division of some 8,000 men and 20 guns reaching Kemnitz – some seven miles west of Hirschberg – increased Pahlen's fear of being enveloped on the left. He intended to hold Hirschberg for as long as possible but believed the French would force him to retreat within twenty-four hours. In this case, he planned to lead his troops ten miles southeast from Hirschberg to Schmiedeberg. As we will see, these three reports threw Langeron into a panic, which in turn caused fits at Army Headquarters.[48]

After reaching Altschönau, fourteen miles northeast of Pahlen's position at Hirschberg, Langeron received Kaysarov's report of the check at Lähn around 8:00 P.M. Believing Macdonald's demonstration marked the start of a general French offensive, Langeron ordered an immediate halt rather than continue the march in accordance with Blücher's "First Disposition." The news that imperial forces had advanced from Löwenberg to Lähn and from Greiffenberg to Berthelsdorf particularly alarmed Langeron. At Goldberg around 10:00 that night, Blücher received Langeron's report, which included Kaysarov's communiqué. In his cover letter, Langeron questioned the wisdom of continuing the advance on the 19th according to the "First Disposition." Blücher responded by explaining that the enemy had apparently made the decision to withdraw his center and left from the Katzbach. Thus, "we should be inclined to doubt a systematic, coinciding movement" by his right. "Meanwhile," continued Blücher, "it is completely possible that the enemy is seeking to halt the advance of our right wing" through a demonstration by his own right. Blücher believed that his push against Ney's left and center would cause Macdonald to abandon the upper Bober. For 19 August, he instructed Langeron to continue the march to Löwenberg according to the "First Disposition," observe the imperial post at Lähn, and report to him every four hours over the situation on the army's left wing. Moreover, Pahlen should continue his march northwest to Marklissa on the Queis. Should he be attacked by superior forces, Blücher wanted him to slowly retreat to the entrenched camp at Landeshut, some twenty miles southeast of Hirschberg. Army Headquarters would reach Löwenberg around 5:00 on the afternoon of the 19th.[49]

Before this response reached Langeron, the corps commander received the reports from Pahlen and Steffens. Anxiety over the proximity of Macdonald's corps prompted Langeron to have his Prussian liaison officer, Lieutenant-Colonel Ende, inform Gneisenau that the Russian corps would march to Löwenberg only on Blücher's express command. He requested instructions on how to proceed, thus implying that he did not intend to march to Löwenberg. Moreover, Langeron communicated the news that he had ordered Pahlen to remain at Hirschberg. However, if that position became untenable, Langeron instructed him to retreat to Schmiedeberg. Although this news threw Gneisenau into a rage and prompted an order for Yorck to halt, Blücher penned a patient response to Langeron at 7:30 A.M. on the 19th:

> From the letter you ordered Ende to write to Gneisenau, I see you are concerned about Pahlen and view the march based on the "Disposition" to be dangerous. I can only believe that the enemy is making a movement with the right wing in order to stop the march of the Silesian Army's right wing because it has been reported to me that the enemy has evacuated Haynau. All news indicates that he has withdrawn his left wing to Bunzlau. Yesterday, a captured French officer interrogated here stated that he did not know how the French army would return, because the infantry is so exhausted that it cannot continue. He as well as many officers had been ordered to round up marauders, which is how he was captured.
>
> If the news that the enemy is marching in force from Löwenberg to Lähn is confirmed, caution demands that this movement be reconnoitered. I have thus halted the march of Yorck's corps until I receive more detailed news over this and I request that you likewise halt your march ... at Schönau. Your vanguard should then proceed toward the Bober to determine if the enemy still stands in force at Lähn or has withdrawn. Furthermore, it must discover if the troops are actually marching this night from Löwenberg to Lähn.
>
> If the enemy has withdrawn, I request that you continue the march according to the Disposition and that you quickly inform me so that I can direct Yorck's corps to Löwenberg. The loss of time means that the corps cannot cross the Bober today, but must remain on the right bank. I request that you instruct Pahlen according to the contents of my letter from last evening; in particular he should retreat to Landeshut if he is forced.[50]

As for Yorck, after receiving little rest his main body trooped west from Goldberg at 5:00 A.M. on the 19th to cover the sixteen miles to Löwenberg. Reaching the Schnelle Deichsel three hours later, he received Blücher's order to halt his two columns at Ulbersdorf (Wojcieszyn) and Pilgramsdorf respectively, and await further instructions. As noted, Langeron's panic over Kaysarov's repulse at Lähn accounted for this pause. Although Army Head-quarters firmly believed that Macdonald's push solely aimed to facilitate Ney's withdrawal, Blücher acknowledged Langeron's concerns by halting Yorck. This affected Blücher's timetable, which called for the entire army to reach the Bober on the 19th. Nevertheless, Blücher prudently chose to conduct another general reconnaissance. To his credit, Langeron ultimately complied with orders and continued his march to Löwenberg before Blücher's response arrived. Rudzevich led the vanguard west from Pilgramsdorf to Petersdorf (Pieszków). A few miles south of Rudzevich, Langeron's main body marched west through Probsthain toward Löwenberg at 4:00 A.M. on 19 August. Less than five miles southeast of Löwenberg, Langeron's forward cavalry found the bridge over the Bober at Zobten (Sobota) destroyed. Grekov's Cossacks located a ford south of Zobten, crossed, and took post on the hills along the left bank. Rudzevich's cavalry followed; the infantry escorted the artillery across the waist-deep water. Rudzevich continued to Siebeneichen preceded by the 12th and 22nd Jäger Regiments. Southwest of Siebeneichen, Grekov led his Cossacks toward Schmottseiffen. Around 10:00 A.M., the Russian Jäger made contact with the imperials at Siebeneichen (see Map 2).[51]

Having come between Macdonald's XI Corps marching down the Bober from Lähn toward Löwenberg and Lauriston's V Corps at Löwenberg, the Russians had a fight on their hands. Despite determined resistance by French skirmishers, the 12th and 22nd Jäger drove Macdonald's troops from the hedgerows before Siebeneichen. Rudzevich moved up the remainder of the vanguard and attacked the village, which the French defended courageously. Three times the Russians took Siebeneichen and three times the imperials drove them out. "After a long and bloody combat," recalled Langeron, "Rudzevich finally took it with the bayonet and held fast." With two dragoon regiments and Prince Nikolay Shcherbatov's 2nd Ukrainskii Cossack Regiment, General Yegor Emmanuel intercepted the remains of the French force after riding around Siebeneichen undetected and taking a position at Mois. While his dragoons cut down 1 battalion and took 200 prisoners, Shcherbatov's Cossacks amused themselves by intercepting Macdonald's baggage, taking 260 prisoners, the marshal's valuables, and numerous supply, hospital, equipment, and baggage wagons as well as the war chest with an estimated 10,000 gold coins. The Russian horsemen also helped themselves to Napoleon's correspondence and the cipher of the French army but neither ever reached Blücher's headquarters.[52]

Rudzevich's men had barely had time to regroup when reports arrived of a French column approaching from the south: the Italians who had attacked Kaysarov at Lähn the previous day. Rudzevich sent Grekov's Cossacks to contain the Italians for as long as possible. At the same time, he learned of the proximity of another French division coming southeast on the road from Mois while a second moved south from Löwenberg along the Bober. Rudzevich held his ground, hoping Langeron's main body would arrive in time to support him. Led by the commander of Lauriston's 19th Division, General Donatien-Marie de Rochambeau, the son of Marshal Jean-Baptiste Donatien Rochambeau of the American Revolutionary War, the imperials attacked the Russians at Siebeneichen.

Meanwhile, Langeron's main body experienced delays. "The horrible, narrow passes of Schönau had retarded the march of my column, which was 25,000 men strong," recalled Langeron. "These passes were so narrow that they could only be passed in single file; at 11:00 [A.M.], the head of my column reached Zobten, where the rear did not arrive until late in the night. By the time I reached Zobten, Rudzevich was attacked by a superior force and hit hard; I immediately ordered General [Aleksandr] Talyzin II to advance with the Moskovskii and Libavskii Regiments, which were at the head of the column ... My vanguard found itself in the greatest danger of being driven into the Bober and losing all its artillery; there was not a moment to lose and, although at that immediate moment I could not dispose of many men, I had to sacrifice as many as I could to save Rudzevich."

After fording the Bober, Talyzin's two regiments managed to reach Siebeneichen and link with Rudzevich's troops. Yet the French division coming from Löwenberg arrived soon after and sent one column through the wooded Bober valley. Approaching unseen, the imperials launched a surprise attack that drove the Russian infantry from Siebeneichen and south along the Bober. According to Langeron, "Talyzin II was pushed back to the meadows that were situated between the Bober and the village; his two regiments were overthrown in an instant, they dispersed and fled, the village was lost, and the enemy energetically pursued our troops. I was witness to this disaster that worsened the situation of my vanguard."

While Langeron attempted to re-form Talyzin's two regiments for another attack on Siebeneichen, General Ivan Witte charged the enemy skirmishers with the 1st and 3rd Ukrainskii Cossack Regiments. Although the terrain did not favor cavalry, Witte reached the hedgerows around Siebeneichen and held the imperials in check for quite a while. Nevertheless, the French managed to direct a considerable volume of fire at Langeron and his entourage. "Several of my orderlies were wounded, and I lost the horse that I was riding, which received two musket [ball] wounds." Meanwhile, to avoid surrendering or being totally destroyed, Rudzevich ordered a retreat. Before encountering the column coming from Lähn, the Russians escaped three miles due south of Siebeneichen to the Frauenberg hills. Yet Langeron had no idea if Rudzevich would find an open ford to flee across the Bober. Witte's charge, which actually allowed Rudzevich to escape, gained enough time for General Pavel Turchaninov's 22nd Division of General Pyotr Kaptsevich's X Infantry Corps to arrive. To create a strong diversion, Langeron, Kaptsevich, and Turchaninov led the 22nd in another assault on Siebeneichen. While the four battalions of the 29th Jäger and Vyatskii Regiments attacked the village, the Starooskolskii, Olonetskii, and 45th Jäger Regiments (five battalions total) turned the village to the north. Siebeneichen fell to the Russians. The turning movement and "the sight of the rest of our troops, who arrived successively and formed into a second and third line, forced the enemy to fall back," explained Langeron.

Led by a peasant, Rudzevich marched less than two miles east from the
Frauenberg hills to ford the Bober at Dippelsdorf (Przeździedza) around
10:00 that night. General Jacques-Pierre Puthod's 17th Division of V Corps
pursued. The Bober's steep banks made the crossing of Rudzevich's artillery
slow and difficult. Fortunately for the Russians, the French did not harass
them. "For a long time I was very uneasy," continued Langeron, "and was
calm only when Rudzevich informed me that all of his forces were on the
right bank: it would have been a sad beginning of a campaign to lose thirty-
six cannon."[53] Incidentally, Blücher had sent Nostitz, who owned an estate
at nearby Zobten, to locate Langeron's corps. He found the Russians just in
time to join Talyzin's charge across the Bober but remained with Rudzevich
after the Russians broke. "Another enemy column emerged from Lähn,"
noted Nostitz. "In this situation, no other means of escape remained than to
ascend the high, steep valley edge of the Frauenberg and to cross the river
near Märzdorf by way of another ford. The order to do this was given and
executed in such a manner that all of the troops, but especially the artillery,
earned great honor. When we saw the spot where this crossing would be
conducted, we could not comprehend how it would be possible to move the
cannon across the almost vertical rock-face." After Rudzevich crossed the
Bober, Nostitz went in search of Langeron's headquarters and learned that
the Russian corps commander would pass the night at Zobten. He reached
his hometown at the same time as Langeron and accompanied him to the
local Schloß. Nostitz continues: "Only when General Langeron ... entered
the completely devastated house did I tell him that I was the owner of the
estate. Up to then I had intentionally kept it secret so that the general would
not be influenced to take any consideration for the ... maintenance of the
village."[54]

Although taking Siebeneichen, Langeron recalled 22nd Division to the
right bank of the Bober after learning that Rudzevich had made good his
escape. "As soon as I knew that the vanguard had recrossed the river,"
commented Langeron, "I withdrew my men from the village but retained
the hedgerows and remained master of the left bank of the Bober. In this
bloody combat that lasted nearly ten hours, all of the troops fought with the
utmost valor and most perfect order."[55] Russian losses during the engagement at Siebeneichen amounted to 68 officers and 1,573 men. Langeron
claimed that the imperials had sustained 800 dead as well as the loss of 600
prisoners, including several staff officers.[56] Rudzevich extracted himself
from a dangerous situation but the risk he took did not please Langeron.
His thoughts on the engagement as well as his view of his former countrymen are worth hearing:

> The excellent dispositions of this brave general, his intrepidness, and that of
> his troops thwarted for a long time every effort of the enemy; his conduct

was perfect in this moment that was so critical for him; one must salute the vanguard for its *sang-froid* and its wonderfully combined operations, but he made the great fault of exceeding my orders and very imprudently attacked the greater part of the enemy's army; he delayed for too long the moment of retreat and tried to do so at the moment when he no longer could; it was the first time that he was the independent commander of a detachment, and this lesson was very useful, but I was obligated to sacrifice myself for him, and lost many men to save him. General Rudzevich committed a great fault in exposing himself too rashly, but the mistake that the French committed by allowing him to cross the Bober, in the dark, is unpardonable, and it proved that their generals truly had little knowledge of this theater of war, although they had been cantoned there for two or three months, and that their outpost troops were far from valuing the importance of our Cossacks. Moreover, the experience proved to me that the French never undertake anything during the night; the close of the day for them is always the end of battle, in whatever position night may find them.[57]

Langeron's engagement at Siebeneichen impacted Pahlen, who loitered around Hirschberg on the 19th in fear of the French troops at Berthelsdorf and Lähn. Langeron's advance prevented the imperials from continuing the offensive against Pahlen's corps. In fact, the Russian presence at Siebeneichen forced the French to abandon Lähn but Pahlen did little to exploit this development.

Sacken's task for the 19th included advancing from Steudnitz through Haynau to Bunzlau, where he would cross the Bober. His van met little resistance at Haynau, from where Sacken reported at around 10:00 A.M. that "the enemy retreats on Bunzlau ... Ney passed through here yesterday morning and Sébastiani passed the night here. Marmont's corps stood at Bunzlau the day before yesterday. We do not know if it marched off." Concluding, he added that a report had just arrived stating that the forty squadrons of Sébastiani's cavalry had taken the road to Löwenberg. Meanwhile, Vasilchikov found Marmont's VI Corps six miles further west between Kreibau (Krzywa) and Wolfshain (Wilczy Las).

After Sacken's main body started to arrive, Vasilchikov resumed the advance around 2:00 P.M., meeting stubborn resistance at Kaiserswaldau (Okmiany). "The vanguard," states the Journal of Operations of Sacken's corps, compiled by the quartermaster-general, Colonel Giuseppe Venançon, "which had passed Haynau, was stopped by enemy positions, of which the right was set on a height covered with woods, the left on a forest, and the center on a hillock full of artillery." Sacken ordered Neverovsky's 27th Division to move south "into the mountains without cannon or caissons" and threaten Marmont's right flank "by filling the woods to the enemy's left with Jäger" while the 8th and 39th Jäger Regiments (four battalions total) from the 3rd Brigade of 10th Division enveloped the marshal's left flank.

Vasilchikov's cavalry along with General Aleksey Voyeikov's 49th and 50th Jäger Regiments (three battalions total) supported by artillery executed a frontal assault on the French center at Kaiserswaldau. Facilitated by the salvos of the 8th Horse Guns that demolished a French battery, the Russian infantry pushed forward, forcing the marshal to withdraw toward Thomaswaldau. "The maneuver succeeded perfectly," wrote Venançon. "Despite the terrain obstacles, Neverovskii ascended the heights, took the enemy in the flank, and repulsed him; then the center acted vigorously, and the Jäger of our right moved forward. A maneuver in peacetime, where distance and time are calculated, could not have been better executed; the enemy's center was forced to cede ground, and as soon as our cavalry was able to deploy in the plain it charged and ... forced them to retreat." Vasilchikov pursued until night put an end to the incessant skirmishing. Sacken's corps bivouacked east of Thomaswaldau, the imperials west of the village.[58]

In the center, Blücher's orders for Jürgaß to lead Yorck's vanguard cavalry and Reserve Cavalry west from Adelsdorf at 2:00 A.M. on the 19th, followed by Lobenthal's infantry, did not reach the colonel until 3:00 A.M., although Army Headquarters had issued them six hours earlier. Within thirty minutes, the diligent Jürgaß placed his lead squadrons on the road with Katzler at their head. Yorck's columns marched three hours later but, as noted, Blücher ordered them to halt around 8:00 as a result of Langeron's report. Should the movement of the French right be more than a demonstration, Blücher did not want the gap between his center and left to increase. By keeping Yorck's main body at the Schnelle Deichsel just west of Goldberg, the Prussians would be eleven miles from Langeron's assumed position at Altschönau. In addition, the presence of imperial troops at Modelsdorf and Steinsdorf made the presence of strong enemy forces on the Haynau–Bunzlau highway extremely likely.

Reports soon clarified the situation on Blücher's left. Around 10:00 A.M., Rudzevich's adjutant reached Army Headquarters at Goldberg with news of the engagement at Siebeneichen and a claim that the imperials had retreated from Lähn toward Greiffenberg. At the same time, a dispatch arrived from Langeron penned at 8:00 A.M. from Probsthain, halfway between Altschönau and Löwenberg, informing Blücher that his corps had been marching since 4:00 A.M. Finally, Nostitz returned around noon, informing Blücher that Langeron had indeed reached the Bober instead of halting at Altschönau. Based on this news as well as the report from Sacken stating that his opponent had retreated *west* from Haynau, Blücher released Yorck's main body to continue its march to Löwenberg. Although Langeron received instructions to remain at Probsthain, his advance to Zobten had already rendered these instructions obsolete. Blücher himself rode to join Yorck's left column and Reserve Artillery, which he found in the process of crossing the Schnelle Deichsel at Pilgramsdorf. Likewise crossing, he and his staff continued west to reach Yorck's vanguard just as it launched an attack.[59]

Between 10:00 and 11:00 A.M., Katzler located Lauriston's rearguard a few miles east of Löwenberg just as Macdonald's troops engaged Rudzevich's Russians at Siebeneichen, four miles south of Löwenberg. French forces stretched from Plagwitz (Płakowice) across the Hirseberg ridge to Ludwigsdorf (Chmielno). Finding the latter occupied, Katzler requested the support of one of Lobenthal's battalions. After deploying its skirmishers to distract the French in the village, the battalion closely followed the cavalry from Deutmannsdorf (Zbylutów) to a point just north of Ludwigsdorf. From there they could see the extent of the French force between Plagwitz and Ludwigsdorf; in cavalry the imperials appeared to have sixteen squadrons. Neither Jürgaß nor Lobenthal knew how far Yorck's columns had progressed, and they had both been instructed to avoid combat with superior forces. At this time, reports arrived of enemy columns moving southwest from Haynau toward the Gröditzberg (Grodziska), a domineering height northwest of the village of Gröditz (Grodziec), which stood to the northeast and thus behind Yorck's vanguard. The Prussians did not know it, but the troops belonged to Ney's III Corps and Sébastiani's II Cavalry Corps. All reports indicated that Ney had led the two corps due *west* from Haynau to Bunzlau. All of Yorck's patrols as well as Sacken's had missed the French turn at Haynau onto the road that ran *southwest* past the Gröditzberg to Löwenberg.[60]

Based on this news, Jürgaß instructed Lobenthal to post his infantry in the wood south of Deutmannsdorf facing the Hirseberg while the cavalry moved onto the hills north of Deutmannsdorf and dispatched patrols to reconnoiter northeast toward the Gröditzberg. Lobenthal deployed a line of skirmishers facing the Hirseberg; the imperials countered by moving up superior numbers of infantry. A firefight ensued during which French cavalry arrived but did not attack. After several hours of skirmishing, the imperials began an orderly withdrawal. Although the French force moving southwest toward the Gröditzberg could come between him and Yorck's main body, Lobenthal made the bold decision to attack. "Those chaps can go to the devil – they must learn to fear us," he purportedly exclaimed to a staff officer. "This is odd: I believe the chaps are more surprised by us than we are by them; nevertheless, I will not allow myself to be disturbed from giving a sound drubbing to whoever is before us."[61]

Leaving a small detachment to guard his rear, Lobenthal advanced. The sudden Prussian assault startled the French, who withdrew all the way to Braunau (Brunów) on the Bober, two miles north of Löwenberg. From Deutmannsdorf, Katzler supported the infantry with the Brandenburg Uhlan Regiment and two horse guns by threatening the enemy's left. After the French broke, his lancers caused havoc at the Braunau bridge while his horse artillery peppered the fleeing imperials. Arriving during this action, the fiery Blücher subjected himself and his staff to heavy artillery fire. In the fog of battle, they found themselves in the midst of a cavalry unit returning to *French* lines. To take in his rearguard, Lauriston moved one division to the left bank of the Bober. In addition to this superior firepower, the French broke the bridges behind them at Braunau and one and one-half miles further north at Sirgwitz (Żerkowice). Toward evening, the main body of Jürgaß's vanguard moved into a bivouac on the Hirseberg under the protection of forward posts on the hills further west along the right bank of the Bober. Blücher established his headquarters at Lauterseiffen. "At this moment, I stoutly cut down the French," he boasted to his wife. "They lost 2,000 men and 6 guns including 300 caissons and many prisoners as well. I am healthy and write this amidst the living and the dying."[62]

East of this action, Prince Karl led Yorck's right column across the Schnelle Deichsel at Ulbersdorf, three miles north of Pilgramsdorf. While marching west, the prince received news of an enemy force with a large body of cavalry hardly one mile from his column. Another patrol reported the presence of more cavalry to the northeast at Großhartmannsdorf. Karl immediately halted the march and deployed his troops at Neudorf-am-Gröditzberg. The 2nd Leib Hussar Regiment drove back the foremost French squadrons to allow the infantry to take a position. Aside from unlimbering horse artillery at the foot of the Gröditzberg and occupying Gröditz on the height's southern slope, the French did little.

Yorck arrived and inspected the situation. He learned that his patrols could not ascertain the size of the enemy forces standing on the northern side of the Gröditzberg. Every patrol had thus far failed to get past the French cavalry screen on the open plain east of the height. To support Karl and protect the rear of the army, Yorck directed his 7th Brigade and Reserve Artillery to Neudorf-am-Gröditzberg while 8th Brigade continued west with the task of occupying Lauterseiffen to secure communication with the vanguard at Deutmannsdorf. Yorck himself rode west to Lauterseiffen and informed Blücher of the situation, insisting that the large French cavalry force had slowed his march because his Reserve Cavalry now served with the vanguard. Blücher authorized him to recall the East Prussian National Cavalry Regiment from Katzler's brigade of the Reserve Cavalry. Yorck ordered the regiment to Neudorf-am-Gröditzberg, where he established his command post. Yorck also concentrated his troops, moving up Horn's 7th Brigade to form his left wing. Around 7:00 P.M., the East Prussian National Cavalry Regiment arrived, providing enough sabers to attack. Yorck decided to begin with a cavalry charge by the East Prussians and Black Hussars. Encouraging the former, who would experience combat for the first time, Jürgaß explained that they could expect to receive a carbine volley at their approach. Nostitz recalled that Jürgaß exhorted his men:

"Do not allow yourselves to be startled by this, but instead strike them right in the mug with your saber." The cavalry gradually gained steam as it approached the Gröditzberg. Not only did the Prussian troopers receive a carbine volley but grenades rained down on them as well. Before contact could be made, the French withdrew; even at a quick trot, the Prussians could not catch them.

As Yorck prepared his infantry to advance, Major Ludwig von Oppen from Blücher's staff reached Neudorf-am-Gröditzberg with a report on the size of the enemy force on the other side of the Gröditzberg. He and Nostitz had reconnoitered to the northern side of the height. "I, who best knew the region," noted Nostitz in his journal, "offered ... to reach the point from where I could see the other side of the *Berg*. Major Oppen of the General Staff accompanied me. The reconnaissance succeeded completely; I reached the point on the high ground that offered an open view as far as the Bober and saw two enemy divisions in bivouac. But enemy cavalry detected us and charged from all sides yet we rode good horses, which quickly brought us to safety. Nevertheless, Oppen lost his beautiful English field-glass during this chase." The presence of these two divisions at Großhartmannsdorf, less than four miles north of Yorck's right wing, appeared to confirm the statements of a prisoner who claimed that Ney's corps of 20,000 men as well as Sébastiani's cavalry corps had moved southwest from Haynau rather than west. Under these circumstances, Yorck did not venture an attack without support from Langeron and Sacken.[63]

However, Ney's subsequent inactivity indicated that he intended to depart shortly. Carefully observing his opponent's every move, Yorck readied his cavalry and artillery to pursue as soon as the imperials withdrew. In the growing darkness, three hussar regiments and one horse battery advanced. Spotting an enemy battery near the village of Gröditz, the Prussians opened fire but received none in return. A patrol discovered that they had shelled some wagons with tree trunks lying across them. Moreover, under the cover of heavy smoke from campfires that they had left blazing, the imperials had retreated northwest toward Bunzlau. Yorck's cavalry attempted to pursue but did not fare well in the choppy terrain that surrounded the Gröditzberg. Four battalions sent from Neudorf-am-Gröditzberg likewise failed to catch the enemy. Yorck's corps bivouacked at Neudorf-am-Gröditzberg, Wilhelmsdorf (Sędzimirów), and Lauterseiffen facing Bunzlau to the northwest while the vanguard remained on the Hirseberg facing Löwenberg to the west. Nightfall on the 19th found Ney and Marmont in retreat; Lauriston's rearguard remained on the west bank of the Bober.

As for Ney, he learned that on the 18th his rearguard had engaged Sacken's advancing troops at Steudnitz. Simultaneously, V Corps evacuated the Katzbach, withdrawing from Goldberg to Löwenberg while Macdonald

6 Marshal Michel Ney, 1769–1815

assembled XI Corps on the upper Bober. Macdonald's strike toward Lähn on the 18th that led to the engagement with the Russians provided clarity on the intentions and strength of the Allied army. To Ney, Blücher's main body appeared to be advancing west through Jauer. Based on this assumption, he wanted to concentrate the army more on his center. For this reason, he decided on 19 August to leave the east–west highway at Haynau and march *southwest* toward Löwenberg rather than continue west to Bunzlau. Reaching the region of the Gröditzberg that day, the marshal found the road to Löwenberg blocked by Yorck's vanguard. Due to the uncertainty of his situation, with the enemy before him, and artillery fire from Sacken's engagement with Marmont at Kreibau behind him, the marshal hesitated to force open the road to Löwenberg. Thus, he did not advance beyond the southern edge of the Gröditzberg, missing a terrific opportunity to catch Yorck's marching columns. Conversely, by not immediately attacking, he allowed Blücher to prepare a powerful strike against him. Moreover, while Ney marched southwest toward Löwenberg on the 19th and Marmont moved VI Corps east, the latter encountered Sacken – who had continued his march through Haynau – east of the Bober. In his isolated position, Marmont did not attempt to stop the Russians despite his numerical superiority. Thanks to a night march on 19/20 August, Ney escaped the dangerous position he had created by isolating himself on the Gröditzberg.

To Blücher's staff, the movements of the French army appeared baffling: its center seemed to be withdrawing *west* on Löwenberg while the wings seemed to be advancing *east* on Lähn and Haynau respectively. Thus, Army Headquarters faced the difficult task of trying to plan an operation to counter these puzzling movements. Despite Gneisenau's attempts to concentrate the army, the distance between the various corps had increased, thus preventing mutual support on the 19th. Blücher's front extended thirty-seven miles from Hirschberg to Thomaswaldau. Occupied at Siebeneichen, Langeron would not have been able to reach the Prussians had Ney's 50,000 troops attacked Yorck's 36,000. Had Marmont held Haynau against Sacken and Ney assailed Yorck, Blücher would have had his hands full. Instead, Marmont withdrew before Sacken's weaker forces while Ney halted before a handful of squadrons. Admittedly, the intelligence Ney received from his cavalry and corps commanders provided no indication of the opportunity to crush Yorck. Thus, Ney did not make Blücher and Gneisenau pay for their underestimation of his forces or their careless overextension. Instead, his retreat indicated that he had overestimated the size of Blücher's army (see Map 3).

Both sides were guilty of faulty intelligence work and security measures. Lobenthal committed a grave error that would have led to the destruction of Yorck's corps if Ney had been aware of the golden opportunity. Before departing from Adelsdorf, Lobenthal failed to act on the news of an imperial column at Haynau. Moreover, he neglected to forward the reports over this column's march toward the Gröditzberg – thus in his flank and rear – to Yorck's main body. Consequently, Yorck did not receive this news until Prince Karl's flank patrol stumbled into the column. Sacken likewise failed to detect Ney's presence on the Gröditzberg in a timely manner. Little did Blücher know how vulnerable he was to a disaster such as the thrashing his army would receive at the hands of Napoleon the following February. Fortunately for Blücher, he was facing Ney rather than the master. The Silesian Army received a pass on this collection of blunders but the time for mistakes was running out.[64]

Notes

1 Lobenthal's command consisted of six battalions, eight squadrons, and one battery each of foot and horse. For this duty, Yorck assigned him the Fusilier Battalions of the 1st and 2nd East Prussian, Leib, and Brandenburg Infantry Regiments as well as two Landwehr battalions; one squadron each from the 2nd Leib and Mecklenburg Hussar Regiments, the four squadrons of the Brandenburg Uhlan Regiment, and two squadrons of the 3rd Silesian Landwehr Cavalry Regiment.
2 Rudzevich commanded the eight battalions of the 15th Infantry Division, the Kievskii Dragoon Regiment and two squadrons of Liflyandskii Jäger for a total

of seven squadrons, seven Cossack Regiments, the Nr. 15 Heavy Battery and Nr. 29 Light Battery, and one Cossack battery: 7,800 men altogether.

3 Blücher to Bernadotte, Würben, 15 August 1813, RA KrA, volym 25, and Add MSS, 20112, 39; Droysen, *Yorck,* II:118; Friederich, *Herbstfeldzug 1813,* I:239–40. Yorck's complete march route is in Höpfner, "Darstellung," 1843:41.

4 According to Jomini, at the time that Tsar Alexander made overtures to him, the armistice had expired and "hostilities would resume on 16 August. Two or three days later, Marshal Ney received many unsolicited promotions for his army; there were no fewer than 500 to 600; my name and that of Captain [Jean-Baptiste Frédéric] Koch, my aide-de-camp, were the only ones absent. Naturally, this new mystification was well suited to double my grievances and make my resolution [to defect] more excusable. However, I must confess that my resolution became irrevocable the day these judgments and this humiliating agenda beat me so cruelly. The reason is very simple; because, as it would have been absurd to impose on a government the obligation to give me the promotion, as deserved as it might have been, I did not think I deserved to suffer an offense serious enough to impair my self-esteem": Jomini, *Lettre du général Jomini à M. Capefigue,* 11. See also Maude, *Leipzig Campaign,* 158.

5 Langeron, *Mémoires,* 225.

6 French writers such as Norvins blame Jomini for Blücher's offensive against Ney: "No doubt instructed on the position of the extremely dispersed troops of Marshal Ney by the reports of General Jomini, a Swiss national and chief of staff of III Corps who had defected to the enemy only a few days before, Marshal Blücher prepared to surprise and attack the positions that the French held along the Katzbach." See Norvins, *Portefeuille de mil huit cent treize,* II:293–94.

7 Blücher to Bernadotte, Würben, 15 August 1813, RA KrA, volym 25, and Add MSS, 20112, 38–39. Bernadotte's response is found in SHAT, C^{17} 132: Charles John to Blücher, Charlottenburg, 19 August 1813, and Add MSS, 20112, 41–42.

8 Müffling, *Die Feldzüge,* 11–12; Vaudoncourt, *Histoire de la guerre,* 141; Nostitz, *Tagebuch,* 53; Höpfner, "Darstellung," 1843:38–39. Blücher was never rebuked by his king or by Allied High Command, which in general believed that the French had violated the neutral zone first, prompting Blücher's reaction.

9 Müffling, *Die Feldzüge,* 11, emphasis added; Höpfner, "Darstellung," 1843:42; Langeron, *Mémoires,* 224.

10 Höpfner, "Darstellung," 1843:42; Freytag-Loringhoven, *Aufklärung und Armeeführung,* 13.

11 These reports are in Höpfner, "Darstellung," 1843:42.

12 Langeron to Barclay, Report on Langeron's operations from 7 August to 2 September, 2 September 1813, GStA PK, VI HA Rep. 92 Nl. Gneisenau, Nr. 18; Höpfner, "Darstellung," 1843:43; Freytag-Loringhoven, *Aufklärung und Armeeführung,* 14; Friederich, *Herbstfeldzug 1813,* I:240–41.

13 Disposition for 16 August 1813, Jauer, 15 August 1813, Add MSS, 20112, 118; Gneisenau to Blücher, Jauer, 15 August 1813, in Höpfner, "Darstellung," 1843:43; Gneisenau to Caroline, Jauer, 16 August 1813, GStA PK, VI HA Rep. 92 Nl. Gneisenau, Nr. 21.

14 Blücher to Hardenberg, Striegau, 16 August 1813, *Blüchers Briefe*, ed. Unger, 173.

15 These reports are in Höpfner, "Darstellung," 1843:44.

16 Höpfner, "Darstellung," 1843:45; Droysen, *Yorck*, II:119.

17 Freytag-Loringhoven, *Aufklärung und Armeeführung*, 44; Maude, *Leipzig Campaign*, 176. Lieven, in *Russia Against Napoleon*, 376, excuses these early mistakes by Blücher and Gneisenau, stating that they needed time "to get into their stride: the Army of Silesia had after all only come together on the very eve of the campaign."

18 Langeron to Barclay, Report on Langeron's operations from 7 August to 2 September, 2 September 1813, GStA PK, VI HA Rep. 92 Nl. Gneisenau, Nr. 18. Pahlen III also conducted a night march on 16/17 August to reach Hirschberg but this had no relation to the snafu at Army Headquarters.

19 Höpfner, "Darstellung," 1843:45.

20 This letter, signed by Gneisenau, informed Sacken that Yorck's corps had reached Jauer and his vanguard stood further west, pushing posts toward Liegnitz. More often than not, Silesian Army Headquarters failed to inform the corps commanders of the status of neighboring corps. Gneisenau makes no mention of Langeron in this letter. Such omissions contrast glaringly with Napoleon's superior practice of keeping his subordinates informed.

21 Gneisenau to Sacken, Jauer, 7:00 A.M., 17 August 1813, in Höpfner, "Darstellung," 1843:46.

22 Gneisenau's column consisted of the 3rd Uhlan Regiment, two squadrons of the 2nd Leib Hussars, two horse guns, and the Fusilier Battalion of the 1st East Prussian Infantry Regiment.

23 The account of the operations on 16 and 17 August is based on Blücher to Bernadotte, Jauer, 18 August 1813, RA KrA, volym 25; Müffling, *Die Feldzüge*, 12–13; Langeron, *Mémoires*, 225; Höpfner, "Darstellung," 1843:44–49; Freytag-Loringhoven, *Aufklärung und Armeeführung*, 16–18, 44; Friederich, *Herbstfeldzug 1813*, I:241–43.

24 SHAT, C² 154: Macdonald to Berthier, 17 August 1813. Pelet, in *Des principales opérations de la campagne de 1813*, 175, castigates the entire Coalition: "Forty-eight hours before the moment when hostilities were to commence, Blücher, Schwarzenberg, and Bernadotte were all in movement. The first [Blücher] surprised our troops who were quietly resting in their cantonments." Norvins, in *Portefeuille de mil huit cent treize*, II:293, thus describes the situation: "On the 14th, Blücher, known since his retreat from Jena to Lübeck to be unscrupulous in honoring his oaths, sent his troops marching into the neutral territory. Marshal Ney was waiting religiously until the last day for the armistice to end." Jomini, in *Lettre du général Jomini à M. Capefigue*, 10–12, also absolves his patron, Ney, of any wrongdoing: "After having rejected my proposal, I thought Marshal Ney might be compromised if Blücher, wiser than him and a great lover of surprises, advanced on the 15th close to the camps to attack at daybreak on the 16th. On my own responsibility, I ordered General [Frédéric-Auguste] Beurmann's light cavalry to march hastily from Lüben to Liegnitz, cross through this town, and place itself on the right bank of the Katzbach to protect headquarters, the parks, and the camps against any surprise. At the same time, I ordered all the artillery train

companies to march day and night to assemble at Liegnitz as soon as possible. All of the marshal's staff can attest to his astonishment in the middle of the night over the fanfare of his own cavalry passing through Liegnitz without his knowledge." At the same time, Jomini indicts Macdonald: "Macdonald, who commanded on our right, thought like me, and pushed reconnaissance in this area. Blücher did much more; he brought 100,000 men." In *Campagne de 1813*, 83–84, Commandant Weil of the French General Staff ignores the entire issue of which side violated the neutral zone first and simply states that Blücher ordered reconnaissance to be conducted early on the 14th. Anon., *Précis militaire de la campagne de 1813 en Allemagne*, 89, makes absolutely no mention of the controversy, stating only that Blücher's troops advanced to Jauer and Bolkenhain on 16 August.

25 Norvins, *Portefeuille de mil huit cent treize*, II:294. This criticism is harsh considering that Napoleon did not appoint Ney to command the forces in Silesia until 15 August.

26 *CN*, No. 20380, XXVI:61–62; SHAT, C¹⁷ 178: Berthier to Ney, 15 August 1813; Maude, *Leipzig Campaign*, 175–76; Pelet, *Des principales opérations de la campagne de 1813*, 175.

27 *CN*, No. 20373, XXVI:45–47; Vaudoncourt, *Histoire de la guerre*, 139; Bogdanovich, *Geschichte des Krieges*, IIa:26.

28 Cathcart, in *Commentaries*, 209, suggested that Napoleon first travelled south probably to confuse Allied spies in Dresden while Odeleben stated: "It has been pretended that he took the road to Bohemia in order to deceive the spies … but that is not probable, for his journey agreed exceedingly well with the arrival of General [Louis] Narbonne, who had returned from Prague in the greatest haste. The fear of spies could not have disturbed him in his plans." See Odeleben, *A Circumstantial Narrative*, I:256–57.

29 *CN*, No. 20389, XXVI:68–69; Bogdanovich, *Geschichte des Krieges*, IIa:22.

30 *CN*, Nos. 20390 and 20392, XXVI:69–71.

31 *CN*, Nos. 20391 and 20392, XXVI:70–71; Odeleben, *A Circumstantial Narrative*, I:258–59.

32 On 17 August, Vandamme received orders to move I Corps from Dresden to Bautzen, from where it would proceed to Görlitz to form Napoleon's Regular Reserve: SHAT, C¹⁷ 178: Berthier to Vandamme, 17 August 1813; *CN*, No. 20410, XXVI:92.

33 *CN*, No. 20398, XXVI:77–78.

34 *CN*, Nos. 20408 and 20410, XXVI:88–89, 93. Napoleon instructed Vandamme to have his 2nd and 3rd Divisions garrison Dresden's Neustadt.

35 SHAT, C¹⁷ 179: Berthier to Macdonald, Mortier, and Latour-Maubourg, 19 August 1813; *CN*, No. 20411, XXVI:95.

36 *CN*, Nos. 20397, 20398, and 20410–20412, XXVI:75–78, 92, 95; SHAT, C¹⁷ 179: Berthier to Mouton, Mortier, Monthion, and Latour-Maubourg, 18 August 1813; Bogdanovich, *Geschichte des Krieges*, IIa:26; Odeleben, *A Circumstantial Narrative*, I:260–61.

37 *CN*, Nos. 20412–20414, XXVI:95–97; Freytag-Loringhoven, *Aufklärung und Armeeführung*, 41; Cathcart, *Commentaries*, 206.

38 *CN*, Nos. 20413, 20414, and 20421, XXVI:96–98, 103–04; Vaudoncourt, *Histoire de la guerre*, 40; Bogdanovich, *Geschichte des Krieges*, IIa:27.

39 CN, Nos. 20414, 20421, and 20437, XXVI:97–98, 104, 111–12; SHAT, C[17] 179: Berthier to Vandamme, 19 and 20 August 1813; Vaudoncourt, *Histoire de la guerre*, 140; Beitzke, *Geschichte der deutschen Freiheitskriege*, II:12–14; Bogda-novich, *Geschichte des Krieges*, IIa:27; Petre, *Napoleon's Last Campaign*, 186–87.

40 Blücher to Bernadotte, Jauer, 18 August 1813, RA KrA, volym 25; Blücher to Sacken and Langeron, Jauer, 17 August 1813, in Höpfner, "Darstellung," 1843:47. Blücher blamed his inability to launch a "primary attack" before the 19th on the time it took to "reunite the principal corps of the army."

41 Sacken to Blücher, Schenk to Yorck, Jürgaß to Yorck, and Rudzevich to Langeron are in Höpfner, "Darstellung," 1843:47–48.

42 "The following are to be sent out as *Streifcorps*: from Langeron's corps: Kaysarov, who will proceed toward Dresden and raid along the highway from Görlitz to Dresden. From Yorck's corps: Major Boltenstern with infantry and cavalry detachments; Major Falkenhausen with cavalry": "The First Dispo-sition for the Continued Pursuit of the Enemy," Jauer, 18 August 1813, Add MSS, 20112, 118.

43 Blücher to Bernadotte, Jauer, 18 August 1813, RA KrA, volym 25.

44 "The First Disposition for the Continued Pursuit of the Enemy," Jauer, 18 August 1813, Add MSS, 20112, 118. The orders reproduced in Friederich, *Herbstfeldzug 1813*, I:242–44, state that the march would continue from 3:00 to 11:00 P.M.

45 Freytag-Loringhoven, *Aufklärung und Armeeführung*, 19–20, 45; Friederich, *Herbstfeldzug 1813*, I:243; Höpfner, "Darstellung," 1843:49.

46 "Journal of Operations of General Sacken's Corps," in Langeron, *Mémoires*, 244.

47 Langeron to Barclay, Report on Langeron's operations from 7 August to 2 September 1813, GStA PK, VI HA Rep. 92 Nl. Gneisenau, Nr. 18.

48 The account of 18 August is based on Langeron, *Mémoires*, 225–26; Höpfner, "Darstellung," 1843:49–51; Bogdanovich, *Geschichte des Krieges*, IIa:23; Frieder-ich, *Herbstfeldzug 1813*, I:242–44; Droysen, *Yorck*, II:120, Freytag-Loringhoven, *Aufklärung und Armeeführung*, 20–23, 38–40.

49 Blücher to Langeron, Goldberg, 10:00 P.M., 18 August 1813, in Höpfner, "Darstellung," 1843:52.

50 Blücher to Langeron, Goldberg, 7:30 A.M., 19 August 1813, in Höpfner, "Darstellung," 1843:52–53.

51 Langeron to Barclay, Report on Langeron's operations from 7 August to 2 September, 2 September 1813, GStA PK, VI HA Rep. 92 Nl. Gneisenau, Nr. 18; Langeron, *Mémoires*, 226–27.

52 Bogdanovich, *Geschichte des Krieges*, IIa:25; Friederich, *Herbstfeldzug 1813*, I:246–47; Müffling, *Die Feldzüge*, 13–14.

53 Langeron, *Mémoires*, 228–31.

54 Nostitz, *Tagebuch*, 54.

55 Langeron, *Mémoires*, 228, 231. Apparently, Talyzin's troops proved the exception: "Had I the choice of my troops, I would not have chosen this brigade, composed of two regiments that I did not know, which had never served under me, and which were terribly commanded by Talyzin II, who lacked both talent and experience of war and who was nearly blind. This Talyzin was five foot ten inches, very thin, and had immense arms: we called him 'the Telegraph'."

56 Sources for the engagement at Siebeneichen are Langeron to Barclay, Report on
   Langeron's operations from 7 August to 2 September, 2 September 1813, GStA
   PK, VI HA Rep. 92 Nl. Gneisenau, Nr. 18; Plotho, *Der Krieg*, II:94–97; Müffling,
   Die Feldzüge, 13–15, Beitzke, *Geschichte der deutschen Freiheitskriege*, II:152–58;
   Bogdanovich, *Geschichte des Krieges*; IIa:25–26; Friederich, *Herbstfeldzug 1813*,
   I:253.
57 Langeron, *Mémoires*, 232. Langeron's after-action report must have concealed his
   true feelings, for Gneisenau lauded Rudzevich in a letter to Hardenberg for
   keeping his head in a situation where "a thousand other generals would have
   despaired. With great courage and prudence, he ordered his troops to repulse all
   enemy attacks and moved them back across the Bober orderly, intact, and
   slowly": Gneisenau to Hardenberg, Jauer, 25 August 1813, GSTA PK, I HA
   Rep. 74 Staatskanzleramt O Ap. Nr. 9, Bd. 3.
58 Freytag-Loringhoven, *Aufklärung und Armeeführung*, 23; "Journal of Operations of General Sacken's Corps," in Langeron, *Mémoires*, 244–45; Bogdanovich,
   Geschichte des Krieges, IIa:23; Vaudoncourt, *Histoire de la guerre*, I:141.
59 Freytag-Loringhoven, *Aufklärung und Armeeführung*, 27.
60 As noted, in his 10:00 A.M. report, Sacken added the news that Sébastiani's cavalry
   had taken this road. Apparently, Sacken's courier did not reach Blücher for
   some time.
61 Quoted in Droysen, *Yorck*, II:121.
62 Blücher to Amalie, [Lauterseiffen], 19 August 1813, *Blüchers Briefe*, ed. Unger,
   174; Unger, *Blücher*, II:68–69; Freytag-Loringhoven, *Aufklärung und Armeeführung*, 23–25; Droysen, *Yorck*, II:121; Friederich, *Herbstfeldzug 1813*, I:249.
63 The account of 19 August is based on Droysen, *Yorck*, II:121–22; Friederich,
   Herbstfeldzug 1813, I:249–52; Müffling, *Die Feldzüge*, 15; Nostitz, *Tagebuch*,
   53–54.
64 Friederich, *Herbstfeldzug 1813*, I:252–54.

4

Löwenberg

The appearance of Ney's two corps in the midst of his columns both surprised and pleased Blücher. Before receiving Yorck's report on Ney's departure, Blücher sensed that the marshal had walked into a trap. He correctly assumed that Sacken had continued his march west to Thomaswaldau, a few miles east of Bunzlau. Should this be the case, Ney's line of retreat through Bunzlau was as good as cut and the marshal as good as encircled; Blücher need only close the net to crush him. His exuberance soared. Reports from Saxony claimed that Ney had been reinforced so that his army numbered six infantry and one cavalry corps, as well as the Young Guard. Completely oblivious to the implications of this French buildup, Blücher boasted to his wife on the morning of the 20th: "Yesterday I fought six French corps for six hours and forced all to retreat. The generals commanding against me were Ney, Macdonald, Marmont, Bertrand, Lauriston, [General Jean-Louis] Reynier, Sébastiani, and Mortier. I march immediately to pursue the enemy."[1]

That evening, Gneisenau drafted an attack disposition that would have led to Ney's destruction if Yorck had been able to hold the marshal at the Gröditzberg long enough for Langeron and Sacken to envelop him. Worded in very simple, straightforward terms, the disposition called for Yorck to fix Ney's front by attacking through Neudorf-am-Gröditzberg at daybreak on the 20th. Likewise at dawn, Langeron's corps would march north from Lauterseiffen against Ney's right flank while Sacken moved his troops south from Thomaswaldau directly to the rear of the enemy corps.[2] Around midnight, shortly after the orderlies sped off with copies of the disposition, Yorck's 10:00 P.M. report on Ney's departure arrived. The whole operation had to be scrapped (see Map 2).

Even if Ney had stood his ground, Blücher's plan would have been ruined by his two Russian corps commanders. Along with the attack disposition, Langeron received orders to *immediately* send a portion of his corps north from Zobten to Deutmannsdorf to block Ney's road to Löwenberg. Then, Langeron would follow with the rest of his corps except the vanguard, which would remain at Zobten. Langeron refused to comply. He responded that the day's combat had fatigued his men; they could not march through the night to Deutmannsdorf.[3] Moreover, his park columns remained in the rear so he could not replenish his ammunition. Thus, his corps could not participate in the expected battle on the 20th. According to Nostitz:

> On this day, the large loss of men, the pressing danger that the vanguard – which had been pushed too far forward – was exposed to for many hours, made an impression on Langeron that detrimentally influenced his behavior during the entire campaign. He reproached himself for having executed Blücher's orders too punctually and too willingly, and henceforth would be more cautious – a resolve that he honored to the slightest detail. That evening he reported to Blücher that his park column had not arrived, the expended ammunition could not be replenished, and the corps was not in a condition to take part in the battle intended for the next day. The enemy withdrew in the night, the battle became impossible, and Blücher's confidence in the talent and goodwill of General Langeron was ruined for good.[4]

According to Müffling, Blücher "found himself in one of the most difficult and unpleasant situations."[5] He and his staff could not understand Langeron's refusal. Was it militarily or politically driven, or was it simply a bold manifestation of his displeasure over being subordinated to a Prussian? More importantly, Blücher had to determine the proper response. Although pursuing a conscious policy of maintaining good relations with his Russian subordinates, Langeron's cheek exasperated him. He firmly and somewhat stubbornly insisted that, if his orders had been followed to the letter, a French corps of 18,000 men would have been destroyed.[6] Bogdanovich judges that not only did Langeron's refusal allow Ney to escape across the Bober at Bunzlau on the 20th, but also that Macdonald received the opportunity to attack Langeron's vanguard with superior forces.[7]

Langeron's actions warranted a court-martial, but at this moment, with the enemy army a few miles away, Blücher had little recourse. The politics of coalition warfare further limited his options. At this early stage of the war and with the "cabal" waiting for him to err, could he even risk a strong reprimand? "If the commander in chief wanted retribution," continued Müffling, "the dissatisfaction that existed in the army could have easily erupted and the entire machine, on whose cooperation the Bohemian Army relied, could have come to a standstill. The Prussian commander also had to consider his Fatherland. In this critical situation, the commander in chief decided to accept Langeron's disobedience as a misunderstanding and to shrug it off lightly. For the future he had no choice but to remain by this corps and await an insubordinate act to orders personally given by himself in which the excuse of a misunderstanding could not be used."[8]

Although not as belligerent as Langeron, Sacken likewise refused to obey Blücher on the grounds that the order made no sense in light of his current position. Receiving the disposition at 4:00 on the morning of the 20th, the Russian responded that opposite him stood a strong corps – Marmont's VI – and that he would have to march backward (east) twelve "long" miles in the face of this enemy to reach the Gröditzberg. Incorrect on two accounts, Sacken could have marched a mere four miles due south from Thomaswaldau to reach the Goldberg–Bunzlau road, which Ney would have been forced to take if Langeron drove through Deutmannsdorf in accordance with Blücher's plans. Although Sacken agreed with Blücher's idea for the battle, he felt that his march to the Gröditzberg would result only in the surrender of hard-won terrain. Moreover, Marmont would surely march to the sound of the guns and follow Sacken, who doubted his Russians could even arrive in time to assist Blücher. He requested further orders but promised to have his reserve of dragoons, infantry, and artillery move toward the Gröditzberg.[9]

No evidence exists that Army Headquarters issued a revised disposition for 20 August despite Ney's escape. Pahlen's corps again did not move from Hirschberg. Langeron's corps remained in the Siebeneichen–Zobten area.[10] On the right wing, Sacken attacked Marmont's rearguard at Thomaswaldau and pursued the French to Bunzlau. Vasilchikov and the vanguard reached Bunzlau just as III and VI Corps retreated across the Bober around 4:00 in the afternoon. As the Russians entered Bunzlau, Sacken's order to withdraw arrived. Bogdanovich speculates that Sacken had probably received a warning from the inhabitants that the French had mined the town to destroy the fortifications they had built during the armistice. Thirty minutes after the French retreated, several explosions rocked the town followed by a thunderous blast that marked the blowing of an enormous powder depot. Bogdanovich claims that "the whole city was showered with grenades, shrapnel, and rocks; fires started in many places. All buildings were severely damaged." Sacken's troops entered Bunzlau that evening; the French maintained possession of the bridge over the Bober a few miles west at Ottendorf, guarding it with numerous batteries erected on the hills along the left bank. Sacken's main body bivouacked east of Bunzlau. Venançon noted in the journal of Sacken's corps: "All of this contributed to the idea that the French plan was to withdraw from Silesia; the reports of their deserters and the measures they took not to be followed supported this assumption."[11]

In the center, I Corps again provided a scene of controversy. During the night of 19/20 August, Gneisenau withdrew Yorck's vanguard from the Hirse hill to a position seven miles east at Hockenau (Czaple), southwest of Neudorf-am-Gröditzberg. The staff chief also directed Hünerbein's brigade northeast from Lauterseiffen to Neudorf-am-Gröditzberg. Blücher repositioned these units before Yorck's report on Ney's departure arrived at midnight. Obviously, these movements, which resulted in a third consecutive night march for the troops involved, indicate the importance Blücher placed on having maximum combat power to pin Ney. After receiving Yorck's report, Blücher most certainly went to bed and Gneisenau probably fell asleep from exhaustion; no one at headquarters remembered to either rescind these particular orders or notify Yorck. The Prussian vanguard had been marching and fighting in streaming rain since 4:00 A.M. on the 19th. After barely two hours of rest during which the men cared for their horses but had yet to eat, the order arrived to ride to Hockenau, and they departed as quickly as possible.[12] As a result, only Katzler's weak forward posts remained along the right (east) bank of the Bober with a few squadrons from the Reserve Cavalry in support at Deutmannsdorf.

Yorck awoke at Neudorf-am-Gröditzberg early on the 20th to find his vanguard only one mile from his headquarters. To his utter disbelief, he learned that Army Headquarters had ordered Lobenthal to abandon the Hirse hill as part of the attack disposition. Indicative of his attitude toward Blücher and Gneisenau, he wrote in the margin of I Corps's Journal of Operations that this movement "violated all of the rules of the art of war, and I know not upon whose order" it was executed. It did not take much to sour Yorck's mood. His demand for perfection permeated I Corps. Already the hostility toward Blücher's staff mounted as Yorck's harsh criticism seeped into the written reports. The journal entry for 19 August reflects the low opinion of Yorck's headquarters toward their compatriots at Blücher's: "partially in march, partially standing under arms since 2:00 A.M. and 5:00 A.M.; from hour to hour expecting the order to continue the march, then again marching, fighting here and marching there, and finally in the middle of the night disturbed from a short rest and sent on poor country roads to different positions."[13] The situation that greeted Yorck early on the 20th threw more fuel on the fire. Hoping the French had yet to occupy the Hirse hill, he immediately dispatched cavalry and horse artillery to reclaim possession of the heights. After reinforcing the vanguard with one heavy battery, he directed Lobenthal to Plagwitz. Later that morning and before Lobenthal could secure the Hirse hill, Yorck learned that French cavalry had again approached the Gröditzberg. His anger mounted. Should Lobenthal find the French on the Hirse hill and if Ney had turned around, Yorck and Langeron ran the risk of being defeated successively in their isolation. Not just I Corps, but the entire Silesian Army would be in jeopardy.

"Thus," Yorck wrote to Blücher, "partial engagements against a concentrated enemy who is advancing on one of two roads ... are best to avoid. I defer the assessment of this comment to your discretion as it depends on the situation of the whole and can only be considered by me according to my narrow view." According to the records of I Corps, "Yorck complained about this manner of immediately following the enemy with the entire army based on any rumor of his retreat. As it lay in the plan of the commanding general to avoid a main battle, the advance of the whole would likewise cause the retreat of the whole, which would ruin the army through marches." The statement goes on to say that, rather than the entire army, Yorck suggested having a strong vanguard remain in constant contact with the enemy. While the vanguard accurately ascertained the enemy's movements, the army could rest and reorganize. After the vanguard provided a clear picture of the situation, the army could lunge forward and grapple with the enemy. "But the gentlemen always fear the enemy will escape them because they attribute to the enemy army their preconception of viewing the movements of an army like the wanderings of travelers." Blücher's terse response that a new disposition would be issued as soon as the relevant reports arrived did nothing to stem the ill-will that already prevailed at Yorck's headquarters. A short memo in Yorck's own handwriting captures his bitter frustration: "The letter remains unanswered, but the true reason lays in the indecisiveness of the General Staff, which does not know whether it should go forward or backward and from time to time hopes for news that the enemy has run away."[14]

Meanwhile, Katzler reported from the right bank of the Bober early that morning that "the enemy holds Löwenberg and guards the destroyed bridge over the Bober. Also, a considerable infantry and cavalry mass still bivouacs on the hills behind [west of] Löwenberg. Now and then convoys leave Löwenberg for Lauban; the enemy is probably moving magazine stores to Lauban. The enemy probably holds Löwenberg only to cover the movement of these convoys. Regarding the bridge at Sirgwitz, only the planks have been thrown down; they can be quickly restored by an advance in this direction."[15] Around noon, Lobenthal found the Hirse hill unoccupied. After securing the high ground, he moved further west to the Weinberg farmstead on the hills along the right bank of the Bober. Gazing across the river at Löwenberg, he observed the imperial camp bustling like a disturbed mound of ants. He estimated 20,000 infantry and 5,000 cavalry. After appearing to be marching west, they suddenly halted and made camp. Lobenthal's reports, which reached Blücher late in the afternoon, also contained astonishing news: according to locals, the imperials expected Napoleon to arrive at any moment. Unconfirmed reports claimed that the emperor had already reached Löwenberg. Blücher rightly doubted that Napoleon had already arrived, yet he could not ignore basic logic. Confirmed intelligence indicated Napoleon's approach. Moreover, the emperor probably would not be traveling alone but instead would be accompanied by reinforcements; prisoners now came in from units hitherto not part of Ney's army.[16]

Five days earlier on 15 August, Blücher conveyed to Bernadotte the news divulged by Jomini that Napoleon would march on Berlin. Ironically, his letter crossed with one penned to him by Bernadotte on the 16th. His note urged Blücher to accelerate his advance because he feared the Army of North Germany would soon suffer a defeat. He based his anxiety on the presence of an imperial army of 100,000 men at Baruth, 35 miles south of his position at Berlin and 150 miles northwest of Bunzlau.[17] Although three days later the crown prince reduced the number of imperials to 60,000 men posted between Baruth and Luckau, his letter of the 16th had to have caused some jaws to drop at Silesian Army Headquarters.[18] Even facing 100,000 men, Bernadotte's army of 125,000 enjoyed an advantage, where Ney's 130,000 soldiers clearly outnumbered Blücher's 100,000. This would not be the last time Blücher heard from the Swedish prince royal. Yet Bernadotte's letter did provide Blücher with additional cause to ignore an order from Schwarzenberg. Communicated via Barclay de Tolly, the Allied commander in chief wanted Blücher to send Pahlen III's corps to Trautenau to relieve Bubna's 2nd Light Division so it could join the Army of Bohemia.[19] With the crown prince in need of support and with reports indicating Napoleon would soon join Ney with reinforcements, Blücher absolutely refused to weaken his forces at such a critical moment. Moreover, the number of days it would take for Pahlen to reach Trautenau via Landeshut would put the corps out of action for an unacceptable amount of time.[20]

Meanwhile, Yorck's corps remained at Neudorf-am-Gröditzberg but patrols ascertained that the approaching imperial cavalry had halted between Mittlau and Altjäschwitz; whether the French horse masked foot could not be determined. Around noon, Blücher received the report of this cavalry's withdrawal toward Bunzlau. At the same time, a report from Langeron reached Army Headquarters at Pilgramsdorf. Langeron held his position at Zobten but the French forced him to evacuate Siebeneichen. That morning, French forces again occupied Siebeneichen as well as the hills that extended to Mois. Langeron estimated the enemy's strength to be thirty battalions and just as many squadrons. Around 10:00 A.M., the majority of these forces trooped north to Löwenberg and the Russians moved back to Siebeneichen. Yet around noon, a strong French column unexpectedly approached the village, forcing the Russians to again withdraw. In the afternoon, the imperials continued their march to Löwenberg and the Russians reoccupied Siebeneichen. Seven miles upstream along the Bober at Lähn, the Russians counted six large enemy columns during the night of 19/20 August but five left before daybreak; their destination remained unknown. Only a weak detachment remained at Lähn. Further south in Pahlen III's sector, Macdonald's detachment at Berthelsdorf withdrew to Greiffenberg but returned soon after. Regardless, Langeron informed

Blücher that the enemy had pulled the majority of his troops from Berthels-dorf, Lähn, and Mois.

Russian claims that the French had evacuated these villages seemed to confirm other reports that Ney intended to continue his retreat across the Queis. Yet other points in the reports confirmed that Ney had received reinforcements. Prisoners professed to belong to IV and VII Corps as well as the Young Guard. Further intelligence placed VIII Corps at Görlitz. Pahlen reported that not Macdonald's corps, but Mortier's Young Guard held Greiffenberg. Intelligence stated that French masses had marched east from Görlitz on the east–west highway to Bunzlau; statements from prisoners identified these masses as Young Guard. Much of this proved to be nonsense: IV and VII Corps were marching on the Prussian capital with the rest of Oudinot's Army of Berlin while VIII Corps remained south of Dresden. Regardless, these reports also suggested a change in the demeanor of Ney's army indicative of the unexpected counterpunch at Siebeneichen.[21]

By late afternoon on the 20th, Silesian Army Headquarters still could not determine whether Ney would continue his retreat to the Queis or, having been reinforced by as many as three corps, would switch to the offensive. Strong imperial forces remained around Löwenberg as well as west of Bunzlau. Opinions differed: some advised preparing for an attack, others for an immediate retreat. Blücher rejected all thoughts of withdrawing before Ney or Napoleon or whomever. He maintained that Yorck and Langeron held an uncommonly strong position that could repulse any frontal attack.[22] Although a French flanking movement remained possible, Sacken blocked the only other permanent bridge over the Bober at Bunzlau. Not fearing a French offensive, Blücher wanted to be ready to exploit a continuation of the French retreat. This meant preparing the army to cross the Bober immediately and simultaneously. With the only crossing points at Bunzlau and Löwenberg, the staff looked for a position that would best accommodate the army's Russian pontoons. Katzler claimed to have found the spot at Sirgwitz, less than four miles north of Löwenberg.

Around 5:00 P.M., I Corps trudged toward Sirgwitz after Yorck granted his men the luxury of a hot meal. That was about all that went right for the Prussians during this ten-mile march. Yorck again formed two columns for the march: the right crossed through Großhartmannsdorf to Gähnsdorf (Gaszów), the left through Deutmannsdorf to Ludwigsdorf. Another summer storm rendered the already drenched roads impassable. Both columns had to clear numerous defiles while the left encountered village after village along a four-mile stretch. It goes without saying that delays led to a fourth consecutive night march. In streaming rain, the lead elements of Yorck's left column finally cleared Deutmannsdorf to reach Ludwigsdorf around midnight.[23]

Yorck's chief of staff, Zielinsky, rode ahead to reconnoiter. His report called into question Katzler's findings. "The position at Sirgwitz," he explained to Yorck, "which should be taken according to the orders of the commanding general, has so many considerable military disadvantages that I hold it as my duty to formally protest against it because the occupation of this point could have the most unfortunate consequences." The staff officer described the position as being hemmed between the Bober and a rivulet that flows into it downstream of Sirgwitz. In addition, it could be observed and flanked by the enemy on the left bank of the Bober. Only one road connected Sirgwitz with Lobenthal's position on the right bank facing Löwenberg, which the enemy still possessed along with the town's stone bridge over the Bober. "This position grants no opportunity to maneuver because only one road runs rearward through Ludwigsdorf. Therefore, I thus suggest halting the corps at Ludwigsdorf, where the Löwenberg–Liegnitz road crosses the Neudorf–Deutmannsdorf road, and await further orders from the commanding general."[24] The final straw for Yorck came when Zielinsky failed to locate a suitable place at Sirgwitz for I Corps to camp. Consequently, Yorck halted his columns at Gähnsdorf and Ludwigsdorf. Straggling units filtered in to the bivouacs throughout the night and into the morning. The rear of the two columns did not arrive until 5:00 A.M. on 21 August. One of Yorck's staff officers, Major Ferdinand Wilhelm von Schack, noted in his journal: "Many stragglers, weary, rain. No one knows where General Blücher will establish his headquarters."[25]

In his report to Blücher, Yorck cited Zielinsky's findings as justification for the halt. This did not deter Blücher, who personally reconnoitered Löwenberg from the hills on the right bank around sunset on 20 August. There he received a second report from Langeron containing intelligence from spies and deserters claiming that Napoleon had reached Löwenberg on the afternoon of the 19th. Langeron noted that the enemy had conducted reconnaissance in force on all points but had withdrawn toward evening and hidden their masses behind the Löwenberg heights.[26] According to the Russian general: "We could see that the enemy's forces were considerably augmented and we learned that Napoleon and Murat arrived at Löwenberg with the French Guard, the Reserve Cavalry, the cuirassiers, and other troops that had come to join the corps of Ney, Lauriston, and Macdonald and Sébastiani's cavalry, which were the original components of the army that we faced."[27]

Blücher either did not want to fall for a French ruse or again allowed his wishes to master his thoughts. The results of his reconnaissance along with other information contained in Langeron's letter – particularly the evacuation of Siebeneichen by the French and the continuous movement of imperial forces to Löwenberg – strengthened Blücher's opinion that Ney would continue to retreat and defend the Bober to conceal his movements.

His assumption that the advance of the Bohemian Army on the left bank of the Elbe would soon impact the imperial forces in Silesia fed this supposition. Moreover, a report from Sacken that arrived in the evening confirmed that imperial forces had evacuated Bunzlau. "The enemy took his retreat on Görlitz," wrote Sacken. "A large number of troops were concentrated here; today, Marshal Ney rode through the ranks at Thomaswaldau and was greeted with music and *"Vive l'Empereur!"*[28]

Passing the night one mile east of Sirgwitz at the Schloß in Hohlstein (Skała) under the immediate protection of one battalion supported by Horn's brigade at nearby Ludwigsdorf, a restless Blücher champed at the bit to launch a rapid offensive across the Bober. He calculated that, by nightfall on the 20th, all of his corps would reach on the right bank of the Bober: Pahlen III at Hirschberg with the left wing; Langeron and Yorck in the center facing Löwenberg; on the right, Sacken before Bunzlau. During the night, Blücher summoned the Russian bridge train to Sirgwitz and occupied the town with one Guard Jäger company and one sharpshooter platoon. The Mecklenburg Hussars moved down the Bober early in the morning to establish contact with Sacken's corps. Meanwhile, the Russians built their bridge at Sirgwitz so Yorck and Langeron could pursue if Ney continued his retreat. Although he was eager to rush forward, a hint of uncertainty gripped Blücher as Barclay's instructions echoed in his ears. Drafting all of Blücher's reports to Frederick William, Gneisenau wrote to the king that "with regard to the enemy army, I follow cautiously in accordance with my instructions so I can avoid becoming entangled in an uneven contest before the Bohemian Army can begin its operations."[29]

During the course of the 20th, Marmont withdrew to Bunzlau's eastern suburb of Gnadenberg (Godnów) in preparation to cross the Bober. Ney placed III Corps and II Cavalry Corps on the hills of Tillendorf (Bolesławice), on the opposite bank of the Bober west of Bunzlau. Marmont's main body then moved through Bunzlau, crossed the river a few miles west at Ottendorf, and headed southwest to link with Lauriston, who stood eight miles further south at Löwenberg. Marmont's rearguard held Bunzlau until evening. As noted, it razed all the fortifications constructed during the armistice, blew the powder magazine, and destroyed every bridge that could be found as far as Eichberg (Dąbrowa Bolesławiecka), five miles north of Bunzlau. In the middle of the French position, Lauriston did little on the 20th. Prussian patrols observed long wagon trains departing from Löwenberg for the Saxon frontier. The imperials partly burned and partly barricaded the bridges over the Bober, making clear they planned to continue their retreat.[30]

History is filled with ironies. In this case, Blücher's most troublesome corps commander, the French émigré Langeron, ordered his corps forward after telling the old hussar he would not move without express orders. As it turned out, the operations of his corps at Siebeneichen on 19 August brought Napoleon racing to Löwenberg with I Cavalry Corps and the Old Guard, altogether around 40,000 men. Odeleben recounts that the movements "suddenly began" on the morning of the 20th as Napoleon "hastened to quit Zittau" and reach Lauban. "It was clearly perceived that this sudden change was the result of the losses the French had suffered in the violent attacks near Lähn, where they had been repulsed the preceding day at the Bober."[31] Somewhere between Zittau and Görlitz the emperor halted after receiving news "that the key for the ciphers of a dispatch sent to one of his marshals [Macdonald] ... had been lost; the officer who was the bearer of it was taken prisoner. It became necessary to directly remedy this matter through immediate orders. The *bureau de la guerre* was established in the open air in a small copse; it consisted of Napoleon, Berthier, and Caulaincourt. Napoleon dictated, walking backwards and forwards; Caulaincourt was seated on the ground and wrote." So many orderlies and officers had to be dispatched that the emperor had few men remaining for further assignments. Odeleben recounts that at both Görlitz and Lauban "an indefatigable activity appeared to be employed during the whole of the day ... and Napoleon expected an important engagement the next day, in which he reckoned completely to defeat the Army of Silesia."[32]

Arriving at Görlitz on the afternoon of the 20th, Napoleon wrote to Ney and Marmont at 2:00 P.M.: "At 5:00 I will be at Lauban. The main business at this moment is to unite and march against the enemy." He then led the Old Guard and I Cavalry Corps to Lauban, where he passed the night planning his offensive against Blücher, whose army the emperor had accurately reassessed to be 80,000–90,000 strong. He intended to attack Blücher on the following day, 21 August: "I plan to fight tomorrow, from noon to 6:00 P.M.," he informed Macdonald. French intelligence still incorrectly placed Kleist with Blücher's army, and the emperor did not know the exact location of Ney and Marmont, nor did he know if French forces still held Bunzlau. Nevertheless, it is difficult to believe Odeleben's claim that Napoleon "was extremely uneasy on being informed that he had to deal with three generals full of energy and experience: Blücher, Kleist, and Langeron, who possibly might prevent his junction with his marshals." Instead, Napoleon wrote Maret at Dresden that the upcoming battle "probably would be a very successful event."[33]

At midnight, Imperial Headquarters issued the attack disposition for 21 August.[34] Ney received instructions to lead III Corps and II Cavalry Corps across the Bober at Bunzlau at 10:00 A.M. If Ney found fewer than 30,000 men before him, he would pursue briskly and then cut sharply south to Giersdorf (Żeliszów) to form the emperor's left wing.[35] Napoleon's belief that the main mass of Blücher's army stood on the upper Bober is stated as the reason for Ney's march southeast rather than due east. Marmont's VI

Corps would advance between Ney and Löwenberg on Napoleon's immediate left. Lauriston's V Corps followed by Macdonald's XI Corps would
cross at Löwenberg and form the emperor's center and right. Napoleon
expected VI Corps and the Old Guard to reach Löwenberg at noon. News
that Ney had ordered the evacuation of the Bober and the retreat west of the
Queis during the afternoon of the 20th unsettled Imperial Headquarters
during the predawn hours of the 21st.[36]

Although reports flooded Blücher's headquarters on the morning of the
21st, the Prussians still could not determine Ney's next move. Thick clouds
that dumped torrential rain on the Bober valley concealed its secrets from
prying eyes. Around 5:00 A.M., the commander of the Mecklenburg
Hussars, Lieutenant-Colonel Ernst Friedrich von Warburg, reached
Bunzlau's southeastern suburb. He reported that "Russian skirmishers are
in the city. At daybreak great movement was heard in the enemy camp.
However, we cannot distinguish anything because of the heavy rain. My
vanguard is close to the Bober; all bridges are down." Forty-five minutes
later, Lobenthal reported from the Weinberg farmstead that "the darkness of
the weather does not allow us to accurately observe the enemy, yet it appears
that the second wave has departed because no campfires are burning. Our
Cossacks have crossed the Bober and have not lost sight of the enemy.
Colonel Neydhardt reported that Siebeneichen is in our hands and the
Cossacks are a good half-hour west of it, patrolling to the right and left."
Halfway between the twelve miles that separated Löwenberg and Bunzlau,
the 4th Squadron of the Mecklenburg Hussars crossed the Bober at
Großwaltitz (Włodzice Wielkie) and continued northwest toward the
Görlitz–Bunzlau stretch of the east–west highway. From Kroischwitz
(Kraszowice) at 6:00 A.M., its commanding officer reported the continued
retreat of imperial forces and that troops of all arms could ford the Bober at
Großwaltitz.[37]

Although the weather prevented Blücher from gaining an overview of
French movements, he remained convinced that Ney would evacuate the
Bober. If not, he thought of exploiting the gap between Ney and Lauriston,
thus between Bunzlau and Löwenberg. Patrols had observed very little
enemy activity in this sector on the 20th. With this in mind, Blücher
considered having Yorck and Langeron cross the Bober at Sirgwitz and then
drive sixteen miles west to Lauban, itself sixteen miles east of Görlitz.
Wanting some definitive news of events on the left bank, Blücher ordered
Major Friedrich Georg von Sohr to lead one Brandenburg Hussar squadron
and the infantry that occupied Sirgwitz across the Bober to reconnoiter
south toward Löwenberg. After repulsing the imperial posts at the river's
edge, Sohr did not get far before his detachment encountered strong forces,
purportedly Württembergers, belonging to Marmont's VI Corps. Pursued
by enemy infantry and cavalry, the Prussians barely had time to recross the

Bober. Imperial infantry reached the bridge, which the Russians managed to dismantle under fire. The little time Sohr spent on the left bank sufficed for him to observe numerous columns marching *east*.[38]

Despite the thick clouds, imperial infantry could be seen massing around Löwenberg at 7:00 A.M. One hour later, a lieutenant reached Army Headquarters with Lobenthal's 7:15 A.M. report: "The enemy camp is in movement; we still do not know whether it will be an attack or a retreat, yet according to the report ... six battalions are now advancing." Within an hour the weather cleared, allowing Lobenthal to see the bustling activity around Löwenberg from his position at the Weinberg farmstead. The hills on the right bank on which the farmstead stood extended northwest to southeast between two dominating heights of equal proportion: the Luften hill to the north and the Stein hill to the south. The Löwenberg–Goldberg highway ran between these twin peaks through a pass 300–400 yards wide before breaking free and cutting through the western portion of Plagwitz. The western face of both heights descended steeply toward the Bober while the eastern cliff of the Stein hill gently stretched its outcrops toward Deutmannsdorf. The smaller Hirse hill rose east of the Luften hill to command the highway running east from Löwenberg to Goldberg as it emerged from the pass. Müffling described the village of Plagwitz as long and considerably intersected, lying between the two mountain ridges.[39]

Almost 100 yards below their position on the Luften hill, the Prussians could clearly see the Bober valley, between 900 and 1,100 yards in width. Löwenberg, a relatively large town, was wedged among the shallow hills on the opposite edge of the valley. Löwenberg's mill race, itself as wide as the Bober, flowed parallel to the river. The Löwenberg–Goldberg road crossed the mill race on a wooden bridge that the French had destroyed. It proceeded to the Bober where a highly arched stone bridge that the French had barricaded carried it across the water. On the right bank, a small stream accompanied the highway, meandering along the foot of the Stein hill to the village of Plagwitz.[40]

It appeared that the French had received considerable reinforcements. The Prussians observed skirmishers deploying along the left bank. Lobenthal unlimbered three batteries on the Luften hill but the height and steepness of the cliff prevented the artillery from having any effect on the Bober defile; Löwenberg and the hills along the opposite bank were out of range. Between forty and ninety yards wide, the Bober could be forded at many places, which likewise did not bode well for the defenders. Around 9:00, the Prussians clearly heard the shout go up in the imperial camp: "*Vive l'Empereur!*" Napoleon had arrived. On receiving Lobenthal's report, Yorck rushed to join his vanguard, which held the Luften hill, the pass, and Plagwitz with the main body some 2,000 yards north of the Luften hill. From his vantage point, he could see Langeron's troops moving north from

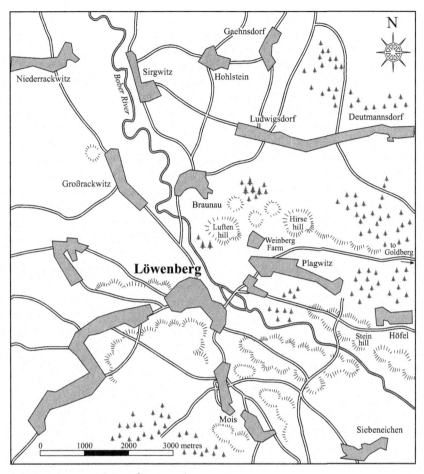

9. Engagement at Löwenberg, 21 August 1813

Zobten toward the Stein hill. Langeron himself soon joined Yorck. Across the river, the Prussians observed Napoleon reviewing the troops. Lobenthal's attempt to enhance the celebration with some shelling had little effect. The French replied, likewise without effect. "They opened a sharp and completely useless cannonade," noted Langeron, "which could only serve to distract us; these batteries, which we could not see and which were firing in parabolic angles, unleashed an immense quantity of balls and shells on the Weinberg, where they inflicted no harm; Yorck had a few advance posts there." Soon the French guns went silent and outpost skirmishing began. Yorck moved his 2nd Brigade into position immediately behind the

Luften hill. One battalion from Langeron's corps occupied the Stein hill while the rest of his vanguard (one Jäger battalion, four squadrons, and four horse guns) moved to Höfel (Dworek), two miles southeast of Plagwitz.[41]

Blücher rode to the Luften hill but Gneisenau remained at headquarters. At 8:45 A.M. the staff chief received a second report from Warburg. Written near Bunzlau, the note stated that Ney "again halted; he positioned much artillery by the rearguard and many [pieces] are concealed in the woods. If this entire mass falls on General Sacken he will be in danger. The enemy is again marching toward Bunzlau; it is around 7:30 A.M." Gneisenau immediately recognized the gravity of the situation. While the Prussians refused to believe Napoleon would launch a frontal assault across the Bober from Löwenberg, they understood that a flanking maneuver posed a serious threat. Should Ney cross the Bober at Bunzlau to attack Sacken or move across the river further south to drive between Sacken and Yorck, the Silesian Army would be forced to wage "a battle under unfavorable circumstances." Therefore, Gneisenau prepared for a general retreat. He instructed Sacken to slowly withdraw before Ney, taking the road from Bunzlau southeast to Modelsdorf. Yorck's corps would take a position on the Gröditzberg while Langeron's corps moved east to Pilgramsdorf. If the French launched a general offensive, the Silesian Army would retreat behind the Katzbach to "provide time for the Bohemian Army as well as the North German Army to ... begin their main drives." As for Blücher's left wing, if the French attempted to outflank it, Yorck would still fall back to the Gröditzberg but Langeron would take a position eleven miles slightly southeast of Löwenberg at Probsthain. From there the Russians would launch a counterattack. Sacken would remain on alert and await orders. If the French withdrew, Gneisenau intended to "follow with caution" but also with enough boldness to slow their march. He believed that, by detaining imperial forces in Silesia, "the operation of the Bohemian Army on the left bank of the Elbe ... can begin in earnest." After dispatching this letter, Gneisenau sent Müffling to inform Blücher and then followed.[42]

Blücher joined Yorck and Langeron on the Luften hill just in time to see the penultimate column of imperial troops reach Löwenberg. Excitement in the imperial camp soon settled down and even the skirmishing subsided. As Blücher maintained, the Allied position appeared formidable. "Our position from Braunau to Zobten is so strong that an attack would cost the enemy many people without obtaining its goal," Gneisenau assured Sacken.[43] Yet rock alone would not stop Napoleon. Perhaps their overconfidence caused the leadership of the Silesian Army to overlook important details. Perhaps Blücher's insistence on launching an offensive through Sirgwitz distracted them. Although Lobenthal's infantry held the pass and Plagwitz, few battalions remained to defend the Luften hill itself. Conversely, Langeron's sole battalion on the Stein hill was virtually worthless, especially without artillery. Inexplicably, the Allies failed to post a ground-level battery to fire on Löwenberg's bridge. Yorck's famed biographer, Johann Gustav Droysen, claims that, in a rare moment of agreement, both Gneisenau and Yorck pleaded with Blücher to change his mind about crossing the Bober at Sirgwitz. Gneisenau conveyed the news he received from Warburg and explained the measures he prepared for the retreat. Blücher could not be convinced that easily. Instead, he watched and waited before returning to his headquarters at noon. The French camp remained quiet but in the distance the Old Guard could be seen marching east from Lauban.[44]

Shortly after returning to Hohlstein, Gneisenau received another disconcerting report from Warburg concerning the advance of considerable French forces on Bunzlau. The 1:00 hour had just struck. With it came the roar of artillery as the French launched their assault from Löwenberg. It appeared that Napoleon planned to fix Blücher's center while Ney turned his right. Despite Gneisenau's planning, Blücher could not escape without a fight. In accordance with Gneisenau's plan, Blücher ordered I Corps to the Gröditzberg. "It is my intention," Blücher informed Yorck, "to avoid the battle that the enemy seeks and to withdraw to the Gröditzberg with your corps. The vanguard will hold the enemy for as long as possible, falling back on the road to Lauterseiffen, and not allowing itself to be thrust aside from it." Langeron received instructions to withdraw to Pilgramsdorf.[45]

Early on the morning of the 21st, Russian and Prussian patrols observed Ney and Sébastiani rendezvous at Tillendorf and march *southwest* toward Naumburg. As Sacken prepared to pursue from Bunzlau, Ney turned around, having received the emperor's attack disposition. In accordance, Ney directed III Corps through Bunzlau to Giersdorf. He ordered Sébastiani to cross the Bober south of Bunzlau and then turn southeast toward Großhartmannsdorf and the Gröditzberg. At 10:00 that morning, the French secured Bunzlau and started repairing the bridge. On its completion, General Joseph Souham's 8th Division led III Corps across the Bober. Venançon's comments in Sacken's journal relate the Russian view of the situation: "At 10:00 A.M., Marshal Ney, reinforced by a cavalry division commanded by General Sébastiani, attacked the village of Bunzlau where General Sacken had some Jäger, who retired to the position that we had taken between Gnadenberg and Bunzlau. The enemy repaired the bridges that they had burned the previous day; at noon, they crossed the Bober; their forces could have been between 30,000 and 35,000 men" (see Map 2).

Sacken formed his corps at the rim of the valley. His 16,000 Russians stood their ground as Vasilchikov's cavalry and the 10th Division fought a textbook rearguard action that kept Sébastiani's troopers at bay.[46] Venançon noted:

> Their plan for this day was easy to divine; their feint against our right, where our cavalry was deployed, did not mislead General Sacken at all; the infantry

that deployed on our left and that outflanked us alerted us to their true intentions. At the beginning of the engagement, we spread ourselves as much as possible. Finally, we were completely outflanked around 6:00 P.M. and General Sacken withdrew his troops. Neverovsky's division took no part in the fighting; according to the disposition, it formed the second line. The 10th Division, commanded by General [Ivan] Lieven, withdrew in echelon by the right and through Gnadenberg. The reserve, composed of two regiments, was thrown in and protected the retreat of the cavalry which, by two consecutive charges, provided time for the reserve to establish itself. After our cavalry withdrew, our reserve followed it. After six hours of fighting, 17,000 men had held against more than 30,000. General Sacken withdrew without being overwhelmed, although he delayed this movement to learn the exact intentions of an enemy whose marches and countermarches left us unable to make any real calculations of his intentions.[47]

Sacken retreated toward Modelsdorf covered by the seven squadrons of the Smolenskii and Kurlandskii Dragoon Regiments. His after-action report to Blücher stated: "Today we had a hard day. The enemy attacked us with a superiority of 40,000–50,000 men. One report claims that the French emperor himself was present. We retreated in good order but not without considerable loss. A portion of the enemy force followed us but the main body of his army went through Thomaswaldau to Haynau; he has much cavalry. I request that you give me a directive and determine how I can maintain contact with you in all situations." Clearly the theory that the retreating soldier counts every enemy twice applies here, for Ney certainly did not cross the Bober with 60,000 to 70,000 men. Moreover, only Ney's 39th Division continued east on the highway to Haynau after his main body turned south. Sacken's vanguard held Alzenau (Olszanica) while his main body camped at Modelsdorf.[48]

Meanwhile, before dawn on the 21st, Napoleon had "hastily repaired to his troops, who were rushing like a torrent along the road to Löwenberg." He reached the outskirts of Löwenberg around 9:00 that morning. After inspecting the troops outside the city, he distributed Eagles for the standards of a few newly formed regiments with great pomp to animate the men, some of whom were seeing him for the very first time. As the emperor rode past his foremost units, he exhorted his warriors: "Forward, forward my children, we must advance!" Entering Löwenberg before noon, he established a temporary command post in the stables of the White Horse Inn. He studied two maps spread on a high bench in a corner. Every so often he would unbutton his signature grey overcoat and then nervously button it up again. His movements revealed restlessness and impatience. Shortly afterward, he put his men to work on the bridges. Sappers of the Guard used requisitioned timber and planks to bridge the mill race. Napoleon then ascended the hills on the left bank of the Bober to observe the unfolding of what he hoped would be a battle. Around noon, General Nicolas Joseph Maison's 16th Division formed to lead Lauriston's V Corps across the Bober. Behind V Corps came units from Latour-Maubourg's I Cavalry Corps followed by the 35th and 36th Divisions of XI Corps.[49]

"At noon," wrote Langeron, "we saw a group of officers on the Löwenberg bridge. It was Napoleon, Murat, and their staffs." One hour later, the intermittent French artillery fire gave way to a massive bombardment, with some guns opening fire from concealed positions along the water's edge. French infantry cleared away the barricades on the Bober bridge, muskets blazing at the Russian skirmishers. Lobenthal's guns responded. Gradually, French skirmishers crossed the Bober either by sprinting across the bridge individually or in small groups that forded the river upstream of the bridge. "A column of light infantry crossed the Bober at the ford, to the left of Plagwitz," continued Langeron; "this column was so weak that at first we did not think it could be a serious attack but rather a reconnaissance. Nevertheless, soon after some strong columns crossed the bridge *au pas de charge* and threw themselves on the village of Plagwitz. We had committed the fault of not sufficiently manning this important position."[50]

Gaining the right bank, the imperials utilized hedges for cover while reinforcements steadily crossed under the protection of their fire. Having sufficient numbers on hand, the French suddenly charged the Stein hill and overwhelmed the single Russian battalion. They chased Langeron's men all the way to Plagwitz, where the Brandenburg Fusilier Battalion had just arrived. Lobenthal had also dispatched the East Prussian Fusilier Battalion to support the Russians on the Stein hill but now ordered it to retake the height. French reinforcements moved onto the hill, making this an impossible task. Maison's main body then moved across the Bober as his artillery unlimbered on the Stein hill. After repulsing the East Prussians, the French drove the Russians and Prussians from Plagwitz. "The enemy's attack was terrible," recalled Langeron, "and I was not content with our defense on this occasion, neither with Colonel Stegemann, nor with his Jäger regiment (the 7th), nor with the Prussian battalion; they all retreated too quickly."[51]

Although the French did not attack the Luften hill, Lobenthal realized he would be trapped and so directed his remaining battalions to Plagwitz. Meanwhile, Blücher arrived at Yorck's command post on the Hirse hill and ordered Prince Karl's 2nd Brigade to open the road to Plagwitz and keep open the road to Zobten. Karl positioned his brigade battery on the Hirse hill, deploying his brigade at the foot of the hill parallel to the highway. One horse battery from Yorck's Reserve unlimbered and sited the guns to fire canister at Plagwitz's exit. Intense combat erupted around the village. Lobenthal ordered several infantry charges through Plagwitz and up the Stein hill; all failed with considerable casualties. Kaptsevich's 7th and 37th Jäger Regiments arrived but Maison already firmly held the Stein hill.[52]

Four Russian horse guns moved up to support the Jäger. As French infantry emerged from Plagwitz in dense columns, the Russian gunners blasted them with canister. Russian and Prussian artillery also managed to clear the imperials from the Löwenberg–Goldberg highway. Lobenthal's vanguard still held the Luften hill, Karl's 2nd Brigade blocked the highway east of Plagwitz, and Kaptsevich's X Infantry Corps took a position at Höfel. Hünerbein's 8th Brigade stood at Lauterseiffen as Yorck's main body retreated toward the Gröditzberg and Wilhelmsdorf. Langeron's main body withdrew toward Pilgramsdorf, expertly covered by Emmanuel's cavalry.[53] The French held Plagwitz and the Stein hill: stalemate ensued.

Müffling provides a glimpse of the situation and decision-making process at Blücher's command post: "Up to now, the general could not fathom the enemy's intentions, but when he saw from the Weinberg hill the entire enemy army defiling with great haste through Löwenberg in attack columns, and great clouds of dust continuously rising above the Lauban–Löwenberg highway, and finally, when a spy found a way to get across the Bober and deliver the news that Bonaparte himself had arrived, no doubt remained that the enemy's intention was to deliver a battle."[54] Gneisenau's report to Hardenberg also offers insight into the thought process at Blücher's headquarters: "On the 21st, the enemy wanted to engage us in a general battle (at Löwenberg). However, we committed only the vanguard and a portion of the prince of Mecklenburg's brigade to the engagement. We held back our remaining masses, Russians and Prussians, and withdrew them to the region of the Gröditzberg unmolested because superior enemy forces advanced against General Sacken's position at Bunzlau and forced him to retreat." The Prussians estimated the strength of Napoleon's force to be six army corps. At 5:00, Blücher reluctantly gave the order for all troops to withdraw from the Plagwitz sector. Although Langeron disagreed, Müffling maintained that "Blücher's position was bad (mainly because Langeron's corps at Zobten was too far from Yorck's left wing) but the terrain favored breaking off the engagement." Covered by General Fyodor Korf's Reserve Cavalry from Langeron's corps, the Silesian Army escaped but French cavalry fiercely pursued Lobenthal's exhausted detachment as well as Karl's 2nd Brigade. Both had to turn around numerous times to repulse the hunters, who finally broke off the chase at Deutmannsdorf. Not one man fell into French hands during this retreat, yet Nostitz claims that Yorck's Landwehr "received many bitter rebukes" at Army Headquarters.[55]

At nightfall, Yorck's 1st, 2nd, and 8th Brigades and the Reserve Cavalry halted at Neudorf-am-Gröditzberg, the 7th Brigade and the rearguard held Wilhelmsdorf and Gröditz. General Denisiyev's Severskii Mounted Jäger Regiment and the sole battalion of the Shlisselburgskii Infantry Regiment covered the retreat of Kaptsevich's X Infantry Corps as it marched to Neuwiese (Nowa Łąki). There it remained as Langeron's rearguard and occupied the passes of Lauterseiffen in conjunction with Yorck's 2nd Brigade. Langeron's main body (Rudzevich's advance guard, VI and IX Infantry Corps) marched to Pilgramsdorf, where Blücher established Army Headquarters. Langeron, who joined Kaptsevich and Karl, noted: "the prince of Mecklenburg found himself directly under my orders; we fought together for more than four hours against very superior forces without losing an inch of ground; on this occasion, I appreciated the merit of this young prince, who at this time was only twenty-three years old, his value, and that of his troops. Nevertheless, the enemy constantly received reinforcements. Nightfall, which we awaited with impatience, finally put an end to hostilities and the French advanced only a short way from Löwenberg."[56]

Both Sacken and Langeron stood on the eastern bank of the Schnelle Deichsel, a small yet "rapid" mountain stream. Covered on both banks by dwellings, gardens, and hedges, the Deichsel's fords did not permit the easy passage of large bodies of troops. In fact, Müffling wrote that only individuals could get across. "Thus, the general was able to wait quietly for the enemy to reveal his measures without being forced into battle." Nevertheless, Yorck's sector at Neudorf-am-Gröditzberg and Gröditz formed a vulnerable salient west of the Deichsel. With difficult defiles between him and the eastern bank, he warned Army Headquarters that his corps could be encircled and destroyed. Blücher's response reveals the purpose of his plan to slowly and methodically withdraw: "If you fear for the retreat of I Corps over the defile of the Schnelle Deichsel in the face of the enemy, I thus leave it to you to select two of your brigades to depart early and take a position behind the defile in order to cover the retrograde march of the others. I do not want the departure of the entire army to occur too soon and before the enemy shows himself because I will not know ... if the enemy has deployed a considerable force against us – even though I completely seek to avoid a general battle." Receiving Blücher's letter at 2:00 A.M. on the 22nd, Yorck sent his 1st and 8th Brigades across the Schnelle Deichsel at Leisersdorf (Uniejowice) and Ulbersdorf respectively. The rest of the corps followed at daybreak. The fighting at Löwenberg had exhausted Lobenthal's vanguard. Yorck dissolved the formation, returning the battalions and squadrons to their parent regiments and organizing a new combined-arms detachment under Katzler's command. Its cavalry took a position on the Gröditzberg while Colonel Heinrich Wilhelm von Weltzien posted its infantry at Neudorf-am-Gröditzberg. Patrols swept both north and south (see Map 2).[57]

The loss of 51 officers and 2,095 men reflected the day's hard fighting. Yorck's Landwehr received its baptism of fire. "It had been a mere skirmish," noted Müffling, "and they proved to be brave yet inexperienced, as was to be expected of young troops. As a result, the loss in dead and wounded was considerable and exceeded 2,000." Despite the opinions expressed at Army Headquarters, Yorck appears to have been genuinely impressed with the militia, which he thought performed just as well as the Line troops. One battalion of Silesian Landwehr twice executed a bayonet attack against imperial forces attempting to advance from Plagwitz; both times it returned to its position under blasts of canister. The story goes that when the commander of this battalion, a Captain Kossecki, received a rebuke for not sending skirmishers against the enemy but instead engaging in line, he answered that "as an old fusilier he knew what had to be done; but the battalion was in fire for the first time; if he dispersed it through skirmishers, he would lose control of it because of the shortage of experienced officers; he would rather die here than see his battalion scattered." After expending its ammunition, the battalion withdrew from the line. As it marched rearward, Yorck solemnly rode past, saluting the men for their bravery.[58]

From the French perspective, V Corps had hardly crossed the Bober "when the general of the Allies refused to accept a decisive battle in that position." Allied artillery, "advantageously posted" along the hills of the right bank, kept the French in check. Napoleon could only watch as the Allies retreated "with the greatest order and coolness" and without losing a prisoner or a gun. "It may now be considered as certain that the retreat had been prudently determined beforehand in the expectation that Napoleon would fall upon that particular army in person." For the moment, Napoleon "appeared to have no suspicion of a plan of operation conceived with so much sagacity and executed with such perseverance." Instead, he "experienced the most lively satisfaction at having repulsed the Allies that day in person and opening the campaign with some success and without sustaining much loss."[59]

Retreat never sat well with the man who eventually earned the epithet "Marshal Forwards," but at least Blücher understood the circumstances. The same could not be said for the average soldier. Concern over morale prompted Blücher to take action. That night, he issued an order of the day from his headquarters at Pilgramsdorf to explain his decision and praise the troops:

> The enemy wants to force us into a decisive battle, but to maintain our advantage we must avoid it. Therefore, we will go back and in a manner that causes him to lose time so the combined Russian, Austrian, and Prussian army gains time to break out of Bohemia and cross the Elbe to his rear while the crown prince of Sweden advances from the Mark and also attacks him from the rear. Thus, the Allied army entrusted to me will view itself as not being forced to retreat, but instead is voluntarily retreating to lead him [the enemy] to his doom. With true pleasure I saw and have learned that the Landwehr troops who participated in the combat today fought bravely and just like the veteran Line troops. I will not fail to inform His Majesty the King of this honorable conduct.[60]

Napoleon continued his quest to destroy Blücher or at least engage and defeat the salty Prussian on the 22nd.[61] Favorable yet incorrect news reached Imperial Headquarters that Blücher had been wounded the day before. To "briskly pursue the enemy in the direction of Goldberg," the emperor ordered XI and V Corps to advance east on both sides of the Löwenberg–Goldberg road. With III Corps and II Cavalry Corps, Ney would pursue the enemy toward Haynau or any other direction the Allies took. Napoleon wanted one of Ney's columns to drive between Haynau and Goldberg in case the opportunity existed to block the Allies from the latter. The emperor also ordered 2nd Guard Cavalry Division supported by two battalions from V Corps to scour the square formed by Löwenberg, Goldberg, Hirschberg, and Friedeberg. "You will send us everything you find and disarm the inhabitants," wrote Berthier to General Philippe-Antoine Ornano, Napoleon's cousin and commander of the division. "You will send forces against the Cossacks and scatter their patrols."[62]

As for the Silesian Army, controversy again accompanied its proceedings on 22 August. From the advantageous position on the eastern (right) bank of the Schnelle Deichsel, Blücher could observe Napoleon's movements. He informed his three corps commanders of his intention to avoid battle but to hold the position on the right bank of the river "until it becomes evident that the enemy is advancing to give battle with superior forces and has deployed these forces before us on the left bank of the Deichsel." In case a further retreat became necessary, Sacken would withdraw through Seifersdorf (Łukaszów) and ford the Katzbach at Schmogwitz (Smokowicka) while Yorck crossed at Dohnau (Dunino) and Kroitsch (Krotoszyce), and Langeron at Röchlitz and Goldberg. Blücher reserved the exclusive right to determine if the situation demanded a retreat. Langeron objected to the halt behind the Schnelle Deichsel. During a meeting at Pilgramsdorf, he informed Blücher that it violated Barclay's directives, which the Russian commander now admitted to knowing. He attempted in vain to persuade Blücher to retreat across the Katzbach. Blücher's refusal mattered little. As soon as the Prussian commander departed to join Yorck's corps around 10:00 A.M., Langeron ordered his corps to retreat to Goldberg (see Map 2).[63]

During the late morning, Katzler reported that imperial forces held Deutmannsdorf, Großhartmannsdorf, and Lauterseiffen. His troopers observed huge enemy columns west of the latter two, yet some of the troops that advanced to Deutmannsdorf the day before had already returned to Löwenberg, where Napoleon passed the night according to locals. Sacken's 8:00 A.M. report from Modelsdorf stated that Ney had moved southeast from Thomaswaldau toward the Allied center. Accordingly, it appeared that the imperial forces that had advanced through Bunzlau the day before had turned off the great highway to march south. This alerted the Prussians to the strong possibility of a renewed French advance toward Goldberg. Because the French tended to depart only after cooking, they could assume the enemy's main columns would not march before noon.[64]

Although Berthier issued the emperor's orders at 6:30 on the morning of 22 August, V Corps and the 35th and 36th Divisions of XI Corps did not commence the advance toward Goldberg until midmorning. From Löwenberg, they sought to catch the enemy's rearguard.[65] While Yorck's rearguard escaped before contact could be made, the French did find the Russians. At 10:00 A.M. on the 22nd, a column of 10,000 men from Macdonald's XI Corps advanced from Deutmannsdorf, attacking Kaptse-vich's X Infantry Corps at Neuwiese one hour later. According to Langer-on's instructions, Kaptsevich slowly retired east toward Pilgramsdorf, contesting every step and skillfully utilizing the terrain. Meanwhile, a second column of 10,000 men from V Corps closed on Pilgramsdorf from the southwest. To take in Kaptsevich, Rudzevich occupied the hills of Pilgrams-dorf with the 2nd Brigade (7th and 37th Jäger and Shlisselburgskii Infantry Regiments) of General Aleksandr Urusov's 8th Division supported by Gen-eral Aleksandr Berdyayev's 3rd Dragoon Division from Langeron's Reserve Cavalry. These units managed to delay the imperials long enough for Langeron's main body to clear the Katzbach at the Goldberg defile and move through Goldberg.

From Yorck's command post on a hill near Ulbersdorf, Blücher gained a clear view of the situation two miles north of him. Müffling claims that, because no imperial forces appeared to be pursuing Yorck and Sacken, "the general took the enemy's movement for a reconnaissance." Around the same time, Blücher received a report from Langeron informing him that consider-able French forces obliged him to retreat through Goldberg. Gneisenau immediately dispatched an adjutant with orders for Langeron to halt. Blü-cher himself rushed to Pilgramsdorf, finding Langeron's main body gone and the imperials challenging Kaptsevich's rearguard for possession of the village. At 3:00 P.M., the main French column surged forward. As French numbers steadily increased, Blücher ordered Kaptsevich to torch the village and fall back to Goldberg but remain near the village and occupy the heights east of it on the road to Jauer.[66]

Although a furious Blücher demanded that Langeron turn around imme-diately, he had little choice but to sign orders for Sacken and Yorck to also retreat. Despite his aggravation over Langeron, Blücher sensed that the situation had changed. From the hills east of Pilgramsdorf, he estimated the strength of the opposing French force to be 20,000 men at most. This certainly did not constitute Napoleon's army. Moreover, they "did not advance with the same zeal they usually displayed when Bonaparte was at their head," recalled Müffling. "He [Blücher] was convinced that Bonaparte had turned back, and sorely regretted that Langeron's premature retreat had frustrated his intentions." To withdraw before Napoleon in accordance with the Reichenbach Plan was one thing, fleeing from an isolated French corps was another. A retreat across the Katzbach now appeared impulsive. After sending orders for Yorck to halt, Blücher himself rushed to Goldberg to find Langeron and drag the Russian general back to his position on the Schnelle Deichsel. Yet not a trace of Langeron's corps could be found. The few locals who remained in the village claimed that the Russians had marched right through Goldberg and kept going on the road to Jauer, which stood fourteen miles to the southeast. Langeron had already covered so much ground that his troops could no longer be seen in the distance. August rains insured wet roads, preventing the dust clouds that normally revealed the march of soldiers.

Despite Blücher's orders, Kaptsevich's X Infantry Corps departed from Goldberg to follow Langeron's main body. Blücher summoned Kaptsevich to return but needed some troops to hold the town. Thus, he redirected Katzler's rearguard to Goldberg around 6:00 that evening. Arriving within an hour, Major Golz occupied the town with four battalions, sending two others to the hills immediately to the south. Nine squadrons under Major Hermann Otto von Stößel covered the right flank between Hohberg (Wyskok) and Goldberg while six squadrons and one battery reinforced by four Russian guns moved behind the hills south of the town. As Golz positioned his battalions, the French moved up to the left bank of the Katzbach. They opened considerable artillery fire that routed Katzler's two Landwehr squadrons as well as one of the militia battalions. This seemed to satisfy the imperials, who ceased firing at dusk. Meanwhile, the lead units of Kaptsevich's rearguard – 2 Jäger battalions and 2,000 cavalry – arrived east of Goldberg.

While Katzler occupied the Goldberg position, Blücher's adjutants chased after Langeron. They finally caught up with the Russians at Seichau, exactly seven and one-half miles from Jauer. Müffling maintains that they delivered Blücher's firm order "'to turn back instantly and resume the position at Goldberg'. The fate of the army hung on this movement: General Langeron executed it." In his journal, Langeron accepted partial responsibility for his actions on this day:

> I withdrew one and one-half miles east of Goldberg toward Seichau. I should have remained at Goldberg but the day before General Blücher had informed me that he intended to withdraw to Hennersdorf.[67] This intention appeared very logical in view of the report that he had received [from Sacken] on the march of Ney's corps but, since this corps never appeared, Blücher decided to remain at Goldberg and found that I was too far from him; the Prussian generals very much would like to present this as a fault on my part, but there is no means of attributing it to me. If it was a fault, it was soon repaired, as during the night I reported to Goldberg: Blücher ordered me to hold the enemy while Yorck's and Sacken's corps made a sharp attack against his left.

Regardless of whether Blücher expressed an intention to withdraw to Hennersdorf, he explicitly ordered Langeron to remain at Pilgramsdorf until further notice. "Thus, it is impossible to justify this high-handed act," judges Friederich. "The explanation for this mistake can only be that he hoped to drag Blücher on a further retrograde movement that he held to be indispensable according to Barclay's directives, which were only partially known to him."[68]

As night fell on the 22nd, Sacken's main body camped at Schmogwitz, a little over nine miles northeast of Goldberg and four miles southwest of Liegnitz. Around 6:00 that evening, Yorck received orders to continue his march to Niederkrayn (Krajów) and Dohnau, the latter being nine miles northeast of Goldberg, the former eight miles east of the town. Late in the night, Yorck's two columns crossed the Katzbach and reached their destinations after completing a fifth night march since the beginning of the campaign. Yorck and Blücher established their respective headquarters at Niederkrayn. Langeron decided to pass the night at Seichau and depart for Goldberg early on 23 August. On the extreme left, Pahlen III's main body withdrew east to Schmiedeberg while Kaysarov's rearguard remained at Hirschberg (see Map 2).

At Niederkrayn, Blücher received a report from Sacken claiming that part of the French army had returned to Bunzlau. His patrols found no sign of the imperials between Haynau and Thomaswaldau on the Bunzlau–Breslau highway. This news further confirmed the inaccuracy of Sacken's earlier report on Ney's southeast march to link with Napoleon's center. Sacken's report, combined with the enemy's lackadaisical performance at Goldberg, reinforced Blücher's belief that the push to the Katzbach had the sole purpose of masking the emperor's departure. Other intelligence claimed that imperial forces had been withdrawing along the Bunzlau–Görlitz highway for the past three days. This news, along with Sacken's report, was wrong and Blücher's assumption proved only partially correct. To compound the situation, a letter from the tsar dated 19 August arrived late in the evening. Alexander communicated his expectation that Napoleon would throw himself on the Bohemian Army. He emphasized the need for Blücher to keep his sword in the back of the imperial army in Silesia but avoid embroiling himself in a general battle.[69]

Although Ney's troops did not march until 3:30 on the afternoon of the 22nd, III Corps and II Cavalry Corps reached Adelsdorf on the Schnelle Deichsel that same day. North of Ney's main body, his 39th Division, which did not depart from Bunzlau until 6:30 P.M., ejected Lanskoy's cavalry from Haynau.[70] During the night, the French occupied Haynau, extending their left wing from Thomaswaldau to Kreibau, and their right wing from Großhartmannsdorf to Adelsdorf. After driving Langeron's rearguard from Pilgramsdorf, the imperials continued toward Goldberg. At nightfall on the

22nd, XI Corps settled in Ulbersdorf and Hermsdorf, the latter being three miles west of Goldberg on the direct highway from Löwenberg; V Corps held the five-mile stretch from Hermsdorf south to Neukirch (Nowy Kościół). At Löwenberg, the Guard, VI Corps, and I Cavalry Corps rested from their recent forced marches.[71]

During the course of the operation on 22 August, Napoleon followed V Corps toward Goldberg. "He had great difficulty in concealing his joy when he learned from the reports that the rearguards of the Prussians and Russians were pursued to the Katzbach, near Goldberg," recalled Odeleben. "He himself went halfway to Goldberg, made his observations on the environs, and the enemies' soldiers who remained on the field of battle, and spoke with the peasants who had had sufficient courage not to quit their homes, conversing affably on indifferent subjects." After receiving news of Blücher's retreat across the Katzbach, the emperor returned to Löwenberg, "his mind being rendered easy with respect to the success of his arms, which had made him gain ground on that side."[72] Napoleon thus described his situation, somehow forgetting that he had started his offensive on the 21st rather than the 20th: "The enemy's Army of Silesia moved against our own, reaching Bunzlau, Goldberg, and Löwenberg on the 20th. I immediately went there and attacked the enemy on the same day, overthrowing him everywhere, and we are now pursuing with the sword in his back. As for my Guard divisions that are destined to join the army I have placed in Bohemia, they rested today and will probably start for Görlitz tomorrow. Nevertheless, if the enemy moves on Dresden, I will arrive in time to fight there and none of my previous dispositions will change: General Vandamme is only two days from Dresden, the duc de Bellune [Victor] is only three days, my Guard divisions are only four days, all of which united with XIV Corps would make a very considerable force."

Statements from prisoners allowed the emperor to draw a conclusive picture of Blücher's army. It consisted of three corps with Langeron commanding a corps of five divisions and Sacken a corps of three divisions. In a letter to Maret, he did not recognize Blücher as the commander in chief, stating only that Blücher and York commanded a corps of four divisions. The entire Army of Silesia amounted to twelve divisions, which Napoleon estimated to total 80,000 to 90,000 men. "What is good is that their infantry is extremely poor," judged the emperor. Moreover, he already sensed that something had to be afoot to account for the enemy's retreat. Instead of attributing it to Allied strategy, he chalked it up to Allied ineptitude and fear. "It seems that their Army of Silesia advanced with more speed than the Allied plan called for and under the belief that we would retreat across the Elbe. They believed that all they had to do was pursue because as soon as they saw our lead columns resume the offensive, terror took them, and we are convinced that their leaders want to avoid a serious engagement. The

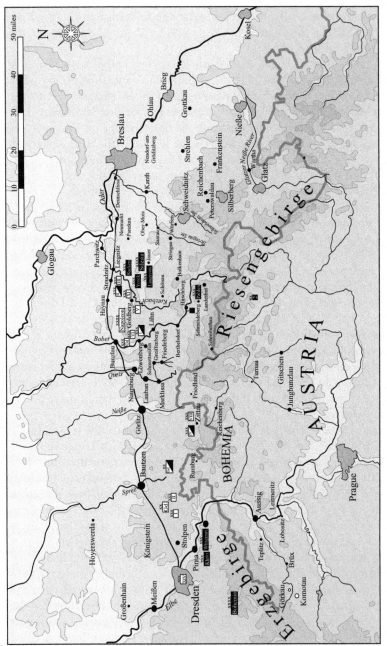

10. Situation, 22 August 1813

whole Allied plan was based on assurances from Metternich that we would retreat across the Elbe, and they are very confused to see otherwise." The only negative aspect of the campaign thus far proved to be the lack of confidence that his subordinates displayed in their own abilities. Left to their own devices, his marshals and generals seemed to always exaggerate the difficulties they faced.[73]

With Blücher on the run, Napoleon's attention immediately switched to Bohemia. Contrary to most histories of the campaign, Napoleon did not receive cries for help from St.-Cyr at Dresden. True, Schwarzenberg did not take the bait. Instead of marching on Zittau as Napoleon expected, the paunchy Austrian directed his army to the left bank of the Elbe from where it would advance on Dresden. However, neither St.-Cyr nor Napoleon knew this on the night of 22/23 August when Berthier issued orders for the return to Görlitz. At 2:30 A.M. on 23 August, the major-general ordered General Jean-Baptiste Corbineau's 1st Light Cavalry Division of I Cavalry Corps to move out of Löwenberg at 4:00 A.M. in order to clear the road between Lauban and Görlitz. The Old Guard would follow thirty minutes later and proceed to Lauban; the Young Guard would strike the same road between 6:00 and 8:00 A.M. At 11:00, the rest of I Cavalry Corps would depart. Marmont's VI Corps likewise received orders to return to Lauban but on another road to prevent its columns from crossing with those of the Guard.[74]

As for the emperor, he first thought of going to Prague and expressed this intention to Ney at 11:00 A.M. on the 23rd, wanting the marshal to accompany him. One hour later he changed his mind, telling Macdonald that he would return to Görlitz that same day but "that his further operations would depend on those of the enemy: if the enemy, on the 23rd or 24th, positively takes the offensive on Dresden, my intention is to leave the initiative to him and immediately go to the fortified camp of Dresden and fight a great battle." Commenting on the refusal of the Allied army in Silesia to accept battle, he informed Maret that nothing would be more fortunate than "an enemy march on Dresden, since then there would be a battle." After reaching Görlitz late in the afternoon of the 23rd, Napoleon received a report from St.-Cyr. Writing at 11:00 P.M. on the 22nd, the marshal explained that a Russian corps (Wittgenstein's) had debouched through the Peterswald (Petrovice) pass with what appeared to be the entire Austrian army following. Napoleon assured him that he would soon arrive at Dresden with 200,000 men.[75]

After sending the Guard, VI Corps, and I Cavalry Corps marching back to the Saxon theater, Napoleon formed the Army of the Bober with the forces that remained in Silesia. He named the 48-year-old Macdonald its commander. Personnel changes needed to be made to aid Macdonald's transition from corps to army commander. Very hard lessons from campaigns in Portugal, Spain, and Russia had taught Napoleon that more than one marshal spoiled the army, meaning that more than one marshal could not be assigned to an army that he did not personally command. Thus, with Macdonald being junior to Ney, the bravest of the brave had to go. Indeed, it was Ney who had been such a thorn in the side of the great André Masséna during the 1810 invasion of Portugal. Determined not to make the same mistake, Napoleon summoned Ney to join him. Souham assumed command of III Corps while Maurice-Étienne Gérard took the helm of XI Corps. Macdonald's army consisted of III, V, and XI Corps as well as II Cavalry Corps: 100,000 men according to Napoleon's estimation. To provide balance and to ease Souham's responsibility of commanding the huge III Corps, he transferred Jean-Gabriel Marchand's 39th Division to XI Corps. Macdonald's corps commanders represented a new crop of battle-hardened divisional generals eager to receive the marshal's baton. For good reason, Napoleon believed he had placed the Army of the Bober in competent hands.[76]

Although Macdonald would prove an utter failure as an independent commander, the instructions he received from the emperor and Berthier cannot be considered either difficult or complicated. Basically, the Army of the Bober would shield Napoleon's operations against the Bohemian Army in Saxony. Equally important, it had to protect the rear of Oudinot's Army of Berlin as it drove on the Prussian capital. Macdonald simply had to hold Blücher at the Bober River long enough for Napoleon to dispose of the Army of Bohemia and return to Silesia with overwhelming forces. However, Napoleon's instructions, confirmed by a second letter from Berthier, referred to the position on the Bober as defensive. In the case of a lost battle on the Bober, Macdonald would retreat to the Queis, which he would hold at all costs. Yet, should Blücher take the offensive, Macdonald did receive the authority to reciprocate. Napoleon encouraged the marshal: if he posted the army in accordance with the emperor's instructions, he could explode from Löwenberg or another point and beat back any enemy offensive. On the 23rd, Napoleon ordered tactical strikes across the Katzbach to drive Blücher beyond the Wütende (Raging) Neiße (Nysa Szalona) and to keep the Prussians guessing. But what would be next for Macdonald? Neither Napoleon nor Berthier made clear whether Macdonald should continue to drive the enemy through Jauer and then return to the Bober position, or whether he should first build the entrenchments to fortify the Bober position and then meet Blücher on a prepared battlefield. Napoleon's oversight in this matter led to the failure of his plan – a failure that ultimately would cost him Germany.[77]

Little did Napoleon know that, as he was emphasizing Macdonald's need to protect the rear of the Army of Berlin, the Prussians were successfully defending their capital against Oudinot with a "pack of bad Landwehr," to quote the emperor. As dawn broke on 23 August, the Army of Berlin converged on the Prussian capital. Tauentzien's IV Corps held Bertrand's IV Corps at Blankenfelde while Bülow's III Corps engaged Reynier's VII Corps at Großbeeren, a village eleven miles south of Berlin. After fierce hand-to-hand combat, Reynier's two Saxon divisions broke, carrying away his lone French division. Darkness fell and the battle ended with VII Corps in full retreat. During the combat, Oudinot's own XII Corps remained idle at Ahrensdorf, facing Bernadotte with his Swedes and Wintzingerode's Russian corps, which likewise did nothing. Casualties on both sides were modest, with Prussian losses numbering 159 dead, 662 wounded, 228 missing, and 6 destroyed guns. Bülow's men captured 14 guns and 52 filled caissons. Reynier's two Saxon divisions lost 20 officers and 1,918 soldiers while the French 32nd Division lost 1,138 men. Despite the low body count, Oudinot, a choice worse than Macdonald for an independent command, ordered a headlong retreat that did not stop until his army reached the safety of Wittenberg on the Elbe.[78]

In Silesia, the Prussians of Blücher's staff knew Napoleon could not pursue them indefinitely and overextend himself from Dresden. As long as the Bohemian Army advanced toward the Saxon capital, the emperor's operations in Silesia would be limited. Blücher believed that, as soon as Napoleon sensed the Silesian Army would not accept battle, he would depart for Saxony to attack Schwarzenberg. To provide time for Schwarzenberg's massive army to reach Dresden, Blücher had to distract Napoleon for as long as possible. "The question now," explained Müffling, "was what would the enemy do next. If he penetrated deeper into Silesia with such a considerable force, he would give the Bohemian Army time to gain Dresden and the line of the Elbe and, since that was the goal of our operations, we could wish for nothing more desirable. But Bonaparte could also turn back from the Bober toward Dresden; thus it was necessary to make him deploy his forces in front of us before we retreated another step."[79]

Notes

1 Quoted in Unger, *Blücher*, II:69.
2 A copy of the attack disposition can be found in Add MSS, 20112, 121.
3 Langeron to Barclay, Report on Langeron's operations from 7 August to 2 September, 2 September 1813, GStA PK, VI HA Rep. 92 Nl. Gneisenau, Nr. 18; Bogdanovich, *Geschichte des Krieges*, IIa:25.
4 Nostitz, *Tagebuch*, 54–55.
5 Müffling, *Die Feldzüge*, 15.
6 Unger, *Blücher*, II:69.
7 Bogdanovich, *Geschichte des Krieges*, IIa:1–25.

8 Müffling, *Die Feldzüge*, 15–16.
9 Friederich, *Herbstfeldzug 1813*, I:255–56.
10 Langeron made no mention in his memoirs of refusing to comply with Blücher's orders.
11 "Journal of Operations of General Sacken's Corps," in Langeron, *Mémoires*, 245; Bogdanovich, *Geschichte des Krieges*, IIa:24.
12 Freytag-Loringhoven, *Aufklärung und Armeeführung*, 31.
13 Reproduced in Droysen, *Yorck*, II:123.
14 Reproduced in Droysen, *Yorck*, II:124.
15 Quoted in Freytag-Loringhoven, *Aufklärung und Armeeführung*, 32.
16 Friederich, *Herbstfeldzug 1813*, I:259–60.
17 SHAT, C[17] 132: Charles John to Blücher, Potsdam, 16 August 1813.
18 SHAT, C[17] 132: Charles John to Blücher, Charlottenburg, 19 August 1813.
19 Barclay to Blücher, Melnick, 18 August 1813, Rossiiskii Gosudarstvennyi Voenno-Istoricheskii Arkhiv (hereafter cited as RGVIA), f. VUA, op. 16, d. 3911, ll. 125–125b.
20 Friederich, *Herbstfeldzug 1813*, I:259.
21 Langeron to Barclay, Report on Langeron's operations from 7 August to 2 September, 2 September 1813, GStA PK, VI HA Rep. 92 Nl. Gneisenau, Nr. 18; Freytag-Loringhoven, *Aufklärung und Armeeführung*, 32–33.
22 Unger, *Blücher*, II:70.
23 Friederich, *Herbstfeldzug 1813*, I:258–59.
24 Quoted in Droysen, *Yorck*, II:125.
25 Quoted in Droysen, *Yorck*, II:126. According to August von Janson of the Historical Section of the German General Staff: "Schack's journal, compared to the original reports and papers, proves ... to be a very reliable source. There exists no reason to assume that the opinion of the situation contained therein as well as the orders received are not completely in accordance with the thought process and the mood of Yorck and his entourage as it actually was at the time ... so the typical critical judgment over Blücher's arrangements is nevertheless completely and clearly genuine. If one had aspired to subsequently embellish the opinions, certainly many of the statements and thoughts would have been omitted." See Janson, "Die Unternehmungen des Yorckschen Korps," Appendix 2, 53. A portion of the journal covering the period from 11 January to 16 February 1814 can be found in GStA, PK, IV HA Rep. 15 A 234.
26 Langeron to Barclay, Report on Langeron's operations from 7 August to 2 September, 2 September 1813, GStA PK, VI HA Rep. 92 Nl. Gneisenau, Nr. 18.
27 Langeron, *Mémoires*, 233.
28 Quoted in Freytag-Loringhoven, *Aufklärung und Armeeführung*, 34.
29 Blücher to Frederick William, 20 August 1813, quoted in Friederich, *Herbstfeldzug 1813*, I:259.
30 Friederich, *Herbstfeldzug 1813*, I:255–56.
31 Odeleben's next statement that this engagement led Napoleon to assume "that the principal strength of the enemy was united there," thus making "his presence to be very necessary at that point," must refer to the concentration of Blücher's army because Napoleon knew by this time that Schwarzenberg's army formed the main host of the Allies: Odeleben, *A Circumstantial Narrative*, I:263.

32 Odeleben, *A Circumstantial Narrative*, I:264.

33 Odeleben, *A Circumstantial Narrative*, I:265; *CN*, Nos. 20425–20428, XXVI:106–07.

34 On the morning of the 21st, III Corps and II Cavalry Corps stood at Tillendorf and Birkenbrück (Brzeźnik); VI Corps at Ottendorf and Rackwitz (Rakowice Małe); V and XI Corps as well as the Young Guard at Löwenberg; the 31st Division from XI Corps at Greiffenberg, and 2nd Brigade from 5th Division of II Corps at Lauban. See Friederich, *Herbstfeldzug 1813*, I:264.

35 Four roads all on the right bank of the Bober, radiating east and south from Bunzlau, were available to Ney. Working clockwise, they were: the main highway that ran through Haynau to Breslau; the Bunzlau–Modelsdorf road, which Sacken had been ordered to take in case he had to retreat; the Bunzlau–Giersdorf road; and the Bunzlau–Löwenberg road.

36 *CN*, Nos. 20428, 20429, and 20435, XXVI:106–10; SHAT, C^{17} 179: Berthier to Ney, Marmont, Mouton, Mortier, Latour-Maubourg, Lauriston, and Friant, 21 August 1813.

37 Warburg's 5:00 A.M. report from the suburbs of Bunzlau is reproduced in reproduced in Höpfner, "Darstellung," 1844:80; Lobenthal to Gneisenau, Weinberg, 5:45 A.M., 21 August 1813, *ibid*.

38 Sohr's group consisted of two hussar squadrons, one Guard Jäger company, and the skirmishers of the 1st Battalion of the Leib Regiment: Müffling, *Die Feldzüge*, 17; Friederich, *Herbstfeldzug 1813*, I:259–60.

39 Lobenthal to Gneisenau, Weinberg, 7:15 A.M., reproduced in Höpfner, "Darstellung," 1844:80; Droysen, *Yorck*, II:126, refers to the northern hill as the Weinberg and the southern as the Plattenberg; Müffling, *Die Feldzüge*, 17–18.

40 Höpfner, "Darstellung," 1844:81; Unger, *Blücher*, II:70–71; Friederich, *Herbstfeldzug 1813*, I:262–63.

41 Langeron, *Mémoires*, 233; Höpfner, "Darstellung," 1844:82.

42 Warburg's 7:00 A.M. report is reproduced in Höpfner, "Darstellung," 1844:82; Gneisenau to Sacken, Hohlstein, 21 August 1813, reproduced *ibid.*, 82–83; Unger, *Blücher*, II:71.

43 Gneisenau to Sacken, Hohlstein, 21 August 1813, reproduced in Höpfner, "Darstellung," 1844:82–83.

44 Droysen, *Yorck*, II:126. Droysen's 1833 *Geschichte Alexanders des Grossen* (History of Alexander the Great) heralded a new school of German historical thought that idealized the power and success held by the so-called great men of history. His work on Yorck has been labeled one of the best German-language biographies. See also Friederich, *Herbstfeldzug 1813*, I:260–63.

45 Blücher to Yorck, Hohlstein, 21 August 1813, reproduced in Höpfner, "Darstellung," 1844:83.

46 Lieven, *Russia Against Napoleon*, 375–76.

47 "Journal of Operations of General Sacken's Corps," in Langeron, *Mémoires*, 245–46.

48 Sacken to Blücher, Modelsdorf, 8:30 P.M., 21 August 1813, reproduced in Höpfner, "Darstellung," 1844:88.

49 Odeleben, *A Circumstantial Narrative*, I:265–66.

50 Langeron, *Mémoires*, 234.

51 Langeron, *Mémoires*, 234.

52 "Having arrived with difficulty on the road from the village of Plagwitz to Höfel, I saw a little before the latter village the 7th Jäger Regiment joined by the 37th that marched up from Höfel attacked sharply on the flank by two (very weak) regiments of French Chasseurs-à-cheval. At the time, I had only two squadrons of the Severskii Mounted Jäger Regiment and their commander, [Luc] Denisiyev, near me. I did not have time to make clear to him the danger that my two foot Jäger regiments faced, before this brave general jumped on his horse, ordered the charge, and with his two brave and beautiful squadrons fell on the enemy cavalry with the speed of lightning, and took them in the flank, overthrew them, and disengaged the infantry": Langeron, *Mémoires*, 234–35.

53 Lieven, in *Russia Against Napoleon*, 376, mistakenly attributes Gneisenau's praise of Rudzevich's action at Siebeneichen on the 19th to the engagement at Löwenberg on the 21st.

54 Müffling, *Die Feldzüge*, 19.

55 Müffling, *Die Feldzüge*, 19; Langeron, *Mémoires*, 235–36; Gneisenau to Hardenberg, Jauer, 25 August 1813, GStA PK, I HA Rep. 74 Staatskanzleramt O Ap. Nr. 9, Bd. 3; Nostitz, *Tagebuch*, 55.

56 Langeron, *Mémoires*, 236–37.

57 Katzler's detachment consisted of eight battalions, twenty-one squadrons, and two batteries: Blücher to Yorck, Pilgramsdorf, 21 August 1813, reproduced in Höpfner, "Darstellung," 1844:89; Müffling, *Die Feldzüge*, 20; Droysen, *Yorck*, II:128.

58 Yorck's corps lost 30 officers and 1,618 men; Langeron's 11 officers and 320 men; and Sacken's 10 officers and 157 men. Langeron estimates the losses to be higher: "We lost 3,000 men, 2,600 of whom were Prussians and 400 were Russians." The account of the combat of Löwenberg is based on Langeron to Barclay, Report on Langeron's operations from 7 August to 2 September, 2 September 1813, GStA PK, VI HA Rep. 92 Nl. Gneisenau, Nr. 18; Höpfner, "Darstellung," 1844:83–87; Müffling, *Die Feldzüge*, 17–20; Beitzke, *Geschichte der deutschen Freiheitskriege*, II:169–73; Vaudoncourt, *Histoire de la guerre*, I:142–43; Bogdanovich, *Geschichte des Krieges*, IIa:28–29; Friederich, *Herbstfeldzug 1813*, I:260–68; Droysen, *Yorck*, II:127, Unger, *Blücher*, II:71–72; Langeron, *Mémoires*, 232–37.

59 Odeleben, *A Circumstantial Narrative*, I:267–68.

60 Order, Pilgramsdorf, 21 August 1813, reproduced in Höpfner, "Darstellung," 1844:89.

61 At nightfall on the 21st, III Corps and II Cavalry Corps halted at Großhartmannsdorf and Giersdorf. Lauriston's V Corps and 3rd Light Division of I Cavalry Corps occupied Deutmannsdorf, Lauterseiffen, and Petersdorf (Pieszków). The Guard, XI Corps, VI Corps and the rest of I Cavalry Corps remained on the left bank of the Bober at Sirgwitz and Löwenberg: Friederich, *Herbstfeldzug 1813*, I:268.

62 SHAT, C[17] 179: Berthier to Macdonald, Lauriston, Ney, and Ornano, 22 August 1813.

63 Müffling, *Die Feldzüge*, 21–22; Bogdanovich, *Geschichte des Krieges*, IIa:31, does not pass judgment on Langeron's actions.

64 Freytag-Loringhoven, *Aufklärung und Armeeführung*, 50.

65 Höpfner, "Darstellung," 1844:90. Per Blücher's initial order to retreat from Löwenberg, Yorck's corps marched in two columns toward Dohnau and Kroitsch, respectively, with two rearguards following. Katzler accompanied the rearguard of the southern column – fifteen squadrons, six battalions, and one battery – whose infantry Major Golz commanded.

66 Müffling, *Die Feldzüge*, 22; Langeron, *Mémoires*, 237–38.

67 Hennersdorf was less than two miles from Seichau on the road to Jauer.

68 Langeron, *Mémoires*, 238; Müffling, *Die Feldzüge*, 22–23; Bogdanovich, *Geschichte des Krieges*, Iia:31; Friederich, *Herbstfeldzug 1813*, I:271–72. Gneisenau makes no mention of this in his report to Hardenberg: Gneisenau to Hardenberg, Jauer, 25 August 1813, GSTA PK, I HA Rep. 74 Staatskanzleramt O Ap. Nr. 9, Bd. 3.

69 Alexander to Blücher, Jungfer-Teynitz, 19 August 1813, RGVIA, f. VUA, op. 16, d. 3399, ll. 7b–8; Bogdanovich, *Geschichte des Krieges*, IIa:33; Freytag-Loringhoven, *Aufklärung und Armeeführung*, 52–53; Droysen, *Yorck*, II:129.

70 Lanskoy, relieved at Polnischlissa by the lead elements of Bennigsen's Army of Poland, crossed the Oder on 20 and 21 August. He received orders to reach Haynau on the 21st with his lead squadrons.

71 Friederich, *Herbstfeldzug 1813*, I:269.

72 Odeleben, *A Circumstantial Narrative*, 268–69.

73 *CN*, No. 20445, XXVI:118–19.

74 SHAT, C^{17} 179: Berthier to Corbineau, Mouton, Mortier, Latour-Maubourg, and Marmont, 23 August 1813.

75 *CN*, Nos. 29437, 20440, 20443, 20445, and 20446, XXVI:112, 114, 117–20; SHAT, C^{17} 179: Berthier to Victor and Vandamme, 23 August 1813.

76 *CN*, Nos. 20440–20442, XXVI:114; SHAT, C^{17} 179: Berthier to Ney, Macdonald, Souham, and Gérard, 23 August 1813.

77 Napoleon's instructions clearly identify Macdonald's position along the Bober as defensive. Three divisions from III Corps would guard Bunzlau; Napoleon wanted all approaches thoroughly entrenched. Three divisions of XI Corps would hold Löwenberg and cover the Hirse, Luften, and Senften hills with entrenchments. For the easy and rapid crossing of the Bober, the emperor ordered the construction of three solid bridges. Lauriston's V Corps would occupy Hirschberg and echelon its divisions toward Löwenberg. With the Bober forming the line of communication between Bunzlau and Hirschberg, Napoleon demanded that the river be carefully guarded against a surprise attack. One division from III Corps would fall back to a fortified position between the Queis and the Bober while Marchand's 39th Division entrenched itself in the principal positions on the Queis: Naumburg, Lauban, and Greiffenberg. Strong combined-arms detachments would be posted on each flank to patrol ceaselessly and prevent Blücher from wheeling around the army. Although the emperor prescribed the building of numerous fortifications on both the Bober and the Queis, he wanted the army to remain mobile and ready to march. All corps would receive eight to ten days of provisions. As Macdonald's main supply depot, Lauban had to be entrenched and defended by redoubts on the surrounding hills. Napoleon did not want Blücher to

exploit the gap between Macdonald's left and the Oder to threaten the Army of
Berlin, or hug the Riesengebirge and squeeze past Macdonald's right to get to
Lusatia and Saxony. Should Blücher attempt to outflank Macdonald's left,
Napoleon instructed the marshal to unite all of his cavalry and one infantry division
on his left wing and as a flying corps have it observe the enemy so he could not
drive toward Berlin between him and the Oder. See *CN*, Nos. 20442 and 20443,
XXVI:115–18; SHAT, C¹⁷ 179: Berthier to Macdonald, 23 August 1813; Jomini, *Vie
politique et militaire de Napoléon*, VI:18–19; Petre, *Napoleon's Last Campaign*,
189–90. Although Jomini claims that Berthier received orders from Napoleon to
instruct Macdonald to take advantage of the opportunity to fall on the Allies with
his forces united, the documentary evidence does not support this.

78 See Leggiere, *Napoleon and Berlin*, 160–77.
79 Müffling, *Die Feldzüge*, 21.

5

Goldberg

As the Reichenbach Plan deferred the initiative to Napoleon, the Army of Bohemia could do little until Allied High Command determined the emperor's intentions. To this end, Austrian intelligence proved totally inadequate during the last weeks of the armistice. Having almost no news of Napoleon, Schwarzenberg could only hope that the emperor would not cross the Erzgebirge before the Russians and Prussians arrived from Silesia. Aside from knowing very little of Napoleon's intentions, the Austrians possessed only a vague idea of his troop dispositions along the Bohemian frontier. After allocating sufficient forces to other theaters, they assumed that 151,000 men out of a total of 413,000 would remain at Napoleon's immediate disposal for an invasion of Bohemia. Yet to everyone's surprise, the French gave no indication of conducting such an operation. By the time a council of war convened at Melnik on 17 August, most Allied commanders believed Napoleon would attack Bernadotte rather than invade Bohemia. Reports confirmed the concentration of large imperial forces for an offensive against Berlin. Although intelligence placed Napoleon at Bunzlau, spies reported that French authorities expected him to arrive at Görlitz from where he would turn north to Cottbus and direct the drive on the Prussian capital. While the emperor conducted his "master plan," imperial forces along the Bohemian frontier and in Silesia would mask the Allied armies facing them. According to the Reichenbach Plan, the Army of Bohemia should respond by crossing the Erzgebirge. While the Army of North Germany retreated ahead of Napoleon's offensive, Schwarzenberg would either take Dresden or march on Leipzig to sever French communications.

At Melnik, however, Schwarzenberg raised the possibility of Napoleon taking a central position at Leipzig. There, he would observe the approach of the Bohemian and North German Armies, waiting to exploit the first mistake made by either Allied army. Just as in Italy in 1796, he would utilize

Zusammenkunft der drei Monarchen bei Prag.
Sie einen sich zu Brüder   Europa athmet wieder

7 The three Allied monarchs at Prague, August 1813

his interior lines to defeat each army in detail. From this supposition emerged the idea that the French would oppose the Allies as they attempted to debouch through the passes of the Erzgebirge where the mountain roads ran almost perpendicular to the vital communication artery that ran from Dresden through Freiberg, Chemnitz, and Plauen to South Germany. In order for Napoleon to maintain communication with his German allies, it appeared logical for him to take a position at either Chemnitz or Freiberg. This led to the decision to divide the Bohemian Army into four columns for an offensive against Leipzig. Three would cross the Erzgebirge and make for the city while the fourth column debouched on Pirna and Königstein to cover Schwarzenberg's right flank (see Map 1).[1]

Both Radetzky and Jomini objected, with the former proposing that Schwarzenberg wait for Napoleon to invade Bohemia and then pounce on his columns as they debouched from the Erzgebirge. Yet at Melnik, Schwarzenberg's views attracted the support of Tsar Alexander as well as the Russian and Prussian generals. But at Prague on 18 August, Allied High Command learned that Napoleon had left Dresden on the 15th and proceeded to Bautzen, presumably to continue through Görlitz to Silesia. News that Napoleon had gone east made it imperative to undertake a more immediate demonstration to relieve the pressure on Blücher.

Thus, a drive on Dresden surfaced in Allied plans as an afterthought to assist the Silesian Army. On 19 August, Alexander, Francis, and Frederick William departed from Prague and reached Komotau (Chomutov). News arrived on the following day of Napoleon's appearance at the Zittau Pass on 18 August. These tidings convinced the Allies to postpone the offensive against Leipzig and instead advance on Dresden. Thus, the "Grand Army" of Bohemia crossed the Saxon frontier in four columns on 22 August. On the far right, Wittgenstein and Kleist led their respective corps through the Peterswald defile, twenty-five miles south of Dresden. After clearing the pass, they struck the great highway that led to the Saxon capital. Running parallel to the Elbe, this direction required the Allies to blockade the fort at Königstein and attack the entrenched camp at Pirna. Wittgenstein accomplished both tasks on the 22nd. After masking Königstein, the Russian vanguard carried the lines of Pirna with the bayonet. The French troops of XIV Corps withdrew to Dresden. Schwarzenberg's three other columns likewise crossed the Saxon frontier; all four converged on Dresden.

In Silesia, the Army of the Bober received the task of pushing across the Katzbach on the 23rd to cover the emperor's departure. Napoleon ordered V Corps to take Goldberg while XI Corps moved across the Katzbach on its left. North of XI Corps, part of II Cavalry Corps would advance directly to Liegnitz while the main body rode to Grosnig (Leśniki) and Rothkirch (Czerwony Kościół), four and five miles southwest of Liegnitz respectively. For reasons unknown, Ney did not receive Berthier's letter summoning him to Imperial Headquarters and transferring command of III Corps to Souham. As a result, he sent three of his divisions marching east on the east–west highway to Liegnitz while the other two joined Sébastiani's cavalry at Rothkirch (see Map 2).[2]

Blücher did not receive word of Lanskoy's mishap at Haynau until noon on the 23rd. Had he learned of it earlier, his plans for the 23rd would have been different. Instead, a report arrived from the single Brandenburg Hussar squadron remaining on the left bank of the Katzbach. According to one of its patrols led by a noncommissioned officer that had circumnavigated the Gröditzberg, the French III Corps had not advanced toward Goldberg. Moreover, the patrol did not encounter any imperial forces behind the French right wing at Ulbersdorf. Consequently, Blücher and his staff made preparations to hold Goldberg and the line of the Katzbach on the 23rd. Just east of the river, Goldberg sat at the foot of the Wolfs hill, an isolated height that mastered the surrounding terrain especially to the east, thus making its

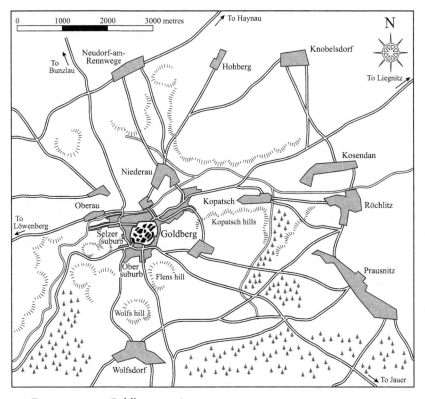

11. Engagement at Goldberg, 23 August 1813

possession invaluable for Goldberg's defense. Ranging between ten and twelve feet in height, Goldberg's medieval wall as well as its accompanying embankment and trench ringed the entire town. Four gates and three emergency exits breached Goldberg's old walls. The roads running west to Löwenberg and Bunzlau converged at the Selzer Gate on the west side of Goldberg. A stone bridge carried the highway from Löwenberg across the Katzbach while the road from Bunzlau spanned a wooden structure. On the southwest side of Goldberg, roads to Löwenberg and Hirschberg departed from the Ober Gate. Roads south could be found outside the Friedrich Gate while the Niederau Gate received travelers from points to the north and east. Between these two gates rose the gentle Flens hill chain that overlooked the eastern side of Goldberg. Extensive suburbs surrounded all four gates. Wooded hills flanked the town to the south and southeast while the terrain leveled to the north to favor cavalry operations. North of Goldberg extended the undulating Silesian plain. Rocky hills bordered the steep valleys of the Katzbach and its tributaries. Dominating points and plateaus randomly jutted upward.[3]

Golz received instructions to occupy the town with four battalions while the remaining three took a position on the Flens hill supported by ten guns. Katzler placed his six squadrons at the eastern feet of the Flens hill. Around 6:00 A.M. on the 23rd, Blücher instructed Kaptsevich to occupy the Flens hill to provide closer support for the Prussians at Goldberg. Langeron's main body, consisting of VI and IX Infantry Corps, moved up to Prausnitz, where the corps commander arrived shortly after daybreak. He placed General Korf's Reserve Cavalry west of the Flens hill. Further west, Rudzevich occupied the Wolfs hill with the four battalions of the 29th and 45th Jäger Regiments. To protect the left flank, the Arkhangelogorodskii and Staroingermanlandskii Infantry Regiments held the village of Wolfsdorf (Wilków) south of the Wolfs hill. Eighteen guns supported the infantry; the three regiments of the 2nd Ukrainskii Cossack Regiment and six squadrons of Mounted Jäger formed echelons between Wolfsdorf and Goldberg. In the open terrain northeast of Goldberg stood two more Jäger regiments, with the rest of X Infantry Corps (four battalions and eighteen guns) somewhat further behind on the Kopatsch hills. Langeron dispatched two infantry regiments to Konradswaldau (Kondratów), seven miles southeast of Goldberg. "As we assumed the enemy wanted to turn our left via Konradswaldau," he recounted, "which is the shortest route to take from Goldberg to Jauer, and since there I had only four squadrons[4] under the orders of General [Andrey] Umanets, I ordered General Talyzin II to march there with the Moskovskii and Libavskii Infantry Regiments, and I put this entire detachment under the orders of General Count Pavel Pahlen [known as Pahlen II]."

Blücher ordered Yorck to post one brigade less than one mile north of Goldberg at Niederau to prevent the enemy from moving into the Katzbach valley between Goldberg and Röchlitz. At 7:00 A.M., Yorck dispatched the 6,400 men and 8 guns of Prince Karl's 2nd Brigade from Niederkrayn. The wet summer weather had been unfavorable for several days but on 23 August the rain fell in torrents, making small-arms fire almost impossible. Morale plummeted as the troops dragged themselves through the clay mud. The Landwehr particularly suffered; many had to surrender their boots to the uncompromising muck. Karl posted one battalion at the Röchlitz cemetery to secure his retreat across the Katzbach. Next, he forwarded the Fusilier battalions of the 1st and 2nd East Prussian Regiments, both commanded by Lieutenant-Colonel Sjöholm, into the steep Katzbach valley west of Niederau; two squadrons of Brandenburg Uhlans and one squadron of Landwehr cavalry joined them. The prince intended to take a position facing west and parallel to the Haynau–Goldberg road with the left wing anchored on Niederau and the right on Hohberg.

This still did not satisfy a restless Blücher. With each hour his anxiety increased as he waited for news that the French army had departed for Saxony. According to Langeron: "Our spies told us that, having failed in his plan to force us into a general battle at Löwenberg, Napoleon had left for Dresden, but we were not at all certain of this." A report from a reliable agent stating that large imperial columns had marched through Bunzlau toward Görlitz provided the last straw for Blücher. At 8:00 A.M., he signed orders changing the day's operation from a defensive to an offensive that sought to envelop the French corps west of Goldberg and place the army in a position to pursue the withdrawing imperials. "Having received the news that one part of the French army that had been facing me at Löwenberg had retired to take another direction," Blücher informed Bernadotte, "I resolved to attack the enemy today to oblige him to deploy his forces."[5]

To envelop the French corps, he directed Yorck to march east to Ulbersdorf on the Schnelle Deichsel from where cavalry and horse artillery would continue to Neuwiese. Yorck's right wing and Reserve Cavalry would move to Pilgramsdorf (see Map 2). Leaving one brigade and one heavy battery in reserve on the hills east of Pilgramsdorf, Yorck instructed both of his wings to descend on the French corps between Pilgramsdorf and Goldberg. Sacken received instructions to march east from Schmogwitz through Adelsdorf to the Gröditzberg. To shield Yorck's rear, Blücher wanted Sacken to take a defensive position, blocking the roads running from Bunzlau and Löwenberg to Neudorf-am-Gröditzberg. Having not yet received news of Lanskoy's troubles, the disposition called for this general to advance from Haynau toward Bunzlau with Sacken's light cavalry. As soon as Yorck's cannonade announced the arrival of I Corps, Langeron, whom Blücher would accompany, would advance against the French from the east.[6] Although the term had yet to be invented, Blücher sought to boil the enemy corps to a pulp in a *Kesselschlacht* (cauldron battle).

A mere hour sufficed to shake Blücher from this beautiful dream. Instead of receiving a confirmed report on the departure of the French army to Saxony, he learned of the approach of large imperial columns toward Goldberg as well as Neudorf-am-Rennwege (Nowa Wieś Złotoryjska), three miles north of Goldberg. Almost at the same time, Sacken reported Lanskoy's setback at Haynau, adding the news of a French advance on Seifersdorf, nine miles north of Goldberg. "Just when I wanted to leave to join the troops," Blücher explained, "I received a report from Sacken that Lanskoy had been attacked at Haynau and driven from the road to Liegnitz; furthermore, that the enemy had directed an attack on Seifersdorf." The *coup de grâce* for Blücher's plans came with the report that very superior forces had engaged Yorck's 2nd Brigade at Niederau. A captured French captain claimed that he had seen Napoleon that morning. "At the same time [that Sacken's report arrived]," stated Blücher in his after-action report, "I received news from Yorck's forward posts that a very large enemy was marching ... toward Neudorf, and the combat by Langeron's corps was growing ever more intense. All of these circumstances indicated that by executing my disposition I could not avoid a battle and, because under the current circumstances I did not know the true strength of my adversary, I decided to remain at the Katzbach and await the deployment of the enemy's forces."[7]

French columns seemed to appear out of nowhere. "Just as we were in the process of executing our attack, the enemy assaulted us at Goldberg while 50,000 men advanced toward Liegnitz," reported Gneisenau. "Our mission made us cautious as a rule." Blücher ordered Sacken to Seifersdorf. If he did not encounter resistance there, he would proceed to Adelsdorf to cover Yorck's left flank and rear. Yorck received orders to move up I Corps to support Karl's 2nd Brigade but to delay committing his brigades until Sacken's corps reached its position. Blücher joined Langeron on the hills east of Goldberg, where he received another report from Sacken written at 11:15 A.M. telling of an enemy column of unknown strength moving against his rear from Liegnitz. Blücher brushed it off, believing that this mystery column could not reach Goldberg on that day or threaten the retreat to Jauer if it became necessary. Obviously, he thought only of a retreat from Goldberg as this column would prevent Sacken from marching in any other direction. Just before leaving Niederkrayn, Blücher dictated a report to Allied Headquarters about the recent events:

> On the 22nd, the entire army stood concentrated with the left wing behind Pilgramsdorf and the right behind Adelsdorf. In this position I expected an enemy attack on Pilgramsdorf, which resulted around noon when the enemy deployed some 15,000 men for the battle. Langeron's corps marched east behind the defile of the Katzbach at Goldberg; I expected any moment the report of an attack on my right wing but that never occurred. Toward evening, I received the news from my advance posts that the enemy had withdrew toward Bunzlau. I awaited confirmation and received this on 23 August through reconnaissance. After receiving it, I issued the accompanying disposition. The troops are already marching and just now the sound of cannon fire by Goldberg signals that the enemy is attacking the six Prussian battalions left behind in the city. I now go to the troops and will send a courier to you immediately after the engagement.[8]

Lauriston's V Corps assaulted both Goldberg and the Wolfs hill. His vanguard crossed the stone bridge over the Katzbach and entered the Selzer suburb only to be repulsed by three Silesian Landwehr companies that were seeing action for the first time. The French fell back to the hills west of the Selzer and Ober suburbs, directing the fire of their skirmishers against the Prussians with little effect. French artillery from the hills on the northern edge of the Katzbach valley poured salvos into the two suburbs. Meanwhile, Rochambeau's 19th Division crossed the Katzbach slightly northwest of the Wolfs hill and drove Rudzevich's two Jäger regiments from the height.

Rochambeau immediately moved his artillery onto the Wolfs hill. From the Flens hill and Wolfsdorf, Russian and Prussian battalions failed on several attempts to retake the Wolfs hill. Each time the Allies drove the imperials against the Wolfs hill, the latter countered with greater numbers. Situated on the Kopatsch hills, Kaptsevich's X Infantry Corps prevented them from passing between Goldberg and Rudzevich's troops at Wolfsdorf. Yet Allied losses mounted: one Silesian Landwehr battalion that started the day with 524 men under arms came back with only 258 survivors.

Russian dragoons, Mounted Jäger, and the 2nd and 3rd Ukrainskii Cossack Regiments executed numerous charges to slow the French advance. Regardless, the imperials mastered Wolfsdorf as large bodies of enemy cavalry started working around Rudzevich's left. Langeron reinforced Kaptsevich with four battalions from General Pyotr Kornilov's 15th Division of IX Infantry Corps and the twelve guns of the heavy artillery battery belonging to VI Infantry Corps. Nevertheless, an attempt to retake the Wolfs hill misfired. An extremely intense firefight ensued for several hours as additional imperial troops arrived. On the other side of Goldberg, combat also lasted for many hours. Finally, as flames engulfed the Selzer and Ober suburbs, the Prussians withdrew to Goldberg's outworks. After expending their ammunition, they retreated into the town. The French followed but withering fire from Goldberg's walls halted their advance. This scene repeated itself at the Friedrich gate. Stalemate ensued on all three sides of Goldberg.

At 2:00, Katzler informed Golz that the Wolfs hill could not be retaken: Goldberg would have to be evacuated. Just before the last Prussian battalion pulled out, Blücher's adjutant, Oppen, arrived with news that 2nd Brigade had held its ground at Niederau. He insisted that Goldberg be held at all costs. Golz turned his men around and reentered the town just as the French broke through the Ober gate. The Prussians fixed their bayonets, huddled shoulder to shoulder, and charged down a narrow lane, driving the French beyond the gate. As Golz secured Goldberg, the fighting around the Wolfs hill still raged. Rudzevich and Kornilov fell back to the Flens hill pursued by imperial infantry and cavalry. Finally, Blücher's orders for a general retreat toward Jauer arrived: the 2nd Brigade could no longer hold on at Niederau.

The action at Niederau began at 9:30 when three large imperial columns approached from Ulbersdorf and Neudorf-am-Rennwege. Having already detached three battalions, the prince deployed his remaining seven in two waves. The first contained two battalions of the 6th Silesian Landwehr Infantry Regiment on the left and two battalions from the 2nd East Prussian Infantry Regiment on the right. In the second wave, a third battalion from the 6th Silesian Landwehr formed on the left while the two remaining battalions of the 1st East Prussian Regiment moved up on the right. Thus, Karl's left wing consisted solely of Silesian militia. He divided his brigade artillery into half-batteries, placing one on each flank. Hardly had the brigade deployed when the French unlimbered thirty guns along the Goldberg–Haynau road and peppered the length of the Prussian position. After silencing the half-battery on the Prussian right, the French concentrated their fire on the Line infantry, which stood completely exposed on the open plain. Horrendous losses rocked the East Prussians until they moved out of range. During the bombardment, a French column drove the skirmishers of the 1st Battalion of the 1st East Prussian Regiment from the burning wreck of Hohberg. French cavalry attacked the East Prussians during their retreat but the Mecklenburg Hussars launched a successful counterattack to save them.

On Karl's left, one French column reached Niederau and continued toward an extensive compound of military barracks that had been used during the armistice. Not only did the compound provide cover, but it also allowed the imperials to work around the Prussian left. Having preserved his ammunition for the decisive moment, the junior officer who commanded the left half-battery – Lieutenant Stern – allowed the column to approach. Firing canister at 400 paces, the Russians sent the imperials reeling back to Niederau. Their blasts quickly attracted counterbattery fire from the French guns. Shell and shot rained down on the half-battery as well as the 4th Battalion of the 6th Silesian Landwehr directly behind it. Its commander likewise pulled his men out of range. Only the frantic efforts of its officers enabled it to resume its position at the end of the line just in time for a shell to exploded in its midst; the men broke and fled in every direction.[9] Despite the collapse of this battalion, the other two militia battalions posted on the left wing held their position while absorbing devastating losses.

Perceiving their adversary to be shaken, the French launched two attack columns, each with between 1,000 and 1,200 men, against the Prussian right wing. Lobenthal ordered the 1st Battalion of the 2nd East Prussian Regiment to fix bayonets. Supported by the second wave's 2nd Battalion of the 1st East Prussian Regiment, it repulsed the French. No sooner had the French infantry yielded when imperial cavalry swarmed the two Prussian battalions. Both suffered considerable losses during this attack. Meanwhile, on the left wing, the French reoccupied the compound and pushed forward skirmishers to harry the gunners of Stern's half-battery. Their steady fire forced the half-battery to withdraw to the rear, where the sole surviving gun from the right half-battery joined it. Stern soon returned to the line, moving from position to position and pouring canister into the ranks of the imperials.

8 2nd Battalion of the 1st East Prussian Infantry Regiment at Goldberg,
23 August 1813

As French guns continued to mow down the Prussians, the infantry
moved up and directed murderous fire at the left wing's remaining battalion –
the 3rd of the 6th Silesian Landwehr Regiment; soon it began to waver. To its
right stood the 2nd Battalion of the 2nd East Prussian Regiment, which also
started to dissolve in chaos. Karl moved up the 2nd Battalion of the 6th
Silesian Landwehr from the second wave into the first. Observing the
approach of three French columns, Karl likewise ordered an advance. The
men of his 2nd Battalion of the 6th Silesian Landwehr fixed bayonets and
marched forward. With its order restored, the 3rd Battalion of the 6th
Silesian Landwehr followed as well as the "shamed" East Prussians.
Together they repulsed the French attack. Close-quarter fighting resulted
in the use of the musket-butt by both sides. The arrival of fresh imperial
forces halted the Prussian advance.

   To end the stalemate, Karl gave Sjöholm permission to attempt to take the
compound and envelop the French right with the Fusilier Battalion of the 2nd
East Prussian Regiment. He also granted Sjöholm's request for the support of
the two Landwehr battalions that formed his left wing. After the militia

9 Prince Carl of Mecklenburg at Goldberg, 23 August 1813

marched south to unite with the fusiliers, a huge gap opened between the four battalions of the right wing and the edge of the Katzbach valley. To close it, Karl ordered a general movement to the valley's edge. Hoping to break the vulnerable Prussians as they marched, French cavalry attacked numerous times. Two large infantry columns also advanced at the double-quick and closed on the Prussians. At the last minute, the East Prussians discharged a full volley into their ranks and then surged forward with the bayonet. The attackers fell back, pursued by the 2nd Battalion of the 1st East Prussian Regiment. The hunters soon became the hunted as French cavalry supported by intense artillery fire drove them back. The four remaining guns of the brigade battery had to be saved by a bayonet attack on the part of the 2nd Battalion of the 2nd East Prussian Regiment. French cavalry immediately descended on the Prussian battalion, which formed a square. Followed by his small staff, Karl came streaming toward it, shouting: "Battalion march!" He then seized its standard and roared: "Now's the time, East Prussians!" With a "Hurrah," the battalion charged and repulsed the French cavalry.[10]

While the prince of Mecklenburg struggled to save his four remaining battalions, Sjöholm broke into the compound. Bitter hand-to-hand fighting ensued until the French detachment withdrew. During the melee, Sjöholm lost control of his men; all three Prussian battalions pursued the imperials onto the open plain. Attacked on all sides by French cavalry, the disorganized Prussians would have been shredded if not for the timely charge of two

Brandenburg Uhlan squadrons supported by a regiment of Don Cossacks. Under their protection, Sjöholm re-formed the battalions as best he could and withdrew across the Katzbach.

The exhausted survivors of Karl's 2nd Brigade made yet another stand at Röchlitz. Yorck moved up to support Karl with his other brigades but less than one hour from Goldberg he received Blücher's order to retreat to the Wütende Neiße, which he had left just a few hours earlier. Indignant by nature, Yorck raged over this order, shouting that "the strength – indeed the very lives – of the men was being treated like 'child's play.'"[11] Leaving Hünerbein's 8th Brigade at Laasnig to receive the 2nd Brigade, Yorck turned his columns south on the road to Jauer. By the time Karl received Blücher's order to retreat – around 2:00 in the afternoon – he had lost 28 officers and 1,747 men. In a five-hour struggle that prevented the enemy from penetrating the Katzbach valley, the Prussian 2nd Brigade repulsed every attack by two French divisions (35th and 36th of XI Corps), supported by 3rd Light Division of I Cavalry Corps, altogether around 18,000 combatants. The brigade earned great praise as well as Blücher's acclaim. According to Gneisenau, the Russian generals spoke with amazement about the performance of the Prussians during this engagement. The next day, Yorck greeted Karl with the solemn words: "Up to now you have worn the Order of the Black Eagle as the king's brother-in-law; yesterday you earned it."[12]

Against Blücher's center, more imperial troops streamed south from Neudorf-am-Rennwege toward Karl's exhausted brigade. On his left, the size of the force attacking the Wolfs hill could not be determined. With French columns reportedly marching to Liegnitz and Seifersdorf on his right, Blücher recognized that retaking the Goldberg sector did not warrant the risk of becoming embroiled in a general battle. He could have committed all of Langeron's corps to retake the Wolfs hill but thought better of escalating the engagement with an adversary whose strength he did not know. Moreover, prisoners claimed that Napoleon remained with the army. Although it tore at every fiber of his being, he ordered the army to retreat along both banks of the Wütende Neiße in the general direction of Jauer. "After having seen the forces that the enemy deployed, Blücher could believe that Napoleon still faced him, and so ordered me to retreat at 3:00 P.M.," recalled Langeron.

From Goldberg, Golz's Prussians and Kaptsevich's Russians withdrew toward Jauer covered by fifteen Prussian squadrons under Katzler as well as Korf's entire Reserve Cavalry. General Yevstafy Udom's 9th Division of General Nikolay Olsufiyev's IX Infantry Corps took a position west of the narrow Prausnitz defile to facilitate the retreat. Olsufiyev, Udom, and their staunch Russian warriors held the imperials for more than two hours before retreating to Seichau, where Langeron's VI Infantry Corps received them. Blücher lingered in the skirmishing line until the very last so that his personal opposition to the retreat would be known to the troops. "I found Langeron's vanguard embroiled in a very intense skirmish," continued

Blücher in his after-action report. "Many times the Russian and Prussian battalions took the Wolfs hill near Goldberg with much bravery, and the affair here probably would have had a positive outcome had not the cohesion of the whole, the nature of the circumstances, and still more the prime directive [Barclay's instructions] demanded that I break off the battle." Langeron claimed that "Blücher, who came over to me during the combat and remained with the rearguard, was full of praise for the bravery and good order of my troops and for the courage, the cold-bloodedness, and satisfactory arrangements of the generals. He continuously shouted: 'Oh, how beautiful,' and clapped his hands. By the second retrograde movement he forgot himself completely, remained immobile, and said repeatedly: 'Oh, how beautiful!' I had to wake him from his admiration and inform him that if he had stayed with the front line five minutes longer, he could repeat his enthusiasm to the enemy. This anecdote perfectly paints the value and love of his work which so eminently distinguished Blücher."[13]

The day's fighting at Goldberg cost the Allies 1,883 men; in round figures: 1,500 Russians and 400 Prussians. Fortunately for them, an intense French pursuit ended at Prausnitz. Altogether, the Silesian Army sustained more than 4,000 casualties during the engagements on the 23rd. The performance of the artillery and the numerous charges by the cavalry favorably impressed Blücher. He claimed imperial losses were "very considerable" and that Cossacks had killed a French general. According to his estimate, the Silesian Army had fought six "sharp" combats in seven days and sustained 6,000 to 7,000 casualties. "The infantry is a little fatigued but the whole army has only one desire: to fight the enemy."[14]

Due to the presence of Ney's infantry and Sébastiani's cavalry around Liegnitz, Sacken received instructions to withdraw to Malitsch, less than five miles due north of Jauer on the main road to Liegnitz. Yorck's corps retreated south to Schlaupe (Słup) on the Wütende Neiße some six miles northwest of Jauer. Gneisenau directed Langeron's corps to Hennersdorf, a few miles southwest of Schlaupe. This order immediately earned Gneisenau the native Frenchman's denigration for having summoned him to Goldberg that morning.[15] Müffling noted that "now, after marching and countermarching the whole night, a strong march again had to be made. This caused much discontent. General Langeron had wanted to stay [at Jauer], but as this did not occur he now believed that this new countermarch clearly proved how completely unnecessary it had been for him to return to Goldberg the previous night."[16] Langeron also expressed renewed concern for his flank and suggested to Blücher that the retreat continue all the way to Schweidnitz. Blücher viewed such a measure as drastic and premature. In addition, he also became suspicious of the goal of this powerful French advance through Silesia under the personal direction of the emperor. Could this be an attempt by Napoleon to reach the Silesian mountain passes into Bohemia, swing south through them, and then march west to catch an unsuspecting Schwarzenberg from behind? In this case, if Blücher withdrew too deep into Silesia a single corps could mask his army while Napoleon turned south and crossed the Riesengebirge without the Prussians knowing. Even if Blücher maintained constant contact with the French while he retreated, Napoleon could gain an advantage of several days (see Map 2).

Based on this concern, Blücher needed to pin the French in Silesia. Consequently, at midnight on 23/24 August, he sent a request to Bennigsen, who had already informed him of his approach, to move all available units of the Army of Poland across the Oder to strike the rear of the French army in Silesia. At the same time, Gneisenau drafted instructions for his successor as military governor of Silesia, Friedrich Wilhelm Leopold von Gaudi, to mobilize the Landsturm and to accelerate work on an entrenched camp at Neiße. This letter is equally instructive as a snapshot of how the Prussians viewed the impact of the other Allied armies on the situation in Silesia:

> The emperor Napoleon has continued the offensive against the combined army in Silesia with six army corps. Accordingly, there have been almost daily combats; those yesterday and today at Goldberg were very considerable and involved large losses on both sides. In compliance with the general operations plan, the combined army will continue to retreat: today it will be in the camp at Jauer; if the enemy deploys considerable strength before my front, it will withdraw from here through Schweidnitz and continue the retreat to Neiße if the operations of the Grand Army of Bohemia do not ultimately cause a change here. As this does not appear to be the case, and both the crown prince of Sweden and General Bennigsen have made no operation to benefit us, we have no choice but to implement every measure at our disposal to offer the enemy as much resistance as possible. Accordingly, I request that you mobilize the Landsturm in those parts of the province that will be in the rear and the flanks of the enemy, and to execute this measure as vigorously as possible.

Regarding the camp at Neiße, Blücher wrote: "I thank you for the appropriate measures you have taken thus far, which your letter of the 22nd mentions, and upon which I return the following instructions: The construction of the main entrenchments of the camp at Neiße must be accelerated as much as possible. General Gneisenau already has discussed this with Colonel [Johann August] von Harroy de Techreaux and explained his ideas to him; the camp will be constructed to accommodate around 50,000 men exclusive of the fortress's garrison." Blücher also explained how he intended to increase the garrisons of Glatz, Neiße, Schweidnitz, Kosel, and Silberberg through both Landwehr and Line battalions. His letter requested the provisioning of the fortresses and the removal of the cavalry depots. All replacements for I Corps were to be directed to Neiße (see Map 7).[17]

On the evening of the 23rd, Army Headquarters decided that Yorck should continue his retreat to Jauer. One of Blücher's adjutants, Count Friedrich Franz von Moltke, delivered the instructions to I Corps at sundown. Not only did this order require another night march but the wording of the letter, which was dictated by Gneisenau, further infuriated Yorck. "Langeron has moved into his camp between Hennersdorf and Seichau, and I thus kindly request that you establish yours by the local gallows." Yorck sensed a degree of spitefulness in being assigned to the "*Galgenberg* [gallows hill]." He did not share this letter with his staff, and the journal of I Corps simply and incorrectly notes: "verbal orders delivered by Count Moltke."[18]

An abominable night march ensued for the men of I Corps. Moving south in the dark, Steinmetz's 1st Brigade struck the wrong roads, veered too far east, and collided with Langeron's baggage en route to Schweidnitz via Jauer. Droysen claims that Steinmetz forced the Russian drivers "to make room for his troops to pass, yet the wagons returned before all had gotten through. One company opened its way with the bayonet but two Landwehr battalions and the East Prussian Grenadiers became cut off and wandered around for a much longer time." While the Prussians most likely did not turn their bayonets against the Russian *traîners*, the resulting mess took hours to clear.[19] Several of Yorck's battalions remained entangled with the Russian wagon trains until late in the night. Order collapsed and many men, especially the Landwehr, dropped from exhaustion. Entire companies dissolved in the chaos. Hungry, tired and soaked, Yorck's soldiers staggered into their bivouacs early on the 24th, finding neither wood nor straw. His rearguard camped at Altjauer (Stary Jawor), the main body on Jauer's *Galgenberg*. Horn and Hünerbein reached the gallows "in the pitch-dark of night and in apparent disorder," wrote Schack in his journal. The Prussian Reserve Cavalry and those units from Steinmetz's brigade that made it through bivouacked with Sacken's men at Profen (Mściwojów) in pouring rain.[20]

The condition of I Corps appalled Yorck. After "an incessant rain had largely inundated the land," innumerable rivulets, swollen by the summer rains, rolled like torrents from the mountains. As a result, the men continuously waded through water that reached their knees. "At night, each bivouac was made in ankle-deep mud and mire while the rain fell without intermission. Supplies could not be brought up and the army suffered privations."[21] Yorck believed that his corps would be completely ruined by the fatiguing marches, incessant exertions, and appalling weather before it saw battle. During the early hours of the 24th, he dispatched every staff officer to help reorganize the troops. In the midst of the confusion, Jürgaß reported the approach of two enemy columns from Liegnitz. Army Headquarters insisted that this had to be a false alarm. Fortunately for Yorck, this proved true, as I Corps was incapable of resistance. Yet, always doubting the news that came from Blücher, Yorck had the 2nd Leib Hussars reconnoiter northwards on the morning of the 24th. Failing to find any trace of the enemy, they returned to Profen. After reading his report, Yorck angrily said to their commander, Major Stößel, "I have no hussars."[22]

During the night of 23/24 August, Langeron's rearguard halted at Seichau, the main body at Hennersdorf. Sacken's rearguard stopped at Malitsch while his main body continued to Profen, less than five miles east of Jauer. Yorck himself went to Profen, quartering in a dilapidated farmhouse while Sacken enjoyed the amenities of the local Schloß. Pahlen III's position did not change from the previous day except that St.-Priest returned to resume command of the corps and Pahlen departed to command the cavalry corps attached to Wittgenstein's army corps. Blücher and his staff spent the night of 23/24 August at Jauer debating what to do next. Around 8:00, Blücher signed his name to orders that instructed Langeron not to yield Hennersdorf without his express order. In particular, a French attempt to turn the army's left concerned the Prussians. With the roads through Konradswaldau and Schönau observed by Langeron's patrols, Blücher emphasized the importance of vigilance and prudence: "Under no circumstance can you abandon your current position before the enemy deploys in strength before your front and I have given the firm and clear order for you to depart. You will inform me of what occurs in your front and your flank in a timely manner. Upon the first artillery round that falls on your front I will mount my horse and quickly join you. Today the enemy showed us weak forces and we cannot provide an answer to our sovereigns for unnecessarily retreating before a weak force." "All is quiet here and all the troops are in camp," responded Langeron at 9:00 P.M. He informed Blücher that four squadrons held Konradswaldau with three Cossack regiments prowling to the north and east. Four battalions and four guns had just departed from Hennersdorf to take post there. He also reported that French forces did not appear to be pursuing from Liegnitz (see Map 2).[23]

One hour after issuing orders to Langeron, Blücher dictated his afteraction report to Allied Headquarters; the letter offers tremendous insight into Blücher's thought process:

> The losses of this day are still not known but they may amount to some 2,000 killed and wounded. Prisoners have been taken from III, IV, V, VI, and XI Corps. Almost all say the French emperor is with the army yet I am still uncertain about this. Five enemy corps and a reserve cavalry would amount to at least 100,000 men. The enemy has not shown this much and his attacks were not intense enough for such a large force. I imagine that, in an attempt to deceive me, the enemy could have left behind a portion of each army corps. I hope to be able to send you news of this quickly because I now have such a position that the enemy must deploy before me.[24]

This report, along with the orders to Langeron, best illustrates the difficulty of Blücher's assignment. To be in position to either evade a general battle with Napoleon or assume the offensive against his marshals required the Silesian Army to maintain constant contact with its adversary. Should Blücher flee before a masking force, Napoleon would have the opportunity to concentrate overwhelming numbers against Schwarzenberg. Conversely, as Barclay's instructions clearly indicated, he had to avoid a confrontation with Napoleon. If Napoleon forced him to deliver a battle and Blücher lost, what would be his excuse for not having retreated in the first place?

It mattered little that Blücher still could not be certain of the size of the imperial army that he faced. Already he could see the telltale signs: offensive operations that "were not intense enough" for a large army commanded by Napoleon himself. Both he and Gneisenau sensed that the retreat should continue only if the imperials displayed the energy that signaled the presence of their master. His growing concern about being deceived reflected not what he and Gneisenau hoped, but what they observed and gleaned from intelligence. During the night of 23/24 August, they proved that hopes and wishes did not govern their thoughts. A report arrived claiming that Napoleon and his Guard had accompanied the advance of the French army. This news, as well as the belief that enemy forces eventually would move south from Liegnitz to threaten Langeron's line of retreat, persuaded the Prussians to err on the side of caution and expect an attack on 24 August.[25] At 7:00 on the morning of the 24th, Gneisenau issued instructions for the Silesian Army to continue the retreat southeast to Striegau. Sacken and Yorck received the order to withdraw to Kohlhöhe (Goczałków Górny); Langeron through Jauer to Großrosen (Rogoźnica).[26]

Following an awful night that granted man and beast little rest, the Army of Silesia resumed its retreat at 9:00 on the morning of 24 August. Showing preferential treatment to the Russians as a rule, Army Headquarters assigned Sacken's corps the direct highway to Striegau while Yorck's exhausted soldiers groped their way along side roads and detours. Summer storms continued to pound the soldiers with unrelenting fury. After marching southeast for six miles, the Russians and Prussians bivouacked at the village of Kohlhöhe, halfway between Jauer and Striegau. After ten days of campaigning, the Army of Silesia stood at almost the exact spot from where it had commenced operations. The exhausted troops desperately needed rest. In less than eight days, the Silesian Army had twice traversed the sixteen-mile stretch between the Katzbach and the Bober – sometimes by way of consecutive marches and countermarches – on washed-out roads, in bad weather, and in constant contact with the enemy. In the past six days, the men endured four night marches; they had not been able to cook during the previous four marches and the horses broke down from lack of fodder. The necessity of sleeping on damp ground, insufficient clothing, and dwindling food supplies prevented the soldiers from recovering. Whenever a halt occurred, exhausted troopers fell out of their saddles asleep. A general demoralization reigned, similar to the mood that accompanied a crushing defeat. The tight bonds of discipline unraveled, ushering in acts of desperation. "The nightly bivouac," noted Professor Steffens, "in the absence of tents, also hardened the feelings of the men. An encampment introduces some regulations of social order but the bivouac fire encourages the license of brigandage."[27]

With its large contingent of militia, Yorck's corps teetered on collapse. The consecutive night marches resulted in much straggling, especially among the Upper Silesian Landwehr, which was fast gaining a reputation for being unreliable. Soldiers became separated from their units; others had to be left behind after they had worn holes in their boots right through to their feet. Noncombat-related losses led to the disappearance of entire Landwehr companies, while Line troops also suffered considerable attrition from exertions and privations. More than 5,000 men disappeared from Yorck's infantry. On 16 August, the 4 battalions of the 2nd Brigade's 6th Silesian Landwehr Infantry Regiment mustered 2,000 men; 8 days later the remnants of all 4 formed 1 battalion of 700 men. Four other battalions disappeared during the night march on 23/24 August and no trace of them could be found; they finally surfaced at Schweidnitz, having been swept away by Langeron's trains. Clothed in uniforms considered sub-par before the war resumed, the Landwehr now appeared more like apparitions of scantily clad Spartan hoplites. One young officer wrote home: "Every day I wish an enemy ball would put an end to me as life is no longer bearable. For three days I have had nothing more to eat than a piece of moldy bread. The horses wander about like skeletons; when looking for oats, they have known nothing for so long that they greedily snatch the leaves from the trees on the street in order to satisfy their hunger. In the completely soaked ground, which is like a sea of filthy mud, we proceed at an dreadful pace. My small, feisty mare has become a meek lamb ... the enemy has it no better."[28]

Blücher hoped that the news his patrols provided on the 24th would help him determine his next move. Early that morning, Jürgaß informed Yorck of the approach of enemy columns from both Liegnitz and Goldberg. Yorck responded by dispatching Stößel's Black Hussar Regiment to Wahlstatt to obtain an overview of the situation seven miles further northwest at Lieg-nitz. Arriving at Wahlstatt, Stößel forwarded a patrol of one lieutenant and forty Hussars to Liegnitz with one squadron following in support. Around 12:30 P.M., Stößel reported the results: the French had occupied Liegnitz at 9:00 P.M. the previous night but had yet to advance from it; their numbers could not be determined. Other patrols found the right bank of the Katz-bach in their vicinity clear of imperial forces. Later that morning, Blücher received the report of a spy claiming that the French had pulled out of

Liegnitz. Aside from contradicting the reports submitted by Jürgaß and Stößel, this intelligence said nothing of where the imperials had gone. Until the situation could be clarified, Blücher decided to keep Army Headquarters at Jauer to be closer to the incoming reports. Langeron posted two battalions at Jauer to cover Army Headquarters; Korf's Reserve cavalry camped just east of the town.[29]

Confusing reports arrived throughout the course of the 24th. Sacken sent not only intelligence, but also a French corporal of the 10th Hussars captured by Cossacks on the 23rd. The prisoner informed Blücher that Napoleon had been present during the engagement at Goldberg but that in the evening he had ridden in the direction of Liegnitz. After finding Ney with III Corps and II Cavalry Corps on the left wing, the emperor had departed for Lauban. This contradicted the statements of another captured French officer who professed Napoleon's determination to continue the offensive in Silesia. This in turn supported Müffling's insistence that the French emperor would not leave Silesia until he had more to show for his efforts. Intelligence from Lauban proved equally vexing. The Prussians learned that Napoleon had passed through there on the 20th going east to Silesia escorted by 10,000 heavy cavalry of the Guard, part of the Guard's light cavalry, 4 horse batteries, and 6,000–8,000 infantry of the Old Guard. The emperor returned to Lauban on the 23rd and traveled west to Görlitz on the 24th. Approximately 15,000 bayonets of Mortier's Young Guard had reached Lauban on the 18th, struck the road south to Zittau on the 19th but returned to Lauban one hour later, departed east on the 20th with Napoleon for Silesia, and then returned to Görlitz on the 23rd. The Allies knew well that Napoleon calculated on making a big impact wherever he went when escorted by his Guard. Thus, they could be confident of his objective when he arrived with his grand reserve. Determining the location of the emperor and his bearskins provided one crucial variable of Blücher's equation.

Around 3:15 P.M. on 24 August, Sacken forwarded a report from Vasilchikov at Malitsch stating that the French had evacuated Liegnitz and marched west toward Haynau. Around 6:00 that evening, Sacken confirmed the enemy's hurried evacuation of Liegnitz. Vasilchikov's Cossacks followed their retrograde movement through Liegnitz, and Sacken's remaining forward troops likewise crossed the Katzbach that evening to reach Rothkirch. Gneisenau sent Lieutenant Wilhelm von Scharnhorst to investigate reports of a large imperial force at Lähn as well as enemy movements up the Bober and Katzbach toward Hirschberg and the passes into Bohemia. At 8:30 P.M. on the 24th, the young staff officer reported that he had not encountered the enemy at Schönau and that nothing indicated that the French had moved south from Goldberg to Hirschberg. All French troops south of Goldberg on the 23rd marched northeast to the Goldberg–Jauer road. According to Langeron, Blücher received confirmed news that evening of Napoleon's departure for Saxony, taking VI Corps with him. Spies also confirmed the rumors of the emperor's departure. That Macdonald's army simply did not do much on the 24th convinced Blücher that Napoleon had left Silesia.

Lauriston's V Corps passed the night of 23/24 August at Goldberg while XI Corps bivouacked between Niederau and Neudorf-am-Rennwege with its cavalry at Hohendorf. As noted, Ney never received Berthier's dispatch and so divided his infantry to follow II Cavalry Corps: three of his divisions went to Liegnitz and two to Rothkirch. Arriving at the latter during the evening, the marshal finally received Napoleon's summons to Görlitz. Misunderstanding the instructions, Ney ordered his entire corps to march west to Bunzlau on the morning of the 24th, which explains Vasilchikov's report. Finally realizing his mistake that evening, Ney turned over command of III Corps to Souham, who spent all of the 25th reinserting his divisions into Macdonald's front line. By forcing Macdonald to wait forty-eight hours before he could commence his operation, Ney's mistake proved fatal to the Army of the Bober. The imperials likewise did little on the 25th. Lauriston extended V Corps to Röchlitz on the right bank of the Katzbach but XI Corps remained on the left bank north of Goldberg.

To Blücher, the energy displayed by the imperials in Napoleon's presence at Löwenberg had fizzled by the 23rd. No appreciable French movements on the 24th could only mean that the emperor had departed, presumably in response to the Bohemian Army's advance on Dresden. The push at Goldberg served to mask his exit from Silesia, just as Blücher had predicted. Some members of his staff, such as Müffling, countered that Napoleon would not have ended the pursuit of the Silesian Army after attaining such paltry results. Blücher shook his head. Around 7:00 on the evening of 24 August, Army Headquarters issued orders with the heading "Provisional Disposition" for 25 August. First and foremost, Blücher wanted to find the French. For this task, "the cavalry of the Reserves and vanguards of all three corps will march with horse artillery to conduct a reconnaissance at daybreak on 25 August." Sacken's men received the task of patrolling through Liegnitz and Haynau; Yorck's across the Katzbach between Liegnitz and Goldberg; and Langeron's toward Goldberg and Schönau. If the imperial army could not be found, Blücher wanted to know where it had gone. Regardless of whether the French had marched south to utilize the mountain passes into Bohemia or marched west toward Lusatia and Saxony, the Silesian Army would follow. "At Jauer around 7:00 A.M.," stated Blücher's cover letter to his corps commanders, "I expect to receive the reports of the reconnaissance over where I can find the enemy. Each corps will send an orderly to my headquarters today to report to General Gneisenau and then deliver the disposition to the corps. PS: If around 8:00 or later three cannon shots fall by Jauer, all infantry will immediately march to Jauer." "I will set in movement 8,000 cavalry to follow the enemy if he retires toward Dresden," Blücher informed the tsar, "and tomorrow, the 25th, I march to attack him at Goldberg if he has plans to march to Bohemia or to pursue him if he retreats toward the Elbe."[30]

On the night of the 24th, Yorck received Blücher's orders for the following day. The thought of turning around and marching back to Jauer made Yorck's blood boil. He believed that his men deserved a full day of rest. A staff officer, Major Christian Karl Dietrich, received the task of going to Army Headquarters at Jauer to verbally deliver Yorck's protest. "Old Blücher was also in an evil mood," explains Droysen, "or Dietrich's statements put him in one; he [Dietrich] was snapped at in the most abject way, threatened with arrest, and being brought before a court-martial. Blücher's order stood." Dietrich paid the penalty in the form of a tongue-lashing for arriving in the midst of one of the few known moments of discord at Army Headquarters. Blücher had always remained fearful of the demoralizing effects of a prolonged retreat. Now he saw his army dissolving around him. Disgruntled and frustrated, he knew that all the exertions had thus far produced no appreciable success. With the haunting memory of the 1806 collapse forever etched on his psyche, he foresaw the army's disintegration if it continued to adhere to Barclay's instructions. Instead of drastic measures, he returned to the idea of a general battle, seeing it as the best solution to the army's problems. Both officers and men would have something to focus on rather than their miserable condition and their frustration with Army Headquarters. A victory would do much to heal the rifts and exorcise the demons of demoralization. Arguably, a defeat could lead to the army's utter collapse but so could the retreat if it continued. For these reasons, Blücher decided to stand and fight. His staff failed in their attempts to change his mind. Blücher countered that he liked the terrain on the Katzbach and the Wütende Neiße, that he was tired of retreating, and that he was determined to fight a battle in that position. If the enemy advanced on Jauer the next day, the Silesian Army would meet him. The old hussar stood firm and for a moment even considered replacing Gneisenau as chief of staff with Katzler, prompting the former to lament to Clausewitz: "You can imagine how difficult my position is. Blücher always wants to go forward and accuses me of being too cautious; Langeron and Yorck hold me back and consider me foolhardy and reckless."[31]

Allied cavalry moved out very early on 25 August. With thirteen squadrons newly assigned to vanguard duty, Katzler rode northwest toward Kroitsch on the Katzbach.[32] He reported at 4:30 A.M. that one of his patrols had made contact with the French around 2:00 A.M. at Röchlitz and had observed numerous campfires around Goldberg. This report reached Blücher before 6:00 A.M. Around 8:30, a second report arrived from Katzler. Writing from Kroitsch at 7:00, he reported the presence of enemy vedettes from Prausnitz to Goldberg. Peasants reported hearing a cannonade at

Haynau. The locals had also seen many campfires between Prausnitz and Goldberg during the previous night.

Meanwhile, Langeron's vanguard cavalry advanced from Peterwitz northwest toward Goldberg but reached only Hennersdorf by 9:00 A.M. The first report that Langeron received came from Pahlen II. Schönau and Lähn, where he observed strong enemy forces on the 23rd, had been evacuated. His patrols rode as far as Probsthain but did not encounter the French. All signs indicated that the imperial forces facing the left wing of the Silesian Army had conducted a retrograde movement. "According to the news that I have received from the mountains that separate Silesia from Bohemia," reported Blücher, "I judge that the enemy is retiring toward the Elbe and that he has renounced his plan to debouch into Bohemia through Landeshut."[33]

By 9:00 A.M., the information at Blücher's disposal appeared very persuasive. On his right, the French had apparently marched to Bunzlau. In his center, the enemy remained at Goldberg while nothing of the imperials could be found on his left. Around 10:00, the three signal shots echoed from Jauer, and the army marched according to new orders based on the assumption that the enemy was in full retreat. Blücher instructed Sacken to cross the Katzbach at Dohnau, Yorck at Kroitsch, and Langeron at Goldberg. If Langeron found Goldberg still in French hands, he would fix their front as Yorck and Sacken enveloped them. If the French retreated before Langeron, the Russian vanguard would pursue and maintain constant contact. Blücher demanded a vigorous pursuit and called for "zeal and activity" from his corps commanders.[34] "Two different plans of the enemy are already ruined," Blücher assured them. "In the meantime, he has lost time that is precious to him. If we act quickly and energetically, this latest plan will be foiled as well." Blücher also wrote to Bernadotte: "The army is marching and if the enemy makes a stand at Goldberg to cover his retreat he will be attacked tomorrow at daybreak."[35]

Three hours into the advance, new reports reached Blücher from the Allied cavalry. Considerable imperial forces remained at Goldberg and several large columns – Souham's III Corps – were marching east from Haynau toward Liegnitz. Sacken reported at 12:45 that his Cossacks had also found the enemy advancing anew from Haynau east toward Liegnitz in numerous columns of considerable strength. For this reason, Sacken planned to halt at Malitsch until he received further orders. Jürgaß, who led Yorck's Reserve Cavalry likewise to Kroitsch, added that "the enemy advances in strength on the road from Haynau to Liegnitz; it could be perhaps 10,000 infantry and they are already at Steuditz. Vasilchikov has only 2,000 infantry and, in case he is very hard pressed, will withdraw to Rothkirch. The Russians still hold Liegnitz" (see Map 2).[36]

By 1:00 that afternoon, Blücher had heard enough; he ordered an immediate halt due to the threat posed to the army's right. The head of I Corps had just marched into Jauer when Yorck received the new orders: "Because I have just received the report of enemy movements on the side of Liegnitz, which must be reconnoitered before the march of the army can continue, I request that your corps remain at Jauer until further instructions. Sacken's corps will halt at Malitsch and Langeron's at Peterwitz." This sent Yorck over the edge. After establishing his headquarters likewise in Jauer, he sought out Blücher.[37]

Blücher, Gneisenau, and their officers had just sat down for a late lunch when the door suddenly flew open and Yorck stormed in, shouting: "You are destroying the troops, you are marching them to no end." An ugly and embarrassing scene unfolded in full view of Blücher's staff, including several Russian and British officers. "I was witness to the most scandalous scene," explained Langeron, "Yorck was in Blücher's room, spewing the most formidable injuries that the German language can furnish on him, Gneisenau, and Müffling; thank God I did not understand a thing because I do not know German but the tone allowed me to judge the ferocity. Yorck's three antagonists made good use of their own voices; the din and the cries of these gentlemen were audible from the street, and I thought they would fight each other, and they were not far from it. I withdrew without uttering a word and retired to my quarters, which offered no such scene."[38]

Gneisenau jumped up and led Yorck to a small antechamber; Blücher followed. Inside, Yorck lambasted Blücher for the reckless leadership of the army and demanded an explanation. He expressed his outrage over the numerous marches and countermarches, which he insisted had crushed the excellent morale of the troops. Yorck concluded by assuring them that the entire army would collapse and that he would no longer accept responsibility for it. He intended to disclose everything in a report to the king. Two accounts exist over what happened next. According to Nostitz as well as Carl Blasendorff, one of Blücher's early biographers, the old hussar responded with surprising fierceness, insisting on the need for unconditional obedience.[39] He ended the conversation with a blistering reality check for Yorck: "The difference between us is that I command and you obey, and that I, and not you, have to bear the responsibility for the orders given." According to Delbrück, who based his account on a letter Gneisenau wrote shortly before his death in 1831, it was Gneisenau who took Yorck to task. "Although he was only a *Generalmajor* and Yorck was a *Generalleutnant*, he concisely recounted to him what had occurred and why, that no matter what they did Yorck always opposed it, and that the old general's obstinacy often bordered on insubordination. He then opened the door and asked: 'Does Your Excellency have any further orders?' Yorck left with a cold bow to Blücher."[40]

While this episode may be amusing, it appears that age and bravado probably played a role in Gneisenau's fanciful account. Regardless, Yorck resolved to resign on the spot and leave the army, but Prince Karl urged him to put the matter to the king's judgment. That night, Yorck wrote to Frederick William:

> Promoting Your Royal Majesty's almighty interests and those of the state to the best of my ability has been my endeavor throughout forty-three years of service. Therefore, please accept as the purest expression of my conviction, if I candidly express the confession that I can no longer be of use to Your Royal Majesty as commander of I Corps. Perhaps my imagination is too narrow to be able to understand the ingenious views that direct the high command of General Blücher. But experience tells me that continuous marches and countermarches in the eight days of the reconvened campaign have already placed the troops entrusted to me in such a condition that a good result cannot be expected if the enemy launches a powerful offensive. That until now he has still not seized the offensive is a stroke of luck, which has protected the combined army here from results similar to those of 1806. Recklessness and inconsistencies in the operations, inaccurate intelligence, and the grasping at any feint by the enemy, thus ignorance of the practical elements that are more important for the leadership of a large army than sublime opinions, are unfortunately the causes well known through experience that can lead an army to ruin before it can achieve its main task. As a subordinate general, my duty demands blind obedience from me. On the other hand, my duty as a loyal subject requires me to strive to counter the evil, and this contradiction has the natural consequence that I stand in the way of the commanding general and on the whole am more harmful than useful. Thus, I turn to Your Royal Majesty with the most humble request to release me from the command of I Corps and to place me in another, be it still a subordinate situation, where I can serve Your Majesty with more utility.[41]

Yorck's frustration represents both a common complaint of corps commanders as well as the relatively recent opposition to the dual-command system of the Prussian General Staff. Regarding the former, corps commanders often felt that army headquarters failed to provide enough insight on the general state of affairs. Viewing the situation only from their limited perspective, they often bombarded army headquarters with requests for more information, complaints and questions about orders, and suggestions for a better way to proceed. Blücher had himself been guilty of this as a corps commander in the Spring Campaign. Yorck's idea to create an advance guard corps to maintain close contact with the enemy rather than wear down the entire army through this task exemplifies the attitude that *those idiots at headquarters don't know what they're doing.* Simple questions immediately render the suggestion indefensible. How large should the advance guard corps be and which corps would provide the manpower? Who would command? Upon which of the three roads being utilized by the imperials would it deploy? If all three, then each detachment would have to be large enough to hold the enemy for at least twenty-four hours so the rest of the army could move up. As for the issue concerning the General Staff, Yorck suspected that Gneisenau ran the army and that Blücher served as his mouthpiece. He resented taking orders from a staff officer junior in rank to him. More than this, he still believed that the commander should command and not forfeit control of the army to his staff. Yorck had a very good relationship with his chiefs of staff, but they took orders from him: dual command did not exist in I Corps.

Following the scene at Jauer, Blücher wanted to determine Sacken's mood. Having yet to meet the Russian in person, he traveled to Malitsch during the afternoon of the 25th. Blücher expressed his satisfaction to the Russian over the performance of his troops and invited him to share his views over the course of the war. Blücher then instructed Sacken's staff and generals on their position for the next morning and ordered them to harass the enemy as much as possible during the night. Müffling claims that Blücher departed "very satisfied after discovering that while the commanders of the other two corps disagreed with him General Sacken was in complete agreement with his views." In a 25 August letter to Hardenberg, Gneisenau praised Sacken even though he had started the campaign with a march that did not comply with Blücher's order. Regardless, Gneisenau labeled Sacken as one of three Russian generals whom the chancellor should mention to Tsar Alexander: "First and foremost is General Sacken. It is not possible to be more active, timely, insightful and determined than he is. He always performs the movements prescribed for him with precision and, when orders cannot reach him, he always arranges the most expedient measures instantly. This is the man who must be placed at the head of an army. At headquarters, we speak of him only with admiration, having become better acquainted with him by observing his measures."[42]

Although this meeting earned Sacken's goodwill and cooperation, disaffection among the Russian generals in Langeron's camp increased to the point of insubordination. Russian discontent over command of the Silesian Army going to a foreigner when they provided the majority of the manpower, which somewhat diminished when Blücher abruptly started the campaign, returned to the fore. Even his first step of the campaign, the premature occupation of the neutral zone, had struck some Russian commanders as inexplicable and undignified. With each day, Langeron's behavior became more obstinate and detrimental to the army as a whole. Naturally, the mood of the Russian commanders impacted their subordinates from general to private. For these reasons, the Prussians had to present a unified front. Any complaint, criticism, or glimmer of distrust toward Blücher's leadership could jeopardize the unity of the army and its ability to function. At this critical juncture of the campaign, Yorck's temper produced an outright scandal, doing much to discredit Blücher and his staff in the eyes of both Russians and Prussians.[43]

Sacken's corps passed the night of 25/26 August at Malitsch; his vanguard withdrew across the Katzbach to a position between Baben (Babin) and Neudorf (Nowa Wieś Legnicka). The infantry of Yorck's vanguard camped at Bellwitzhof (Bielowice), pushing detachments to the crossings over the Wütende Neiße at Niederweinberg (Winnica) and Schlauphof.[44] After stationing cavalry posts on the left bank of the Katzbach and in support of the infantry at the Wütende Neiße, Katzler's vanguard cavalry bivouacked on the high plateau east of the Wütende Neiße. Jürgaß also moved Yorck's Reserve Cavalry onto the plateau, south of Katzler. In terrible weather, patrols from the cavalry posts that remained on the left bank of the Katzbach detected the bivouac fires of the imperials extending from Rothkirch along the Goldberg–Liegnitz road to Liegnitz itself. The French did not move into the towns immediately along the Katzbach. Yorck's main body camped between Grögersdorf (Grzegorzów) and Jauer, with corps headquarters at the latter.[45]

The reports from Langeron's troopers stated that, as of noon on the 25th, the French still held Prausnitz and that many infantry regiments could be seen east of the Katzbach between Prausnitz and Goldberg. Artillery crowned the hills on both sides of Goldberg and behind them the Russians could see smoke rising, indicating the presence of more bivouacs. Yet the imperials gave no signs of advancing or withdrawing. Langeron's vanguard reached Seichau and pushed its Cossacks toward Röchlitz and Prausnitz; the main body of the corps camped at Hennersdorf. Pahlen II's detachment secured the left flank at Konradswaldau.[46] Nothing changed on the 25th for St.-Priest, yet he did report that Napoleon had returned to Saxony on the 23rd by way of Lauban and that many troops had followed the emperor.

Gneisenau issued orders to Yorck around 10:00 P.M. to move I Corps at 5:00 on the morning of the 26th from Jauer to a concealed position at Schlauphof to be abreast of the other corps. As soon as Yorck reached this point, all three corps would proceed to the Katzbach along three roads that did not offer mutual support until the army reached the opposite bank of the river. On the left, Langeron would proceed on the Jauer–Goldberg highway to the latter. In the center, Yorck's corps would cross the Katzbach at Niederkrayn, while on the right Sacken marched from Malitsch to Dohnau. For much of their respective marches, Yorck and Langeron would be separated by the Wütende Neiße and the high plateau that this narrow but turbulent brook bordered to the west and the Katzbach bordered to the north. Although Yorck and Sacken initially would march along parallel roads on the plateau, Yorck would turn northwest and debouch from the plateau to get across the Wütende Neiße and then the

Katzbach while Sacken continued due north to the latter river. As soon as Yorck exited the plateau, Sacken would be isolated, as would Yorck until he crossed the Katzbach. What an opportunity for a skilled enemy commander! Moreover, it appears that Army Headquarters had not taken into account the weather. Heavy summer storms continued their assaults. By the evening of the 25th, most of the watercourses in Blücher's area of operations rose above their banks, flooding the lowlands and fouling the roads.[47]

While anger drove Yorck's quill on the evening of the 25th, pure optimism guided those of Gneisenau and Blücher. Again, Gneisenau's correspondence grants us a look into the thought process at Silesian Army Headquarters: "If the enemy further continues his retreat to Saxony, then obviously he has failed to attain his objective against us. With his superior forces, he has failed to engage us in a battle and the partial attacks have cost him much blood. Our losses are not slight. His retreat can still cost him much. Nothing shall lack in our efforts to exploit his retreat."[48] Blücher's letter to his wife is worth citing in full, because it perfectly captures Blücher's understanding of his role and that of his army:

> The tide has turned! For three days the emperor Napoleon attacked me with all his forces and tried everything to bring me to battle; I successfully thwarted all of his plans. He retreated yesterday evening; I will follow him immediately and I hope Silesia is now safe. I have saved Berlin by drawing the emperor of France here and delaying him for seven days, during which the Grand [Bohemian] Army invaded Saxony from Bohemia. The crown prince of Sweden is marching from Berlin to likewise invade Saxony. Both large armies advance in the rear of the enemy while I now follow close on his heels and will attack him wherever I find him.
>
> They will bless us in Berlin. I am well and very pleased that I have led the great man around by the nose; he will be very angry that he could not force me to fight. Both sides have suffered casualties; the enemy has lost three times as many as us. We have already captured 1,500 men; the enemy has taken fewer than 100 from us.[49]

Blücher's casualty estimates fell far short of the truth. During the engagements on 21, 22, and 23 August, the Silesian Army had lost some 6,000 to 8,000 killed, wounded, and missing. Imperial losses since 17 August numbered just as many. Limited operations on the 24th and 25th did much good for both armies, but especially the Silesian, which according to Gneisenau had fought seven large engagements in the five-day period from 19 to 23 August. Although these two days allowed the troops to rest, repair their weapons, and restock ammunition and food, Blücher knew he needed to end the continuous back-and-forth marches. Likewise, he knew that only a battle would heal the army. Only a battle would reconcile Langeron and his Russians as well as Yorck and his Prussians. "Discontent among the foreign troops and inexperience among his own," noted Müffling, "dissatisfaction among their commanders, and demands that could not be fulfilled – truly the situation required speedy help, and only in a great and successful military event could such be sought." Encouraged by the news that Napoleon and his Guard had departed for Saxony, Blücher intended to find battle the next morning, regardless of the situation.[50]

Following Napoleon's Löwenberg offensive, Blücher suspected he would mask his departure through tactical offensive strikes by his marshals. Thus the dilemma: because the situation could change any day as a result of Napoleon's departure, the Silesian Army had to maintain constant contact with the French to be able to immediately exploit his absence. Yet, this meant executing a methodical, fighting withdrawal in the presence of the master of operations, of the *manoeuvre sur les derrières*, and of the *manoeuvre sur position centrale*. Blücher simply could not flee before advance guards, but had to find a way to force the imperials to deploy for battle, determine if the energy they displayed indicated the emperor's presence, and then react accordingly by either continuing the retreat or assuming the offensive. The complexity of his task cannot be underestimated, particularly considering his penchant to attack. With no choice but to surrender the initiative, his opponent's actions would dictate his own. If the French advanced, he had to retreat. If the French withdrew, he had to follow. If they stood still, he had to determine the reason for their halt: was it temporary or was it the prelude to an extensive operation?

Blücher's position became all the more difficult after the French appeared to be marching back and forth between the Katzbach and the Bober. For this reason, the cavalry of his advance guards traversed the area between the Schnelle Deichsel and the Bober three times within a 24-hour period. To accurately assess the intent of his adversary, Blücher's army had to remain in close contact with the enemy at all points along its front. This required exhausting marches and countermarches regardless of the time of day, and with apparent indifference to the needs of man and horse. Although the Allied army was well provided with intelligence, errors in judgment could be made just as easily while on patrol as at Army Headquarters. At times, Blücher's orders appeared haphazard or contradictory to his corps commanders, who never appreciated the difficulty of a task he never felt inclined to explain.

Allied High Command kept the Reichenbach Plan secret, never explaining to the corps commanders its principles prior to the commencement of hostilities. Müffling explains: "Peculiar circumstances, especially the difficult task of never losing sight of the enemy yet never engaging in a decisive action with him, had demanded great exertions from the army. Moreover, this often caused very contradictory orders to be issued in the course of a few hours according to the incoming reports." Yorck certainly did not know of the plan, nor was he privy to the discussion between Blücher and Barclay. Thus, the corps commander based his judgments only on what he could observe from his limited perspective. Although Yorck had little confidence in Blücher and Gneisenau from the start, the increasing illogic of their leadership eroded any trust he had in his countrymen. Failing to see the pursuit of a consistent plan, he attributed the excessive night marches to blind ignorance and folly. As noted, neither Blücher nor Gneisenau felt inclined to explain their decisions to Yorck.[51] Although Nostitz adored Blücher, he had a solid relationship with Yorck, making the following account nearly unbiased:

> Due to the events of the latter day [23 August], Yorck had become very vexed. He saw in the deficient leadership of the army's high command the real and only cause of the losses suffered. The many night marches and exertions negatively impacted the good morale of the troops. The general loudly expressed the bitterest censure and depicted the entire dissolution of the corps as unavoidable if Blücher continued to place his trust in men, who, without practical training and experience, gave advice on the arrangements of the operations based merely on their brilliance and fantasies. He considered Blücher himself a brave soldier and harbored feelings of gratitude for him from earlier times in his career, but he hated the advisors, finding himself pushed to the background and Gneisenau and Müffling exercising greater influence on the direction of affairs than did he. This always provided his evil temper with new sustenance and increased the bitterness and asperity of his nature. Thus, Yorck was wrong in the affair itself, and the rebuke he received is justifiable because through his behavior Blücher's relationship with the Russian corps commanders became more difficult and uncertain. Nevertheless, none can deny that the army command did not always observe the formalities that Yorck felt were completely legitimate based on his experience. The reciprocal antipathy and mistrust that had already sunk deep roots before and during the armistice increased daily. Thus, it came to pass that both sides observed only the respect toward each other that the regulations required as indispensable. Already, the general had been informed several times of how Yorck's behavior had negatively impacted the mood of the army. Now, he was formally ordered by way of a serious and clear-cut reprimand to end the bad state of affairs.[52]

Already suspicious of Blücher's compliance with Barclay's instructions, Langeron became increasingly indignant over the pointless marches and countermarches as well as the seemingly endless cycle of turning around, making front, and marching away only to repeat the process a few miles down the road. In describing Langeron, Nostitz noted: "Meanwhile, the first unfavorable combats at the beginning of the campaign made him skeptical. As the senior general of the two Russian corps under Blücher's command, he felt a great responsibility in terms of scrutinizing the orders he received, striving to limit Russian participation in the operations to those principles that appeared compatible with his individual views. Also, he had loudly and often stated his disapproval and complaints; only intelligence and the considerations that were necessary to observe prevented Blücher from reprimanding him as he did General Yorck."[53]

In evaluating Blücher's fulfillment of his primary responsibility – maintaining constant contact with the enemy army in Silesia – we find a mixture of success and problems stemming from the nature of the task as well as some flaws inherent to the new Prussian army. As for the latter, Frederick William issued instructions for the composition of vanguards on 29 July 1813: "I determine that, when advance guards must be formed in the field, entire brigades, whose composition is not calculated for this, should not be used. Instead, in accordance with regulations, only fusilier battalions from the brigades and likewise battalions from the Reserve Infantry regiments should be used. These should be taken in the manner that only one battalion from each regiment should be designated for this duty until the Landwehr is far enough along in field experience for it to also be used for advance guard service. As for cavalry, hussars and uhlans from the brigade cavalry should be used as much as possible, but additional requirements should be met by the reserve cavalry, yet not the cuirassiers."[54] Thus, the Prussians placed great emphasis on the combined-arms composition of their vanguards, meaning infantry would be used in addition to cavalry and horse artillery. In their post-Jena zeal to modernize the army, the Prussians in fact went overboard in adopting and modifying the tenets of combined-arms units so that they both forgot the Frederician principle of employing the cavalry en masse for shock and seemingly ignored the Napoleonic principle of the great cavalry reserve to ensure the decisive victory, just as Murat's sabers had demonstrated in October 1806.

The combined-arms composition of the vanguard in which each branch received commensurate representation meant that the cavalry never contained enough sabers to operate independently. Thus, it could not get too far ahead of its infantry. "The combination of cavalry with infantry units has always proven to be a ball and chain for the cavalry arm," explains Freytag-Loringhoven. "Only complete freedom of movement assures good performance."[55] In addition, the lack of reconnaissance in the right flank of Yorck's corps on the 19th resulted from the constraints placed on the cavalry associated with being part of the combined-arms advance guard, which in turn could not conduct a uniform reconnaissance of the entire front of the army. Moreover, patrolling and reconnoitering led to the dispersal of the advance guard cavalry and the corresponding erosion of combat strength in the frontline regiments. Consequently, they remained glued to their own infantry as soon as they made contact with the enemy. For example, on the

18th, Katzler sacrificed contact with the French to return to the bivouac at Adelsdorf and the protection of the advance guard infantry.

Basing operations on the task of maintaining constant contact with the adversary meant that Gneisenau employed the majority of Blücher's cavalry in front of the army.[56] In the situation in which the Prussians found themselves, an encounter battle appeared much more probable than a pitched battle. With the cavalry proliferating before the front of the army, the numerical advantage enjoyed by the Allies in this arm would have had little to no effect on the course of an encounter battle. "This abortive arrangement immediately asserted itself," continues the prolific Prussian historian and deputy chief of the German General Staff during the First World War, Baron Hugo von Freytag-Loringhoven, "and was the reason the 24,000 cavalry of the Silesian Army did not completely make itself felt."[57] Two examples support this argument. First, on the 18th, Sacken could not exploit his success at Steudnitz due to Lanskoy's continued absence. Second, after Jürgaß's Reserve Cavalry joined Yorck's advance guard on the 17th, the corps commander lacked adequate cavalry to contend with Ney after the marshal suddenly appeared on the Gröditzberg two days later. Yorck had to request that Blücher allow the East Prussian National Cavalry Regiment to rejoin the main body of the corps before he could take action.

The seriousness with which Blücher approached his task of remaining in constant contact with the French in Silesia did not always have a positive impact on the army. For example, on the 21st, when it became crystal clear that the imperials had concentrated along the left bank of the Bober, he could not break free from his belief that the French would retreat. Admittedly, most Allied commanders from Bernadotte to Schwarzenberg to Alexander believed that Napoleon would summon his forces from Silesia to turn against either Berlin or Prague. Regardless, Blücher tended to interpret the intelligence to indicate a French retreat. This led to the frequent revisions of directives that his headquarters did not always draft and issue punctually. As a result, orders sometimes reached the troops so late that their objective could be attained only through strenuous night marches. Also, in a very marked contrast to the Napoleonic system, Gneisenau's orders failed to inform corps commanders of the instructions issued to the neighboring corps. At times, he sought a quick fix to the difficulties that resulted from this negligence by ignoring the corps commander and issuing orders directly to individual units, as we saw with I Corps on the 20th.[58]

Despite these numerous difficulties, which worsened before they improved, Blücher had passed his first major test. Overcoming his instinct to attack the French army, especially one commanded by Napoleon himself, he complied with the tenets of the Reichenbach Plan. According to Gneisenau, Headquarters proceeded according to a very basic principle: as soon as the French threatened one of his flanks, Blücher broke off the engagement and retreated.[59] Moreover, Blücher accepted the principles of the Allied strategy: he would fix Napoleon's attention on himself to provide Schwarzenberg and Bernadotte with time to cross the Elbe and reach Saxony from Bohemia and Brandenburg respectively. Indeed, he accomplished much by boldly advancing. Not only did he throw Ney's army into disarray, but he brought the emperor to Silesia with his Guard and I Cavalry Corps. Blücher certainly did his part to facilitate Schwarzenberg's offensive.

Blücher and Gneisenau never lost sight of the best way to liberate Silesia: by crushing the French army in a decisive battle. Such a battle could be sought as soon as the emperor departed. Retribution for Jena-Auerstedt remained ever present in their minds. Not for one moment did they believe the retreat would be indefinite, again because they understood how the operations of the two other Allied armies would facilitate their own. After conducting a slow, fighting withdrawal, Blücher was about to see his patience rewarded.

Notes

1 Friederich, *Herbstfeldzug 1813*, I:154–60.
2 The orders issued to the Army of the Bober for 23 August have been lost. The description is based on the operations that took place on the 23rd.
3 Friederich, *Herbstfeldzug 1813*, I:272–73; Freytag-Loringhoven, *Aufklärung und Armeeführung*, 53; Müffling, *Die Feldzüge*, 24; Bogdanovich, *Geschichte des Krieges*, IIa:33.
4 The Kinburnskii Dragoon Regiment and Dorpatskii Mounted Jäger Regiment, each consisting of two squadrons.
5 Blücher to Charles John, Jauer, 23 August 1813, RA KrA, volym 25; Gneisenau to Hardenberg, Jauer, 25 August 1813, GSTA PK, I HA Rep. 74 Staatskanzleramt O Ap. Nr. 9, Bd. 3; Langeron, *Mémoires*, 238; Bogdanovich, *Geschichte des Krieges*, IIa:35; Friederich, *Herbstfeldzug 1813*, I:272–75.
6 Attack Disposition, Add MSS, 20112, 122.
7 Blücher to Barclay, Jauer, 9:00 P.M., 23 August 1813, RA KrA, volym 25; Müffling, *Die Feldzüge*, 24.
8 Blücher to Barclay, Niederkrayne, 11:00 A.M., 23 August 1813, RA KrA, volym 25. Reports such as these were written in fours, with one each going to Alexander, Frederick William, Barclay, and Bernadotte. The salutations and pronouns were changed accordingly. Silesian Army Headquarters did not report to Schwarzenberg or the headquarters of the Bohemian Army. In fact, Blücher wrote several letters to Bernadotte between 12 August and 14 October but only three to Schwarzenberg.
9 The battalion was never re-formed and its manpower was distributed to other battalions.
10 Quoted in Höpfner, "Darstellung," 1844:98–99. "The demeanor of these four battalions during the continuous attacks by a strong cavalry was downright exemplary," judges Friederich in *Herbstfelduzg 1813*, I:280.

11 Droysen, *Yorck*, II:132.

12 The account of the combats on 23 August is based on Blücher to Barclay, Jauer, 9:00 P.M., 23 August 1813, RA KrA, volym 25; Gneisenau to Hardenberg, Jauer, 25 August 1813, GSTA PK, I HA Rep. 74 Staatskanzleramt O Ap. Nr. 9, Bd. 3; Stern-Gwiazdowski, *Das Gefecht bei Goldberg-Niederau*; Höpfner, "Darstellung," 1844:97–100; Friederich, *Herbstfeldzug 1813*, I:275–285; Droysen, *Yorck*, II:130–33; Beitzke, *Geschichte der deutschen Freheitskriege*, II:179–83; Bogdanovich, *Geschichte des Krieges*, IIa:35–40; Langeron, *Mémoires*, 240; Vaudoncourt, *Histoire de la guerre*, 144; Wagner, *Plane der Schlachten*, II:12–18.

13 Langeron, *Mémoires*, 243; Blücher to Barclay, Jauer, 9:00 P.M., 23 August 1813, RA KrA, volym 25; Freytag-Loringhoven, *Aufklärung und Armeeführung*, 55–56; Bogdanovich, *Geschichte des Krieges*, IIa:39–40; Friederich, *Herbstfelduzg 1813*, I:281–82.

14 Blücher to Alexander, Jauer, 24 August 1813, RA KrA, volym 25.

15 Bogdanovich, *Geschichte des Krieges*, IIa:40, maintains that Blücher ordered Langeron to Jauer but the Russian corps commander refused. Claiming his men were exhausted and needed rest, Langeron united his corps at Hennersdorf, where it passed the night.

16 Müffling, *Die Feldzüge*, 24–25.

17 Bogdanovich, *Geschichte des Krieges*, IIa:42; Blücher to Gaudi is in Höpfner, "Darstellung," 1844:106–07.

18 Quoted in Droysen, *Yorck*, II:133. Delbrück describes Yorck as being "incapable of grasping great plans; melancholic, grim, and morose; he rebuked all their steps, interpreting them as personal, intentional slights, and seeing in them the downfall of the army, a second edition of Jena and Auerstedt ... Unfamiliar with the contents of the secret instructions [Reichenbach Plan], seeing only the suffering and privations of the troops ... namely the young Landwehr, he engaged in acrimonious and bitter outbursts against the leadership, not only with denouncements, but claims that he could virtually foresee the destruction of his corps. Admittedly, he compensated for these vices and his inflexible, insubordinate refusal to obey unpleasant orders with the greatest bravery and a stamina that earned him the utmost respect from subordinate and superior, from friend and enemy": Pertz and Delbrück, *Gneisenau*, III:197.

19 Freytag-Loringhoven, *Aufklärung und Armeeführung*, 58, claims that Steinmetz's brigade "had to forcibly carve a path through the Russian trains." It is not known if he is merely echoing Droysen. Friederich says nothing about the Prussians having to cut their way out. Bogdanovich, *Geschichte des Krieges*, IIa:41, who cites Müffling as his source for this account, states that the Prussians "lost patience and so made use of the musket-butt to clear a path."

20 Droysen, *Yorck*, II:133; Freytag-Loringhoven, *Aufklärung und Armeeführung*, 58; Friederich, *Herbstfeldzug 1813*, I:284–85.

21 Gneisenau, *Blücher*, 162.

22 Quoted in Droysen, *Yorck*, II:133. See also Müffling, *Die Feldzüge*, 25.

23 Langeron to Blücher, Hennersdorf, 23 August 1813; Blücher to Langeron, 8:00 P.M., 23 August 1813; and Langeron to Blücher, Hennersdorf, 9:00 P.M., 23 August 1813 are in Höpfner, "Darstellung," 1844:105.

24 Blücher to Barclay, Jauer, 9:00 P.M., 23 August 1813, RA KrA, volym 25.

25 Blücher to Alexander, Jauer, 24 August 1813, RA KrA, volym 25.

26 Friederich, *Herbstfeldzug 1813*, I:285–86. Bogdanovich asserts that Blücher's failure to concentrate the army on the 23rd led to the continuation of the retreat on the 24th: Bogdanovich, *Geschichte des Krieges im Jahre 1813*, IIa:41–44.

27 Steffens, *Adventures*, 111; Droysen, *Yorck*, II:133–34.

28 Quoted in Kähler, *Litthauischen Dragoner-Regiments*, 363; Müffling, *Die Feldzüge*, 25; Unger, *Blücher*, II:73; Friederich, *Herbstfeldzug 1813*, I:286.

29 The rest of Langeron's corps moved into a bivouac at Großrosen, between Jauer and Striegau. Langeron's rearguard held Peterwitz, two miles west of Jauer. Likewise from Langeron's corps, Pahlen II covered the army's left flank from Pläswitz to Falkenberg with his detachment while a detachment of one dragoon and one Cossack regiment under Dmitri Yuzefovich went to Bolkenhain. Blücher's two other corps bivouacked at Kohlhöhe: Sacken in the first line, Yorck in the second. To secure the right flank of the army, the Mecklenburg Hussar Regiment took a position eleven miles east of Jauer at Kuhnern (Konary) while Katzler and fifteen squadrons stood halfway between the two at Profen. Jürgaß secured the northern perimeter of Jauer with Yorck's Reserve Cavalry; north of him, Vasilchikov stood with Sacken's rearguard at Malitsch on the Jauer–Liegnitz road so that between Jürgaß and Vasilchikov 6,000 Allied cavalry blocked the road south from Liegnitz. See Freytag-Loringhoven, *Aufklärung und Armeeführung*, 59; Friederich, *Herbstfeldzug 1813*, I:286–87.

30 Preparatory Disposition, Jauer, 7:00 P.M., 24 August 1813, Add MSS, 20112, 123; Blücher to Alexander, Jauer, 24 August 1813, RA KrA, volym 25; Gneisenau to Hardenberg, Jauer, 25 August 1813, GSTA PK, I HA Rep. 74 Staatskanzleramt O Ap. Nr. 9, Bd. 3; Pertz and Delbrück, *Gneisenau*, III:198–99; Unger, *Blücher*, II:73–74; Freytag-Loringhoven, *Aufklärung und Armeeführung*, 59–62; Langeron, *Mémoires*, 247; Bogdanovich, *Geschichte des Krieges*; Vaudoncourt, *Histoire de la guerre*, 144; Petre, *Napoleon's Last Campaign*, 150.

31 Droysen, *Yorck*, II:134; Gneisenau to Clausewitz, Goldberg, 28 August 1813, GStA PK, VI HA Rep. 92 Nl. Gneisenau, Nr. 21; Unger, *Blücher*, II:73.

32 Lobenthal's battalions likewise returned to their parent regiments and were replaced by fresh units. Major Johann Friedrich August von Hiller replaced Lobenthal as commander of the advance guard infantry.

33 Blücher to Charles John, Jauer, 12:00 P.M., 25 August 1813, RA KrA, volym 25; Freytag-Loringhoven, *Aufklärung und Armeeführung*, 63–64; Friederich, *Herbstfeldzug 1813*, I:289–90.

34 From the Katzbach, Blücher planned to march to the Bober. Sacken's corps would cross at Großwalditz (Włodzice Wielkie), halfway between Bunzlau and Löwenberg, but its light cavalry was to pursue the French through Bunzlau. Yorck's corps would return to Sirgwitz and cross the river. Langeron's corps would move across the Bober at Löwenberg, with a detachment crossing further south at Lähn to secure the army's left and cut off any imperial forces that had reached Hirschberg. See Friederich, *Herbstfeldzug 1813*, I:290–91.

35 "Disposition," Jauer, 25 August 1813, Add MSS, 20112, 124–25; Blücher to Charles John, Jauer, 12:00 P.M., 25 August 1813, RA KrA, volym 25.

36 Quoted in Freytag-Loringhoven, *Aufklärung und Armeeführung*, 66.
37 Blücher to Yorck, Jauer, 1:00 P.M., 25 August 1813, in Friederich, *Herbstfeldzug 1813*, I:291.
38 Henderson, *Blücher*, 126; Langeron, *Mémoires*, 247; Bogdanovich, *Geschichte des Krieges*, IIa:43, cites Droysen as the source of his account.
39 Blasendorff, *Blücher*, 204. Droysen can probably be added to this group. According to his version, "He [Yorck] personally went to Blücher; there was a very ugly scene; Blücher's anger appears to have been pushed to the extreme limit": Droysen, *Yorck*, II:135.
40 Nostitz, *Tagebuch*, 56; Pertz and Delbrück, *Gneisenau*, III:200.
41 Quoted in Droysen, *Yorck*, II:135–36.
42 Müffling, *Die Feldzüge*, 26–27; Gneisenau to Hardenberg, Jauer, 25 August 1813, GSTA PK, I HA Rep. 74 Staatskanzleramt O Ap. Nr. 9, Bd. 3. Rudzevich and General Ivan Witte were the other two. Although Gneisenau could speak frankly to Hardenberg, it is possible that he exaggerated his praise of Sacken to cause the absence of Langeron's name to appear more glaring.
43 Bogdanovich, *Geschichte des Krieges im Jahre 1813*, IIa:42–43; Blasendorff, *Blücher*, 204; Unger, *Blücher*, II:73.
44 Kaemmerer, *Ortsnamenverzeichnis der Otschaften jenseits von Oder und Neiße*, 144, lists Słup for Schlauphof as well as Schlaupe, but modern maps do not provide a Polish name for the small town south of Winnica that was referred to as Schlauphof.
45 Henckel von Donnersmarck, *Erinnerungen*, 212–13.
46 This detachment consisted of the two squadrons of the Kinburnskii Dragoon Regiment, the two squadrons of the Dorpatskii Mounted Jäger Regiment, and the Moskovskii and Libavskii Infantry Regiments.
47 Müffling, *Die Feldzüge*, 27–28; Freytag-Loringhoven, *Aufklärung und Armeeführung*, 66–67; Bogdanovich, *Geschichte des Krieges*, IIa:49.
48 Gneisenau to Hardenberg, Jauer, 25 August 1813, GSTA PK, I HA Rep. 74 Staatskanzleramt O Ap. Nr. 9, Bd. 3.
49 Blücher to Amalie, Jauer, 25 August 1813, *Blüchers Briefe*, ed. Unger, 174–75.
50 Müffling, *Die Feldzüge*, 26; Gneisenau to Hardenberg, Jauer, 25 August 1813, GSTA PK, I HA Rep. 74 Staatskanzleramt O Ap. Nr. 9, Bd. 3; Vaudoncourt, *Histoire de la guerre*, 144; Bogdanovich, *Geschichte des Krieges*, IIa:47.
51 Friederich, *Herbstfeldzug 1813*, I:287; Müffling, *Die Feldzüge*, 25; Droysen, *Yorck*, II:136; Henderson, *Blücher*, 126.
52 Nostitz, *Tagebuch*, 55.
53 Nostitz, *Tagebuch*, 56. Lieven, in *Russia Against Napoleon*, 377, contends that Langeron had been unfairly placed in a difficult position, believing that his opposition to Blücher corresponded to the tsar's desire that the Prussian obey the Reichenbach Plan.
54 Quoted in Freytag-Loringhoven, *Aufklärung und Armeeführung*, 11–12.
55 Freytag-Loringhoven, *Aufklärung und Armeeführung*, 43.
56 Gneisenau likewise understood the role of the Silesian Army, as seen in this 25 August letter to Hardenberg: "Finally I have a free moment to inform you that we have opened the campaign with much activity, and the difficult task that

we received – to never lose sight of the enemy, to engage him constantly, to initiate combat with him and yet avoid a battle – up until now has been fulfilled." See Gneisenau to Hardenberg, Jauer, 25 August 1813, GSTA PK, I HA Rep. 74 Staatskanzleramt O Ap. Nr. 9, Bd. 3.

57 Freytag-Loringhoven, *Aufklärung und Armeeführung*, 42.
58 Freytag-Loringhoven, *Aufklärung und Armeeführung*, 45–46.
59 Gneisenau to Hardenberg, Jauer, 25 August 1813, GStA PK, I HA Rep. 74 Staatskanzleramt O Ap. Nr. 9, Bd. 3.

6

The Katzbach

Including most of III Corps, Macdonald's army held a twelve-mile line stretching northeast to southwest along the Katzbach between Goldberg and Liegnitz on the evening of the 25th. Souham's main body camped at Rothkirch, with one division still marching east from Haynau to Liegnitz, which the French occupied. Sébastiani's cavalry passed the night at Hohendorf, some nine miles southwest of Liegnitz and four miles northeast of Goldberg. Lauriston's V Corps maintained Goldberg itself, with a vanguard at Prausnitz. Gérard's XI Corps stood just west of Goldberg; his 31st Division held Schönau, eleven miles south of Goldberg. After losing two days because of Ney, Macdonald eagerly prepared to move against Blücher's suspected position north of Jauer. He wanted to drive the Allied army deeper into Silesia and believed the mere advance of his own army would suffice to achieve this goal (see Map 2).

Just as Blücher needed a battle to save his army, Macdonald likewise needed to improve the situation of his own. Supply became a headache that worsened with each passing hour. Sitting in a region sucked dry during the armistice, his army desperately needed to move across the Katzbach and the Wütende Neiße in the hope of finding food in the untouched region of the former neutral zone. The region as far west as the Queis offered little for the masses that concentrated along the Katzbach. Inadequate supply forced the individual soldier to survive as best he could, inflicting devastation and violence on the inhabitants. The complete breakdown of discipline led to the victimization of the civilian population through plunder, robbery, burning, rape, and murder. Now the time had come for this army to conduct a military operation: could discipline be restored with the flip of a switch?

Macdonald could not worry about the answer: the marshal felt he had no choice but to move east on 26 August. From Goldberg, he issued an "Order of Movement" at 11:00 on the night of the 25th. Like Wittgenstein a few

10 Marshal Étienne-Jacques-Joseph-Alexandre Macdonald, 1765–1840

months earlier, the newly minted French commander drafted lengthy, complicated, and partly unclear instructions. For the next day, Gérard's XI
Corps, minus François Ledru's 31st Division, would form the center of the
imperial army and proceed from its positions west of Goldberg through
Röchlitz and Seichau to Jauer. Macdonald instructed Ledru to unite his
division at Berthelsdorf on the 26th to attack the Allied corps at Hirschberg
on the 27th. On the right wing, V Corps, less Jacques-Pierre Puthod's 17th
Division, would take the military highway southeast from Goldberg
through Prausnitz and Seichau to Jauer. On his far right, the marshal wanted
17th Division to reach Schönau on the 26th. From there, Puthod would send
one brigade to unite with the 31st Division in the assault on Hirschberg.
With his main body, Puthod would push through Jägendorf (Myślinów)
toward Jauer on the 27th to threaten Blücher's line of operation.

  While the instructions for XI and V Corps are fairly concise in the sense
that Macdonald at least provided clear objectives for his right and center,
those for his left wing – III Corps and II Cavalry Corps – are based on
conjecture and in consequence are extremely vague. All that clearly emerges
is the marshal's desire for the close cooperation of the units on his left wing.
Macdonald wanted III Corps marching by 7:00 "to pursue the enemy in the
supposition that he is retreating on Jauer, but whether he takes one or several
directions, Souham will limit himself to demonstrations with some of his
army corps and, as far as possible, with troops in proportion to the enemy's
forces, and with the rest he will threaten Jauer, heading toward this town by

the regular road from Liegnitz. Understanding the importance of always being in communication, Souham will remain in contact with Sébastiani and the troops he considers sufficient to leave at Liegnitz as well as those facing the enemy. Souham will echelon his corps and reach an agreement with Sébastiani over the amount of cavalry forces that will be appropriate to move to the left [east] of III Corps for flank coverage." Although less vague than Souham's, the instructions for Sébastiani indicate that Army Headquarters had little knowledge of the terrain: "After providing Souham the cavalry he will need to attain the dual objective noted above, Sébastiani will depart at 7:00 in the morning to move through Kroitsch on Jauer, using the Bunzlau–Jauer road. This general will remain in contact with Gérard and Souham through detachments. If Sébastiani has to cross defiles to pass, Souham will provide a few battalions to cover the cavalry."

With this, Macdonald's instructions came to an end. To his credit, the marshal invited scrutiny: "If this order of movement is susceptible to some observations or modifications, the commanding generals will share them with me immediately." He also recognized the possibility that his corps commanders would be unable to offer each other mutual support. Thus, to prevent his corps from becoming isolated, he reserved the right to determine the point of attack. Based on the army's movements as well as the numerous after-action reports, we can deduce how the corps commanders, mainly Souham and Sébastiani, interpreted their orders. Both believed they had to cross the Katzbach at Liegnitz and Kroitsch respectively. Souham would then strike the highway to Jauer and proceed south to Malitsch while Sébastiani crossed the Katzbach and Wütende Neiße in the region of Kroitsch and debouched on the plateau, seeking the Liegnitz–Jauer road.[1]

Because the marshal believed Blücher either would be caught south of Jauer or would continue to retreat deeper into Silesia, he departed from Goldberg without making any contingency plans in case the enemy should appear north or west of Jauer. His center, XI Corps, marched at 6:00 from Neudorf-am-Rennwege on the morning of 26 August "to reach Jauer through Röchlitz and Seichau." Macdonald accompanied V Corps, which advanced from Prausnitz along the left bank of the Wütende Neiße on the Goldberg–Jauer road at 7:00 A.M. Likewise at 7:00, Sébastiani's II Cavalry Corps filed out of Rothbrünnig (Brennik) en route to Kroitsch. Macdonald expected III Corps to also commence its operation at 7:00 in order for Souham to reach the plateau at the same time as Gérard and Sébastiani.[2]

Macdonald's courier left Army Headquarters at 11:00 P.M. on the 25th but did not reach Souham at Rothkirch until 9:30 on the morning of the 26th: two and one-half hours *after* III Corps should have departed. Souham then required an additional two hours to assemble his divisions.[3] In addition, Souham directed III Corps to Kroitsch rather than across the Katzbach at Liegnitz, claiming that the heavy rains had rendered the river impassable there. The results of a grossly delayed march to the wrong objective would prove disastrous for the marshal: the left wing of his army failed to reach the battle in time to influence its outcome. Macdonald could never have foreseen that III Corps would play such a limited role in the battle.

Terrain played a prominent role in the upcoming clash. The area of Silesia where the battle occurred formed a triangle between Goldberg, Liegnitz, and Jauer. To the west, the Katzbach between Liegnitz and Goldberg formed one side of the triangle. Main crossing points existed at Goldberg, Niederau, Röchlitz, Kroitsch, Schmogwitz, the Teichmann estate, and Liegnitz. Half-way between Goldberg and Liegnitz, the Wütende Neiße, a mountain stream, flowed into the Katzbach, thus cutting the battlefield in two. The Brechelshof estate, Schlaupe, Schlauphof, and Niederkrayn provided the main points of passage between the stream's steep banks. At Niederkrayn in particular, the right bank dominated the streambed. While both the Katzbach and the Wütende Neiße could be forded at many points in the dry season, they often overflowed their banks in rainy weather, carrying away the bridges and providing considerable obstacles. Having a large waterfall and absorbing several other mountain streams when in flood, the Wütende Neiße bore the well-deserved reputation of *wütende* (raging). The rainy season affected not only the watercourses, but the clay soil as well. Heavy summer storms turned roads into muddy quagmires, making the movement of military forces almost impossible: the unrelenting mud swallowed artillery up to the axles.

Along the right bank of the Wütende Neiße, on the eastern half of the battlefield where Yorck and Sacken would fight, the undulating plain of the mile-wide plateau extended north for two miles before descending to the Katzbach at Dohnau. On the western spur of the plateau, the hill chain that extended to Goldberg squeezed the Wütende Neiße into a narrow but steep gorge extending north from the Brechelshof estate to its junction with the Katzbach. Thus, the Wütende Neiße's sloping valley formed the western edge of the plateau as it snaked its way past Schlauphof, Niederweinberg, and Niederkrayn to just west of Dohnau. From the Brechelshof estate to the influx of the Wütende Neiße in the Katzbach, the flat, treeless plateau towered from 100 to 200 feet above the valley floor. Narrow, precipitous, overgrown ravines descended into the valley. Between Eichholtz (Warmątowice) and Bellwitzhof on one of the gentle hills that rolled across the plateau stood a colossal *Linde* (lime tree) later called the "*Blücherlinde*" because the Prussians established Blücher's command post under its boughs. Two main roads traversed the eastern half of the battlefield. The first ran northwest from Jauer through Brechelshof, Oberweinberg, and Niederweinberg[4] to Niederkrayn, where it crossed the Wütende Neiße and led to Kroitsch. There, the road forked: one branch continued northwest to Bunzlau while the other extended southwest through Röchlitz to Goldberg. The second road extended almost due north from Jauer through Neudorf to Liegnitz.

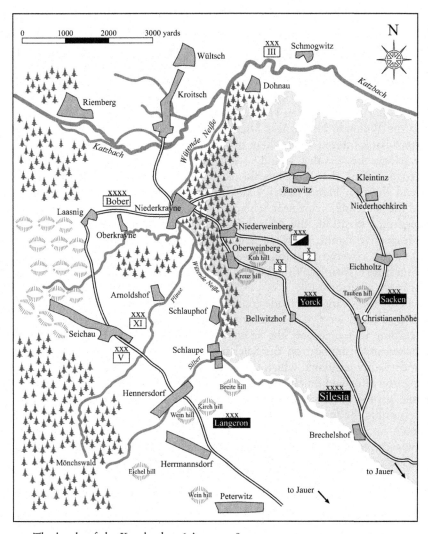

12. The battle of the Katzbach, 26 August 1813

Along the left bank of the Wütende Neiße, the western half of the battlefield bore little resemblance to the eastern portion. Less than three miles west of the Wütende Neiße rose the Mönchswald (Monks Forest) on a steep outcrop of the Sudeten Mountains called the Fulnigsberge. From this hill chain sprang numerous streams of varying depth that fed both the Wütende Neiße and the Katzbach. The intervals between these water courses formed excellent terrain sectors in the hilly region that provided very favorable defensive positions for Langeron's corps. The Goldberg–Jauer road, which ran northwest passing Hennersdorf and Seichau, cut through a valley located between the Mönchswald and the Wütende Neiße. This road intersected at right angles two advantageous terrain features found in this valley: a hill chain south of Hennersdorf and the swampy Plinse stream, which practically covered Langeron's entire front. Flowing southwest to northeast between Hennersdorf and Seichau, the Plinse discharged into the Wütende Neiße near Niederweinberg. A slight ridgeline along its eastern bank offered an excellent position for Langeron's vanguard. Behind this ridge, his cavalry found a suitable plain between Herrmannsdorf (Męcinka) and the Mönchswald. A second stream, the marshy Silber, passed through Hennersdorf, likewise flowing southwest to northeast to feed the Wütende Neiße near Schlaupe. While the Plinse covered the front of Langeron's position, the Mönchswald and the Wütende Neiße guarded its respective flanks. Between Seichau and the Plinse, the terrain offered a forward, covered position for defenders, while the hill chain south of Hennersdorf – primarily the Eichel, Wein, Kirch, and Breite hills – provided a primary position.

Lauriston's vanguard made contact with Langeron's advance posts on the hills north and west of Seichau around 9:00 on the morning of 26 August. According to Langeron: "the enemy advanced against me; strong columns attacked my vanguard on the Seichau heights, and others moved into the woods on my left flank, which they obviously sought to turn." At 9:30 A.M., Langeron informed Blücher that the enemy had engaged Rudzevich's forward posts, but the thick woods of the Mönchswald prevented the Russians from determining the size of the attacking force. Thirty minutes later, at 10:00, the French attacked the Russian post at Seichau itself; Lauriston's vanguard slowly drove back the Russians. At 11:00, Langeron ordered his forward posts to withdraw across the Plinse and reunite with Rudzevich's vanguard.[5]

Turning to the Prussians, Katzler passed the night slightly northwest of Bellwitzhof on the hills of Niederweinberg with Yorck's vanguard: six battalions, twelve Reserve Cavalry squadrons, and one battery each of horse and foot. Cavalry posts extended to the villages of Kroitsch and Wültsch (Wilczyce) situated close together on the left (western) bank of the Katzbach.[6] Early that morning, three East Prussian Jäger companies, 100 skirmishers from the Brandenburg Regiment, the Brandenburg Uhlan Regiment, and the 3rd and 4th Squadrons of Lithuanian Dragoons moved into the two villages; the rest of the cavalry and the horse battery remained on the right bank. Hiller, the commander of the vanguard infantry, sent small detachments to occupy the defiles of the Wütende Neiße from Schlaupe downstream to Niederkrayn while the main body held positions at the Niederweinberg mill, on a hill close to Niederweinberg, at the bridge over the Wütende Neiße at Niederkrayn, and along the bank downstream of this bridge.[7] The six-pound guns of Light Foot Battery Nr. 24 unlimbered on a steep hill that commanded the road from Niederkrayn to Jänowitz.

Meanwhile, Sébastiani's II Cavalry Corps approached Kroitsch. His 4th Light Cavalry Division under Rémy-Joseph Exelmans advanced in squadron columns to the left of the road while Nicolas-François Roussel's 2nd Light Cavalry Division proceeded along the right; Antoine-Louis St.-Germain's 2nd Heavy Cavalry Division followed behind the center of the two lead divisions. Roussel's detachments established and maintained communication with XI Corps to the southwest while Exelmans did the same with III Corps to the northeast. Inexplicably, neither reconnoitered the front toward Kroitsch, thus enabling the Prussians to spot their approach at 10:00.[8]

Around 11:00, Katzler observed Langeron's advance posts retreating southeast. With his left flank exposed by the Russian retreat, he withdrew the cavalry across the Wütende Neiße; two uhlan squadrons remained to take in the Jäger posted at Kroitsch and Wültsch. Meanwhile, Sébastiani's cavalry steadily closed on Wültsch. Waiting until the head of the column came very close, the Prussian Jäger opened fire, ripping holes in the ranks of the imperials. The well-aimed volleys at such close range forced the French to fall back. To blast the Prussians from their position, French horse artillery attempted to unlimber, but the Jäger inflicted so many casualties on the gun crews that the battery had to withdraw several hundred yards before opening an ineffective bombardment. After streaming rain fouled their muskets, the Prussian Jäger evacuated Kroitsch, crossed the Katzbach, and took position at Niederkrayn. The commander of the Jäger, Major Franz Karl von Klüx, described the action:

> I had hardly occupied the villages for five minutes when the outposts were thrown back in full gallop on Kroitsch by six or eight cavalry regiments mixed with artillery that were already getting close to the village. The enemy appeared to want nothing more than to reconnoiter and march through our outposts when he received fire from the Jäger at fifty paces. The resulting terror caused an about-face that rolled up the enemy and made such a great mass that no shot could miss. They withdrew somewhat, unlimbering a battery facing Wültsch and firing caseshot against the Jäger without great effect; they did likewise at Kroitsch, which they set ablaze with grenades. Because no infantry faced me and the thickly overgrown Katzbach was close in my rear, I viewed the villages as fortresses to be occupied as long as I could still fire a shot from the bushes in the strong rain, and only then moved across the water straight backwards.[9]

As soon as the Prussians withdrew from the villages, Sébastiani's cavalry continued its advance. At this time, the lead brigade of XI Corps' 35th Division marched through Riemberg (Rzymówka) and reached Kroitsch from the west just as Sébastiani's troopers entered the village from the north.

Infantry and cavalry collided. Both columns rolled pell-mell through the village and across the bridge, causing needless confusion that could have been avoided had Macdonald directed II Cavalry Corps to Dohnau. A portion of Sébastiani's cavalry took this road, but the majority rode through and sometimes over the infantry.[10] The awful weather made matters worse: pouring rain obscured the horizon, turned the rivers into swollen torrents, and washed out the roads. Both sides experienced difficulties executing movements.

Around this same time, Macdonald and Gérard rode into Laasnig with the head of XI Corps: General Claude-Marie Meunier's 2nd Brigade from 36th Division. Hearing musket fire to his left, Gérard rode northeast to investigate. Observing about a dozen Prussian squadrons in the valley south of Kroitsch facing Sébastiani's cavalry, he summoned three battalions and two guns from Meunier's brigade to scatter the enemy horse and take possession of the bridge over the Wütende Neiße at Niederkrayn. According to Gérard's report, his infantry moved to within fifty paces of the enemy cavalry line without being noticed. Behind the Prussians, the French infantry could have wreaked havoc, but the heavy rain had fouled the powder so that only forty muskets discharged. Nevertheless, Gérard maintains that this sufficed to convince the Prussian horse to hastily retreat to Niederweinberg. After a short resistance, the Prussians yielded that hamlet as well as the entire stretch between the Katzbach and the Wütende Neiße. Macdonald instructed Gérard to open the Oberkrayn–Niederweinberg road for II Cavalry Corps. The marshal wanted Sébastiani to re-form his regiments south of Kroitsch and then ascend the Niederweinberg defile as soon as Meunier's brigade had crowned the plateau with its infantry and artillery as well as the battery of twelve-pound guns belonging to XI Corps and now attached to 36th Division. Macdonald planned to support V Corps against Langeron with the rest of 36th Division as well as all of 35th, the corps cavalry, and reserve artillery.[11]

Despite the disorganized rabble on the opposite bank, Katzler realized he would not be able to resist the enemy's growing numbers. Hiller methodically withdrew his infantry to Niederkrayn, pursued by the three lead battalions of Meunier's brigade. Firing both too high and too low, Light Battery Nr. 24 failed to slow the French advance. Hiller retreated across the Wütende Neiße bridge, moving upstream in the valley (south) to the Niederweinberg defile. Pursued by Meunier's infantry, the Prussians defended the gorge for almost one hour. Without artillery support, the French could not dislodge Katzler's combined-arms vanguard from the slopes above Niederweinberg. Fortunately for the Allies, the Prussians eventually retreated and opened the passes to the French, thus allowing the ensuing battle on the plateau.

According to Hiller, imperial forces, "whose strength I estimated to be 40,000 men, pressed forward with uncommon zeal." Macdonald's troops

appeared everywhere. Besides pressing Hiller, the French reached Schlauphof south of Niederweinberg while to the north Sébastiani's cavalry moved
west toward Dohnau. As far as the eye could see, cavalry, infantry, and
artillery advanced across and through the ever-swelling waters of the
Wütende Neiße to the sunken roads and ravines of the valley. The French
finally unlimbered their artillery. Hiller continues:

> Three to four batteries, which came closer and closer to the defile, bom-
> barded me very intensely; some balls, which fell in Kempsky's [Oppeln's]
> Landwehr battalion, broke it, and the wild mass wanted to throw itself on the
> next battalion. Along with me, the brave commander of the battalion ...
> attempt to halt and re-form this battalion, which consisted only of raw Upper
> Silesians. Regardless, we were not successful until I pointed some cannon at
> them and gave my word of honor that I would fire on them. This worked,
> and from that moment on the battalion was so brave that, when a shell
> suddenly struck down fourteen men, it maintained order.[12]

Earlier that morning, I Corps had departed from Jauer at 5:00 and
marched northwest toward Schlauphof to fill the gap between Sacken and
Langeron.[13] In two columns, Yorck's soldiers trudged out of their bivouac
under heavy downpours and in the face of an unrelenting north wind. To
add to their misery, a portion of the march ran through fields that the
merciless rain had turned into bogs: many a soldier emerged without his
footgear. The mood of the troops matched the grey sky: with heavy hearts
they dragged themselves through the clay sludge. Following the right bank
of the Wütende Neiße, the Prussians trudged north through the Brechelshof
estate toward Bellwitzhof directly opposite Schlauphof; the Reserve Cavalry
moved right (northeast) to the Christianenhöhe farmstead 2,000 yards from
Bellwitzhof. In streaming rain, Yorck's lead brigades halted between Brechelshof and Bellwitzhof around 10:00 to await further orders; reports
arrived that Katzler's vanguard could not hold the enemy at the Katzbach.
Finally overpowered, Hiller conceded the Niederweinberg defile.

Reaching Brechelshof around 10:30 that morning, Blücher planned to
cross the Katzbach and attack Macdonald.[14] Starting around 9:00, intermittent firing could be heard from the direction of Seichau, but Headquarters
attributed this to outpost skirmishing. The Allies could see little: "A most
tremendous, continuous rain and a lowering sky had so darkened the horizon that every movement was difficult and any kind of reconnoitering
almost impossible."[15] Thus far, all reports had indicated the concentration
of enemy forces at Liegnitz and Goldberg. Between the two, a large body of
cavalry camped at Rothbrünnig. According to informants, Macdonald's
right wing did not move on the 25th while the left had fallen back to Haynau
on the 24th, but again moved forward on the 25th. Based on this information, Blücher and Gneisenau concluded that the imperials would

maintain a defensive position west of the Katzbach. Having no idea that Macdonald intended to take the offensive, they decided to proceed with their advance. Some accounts mistakenly claim that Blücher convened a council of war. Per his tradition, the general did speak openly with Gneisenau in the presence of the General Staff officers, especially those charged with writing and delivering his orders. In 1817, Blücher himself refuted this, telling an associate "that a dumb chap had just written a book" on the history of the Katzbach "in which he said that before the battle he [Blücher] had held a council of war. This was not true – never in his life had he [Blücher] held one."[16]

Around 11:00 A.M., Blücher issued the orders he hoped would bring him the battle he so desperately needed. For a diversion, he instructed Langeron to dispatch his left wing detachment (Pahlen II) from Schönau and Konradswaldau to attack the enemy at Goldberg. Langeron's vanguard would maintain a defensive posture at Seichau, shielding the main body as it marched north to cross the Katzbach at Riemberg and if possible Röchlitz as well. After crossing the river, Blücher wanted Langeron to form columns with the cavalry pushed northwest toward the Schnelle Deichsel. Meanwhile, the main blow would fall on Macdonald's left wing.[17] Yorck would lead I Corps across the Katzbach at Kroitsch and Dohnau. Marching northwest, he would take a position at Steudnitz, halfway between Liegnitz and Haynau, cutting off the enemy from the latter and attacking his rear at the former. To gain time for Yorck to complete the envelopment, Sacken had to fix the French at Liegnitz and gradually swing south, moving his corps across the Katzbach to "intensely" attack the enemy's right flank. The disposition ordered Sacken to send his light cavalry across the Katzbach downstream of Liegnitz to slam the enemy's left flank and cut off his retreat to Glogau. All corps should begin the march at 2:00 that afternoon. Blücher later extended the time to 3:00 for reasons that we shall soon see. "As soon as the enemy retreats," concluded Blücher's orders, "I expect the cavalry to proceed with boldness. The enemy must learn that he cannot retreat before us unscathed."[18]

After crossing the Katzbach, French officers restored enough order to form two main columns and send them in different directions. Sébastiani's cavalry mainly crossed the Wütende Neiße at Niederkrayn, ascended the plateau by various paths, and converged on the road that ran east to Jänowitz. The smaller column – Meunier's brigade and some of Sébastiani's regiments – turned south at Niederweinberg to move through Oberweinberg and debouch on the plateau by the Kuh hill. Although Meunier's infantry led the march, Sébastiani's troopers strove to reach the plateau first. Carelessly cutting their way through the foot soldiers, the impetuous riders completely shattered the cohesion of the infantry as it attempted to get through the pass. Meunier's battalions disintegrated as companies became separated. As soon as the officers restored order in one battalion, it continued to plod up the steep slope. Consequently, only individual battalions gradually cleared the pass to reach the plateau, which meant the French never gained numerical superiority over the retreating Prussians. The defile delayed the advance of the imperial infantry for some time, but Katzler knew his small vanguard could not stop the enemy from deploying. Moreover, his position at Niederweinberg became increasingly dangerous after French forces cleared the Niederkrayn defile and struck the road to Janöwitz, thus threatening his right flank.

Katzler formed the rest of Hiller's infantry in two lines on the road to the Christianenhöhe farm. Soon joined by the cavalry, the Prussians withdrew en echelon with the left wing remaining forward of the right. Light Battery Nr. 24 somewhat redeemed itself by placing four guns on each wing and skillfully using the terrain to destroy one gun and one mortar from a French battery. Heavy rains continued to foul the muskets so that the pursuing imperials could only fire curses at the Prussians. In his report, Hiller claimed that they "made front every 100 paces in order to give the army time to position itself." Around 1:30 P.M., the first French infantry – Meunier's battalions – reached the plateau. They immediately dispatched swarms of skirmishers, who soon discovered that the weather had rendered their muskets useless. "Believing we were retreating," continued Hiller, "the enemy mocked us with swear-words, deployed quickly, and pushed forward a mass of skirmishers, but they were hardly effective because of the continuous rain."[19]

Although the French infantry posed little threat, the main mass of Sébastiani's cavalry as well as his horse artillery also debouched onto the plateau after climbing the slopes of the Wütende Neiße valley in columns of twos. His lead division, Roussel's 2nd Light, turned southeast, placing its left wing at Kleintinz (Tyńczyk Legnicki) and arranging its regiments in three lines: 11th and 12th Chasseurs and 2nd Lancers formed the first; 2nd and 4th Lancers and 5th Hussars the second; and 3rd and 9th Hussars the third. Next, the twenty-four guns of II Cavalry Corps moved up and unlimbered between the right wing of the 2nd Light Cavalry and the left wing of Meunier's brigade near the Kuh hill.[20] The French completed this deployment by 2:00; Sébastiani's troopers wasted no time in harrying Hiller's infantry. Again the Landwehr performed admirably. "Later," reported Hiller, "when no man could fire any longer, the battalion held together in square when it was beset by enemy cavalry. Throughout the entire engagement, the Seydlitz [Schweidnitz] Landwehr Battalion maintained itself with the order and calm of a veteran battalion."[21] To take in the advance guard, Jürgaß formed the Reserve Cavalry between Christianenhöhe and the Oberweinberg–Bellwitzhof road; his Nr. 1 and Nr. 2 Horse Batteries went into action against the French artillery. Thus covered, Katzler's troops continued their retreat. Around 2:00, they reached a position between Bell-witzhof and Christianenhöhe while Yorck's main body moved up between Bellwitzhof and Brechelshof.

Macdonald did not follow the troops to the plateau, but instead established his command post near the Bunzlau–Jauer road purportedly "awaiting from one moment to the next the arrival of III Corps." To the east, a few enemy battalions appeared to be retreating on the plateau. However, V and XI Corps seemed to be intensely engaged to the south, leading the marshal to believe that the main action would occur on his right. Hearing the increasing intensity of Lauriston's guns, the marshal rode toward his right wing. En route, he met Souham, who "announced the arrival of III Corps behind II Cavalry Corps." Although two battalions from III Corps had been at Liegnitz since the 25th, they had taken no measures to reconnoiter that sector of the Katzbach to determine the condition of the bridges and crossing points. Not until the march commenced on the 26th – albeit four and one-half hours late – did the French evaluate these points of passage. The commander of Souham's engineers reported that he could not find one passable bridge over the Katzbach in the Liegnitz region. "I took all the information on the crossings of the Katzbach that I could get in that short time, which did not allow reconnaissance to be conducted," stated Souham in his after-action report to Berthier. "I learned that all the bridges at Liegnitz were down, and the only one that existed vis-à-vis the position was at Kroitsch." To save time, Souham directed III Corps to Kroitsch. Instead of the entire corps, only the 39th Division marched to Liegnitz to cover the engineers as they rebuilt the bridge on the Liegnitz–Jauer road.[22]

With his right wing leading the march, Souham's lead division – General Michel-Sylvestre Brayer's 8th – reached Kroitsch at 2:30 P.M., just as II Cavalry Corps finished crossing the Katzbach. "Because the marshal told me to maintain direct contact with the cavalry corps of General Sébastiani," continued Souham, "I thought it necessary to direct the right of the army [corps] to this village to fulfill this goal, and at the same time not act alone and not become involved in a separate affair, which the marshal had warned each corps against." Macdonald expressed his understanding of Souham's predicament but, in view of the smooth deployment of the army, III Corps had arrived at a terrible moment. Thus, he insisted that only 8th Division cross the Katzbach at Kroitsch and climb the valley wall at Niederkrayn. But what of the rest of the corps: 9th, 10th, and 11th Divisions?

An unexpected opportunity to redress Souham's mistake became available to Macdonald. Only the commander in chief had the authority to prevent III Corps and II Cavalry Corps from becoming entangled. Indecision momentarily froze Macdonald; he limited himself to mere recommendations. Before continuing to Lauriston's sector, he advised Souham to move one division onto the plateau while two others turned it by seeking a point of passage across the Katzbach further downstream, and the fourth remained in reserve. Souham's version slightly varies, yet the corps commander's report to Berthier and thus the emperor provides sufficient evidence to conclude that Macdonald did not make a decisive decision on the spot: "The affair was already heavily engaged, the other three divisions were placed in a position on the left bank to be able to turn the enemy's right wherever the marshal judged necessary. The 8th Division formed at the foot of the plateau on which the engagement was taking place."[23]

Thirty minutes later, Macdonald finally made a firm decision.[24] After observing the combat on his right wing, he sent orders for Souham's 9th, 10th, and 11th Divisions to "move rapidly to the left along the right bank of the Katzbach to take the enemy in the flank and force him to abandon his position [on the plateau]." The marshal hoped this movement would open the defiles of the Wütende Neiße. French staff officer and historian Gabriel Fabry criticizes the marshal for not throwing all of III Corps against Langeron, whom the Wütende Neiße and the hills south of Oberkrayn separated from the rest of Blücher's army. Moreover, how could the marshal expect the divisions of III Corps, whose head arrived at Kroitsch at 2:30, to march on a single road and get across the Katzbach in time to intervene on the plateau with force? Even if they cleared the river in good time, Souham's divisions would then have faced the possibility of having to master enemy-occupied heights just to climb on the plateau. Indeed, according to the journal of the III Corps, by the time 9th Division, which was closest to the battlefield, changed direction, marched left (east), and "boldly climbed the mountain" at Dohnau, the Allies had already driven the French from the plateau. Thus, 9th Division "was received by an artillery fire that its own could not answer." While the first and second points of Fabry's critique are legitimate arguments, this last criticism, which relies exclusively on hindsight, is undeserved: Macdonald had no way of knowing that the situation on the plateau would end with the rout of his left wing.[25]

Returning to Blücher's left wing, Langeron completed the deployment of his army corps around noon. North of Hennersdorf, Rudzevich's ad hoc vanguard division held the ridgeline along the left bank of the Plinse, with 1st Brigade of 8th Division of X Infantry Corps (Staroingermanlandskii and Arkhangelogorodskii Infantry Regiments, four battalions total) to the left (west) of the Goldberg–Jauer road, the two battalions of the 45th Jäger Regiment in the center holding the left bank of the Plinse itself, and the two battalions of the 29th Jäger Regiment to the right (east) of the Goldberg–Jauer road.[26] Regarding the cavalry and artillery, Rudzevich's disposition reflects Langeron's concern about being enveloped on the left. While the three squadrons of the 2nd Ukrainskii Cossack Regiment covered the extreme right wing, the two squadrons of the Litovskii Mounted Jäger

Regiment and the five squadrons of the Kievskii Dragoon Regiment held the extreme left, supported by the 3rd Ukrainskii Cossack Regiment, which took a position behind (south of) 1st Brigade of 8th Division. On a hill north of these two regiments, the ten guns of the Don Cossack 2nd Artillery Battery unlimbered. Forward posts stood north and west of Seichau.

Langeron's main body deployed along the curve formed by Herrmannsdorf, Wein hill, Kirch hill, Breite hill, and Schlaupe, with Olsufiyev's IX Infantry Corps and General Aleksey Shcherbatov's VI Infantry Corps forming the respective left and right wings. Langeron posted his reserve behind the right wing of his position between Herrmannsdorf and Breite hill, Korf's cavalry on the left east of Herrmannsdorf, and two brigades as well as the artillery of Kaptsevich's X Infantry Corps on the right west of Breite hill. "My other [infantry] corps," noted Langeron, "occupied the three heights of Wein, Kirch, and Breite, between Herrmannsdorf and Schlaupe, having in front of them the village of Hennersdorf, which was occupied by my Jäger; Schlaupe was occupied by the 11th Jäger, supported by the 2nd Ukrainskii Cossack Regiment ... and by some Prussian cavalry squadrons from the left flank of Yorck's corps, on which my right flank rested; my left flank was secured by the movement I [eventually] ordered Rudzevich to make."[27]

With more than thirty battalions, eleven squadrons of regular cavalry, and seventy-eight guns at his disposal, Langeron could have offered considerable resistance.[28] With his right anchored to Schlaupe on the Wütende Neiße and his left on the Mönchswald, Langeron's front extended a manageable 5,000 yards. At Schlaupe, the Russian right connected with Yorck's left on the eastern bank of the Wütende Neiße while the thick wood of the Mönchswald prevented any sizeable force from turning his left in a tactical envelopment. However, a strategic envelopment of his left through Jägendorf concerned the Russian corps commander, although he hoped Pahlen II's detachment at Konradswaldau would inform him in time of such a movement.

By noon, Langeron's vanguard was in position on the left bank of the Plinse while his main body stretched from Herrmannsdorf to Schlaupe along the curve of the Silber. Facing it, Lauriston deployed his two divisions – Maison's 16th and Rochambeau's 19th – in the one-mile gap between Seichau and Arnoldshof (Sichówek). To envelop the Russians, a flanking detachment consisting of two battalions and two guns took a position on the Kreuz hill – the northern gateway to the Mönchswald – with orders to proceed through the forest by way of a ravine. At this time, Blücher's courier, Lieutenant Ludwig Friedrich Leopold von Gerlach, delivered the attack disposition that had been drafted at 11:00. "At noon," Langeron recalled, "Blücher shared with me a brilliant and daring plan that he had conceived to attack the enemy with his right. He ordered me to move to my right via Bromberg to support his attack if possible but, if I could not execute this movement, to content myself with holding the enemy to their right; he added that my corps would be the pivot in the great maneuver that he was projecting."

According to Langeron, the scribe – probably Müffling – had used a thin sheet of paper that the rain reduced to pulp. Langeron asked Gerlach if he knew the contents. Gerlach had been listening while Gneisenau dictated the orders, but could not recall his instructions verbatim. Langeron ordered the lieutenant to recite what he knew several times before witnesses, explaining in his memoirs that "I had to use extreme caution with a man like Gneisenau who, in fact, commanded our army and wanted a German and not a Frenchman to command my corps." Not able to contain his discontent, the corps commander blurted: "Your general [Blücher] is a good swordsman, but that is all." He explained to Gerlach the difficulty of his situation and, according to German sources, added: "We must be prudent and, you must admit, prudence is not the strongpoint of General Gneisenau."[29]

Blücher's instructions – based on the assumption the French would remain at Goldberg, thus allowing Langeron to march north – no longer appeared feasible. Even worse, the imperials had taken the offensive. Believing that Lauriston's advance had completely changed the situation, the Russian commander understandably felt he could not execute his orders. Should he attack Lauriston? Headquarters made no mention of this circumstance in the recent correspondence, and the disposition stated that the advance would not begin until 2:00. Langeron noted that "the considerable forces I had before me and the clear intention of the enemy to turn my left did not permit me to abandon my position and march to my right without opening the Jauer road, but I assured Blücher that I would not lose an inch of terrain and that I would continue to tie down a large number of the enemy's forces, although I was weakened by the detachment of X Infantry Corps. I had not overstretched myself in giving this assurance to Blücher, considering the excellent troops that I commanded."[30]

Meanwhile, Lauriston ordered V Corps to advance around 12:30. He positioned his left wing – all of Rochambeau's 19th Division – to move across the Plinse ravine. On his right, Maison's 16th Division prepared to turn the Russian left. Led by the flank detachment of two battalions and two guns, Maison's main body surged forward. After moving straight through Seichau, Rochambeau's division divided into several battalion columns south of the village to advance in a broad front across the Plinse. According to the French corps commander: "The enemy appeared on the hills of Hennersdorf: lots of artillery and cavalry, but few infantry. In cavalry, I had [Paul Ferdinand] Dermoncourt's brigade, which did not contain more than 600 horses. When I heard the first shots of XI Corps, I began the attack for the passage of the ravine. I placed a battery of six twelve-pound guns and two six-pound howitzers, which took the enemy's batteries obliquely. I also established other batteries in advantageous positions. General Maison brought up the troops with his usual vigor."[31]

Lauriston's advance settled the issue in Langeron's mind: the situation called for a retreat. He immediately dispatched an officer to Blücher armed with a lie. To justify his intended retreat through Jauer on Striegau, Langeron reported that he faced superior forces in his sector. In response to Blücher's 11:00 attack disposition he wrote: "Two columns that want to turn my left flank are moving toward the woods followed by three others. In addition, I can see the columns debouching from Seichau to attack the vanguard. If I execute the ordered movement, the vanguard will be forced to immediately withdraw to Jauer because it will be attacked by a superior enemy force. The enemy has taken Seichau."[32] Although correct in the assumption that he could not execute Blücher's order, Langeron's desire to retreat superseded his military judgment. In dictating his letter to Blücher's liaison officer, Ende, Langeron caused a scene. Purportedly, he originally stated: "Two strong columns have turned my left." Ende asked Langeron to clarify what he meant by the term "strong." Langeron requested clarification from the officer who delivered the report. In turn, the Russian replied that at most the columns consisted of two battalions each. "Very well," exclaimed Langeron, "write two columns." Ende then questioned the use of the phrase "have turned my left," "Very well," retorted Langeron, "write: 'want to turn.'"[33]

Lauriston's steady pressure prompted Langeron to withdraw Rudzevich's vanguard from its positions between the Plinse and Hennersdorf. "I pushed the enemy to the heights of Seichau," stated Lauriston in his after-action report; "he took a few cannon shots, but as this produced no effect, we made the enemy cross the deep ravine that separated Seichau from Hennersdorf. I halted in this position, both to make my dispositions for the passage of the ravine and to await the divisions of XI Corps, whose attack was to take place simultaneously."[34] After exchanging a few shots with the French, Rudzevich received instructions to withdraw southwest of Hennersdorf to a position west of Herrmannsdorf and form Langeron's new left wing. Thus, Langeron abandoned the advantageous ridgeline along the left bank of the Plinse. His front now consisted of Rudzevich's vanguard division on the left, west of Herrmannsdorf; Olsufiyev's IX Infantry Corps in the center between Herrmannsdorf and the Kirch hill; and Shcherbatov's VI Infantry Corps on the right wing, extending northeast from the Kirch hill across the Breite hill to Schlaupe. In his memoirs, Langeron attempted to justify this decision:

> After two hours of cannon and musket fire from the skirmishers, and seeing the majority of the enemy's forces moving to their right and turning the left of my vanguard through the woods, I ordered Rudzevich, whom I had been

with since the beginning of the engagement, to quit the Hennersdorf heights and place himself to the left of my line between the woods and the village of Herrmannsdorf, in a plain through which the enemy could easily turn my left flank, which was totally unsupported. This movement ... was made just in time; if I had delayed for only thirty minutes, I would have been completely outflanked and forced to quit my position.

Langeron's next move likewise caused controversy. He ordered Kaptsevich's X Infantry Corps to march south and take a position just north of Peterwitz, forming its battalion lines facing west on another height called Wein hill. According to Langeron, after he "received from Yuzefovich the news that an enemy corps was moving on Schönau, and seemed to wish to move to Jauer (which Macdonald had effectively ordered), I detached X Infantry Corps from the rear that formed my second line, and I ordered General Kaptsevich to move on Peterwitz and, if it was necessary, on Mois-dorf to stop the enemy's advance on Jauer. Having detached X Infantry Corps, which also served as my reserve, I remained with a highly extended line."[35] Macdonald had indeed ordered Puthod to march on Jauer, but not on 26 August. As noted, the marshal wanted the 17th Division to march from Steinberg to Schönau on the 26th. From there, Puthod would push through Jägendorf toward Jauer on the 27th. Moreover, Steinberg was located five miles west-southwest of Goldberg. Puthod did not begin his march until 12:30 P.M. and Yuzefovich did not receive news of it until the evening. Nevertheless, Langeron ordered Kaptsevich to withdraw to Peterwitz some-time before 1:00 P.M. This can only mean that Langeron was preparing for a general retreat.

On the eastern side of the battlefield, Yorck's rear echelon reached the Brechelshof estate around 11:00. Shortly afterward, he received the attack disposition along with instructions to have the troops cook. Yorck's mood, no doubt soured by the march, certainly did not improve by what appeared to be a bad joke: how could his men cook in such weather? Some accounts claim that, like Langeron, Yorck also refused to comply with Blücher's attack disposition. With an eye toward Gneisenau, the crotchety man of Tauroggen supposedly swore that he would rather break his sword than cross the Katzbach. Although this tale undoubtedly captures Yorck's foul mood, it is only partially correct. To comply with Blücher's attack dispos-ition, Yorck issued a "Special Disposition" to his corps.[36] Yet, starting around noon, he "heard a quickly approaching fire." To his left on the other side of the Wütende Neiße, individual cannonballs falling on the road to Goldberg came closer and closer. Around this time, Gneisenau requested that I Corps be ready to send one column downstream along the Wütende Neiße and a second to the plateau north of Bellwitzhof at 2:00. Yorck's biographer, Droysen, claims that "Yorck's refusal was evident." One of

Blücher's biographers, Blasendorff, maintains that Yorck demanded two days of rest before the army launched an offensive. Moreover, Droysen attributes the delay of the attack from 2:00 to 3:00 to the debate triggered by Yorck's refusal.[37]

After receiving Hiller's report that the advance guard had withdrawn onto the plateau, Yorck retracted the "Special Disposition," mounted his horse, and prepared to ride north. Ordering the columns to follow, he shouted, "I will decide the rest on the spot." Before his horse could break into a gallop, an officer, Captain Karl Otto von Brünneck, approached from Army Headquarters. Although described as "very brave and capable," Brünneck tended to irritate Yorck. The major presented himself to Yorck and recited: "'General Blücher orders General Yorck to allow as much of the enemy to move up as he believes he can still defeat and then he will attack.' Yorck responded to the pretentious Junker blueblood: 'You ride out there and you count; I can't even count my fingers in this rain.'" With enemy shells falling increasingly closer to his thick columns, Yorck ordered the infantry to form lines to spare the men from having to execute this maneuver under fire. He also instructed Colonel Schmidt to unlimber the artillery on the Tauben hillock between the Christianenhöhe estate and Eichholtz. Although only a slight elevation, the Tauben hill commanded the entire plateau. Before the Prussian guns arrived, the twelve-pound pieces of Sacken's Nr. 13 Heavy Battery blazed from this same position. Recognizing the importance of the hill, Sacken had directed his heavy guns there, although the point was not situated on his line of march. This earned the Russian commander Blücher's highest praise as well as the "lasting esteem and attachment" of Yorck's men. Upon receiving Blücher's orders, Sacken purportedly exclaimed: "Tell the general my only answer is 'Hurrah!'"[38]

To the right (east) of I Corps, Sacken's troops marched northwest from Malitsch toward the space between Niederhochkirch (Kościelec) and Eichholtz, the latter being one and one-half miles northeast of Bellwitzhof. Sacken's foot consisted of the three divisions (27th, 16th, and 10th) of XI Infantry Corps. The four battalions of the 8th and 39th Jäger Regiments that constituted one of 10th Division's three brigades occupied Eichholtz with Karpov's six Cossack Regiments roaming north of the village. Sacken moved up Neverovsky's 27th Division and the remaining two brigades of 10th Division, commanded by General Lieven, to a position just south of Eichholtz. From these positions, Sacken ordered 27th Division along with the Okhotskii and Kamchatskii Infantry Regiments (two battalions *total*) of the sole brigade of 16th Division to form the first line; Lieven's 10th Division provided the second. General Sergey Ushakov posted the Kurlandskii and Smolenskii Dragoon Regiments south of Eichholtz on the right flank of the second line while Vasilchikov led the 2nd Hussar Division to a position just east of Eichholtz.

In the meantime, Gneisenau and Müffling left Brechelshof to reconnoiter the plateau. At Christianenhöhe they met Hiller, who reported that the enemy had crossed the Katzbach in considerable strength, pursued through Niederkrayn, and ascended the plateau. Katzler remained behind with the cavalry. Unable to see more than 500 yards in front of them, Gneisenau and Müffling managed to ride north for a long way because the French neglected to deploy a cavalry screen. "We saw nothing before us," recalled Müffling; "we did not hear a shot." Finally they met up with Katzler, who claimed the enemy to be "close on my heels. More he could not tell, for in his irresponsible hussar manner he had called in all his flankers." Müffling started to censure Katzler, but Gneisenau cut him short, stating that the mistake had been made and they had to move on. Gneisenau started to move forward with Katzler and the officers of the advance guard cavalry. Müffling insisted that such a large suite would not be effective for reconnaissance work and offered to go alone. Gneisenau accepted and the colonel sped toward the Kuh hill.

"I was mounted on a chocolate-colored horse," continues Müffling, "and I wore a grey cloak, so that in the pouring rain I was not visible at 100 paces. Moreover, I took a good map of the district with me, which I had already learned by heart." Reaching the Kuh hill, "not one man was to be seen on the plains toward Kleintinz or anything to be heard in the valley toward Oberweinberg." Müffling then rode toward the Niederweinberg–Jänowitz road. Reaching the latter, he found himself so close to enemy cavalry that he had to take cover "behind a leafy tree to remain undiscovered. I saw some batteries follow the cavalry on the road from Niederkrayn to Jänowitz. Behind me I heard shouts in French, and saw in the valley of Niederkrayn an enemy infantry column marching, whose head had almost reached the plateau." Müffling quietly slipped away. Gaining the Niederkrayn–Brechelshof road, he looked back. As much as the rain would permit an estimate, he observed 3,000 cavalry and several batteries moving east in the direction of Jänowitz.[39] Imperial infantry followed on the same road, but only a few battalions appeared to be moving south. Owing to the streaming rain, the Prussian officer could not ascertain if more French columns stood further north. In all, it appeared that 10,000–12,000 enemy troops had ascended the plateau.

Returning to Blücher's command post, Gneisenau explained that the French apparently intended to overwhelm the few battalions of Yorck's vanguard on the plateau in order to double-envelop Langeron's corps.[40] If a second column debouched through Dohnau – which the Prussians could not reconnoiter – enemy forces could increase to between 35,000 and 40,000 combatants. Thus, Müffling suggested that Blücher order Yorck to immediately attack with three and one-half brigades, leaving the other half-brigade to maintain contact with Langeron's corps; Sacken should be directed to Eichholtz. Although Yorck and Sacken outnumbered the enemy, Müffling advised against giving the imperials time to move additional forces onto the plateau. Not knowing if French forces stood north of Jänowitz, the colonel insisted that the best option would be to drive the imperials into the defiles and onto their approaching reinforcements. Purportedly with watch in hand, Müffling assured Blücher "that, if General Yorck moves out immediately and continues to march in column uninterrupted, in fifty-one minutes he can reach the point on the plateau where I saw the enemy infantry column. Because they must march through a narrow defile, General Yorck cannot possibly find more than 10,000 infantry." No one doubted that Langeron could maintain his strong position to cover Blücher's flank and rear. With the Wütende Neiße and the Katzbach in their rear, the French could not avoid a catastrophe.

Blücher approved with gusto. Headquarters again cut new orders for Yorck: instead of waiting, I Corps would establish its artillery line and right wing on the hills between Bellwitzhof and Eichholtz to engage the enemy approaching from Niederweinberg and Kleintinz. His left wing, concealed on the high western edge of the plateau, would advance north, hugging the edge of the Wütende Neiße valley. Gneisenau accepted Müffling's contention that in one hour Yorck's left could reach the point where the sunken road from Niederkrayn opened onto the plateau. From there, this wing could envelop the enemy's right flank while Sacken executed a similar movement against the opposite flank. Müffling received the task of leading Yorck's corps to its designated position.[41]

Yorck had already arranged his corps to comply with the original attack disposition Blücher had issued at 11:00. His left wing consisted of 8th and 7th Brigades as well as the Reserve Artillery; 2nd and 1st Brigades and the Reserve Cavalry formed the right. According to Blücher's new instructions, 2nd and 7th Brigades as well as the majority of 8th Brigade would form the first wave while 1st Brigade followed in reserve; battalions from 8th Brigade would secure Schlaupe, maintain contact with Langeron, and cover Yorck's flank. Yorck disregarded these instructions to place three brigades in his first line and marched with his corps in two wings.[42] As the infantry slogged across the sopping fields between Brechelshof and Bellwitzhof, the Nr. 3 Light Battery unlimbered next to the Russian artillery on the Tauben hill while the Nr. 1 Heavy Battery (twelve-pound guns) and the Nr. 15 Light Battery formed a line next to the Nr. 2 Horse Battery of the Reserve Cavalry northwest of Christianenhöhe to cover the deployment. A total of ninety-two Allied guns dueled with forty pieces of French artillery. To occupy the imperials while Yorck's infantry moved up, the 1st, 2nd, and Jäger Squadrons of the Lithuanian Dragoon Regiment dismounted on the left to provide covering fire.

During the march, Yorck ordered Horn's 7th Brigade to change places with Karl's 2nd, so that the former would move from the second wave of the left wing to form the first wave on the right wing, and the latter would move from the first wave of the right wing to form the second wave of the left wing. Following this switch, I Corps would be arranged so that 8th Brigade followed by the 2nd formed the left and 7th Brigade followed by 1st the right. Yorck's reasons for altering the march formation are not known. Inexplicably, not all of the brigade commanders received this order. As the two wings of I Corps approached the Bellwitzhof–Christianenhöhe line, Yorck found both brigades in their original position: the 2nd on the right in the first wave and the 7th on the left in the second wave. The Prussians then wasted considerable time crossing the two brigades in compliance with Yorck's instructions. Moreover, Horn and Karl purportedly argued over whose brigade would receive the place of honor in the front line. During this interval, Yorck received word of two large enemy columns approaching Schlaupe. With orders to hold this vital position at all costs, he sent the 4th Battalion of the 14th Silesian Landwehr and the Silesian Grenadier Battalion to reinforce the Brandenburg Fusilier Battalion. Moreover, one of Blücher's staff officers, Major Oppen, informed Yorck that at most the enemy force on the plateau consisted of four battalions, eight guns, and some cavalry. Concluding that he would not encounter strong resistance on the plateau, Yorck dispatched 8th Brigade's commander, Hünerbein, to direct the defense of Schlaupe.

As noted, Yorck deployed his brigades in lines to enable his inexperienced battalions to attain the proper extension along the length of the front. After rearranging the brigades to his liking, 7th and 8th formed the first wave, 2nd the second, and 1st remained in reserve. Each brigade formed two echelons. On Blücher's orders, Müffling arrived to guide I Corps to its correct position. Seeing the infantry formed in lines, he reminded Yorck that the approach march should be executed in columns. Although linear formations would reduce the deadly and terrorizing effects of French shelling, advancing in line required more time than an advance in column. Müffling argued that the imperials would use this time to move more troops onto the plateau. Moreover, he insisted that the soaked ground and the inexperience of the Landwehr had rendered a linear advance impractical. Yorck resisted, furiously protesting against this staff officer's interference. "Müffling became excited over the loss of time," explains Droysen, "but the practitioner [Yorck] placed no value on winning time if it was purchased with the lack of tactical security." Purportedly "foaming with rage," Müffling rode off to find Blücher, eventually returning with a direct order for I Corps to advance in column. "The general deliberated sullenly, but at last obeyed though not without signs of anger," recalled Müffling.[43]

Blücher and Prince William rode before the front of each battalion, inciting the men and demanding that they attack with cold steel rather than try to fire their muskets in the rain. "My brave lads," Blücher shouted, "this day decides it! Prove to your king and to your country that your courage is equal to your devotion. Prove it, I say, at the point of your bayonet. Look yonder, there's the enemy. Now march and prove yourselves to be gallant Prussians."[44]

Delayed by its collision with 2nd Brigade, Horn's 7th Brigade had not completed the formation of its columns when Yorck commenced the advance. Thus, only the six remaining battalions of 8th Brigade – commanded by Lieutenant-Colonel Borcke – moved forward on Yorck's left; even the brigade cavalry remained behind because Yorck ordered it to move south of Bell-witzhof in case Hünerbein needed support at Schlaupe. "The ground was undulating," wrote Müffling in 1824, "and the rain so violent, that both combined to prevent the French army from detecting the approach of our infantry until the village of Bellwitzhof was far to our rear." Meanwhile, on Yorck's right, the Reserve Cavalry moved through the intervals of the artillery: the eight squadrons of the 5th and 10th Silesian Landwehr Regiments pos-itioned themselves to the right of the artillery line to cover the guns while the Brandenburg Uhlans secured the link with Sacken. The Nr. 24 Foot Battery and Nr. 1 Horse Battery formed the left of the artillery line. Jürgaß placed the remainder of the Reserve Cavalry between the 7th and 2nd Brigades.

From left to right, the first wave of 8th Brigade consisted of the 2nd Battalion of the 12th Reserve Regiment, the 3rd Battalion of the 14th Silesian Landwehr Regiment, and Major Karl Thomas von Othegraven's 2nd Battal-ion of the 2nd Brandenburg Regiment; the 3rd and 1st Battalions of the 12th Reserve and the 2nd Battalion of the 14th Silesian Landwehr formed the second wave. Platoons of skirmishers preceded the battalions, but they remained bunched in groups for safety because their muskets could not fire. The rain fell so violently that they did not see the French. Marching in complete isolation, with its left wing pressed against the edge of the Wütende Neiße valley, 8th Brigade unknowingly came within range of a French half-battery on the Kreuz hill. "I led the left wing of the two brigades toward the Kuh hill," explains Müffling, "behind which the enemy cavalry was posted with five or six batteries that were firing at great dis-tances. Nothing else was to be seen of the enemy. Completely unexpectedly, enemy infantry with some cannon appeared on the Kreuz hill this side of the Kuh hill."[45]

Moving ahead of the rest of the first wave, Othegraven's battalion soon received flesh-tearing canister fire: many men fell, but the survivors con-tinued to advance. In addition to the enemy guns, the Prussians soon discerned Meunier's three battalions cresting the Kuh hill. On seeing the Prussians, two of Meunier's battalions retraced their steps to avoid a skir-mish but the third moved down the slope and formed a square. From the French viewpoint: "The enemy [Katzler] had continued his retrograde movement, and we believed very much he was in full retreat when we saw columns to our left, which we initially took for III Corps, which was supposed to debouch in that direction. A moment later, enemy artillery and infantry appeared in front of us."[46] Coming within range of French muskets, the Prussians increased their march but had little to fear because the enemy could not fire. Othegraven, marching with the first rank of his battalion, ordered his men to fix bayonets. Unable to fall back, the French offered fierce resistance. Supported by the 2nd Silesian Landwehr Battalion from the second wave, the Prussians encircled the square. An extremely bloody struggle ensued: musket-butt clubbed and bayonet stabbed. One Prussian officer recalled:

> We now doubled our pace, lowered our muskets, and attacked the middle square of French grenadiers with fixed bayonets amid terrifying cries of "Hurrah." The square stood like a wall. We came within two paces. For a moment our people stood across from the French so that both sides could see each other. We officers shouted: *"Drauf, drauf!* [On them, on them!]" and now the soldiers reversed their muskets and drove into the French with the butt of their muskets. Because we stood in line, the square was quickly encircled on the left and right and thus attacked from all sides with the bayonet and the musket-butt. No one thought of giving quarter; after ten minutes the entire square was shattered and transformed into a pyramid. Some 150 unscathed and lightly wounded found themselves among heaps of dead and wounded; they were sent back as prisoners.[47]

Othegraven lost 3 officers and 188 men; the Prussians captured 7 officers and 165 men; French killed and wounded are not known.

Meanwhile, the other two battalions of the first wave turned against the half-battery on the Kreuz hill. After driving the infantry escort down the reverse slope, the Prussians took one gun but the other three attempted to escape. Yorck's men would not have it: they tracked down and captured the pieces. A French Chasseur squadron approached the right flank of the 3rd Silesian Landwehr Battalion, which had become completely disordered during the melee. French officers offered quarter, but the commander, Colonel Gaza, managed to re-form the militia. With bayonets fixed the Prussians advanced toward the French troopers, who decided it would be best to follow their infantry. "The Landwehr battalion was surrounded by enemy cavalry and ordered to surrender," recounts Gneisenau. "'No! No!' shouted the Landwehr and attempted to fire. Few muskets could fire due to the heavy rain, yet the brave men staved off the cavalry with the bayonet. When the cavalry retreated, the men immediately fell on a pair of cannon and took them. This is what veteran, experienced soldiers would do, which makes this even more noteworthy because it was done by freshly raised infantry."[48] Unable to pursue due to their lack of cavalry, Borcke's first wave fell back to the Kreuz hill to reorganize while the battalions of the second wave formed squares.

During this action, the Prussians moved two more batteries into the artillery line on the Tauben hill: Heavy Battery Nr. 2 and Light Battery Nr. 12. "The enemy reestablished his line and began a bombardment of the most vivid that lasted over five hours," stated Gérard in his after-action report.[49] Meanwhile, Horn and Karl did their utmost to realign the 7th and 2nd Brigades. Gradually, the battalions formed columns and the 7th Brigade cleared the Bellwitzhof–Christianenhöhe line. Katzler's vanguard battalions formed on Horn's left wing; the Reserve Cavalry came next, followed by 2nd Brigade. Behind the guns, all surged forward, advancing north through the intervals of the artillery.

In the meantime, Sacken's infantry had continued to move up. To oppose the progress of the Russian columns at Eichholtz that threatened the French left, Roussel positioned the second line of his 2nd Light Cavalry Division opposite the village gallows. French reinforcements arrived only slowly. Following Roussel through the defile at Niederweinberg, Exelmans's 4th Light Cavalry Division encountered tremendous difficulties ascending the slope. Trodden by the horses of the 2nd Light, the slippery and treacherous ground forced the troopers to dismount and lead their steeds. In this manner, General François-Isidore Wathiez deployed the eleven squadrons of his 2nd Brigade from Exelmans's 4th Light on the plateau at the exit of the defile; General Antoine Maurin followed with the seven squadrons of 1st Brigade. Sébastiani's after-action report provides a glimpse of this period of the battle from the French perspective: "Around 4:00, enemy infantry and cavalry debouched on us all along our front, but stood en masse and marched slowly. During this time, Wathiez's brigade from Exelmans's division crossed the defile and formed in squadron columns in front of the defile and Maurin's brigade was following."

At the same time, additional French infantry started to arrive on the plateau: the head of the 1st Brigade of Brayer's 8th Division. A bottleneck at Kroitsch caused by Sébastiani's baggage had forced Brayer to leave behind all of his artillery. For the same reason, St.-Germain's 2nd Heavy Cavalry Division failed to get across the Katzbach and remained idle at Kroitsch throughout the day. The journal of III Corps grants us a view of the scene Brayer's men found: "Forming the head of the column, 8th Division left its position at noon. The weather was awful. It arrived at the defile of Kroitsch at 2:30. The II Cavalry Corps had crossed the defile but obstructed and greatly delayed the march of 8th Division. A considerable number of wagons cluttered the road and we made some effort to unblock it but it became necessary to give up on moving the artillery. The infantry debouched into the marshy valley formed by the foothills of the position occupied by the enemy who, perceiving the confusion that reigned in the defile, had returned with an imposing force."[50]

Just as the Prussian Reserve Cavalry reached the artillery line, Major Count Friedrich Wilhelm von Brandenburg of the General Staff informed

Jürgaß of the enemy's retreat – referring to the repulse of Meunier's three leading battalions. "Therefore," stated Jürgaß in his report, "the moment appeared favorable for the troopers to sharply attack him."[51] He led Yorck's Reserve Cavalry with seven squadrons in the first line north and to the right of 8th Brigade. The second wave – three squadrons from the East Prussian National Cavalry Regiment – wheeled left (west) to contend with imperial forces moving onto the plateau from Niederweinberg. The heavy battery from XI Corps escorted by two Chasseur squadrons had just debouched when the East Prussians charged. Attempting to turn around, some of the guns and caissons overturned; the Prussians attempted to ride off with the guns that could not escape.

Unfortunately for the attackers, infantry fire from nearby hedges and the appearance of three battalions – the 1st Brigade of Brayer's 8th Division – forming near the Kuh hill and thus behind the East Prussian troopers distracted them from their prey. The journal of III Corps grants a view of the action: "A swarm of Prussian lancers charged the reserve park of XI Corps and took possession of it. At once 1st Brigade of 8th Division formed battalion masses. One of them, the 4th Battalion of the 34th, fired at the park and the cavalry. It had been raining since morning and the weapons were wet; barely one-sixth could ignite. However, this proved sufficient to end the melee. The cavalry was shaken. This battalion saw this and put it to flight by charging it with the bayonet. Master of the park by [virtue of] this vigorous blow, the 4th Battalion reorganized and remained in that position 200 or 300 yards from the rest of the brigade." Exelmans's troopers moved up in support. "While this occurred on the right," continues the journal, "II Cavalry Corps debouched on the left through a rather narrow gorge. As the squadrons cleared the defile in twos and formed for battle, they fell on the enemy cavalry that threatened to charge and retake the park of XI Corps."[52]

Thus, without infantry support and receiving sporadic fire from the 4th Battalion of the French 34th Line, the Prussian troopers fell back just in time to support a fourth squadron of the National Cavalry Regiment, which had been left behind to cover the left wing of the artillery line. Seeing an opportunity to charge a French battery that had unlimbered opposite Yorck's line, the East Prussian horsemen charged the gunners, but two imperial cavalry regiments moved up to challenge them. At risk of being severely handled by the more numerous imperials, all four squadrons retreated behind Horn's 7th Brigade.

The East Prussians reached the safety of the infantry at almost the same time as the seven squadrons of the first wave returned. Joined by a half-battery of horse guns, the first wave had continued north after the East Prussians turned west. In the distance, the Prussians observed a small infantry column advancing toward their left wing. Accelerating to a gallop, the Prussians closed in for the kill. To their disappointment, they found that the column consisted of Othegraven's prisoners being escorted to the rear. Regrouping became problematic: the long gallop had broken the cavalry's cohesion as the weaker horses had to be left behind after the boggy fields sapped their strength. Although the officers failed to close the gaps in the line, individual squadrons launched numerous charges against the French batteries that had now started to mass. Henckel von Donnersmarck's brigade of West Prussian and Lithuanian Dragoons charged straight into the imperial artillery line, overwhelming the cavalry escort. Yet, the numerous charges and sharp melees completely disordered the Prussian troopers. Now in the midst of the imperial line, the Prussians found themselves attacked on all sides by fresh forces and superior cavalry, mainly Wathiez's 2nd Brigade. With retreat or surrender the only options for survival, the Prussians turned their steeds south as quickly as the tired beasts could move. Watching his Reserve Cavalry flee behind the 2nd Brigade, Yorck believed all was lost. Screaming curses at "those who wanted to acquire fame" (Gneisenau), the corps commander went straight to Jürgaß, lambasting the colonel with a tapestry of insults for losing control of his cavalry.[53]

Closely pursued by Wathiez's troopers, the Prussian riders hoped to reach the safety of their infantry. After catching the Prussian half-battery, the French cavalry split: a portion slammed into the left wing of Yorck's artillery line – taking nine guns according to French sources – while the rest headed for the four battalions of the advance guard infantry, which had just come abreast of the artillery. "At 5:00," reported Sébastiani, "the enemy debouched from Brechelshof with fifteen squadrons and passed in column between the wood and the right of General Henri-François Charpentier, charging Wathiez's brigade. This brigade, which went to meet the enemy, repulsed and pursued him beyond Bellwitzhof and took nine guns. The 23rd and 24th Chasseurs and the 11th Hussars executed this charge, taking more than 200 prisoners and leaving the battlefield covered with dead."[54]

Sébastiani's cavalry formed to move along a broad front between Kleintinz and the edge of the valley against the Allied artillery and Yorck's infantry. Hiller hurried to the batteries with the lead unit: the 1st Battalion of the Brandenburg Regiment. The three others fixed bayonets and charged the French cavalry. Still, if not for the intervention of Army Headquarters, the artillery would have been lost and the infantry severely shaken. At this critical moment, Blücher ordered four battalions from 2nd Brigade to fill the gaping hole between the 8th and 7th. Behind them, Karl moved forward the rest of the brigade. Their horses now exhausted, the French refrained from attacking four fresh battalions. A period of fifteen minutes passed during which Yorck's infantry and Sébastiani's cavalry faced each other but neither side attacked.

Just prior to this point, Müffling, after observing the loss of the half-battery of horse guns and the flying retreat of the East Prussian National

Cavalry, raced back to Brechelshof to alert Blücher and Gneisenau. After listening to the colonel's description of the dire situation, Blücher tasked Gneisenau with investigating Müffling's allegations. On finding Yorck, Gneisenau learned that everything thus far had occurred according to plan, although the prickly corps commander did admit that the situation was not wonderful. Despite their utter disdain for each other, the two officers planned the next steps for I Corps, with Gneisenau mainly telling Yorck what had to be done. Exchanging Müffling for Gneisenau did nothing for Yorck's demeanor. He struck Gneisenau as extremely grumpy, more so than usual, which Gneisenau did not attribute to the battle, but to Yorck's ill-feelings over the events of the previous days. Yorck did not help his case when he exclaimed that the army would not see a victory on this day and that victory had been ripped from his hands. Gneisenau took the trouble to offer a rebuttal, but sensing Yorck's negativity, resorted to admonishing him to execute their arrangements as if they had the force of Blücher's orders. Yorck restored order and reassembled the cavalry. Fortunately for the Allies, the French were unable to either carry off or spike his guns. Soon, the entire arsenal of I Corps – some 100 pieces – opened against the French right wing as well as the defiles.[55] Blücher knew he could count on Yorck. "He is a venomous chap," the old hussar once remarked; "he does nothing but complain; but when he bites, nobody bites harder."[56]

While Yorck reassembled the Prussians, the stalemate along his front ended thanks to a massive Allied cavalry charge. From his position at Eichholtz, Sacken observed a golden moment present itself on his left. By charging the Prussians, Sébastiani exposed his own left flank. After Vasilchikov's scouts did not find any imperial infantry in the villages north of Eichholtz, Sacken gave the signal to charge around 5:00. At the same time, Karpov moved his Cossacks north through Kleintinz to attack the enemy's rear. Supported by Ushakov's Dragoon Brigade (seven squadrons total), General Anastasy Yurkovsky smashed into Sébastiani's front with the 2nd Brigade of the 2nd Hussar Division.[57] Soon afterward, the Allies overran his left flank between Kleintinz and Eichholtz with the 1st Brigade of the 2nd Hussar Division led by Lanskoy, along with the Brandenburg Uhlans and two squadrons of Lithuanian Dragoons.[58] With six Cossack Regiments, Karpov fell on Sébastiani's rear between Kleintinz and Jänowitz. Neverovsky's 27th Division followed Yurkovsky's troopers while Lieven moved his 10th Division into the first line and advanced toward the enemy "with impetuosity and a defiance of danger that baffles all description, as if animated by one soul, and impelled by one spring of action."[59] "A great cavalry combat began with alternating results," wrote Gneisenau, "mostly occurring in one long line. For a moment, the venture hung in the balance." From three directions, the Allied cavalry fell on Sébastiani's troopers and drove them back upon the imperial infantry. "The enemy returned with thirty squadrons against this division [Exelmans], and with more than forty against Roussel's division, while twenty squadrons debouched through Jänowitz," attested Sébastiani's after-action report. "We were obliged to charge the enemy in three different directions: we were surrounded. He was overthrown twice, but at 6:15 more than 12,000 line cavalry and 2,000 or 3,000 Cossacks supported by 30,000 infantry and formidable artillery came upon us."[60]

In the meantime, after being gone for thirty minutes, Gneisenau returned to inform Blücher of Yorck's status. Around the same time, the report arrived that Sacken's cavalry had attacked the enemy's left flank. Together with Katzler, the Allied horse had forced the imperials to retreat. Blücher now gave the order for the general advance; with sword drawn he placed himself at the head of Yorck's Reserve Cavalry, which had re-formed behind 2nd Brigade. Reinforced by the sixteen squadrons of the 5th and 10th Silesian Landwehr Cavalry Regiments, the 1st Neumark Cavalry Regiment, and the Brandenburg Uhlans, the troopers headed north toward Jänowitz. Behind the cavalry, Yorck led the thick attack columns of infantry. As Yorck's corps moved north, Sacken's infantry formed on either side of Eichholtz and likewise advanced. While additional artillery unlimbered on the Tauben hill and its northeastern slope, the Russian cavalry linked with the right of the Prussian horse between Eichholtz and Niederhochkirch.

Although Macdonald had hoped III Corps would be up by now, all Sébastiani could do was call on 1st Brigade of Brayer's 8th Division for assistance. Preceded by three light cavalry regiments, 1st Brigade sliced through the disordered Russo-Prussian cavalry and momentarily drove them back. The journal of III Corps captures the action: "Our squadrons, constantly swamped [and] having to deal with much larger forces, were always rejected and finally driven back in disorder. General Sébastiani, who commanded them, ordered 1st Brigade of 8th Division to move forward to support them. By that time it had not 100 muskets that could fire. In a broad valley, the arrival of this brigade was of very little help to the cavalry. Isolated, unable to make use of its musketry and without artillery, it just narrowed the vast field upon which the enemy maneuvered; very soon it had to be ready to receive the charge he threatened to make."

After Brayer's 1st Brigade advanced, his 2nd moved up and took its position, sending a battalion to clear the Niederweinberg defile, which the Prussian cavalry had already reached. Apparently, the Prussians had also moved behind 1st Brigade and again seized XI Corps's heavy battery. Brayer's 2nd Brigade wrestled it back. Pressure mounted on the French foot and horse, with the former unable to support the latter. "The action became more obstinate," continues the journal of III Corps, "and our squadrons were exhausted in vain efforts; their partial charges were repulsed by the

11 Blücher at the battle of the Katzbach, 26 August 1813

enemy, who stood forty to fifty paces from 1st Brigade, which could not provide any help. This difficult situation made them throw themselves in the gorge, which they entered pell-mell with the enemy."[61]

To make matters worse for the imperials, Yorck's infantry caught up with the action. Supported by canister from a horse battery, the Prussians drove back Brayer's troops, especially because the French infantry could not exchange fire. While Sébastiani does not admit that his warriors flew down the defile "pell-mell" with the Prussians, his after-action report roughly agrees with III Corps's journal: "I retired to the left of the infantry division of III Corps, which was beginning to form in front of the defile, where I directed all my guns. This 8th Infantry Division would have supported us against the shock of this mass, but a horrible rain that had lasted for eighteen hours had rendered its efforts useless and paralyzed its courage. The weapons were in such a state that each square got off no more than twenty shots. We were forced to descend into the ravine."[62]

With his left exposed and his right battered by fifteen Allied guns, Brayer struggled to restore order. Against his center advanced two large Prussian columns preceded by twelve guns. To evade the Prussian infantry, Brayer withdrew to the edge of the plateau, where he labored to steady his men and buy time to cover Sébastiani's retreat. As the Prussian columns came within musket range, their artillery fired several times at point-blank range. This proved too much for the French, who threw themselves down the slope in search of cover amongst the undergrowth. We hear a final word from the journal of III Corps concerning the struggle on the plateau: "A battery of fifteen pieces placed at the tip of a mountain in front of the ravine struck the right side of the division while two strong columns of infantry supported by twelve guns prepared to take it obliquely. It continued to rain: night was approaching. Recognizing the danger of this position ... General Brayer united 8th Division on the crest of the hill to protect the retreat of II Cavalry Corps. But the two enemy columns that we had sought to avoid engaging ... took a position within gunshot of our small mass and fired several artillery volleys at close range, which forced us to retreat into the thicket that covers the side of the mountain." Gneisenau provides the Prussian view: "The infantry masses, which remained standing to await the outcome of the cavalry combat, were led against the enemy infantry. Finally, the enemy, whose rear was pressed against the deep valley edge of the Wütende Neiße and the Katzbach, was driven over it, after which we shelled him with canister."[63]

Around 6:30 P.M., II Cavalry Corps, Brayer's 8th Division, and Meunier's 2nd Brigade collapsed. While only a few imperial battalions managed to withdraw in squares to the other side of Niederkrayn, the after-action reports submitted by III and XI Corps contest the notion of a collapse. Souham's report, based on Brayer's account, purposely downplays the division's disaster on the plateau:

> The 8th Division had formed on the crest when the Russian [Prussian] cavalry charged and shattered ours, forcing it to retreat behind the infantry. After forming squares without flinching, the infantry countered the efforts of the enemy and, if it had been able to make use of its arms that evening, victory would have been assured by the wise arrangements made by the marshal. But the rain, which had fallen in torrents since the morning, put the weapons temporarily out of service and from whole squares only a few could fire. At that moment, the light cavalry yielded to the efforts of the enemy, whose number was growing. It was then vital to yield to necessity and escape the fire of the batteries that poured canister on the masses of infantry. The 8th Division effected its retreat in order, always firmly repulsing the attempts made by the enemy to engage and disorder our ranks. Nightfall ended the battle.

Gérard's after-action report, which appears slightly more credible than Souham's, describes the fate of the five battalions of Meunier's 2nd Brigade after the Allied cavalry charge:

> They charged Sébastiani's cavalry at the same time that they directed the columns of infantry supported by two lines of cavalry and artillery on the

battalions of General Charpentier [Meunier]. Sébastiani's corps made a retrograde movement; the enemy seized the opportunity to direct numerous cavalry on the left and the rear of the infantry. They charged our squares which were unable to fire because of the excessive rain that had made the weapons incapable of service. The squares presented bayonets and this attitude intimidated the enemy, who dared not undertake anything.

The Russian [Prussian] infantry had closely followed their cavalry; they marched to a square of the 14th [Light Infantry Regiment] and engaged in a bayonet melee. The soldiers of the battalion made the most vigorous resistance: they did not allow themselves to be overwhelmed, repelled the attack, and kept their ranks in the greatest order. The cavalry charges were successful on both sides. Sébastiani, despite his best efforts, was unable to resist the enemy and made his movement to the rear. No longer having support, Charpentier's infantry withdrew to the woods in great order; it crossed the woods and the ravine near Oberkrayn [Oberweinberg]. The only road to retreat was blocked by the equipment of II Cavalry Corps; none of the guns of Meunier's brigade nor the twelve-pound battery could pass. I drew all these details from General Charpentier's report. I enclose the original so that Your Excellency can judge the facts.

Even Sébastiani's account of the battle's climax is somewhat sanitized:

In the position I found myself, I felt that retreat was impossible. Thus, for six hours I stood under a horrible cannonade in front of forces that were way out of proportion to mine. We always charged, repeating the cry *"Vive l'Empereur!"* and we inflicted a lot of damage on the enemy. A detachment of Cossacks had passed the ravine far below us and attacked St.-Germain's Cuirassier Division, from which two squadrons charged and killed many. Our losses are very considerable; our artillery remained stuck in the mud. Without taking one step backward, the 11th and 12th Chasseurs and the 2nd Lancers lost about 80 and 100 horses each to the cannon. Generals Exelmans and Roussel distinguished themselves by their courage as much as by their goodwill.[64]

If French forces did not collapse in a rout on the plateau itself, they certainly disintegrated in the defiles and valleys. Infantry, cavalry, guns, and caissons rushed down the steep gorges that led from the plateau to the Wütende Neiße valley and from there to the Katzbach. In the chaos, wagons and guns overturned, horses lost their footing and tumbled down the slopes, men crawled over each other seeking to escape. In a short time, the gorges became blocked by the wreck of Macdonald's left wing. A mass of 15,000 men rushed in disorder from the hills after having abandoned all resistance. Leaving behind their weapons and equipment, survivors struggled to reach the bridges and fords of the Wütende Neiße and Katzbach. Many soldiers and horses reached the valley floor dazed and injured, as ruin fell from the sky in the form of enemy shells. Langeron recalled:

While the sharp and brilliant charges of Sacken's and Yorck's cavalry forced the enemy into partial retreats, which, soon thereafter, became a general flight, troops of deserters rushed into the valley of Wütende Neiße. The cannon, caissons, equipment, etc., were all overthrown and fell down the sunken roads, or thrown from the steep heights, that lined the right bank of the Wütende Neiße: this brook and the Katzbach, swollen by the rain, offered no fords, and drowned the men and the horses that tried to cross them in the same places as the day before and that morning, places where they had not found a foot of water. There was a bridge at Niederkrayn, but it was not sufficient for the quantity of deserters, and those that remained on the right bank were smashed by the Russian and Prussian batteries established on the heights.[65]

As Langeron indicated, the elements themselves appeared to have conspired against the French. Within a matter of hours, the constant, streaming rains had transformed the shallow mountain streams into raging rivers; the swollen Wütende Neiße and Katzbach became ferocious tempests. Their maelstrom swept away the imperials who attempted to wade across. The bridges at Niederkrayn and Dohnau could not be crossed safely by the masses that attempted to push across. Hundreds fell into the water and drowned in their panic-stricken attempts to swim. Thousands wandered along the banks of both rivers seeking a way to cross with many men and horses finding death beneath the waves. The whirlpool of the general flight carried away most of the imperial foot. Again, while maintaining that the withdrawal from the plateau had been orderly, III Corps's journal provides a glimpse of the chaos that ensued: "Despite the night and the rain, the ground was disputed step by step. The retreat was orderly up to the first arm of the Katzbach [the Wütende Neiße], which has very steep banks and is very deep. Its wooded bank was still crowded with wagons; our soldiers crossed the water under the fire of the enemy, and reached the other side in disorder. We wanted to rally after the passage of the second arm of the river [the Katzbach], but we could not do it. The night was so dark and the weather so bad we could not recognize each other. Part of the division got lost."[66]

In pursuit, Yorck's corps turned west toward the Niederweinberg and Niederkrayn defiles while Sacken's troops continued north toward Dohnau. From the hills, Yorck's Nr. 12 Horse Battery, the howitzers of the Nr. 2 Heavy Foot, and one Russian twelve-pound battery pounded the enemy with canister before switching to shells. Finding an open path, Katzler himself led the Black Hussars followed by two East Prussian battalions to Niederkrayn, taking the village and its bridge across the Wütende Neiße. Fortunately for the imperials, exhaustion quickly ended the Prussian pursuit while the onset of darkness silenced their artillery. Displeased by the cavalry's lackluster pursuit, Gneisenau recalled Katzler to the plateau; only sixty hussars and the sharpshooter platoons from two East Prussian battalions occupied the ruins of Niederkrayn.[67]

Late in the afternoon, Antoine-Guillaume Delmas's 9th Division, led by Souham himself, ascended the plateau at Dohnau. Although his artillery could not negotiate the muddy slopes and his infantry could not fire their muskets, Souham sought to turn the enemy's right. Receiving heavy artillery fire from the Russians, he resolved to have his men fix bayonets and charge. However, Delmas protested, calling it suicide. Conceding, Souham opted to maneuver beyond the range of Sacken's guns, which destroyed six French pieces that had managed to climb the plateau after "incredible efforts." Seeing nothing of the 10th and 11th Divisions on his left and certain of the failure of Macdonald's center to his right, Souham ordered Delmas to retreat to Kroitsch, where St.-Germain's division of cuirassiers and carabineers stood all day. The 9th Division recrossed the Katzbach and took a position on the hills north of Kroitsch; one of its brigades covered the park of III Corps.[68]

Sacken halted on the hills of Kleintinz, but soon learned of the approach of large enemy columns from Liegnitz. This force – the 10th and 11th Divisions of III Corps – sought to cross the Katzbach at Schmogwitz and move onto the hills between Dohnau and Kleintinz. On finding the bridge swept away, Souham's staff chief, General Jean-Joseph Tarayre, ordered the soldiers to wade across the waist-deep water; twelve guns as well as the 10th Hussar Regiment and Badenese Light Dragoon Regiment likewise reached the opposite bank. According to the journal of III Corps, the Russians observed the movement but did nothing to hinder it, "probably not suspecting that we would undertake a serious attack on this side, or perhaps too heavily occupied on the right to notice." In his report to Blücher, Sacken described one infantry brigade with sixteen cannons that came from Liegnitz reached the Katzbach "to harass my right flank and to cover the retreat of the enemy. The night assisted this operation, our people remained in their places, but we could not judge the strength of the enemy and his position."[69]

Both French divisions formed brigade masses with artillery in the intervals and struck the road south toward the hills of Kleintinz. While trying to determine why the enemy was so far north, Étienne-Pierre Ricard, the senior general of division, observed a column cresting the hill to his right, which he believed to be Delmas's 9th Division. He then noticed several squadrons on the plain. "The fire on the right was slowing," continues the journal. "We saw a strong column of infantry filing on the crest of the mountain at the time when we assumed General Delmas would be chasing the enemy before him. Almost immediately we saw several squadrons on the plain to the right: new reason to believe that the column was ours." Taking them to be French, Ricard decided to attack. Before the French assault could get under way, however, scouts brought back the perplexing news that the cavalry happened to be Prussian hussars – the column to his right: Russian infantry. "Therefore, there was no doubt about the purpose of the march of the column that we found a quarter of an hour earlier: it was the corps commanded by [Sacken] who, after getting rid of everything before him, had just reinforced the right wing of the combined army, which he thought was being attacked by reserves coming from Liegnitz."⁷⁰ Russian skirmishers greeted the French around 7:00. Supported by numerous guns, Sacken's 27th and 10th Divisions advanced.

In Fabry's opinion, an immediate attack would have been the best option for Ricard. However, Macdonald's instructions had explicitly warned against becoming entangled in an isolated engagement. "As elsewhere, extremely serious responsibility had to be taken at this point, [but] no one took charge," laments Fabry. "General Souham certainly was not there. We note his [Ricard's] indecision; the enemy infantry descended to mid range, the artillery to the left forced our masses to fall back." The journal of III Corps is just as critical of Ricard:

Night was falling and the rain increased. In the position that our two divisions were in they had to attack quickly. They advanced at the double, under arms, and in silence. When they were within range of artillery, the enemy unmasked all his batteries and had them play on our masses; our people responded with their best. Yet just as the infantry began to suffer, the enemy artillery changed direction. Small-arms firing began and was sustained by both sides with as much vivacity as time permitted. Before ordering the two divisions to take the position with the bayonet, General Ricard wanted to know what was happening to his right. Regardless, the undertaking appeared too risky to accept responsibility; he remained for almost twenty minutes in that position, where he was protected from enemy fire. We saw his irresolution. The enemy infantry descended halfway: the artillery moved left to take our masses in the rear. Even our skirmishers were repulsed. We were going to be charged, unless we ourselves charged.

At that moment, news of Macdonald's disaster arrived to convince Ricard of the futility of attacking. "An energetic man at least would have attempted an attack; General Ricard saw a reason to retreat," decries Fabry. Around 7:30 that evening, the two divisions retreated in good order across the ford. The French claim that Sacken did not pursue. "After some shots were exchanged, he withdrew," maintained Sacken in his after-action report. "In the pursuit, General [Louis] Suden, chief of a brigade of III Corps, was wounded and captured." Within thirty minutes, the head of 10th Division lost contact with the rear of 11th. En route to Kroitsch, the 11th lost its way several times before bivouacking between 1:00 and 2:00 A.M. on a farm located at the junction of the roads coming from Bunzlau, Haynau, and

Liegnitz. Halting north of Schmogwitz, 10th Division eventually took the road northwest to Haynau around 2:00 A.M. after being swarmed by Sacken's Cossacks.[71]

Returning to Langeron's sector, the columns of Rochambeau's 19th Division pushed across the Plinse shortly after 2:00. "The fire became very intense," noted Lauriston, "we silenced the enemy's batteries and forced them to withdraw. Our troops drove out the infantry established in the depths of the ravine and reached the hill on the opposite side. The transition was difficult; I reconnoitered for the artillery; we found a position. My batteries forced those in the center of the enemy line to move away; I sent Rochambeau's division on the road from Seichau to Hennersdorf." To Lauriston's left (northeast), units from XI Corps – 35th Division, the rest of the 36th, and the corps cavalry – began moving through Seichau. Directed by Macdonald, Gérard advanced toward the gap between Hennersdorf and Schlaupe. "The enemy has thus far offered little resistance," noted Gérard in his report to Macdonald, "but we found him in position and in force on the hills behind Hennersdorf, occupying this village strongly. Your Excellency ordered me to attack it."[72]

The situation on Lauriston's right did not unfold so well. Unable to move up the cannons, Maison's men advanced toward the Russian left without artillery support. Lauriston tells us that 16th Division lost "many men by attacking it head on. In fact, I could not find positions in the center favorable for my guns." Maison directed two columns toward the forest edge to work around the Russian left as a third marched on Herrmannsdorf. A successful charge by Emmanuel with the Kievskii Dragoons and Colonel Philip Paradovsky's Liflyandskii Mounted Jäger brought the advance of the first two columns to a standstill while Witte stopped the third column with a bold charge by his 4th Ukrainskii Cossack Regiment. According to Langeron: "the enemy made his principal attack on my left around 2:00 P.M. Rudzevich received it and held with great valor; Emmanuel and Paradovsky charged and cut down two enemy columns that tried to flank our skirmishers. The Ukrainian horsemen charged a third time toward Herrmannsdorf; these charges met with great success; but unfortunately I lost Colonel Paradovsky, who was killed by a cannonball; he had been wounded on 23 August, but his zeal already had him back in the saddle leading his regiment." "The position would have been easily taken if the fire of our infantry had not been somewhat extinguished by the rain that had not ceased since the early morning," lamented Lauriston. "Perceiving our inability to fire, the cavalry charged so many times that our infantry could not hold. It returned to charge more than ten times."

Finally, one last effort by Maison's warriors, supported by an attack on Langeron's center by one of Rochambeau's brigades, overwhelmed and routed the Russians. Langeron described the situation:

From the hills by Schlaupe, I soon saw the brilliant and fortunate attack ordered by Blücher, and so well executed by Yorck's and Sacken's corps, and the complete victory that we owe to this beautiful movement, so well calculated, so rapid, and so unexpected by the enemy, who, the attackers having become the attacked, were flung into a horrible confusion within a half-hour: the cavalry from Yorck's and Sacken's corps immortalized themselves on this occasion. I then prepared to second this great attack by attacking General Lauriston who faced me; but this general (whose conduct in battle is worthy of the highest elegies) had pushed forward his reserve, anticipated me, and made (apparently to make a diversion in favor of the left of his army) one of the sharpest and most vicious attacks that I saw during the war.

"We managed to drive the enemy from the side, pushing and even routing him," continued Lauriston. "Our troops pursued three guns, passing their bayonets through several enemy gunners, but could not reach the pieces." Lauriston moved forty heavy guns onto the hills northwest of Hennersdorf. This battery silenced the lighter caliber Russian artillery on the slopes of the Wein hill and then covered the storming of Hennersdorf by General François Hénin's 1st Brigade of 35th Division. Without artillery, the two battalions (10th and 38th Jäger Regiments) that comprised the 3rd Brigade of Olsufiyev's 9th Division could not hold Hennersdorf. The village fell around 4:00.

After taking Hennersdorf, Hénin drove the Russians from Stein hill, which stood between Schlaupe and Hennersdorf. "With his 1st Brigade, General Hénin marched on the village of Hennersdorf with the charge beating as two battalions of the 22nd headed to the heights on the left," declared Gérard. "Everywhere the enemy was overthrown: we not only captured the village, but we also drove the enemy from a hill [Stein], which was carried by the bayonet." The Russian 28th and 32nd Jäger Regiments withdrew behind the ravine at Schlaupe while the 10th, 12th, and 38th Jäger retreated to the second line south of Wein hill. Lauriston quickly exploited the situation, concentrating all of his artillery against Wein hill. According to Langeron:

Despite the fire of my batteries placed on the three heights by my artillery commander, General [Gavriil] Veselitsky, General Lauriston placed a battery of forty cannons on the heights between Seichau and Hennersdorf, and the fire of this battery directed against my center silenced my batteries on the Weinberg to the right of Herrmannsdorf. Under the protection of this fire, strong columns appeared from the hedgerows of Hennersdorf and pushed back the troops that were defending the Wein hill and occupied it themselves. This moment was critical; this height was the key to my position, the battle was already lost on my flank unless I reoccupied it; in the contrary case, I would be forced to refuse my entire left, to open all of the roads to Jauer and to compromise Pahlen's detachment.

At this point, with both of Langeron's flanks hard pressed, cooperation between the French V and XI Corps ended. Apparently, all of Rochambeau's division became embroiled in the attack on the Russian center and left, mainly between Hennersdorf and the Mönchswald. Consequently, no elements of V Corps supported Gérard's advance. Uninformed about the events to his right, Gérard simply halted. "This movement was not supported by the troops who were on our right, and who remained in the same position," explained Gérard. "I decided not to continue. We remained in that position until dusk." Around this time, 6:00 P.M., Macdonald arrived and undertook to restore command and control on his right. Unfortunately, at this critical juncture, he learned of the disaster that had befallen his left.[73]

From the plateau, the weather prevented Blücher and his staff from gaining a complete overview of Langeron's situation, but it appeared that the Russians could not hold their position. "The firing on the left bank of the Wütende Neiße was moving further and further away toward Jauer," reports Müffling, "and had already become very faint." Blücher and Gneisenau grew extremely indignant: Langeron appeared to abandon one good position after another. "During a discussion near Niederkrayn," continues Müffling, "General Langeron was called a miserable coward who should be denounced to the tsar and cashiered. His (cowardly) behavior was contrasted with ours, through which we considered ourselves heroes." As Lauriston advanced further and the flashes of his artillery moved closer to Blücher's line of retreat to Jauer, Müffling became convinced that Langeron faced Macdonald's main force. Arguing that Yorck and Sacken had engaged merely "left-wing patrols," Müffling implored Blücher to commit Yorck's reserve – Steinmetz's 1st Brigade – to save Langeron. Blücher and Gneisenau rejected all of the future field-marshal's points. Nevertheless, Müffling did not relax his pressure, especially after Gneisenau left the command post. Observing Lauriston's push to the Weinberg, Müffling hounded Blücher. Finally, the old man reluctantly approved: "In the name of the devil, advance with the brigade, now!"[74]

Around 6:00, after the issue had been decided on the plateau, Müffling along with Captain Stosch and Lieutenant Gerlach hurried to Langeron's command post. As they rode through Schlaupe, fighting between the Prussians and units of XI Corps erupted. At the same time, 1st Brigade received orders to cross the Wütende Neiße between Schlaupe and Schlauphof to operate against Lauriston's rear and flank. "To somewhat shame him," states a note in the margin of Blücher's Journal of Operations, "Colonel Müffling and several other officers from Headquarters very triumphantly informed General Langeron of the successful results – we had taken twenty cannon, Sacken is a brave general, Steinmetz's brigade would advance against the enemy's left flank – because otherwise nothing would have occurred."[75]

Thus informed by Müffling of Blücher's success on the plateau, Langeron realized his folly. His conduct had jeopardized the day's success and could have threatened the very existence of the Silesian Army if the imperials had driven Blücher from the plateau. Embarrassed by his mistakes, the French émigré accepted responsibility for them, stating that he was extremely disappointed with himself. Again, he claimed to have based his actions on his knowledge of Barclay's instructions. To believe Langeron, around 6:00, when the French attack stopped, he thought of resuming the offensive. Müffling claims the contrary: "I found General Langeron engaged in withdrawing." With Shcherbatov, Olsufiyev, Rudzevich, Ende, and several other officers looking on, Müffling purportedly cried: "In the name of God, general, you beat a retreat while we have won a brilliant victory? Delivered from our enemies, our reserves are in full march to cross the Wütende Neiße and to take back everything that is before you." Embracing him, Langeron supposedly replied: "Colonel, you are my savior." "Let's attack immediately," continued Müffling, "I will stay with you. I need to witness your glory just as I witnessed General Sacken's." Ende interrupted this scene by interjecting: "We have nothing left here but the rearguard; 100 guns were sent back a long time ago." "Recall everything," Müffling cried out, "and attack with what you have." Although the officers of his suite voiced their support for Müffling, Langeron raised one final objection: "Colonel, are you sure that the commander in chief does not need my corps to cover his retreat?" "I'm sure, sir," responded Müffling, "the commander in chief will cross the Wütende Neiße to crush the enemy who has attacked you: we must stand firm, we must correct the mistakes, and we must intimidate the presumptuous by attacking them with drums beating." Gazing through the rain toward the plateau, Langeron suddenly saw the imperials scrambling to get across the Wütende Neiße. "Good God, they are running," he purportedly exclaimed.[76]

To make good his mistakes, Langeron ordered the retaking of Wein hill. Udom stormed the height with the 1st and 2nd Brigades of Olsufiyev's 9th Division. "I ordered General Olsufiyev to retake this height at all costs," recounted Langeron, "which he executed with as much celerity as courage: the Nasheburgskii, Ryazhskii, Yakutskii Regiments, under the orders of General Udom ... moved in dense columns onto the heights, chasing away the enemy and following them into the village. The rain had so dampened the muskets that none could fire and so the fighting was hand to hand, with musket-butts and bayonets." Not expecting the counterattack and completely unprepared, the French streamed back to Hennersdorf.

As darkness descended, Langeron's right wing – Shcherbatov's VI Infantry Corps – likewise advanced to link with Steinmetz's 1st Brigade. "To the right," continues Langeron, "Shcherbatov perfectly contained the enemy, despite their reiterated attacks: after the success of Olsufiyev's attack,

I ordered Prince Shcherbatov to advance with VI Corps and attack the enemy, by moving to his right, and thereby to link up with the Prussians, which he did instantly and with great resolution. The 7th and 18th Divisions, commanded by General Stepan Talyzin I and Benardos, forced the enemy to retreat." Despite the Allied pressure, Lauriston held a portion of Hennersdorf as well as the terrain north of the village. Between Hennersdorf and Schlaupe, General Vasily Meshcherinov drove the French from the domineering Stein hill.[77] Master of this height, Shcherbatov moved the 34th Light Battery onto it to take Lauriston's great battery in the flank; soon after the French guns withdrew. "The VI Infantry Corps established itself on the left of Hennersdorf," affirmed Langeron, "and Meshcherinov, with his brigade of Jäger, chased the enemy from a height between Hennersdorf and Schlaupe, where Shcherbatov posted the Nesterovskii light artillery company, which opposed the great French battery, scattering and silencing it … Neither the darkness nor the rain ended the fighting; it lasted until 11:00 P.M. in the village of Hennersdorf."

Meanwhile, Steinmetz directed four battalions to Schlauphof and three to Schlaupe, forcing the imperials to form a flank to oppose the Prussian advance.[78] Steinmetz himself forded the Wütende Neiße with two battalions and took the hills on the left bank. His brigade artillery unlimbered on the hills of the Wütende Neiße's right bank; its fire drove the French from the opposite bank. Around 8:00 P.M., Langeron finally summoned his heavy artillery and Kaptsevich's X Infantry Corps to return to the battlefield. He also ordered Pahlen II to advance toward Konradswaldau. In his memoirs, Langeron defended his original decision to send Kaptsevich's infantry to Jauer: "Having seen the success of the day and having nothing to fear for Jauer, I was joined by Kaptsevich's X Infantry Corps at 8:00 P.M., which took no part in the action; he would have been very useful to me, but he would have been more useful where I sent him." Macdonald's report the day after the battle maintains that Langeron's counterattack severely shook XI Corps. Yet, other French reports claim that no one left this sector of the battlefield with a sense of defeat. In fact, Lauriston, in his report written two days after the battle, maintained that his "position at the close of the day was beautiful; we were masters of the heights and could have remained there." French troops remained at Seichau until as late as 4:00 on the morning of the 27th.[79]

Blücher's exhausted troops remained where they stood when darkness fell, with only the Reserve Cavalry moving back behind the hill at Brechelshof. "The contest completely had the look of a battle in antiquity," wrote Gneisenau. "During it, small-arms fire was completely silenced until we were able to move our artillery through the soppy ground. Only the cries of the warriors filled the air; the polished weapon decided the affair." "The strong rain prevented the infantry from firing and so we fought almost exclusively with cannon, bayonet, and cold steel," confirmed Henckel. The losses of the Silesian Army amounted to 1,400 men from Langeron's corps, 874 from Yorck's, and 575 from Sacken's. Two days later, on the 28th, Blücher signed his second report on the battle: "Perhaps never has a victory been purchased with so little blood for, although I still have no report over the losses, at most they amount to 1,000 men." The fruits of the victory remained equally uncertain; his initial report on the 28th stated that 36 guns, 110 caissons, 2 medicine wagons, 4 field forges, and 1,200–1,400 prisoners as well as numerous officers had fallen into Allied hands. Regardless of the numbers, Maude concludes that "this brilliant victory was the making of Blücher and the Prussian army." While such an epithet may be too bold, the victory on the Katzbach certainly marks the rise of Blücher as the mover and shaker of the Sixth Coalition.[80]

In a private letter written on the night of the battle, Gneisenau estimated that "the booty of this battle is 30 cannon, 300 caissons, field forges, etc., and 15,000 prisoners. The battle lasted one hour into the night. The darkness did not allow us to determine the extent of our victory. Therefore, the after-action report written immediately after the battle states only the cannon captured with the sword and bayonet without mentioning those the enemy have left standing on the field or which toppled into the steep valley." The number of prisoners – 15,000 – is just part of the myth that surrounds the battle's conclusion. German accounts tell of a complete rout on the plateau: "We have won a very glorious battle on the Katzbach," continued Gneisenau, "so decisive that the French have never suffered such a defeat in battle. The road between the Katzbach and the Bober shows the terror that had seized the enemy. Everywhere run-over corpses are stuck in the mud. Regarding the enemy army, few organized units remain available. The French who were cut off from the river crossings wander around in the woods and commit offenses."[81]

French reports stated the exact opposite. Certainly, the French argument can be used to correct the exaggerated notion that Macdonald's entire army collapsed on the plateau. Yet, reports from division and newly appointed corps commanders – most of whom still dreamed of attaining the marshal's baton – to a green army commander naturally would paint a defeat in the best light. Thus, according to Souham, "8th Division conducted its retreat in order and always firmly rejected the enemy's attempts to engage and bring disorder in our ranks. Night ended the battle." Gérard, who relied on Charpentier's account, stated in his after-action report: "Unable to resist the enemy despite the best efforts, Sébastiani executed his movement to the rear. From then on without support, Charpentier's infantry retired to the woods in the greatest order. It passed the woods and the ravine near Ober-krayn and re-formed on the hills close to where one of Souham's divisions had taken a position." Not only did Fabry allow himself to be influenced by such reports, but he also looked for proof of French resistance in the actions of the Allies: "It is three kilometers from Brechelshof to Bellwitzhof, and less than two from the latter to Niederkrayn. Yorck's corps needed nearly five hours to win this stretch of terrain; it only had to contend with Meunier's brigade, a part of the 8th Division, two divisions of II Cavalry Corps, and thirty-six guns. Nevertheless, the intervention of Sacken's whole corps was necessary to break our resistance."[82]

An unexpected encounter by two opposing armies advancing simultaneously resulted in the battle of the Katzbach. Both army commanders believed they could get their forces across the Katzbach without interference from the other. The weather, which severely limited visibility, contributed to this erroneous idea. While Macdonald planned to engage the Silesian Army at Jauer, Blücher believed he would find his opponent at Goldberg and Liegnitz. Macdonald intended to envelop the Army of Silesia concentrically while Blücher wanted to separate the individual corps of the Army of the Bober and defeat them in detail. Preparing for battle, Blücher concentrated his army. Preparing for envelopment and pursuit, Macdonald stretched his army. Having no overview of the situation rendered Blücher just as blind as Macdonald. The two armies moved toward each other without knowing it. This much the Prussians knew: having met gutsy yet brief resistance, the imperials pursued what they perceived to be Yorck's rearguard without having any idea of the proximity of the entire Silesian Army. In his memoirs, Henckel von Donnersmarck provides some astute observations: "Emboldened by our previous retreats, the enemy believed that we were once again withdrawing, and thus, holding our vanguard to be a rearguard, attacked it, drove it across the Katzbach, and crossed this river, which later led to his actual destruction. On our left, General Langeron was also engaged. Because of the terrible roads, he had already sent back most of his artillery and had on hand only a few light pieces while the enemy deployed ten[-] and twelve[-pound] guns; to the enemy, all of this reinforced the idea that we were retreating and he only had to deal with a rearguard." "All of his prior retreats actually gave Blücher an advantage: it made the French imprudently advance onto the plateau," observed Blücher's authoritative German biographer, General Unger. According to Langeron: "We were all surprised to see Macdonald, one of the most distinguished generals of the French army, due equally to his talent and his bravery, risk and lose – by his own fault – such a decisive battle. His supporters claim that Napoleon said he had only 50,000 men facing him: this assertion does not accord with the instructions Napoleon gave him. Moreover, it is very true that, in this campaign as in 1812, he always believed that we were much weaker than our actual effective strength."[83]

After Macdonald's advance rendered the 11:00 A.M. attack disposition obsolete, Blücher decided to use the opportunity to allow part of the enemy army to ascend the plateau, then fall on it and drive the imperials over the cliffs. Written a few hours after the battle, Gneisenau's letter to Count Ernst Friedrich Herbert von Münster, the Hanoverian minister in London, captures the thinking of Blücher's headquarters: "We made the disposition for the attack and were in the process of executing it when the report arrived that enemy columns were advancing over the Katzbach against us. We quickly changed our plan of attack, hiding our columns, showing only our vanguard, and positioning ourselves as if we were falling back on the defensive. Now the cocksure enemy pressed forward. All at once we emerged." To Clausewitz he explained: "Our plan for the attack and the circumstance that we had been marching early saved us from ruin. We could now make our dispositions calmly. The enemy was approaching over the Katzbach and had the defile to his rear."[84]

"Also, the heavy rain hindered reconnaissance," added Unger, "and negated French effectiveness with the musket, and brought the unleashed fury of Germanic and Slavic warrior into the struggle of man against man." While this last statement represents the nationalistic fervor that besieged Europe when General Unger published his work at the beginning of the twentieth century, Blücher's men won him the battle he so desperately sought. He lauded the bravery of the Prussian troops: "Particularly praiseworthy was the conduct of the infantry, which mostly consisted of very raw soldiers." Gneisenau likewise could not conceal the pride he felt about the performance of the Silesian Army in general and the Prussian foot specifically. Regarding the latter, Gneisenau informed Alexander Gibsone that "after the combat of this day, the infantry, which overall remained in noteworthy order throughout the entire battle, stood in well-ordered, complete squares. This day marks the triumph of our newly-created infantry." Concerning the army on the whole, he wrote: "The Silesian Army has performed great service. In eight days it has had seven large engagements and one battle – engagements that have cost us (Prussians alone, without the Russians) 1,800–2,000 men in dead and wounded."[85]

Napoleon's 23 August directive advised Macdonald to execute a short offensive strike through Jauer. Macdonald would have achieved his goal had he conducted his operation on either the 24th or 25th, when Blücher, still uncertain of Napoleon's whereabouts, had decided to retreat east-southeast toward Striegau. Ney's hijacking of III Corps prevented Macdonald from maintaining the army's momentum and commencing the offensive during this crucial 48-hour period. During these two days, Macdonald also failed to direct Ledru's 31st Division to Hirschberg and in line with the army to provide right-flank coverage. Had Ledru advanced toward Hirschberg on the 25th, he would have learned that St.-Priest had withdrawn from there on the 24th and made for Landeshut. With this information, Macdonald would not have had reason to send Puthod's 17th Division to Schönau with the task of forwarding one brigade to Hirschberg and the other to Jauer. These mistakes ultimately deprived Lauriston of his 17th Division on the day of battle. Considering the events in Lauriston's sector, an additional division may have sufficed to send Langeron running and to roll up Blücher's right and rear.[86]

Macdonald's intentions have come under scrutiny. Writing in 1886, the retired French cavalry officer, Commandant Maurice-Henri Weil, asserts that Macdonald's orders for 26 August reflected the marshal's hope of using maneuver rather than battle to force his adversary to withdraw into the heart of Silesia. Less than twenty years later, Friederich argued that "obviously Macdonald expected to engage his adversary in a position at Jauer; on the 26th he thought to continue his advance up to the plateau of Jauer and attack on the 27th in case the Silesian Army had not voluntarily retreated." By 2:00 on the 25th, Macdonald himself remained uncertain over his next move, initially because he did not know the whereabouts of III Corps thanks to Ney's error, and then because he could not be sure if Blücher would make a stand. During the course of the morning, much enemy cavalry prowled around the front of V and XI Corps, while the sound of artillery to the north indicated that Sacken had pursued III Corps. Macdonald did not believe this activity signaled an imminent Allied offensive, but did assume Blücher thought the rest of the Army of the Bober would "retreat" like III Corps. "We are ready to receive him or march on him, if he retires," he assured Napoleon at 2:00 P.M. If III Corps returned, he planned a demonstration against Jauer. If not, he would fall back to the Bober, reorganize the army, and resume the offensive. In a report drafted two hours later, the marshal informed Napoleon that III Infantry and II Cavalry Corps had returned to their positions. In the next line, the marshal exclaims: "I will prepare an offensive movement on Jauer." He concluded: "I do not worry about the forces opposite me; I will march against them without hesitation." But to Berthier he confided: "I am organizing the army and then I shall present battle to the enemy but I doubt it will be accepted." Therefore, Macdonald believed Blücher would retreat or was in the process of retreating.[87]

To be fair to Macdonald, his operation complied with Napoleon's instructions and, although advancing, he did not seek battle. Perhaps being better acquainted with Blücher would have triggered the idea that the impetuous Prussian might launch his own offensive. Such a consideration can only be made with the benefit of hindsight. As of August 1813, Blücher remained the man who had recklessly squandered the Prussian cavalry at Auerstedt, the man who had surrendered at Lübeck, and the septuagenarian loudmouth whom the emperor had cashiered. If the Russians doubted Blücher's abilities, how could the French not? Indeed, he had followed the French when they retreated west, but fled before the emperor. If the

Prussian commander's marches and countermarches had infuriated and dumbfounded his subordinates, they must have looked just as erratic to the French as those of the Prussian commander in chief, Duke Charles William Ferdinand of Brunswick, in 1806. Although Langeron and Sacken remained in contact with Macdonald's wings, what reason did the marshal have to assume they would not follow Blücher's center and retreat deeper into Silesia?

To secure his right, Macdonald allocated 12,000 men (the 31st Division and one brigade of the 17th) to contend with St.-Priest's VIII Infantry Corps in the Hirschberg region. With 45,000 men (V and XI Corps), he would fix Blücher at Jauer by sending two of Lauriston's divisions southeast from Goldberg directly on Jauer, while half of the 17th Division trekked east from Schönau. Meanwhile, the rest of the army, another 45,000 men (III Infantry and II Cavalry Corps), would cross the Katzbach and the Wütende Neiße to flank Blücher's position at Jauer. As the emperor's instructions had stressed the importance of keeping open the army's communications, Macdonald left the 31st Division in its positions at Kemnitz and Berthelsdorf and moved Puthod's 17th along with Lauriston's 6th Light Cavalry Brigade to the left bank of the Katzbach to observe the river crossings south of Goldberg.

On the surface, all are textbook maneuvers, but Macdonald should have employed a sharper eye for judging the terrain and should have followed his master's habit of interrogating the locals. Terrible weather and false assumptions about Blücher led to inefficient reconnaissance. He directed his army to descend on Jauer in two groups separated by the Katzbach and the Wütende Neiße. Moreover, his center first had to cross the Katzbach, followed by the Wütende Neiße, and then ascend the steep slope that towered over its right bank before XI Infantry and II Cavalry Corps could debouch onto the plateau. For good reason the locals referred to the latter watercourse as "raging." With the water level constantly increasing due to the summer rains, the Wütende Neiße could become an impassable obstacle in a matter of hours. The few bridges found in the tiny villages along its banks hardly provided the opportunity for mutual support between Macdonald's right and center. No doubt to the marshal's horror, the situation that unfolded led to the isolation of the 27,000 men from II Cavalry Corps and elements of XI Corps on the plateau east of the Wütende Neiße. There they would face the 55,000 men under Yorck and Sacken concentrated along a four-mile front between Bellwitzhof and Eichholtz. On the other side of the Wütende Neiße, Lauriston's corps – reduced to 17,000 men – confronted Langeron's 24,000 Russians.

Regardless, Macdonald's measures could have led to victory. He intended to unite 60,000 men on the plateau, who would have confronted the 55,000 men of Yorck's and Sacken's corps. The reason this plan failed is simple: his subordinates failed to provide on-the-spot leadership and cooperation.

Columns belonging to Gérard and Sébastiani collided at Kroitsch, where they simultaneously engaged Yorck's vanguard. Due to the enemy's presence, the French should have taken security measures for the advance to Jauer. Instead of one corps waiting for the other to pass, both corps continued the march intermingled, pushing through each other to reach Niederkrayn. Although Katzler withdrew onto the plateau, French leadership dissolved in the face of the adverse weather and imposing terrain. Imperial units disintegrated into numerous small columns, which chaotically sought to win the plateau. Intending to cover the deployment of Gérard's infantry, Sébastiani's cavalry mistakenly pressed forward. Having already encountered resistance at the Katzbach, the infantry should have taken the lead, opening the defiles and pushing up the slopes to the plateau. Under their protection, Sébastiani's troopers should have ascended the plateau and deployed with the artillery following. Instead, cavalry, infantry, and artillery all emerged on the plateau haphazardly and in isolated pockets. Numerous batteries unlimbered along the Kuh hill–Kleintinz line; the cavalry gradually re-formed north of the guns, while the infantry slowly deployed on the plateau. Not one French commander on the spot sought to determine if Souham's III Corps had come on line. After a considerable artillery duel, Jürgaß charged the French guns with part of Yorck's Reserve Cavalry but Sébastiani's cavalry forced him to fall back. Sacken's cavalry attack on the flank and rear of the French line decided the battle, which on the right bank of the Wütende Neiße was essentially only a cavalry engagement. Driven from the plateau and back down the defiles, the retreating French slammed into their approaching reinforcements, disordering them and eventually sweeping them away. This enabled Blücher to send Steinmetz's brigade across the Wütende Neiße to threaten Lauriston's left. In this sector of the battlefield, we saw the fatal lack of cooperation between the French V and XI Corps. With both of Langeron's flanks hard pressed and his center suffering under the withering fire of the French grand battery, Lauriston and Gérard stopped collaborating. With Rochambeau's division attacking the Russian center and left between Hennersdorf and the Mönchswald, no elements of V Corps supported the advance of XI Corps, prompting Gérard to simply halt.

It must be noted that the same factors that plagued Macdonald could have worked against Blücher. Believing he had found the Army of the Bober split in two groups at Goldberg and Liegnitz, he wanted to destroy one of them. The distance between Goldberg and Liegnitz amounted to eight miles, meaning that the portion of Macdonald's army that he attacked would not receive support from the other for several hours. Thus, the decisive blow would have to fall within this timeframe. Blücher and Gneisenau decided to envelop Souham's corps at Liegnitz by having Yorck's corps cross the Katzbach at Kroitsch and Dohnau and turn toward Steudnitz by passing

to the left of Rothkirch. At Steudnitz, Yorck would strike the Liegnitz–
Haynau road and thus sever Souham's line of retreat. Yet, Souham could
have held the line of the Katzbach with two of his divisions and simultaneously attack Yorck's right with the remaining three. This would have
forced Yorck to make front to the northeast, allowing Sébastiani's cavalry
at Rothbrünnig to attack the Prussian's left flank and rear. Langeron
received the task of securing Yorck's left flank and rear, but the imperial
forces at Goldberg would have kept the Russians in check. Cut off from
Sacken by the Wütende Neiße and the Katzbach and with Langeron
neutralized, Yorck's corps could have been destroyed, especially considering the morale of his men. As Friederich concludes, "certainly, to say
that Blücher's disposition was impossible to execute goes too far. Yet its
success depended on a series of contingencies, and we can only view it as
fortunate that the circumstances made the execution of his intentions
unnecessary."[88]

Notes

1 "Ordre de mouvement," Goldberg, 25 August 1813, reproduced in Fabry, *Étude
sur les opérations du maréchal Macdonald*, 50–51; SHAT, C^2 154: Lauriston to
Macdonald, 26 August 1813; Sébastiani to Macdonald, 27 August 1813; Macdonald
to Berthier, 27 August 1813; Souham to Berthier, 29 August 1813; and Gérard to
Macdonald, 31 August 1813. Weil offers a different interpretation of Macdonald's
orders. According to Weil, Macdonald directed V Corps to take the direct road
southeast from Goldberg through Seichau to Hennersdorf. To its left, II Cavalry
Corps had to cross the Katzbach at Kroitsch and move south along the left bank of
the Wütende Neiße. In the center, Gérard's XI Corps would ford the Katzbach at
Schmogwitz and proceed south along the western edge of the plateau to
Brechelshof (Brachów). On the left wing of the army, III Corps received instructions to cross the Katzbach at Liegnitz and proceed south to Malitsch. On his far
right, he wanted Puthod's 17th Division at Schönau on the 26th, from where he
would send one brigade through Jägendorf to Jauer while the second brigade
united with the 31st Division to contend with the enemy corps at Hirschberg.
Because of the roads that existed in the region at that time, Weil's supposition that
XI Corps would cross the Katzbach at Schmogwitz was impossible based on the
march direction it took on the morning of the 26th. See Weil, *Campagne de 1813*,
103; see also Friederich, *Herbstfeldzug 1813*, I:295.
2 SHAT, C^2 154: Gérard to Macdonald, 31 August 1813.
3 Souham's report to Berthier claims that III Corps moved out at 11:30 A.M., yet the
journal of III Corps puts the start time at noon: SHAT, C^2 154: Souham to
Berthier, 29 August 1813; Fabry, ed., *Journal des opérations du IIIe Corps*, 55.
4 During the course of the nineteenth century, Oberweinberg and Niederweinberg
became the town of Weinberg, which is now Winnica in Poland.
5 Langeron, *Mémoires*, 248; Langeron to Blücher is in Höpfner, "Darstellung,"
1844:123; Friederich, *Herbstfeldzug 1813*, I:298.

6 Nineteenth- and early twentieth-century sources refer to Wildschütz as Wöltsch and Wültsch.

7 Specifically: 50 skirmishers and a Jäger detachment from the Silesian Grenadier Battalion at Schimmelwitz; 150 skirmishers at Niederkrayn; the 4th Battalion of the Brandenburg Regiment at the Niederweinberg mill; the 2nd and 3rd Battalions at the bridge over the Neiße at Niederkrayn; and the 1st Battalion on the bank downstream this bridge. The Thuringian Battalion placed its 1st and 3rd Companies astride Niederweinberg. The two Landwehr battalions and the Silesian Grenadier Battalion formed the reserve on the hills east of Weinberg. See Höpfner, "Darstellung," 1844:124–25.

8 SHAT, C² 154: Sébastiani to Macdonald, 27 August 1813; Friederich, in *Herbstfeldzug 1813*, I:299, incorrectly states that the enemy column consisted of infantry. He corrects this error in *Die Befreiungskriege*, II:124.

9 Quoted in Droysen, *Yorck*, II:139–40.

10 Friederich, *Herbstfeldzug 1813*, I:300. French reports make no mention of this collision.

11 SHAT, C² 154: Gérard to Macdonald, 31 August 1813.

12 Quoted in Droysen, *Yorck*, II:140–41.

13 Yorck's 1st and 2nd Brigades formed his right column, which marched toward the Weinberg villages, passing east of Altjauer and Brechelshof. The left column – 7th and 8th Brigades and Reserve Artillery – marched through Jauer, Altjauer, and Brechelshof likewise toward the Weinberg villages: Fabry, *Étude sur les opérations du maréchal Macdonald*, 67.

14 "We had made the plan to cross the Katzbach with the combined army and attack the enemy. We were two [eight] miles closer to the enemy than he expected us. The headquarters directed itself to Brechelshof in a timely manner to be closer to all the reports": Gneisenau to Gibsone, Brechelshof, 26 August 1813, GStA PK, VI HA Rep. 92 Nl. Gneisenau, Nr. 21.

15 Gneisenau, *Blücher*, 162.

16 This statement is from a letter written by Johann Friedrich Benzenberg to Gneisenau on 11 March 1817, quoted in Pertz and Delbrück, *Gneisenau*, III:204.

17 In *Mémoires*, 250, Langeron states that Blücher informed him that he intended to attack the French army with his right. In *Étude sur les opérations du maréchal Macdonald*, 68, Fabry concludes that Blücher's orders state the exact opposite. Instead, the French staff officer claims that by directing Yorck to Steudnitz, Blücher intended to crush Macdonald's center and then have Yorck fall on the rear of the enemy force supposedly marching from Haynau to Liegnitz. This assertion cannot be supported because Blücher knew of only a French cavalry force posted between Macdonald's two wings.

18 "Disposition," Brechelshof, 11:00 A.M., 26 August 1813, Add MSS, 20112, 128.

19 Quoted in Droysen, *Yorck*, II:140.

20 SHAT, C² 154: Sébastiani to Macdonald, 27 August 1813.

21 Quoted in Droysen, *Yorck*, II:141.

22 SHAT, C² 154: Macdonald to Berthier, Goldberg, 27 August 1813; Fabry, ed., *Journal des opérations du IIIe Corps*, 55.

23 SHAT, C² 154: Souham to Berthier, 29 August 1813 and Macdonald to Berthier, Goldberg, 27 August 1813.

24 Fabry, ed., *Journal des opérations du IIIe Corps*, 58, states that Brayer's division reached Kroitsch at 2:30 and that "the duc de Tarente [Macdonald], who was observing the progress of the enemy on the right [Langeron] at the moment when III Corps debouched, around 3:00 sent General Tarayre to the 9th, 10th, and 11th Divisions that followed the 8th with orders to execute an attack on the left to create a diversion and disengage those forces that presented us with so many disadvantages in the defile of Kroitsch."

25 SHAT, C² 154: Souham to Berthier, 29 August 1813; Fabry, ed., *Journal des opérations du IIIe Corps*, 56, 58.

26 The 29th and 45th Jäger Regiments formed the 2nd Brigade of the 22nd Division of Kaptsevich's X Infantry Corps.

27 Langeron, *Mémoires*, 248. Starting with Olsufiyev's IX Corps on Langeron's left, Kornilov split the 3rd Brigade of his 15th Division, sending the two battalions of the 12th Jäger Regiment to defend the Silber west of Hennersdorf and the sole battalion of the 22nd Jäger to occupy Herrmannsdorf. Udom, the commander of Olsufiyev's 9th Division, instructed his 3rd Brigade (10th and 38th Jäger Regiments, two battalions total) to occupy Hennersdorf. The four remaining brigades (nine battalions total) of 9th and 15th Divisions formed south of the Weinberg, extending from Herrmannsdorf on the left (west) to the Kirchberg on the right (east). On Langeron's right wing, the 1st and 2nd Brigades (four battalions total) of General Panteleimon Benardos's 18th Division of Shcherbatov's VI Infantry Corps extended northeast from the Kirchberg to the Breiteberg, where the 1st and 2nd Brigades (five battalions total) of General Stepan Talyzin I's 7th Division deployed. Benardos's 3rd Brigade, consisting of the 28th and 32nd Jäger Regiments (two battalions total), held the hills just east of Hennersdorf between Schlaupe and the Breiteberg, while the three battalions of Talyzin's 3rd Brigade (11th and 36th Jäger Regiments) secured Schlaupe on the extreme right.

28 Subtracting Pahlen II's detachment, which consisted of the two squadrons of the Kinburnskii Dragoon Regiment, the two squadrons of the Dorpatskii Mounted Jäger Regiment, and the Moskovskii and Libavskii Infantry Regiments, Langeron had at his disposal: the eight battalions, six squadrons, two Cossack regiments, and ten guns of Rudzevich's vanguard; the twelve battalions and twenty-four guns of Shcherbatov's VI Infantry Corps; the eleven battalions and twenty-four guns of Olsufiyev's IX Corps; the eight battalions and twenty-four guns of Kaptsevich's X Corps; and the eleven squadrons and six guns of regular cavalry belonging to Korf's reserve. The historian of the Russian General Staff, Bogdanovich, describes Langeron's position as very advantageous. See Bogdanovich, *Geschichte des Krieges*, IIa:57–58, 66–67; Friederich, *Herbstfeldzug 1813*, I:297–99.

29 Langeron, *Mémoires*, 250, quoted in Höpfner, "Darstellung," 1844:126. These sentences are not included in Langeron's memoirs.

30 Langeron, *Mémoires*, 250.

31 SHAT, C² 154: Lauriston to Macdonald, 28 August 1813.

32 Langeron to Blücher is in Höpfner, "Darstellung," 1844:127. In his memoirs, Langeron claims to have responded to Blücher that he could not leave his position to execute a movement to the right because of the enemy's attempt to turn his left, but promised he would not yield an inch of terrain. See Langeron, *Mémoires*, 250.

33 Höpfner, "Darstellung," 1844: 127.
34 SHAT, C² 154: Lauriston to Macdonald, 28 August 1813.
35 Langeron, *Mémoires*, 248.
36 The disposition, which is in Höpfner, "Darstellung," 1844:127, calls for I Corps to form two massive columns. The left wing would be composed of 7th and 8th Brigades. Horn's 7th Brigade would be arranged so that the brigade cavalry would be at the head followed by one battalion, the brigade artillery and one twelve-pound battery, and then the remaining battalions. Hünerbein's 8th Brigade would be arranged so that the lead battalion would be followed by the brigade artillery, one twelve-pound battery, the remaining battalions, and the brigade cavalry at the rear. This column received the task of marching through Schlauphof and Niederkrayn to Kroitsch, where it would cross the Katzbach and passing Rothkirch on the right proceed to Steudnitz. The right wing column would consist of 1st and 2nd Brigades and the Reserve Cavalry. The brigade cavalry of both units would form the head followed by one battalion of the 1st Brigade, one twelve-pound battery, and the brigade battery, and the remaining battalions of 1st Brigade followed by 2nd Brigade in the same order but without a twelve-pound battery; the Reserve Cavalry would form the rear. This column would march through Jänowitz to Dohnau, where it would cross the Katzbach and march through Rothkirch to Steudnitz. To secure the two points of passage across the Katzbach, Yorck split his vanguard.
37 Blasendorff, *Blücher*, 206; Droysen, *Yorck*, II:139.
38 Müffling, *Die Feldzüge*, 31–32; Bogdanovich, *Geschichte des Krieges*, IIa:60.
39 Müffling, *Die Feldzüge*, 29–30, and *Aus meinem Leben*, 59–61. Written in 1824 before Gneisenau's death six years later, the former provides an excellent operational history without the backbiting and self-promotion found in the latter. Because Gneisenau was still alive at the time of the publication of the former, we can assume that the account is accurate.
40 "A quarter-mile from us, the enemy was just in the process of taking the corps of General Langeron in the right flank as he had already done in the left. He wanted to bowl over the few battalions of our vanguard": Gneisenau to Gibsone, Brechelshof, 26 August 1813, and Gneisenau to Clausewitz, Goldberg, 28 August 1813, GStA PK, VI HA Rep. 92 Nl. Gneisenau, Nr. 21; Pertz and Delbrück, *Gneisenau*, III:206.
41 Müffling, *Die Feldzüge*, 28–31, and *Aus meinem Leben*, 61–62.
42 Yorck decided that the narrow stretch between the plateau's edge and Eichholtz – hardly 2,000 paces in width – did not suffice for a front of three brigades to deploy, especially since Sacken's artillery extended west of Eichholtz.
43 Droysen, *Yorck*, II:142; Müffling, *Aus meinem Leben*, 62.
44 Quoted in Gneisenau, *Blücher*, 163.
45 Müffling, *Die Feldzüge*, 32, and *Aus meinem Leben*, 63.
46 SHAT, C² 154: Gérard to Macdonald, 31 August 1813.
47 Quoted in Droysen, *Yorck*, II:143.
48 Gneisenau to Gibsone, Brechelshof, 26 August 1813, GStA PK, VI HA Rep. 92 Nl. Gneisenau, Nr. 21. In his letter to Clausewitz written two days later, Gneisenau claims that only one musket fired.

49 SHAT, C² 154: Gérard to Macdonald, 31 August 1813.

50 Marbot, *Mémoires*, III:285; SHAT, C² 154: Sébastiani to Macdonald, 27 August 1813; Fabry, ed., *Journal des opérations du IIIe Corps*, 55–56.

51 Quoted in Droysen, *Yorck*, II:143.

52 Fabry, ed., *Journal des opérations du IIIe Corps*, 56.

53 Unger, *Blücher*, II:80; Droysen, *Yorck*, II:142.

54 SHAT, C² 154: Sébastiani to Macdonald, 27 August 1813.

55 Blasendorff, *Blücher*, 206; Pertz and Delbrück, *Gneisenau*, III:207. Blasendorff claims that Yorck "only slowly deployed his troops to support the vanguard" and "withheld his serious cooperation." Such allegations can be dismissed.

56 Unger, *Blücher*, II:80. "It was typical for General Yorck to be irresolute before he determined on an attack," wrote Steffens; "but, once resolved, he held back nothing": Steffens, *Adventures*, 120.

57 The Aleksandriiskii and Mariupolskii Hussar Regiments, eleven squadrons total.

58 The 1st Brigade of the 2nd Hussar Division consisted of the Akhtyrskii and Belorusskii Hussar Regiments, twelve squadrons total.

59 Gneisenau, *Blücher*, 164.

60 Gneisenau to Gibsone, Brechelshof, 26 August 1813, GStA PK, VI HA Rep. 92 Nl. Gneisenau, Nr. 21; SHAT, C² 154: Sébastiani to Macdonald, 27 August 1813.

61 Fabry, ed., *Journal des opérations du IIIe Corps*, 56–57.

62 SHAT, C² 154: Sébastiani to Macdonald, 27 August 1813.

63 Fabry, ed., *Journal des opérations du IIIe Corps*, 57; Gneisenau to Gibsone, Brechelshof, 26 August 1813, GStA PK, VI HA Rep. 92 Nl. Gneisenau, Nr. 21.

64 SHAT, C² 154: Souham to Berthier, 29 August 1813; Gérard to Macdonald, 31 August 1813; and Sébastiani to Macdonald, 27 August 1813.

65 Langeron, *Mémoires*, 254.

66 Fabry, ed., *Journal des opérations du IIIe Corps*, 58, 60.

67 "Tagebuch der reitenden Batterie Nr. 12 des I AK," GStA PK, IV Rep. 15a Nr. 376; Freytag-Loringhoven, *Aufklärung und Armeeführung*, 83.

68 Fabry, ed., *Journal des opérations du IIIe Corps*, 58; SHAT, C² 154: Souham to Berthier, 29 August 1813.

69 Sacken to Blücher, Großjänowitz, 10:00 A.M., 27 August 1813, is in Pertz and Delbrück, *Gneisenau*, III:236.

70 Fabry, ed., *Journal des opérations du IIIe Corps*, 59. The journal incorrectly states that this Russian corps was commanded by General Nikolay Rayevsky.

71 Fabry, *Étude sur les opérations du maréchal Macdonald*, 90–91; Sacken to Blücher, Großjänowitz, 10:00 A.M., 27 August 1813, is in Pertz and Delbrück, Gneisenau, III:236; Fabry, ed., *Journal des opérations du IIIe Corps*, 59–60.

72 SHAT, C² 154: Gérard to Macdonald, 31 August 1813.

73 SHAT, C² 154: Gérard to Macdonald, 31 August 1813, and Macdonald to Berthier, 27 August 1813; Langeron, *Mémoires*, 251–52.

74 Müffling, *Aus meinem Leben*, 64–67. Müffling disagreed with both the harsh criticism of Langeron and the notion that victory on the plateau had elevated them to hero-like status. Posing as the savior, he notes in his memoirs: "Accordingly, here again fell to me the difficult task of disturbing self-satisfying delusions by using plain truths to eradicate the consequences of such hallucinations." In

Étude sur les opérations du maréchal Macdonald, 96, Fabry criticizes Blücher for neither leading 1st Brigade himself nor going to Langeron's command post: "There is no doubt that the intervention of a leader as energetic as Blücher would have given Steinmetz's attack another character. Because the commander in chief was concerned about what was happening to Langeron's corps, his true place was with it. He would have found a favorable opportunity to intervene by launching the 1st Brigade through Schlaupe against the left of XI Corps and to reestablish the combat of the Russian corps he claimed was lost by the incorrect measures of its commander." Blücher had to decide between the lesser of the two evils: Yorck or Langeron. Had he accompanied the latter, the former may have been the one to retreat to Jauer, leaving Sacken's corps to absorb the full weight of III Infantry and II Cavalry Corps.

75 Quoted in Droysen, *Yorck*, II:145, but the journal itself was lost during the Second World War.

76 Quoted in Lieven, *Russia Against Napoleon*, 384–85; Langeron, *Mémoires*, 252; Müffling, *Aus meinem Leben*, 67–68. Gneisenau's adjutant, Captain Stosch, attested to the accuracy of Müffling's testimony regarding this assignment. See Pertz and Delbrück, *Gneisenau*, III:208.

77 Meshcherinov led the 28th and 32nd Jäger Regiments of the 3rd Brigade of 18th Division, supported by the 11th and 36th Jäger Regiments of 7th Division's 3rd Brigade.

78 As noted, Gneisenau wrote that Langeron "was saved when some battalions from Steinmetz's brigade crossed the Wütende Neiße and took the enemy in the left flank." Moreover, Nostitz asserts that, "through the appropriate maneuver, a Prussian brigade prevented the enemy from making use of his superior numbers against Langeron's corps. In this case it was Steinmetz's brigade, which through its crossing of the Neiße and victorious advance between Schlaupe and Schlauphof forced the French to disengage from Langeron's corps." Fabry firmly rejects the Prussian claim that Steinmetz saved Langeron. According to the French officer, Steinmetz "himself forded the river with two battalions and took the heights on the left bank. His movement was supported by the battery of his brigade, half of the Nr. 1 Horse Battery, the Grenadier Battalion that had been assigned as an escort. In fact, the support provided by Steinmetz's brigade was reduced to two battalions. Therefore, Gneisenau had no right to claim to have saved Langeron by jumping on the rear of the French corps that was attacking him." See Gneisenau to Clausewitz, Goldberg, 28 August 1813, GStA PK, VI HA Rep. 92 Nl. Gneisenau, Nr. 21; Nostitz, *Tagebuch*, 57; Fabry, *Étude sur les opérations du maréchal Macdonald*, 98.

79 Langeron, *Mémoires*, 252–54. While Fabry is quick to point out that Müffling maintained that three French battalions retreated from the plateau in order, he fails to mention that the Prussian claimed the imperials "behaved without energy and irresolutely" after the Russian counterattack: SHAT, C² 154: Macdonald to Berthier, 27 August 1813 and Lauriston to Macdonald, 28 August 1813; Müffling, *Aus meinem Leben*, 68.

80 Gneisenau to Clausewitz, Goldberg, 28 August 1813, GStA PK, VI HA Rep. 92 Nl. Gneisenau, Nr. 21; Henckel von Donnersmarck, *Erinnerungen*, 214; Blücher

to Charles John, Goldberg, 28 August 1813, RA KrA, volym 25; Maude, *Leipzig Campaign*, 178.

81 Gneisenau to Gibsone, Brechelshof, 26 August 1813, GStA PK, VI HA Rep. 92 Nl. Gneisenau, Nr. 21. Freytag-Loringhoven, in *Aufklärung und Armeeführung*, 83, states: "With regard to the trophies and the losses of the French, it can no longer be determined what fell into Allied hands during the battle itself and what they captured in the pursuit." Although vicious attacks on Gneisenau abound in his memoirs, Müffling, in *Aus meinem Leben*, 73–74, offers a possible explanation for the inflation of numbers: "He [Gneisenau] was anxious that the victory on the plateau should be considered by all of Europe as a general defeat of the whole of Macdonald's army, because this suited his 'electrifying system.'" It is more plausible based on his correspondence with Münster that Gneisenau sought to portray the victory as decisive to earn more British monetary and material support for Prussia in general and the Silesian Army in particular.

82 SHAT, C² 154: Souham to Berthier, 29 August 1813, and Gérard to Macdonald, 31 August 1813; Fabry, *Étude sur les operations du maréchal Macdonald*, 89.

83 Henckel von Donnersmarck, *Erinnerungen*, 213; Unger, *Blücher*, II:79; Langeron, *Mémoires*, 260.

84 Gneisenau to Münster, Brechelshof, 26 August 1813, GStA PK, VI HA Rep. 92 Nl. Gneisenau, Nr. 20b; Gneisenau to Clausewitz, Goldberg, 28 August 1813, *ibid.*, Nr. 21. Not surprisingly, Gneisenau's assessment in his letter to Münster agrees with Blücher's initial after-action report to the king, which Gneisenau drafted: "I had decided to attack the enemy today but at the moment when my orders were about to be executed the enemy crossed the Katzbach opposite me. I concealed my troops and initially brought only my vanguard into combat; but when all of his troops had crossed the Katzbach, I led the army entrusted to my command against them and I soon had the fortune of achieving a complete victory." A copy of Blücher's letter to Frederick William, written in German at Brechelshof on 26 August 1813, is in RA KrA, volym 25.

85 Unger, *Blücher*, II:79; Gneisenau to Gibsone, Brechelshof, 26 August 1813, GStA PK, VI HA Rep. 92 Nl. Gneisenau, Nr. 21.

86 Sources for the battle of the Katzbach are: Höpfner, "Darstellung," 1844:123–27; Vaudoncourt, *Histoire de la guerre*, 144; Plotho, *Der Krieg*, II:107; Gneisenau, *Blücher*, 163–64; Bogdanovich, *Geschichte des Krieges*, IIa:50–70; Pertz and Delbrück, *Gneisenau*, III:201–08; Müffling, *Die Feldzüge*, 28–37; Unger, *Blücher*, II:76; Droysen, *Yorck*, II:138–46; Fabry, *Étude sur les opérations du maréchal Macdonald*, 72–79, 90–99; Weil, *Campagne de 1813*, 104; Friederich, *Herbstfeldzug 1813*, I:297–311; Blasendorff, *Blücher*, 205–07; Henckel von Donnersmarck, *Erinnerungen*, 213–14; Unger, *Blücher*, II:77–78; Lieven, *Russia Against Napoleon*, 380–83.

87 SHAT, C² 154: Macdonald to Berthier, 4:00 P.M., 25 August 1813, and Macdonald to Napoleon, Goldberg, 2:00 P.M. and 4:00 P.M., 25 August 1813.

88 Friederich, *Herbstfeldzug 1813*, I:312–14.

7

Blücher's hare hunt

In the streaming rain, Blücher rode back to Brechelshof accompanied by Gneisenau. Initially silent, he then joked with his companion. "No, Gneisenau," he purportedly exclaimed, "we have won the battle and nobody can deny us that. Now, they will demand to know how we did it so well and I will have to teach them!" Unable to find a structure large enough to accommodate Army Headquarters because the few buildings on the estate housed the wounded, they went to the *Rittergut* (manor), which now served as the army's main hospital. Karl Ernst Friedrich, Baron von Richthofen, had purchased the estate, previously the Leubus Seminary, in 1811 during Prussia's liquidation of religious holdings. At a long table in the large, arched great room, Blücher and his staff sat down to a meager victory dinner consisting of boiled potatoes served in large clay bowls. Although the potatoes were freshly dug, no spices could be found to add flavor. Seated at the far end of the table, young Scharnhorst seemed restless and looked around disappointingly. Blücher noticed and asked the lieutenant what troubled him. When Scharnhorst declared he desired salt, Blücher bellowed: "He is such a gourmand that he even needs salt!"[1]

After dinner, work continued deep into the night. Blücher wrote his own report to the magistrate of Breslau announcing the victory as well as requesting care for the wounded and food for his troops. Despite his exhaustion, he also penned private letters. "Today was the day that I have so long wished for," he divulged to his wife; "we have completely defeated the enemy, capturing many cannon and taking many prisoners. I expect even more prisoners will be taken tomorrow because I will pursue the enemy with all my cavalry." He briefly summarized the campaign in a letter to a friend:

Being moved by the insolence of the French, I started hostilities two days before the expiration of the armistice. I drove the French army under Ney back to the Bober, where the great Napoleon appeared with six marshals and six different corps. I was forced to yield before this great superiority. In constant combat, I withdrew behind the Katzbach to Jauer. Then I learned that the emperor had returned to Saxony, taking with him Marshal Marmont and his corps. I now made the decision to seize the offensive and on the 26th marched against the enemy to attack him. The enemy had made the same decision and had already crossed the Katzbach. We met each other at Brechelshof. I attacked: the combat lasted from 2:00 P.M. until the evening. The enemy was completely defeated: more than forty cannon and most of his ammunition have fallen into my hands. Not too many prisoners were taken: the troops were too bitter and cut down everything. We are in pursuit of the enemy and I promise even greater gains. It rained the entire day and toward evening the muskets could no longer fire. My infantry fought with bayonets; Prussians and Russians competed with each other and neither wanted to concede the advantage. Our troops fought with great bravery. I still cannot determine my losses yet they are not great compared to the victory that we have won.[2]

As of midnight, Blücher likewise could not estimate the extent of Macdonald's losses. "We have taken a considerable number of cannon and caissons," stated Blücher's initial account to Bernadotte, "but at this moment, I cannot determine the exact number. Before daybreak, the light cavalry supported by infantry will again attack or intensely pursue the enemy." A copy of this report never reached the king because the courier, Count Moltke, drowned crossing the Elbe at Arbesau (Varvažov) in Bohemia.[3]

A name for the battle still needed to be chosen. Ironically, Blücher eventually selected "the battle of the Katzbach" as a form of damage control to placate an offended corps commander. Instead of Yorck or Langeron, this time Blücher had to contend with Sacken, whose performance in the battle had unequivocally pleased Army Headquarters. On the night after the battle, Blücher informed Bernadotte that Sacken had worked wonders. On the 27th, Blücher exclaimed to his entourage: "We owe a great deal to General Sacken; his twelve-pound guns on the Eichholtz hills facilitated our work; his cavalry in Sébastiani's rear completed the victory. Let us regard this man with honor." Blücher's words stuck – the Prussians held Sacken in esteem. Shortly after this, Sacken accidentally appeared in the midst of Yorck's columns. Per their tradition, the Prussian officers saluted him in silence as he passed, while the soldiers greeted him with a hearty "hurrah" per theirs. Sacken recognized the value of such approbation from his allies.[4]

"General Sacken participated with fortitude and strength in the fate of the day, and in a noteworthy manner put behind him all of the bitter accusations that had been made against him in the previous campaign [1812]," declares Nostitz. "Alluding to this, Blücher said to him the day after the battle with a hearty handshake: 'My dear Sacken, yesterday you defeated the tsar's enemy as well as your own personal enemy.'"[5] Neverthe-less, Blücher learned that his brief after-action report to the king had irked Sacken and offended his officers. Apparently, the Russians felt that Blücher had failed to adequately highlight their performance and contribution to the victory. "Modesty," sneered Gneisenau, "attires well those who have been miserable for so long."[6] Regardless, Blücher sought to make amends in a second, more comprehensive report to the king on the 28th: "I owe this important victory first to Baron Sacken, who occupied the hills between Brechelshof and Eichholtz quickly and spontaneously with a twelve-pound battery, which made it possible for me to immediately direct the formal attack on the enemy's right wing. Gneisenau and Müffling arranged the attack ... while Yorck held the center." To further satisfy Sacken, Blücher officially informed him on 30 August that, "to honor you, this battle will be called the battle of the Katzbach because your brave troops advanced to this stream amidst constant fighting."[7]

Indeed, the Prussians not only lauded Sacken's conduct, but exploited the effects of his actions to paint an ugly picture of Langeron: "The battle has been named the battle of the Katzbach to honor the brave and insightful Russian general Sacken," wrote Gneisenau, "whose right wing extended up to this river while we were on the Wütende Neiße. These two rivers mainly united before our front and in the rear of the enemy position. Through our victory, General Langeron, who hovered in great danger throughout, was ultimately saved." Blücher's two reports to Allied Headquarters made no mention of Langeron. The only reference to the action on his part of the field occurred when Blücher noted that Lauriston's "still unbeaten V Corps" remained north of Hennersdorf during the night of 26/27 August. To Bernadotte he wrote: "Langeron's corps was on my left. It remained on the defensive and did not quit its position." Nostitz provides insight into how Army Headquarters viewed Langeron's performance in the battle:

> The conduct of General Langeron on this day deserved the well-earned rebuke. If the day had not ended so gloriously, he would have been held accountable. Out of timidity and against orders, he sent his Reserve Artillery so far back that when the battle began he had no batteries to employ against the enemy. As decisive as these almost unprecedented proceedings certainly would have been in any other battle, the negative impact was only slight and soon overcome by a Prussian brigade that maneuvered to prevent the enemy from making use of his superior numbers against Langeron's corps. The jubilation and universal joy over the victory in part stifled the reprimand that the general expected and earned.[8]

According to nineteenth-century German sources as well as the main Russian authority on the 1813 campaign, Bogdanovich, Langeron did not intend to either attack the French or defend his position. They claim that, knowing of the task assigned to Blücher but not the secret concessions granted to him by Barclay, Langeron thought Blücher would order the army to retreat in the face of the enemy's advance. Langeron himself decided that a retreat to Striegau would best comply with Barclay's directives. As a result, he sent almost all of his heavy artillery – forty-eight pieces – retreating through Jauer toward Striegau. After describing the strength of Langeron's position, Bogdanovich notes: "Langeron, who not in the slightest considered a defensive battle, directed his entire attention only toward securing a retreat to Silesia's interior; for this purpose, he left behind all his battery artillery at Jauer, believing that in the case of a march on poor roads it would be more of a hindrance than a use. These measures were taken unbeknownst to the commander in chief, but Langeron took the opportunity to defend his position. His situation would have been extremely dangerous if Sacken and Yorck had not won a glorious victory."[9]

In addition, Langeron instructed Kaptsevich to take a defensive position at Peterwitz to receive the army corps as it retreated and to guard against enemy forces approaching from the Schönau–Jägendorf region.[10] Langeron also claimed that his artillery commander, "General Gavriil Veselitsky, an excellent officer, but sharing in the highest degree the weakness that affects all Russian artillery commanders, which is the belief that the loss of one gun is a great dishonor, believing that the battle was lost (he was unaware of the success of our right) and providing that the rain could make the roads impassable, hastened to withdraw, *without my orders*, all the spare batteries to Jauer, where their arrival caused the greatest alarm."

Aware of how the Prussians of Blücher's staff viewed these proceedings, Langeron added:

> Gneisenau wished to make me responsible ... it seemed to him to be an excellent opportunity to rid himself of a Frenchman who offended him and to obtain some *Tudesque* [Teuton (German)] from our army; he convinced Blücher to send the tsar a report against me which undoubtedly would have caused the loss of my sovereign's confidence had it arrived at Allied Head-quarters, but the adjutant, Count Moltke, who was charged with its delivery, drowned while crossing the Elbe at Arnau in Bohemia and all of his papers were lost. The success that the troops under my command constantly enjoyed, especially after the battle of the Katzbach, inhibited Monsieur Gneisenau from renewing his attacks against me; he never wished me well but at least he kept up appearances; Müffling was more just in his treatment of me.[11]

Nostitz delivered Gneisenau's after-action reports to Hardenberg as well as to the king's adjutant, Major Ludwig Gustav von Thile. In both, the staff chief praised Sacken and chastised Langeron, reiterating his request that the former receive command of the latter's larger corps and for Langeron to be transferred elsewhere. "I will make good use of all your remarks concerning the Russian generals," responded Hardenberg on the 30th. Thile answered from Teplitz on the 31st: "I wish ... that your request referring to Langeron and Sacken will soon be fulfilled. Concerning them and you, I can say nothing except that we know what is happening." Much to the chagrin of the Prussians, Langeron would remain at the head of his corps for the rest of the war.[12]

In his duel with Yorck, Blücher waged everything on this battle. "The Prussian corps played the decisive part in the victory," Nostitz recorded in his journal; "this conviction removed for a time all the wrinkles from the forehead of its heroic commander." Yorck did indeed send the letter of complaint he had written to the king the day before the battle. Droysen claims to have found the fragment of a recantation that Yorck never finished. Writing sometime before the end of August, Yorck stated: "After the glorious victory on the 26th of this month, it may appear that I was incorrect to criticize the operations as such. I would commit an injustice to both myself and the truth if I argued that wise arrangements based on proper judgment procured for us that great success. On the contrary, this success is attributable only to good luck. This inept operation, in which the enemy opposite us frustrated our offensive operations, probably would have led us to a mishap like the enemy himself suffered." Work on this essay probably ceased as a result of two cabinet orders issued by the king from Teplitz on 31 August to sooth Yorck. Frederick William's first note rewarded Yorck's performance at the Katzbach with Prussia's highest civil-military award: the Order of the Black Eagle. The king's second letter firmly but gently sided with Blücher:

> I quite believe that the movements executed by I Army Corps since the resumption of the campaign have exhausted the troops and I do not fail to recognize in the concerns you expressed on the 25th of this month your praiseworthy care for the preservation of the good condition of the troops subordinated to you. Nevertheless, these movements cannot be avoided because they are based on the plan that has been agreed upon by my allies and me for the operations of the Allied armies. As you already know, the execution of this plan generally has had the best results. Therefore, I request that you persist in the zeal with which you have up to now supplied the state with the most laudable services. The status of your health will hopefully be bolstered as much as possible by the preservation of your goodwill, and through the fulfillment of this, which is my wish, you will acquire new claims on my particular gratefulness.[13]

Victory certainly provided Blücher with the moral edge over the hero of Tauroggen, especially in view of Yorck's behavior at the start of the battle. "Yorck held everything to be lost," Gneisenau explained to Clausewitz. "'We are lost!' he shouted. 'Now you can collect your laurels. We will be beaten into the ground; victory will be ripped from our hands,' and things to that effect. Nevertheless, our entire infantry stood in the most superb order. 'The march from behind Jauer should not be made,' he said. 'You needlessly fatigue the troops,' he said. Thus we had to obtain this victory by force, success is sweet for us, and the just cause was victorious despite all jealousy. Success is so sweet for me!"[14]

Many historians incorrectly follow the contention stated by Blücher's biographer, Unger, that "this victory restored the trust in the army's high command that threatened to completely collapse. This victory completely justified all of the recent hardships as well as the incomprehensible back-and-forth marches."[15] "The battle at the Katzbach was fought," recorded Nostitz. "Among the many and great results that the glorious victory produced was the restoration of harmony among the commanding generals and the rejuvenation of troop morale; the losses and hardships of the previous days passed into oblivion."[16] In his 1827 work, Müffling showered Blücher with praise: "The general in chief demonstrated that he knew well the proper moment to switch from a cautious defense to a bold attack, which would produce great results. Thus, one day's work removed all discord and all ill-humor from the heart of the Silesian Army."[17]

Claiming that the victory had reestablished trust between Army Head-quarters and Yorck and Langeron is certainly a stretch considering the two corps commanders had never trusted Blücher's staff in the first place. More-over, asserting that the victory vindicated Army Headquarters for what appeared to the corps commanders to be two weeks of incomprehensible, exhausting tramps across Silesia is hagiographic. In fact, the lauding of Sacken in the reports over the battle sickened Yorck, who from that time on referred to the Russian as "General Hurrah." Langeron, whom the reports purposefully did not mention at all, was all the more displeased. To console him, Blücher submitted for publication Langeron's full account of the pursuit after the battle as the army's official report. In both cases – the army report over the battle and the army report over the pursuit – Army Headquarters ignored the part played by Yorck's corps based on his report because it did not correspond to the Russian versions. "It lay in the nature of the relationship," explains Droysen, "that Blücher's headquarters avoided with most abject care anything that could give the Russian generals and troops cause for ill-feeling and jealousy."

While the victory did not heal the rifts, it is accurate to view the day of the Katzbach as the emergence of Blücher, the birth of Marshal *Vorwärts*. From this point on, the magic that the troops affixed to Blücher's personal-ity – just like the charisma of Napoleon – unfolded its full power. Behind the field commander, Gneisenau's boldness of thought and complete devotion enabled Blücher to soar increasingly higher. Even Droysen declared that the Katzbach "decided the high moral and intellectual preponderance that from this time on characterized the leadership of the Silesian Army."[18]

Gneisenau appears to have been much more affected than Blücher by the hostile demeanor of the corps commanders. Proof emerges from the battle-field that very night when Gneisenau rode over to Yorck, removed his cap, and offered his congratulations in the hope of restoring good relations. "I commend Your Excellency on the victory," stated Gneisenau. "Yea, which I have won for you," responded the curmudgeon, "but where are the provisions? The poor soldiers are dying of hunger." Gneisenau retorted sharply: "You still have bread for two days, fat stock for one; here [pointing at the potato field], where they stand, potatoes are in abundance as well as wood for the cooking; twigs are on the wagons. Therefore, if the soldiers are starving, it is your fault!" Gneisenau turned his horse and sprang forward. After this exchange, the two officers spoke no more. A few years later, during a commemoration of the battle, both tried in vain to reconcile. Gneisenau simply explained that "regarding old, coarse Yorck, it is best if one does not speak to him at all."[19]

From Gneisenau's own melodramatic letters it emerges that Langeron and Yorck directed the brunt of their anger, criticism, and jealousy at him, which compounded the pressure applied by Blücher. "Both consider me to be an aspiring daredevil, and my commander always wants an attack dispos-ition from me. It actually takes a degree of good luck to emerge unscathed from such dangerous situations. Thus far, fortune has favored me, but will it always be sweet to me? When it does abandon me, reproach and disgrace will fall on me alone; think of me from time to time: I do not at all share in the glory of the success."[20] To Knesebeck he wrote: "My position is critical. The commanding general wants me to go forward, others pull me back, making difficulties, evading or not following orders. The palm of victory was forced into the hands of the corps commanders. My value to them is slight. I have only decisiveness and mental fortitude. Fortune again showed me its favor. The bravery of the infantry and artillery completed what we planned. Hatred, envy, and resentment are humbled; and the slander may now go its own way. This time it went well; but do not always count on my good fortune, even less on my merit. It will not always be possible for me to extricate myself from the difficult situation in which the will of the king has placed me."[21]

Mounting tension between Gneisenau and Müffling did not make matters any easier for the staff chief. During the Spring Campaign, the latter had become sensitive to the issue of spinning battle accounts for public consumption. He alleged that the Prussian newspapers published accounts "that partly gave a distorted picture of events" and frequently compromised the Prussian army to please the Russians. Despite a public hungry for news of the war, the government possessed no official bureau for providing infor-mation to the press. This made the media dependent on news provided by volunteers, mainly private letters usually written by officers to their relations with the intent of having the contents forwarded for publication. Recognizing that this type of report could positively impact public morale, Frederick William preferred this method of disseminating information. However, explaining that private letters "often unintentionally state the most insignificant facts as the most important" and thus "provide a false picture of the situation of the belligerent armies," Müffling preferred a formal method of channeling the fullest account of an event as possible. "Therefore," he argued, "the acceptance of unauthenticated reports from the army by newspaper correspondents must be prohibited by the censorship; but at the same time something else must be substituted, namely official articles, simple and true rather than lying bulletins like Napoleon's." Moreover, by parroting criticism of Allied leaders without providing a balanced description of events, such letters could in fact undermine the war effort. "By such inconsiderate communication is public opinion formed," he lamented.

With Gneisenau wanting to capitalize on the victory as much as possible both abroad and at home, Müffling found his personal view of the battle, particularly "that the engagement on the plateau had been an insignificant encounter," ran counter to that of his superior. Müffling's first attempt to draft an account of the battle for the media earned Gneisenau's censure for being "too cold, measured, and pedantic." Blücher rejected it for failing to praise "his brave comrades in arms, which, to be just, he could not deny them." Responding to Gneisenau's criticism, Müffling insisted that he had "studied the prose of our official style," that he knew no other way to write, and that no other style would be suitable. To Blücher he stressed the need to keep the press releases short and to minimize praise or blame to avoid offending allies and encroaching on the rights of the sovereigns. He added that Blücher's account would be published long before the official reports that included comments on particular commanders reached the monarchs, who had the sole right to mete out punishment or rewards. "All these arguments availed to nothing," wailed Müffling. "Gneisenau adorned my paper with phrases and flowers; General Blücher introduced Prussian names." Müffling of course claimed that he had staunchly held his ground, challenging Gneisenau to submit the matter to the king's judgment. "Gneisenau yielded, not wishing that the affair be referred to the king for judgment. Blücher fell quiet when I told him that military achievements, conveying in them the highest praise, might be related as facts, and the names of the actors mentioned as a matter of course, without laudatory additions."

Müffling wrote a second draft, attributing victory to three events: (1) the struggle on the plateau; (2) Steinmetz's attack at Schlaupe; and (3) Langeron's counterattack at 6:00 P.M. Gneisenau objected to the second and third points because, according to Müffling, they weakened the impression of the first.

Müffling overcame these objections by countering that, if the report ignored Langeron's operations, "the partial struggle on the plateau could not be designated as a battle of the Silesian Army." Similar to Blücher's report to the king, Müffling's third draft, written on the night of the 27th, attracted the enmity of the Russians. Sacken objected because the account said too little of his corps, and Langeron because it said nothing of his. Müffling included the statements of both Russian corps commanders in a fourth version, which of course angered Yorck because the account contained nothing from his mouth. "General Blücher and Gneisenau always catered to the discontented party, and I could expect no defense from them," noted Müffling. Although he made no mention of a fifth draft, this statement leads us to believe that he returned to his quill yet again.

While everything Müffling claims must be carefully measured, circumstantial evidence, particularly Gneisenau's propagandizing correspondence, suggests that this fracas occurred at Army Headquarters. In fact, it is just as easy to see Müffling caught between Gneisenau and Blücher in regards to reporting as it is to see Gneisenau caught between Blücher and Yorck concerning operations. According to Müffling, the confrontation with Gneisenau by no means settled this issue. "Each report gave rise to fresh contests of the same nature. Although my opponents had yielded, I had not convinced them. Gneisenau accused me of viewing all the achievements of the Silesian Army as trifles not worth mentioning. Blücher wished to see every well-executed commission mentioned and praised as a martial exploit. In this continued conflict, Gneisenau feared that in the next report I would present the combat on the plateau as a *Cossack hurrah*; and he strove incessantly to get me to acknowledge its more extensive importance." The only closure Müffling provides is the following quip: "My experience at this time taught me that it is impractical to take away from the commanding general the charge of drafting such army reports."[22]

Following the battle, providing security for the local inhabitants became a concern. "The French, who were cut off from the river crossings, wander around in the woods and commit offenses," Gneisenau explained. "I have ordered the alarm sounded in order for them to be killed or captured by the peasants." On the evening of the 26th, he instructed Müffling to issue orders for the mobilization of the Landsturm in the districts along the flanks and rear of the Army of the Bober but particularly at Jauer. Müffling wrote to the military governor of Silesia, General Gaudi, requesting the immediate mobilization of the Silesian Landsturm to collect the routed bands of imperials, the stragglers and deserters, the sick and wounded, and the arms, cannon, and wagons that littered the fields as far as the eye could see. All should be sent to the Silesian fortresses. Ironically and inexplicably, Gaudi issued a memorandum that same day announcing the retreat of imperial forces from Silesia *before* receiving any news of Blücher's victory. Later

12 French lancers marauding

claiming that Müffling's letter had never reached him, Gaudi did not decree a general mobilization of the Landsturm. Only Hirschberg, a district directly instructed by Blücher to deploy its Landsturm, contributed in the way Gneisenau envisioned.[23]

To avoid a second battle, Blücher and Gneisenau wanted to destroy Macdonald's army before it escaped from Silesia. "I shall do everything in my power to complete the destruction of this army," Gneisenau assured Clausewitz. Of course, delivering the *coup de grâce* to the Army of the Bober required more than the mobilization of teenaged peasants and middle-aged burghers. According to the reports, French forces occupied Liegnitz and the left bank of the Katzbach as far as the influx of the Wütende Neiße. West of Hennersdorf, which the imperials still held, stood Lauriston's V Corps. Between these two points – Hennersdorf and the influx of the Wütende Neiße – XI Corps and some elements of III Corps, including Sébastiani's cavalry, withdrew toward Haynau through Goldberg, Kroitsch, and Rothkirch.[24]

At 9:30 on the night after the battle, Gneisenau drafted extremely detailed instructions for the pursuit. The wording made it crystal-clear that Blücher sought retribution for the lethal hunt Napoleon had unleashed in October 1806 following the battles of Jena–Auerstedt. Gneisenau directed Sacken's corps to Haynau, Yorck's corps to Kroitsch, Langeron's corps to Röchlitz and Goldberg, and St.-Priest's corps to Greiffenberg. He instructed Yorck to

attempt to move one infantry brigade across the Katzbach at Kroitsch around
2:00 A.M., "followed by the majority of the Reserve Cavalry with horse
artillery; both should ruthlessly fall on the enemy with cold steel and push as
far as the Schnelle Deichsel. The infantry was to cross in battalion masses
and observe the greatest quiet. No soldier may relieve himself or dare smoke
tobacco." Gneisenau further declared that, "if the infantry encounters the
enemy, they will attack with fixed bayonets and without firing. At the head
of this infantry will be the majority of the Reserve Cavalry. The bravest and
most resolute people will be placed at the head of the column."

If Yorck's brigade found enemy forces on the left bank of the Katzbach,
Blücher wanted the Prussians to repulse them and then take the most direct
route to the hills at Ulbersdorf. Sacken would send his cavalry across the
Katzbach at Schmogwitz to reach the great east–west highway; if the
cavalry needed support for this task, the infantry should follow. A portion of
his cavalry also had to cross the Katzbach below Liegnitz in order to win the
road from Liegnitz to Lüben. As for Langeron, Gneisenau wanted him to push
Rudzevich's vanguard, supported by the majority of the Russian cavalry and a
"suitable infantry corps," toward Röchlitz on the Jauer–Goldberg road, seeking
to cross the Katzbach and take Goldberg. He further instructed Langeron to
dispatch orders for St.-Priest to advance in forced marches toward Greiffenberg.
"The rest of the troops will remain ready to follow the enemy tomorrow as soon
as they have eaten. Because night combat is a possibility, the password for the
troops of both nations will be Alexander and Frederick William."[25]

Müffling sharply opposed these orders, which Gneisenau had issued before
his subordinate returned to Brechelshof sometime after 11:00 P.M. on the 26th.
Near the end of the battle, Müffling had suggested occupying Niederkrayn
with as many brigades as possible. He departed for Langeron's command
post to deliver the news of the victory on the plateau believing his recommendation had been accepted. Instead, Gneisenau decided to have only one
of Yorck's brigades secure Niederkrayn at 2:00 A.M. and then attempt to
cross the Katzbach at Kroitsch. Condemning this plan as "censurable in
every respect and ill considered," Müffling claimed that Gneisenau had
based this decision on the mere assumption that the French V and IX
Corps – 30,000–40,000 men according to Müffling – had already retreated
to Goldberg. "The very contrary should have been assumed," he noted in his
memoirs. In his opinion, before retreating from Hennersdorf, the enemy
first had to secure it, which meant occupying Niederkrayn because the
Hennersdorf–Goldberg road came within 3,000 paces of this key position.
"Such impractical orders," he continues, "have the effect of undermining
obedience and destroying the army's confidence in its commander. My
remonstrance, however gentle, was very ill received by General Gneisenau."

The degree to which Müffling complained to Gneisenau certainly falls in
the realm of speculation as no other sources support this account. Yet we do

find agreement in his contention that Yorck refused to comply with any order he felt could not be executed. Instead, he would, according to Müffling, "inquire about everything to be relieved of the responsibility." Yorck would indeed find excuses to avoid executing his orders. Army Headquarters viewed his alleged inability to carry out orders as passive-aggressive disobedience. This tension between Army and Corps Headquarters provided the backdrop to the pursuit and caused a "vexatious" correspondence between Yorck and Gneisenau, with Blücher serving as the conduit.[26]

Meanwhile, the rain streamed down on the exhausted troops and horses, almost all of whom remained where the end of the battle and the onset of darkness found them. With a cold north wind howling, they mainly camped on the open fields where no fires would light. Yorck's soldiers passed the miserable night sleeping on the drenched ground; the Landwehr in particular suffered. With his men soaked to the skin, without provisions or straw, clad in thin, linen trousers, lacking proper clothing and overcoats, and many without footgear, Yorck observed only the hardiest muster the following morning.[27] Hünerbein's 14th Silesian Landwehr Regiment provided an appalling example of the attrition. Of the 577 men of the 1st Battalion, only 271 reported for duty the next day; of the 3rd Battalion's 510 men, only 202 could muster; and the 4th Battalion provided only 407 men out of 625. On the other hand, the 2nd Battalion, which along with Othegraven's 2nd Battalion of the 2nd Brandenburg Regiment had taken overcoats and shoes from dead and captured imperials, lost only 53 men.[28] Under such conditions, it is hard to believe Gneisenau's claim that despite all the hardship the mood of the troops remained positive:

> The army fought through hardships, difficulties, and shortages; the soldier waded through rain-swollen waters up to his belt. Deprived of wagons by both friend and foe, with villages evacuated by their inhabitants, neither the means of transport nor nourishment could be found. Because of this lack of wagons and because of the muddy roads, food could not be supplied. Many, very many, soldiers go barefoot. Nevertheless, the stout soldier endures all hardships and all privations with patience, without grumbling, and with pleasantness. Is there anything more honorable when such toleration mates with such bravery? At such times, the soldier rises high above his fellow citizen who remains at home.[29]

Inconceivably, Blücher's orders did not reach Yorck until 5:00 A.M., three hours after his troops should have commenced the pursuit across the Katzbach. Yorck read the instructions in disbelief. Cynics at Yorck's headquarters questioned why only one brigade would conduct the pursuit. "The commanders must have a special reason for not advancing," they murmured. Now, at the end of a long day, he had to dispatch one brigade in streaming rain to navigate a steep defile under a black sky and then cross an extremely swollen river, quite possibly having to fight the enemy in the process. Aside from the weather, Lauriston's presence at Hennersdorf justified Yorck's concerns about moving down the plateau that night. Instead, he preferred to reassemble all of his brigades on the plateau and allow man and horse to rest. Lecturing his entourage that the victory could not be secured until he had several combat-ready battalions at hand, Yorck issued orders for the troops to be reorganized as quickly as possible and prepared to renew the struggle. His adjutants rode off in the downpour to assemble the units as best they could.[30]

Although they were ambitious and appropriate, nature ultimately stymied Blücher's plans. Rain fell continuously for twenty-eight hours in Silesia, Lusatia, and Saxony, turning small streams into raging rivers everywhere. At Kosel, the Oder purportedly rose twenty-four feet above its highest water mark, carrying away part of the fortress's outworks. With the Katzbach still rising, Sacken's Cossacks under Karpov failed to get across the river at Schmogwitz. Forced to detour downstream to Liegnitz, they finally reached the town around 2:00 on the afternoon of the 27th. Around the same time that Karpov's Cossacks arrived, the French garrison received orders to withdraw on Haynau. However, Karpov had already informed Sacken that enemy forces still held the town. Consequently, the Russian corps commander dispatched his vanguard under Vasilchikov to Liegnitz but the main body of the corps did not move, allowing his prey to make good progress. West of Sacken, *Streif-korps* under Falkenhausen and Rakhmanov harassed the French retreat on the Liegnitz–Bunzlau stretch of the east–west highway. With one squadron and some Cossacks, Falkenhausen pursued Marchand's 39th Division as it retreated from Haynau to Bunzlau. Falkenhausen captured only thirty-five men but spread terror among the demoralized imperials. With Falkenhausen's other squadron and eighty Cossacks, Rakhmanov followed the portion of III Corps that had retreated in good order from the Katzbach. In a successful attack in the region of Haynau, he inflicted 150 casualties.

Opposite Langeron, Lauriston retreated from Hennersdorf to Goldberg during the night of 26/27 August; his rearguard followed at daybreak. Numerous fugitives both preceded and followed V Corps as discipline unraveled. Before the battle on the 26th ended, absconders had already made their way to Goldberg: at first lone soldiers, then groups. Utter confusion reigned as throngs of soldiers pushed through the town to escape across the Katzbach by way of Goldberg's sole bridge. Units became mixed and all order collapsed. Demoralized by the weather and their empty bellies, the soldiers refused to obey commands. Officers went to great lengths to drive them from Goldberg's houses and force them to continue the retreat. The arrival of Lauriston's main body worsened the situation as the corps com-mander ordered his soldiers to employ violence to drive through their countrymen and allies to get across the bridge. By noon on the 27th, most of the imperials had left Goldberg; almost all struck the highway west to Löwenberg.

Rudzevich led Langeron's vanguard – reinforced by Kaptsevich's fresh X Infantry Corps and regiments from Korf's Reserve Cavalry – toward Goldberg prior to sunrise on the 27th. All along the road the Russians found corpses as well as wounded and dying soldiers; discarded equipment, artillery, and caissons likewise guided the way to Goldberg. Scores of imperial soldiers surrendered. "Before daybreak on the 27th and during a frightful rain," recalled Langeron, "Rudzevich moved toward Prausnitz and the Wolfsberg with the vanguard; I followed him with all the other corps. At each step, we found the dead, dying, and wounded thrown and abandoned in the mud, a multitude of dead horses, overturned wagons, equipment, cannon, caissons; at each step, we took prisoners; the loss and the disorder of the enemy moment-arily reminded me of the flight from Moscow to the Vistula."[31]

Making for Goldberg, Grekov advanced through Prausnitz with Langer-on's Cossacks while Emmanuel moved on the highway toward Röchlitz with the van's regular cavalry. As Emmanuel's troopers continued west, Yorck's Black Hussars emerged on the road in front of them. Taking the initiative, its commander, Major Stößel, had commenced the pursuit from Niederkrayn as soon as his patrols reported the enemy's departure from Hennersdorf. At Röchlitz, the Prussians found a French rearguard of some 1,000 men. Seeing Emmanuel immediately following, Stößel attacked without delay. More than 400 French soldiers, many whose muskets could not fire, surrendered to the Prussians. The major then crossed the Katzbach by way of the bridge on the Goldberg–Liegnitz road and turned northeast after receiving a report of enemy columns marching from Kroitsch toward Haynau.

With a portion of his cavalry, Emmanuel followed Stößel across the bridge but continued west to Goldberg, enveloping the town from the north. His remaining squadrons advanced through Goldberg as soon as the French departed. Reuniting his cavalry, Emmanuel continued the pursuit west to Pilgramsdorf, where his Kharkovskii and Kievskii Dragoon Regiments cap-tured 200 men and 6 guns. Meanwhile, Grekov's Cossacks collected 700 exhausted imperial soldiers and 5 guns as they pursued the three battal-ions of Lauriston's rearguard on the road to Prausnitz. On seeing Emmanuel's cavalry already in possession of Goldberg, the French com-mander, Colonel Jean-Pierre Maury, turned south in an attempt to cross the Katzbach upstream of Goldberg. Maury's rearguard had originally pos-sessed four cannon but three had to be abandoned in the valleys of Prausnitz.

With the Severskii and Chernigovskii Mounted Jäger Regiments and Tverskii Dragoon Regiment, General Ivan Panchulidzev I caught Maury at the Wolfs hill. Denisiyev's Mounted Jäger enveloped the enemy's right flank to prevent the French from reaching the woods, where they would have been more difficult to attack. On the French left, Berdyayev's

Dragoons moved around their flank to block the escape route to Löwenberg. The Chernigovskii Mounted Jäger took a position directly facing the French. Despite the fact that many of their muskets could not fire, the French prepared to resist. After the enemy greeted a Russian negotiator with small-arms fire, Panchulidzev gave the order to attack from all three sides. Langeron described the situation:

> This attack was not necessary and even became difficult given the disadvantages of the marshy terrain and the plowed earth after thirty-six hours of pouring rain, but we needed to make an account, to task ourselves to create cordons, crossings, etc., which the great talents of the two Panchulidzevs[32] and their warriors demonstrated in all their brilliance; no one offered them any resistance; they penetrated at the *petite trot* the ranks of the discouraged soldiers, exhausted from fatigue and hunger, whose muskets could not fire and who did not have enough energy to make use of their bayonets. The attack was an act of cruelty more deserving of punishment than reward. In five minutes, more than 500 men were cut down and laid to rest on the spot; we took the enemy's remaining cannon and 950 prisoners; Colonel Maury, the commander of this brigade, and 30 officers fell into our hands.

Altogether, Panchulidzev I captured 1,156 men and 1 gun. That afternoon, Langeron transferred his headquarters to Goldberg, which contained a French hospital with 1,200 wounded, including 200 Russians and 400 Prussians. His main body bivouacked there as well while Rudzevich halted the vanguard at Pilgramsdorf. On the army's far left at Schmiedeberg, St.-Priest's van detected the presence of Puthod's division north of Hirschberg but could do little due to the flood of the upper Bober.[33]

In the center, Yorck formed a strong vanguard for the pursuit.[34] Despite being ill, Katzler volunteered to lead the cavalry while Horn commanded the entire advance guard. Whether or not Yorck objected to Blücher's order mattered little at this stage because practical reasons prevented its execution. Overturned caissons and artillery blocked all the roads leading down the plateau to the valley. Rather than commencing the pursuit, Yorck's troops started clearing the defile that led to Niederkrayn. Around 6:00 on the morning of the 27th, Yorck finally authorized Katzler to proceed with the vanguard cavalry followed by Horn's 7th Brigade. Although the defile had been cleared, the ruined roads could hardly support the passage of almost 10,000 men. More delays ensued.

At 8:00 A.M., the Prussian van started crossing the Wütende Neiße; the infantry waded in water up to their chests. A detachment of Black Hussars left behind at Niederkrayn reported that imperial forces still held Kroitsch and its bridge over the Katzbach. Large infantry and cavalry units – Delmas's 9th Division and part of Sébastiani's cavalry – could be seen on the hills of the left bank of the Katzbach apparently covering the retreat of

French forces (10th and 11th Divisions) to the Liegnitz–Haynau road. South of this position, the Black Hussars observed enemy columns – XI Corps – retreating through Adelsdorf toward Alzenau. Katzler took the bridge at Kroitsch after a short combat; the imperials had neglected to destroy the structure. Around 10:00 A.M., the French evacuated Kroitsch and started the retreat northwest to Rothkirch. To reach the bridge, Horn's infantry waded through a good stretch because of the flooding river. Finally, at noon, the Leib Fusilier Battalion crossed the Katzbach and entered Kroitsch. "But the march of my brigade," Horn reported to Yorck, "took so long that I had no more than three cavalry regiments and one battalion through Kroitsch. The Katzbach is rising so much that according to farmers it will no longer be passable by nightfall. The bridge here at Kroitsch is useless because we have to cross through the water that is overflowing its banks." Although concerned that the Katzbach would cut him off from the rest of I Corps, Horn authorized the pursuit to continue.[35]

In a short time, Horn's troops captured more than sixty wagons, a herd of cattle, and numerous stragglers, yet Katzler's cavalry inflicted only minimal damage on the retreating imperials. Horn's infantry reached Wildschütz but the imperials outdistanced him en route to Haynau and Alzenau. Two enemy cavalry regiments supported by numerous horse guns faced down the Lithuanian Dragoons, one Landwehr Cavalry Regiment, and the Brandenburg Hussars of the 7th Brigade. Fulfilling Müffling's prophecy, Yorck requested instructions after Horn reported that he could not move his horse artillery across the Katzbach. In response, Gneisenau issued the verbal order "to cross the Katzbach wherever he could, to give the enemy no rest either in his cantons or in his bivouacs, and to proceed between Sacken's and Langeron's vanguards in communication with both." With the bridge at Kroitsch already under water and in constant danger of being ripped apart, Horn lacked secure communication with the rest of I Corps. Thus isolated, he did not want to venture too far. He sent his two batteries back across the Katzbach and in the evening recalled Katzler's cavalry from Rothkirch to Wildschütz, leaving only fifty Brandenburg Hussars under Captain Theodor Franz Sartorius von Schwanenfeld to maintain contact with the enemy. The two orderlies Horn dispatched to deliver his report to Yorck had to swim across the Katzbach.

Sacken reported finding enemy infantry at Liegnitz but Cossacks prowled the suburbs and closed the roads leading to the town. Although the enemy appeared to have evacuated the right bank of the Katzbach, Sacken contended that his troops could not cross the swollen river. "I have ordered the Cossacks to do everything possible to get across the Katzbach," he assured Blücher. "According to the statements of a captured officer from the horse artillery, Marshal Macdonald has been the commander since Marshal Ney's departure; he believes the following units fought here: the corps of Macdonald and Lauriston, and two divisions of Ney's corps under

General Souham, and the entire cavalry under General Sébastiani. This cavalry marched here very quickly from eight miles behind Bunzlau; the twenty-four cannon that were all captured or demolished yesterday belonged to this cavalry as did this artillery officer." In a postscript, Sacken added that a report from Colonel Valerian Madatov had just arrived claiming "that the enemy has sent a great portion of his troops to Saxony. Only two regiments should remain at Bunzlau and only one at Haynau."[36]

Sensing his enemy slipping away, Blücher signed orders around 2:00 P.M. on the 27th for Yorck to forward the rest of the Reserve Cavalry to Horn's position. Two hours later, he issued instructions for the rest of I Corps to cross the Katzbach and advance one hour west of the river. This order, which reached Yorck at 5:00 P.M., earned the following comment in the log of Yorck's headquarters: "Here it can be observed that Sir Gneisenau and Sir Müffling have no idea how to move an army." With the lowland between the Wütende Neiße and the Katzbach a veritable swamp and the rain still streaming down, Yorck foresaw only difficulties if he attempted to cross the Katzbach on washed-out roads with troops he considered exhausted. Yet if he did not cross the river, Horn would be cut off. Moreover, the vanguard risked losing contact with the enemy unless support arrived. Therefore, Yorck issued orders to commence the march but sent Zielinsky to the Katzbach to determine if the river could be crossed. As he waited for the staff officer's verdict, Yorck factored in other considerations. Crossing the Wütende Neiße required the brigades to march in tight columns and the same would be true to get across the Katzbach. In this formation, it would take hours for the entire corps to reach a position one hour west of the Katzbach. In addition, dry ammunition could be in neither the pouch or the caisson. Finding the water rising quickly, Zielinsky reported that the Katzbach could not be crossed at either Kroitsch or Röchlitz. Should the tired, starving troops swim the Katzbach in the dark to comply with Blücher's order? Yorck did not have to think twice about the answer. In his mind, nature left him no choice. Thus, after having made little progress, Yorck ordered a halt: the portion of the Reserve Cavalry still with I Corps passed the night at Niederkrayn; the infantry never moved off the plateau. From his headquarters at Niederkrayn, Yorck wrote Blücher at 7:45 that evening describing his inability to cross the Katzbach. With the river passable only at Liegnitz and Goldberg, he suggested that Blücher direct Horn to the latter, where he could link with Langeron.[37]

After receiving a second report from Sacken concerning the enemy's evacuation of Liegnitz, Blücher dispatched a third order to Yorck around 6:30 that evening. Assuming I Corps had already started the march to reach a position one hour west of the Katzbach, Blücher allowed Yorck to quarter his troops with the exception of the vanguard, which would bivouac. If the French corps that the Allies had repulsed on the plateau retreated on Bunzlau, Yorck's van and Reserve Cavalry would pursue and attack it. In addition,

Blücher wanted the communication cut between this corps and the corps that had attacked Langeron. For this task, he wanted Yorck to push his cavalry toward the Gröditzberg. A few hours later, Blücher received Yorck's 7:45 P.M report informing him that I Corps had not crossed the Katzbach. The frustrated commander in chief issued verbal orders for Yorck to "cross the Katzbach wherever he can, not exposing Horn but having him pursue along with Sacken's and Langeron's vanguards." Thus, the main body of the corps had to cross the river wherever it could. He demanded that Horn continue the pursuit and not allow the enemy any rest. This response and its key phrase of crossing the Katzbach "wherever he could" did little to help Yorck. Should he march to Goldberg or Liegnitz and risk becoming entangled with Langeron or Sacken? Unfortunately for Yorck, written instructions assigning a point of passage to I Corps did not follow Blücher's gruff response until much later.[38]

The euphoria of the previous night turned to disgust in less than twenty-four hours. "Regarding our cavalry," complained Gneisenau to Clausewitz, "they did not pursue because they no longer understood their craft ... in part the commanders could not be found, others were not in the mood." In Blücher's official report on the 28th, the staff chief retracted his claws: "The darkness of night and the obstruction of all defiles by cannon and caissons hindered the execution of this order [to pursue]; only toward noon did General Horn take the village of Kroitsch and its bridge and follow the enemy with his brigade and half of the Reserve Cavalry. The Wütende Neiße and the Katzbach rose so much that the former was very difficult to cross and the latter thoroughly impossible. Despite all of the army's efforts, it could not pass the Katzbach at Goldberg and Liegnitz on the 27th because of the continuous rains." "We crossed through swollen waters up to the chest," Gneisenau informed Clausewitz. "We hope to find the enemy at the Bober and to find this river so swollen that he cannot escape."[39]

Despite attributing the army's difficulties to nature in this report, Blücher remained less than satisfied with the energy displayed by Sacken and Yorck.[40] The former's vanguard reached only Liegnitz while his main body did not move from Kleintinz. Horn halted at Wildschütz and the main body of I Corps remained around Niederkrayn. To make up for his actions the previous day, Langeron reported that, after occupying Goldberg, he had pursued the imperials another four miles toward Löwenberg. The Russian corps commander pushed the cavalry of his vanguard to Pilgramsdorf while the main body of his corps camped around Goldberg. On this day, Langeron's Russians captured 5 guns, 20 caissons, and more than 1,000 prisoners. On the far left, floods forced St.-Priest's corps to remain inactive with its vanguard at Schmiedeberg and main body at Landeshut.[41]

At least in the case of Yorck, Army Headquarters deserves some of the blame for the slow progress of the pursuit. The 4:00 P.M. orders for all of I Corps to cross the Katzbach should have been issued no later than noon.

Had this occurred, Yorck could have crossed the Katzbach before the waters made this an impossible task. Supported by the entire corps, Horn's brigade could have maintained contact with the enemy. Regardless, a furious Blücher ordered Gneisenau to write to Yorck early on 28 August and rebuke the corps commander.[42] "I have received your letter from 7:45 P.M. on the 27th and cannot conceal my displeasure over the cavalry. You know its assignment: to maintain contact with the enemy and to inflict damage on him where it can. Instead of this, the cavalry wants to observe and to postpone orders. It is not enough to be victorious: one must also know how to exploit the victory. If we do not press the enemy hard, he will naturally make another stand and we will have to fight another battle to achieve what we could have obtained from this one had we acted with energy. I request that you proceed according to this view and to make this known to the vanguard and Reserve Cavalry." A second letter written on the evening of the 28th states:

> By the present retreat of the enemy, our entire effort must be to inflict so much damage on him that it is impossible for him to again oppose us. This important goal can be achieved only through a rapid and bold pursuit of the enemy. Yet I see with regret that the conduct of our cavalry in no way corresponds with this goal, that it has taken no prisoners, and that it generally acts with such wariness that it seems as if it faces a victorious rather than a defeated foe. You will thus make each of your cavalry commanders responsible for pursuing with the zeal and the untiring activity that the importance of the task assigned to them demands. Also, make them aware that they must act according to their own judgment because of their distance from the army's main body. On no occasion should they stop to request instructions and waste precious time they could be using.[43]

Despite the fatigue of man and horse, Blücher would not be satisfied until his cavalry had pursued the imperials in the same manner as the French had hunted the Prussians in 1806. Disgusted by Langeron's conduct on the day of the battle followed by Yorck's passive-aggressive disobedience during the pursuit, Gneisenau drafted an Army Order that Blücher promulgated. One of the harsher decrees to emerge from Army Headquarters, it illustrates the mounting frustration over the seemingly lethargic pursuit:

> After receiving a march or supply order, every brigade chief and every detached commander will immediately report where and when he received this order. Even if he is at a post or a bivouac, he will immediately send an officer or at least a noncommissioned orderly to General Gneisenau with a status report. This officer will remain with General Gneisenau. If a brigade chief or another detached commander cannot reach his destination in a timely manner, he must immediately report this to Headquarters. Any brigade chief who receives no supply according to the general arrangements or who has not procured any shall be held responsible because he has complete authorization to use all means

for the completion or the procurement of supply. If negligence therein occurs, the brigade commissariat likewise will be punished. As soon as the brigade halts, the senior officers of the General Staff attached to the brigade must inform General Gneisenau and always report the location of the brigade.[44]

"General Blücher was fixated on the notion that he had totally defeated the French army," opined Müffling, "and all that remained was to pursue it hotly, for which the cavalry would suffice." Contrary to the sage advice offered by Müffling, "Gneisenau ... agreed with General Blücher's notion, assented to all that he wished, and admitted that through this hussar pursuit Macdonald would reach Dresden *alone*." Regardless, Yorck and his officers did not deserve such treatment. Based on the circumstances, the Prussian cavalry could not have achieved much more than it did. Aside from the men, the horses had become horribly rundown from the exertions and privations of the previous two weeks. On the morning of the battle, Katzler had requested rest for man and horse. Instead, they spent the day in combat while the rainy night granted little relief. By the next morning, Katzler himself needed bed rest. "Although I find myself extremely ill," he wrote Yorck early on the 27th, "the motive of hurting the enemy with all our strength is too splendid a thought for me to remain behind." Somehow finding the strength, he again assumed command of the advance guard cavalry. Yet, by early on the 28th, the exhaustion of his horses forced Katzler to report that he could no longer catch the enemy despite riding far with the Cossacks "to take part in this hare hunt."[45]

On the French side, by the night of the 27th, the heads of Macdonald's army had cleared the Bober River while the rearguards remained at the Schnelle Deichsel. Marchand's 39th Division retreated from Liegnitz to Bunzlau, picking up fugitives from all four corps along the way. East of the 39th, III Corps and most of II Cavalry Corps reached Haynau. Gérard's XI Corps retreated across the Schnelle Deichsel at Adelsdorf and continued northwest toward Bunzlau. Lauriston's rearguard halted at Neuwiese, his main body at Lauterseiffen. Ledru's 31st Division remained at Spiller; and a large mass of refugees from all corps sought salvation at Löwenberg. Because the bridge over the Bober at Löwenberg could no longer be used, the imperial troops stranded on the right bank turned downstream toward Bunzlau, where they arrived east of the city on the following night. Puthod led his 17th Division from Hirschberg to Grunau on the 27th in an attempt to escape across the Bober but found the water so far over its banks that he turned back and sought to go further downstream along the right bank of the river. From Grunau, he reported his intent to march through Lähn to Zobten on the 28th. General Yuzefovich's Cossacks, which closely pursued and had already netted numerous prisoners, intercepted the letter. Thanks to the terror caused by the Cossacks and the feeling of not being able to escape, most of Puthod's division had scattered in the woods or hid in the small

General Langerons Gefecht mit der Division Puthod vor Löwenberg.

13 The destruction of Puthod's division on 27 August 1813

villages. The Cossacks hauled in numerous stragglers – many of whom had to be forcibly retrieved from the houses. "Yuzefovich," explained Langeron, "an intelligent and active officer, never lost sight of him [Puthod], followed him and, although he had neither infantry nor cannon, disordered the enemy's rearguard, taking 1,200 prisoners." Puthod's report to Macdonald stated "that, despite my efforts and exertions and those of their chiefs and officers, three-quarters of the soldiers have thrown themselves in the woods and houses. Kindness, threats, and blows have no effect on them and they answer that it is better to be captured than to succumb to misery."[46]

Although pressured only by Langeron, Macdonald decided to run for it rather than attempt to rally. He hoped to outdistance the Allies and reach Lusatia where he could reorganize his army close to the emperor's legions. Resorting to a survival-of-the-fittest mentality, he accepted the harsh reality that thousands would be lost to straggling and desertion. Yet by escaping with the core of his army largely intact, he stood the chance of avoiding the emperor's fury. Unfortunately for Macdonald, the current state of his army rendered this hope fanciful. It is important to remember that, like the men of the Silesian Army, the soldiers of the Army of the Bober had also marched and counter-marched continuously for two weeks sustained by food supplies that were approaching exhaustion before hostilities had resumed. Many imperial battalions consisted of young conscripts unaccustomed to the rigors of campaigning – very similar to the harsh baptism experienced by the Prussian Landwehr. As the Allied pursuit gained steam, the Army of the Bober resembled a forlorn mob driven by fear, cold, sickness, and hunger. Those who pushed on faced the streaming rain, drenched roads, violent mountain streams, and bridges smashed or weakened by flood waters. Order and discipline crumbled, hundreds remained skulking about the fields and scattered in the villages, producing horrible desolation. All over the fields lay discarded weapons and backpacks, cannon, and caissons as well as the dead and dying. Units that maintained order found themselves herded like cattle by the Allied vanguard. With canister and roundshot, the lance and the bayonet, the victors wreaked havoc on the imperial formations. Allied detachments led away prisoners in the hundreds. "Despite the fact that some people do not understand how to exploit a victory," continued Gneisenau in his letter to Clausewitz, "the results of ours – at least what is known – are considerable nonetheless. Some 60 cannon, 200 caissons, 8 field forges, and 6,000–7,000 prisoners are the fruits of the victory. What we have seen in corpses, wagons, etc., during our march from Eichholtz, and what we have heard about the disorder and composition of the [enemy] rearguard, which consists of the fugitives of many regiments, tells us that Macdonald's army has completely collapsed."[47]

Silesian Army Headquarters moved only a few miles to Eichholtz during the afternoon of 27 August. Good tidings from abroad helped ease the mounting aggravation at Army Headquarters but increased Blücher's impatience. A message arrived confirming that the Prussians of the Army of North Germany had stopped Oudinot's Army of Berlin at Großbeeren on the 23rd. The bravery of the Landwehr units that had fought in Bülow's III and Tauentzien's IV Corps earned great praise. According to this preliminary report, the entire imperial army had retreated toward Torgau in the aftermath.[48] Blücher believed that the crown prince of Sweden would closely follow Oudinot, so this news only inflamed his desire to launch a relentless pursuit of Macdonald. He had already envisioned the possibility of the Silesian and North German Armies cooperating in an offensive across the Elbe. Through St.-Priest, who established communication with the Austrian 2nd Light Division, Blücher received word that the Bohemian Army had moved across the Saxon frontier on 22 August and that Wittgenstein had stormed the imperial camp at Pirna on the 23rd. The temporary commander of the Austrian 2nd Light Division, General Adam Albert von Neipperg, speculated that Schwarzenberg's crossing of the Erzgebirge prompted Napoleon to withdraw from Silesia. This report confirmed news that had arrived the day before, telling of the Bohemian Army's entry into Saxony. Due to Neipperg's report, Blücher believed Schwarzenberg would continue his offensive. He had no idea that, while the Silesian Army engaged Macdonald's forces on the 26th, Schwarzenberg was assailing Napoleon at Dresden. After a second day of fighting on the 27th, the Allies broke off the attack and retreated. Not knowing this, Blücher incorrectly concluded Napoleon would withdraw to Torgau before Schwarzenberg's onslaught.[49]

Based on these thoughts, Blücher and Gneisenau decided to direct the Silesian Army through Görlitz and Bautzen to Dresden, finishing off the Army of the Bober in the process. "I must assume that the enemy marches to Torgau," Blücher explained to Langeron, "because after the loss of the camp at Pirna it will be difficult to maintain Dresden as his central point. Thus, it is necessary to destroy Macdonald's army without delivering a new battle." Early on the 28th, Army Headquarters issued orders to intensify the pursuit. To Langeron went instructions for St.-Priest to circumvent the upper courses of the rivers that slowed the army – the Katzbach, Schnelle Deichsel, Bober, and Queis – and attempt to block the enemy's retreat to Marklissa and Görlitz. Blücher also hoped that the 6,000 men of Neipperg's light division would advance toward Görlitz and Bautzen. "Without doubt," continued Blücher in his dispatch to Langeron, "you are already moving toward Löwenberg with the army, which is going in this direction. Today I move my headquarters to Goldberg." "Forward, always forward, my children," bellowed Blücher. "If you start out hard, you can spare yourselves another battle." In response, the soldiers shouted: "Long live Father Blücher!" But again he would be disappointed: nature and Langeron's obstinacy continued to slow the Silesian Army.[50]

Learning that Gaudi had yet to summon the Landsturm, Blücher issued a second letter: "I kindly request that you inform me, why ... the Landsturm still has not been mobilized in the rear and flanks of the enemy and the tocsin still has not been sounded in the manner that I instructed you through General Gneisenau. If this measure had been carried out, the enemy's losses in the battles on the 26th and 27th would have been much greater because the Landsturm would have captured the stragglers and taken the enemy's wagons, which would have been easy because of the poor roads and swollen waters." On the next day, the 29th, Gaudi attempted to excuse himself by claiming he had never received the instructions. Gneisenau smelled a rat. It appeared that Gaudi was dragging his feet in hesitating to issue general mobilization orders. When he finally did, his couriers could not get across the rain-swollen rivers of Silesia to deliver the summons. Gneisenau drafted a sharp response that Blücher signed. "If you had carried out the assignment that my quartermaster-general gave in my name for the immediate sounding of the tocsin at Jauer, which he requested that you do, the impassable waters at that time would not have hindered your orders from being executed. Thus, much time was lost and the waters swelled forty-eight hours later. However, this measure has met with success where it was received and executed; yesterday, the peasants of the Hirschberg District seized 700 prisoners. Had this measure been enacted earlier, we could have captured several thousand, whom we now must fight again because they escaped."[51]

Returning to operations, during the morning of the 28th, Katzler and Karpov resumed the pursuit of Souham's rearguard in the direction of Haynau. Around 8:00, Karpov's Cossacks arrived after capturing 180 stragglers. Katzler's troopers reached Haynau thirty minutes later. Around 9:00, the Prussian officer reported to Blücher and Yorck that "the enemy flees so quickly it is impossible for me to catch up with them with the exhausted horses of my cavalry. Today they evacuated Haynau around 6:00 A.M. and yesterday from 9:00 A.M. until 10:00 P.M. they fled through here in the greatest disorder, meaning cavalry and infantry all mixed together. They broke the bridge over the Schnelle Deichsel at Haynau, but I have instructed the local magistrate to use all means for its restoration as soon as possible." Katzler complained that he had to rest his horses while the better steeds used by the Russians allowed the Cossacks "to take the butter from our bread." Despite the exhaustion of their mounts, he and 100 of his Hussars joined the Cossacks in pursuing the enemy toward Bunzlau.[52]

Around 6:15 P.M., Katzler reported from Wolfshain that the horses "are very fatigued and absolutely must have an hour to feed." Souham's rearguard of six battalions, some cavalry, and two guns fell back in good order and took a position first at Kreibau and then on the hills of Thomaswaldau to cover the crossing of the Kleinen Bober (Bobrzyca). "All statements of the inhabitants agree that the enemy is retreating in disorder. Only the rearguard remains organized, as I myself have seen." According to Katzler, the route to Thomaswaldau offered a gruesome sight: "The road is covered with dead enemy soldiers and dead horses; some may have been killed in earlier engagements because they are already decomposing." Without artillery, the Allied horse could do little except observe the imperials retreat.[53]

East of Katzler and Karpov, Sacken's vanguard under Vasilchikov pushed through Haynau around noon and camped on the east–west highway between Wolfshain and Haynau. Horn's 7th Brigade arrived one hour later. Both commanders decided not to proceed any further on this day. Behind them, Sacken's main body halted at Liegnitz, thus moving only one hour west from the battlefield in the two days that followed the struggle on the 26th. In this completely exhausted region, the Russians and Prussians as well as the imperials suffered from the lack of provisions. On this day, 700 prisoners lumbered toward the rear – they had even less to eat. Around 7:00 P.M., Katzler received a report from his picket at Thomaswaldau on the departure of the enemy from the hills on the right bank of the Kleinen Bober. Katzler tasked the reporting officer, Captain Friedrich von Eisenhart, with ascertaining the status of the bridge over the Kleinen Bober as fast as possible. If the enemy had destroyed it, Eisenhart would repair it immediately.[54]

Yorck's corps lost time crossing the Wütende Neiße at Niederkrayn and then the Katzbach at Röchlitz. Not only did the cresting rivers force the infantry to wade through water up to their chests, but the ammunition of the brigade artillery became soaked and unusable. Nevertheless, I Corps cleared the Katzbach. Horn's two batteries moved northwest toward Haynau escorted by the Brandenburg Uhlans while the rest of the corps trudged west through Goldberg. Major Stößel again seized the initiative with his Black Hussars. Of his own accord, he hunted French stragglers between the Katzbach and the Bober. If the reports to Yorck were accurate, Blücher's wish in part came true. One lieutenant with 15 troopers of the Jäger squadron captured 144 men while 1 corporal with 2 hussars purportedly captured 50 more. Another squadron apprehended 150 imperials. One captain with 60 Hussars brought back 55 prisoners. Near Adelsdorf, they salvaged four of six guns found stuck in the mud. "Today," Blücher informed Bernadotte, "Yorck's corps has taken 4 cannon, a number of wagons, and some 700 prisoners. His vanguard has united with Sacken's at Haynau and pursues toward Bunzlau. More important than anything else is the disintegration of the enemy army, which all reports confirm. I have learned that during the affair at Goldberg General Ricard was killed and General Maison lost a leg." By the end of the day, Jürgaß reached Neudorf-am-Gröditzberg with the Reserve Cavalry. Further east, 2nd Brigade reached Leisersdorf and Ulbersdorf on the Schnelle Deichsel late in the evening. Hünerbein's 8th Brigade did not arrive at the Schnelle Deichsel until the morning of the 29th while Steinmetz's 1st Brigade pulled in during the afternoon.[55]

On the left wing of the Silesian Army, Rudzevich's vanguard moved west from Pilgramsdorf to Lauterseiffen, forwarding its Cossacks to the Bober. Shcherbatov's VI Infantry Corps followed as far as Pilgramsdorf but the rest of Langeron's corps remained at Goldberg. Langeron had planned to continue west toward Löwenberg in accordance with Blücher's orders until Yorck informed him that, rather than continue west, I Corps would turn north at Ulbersdorf and thus remain behind Langeron's corps. Not wanting to advance on Löwenberg until Yorck came on line with him, Langeron decided to give his main body a day of rest at Goldberg, completely disobeying Blücher's instructions. "In the meantime," stated his report to Blücher, "the enemy is in such a rout that the light troops almost suffice and I do not doubt that they will bring in many prisoners."[56]

As noted, Blücher had already written to Langeron from Eichholtz expressing the necessity of maintaining close contact with the enemy, requesting that the corps commander order St.-Priest to cross the Katzbach, Schnelle Deichsel, Bober, and Queis at their upper courses, and stating his expectation for Langeron to march on Löwenberg. This order induced the general neither to move his corps further west from Goldberg nor to push his advance guard to the Bober, despite the "rout" of the enemy mentioned in his report. Consequently, Langeron missed a great opportunity to trap elements of XI Corps at Löwenberg. Unable to repair the bridge due to the Bober's swift current, the imperials backtracked to Plagwitz. That evening, they departed for Bunzlau, hoping to find passage across the Bober there. Langeron could have caught at least part of these troops, yet only his Cossacks reached the Bober. St.-Priest succeeded in crossing the upper Bober on temporary bridges and reaching Schmiedeberg with his main body; Bistrom occupied Hirschberg with the vanguard. According to Blücher's report to the king, Langeron's corps still managed to harvest 6 guns, "a great number of caissons," and approximately 2,000 prisoners.

As for Macdonald's army, early on the morning of the 28th Puthod led his 17th Division from Grunau down the Bober, seeking a crossing in vain. Losing many stragglers to Yuzefovich's Cossacks, the French halted for the evening at Zobten. West of Puthod, Ledru's 31st Division marched unhindered northwest from Spiller to Greiffenberg. Meanwhile, Macdonald's main body continued to flee westward: Marchand's division and thousands of refugees from other corps crossed the Bober on makeshift bridges at Bunzlau and reached Paritz (Parzyce) on the right bank of the Queis. Units of V and XI Corps that marched down the right bank of the Bober from Löwenberg to Bunzlau on the 27th likewise escaped across the river on the 28th and made for the Queis; detachments of XI Corps remained at Löwenberg. The III Corps and II Cavalry Corps cleared the Kleinen Bober and reached Bunzlau, leaving a rearguard at Thomaswaldau facing Katzler and Karpov.[57]

An intercepted letter written on the 30th by a French officer to his wife in France describes the travails of the imperial army:

> Up until the 25th we defeated the enemy continuously; Goldberg was taken by storm after inflicting great losses on the enemy. But with the 26th, despite a horrible rain from early morning on ... we fought from 8:00 A.M. until the night. Our infantry was drenched to the bone, the muskets would not fire, and they gave way in disorder. This forced us to likewise retreat up to this city [Löbau], which lies in Saxony. The emperor must come to help us reorganize the three defeated corps. As brave as all our young soldiers are, when they are pressed by the enemy, they are good for nothing but to retreat. Terror masters them. Also, the rain has continued uninterrupted for four days and nights, making the men sick, the weapons useless. We have not had a day of rest – the enemy has not granted us any. My boots have not come off since the 15th; I have not had anything to eat since the 20th except for biscuit, which I have to soak because it is so hard. No meat or brandy, and I am on my horse from 3:00 A.M. to 6:00 P.M. The horse has had nothing to eat except for some straw – fortunately it has this – and the men likewise fall from hunger. We arrived here around 3:00. I will try to reach headquarters on the great highway; my strength and my courage abandon me. Hopefully they will soon return but the enemy has three cavalry troopers to our one.[58]

The rain finally ended during the night of 28/29 August and beautiful weather returned. On 29 August, Langeron again advanced. After receiving Puthod's intercepted letter from Yuzefovich, the corps commander claimed

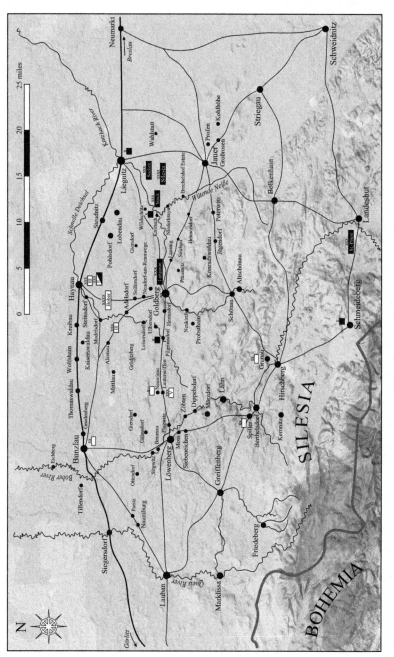

13. Situation, 27 August 1813

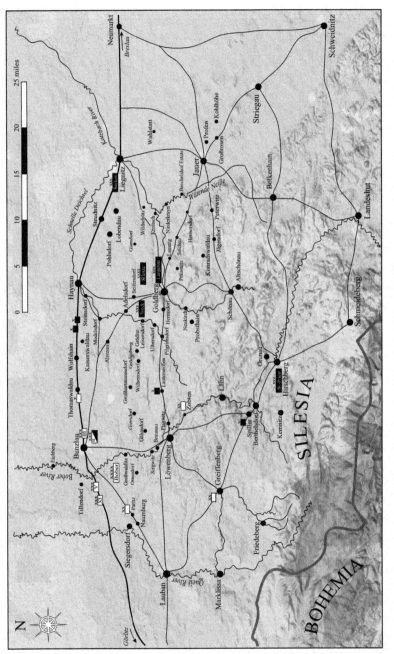

14. Situation, 28 August 1813

that he "conceived the hope of cutting off and surrounding" the 17th Division. From his position in the valleys and woods between Pilgramsdorf and Lauterseiffen, Rudzevich pushed Emmanuel's cavalry westward to block Puthod's route to Löwenberg, where the French could have escaped across the town's stone bridge and the rafts being hastily constructed there. In addition, Korf led Langeron's Reserve Cavalry west from Lauterseiffen to Zobten.

Meanwhile, Puthod continued with his plan to march downriver from Zobten through Höfel to Bunzlau. He cleared Zobten but did not know Korf's cavalry was behind him. Hoping to find a passage through the flooded terrain east of Löwenberg, Puthod turned west toward Plagwitz around 8:00 on the morning of the 29th. At Löwenberg, two battalions and five guns from Ledru's 31st Division waited on the opposite bank of the Bober to take in the beleaguered 17th. To obtain building material for a bridge, Puthod's soldiers demolished several of Plagwitz's houses. Despite their strenuous work, they could not bridge the river. To make matters worse, their security posts reported the approach of Russian forces from the east. Around 9:30, Emmanuel reached Plagwitz with Rudzevich's vanguard cavalry. At the same time, Stößel's Black Hussars arrived. Resolving to cut his way through to Bunzlau, Puthod ordered the firing of seventy caissons and almost all the baggage. To defend against the enemy cavalry, he assembled his division on the Stein hill. Soon, however, Rudzevich's infantry arrived and by 11:30 the Russians held Plagwitz. Skirmishing fixed the French and prevented them from marching down the Bober while Shcherbatov's VI Infantry Corps closed in from Pilgramsdorf, and Korf reached Zobten with Langeron's Reserve Cavalry to completely block Puthod's escape route. Ordered by the Russians to surrender, the French chose honor over shame.

Around 2:00, the Russians commenced a general assault on the Stein hill supported by one battery each on the Hirse and Luften hills. With the Kharkovskii and Kievskii Dragoon Regiments, Emmanual enveloped Puthod's left. Korf led the Tverskii and Kinburnskii Regiments as well as the Don Artillery Company to Zobten and then moved around Puthod's right. On arriving, Shcherbatov's 34th Light Artillery Company unlimbered on the hills overlooking Stein hill. Several well-aimed shots disordered the French. According to Langeron, "Nesterovsky's battery ravaged the squared ranks and forced them to retire dispersed." One hour into the engagement, General Vasily Meshcherinov ordered the 11th, 28th, 32nd, and 36th Jäger Regiments (five battalions in total) to fix bayonets and charge up Stein hill. Behind the infantry thundered the Russian cavalry. Puthod's line broke. Some soldiers threw down their muskets; others joined the many officers who jumped into the river and attempted to swim to the other bank. Almost all drowned – 400 according to Russian estimates – including Benoît-Prosper Sibuet, the commander of Puthod's 2nd Brigade, who had received his promotion to general only one week earlier on the 22nd. Altogether,

120 officers including Puthod, 3,500 soldiers, and 16 guns fell into Allied hands. Two officers – Lieutenant Aleksandr Kalinin and Ensign Aleksandr Bogdanov – from the sole battalion of the 28th Jäger Regiment captured the Eagles of the 146th and 148th Infantry Regiments; the French threw the Eagles of the 134th and the 147th into the Bober. Langeron's men found the Eagle of the former after the Bober's waters receded. At the start of the campaign, Puthod's division numbered 8,237 men: only 254 managed to recross the Bober. The Russians purportedly lost between 80 and 200 men on this day.[59]

Gneisenau proudly tallied the results of the "hare hunt." In the first three days of the pursuit, Stößel's Black Hussars alone captured 7 cannon, 36 caissons, field forges, several hundred horses, 26 officers, and 335 men. "Some 80 guns, 300 caissons, wagons, mobile forges, etc., 11,000–12,000 prisoners are the trophies that we have ripped from the enemy," boasted the staff chief. "The swollen waters halted our pursuit but we followed as best we could. The consequences of the terror that seized the enemy are visible everywhere on the roads from the Katzbach to the Bober: corpses stuck in the mud, overturned wagons, and heaps of prisoners. I hope to completely destroy Macdonald's army. Long live the king! His throne is now safe and we will bequeath national independence to our children. Now I go to sleep a happy man."[60]

While the left wing had success on the 29th, Blücher's right wing and center stalled completely. On the extreme left, St.-Priest's main body remained at Schmiedeberg but his vanguard reached Spiller and made contact with Ledru's division at Langwasser (Chmieleń). In the early hours, Souham's rearguard exchanged its position at Thomaswaldau for one behind the defile at Gnadenberg to secure the passage across the Bober at Bunzlau. Receiving news of this, Katzler and Karpov continued the pursuit followed by the cavalry of Sacken's van, Horn's 7th Brigade, and Vasilchikov with Sacken's vanguard infantry. En route, two Prussian squadrons and the Cossacks collected another 600 imperial stragglers. Reaching Gnadenberg, the Allied cavalry again halted before six French squadrons supported by three guns. Discerning additional French forces west of the cavalry, Katzler and Karpov decided to wait until Horn and Vasilchikov came up. On arriving, Vasilchikov and Horn together scouted the enemy. Covered by the six squadrons, the imperials held a position extending from Looswitz (Łaziska) to Neuschönfeld (Chościszowice). Although unable to determine the enemy's strength, Horn and Vasilchikov did not believe their own forces sufficed to attack. Horn requested cooperation from Sacken. The Russian commander "would commit himself to nothing, but promised to advance immediately if Yorck, who stood four hours away on the left [south], showed some sign of life" (see Map 2).[61]

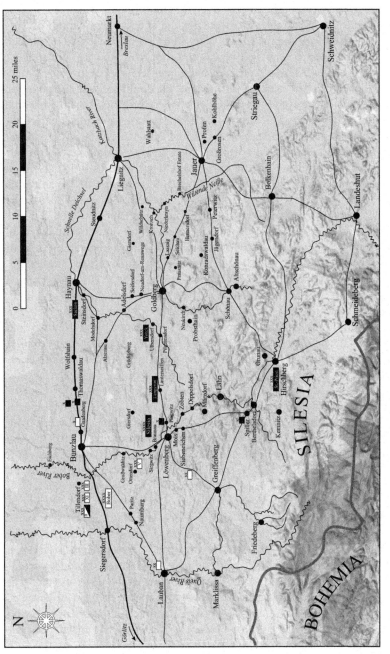

15. Situation, 29 August 1813

Around 11:00 A.M., Horn sent his adjutant, Lieutenant Karl Friedrich von Reibnitz, to Yorck with a report over the situation, assuring him that "if it is possible for you to make an attack on the enemy's right flank on this day, we will have a glorious affair. The affair will be decided in fifteen minutes. As soon as we hear the first cannon shot from you we will attack." While Horn awaited Yorck's answer, Schwanenfeld's detachment of fifty Hussars reached the Bober north of Bunzlau. He could see that considerable French forces had already crossed the Bober there but the river had risen so much in the past twenty-four hours that a point of passage no longer could be found. Therefore, the imperial units east of Bunzlau on the right bank of the Bober could not escape. Cut off from Macdonald's main body on the left bank, these troops appeared to be easy prey. "The Bober is unusually high and almost impossible to cross," explained Schwanenfeld. "Confirmed reports claim that before the water rose several crossings existed for the corps of the enemy army; but the troops who arrived yesterday are in the greatest predicament and must surrender as soon as they are attacked in earnest." Horn forwarded this report to Yorck, again requesting a joint attack on the imperial forces stranded on the right bank east of Bunzlau.[62]

Meanwhile, a portion of the Reserve Cavalry under Jürgaß remained with I Corps in and around Neudorf-am-Gröditzberg. Jürgaß sent only officer patrols northwest toward Bunzlau and southwest to Löwenberg. In the first direction, the Prussians encountered French cavalry at Neuwarthau (Warta Bolesławiecka) which withdrew to Looswitz, less than three miles southwest of Bunzlau. Pursuing, the Prussians learned that the imperials stranded on the right bank of the Bober at Bunzlau could cross the river only by boat. Meanwhile, Major Stößel led his 2nd Leib Hussar Regiment north-west from Großhartmannsdorf toward Bunzlau, encountering four imperial cavalry regiments and several battalions. With man and horse still weak from the preceding exertions, Stößel deferred attempting an attack. Yet he too reported to Yorck that the Prussians could "take thousands of prisoners if several cavalry regiments advance. The enemy appears to remain holding on *coûte que coûte* [at all costs] because he cannot cross the swollen water."[63]

Around 4:00 P.M., Reibnitz delivered Horn's report to Yorck at Leisersdorf. Despite the brigadier's urging, Yorck did not depart northwest for Bunzlau with 2nd Brigade, which had been resting for almost twenty-four hours. Instead, he ordered Stößel to lead the Black Hussars southwest toward Löwenberg because the corps commander believed the Bober cross-ing at Sirgwitz could be utilized. The only clue we have to explain this puzzling decision is a note that Droysen found in the column of Schack's journal: "General Gneisenau told Colonel Valentini, Colonel Müffling, and Major Schack that the direction of I Corps is Sirgwitz." Compounding the problem, Blücher's instructions for Yorck to march to Bunzlau on the 29th did not reach the corps commander until 6:00 on the morning of the 30th.

Droysen tells us that Schack's journal contains a morning entry for the 30th stating: "Waiting for march orders since yesterday." Consequently, late on the afternoon of the 29th, Yorck simply forwarded Reibnitz to Blücher at Goldberg with Horn's reports and a request for instructions. Before Reibnitz could reach Goldberg, Army Headquarters departed for Hohlstein, north of Löwenberg and less than two miles east of Sirgwitz. Of course, neither Yorck nor Reibnitz knew of this until the latter rode four miles east from Leisersdorf to Goldberg and then had to backtrack through Leisersdorf and cover another fifteen miles west to reach Hohlstein. After being in the saddle for fourteen hours, the good lieutenant finally delivered his report to Army Headquarters around 6:00 A.M. on 30 August – the very same time Blücher's courier delivered the 29 August order for Yorck to cross the Bober at Bunzlau.[64]

Meanwhile, back at Löwenberg on the 29th, the patrol dispatched there by Jürgaß received infantry fire from the opposite bank. The officer learned that large numbers of imperial soldiers had reached Löwenberg but found the Bober impossible to cross. As a result, they continued marching north toward Bunzlau. Major Schenck from the Black Hussars confirmed this news in a 10:00 A.M. report to Yorck. According to Schenk, the last of the units still east of Löwenberg on the right bank of the Bober marched toward Bunzlau between 5:00 and 7:00 that morning. However, locals alerted the Prussians to the approach of an enemy column – Puthod's division – from the upper Bober along the river's right bank. This news accounted for Stößel's arrival in time to participate in the destruction of Puthod's corps. Schenk likewise expressed his opinion that a mere advance by I Corps would force the enemy to surrender in droves. Despite all of this inviting news, Yorck did nothing on the 29th, meaning that Horn and Vasilchikov likewise remained inactive all day. Sacken's main body arrived at Haynau around 3:00 P.M. After receiving Vasilchikov's report on the situation east of Bunzlau, Sacken informed Blücher that he remained ready to support the vanguard if needed. What accounted for Yorck's behavior?[65]

As noted, the victory on the 26th did little to alter Yorck's negative view of the army's leadership. Although the Silesian Army had won a major victory, the repercussions of it resembled a defeat for I Corps. While inclement weather and supply shortages exhausted and spread illness among the well-clad line troops of both armies, it devastated the insufficiently uniformed and sometimes barefooted Landwehr. Desertion, straggling, and sickness soared as the inevitable result. Even Langeron described his stout Russians as being "utterly crushed by fatigue."[66] In the days following the Katzbach, Yorck's anger intensified as starvation took its toll on his exhausted soldiers.[67] "Two hundred loaves of bread weighing ten pounds each," reported Horn on the morning of the 29th, "is all that I have been able to obtain from the city [Haynau] and surrounding region." He claimed that the 4th Battalion of the 15th Silesian Landwehr and the 2nd Battalion of the 4th Silesian Landwehr could muster only 100 men each. According to the majors who commanded them, these survivors could no longer march because of exhaustion and the lack of food. Horn found them so malnourished and fatigued that he had to leave them at Haynau. He informed Yorck that the other battalions of these regiments appeared very weak; he feared the majority would desert because of hunger. The four battalions of the 15th Silesian Landwehr had started the campaign with a total of 3,200 men but now numbered only 320. Horses suffered as well from the acute shortage of fodder. "The enemy has so thoroughly foraged everything here that neither horse nor man can get anything," concluded a report from Jürgaß. "This forces me to put down many horses and I am also forced to send back many sick men. Thus, I urgently request that you provide me with provisions and fodder as soon as possible because otherwise I cannot guarantee that the regiments will be able to do what you so urgently desire."[68]

In a controversial report to Blücher on the 29th, Yorck unfairly questioned the fortitude and commitment of his Landwehr troops: "With regret, I have the honor to inform you that, due to the extraordinary poor weather in these days and due to the utter lack of uniforms, the Landwehr, especially the Landwehr battalions attached to Prince Carl von Mecklenburg's brigade, are quickly beginning to dissolve. In part from exhaustion, but also in part from ill-will, hundreds remain behind and because sufficient measures cannot be taken in the rear of the corps they might scatter in the countryside or return to their homes."[69] Major Reiche, the war commissar assigned to I Corps, could do little to overcome the obstacles caused by the weather. On the 29th he informed Yorck that the flooding made it completely impossible to quickly move up provisions for the troops:

> To the degree that the glorious victory has made you happy, in the same degree I feel miserable that the current weather makes it completely impossible to quickly deliver the food supplies to the troops. We wage war in a land where hands are for work and threshing, where the means for transport are completely lacking. In order to provide one day's supply of fodder, we need more than 300 wagons, and no magazine is available from which we can fulfill the need of 3,000 bushels a day. My arrangements and efforts apparently do not interest God, yet I cannot hide the impossibility that I can neither forage the hay in the fields nor the corn in the sheaves from the barns. In my situation, where the best intentions cannot help, I am so miserable that I no longer have joy, and I dread seeing any more since everything weighs on me and because it is certainly very embarrassing to suffer underserved statements of discontent and complaints.

Resupplying the ammunition proved no less challenging. "The continuous rains," stated a report by Lieutenant-Colonel Schmidt, "thoroughly soaked all cartridge pouches, completely ruining the ammunition found therein. The regiments flooded me with the request to replace this ammunition and by calculation I found that all my columns did not suffice to replace half of the ammunition that had been ruined by moisture. Had events ... led to a new, serious engagement or a full battle, the Silesian Army probably would have been very unfortunate due to the lack of ammunition." On the 26th, the day of the battle, a Lieutenant Peucker went to the fortress of Neiße to organize and bring back munitions columns. Not only should this task have been completed earlier in the month, but Army Headquarters should have established an ammunition depot closer to the area of operations such as at Schweidnitz. Nevertheless, Peucker executed his task efficiently, prompting Prince August of Prussia, the chief of artillery, to exclaim that "his ideal example can serve every young officer in a similar situation."[70]

Confronted by these interrelated crises, Yorck gave his men another day of rest on the 29th. "The roads are so bad and the rivers so extremely difficult to cross," he explained to Blücher, "that the majority of the troops did not reach their assigned destinations until last night and many still have not arrived. The Schnelle Deichsel is so swollen that it can be crossed only by way of the bridge at Pilgramsdorf. We will know tomorrow whether the water level will allow some footbridges to be built. For these reasons, only the forward cavalry will ride toward the Bober today and I will remain behind with the main body because neither General Langeron nor General Sacken are on line with me." On the previous day, Langeron had not advanced because Yorck failed to come on line with him, now Yorck would not advance because Langeron and Sacken remained behind him. We can only imagine the angst that this caused at Army Headquarters.[71]

Not having received formal instructions from Blücher of where to cross the Bober on the 29th, Yorck opted to wait until the French made their next move. He had already decided to grant the day of rest before he received the reports from Stößel, Schenk, and Horn, which did not arrive until around 4:00 in the afternoon. This certainly did not correspond to Blücher's demand "to pursue and to harm the enemy unceasingly." Blücher's style of command, although much more decentralized than Napoleon's, established the principle that the corps commanders had to proceed according to the spirit of the general instructions, establish communication with neighboring corps, and find material to build bridges. He rejected the notion of sacrificing time to reorganize brigade-level units. The pursuit itself should consume all efforts. "What is behind will remain behind and must follow," he declared. Although satisfied with the troops for enduring the strains and privations, by no means did Blücher believe the hardships had been extreme: more could have been asked and accomplished. The cavalry had to be utilized with ruthlessness. Yorck either did not believe he could take the initiative, or thought the actions of Langeron and Sacken would dictate his own, or simply cited these reasons as excuses for his continued defiance. Even Yorck's biographer, Droysen, has little ammunition to defend the corps commander: "Those at Blücher's headquarters recognized this evil situation, but according to the audacious and grandiose view that reigned there, they appreciated the significance of the victory and its costs more than Yorck could in his position and possibly according to his nature."[72]

In Blücher's response to the report made by Reibnitz, we can feel his fury over Yorck's failure to march on Bunzlau, especially because the dispatches from Horn that Yorck included with his letter claimed that the enemy forces on the eastern bank of the Bober would be forced to surrender. "You asked me what to do about Horn's report," seethed Blücher. "According to my previous letters, I expressed the desire that you make a decision without inquiry. Now, so much time has been lost that any measure will be too late. Moreover, I asked that in all cases any question should be resolved according to the general disposition that was issued. Because the enemy has directed all of his columns toward Bunzlau to cross the Bober there, you will thus depart for Bunzlau and cross the Bober there. Should the enemy still be at Gnadenberg you will attack him immediately."[73]

Yorck fired back. His response, which Gneisenau read before passing it to Blücher, contained the staff chief's comments in the margin, which capture the friction between Army and Corps Headquarters. Yorck begins by maintaining that the first order he received from Blücher to march on Bunzlau only arrived at 6:00 that morning – the 30th – and not the 29th. He then addressed the events of the 29th directly: "I did not depart immediately after receiving Horn's report because the majority of Steinmetz's and Hünerbein's brigades still had not reached their designated points." Gneisenau remarked: "The brigades did not have to fight, but send only a few battalions for support." "I found myself in the unfortunate situation of having to cross extraordinarily swollen rivers without bridges," continued Yorck, "because the corps of Generals Sacken and Langeron are operating on the two main highways where bridges are available." Remarking on Yorck's "unfortunate situation," Gneisenau retorted: "The enemy found himself in an even worse situation because he was defeated." As for Yorck's claim that he could not cross the swollen rivers, Gneisenau scribbled: "One can find appropriate measures to get across water if one wants to." The corps commander then raised an issue that constantly plagued Blücher's operations – an issue that caused Napoleon comparatively few problems because of his superior system of communication. "Had I," asserted Yorck, "remained in movement with the corps without awaiting orders from Your Excellency, it would have become extremely necessary for me to be informed of the existing situation of the two adjacent corps." In the margin next to Yorck's statement "Had

I remained in movement," Gneisenau, now quite exasperated, snapped: "Yea, since it was already ordered." Concerning Yorck's insistence that Army Headquarters should have informed him of the situation of Langeron and Sacken, Gneisenau scrawled: "This is the responsibility of the general-lieutenant. Only he can maintain communication because we do not know where the corps are situated." By comparison, the orders issued by Napoleon and Berthier always contained a status report of the friendly units – mainly corps and divisions – operating in the area. Napoleon's orders constantly stress the need for the corps commanders to establish and maintain communication with each other.

"Had I marched yesterday with a small portion of the corps to Löwenberg," persisted Yorck, "which was my direction to take, I thus would have made a futile march, and the corps would have been completely fragmented." "False assertion," noted Gneisenau, "not at all futile. The corps could have gone to Sirgwitz. No! Not fragmented, but divided in columns to facilitate the march and to arrive between the enemy's columns." Yorck continued: "General Horn's brigade, including the Reserve Cavalry, was sent forward to pursue the enemy. Wherever Horn went the main body [of the corps] had to follow; whether it would be Löwenberg or Bunzlau depended on the operations of the two flank corps [Sacken and Langeron] and I believed I had to await either a request from one of the imperial Russian corps commanders or an order from Your Excellency to determine where I should march with the main body of the corps because the arrival of many corps on one point can only be disadvantageous." Next to Yorck's line that stated he had to await an order from Blücher, Gneisenau wrote: "Whoever wants to pursue zealously does not wait for an order." Gneisenau's blood had started to boil. Remarking on Yorck's comment about all corps arriving at the same point, he penned: "Above: not fragmented, here: not united!"

"Early yesterday I reported to Your Excellency that the majority of the corps still had not reached the designated point of the Schnelle Deichsel, thus making a further march impossible," explained Yorck. "And why?" asked Gneisenau. "Could not a part [of the corps] have advanced and the other followed?" Yorck continued: "Moreover, I proved on the 26th that I will gladly do all that is feasible and that the troops can achieve everything that is in their power." Gneisenau could not resist reminding Blücher that Yorck had insisted on giving the troops a day of rest on the 26th: "If we had waited a second twenty-four hours as he demanded, we would have been defeated. Now we should be thankful that he came to the battle?" Yorck concluded by emphasizing the exertions of the troops, "in particular during the march of the 28th, which lasted for thirty-six hours, in which the troops had to wade through the waters." Gneisenau's final response mirrored the sentiment at Army Headquarters: "Had he crossed the river on the 27th, they would not have had to wade through the flooded waters on the 28th. If one does not pursue the enemy with exertions, one will find himself in the situation where the enemy, whom one could have destroyed, has to be fought again. Because he had shunned exertions, Prussian blood will again have to be shed."[74]

Based on Gneisenau's comments, Colonel Johann Georg (Gustav) von Rauch drafted a reply that the former proofread and Blücher signed: "I received your letter of the 30th in which you compare for me the exertions of the troops and the difficulties that you encountered by advancing. It gives me so much pleasure each time to have the same opinion as you, yet I see myself forced to explain to you that although I am content with the goodwill and the manner in which the troops have endured all exertions, I nevertheless in no way find that the exertions have been carried to the extreme and that more still could not have been achieved." Concerning this point, we again hear from Müffling: "This corresponded with his [Gneisenau's] principle that you must always require from the men more than they can perform, because in execution less is invariably accomplished than is demanded – a principle that I have always considered as dangerous as it is incorrect."[75] Returning to Blücher's letter:

> The instructions issued to you during the night of 26/27 [August], then later to General Horn, and the orders issued to you in the afternoon, expressed with the greatest clarity my intention to pursue and harm the enemy without delay. Three corps received orders from my headquarters. As soon as these were issued, it became the business of the corps commanders not only to act according to the general instructions, but to observe everything that pertains to these orders. I cannot maintain communication between them: the corps themselves must maintain it; where a bridge is lacking, it must be built quickly and at such an important moment one should raze the nearby houses to obtain lumber. The corps are provided with the necessary personnel for this. In the pursuit of a fleeing enemy who is weakened every hour by the loss of prisoners and fugitives, it is not necessary to march against the enemy with whole brigades or even with whole battalions and squadrons. What remains behind must be left behind and brought up.
>
> One must not heed the complaints of the cavalry, because if one can achieve an objective as great as the destruction of an entire enemy army, the state can spare a few hundred horses that fall from exhaustion. Instead of settling the affair with some energy, the immediate consequence of failing to exploit a victory is that a new battle must be delivered. Yesterday's engagement at Bunzlau should be viewed in the same way, in which a failure in the pursuit of the enemy is to blame.[76]

Claiming that this lecture convinced Yorck of the error of his ways would misrepresent the curmudgeon's character, but he remained silent and the unpleasant correspondence between the Prussians temporarily ceased.

To summarize the movements of the 29th, Macdonald's army crossed the Bober and halted west of the river while the van of the Army of Silesia reached the Bober.[77] After receiving the news of Langeron's engagement with Puthod east of Löwenberg, Blücher moved his headquarters to Hohlstein, north of Löwenberg. There he received letters from Tsar Alexander and Barclay, both dated 25 August, informing him that the Bohemian Army had reached Dresden. Moreover, Allied Headquarters assumed that Napoleon and the Grande Armée stood in Lusatia. Although both Alexander and Barclay warned Blücher to avoid a serious engagement, they both expressed the desire of seeing the Silesian Army approach the Elbe and thus the Bohemian Army as soon as possible.

During the night of 29/30 August, Souham's rearguard withdrew from Gnadenberg to the opposite bank of the Bober, leaving Bunzlau occupied only by light infantry. Allied patrols immediately detected the French retreat; Horn and Vasilchikov decided to take the town without delay. To minimize losses, the Allies maneuvered the imperials out of Bunzlau, which stood east of the Bober. With the Brandenburg Uhlans, one horse battery, the Jäger detachments of the Leib Regiment, and the skirmishers of the Leib Fusilier Battalion, Katzler enveloped the city to the southwest and reached the Kessel hill. As soon as the Nr. 2 Horse Battery started shelling Bunzlau, Horn led the 7th Brigade against the eastern side of the town. The French skirmishers evacuated the city after attempting to ignite a magazine. To guard the Bober bridge, the French posted one battalion southeast of the Bunzlau mill race. Shelled by the Prussian horse guns and attacked in the flank by the Jäger and skirmishers, the battalion fell back after setting fire to the bridge over the mill race. Jäger and Uhlans sought to put out the flames and save the bridge. This delay allowed the imperials to rip up the planking on the large bridge over the Bober and fire the structure itself. French troops started to deploy on the hills along the western bank but a Russian battery numbering twelve guns unlimbered further west on the Kessel hill and fired so effectively that they retreated. As this unfolded, two guns from the Prussian horse battery moved from the hill to the mill race and pelted the French skirmishers with caseshot to force them to withdraw. Horn's battalions finally reached the bridge to reinforce the Jäger. With sufficient manpower, the Allies drove off the remaining enemy skirmishers and extinguished the flames on the bridge. However, heavy fire from Tillendorf prevented them from repairing it. A heated firefight ensued between the banks of the river, until the Prussians suffered from the effects of their ammunition shortage. Additional cannon arrived but French guns unlimbered as well so that the exchange intensified and continued for quite some time, until the imperials began to withdraw around 10:30 A.M.

After repairing the bridge, the Allies moved across the Bober with Cossacks leading the way. Horn ordered the skirmishers of the Leib

Regiment and two Landwehr battalions to follow and occupy Tillendorf as well as the hills along the western bank while two other battalions moved into the outskirts of Bunzlau. Horn and Vasilchikov believed that the imperials had retreated, and the situation remained quiet until 2:00. Around that time, the French rearguard emerged from a concealed position in the woods west of Tillendorf, attempting to eject the Cossacks and Landwehr battalions posted in the village. Unable to fire their muskets because they lacked ammunition, the Landwehr withdrew east across the Bober bridge. Prussian skirmishers and a few companies of the Leib Regiment ended the French charge but the bridge remained in enemy hands. Out of ammunition, the Prussians could do nothing but watch as the enemy went to work destroying the vital structure. Finally the ammunition wagons arrived and distributed the last remaining supplies. Then, all soldiers with cartridges attacked the bridge. A stalemate ensued until a bayonet attack by the two battalions of Sacken's Ochakovskii and Kamchatskii Infantry Regiments drove the French from the bridge. Although the Russians could not secure Tillendorf, they managed to maintain possession of the damaged bridge over the Bober.[78]

To Yorck's credit, he immediately issued the necessary orders to "depart for Bunzlau and cross the Bober there" on the 30th after he received Blücher's letter from 29 August. Yet despite Blücher's insistence on speed, I Corps did not march until around noon due to delays in crossing the Schnelle Deichsel. Although its waters had subsided, safe passage still required bridges, which slowed the crossing. Yorck's main body reached Bunzlau around 5:00 P.M. on the 30th, bringing additional supplies of ammunition; three battalions from 2nd and 8th Brigades relieved the troops guarding the Bober bridge. Small-arms fire continued late into the night. Vasilchikov's troops occupied Bunzlau while Sacken posted his main body west and north of the town. Yorck positioned two brigades west and south of Bunzlau while the rest of the corps camped to the southeast at the Drüssel Estate. Horn's losses amounted to 8 officers and 354 men; Russian and French losses are not known. The Allies made good use of the large magazine at Bunzlau that the French had attempted but failed to burn, yet the horses still continued to suffer from lack of fodder.

Prisoners claimed that troops from the French III Corps formed the rearguard at Bunzlau. On the evening of the 30th, Yorck received a report from Schwanenfeld written at 3:00 P.M. near Görlitz, where he arrived after crossing the Bober north of Bunzlau. According to the intrepid captain, after completely collapsing in its retreat across the Queis, the Army of the Bober had continued toward the Neiße. The portion that reached Görlitz camped in the greatest disorder. A French staff officer captured by Schwanenfeld's troopers alleged that Napoleon could be found seventy miles east of Bunzlau at Stolpen. South of Schwanenfeld's detachment, Russian *Streifkorps* under

Madatov and Rakhmanov also crossed the Bober, sending a portion of their Cossacks toward the Bunzlau–Siegersdorf road. With their main bodies, they crossed the Queis and the Neiße, destroying the bridges over the latter between Görlitz and Penzig (Pieńsk). Madatov reached the region of Löbau on the 30th. Falkenhausen had not been able to follow the Cossacks because of the weaker horses that carried his Landwehr troopers. Then, he could not find any bridges across the Neiße. On the 31st, he finally managed to cross the Neiße at Penzig and unite with Schwanenfeld near Görlitz.

On the left wing of the Silesian Army, Langeron attempted to cross the Bober on the 29th but high water levels frustrated his plans. For the 30th, he intended to cross downstream (north) of Löwenberg at Braunau in the morning. Coming from Lauterseiffen, his pontoons reached the bridging site at 8:00 A.M. Around the same time, the 35th and 36th Divisions from Gérard's XI Corps reached Löwenberg, taking a strong position on the Popel hill opposite the bridge site. After retreating through Bunzlau, Gérard had reorganized the two divisions east of Naumburg and then marched back to the Bober. Now unable to build the bridge at Braunau, Rudzevich attempted to throw a bridge thirty minutes upstream of Löwenberg but encountered elements of Ledru's 31st Division that foiled his efforts. The Russians decided to make a third attempt to cross the Bober, this time at Zobten. While the vanguard and Olsufiyev's IX Infantry Corps remained at Plagwitz, Langeron's main body marched south only to find difficulties of another sort. After reaching Zobten, the Russians could not move the pontoons over the muddy and flooded ground to reach the Bober. Transferring the pontoons to Dippelsdorf, they managed to build a bridge only to see the Bober's raging current tear it apart on three occasions. Toward evening, Rudzevich informed Langeron that the behavior of the French at Löwenberg indicated that they would depart soon. As the French proved him correct, the Russians started building a bridge there at daybreak on the 31st.

On Blücher's far left, Bistram led St.-Priest's advance guard toward Greiffenberg, where he encountered Ledru's main body. Following a sharp combat, the French withdrew into Greiffenberg, successfully defending the town's barricaded gate against Russian attacks. After night fell, Bistram withdrew to Ottendorf (Radoniów). St.-Priest's main body reached Spiller that evening. Ledru's 31st Division evacuated Greiffenberg on the following day and took a position behind the Queis with two brigades at Marklissa and a third at Lauban.

The day of 30 August thus ended with Yorck's and Sacken's corps at Bunzlau, and Langeron's vanguard at Plagwitz and Braunau; the latter's main body at Dippelsdorf and Zobten. While the Silesian Army failed to get across the Bober with the exception of St.-Priest, Macdonald's army remained between the Queis and the Bober, with the majority at points along the former. Souham instructed his rearguard to hold Tillendorf but echeloned the rest of III Corps westward. Macdonald's center – XI Corps and II Cavalry Corps – halted at Siegersdorf and Naumburg, both on the Queis. To his right, Lauriston's V Corps and Marchand's 39th Division likewise stood at the Queis in and around Lauban. Ledru's 31st Division held Greiffenberg. As noted, Souham's rearguard evacuated Tillendorf during the night of 30/31 August and the entire III Corps withdrew across the Queis to Lauban, destroying the bridges at Naumburg and Siegersdorf. From Lauban, Marchand's division commenced the march due west to Görlitz, sending one brigade southwest to Ostritz to link with VIII Corps.[79] Macdonald's headlong flight continued as described by Gneisenau:

> Our victory on the 26th was far more complete than I was able to tell you in my last letter. In the steep, wooded valleys of the Wütende Neiße and the Katzbach we found overturned guns and military wagons on the next day. We have captured more than 100 cannon, 300 caissons, and field forges; 15,000 prisoners have been brought in, many come in hourly. All roads between the Katzbach and the Bober show the effects of our enemy's terror; corpses run over and stuck in the mud, overturned wagons, and burned villages. The majority of Macdonald's army has dissolved. Cut off from the crossings over the swollen rivers, the stragglers wander around in the forests and mountains, succumbing to delirium from hunger. I have sounded the tocsin against them and summoned the peasants to kill them or take them prisoner. Yesterday, Puthod's division met its end in this vicinity. It was overtaken and had to fight with its back against the Bober. Initially, we shelled it with canister and then attacked with the bayonet. Some were killed, others driven into the water; the rest – generals and officers – were taken prisoner and two Eagles captured. Some 20,000 men are all that remain of Macdonald's 80,000-strong army. If the orders that have been issued are executed, they also will be eliminated.[80]

On the 30th, Blücher charged Gaudi with ensuring that the liberated districts of Silesia resume the delivery of manpower, horses, and war materiel. Officials needed to be appointed to administer Liegnitz, Löwenberg, Bunzlau, and especially Goldberg, which contained 800 wounded soldiers from both armies. Blücher instructed Gaudi to assist the postmaster in restoring the mail system. Probably fearful that his predecessor, Gneisenau, would report him to the king, Gaudi did not let this opportunity slip away. The military governor responded that he had already placed an order for 20,000 pairs of shoes to meet the needs of the army: 10,000 each would come from Neiße and Breslau. A convoy had already left Breslau for Goldberg with doctors and surgeons to care for the wounded and transport them to a military hospital. The Landsturm of the surrounding districts had been summoned to procure horses, round up Allied stragglers, and apprehend enemy fugitives. Finally, district authorities decreed the collection of all arms, which would be delivered to Jauer and Schweidnitz.[81]

That evening, Blücher instructed Yorck to cross the Bober "if possible" on the 31st and attack or pursue the imperials. Sacken received orders to march on Siegersdorf, which meant at least a part of Yorck's corps would have to take the road to Naumburg because the two corps could not operate on the same road. Blücher expected Langeron to cross the Bober that same night at Zobten and attack the enemy. Sometime after midnight, Gneisenau drafted Blücher's report to the king explaining that the army still could not cross the Bober in the vicinity of Löwenberg. "This hinders the complete destruction of the enemy. But in the meantime, if St.-Priest can execute the orders repeatedly issued to him, the enemy will be attacked from the rear at Marklissa and thus destroyed. He, St.-Priest, will then stand on the shortest road to Dresden and can unite with Neipperg. If all our subordinate commanders execute the orders that have been issued, Your Royal Majesty can consider the army of Marshal Macdonald as practically destroyed."[82] Blücher signed similar letters addressed to Alexander and Barclay.

Early on the morning of the 31st, Sacken's corps commenced the crossing of the Bober at Bunzlau. Vasilchikov reached the Queis at Paritz but found the bridge destroyed and the French guarding the opposite bank. Organizational issues again delayed Yorck's march. This time the creation of a new vanguard at Tillendorf consumed several hours. After Sacken's corps cleared Tillendorf around 3:00 P.M., Katzler departed for Naumburg at the head of an impressive vanguard: seven and three-quarters battalions, eighteen squadrons, twenty guns, and per his request a pioneer detachment. At 4:30, its lead elements entered Naumburg. Of course they found the bridge over the Queis down and the opposite bank lined with French skirmishers. Behind them, the Prussians could see a large bivouac. Hiller, who again commanded the van's infantry, moved three Jäger companies to the eastern bank. He scattered skirmishers among the terrain and in the houses of Ullersdorf (Oldrzychów). Katzler's cavalry occupied Naumburg along with two battalions; the rest of the vanguard camped south of the town. Patrols established communication with the vanguards of both Russian corps: Rudzevich eight miles upriver at Bertelsdorf (Uniegoszcz) and Vasilchikov three miles downriver at Paritz. East of Katzler, Yorck's main body crossed the Bober around 4:00 P.M. to bivouac one mile east of Naumburg at Herzogswaldau (Milików) after sunset. The repair work on the bridge at Naumburg proceeded slowly during the night of 31 August–1 September because the imperials had burned the pylons. Patrols reported that the river could not be crossed without a bridge due to the high water level.

In Langeron's sector, the French forces that had opposed his bridge-building attempts near Löwenberg likewise withdrew in the night to Lauban. Thus, on the morning of the 31st, the Russians finally bridged the Bober at Löwenberg and Dippelsdorf. Rudzevich's vanguard crossed the river around 8:00 A.M. and commenced the march to Lauban. Arriving there,

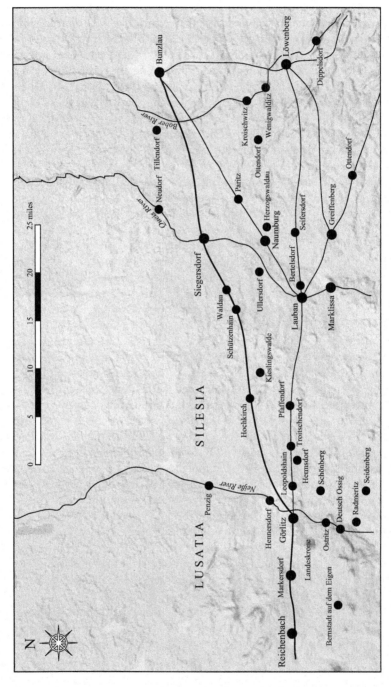

16. Region between the Bober and the Neiße Rivers

the Russians found both of its bridges over the Queis destroyed and a large imperial force holding the opposite bank. Rudzevich posted the vanguard in the region of Bertelsdorf while Langeron's main body reached Seifersdorf (Mściszów), five miles east of Lauban. Langeron informed Blücher that, after destroying the bridges, the imperials had taken a position on the hills of the left bank that surrounded Lauban in a semi-circle facing east. According to prisoners, Lauriston had arrived from Bunzlau with V Corps to unite with Marchand's 39th Division, the 2nd Brigade of Ledru's 31st Division, 3,000 cavalry, and 24 guns. Further south, the rest of Ledru's division evacuated Greiffenberg and retreated to Marklissa on the Queis, seven miles upriver of Lauban. As soon as the townspeople of Greiffenberg informed St.-Priest of the French departure, Bistrom's vanguard marched. Pursuing west toward Marklissa and northwest toward Lauban, Bistrom established communication with Rudzevich; St.-Priest's main body moved into Greiffenberg. By nightfall on the 31st, only the Queis separated the main bodies of the two armies.

As for Blücher, the 31st found him feeling "very sick." Nostitz tells us that normally Blücher's health "left nothing to be desired. His strong, powerful body endured with ease all the fatigues of war and although seventy years old his spirit maintained a juvenile cheerfulness. He accompanied all marches on horseback." Learning about the loss of Moltke may have contributed to his condition. "But all luck is accompanied by misfortune: my good Count Moltke is no more," wrote Blücher to his wife. "I sent him to the king with news of the victory, where he certainly would have received a considerable reward. On the way, he drowned in high water [the Elbe] and here we grieve his loss."[83]

Before transferring his headquarters from Hohlstein to Löwenberg on the afternoon of the 31st, he received a discomforting report from Major Oppen, his intelligence chief. Apparently, rumors had reached Löwenberg as early as the afternoon of the 28th of a great French victory over the Austrians at Dresden. A captured Westphalian officer added that his unit had been informed of the emperor's decisive victory over the main Allied army during an epic struggle at Dresden on 26 August. According to the prisoner, Schwarzenberg lost 12,000 prisoners, 15 guns, and 8 flags. Blücher and Gneisenau immediately recognized the serious implications of this news should it be true. Leaving the pursuit of Schwarzenberg to his marshals, Napoleon would return to Silesia with reinforcements to crush Blücher and drive him into Bohemia.[84] By maneuvering Blücher into Bohemia, Napoleon could surround and destroy both the Bohemian and Silesian Armies in one great battle, similar to the situation that would lead to Königgrätz (Hradec Králové) during the 1866 Austro-Prussian War. Consequently, Army Headquarters took precautions to prepare a fallback position in case Napoleon forced a retreat. Before the defile of Wartha near Frankenstein, in the vicinity of the three fortresses of Glatz, Silberberg, and Neiße, Gneisenau identified a position that would allow the Silesian Army to stand against a superior enemy and to close the southeastern passes into Bohemia. "If I am pressed by superior forces," Blücher assured Schwarzenberg, "I will move into this position and accept battle in it if I am attacked."[85]

That same day, the 31st, Blücher instructed his corps commanders to have their light cavalry maintain constant contact with the enemy. Their vanguards would remain within supporting distance of the forward cavalry but their main bodies would not cross the Queis until further notice. Recognizing the need to proceed with caution, similar to the operations before the 26th, Blücher wanted his vanguards to continue to pressure and unsettle Macdonald's forces. At the same time, he halted the main body of the army and concentrated his corps. In this way, he planned to be battle-ready when Napoleon arrived with superior forces. He also informed his corps commanders of the news he had received. Acting on this information, Yorck ordered bridges thrown across the Bober at Wenigwalditz (Włodzice Małe) and Kroischwitz to avoid colliding with Sacken's corps at Bunzlau. A road from both points had to be cut through Ottendorf (Ocice).

While Blücher prepared to retreat eastward, Macdonald continued his retreat westward. During the night of 31 August/1 September, the Army of the Bober left its position on the Queis, crossed the Neiße at Görlitz, and took a position on the hills to the west. A single brigade reinforced by some cavalry remained on the hills of the eastern bank until it crossed the Neiße and occupied Görlitz on the evening of the 1st. On the opposite end, Macdonald's vanguard, Marchand's 39th Division, reached Reichenbach. We do not know why Macdonald united his army at Görlitz on 1 September. If he wanted to defend the Neiße, a position at Görlitz would prove useless because the Allies could cross the river at several other points. If he wanted to continue the retreat, uniting his army on the hills west of Görlitz to conduct a retrograde march on a single road made little sense.

On the morning of 1 September, Blücher repeated the order for the cavalry to maintain contact with the enemy and for the infantry of the vanguards to follow at a suitable distance. "The army has a day of rest," concluded the order. "At 6:00 this evening will be a religious service, both by the corps as well as by the vanguards. Following it, a volley will be fired from large and small cannon to celebrate the victory on the Katzbach and the liberation of Silesia." "So, one day of rest and a religious service! Then, we will certainly get a good beating," scoffed Yorck after receiving this order. In compliance with Blücher's orders, the main bodies of all three corps remained on the eastern bank of the Queis that day while the van-guards continued west. Around 7:00 A.M., Sacken reported that his light cavalry had made contact with the enemy retreating toward Görlitz. From Löbau, Madatov reported large French forces assembling at Görlitz,

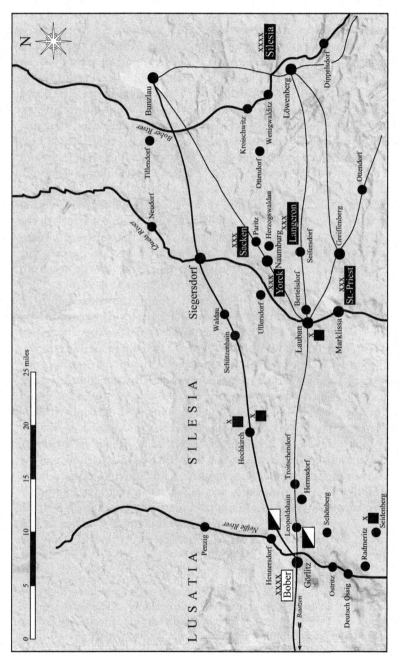

17. Situation, 31 August 1813

333

fourteen miles east of his position. Yet imperial troops had already started the retreat from Görlitz toward Bautzen. Twenty miles south of Görlitz, Poniatowski's VIII Corps held a fortified position at Zittau. Later in the day, around 3:00, Sacken's engineers repaired the bridges over the Queis downstream of Paritz at Siegersdorf (Zebrzydowa-Wieś) and Neudorf (Nowa Wieś), allowing Vasilchikov's vanguard to reach Hochkirch (Przesieczany) ten miles east of Görlitz. Sacken's main body remained at Paritz. The corps commander's 3:00 P.M. report expressed his intention to continue to Görlitz. Without considering the general circumstances, Sacken suggested attacking Macdonald immediately. Doubtless Sacken's aggressive attitude pleased Blücher, but the news about Dresden made the stakes much higher than the old Prussian could afford. Around 8:30 P.M., Sacken communicated Karpov's report that large enemy forces indeed stood at Görlitz.[86]

In the center, Yorck's men did not repair the bridge over the Queis at Naumburg until 10:00 A.M. on the 1st. Not wanting to lose contact with the imperials, Katzler had ordered six squadrons of the Brandenburg Uhlans and Black Hussars to swim the river four hours earlier. He pursued the enemy to Hennersdorf (Jędrzychowice) on the Neiße downriver from Görlitz. Aided by the Cossacks, his patrols rode close to Görlitz. They learned that the main body of Macdonald's troops had moved into an entrenched camp west of Görlitz: only weak imperial forces remained on the east bank. Meanwhile, Hiller and the rest of Yorck's vanguard joined Vasilchikov at Hochkirch. On the left wing, the imperial units facing Langeron's corps at Lauban likewise departed early in the morning for Görlitz pursued by the Cossacks. As soon as the Russians completed the pontoon bridge, Rudzevich's vanguard cavalry crossed the Queis and advanced to the Neiße. Rudzevich's infantry remained at Lauban while Langeron's main body rested at Seifersdorf. St.-Priest's vanguard, now commanded by General Nikolay Borozdin II, moved to Seidenberg (Zawidów), eleven miles southeast of Görlitz. Leading his main body to Marklissa on the Queis, St.-Priest reestablished communication with Neipperg's Austrians at Liebenau (Hodkovice nad Mohelkou) and delivered Blücher's instructions.[87]

With his vanguard in Upper Lusatia, Blücher's first campaign as an independent army commander ended with the liberation of Silesia in just fourteen days. To celebrate, he issued a general order to the army on 1 September courtesy of Gneisenau's quill:

Silesia is now liberated from the enemy. To your courage, brave soldiers of the Russian and Prussian army under my orders, your exertions and perseverance, your patience in the endurance of hardships and shortages, I owe the good fortune of having ripped a beautiful province from the hands of a greedy foe.

During the battle of the Katzbach, you defiantly opposed the enemy. Courageously and with the speed of lightning you broke forth from behind the hills. You spurned attacking him with musket fire; without hesitating you advanced, [and] your bayonets drove him over the steep valley edges of the Wütende Neiße and the Katzbach.

Since then you have waded through rivers and swollen streams. Some of you have suffered from the shortage of provisions because the washed-out roads and lack of wagons prevented their transport. You have struggled with cold, wet, privations, and some of you lack sufficient clothing; nevertheless, you did not grumble and you pursued your defeated enemy with effort. I thank you for such praiseworthy conduct. Only he who combines such characteristics is a natural-born soldier.

In our hands are 103 cannon, 250 caissons, the enemy's hospital equipment, his field forges, his flour wagons, 1 general of division, 2 generals of brigade, and a large number of colonels as well as staff and other officers, 18,000 prisoners, 2 Eagles, and other trophies. The remainder of those who faced you in the battle of the Katzbach have been so seized by the terror of your arms that they can no longer bear to see your bayonets. You have seen the roads and fields between the Katzbach and the Bober; they bear the signs of the terror and confusion of your enemy.

Let us sing praises to the Lord of Hosts, through whose help you have defeated the enemy and in religious service let us publicly thank him for the glorious victory. A threefold salvo of artillery will conclude the hour that you consecrate to prayer. Then, after your enemy anew![88]

Feeling better than the previous day, Blücher boasted: "Yesterday I chased the last Frenchman across the Saxon frontier. The fruits of our victory you will see ... 103 guns, 250 caissons, 18,000 prisoners, 2 Eagles, and other trophies. This evening around 6:00 P.M. will be a general religious service and early tomorrow morning the bridges over the Queis, which the enemy burned and destroyed, will be repaired and I will pursue." Although Blücher had reason to celebrate, losses among the Prussians had not been slight. Yorck's corps had lost some 12,925 men and 1,119 horses since hostilities had commenced. On 31 August, I Corps numbered 25,296 men and 6,248 horses. The Russians had fared better: Sacken reported the totals of his musters to be 15,119 men indicating a loss of 2,793 men after hostilities resumed. After sustaining a loss of 6,648 men since the armistice expired, Langeron reported his corps to number 28,340 men on 1 September. St.-Priest's army corps totaled 13,320 men by 1 September. In round figures, the Silesian Army had lost some 23,000 men in less than three weeks of campaigning; 82,000 men remained for the next stage of the war.[89]

Harmony rarely existed between the leading figures of the Silesian Army, as Gneisenau explained:

The two subordinate generals, Langeron and Yorck, are poor commanders. The former is nervous and faint-hearted to the extreme, the latter always pessimistic; both lack mental fortitude. Moreover, the latter hates me wholeheartedly and censures all of my measures. If it had been up to these two, instead of being victors, we would have been completely defeated on 26 August. From the brilliant position assigned to him, Langeron sent back almost all of his artillery so he would not have to fight. Nevertheless, because of the victory of our wing, he was saved, barely. The latter wanted twenty-four hours of rest. Had he been granted this, his corps would have stood five miles behind Langeron's, and when Langeron was overwhelmed we would have been defeated.[90]

Gneisenau remained embittered by the conduct of Yorck and Langeron. "I gave the disposition for the pursuit of the enemy immediately after the battle. Had it been followed, nothing of Macdonald's army would have survived. At that time, the waters of the heavens were in league with us, discharging so that all streams were swollen and the rivers overflowing their banks. No enemy would have been saved. But the pursuit was postponed by the subordinate commanders and for the most part the enemy escaped."[91] "Such were the results of the battle on the Katzbach," explained Müffling in his 1827 work, "which although not bloody, was as important in its consequences as the most bloody of battles. Until 3 and 4 September, prisoners continued to be brought in from all sides; the Landsturm in the mountains on our left flank took an active part in this. From 18,000 to 20,000 prisoners, over 100 guns, more than 300 caissons, the hospital wagons, and baggage of the army remained in our hands. More important than this was the spirit that now pervaded the army, which must be viewed as the result of this battle. The army itself was amazed about the great results, as each individual part could only see a small portion of the results of the pursuit. All united in praise of the field commander and the acclamation for rescuing Silesia was itself a satisfying reward for the Russian soldiers."[92]

On reaching the Neiße after liberating Silesia, Blücher had much to be proud of: energy, controlled aggression, and commitment to defeating the enemy army marked his leadership. His army had remained in constant contact with the imperials since it moved across the neutral zone. Almost no day went by in which some part of his army did not engage the enemy. While the need for the numerous combats, countermarches, and night marches can be debated, it is difficult to imagine how Blücher could otherwise have fulfilled his charge at a time when information, which was not always accurate, traveled only as fast as a horse could gallop. Blücher often had to overcome the passive resistance, preconceived opinions, jealousies, and biases of his corps commanders, who habitually saw only difficulties in the task at hand. Rather than consider the far worse situation of the French army, Yorck and Langeron only looked at the situation of their own troops. According to Freytag-Loringhoven: "In the creation of this contrast between the army leadership and the subordinate commanders lies no reproach for otherwise reliable men because they conducted the war as they had learned it, but in this is a claim to glory for the leadership of the Silesian Army and the proof of how high they stand out above the mass of their contemporaries."[93]

As for Macdonald, his biggest mistake occurred on the night after the battle itself. Rather than withdraw during the night, he should have allowed the army to rest along the left bank of the Katzbach throughout the night of 26/27 August. For this to have been possible, imperial command and control needed to have been more efficient in reordering the troops coming from the plateau. Niederkrayn could have been held by at least one division to stop the Allies from debouching. As we have seen, the disaster on the plateau in no way resembled Prussian accounts of a complete rout. Besides, two cavalry divisions, one infantry division, and one infantry brigade supported by three batteries did not constitute Macdonald's army. After Lauriston stopped Langeron's late push, Macdonald had little to fear from Blücher's army considering the weather, terrain, and time of day. Regardless, Macdonald ordered a general retreat during the night, which further disrupted his command and control. Worse for the Army of the Bober, Macdonald overtaxed the physical limits of his starving and exhausted soldiers. For this reason, the men of Lauriston's V Corps, who had arguably scored a victory against Langeron's Russians, fell apart on the road to Goldberg. In such a state of exhaustion, they could no longer fight or march. Thus, we see Langeron's soldiers take the lion's share of the spoils. Although this argument is based on speculation, twelve hours of rest and reorganization followed by a coordinated retreat commencing at 7:00 on the morning of the 27th could have saved Macdonald's army from the dissolution that overcame it.[94]

Notes

1 Quoted in Blasendorff, *Blücher*, 207–08. According to Delbrück, in *Gneisenau*, III:214, Dr. Karl Otto Johannes Theresius, Baron von Richthofen (1811–1888) communicated this story to Hans Delbrück. Only two years old in 1813, Karl no doubt heard this story from his father, Karl Ernst (1747–1841). Manfred von Richthofen (1892–1918), the famous Red Baron of the First World War, was a distant cousin.

2 Blücher to Amalie, Brechelshof, 26 August 1813, and Blücher to Bonin, at the Katzbach, 27 August 1813, *Blüchers Briefe*, ed. Unger, 175–76; Blassendorf, *Blücher*, 208.

3 Blücher to Bernadotte, Brechelshof, 26 August 1813, is RA KrA, volym 25. Scharnhorst delivered a copy of the same report to Bernadotte. Moltke bore victory reports to Alexander, Frederick William, and Barclay but nothing for Schwarzenberg.

4 Quoted in Müffling, *Die Feldzüge*, 32.

5 Quoted in Nostitz, *Tagebuch*, 57.

6 Quoted in *Droysen*, Yorck, II:147.

7 Bogdanovich, *Geschichte des Krieges*, IIa:83; Blücher to Frederick William, Goldberg, 6:00 P.M., 28 August 1813, RA KrA, volym 25; Blücher to Sacken, Hohlstein, 30 August 1813, RGVIA, f. VUA, op. 16, d. 3851, ll. 266–266b. Although
Gneisenau stated this to be the case in his 26 August letter to Gibsone, it is
unclear why Blücher waited until the 30th to make it official.

8 Gneisenau to Gibsone, Brechelshof, 26 August 1813, GStA PK, VI HA Rep. 92
Nl. Gneisenau, Nr. 21; Blücher to Bernadotte, Brechelshof, 26 August 1813, RA
KrA, volym 25; Nostitz, *Tagebuch*, 56–57.

9 Bogdanovich, *Geschichte des Krieges*, IIa:66–67. According to Droysen in *Yorck*,
II:138, "On receiving this disposition, Langeron declared he would not follow it.
'He spoke of secret instructions he had to obey and that he could not risk his
corps.'" Later German scholars retreated from their nationalistic assault on
Langeron. Writing in 1900, Freytag-Loringhoven argued that Langeron's "actions
appear less ambiguous than they have been described up to now by German
sources. In view of the continued back-and-forth marches of the recent days,
which must have been blamed on the army's leadership, Langeron's measures
appear comprehensible in a purely objective military assessment of the situation,
at least from the standpoint of a Russian commander, all the more so when
Langeron's corps was attacked by Lauriston's V Corps. Regardless, Langeron's
behavior cannot be justified by hindsight": Freytag-Loringhoven, *Aufklärung
und Armeeführung*, 81.

10 According to Langeron, "At noon, despite the rain that had fallen in torrents
since nine in the morning, the enemy sharply attacked my front but, having seen
that their principal columns were still moving on my left and into the woods, and
having received from Yuzefovich news that an enemy corps was moving on
Schönau, and seemed to wish to move on Jauer (which Macdonald had effectively
ordered), I detached X Infantry Corps from the rear ... and ordered Kaptsevich
to move on Peterwitz and, if necessary, on Moisdorf, to stop the enemy from
advancing on Jauer. Having detached X Infantry Corps, which also served as my
reserve, I remained with one extremely extended line": Langeron, *Mémoires*, 253.

11 Langeron, *Mémoires*, 253, emphasis added.

12 Gneisenau to Hardenberg, Brechelshof, 26 August 1813, GStA PK, VI HA
Rep. 92 Nl. Gneisenau, Nr. 20b, and Hardenberg to Gneisenau, Laun an der Eger
(Louny nad Ohří), 30 August 1813, *ibid.*, Nr. 24; Thile to Gneisenau, Teplitz,
31 August 1813, *ibid.*, Nr. 21.

13 Nostitz, *Tagebuch*, 56, quoted in Droysen, *Yorck*, II:159.

14 Gneisenau to Clausewitz, Goldberg, 28 August 1813, GStA, PK, VI HA Rep. 92
Nl. Gneisenau, Nr. 21.

15 Unger, *Blücher*, II:81. Unger followed Blasendorff's assessment: "Blücher
achieved great success through the victory at the Katzbach and the restless
pursuit. It became even greater through the influence that it had on the victorious
army. Now, the defiant corps commanders had to admit that Headquarters' plan
had been more than the sudden bright idea of an ingenious mind." See Blasendorff, *Blücher*, 211.

16 Nostitz, *Tagebuch*, 56.

17 Müffling, *Die Feldzüge*, 40–41. Despite the balanced approach to this work as opposed to his *Aus meinem Leben*, Müffling continues with a blatant lie to shield the image of the Silesian Army: "In the subsequent seven months, until its demobilization after the peace, no complaint and no discontent occurred again. Everyone served willingly under General Blücher, and the deeds performed by this army in 1813 and 1814 will sufficiently prove to posterity that it must have been animated by a rare spirit of unity and trust." Droysen, in *Yorck*, II:148, calls this comment "inaccurate."

18 Droysen, *Yorck*, II:198.

19 Quoted in Pertz and Delbrück, *Gneisenau*, III:214.

20 Quoted in Droysen, *Yorck*, II:149. According to Droysen, Gneisenau wrote this letter in early September and obviously before he had received the king's letter of 31 August stating: "General Blücher's report informed me of the part you have had in the operations of the Silesian Army and especially in the success of the attack on 26 August and the defeat of the enemy." Thanks to Blücher's praise, Frederick William awarded Gneisenau the Iron Cross, First Class. See Frederick William to Gneisenau, Teplitz, 31 August 1813, GStA PK, VI HA Rep. 92 Nl. Gneisenau, Nr. 16.

21 Gneisenau to Knesebeck, Hohlstein, 31 August 1813, in Droysen, *Yorck*, II:148–49.

22 Müffling, *Aus meinem Leben*, 73–79.

23 Gneisenau to Gibsone, Brechelshof, 26 August 1813, GStA, PK, VI HA Rep. 92 Nl. Gneisenau, Nr. 21; Gneisenau to Gaudi, Jauer, 26 August 1813, *ibid.*, Nr. 16; Pertz and Delbrück, *Gneisenau*, III:239–40; "Generalmajor von Gaudi über den Abzug der Franzosen aus Schlesien," Frankenstein, 26 August 1813, in Pflugk-Harttung, *Das Befreiungsjahr 1813*, Nr. 202, 282.

24 Gneisenau to Clausewitz, Goldberg, 28 August 1813, GStA, PK, VI HA Rep. 92 Nl. Gneisenau, Nr. 21; Blücher to Frederick William, Goldberg, 6:00 P.M., 28 August 1813, RA KrA, volym 25.

25 Army Order, Brechelshof, 9:30 P.M., 26 August 1813, in Höpfner, "Darstellung," 1844:126; see also Friederich, *Herbstfeldzug 1813*, I:316; Unger, *Blücher*, II:83.

26 Müffling calls the disposition for the 27th "impractical" and "impracticable": Müffling, *Aus meinem Leben*, 69–70.

27 During the morning just before the battle, Blücher wrote to the magistrate of Breslau requesting a loan of 150,000 thaler from the city so he could purchase cloth for better uniforms: Blücher to Kospoth, magistrate of Breslau, Jauer, 26 August 1813, Blücher, "Aus Blüchers Korrespondenz," ed. Granier, 159–60. Kospoth responded that the city was not in a position to make large loans.

28 Droysen, in *Yorck*, II:147, took these figures as well as the description of the militia being "almost all without shoes and trousers; all without coats, in the worst condition" from Hiller's comments on 1st Battalion of 14th Silesian Landwehr.

29 Gneisenau to Gibsone, Brechelshof, 26 August 1813, GStA, PK, VI HA Rep. 92 Nl. Gneisenau, Nr. 21.

30 Droysen, *Yorck*, II:150; Müffling, *Die Feldzüge*, 37.

31 Langeron, *Mémoires*, 261; Pertz and Delbrück, *Gneisenau*, III:234; Freytag-Loringhoven, *Aufklärung und Armeeführung*, 85–86; Bogdanovich, *Geschichte des Krieges*, IIa:73–75.

32 Ivan Panchulidzev, known as Panchulidzev I, and his younger brother Semyon, known as Panchulidzev II. However, it does not appear that the younger Panchulidzev participated in this engagement.

33 Blücher to Charles John, Goldberg, 6:00 P.M., 28 August 1813, RA KrA, volym 25; Müffling, *Die Feldzüge*, 38–39; Bogdanovich, *Geschichte des Krieges*, IIa:75–76; Friederich, *Herbstfeldzug 1813*, I:322; Freytag-Loringhoven, *Aufklärung und Armeeführung*, 89–90; Gneisenau, *Blücher*, 168; Lieven, *Russia Against Napoleon*, 386–87; Langeron, *Mémoires*, 261–63. In *Geschichte des Krieges*, IIa:31, Bogdanovich puts the loss of French officers lower, at seventeen including Maury.

34 The vanguard consisted of Horn's 7th Brigade, the 4th Company of the Guard Jäger Battalion, and a portion of the Reserve Cavalry: the Lithuanian Dragoons, the 5th and 10th Silesian Landwehr Cavalry Regiments, and one horse battery.

35 Horn to Yorck is in Höpfner, "Darstellung," 1844:139; see also Müffling, *Die Feldzüge*, 37; Freytag-Loringhoven, *Aufklärung und Armeeführung*, 86.

36 Pertz and Delbrück, *Gneisenau*, III:210, 235–36; Friederich, *Herbstfeldzug 1813*, I:317–18; Freytag-Loringhoven, *Aufklärung und Armeeführung*, 87.

37 Blücher to Yorck, Brechelshof, 2:00 P.M., 27 August 1813, in Höpfner, "Darstellung," 1844:139; Droysen, *Yorck*, II:150; Friederich, *Herbstfeldzug 1813*, I:319; Yorck to Blücher, Niederkrayn, 7:45 P.M., 27 August 1813, GStA PK, IV HA Rep. 15 A 324.

38 Blücher to Yorck, Eichholtz, 6:30 P.M., 27 August 1813, in Höpfner, "Darstellung," 1844:140–41; Friederich, *Herbstfeldzug 1813*, I:318–19; Freytag-Loringhoven, *Aufklärung und Armeeführung*, 88.

39 Blücher to Frederick William, Goldberg, 6:00 P.M., 28 August 1813, RA KrA, volym 25; Gneisenau to Clausewitz, Goldberg, 28 August 1813, GStA, PK, VI HA Rep. 92 Nl. Gneisenau, Nr. 21.

40 Sacken's performance certainly had nothing to do with goodwill. On the morning after the battle, he wrote to Blücher that "the victory that Your Excellency won over the enemy yesterday will find a distinguished place in our history. It has gloriously reopened the campaign. Our descendants will read with compassion how hand in hand the Allies defeated the destroyer of human peace, and they will say: that was their strength": Sacken to Blücher, Großjänowitz, 10:00 A.M., 27 August 1813, in Pertz and Delbrück, *Gneisenau*, III:235.

41 Blücher to Charles John, Goldberg, 6:00 P.M., 28 August 1813, RA KrA, volym 25; Höpfner, "Darstellung," 1844:148–49; Friederich, *Herbstfeldzug 1813*, I:320; Pertz and Delbrück, *Gneisenau*, III:236–37.

42 According to Droysen, in *Yorck*, II:152: "Both letters were written by Gneisenau, and whoever recalls the pursuit after the battle of Belle-Alliance [Waterloo] can recognize that they breathe his spirit."

43 The first letter is in Höpfner, "Darstellung," 1844:141, while the second is in Droysen, in *Yorck*, II:151–52.

44 Quoted in Pertz and Delbrück, *Gneisenau*, III:213.

45 Quoted in Unger, *Blücher*, II:84; Müffling, *Aus meinem Leben*, 70–71.

46 Quoted in Friederich, *Herbstfeldzug 1813*, I:322–23; Langeron, *Mémoires*, 263; Freytag-Loringhoven, *Aufklärung und Armeeführung*, 90.

47 Lieven, *Napoleon Against Russia*, 387; Pertz and Delbrück, *Gneisenau*, III:212; Gneisenau to Clausewitz, Goldberg, 28 August 1813, GStA, PK, VI HA Rep. 92 Nl. Gneisenau, Nr. 21.

48 Oudinot later changed course and took the direct road to Wittenberg. See Leggiere, *Napoleon and Berlin*, 160–76.

49 Blasendorff, *Blücher*, 212; Freytag-Loringhoven, *Aufklärung und Armeeführung*, 96.

50 Blücher to Langeron, Eichholtz, 28 August 1813, in Höpfner, "Darstellung," 1844:149; Varnhagen von Ense, *Blücher*, 191–92.

51 Blücher to Gaudi, Eichholtz, 28 and 29 August 1813, GStA, PK, VI HA Rep. 92 Nl. Gneisenau, Nr. 16.

52 Katzler to Blücher and Yorck in Höpfner, "Darstellung," 1844:145.

53 Katzler to Blücher in Freytag-Loringhoven, *Aufklärung und Armeeführung*, 93.

54 Horn to Yorck in Höpfner, "Darstellung," 1844:146; Freytag-Loringhoven, *Aufklärung und Armeeführung*, 93.

55 Blücher to Charles John, Goldberg, 6:00 P.M., 28 August 1813, RA KrA, volym 25; Friederich, *Herbstfeldzug 1813*, I:324–25.

56 Langeron to Blücher in Höpfner, "Darstellung," 1844:149.

57 Blücher to Frederick William, Goldberg, 6:00 P.M., 28 August 1813, RA KrA, volym 25; Droysen, *Yorck*, II:151; Friederich, *Herbstfeldzug 1813*, I:325–27; Freytag-Loringhoven, *Aufklärung und Armeeführung*, 94–99.

58 In Pertz and Delbrück, *Gneisenau*, III:241–42.

59 This account is based on Langeron, *Mémoires*, 264–65; Plotho, *Der Krieg*, II:116–17; Müffling, *Die Feldzüge*, 39–40; Vaudoncourt, *Histoire de la guerre*, 147–48; Bogdanovich, *Geschichte des Krieges*, IIa:79–80; Friederich, *Herbstfeldzug 1813*, I:332; Pertz and Delbrück, *Gneisenau*, III:240; Gneisenau, *Blücher*, 170; Six, *Dictionnaire Biographique*, II:455.

60 Freytag-Loringhoven, *Aufklärung und Armeeführung*, 100; Gneisenau to a friend, Hohlstein, 29 August 1813, in Pertz and Delbrück, *Gneisenau*, III:242–43.

61 Droysen, *Yorck*, II:154.

62 Freytag-Loringhoven, *Aufklärung und Armeeführung*, 98; Horn to Yorck, Gnadenberg, in Höpfner, "Darstellung," 1844:151; Friederich, *Herbstfeldzug 1813*, I:330.

63 Quoted in Freytag-Loringhoven, *Aufklärung und Armeeführung*, 98–99.

64 Quoted in Droysen, *Yorck*, II:154–55. After the war, Schack compiled the "Tagebuch of I Armeekorps während des Feldzuges von 1814," which for the most part is reproduced in the essay "Der Verluste der Armeen in den neueren Kriegen," 1841:143–82, 192–208, without the source being specified.

65 Freytag-Loringhoven, *Aufklärung und Armeeführung*, 99–100; Friederich, *Herbstfeldzug 1813*, I:330–31.

66 Langeron, *Mémoires*, 263.

67 Gneisenau maintained that these severe conditions did not impact morale: "The soldier went through water up to his chest; he sank in the mud; many are barefoot and their number increases. In this ravaged region is a lack of foodstuffs and the supply wagons cannot follow because of the muddy roads. Also, the evacuated villages lack wagons. Regardless, instead of complaining, the soldier bears these

hardships with joy." See Gneisenau to a friend, Hohlstein by Löwenberg, 29 August 1813, in Pertz and Delbrück, *Gneisenau*, III:242–43. Regarding the internal conditions of the Russian corps, the available sources say little, yet the Russians who were weather-beaten, hardened by the tremendous march from the Russian interior, and much more well clothed and outfitted, appeared to have better endured the exertions and privations of these days.

68 Jürgaß to Yorck in Höpfner, "Darstellung," 1844:150–51; Droysen, *Yorck*, II:152; Friederich, *Herbstfeldzug 1813*, I:328.

69 Yorck to Blücher, Leisersdorf, 29 August 1813, GStA PK, IV HA Rep. 15 A 324. Friedrich explains: "according to the conditions among the Landwehr, we must find it understandable that goodwill was not sufficient to surmount the unexpected exertions when the men were insufficiently clothed and fed. How important at that very moment good clothing is for the endurance of extraordinary hardships is proven by the circumstance that those battalions who obtained overcoats and shoes from dead or captured French soldiers fared much better." See Friederich, *Herbstfeldzug 1813*, I:328.

70 Quoted in Droysen, *Yorck*, II:153–54.

71 Yorck to Blücher, Leisersdorf, 29 August 1813, GStA PK, IV HA Rep. 15 A 324.

72 Unger, *Blücher*, II:85–86; Droysen, *Yorck*, II:154.

73 Blücher to Yorck, Hohlstein, 30 August 1813, in Höpfner, "Darstellung," 1844:154–55.

74 Yorck to Blücher, Leisersdorf, 30 August 1813, GStA PK, IV HA Rep. 15 A 324; Blücher to Yorck, Hohlstein, 31 August 1813, in Höpfner, "Darstellung," 1844:155–56; Pertz and Delbrück, *Gneisenau*, III:243–45.

75 Müffling, *Aus meinem Leben*, 71.

76 Blücher to Yorck, Hohlstein, 31 August 1813, in Höpfner, "Darstellung," 1844:155–56.

77 Souham's rearguard halted at Gnadenberg with his main body on the west bank of the Bober at Tillendorf along with XI Corps and II Cavalry Corps. In the center, Lauriston's V Corps bivouacked west of the Bober at Ottendorf while Ledru's 31st Division extended between Löwenberg and Greiffenberg. Clearing the Queis, Marchand's 39th Division reached Lauban. St.-Priest's main body reached Hirschberg, his van Spiller. Yorck's and Sacken's vanguards remained united at Schwiebendorf (Świeborowice) while the main bodies of the corps stood at Ulbersdorf and Haynau respectively. Langeron's van held Plagwitz; the main body halted at Lauterseiffen.

78 These two "regiments" comprised the 1st Brigade of Sacken's 16th Division.

79 The account of the action on 30 August is based on Bogdanovich, *Geschichte des Krieges*, IIa:81; Freytag-Loringhoven, *Aufklärung und Armeeführung*, 100–05; Friederich, *Herbstfeldzug 1813*, I:336–39.

80 Gneisenau to Münster, Hohlstein by Löwenberg, 30 August 1813, GStA, PK, VI HA Rep. 92 Nl. Gneisenau, Nr. 20b. Whether Gneisenau actually believed that only 20,000 men remained at Macdonald's disposal or he meant for such statements to be used as political capital in London matters little. The disintegration of Macdonald's army unquestionably helped erase the memory of the destruction of the Prussian army in 1806. Yet Gneisenau, a political animal, knew that Münster,

the former Hanoverian minister, enjoyed a close relationship with the British royal family. He took this opportunity to lobby for more support, mainly material aid, based on the merit of the Silesian Army: "The weather is awful, the rain incessant. The soldier spends the night in the open air, sinks in the mud, lacks shoes, and wades after the enemy in swollen waters up to his chest. He goes without food because the abandoned villages contain nothing edible. Due to the lack of wagons, nothing can be delivered. Often, he is barefoot and wades through the muck. Most of the militia have only linen trousers and lack overcoats. Due to the expansion of the army from 40,000 men to 270,000 men and because of the exertions of the state, neither material nor money is available to purchase cloth. Nevertheless, the soldier does not complain, but endures with patience all these difficulties and goes joyfully and decisively against the enemy. The militia rivals the standing army. Give my regards to the prince regent and the duke of York."

81 Pertz and Delbrück, *Gneisenau*, III:247–48.
82 Blücher to Yorck, Hohlstein, 30 August 1813, in Höpfner, "Darstellung," 1844:161; Blücher to Frederick William, Hohlstein by Löwenberg, 31 August 1813, in Pertz and Delbrück, *Gneisenau*, III:251–52.
83 Nostitz, *Tagebuch*, 59; Blücher to Amalie, Hohlstein by Löwenberg, 1 September 1813, *Blüchers Briefe*, ed. Unger, 177; Bogdanovich, *Geschichte des Krieges*, IIa:81–82; Freytag-Loringhoven, *Aufklärung und Armeeführung*, 106–07.
84 Blücher to Gaudi, Hohlstein by Löwenberg, 31 August 1813, GStA, PK, VI HA Rep. 92 Nl. Gneisenau, Nr. 16: "The enemy could win advantages against the Grand [Bohemian] Army, wanting to make himself master of Bohemia, concentrate against our Silesian Army with superior forces, endeavor to defeat us, and then seek to win additional passages into Bohemia. This is the case we must keep in mind."
85 Blücher to Schwarzenberg, Hohlstein by Löwenberg, 2 September 1813, Add MSS, 20112, 5.
86 Sacken to Blücher, Paritz, 7:00 A.M., 3:00 P.M., and 8:30 P.M., 1 September 1813, in Höpfner, "Darstellung," 1844:165–66; Droysen, *Yorck*, II:160; Freytag-Loringhoven, *Aufklärung und Armeeführung*, 106–08.
87 Blücher to Neipperg, Hohlstein by Löwenberg, 31 August 1813, Österreichisches Staatsarchiv Kriegsarchiv (hereafter ÖStA KA), FA 1530, 66a; Friederich, *Herbstfeldzug 1813*, I:338–41.
88 Order of the Day, Hohlstein by Löwenberg, 1 September 1813, in Höpfner, "Darstellung," 1844:168.
89 Blücher to Amalie, Hohlstein by Löwenberg, 1 September 1813, *Blüchers Briefe*, ed. Unger, 176; GStA PK, VI HA Rep. 92 Nl. Gneisenau, Nr. 108; Höpfner, "Darstellung," 1844:169–70. The loss of 12,925 men from I Corps is broken down as follows: 11,132 infantry; 1,617 cavalry; 192 gunners; and 14 pioneers. Of the 12,955, the Landwehr accounted for 7,092. The Prussian General Staff estimated that 5,000 of the 12,955 had been lost prior to the Katzbach, 874 during the battle itself, 354 during the engagement at Bunzlau, and the rest during the pursuit to the Neiße. Of the 25,296 men still under arms, 18,785 served with the infantry; 4,101 cavalry; 1,755 artillery, and 135 pioneers. Sacken's corps lost 575 men at the Katzbach. Of Sacken's remaining 15,119 men, 7,454 were infantry; 6,700 cavalry,

and 965 gunners. Langeron reported a loss of 1,400 men at the Katzbach but this number appears too low. His remaining 28,340 men are broken down thus: 19,769 infantry; 5,789 cavalry; and 2,782 artillery and pioneers. St.-Priest commenced the campaign with 13,586 men but received one cavalry regiment numbering 500 troopers. Thus, his losses in August amount to some 856 men.

90 Gneisenau to Münster, Bautzen, 18 September 1813, GStA PK, VI HA Rep. 92 Nl. Gneisenau, Nr. 20b.

91 Gneisenau to Maria von Clausewitz, 7 October 1813, GStA PK, VI HA Rep. 92 Nl. Gneisenau, Nr. 21.

92 Müffling, *Die Feldzüge*, 40–41.

93 Freytag-Loringhoven, *Aufklärung und Armeeführung*, 125.

94 Müffling, *Aus meinem Leben*, 71–73.

8

"Nothing more remains than to have them shot dead"

The triumphant proclamation Blücher issued to the troops on 1 September masked the anxiety of Silesian Army Headquarters, which only increased on the 2nd. On this day, Blücher received Barclay's letter from Altenberg dated the 29th, which reported the failed attempt on Dresden and the advance of Vandamme's I Corps from Königstein around the right flank of the Bohemian Army. In response, Schwarzenberg decided to retreat over the Erzgebirge and back into Bohemia. Still, the Allies held all the mountain passes and Barclay predicted Schwarzenberg would advance again soon. He added that the Prussian troops had distinguished themselves through discipline and courage. Later that day, Major Wenzel Liechtenstein arrived from Schwarzenberg's headquarters to present a verbal report based on extensive instructions from the Austrian staff. Not only did Liechtenstein provide news of the battle of Dresden, but he also requested that Blücher march to Bohemia with 50,000 men to reinforce the main army. The Austrian major also delivered Gneisenau a letter from Neipperg at Liebenau urging him to support Schwarzenberg's request. "In the name of the good cause," wrote Neipperg, "please do what is possible. By doing this, you will only bring more military renown to your glorious army."[1]

As noted, the Bohemian Army had moved across the Saxon frontier on 22 August, storming the imperial camp at Pirna on the 23rd. As the Silesian Army engaged the Army of the Bober on the 26th, Schwarzenberg assailed Dresden. However, the three days Schwarzenberg used to cover the twelve miles that separated Pirna from Dresden cost him dearly. Although not present, Langeron provides interesting commentary:

> While Napoleon arrived to attack us at Löwenberg, the main army of the sovereigns moved on Dresden. By moving against the Army of Silesia with the majority of his forces and leaving only a small contingent at Dresden,

Napoleon appeared to count more on slowness – always justified regarding the Austrians – than on a real calculation based on the rules of the military art. According to these rules, he should have lost Dresden. Encircled by our armies, deprived of his base, deprived of his lines of operation, and cut off from his reserves, he should have been destroyed.

The plan to liberate Dresden adopted by the chiefs of the main Allied army was perfectly conceived and would have unfailingly succeeded had its execution corresponded to the dispositions; but Schwarzenberg and his quacks totally ignored the great principle of war that a moment can never be lost, or to put off until tomorrow what can be done today. Had Schwarzenberg pushed his attacks on the same day that he appeared before Dresden, even if he had pushed them vigorously the next morning, undoubtedly Marshal St.-Cyr would have been forced to surrender or evacuate the Saxon capital by the Dresden bridge, but Schwarzenberg wanted to wait ... It is due to their incurable slowness that the Austrians always suffered reverses, because their troops (especially the Hungarians) are very brave, their officers instructed and susceptible to serve well, although they are too pedantic and too attached to old principles ... They provided time for Napoleon to arrive and completely change the situation.[2]

Thus, Napoleon arrived with the Guard to repel Schwarzenberg's assault. During the night of 26/27 August, the French II and VI Corps came up, increasing Napoleon's combatants to 135,000 men against 215,000 Allied soldiers. Continuing the battle on the 27th, Napoleon enveloped Schwarzenberg's left, crushing two Austrian corps. With Vandamme's I Corps steadily working around his right, Schwarzenberg ordered the retreat. The Army of Bohemia withdrew after losing 38,000 killed, wounded, and missing along with 40 guns. Although the imperials sustained far fewer casualties in comparison (10,000), decisive victory again eluded Napoleon. Illness forced the emperor to leave the field rather than personally coordinate the pursuit. Vandamme's I Corps followed by XIV and VI Corps closed on Schwarzenberg's demoralized army.

Allied Headquarters feared Napoleon would invade Bohemia along the left bank of the Elbe. Planning to take a position on the right bank of the Eger in the region of Budin or Laun (Louny), Schwarzenberg sought substantial reinforcements to stop the French emperor. Thus, he petitioned Blücher on 30 August to personally hurry to aid him by leading the majority of the Silesian Army, at least 50,000 men, through Theresienstadt (Terezín), while 5,000–6,000 of Blücher's Cossacks should be sent across the Elbe to operate against the enemy's communications in Saxony. Schwarzenberg stipulated that the rest of the Silesian Army should unite with the Austrian 2nd Light Division and take a position around Zittau. He also expressed hope that Bernadotte's Army of North Germany had already crossed the Elbe and would close on the rear of the Grande Armée as it penetrated

Bohemia.[3] Although flawed, the logic behind Schwarzenberg's request is clear: thinking that his own advance on Dresden had compelled Napoleon to concentrate the majority of his forces at the Saxon capital, Schwarzenberg incorrectly assumed that nothing stood in Blücher's path. Second, he supposed that Napoleon would ignore the Silesian Army in order to pursue the Bohemian Army with all of his forces. His being wrong on both accounts made it impossible for Blücher to comply with Schwarzenberg's request even if he had desired to do so.

Before examining and assessing the evasive yet insightful response the Prussians made to Schwarzenberg, it is useful to scrutinize a letter drafted by Gneisenau to Bennigsen, the commander of the Army of Poland. Arriving almost simultaneously with Liechtenstein, a Russian orderly delivered a communiqué from Bennigsen stating that he would reach Breslau on 31 August with his left wing: General Dmitry Dokhturov's corps of 26,000 men. His right wing, Pyotr Tolstoy's corps of 16,000 men, standing only one march from the Silesian frontier, would observe Glogau on the right bank of the Oder and maintain communication with Bernadotte. Bennigsen planned to remain at the Silesian capital until an evaluation of the situation determined where he should direct his force.[4] Schwarzenberg's letter prompted Blücher's response to Bennigsen's dispatch; its contents reveal how the Prussians planned to handle Schwarzenberg:

> Just now the imperial Austrian major, Prince Liechtenstein, arrived with instructions for me in the name of Field-Marshal Prince Schwarzenberg; I have the honor of sending you a copy. Because it is known to me that His Majesty Tsar Alexander commands the Allied armies and up to now I have received my operational orders only from him, I believe that on these grounds I do not have to implicitly obey the request of Prince Schwarzenberg. I will especially refuse to obey it because this request is based solely on an assumption, mainly on the concern that the emperor Napoleon will pursue the Bohemian Army into Bohemia with his main force. Yet, it can just as likely be his intention – as he has already done on 21 August at Löwenberg – to suddenly turn against me with the majority of his forces, defeat me, and win all the debouches from Silesia into Bohemia. Thus, I consider it absolutely necessary to keep my army together until the enemy's movements remove all doubt over his intentions. However, in case Prince Schwarzenberg's assumption comes true, I want to satisfy his immediate desire and so I request that you issue orders to General [Yevgeny] Markov, whom you stated you would send to me, so I can send Langeron's corps to join the army in Bohemia. Furthermore, I see myself induced to urgently and insistently request that if the emperor Napoleon actually pursues the army in Bohemia with his main force that you will unite with me in a joint offensive operation against the Elbe, which ... will be of decisive service for the good cause.[5]

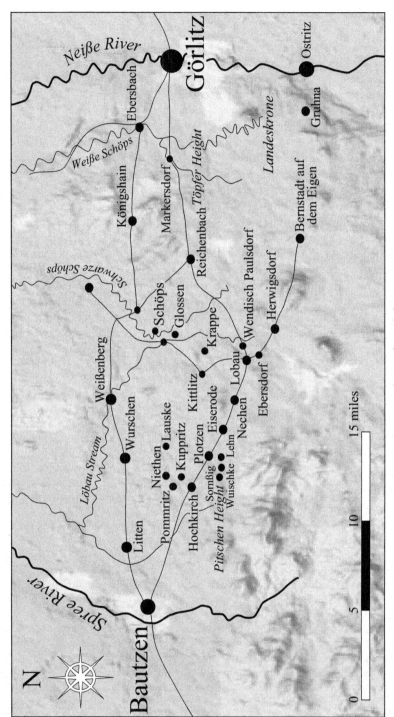

18. Region between the Neiße and the Spree Rivers

In this letter to Bennigsen, four points clearly emerge. First, Blücher would accept direct orders only from Alexander. Second, he did not agree with Schwarzenberg's assumption that Napoleon would pursue the main army into Bohemia. Third, he wished to rid himself of Langeron by transferring his corps to the Bohemian Army in return for Markov's corps from the Army of Poland.[6] Fourth, Blücher wanted to drive to the Elbe in unison with Bennigsen.[7]

Keeping these intentions in mind, let us look at his response to Schwarzenberg. "In your desire for me to detach 50,000 men from my army corps," stated Blücher, "Your Excellency assumes that the French emperor will follow the Allied army into Bohemia with his main force." Reminding Schwarzenberg that this scenario "is still not certain," Blücher speculated that "an offensive movement by my army to the Elbe on indirect roads may perhaps be a more effective response than a straight march of 50,000 men to Bohemia, a number that will hardly increase the actual strength of the Allied army in Bohemia compared to the strategic and morale advantages of keeping my army together and having it make an offensive movement to the Elbe." He then stated his main concern: "We also can foresee the case that the French emperor will once again unite his main force against us here to defeat us or at least to drive us back and through this win the passage from Silesia to Bohemia and reach the Allied rear. In this case it is undoubtedly better to maintain the local [Silesian] army in an imposing condition instead of dismembering it and sending it where it will not be much help."

The letter continued by stressing that "much hard fighting" had reduced the Silesian Army to fewer than 70,000 men. By detaching 50,000 soldiers, "the existence of an army here would disappear." Blücher then emphasized two advantages of preserving the Silesian Army. First, it offered the only direct protection for Silesia if the French emperor decided to invade the province. Second, it offered "the advantage of an offensive movement to the Elbe if he should pursue the Allied army into Bohemia." Staying with his pet project, Blücher assured Schwarzenberg that a march to the Elbe would place him "in position to unite with the crown prince of Sweden," who otherwise "would be difficult to convince to advance toward the Elbe." He also informed Schwarzenberg of his plans to withdraw to the entrenched camp near Frankenstein if Napoleon advanced against the Silesian Army: "As soon as I learned yesterday of the disaster of the Allied army, I immediately instructed my quartermaster-general to entrench the strong position at Frankenstein and provide it with heavy caliber guns. I will move into this position if I am pressed by superior forces and there I will accept a battle if attacked by a large superiority." Blücher assured the Allied generalissimo that he would immediately write to Bennigsen. "Because he has promised to help me, I will ask him to move General Markov closer to me. If this happens, a portion of my Russian troops can move to you, although here I must again repeat that an offensive movement toward the Elbe from my position will be far more certain to free the Allied army in Bohemia than a flank march by a part of my army through the mountains and defiles."

Blücher concluded with a plea for Schwarzenberg to act sensibly: "a psychological reason supports my opinion, mainly that it is not good to separate a victorious army, where the troops have mutual trust in each other and with whom the memory of their victory is still fresh." If this logic failed to sway the Austrian, then Gneisenau designed the last sentence to send a message: "From Tsar Alexander and the king, my master, I have heard nothing." This is an example of Gneisenau's "diplomatic acuteness," employed to emphasize "that an order as decisive as the directive to march to Bohemia and thus abolish all the decisions made at Trachenberg and Reichenbach had to be communicated at least by one of the monarchs of Russia or Prussia." In the end, this last line clearly implied that the commander of the Silesian Army would comply with a direct order from Alexander or Frederick William only and not the Allied commander in chief.[8]

Fortunately for the Prussians, an unexpected victory near the town of Kulm (Chlumec) in northern Bohemia on 30 August helped make Schwarzenberg's request superfluous. On the 29th, Vandamme caught Russian general Aleksandr Osterman-Tolstoy's ad hoc army corps just inside the Bohemian frontier at Kulm, thirty-five miles south of Dresden.[9] Neither side gained an advantage despite savage fighting. With the battle continuing on the 30th, Kleist's Prussian II Corps marched east to Nollendorf (Nakléřov), six miles north-north-east of Vandamme's position. While the Prussians attacked the rear of Vandamme's I Corps, the Russian Guard pushed against its front and an Austrian corps enveloped its left. With XIV and VI Corps too distant to support, Vandamme attempted to drive through the Prussians but failed. Imperial losses on 29 and 30 August amounted to 25,000 killed, wounded, and captured along with 82 guns; Allied casualties numbered 11,000 men. We return to Langeron's commentary:

> A few of his [Napoleon's] victories have been highly vaunted, and they well deserve to be: Marengo, Austerlitz, Jena, Ratisbon, Friedland, and some ten battles in Italy were greatly appreciated by the men of the military arts, but less has been said of Dresden, which I regard as one of his greatest victories. Encircled and outnumbered by a force double the size of his own, confined in a tightly packed city, he struck from all sides, overthrew the masses that opposed him, cut off the left wing of his enemy and took it all prisoner, smashed its center and right and pushed them back into the gorges and mountains where everything was an obstacle and a danger for them: he had foreseen this victory, designating the place where he would drive back his enemy; he detached Vandamme to guard the outlets, and by that he should

have destroyed all of the Coalition's equipment and precluded the flight of the Allies across the narrow, mountainous road that was bordered by precipices, where the men were isolated and dispersed. The failures of Vandamme and the heroic resistance of the Russians, especially the Guard, saved our armies and our cause.[10]

By refusing Schwarzenberg's 29 August request to march to Bohemia with 50,000 men, Blücher has been accused of letting pride cloud his judgment. While his character, temper, and past behavior suggest that he sought only to preserve his independence of command and avoid being directly subordinated to Schwarzenberg, the reasons for the snub were military rather than personal. Certainly human nature and egotistical interests cannot be entirely dismissed but Blücher wanted to maintain the independence of his army because he and Gneisenau foresaw the ruinous consequences of a union with the Bohemian Army. They knew enough about the Austrians to suspect that they would paralyze the offensive spirit that the Prussian leadership of the Silesian Army had labored to instill in its officers and men. Intertwined with the great mass of the Bohemian Army and subordinated to the hydra formed by the combined staffs of the monarchs, Schwarzenberg, and Barclay, they instinctively recognized that their ability to wage a war of revenge to defeat the French would be impossible. By 9 September, Gneisenau had heard enough about the battle of Dresden to reach the following conclusion: "At Dresden on 26 and 27 August, our arms suffered a defeat more through misunderstanding or lack of agreement than through the superiority of enemy arms."[11] Of course, hindsight allows us to use the results Blücher achieved during the war to justify his refusal. Yet these results would not have occurred had he and Gneisenau lacked the foresight in September 1813 to resist Schwarzenberg's cries for help.

Schwarzenberg's request also violated the tenets of the Reichenbach Plan. According to the plan, if Napoleon launched a major offensive into Bohemia, Schwarzenberg would simply withdraw behind the Eger River and all the way to Prague if necessary. Thus, the Army of Bohemia would yield as much ground as possible until the advance of the Silesian and North German Armies against the rear and flank of Napoleon's army forced him to break off his pursuit. In Schwarzenberg's defense, hopelessness pervaded Grand Allied Headquarters in the wake of the mauling the Bohemian Army had suffered at Dresden. Had Napoleon actually advanced into Bohemia with his entire army, the results could have been colossal. Thus, for good reason, and not for the last time, Schwarzenberg viewed Blücher's army as his only means of salvation. Yet the union of the Bohemian and Silesian Armies would have created a mass of more than 300,000 men. Schwarzenberg would not have had the luxury of squatting on the foothills of the Erzgebirge for an extended period before supply shortages and disease ravaged his ranks.[12] Thus, he would have been obliged to advance into Saxony, where Napoleon would have displayed his operational mastery. It is highly unlikely that the combined Silesian and Bohemian Armies would have succeeded in forcing Napoleon to accept battle around Chemnitz or at Leipzig on Schwarzenberg's terms.

Although a request and not a direct order, Blücher's refusal certainly bordered on insubordination in view of Schwarzenberg's position as Allied commander in chief. Blücher's rejection of Schwarzenberg's request did jeopardize the Bohemian Army and thus the Sixth Coalition itself. Although correct in their assumption that Napoleon would not advance into Bohemia, neither Blücher nor Gneisenau could predict the emperor's next move with absolute certainty. Conversely, while they again correctly assumed he would return to Silesia, the probability of such an operation remained no greater than his pursuit of Schwarzenberg's army. Finally, while Blücher's contention that his army had to remain in Silesia to protect the province probably resonated with those at Allied Headquarters still entrenched in eighteenth-century principles, it hardly related to Napoleonic warfare. Guarding Silesia would become unnecessary as soon as the Silesian Army departed for Bohemia because Napoleon ultimately would target the army and not the province. Macdonald's army – defeated, demoralized, and exhausted – could be held in check by 30,000 men. By refusing Schwarzenberg's appeal, Blücher was clearly gambling with the future of the Coalition. Regardless, Schwarzenberg's request and Blücher's response, news of which quickly circulated throughout Allied Headquarters and became known to Frederick William, eventually earned the Prussians an apology. Per Schwarzenberg's 4 September request, General Karl George von Hake, the Prussian attaché assigned to Austrian Headquarters, sought Blücher's pardon for an appeal made under extreme duress. He also conveyed "expressions of the utmost admiration from Schwarzenberg."[13]

After dispatching the letters to Allied Headquarters and Bennigsen on 2 September, Blücher left Löwenberg for Lauban. After granting the main bodies of his three corps a day of rest on 1 September, Blücher ordered the army to cross the Queis and proceed to Görlitz on the 2nd. Langeron's corps struck the Lauban–Görlitz highway, Sacken's remained on the great east–west highway, and in the middle Yorck's corps proceeded west from Naumburg. Blücher ordered the pontoon train to march in front of the Prussians so a bridge could be thrown across the Neiße as quickly as possible. If Macdonald placed a strong rearguard west of Görlitz, the columns would halt at the Neiße and await further orders.[14]

All three vanguards crossed the Neiße on 2 September. Finding Görlitz free of imperial forces, Katzler led Yorck's vanguard across the river by way of a ford and a quickly built trestle bridge. Followed by the vanguards of both Russian corps, the Prussians occupied Görlitz. Blücher instructed them to continue to Hochkirch, some twenty miles west of Görlitz and less than seven miles east of Bautzen. All three corps commanders established their headquarters at Görlitz, where Blücher and his staff also passed the night. Eight miles due south of Görlitz, St.-Priest reached Radmeritz (Radomierzyce). Fifteen miles southwest of Radmeritz, Poniatowski's VIII Corps evacuated Zittau, which the Austrian 2nd Light Division promptly occupied. Allied patrols reported that the imperials had formed two columns at Reichenbach. By the evening of the 2nd, the northern column stood echeloned between Bautzen and Wurschen while the southern column extended between Bautzen and Hochkirch. Poniatowski withdrew just inside the Austrian frontier to Schluckenau, posting a rearguard at Rumburg.[15]

Blücher prepared to either continue the pursuit of Macdonald or revert to the defensive should Napoleon assail the Silesian Army. On the 2nd, Gneisenau drafted general orders for 3 September. "After a failed attempt on Dresden," stated Blücher's cover letter, "the Grand Bohemian Army has withdrawn to Bohemia and it is still completely uncertain whether the enemy will pursue it with all of his forces or direct them against the Silesian Army. Thus, I must proceed with caution yet make the enemy believe that we are pursuing him with all energy and attack so that he will be forced to direct a portion of his forces against us and to disengage from the Bohemian Army. Enclosed is a disposition through which I hope to achieve this goal and which will be communicated to the commanders of the vanguards and St.-Priest."

According to the disposition, Blücher finally complied with a request from Yorck to form an "advance guard corps" by uniting the vanguards of all three army corps. After the Katzbach, the Silesian Army faced a much smaller, demoralized army that was marching on two roads from Görlitz to Bautzen along a narrow front. These very different circumstances that confronted the Silesian Army allowed for the formation of the advance guard corps that would separate Blücher's main body from the French, allowing it more rest and more room to maneuver without losing contact with imperial forces. Consisting of the 18,000 men belonging to the combined vanguards of Sacken, Yorck, and Langeron with the addition of a mass of horse artillery, the vanguard corps would be under the direct orders of the commander in chief. Its commander would report directly to Blücher. Command went to the most senior general officer: General-Lieutenant Vasilchikov. He received the task of constantly maintaining contact with the French. In addition, the *Streifkorps* would continue to operate on the flanks and rear of the enemy to obstruct imperial communications. The main body of the Silesian Army, including Army Headquarters, would follow the vanguard at a distance of one day's march, standing ready to take in Vasilchikov should he be driven back. With this constant pressure, Blücher and Gneisenau hoped to distract Napoleon from his pursuit of the Bohemian

Army. "This advance corps," stated Blücher, "will remain on the enemy and always seek to disrupt his march with horse artillery; if the enemy unlimbers artillery, he must immediately be attacked by our superior numbers. The advance corps will take pains to determine the strength of the enemy, his positions, and his movements, and immediately report them to me." For 3 September, Vasilchikov received orders to march on Bautzen in unison with St.-Priest and Bubna, who had resumed command of the Austrian 2nd Light Division. Meanwhile, Blücher's three army corps would take positions west of Görlitz. Gneisenau directed Langeron's corps, which still formed the army's left wing, to the Landskrone, with the great east–west highway separating it from Yorck's corps in the center. In addition, Langeron had to throw a bridge across the Neiße downstream of Görlitz. Sacken's corps would remain on the right wing.[16]

Early on the morning of the 3rd, Vasilchikov assumed command of the vanguard corps. Placing all Russian cavalry on the right wing, the Allied infantry in the middle, and all Prussian cavalry on his left, he prepared to pursue Macdonald's army on the road to Bautzen. Vasilchikov did not go far before his Prussian scouts reported a French rearguard entrenched at Hoch-kirch. The Russian commander opted to postpone the attack until the following day. He moved into positions along the Weißenberg–Löbau road that ran perpendicular to the east–west highway. East of the vanguard, the main body of the Silesian Army marched around 7:00 A.M., crossed the Neiße on pontoon and trestle bridges, and camped along the Ebersbach–Landskrone line that evening. St.-Priest's small corps and Bubna's division maintained their positions but their cavalry raided north toward Reich-enbach and south toward Rumburg. The Russo-Prussian *Streifkorps* turned the left wing of Macdonald's army. At Wurschen, behind the imper-ials, Madatov's forces surprised an ammunition column on the Bischofswerda–Bautzen road, taking 500 men prisoner, blowing 100 cais-sons, and pilfering numerous horses. Falkenhausen scattered an imperial detachment between Görlitz and Bautzen, capturing one gun.[17]

A communiqué from Barclay's headquarters at Teplitz reached Görlitz announcing the victory over Vandamme's I Corps at Kulm. Barclay con-cluded his letter with the news that Allied "parties raid as far as Pirna and Königstein, and Marmont, who attempted to drive through Altenberg, is now being pursued by Wittgenstein. In a few days we will follow and operate with energy against the enemy."[18] This news confirmed Blücher's assumption that Napoleon would not pursue Schwarzenberg into Bohemia. Yet Barclay did not provide any insight into Napoleon's next move. Of the Silesian and North German Armies, undoubtedly the former posed the greater threat to the emperor. Thus, just as they expected, the Prussians had to prepare for another offensive by Napoleon himself. That night, Blücher informed Frederick William of his inability to issue further orders until he ascertained Napoleon's intentions. Apparently, he had received instructions from the king to move his left wing closer to the Bohemian Army. He assured his monarch that he would comply with these instructions and remain in close communication with Schwarzenberg, "especially because the army of the crown prince of Sweden is still too far back for me to link with it in any effective way." Moreover, he declared that should the enemy "throw himself on the Silesian Army, I will avoid a battle against superior forces, but hold him up as long as possible through chicanery to give the Bohemian Army time to begin its operations."[19]

Aside from Napoleon's victory at Dresden, the first two weeks of the Fall Campaign proved devastating for imperial arms. Macdonald and Oudinot failed miserably as army commanders. Many historical accounts claim that Macdonald's army collapsed in the days following the battle of the Katzbach. This is incorrect. As we will see, the Army of the Bober resumed offensive operations on the 4th at the mere rumor of the emperor's arrival. An army that has collapsed simply cannot go from the defensive to the offensive at the flip of a switch. Nevertheless, Macdonald had lost 30,000 men since the expiration of the armistice. In terms of materiel, the Army of the Bober had likewise suffered staggering losses: 103 guns could not be replaced overnight. As for Oudinot, the marshal let his minor defeat at Großbeeren on 23 August drive his Army of Berlin (IV, VII, and XII Corps and III Cavalry Corps) completely from the theater of war. Unmolested by the Army of North Germany, Oudinot conducted a headlong retreat to the safety of Wittenberg's guns. In so doing, he exposed General Jean-Baptiste Girard's division as it moved up from Magdeburg to support him. On 27 August, a brigade of mostly Landwehr from Tauentzien's IV Corps destroyed Girard's force at Hagelberg.[20] Three days later came Vandamme's disaster at Kulm.

In addition to the loss of men, materiel, and morale, Napoleon's strategic situation had worsened considerably. Allied *Streifkorps* tore at his communications, shortages of all kinds had already taken a toll on the army, and the master had failed to maneuver one of the enemy armies into a decisive battle. Moreover, Oudinot's demoralized army stood where it started the campaign, while Macdonald's army had been driven from Silesia. Napoleon thrived on adversity and made a sport of exploiting his adversary's mistakes. Rather than taking advantage of his enemy's missteps, he now had to contend with his subordinates' blunders, which had devastating effects on his strategy. On 28 August, the day after the battle of Dresden, Napoleon left the pursuit of Schwarzenberg to his marshals and returned to the Saxon capital to contemplate his next move. No sufficient answer exists to explain why he left the army on the 28th. Two days later, in an extensive essay simply titled "Note sur la situation générale de mes affaires," Napoleon decided against converting the pursuit of Schwarzenberg into a full-scale invasion of Bohemia.

Instead of an operation against Prague, he returned to his pet project: taking Berlin, relieving Stettin and Küstrin, and moving the theater of war to the lower Oder. "By marching on Berlin, I will immediately attain great results," predicted the emperor. In part, he envisioned Oudinot's army at Berlin and Davout's XIII Corps at Stettin. Yet two requirements had to be met in order for him to personally implement the master plan. First, with I, II, VI, and XIV Corps and I Cavalry Corps, Murat had to be able to defend Dresden along both banks of the Elbe by containing Schwarzenberg for at least two weeks. Second, Macdonald had to hold the Queis against Blücher. Having thus secured his communications, Napoleon and the Guard could join the Army of Berlin and march on the Prussian capital.[21]

Within thirty-six hours, events unfolded that impacted Napoleon's timetable as well as his ability to personally execute the master plan. While Vandamme's mauling at Kulm would appear to be the culprit, his defeat simply marked the end of the pursuit of Schwarzenberg's army. Although a devastating blow, its strategic impact was minimal because Napoleon had already decided against invading Bohemia. Instead, Macdonald's retreat proved much more detrimental to Napoleon's plans. On 1 September, the emperor learned that the Army of the Bober had abandoned the line of the Queis in the face of Blücher's pursuit. With Macdonald now at Görlitz on the Neiße, Napoleon feared the marshal would continue his retreat. He informed Murat that, should Macdonald continue his retrograde movement, "it will be necessary for me to march to reestablish my affairs there." Above all, he could not let Macdonald retreat west of Bautzen.

Berthier cut orders for Macdonald to hold his position at Görlitz. To discourage him from retreating to Bautzen, Napoleon instructed the major-general to write that "the area around Bautzen is quite ruined." Suspecting Macdonald would not heed these orders, Napoleon assumed the Army of the Bober would reach Bautzen on 3 September. Should this be the case, he resolved to go there himself. Thus, he had to postpone taking personal leadership of the Berlin offensive. Moreover, not knowing the exact condition of Macdonald's army or Blücher's proximity, Napoleon wanted a substantial reserve available to take in the Army of the Bober. For this reason, he summoned the Young Guard, VI Corps, and I Cavalry Corps from the Bohemian frontier to Dresden. To monitor the passes into Bohemia in Dresden's vicinity, Napoleon placed St.-Cyr's XIV Corps at Pirna and Victor's II Corps at Freiberg.[22]

In addition, Ney departed to replace the incompetent Oudinot as commander of the Army of Berlin. Two letters from Berthier on 2 September explain the purpose of Ney's mission as well as Napoleon's commitment to the master plan. According to the first, Napoleon wanted Ney to assume command of the army, which he believed stood at Jüterbog, twenty-five miles northeast of Wittenberg and forty-five miles south of Berlin. The news that Bernadotte had sent considerable reinforcements from the Berlin sector to support Wallmoden on the lower Elbe against Davout is the only justification cited by Berthier for the change in command. "You know how important it is that the prince d'Eckmühl [Davout] can continue his movement to relieve Stettin," concluded the major-general. According to his instructions, Ney should have the army marching toward the Prussian capital by 4 September. "His Majesty will be on the right bank of the Elbe and take an intermediate position between Berlin and Görlitz, not too far from Dresden."[23] While Berthier did not reveal what Napoleon planned to do from this intermediate position, we can assume he intended to proceed to Berlin.

In the second missive to Ney, which can be traced to a letter from Napoleon to Berthier earlier that day, the emperor further developed his thoughts and demanded a speedier implementation of the master plan. Apparently, after writing the first dispatch to Ney, Berthier received Oudinot's report on his retreat to Wittenberg. Incensed, Napoleon declared that Oudinot's movement had ultimately allowed "Tauentzien's corps and a strong party of Cossacks to move on Luckau and Bautzen and harass Macdonald's communications."[24] Napoleon recognized that this development would do little to halt Macdonald's retrograde movement. To fill the gap between Oudinot and Macdonald, secure the latter's communications, and place himself in a position to lead the Berlin offensive, Napoleon selected Luckau as the "intermediate position between Berlin and Görlitz, not too far from Dresden." "The emperor instructed me to inform you that everything here is preparing to move to Hoyerswerda," Berthier explained to Ney, "where His Majesty will have his headquarters on the 4th. Thus, it is necessary for you to start your march on the 4th so that you are at Baruth on the 6th" (see Map 1).

Napoleon planned to have one corps at Luckau on the 6th to establish contact with Ney's army. After securing this communication, he wanted the marshal to continue the march on Berlin and assail the Prussian capital on 9 or 10 September. Referring to the Army of North Germany as "all this cloud of Cossacks and pack of bad Landwehr," he predicted that Bernadotte's forces would flee before Ney as long as his army proceeded forcefully. Berthier reiterated Napoleon's admonition: "You know well the necessity of maneuvering rapidly to take advantage of the disarray of the Grand Bohemian Army, which will make its movements as soon as it notices those of the emperor." Berthier then issued orders for the Guard and II Cavalry Corps to march to Stolpen on 3 September and from there to Hoyerswerda.[25]

Thanks to Blücher's steady pressure on Macdonald, Napoleon canceled the march to Hoyerswerda on the 3rd. Up to this point the marshal had concealed the destitute condition of his army from Imperial Headquarters.

Only Lauriston made two appeals for assistance to Berthier, both on 31 August, but based his reasoning more on supply problems than combat-effectiveness: "This army is extremely reduced, I have almost 8,000 men and 42 guns, and 2 are out of service. We cannot replenish our ammunition; I have found that, since the 26th, [each] soldier has had only three or four cartridges. If His Majesty wants to move this army forward, it is necessary to send a new corps. Simply its march would bring back many men who have gone astray." His second missive stated: "To raise the spirit and confidence of the army, it would be necessary for His Majesty to send a corps such as the Young Guard to meet us. This march would collect a large number of fugitives. Yet no discouragement exists. The troops know they are superior to the enemy in combat, and ... I am sure of success."[26]

The further west Macdonald withdrew, the more accountable he became. After offering no resistance at the Queis and evacuating the river line against orders, he finally shed light on the condition of his army. "We have rallied 5,000 men of all arms and from all corps," stated his 1 September report to Berthier. "I intend to retrieve double this number between here and Dresden. I must have 60,000 to 70,000 men; many lack weapons and the corps lack ammunition. The enemy picks up the marauders whom no discipline can keep in the ranks where, to be frank, there is great indifference." Writing to Berthier at 5:00 A.M. on the 2nd, the marshal already knew that his retreat would persist on the 3rd: "Tomorrow our march will continue on Bautzen. We cannot reach a position soon enough where we can rest and rearm the soldiers who lack weapons and cartridges, which cannot be found anywhere in the army. They were all consumed on the days of the 21st, 23rd, and 26th and not replaced." Later on the 2nd, after receiving Napoleon's 1 September instructions to hold his position at Görlitz, the hapless marshal could no longer avoid full disclosure. Aside from requesting to be replaced as army commander, Macdonald took the low road by blaming his officers and soldiers:

> I also thought of remaining at Görlitz but I must say that the indifference of the chiefs, the indiscipline, the pillaging, and the lack of weapons and ammunition for perhaps 10,000 men are all reasons that should prompt His Majesty to move closer to his army in order to completely reorganize it and restore its morale. I resent the lack of zeal and interest that [officers have] for the service. I put all the energy and strength of character that I can into the very difficult circumstances that I find myself. I am neither supported nor imitated. I pray that you earnestly solicit from His Majesty another commander for this army and let me command XI Corps only. I will give the others an example of obedience, zeal, and dedication. In the present state of affairs, it is preferable to concentrate the army by establishing a camp where it can rest and then resume the offensive because, if it is exposed to a failure at this moment, it will completely dissolve.[27]

Believing he would leave Ney on his own only momentarily, Napoleon planned to take in the Army of the Bober, quickly demolish the Silesian Army, and then "march in great haste on Berlin."[28] Thus, Macdonald's bleeding stopped on the 3rd. On this day, the emperor ordered the Guard, VI Corps, and I Cavalry Corps to unite at Bischofswerda and proceed to Bautzen. He informed the marshal that arms and ammunition would be transported from Dresden to Bautzen on the following day. Napoleon instructed Macdonald to tightly concentrate the Army of the Bober so that the emperor could ride across its front in thirty minutes. Planning to engage Blücher on the evening of the 4th or the morning of the 5th at the latest, Napoleon passed the night of 3/4 September at Großharthau.[29] He woke early on the 4th and rode toward Bautzen. While he expected to find Macdonald's army in disarray, the extent of the army's disorder caught him by surprise. Hoards of starving, unarmed, barefooted soldiers marauded along the road. A convoy of provisions and ammunition he had sent to resupply Macdonald fell prey to Blücher's *Streifkorps*; its smoking ruins remained by the roadside. The whole scene so rocked the emperor that he lost his composure. A small dog barking incessantly at his horse earned Napoleon's ire. He drew his pistol and attempted to fire but the weapon fouled. In a fit of rage, he hurled the pistol at the animal and rode off in silence.

Around 11:00 A.M., he reached the outskirts of Bautzen, where Macdonald and his staff received him. Not Macdonald but Sébastiani became the victim of such a tongue-lashing that the emperor's staff circled around the two to conceal the undignified scene. Napoleon purportedly greeted Sébastiani with the words: "You command a mob, not soldiers." Sébastiani responded that his men had suffered much and nothing more could be demanded of them; Macdonald attempted to support him as best he could. The emperor then tore into Sébastiani's regimental commanders. After venting, Napoleon proceeded to Hochkirch from where he could see the heads of Blücher's columns. Macdonald's rearguard, which had departed from Hochkirch at 5:00 that morning, received the order to halt. After orienting himself with regard to Blücher's position, the master ordered Murat to form the left wing with III Corps and I Cavalry Corps. At noon, the king of Naples commenced his advance from Bautzen toward Görlitz on the great east–west highway. Macdonald received instructions to form the emperor's right wing with V and XI Corps, II Cavalry Corps, and the Guard. Accompanied by the emperor, Macdonald struck the Hochkirch–Löbau–Görlitz road. With VIII Corps and IV Cavalry Corps, Poniatowski marched from Zittau to Löbau to slam Blücher's left flank. General Samuel François Lhéritier's V Cavalry Corps and the remains of I Corps, now commanded by General Georges Mouton, would hold Dresden while II Corps remained at Freiberg and XIV Corps at Pirna.[30]

For the 4th, the main body of the Silesian Army continued west toward the Wurschen–Hochkirch line around 6:00 A.M. The disposition called for the army to march in three columns at 6:00 A.M. For march goals, Sacken received Wurschen, Yorck a position north of Hochkirch between Pommritz and Niethen, and Langeron Hochkirch. Blücher planned to accompany Yorck's corps and establish his headquarters at Lauske. He directed St.-Priest through Löbau to Schirgiswalde on the Spree, eight miles upstream of Bautzen. Temporarily under Blücher's command, Bubna marched through Neustadt in Sachsen toward Stolpen far southwest of Bautzen to envelop the enemy's right flank. In front of the army, Vasilchikov closed on Macdonald's rearguard. Initially, the imperials fell back slowly but then something changed. Large dust clouds could be seen rising from the plains of Bautzen moving *toward* the Army of Silesia. "All of a sudden," recounted Langeron, "the enemy, who had retired from Hochkirch and seemed to want to abandon Bautzen, reappeared in force and repulsed our advance posts and my quartermasters. I immediately went to the vanguard and I saw near Hochkirch several strong columns advancing toward us. I was able to observe that the French Guard and the cuirassiers were part of this contingent and, as the forces that deployed in front of us could be estimated at more than 50,000 men, and we could see near Bautzen dust clouds that announced other strong columns moving toward Weißenberg, I no longer doubted Napoleon had arrived from Dresden a second time to fight us with superior forces." Fortunately, a snafu at Langeron's headquarters prevented Blücher's orders from being forwarded to St.-Priest, "who would have found himself behind the enemy army's left flank, and completely cut off from us, could have suffered a total defeat or been forced to push into the Bohemian mountains."[31]

Katzler led eight squadrons of the Prussian vanguard west of Hochkirch but soon encountered imperial skirmishers. He received heavy fire from Hochkirch as well as an adjacent hill where the French unlimbered a battery of heavy mortars and numerous cannon. Ten enemy battalions moved up and drove him east. As the Jäger and fusiliers of the vanguard hurried forward, they too failed to hold the village. While Katzler attempted to contain the enemy at Hochkirch, Vasilchikov posted the left wing of his Prussian infantry on the Hochkirch–Löbau road and the right wing at the village of Kuppritz. Imperial troops continued to advance in force. From the right wing soon came the report that a considerable mass of imperial infantry likewise was advancing toward Hochkirch. To hinder the impending breakout from Hochkirch, Vasilchikov issued orders to Hiller around 8:00 A.M. to move the six battalions of Prussian infantry onto the advantageous Pitschen height and defend it to the last man. Hiller posted his battalions on both sides of the height, covered by Landwehr cavalry on the plain to the left (south). Four miles north of Hochkirch, the Russian infantry encountered fierce resistance at Wurschen. Specifically designed to perpetually and ener-getically harass the enemy, the vanguard corps managed to fight well on the defensive, holding the imperials until 3:00 P.M. At that time, the French surged from Hochkirch and blasted through the forward troops; Katzler fell back to the Pitschen hill.

Meanwhile, Blücher reached Glossen where reports streamed in not only of the French advance, but also of the arrival of Napoleon and his Guard. This seemed to confirm the numerous rumors that Napoleon had crossed the Elbe at Pirna with masses of reinforcements to support Macdonald. Cossacks apprehended an Italian courier, who claimed to have been at Imperial Headquarters earlier in the day. He reported that Napoleon had reached Bautzen at the head of the Guard. A young man from Bautzen likewise maintained that he had observed the emperor ride into Bautzen around noon. Again Blücher demonstrated that going backward could be just as valuable as going forward. Again he proved that he could control his emotions and instincts. Without hesitating, he ordered the army to retreat east of the Löbau stream, from where it would fall back to a position on the Landskrone, slightly southwest of Görlitz. Headquarters would remain at Görlitz. Blücher decided he would continue the retreat only if the enemy army drove through Reichenbach. "I will avoid a serious engagement," Blücher wrote to Barclay. "Should the enemy go through Zittau to Bohemia, I will attack him and follow to Bohemia as long as he does not leave behind too great a force against me."[32]

To cover the army's retreat, Blücher tasked Vasilchikov's corps with holding the Pitschen hill until evening. At 5:00 P.M., large imperial infantry and cavalry columns debouched from Hochkirch and formed east of the village. One hour later, they advanced in three columns on the Löbau road to attack the Pitschen height. A fourth column moved on the east–west high-way from Bautzen to Görlitz to overwhelm the Russians. "When I left the vanguard," continued Langeron, "it was 4:00 P.M.; we were very lucky that Napoleon had arrived so late. Nightfall needed to arrive soon to protect us. Without it, Vasilchikov would have found himself in a critical position. This brave and capable general, who was so well seconded by Lanskoy, Rudzevich, and Katzler, certainly could have withdrawn with honor but he needed to protect our retreat and, consequently, as he could retire only slowly, risked encirclement, and we could help him only by risking a general battle, which we had to avoid." Despite French numerical superiority, the Prussians managed to hold the Pitschen hill until Vasilchikov withdrew the Russian infantry in order. An intense engagement first to hold the Pitschen height, then to hold back the press of the enemy during the retreat, con-tinued until long after sunset. Attacking from all sides, the imperials sorely pressed the Prussian rearguard. Numerous cavalry charges were repulsed with the bayonet as the Prussians cut crosscountry due west to Krappe.

In complete darkness, the retreat continued to positions west of Glossen and the Löbau stream. Prussian losses reached 400 men on this day; Russian and French casualties are not known.[33]

Blücher's retrograde march encountered difficulties: mainly narrow gorges and poor roads blocked by baggage and supply wagons. Langeron described the conditions: "I immediately ordered my column to halt before becoming too engaged in the Löbau defiles from which we could not escape without great difficulty and losses if attacked. These passes were so narrow that a single cannon could not be turned in them and, if my column had advanced, I would still, even without being attacked, have lost precious time. Fortunately, Shcherbatov, who commanded at the head of the column, foresaw the orders that I would send him and stopped the column while the artillery was still in the plain. After that, my retreat, which I ordered soon afterward, was easy. On this occasion, I owe a great deal to Shcherbatov's resolution and foresight." Langeron failed to mention that a Russian hospital train, followed by Russian troops and baggage including a host of Cossacks, had driven right through Yorck's columns. Around 10:00 that night Yorck's corps commenced the retreat to Görlitz. The hasty nature of the retreat only magnified the chaos the collisions with the Russians had caused in I Corps. Again, many soldiers, particularly Landwehr, dropped from exhaustion and hunger. After marching for the majority of twenty-four hours, the last units reached the bivouac at the Landskrone late on the morning of the 5th. According to Schack's journal, "abominable night march; ran into Sacken's [Langeron's] Russian column at Schöps; innumerable wagons clogged the defile of Reichenbach; a halt was made behind [east of] Reichenbach until all [the wagons] were in order. The troops did not reach camp until 10:00 A.M."

"At 9:00 P.M.," explained Langeron, "Blücher warned me that Napoleon had come from Dresden with a great portion of his forces; he learned this from his spies, from deserters, and from prisoners that our advance posts had taken. At the same time, he told me that he did not wish to engage in a general battle with forces greatly superior to his own, and so he would revert to his wise system of retreat to foil the enemy's new plans, pull him once again far from Dresden, and once again make him lose precious time. We marched at 10:00 P.M. and returned to the position on the Landskrone, west of Görlitz." Ten miles further west, Vasilchikov's corps passed the night around Glossen while St.-Priest fell back to Bernstadt auf dem Eigen. Southwest of the army, Bubna's division extended between Zittau and Rumburg, too far removed to play a role in the current affair. "Since yesterday," stated Blücher in a letter to Knesebeck early on the 5th, "the emperor Napoleon has been ready to fall on me with all of his forces. As long as he has everything assembled here, he shall not tempt me to accept battle; should he turn and go to Bohemia, he shall find in me a true companion and the devil will take the hindmost ... I will not fight the entire force of our enemy and he will have to divide his forces. Thus, I will keep myself strong enough to destroy a portion. It is 6:00 A.M. and the enemy is still resting."[34]

Early on 5 September, Silesian Army Headquarters issued instructions for the troops to cook, rest, and feed the horses. Gneisenau wanted the soldiers supplied with provisions to see them through the next twenty-four hours at least. All wagons moved east across the Neiße to facilitate a further retreat if necessary. Exhausted from six weeks of hard campaigning, the soldiers of the Silesian Army no doubt welcomed the rest. Although it was a pursuit of only ninety miles, the exertions and privations encountered during the march from the Katzbach to the Spree eroded discipline and morale. After the army advanced west, its magazines followed only to the Bober. The stores received continuous replenishment from further east, but poor roads and difficult terrain prevented the supply columns from keeping pace with the army. Blücher's vanguard, pushed far to the west, suffered the most. The troops received permission to seek help from the locals but the unfortunate inhabitants of western Silesia and Upper Lusatia had little to offer. Impoverished from weeks of being sacked by the imperials, those who still cared to help a man in uniform could offer hardly anything more than potatoes. The arrival of the Cossacks only worsened their plight. Despite Blücher's threats, the Russian warriors surpassed the French in the unprecedented pillaging and mistreatment of both peasant and burgher. Prussian authorities did not manage to establish the orderly arrival of supplies from Löwenberg until mid September.[35]

While the Russians persevered, Yorck's Landwehr continued to disappear. Several militia battalions from Yorck's 1st Brigade completely dissolved during the night march of 4/5 September. To collect stragglers and round up marauders, flying columns scoured the rear areas. By the end of the month, 2,000 Landwehr remained missing and had probably deserted. Gneisenau also called on the Military Government of Silesia to issue proclamations recalling the militiamen who had returned to their homes: "The districts that harbor such deserters will be punished; the deserters themselves will be punished through harsh treatment and poor fare, and their names will be dragged through the mud. If you do not employ strict measures, I fear that the majority of the Silesian Landwehr will dissolve because aside from combat there is not enough discipline among them to hold them together; discipline can be produced mainly only through severity, and only through severity will the soldier know that returning home will not be tolerated."[36]

Incensed by the desertions, Blücher demanded that the regimental commanders report to Yorck on its causes. They claimed to have done their utmost to maintain order but the Landwehr battalions had too few officers to assist them. They accused the available company and battalion officers of being too old and too unfamiliar with regulations to be effective. Dead tired and physically drained, the soldiers fell to the ground and remained lying in the muck believing that a little sleep would restore their strength to look for potatoes and then continue the march.[37] An explanation from the brigade commander, Steinmetz, confirmed these reports:

> During a night march, when many columns cross with each other, it is not possible to keep together troops who are completely exhausted by repeated deployments in the night and by hunger, and who are suffering on their feet because their clothing is incredibly poor. The officers took great pains to maintain proper order but this was impossible because of the weakness, youth, and inexperience of the general Landwehr man and the lack of good officers opposite them. I cannot in any way guarantee that henceforth straggling will not occur because I have already taken pains to prevent this evil through punishment and very harsh punishment at that. *The battalion commanders have been punished by way of severe reprimands, several officers have been arrested, and by far the majority of the Landwehr has been demoted to second class, paraded through the ranks with their caps turned upside down, punished with hunger and blows from the cane, and nothing more remains than to have them shot dead.*[38]

As for Napoleon, after spending the night of 4/5 September at Hochkirch, he personally reconnoitered the Allied position east of the Löbau stream early on 5 September and then ordered a general advance through Löbau and Reichenbach. Expecting to encounter considerable resistance at Reichenbach, the emperor instructed Macdonald to attack the front of the assumed Allied position while Poniatowski marched northeast through Löbau to envelop the left and Murat with the northern column enveloped Blücher's right. Napoleon joined the forward cavalry but would be disappointed on this day as Blücher continued his retreat across the Neiße. Not wanting to waste any more time on Blücher – or Macdonald – the emperor hoped to finally be able to participate in the Berlin offensive. However, he received reports from St.-Cyr concerning the movement of Schwarzenberg's army. Leaving behind Murat and Macdonald with approximately 70,000 men to continue the offensive against Blücher, Napoleon returned to Bautzen that same evening with the Guard and VI Corps. He selected Bautzen because it allowed him to return to Dresden if Schwarzenberg moved on it or to march north and support Ney's operation against Berlin.[39]

To obtain a precise view of the enemy's movements and intentions, Gneisenau and Lieutenant Scharnhorst went to Reichenbach on the morning of the 5th, with Blücher and Müffling posted on the Landskrone to observe the enemy. Blücher would not give orders for the further retreat until he saw for himself large enemy columns advancing from Reichenbach. As soon as he received confirmation of the enemy's advance around 10:00 A.M.,

Gneisenau drafted a report to Allied Headquarters in Blücher's name: "The news has been confirmed that Napoleon has joined the army facing me and has reinforced it with the Guard, Poniatowski's corps, and several cavalry divisions. At this moment, I received the report that the enemy is marching toward me through Löbau and Glossen. If he remains before me in superior strength, I will avoid the decisive battle that he appears to seek. Nevertheless, I will harass his movements and exploit any advantage, especially if he should go through Zittau and Annaberg-Buchholz to Bohemia." A similar letter went to Bernadotte, whom Blücher implored to act: "The offensive movement that you seemed to want to make against the enemy's left flank is sure to hamper him quite prodigiously. It is possible that the emperor Napoleon's intention is to enter Bohemia by way of Zittau."[40]

Denying Napoleon the opportunity to envelop him, Blücher continued the retreat of his main body that again lasted late into the night. The Allies utilized three bridges to escape across the Neiße: one upstream of Görlitz, another at Görlitz, and the third downriver from the town. By evening, the main body of the Silesian Army reached the right bank of the Neiße thanks to the sacrifices of the vanguard.[41] While his cavalry remained on the right bank of the Löbau stream, Vasilchikov withdrew his infantry and artillery to Reichenbach at daybreak on the 5th. From there, his main body took a position on the Töpfer height east of the town. West of Reichenbach, the rapid advance of the imperials forced the Allies to turn and fight at 11:00 A.M. Prussian and French sources disagree over the events that followed. On the left, Katzler charged the thirteen squadrons of the 3rd Light Cavalry Division of I Cavalry Corps with sixteen Prussian squadrons led by the West Prussian Dragoons. According to the French staff officer and historian Gabriel Fabry, a French volley broke the dragoons, who fell back in disarray and prevented the approaching Prussian 1st and 2nd Hussar Squadrons from charging. At the same time, a blast of grape ripped through the Prussians. Fabry maintains that the charge of the Prussian 3rd and 4th Hussar Squadrons stabilized the situation and allowed Katzler to reorganize.[42] On the right wing, Emmanuel engaged four regiments of enemy light cavalry supported by two regiments of cuirassiers that attempted to cut off his retreat and take six guns that supported his right. After bloody hand-to-hand combat, Emmanuel repulsed the imperial horse. Langeron described the action:

> Emmanuel distinguished himself again during this sharp and unequal fight. The enemy cavalry was superior to that of our vanguard; it wanted to turn their flank, cut them off from the pass at Reichenbach, and take six pieces of cannon that Emmanuel had placed on his right. Four regiments of French light cavalry, supported by two regiments of cuirassiers, advanced to attack these cannon, but were repulsed by Emmanuel, who charged them with the

Kievskii Dragoon Regiment and Prince Nikolay Shcherbatov's[43] 2nd Ukrainskii Cossack Regiment to which was attached two squadrons of the Aleksandriiskii Hussars ... The enemy cavalry was repulsed; the engagement was long and costly for both sides; each of our squadrons attacked several times, and each time with the same audacity and success; the cannon were saved, the pass was not outflanked, and General Vasilchikov withdrew, fighting all the while to the Neiße, which he recrossed after our columns: the wooden bridge was burned and the pontoon bridges raised, despite the enemy efforts to stop it.[44]

During this cavalry combat, Vasilchikov directed two Prussian battalions to Reichenbach with orders to hold the town to their last drop of blood. He then changed his mind and started the retreat east from the Töpfer height shelled by French cannon and mortar fire. Under intense fire, the Allies experienced many difficulties retreating through the elongated village of Reichenbach. At the Landskrone, Vasilchikov again turned to face his pursuers and buy time for Blücher's main body to cross the Neiße. Vasilchikov ordered Katzler, who had already passed through Markersdorf, to turn around and again charge the imperials. Katzler and his Brandenburg Hussars could not hold the French cuirassier regiments indefinitely but they slowed the imperials long enough to allow Vasilchikov's rearguard to clear the narrow defile at Markersdorf and reorganize west of Görlitz and continue the retreat. As soon as the sound of the guns approached Görlitz, Blücher gave the order to depart. Yet because of the late arrival of Yorck's corps to its bivouac, many of the chuck wagons that had come up to distribute provisions had not returned to the rear. This caused a bottleneck as Schack noted: "The wagons became entangled in and close to the city; confusion on all sides; wagons driving through the river, many getting stuck. Disorderly retreat. The situation looked desperately dangerous and would have been if the enemy had followed."[45] Langeron provides a different perspective:

> The retreat was momentarily obstructed by a crowd of Prussian wagons, overburdened by all those foul creatures by which the Prussian army is infested; there were more than 200 women on these wagons, which should have retired long before. They let loose horrible cries and wanted to move ahead of our troops; they were forced to remain on the left bank, and when our men had passed, burned the bridge, and raised the pontoons, all these women went to charm the leisure time of the French. I only mention this event on our part to be honest, but not to suggest that it was humane yet it did great good to free our army of these miserable wretches.

According to Friederich, "poor execution of the order to move out the trains had caused a bottleneck at the bridge, which was only cleared up when old Blücher, in order to provide the troops with an example, went through the river at the head of the cavalry." Müffling of course assumed credit for resolving the situation. First, he claimed that, while on the Landskrone, he had advised Blücher of the correct moment to depart and cross "the Neiße bridges without any serious fighting, but some unnecessary delays in Yorck's corps produced a stoppage at the bridge and an engagement at a disadvantage became unavoidable, unless all the cavalry of the rearguard could cross a ford, yet they had no inclination to do so because of its depth." Refusing to listen to their officers, the huddled troopers continued to block the infantry from gaining access to the bridge. Second, Müffling maintains that, "in this quandary, I suggested to the commander in chief that he set the example. Without a moment's hesitation he plunged into the water that rose up to his saddle-bow. All the cavalry had to follow and, covered by a twelve-pound battery, we reached the right bank without losing one man. The soldier happily and willingly will follow a field commander who thus shares the hardships of the common trooper."

Soon Vasilchikov's corps reached Görlitz; Hiller's infantry covered the retreat through the town. On the eastern bank, Yorck's 2nd Brigade and Langeron's VI and X Infantry Corps formed to take in the vanguard. Imperial artillery continued to pound the retreating Allies. After crossing the river, Vasilchikov posted his rearguard along the hills on the right bank. His main body halted on a line extending from Leopoldshain, some four miles east of Görlitz, to Hermsdorf, situated upstream of Görlitz on the right bank. Further south, St.-Priest's corps probably reached Seidenberg but its vanguard remained on the left bank of the Neiße. Bubna's division withdrew to Georgenthal with its vanguard stretched along the Zittau–Rumburg line.[46]

Imperial forces followed to the Neiße. That same evening, Murat attempted to cross the bridge upstream of Görlitz with the lead elements of I Cavalry Corps packed in a tight column. Only one Prussian cavalry regiment guarded the opposite bank. To cover his crossing, Murat directed two horse batteries to open fire on the Prussians from 700 paces. After the first shots fell, half the Prussian squadrons peeled off to the right, the other half to the left, revealing a line of Russian heavy artillery. The Allied guns opened an intense bombardment that shattered the morale of the unsuspecting French. In a matter of moments, some 150 men and even more horses fell; well-aimed fire disabled two of Murat's guns. Langeron recalled: "Shcherbatov placed twelve twelve-pound guns from Nesterovsky's company on the right bank of the river; they conducted such a sharp and well-fed fire that the enemy, who had advanced to the left bank, was forced to pull back with loss, and even momentarily abandon two pieces of cannon, that we could not take, the bridges already having been razed." Such losses did not deter the king of Naples. He issued orders for one cavalry regiment to ford the river and flank the enemy guns. His subordinate generals begged him to rethink the wisdom of such bravado. They reminded Murat that during the last review the emperor had demanded that his officers manage the cavalry with greater prudence. Murat conceded, ordering his troopers to withdraw to the opposite side of Görlitz. Macdonald directed three battalions from Meunier's brigade to occupy Görlitz. Encountering no opposition, the French pushed east and occupied the suburb on the left bank of the Neiße.

By the end of the day's fighting on 5 September, Murat's vanguard stood in and around Görlitz, the main body on the Landskrone. Poniatowski's corps camped at Löbau, with its van at Ebersdorf. Thus, his forward troops passed the night along the Weißenberg–Löbau line; Murat departed and command of the Army of the Bober reverted back to Macdonald. Owing to Blücher's tenacity, Macdonald did not relish his task. Yet the marshal hoped his opponent would not learn of the emperor's departure for a few more days. For this reason, he counted on the Silesian Army continuing its retreat. To deceive Blücher into thinking that the offensive would continue, Macdonald ordered his vanguard to cross the Neiße in several small columns on 6 September; his main body remained on the Landskrone. Only Poniatowski's vanguard skirmished with Bubna's troops and St.-Priest's Cossacks. "On this day," concluded Gneisenau in his report to the king, "they [the French] showed 30,000–40,000 men between the Landskrone and Görlitz, having some detachments cross the river, yet again withdrew, whereupon Blücher had the advance corps move back to the Neiße in order to exploit the first favorable moment in case Napoleon should again disengage his main force from the Silesian Army."[47]

Obliging Macdonald, Blücher ordered the retreat to continue east of the Queis during the night of 5/6 September. Moreover, he dissolved the advance corps. Its inability to protect the army from either unnecessary engagements or night marches led to its demise after a mere three days. Unfortunately for Army Headquarters, this experiment did not yield the results it desired, such as increased flexibility for the army's main body. At the least, its creation demonstrates that Blücher and his staff recognized the need to conform to the changing conditions of war instead of remaining static. With the army now operating in an area where Blücher could disperse his corps, each again formed its own vanguard. Operations continued on the 6th with Sacken retreating across the Queis at Siegersdorf and proceeding southeast to Paritz with considerable enemy forces in view. "The French army is very strong," he reported to Blücher. "The Old and New Guard are here and many cuirassiers. Marshals Mortier and Macdonald are with them."[48] Yorck crossed at Ullersdorf and marched to Naumburg; Langeron passed the Queis at Lauban and halted; and St.-Priest remained at Seidenberg. The respective vanguards of each corps halted halfway between the Neiße and Queis, with their forward posts remaining very close to the former. "On 7 September," noted Langeron, "we withdrew to Lauban and behind the Queis; the vanguard was separated once again ... but the advance posts remained at the Neiße. Some French skirmishers crossed the river and stationed themselves several paces from our front but refrained from sticking out their necks too far. Nevertheless, the enemy was preparing materials for the construction of a bridge and even had it halfway built, thereby announcing the offensive intentions that they were far from being able to support."[49]

After two marches, the Silesian Army stood east of the Queis with headquarters at Lauban. "Here the page has again turned," Blücher explained to his wife, "the emperor Napoleon, angry about the destruction of the Army [of the Bober], is again marching against me with his main army. For two days he did everything possible to make me accept battle because he is twice as strong as me. All his maneuvers have been in vain; I will withdraw before him until he has to again go back: and then I will warmly embrace him."[50]

Meanwhile, Gneisenau received a report written by Knesebeck from Allied Headquarters at Teplitz on 3 September. Knesebeck described the battle of Kulm on the 30th as the opportunity "to avenge the stain of Dresden." Indeed, the destruction of Vandamme's I Corps had made quite an impression on Allied High Command, as Knesebeck's account demonstrates: "Thus, on the 29th, 8,000 Russian Guards under Osterman-Tolstoy fought with Vandamme's corps – which numbered 43,000 men according to the muster that was found – at Kulm like the Spartans at Thermopylae, and yielded not a foot, although they were attacked the entire day in the front and on both flanks. Thus the brave Osterman-Tolstoy lost an arm. Overall, our losses were considerable, especially by Kleist on the 30th." Kleist led his II Corps straight into the enemy's rear at Nollendorf, fighting "for three long hours [and] having to cut his way through the enemy; thus Grolman was wounded in the hip ... Kleist lost almost all his adjutants." Similar to the experience of Yorck's I Corps, the majority of Kleist's Landwehr "was scattered," causing Knesebeck to consider reassembling them in Silesia. "We would be inconsolable over these losses had the results not have been so good because of Kleist's resolve." According to the most recent figures, the Allies captured 83 guns, numerous caissons, and 10,000–12,000 prisoners as well as Vandamme himself and four other French generals.

Despite the victory at Kulm, Knesebeck explained that the fatiguing marches during the retreat from Dresden to Bohemia as well as "the great loss in baggage and draft horses has prevented us from driving back over the mountains with force." Although Kulm relieved the pressure on Schwarzenberg's army, the Allied commander in chief wanted to resupply and reorganize his army before taking another step. Attrition from combat and illness reduced the Bohemian Army by some 45,000 men. A complete collapse of the commissariat demoralized the soldiers and turned the

Das große Dankfest der drei verbündeten Monarchen zu Töplitz am 2ᵗ September 1813.

14 The three Allied monarchs at the Festival of Thanks for the victories at Großbeeren, the Katzbach, and Kulm, Teplitz, 2 September 1813

Cossacks against the local population. Yet Schwarzenberg's forces retained control of the passes through the Erzgebirge and his *Streifkorps* raided downstream the Elbe as far as Meißen and along the Saale. Knesebeck stated that the further plans and movements of the Bohemian Army "will probably be determined by the direction we see the enemy take." He informed Gneisenau of his opinion that, if Napoleon made a stand at Bautzen to confront Blücher, Schwarzenberg should reinforce Bubna with 30,000 to 50,000 men for an immediate operation against his flank. Should Napoleon concentrate all his forces west of the Elbe, Knesebeck offered a typical eighteenth-century response: "our plan must thus proceed to further divide him. We will achieve this if we attempt to cut him off from his ammunition at Erfurt, while the crown prince of Sweden does the same with Magdeburg. Because Napoleon has expended much ammunition and has lost even more, he cannot abide this and therefore this will force him to detach [forces] and through this we will find an opportunity to again defeat him in detail and to fall on one of his corps with superiority."

Although Knesebeck's views on strategy and operations belonged to the past, his take on some of the personalities at Allied Headquarters is worth citing in full at least for its comedic value. "The tsar of Russia is surrounded by many young advisors who always argue against maneuvering – others have eccentric movements in mind, like those of the Austrians in 1809. Jomini appears suspicious to me; he can offer six different suggestions in just one minute; he always puts himself in a position where it is not easy to reproach him; he seeks to increase disunity; he blames everyone else; in short, he is completely useless.[51] Schwarzenberg and Radetzky are good people but have no control over the Russians. Barclay de Tolly is inert: just as you know him to be. Thus, the situation of our overall command; but when the troops fight they make everything right through their bravery."[52]

Two days later on 5 September, Blücher's refusal to lead 50,000 men of the Silesian Army to Bohemia reached Allied Headquarters.[53] Schwarzenberg's reaction justified the moniker *"l'homme de la coalition."* In two letters addressed to Blücher that same day, the Allied commander in chief not only expressed his agreement with the Prussian's views, but also officially attached Bubna's 2nd Light Division to the Silesian Army. Schwarzenberg explained that, following the "partial check" Napoleon suffered at Kulm, the emperor had concentrated all his forces around Dresden "in order to attack with overwhelming superiority any army that offers him the greatest advantages through its situation." This circumstance required mutual support between the Bohemian and Silesian Armies. Planning his preliminary steps, Schwarzenberg informed Blücher of his intention to throw two bridges across the Elbe at Außig and repair the roads that ran from this point to Rumburg and Zittau. He also pledged to allocate between 50,000 and 60,000 troops to support the Silesian Army. The Austrian commander planned to issue explicit orders for Bennigsen to advance and support Blücher. Finally, the former Saxon general, Johann von Thielmann, received the task of harassing French lines of communication with the objective of cutting off Napoleon from the resources of his German allies. For this last point, Schwarzenberg informed Blücher that Thielmann's 3,000 men would not suffice and the Bohemian Army could spare few of its troops. Consequently, Schwarzenberg wanted Blücher to forward all of his Cossacks to Thielmann. Blücher neither responded nor forwarded his Cossacks to Thielmann. In his opinion, Schwarzenberg's memo represented an extension of the same thinking that had formulated the Reichenbach Plan. Based on this frame of mind, the Allies perpetually ceded the initiative to Napoleon; instead of acting, they reacted.[54]

Still, on 5 September, enough information reached Allied Headquarters to confirm reports that Napoleon had gone to Bautzen with his Guard. Believing this heralded an offensive against Bernadotte or Blücher, Schwarzenberg prepared a serious demonstration against Dresden. A few hours after writing his first letter to Blücher, Schwarzenberg dictated the second that warned of Napoleon's march from Dresden to Bautzen. Moreover, considerable French forces marched northeast through Pirna and Königstein toward Stolpen on the road to Bautzen. "I thus hurry to inform you of this and to notify you that I will depart immediately with 50,000 to 60,000 Austrians and debouch through Zittau by the 13th of this month. Until then, you will probably face superior forces." Bubna's division would now serve as Schwarzenberg's vanguard; the Allied generalissimo "urgently" requested that Blücher provide Bubna with news of the Silesian Army's whereabouts twice a day.[55]

While the Erzgebirge shielded Schwarzenberg's legions, the mountains also inhibited the timely flow of reports to Allied Headquarters. Intelligence generally arrived too late, thus rendering Schwarzenberg's arrangements inappropriate by the time his couriers reached their destinations. Moreover, the inertia that reigned at Allied Headquarters and in the Austrian army itself prevented the Bohemian Army from reacting to any situation in a timely manner. Schwarzenberg did indeed seek to exploit the success at Kulm but his timetable paled in comparison to that of Napoleon. Per the intentions he had expressed to Blücher, Schwarzenberg detached 60,000 Austrians and personally led them in two columns along the right bank of the Elbe with the goal of reaching Lusatia by 11 September. Simultaneously, Barclay's Russo-Prussian troops marched on Dresden. Barclay also received command of the Austrian troops that remained on the left bank of the Elbe: IV Corps and 1st Light Division. Because these units stood on the far left wing of the Bohemian Army, they did not participate in the demonstration against Dresden but instead advanced from Komotau toward Freiberg.[56]

Although noble, Schwarzenberg's decision to divide his army and march to support Blücher was extremely dangerous. Neither Schwarzenberg nor Alexander instructed Blücher to hold his ground and thus fix Napoleon in Lusatia. Consequently, if Blücher adhered to the Reichenbach Plan and retreated into Silesia to avoid Napoleon's blow, Schwarzenberg would suddenly emerge in Lusatia with only one-third of his army. Depending on how fast both Napoleon and Schwarzenberg reacted, the former would have the opportunity to catch the latter before he could escape to Bohemia. Based on Napoleon's mastery of operations, Schwarzenberg could very easily find himself surrounded by 200,000 imperials.

Meanwhile, Barclay's demonstration against Dresden looked like a full-scale offensive. On 5 September, his troops commenced the march north: General Andrey Gorchakov's Russian I Infantry Corps and General Hans Ernst von Zieten's Prussian 11th Brigade marched from Nollendorf toward Peterswald. Some twenty miles south of Dresden, Zieten's vanguard took Hellendorf on the left bank of the Elbe from the reconstituted French I Corps after a sharp engagement. A few miles southwest, Prince Eugen of Württemberg's Russian II Infantry Corps took the hills of Ölsen. Two days later, the rest of Kleist's main body moved north from Teplitz to Altenberg. On the right wing, 60,000 Austrians crossed to the right bank of the Elbe at

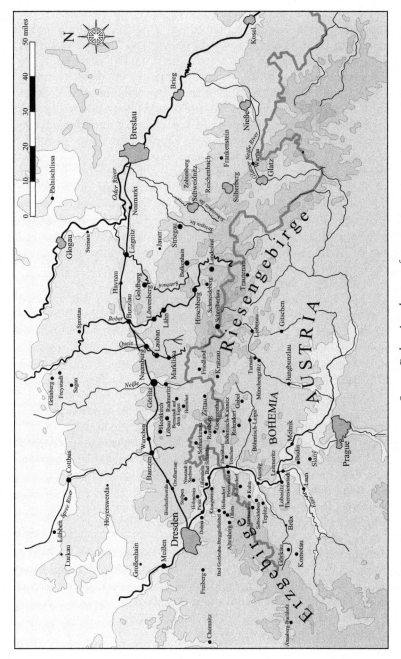

19. Saxon–Bohemian theater of war

Außig and proceeded to Lewin (Levín) on 7 September "ready to march on the road to Rumburg and operate in unison with the army from Silesia." By nightfall, the Army of Bohemia's center stood at Altenberg while its left wing moved north from Komotau toward Freiberg and Marshal Victor's II Corps. Allied Headquarters prepared to relocate from Teplitz to Außig.[57]

These movements alarmed St.-Cyr, whose XIV Corps was divided between Pirna and Lilienstein on the right bank of the Elbe while the small I Corps retreated to Dresden. The marshal's cry for help brought Napoleon racing back to Dresden. He initially sent VI Corps and I Cavalry Corps marching northwest to Hoyerswerda early on the morning of the 6th in the hope of finally taking part in the Berlin offensive. However, at 10:00 A.M., he recalled them and sent them southwest to Dresden in response to St.-Cyr's reports of the advance of the Bohemian Army. Again forced to at least postpone his participation in the master plan, Napoleon and the Guard returned to Dresden that night. Little did he know that earlier in the day the Prussian III and IV Corps of Bernadotte's Army of North Germany had smashed Ney's Army of Berlin at the small village of Dennewitz, some ninety miles northeast of Dresden. As a result of Macdonald's plight, Napoleon could not execute the Berlin offensive as planned in his "Note" of 30 August. He neither marched north nor sent reinforcements. Ney, who had assumed command of the Army of Berlin on 3 September, never received word of the emperor's change of plans. Therefore, when the marshal began his operation on the 4th, he ordered the Army of Berlin to march east to unite with Napoleon, who, according to Ney's information, would reach Luckau on the 6th.[58] Instead of the emperor, Ney found Bülow and Tauentzien. Left to his own devices, Ney succumbed to his own fiery personality, which cost him the victory. Approximately 45,000 Allied soldiers defeated four imperial corps commanded by one of the period's most charismatic leaders.

Two days later, on 8 September, Barclay's vanguards approached Napoleon's headquarters at Dohna, only ten miles southeast of Dresden. Around 2:00 that afternoon, the imperials launched a fierce counterattack. Led by Napoleon himself, St.-Cyr's troops crossed the Elbe at Pirna and assaulted the Allied rear, killing, wounding, and capturing some 1,000 men mostly from Zieten's brigade. At this point, Allied Headquarters did not know the extent of Ney's defeat at Dennewitz, meaning its strategic repercussions had yet to be felt. Thus, Schwarzenberg, who on the 7th learned of Napoleon's march from Bautzen to Dresden, returned Allied Headquarters to Teplitz on the 8th, ordered a general halt, and recalled the 60,000 Austrian troops who had crossed the Elbe en route to Rumburg to support Blücher.

As for Napoleon, he returned to his headquarters at Dohna on the evening of the 8th escorted by the Guard. Although dining with Murat and St.-Cyr and having a long conversation with them, the master said nothing about his next step. During the course of dinner, Napoleon's aide-de-camp, General Anne-Charles Lebrun, arrived with a detailed account of Ney's defeat at Dennewitz. With "unshakable composure," the emperor listened to every detail and then interrogated Lebrun. Despite maintaining his poise, Napoleon quickly realized that Oudinot, Macdonald, Vandamme, and Ney had squandered the fruits of his victory at Dresden. Recognizing the mounting threat to his position in Central Europe, he sought to insure the readiness of his Rhine fortresses for a defensive war. Yet even this precautionary step added to his dilemma: France's German allies certainly would view this as a precursor to a French withdrawal from Central Europe that would leave them at the mercy of the Allies. The Coalition itself would certainly exploit the propaganda value of such a desperate move by portraying it as further proof of his vulnerability. To keep the preparations as secret as possible, that night he ordered his foreign minister, Maret, to send a dispatch in code to Minister of War Henri Clarke in Paris with instructions to place the fortifications on the Rhine in a state of defense.[59]

From Teplitz, Knesebeck penned a morose update on 8 September describing Schwarzenberg's operations. Napoleon's arrival had caused panic and disagreement at Allied Headquarters. According to Knesebeck, decision-making approached the impossible for a variety of reasons: "We know little for certain about the enemy. His outposts have fallen back and it appears that he wants us to advance on Dresden. To say what we will do is very difficult, because as always we do not proceed according to sound military principles. Schwarzenberg is a sensible man but does not enjoy the confidence of the monarchs and lacks faith in himself. The tsar issues orders occasionally; Toll, Volkonsky, Jomini, and Diebitsch blunder in threes. As a result, we receive counterorder after counterorder, and nobody knows who is the cook and who is the waiter. As a result, up to now we have done much too little according to our strength." Despite this vacillation, Knesebeck felt confident enough to promise that, should Blücher advance or be pressed by Napoleon, Schwarzenberg would support him.

Knesebeck concluded with a plea for an update: "We have heard nothing from the Silesian Army since the 5th, and nothing from the crown prince [of Sweden] since the 30th. A report from the 31st from Berlin said that Oudinot concentrated at Wittenberg and the crown prince would deliver a second battle. Whether it has occurred or not is unknown. Send some news of yourself soon. Your deeds will set us in motion." Just after signing his name, Knesebeck added that, according to new intelligence, "it appears absolutely necessary to hasten to the aid of the crown prince." Knesebeck related that, twelve days earlier, Bernadotte had ordered 20,000 *biscuits* to be baked for Wallmoden's troops facing Davout's XIII Corps on the lower Elbe. He notified Wallmoden that a large quantity of wagons would be en route and made this news very public. French spies obtained this information but somehow confused biscuits with men. Thus, as noted, Berthier informed Ney on 2 September that Bernadotte had detached considerable reinforcements from his main body at Berlin to send to Wallmoden. This letter, a copy of which the Allies intercepted, instructed Ney to take command of the Army of Berlin and have it marching on the Prussian capital by 4 September. Thus, Knesebeck's desperate cry for Blücher to rescue the crown prince.[60]

Schwarzenberg convened a council of war at Teplitz on the 9th. Debate focused on finding an explanation for the emperor's return to Dresden. Some believed he intended to hold the line of the Elbe while others insisted that this marked the start of his evacuation of the right bank of the Elbe and retreat to Leipzig. In either case, the Allies agreed that the best counter-operation would be an offensive movement by the Bohemian Army fifty miles north-northwest of Teplitz to Chemnitz. To protect Bohemia and cover the army's communications, the Silesian Army would move to Bohemia, linking with Schwarzenberg's right wing at the Elbe to facilitate his advance into Saxony.[61]

Volkonsky prepared a summary of the council of war for Blücher that provided a view of the thought process at Allied Headquarters:

> All reports lead us to believe that the French army is considering a movement on Leipzig. Nevertheless, it should be assumed that only the most compelling circumstances will prompt the emperor Napoleon to abandon the Elbe and so he will leave his forces concentrated at Dresden for as long as possible. In both cases, we recognize that the best means of operating against him is for the Silesian Army to move closer to our right wing in order to secure our communications and to cover and support an offensive movement by our left wing in the direction of Chemnitz.
>
> Blücher will recognize the importance of this assignment and is experienced enough to decide how far he can risk this movement in the face of the enemy . . . it is up to him to select the way he prefers and even to refrain if it is completely impossible.[62] Bennigsen's army will follow Blücher's movement as far as Görlitz, where it will take a position and observe the enemy. His light troops will raid as far as possible in the direction of Dresden in order to secure Blücher's march on Rumburg. However, whatever Blücher decides, he will upon receipt of this order immediately dispatch six Cossack regiments on the shortest road through Leitmeritz to Teplitz, from where they can fall on the enemy's communication with Leipzig and Erfurt. Prince Schwarzenberg will send Blücher a bridging train to facilitate his arrival, be it through Pirna or by way of another point. He himself should be equipped with a similar bridging train.[63]

To avoid any ambiguities, a cover letter from Tsar Alexander accompanied Volkonsky's minutes. Alexander wrote nothing about Blücher's deciding for himself on the necessity of this march. According to a Saxon officer who defected, Napoleon held Dresden with 100,000 men, making a march to Pirna too dangerous. For this reason, Alexander insisted that Blücher utilize the road to Leitmeritz. Bennigsen likewise received Volkonsky's memo along with a cover letter from Alexander that ordered him to march directly to the Elbe. Should the French evacuate its right bank, Bennigsen would besiege Dresden, Königstein, and Torgau. In the opposite case, he would avoid an engagement with superior enemy forces. Blücher received the tsar's letter on 11 September. Alexander's participation in this correspondence served to reinforce Blücher's belief that he did not have to obey orders from Schwarzenberg. In this latest round of letters, the Allied commander in chief remained conspicuously silent. Rather than an agreement between Alexander and Schwarzenberg to have the former handle recalcitrant subordinates, most likely the Allied commander in chief had no knowledge of the detailed arrangements issued by the tsar.[64]

Returning to Napoleon, on 9 and 10 September he made a futile attempt to double-envelop Barclay and cut him off from the Erzgebirge passes before the Austrians, who had crossed the Elbe en route to Rumburg, could return to the right bank. Unfortunately for the imperials, Barclay observed their movements, divined the intent, and ordered a general retreat across the Erzgebirge. Only two Prussian uhlan regiments and two Russian Cossack regiments remained on the hills of Nollendorf; the rest of the Allied troops moved into two lines at Sobochleben (Soběchleby) between Kulm and Teplitz on the 10th. By the end of 10 September, St.-Cyr's XIV Corps had reached Ebersdorf (Habartice) with its vanguard at Mariaschein (Bohosudov), less than four miles northeast of Allied Headquarters at Teplitz. On the 11th, Napoleon observed the Army of Bohemia assembled at Sobochleben. With his troops unable to enter the Teplitz valley, he could not go any further. Frustrated, he departed for Pirna.[65]

That night, Napoleon addressed the strategic repercussions of Ney's defeat at Dennewitz. He believed the current operation would suffice to convince Schwarzenberg to withdraw all his troops from Saxony: "I have reason to believe that the enemy, who appears very alarmed [and] who has lit alarm fires all across the mountains of Bohemia, will recall all detachments and thus the whole of Saxony will be purged of enemy parties." Should Bernadotte advance toward Großenhain as part of a combined movement with Blücher against Dresden, Ney would threaten the Army of North Germany by debouching from Torgau against its flank. He instructed Macdonald to hold Bautzen and the right bank of the Spree. Concerns over both Ney and Macdonald prompted him to order two Young Guard divisions as well as 1st Guard Cavalry Division to prepare to march to Bautzen. Although the orders to commence the march did not come, the gendarmes received instructions to collect the stragglers of Macdonald's army and return them to their respective corps.[66]

The mood at Allied Headquarters during the night of 11 September remained so somber that Alexander sent another letter to Blücher, which the Prussian commander received on the morning of 13 September. Claiming that the Army of the Bober had retreated to the Elbe to unite with the Grande Armée for an offensive against the Army of Bohemia, the tsar explicitly ordered Blücher to lead the Army of Silesia to Bohemia along the road that ran through Rumburg to Leitmeritz. He explained that "the emperor Napoleon has crossed the Elbe at Dresden with the majority of his forces and is moving on the highway to Teplitz against the Army of Bohemia – his vanguard has reached the defile of Nollendorf. It is probable that the corps of Ney, Lauriston, Poniatowski, and Sébastiani will attempt to reunite with the emperor Napoleon by way of Königstein." Schwarzenberg also requested that Bubna convey to Blücher the Allied commander in chief's pressing desire "to know the decision General Blücher has made regarding the union with this army and what movements he plans to make." Bubna forwarded a copy of this letter to Silesian Army Headquarters, where it arrived around 10:00 P.M. on 12 September.[67]

While the generals wrung their hands, the diplomats at Teplitz achieved success on the 9th with the signing of bilateral alliance treaties between Russia, Austria, and Prussia. The general terms called for the material restoration of Austria and Prussia to their pre-1805 status; the restoration of the states of northwestern Europe to their 1803 status; the dissolution of the Confederation of the Rhine; the independence of the German states between the Rhine and the western frontiers of Austria and Prussia; and the partition of the Grand Duchy of Warsaw along lines that would be determined later. The three Eastern powers vowed not to make a separate peace with Napoleon, and each agreed to keep an army in the field until the end of the war. Although something could be found in the Teplitz Accords that satisfied each Eastern power, Metternich achieved another victory. The stated goal of the alliance was not the ultimate destruction of France. For Austria's geopolitical interests, Metternich needed to retain a powerful and preferably Napoleonic France to help contain Russia. The accords ignored Italy, Holland, and Spain; Metternich figured he could use these issues later to coerce the British into accepting his designs for Central Europe. Yet Teplitz was not a total victory for the Austrians; Tsar Alexander recovered some of the diplomatic initiative he had lost to Metternich during the Armistice. Both Prussia and Austria remained dependent on Russia to secure their postwar objectives. For Prussia, Frederick William could take comfort that, as long as he remained loyal to the tsar, Prussian influence in Germany would increase, despite Austrian opposition.[68]

As for Blücher, by nightfall of 6 September he had received numerous reports stating that the French did not appear inclined to pursue across the Neiße, despite their work on a bridge at Görlitz. His staff quickly concluded that such idleness signaled Napoleon's departure. Moreover, the various *Streifkorps* operating in the region reported that the emperor had returned to Bautzen on the evening of the 5th with numerous troops. Sacken also provided

15 Russian Cossacks attacking a French soldier

confirmation of Napoleon's departure. Around 5:00 P.M. on the 5th, his Cossacks raided along the Reichenbach–Bautzen stretch of the east–west highway and intercepted Caulaincourt's secretary. The terrified captive declared that the emperor would soon ride to Bautzen. According to Sacken's 8:00 P.M. report on 6 September, "Colonel Figner, one of my partisans, has just arrived with General Caulaincourt's secretary. He was captured yesterday afternoon between Reichenbach and Bautzen; he had been sent from the former to arrange his master's lodgings at Bautzen. At that moment, both the emperor Napoleon and the king of Naples were still at Reichenbach but both planned to go to Bautzen." "We soon learned," noted Langeron, "that having failed a second time to achieve his goal, which was to engage us in a general battle with forces superior to our own, Napoleon had again returned to Dresden with all the troops he had brought. He left facing us the same corps that had faced us previously, of which three had been manhandled at the Katzbach."[69]

Nevertheless, Langeron continued to act arbitrarily, thus undermining Blücher. On this day, 6 September, he again sent his heavy artillery far to the east, purportedly spreading terror in the countryside and preventing Blücher from resuming the offensive. Consequently, the army received a day of rest on the 7th so the Russian guns could return. Blücher sent Langeron a pointed reproach, demanding that the corps commander strictly obey orders. A repeat of such behavior would prompt Blücher to complain to the tsar. Gneisenau, in turn, wrote to Stein at Allied Headquarters, explaining his thoughts on the military situation as well as the Silesian Army's imminent plans and measures. Knowing Stein would share the contents of the letter with Alexander, Gneisenau sought assistance with countering the opposition posed by Yorck and Langeron. Three days later, after no change could be seen in Langeron's conduct, Gneisenau drafted a long complaint to the king that Blücher signed. Describing in detail the infractions committed by Langeron as far back as 19 August, it requested that the king seek the recall of the native Frenchman. Blücher explained that "ill-will is not the reason why Count Langeron acts like this, but it is because he momentarily loses his head and has no military judgment."[70] Although Allied Headquarters did not take immediate action, Langeron's behavior created an issue that had to be monitored and rectified if needed. A letter of 28 September from the king's adjutant, Major Thile, to Yorck provides the evidence. Accordingly, Thile requested that Yorck confidentially comment on Langeron's performance as a corps commander: "Both monarchs are – which I am telling you in the strictest of confidence – in agreement that General Langeron can be replaced by another general if the interest of the good cause demands it. His Majesty the King, however, also wishes to know your opinion on this, which is an issue of consequence with the tsar, and which requires acuteness and impartiality. I thus ask you to communicate to the king your confidential views on the leadership of Langeron's corps, but to keep the knowledge of this request to yourself out of consideration for General Count Langeron and to expedite the affair as much as possible because the monarchs believe that, if an evil remedy is needed, it is [better] done sooner than later."[71]

Concerning Yorck, the retreat behind the Queis had perturbed him and his staff. Although believing that the larger strategic plan required the retrograde march, they complained that it could have been conducted with more composure and less loss. Lieutenant-Colonel Georg Wilhelm von Valentini recorded in his journal: "Precipitate retreat from Görlitz; humiliating to see that we are chased by a handful of enemies." The 6 September entry in Schack's journal states: "The enemy still has not occupied Görlitz, proof that the poor affair merely was caused by the poor measures." Hiller's infantry lost 520 men and again the corps made consecutive night marches in heavy summer rains. The troops were "extremely exhausted, the horses deteriorating, the supply continuously difficult, the clothing poor beyond all measure." Fortunately for the men, they found some potato fields.[72]

Also arriving on 6 September was Frederick William's 31 August congratulations for the victory at the Katzbach, which somewhat lightened the mood of the Silesian Army's key players. Blücher received the Great Cross of the Iron Cross; Yorck and Sacken the Black Eagle; Gneisenau, Müffling, and Prince Karl the Iron Cross, First Class; Majors Othegraven, Bieberstein, Thiele, and

Lieutenant-Colonel Warburg the Iron Cross, Second Class. While Kaiser Franz named Blücher a commander of the Order of Maria Theresa, Tsar Alexander awarded him the Order of St. Andrew, removing the pin from his own uniform and sending it to the Prussian general with this flattering letter:

> Among the most agreeable moments of the campaign, I recognize those in which I can give you proof of the particular satisfaction I feel in doing justice to your brilliant courage, the activity of your operations, and the energy of your movements. At this moment when we for our part have won a brilliant victory [Kulm], I detach from my coat the insignia of the Order of St. Andrew, which I award to you. I do not believe that this circumstance will increase the value of this sign of my satisfaction but it will at least prove to you that I have not wasted one moment in assuring you as well as those brave soldiers under your orders of the pleasure your success has brought me. The soldier reflects the glory of his commander, just as the commander reflects that of his soldiers. Tell them, general, how much I appreciate their deeds and accept the assurances of my best wishes.

More rewards followed. Alexander promoted Sacken to general of infantry, awarding him the Order of St. George, Second Class. On their shakos, the troopers of Sacken's Mariupolskii, Aleksandriiskii, Akhtyrskii, and Belorusskii Hussar Regiments received the inscription commemorating the battle of the Katzbach dated according to the Russian calendar: "Distinguished on 14 August 1813." For his role in the Allied victory, Langeron received 30,000 rubles as well as the imperial *Wenzel*: the practice of granting to distinguished individuals or entire units the right to wear the Russian imperial monogram represented by the first letter of the ruler's name.[73]

After granting his soldiers a day of rest on the 7th mainly so Langeron could recall his artillery, Blücher resumed the offensive on the 8th. Gneisenau issued orders to commence a two-day operation that Blücher hoped would force the imperials to either retreat on Bautzen or accept battle at the Neiße. The terrain between the Neiße and the Queis consisted of rolling, wooded hills with valleys deep enough to hide their contents from prying eyes on the banks of the former. Based on this advantage, Gneisenau planned to move the left wing of the army unnoticed around Macdonald's right to attack his rear. For the 8th, the vanguards would remain in their positions to occupy Macdonald's front while the army's main body marched southwest: Langeron to Ostritz, Yorck to Radmeritz, and Sacken toward Görlitz. Gneisenau wanted St.-Priest to cross the Neiße at Ostritz and proceed six miles west to Bernstadt auf dem Eigen, where his corps would serve as Langeron's new vanguard. On the 9th, Sacken would pin the imperials at Görlitz with his corps as well as Yorck's vanguard under Katzler while Langeron and Yorck crossed the Neiße at Ostritz to envelop Macdonald from the south; Bubna's division would sever the marshal's line of retreat.

This operation appeared all the more secure because Bennigsen's Army of Poland could reach the Katzbach by the 8th and 9th meaning that, in case of a setback, the Silesian Army could retreat to Bohemia knowing that Bennigsen could defend Silesia.[74]

"I am resuming my offensive movement," Blücher declared with confidence on the 8th, "and have reinforced my left to cross the Neiße today at Ostritz. I count on turning the enemy's right by marching on Löbau." At daybreak, he received a report stating that the enemy skirmishers on the east bank of the Neiße at Görlitz had withdrawn to the opposite bank. Moreover, the imperials had partially restored one of Görlitz's bridges and numerous campfires still burned west of the town. St.-Priest reported that Yuzefovich's patrols along the west bank of the Neiße had brought back prisoners who stated that Napoleon and most of the imperial cavalry had departed for Dresden on the 5th. With only weak detachments opposite him, St.-Priest confirmed that he would commence the march to Bernstadt auf dem Eigen around 4:00 that morning.[75]

However, a letter from Bubna, written shortly after midnight on the night of the 7th/8th, seemed to challenge the statements made by Yuzefovich's prisoners. According to the Austrian, Napoleon was marching to Bautzen with 50,000 men, and Poniatowski's VIII Corps again occupied Schluckenau. Blücher doubted the accuracy of Bubna's claims. After the operation commenced on the 8th, the Prussian commander received Schwarzenberg's two letters from 5 September warning of Napoleon's march from Dresden to Bautzen and promising to lead 60,000 Austrians through Zittau by the 13th. Blücher immediately responded: "Your Excellency should already have been notified that on the afternoon of 4 September the emperor Napoleon turned around his retreating troops at Bautzen and seized the offensive. I halted the army, learned at 6:00 of the arrival of the emperor and his reinforcements, and avoided a battle on the 5th by withdrawing across the Neiße." Blücher then provided an account of his operations on 6 and 7 September as well as the news that several reports had confirmed Napoleon's return to Dresden with his reinforcements. "An enemy force still stands on the left bank of the Neiße by Görlitz, but I am ready to deal with it and already today I have commenced an offensive movement ... If the enemy maintains his position at Görlitz he will be forced to engage me under very unfavorable circumstances. Whether based on this news Your Excellency finds it necessary to continue your march or instead turn around and considerably reinforce the offensive of the Bohemian Army I leave to your judgment." Blücher's failure to inform Schwarzenberg earlier of Napoleon's return to Dresden is indicative of the inadequate system of communication at Silesian Army Headquarters.[76]

Meanwhile, Blücher's vanguards quietly faced the enemy at Görlitz while his three corps swung southwest. St.-Priest crossed the Neiße at Ostritz and repulsed a French detachment but pushed only his vanguard to Bernstadt auf dem Eigen rather than his entire corps per Gneisenau's instructions. Langeron's corps moved into Ostritz, Yorck to Kieslingswalde, and Sacken to Hochkirch. According to Gneisenau's plan for the 9th, St.-Priest would march straight to Löbau, where reports placed Poniatowski's VIII Corps as it covered Macdonald's right flank between Bautzen and Pirna. While St.-Priest engaged the Poles, Langeron would support this attack and then march to Reichenbach and attack the rear of the enemy forces at Görlitz. Blücher would lead Yorck's corps from Ostritz against Macdonald's right flank while Sacken assaulted his center. Gneisenau designed this plan to attain considerable results but again Langeron's carelessness ruined its execution. Although Blücher wanted Langeron's corps to remain in the concealed valleys east of the Neiße, Langeron led Kaptsevich's X Infantry Corps across the Neiße on the 8th. Moreover, by failing to prevent his troops from lighting campfires west of Ostritz, Langeron revealed the approaching danger to Macdonald. Some of Blücher's staff firmly believed that Langeron intentionally presented himself to the enemy in order to induce Macdonald to retreat and avoid a battle. According to Müffling,

> We again assumed the offensive with a view to take the king of Naples in the flank and rear; everything depended on our concealing from the enemy the flank march to the left; Langeron received strict injunctions to allow no fires to be kindled at night in the bivouac at Ostritz, which could be seen from the Landskrone. Langeron was not aware that Napoleon had returned to Dresden, and considered the passage of the Neiße at Ostritz an extremely hazardous undertaking. He did not follow the injunction not to allow any fires to be lit, and thus drew upon himself the suspicion that this fresh instance of disobedience, which deprived us of the fruits of this movement, was not unintentional. He received a well-deserved reprimand, but I had to defend him against the suspicion of any bad intention.[77]

"You will demand a written explanation from St.-Priest as to why he did not follow my orders to advance to Bernstadt auf dem Eigen," a frustrated Blücher wrote to Langeron. "Furthermore, it was my intention that you place yourself behind this place [Ostritz], as the disposition clearly states. Your position is such that from the Landskrone one can see all your campfires. I must admit my discontent with you." Naturally, Langeron denied any wrongdoing:

> I only waited for the arrival of Yorck's corps, which was marching from Kieslingswalde to Ostritz, to move rapidly on Reichenbach, but despite the precautions that we had taken, the enemy observed our march from the mountain of the Landskrone, from where one can see the entire country, and withdrew quickly from Görlitz to Reichenbach: my cavalry took some prisoners. Sacken's corps entered Görlitz and moved on Reichenbach.

The plans that directed all of these movements were well conceived but the dispositions were not made well and the march was not concealed: some uncertainty and confusion existed at headquarters. Sir Gneisenau dared say nothing less than that it was the campfires of my corps that aroused the enemy; nothing is more false and he himself is alone responsible for the disposition and delivery of orders.[78]

Regardless of who was at fault, Macdonald recognized the danger to his right. To Blücher's dismay, the marshal wasted no time withdrawing his troops from Görlitz to Reichenbach. Poniatowski's VIII Corps covered the march of Macdonald's right wing by holding firm at Löbau. Some five miles northwest of Bernstadt auf dem Eigen, the Polish vanguard took post at Herwigsdorf. With his left wing falling back westward to Weißenberg and Glossen, the marshal swung his right wing to the northwest so that the Army of the Bober faced south.

As the French army retreated, Borozdin led the main body of St.-Priest's vanguard northwest from Bernstadt auf dem Eigen before dawn on the 9th. St.-Priest's main body marched at daybreak; Langeron himself led Kaptsevich's X Infantry Corps from Ostritz. Borozdin found the Poles holding the heights and thick woods just south of Herwigsdorf. Although the Poles welcomed the Russians with the hatred that marked almost every confrontation between these deadly foes, the Moskovskii Dragoons supported by several Chernomorskoye Cossack Regiments pushed back their advance posts. Bistram directed the 1st and 33rd Jäger Regiments (three battalions in total) through the woods, turning the enemy's left flank and reaching the road to Reichenbach. Outflanked, the Poles withdrew two and one-half miles west to Ebersdorf, where their rearguard took a position on the hills east of this village. The native Livonian, General Rodion Gerngross, moved up with the 1st Brigade of the 1st Dragoon Division; his Kargopolskii and Mitavskii Dragoons dispersed the Poles. Poniatowski's rearguard fought hard to hold Ebersdorf as French infantry and cavalry support could be seen advancing from Löbau. To take Ebersdorf before the Poles could be reinforced, Borozdin committed the Ryazanskii Infantry Regiment supported by the Kargopolskii and Mitavskii Dragoons; a well-placed battery silenced the Polish cannon and ignited several fires in Ebersdorf. The Polish infantry desperately sought to hold their ground but mounting flames forced them to finally abandon the position.

Poniatowski established a new position north of Löbau but his rearguard continued to occupy the village. From Ebersdorf, Borozdin directed his men northeast to a 400-meter-tall height just east of Löbau. As soon as the Russians reach the domineering hill, the Poles sortied from Löbau. But around this time, St.-Priest's 17th Division arrived from Ebersdorf to attack the right flank of the advancing enemy columns while Borozdin attacked their front. Although Poniatowski recalled his columns to Löbau, the Russians observed elements of Lauriston's V Corps moving southwest toward their rear from the direction of Reichenbach. Any joy on the part of the Poles proved illusory as timing favored St.-Priest on this day. Before the French could reach their allies, Kaptsevich's infantry arrived. The 29th and 45th Jäger Regiments blocked the Reichenbach road and chased the imperials from Wendisch Pauls-dorf. Around 4:00 P.M., Poniatowski finally ordered a withdrawal; the blood of his countrymen had bought enough time for Lauriston's V Corps to pass west. After evacuating Löbau, the Poles took a position a few miles northwest of the town on line with Lauriston's corps, which halted on the hills of Kittlitz. Kaptsevich pushed north and deployed his infantry on the hills facing V Corps. Skirmishing continued until around 9:00 P.M., at which time the Poles withdrew under the protection of IV Cavalry Corps – likewise an all-Polish unit except for its commander, General François-Étienne Kellermann – six miles northwest to Hochkirch on the road to Bautzen, leaving their rearguard at Plotzen. At nightfall, V Corps halted at Hochkirch with III and XI Corps and II Cavalry Corps between Glossen and Weißenberg.[79]

Thus, Macdonald's army escaped to Bautzen largely unscathed on 9 September; each side lost some 500 men. Borozdin pursued the Poles for a few miles before establishing a camp between Eiserode and Nechen; St.-Priest's main body bivouacked between Nechen and Löbau. Langeron's corps camped at Bernstadt auf dem Eigen, Yorck's just west of Ostritz at Gruhna, Sacken's at Görlitz, and Bubna's division at Rumburg. Blücher portrayed the day as a success to Bernadotte: "This maneuver was so very successful that at this moment the enemy is in full retreat on Bautzen. I hope my vanguards will attain still more."[80]

On 10 September, the day that his *Streifkorps* reached the Elbe and the rear of the French army, Blücher granted Langeron and Yorck a day of rest; only the vanguards continued the pursuit west from the banks of the Neiße toward Bautzen. Long before dawn Katzler ordered the hussar regiment commanded by Prince Friedrich of Hesse forward to seek an advantage where possible. Katzler followed at daybreak with the vanguard's main body, taking a north-west direction with Reichenbach to the right (north). To his northwest, Vasilchikov led Sacken's vanguard through Glossen and Wurschen, halting at the latter and pushing his outposts toward Bautzen. His forward units found the imperials retreating in two columns: one through Weißenberg, the other through Hochkirch.[81] Sacken's main body trooped from the Land-skrone to Schöps, with corps headquarters taken at Reichenbach. Yorck's corps remained at Gruhna and Langeron's at Bernstadt auf dem Eigen.

Continuing through Hochkirch and Weißenberg on 10 September, the majority of Macdonald's army halted on the hills east of Bautzen while the Poles – VIII Corps and IV Cavalry Corps – marched thirteen miles southwest from Bautzen to Putzkau. Again, the Russians on Blücher's left wing endured intense fighting. At 4:00 A.M. on the 10th, St.-Priest pushed his corps

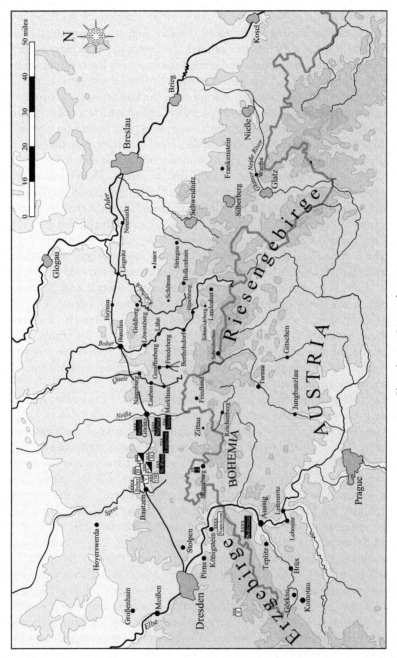

20. Situation, 9 September 1813

northwest toward Hochkirch on the Bautzen–Löbau road. Leading St.-
Priest's vanguard, Borozdin made contact with Poniatowski's posts south
of Plotzen. While Yuzefovich's dragoons pinned the Poles, Bistram's Jäger
brigade turned their right by reaching Lehn. Thus taken in the flank, the Poles
withdrew on Plotzen, where Poniatowski committed a sizeable force supported by eight guns. Other columns – Lauriston's V Corps – could be seen
moving south from Hochkirch toward Lehn, Sornßig, and Wuischke, which
the Poles also held. Poniatowski posted his main body in battle order on the
hills of Hochkirch less than one mile northwest of Plotzen. St.-Priest moved
up General Yegor Pillar's 17th Division to take Plotzen while Gerngross led
the Ryazanskii Infantry Regiment and Novorossiiskii Dragoons west to
support Bistram's Jäger at Wuischke. After the Russians took both Plotzen
and Wuischke, Pillar continued northwest toward Hochkirch. The Poles
evacuated the village around 1:00 in the afternoon and withdrew on Bautzen.
Yuzefovich's dragoons pursued some four miles to the defile at Jenkwitz,
itself less than three miles southeast of Bautzen, before withdrawing to
Niethen for the night. Borozdin bivouacked at Hochkirch; St.-Priest led his
main body to Eiserode, three miles southeast of Hochkirch. Behind him,
Kaptsevich's X Infantry Corps halted at Löbau. Both sides again lost around
500 men with the Russians taking an additional 400 prisoners.[82]

Although Blücher failed to pin Macdonald at the Neiße for a second battle
on 8 or 9 September, he forced the Army of the Bober to retreat to Bautzen. In
reflecting on the overall situation, we again see the magnitude of Blücher's
operations. His constant pressure prevented Macdonald from rallying his
army at the Bober, the Queis, or the Neiße. By driving the marshal to
Bautzen, Blücher completely disrupted Napoleon's timetable and planning.
From 31 August to 3 September, the emperor sat at Dresden uncertain if he
could lead the Berlin offensive because of Macdonald's steady flight westward.
Forced to stop the Army of the Bober from retreating across the Spree,
Napoleon transferred VI Corps and I Cavalry Corps from the Bohemian
frontier to Bautzen, to where he proceeded with his Guard on 4 September.
Hoping to quickly engage Blücher and destroy his army, Napoleon lunged
but missed. Again proving that going backward could be just as beneficial as
going forward, Blücher retreated across the Neiße to the Queis.

Not only did Blücher conform perfectly to the tenets of the Reichenbach
Plan, but his drive against Macdonald both spared Bernadotte a confrontation with Napoleon and took the pressure off Schwarzenberg. To take in
Macdonald's beleaguered army, Napoleon assembled the Guard, VI Corps,
and I Cavalry Corps at Dresden. Instead of marching on Berlin, he went to
Bautzen to personally restore Macdonald's command. Thus, while a great
victory for the Allies, Kulm only managed to pull the imperials out of the
passes of the Erzgebirge. The return of VI Corps and I Cavalry Corps to
Dresden, and the posting of II and XIV Corps at Freiberg and Pirna

respectively – all precautionary measures taken as a result of Macdonald's flight – relieved the pressure on the Army of Bohemia. Sensing that he no longer had a sword at his back, Schwarzenberg managed to generate enough steam to alarm St.-Cyr and bring Napoleon racing back to Dresden, which in turn took the pressure off Blücher.

While Schwarzenberg deserves credit, the damage to Napoleon's strategy had already been done by 6 September. Owing to Blücher's pressure, Macdonald's retreat obstructed Napoleon from taking command of the Berlin offensive from 31 August to 3 September. Then, his pursuit of the Silesian Army cost the emperor another three days and culminated with his returning to Dresden rather than marching on Berlin. Thus, Napoleon squandered an entire week contending with the difficulties caused by Blücher. While Napoleon secured Macdonald, Ney continued his operation and met with defeat at Dennewitz on the 6th. Detaining Napoleon in Saxony from 31 August to 6 September must be counted as one of Blücher's major achievements in the Fall Campaign. Had Napoleon and the Guard united with Ney's army it is difficult to imagine Bülow and Tauentzien winning the battle of Dennewitz. Warned of the emperor's approach, Bernadotte would have retreated to Swedish Pomerania. The campaign in Brandenburg then would have depended on how well Napoleon could maneuver in conjunction with Davout and how well the prince royal could counter their movements. While the Swedes and Russians followed the crown prince, Bülow and Tauentzien would have made a stand somewhere to bravely sacrifice their corps rather than continue a shameful retreat. If Murat and Macdonald held up against Schwarzenberg and Blücher, Bernadotte would eventually have to fight or risk being driven across Swedish Pomerania and into the Baltic. By maintaining constant pressure on Macdonald and then going backward at the right moment, the future Marshal Forwards prevented this scenario altogether. Instead of triumphantly entering Berlin as he did in 1806, Napoleon returned to Dresden after having achieved nothing.

Taking stock of the situation, Gneisenau considered a further pursuit pointless and even detrimental to the overall situation. Favorable results could easily drive Macdonald's army across the Elbe and into Napoleon's arms, allowing the emperor to again fall on the Bohemian Army with superior forces before the Silesian Army could rush to its support. Indignant about the lost opportunity to deliver a decisive blow, Blücher demanded that the army press forward. Gneisenau and Müffling countered that a further advance would serve no purpose. "Bonaparte stood with his principal forces in and near Dresden," recalled Müffling. "Although he had detached a portion to oppose the main army and another against the Silesian Army, he could still reunite all his forces in one night and attack with superior numbers whichever of the two armies exposed itself to him. This reason alone would have prevented General Blücher from moving any closer to

Dresden than Bautzen, and thus risk an unequal engagement; but there were other reasons besides." By driving Macdonald across the Elbe, Blücher would then be obliged to post the Silesian Army along the river. "In that case, it would be in a barren district," continued Müffling, "amidst forests in which it was impossible to live." Worse, "the army would be immediately obliged to fall back on the defensive." Unable to cross the Elbe at Dresden, another point of passage from the eastern to the western bank of the Elbe would be needed. Even if Blücher found a secure crossing, the Silesian Army would not be able to cross to the left bank undetected. Napoleon would then make "counterarrangements to impede a new movement."

Blücher could hardly reconcile himself to this unnatural way of war; his instinct told him to strike. His constant demand to go forward led to another disagreement with Gneisenau. Like Napoleon, Blücher believed that the problems of warfare could not be solved through inactivity. Yet, on this occasion, Gneisenau refused to compromise. As with most of their clashes, Gneisenau emerged the victor because Blücher trusted his subordinate's grasp of strategy and operations much more than his own. "All of these reasons combined to make General Blücher decide against proceeding further," wrote Müffling, "and instead to take a position so that, if Bonaparte advanced against him, he could evade the blow."[83]

Blücher's report to the king, drafted by Gneisenau at 11:00 A.M. on the 10th, grants insight into their view of the situation as well as their solution, which explains the day of rest for Yorck and Langeron. Rather than drive Macdonald into Napoleon's arms, Gneisenau suggested the opposite: force Napoleon to rescue the marshal. In this way, the Bohemian Army would have time to take Dresden or cut French communications. "Because the opportunity to force the enemy into a battle has escaped me, the continuation of my offensive operation in my opinion appears to be of no use to the Bohemian Army. On the contrary, if I drive the corps facing me (Poniatowski, XI Corps, with part of III and V Corps) across the Elbe, they can then easily unite and fall on the Bohemian Army before I have time to come to its assistance. In general, nothing would be more advantageous than if my operations again induce the emperor Napoleon to come to the aid of the Army of the Bober with a considerable force." The letter continued by stressing the advantageous nature of Napoleon's "strategic position" at Dresden but asserted that a weakness could be found: "so risky would it be if he lingered there for some time and exhausted himself." With this, Gneisenau began constructing an argument in favor of a strategy of attrition. In Napoleon's current situation, Gneisenau maintained that "the most advantageous move he can make is to quickly throw the army that faces the crown prince of Sweden onto the Saale and use it to reopen all communication. If this does not occur, in my humble opinion an offensive against the subsistence of the enemy and a defensive against his forces will most certainly lead

to a favorable result. I await most humbly Your Royal Majesty's orders over
the further operations and until then will continue to hurt the enemy through
the *kleinen Krieg*." Müffling further explains this thought process:

> By all accounts, we can assume that the French armies were weaker than
> those of the Allies at the beginning of the campaign. As the former suffered
> much greater losses in battle, Allied forces (including Bennigsen's army
> marching from Poland through Silesia) must have exceeded them by
> 100,000 men. The Allies had, namely, 400,000 men; Napoleon 300,000 men,
> or 4 to 3. Therefore, the surest means of successfully ending the war was to
> engage in daily combats, even if they decided nothing. If after some time, an
> equal number of men were killed (say 100,000 men on each side) in this
> manner, the Allies would have a 3 to 2 ratio and it would then be the time to
> completely crush Bonaparte in a great battle. This was the general opinion at
> General Blücher's headquarters. Officers were dispatched by him to the
> headquarters of the main army and of the crown prince of Sweden to learn
> the opinions that prevailed there.[84]

Gneisenau's suggestion to halt the advance and allow the effects of the
kleinen Krieg to exhaust Napoleon appears to have been influenced by
Knesebeck's letter of 3 September and marks a change in the outlook of
Silesian Army Headquarters. When not retreating from Napoleon, Blücher
and Gneisenau had pursued a strategy to overwhelm their enemy, a
Niederwerfungsstrategie (strategy of annihilation) that would culminate in a
Vernichtungsschlacht (battle of annihilation). Up to this point, Blücher had
distinguished his way of war with extraordinary energy and activity, missing
no opportunity to attack and damage the enemy. Now, he reluctantly
endorsed a strategy of exhaustion, an eighteenth-century *Ermattungsstrategie*
akin in principle to the ideas that mastered the Reichenbach Plan. Gneisenau's
logic for halting the offensive against the Army of the Bober – because it
would unite with Napoleon's Grande Armée, thus increasing the forces facing
the Bohemian Army – defies explanation. It certainly ignores the fact that the
Silesian Army would maintain complete independence, meaning it could
either march on Napoleon's vital base at Dresden or unite with the Army of
North Germany, cross the Elbe, and operate against the rear of the Grande
Armée. Moreover, as the Prussians knew well, the Reichenbach Plan stipulated that, if the Bohemian Army faced a superior enemy force,
Schwarzenberg could withdraw deep into Bohemia. "But it appears even
more disconcerting to us," bemoans Friederich, "to hear from the mouths of
Blücher and Gneisenau the view that the defensive against the enemy's forces
and the offensive against his rearward-lying communication was the best
guarantee for a favorable result." While we cannot account for this "disturbing" change, as Friederich terms it, it is useful to understand that the cult of the
Frederician army had not disappeared entirely – and could not. Thus, we must

judge the degree to which Blücher and Gneisenau – a rookie combination of commander and staff chief co-leading a multinational army for the first time – successfully reconciled their institutional heritage with Napoleon's new way of war in the midst of the largest conflict Europe had ever seen.[85]

After writing the report to Frederick William at 11:00 A.M. on 10 September, Blücher and his staff traveled thirteen miles west from Radmeritz to Herrnhut. Two interesting letters arrived. The first, Knesebeck's gloomy report from Teplitz on 8 September, described Napoleon's sudden arrival at Dresden and warned that "it appears absolutely necessary to hasten to the aid" of Bernadotte. Blücher and Gneisenau knew better thanks to the second letter that arrived on 10 September. Sent from Bernadotte's headquarters at Jüterbog, it announced the Army of North Germany's victory over Ney at Dennewitz on the 6th. In describing Ney's defeat, the crown prince praised the heroism of the Prussian III and IV Corps but spitefully and incorrectly attributed the victory to the Russian and Swedish corps attached to his army. By thus destroying his relationship with Bülow and Tauentzien, Bernadotte created conditions that would facilitate Blücher's march down the Elbe. For now, however, the Army of North Germany's booty could not have been better: 5,000 prisoners, at least 40 guns, 200 caissons, and 3 flags. Two days later the number of prisoners jumped to 15,000. Like the disintegration of Macdonald's army, this number increased over the course of the next week as Ney retreated to Torgau, producing a total loss of 23,215 men, 53 guns, 12,000 muskets, 412 wagons, and 4 flags.[86]

Consequently, Knesebeck's alarm over the crown prince of Sweden did not resonate at Blücher's headquarters. Instead, Blücher and Gneisenau believed the time had come for Bernadotte to cross the Elbe and enter the main theater of war. A subsequent letter from the crown prince dated 9 September raised their hope that the Army of North Germany would be led across the Elbe by its commander without much goading. "According to the news I receive from you," wrote the prince royal, "I am prepared either to march against the flank of the emperor Napoleon if he goes to Silesia or to cross the Elbe if he withdraws before you." Bernadotte explained that he had sent 10,000 men to Luckau, seventy miles northwest of Bautzen, and could have another 10,000 follow. If Napoleon crossed to the right bank of the Elbe to attack Blücher, Bernadotte pledged to march up (south) the Elbe to attack the emperor's left flank. Should Napoleon withdraw before the Silesian Army, he still planned to lead the Army of North Germany south, cross to the left bank of the Elbe, and proceed against the Grande Armée.[87]

Although Bernadotte's plans sounded promising, the Prussians remained skeptical. "The correspondence of the crown prince of Sweden," noted Müffling, "which was entrusted to me, required very unique attention, being more diplomatic than military. Every word had to be weighed and considered, with a view toward the conclusions that might be drawn from them.

We found by experience that the written communications of the crown prince did not at all agree with his verbal expressions, which we learned through the Prussian officers at his headquarters." Nevertheless, the Prussians felt that "the time had come to arrange a new plan of operations. At the beginning of the campaign after the armistice, each field commander acted on his own, observing some important general principles, but the army's approach to the Elbe made it necessary for arrangements for all operations to be made in time so the Allies could take full advantage of the superiority in manpower and so that no army be exposed to the danger of being defeated individually."[88] With this thought in mind, the Prussians started planning one of the most unorthodox yet decisive operations of the campaign.

Notes

1 Barclay to Blücher in Höpfner, "Darstellung," 1844:168, quoted in Pertz and Delbrück, *Gneisenau*, III:254.

2 Langeron, *Mémoires*, 254–56.

3 Peter Duka von Kádár on behalf of Schwarzenberg to Blücher, Dux, 30 August 1813, Add MSS, 20112, 2–3.

4 Friederich, *Herbstfeldzug 1813*, II:241; Pertz and Delbrück, *Gneisenau*, III:256.

5 Blücher to Bennigsen, Löwenberg, 2 September 1813, in Höpfner, "Darstellung," 1844:208.

6 Markov commanded an advance corps of around 9,246 infantry, 2,197 cavalry, 3,255 Cossacks and Bashkirs, and 689 gunners to man 38 guns. Dokhtoruv commanded the right wing corps of Bennigsen's army consisting of 19,924 infantry, 3,424 cavalry, and 120 guns for a total of 26,571 combatants. Tolstoy commanded the left wing corps of mainly militia and cavalry: 15,995 men and 40 guns. In all Bennigsen's army numbered 59,052 men and 198 guns. See n. 63, lxxiii–lxxix, in the appendix of volume II of Bogdanovich, *Geschichte des Krieges*.

7 Continuing to Bernadotte's headquarters, Liechtenstein was to also request that the Army of North Germany execute a general movement toward the Elbe. Purportedly, Blücher had Liechtenstein deliver a letter to Bernadotte likewise requesting that he cross the Elbe.

8 Blücher to Schwarzenberg, Löwenberg, 2 September 1813, ÖStA KA, FA 1530, ad83; RA KrA, volym 25 and Add MSS, 20112, 4–5.

9 Tolstoy's command consisted of one Guard Cavalry brigade, one regular cavalry corps, V Guard Corps, and II Infantry Corps.

10 Langeron, *Mémoires*, 256.

11 Gneisenau to Caroline, Radmeritz, 9 September 1813, *Gneisenau*, ed. Griewank, 250–51.

12 Supply difficulties and the effects of the bivouac on the health of the army would take their toll. By the second week of September, the Austrian army alone tallied a sick list of 209 officers and 15,132 men.

13 Quoted in Pertz and Delbrück, *Gneisenau*, III:258.

14 "Disposition for 2 September," Löwenberg, 1 September 1813, Add MSS, 20112, 129.

15 Bubna to Schwarzenberg, Gabel, 3 September 1813, ÖStA KA, FA 1530, 66; Müffling, *Die Feldzüge*, 44; Droysen, *Yorck*, II:160–61; Friederich, *Herbstfeldzug 1813*, II:244.

16 Blücher to Langeron, Yorck, and Sacken, Lauban, 2 September 1813, Add MSS, 20112, 141; Blücher to Langeron, Lauban, 2 September 1813, RGVIA, f. VUA, op. 16, d. 3912, chast 2, l. 432; Disposition, Lauban, 2 September 1813, Add MSS, 20112, 130; Bubna to Schwarzenberg, Gabel, 3 September 1813, ÖStA KA, FA 1530, 66; Friederich, *Herbstfeldzug 1813*, II:245–46; Pertz and Delbrück, *Gneisenau*, III:265.

17 Vasilchikov's report is in Höpfner, "Darstellung," 1844:212; Bubna to Schwarzenberg, Gabel, 3 September 1813, ÖStA KA, FA 1530, 66; Blücher to Charles John, Lauban, 8 September 1813, RA KrA, volym 25; Müffling, *Die Feldzüge*, 44; Bogdanovich, *Geschichte des Krieges*, IIa:306.

18 Quoted in Höpfner, "Darstellung," 1844:212.

19 Blücher to Frederick William, Görlitz, 3 September 1813, GStA PK, VI HA Rep. 92 Nl. Gneisenau, Nr. 16.

20 See Leggiere, *Napoleon and Berlin*, 181–83.

21 *CN*, No. 20492, XXVI:153–57; Yorck von Wartenburg, *Napoleon as a General*, II:307.

22 *CN*, Nos. 20496, 20498, and 20499, XXVI:159–61; SHAT, C^{17} 180: Berthier to Macdonald, Murat, Mortier, Marmont, Victor, St.-Cyr, and Latour-Maubourg, 1 September 1813.

23 SHAT, C^{17} 180: Berthier to Ney, 2 September 1813.

24 While dictating the letter for Berthier, the emperor instructed his scribe to use quotation marks so the staff chief would know to copy those exact words. While copying much of Napoleon's note verbatim, the major-general did omit the line: "It is really difficult to have fewer brains that the duc de Reggio [Oudinot]." See *CN*, No. 20502, XXVI:162.

25 SHAT, C^{17} 180: Berthier to Ney and Mortier, Dresden, 2 September 1813.

26 SHAT, C^2 154: Lauriston to Berthier, 31 August 1813.

27 Macdonald's reports to Berthier are in SHAT, C^2 155.

28 *CN*, No. 20508, XXVI:165; SHAT, C^{17} 180: Berthier to Ney, 3 September 1813.

29 *CN*, Nos. 20507, 20516, and 20517, XXVI:164–65, 171–72; SHAT, C^{17} 180: Berthier to Marmont, Latour-Maubourg, and Mouton, 3 September 1813.

30 Odeleben, *A Circumstantial Narrative*, I:182–83; *CN*, No. 20510, XXVI:166–67.

31 "Disposition," Görlitz, 3 September 1813, Add MSS, 20112, 132; Bubna to Schwarzenberg, Gabel, 5 September 1813, ÖStA KA, FA 1530, 83; Müffling, *Die Feldzüge*, 44–45; Langeron, *Mémoires*, 268–70.

32 Blücher to Barclay, Glossen, 6:30 P.M., 4 September 1813, RGVIA, f. VUA, op. 16, d. 3912, chast 2, ll. 545–545b; Höpfner, "Darstellung," 1844:217; Plotho, *Der Krieg*, II:260; Beitzke, *Geschichte der deutschen Freiheitskriege*, II:290–91; Bogdanovich, *Geschichte des Krieges*, IIa:307–08; Droysen, *Yorck*, II:161–62.

33 The account of 4 September is based on Blücher to Barclay, Glossen, 4 September 1813, RGVIA, f. VUA, op. 16, d. 3912, chast 2, ll. 540–541; Müffling, *Die Feldzüge*, 44–45; Plotho, *Der Krieg*, II:261; Höpfner, "Darstellung," 1844:215–19; Beitzke, *Geschichte der deutschen Freiheitskriege*, II:291–92; Bogdanovich, *Geschichte des Krieges*, IIa:308; Droysen, *Yorck*, II:161–63; Pertz and

Delbrück, *Gneisenau*, III:289; Friederich, *Herbstfeldzug 1813*, II:247–48; Langeron, *Mémoires*, 269.

34 Langeron, *Mémoires*, 269–70; Blücher to Knesebeck, Görlitz, 5 September 1813, *Blüchers Briefe*, ed. Unger, 178; Bubna to Schwarzenberg, Gabel, 5 September 1813, ÖStA KA, FA 1530, 83; Pertz and Delbrück, *Gneisenau*, III:291; Droysen, *Yorck*, II:162–63.

35 Blücher to Sacken, Langeron, and Yorck, Görlitz, 5 September 1813, GStA PK, VI HA Rep. 92 Nl. Gneisenau, Nr. 18; Friederich, *Herbstfeldzug 1813*, II:260.

36 Gneisenau to Gaudi, Lauban, 3 September 1813, GStA PK, VI HA Rep. 92 Nl. Gneisenau, Nr. 16.

37 Pertz and Delbrück, *Gneisenau*, III:291, 301.

38 Steinmetz to Gneisenau, Herzogswaldau, 7 September 1813, GStA PK, VI HA Rep. 92 Nl. Gneisenau, Nr. 24, emphasis added.

39 SHAT, C[17] 180: Berthier to Macdonald, 5 September 1813; Fabry, *Étude sur les opérations de l'empereur*, 1; Vaudoncourt, *Histoire de la guerre*, I:177; Norvins, *Portefeuille de mil huit cent treize*, II:345; Maude, *Leipzig Campaign*, 213.

40 Blücher to Barclay, Görlitz, 2:00 P.M., 5 September 1813, RGVIA, f. VUA, op. 16, d. 3912, chast 2, l. 516; Blücher to Charles John, Görlitz, 2:00 P.M., 5 September 1813, RA KrA, volym 25; Müffling, *Die Feldzüge*, 45; Pertz and Delbrück, *Gneisenau*, III:289.

41 Müffling, *Die Feldzüge*, 46. Sacken's corps and Yorck's 1st and 2nd Brigades crossed the Neiße on a pontoon bridge downstream of Görlitz; Langeron's corps and Yorck's 7th and 8th Brigades crossed by way of a bridge of boats upstream of the city. Olsufiyev's IX Infantry Corps and Langeron's Reserve Artillery reached Pfaffendorf (Rudzica) while the latter's VI and X Infantry Corps remained on the right (east) bank of the Neiße along with Yorck's 2nd Brigade to take in Vasilchikov's advance guard corps. Upstream of Görlitz, the rest of Yorck's corps crossed the river and reached Kieslingswalde (Sławnikowice). Sacken's corps halted on the great east–west highway north of the Prussians. Further south, St.-Priest's corps escaped across the Neiße to Seidenberg but its van remained at Radmeritz on the western bank. Bubna's division withdrew to Georgenthal (Jiřetín pod Bukovou) inside the Bohemian frontier.

42 Fabry, *Étude sur les operations de l'empereur*, 3–4. According to the Prussian account, carbine fire from Katzler's West Prussian Dragoons broke the French. The Brandenburg Hussars and Uhlans followed the dragoons and charged the enemy troopers, driving them into the undergrowth and gorges until two cuirassier regiments belonging to the 1st Heavy Cavalry Brigade of I Cavalry Corps moved up in tight formation. Poorly mounted, they too were thrown back. See Gneisenau to Frederick William, Lauban, 6 September 1813, GStA PK, VI HA Rep. 92 Nl. Gneisenau, Nr. 16; Droysen, *Yorck*, II:163.

43 The younger brother of the commander of X Infantry Corps: Aleksey Shcherbatov.

44 Langeron, *Mémoires*, 271–72. Not providing a rebuttal to Langeron's account concerning Emmanuel's repulse of the four light and two heavy squadrons of French horse, Fabry merely states: "if we are to believe Langeron, they were rejected by the Kievskii Dragoons, the 2nd Ukrainskii Cossack Regiment, and two squadrons of the Aleksandriiskii Hussars." See Fabry, *Étude sur les operations de l'empereur*, 3.

45 Quoted in Droysen, *Yorck*, II:163–64.

46 Bubna to Schwarzenberg, Gabel, 10:00 P.M., 5 September 1813, ÖStA KA, FA 1530, 83.

47 Gneisenau to Frederick William, Lauban, 6 September 1813, GStA PK, VI HA Rep. 92 Nl. Gneisenau, Nr. 16. The account of 5 September is based on Blücher to Charles John, Görlitz, 5 September 1813, RA KrA, volym 25; Blücher to Barclay, Görlitz, 5 September 1813, RGVIA, f. VUA, op. 16, d. 3912, chast 2, l. 516; Bubna to Schwarzenberg, Gabel, 6 September 1813, ÖStA KA, FA 1530, 178; Müffling, *Aus meinem Leben*, 79–80; Langeron, *Mémoires*, 271–72; Plotho, *Der Krieg*, II:262–63; Höpfner, "Darstellung," 1844:217–21; Beitzke, *Geschichte der deutschen Freiheitskriege*, II:338–42; Bogdanovich, *Geschichte des Krieges*, IIa:308–10; Droysen, *Yorck*, II:163–65; Friederich, *Herbstfeldzug 1813*, II:249–51; Fabry, *Étude sur les operations de l'empereur*, 3–6.

48 Sacken to Blücher, Paritz, 8:00 P.M., 6 September 1813, RGVIA, f. VUA, op. 16, d. 3912, chast 2, l. 544.

49 Langeron, *Mémoires*, 273.

50 Blücher to Amalie, Lauban, 6 September 1813, *Blüchers Briefe*, ed. Unger, 178–79. The account of 6 September is based on Blücher to Barclay, Görlitz, 6 September 1813, RGVIA, f. VUA, op. 16, d. 3912, chast 2, ll. 543–543b; Bubna to Schwarzenberg, Gabel, 6 and 7 September 1813, ÖStA KA, FA 1530, 178 and 194; Plotho, *Der Krieg*, II:262–63; Beitzke, *Geschichte der deutschen Freiheitskriege*, II:341–42; Bogdanovich, *Geschichte des Krieges*, IIa:310.

51 Langeron's appraisal of Jomini was no more flattering: "He had no influence over the plans for the campaign and the little counsel that he was asked to give was all very timid, which might be surprising, coming from a writer who had attributed (and rightly so) all of Napoleon's success to his audacity and the calculated temerity of his operations. Moreover, all of these great geniuses, pen in hand, (and this is only referring to contemporaries) starting with Mack and Jomini, failed as soon as it became necessary to drop the pen and take up the sword." See Langeron, *Mémoires*, 225. Austrian general Karl Mack von Leiberich (1752–1828) capitulated to Napoleon at Ulm on 20 October 1805.

52 Knesebeck to Gneisenau, Teplitz, 3 September 1813, GStA PK, VI HA Rep. 92 Nl. Gneisenau, Nr. 23; Bogdanovich, *Geschichte des Krieges*, IIa:302; Maude, *Leipzig Campaign*, 216.

53 Janson, in *Friedrich Wilhelm*, 211, does not comment on Frederick William's reaction to Blücher's response.

54 Schwarzenberg to Blücher, Teplitz, 5 September 1813, Add MSS, 20112, 6–8, 11. In *Geschichte des Krieges*, IIa:302, Bogdanovich notes that "with the exception of Blücher, none of the Allied commanders exploited the favorable circumstances following the battles they won."

55 Schwarzenberg to Blücher, Teplitz, 5 September 1813, Add MSS, 20112, 12.

56 Bernhardi, *Toll*, III:302.

57 Knesebeck to Gneisenau, Teplitz, 8 September 1813, GStA PK, VI HA Rep. 92 Nl. Gneisenau, Nr. 23; Schwarzenberg to Blücher, Teplitz, 7 September 1813, ÖStA KA, FA 1530, 210; Bogdanovich, *Geschichte des Krieges*, IIa:311; Plotho, *Der Krieg*, II:185; Bernhardi, *Toll*, III:302.

58 SHAT, C¹⁷ 180: Berthier to Marmont and Latour-Maubourg, 6 September 1813; *CN*, No. 20502, XXVI:162–63.

59 St.-Cyr, *Mémoires*, IV:141–50; Plotho, *Der Krieg*, II:192; Bogdanovich, *Geschichte des Krieges*, IIa:312–13; Yorck von Wartenburg, *Napoleon as a General*, II:314. Napoleon's 8 September letter to Maret is in Thiers, *Histoire du Consulate et de l'Empire*, XVI:441–42.

60 Knesebeck to Gneisenau, Teplitz, 8 September 1813, GStA PK, VI HA Rep. 92 Nl. Gneisenau, Nr. 23, emphasis added. Knesebeck claimed that Berthier's letter to Ney stated that Wallmoden would receive 20,000 *men* from the Army of North Germany rather than 20,000 *biscuits*. Berthier actually wrote: "*Il paraît que l'armée ennemie de Berlin fait un fort détachement contre le prince d'Eckmühl [Davout] qui se trouve du côté de Wismar et de Schwerin* [It appears that the enemy army at Berlin has sent a strong detachment against the prince d'Eckmühl, who is between Wismar and Schwerin]." No letter from Napoleon to Berthier that would have prompted the latter to send this information to Ney is contained in the *CN*. Moreover, Napoleon makes no mention of these reinforcements in his letter to Berthier concerning Ney on 2 September. It was this letter that prompted Berthier to issue instructions to Ney. See *CN*, No. 20502, XXVI:162; SHAT, C¹⁷ 180: Berthier to Ney, 2 September 1813.

61 Janson, *Friedrich Wilhelm*, 212–13.

62 The minutes also stated: "There are two routes to effect this union. The first would be if Blücher's army is near Bautzen: from there it would proceed through Neustadt to Pirna or Königstein. This would be the best way and Blücher will prefer it as soon as he is certain that the main body of the enemy army and the emperor Napoleon have evacuated the right bank of the Elbe or have turned against the crown prince of Sweden. In the opposite case, this movement is not feasible. The second would be for Blücher to have his vanguard advance as far as possible toward Dresden and, thus covered by Bubna's division, he can decide whether to march on Leitmeritz either through Rumburg and Böhmisch-Kannitz [Česká Kamenice] or through Zittau and Böhmisch-Leipa. Blücher will send two intelligent staff officers, the first through Rumburg, who then will return through Zittau, the other through Leitmeritz and Böhmisch-Leipa to Zittau, who can then report on the condition of the roads and the possibility of executing a movement on them" (see Map 19).

63 "Opérations arrêtées pour les armées combinées," Volkonsky, Teplitz, 9 September 1813, in Höpfner, "Darstellung," 1844:244.

64 Alexander to Blücher, Teplitz, 9 September 1813, in Mikhailovsky-Danilevsky, *Denkwürdigkeiten*, 336–37.

65 *CN*, No. 20534, XXVI:182–83; Friederich, *Herbstfeldzug 1813*, II:63–64; St.-Cyr, *Mémoires*, IV:151–58; Marmont, *Mémoires*, V:155–61; Plotho, *Der Krieg*, II:198; Bernhardi, *Toll*, 313–18; Bogdanovich, *Geschichte des Krieges*, IIa:315–18; Thiers, *Histoire du Consulat et de l'Empire*, XVI:445–50; Yorck von Wartenburg, *Napoleon as a General*, II:314–16.

66 *CN*, No. 20538 and 20540, XXVI:185–86; SHAT, C¹⁷ 180: Berthier to Ney and Macdonald, 11 September 1813.

67 Alexander to Blücher, Teplitz, 11 September 1813, in Höpfner, "Darstellung," 1844:248–49; Schwarzenberg to Bubna, Teplitz, 11 September 1813, *ibid.*, 247.

68 See Leggiere, *Napoleon and Berlin*, 218–19. The full text of the treaty can be found in F. F. Martens, *Recueil des traités et conventions, conclus par la Russie*, III:117–26.

69 Sacken to Blücher, Paritz, 6 September 1813, RGVIA, f. VUA, op. 16, d. 3912, chast 2, l. 648; Sacken to Blücher, Paritz, 8:00 P.M., 6 September 1813, *ibid.*, 544. See also Müffling, *Die Feldzüge*, 46; Unger, *Blücher*, II:89; Langeron, *Mémoires*, 273. "Langeron," notes Droysen in *Yorck*, II:164, "again in his unnecessary caution, sent back his Reserve Artillery."

70 Quoted in Friederich, *Herbstfeldzug 1813*, II:261.

71 Blücher to Langeron, Lauban, 7 September 1813, in Höpfner, "Darstellung," 1844:229; Gneisenau to Stein, Lauban, 7 September 1813, GStA PK, VI HA Rep. 92 Nl. Gneisenau, Nr. 20b; Thile to Yorck, 28 September 1813, GStA PK, IV HA Rep. 15 A 268. Unfortunately, Yorck's response has been lost. Droysen, *Yorck*, II:168. See also Bogdanovich, *Geschichte des Krieges*, IIa:310; Plotho, *Der Krieg*, II:263; Pertz and Delbrück, *Gneisenau*, III:303–04.

72 Quoted in Droysen, *Yorck*, II:164–65.

73 Frederick William to Blücher, Teplitz, 31 August 1813, GStA PK, VI HA Rep. 92 Nl. Gneisenau, Nr. 16; Alexander to Blücher, Teplitz, 30 August 1813, in Mikhailovsky-Danilevsky, *Denkwürdigkeiten*, 331; Bogdanovich, *Geschichte des Krieges*, IIa:83–84. In this case, Alexander granted Langeron the right to wear an embroidered Wenzel in the shape of the letter "A" on his epaulette: a sign of great honor.

74 See Müffling, *Die Feldzüge*, 47–48; Friederich, *Herbstfeldzug 1813*, II:252; Bogdanovich, *Geschichte des Krieges*, IIa:310, 319–20; Disposition for 8 September, Lauban, 7 September 1813, Add MSS, 20112, 134; Blücher to Bubna, Lauban, 7 September 1813, ÖStA KA, FA 1530, 229a, and Add MSS, 20112, 133.

75 Blücher to Charles John, Lauban, 8 September 1813, RA KrA, volym 25; Höpfner, "Darstellung," 1844:231–32.

76 Bubna to Blücher, Grottau, 8 September 1813, ÖStA KA, FA 1530, 229b; Blücher to Schwarzenberg, Lauban, 10:00 A.M., 8 September 1813, *ibid.*, FA 1531, 329.

77 Bubna to Schwarzenberg, Gabel, 8 September 1813, ÖStA KA, FA 1531, 294; Disposition for 9 September, Lauban, 7 September 1813, *ibid.*, FA 1530, 266, and Add MSS, 20112, 135; Droysen, *Yorck*, II:165; Friederich, *Herbstfeldzug 1813*, II:252; Müffling, *Aus meinem Leben*, 80.

78 Blücher to Langeron, Radmeritz, 10:00 P.M., 8 September 1813, in Höpfner, "Darstellung," 1844:233; Langeron, *Mémoires*, 275. In *Herbstfeldzug 1813*, II:252, Friederich makes no mention of Langeron's culpability, stating only that from the Landskrone the enemy observed Allied movements.

79 The account of 9 September is based on Blücher to Frederick William, Radmeritz, 11:00 A.M., 10 September 1813, GStA PK, VI HA Rep. 92 Nl. Gneisenau, Nr. 16; Bubna to Schwarzenberg, Rumburg, 9 September 1813, ÖStA KA, FA 1530, 266; Langeron, *Mémoires*, 275–77; Müffling, *Die Feldzüge*, 32; Bogdanovich, *Geschichte des Krieges*, IIa:320–21; Beitzke, *Geschichte der deutschen Freiheitskriege*, II:344–45; Friederich, *Herbstfeldzug 1813*, II:252–53.

80 Blücher to Charles John, Radmeritz, 9 September 1813, RA KrA, volym 25, and Add MSS, 20112, 48.

81 Sacken's report to Blücher is in Höpfner, "Darstellung," 1844:238.

82 The account of 10 September is based on Blücher to Charles John, Hernnhut, 11 September 1813, RA KrA, volym 25, and Add MSS, 20112, 49; Langeron, *Mémoires*, 277–78; Bogdanovich, *Geschichte des Krieges*, IIa:320; Beitzke, *Geschichte der deutschen Freiheitskriege*, II:346–48; Höpfner, "Darstellung," 1844:238; Friederich, *Herbstfeldzug 1813*, II:253–54.

83 Müffling, *Die Feldzüge*, 49–50; Unger, *Blücher*, II:89.

84 Müffling, *Die Feldzüge*, 51–52; Blücher to Frederick William, Radmeritz, 11:00 A.M., 10 September 1813, GStA PK, VI HA Rep. 92 Nl. Gneisenau, Nr. 16. Based on Gneisenau's letters and Müffling's analysis, Delbrück validated this argument, pointing out that "up to now the results of the *kleinen Krieg* had far surpassed all expectations": Pertz and Delbrück, *Gneisenau*, III:300.

85 Friederich, *Herbstfeldzug 1813*, II:253–54.

86 Charles John to Blücher, Jüterbog, 7 September 1813, Add MSS, 20111, 114–15; Unger, *Blücher*, II:90; Leggiere, *Napoleon and Berlin*, 216. Lowe noted the ferocity with which the Prussians fought: "It is accounted for as a reason for so few prisoners being taken at Jüterbog [actually Dennewitz], in the same way as it was with General Blücher in Silesia, that the Prussians are particularly averse to giving quarter." See Lowe to Bunbury, Stralsund, 9 September 1813, Add MSS, 20111, 117.

87 Charles John to Blücher, Jüterbog, 9 September 1813, Add MSS, 20111, 116.

88 Müffling, *Aus meinem Leben*, 84, and *Die Feldzüge*, 49–50.

9

Lusatia

For 11 September, Blücher again planned to push forward only the vanguards. In fact, he remained quite wary, writing to Yorck over the "extreme" necessity of being able to withdraw through the defiles in the region of Bernstadt auf dem Eigen and Herrnhut "in the case that a rapid advance by a superior enemy forces a retreat toward the Neiße." The reports that arrived early on the 11th indicated that Macdonald's army remained on the hills both east and west of Bautzen. Before daybreak, Katzler crept as close as possible to the imperial outposts. At first light, he estimated having some 20,000 men in sight. Prisoners confirmed that the troops in front of the Silesian Army belonged to XI, III, and V Corps in addition to Poniatowski's VIII Corps. Based on these statements, Katzler estimated the total size of Macdonald's force to be 50,000 men. North of Katzler, Vasilchikov planned to lead Sacken's vanguard from Wurschen through Litten toward Bautzen in an attempt to move around Macdonald's left. However, he halted at Litten after observing that Borozdin had not led St.-Priest's vanguard from Hochkirch toward Bautzen.[1]

Blücher's commitment to the *kleinen Krieg* ended in less than thirty-six hours. He changed his mind after receiving several reports including many dispatches found on one of Poniatowski's captured adjutants claiming that Napoleon had resumed the offensive against Schwarzenberg; Gneisenau agreed. Around 10:30 A.M. on the 11th, Army Headquarters issued new orders. "According to reports," stated Blücher's cover letter, "the enemy has turned against the Bohemian Army with his main force. My intention is to drive what stands before me away from Dresden. I know from an intercepted letter that Poniatowski wants to take a position at Neustadt in Sachsen to cover Macdonald's flank. He must be attacked quickly and destroyed so that the army can turn right and drive the enemy northwest from Bautzen toward Kamenz. With this intent . . . each commanding officer will proceed and attack the enemy where he finds him."[2]

Covering 11 and 12 September, the accompanying disposition called for the Silesian Army to pivot on Bautzen with its right wing (Sacken) while its left wing (St.-Priest, Langeron, and Yorck) executed a sweeping movement to the west in the spirit of Blücher's earlier plans. While Sacken's corps advanced directly on Bautzen, St.-Priest's main body would move west from Hochkirch to Großpostwitz on the eastern bank of the Spree less than five miles south of Bautzen. Blücher ordered St.-Priest's light cavalry to make for Bischofswerda on the great east–west highway twelve miles west of Bautzen. South of St.-Priest, Kaptsevich's X Infantry Corps would march west from Löbau through Schirgiswalde to the region of Ringenhain, pushing its light cavalry to Neustadt in Sachsen, some seventeen miles southwest of Bautzen and twenty-three miles due east of Dresden. Behind these forward troops, Langeron would lead the rest of his corps from Bernstadt auf dem Eigen to Neusalza, twelve miles south-southeast of Bautzen. Yorck's corps received the task of marching west-southwest from Ostritz to Rumburg. Katzler's vanguard remained temporarily under Sacken's command for the operation against Bautzen. "Should the enemy evacuate Bautzen, the vanguards must fall on him from all sides and engage him in serious rearguard combat so that the enemy breaks in disorder," concluded Blücher's orders. Typical of Silesian Army Headquarters, this ambitious plan called for marches in excess of twenty miles. Also typically, concern about a night march played no role in the planning.[3]

One hour after issuing the 10:30 A.M. disposition for 11 September, Blücher received Volkonsky's minutes and the tsar's letter dated 9 September that again summoned the Silesian Army to Bohemia. Alexander's letter arrived at a time when the leadership of the Silesian Army gazed at the crown prince of Sweden with increasing suspicion and disdain. According to that erstwhile bard, Müffling, "important transactions took place at Bautzen, where Blücher moved his headquarters on 15 September. General Bülow, who had never placed any faith in the [French] marshal who had been summoned to Sweden, observed the machinations at the headquarters of the crown prince, and putting together his indiscretions with his deliberate insinuations, soon saw through the threads of the web. He warned Tauentzien and Blücher, and made a secret agreement with Wintzingerode as to how far they should obey and in what cases they must refuse obedience to avoid irreparable disasters. These views and agreements explain Bülow's behavior . . . and provide a complete explanation of Blücher's measures from the time he arrived at Bautzen." Shortly after the battle of Dennewitz, Bülow sent a confidential report to Blücher detailing "the daily progressive measures that the crown prince of Sweden adopted to prove to the French army that he acted not only as their countryman, but their friend; and how far he was from wishing to destroy them with his Swedes or to shed their blood. These proofs were very comprehensive, and of such recent date that they could not yet have reached Allied Headquarters. They convinced General Blücher to resolve to obviate all political high treason by a rapid flank march to the right; and he persisted in this resolution, even when, at almost the same time, he received orders from the sovereigns to move closer to them on the left, toward Bohemia."

Müffling tended to exaggerate his own influence on Blücher's decision-making, but his testimony about Bülow's report needed no embellishment. Bernadotte's conduct exasperated both Bülow and Tauentzien. According to the former, they were tired of seeing themselves inhibited "by the timidity and egotistical politics of a foreigner."[4] Not only Bülow and Tauentzien, but also Wintzingerode and even the commander of the Swedes, Stedingk, considered Bernadotte a charlatan. This sentiment reached the Silesian Army and considerably influenced its Prussian leaders. Commenting on Bernadotte's lethargic operations following the victories at Großbeeren and Dennewitz, Müffling noted that Blücher's headquarters knew the crown prince could have exploited both victories to make them decisive. "Not only was this not done, but the report spread that he had prevented General Bülow from undertaking a pursuit that would have produced the greatest results. These opinions and rumors spread the notion in the Russian and Prussian armies that the crown prince or perhaps the Swedish government had a special agreement that included the obligation of sparing the French."

Müffling maintains that Blücher received accurate information of all that occurred in Bernadotte's army. "Thus, he thought it necessary and conducive for the good cause to remain in the vicinity of the Army of North Germany for future operations." On account of Bernadotte's idleness, Blücher assumed that no activity could be expected from him as long as he remained isolated in a separate theater of war. "Thus, General Blücher was disposed ... to turn to the right and toward the crown prince, and with him cross the Elbe." The Prussians presumed that if the crown prince crossed the Elbe between Wittenberg and Magdeburg, Napoleon would most likely abandon his position at Dresden to confront his former marshal. In this case, the Silesian Army would cross the Elbe between Dresden and Torgau to link with the Bohemian Army, which Blücher believed would direct its main body to the plain between Altenburg and Leipzig. Consequently, the Prussians viewed a march down the Elbe as imperative to force Bernadotte to assume an active role in the war rather than remain on the passive defensive.[5]

On that same day, 11 September, Blücher took the initiative and wrote directly to Bernadotte. Calling the victory at Dennewitz "brilliant," he devoted a long paragraph to flattering and praising the crown prince of Sweden. "I learned with a pleasure that is difficult to express that the Prussian troops conducted themselves well in this battle but I am not surprised because of the happiness they must have had to fight under a prince who has earned the admiration of all soldiers and whose fame is known throughout Europe." Then, after describing his Army of Silesia as "principally destined to support the Grand Army in Bohemia" by marching against the enemy's bridges at Lilienstein and Pirna, he stated his belief that an offensive movement along the left bank of the Elbe by the Army of North Germany "would have the most pernicious results for the enemy." Blücher assured the prince royal that he did not have to fear for the Army of North Germany's left: "Bennigsen has received the order from his sovereign to enter on line on the Neiße with his 40,000 men."[6]

As for the tsar's dispatch, Gneisenau drafted Blücher's response, which stated only that "the 9 September letter from Your Imperial Majesty reached me today and I have the honor to lay at your feet the considerations I suggest for my movements. Today, the enemy has taken a position behind the Spree. My outposts stand before the gates of Bautzen. I have sent St.-Priest to Großpostewitz and Kaptsevich to Schirgiswalde; they will cross the Spree at these points. The corps will follow these movements. I hope to fix the enemy but according to all that we have learned this evening I believe he will depart for Dresden tonight. If this is the case, I will attack him either tomorrow evening or the following morning." In addition, the Silesian Army's ammunition and supply wagons remained on the other side of the Neiße. In light of this and with the army extended between Kamenz and Neustadt in Sachsen, it could not reach Leitmeritz for at least eight days. Blücher suggested that he continue his drive into Saxony without sending any reinforcements to Bohemia. He also informed the tsar that Bernadotte would do nothing if the Silesian Army moved away from the Army of North Germany.[7]

A lengthy "Mémoire" written by Gneisenau and signed by Blücher, purportedly with a sly grin, accompanied the letter to Alexander; the Prussians also sent a copy to Bernadotte with a request for him to approve their measures. Once again, Gneisenau's mastery of the quill emerged. Although Alexander's 9 September orders allowed Blücher to choose the route he would take to Bohemia, the tsar suggested that he march through Leitmeritz. Instead, Silesian Army Headquarters presented choices completely different from those listed by the monarch. Reading between the lines of Gneisenau's memo, the fact that Blücher and his staff did not consider a union with the Bohemian Army their first priority clearly emerged. Although claims by Friederich that they wanted to avoid becoming "tangled in the listless strategy of Allied Headquarters" are premature, Blücher and Gneisenau certainly wanted to maintain their freedom of movement.

Completely ignoring the fact that Alexander had not sent a request, Gneisenau wrote: "His Majesty the Tsar of All the Russias has given us the choice between two proposed operations: (1) to march through

Rumburg, Bohemian-Leipa, and Leitmeritz and unite with the Bohemian Army or (2) to advance toward the Elbe and establish communication on Saxon territory." Gneisenau then explained the considerations that would determine "which of the two operations would offer the two armies the greatest advantage." Accordingly, the Army of North Germany's "brilliant victory" at Dennewitz on the 6th paralyzed Ney's Army of Berlin. This allowed the crown prince of Sweden to inform Blücher that the Army of North Germany could advance anywhere it was needed. Blücher, stated the memo, responded that a crossing of the Elbe by the Army of North Germany "would have disastrous consequences for the enemy. If this victorious army crosses the Elbe between Wittenberg and Magdeburg at this moment and drives on Leipzig, it would be very probable that through this movement the emperor Napoleon would be forced to abandon his position at Dresden to oppose the crown prince's army. In this case, the Silesian Army would seek to cross the Elbe without delay between Torgau and Dresden to link with the Bohemian Army, which without doubt would proceed to the plains of Altenburg and Leipzig." Indirectly referring to the order to transfer the Silesian Army to Bohemia, Gneisenau noted that, while the battle of Dennewitz had changed the situation, the crown prince "probably will immediately lapse into a completely justified idleness if he perceives that the Silesian Army is distancing itself from him along a very wide stretch." Viewing Napoleon's return to Bautzen as an indication of another offensive against Schwarzenberg, Gneisenau added that, if the emperor attacked the Bohemian Army, the crown prince would halt the Army of North Germany until the results of this operation became known. In light of this argument, Gneisenau suggested that "His Majesty the Tsar of All the Russias will probably be inclined to give his authorization to Blücher to drive the enemy toward the Elbe rather than march to Bohemia."

Gneisenau also insisted that, although the Army of the Bober numbered only 40,000 to 50,000 men, the closer it moved to Dresden, the more Blücher needed to be on his guard against Napoleon advancing against him with superior forces. To be secure against any attack, he advocated a central position between Bautzen and Schluckenau with forward posts pushed to the Elbe. As soon as Bennigsen's Army of Poland reached the line of the Neiße, the Army of Silesia could resume offensive operations by either marching north to link with the Army of North Germany or immediately crossing the Elbe should Napoleon invade Bohemia. If the emperor decided to operate against the Silesian Army, Blücher could withdraw either through Zittau to Bohemia or across the Neiße and into Silesia. Gneisenau speculated that, if the Army of Poland could reach the Neiße, the Silesian Army's withdrawal through Zittau would force the enemy to divide his forces or expose his flank to either Blücher or Bennigsen depending on which Allied army he pursued. Concluding the "Mémoire," Gneisenau simply stated that the same advantage would exist if the Army of North Germany crossed the Elbe and the Silesian Army marched on Elsterwerda to link with it. Neither Blücher nor Gneisenau knew that, at Trachenberg in July, the tsar had pledged to subordinate Blücher to Bernadotte if the North German and Silesian Armies came together. Had they known, the Prussians would not have refrained from pursuing this operation. As we will see, they planned to completely circumvent Bernadotte by getting his Prussian corps commanders – Bülow and Tauentzien – to follow Blücher across the Elbe, despite the crown prince's orders.[8]

We left the Bohemian Army facing large imperial forces at Sobochleben in the Teplitz valley on 11 September. Much to the surprise of Allied Headquarters, Napoleon did not attack on 12 or 13 September, thus allowing Schwarzenberg to hold his position. Patrols even reported the enemy's withdrawal along the entire front: an imperial outpost remained only at Nollendorf. The enemy's unexpected withdrawal along with news of the victory at Dennewitz convinced Schwarzenberg that Napoleon would commence a general retreat of all imperial forces to Leipzig. In his opinion, the French posts at Nollendorf and on the ridge of the Erzgebirge served to mask the departure of the Grande Armée. He assumed the Silesian Army's proximity to the Elbe had contributed to Napoleon's decision. Moreover, he figured that by now Blücher had received the order to march to Bohemia and had taken the road to Pirna. Based on these considerations and assumptions, Schwarzenberg decided to drive back the weak French forces left behind by Napoleon, pursue them into Saxony, and establish communication with Blücher. Then, he planned to advance on Leipzig in unison with the Army of North Germany. This plan differed slightly from the one made during the 9 September council of war: now the march to Saxony would begin immediately and before Blücher's army reached Bohemia. Moreover, the plan of 9 September envisaged a strategic flanking maneuver with the purpose of forcing Napoleon to evacuate Dresden and abandon the Elbe. Schwarzenberg now advocated a pursuit of the enemy, who he believed would be withdrawing on Leipzig. A council of war at Teplitz on the 13th produced general support for Schwarzenberg's proposals. After repulsing the enemy forces on the foothills, the main body of the Army of Bohemia would march northwest in the direction of Chemnitz and Leipzig while Barclay guarded Bohemia with the corps of Wittgenstein and Kleist until the Silesian Army arrived.

The 13 September council of war had barely ended when Blücher's 11 September response to Alexander's 9 September order to march to Bohemia arrived, prompting the monarchs and generals to reconvene. During the first council of war earlier that day, the Allies had decided that Schwarzenberg would immediately commence his army's march to Chemnitz before the Silesian Army reached Bohemia. They based this decision on the assumption that Blücher would soon pass Pirna, move into Bohemia, and thus cover Schwarzenberg's communications as his army marched. Yet Blücher's reply placed the Silesian Army at Bautzen, thirty miles northeast of Pirna. Moreover, Blücher faced the Army of the Bober, making it unlikely that he would offer his flank and rear to Macdonald by marching to Bohemia. Consequently, Allied Headquarters had little choice but to view the arrival of the Silesian Army in Bohemia as very unlikely or delayed indefinitely. Thus, during the second council of war on the 13th, Schwarzenberg decided to postpone the advance to Chemnitz.[9]

But what of Blücher? Despite Gneisenau's finesse, Allied Headquarters remained far from satisfied with his rejection of the tsar's direct order, which had offended Alexander. Blücher's apparent refusal to march to Bohemia incensed those who saw numerical superiority as the only means to defeat Napoleon. Yet those who understood operational warfare recognized Gneisenau's wisdom. Even Radetzky, whose memorandums of 4 and 5 September called for the Silesian Army to march to Bohemia, now rejected the idea of uniting the two armies. "Any immediate union with the crown prince of Sweden or General Blücher would make us a clumsy colossus," he wrote on 14 September, "which only a God-like will and God-like obedience could inspire. United we would be the army of Xerxes." Frederick William also agreed with Gneisenau. During the second council of war on the 13th, he endorsed the idea for the Silesian Army to march down the Elbe to link with the Army of North Germany. The king likewise agreed that Bennigsen's Army of Poland should take the place of the Silesian Army in Upper Lusatia. His arguments failed to impress Alexander, who turned to Knesebeck. He instructed the Prussian officer to compare the pros and cons of Blücher's proposed movement to the middle Elbe with those of his movement to Bohemia. Support for the latter operation still held sway by the time the meeting concluded at 8:00 P.M. Nevertheless, Frederick William managed to snatch victory from the jaws of defeat by convincing Alexander to allow Blücher the latitude to decide for himself.[10]

Knesebeck recorded the minutes of the second council of war on the 13th and dispatched them to Blücher that same night. Before examining the memo, it is useful to consider the contents of the cover letter Knesebeck wrote Gneisenau: "At a conference held today, His Majesty the Tsar tasked me with drafting a memo containing the various reasons that would emerge for and against a movement of the Silesian Army to the middle Elbe or to Bohemia. I did this, but had to stop writing about the main reason, which I can mention to you only in the confidentiality of friendship. With the knowledge of the sovereigns, I will explain myself to you." Knesebeck continued by describing that in the Army of North Germany's two victories – Großbeeren on 24 August and Dennewitz on 6 September – the crown prince of Sweden had sacrificed the Prussian III and IV Corps, leaving them to face the French alone. In addition, Bernadotte failed to exploit either victory. "We have been informed of this," admitted Knesebeck, "and the Russians and Swedes are angry and aggrieved over this." "Choose now from the alternatives available to General Blücher," he declared. Yet he cautioned against advancing to the region of Torgau and Mühlberg to attempt a passage of the Elbe because it would bring the Silesian Army too close to Bernadotte. Knesebeck finally revealed to Blücher the pledge Alexander had made to Bernadotte in July: "According to the arrangements made at Trachenberg, the crown prince of Sweden could place the entire Silesian Army under his command temporarily." Showing acute foresight, Knesebeck predicted that Bernadotte would cross the Elbe only under this condition. "Therefore, it is quite possible that the entire effort of the Silesian Army would be paralyzed by this. It would be risky for you to cross the Elbe alone because you are not strong enough for this. Consider this important point and those contained in the memo and then decide."

As for the memo, Knesebeck's first sentence stated that only Blücher could decide whether the Silesian Army should march to Bohemia or march down the Elbe and cross the river near Torgau in unison with the Army of North Germany: "Therefore, he alone must make the choice." Enumerating three reasons that supported the movement down the Elbe, Knesebeck contended that the march could commence immediately without having to await the arrival of Bennigsen's army; the gap that would emerge because of Blücher's movement could be filled by a masking force. Second, the Silesian Army would be able to remain closer to its resources and, third, Blücher could extend his hand to Bernadotte. Next, Knesebeck listed five reasons against Blücher's proposed march down the Elbe:

(1) A reinforcement of Allied forces on the middle Elbe or in the region of Torgau would push the enemy back upon his resources and his motherland, thus strengthening him; increasing Allied forces in Bohemia would pull him away from his resources and therefore would work in our favor.

(2) If Blücher does not move his army to Bohemia, the Bohemian Army is not strong enough to both venture toward Chemnitz against the enemy's communications and leave behind 50,000 men to cover its *point d'appui* on the Elbe [Dresden] because it will be weaker than the enemy on the other side of the Erzgebirge. Because Napoleon needs only three marches from Dresden to reach Teplitz, the Bohemian Army cannot distance itself further than three marches ... from Teplitz in order to have enough time to be able to return to defend this point if necessary. Therefore, it will not be able to operate against Napoleon's communications with entire army units but instead with only insufficient raiding parties. In contrast, if the Silesian Army assumes guard over the Elbe, then the Bohemian Army can confidently move into Saxony.

(3) The Silesian Army will encounter great difficulties crossing the Elbe in the region of Torgau. If it cannot effect the crossing, it will be outside its sphere of effectiveness and, because the Army of North Germany will find itself in the same situation, the strength of the enemy will fall on the Bohemian Army alone.

(4) If the Silesian Army manages to cross the river, it will find itself quickly forced to accept battle because with the river behind it, it will no longer be able to avoid a blow as it has up to now. A battle before the union with the Army of North Germany would be very risky.

(5) United with the crown prince of Sweden, the Silesian Army would lose its independence, which would be quite contrary to its basic purpose.

Concluding, Knesebeck wrote: "These are the reasons that support the movement to Bohemia as soon as Bennigsen is in the vicinity to take the place of Blücher's army. Because we cannot predict the situation of General Blücher's corps or of the enemy standing on the right bank of the Elbe – and this must have a large bearing on the decision – at the time this letter arrives, the choice of what part he will play must be left to the insight of this general." Perhaps foreseeing Blücher's decision, Alexander wrote to Bennigsen that same day, ordering the Army of Poland to march to Bohemia to cover Schwarzenberg's communications. For reasons unknown, Knesebeck's memo did not reach Blücher until 15 September. By that time, Alexander and Frederick William had reached a definitive decision concerning Blücher.[11]

Returning to Blücher's front, the vanguards of the Silesian Army advanced toward Bautzen on 11 September followed by their parent corps. Toward evening, Prussian patrols reported a French withdrawal but soon found the movement to be an extension of Macdonald's right wing further south toward Oberkaina and Singwitz. Yorck received the disposition at 4:00 P.M. Although the corps marched immediately, it did not reach the defiles of the Neiße at Ostritz until nightfall. Difficult terrain permitted the corps to proceed only in a single column with the Reserve Cavalry at the head. The tip of Yorck's column did not reach Großhennersdorf until after 10:00 P.M.; the corps bivouacked there in the order of its march columns. Sacken received the orders even later than Yorck and thus reached Glossen late on the 11th. St.-Priest's troops crossed the Spree to reach Neukirch, detecting the enemy at Putzkau some four miles further west. Kaptsevich's troops took a position at Ringenhain.

During the course of the 11th, Macdonald's forces remained in their positions east and west of Bautzen while Poniatowski led the Polish infantry and cavalry southwest from Putzkau to Neustadt in Sachsen. Macdonald's army commenced the retreat from Bautzen around 2:00 A.M.

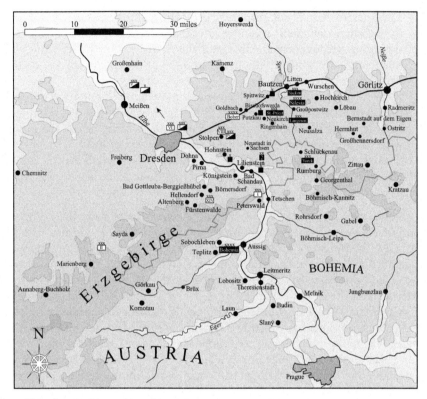

21 Situation, 12 September 1813

on 12 September. In two columns, the imperials trooped thirteen miles southwest to Bischofswerda and Putzkau respectively. A strong rearguard held the former; Macdonald's main body bivouacked between there and Goldbach. Poniatowski's Poles continued their march, reaching Stolpen, eight miles southwest of Bischofswerda and eighteen miles east of Dresden.

Around 5:00 on the morning of 12 September, the French rearguard evacuated Bautzen; Katzler's Prussians pursued. After uniting most of Yorck's vanguard at Bautzen, Katzler forwarded the cavalry, horse artillery, and light infantry toward Bischofswerda. The Prussians did not advance very far before they encountered Macdonald's rearguard, which kept them at bay until nightfall; Katzler halted at Spittwitz, seven miles west of Bautzen. Sacken's corps and the majority of Katzler's infantry under Hiller remained at Bautzen and did not follow the Prussian vanguard because a spy informed Sacken that Napoleon had reached Bischofswerda with his Guard.

Vasilchikov led Sacken's vanguard northwest toward Hoyerswerda and Kamenz to reconnoiter that region.

From Großposterwitz, St.-Priest reported the enemy's retreat from Bautzen. He informed Blücher that he planned to lead his Russians through Neukirch straight to Bischofswerda to take Macdonald in the flank and sever Poniatowski's line of retreat. His vanguard commander, Borozdin, encountered strong imperial forces at Putzkau, three miles southeast of Bischofswerda. With Sacken's corps still too far to the northeast to support him, St.-Priest ordered Borozdin to remain near Putzkau and halted the main body of the corps three miles to the east at Neukirch. Rudzevich led Langeron's advance guard to Neukirch as well; Kaptsevich's X Infantry Corps halted at Ringenhain, some two miles southeast of Neukirch. On the army's left, Yorck's corps marched at daybreak on the 12th in the direction of Rumburg, where the main body arrived long after nightfall. West of Yorck, Bubna moved his main body from Schluckenau to Ulbersdorf in Saxony, but he also heard rumors that Napoleon had led massive columns east after crossing the Elbe at Dresden.[12]

Blücher's thoughts on the situation are best illustrated in his reply to a letter from Bennigsen notifying him that the vanguard of the Army of Poland had crossed the Oder at Breslau and Steinau. "Early this morning, the enemy evacuated Bautzen and fell back on Dresden," responded Blücher. "According to intelligence reports, a strong enemy column has defiled from Dresden toward Bautzen, which is to join another enemy offensive operation." He notified Bennigsen that the Silesian Army would take a central position between Bautzen and Schluckenau, pushing its vanguards toward the Elbe. In the meantime, Blücher planned to await either the approach of Bennigsen's army, the crossing of the Elbe by the Army of North Germany, or orders from Allied Headquarters. He did not fail to note that Bernadotte had been requested to cross the Elbe after his victory at Dennewitz. "Should the emperor Napoleon fall on us with superior numbers," concluded his letter, "I will avoid his blow through a prepared retreat across the Neiße at Ostritz."[13]

As noted, Blücher received the copy of Schwarzenberg's 11 September letter to Bubna late on the 12th and responded immediately to the former. Using the same logic employed by Gneisenau in his "Mémoire" of 9 September to Alexander, Blücher explained that the Army of North Germany's victory at Dennewitz had convinced him that the best service the Silesian Army could provide to Schwarzenberg would be to drive the enemy across the Elbe and in this way relieve any pressure on the Bohemian Army. In a more forceful tone, the Prussian informed Schwarzenberg "that it is extremely unlikely that the emperor Napoleon would move more than one march into Bohemia ... Nevertheless, should this occur against all probability, I will throw myself onto the left bank of the Elbe and against the enemy's rear in unison with the crown prince of Sweden." To conclude, Blücher returned to numbers. Pointing out that Macdonald's army numbered at least 50,000–60,000 men, he assured Schwarzenberg that Napoleon could not invade Bohemia with more than 100,000 men. "Because your forces are superior in number," he reminded Schwarzenberg, "there is absolutely no probability of a successful outcome for the emperor Napoleon."[14]

Sacken's reports on 12 September concerning a renewed offensive by Napoleon prompted Blücher to halt the advance of his main body on the 13th; only the vanguards pushed forward. No evidence could be found of an advance by the French emperor. Instead, the initial reports that reached St.-Priest indicated a continuation of Macdonald's retreat. Learning that the Poles had withdrawn further west from Putzkau, St.-Priest ordered Borozdin's vanguard to pursue and occupy the heights and woods near the village of Großdrebnitz, less than five miles west-southwest of Putzkau. Before Bistram could lead the head of the vanguard from Putzkau toward Großdrebnitz, Poniatowski's rearguard sortied from the thick woods between the two villages. With one battalion of the 48th Jäger, Bistram held his position on the outskirts of Putzkau and sent the other battalion of the 48th into the woods to the south toward the heights of Oberottendorf. Satisfied with repulsing the Russians, the Poles halted and commenced the march back to the woods, leaving their skirmishers and artillery to cover the retreat. Despite their steady fire, Yuzefovich's Kharkovskii Dragoon Regiment navigated the marshy terrain and charged the Polish skirmishers, cutting down several. After clearing the line of skirmishers, the Russian troopers caught up with the main body of Polish infantry. Again charging, the Russians forced the Poles to seek shelter in the woods of Großdrebnitz, where they re-formed and again sortied supported by several guns. By this time, a Russian battery unlimbered to answer the imperial artillery. To support Bistram, St.-Priest moved up the two battalions of the Vilman-strandskii Infantry Regiment from his 17th Division. On arriving, the Russians fixed their bayonets and charged the Poles in conjunction with Yuzefovich's dragoons. This audacious attack on the numerically superior Poles surprised and disordered Poniatowski's usually stout warriors, who again withdrew into the Großdrebnitz woods. To counter the Russians, a second Polish column attempted to turn St.-Priest's left by marching north-east toward Bischofswerda. General Ivan Poll repulsed this column with his Kargopolskii Dragoons and a regiment of Don Cossacks. Despite this success, fighting lasted until 11:00 P.M. and St.-Priest ultimately failed to dislodge the Poles from Großdrebnitz. Hearing the sound of St.-Priest's cannon, Yorck marched I Corps to Schluckenau but Sacken and Langeron maintained their positions at Bautzen and Neusalza respectively.[15]

On the morning of the 13th, Blücher received Alexander's letter of 11 September claiming that Macdonald's army would unite with Napoleon for an offensive against the Army of Bohemia. Thus, the tsar ordered the Silesian Army to immediately march through Rumburg to Leitmeritz. Blücher's response, again a fine essay written by Gneisenau, assured him of the Silesian Army's preparations to march to Rumburg in accordance with the monarch's instructions. However, the Prussians presented three counterarguments meant to convince the tsar to rescind his order. Similar to their 12 September response to Schwarzenberg, the Prussians first discussed the numbers at Napoleon's disposal for an offensive against the Bohemian Army. "The news of the change in the enemy's situation will induce Your Imperial Majesty to change the direction given to me. The enemy force that my forward troops observed withdrawing yesterday from Bautzen to Neustadt in Sachsen [and] toward Bischofswerda and Stolpen is very considerable. Marshal Macdonald and Generals Lauriston and Sébastiani evacuated Bautzen around 1:00 A.M.; Prince Poniatowski moved to Neustadt in Sachsen." Moreover, the Prussians claimed that the Army of Berlin, which Bernadotte had defeated at Dennewitz, numbered between 60,000 and 70,000 men. "Therefore, the force that the emperor Napoleon can lead against the main army in Bohemia can be only 100,000 men."

Logistics and timing provided Blücher's second point. "My ammunition transports and my supply trains have yet to cross the Neiße, and because the army is extended from Kamenz to Schandau it is unlikely to reach Bohemia through Rumburg before 15 September and thus the heads of the columns will not reach Leitmeritz before 19 September." His third reason centered on Bernadotte: "I have the honor to inform Your Imperial Highness that I have summoned the crown prince to cross the Elbe." He guaranteed that the Army of North Germany would "encounter no difficulties because the defeated army has withdrawn across the Elbe and according to the latest report has taken the road to Leipzig. I will not mention to the crown prince my preparations to march to Bohemia until a second courier arrives from your Imperial Majesty to avoid providing him a reason to halt his operations."[16]

Gneisenau expressed his concern that Allied Headquarters might interpret their counterproposals to be the work of the staff chief alone. To be clear that Blücher totally supported the march north and the crossing of the Elbe, Gneisenau convinced him to personally write a note to Knesebeck. "For the general good," wrote Blücher, "I must warn against a union with the Grand [Bohemian] Army. What will such an enormous mass achieve in such a wasteland? Here, I will be effective and I can be useful. If I deviate from the plan of operations communicated to the crown prince of Sweden, he will crawl forward instead of proceeding with forceful steps. If Napoleon wants to invade Bohemia, he must be destroyed in Bohemia, but I believe he will abandon the Elbe if we maneuver well."[17] Major August Otto Rühle von Lilienstern, a former classmate of Carl von Clausewitz in Scharnhorst's courses for staff officers, received the task of delivering these letters to Allied Headquarters. Blücher also authorized him to make a verbal report to Alexander and Frederick William concerning the strategic situation of the Silesian Army and the views of its leadership.

To relieve the pressure on Schwarzenberg, Blücher considered crossing the Elbe at Herrnskretschen (Hřensko) and Tetschen, twenty-eight and thirty-three miles upstream of Dresden respectively; Bubna received orders to conduct the necessary reconnaissance. For the 14th, Blücher ordered the vanguards to continue toward Dresden: their patrols should seek to cross the Elbe. Blücher again kept the main bodies of his three corps in their positions: Sacken at Bautzen, Langeron at Neusalza, and Yorck at Schluckenau. He insisted on the continuous flow of information to headquarters: "For everyone it is determined that the outposts will report all morning, all afternoon, and all evening when their patrols bring in news of the enemy even if nothing is new. In this way, the commander in chief expects regular reports because he must then direct all the movements of the army."[18]

Early on the 14th, Katzler reported the evacuation of Bischofswerda by the imperials. He followed but soon found the French holding a position on the hills along the Wesenitz River, a right tributary of the Elbe. In fact, the imperials had settled down to cook, making their continued retreat seem unlikely. Escorted by one platoon of troopers, Katzler rode into an ambush, which prompted the Prussians to retreat. Katzler returned to where the vanguard had bivouacked the night before and received the disposition from Army Headquarters that directed him to Stolpen. While en route, he reported to Blücher that in no way did the enemy appear to be retreating to the Elbe. Unable to take the direct road from Bischofswerda to Stolpen, Katzler led his brigade through Neukirch to Oberottendorf, seven miles east of Stolpen, and halted. St.-Priest also reported to Blücher that, after withdrawing from Bischofswerda and Großdrebnitz, the imperials had taken a position behind the Wesenitz extending from Bischofswerda through Goldbach and Großharthau to Schmiedefeld. As a result of this movement, St.-Priest remained in his position at Putzkau. He again forwarded to Blücher a spy's report claiming that Napoleon and his Guard had reached Stolpen, less than eight miles south of Bischofswerda. To the southwest, Bubna informed Blücher from Ulbersdorf that across the Elbe from his position the enemy did not appear to be advancing through Nollendorf into Bohemia. Moreover, the intelligence he collected indicated Napoleon had left Pirna with his Guard and returned to Dresden on the 12th. Blücher likewise received information from spies claiming that large French forces including Marmont's VI Corps had marched from Dresden toward Großenhain on 12 and 13 September. Finally, a message from *Streifkorps* commander Major Falkenhausen noted the departure of large forces from Dresden north toward Großenhain. Thus, the reports that Blücher received on the

14th completely contradicted the news from Allied Headquarters concerning the retreat of Macdonald's army.[19]

In addition to his report, Bubna forwarded to Blücher a letter written by Schwarzenberg on the 12th. Based on Bernadotte's victory over Ney at Dennewitz, the Allied generalissimo informed Bubna that Napoleon had commenced a general retreat to Leipzig. Schwarzenberg believed that the forces standing in front of him simply served to mask the withdrawal from Dresden. He explained his plan to attack and drive back the imperials holding the passes of the Erzgebirge in order to closely cooperate with Blücher's army, which Schwarzenberg placed in the vicinity of the Elbe. He intended to move a pontoon train to the Elbe as soon as possible to establish direct communication with Blücher.[20]

Rejecting Schwarzenberg's optimistic hope that Napoleon would retreat to Leipzig, Blücher and his staff correctly interpreted these movements as Napoleon's preparations for an offensive. A letter from Teplitz written by Frederick William's adjutant, Major Thiele, reached Blücher early on the 15th; it echoed Schwarzenberg's statements about the enemy's withdrawal from the passes of the Erzgebirge to Dresden but warned that this probably indicated Napoleon's plans to target the Silesian Army. Reports from Blücher's forward troops concerning French movements along their front likewise reinforced the idea of an enemy offensive but the target remained the question. In addition, more information arrived concerning the concentration of imperial forces at Großenhain, twenty-one miles north of Dresden. Thus, the situation appeared to require the exact opposite of Schwarzenberg's plans. Rather than concentrate the Silesian Army on its left wing as the preliminary step for close cooperation with the Army of Bohemia, Blücher wanted to concentrate the Silesian Army on its right wing to prevent Napoleon from attempting a bold flanking maneuver such as the one Ney had executed at Bautzen. The easing of the pressure on Schwarzenberg supported this idea. Moreover, Blücher's own "master plan" of marching down the Elbe would not be served by a concentration on the upper Elbe. As a result, Sacken received orders to push his light cavalry toward Königsbrück and to move his main body to the St. Marienstern Convent at Panschwitz-Kuckau, approximately ten miles northwest of Bautzen, while Yorck led his corps north to Bautzen (see Map 4). The portion of Langeron's corps that stood at Neusalza likewise would march to Bautzen. All remaining troops would maintain their positions facing the enemy in accordance with the disposition of 13 September. In the case of a general French offensive against the Silesian Army, Sacken, Yorck, and Langeron would withdraw from Bautzen toward Görlitz while St.-Priest withdrew through Herrnhut and across the Neiße at Ostritz; Bubna would remain parallel to St.-Priest.[21]

After working out the disposition with Müffling and Gneisenau, Blücher drafted an explanation of his plans for Tsar Alexander. He claimed that the reports from Falkenhausen as well as the news that the French had disengaged from the Army of Bohemia had convinced him to immediately concentrate the Silesian Army on its right wing at Bautzen, pushing Sacken to Kamenz. "Will the enemy move across the Elbe? Will he march to Torgau or perhaps against the crown prince to prevent him from crossing the Elbe? Will he take the Silesian Army in the right flank? I will be able to answer these questions in forty-eight hours." Blücher also wrote a short note to Bernadotte regarding confirmed reports of a French concentration at Großenhain. "It is difficult to judge the enemy's intentions because a march against you or against the Army of Silesia is just as likely. To be *à portée* to all, I am having Sacken's corps march to Kamenz and I am uniting my forces at Bautzen to be able to follow the enemy as soon as I receive news that he is marching against you."[22]

As for Napoleon, late on the night of the 11th he entertained the idea of going to Großenhain to contend with Bernadotte. For this reason, he did not want Macdonald to abandon Bautzen. At 3:00 A.M. on the 12th, the emperor decided to send V Cavalry Corps and the cavalry brigade from VI Corps to Großenhain. Two immediate factors converged to prompt this movement. First, the shortage of flour at Dresden had become acute, forcing Napoleon to decrease the daily ration from eight ounces of bread to four ounces of rice supplemented by potatoes if possible. For relief, he arranged the transfer of mainly flour from Torgau to the Saxon capital. With Blücher and Bernadotte closing on the right bank of the Elbe, barges could not safely sail up the river from Torgau to Dresden. To protect transportation on the river, Allied forces had to be driven from the right bank. Second, the emperor wanted to secure communication with Ney's army at Torgau, especially if Bernadotte were to link with Blücher on the right bank of the Elbe north of Dresden. Later on the morning of the 12th, he decided to recall his forces – namely the Guard, I, II, and XIV Corps – from Bohemia.[23]

Returning to Dresden on the night of the 12th, he instructed Berthier to send the remaining units of VI Corps to Großenhain early on the 13th with orders "to chase the enemy from the right bank of the Elbe, between Torgau and Dresden, and aid a convoy of 15,000 hundredweights of flour that soon will be moving from Torgau to Dresden. The arrival of this convoy is of utmost importance because it will provide subsistence for several months at our central supply depot of Dresden." Murat likewise received instructions to depart for Großenhain on the 13th with I Cavalry Corps. On arriving, he would take command of V Cavalry Corps as well. With VI Corps, he would "maneuver to free the Elbe so that the convoy of 15,000 hundredweights of flour that is embarking at Torgau can reach Dresden." An officer departed from Dresden for Torgau with orders for Ney to immediately send the flour convoy and coordinate with Murat to assure its safe passage. The convoy left Torgau on 13 September. "The important business is the convoy that will deliver 15,000 hundredweights of flour," Napoleon anxiously explained to Murat on the 14th. "I hear it left Torgau on the 13th, and I think the wind was favorable, so it should not be far off, and it must have passed the difficult points."[24]

Napoleon then busied himself with preparations for an offensive against the Army of North Germany. Should Bernadotte cross the Elbe and repulse Ney a second time, he could then operate against Napoleon's communications with France. In view of this threat, Napoleon conceived a bold operation. First, he would cross the Elbe at Pirna to attack Blücher's left wing. After he drove back the Silesian Army, the road would be open for him to unite with Murat and Marmont in the Großenhain–Königsbrück region. Second, while St.-Cyr and Victor masked Schwarzenberg, Napoleon would lead the Grande Armée down the Elbe toward Torgau to unite with the remnant of Ney's army and seek a decisive battle with Bernadotte. Informing Ney that he had driven the Army of Bohemia back to Teplitz, the master revealed that he would now contend with Bernadotte. "Be prepared to follow the movement of the emperor and tell us the number of infantry, cavalry, and artillery with which you can rejoin His Majesty," wrote Berthier.[25]

To secure his rear and flank while he hunted his former marshal, Napoleon took painstaking measures to stiffen Macdonald's resolve. Around 4:00 on the morning of the 14th, he sent his orderly, Captain Caraman, to deliver a letter from Berthier to Macdonald as well as the master's verbal instructions extolling the benefits of the terrain at Bautzen. Napoleon wanted the Army of the Bober "well situated in open country, on the hills where the whole army can give battle." "The hills behind Bautzen provide the best positions," he advised. Napoleon tasked Macdonald with placing a strong combined-arms vanguard on the east–west highway, and securing his flanks with detachments that would reconnoiter to the north and the south. "In this way," lectured the emperor, "the army will be in a good position, protected against any surprises, and ready for combat or to do whatever it wants."[26]

Events during the 14th turned Napoleon's attention away from Bernadotte and back to Bohemia. On this day, Schwarzenberg's army conducted a reconnaissance in force along the Austro-Saxon frontier. Barclay easily repulsed elements of I Corps at Nollendorf and then again at Hellendorf on the Saxon side of the frontier, eleven miles south of Pirna. Despite Barclay's advance, the emperor did not believe it signaled a general Allied offensive. He explained to Murat that, although 15,000 to 20,000 men had debouched through Peterswald, the Allies had not challenged XIV Corps at Borna, eight miles northeast of Hellendorf. According to the emperor, I Corps "fell back to the only position it could defend, that of Berggießhübel. The enemy arrived there at 1:00. After a few shots he stopped in front of this position and remained quiet." "It is unclear what will happen today," concluded Napoleon early on the 15th. He planned to lead the Guard south from Dresden to see if the Allies had the stomach for an engagement.[27]

On the other side of the Erzgebirge, Rühle's arrival at Teplitz on the evening of the 14th started a chain reaction. Delivering the letters drafted at Silesian Army Headquarters on the 13th, the major made a persuasive verbal report that proved more effective than Blücher's written response. Rühle rationalized the necessity of having the Silesian Army march down the Elbe, arguing "that, because of the crown prince's politics, we should expect no activity from him while he stands alone with his army and is assigned to a separate theater of war. Thus, after leaving behind a few troops to conceal his departure and to cover his main communication with Silesia, General Blücher intends to turn right [north] toward the crown prince and to cross the Elbe with him." Based on Rühle's persuasive presentation, the tsar now completely understood and approved Blücher's proposal. Considerations over what to expect from the crown prince of Sweden influenced Alexander and Frederick William. Both agreed that Blücher had to take the lead; he would set the ball rolling. They regarded the issue as their personal business, thus earning the enmity of the Austrians at Allied Headquarters.[28]

Early on the 15th, Alexander and Frederick William officially rescinded the order for the Silesian Army to march to Bohemia. It is unclear if the monarchs issued an official letter repealing the orders that same morning. Yet it is clear that the Austrians did not have any say in the matter. As an explanation, Schwarzenberg and the rest of Allied Headquarters received the lame excuse that the Silesian Army already stood too close to the Elbe and could not march to Bohemia unnoticed by the enemy. Rühle eventually departed from Teplitz on the afternoon of the 17th with an extremely confidential communiqué from Knesebeck that expressed the two monarchs' secret approval for Blücher to march down the Elbe to the region of its juncture with the Black Elster River.[29]

After reports of the success at Nollendorf and Hellendorf reached Teplitz, the council of war reconvened on the 15th to debate Schwarzenberg's next move. In addition to the likelihood that Blücher would not come to Bohemia, Bennigsen's Army of Poland remained much further east than Allied Headquarters had anticipated: his lead elements could not reach Zittau until 17 September while his rear echelon would not arrive until the 26th. This meant that, if the Bohemian Army marched to Chemnitz, it would do so without support from either Blücher or Bennigsen. On the other hand, the success at Nollendorf and Hellendorf reinforced the conviction that Napoleon's retreat to Leipzig had commenced or simply needed a slight nudge. In turn, this led some to argue that the Bohemian Army no longer needed support. Despite Schwarzenberg's opposition, the Allies decided to immediately commence the march to Chemnitz without awaiting reinforcement from another army. As a result, the Bohemian Army received orders to begin the march northwest on the 15th.[30]

This came to naught after Schwarzenberg misread the situation. Still fearing a general invasion of Bohemia, he quickly rescinded the orders after Napoleon's tactical strike on the 15th. During the course of the day, I Corps and the Guard pushed Barclay across the Bohemian frontier. Although Schwarzenberg concentrated his army and stood his ground, he missed a golden opportunity to counterattack when imperial troop strength had markedly declined due to the need to safeguard the flour convoy from Torgau. As of the morning of the 15th, VI Corps stood at Großenhain while Murat maneuvered between Torgau and the Black Elster with the cavalry.[31]

Following the operation on the 15th, Napoleon went to Pirna and issued directives for the building of a pontoon bridge to improve communication with Macdonald. On the 16th, the emperor endeavored to reach Peterswald inside the Bohemian frontier with I Corps, while XIV Corps advanced on his right. En route, his cavalry dispersed a mass of Allied horse from Peterswald and Nollendorf. A wounded Lieutenant-Colonel Franz von Blücher numbered among the prisoners taken by the Polish Lancers.[32] Reaching Nollendorf late in the day, Napoleon obtained little information due to a heavy mist that blanketed the valleys of the Erzgebirge. Remaining at Peterswald throughout the 17th, the emperor did little other than instruct Ney as well as the commandants of Wittenberg and Magdeburg to refuse any attempts by Bernadotte to open negotiations; all communication with the Allies would be conducted through Schwarzenberg's army. At 5:00 on the morning of the 18th, he expressed his intention to resume the master plan despite the attrition of Ney's Army of Berlin. Berthier explained to Ney that Murat and Marmont remained on the right bank of the Elbe between Torgau and Dresden for the purpose of operating against Berlin and the Army of North Germany. In case of a setback, Ney would "do everything possible to save Leipzig."[33]

Unfortunately for the emperor, Macdonald did not do everything possible to hold his ground against Blücher. Napoleon assigned him the "indispensable" task of guarding the roads on his left (north) to assure the safe arrival of the flour convoy. This prompted Napoleon to continue his plan to bridge the Elbe at Pirna to facilitate communication with the marshal, some thirty miles northeast at Bautzen. Twenty miles southwest of Bautzen, Macdonald started building redoubts between Neustadt in Sachsen and Hohnstein. This signaled to Napoleon the marshal's intention to continue his retreat. With the latter point only eleven miles east of Pirna and twenty miles southeast of Dresden, Napoleon could not allow Macdonald to withdraw into this position with Blücher following. He demanded that the marshal hold Bautzen and inform him "of the movements he can execute to hurt the enemy." With Murat and Marmont between Großenhain and Torgau, Napoleon expected the Army of the Bober to make some type of stand.[34]

Encouraged by the proximity of the emperor, Macdonald ordered a general reconnaissance on the 15th; imperial patrols clashed with Allied posts all along Blücher's front. In some sectors the engagements became intense: St.-Priest barely managed to hold Putzkau. At 5:00 that morning, the Poles launched an energetic attack against Borozdin's vanguard while a flanking column moved toward Oberottendorf and St.-Priest's left flank. With the Karkovskii and Novorossiiskii Dragoon Regiments, the Don Cossacks, and the 1st Jäger Regiment, Yuzefovich held his ground against the Polish columns that emerged from the woods between Großdrebnitz and Putzkau. As the enemy "ceaselessly reinforced himself," it became apparent to the Russians that this was not a mere demonstration to cover a retreat. Borozdin moved up reinforcements, thus allowing Yuzefovich to arrange a counterattack. Yet more Polish support arrived, including one battery that opened fire on the Russian center. Borozdin summoned Bistram from Putzkau with the 33rd Jäger Regiment, one battalion of the 48th, and two companies of the 30th.

After observing Borozdin fail to make headway with these additional troops, St.-Priest moved up all available artillery as well as the Moskovskii Dragoon Regiment. Soon after, he committed the Yeletskii, Vilmanstrandskii, and Ryazanskii Infantry Regiments as well as the remaining battalions of the 30th Jäger. Borozdin deployed the Polotskii Infantry Regiment and the other battalion of the 48th Jäger to defend the Oberottendorf heights. Well-aimed fire from St.-Priest's thirty-six guns soon took its toll on the Poles, dismounting several cannon and forcing them to momentarily retreat. After re-forming, the Poles again moved against St.-Priest's left flank and renewed their attacks on the Oberottendorf heights. "It is difficult to determine their intentions," recalled Langeron; "they fought ferociously and without an objective, as the position that they occupied was not sufficiently valuable to sacrifice as many men as they did to maintain it, while their army was too weak to resist our own, and at the moment had to await the order before it could retreat. Our artillery moved with audacity until it reached the skirmishing line, crushing with grapeshot the heads of the enemy columns that were trying to deploy from the woods under the protection of their cannon, which were soon forced to retire." After sixteen hours of "ferocious fighting," the Poles finally conceded the field. They withdrew altogether on the following day, 16 September, retreating eight miles southwest to Stolpen on the road to Pirna. St.-Priest occupied Großdrebnitz and the steep Bühlau heights three miles to the west from which he could observe and dominate every enemy position. Losses amounted to 400 for each side.

While attempting to move Yorck's vanguard west from Oberottendorf to Stolpen, Katzler collided with a column from Poniatowski's corps at Rückersdorf, less than three miles south of Großdrebnitz. Forced to retreat four miles southeast to Neustadt in Sachsen, the Prussians found General Emmanuel from Langeron's corps engaged with a second column of Poles. Together, Katzler and Emmanuel managed to drive the Poles northwest on the road to Stolpen. Less than two miles from Stolpen, the Allies took the village of Langenwolmsdorf but could not hold it and eventually withdrew southeast to the hills at Rückersdorf. Around noon, Sacken informed Blücher that the imperials still held firm at Bischofswerda and that all reports as well as prisoners' statements confirmed the movement of large enemy forces to Großenhain.

As for the main body of the Silesian Army, Blücher's disposition for 15 September did not reach the corps until that afternoon. Sacken immediately dispatched Vasilchikov with the van toward Kamenz and followed with the rest of the corps as far as the St. Marienstern Convent. Yorck's corps marched through Sohland and Schirgiswalde toward Großpostwitz but became entangled with Langeron's Russians and lost several hours. After reordering the columns, Yorck continued to Bautzen. His lead elements did not bivouac until 2:00 on the morning of the 16th; the main body around 7:00 A.M. Langeron's corps likewise trudged into the bivouac very late: the two corps camped astride the great east–west highway on the eastern side of Bautzen.[35]

A report from Sacken written on the evening of the 15th confirmed that Murat had arrived at Großenhain with 50,000 men on the 14th. As for the Army of North Germany, Bülow's III Corps reached Wittenberg on the 14th; his engineers started work on bridging the Elbe ten miles upstream of the fortress at Elster. On the 15th, elements of Tauentzien's IV Corps destroyed the bridge over the Elbe near Torgau.[36] Northwest of the Prussians, the remainder of the Army of North Germany moved west to Roßlau and Zerbst while Chernishev crossed the Elbe with 2,000 Cossacks. Blücher received Tauentzien's request to drive through Kamenz toward Großenhain and secure communication with Bernadotte. A letter from Bennigsen indicated that, on the 16th, General Pavel Stroganov's division of the Army of Poland would reach Görlitz while Dokhturov's corps would extend to the Queis.

The activity along the length of Blücher's front throughout the course of 15 September again demonstrated the futility of continuing the dance with Macdonald. His close proximity to Dresden allowed the marshal to double his forces on the right bank of the Elbe in less than twenty-four hours. If Blücher still managed to drive him back, Macdonald could simply withdraw into Dresden's fortified camp. Pinning Macdonald at Dresden would not grant the Silesian Army any greater degree of flexibility. With considerable French forces rumored to be at Großenhain, Blücher could not march down the Elbe. Moreover, he could not risk crossing the Elbe immediately down-stream from Dresden at Meißen or Mühlberg because of the proximity of the Grande Armée.[37] Conversely, the situation upstream of Dresden offered little chance for a successful crossing, as Langeron noted:

> We knew that Napoleon was at Pirna with all of his forces; that there were two bridges across the Elbe; and that the old Schloß and the heights of Stolpen – which had been repaired and fortified – offered him an excellent point of support. A good, freshly paved road took him from Pirna, and, because of his position, Napoleon could move with his entire army either against the army [of Bohemia] ... via Peterswald or against us via Stolpen. This reason, as well as the passes and the woods that rendered offensive operations extremely difficult, caused General Blücher to wait for several days near Bautzen to see the results of the movements behind the Elbe of the Grand Army of Bohemia and that of the prince royal of Sweden while the reserve army under Bennigsen, which had already reached the Neiße, marched through Zittau to Teplitz in Bohemia.[38]

In view of these considerations, Blücher and Gneisenau wisely decided to watch and wait. They hoped a few days would provide time for Bennigsen's army to pass unobserved behind the Silesian Army and into Bohemia. By that time, the French presence at Großenhain would be clarified and Blücher could commence the march down the Elbe to cross the river somewhere between Torgau and Wittenberg. The next few days remained relatively quiet along Blücher's front.

On the 16th, Blücher received a message from Tauentzien that communicated his desire to cooperate with the Silesian Army. "Nothing good comes from our operations," wrote the Prussian general; "we lose time and do nothing. Because it appears that Napoleon wants to exploit the weakness of our left wing by sending a corps (supposedly under the king of Naples) to Luckau, I urgently request that you detach something to Großenhain [see Map 4]. My most ardent wish is to unite with you. I urgently request that you inform me of your position and your future plans so I can act in concert with them." Responding that same day, Blücher wanted to know how fast Tauentzien could join him to attack the imperial forces at Bischofswerda. "I am of the mind to quickly concentrate and attack the enemy standing before me. If you cooperate, I can be even more certain of success. There-fore, I am responding to your declaration with the request that you inform me when you can arrive in this region."[39]

Tauentzien's courier also delivered a letter from Bernadotte dated 14 September. Written from Coswig on the right bank of the Elbe 110 miles northwest of Bautzen, the letter stated that the crown prince had received Blücher's 11 September memo, itself a version of the letter the Prussians wrote to Alexander in protest to the Silesian Army being summoned to Bohemia.

Bernadotte expressed his complete agreement with Blücher's suggestion that the Army of Silesia march down the Elbe to cross the river in unison with the Army of North Germany. Nevertheless, he attempted to scare the Prussians with the thought of losing Berlin *should* his army cross the Elbe:

> I recognize in this the wisdom of an experienced general and the talent that corresponds to the current principles of war. A few days ago, I was in a critical situation with 70,000 men facing me, the Oder fortresses behind me, Magdeburg, Wittenberg, and Torgau in front of me, and 10,000 men on my right flank. The day of the 6th [the battle of Dennewitz] has done much to improve our situation. The enemy no longer holds the region of the right bank [of the Elbe] in front of us and Marshal Davout has withdrawn to the right bank of the Stecknitz.
>
> Nevertheless, all of this does not eliminate the difficulties of crossing the Elbe. The line that I have to hold is immense; it spreads from Hamburg to Torgau. Behind me I hold only Spandau, which is a cesspool. Moreover, its distance from the Elbe hinders us from using it and the enemy has three crossings over this river. While I march on Leipzig, he can march on Berlin from Magdeburg. I do not attach the fate of monarchies to that of their capitals but the case of Berlin is an exception. If the French advance there, they would find immense resources, and would fully destroy the means to recruit and equip the Prussian army. Nevertheless, I am determined to cross the Elbe and will make the necessary preparations.

Bernadotte continued by citing his orders for Tauentzien to build a bridgehead near Torgau and for Bülow to besiege Wittenberg. He also mentioned his intent to bridge the Elbe at Roßlau, less than twenty miles downstream of Wittenberg. With the bulk of the Army of North Germany west of Wittenberg, the crown prince requested that Blücher extend a hand to Tauentzien at Torgau, thirty miles upstream of the city made famous by Martin Luther. Moreover, Bernadotte claimed to have received confirmed reports of Napoleon's march on Großenhain. In light of this, he suggested that Blücher assist Tauentzien by advancing a large column through Kamenz to Großenhain. In a postscript he added with a note of panic: "I just received a report confirming that Napoleon has advanced his army to Großenhain. Now do you see how difficult it is for me to cross the Elbe in force with my left flank thus threatened?"[40]

In response, Blücher assured Bernadotte that he had directed the Silesian Army to assemble on its right and that Sacken's corps had already struck the road to Kamenz: "You will be informed the very moment that I hear of the enemy's march on Großenhain. The enemy is still in front of me at Bischofs-werda, which I am planning to attack if he continues his march on Großenhain; but if he retires from Großenhain to Dresden, the concentration of all forces on this side will force me to act only in conjunction with the Grand Army; but I will not fail to attract to me all so that I can deliver a great blow." He informed the crown prince that "numerous prisoners" attested to "the pitiable state and demoralization of the French army. Bennigsen has received the order to march with his army of 75,000 men in two columns through Zittau and Rumburg and occupy the position of the Grand Army, which will march to its left to completely cut off the emperor Napoleon from his resources."[41]

A few days later, the Allies learned that the French force at Großenhain mainly served to protect a supply convoy moving south from Torgau to Dresden. Committing 50,000 men under the king of Naples to ensure the safe delivery of flour certainly revealed the severe supply problems Napoleon faced just one month into the Fall Campaign. Whether this force intended to launch an offensive or guard flour mattered little to Blücher; he wanted to inflict as much damage as possible: "If only the crown prince of Sweden would advance as I have incessantly requested him to do, the situation would go well. Yesterday I received the news that 50,000 men were marching to Großenhain and only the Guard remained at Dresden; today I learned that all would return to Dresden. To deceive us, Napoleon goes here and there; with God's help this will do him no good; he is on the move and we must be off."[42]

Blücher's forward troops under St.-Priest, Bubna, and Katzler spent the 16th and 17th locked in minor clashes with Macdonald's rearguards but the main bodies of the two armies did not change position. On 18 September, Army Headquarters received confirmed reports that two days earlier an imperial detachment of approximately 1,000 infantry and 2,000 cavalry had marched toward Elsterwerda while an army of 40,000 men and 32 guns had camped at Großenhain.[43] From a letter to Sacken, we know the conclusion Blücher drew from these reports: the French held Großenhain and its environs in part to obtain food and fodder for Dresden and in part to relieve the supply problems at the Saxon capital by forwarding 40,000 men to a relatively untouched region. Still contemplating an operation against Großenhain, Blücher ordered Sacken to determine the exact position and strength of the enemy. In his opinion, until the Bohemian Army launched an offensive, the most appropriate step for the Silesian Army would be to drive the imperials from Großenhain. That evening, the Russian corps commander sent patrols west from Kamenz toward Großenhain, moving northwest toward Elsterwerda and southwest in the direction of Radeburg. Sacken's presence twelve miles north of Bischofswerda apparently prompted Macdonald to move closer to Dresden. Evacuating the Bischofswerda–Frankenthal area, the imperials moved half a day's march westward to the Großharthau–Arnsdorf line. Blücher's troops occupied Pulsnitz; Russian cavalry pursued as far Arnsdorf (see Map 4).[44]

Rühle returned from Allied Headquarters with Knesebeck's secret letter confirming that the Russian and Prussian monarchs had granted Blücher complete freedom of action. As soon as the Army of Poland reached Bohemia, the Prussian commander could march north to cross the Elbe at an appropriate point. That same evening, the 18th, Gneisenau issued orders to invest Glogau on the left bank of the Oder and to secure the army's rearward communications. On the 19th, Blücher received the results of Sacken's reconnaissance: Großenhain contained a camp of 30,000 men, mostly infantry, and 6 guns as well as Murat's headquarters.[45] That night, confirmation reached Blücher concerning the Army of Poland's march to Bohemia: Bennigsen planned to reach Zittau on the 20th.

More importantly, Tauentzien's response to Blücher's letter of the 16th arrived. "It is my most sincere wish to join you and to operate against the enemy in unison with your army," wrote the commander of the Prussian IV Corps. To accomplish this with as much strength as possible, Tauentzien suggested that Bernadotte order Borstell's 5th Brigade from Bülow's III Corps to occupy the defiles at the village of Elster. "If this occurs, I will be strong enough to move through Elsterwerda against the enemy at Großenhain and to link with you through Elsterwerda and Ortrand. Should the crown prince reject my suggestion, I will be forced to leave behind [General Karl Georg von] Wobeser's brigade at Elster and facing Torgau. I then will have only 10,000–11,000 men at my disposal." Even with 10,000 men, Tauentzien pledged his readiness to link with Blücher and only awaited his orders. "In the meantime, I am very weak in cavalry and especially in artillery and thus humbly request that you support me with some cavalry and if at all possible with some horse artillery or at least heavy artillery" (see Map 4).

Although Blücher's one-time rival for command of the Prussian army appeared ready to operate in unison with the Silesian Army, he offered no prediction regarding Bernadotte's possible reaction. Blücher harbored little concern for protocol or the manner in which this cooperation would be viewed by the crown prince. "As soon as you can," stated his reply, "I request that you march on Elsterwerda and inform me of your arrival. Then, I will direct a corps from Königsbrück to Großenhain so that it reaches the enemy at the same time you do. I will send you cavalry and artillery; expect to meet it halfway between Elsterwerda and Großenhain. If the enemy makes a stand at Großenhain, we can probably cut him off from Dresden." According to the rumors that reached Silesian Army Headquarters, Bülow likewise prepared to proceed with or without Bernadotte's approval.[46] Steffens noted the positive mood that permeated Blücher's headquarters over this news:

> During our stay at Bautzen important negotiations ensued between the Silesian and the main armies. I almost always dined with Gneisenau, together with many officers of the staff. One day he was in great spirits;

the conversation turned to the victories we had already won at Dennewitz, Jüterbog, and Kulm; at length Gneisenau said, with the most confident air, "Gentlemen, we shall taste this year's grapes on the Rhine; but do not mistake me, I mean the last grapes which, in November, will yet be hanging on the vines." I guessed that this decided belief sprang from some great intended enterprise of the success that he felt assured. Yet Napoleon was still mighty; he ruled not only over France, but great parts of Germany, Italy, Belgium, and the Netherlands; and though his fortunes seemed dire in Spain, his resources were enormous. Therefore, Gneisenau's positive prediction was startling.[47]

Blücher's confidence, especially in the troops, also remained high: "You will not believe how brave our Landwehr is," he wrote a friend; "the Russians I have with me are also very brave but the Cossacks steal like ravens." However, the campaign continued to take a toll on the soldiers, which in turn eroded discipline and increased attrition. By 25 September, the Landwehr of Yorck's corps mustered 8,012 men and 528 officers, while an additional 2,410 lay in the hospitals and 386 men had died. Thus, from the militia's original strength of 13,370 men, some 2,034 were still missing. Some had been captured by the French but others deserted. Of the 16,741 men of the Line infantry at the expiration of the armistice, only 12,058 were still under arms despite the arrival of more than 3,000 replacements. The total strength of the corps on 25 September 1813 numbered 20,588 infantry and 4,043 cavalry.

With its magazines still on the Bober, the Army of Silesia was barely receiving enough food. Official reports to the king by Gneisenau and Blücher claimed that the Silesian Army did not lack bread, meat, or brandy, but fodder. Consequently, foraging parties had to be dispatched miles away from the camps to find food for the horses, yet discipline in general remained satisfactory. Some disagreement existed over this last issue. Major Oppen, who administered the army's military police, reported that "order is maintained by mobile columns, a superb spirit reigns in the army, and an excellent understanding exists between the allies." However, Müffling took issue with this appraisal and spoke openly of the lack of discipline in the Silesian Army. In a letter to his friend, Knesebeck, he reiterated Blücher's sentiments regarding the Cossacks but also implicated the Prussian soldiers as well as the army's leadership for not taking a tougher stand against marauding:

The momentary pause in our operations was absolutely necessary to avoid degenerating into a wretched state. A great convoy of shoes has finally reached us and 4,000 pairs have been distributed to each brigade. Half of the men in many battalions went barefoot. Regarding the provisions, up to now the system is still functioning; but soon everything will be consumed because the disorder caused by the Cossacks is indescribable. It is not enough that they destroy everything that they cannot take with them, but they steal all horses and livestock so that transports are no longer possible. Due to recurring robberies on the public highways, which everyone is exposed to and defenseless against, deliveries no longer come from Silesia. Deputies who came from many cities from inner Silesia and wanted to bring the army gifts of food were robbed, and their boots stolen; they had to return home barefooted. The severest punishment of the marauders by means of compliance with the judgment of martial law is the only means to restore discipline and safeguard our subsistence. But for this our generals and especially Blücher cannot decide. If we remain idle any longer it will then be possible to gradually get through this and restore order but it will be impossible if we move. Almost all the Cossacks are behind the army. With them is a portion of the Landwehr and even our best cavalry regiments have numerous marauders who plunder and steal. This disorder has caused me much concern and it still does, for if we move ten miles further without a halt, it will be just as bad as it was.[48]

Supply shortages did indeed exist in the Silesian Army. While marching to Bohemia, Bennigsen's army moved across Blücher's rear, thus severing the latter's supply lines. The stoppage of provisions from Silesia drove the men of the Silesian Army to take steps necessary for their survival. Thus, only the strict enforcement of the regulations could end the increasing crimes committed by the starving soldiers. Yet the generals, especially Blücher, could not bring themselves to punish the soldiers, especially because time would improve the situation. Actual complaints to the king and his entourage over shortages concerned the critical dearth of hard currency. Officers had not received pay since July. Asserting that this made the officers indignant, Gneisenau urged Hardenberg to remedy the problem. He explained that, unable to purchase new boots and uniforms, officers had to have the former resoled and the latter patched. Replacing footgear in general became vital. In some battalions, only half the manpower still possessed footgear. Army Headquarters did not have the funds to cover the needs of thousands. "One speaks of English subsidies," complained Gneisenau, "but no one sees any money." The state chancellor responded two days later:

That the army suffers from the lack of funds and has received no pay since the month of July arouses an extremely unpleasing feeling in me, dear friend. But I confess that I do not understand this since 250,000 thaler has been designated for this army since the outbreak of hostilities [150,000 thaler from the national government and 100,000 from the Silesian provincial treasury]. When I received your letter, measures already were being taken to make a further 175,000 thaler available, as you can see from the copy of my letter to General Blücher. "One speaks of English subsidies, but no one sees any money," you wrote. From where, then, did those payments come, as well as the great variety of other things that I have supplied, other than from this source? It is only bad in the sense that it is difficult to turn the English credits into hard currency and that the movement to and fro is poor and much time is lost. It has been much more difficult to procure the necessary funds for this war and for our great exertions than the uninformed multitude believes ... If I have enemies, dear friend, my conscience tells me that I do not deserve them and this awareness raises me above their judgment.[49]

Resentment and concern over the pause at Bautzen mastered the Prussians at a time when many anxiously awaited the outcome of a war they thought would soon be over. Should all the sacrifice and strains be in vain because the Allied commanders delay out of fear of Napoleon's genius? "If we cannot do anything now, then when can we really do something?" asked Clausewitz. "Who is the huntsman; who will take the redemptive shot?"[50]

Blücher's movements, which had caused panic at Macdonald's headquarters, finally caught Napoleon's attention. Shortly after learning on the morning of the 19th of Macdonald's retreat, Napoleon received a proposal from Murat that appealed to the emperor: unite Murat's command (VI Corps and I and V Cavalry Corps) with Ney's army between Herzberg and Torgau, drive all enemy forces east, turn northwest to destroy Bernadotte's army, and then continue to Berlin. "Your plan," responded the emperor at 10:00 A.M. on the 19th, "would not, I believe, encounter any great obstacle." Yet Macdonald's situation and more importantly Blücher's proximity frustrated Napoleon. "It seems that the enemy has pushed a sufficiently strong detachment [Sacken's vanguard] from Pulsnitz to Radeberg, and that the duc de Tarente [Macdonald] is very worried." Seeking a way to kickstart Macdonald, Napoleon explained to Murat that the latter's movement from Großenhain to Königsbrück and Kamenz would enable Macdonald to resume the position at Bautzen. Nevertheless, Napoleon hesitated. He could not decide between endorsing Murat's suggestion to implement the master plan or to conduct a general operation against Blücher in conjunction with Murat and Macdonald. Odeleben claims that the news of Bernadotte's crossing of the Elbe at Dessau caused consternation: "A dismal silence reigned at French headquarters. The majority of the army had been harassed by useless marches and countermarches; a painful expectation continually prevailed. The blinds of Napoleon's cabinet remained drawn, as was the case during all emergent business." Napoleon speculated to Murat: "If I decide to march on Stolpen, Bischofswerda, and Bautzen tomorrow, your movement on Kamenz ... would cut off several detachments and even the enemy's infantry. Get yourself and the duc de Raguse [Marmont] ready to execute the movement you suggested."[51]

The fact that Allied *Streifkorps* were gnawing at Napoleon's communications exacerbated the situation. In particular, the renegade Saxon general, Thielmann, now in Russian service, had severed the French lifeline to Erfurt and thus Paris. To restore his communication, the emperor dispatched the Guard Cavalry's 2nd Division. "It is of utmost importance to drive the enemy from Naumburg and Weißenfels, reopen communication with Erfurt ... and restore freedom to the debouches of the Saale," he wrote to the cavalry commander, General Charles Lefebvre-Desnouettes. "Several of my couriers are missing. Send all my cavalry depots and wounded as well as all the materiel at Leipzig to Erfurt and Gotha. All of this is of utmost importance." To secure his communication across the Saale, Napoleon ordered Marshal Charles Pierre Augereau's IX Corps to march from Würzburg to either Erfurt or Jena (see Map 1).[52]

One hour after replying to Murat, Napoleon moved closer to making a decision. According to Yorck von Wartenburg, Blücher's advance on Kamenz brought the Silesian Army "so close to the central position of the French army that the whole strategical [sic] edifice was shaken." Consequently, Napoleon ordered two divisions of Young Guard as well as the Guard Cavalry to cross the new bridge at Pirna. Masked by the Poles of VIII Corps and IV Cavalry Corps a few miles east at Stolpen, the master instructed his shock troops to take positions in the triangle formed by the villages of Lohmen, Röhrsdorf (Dürrröhrsdorf-Dittersbach), and Stürza. The northern point of the triangle – Röhrsdorf – lay seven miles south of the Großharthau–Arnsdorf line, which Macdonald held that day. "If the weather is less terrible tomorrow," wrote Napoleon at 11:00 A.M., "I am inclined to march on the enemy and push him beyond Bautzen." He gave the Poles strict orders to ensure that Blücher remained completely ignorant of the approach of the Imperial Guard: "Conceal your troops with your cavalry so the enemy sees nothing and remains absolutely ignorant of this movement" (see Map 4).[53]

Drenched by the downpours of late summer, the Young Guard and Guard Cavalry crossed the eight or so miles to reach the triangle formed by Lohmen, Röhrsdorf, and Stürza on the 19th. Orders to continue to Bautzen did not follow that day or the next. Napoleon postponed operations simply because of the bad weather and its impact on the troops. He passed the night of 19/20 September at Pirna. Little had changed by 4:00 A.M. on the 20th. "Yesterday and last night were so awful that it was impossible to move," he informed Marmont at Großenhain. "The duc de Tarente [Macdonald] gave a false alarm. You must remain in your position until further notice. It is unlikely that the enemy infantry will dare to advance. If it does, I will arrive to reinforce you and we will give battle, which would be very advantageous, but that appears to be opposed to their system. The major issue at the moment seems to be to conserve the weapons and cartridges as much as possible." This letter suggested that, in addition to the foul weather, the Reichenbach Plan had impacted Napoleon's thinking and contributed to his forfeiture of the initiative. After concluding his letter to Marmont, the emperor decided that the adverse weather ruled out operations on the 20th. "The dreadful weather that has continued today makes all movement impossible," he explained to Berthier; "if the weather is better tomorrow, we will be ready the day after."[54]

Returning to Blücher, he estimated that perhaps 50,000 imperial soldiers spread between Bischofswerda, Stolpen, and Großenhain faced his army. Aside from a small skirmish at Großharthau, 20 September passed quietly. Sacken's intelligence service provided numerous reports on the situation at Großenhain. Estimating the Silesian Army to number 120,000 men, the imperials appeared to be bracing themselves for an attack but had returned the majority of their artillery to Dresden. According to deserters, Murat himself commanded between 45,000 and 50,000 men at Großenhain. Insufficient food, lack of shoes, and exhaustion sapped their strength and morale. Considerable unrest reigned in the imperial army as a whole, especially among the Germans.[55]

On the extreme left wing, Bubna conducted reconnaissance toward Pirna based on a request from Gneisenau.[56] He reported from Langburkersdorf near Neustadt in Sachsen that a spy placed the main French army eleven miles south of Dresden along a twelve-mile stretch between the villages of Dohna and Dippoldiswalde; Napoleon was quartering at a mill near Pirna. To cover the bridge over the Elbe at Pirna, the imperials extended their line along the right bank of the Elbe through Lohmen to Stürza. Bubna estimated the detachment at Lohmen to number 500–600 men. Aside from the smaller garrison at Stürza, he remained certain that no considerable imperial forces had crossed the bridge at Pirna. A large garrison occupied Pirna itself exclusive of the 1,000 men of the Imperial Guard who defended the bridge.[57]

Around noon on the 21st, Blücher received Tauentzien's response from Bad Liebenwerda, sixty miles northwest of Bautzen, written at noon on the 20th. Finding the imperials concentrated at Großenhain, twenty miles south of his main position, Tauentzien urgently requested information on Blücher's next move. As a result of this communiqué, Gneisenau and Müffling issued the extremely detailed "Secret Disposition" for 21 through 24 September to envelop the enemy forces facing the Silesian Army on the highway to Dresden. Quite simply, Yorck and Langeron would fix Macdonald in the region of Radeberg while Sacken and Tauentzien attacked Murat at Großenhain. To honor his pledge to Tauentzien, Blücher instructed Jürgaß to lead three Prussian cavalry regiments and two horse batteries across the Spree downstream from Dresden and proceed to Rosenthal. On the 23rd, the detachment would continue northwest to Ortrand and await Tauentzien's orders. During these two days, the Silesian Army would move west: Sacken to Königsbrück, Yorck ten miles behind him at Kamenz, and Langeron to Förstchen. On the afternoon of the 24th, Army Headquarters planned on Sacken and Tauentzien attacking Murat at Großenhain and preventing his forces from retreating to Dresden. Meanwhile, Langeron's vanguard would execute a feint attack on Macdonald's position at Großharthau as Yorck's vanguard did the same at Lotzdorf and Radeberg. Should Sacken and Tauentzien succeed at Großenhain, Blücher instructed them to remain there. In the opposite case, both would withdraw either northeast to Ortrand or southeast through Königsbrück.[58]

Although reports clearly indicated that Murat would have a slight numerical advantage over Tauentzien's 11,000 men and Sacken's 25,000 including the cavalry under Jürgaß, Blücher remained confident of a victory at Großenhain. Time represented one inherent flaw in the "Secret Disposition" that the Prussians could not control. They could hardly count on the situation of the imperials to remain the same from the evening of the 21st to the afternoon of the 24th. Indeed, late on the morning of the 22nd, a report from Sacken arrived: Murat had evacuated Großenhain. Acting on Napoleon's orders, the king of Naples had withdrawn eleven miles southwest to Meißen with his main body. Blücher requested confirmation from Sacken. If this was true, the Russian commander had to inform Tauentzien and attack Macdonald's left wing at Radeberg either alone or with him. Despite the uncertainty of the situation, Blücher's optimism mounted. "I stand with Dresden under my nose and I think I will soon go there," he wrote on the morning of the 22nd. "The French emperor stands at Pirna with his main force. Facing me at Großenhain stands the king of Naples; I think I will attack him in a few days." So confident was Blücher that he spoke of peace and retirement: "The situation now goes well. We will certainly reach the Rhine before winter and then there will be peace. If I live to see this, I will say farewell to the service and live a few days for myself."[59]

Yorck's main body camped in tight cantonments between the Spree and the Bautzen–Weißenberg road; Prussian veterans recalled the narrow escape from that very place five months earlier. Late in the morning, Yorck rode west with Schack to the outposts to reconnoiter the terrain. Bischofswerda lay completely in ruins. From a hill on the opposite side of the town he observed the enemy position at Großharthau and on the Kapellen hill; the outposts of both sides stood very close to each other. The wood to the north particularly concerned Yorck because it could conceal a force approaching Bischofswerda. Returning, he had barely had time to dismount when he received Katzler's report of a general enemy advance.[60]

Returning to Napoleon, he limited his movements on the 21st to recalling one division of Young Guard to Pirna while he himself went to Dresden with the Old Guard. His purely defensive arrangements aimed to secure the line of the Elbe and grant the army some rest. He transferred V Corps from Macdonald's purview to that of St.-Cyr. With V, I, and XIV Corps – in Napoleon's estimate 40,000–50,000 men – St.-Cyr not only had to hold the Elbe from Pillnitz to Königstein, but guard all the debouches from

Bohemia between Königstein and Freiberg. He directed VI Corps to Freiberg and II Corps to Chemnitz: together they would observe the Bohemian
frontier from the left bank of the Elbe to the right bank of the Saale. Stripped
of command of all but his XI Corps, Macdonald received instructions to fall
back to the woods west of Dresden. Returning III Corps to Ney, Napoleon
tasked the bravest of the brave with the defense of the Elbe from Magdeburg
to Torgau with this corps as well as the remains of the Army of Berlin: IV
and VII Corps and III Cavalry Corps. This assignment received particular
emphasis because of the news that reached Imperial Headquarters concerning Bernadotte's efforts to bridge the Elbe in the Dessau–Roßlau region.
Between the sectors of the Elbe held by Ney and St.-Cyr, Murat received
orders to cross to the left bank of the Elbe at Meißen early on the 22nd with
I and V Cavalry Corps and VI Corps. If he received confirmation that the
Army of North Germany had crossed at Dessau, Napoleon wanted him to
lead his army group directly to Torgau. Regardless of the situation further
downstream, Murat would dispatch detachments along the left bank to
Torgau. As for VI Corps, if reports confirmed Bernadotte's crossing of the
Elbe, presumably to make for Leipzig, the master wanted Marmont to
occupy the bridgehead at Meißen and to be ready to march on Torgau rather
than move his corps to Freiberg.[61]

   While these orders addressed the threats posed by Schwarzenberg and
Bernadotte, they ignored Blücher. However, later on the 21st, Napoleon
received news from Poniatowski at Stolpen over the approach of Blücher's
army. The emperor insisted that Macdonald support the Polish prince "so
that under no circumstances will he be obliged to evacuate Stolpen." Early
on the 22nd, Blücher's operations finally forced Napoleon to take action.
His letter to Berthier provides an interesting snapshot of the extent to which
Blücher's movements bedeviled Macdonald and, by extension, Napoleon.
"The situation of the enemy between the Spree and Bischofswerda appears
uncertain," wrote the emperor. "The duc de Tarente [Macdonald] indicated
in his letter of the 14th that the corps of Langeron and St.-Priest ... had
maneuvered to the right [south], and that he decided to concentrate on his
position. Since then, he has claimed in his letter of the 19th that he feared
taking a position at Weißig because the enemy, after operating on his right,
now maneuvered on his left and threatened to reach Dresden before him.
Finally, according to yesterday's report, the duc de Tarente's spies
announced that 15,000 men from Yorck's corps are on the far left [north],
and that another Russian or Prussian corps is following, always in the
direction of the Elbe."

   In addition, Müffling maintained that on 21 September Blücher wrote a
letter to his son, Franz; a Prussian trumpeter delivered it to the nearest
imperial outpost. To deceive Napoleon about his whereabouts, Blücher
dated his letter from Bischofswerda.[62] Langeron confirmed this story:

This was a ruse by Blücher, who made Napoleon believe that our army had advanced as far as Bischofswerda. Blücher's son, who was serving with the main army, had been wounded and taken prisoner near Dresden. Napoleon advised Blücher of these events and proposed exchanging his son for Colonel Edmond de Perigord, who had been taken by Tauentzien's light troops, whom Napoleon believed to be from our army. Blücher thanked Napoleon for his concern and dated his letter from Bischofswerda, where Napoleon had hoped to surprise us and thus lost five precious days that he needed. Blücher also noted that Perigord was not held by our army but could have been taken prisoner by the light troops of the prince royal of Sweden, or by those of Bennigsen, who was still far away from us; Blücher wanted to make him believe that we had all united and he succeeded in this for a short while.[63]

Revealing his frustration with Macdonald, Napoleon put down the imperial foot: "In this situation, the emperor now orders the duc de Tarente to attack between 11:00 A.M. and 1:00 P.M. on the 22nd with his left, center, and right, approaching the enemy in all of his positions and carrying everything before him until he finds himself in a position facing an army ready for battle and in strength equal to or greater than his. He will try to take prisoners; he will interview the inhabitants to gather as much information as possible about the enemy's movements." Napoleon hinted that he would probably follow Macdonald, ready to unite with the marshal according to circumstances and to attack Blücher the next day "if we find the enemy line." Per the norm of Imperial Headquarters, Napoleon wrote these instructions to Berthier, who then generated a second letter to Macdonald. However, per Napoleon's original letter, the major-general included the admonition: "Today's attack for a grand reconnaissance is ordered by the emperor as part of the general affairs of the whole and should not be postponed for any pretext whatsoever, unless the weather is as bad as it was on the 20th; but, if the weather is like it was on the day of the 21st, the attack should proceed."[64]

Macdonald received these orders at 9:30 on the morning of the 22nd. Not expecting to be called to launch an offensive, he had already dispatched large foraging parties. Responding with a request to postpone the operation until the following day, Macdonald learned that the emperor himself would reach the vanguard "between 12:00 and 1:00 P.M. I want you to unite all the cavalry, infantry and artillery that you can. If the artillery cannot move on the highway, it will be the same for the enemy. Today I want to know positively what the enemy is doing. Between noon and 2:00 we will make a sudden attack and take some prisoners. We will also obtain some information at Bischofswerda, and then, depending on the circumstances, we will be able to act strongly tomorrow. I warned you that my intention was to attack as long as the weather was not so bad." Despite having wasted the days of the 19th, 20th, and 21st, the emperor concludes: "In a war like this,

days are of great importance. Please, make your dispositions." With orders
for its dissolution already issued, the Army of the Bober would advance one
last time.⁶⁵

Napoleon himself arrived at Macdonald's headquarters accompanied by
only one battalion of Old Guard, one squadron of Chasseurs-à-cheval, and
sixty gendarmes. Per his tradition before a decisive battle, the emperor
reviewed the battalions on hand, awarded the Legion of Honor, and conse-
crated the standard of the 49th Line with the usual pomp. Around 2:00 P.M.,
Macdonald's subordinates received their marching orders: III and XI Corps
toward Bischofswerda, and V Corps on Neustadt in Sachsen. Suspected
enemy forward positions at Goldbach, Großdrebnitz, and Pulsnitz should
be attacked immediately. Slightly after 2:00, imperial squadrons supported
by one battalion advanced from Großharthau. Intense fire from the heavy
artillery that supported the Prussian outposts kept them at bay. "Then one
saw many fire signals go up; immediately after, columns advanced from a
concealed position north of the Kapellen hill; all proceeded with such
intensity and the *en avant* was so strongly shouted that one immediately
concluded that Napoleon was present."⁶⁶

Extensive columns – some 20,000 to 30,000 men according to Blücher –
advanced from the Kapellen hill west of Großharthau as well as from the
Massenei wood to the northwest. Artillery unlimbered on the hill east of
Großharthau. The Allied outposts gradually withdrew east toward Goldbach. Two miles south of Großharthau, Langeron watched as the imperials
deployed:

> From the hills of Bühlau, where I had gone with Count St.-Priest to observe
> the enemy positions, I noticed at 4:00 P.M. on 22 September that they were
> once again advancing toward us with large forces. At 5:00, I saw all these
> columns move quickly on the Bischofswerda road; they defiled 1,000 paces
> from us, and we knew, by means of a deserter, that Napoleon had arrived
> from Pirna that morning with large forces, and that he himself was at their
> head to direct the attack that he planned. I estimated the forces he deployed
> against my advance guard to be around 40,000 men. Earlier that morning, he
> had driven Sacken's Cossacks from Pulsnitz. Thus secured on his left flank,
> he wished to once again attempt to engage our army in a general battle,
> believing us to be at Bischofswerda. At 6:00 P.M., he made an impetuous
> attack on the vanguards of Borozdin, Rudzevich, and Katzler.

Emmanuel, commanding Rudzevich's vanguard cavalry, and Katzler with
Yorck's agreed to stop the French at Goldbach. Should this attempt fail,
they hoped to slow the enemy as much as possible before making a stand
east of Bischofswerda. With his forward infantry east of Goldbach and his
cavalry on the right wing, Katzler covered the eastern exits of the village
with four batteries. His main body remained in reserve at Bischofswerda.

Emmanuel placed his troops on Katzler's left wing; Borozdin stood west of Bühlau with St.-Priest's advance guard.

With an intensity befitting their emperor's presence, Macdonald's troops pursued the Prussians east from Großharthau. Two miles to the north, a second column plowed southeast through Frankenthal toward Goldbach, unlimbering several batteries on the hills west of the latter village. To the south, Lauriston's V Corps converged on Bühlau, gradually pushing the Russians east to Großdrebnitz. Langeron continues:

> I again found myself with Count St.-Priest, Borozdin, and many officers on the heights of Bühlau, from where I observed all the French columns and examined their movements. They stopped near us, and I saw Napoleon (whom we easily recognized) enter the farm of Großharthau. At the same moment, his light troops quickly moved against our advance posts and they managed to get ahead of us in the woods, even though we were retreating at a gallop. They fired many musket shots close to us and for a moment I thought they had cut off my retreat on the Bautzen road ... had they killed my horse, I would not have had any means to escape capture; we had remained, very imprudently, too long on the mountain of Bühlau, and the speed of our horses alone saved us from this unfortunate fate. The French light troops are truly unbelievable.

North of Großdrebnitz, Prussian canister confined the imperials at Goldbach for approximately thirty minutes. That is all the time Katzler could buy before the column coming from Frankenthal threatened to envelop his left. To cover the retreat east to Bischofswerda, the Prussian cannon withdrew from the firing line individually, thus maintaining the shelling for as long as possible. Despite the deadly effects of Prussian grape, the imperials seemed to sprint across the two miles that separated Goldbach and Bischofswerda. Bitter street fighting ensued in the latter, with Katzler's rearguard barely holding the town. "The enemy burned Goldbach and attacked Bischofswerda, which the Prussian infantry of Katzler's vanguard defended with the greatest courage," noted Langeron. "After having lost many men, Napoleon was obliged to employ great forces to take this little village, which had burned three months earlier during the retreat from Dresden to Bautzen, and he could not advance further ... The Prussian major Hiller, who commanded at Bischofswerda, earned great honor with his stubborn defense."[67]

Although the imperials finally took the town, Katzler's guns east of Bischofswerda prevented them from debouching. Fighting persisted until 10:00 P.M., at which time the Allies retreated five miles northeast to Rothnaußlitz. Katzler lost 252 killed and wounded; Russian and French losses are not known. Macdonald did not pursue beyond Bischofswerda: III and XI Corps camped on the western edge of the town while V Corps halted at

Großdrebnitz and Lauterbach opposite Langeron's rearguard. Napoleon spent the entire afternoon on the Kapellen hill receiving reports but passed the night at Großharthau. He sent for the mayor of Bischofswerda and made inquiries over the whereabouts of Blücher himself. Although Napoleon could not find his Prussian adversary, he obtained the desired information regarding the Silesian Army. To his foreign minister, Maret, he wrote: "I attacked and drove the enemy, who withdrew to Bautzen. My vanguard moved beyond [east of] Bischofswerda. It appears the enemy is divided into three corps: that of Langeron forward [east] of Stolpen, to turn our right; that of Sacken at Kamenz, to turn our left; Yorck at Bischofswerda. The column of 20,000 men that marched on our left was that of Sacken. It appears that the bulk of the enemy army is at Hochkirch on the right bank of the Spree."[68]

Not knowing the number of reinforcements Napoleon had brought with him and expecting the emperor to continue the offensive, Blücher ordered a limited but general retreat for 23 September. Katzler, Borozdin, and Rudzevich received explicit instructions to avoid serious engagements and withdraw on Bautzen but to slow the imperials as much as possible while observing all their movements. Army Headquarters tasked Sacken with notifying Tauentzien that, rather than an operation against Großenhain, the Silesian Army would concentrate at Bautzen. Should the imperials seek a battle, Sacken's corps and Jürgaß's detachment would withdraw on the great east–west highway to Bautzen. On the left wing, St.-Priest would also avoid a serious engagement and march east to Herrnhut, twenty miles southeast of Bautzen "to be on line with the other corps." South of St.-Priest, Kaptsevich and Bubna would retreat from the Stolpen–Neustadt in Sachsen region to Rumburg. Gneisenau dispatched staff officers to insure the availability of all the crossings over the Neiße. Although preparing for a further retreat, Blücher planned to wait at Bautzen before determining his next move. "If our Grand [Bohemian] Army does not operate soon," Blücher warned Knesebeck, "I will be paralyzed here and winter will come before we have achieved anything considerable with a half-million men under arms."[69]

Around 11:00 A.M. on 23 September, the Army of the Bober resumed its advance in three huge columns. Consisting of all arms, the left or northern column marched through Geißmannsdorf, less than two miles north of Bischofswerda. Macdonald's middle column, exclusively infantry, negotiated the marshy terrain between Geißmannsdorf and Bischofswerda. His right or southern column of cavalry and artillery pushed through Bischofswerda itself. Katzler commenced the retreat northeast on the road to Bautzen with the imperials closing fast. Using a large, dense wood east of Bischofswerda for cover, Prussian skirmishers managed to slow the French long enough to allow the infantry to withdraw in order. On the other side of the grove, Katzler took a position on the high ground west of Wölkau and Demitz-Thumitz, almost four miles northeast of Bischofswerda, to ascertain the size of the enemy force that had cleared the wood. Time did not permit the colonel to be an observer. Threatened on both flanks by the huge imperial columns, he withdrew another three miles northeast to Kleinpraga.

Battalion-sized swarms of skirmishers followed by their organic units pursued but the advance of the main column broke on the forest. Katzler, Emmanuel, and Witte utilized this moment to charge the French van with nine Prussian and six Russian squadrons. Led by the East Prussian National Cavalry Regiment, the Allies drove most of the skirmishers northwest from the Bischofswerda–Bautzen road toward the village of Pottschapplitz. Those who escaped fled south of this road to Rothnaußlitz. The other Allied squadrons remained on the road, passing Rothnaußlitz and charging three imperial cavalry regiments that emerged from the wood to support the infantry of the vanguard. Only one rode forth to meet the Allies; soon, its terrified troopers came flying back, disordering the other two. All three sought shelter behind three fresh infantry regiments of the main body that had finally moved up from the wood. Although tiring, the Allied horse successfully charged this infantry and pursued almost to the wood's edge, where fresh imperial foot debouched to end the hunt. The Russian and Prussian troopers slowly withdrew to Kleinpraga and from there to Göda, five miles due west of Bautzen. They brought with them the trophies of the engagement: 10 officers and 360 men. Langeron described the action:

> Noticing that after crossing the defiles of Bischofswerda, the enemy sent forth numerous skirmisher battalions but did not support them with massed troops, Rudzevich and Katzler attacked with their cavalry. Emmanuel, with the 1st and 3rd Ukrainskii Cossack Regiments, two squadrons of the Kievskii Dragoon Regiment, the Prussian cavalry, and supported by General Udom and Major Hiller with the infantry of the two vanguards, fell on the skirmishers; this attack, made sharply and at the right moment, was a complete success: almost all of the enemy Chasseurs were cut down; 360 Westphalians, some of whom were from the Guard, were taken along with many officers. The French cavalry, which remained in columns too far to the rear, was unable to arrive in time to save its skirmishers who had advanced too far forward.

After the Russo-Prussian cavalry charge, the French formed an artillery line of twenty-four guns; both sides exchanged salvos for a few hours until the imperials moved up sufficient numbers of infantry. Funneling through the Bischofswerda wood consumed so much time that they did not reach Göda until nightfall. After shelling the village, French infantry surged forward in an attempt to double-envelop Göda. A heated and confused struggle ensued for possession of the village. Realizing the futility of their efforts, Rudzevich and Katzler evacuated Göda, taking a position on the hills to the east with outposts close to the village. Russo-Prussian losses amounted to 6 officers and more than 200 men killed and wounded.

Throughout the day of the 23rd, Yorck's and Langeron's corps remained in their bivouacs close to Bautzen's eastern edge on either side of the road to Weißenberg. On the left wing, St.-Priest's main body reached Wilthen, six miles south of Bautzen. After receiving Blücher's orders for the general retreat at the late hour of 3:00 P.M., Bubna arranged with Kaptsevich to withdraw east that evening to Hainsbach (Lipová/Hanšpach), inside the Austrian border and nine miles south of Wilthen. However, before they could execute this movement, Lauriston's V Corps deployed on the hills between Lauterbach and Langenwolmsdorf facing Kaptsevich's outpost at Rückersdorf, six miles south of Bischofswerda. After repulsing two attacks by a French division, the Austro-Russian force retreated. Unmolested by the imperials, they bivouacked at Hainsbach around midnight.[70]

As for Napoleon, he passed the night of 22/23 September at Großharthau, where he learned that Bernadotte's troops had completed a bridge across the Elbe near the mouth of the Black Elster. He spent most of the day of the 23rd at Großharthau, purportedly in a fit of indecision over whether he should return to Dresden or continue his offensive to take Bautzen. Finally joining Lauriston around 4:00 P.M., he observed V Corps give a final push to Bubna's retreating Austrians. At sunset, he returned to Großharthau. To his great relief, Napoleon learned that Lefebvre-Desnouettes had defeated Thielmann and restored communication with Erfurt, which allowed seven couriers from Paris to continue on to Imperial Headquarters. Although his cavalry had reestablished rear-area security, the emperor made a decision: he would evacuate all territory east of the Elbe.[71]

Frustrated by the Reichenbach Plan in general but specifically by Blücher's refusal to accept battle, the master decided on a purely defensive strategy that would allow his troops to rest along the left bank of the Elbe. The dismal state of Macdonald's 60,000 men contributed to his decision. Tightly confined in the desolated area between the Elbe and the Spree,[72] the exhausted imperial soldiers suffered from severe shortages of food. Surrounded by Allied light troops, the French commanders could not allow their soldiers to go too far afield to forage. After consuming the immediate area's meager resources, tens of thousands faced starvation as food simply could not be found. Marauding reached unprecedented levels and the situation would only become worse as summer steadily yielded to autumn. Because his men could not supplement their scanty provisions by foraging, they again deserted in droves, thus thinning Macdonald's ranks. To compensate for the loss of manpower, the French impressed captured native Poles who served in the Allied armies. Conversely, Austrian, Prussian, and Russian prisoners volunteered to fight for the French in Spain to escape death by starvation in prison camps. Meanwhile, the Allied armies closed in from all sides, slowly suffocating Napoleon and his Grande Armée.[73]

The condition of the troops only accentuated the dire need for Napoleon to attain a decisive victory. To increase the chances of waging such a battle, he offered the right bank of the Elbe as bait, particularly to attract Blücher. Macdonald, who had retained command of III and V Corps a bit longer, would withdraw across the river but remain ready to return to the right bank as soon as the Prussians came closer. Still clinging to Dresden as his base, Napoleon ordered the construction of two formidable redoubts: one on the highway leading to Berlin and the other on the great east–west highway coming from Bautzen. In fact, Napoleon based his strategic defensive on the same logic he had applied at the start of the campaign: the ability to debouch at will across the Elbe. In the immediate theater of operations, he possessed no fewer than seven bridges: three at Dresden and one each at Pirna, Königstein, Pillnitz, and Meißen. "All these bridges will be defended by good bridgeheads," he explained to Murat, "and we will occupy all the outlets of the Dresden Forest. In this position I will closely watch the enemy and, if he engages in an offensive operation, I will fall on him so he cannot avoid a battle." Although the execution of his plan had failed in August thanks to Oudinot and Macdonald, the logic remained sound. Now, one month later, he dispensed with detaching independent army groups that operated far from his support. He would concentrate and let the Allies come to him using the Elbe first to lure them into his lair and then as a trap for a strategic envelopment.

Claiming that Blücher had retreated across the Spree in "disorder" and that Macdonald "must be moving on Bautzen," the master revealed more of his thinking and plans to Marmont. He placed I Cavalry Corps under the marshal's orders and planned to send III Corps to Meißen on the 25th or 26th. Thus, with III and VI Corps as well as I and V Cavalry Corps, "you will have a strong army to move wherever circumstances require." Resuming his plans to disestablish the Army of the Bober, he charged Macdonald's XI Corps with guarding the entrenched camp at Dresden as well as all the outlets of the wood west of the Saxon capital. "Therefore, I can have III, V, and VIII Corps and the majority of II Cavalry Corps and all of my Guard; with these forces I will watch the enemy closely and exploit the first error he makes." Such thoughts comforted Napoleon at a moment when he had completely surrendered the initiative to his foes: the Allies would now dictate his next move.[74]

The withdrawal across the Elbe commenced on 24 September. Napoleon himself again rode east almost as far as Bischofswerda before returning to Großharthau. At 5:00 that evening, he made preparations for the continued retreat. Napoleon directed XI Corps to Großharthau, V Corps to Stolpen, and III Corps to Weißig. For the 26th, he wanted III and V Corps at

Dresden and XI Corps at Weißig. "The duc de Tarente will remain at Weißig the 27th," Napoleon instructed Berthier. "He must make his movement in a manner that does not tire his troops and does not lose any men. I noticed on the road a few French corpses; the duc de Tarente must bury them and leave no trace." One hour later, Napoleon expressed his belief to Macdonald that Blücher would "beat a retreat this night and recross the Spree." If he did not recross that night, the emperor planned to "deploy large forces against him" to force Blücher to recross on the 25th. Yet he admitted that such an operation would cost him several days "with no hope of any result." As if thinking aloud, he changed his mind. "Send III and V Corps to me at Dresden right now," he snapped. Napoleon wanted Macdonald himself to remain at Weißig until the 28th with XI Corps and II Cavalry Corps. He also challenged the marshal to show some initiative: "nothing prevents you from coming to Dresden to confer with me and acquainting yourself with the entrenched camp and all the outlets of the forest. You are responsible for guarding the part of the fortified camp on the right bank and all the outlets of the forest within two leagues of Dresden. You will have time to reconnoiter all the outlets of the forest, so that when you leave Weißig you can cover all debouches."[75]

After returning to Dresden during the night, the master received a message from Macdonald at noon on 25 September. He responded with admirable patience: "I see by your letter that you think the enemy has been reinforced and is in a position to give battle. If this is the case, I think it is acceptable if you retain III, V, and XI Corps on the heights of Weißig, and that you take a good position." With his interest somewhat piqued, Napoleon speculated: "We shall see what the enemy wants to do in this situation." Stating the obvious, he suggested that Macdonald's "retrograde movement may have emboldened him." Nevertheless, he assured the marshal that, should Blücher force him to retreat across the Elbe, several divisions would be available to support him. "I think this plan will further frustrate the enemy army, better cover Dresden, and will be more suitable for troops that are encamped on the heights all together. You can take this position tomorrow. I will find you tomorrow and we will reconnoiter. In response to any movement the enemy makes, I can reinforce you with 40,000 men in one night, debouching at daybreak."[76]

Later on the 25th, Napoleon rode to Bischofswerda, apparently expecting to be attacked. Odeleben comments that Blücher's march had "seriously threatened the flank of the French army. I have no doubt that considerable losses could have been inflicted on him, yet a mere demonstration was made." As night approached, he left Bischofswerda and made his way back to Dresden. The reconnaissance he mentioned to Macdonald never occurred. "At Dresden," continues Odeleben, "he watched the maneuvers of his opponents, always hoping to discover a weak spot and exploit it.

He sometimes occupied himself with the business of his cabinet, sometimes with the fortifications of Dresden ... so that the days passed in weariness and care."[77] As unlikely as it seems, Napoleon ignored Blücher for the next several days thanks to Schwarzenberg's decision to advance on Leipzig.

Returning to Blücher, Silesian Army Headquarters correctly assumed on 23 September that Napoleon was no longer accompanying the Army of the Bober, meaning that Macdonald no longer sought battle. Blücher hoped to exploit this transition of command with a surprise attack on Macdonald's left. For this purpose, the Prussians made plans for Sacken to drive the enemy from the St. Marienstern Convent that same night. Yet the staff's recurring problem of cutting orders too late rendered this operation impracticable. As a result, Blücher placed Katzler at Sacken's disposal and instructed the Russian corps commander to take a concealed position two miles north of Göda on the 24th. If the opportunity arose, Sacken could attack the enemy's flank.[78]

Unfortunately for Blücher, 24 September does not stand out as a shining example of his staff's work. Quite the contrary, it serves more as a precursor to his sloppy operations in February 1814 during the campaign in France. Communication and reconnaissance – hallmarks of Napoleon's successful system of command and control – are conspicuously missing from the Allied operation. Again, the belated issuing of orders as well as the poor coordination of the march columns in difficult terrain prevented Sacken from executing his task. Joining Yorck's vanguard, Blücher watched and waited throughout the morning of the 24th, but Napoleon ordered the retreat to the Elbe. "On 24 September," recalled Langeron, "the enemy made no serious movements. Nevertheless, numerous columns advanced against us, but at noon these columns retreated toward Dresden, and we soon knew that Napoleon had received reports that forced him to make this retreat." Consequently, Blücher decided to have his vanguards attack the enemy's front at Göda while Sacken's corps advanced in the direction of Bischofswerda to cut his line of retreat. Receiving the order at 5:00 P.M., Sacken did not commence the operation because he did not think his troops could reach the enemy before sundown. After waiting in vain at Yorck's outpost for four hours to observe Sacken's movement, Blücher returned to Bautzen "very dissatisfied," according to Schack's journal.[79]

Around midnight, Sacken finally launched a surprise attack from Pottschapplitz but found Bischofswerda abandoned. Meanwhile, a few miles east of Sacken, Katzler's men passed the entire night under arms waiting in vain for the Russian commander's signal to advance. At 4:00 on the morning of the 25th, the Prussian forward posts reported the enemy's evacuation of Göda. Katzler made contact with the imperial's rearguard at Demitz-Thumitz but Sacken did nothing. On the left wing, Bubna and Kaptsevich advanced west before Blücher's orders arrived. Encountering no resistance, the Austro-Russian force-marched to Neustadt in Sachsen, twenty-three miles east of Dresden, on the 25th. St.-Priest also moved west, occupying his former positions stretching from Bühlau to Putzkau just south of Großharthau and Bischofswerda.

According to intelligence provided by Katzler, Napoleon had gone to the hills of Bischofswerda on the afternoon of the 24th. There, he received reports from Dresden that caused him not only to return to the Saxon capital, but also to order the Army of the Bober to retreat to the Elbe. Macdonald withdrew during the night of 24/25 September. By 8:00 on the morning of 25 September, Silesian Army Headquarters still remained unclear over the meaning of these movements. "Last evening," Gneisenau explained to Knesebeck on the morning of the 25th, "the enemy quickly withdrew from us. This rearward movement had already started yesterday afternoon. Meanwhile, until noon yesterday, the enemy's troop movements toward us extended to our left wing but he then began this rearward movement. We do not know whether this was prompted by the march of Sacken's corps or by events on the other side of the Elbe. During the night, we received news only of the retreat of the left wing, which Sacken had alarmed but now no longer can be found. Our forward troops are scouting and pursuing the enemy, but up to now we have no news of the results."

Although the reports had yet to arrive, the Prussians believed these movements indicated that Napoleon had finally relinquished the offensive against the Silesian Army. Blücher and his staff even speculated that he had decided to completely evacuate the right bank of the Elbe. Furthermore, the last troops of Bennigsen's army presumably would clear Zittau on the 25th.[80] By focusing on Blücher, Napoleon's short two-day offensive against the Silesian Army allowed the Army of Poland to reach Bohemia unnoticed and unmolested. Based on these circumstances, the situation appeared ideal for the Silesian Army's march down the Elbe. Should Macdonald withdraw as far as Dresden, the Silesian Army would "prepare to move closer to the Elbe through a march to the right," continued Gneisenau. "We do not believe this will expose Silesia to danger, either in regard to the general state of affairs which will not permit the emperor Napoleon from making such an overextended invasion [of Silesia], or in our particular position, where it would be extreme audacity for him to drive to Bohemia or Silesia in front of our face." Returning to the issue of supply, he conceded that "the lack of fodder itself justifies such a movement."

In this letter to Knesebeck on the morning of the 25th, Gneisenau insisted "that we must freely conform to the war of maneuver but we must conduct it in a manner that leads to great results in order to reward ourselves for the dangers that we thus have to endure. The crown prince of Sweden acts as if he will cross the Elbe. Sending 20,000 men across, like he wants, will frighten nothing. But if we execute the crossing with the Silesian Army and the majority of the Army of North Germany, we will attain a completely different result. We would then be in position to deliver a great battle, which could decisively influence the war." Gneisenau asserted that Blücher could afford to take risks: "A defeat will not be very dangerous to us, since your army [the Bohemian] will stifle the enemy's pursuit." Moving to the heart of his argument, Gneisenau exclaimed: "I repeat that I do not think it is likely that the crown prince of Sweden will cross the Elbe with his army. An invitation from us to do this is merely a polite request. What if he answers with beautiful phrases and does nothing? Should we then leave splendid forces unused in his hands even longer? The duty to our master demands that we work to prevent such a paralysis. We must strive to unite with Bülow (Tauentzien is already prepared to operate in unison with us) so that we are in a position to deliver a battle on the plains of Saxony along the left bank of the Elbe." Pointing to the "dissatisfaction that reigned among the generals of the Army of North Germany," Gneisenau reasoned that Wintzingerode could likewise be swayed to unite with Blücher. "If we win the battle, the crown prince can then pursue his personal and his purely Swedish plans because we will need him no more."

Gneisenau's opinion of Bernadotte, which prevailed throughout the Silesian Army, could not have been much lower. "He has a weak character and is surrounded by many intriguers. Much pro-French sentiment still reigns in Sweden. To him, his purely Swedish goals must come first because only through their attainment can he expect to maintain himself on the Swedish throne." Ignoring the simple fact that Napoleon's hegemony had to be reduced considerably in order for Bernadotte to take Norway from Denmark, Gneisenau argued that, "as great as his hate toward the French emperor may be, his goal can never be to proceed in the extreme against him or destroy the system to which he owes his elevation. We must not forget that the crown prince of Sweden is a son of the Revolution. If the French system falls, the Swedish nobility will not suffer General Bernadotte on their throne." Conceding that Bernadotte possessed the talents of a field commander, Gneisenau insisted that the strategic situation now rendered him superfluous. Referring to 1812, he noted that "the appearance of a bold field commander on the German coast with 35,000 Swedes, 25,000 Russians, and 10,000 British could have had a decisive result for the war in Russia; now the help of 25,000 Swedes is of little importance." Predicting that a decisive victory in Saxony would lead to the defection of several German states from Napoleon's fold, he insisted that Allied forces would be increased by 100,000 men – more than enough to replace Bernadotte's 25,000 Swedes. He hoped that by detaching Bülow and Tauentzien from the Army of North Germany, either officially or unofficially, "the crown prince would return home out of annoyance. But he will not do this because he does not want to lose his British subsidies and his chances to secure Norway."

Expressing the imperativeness of quickly executing this plan, Gneisenau revealed his intention to secretly communicate Blücher's plans to Bülow. "The appearance of a great force on the left bank of the Elbe will undoubtedly and immediately give the war a different turn and everything that we do there will in no way disturb the movements of the Bohemian Army. Instead, it will facilitate everything you undertake." Gneisenau certainly walked a fine line. Ignoring treaty obligations and diplomatic concerns, he justified his request for Bülow and Tauentzien to disregard Bernadotte's orders in favor of Blücher's by telling Knesebeck that loyal service to Frederick William demanded such insubordination. He then had the pluck to seek Knesebeck's endorsement of his scheme.[81] "If my plans are not approved," he warned, "we will continue to endure the frustration of seeing a great army whirling about between the Spree and the Elbe after two victories [Großbeeren and Dennewitz], and through this it holds back a neighboring army [the Silesian] on the latter river."[82] To Clausewitz he wrote: "Tauentzien is in agreement with us and will operate in unison with us. Because of his well-known personal interests, I hope Bülow will likewise do this without being too troubled by the paralyzing effects of the crown prince. If he cannot follow our invitation, we believe we are ready for the undertaking even without him."

Gneisenau could not conceal his excitement about the upcoming operation. "We will break on the scene and assume the main role because the others do not want it," he informed Clausewitz. "In the main army they constantly draft new plans and nothing gets done; after two victories, the crown prince of Sweden loiters between the Nuthe and the Elbe."[83] At 8:00 P.M. on the 25th, Gneisenau drafted Blücher's report to the king with pride about the events of the previous days and the ensuing march down the Elbe:

> I have the honor to report the failure of the enemy's third offensive operation against the Silesian Army. Because Bennigsen's army will have completed its march to Zittau and my assignment – to cover this march – is complete, I will begin my rightward movement and attempt to cross the Elbe and in unison with the army of the crown prince to draw the enemy onto the plains so the Bohemian Army can execute its operations with greater ease. Bubna and a small corps of the Silesian Army will remain behind to observe the enemy, maintain communication with Bohemia, and prevent the enemy from operating against Bohemia or Silesia. Should he attempt such an improbable movement, I will stop him through a flank position at the Black Elster and, if this should not suffice, through a march against Dresden to cut him off.[84]

Rühle's masterful argument in favor of Blücher's proposed march down the Elbe convinced Alexander and Frederick William to discard the plan of transferring the Silesian Army to Bohemia. Instead, Bennigsen received orders to lead the Army of Poland to Bohemia. Masked by the Silesian Army, Napoleon received no intelligence concerning Bennigsen's march. For these two reasons, the decision made at Allied Headquarters on the night of 14 September to accept Blücher's proposal proved to be one of the most profound and consequential judgments of the campaign.

While Allied Headquarters approved Blücher's bold plan, Napoleon's relative inactivity in the month of September is conspicuous. As one contemporary noted, "The Grand Combined Austrian, Russian, and Prussian Army under the supreme command of Marshal Prince Schwarzenberg had remained for a long time inactive in the vicinity of Teplitz, watching the movements of the French Grande Armée under Napoleon in person who, after the disaster that had occurred to General Vandamme, appeared to limit his operations, principally to his own security, the defense of Dresden, and the preservation of his line of communication along the Elbe."[85] After disengaging from Blücher and returning to Dresden on 7 September, Napoleon bounced between the Saxon capital and Peterswald: a line of twenty-three miles between the former and the latter. Although Napoleon did not confirm until the 18th that Schwarzenberg did not intend to launch a general offensive, the other two Allied armies did not remain idle. As Blücher and Bernadotte gradually closed on the Grande Armée, they threatened to negate Napoleon's strategic advantage of interior lines by tactically surrounding all of his forces.[86]

It is hard to believe that the general who waged the 1796 Italian Campaign so willingly forfeited the initiative in 1813. The indecisive, almost listless activity that had first become noticeable during the Russian campaign continued. Instead of action, we hear Napoleon's excuses: "I will await the news of this day ... I will send orders tonight," he wrote Murat on the morning of 19 September. "The weather is horrible. The prince de Neuchâtel [Berthier] is sick; I do not know if it is his gout or only a fever." Between 3:00 and 4:00 A.M. on the 20th, he instructed Berthier to explain to Macdonald that "it is unfortunate he made an unnecessary movement and relocated his bivouacs and camps on such a horrible day, which causes infinite suffering among the troops."[87]

Until the end of September, the Allied armies operated at considerable distances from each other. After reaching Bautzen, Blücher closed the distance between his army and the Bohemian Army at Teplitz to a mere fifty-five miles as the crow flies over the Lusatian highlands, a branch of the Sudetes. However, the closest road for Blücher to take over the mountains – Bautzen–Zittau–Gabel–Leitmeritz–Teplitz – increased the actual distance to ninety-five miles. Moreover, some 125 miles still separated the main forces of the Silesian and North German Armies. Schwarzenberg's army was operating on the left bank of the Elbe, while Blücher's and Bernadotte's remained on the right. Between the three Allied Armies, Napoleon maintained his strong central position on the Elbe with fortresses protecting his main points of passage. Conversely, to unite with Schwarzenberg, Blücher and Bernadotte could rely only on bridges that had to be built within reach of Napoleon's forces or in the vicinity of a French stronghold. Yet only the simultaneous advance of all three Allied armies against Napoleon's communications would deny him the advantages offered by his central position on the Elbe and force him to accept battle under extremely unfavorable conditions. Blücher took it upon himself to make this happen by resolving to cross the Elbe and drag Bernadotte's army with him.[88]

Notes

1 Höpfner, "Darstellung," 1844:241.
2 Blücher to Langeron, Sacken, Yorck, St.-Priest, Kaptsevich, and Bubna, Herrnhut, 11 September 1813, Add MSS, 20112, 136.
3 Disposition, Herrnhut, 11 September 1813, Add MSS, 20112, 137.
4 Bülow to Blücher, Nudersdorf, 1 October 1813, in Höpfner "Darstellung," 1844:301–02.
5 Müffling, *Die Feldzüge*, 51–54; Unger, *Blücher*, II:91.
6 Blücher to Charles John, Herrnhut, 11 September 1813, RA KrA, volym 25, and Add MSS, 20112, 49.
7 Blücher to Alexander, Herrnhut, 11 September 1813, ÖStA KA, FA 1531, 419b.
8 Blücher to Charles John, Herrnhut, 11 September 1813, RA KrA, volym 25; "Mémoire," Herrnhut, 11 September 1813, ÖStA KA, FA 1531, 419b, and RA KrA, volym 25.
9 For the best accounts of the deliberations at Allied Headquarters, see Bernhardi, *Toll*, III:327–29; Bogdanovich, *Geschichte des Krieges*, IIa:345–46; Friederich, *Herbstfeldzug 1813*, II:64–72.
10 "Über die Grundsätze damit die, aus vielen Körpern bestehende Armee der Alliirten, nicht in einen Koloß zusammengedrängt, sondern theilweise, mit vereinten Kräften auf den Feind loszugehen habe, und dadurch die eine Armee die andere zu unterstützen vermöge," Teplitz, 14 September 1813, in Radetzky, *Denkschriften*, 172; Janson, *Friedrich Wilhelm*, 214.
11 Knesebeck to Gneisenau, Teplitz, 8:00 P.M., 13 September 1813, GStA PK, VI HA Rep. 92 Nl. Gneisenau, Nr. 23; Alexander to Bennigsen, Teplitz, 13 September 1813, in Mikhailovsky-Danlivesky, *Denkwürdigkeiten*, 341–42. The tsar instructed Bennigsen to take a position north of Teplitz facing Kulm with his vanguard pushed north to Nollendorf or Peterswald. Alexander explicitly stated that, aside from covering the rear of the Bohemian Army, Bennigsen would "facilitate General Blücher's passage of the Elbe." See also Bogdanovich, *Geschichte des Krieges*, IIa:346–47.
12 The account of the operations on 11 and 12 September is based on Zychlinski, *Geschichte des 24sten Infanterie-Regiments*, I:91–92; Henckel von Donnersmarck, *Erinnerungen*, 220–21; Ollech, *Reyher*, 216–17; Höpfner, "Darstellung," 1844:242–46; and Friederich, *Herbstfeldzug 1813*, II:54–56. On this day, Bubna

detached General Theophil Zechmeister's brigade to Altendorf to observe the Elbe from Bad Schandau to Lilienstein and Neipperg's brigade to Hohenstein to monitor the river from Porschdorf to Rathen. With the remaining brigade of 2nd Light Division, Bubna moved to Ulbersdorf: Bubna to Schwarzenberg, Ulbersdorf, 12 September 1813, ÖStA KA, FA 1531, 474.

13 Blücher to Bennigsen, 12 September 1813, in Höpfner, "Darstellung," 1844:246–47.

14 Blücher to Schwarzenberg, Herrnhut, 10:00 P.M., 12 September 1813, ÖStA KA, FA 1531, 419a, and Add MSS, 20112, 16.

15 The account of the operations on 13 September is based on Langeron, *Mémoires*, 279; Höpfner, "Darstellung," 1844:250–52; Bogdanovich, *Geschichte des Krieges*, IIa:320–21; Friederich, *Herbstfeldzug 1813*, II:256–57; Vaudoncourt, *Histoire de la guerre*, 177–78; Beitzke, *Geschichte der deutschen Freiheitskriege*, II:346–58.

16 Blücher to Alexander, Herrnhut, 13 September 1813, in Höpfner, "Darstellung," 1844:249.

17 Blücher to Knesebeck, Herrnhut, 13 September 1813, *Blüchers Briefe*, ed. Unger, 179–80.

18 Gneisenau to Bubna, Herrnhut, 5:30 P.M., 13 September 1813, ÖStA KA, FA 1531, ad 497a; Bubna to Schwarzenberg, Ulbersdorf, 14 September 1813, *ibid.*, 497; Disposition, Herrnhut, 13 September 1813, *ibid.*, ad 474; and Add MSS, 20112, 138–39. Blücher issued these orders on the night of the 13th before reports from Katzler and St.-Priest arrived.

19 Bubna to Schwarzenberg, Ulbersdorf, 14 September 1813, ÖStA KA, FA 1531, 497; Friederich, *Herbstfeldzug 1813*, II:257; Höpfner, "Darstellung," 1844:253–54. Falkenhausen stumbled on a French hospital at Kamenz. He arrested a Saxon major who had brought his sick wife there for treatment. Falkenhausen had him escorted to Bautzen, where he was interrogated at Sacken's headquarters. According to his statements, Napoleon and the Guard had returned to Dresden during the afternoon of the 12th; other French troops, probably coming from Pirna, had likewise arrived at Dresden that afternoon but had continued without delay to Großenhain. Moreover, all Guard personnel at Dresden received orders to be ready to march to Großenhain at 4:45 A.M. on 15 September. Reporting from Pulsnitz at 4:00 A.M. on the 14th, Falkenhausen confirmed the statements of the Saxon officer that considerable troop masses had marched from Dresden toward Großenhain on the morning of 13 September and that Napoleon had followed around 7:00 A.M. The two enemy camps in the Dresden moor likewise departed and were probably marching toward Großenhain. According to the rumors circulating through the imperial army, Napoleon would go to Torgau and cross the Elbe but not to conduct an offensive against the crown prince of Sweden.

20 Bubna to Schwarzenberg, Rumburg, 11:00 P.M., 10 September 1813, ÖStA KA, FA 1531, 316; Schwarzenberg to Bubna, Teplitz, 12 September 1813, in Höpfner, "Darstellung," 1844:254; Bubna to Blücher, Ulbersdorf, 15 September 1813, ÖStA KA, FA 1531, 500a.

21 Disposition, Herrnhut, 10:30 A.M., 15 September 1813, ÖStA KA, FA 1531, 500b, and Add MSS, 20112, 140.

22 Höpfner, "Darstellung," 1844:256; Blücher to Alexander, Herrnhut, 11:00 A.M., 15 September 1813, RGVIA, f. VUA, op. 16, d. 3913, ll. 39–40; Blücher to Charles John, Herrnhut, 15 September 1813, Add MSS, 20112, 52.

23 *CN*, Nos. 20542, 20544, and 20545, XXVI:187–89; SHAT, C^{17} 180: Berthier to Ney, Macdonald, and Daru, 11 September 1813. By that evening, the Young Guard reached Cotta, just west of Dresden while to the south I Corps held the Nollendorf–Peterswald line; XIV Corps Börnersdorf to Fürtsenwalde; and II Corps between Sayda and Marienburg. See Yorck von Wartenburg, *Napoleon as a General*, II:315–16.

24 *CN*, Nos. 20552, 20553, 20562, XXVI:192–93, 200; SHAT, C^{17} 180: Berthier to Marmont, Murat, and Ney, 12 September 1813, Berthier to Piré, 13 September 1813. Approximately 10,000 hundredweights of wheat that could be ground into flour would remain at Torgau. Napoleon likewise ordered the transfer to Dresden of some 2,800 hundredweights of flour from Leisnig, 2,300 from Rochlitz, and 1,300 from Colditz.

25 SHAT, C^{17} 180: Berthier to Ney, 12 September 1813.

26 *CN*, No. 20560, XXVI:198; SHAT, C^{17} 180: Berthier to Macdonald, 14 September 1813.

27 *CN*, Nos. 20567 and 20568, XXVI:202–03; Friederich, *Herbstfeldzug 1813*, II:73.

28 Quoted in Pertz and Delbrück, *Gneisenau*, III:319–20; Janson, *Friedrich Wilhelm*, 215.

29 It is not clear when Blücher received notification of the monarchs' approval prior to Rühle's return to Silesian Army Headquarters on 18 September. Friederich maintains that the official cancellation was sent to Blücher early on the 15th but "we do not know the exact contents of the letter; Blücher immediately destroyed it on the express order of the monarchs": Friederich, *Herbstfeldzug 1813*, II:77. However, in a letter written by Gneisenau to Knesebeck on 18 September, the staff chief states, "We expect at any hour Major Rühle, who will bring to us the treatise you have completed on the order of the tsar. According to a report from Major Rühle, I already know that my suggestion to utilize Bennigsen's army for the posting on the Eger has been accepted": Gneisenau to Knesebeck, Bautzen, 18 September 1813, in Pertz and Delbrück, *Gneisenau*, III:343–44. Knesebeck's letter to Gneisenau was likewise destroyed probably because of the derogatory comments concerning Bernadotte: Janson, *Friedrich Wilhelm*, 215.

30 For the best accounts of the events at Allied Headquarters, see Bernhardi, *Toll*, III:331–39; Bogdanovich, *Geschichte des Krieges*, IIa:351–53; Beitzke, *Geschichte der deutschen Freiheitskriege*, II:355–59; Friederich, *Herbstfeldzug 1813*, II:75–78.

31 *CN*, No. 20568, XXVI:203.

32 Odeleben, *A Circumstantial Narrative*, I:306–07. Odeleben and thus Petre, who follows him, mistakenly state that the younger Blücher was captured on 11 September: Petre, *Napoleon's Last Campaign*, 284–85.

33 *CN*, Nos. 20569, 20577, and 20582, XXVI:203, 209, 211; SHAT, C^{17} 180: Berthier to Ney, 17 and 18 September 1813. On the 17th, Berthier informed Ney of the emperor's decision to dissolve XII Corps and divide its remains among IV and VII Corps as well as the garrison at Dresden.

34 *CN*, Nos. 20568 and 20573, XXVI:203, 207; SHAT, C¹⁷ 180: Berthier to Macdonald, 16 September 1813.

35 The account of 15 September is based on Langeron, *Mémoires*, 280–81; Höpfner, "Darstellung," 1844:256–59; Vaudoncourt, *Histoire de la guerre*, 178; Beitzke, *Geschichte der deutschen Freiheitskriege*, II:358; Friederich, *Herbstfeldzug 1813*, II:257–59.

36 Müffling, *Die Feldzüge*, 54. Tauentzien operated with only 2 of his 4 brigades, altogether about 20,000 men. The other 2 brigades were conducting sieges.

37 Friederich, *Herbstfeldzug 1813*, II:258; Höpfner, "Darstellung," 1844:259; Leggiere, *Napoleon and Berlin*, 234.

38 Langeron, *Mémoires*, 282.

39 Tauentzien to Blücher, Herzberg, 15 September 1813, and Blücher to Tauentzien, Bautzen, 16 September 1813, are in Höpfner, "Darstellung," 1844:262–63.

40 Charles John to Blücher, Coswig, 15 September 1813, Add MSS, 20112, 50–51.

41 Blücher to Charles John, Bautzen, 16 September 1813, RA KrA, volym 25, and Add MSS, 20112, 53–54.

42 Blücher to Hardenberg, Bautzen, 16 September 1813, *Blüchers Briefe*, ed. Unger, 181.

43 Bubna to Schwarzenberg, Langburkersdorf, 16 and 17 September (2) 1813, ÖStA KA, FA 1532, 531, 561, and 565; Höpfner, "Darstellung," 1844:264–65; Friederich, *Herbstfeldzug 1813*, II:259. At 10:00 A.M. on the 17th Katzler reported to Blücher that Napoleon and his Guard stood at Pirna, where the French threw two bridges across the Elbe. After reaching the Bischofswerda–Bautzen road around 2:00 in the afternoon, Katzler again reported at 4:00 P.M. that Macdonald's XI Corps stood at Schmiedefeld, Großdrebnitz, and Goldbach while III and V Corps camped at Geismannsdorf, Rammenau, and Frankenthal with VIII Corps at Stolpen. Altogether, he estimated this force to number 50,000 men. On Blücher's left wing, Bubna sent patrols from Hohenstein to Lohmen and Wehlen to closely monitor the French pontoon bridges at Pirna in case Napoleon should cross to the right bank of the Elbe. He reported to Blücher that on the 16th the imperials had driven back Zieten's brigade from Nollendorf toward Kulm but a flanking maneuver on the 17th forced the French to retreat to Hellendorf. From Tetschen on the Elbe, *Streifkorps* commander Major Boltenstern reported to Blücher that Napoleon had been present during the fighting at Nollendorf on the 17th.

44 Blücher to Alexander, Bautzen, 5:00 P.M., 19 September 1813, RGVIA, f. VUA, op. 16, d. 3913, l. 116; Friederich, *Herbstfeldzug 1813*, II:263; Blücher to Sacken, Bautzen, 18 September 1813, in Höpfner, "Darstellung," 1844:265; Pertz and Delbrück, *Gneisenau*, III:345–46.

45 *Streifkorps* under Prince Valerian Madatov and Major Falkenhausen repulsed a Saxon cuirassier brigade from General Étienne Bordessoulle's 1st Heavy Cavalry Division of I Cavalry Corps at Böhla as it advanced toward Ortrand, seventeen miles northwest of Sacken's position at Kamenz.

46 Tauentzien to Blücher, Herzberg, 18 September 1813, and Blücher to Tauentzien, Bautzen, 5:00 P.M., 19 September 1813, are in Höpfner, "Darstellung," 1844:267–68; see also Müffling, *Aus meinem Leben*, 80–81.

47 Steffens, *Adventures*, 114–15.
48 Blücher to Bonin, Bautzen, 22 September 1813, *Blüchers Briefe*, ed. Unger, 183; Droysen, *Yorck*, II:172; Droysen, *Yorck*, II:171–72; Unger, *Blücher*, II:94; Müffling's letter to Knescbeck is in Friederich, *Herbstfeldzug 1813*, II:260.
49 Gneisenau to Hardenberg, Bautzen, 25 September 1813, GStA PK, VI HA Rep. 92 Nl. Gneisenau, Nr. 20b. Hardenberg to Gneisenau, Teplitz, 28 September 1813, GStA PK, VI HA Rep. 92 Nl. Gneisenau, Nr. 24.
50 Quoted in Unger, *Blücher*, II:95.
51 SHAT, C² 156: Macdonald to Berthier, 18 September 1813; *CN*, No. 20593, XXVI:218; Odeleben, *A Circumstantial Narrative*, I:314–15.
52 *CN*, Nos. 20581 and 20583, XXVI:210–11.
53 Yorck von Wartenburg, *Napoleon as a General*, II:321; *CN*, No. 20594, XXVI:219.
54 *CN*, Nos. 20601 and 20601, XXVI:224.
55 Blücher to Charles John, Bautzen, 19 September 1813, RA KrA, volym 25; Höpfner, "Darstellung," 1844:268–69.
56 Gneisenau to Bubna, Bautzen, 6:00 P.M., 19 September 1813, ÖStA KA, FA 1532, ad661. Gneisenau's letter was in response to a letter written by Schwarzenberg at 11:00 on the night of the 17th to Bubna. According to a captured French general, Napoleon was preparing to invade Bohemia. Schwarzenberg wanted Blücher to be ready to support the Bohemian Army by immediately marching against Napoleon's communications and rear.
57 Bubna to Blücher, Langburkersdorf, 20 September 1813, ÖStA KA, FA 1532, 727c, and Bubna to Schwarzenberg, Langburkersdorf, 20 September 1813, *ibid.*, 661.
58 Secret Disposition for 21–24 September, 21 September 1813, ÖStA KA, FA 1532, 727b, and Add MSS, 20112, 142; Höpfner, "Darstellung," 1844:270.
59 Blücher to Bonin, Bautzen, 22 September 1813, *Blüchers Briefe*, ed. Unger, 182–83.
60 Droysen, *Yorck*, II:175; Friederich, *Herbstfeldzug 1813*, II:265–66; Höpfner, "Darstellung," 1844:272.
61 *CN*, Nos. 20603 and 20604, XXVI:224–26.
62 *CN*, Nos. 20607 and 20609, XXVI:226–28; Müffling, *Die Feldzüge*, 56–57.
63 Langeron, *Mémoires*, 284–85.
64 SHAT, C¹⁷ 180: Berthier to Macdonald, 22 September 1813.
65 *CN*, No. 20612, XXVI:229.
66 Droysen, *Yorck*, II:175.
67 Langeron, *Mémoires*, 284–85.
68 *CN*, No. 20615, XXVI:232–33. The account of 22 September is based on Blücher to Bubna, Bautzen, 8:30 P.M., 22 September 1813, ÖStA KA, FA 1533, 887c; Höpfner, "Darstellung," 1844:273–75; Friederich, *Herbstfeldzug 1813*, II:264–65; Bogdanovich, *Geschichte des Krieges*, IIa:332–33; Vaudoncourt, *Histoire de la guerre*, 181; Marmont, *Mémoires*, V:161; Müffling, *Die Feldzüge*, 57.
69 Quoted in Unger, *Blücher*, II:93; Blücher to Bubna, Bautzen, 8:30 P.M., 22 September 1813, ÖStA KA, FA 1533, 887c.
70 The account of 23 September is based on Blücher to Frederick William, Bautzen, 25 September 1813, GStA PK, VI HA Rep. 92 Nl. Gneisenau, Nr. 16, and ÖStA

KA, FA 1533, 832; Langeron, *Mémoires*, 285–86; Höpfner, "Darstellung," 1844:275–77; Friederich, *Herbstfeldzug 1813*, II:265–69; Beitzke, *Geschichte der deutschen Freiheitskriege*, II:409–12; Bernhardi, *Toll*, III:342–43; Droysen, *Yorck*, 176; Langeron, *Mémoires*, 286–87; Bubna to Schwarzenberg, 25 September 1813, ÖStA KA, FA 1533, 814.

71 SHAT, C² 156: Ney to Berthier, 22 September 1813; *CN*, No. 20617, XXVI:235; Odeleben, *A Circumstantial Narrative*, I:315–16; Bogdanovich, *Geschichte des Krieges*, IIa:333.

72 At Großharthau on the great east–west highway, Macdonald's three infantry corps (III, V, and XI) stood some eighteen miles east of Dresden and sixteen miles west of Bautzen. Poniatowski's VIII Corps held Stolpen. The marshal established his headquarters at Fischbach, likewise on the east–west highway but four miles west of Großharthau. With VI Corps and I and IV Cavalry Corps, Murat established his base at Großenhain, twenty miles north of Dresden. See Vaudoncourt, *Histoire de la guerre*, 177; Marmont, *Mémoires*, V:161.

73 *CN*, No. 20618, XXVI:236; Yorck von Wartenburg, *Napoleon as a General*, II:323; Petre, *Napoleon's Last Campaign*, 291; Beitzke, *Geschichte der deutschen Freiheitskriege*, II:400–06; Bogdanovich, *Geschichte des Krieges*, IIa:333.

74 *CN*, Nos. 20616–20618, XXVI:233–36; Yorck von Wartenburg, *Napoleon as a General*, II:324.

75 *CN*, Nos. 20625 and 20626, XXVI:241–43; SHAT, C¹⁷ 180: Berthier to Macdonald, 24 September 1813.

76 *CN*, No. 20632, XXVI:246–47.

77 Odeleben, *A Circumstantial Narrative*, I:318–20.

78 Gneisenau to St.-Priest, Bautzen, 10:00 P.M., 23 September 1813, ÖStA KA, FA 1533, ad871; Blücher to Sacken, Bautzen, 24 September 1813, in Höpfner, "Darstellung," 1844:278.

79 Langeron, *Mémoires*, 287; Droysen, *Yorck*, II:177 and 198; Müffling, *Die Feldzüge*, 57–59.

80 Gneisenau to Bubna, Bautzen, 9:00 P.M., 24 September 1813, ÖStA KA, FA 1533, ad814; Bubna to Schwarzenberg, Langburkersdorf, 25 September 1813, *ibid.*, 814; Blücher to Alexander, Elsterwerda, 29 September 1813, RGVIA, f. VUA, op. 16, d. 3913, l. 268; Friederich, *Herbstfeldzug 1813*, II:269–70; Höpfner, "Darstellung," 1844:277–80.

81 Realizing that his three-volume study would be a training tool for the officers of the Second Reich, Friederich counsels that "Gneisenau's attempts to coerce the dissatisfied generals of the North Army to join the Silesian Army against the will of their commander in chief was without doubt – even if emerging from patriotic endeavors – ill judged and dangerous. They could have had the most ill-fated results, and indeed could have led to the complete collapse of the alliance. Thus, we can only see it as a fortunate chance that the general's letter reached the hands of King Frederick William, whose judgment on the crown prince was doubtless more impartial and correct, and who also did not fail to intervene." While it is doubtful that the Sixth Coalition would have fallen apart had Bülow and Tauentzien followed Blücher across the Elbe without Bernadotte's authorization, problems that Frederick William did not need predictably would have arisen. See Friederich, *Herbstfeldzug 1813*, II:273.

82 Gneisenau to Knesebeck, Bautzen, 8:00 A.M., 25 September 1813, in Pertz and Delbrück, *Gneisenau*, III:371–75.
83 Gneisenau to Clausewitz, Bautzen, 8:00 A.M., 26 September 1813, GStA, PK, VI HA Rep. 92 Nl. Gneisenau, Nr. 21.
84 Blücher to Frederick William, Bautzen, 8:00 P.M., 25 September 1813, GStA PK, VI HA Rep. 92 Nl. Gneisenau, Nr. 16, and ÖStA KA, FA 1533, 832.
85 "Battles of Leipzig," Lowe, Add MSS, 20111, 161.
86 *CN*, No. 20585, XXVI:212; Petre, *Napoleon's Last Campaign*, 288–89.
87 *CN*, Nos. 20593 and 20602, XXVI:218, 224.
88 Bogdanovich, *Geschichte des Krieges*, IIb:35.

10

The Middle Elbe

Breaking onto the scene momentarily appeared more difficult than Gneise-nau had imagined due to the backlash in the Silesian Army caused by the unveiling of the plan to march north. Although it had long been contem-plated, the staff had kept this idea so secret that its announcement caused incalculable surprise in every quarter. The boldness of the plan did not receive general approval. General Dideric Jacob Teyl van Seraskerken, the Dutch-born Russian war commissar attached to Blücher's staff, provided surprising, vehement protest. Having emigrated to Münster after the 1794 French conquest of the Netherlands, Teyl had become close friends with Blücher, even being a house and table companion for years. For this reason, Tsar Alexander selected Teyl for the post on Blücher's staff. In August, Blücher received him as an old friend. Müffling described him as "a brave man, but cautious in the extreme." After Blücher issued orders at 7:00 P.M. on 25 September for the march down the Elbe, Teyl argued that the operation would violate the principles of the Reichenbach Plan and selfishly jeopardize the results of the entire campaign thus far. "He availed himself of his *grandes entrées* to the general," maintained Müffling, "to make the most urgent remonstrance against allowing himself to be carried away by Gneisenau and me into such hazardous undertakings. Blücher answered: 'Be quiet, old friend; everything has been maturely considered'." Teyl continued his protest, insisting that Blücher solicit the opinion of the army's generals. Blücher looked at him in astonishment. "I do not hold councils of war," roared the hoary Prussian. "Colonel, the tsar, your master, sent you here to report to him, for which purpose I furnish you with all the necessary materials with the greatest readiness. When you protest against my pub-lished orders, you depart altogether from your instructions; you are not my appointed advisor! Therefore, I will not listen to you and I take my leave." With that, Blücher walked out of the room.

Lingering eighteenth-century conceptions of warfare also prompted concern over Silesia. General Rauch, whose special assignment consisted solely of overseeing the security of Silesia, drafted a memo describing the poor condition of the province's fortresses and all the danger entailed in Blücher's march north. After failing to force his opinion on Gneisenau, he attempted to persuade Blücher. Müffling claimed that Rauch fared worse than Teyl in this endeavor. "General Blücher made no mystery of these conversations, and the result was that these two officers sought and obtained other appointments; at the same time, his opponents became more cautious." Still others opined that abandoning the ties to Silesia's supplies of food and war materiel appeared extremely risky. Blücher's strength of character weathered the storm.[1]

Blücher and Gneisenau recognized the risks entailed in this operation. The crossing of the Elbe would occur within Napoleon's reach. If the Silesian Army won the left bank, Blücher would enter his lair and face the Grande Armée itself: a force far superior in numbers and morale than the Army of the Bober. Even if he had wanted to cooperate, Schwarzenberg's ability to do so seemed doubtful based on the chaotic descriptions of the daily business at Allied Headquarters that Blücher received. Bernadotte's cooperation appeared even more doubtful. Tauentzien seemed committed to following Blücher even if it meant ignoring the crown prince's orders. That night, Blücher wrote to Tauentzien instructing him to inform the crown prince of the march of the Silesian Army but to say nothing of a resolute decision to cross the Elbe. As for Bülow, after numerous disagreements with Bernadotte about the defense of Berlin as well as the correct way to exploit the victories at Großbeeren and Dennewitz, the crown prince's threat to arrest him completely alienated the Prussian corps commander. Assigned to the pointless siege of Wittenberg, Bülow viewed this task as the crown prince's punishment for his outspokenness, as well as an excuse for the Army of North Germany to remain idle on the right bank of the Elbe. Gneisenau tempted Bülow with the prospect of receiving independent command of an army if he cooperated with Blücher on the left bank of the Elbe. The staff chief also hoped to win over Wintzingerode, whose Russian corps likewise belonged to the Army of North Germany. Regardless, with or without cooperation, Blücher and Gneisenau committed themselves and the Army of Silesia to crossing the Elbe. "Neither your general [Bülow]," Gneisenau wrote to Boyen on the 25th, "nor mine, nor you, nor I shun any great accountability. If one wants to render his master an important service, one must have the courage to do something. Besides, one victory will justify everything."[2]

"At this moment," responded Boyen, "I have received your letter dated the 25th and hasten to reply in detail over it. I gave your letter to Bülow to read. Based on the character of the general as well as the circumstances, you can be assured that he is in complete agreement and I can give you my word that Bülow fought and won the two victories at Großbeeren and Dennewitz despite all sorts of obstacles and even against the actual will of the crown prince. Since Dennewitz, Bülow has repeatedly asked the crown prince to cross the Elbe but all has been in vain; the king knows of this. Of all that we could reasonably do, nothing has happened." Despite the enthusiasm, Boyen posed some tough questions: "Where will we undertake the crossing to achieve our union? In a possible march to our left [southeast], we would approach you on the Elbe but we will be weakened considerably by a major detachment that we would have to leave before Wittenberg; also our food supply is so bad that we often have nothing to eat for several days. Please do not view these questions as evasive complaints; our will is resolved; our only question is what means do you have to overcome these difficulties, what is your plan – then I can see what is possible." Boyen also relayed Bülow's belief that Blücher would not be able to hijack both Prussian corps from Bernadotte. Bülow suggested leaving Tauentzien, his rival, with Bernadotte. According to Bülow, "it would be best if we allocate only 27,000 men for use by the Swedes; Tauentzien can be placed at the disposal of the crown prince and we can support you, then everything can be accomplished with ease." Moreover, Bülow did not realize that Blücher planned to conduct this operation behind the back of the crown prince. Instead, he advised Blücher to make a proposal to Bernadotte in the hope of getting him to cooperate. Blücher and Gneisenau needed time to consider these points.[3]

Regardless, on 26 September 1813, Yorck's birthday, the Silesian Army commenced the fifty-mile march northwest from Bautzen to Elsterwerda, from where it would continue another forty-five miles to the village of Elster.[4] After striking out at daybreak on the 26th, Sacken's corps pushed six miles west through Kamenz to Schwosdorf on the road to Königsbrück. To conceal the army's movement, Gneisenau tasked the Russian commander with taking a position between Königsbrück and Großenhain. Behind the Russians, Yorck's corps departed at 6:00 A.M. and marched seventeen miles northwest from Bautzen to Kamenz. Three hours later, Langeron's soldiers started their twelve-mile march to the St. Marienstern Convent at Panschwitz-Kuckau while St.-Priest's main body covered the army's rear from Bischofswerda. Kaptsevich moved into St.-Priest's former position at Putzkau and established communication with Bubna. For his part, the Austrian general continued to observe the region of Neustadt in Sachsen, guarding the road through Rumburg and maintaining communication between the Silesian and Bohemian Armies. Patrols extended west to the Elbe, ever vigilant of enemy movement from the directions of Meißen and Torgau. East of the army, 2 Russian companies escorted 100 canvas pontoons from Görlitz to Bad Liebenwerda. To both deceive the imperials and guard communication along the great east–west highway to Silesia, the two divisions of Shcherbatov's VI

Infantry Corps remained at Bautzen. Reinforced to more than 9,500 men by the addition of cavalry commanded by Panchulidzev I, Shcherbatov received orders to follow the French to the Elbe if they continued to retreat.[5] If they advanced, Blücher instructed him to do all that he could in unison with Bubna's 10,000 Austrians to block the enemy's path to Silesia. In the worst-case scenario, he could retreat through the province to the entrenched camp at Landeshut but Blücher would not turn back. South of the Silesian Army, Bennigsen reached Zittau with 198 guns and almost 60,000 men, reportedly in "excellent condition." Three days later, he informed Blücher of his arrival at Außig and the Bohemian Army's impending departure for Chemnitz. Bennigsen noted that he would begin his advance on 1 October to distract the imperials and thus support Blücher's crossing of the Elbe.[6]

At 7:00 on the morning of the 26th, Gneisenau penned another epistle for Knesebeck that was meant for the king's eyes. "Today," he wrote, "our army has started its march to the right; headquarters will remain here today but in a few marches we will reach the Elbe. Regarding the execution of the plan that I communicated to you yesterday, I have consulted with Müffling and Rühle. The result is the following. As soon as we cross the Elbe, we must expect a battle. Of course we can again play the same role that we did on this side of the river but ultimately it will come down to a decisive day ... The task is now to deliver it because we can accept battle with the highest probability of victory." Recognizing the danger of fighting with a river behind them, Gneisenau formulated the ingenious idea of building an entrenched camp on the right bank of the Elbe complete with bridges to the opposite bank. However, the army would actually cross from the right to the left bank at a different point along the river. In so doing, he hoped to confuse the French in case the Silesian Army should suffer a defeat in the field. The French would naturally believe that the Silesian Army's line of operation would extend across the bridges that it had utilized to cross the Elbe. Yet, in the case of a defeat, Gneisenau planned to abandon this line of operation and instead withdraw to the entrenched camp. He selected the confluence of the Black Elster and the Elbe, thirty miles downstream of Torgau and ten miles upstream of Wittenberg, where "the latter river in its course to the north makes a sharp bend to the west, as the site for this camp. We will use this angle for an entrenched camp and build our bridges there, not to cross the Elbe there, but to have the complete freedom to quickly return to this bank should it become necessary for us. While we build this entrenched camp, we will move further upstream along the Elbe and seek to quickly cross." Gneisenau identified Mühlberg, fifteen miles upstream of Torgau and thirty-seven miles upstream of the confluence of the Black Elster and the Elbe, as the location for the army to cross the river.

Gneisenau also explained to Knesebeck how the Silesian Army would resume its role on the left bank of the Elbe in accordance with the

Reichenbach Plan: "we will place ourselves in the vicinity of the enemy and withdraw before him if he moves against us with his forces united. If we can, we will engage his detachments because we are of the opinion that these engagements must be deadly for him. With all our means, we will conduct our operations so that we become a heavy burden for him and to entice him to move against us with all his forces. If he does this, we will withdraw as slowly as possible to our entrenched camp. If he attacks us in it, we can only hope the camp is built well enough to guarantee us victory. We hope to build it so that 50,000 men will suffice for its defense and the remaining troops can be used as a reserve."

Demonstrating his knowledge of modern war, Gneisenau offered a lesson for Knesebeck, whose views tended to reflect Frederician warfare. "Not the immediate coverage of a province," he lectured, "but the destruction of enemy forces must be the goal that a general must strive to achieve. During the next few days, we will try to convince the enemy that we want to concentrate toward Dresden so we can win a few days to build the entrenched camp; then, we will quickly turn to the crossing point." Somewhat prophetically, he concluded: "I hardly believe that another [plan] can be found that promises the Bohemian Army so many advantages and such wide room to maneuver while giving our army the possibility to torment the enemy, first through back-and-forth marches, and then by delivering a decisive battle with a high probability of success. Also, it is very necessary to bring into play the forces that are in the hands of the crown prince of Sweden."[7]

From this letter, we see that Gneisenau recommended crossing the Elbe between Dresden and Torgau, presumably at Mühlberg. He based this suggestion on the assumption that the Grande Armée would exchange Dresden for Leipzig. If Napoleon's main army moved to Leipzig, Mühlberg offered Blücher the most expedient means of maintaining communication with Schwarzenberg. As yet, no sign indicated that Napoleon had evacuated Dresden. Should the emperor hold Dresden and presumably defend the Elbe, the Silesian Army would then cross the river closer to the entrenched camp and unite with Bernadotte. Consequently, Gneisenau dispatched Rühle and Captain Johann Christoph Lölhöffel von Löwensprung to find a suitable crossing point downstream of Mühlberg. The staff chief carefully explained his thought process to the major. He believed Murat's "army" had crossed to the left bank to take a position at Lommatzsch, twenty-five miles northwest of Dresden. He speculated that Murat would guard the Elbe along the 32-mile stretch between Lommatzsch and Torgau while the Grande Armée held the 40 miles of river line that extended from Lommatzsch to Königstein. "The Silesian Army," stated Gneisenau in his instructions to Rühle, "will fail in its purpose if it seeks a crossing between these points."

Should Murat hold his position, Gneisenau understood that a crossing between Torgau and Wittenberg would not only be easier, but would also allow the army greater flexibility to react to adverse situations or escape to the right bank in the event of unforeseen enemy movements. As a result of these considerations, Rühle received the task of reconnoitering the right bank of the Elbe from Torgau toward Wittenberg "to locate a point where we can cross the Elbe with our pontoons and without counting on the help of rafts or boats. Moreover, it is of the greatest importance to select an opposite point that offers the advantage of a bridgehead so that an army of 50,000 men, with both wings leaning on the [left bank of the] Elbe, can advantageously accept a battle against a force three times its strength. The curves of the Elbe near Elster appear to best combine these advantages."[8] A sortie up the right bank of the Elbe from French-occupied Torgau could force the Silesian Army to abandon the bridgehead and entrenched camp on the left bank. Thus, Gneisenau called for the construction of a second entrenched camp, this one on the right bank of the Elbe, that would allow 20,000 men to "fight with advantage against a superior force. The confluence of the Black Elster with the Elbe appears favorable for the construction of such an entrenched camp." Lastly, he stipulated that all entrenchments had to be battle-ready within five or six days of the start of construction.

As soon as Rühle completed the reconnaissance, he would seek Tauentzien and Bülow. Concerned that the Army of Berlin might be close enough to the Elbe to attack the Silesian Army, Gneisenau instructed Rühle to request their assistance. At the least, Gneisenau wanted them "to remain close enough until the Silesian Army reaches the point where it can protect the works." Verbally, he tasked Rühle with pointedly asking Tauentzien and Bülow if they would follow the Silesian Army across the Elbe without the crown prince's approval.[9]

To dupe the imperials, Army Headquarters lingered at Bautzen for as long as possible on the 26th. Throughout the day, Blücher received reports confirming Macdonald's retreat to the Elbe. After evacuating Radeberg, imperial forces held only the river's crossings. Numerous rumors also reached the Prussians. From Dresden, Napoleon had purportedly transferred many units along the right bank of the Elbe to Meißen, reinforcing his troops with 4,000 impressed Austrian prisoners and his Guard with 6,000 Poles. At Dresden, where 30,000 imperial soldiers filled the hospitals, the French had supposedly burned 3,500 bushels of hay. Rumors also spread that 30,000 Bavarians had defected, giving more reason for the Prussians to envision winter quarters on the Rhine. For the 27th, Blücher ordered Sacken's main body to march fifteen miles west from Schwosdorf to Schönfeld, pushing its vanguard an additional eight miles toward Großenhain. Uncertain of the status of the latter, Blücher wanted Großenhain observed if the imperials held the town in strength. In the opposite case, he authorized the Russians to inflict as much damage on the enemy as possible.[10]

Around 2:00 A.M. on 27 September, the imperials withdrew from Großenhain leaving behind a rearguard, which Sacken's vanguard attacked seven hours later. Pursuing south toward Meißen, Vasilchikov's cavalry overtook Lhéritier's cavalry division at Medessen, plucking 200 prisoners and inflicting 200 casualties. Continuing south, the Russians halted at Wantewitz, the midpoint between Großenhain and Meißen. With imperial forces so close, Sacken led his main body back to Großenhain. Yorck's corps pressed nineteen miles west through Königsbrück to Radeburg while Langeron's corps halted at Königsbrück, St.-Priest moved from Bischofswerda to Schwosdorf, and Kaptsevich pulled into Kamenz. That same day, Shcherbatov occupied Schmiedefeld and Bubna moved into Stolpen: both less than twenty miles west of Dresden. Although their right wing extended through Dresden and their left through Meißen, the French gave every indication that they intended to evacuate the right bank of the Elbe. Locals stated that the imperials had driven all the livestock they could find on the right bank to Meißen. On the left bank, long columns could be seen marching from Dresden to Meißen. Unless the circumstances changed, Blücher planned to march through Bad Liebenwerda to Herzberg, with headquarters reaching Elsterwerda on the 28th (see Map 4).[11]

After crossing the Elbe, Blücher expected to encounter Ney's Army of Berlin before the Silesian Army could reach Leipzig. Following his defeat at Dennewitz, Ney maneuvered the wreck of his army between the Elbe and the Mulde. He then spent the next five days (17–21 September) reorganizing the Army of Berlin based on Napoleon's instructions. Mainly, he dissolved XII Corps, transferring its remaining manpower to IV and VII Corps.[12] Oudinot went to Dresden, where he assumed command of I Young Guard Corps, consisting of the 1st and 3rd Divisions of Young Guard. Like Macdonald in the wake of his defeat on the Katzbach, Ney requested Napoleon's personal intervention to prevent the multinational Army of Berlin from disintegrating. Friction between the French and their Italian, Saxon, Württemberger, Westphalian, and Bavarian allies mounted. On the night of 22/23 September, an entire Saxon battalion of 300 men defected to the Army of North Germany. Reynier also reported that 1,019 cavalry troopers deserted. Ney lamented that "this example of mass desertion requires a prompt remedy." Unable to answer Ney's pleas, the emperor left the marshal on his own. As a result, Ney continued to maneuver the 35,000 men and 96 guns of his army between the Elbe and the Mulde.[13]

Although Bernadotte did not exploit the victory at Dennewitz according to the demands of his Prussian subordinates, he did not remain idle. On 16 September, the Swedes crossed the Elbe at Roßlau and started building a bridgehead on the left bank. They entered Dessau on the 18th, where their engineers threw a bridge across the Mulde on the 20th. Construction of a second bridge over the Elbe began twelve miles downstream of Roßlau at

Aken on the 21st. Thirty-two miles upriver from Roßlau, Bülow besieged Wittenberg from the right bank with the main body of III Corps while his 3rd and 5th Brigades camped fifteen miles to the east at Seyda to cover the construction of a bridge at Elster. After his engineers completed the bridge on the 21st, the Prussians occupied the bridgehead near the village of Wartenburg on the left bank across from Elster (see Map 5).[14]

On 21 September, Ney learned that Bülow's corps had completed a bridge near Wartenburg. The marshal doubted the accuracy of the report and demanded more information. For the 23rd, he instructed General Charles-Antoine Morand's 12th Division of IV Corps to drive the Prussian detachment back across the Elbe and destroy the bridge while the rest of the army marched toward Dessau to contend with the crown prince of Sweden. On the morning of the 23rd, the three battalions and Westphalian light cavalry that formed Morand's vanguard easily drove the Prussian post from Wartenburg. Yet Morand's attack did not catch the Prussians by surprise. On the previous day, 22 October, Bernadotte had informed Bülow that, according to intercepted dispatches addressed to Ney and Reynier, the imperials would attempt to destroy the bridge at Elster. Thus forewarned, the Prussian commander, Major Hellwig, made a stand in the thick woods between Wartenburg and the left bank. Prisoners informed Morand that the pioneers had finished the bridge and that Bülow's corps had started crossing the Elbe. This misinformation caused Morand to reconsider his mission. With Bülow's entire corps supposedly defiling across the river, he did not want to risk becoming entangled in the overgrown terrain east of Wartenburg. Rather than drive Hellwig across the river, Morand decided to await support. At dusk, he broke off the firefight with the Prussians and withdrew less than one thousand paces west of Wartenburg, which Hellwig immediately reoccupied.[15]

Sometime during the night of 22/23 October, Ney received the emperor's orders dated 4:00 A.M. on 22 September to concentrate his forces at Wittenberg and not for any reason allow himself to be cut off from Torgau. These directives, along with the enemy's activity at Wartenburg, convinced Ney to renounce his plan to march on Dessau. Instead, he decided to take a position that allowed him to cover both Wittenberg and Torgau as well as to monitor Allied movements, especially through Dessau. To support Morand, he directed Bertrand's 38th Division, all Württembergers commanded by General Friedrich von Franquemont, to Bad Schmiedeberg. Yet the news Ney received of Morand's situation caused him also to send Bertrand's 15th Division – Italians commanded by General Appiani Fontanelli – to Pretzsch, less than ten miles south of Wartenburg.[16]

On the Allied side of the Elbe, Bülow learned from Hellwig on 23 September of the march of French forces toward Wittenberg and assumed Ney would attempt to advance through the fortress and raise the siege.

Consequently, he summoned his 3rd Brigade from Elster to Wittenberg and ordered General Borstell's 5th Brigade to backtrack from Jeßen to Elster. These movements took place on the 24th, with Borstell arriving just as Hellwig withdrew from Wartenburg after skirmishing with Morand's troops for several hours. Nevertheless, Prussian resistance convinced Bertrand, who had arrived in the evening, that he faced the vanguard of an enemy corps of between 15,000 and 20,000 men who probably planned to cross the Elbe the following day. His report persuaded Ney to concentrate IV Corps at Wartenburg to prevent Bülow from crossing.

On the 25th, Ney himself went to Wartenburg to greet Bülow's Prussians when they crossed the river. He waited but the Prussians never showed. "It appears that the bridge was built too hastily," he explained to Marmont at noon, "and that the enemy will not dare move his cannon across until it is reinforced, which will take several days." By 4:00 P.M., no attack had come but the situation still did not please the marshal. "My position is extremely hazardous," he complained to Berthier, "because if the enemy debouches from Dessau on Kemberg and at the same time through Elster, I would have no choice other than to quickly retire to avoid being cut off from Torgau, which, if this happens, would require me to fall back under the protection of Wittenberg's guns." Interestingly, Ney took responsibility for the presence of the bridge at Elster: "The bridge that the enemy has vis-à-vis Elster, as poor as it is, is still very disturbing, and it is even more unfortunate that we did not oppose its establishment but I never obliged Reynier to approach it." As for the emperor, he could not understand why the Elster bridge caused his subordinates such fits: "His Majesty has charged me with telling you that he cannot fathom why Bertrand does not launch rafts to destroy the enemy's bridge. Launching them in the middle of the night is likely to succeed." This would not be the first mistake that either Ney or Bertrand would make at Wartenburg.[17]

With only General Jean-Marie Defrance's 4th Heavy Division of III Cavalry Corps and General Jan Henryk Dąbrowski's all-Polish 27th Division (four battalions, eight squadrons, and eight guns) facing the Swedes and Russians of his right wing, Bernadotte could easily have driven across the Elbe. Instead, reports of Ney's march toward Wittenberg had the same effect on Napoleon's former marshal as it did on Bülow. Thinking that this movement heralded an attempt by Ney to break out of Wittenberg, Bernadotte issued inexplicable orders to Bülow on the 24th. Referring to the bridge at Elster "as an object of secondary importance," the prince royal instructed him to recall his troops from the left to the right bank of the Elbe, dismantle the bridge, and unite his corps at Wittenberg to support the Swedes. Extremely bitter, Bülow forwarded the instructions to Borstell, who received the dispatch early on the 25th. With the imperials holding Wartenburg, he prudently delayed its execution until dark. During the night of 25/26 September, he sailed as many of the boats as he could up the Black Elster and sank the remainder. On the morning of the 26th, his 5th Brigade departed for Wittenberg, leaving five companies, one squadron, and four guns at Elster to observe the French on the opposite bank.[18]

After the Prussians failed to appear at Wartenburg, Ney quickly turned his attention to Dessau. On the 26th, he led VII Corps west to Oranienbaum while IV Corps temporarily remained at Wartenburg. All three of Reynier's divisions encountered Cossacks and small detachments from Bernadotte's army during the course of the day but all withdrew. This convinced Ney that he had nothing to fear of an Allied crossing of the Elbe in strength. He reported to Berthier that, aside from 6,000 men who held Dessau, the crown prince of Sweden's entire army remained north of the Elbe in camps around Roßlau; Bernadotte's headquarters stood at Zerbst, some ten miles north-west of Roßlau. After learning that the Prussians had dismantled the bridge at Elster, Ney drew down his forces at Wartenburg so IV Corps could better support VII Corps at Dessau. Eventually, only a weak post of thirty troopers remained at Wartenburg to observe the Elbe.

On the 27th, IV Corps extended from Kemberg to Schleesen while Reynier conducted further reconnaissance toward Dessau, which prompted the Swedes and Cossacks to abandon the right bank of the Mulde. In fact, 1st Brigade of 1st Division of Bernadotte's Swedish corps fled across the Elbe, leaving only Cossacks to hold the portion of the town situated on the Mulde's left bank; two companies of French voltigeurs occupied the part of Dessau on the right bank. Pleasantly surprised by the withdrawal of the enemy's regular forces, Ney planned to take the rest of Dessau on the 28th, drive any remaining Allied troops across the Elbe, and destroy the bridge at Roßlau.[19]

Although Bernadotte had ordered the commander of the Swedish 1st Brigade, Conrad Theodor von Schulzenheim, to avoid a serious engagement, the general's retreat across the Elbe and the evacuation of Dessau did not please the prince royal, particularly because he had given his word to Blücher that the Army of North Germany would cooperate with the Army of Silesia within three days of the latter's crossing the Elbe. Thus, he ordered Stedingk to send a detachment to reoccupy Dessau on the morning of the 28th. To distract Ney, relieve the pressure on his own right wing, and prepare for Blücher's crossing, Bernadotte ordered Bülow to send a few battalions and some artillery to rebuild the Elster–Wartenburg bridge on the army's left. On the 28th, the Swedes failed to retake Dessau but managed to prevent the imperials from reaching Roßlau. The following day, Ney launched an attack on Roßlau from the east with VII Corps supported by IV Corps. Although avoiding a frontal assault on the Swedish position, the imperials could do little against the entrenched bridgehead. Outnumbered five to one, the Swedes admirably maintained their positions under the protection of batteries posted on the right bank of the Elbe. Failure convinced Ney that the entrenchments could not be taken by storm.[20]

Early on the morning of the 28th, Ney received extensive instructions from Imperial Headquarters. The contents assured Ney that Bernadotte would not dare move on Leipzig and expose his flank. Napoleon thought it even less likely that Bernadotte would make such a move until Schwarzenberg launched an offensive through Chemnitz. Should the Army of North Germany launch an offensive on Leipzig, the emperor instructed Ney to destroy Bernadotte's bridges over the Elbe and sever his line of retreat to Berlin. If Bernadotte remained in his position, Ney should cross the Elbe at Wittenberg, raise Bülow's siege, and from the right bank threaten Bernadotte's bridges, "which will oblige him to quickly recross" the Elbe. For this operation, the emperor grossly overestimated Ney's force to number 80,000 men.[21]

Based on these instructions and after failing to drive the Swedes from Roßlau, Ney decided to dig parallels and formally besiege the bridgehead. With the arrival of Marmont's VI Corps at Leipzig and Latour-Maubourg's I Cavalry Corps at Wurzen, Ney planned to guard the debouches of the Mulde and contain the Allies at Roßlau while he moved on Wittenberg. On the 30th, however, he learned of renewed enemy activity at Elster. In fact, Bülow's Prussians had rebuilt their bridge during the night of 29/30 September but only 200 Jäger had thus far crossed. Bertrand responded by instructing Franquemont to send one brigade to reconnoiter and drive off any Prussians it found on the left bank.[22]

In addition to having to contend with Bernadotte and Bülow, Ney somehow had to lift the siege of Wittenberg in accordance with Napoleon's orders. To fulfill this task, he demanded more manpower, and so the emperor instructed him to utilize Marmont's VI Corps.[23] However, as in previous campaigns, the inability of the marshals to work together hampered operations. By sending mixed messages, Napoleon bears much of the blame in this case. On the 30th, he placed VI Corps and I Cavalry Corps in an army group commanded by Marmont to counter a supposed Allied operation from Bohemia to Altenburg. "Did the enemy send 25,000 infantry to Altenburg?" the emperor asked Marmont. "If this is the case, this corps must be cut off and destroyed. If they sent cavalry as well, this corps must still be harassed and forced to withdraw. The prince de la Moskova [Ney], with IV and VII Corps, III Cavalry Corps, and Dąbrowski's division, has 40,000 men. The VI, VIII, and V Corps, I and IV Cavalry Corps, and Margaron's division will give you nearly 60,000 men." Consequently, Napoleon informed Ney that he should utilize Marmont for his operations on the middle Elbe while at the same time he offered Marmont an independent command south of Leipzig. Until Marmont determined the situation at Altenburg, he offered little assistance to Ney.

On 1 October, Ney instructed Marmont to send one division to Bad Düben, another to Bitterfeld, and the third to Wurzen, where it could cover communication with Dresden along with I Cavalry Corps. He explained that this disposition would fulfill Marmont's dual requirement of covering Leipzig and supporting Ney's own operation. Ney sensed that Marmont would be a difficult subordinate. Before giving Marmont time to respond, he explained to Berthier that he did not think Marmont would cooperate because "I do not know if the marshal deems it appropriate to carry out the provisions that I will take." Marmont did not reply to Ney. This prompted a complaint to Imperial Headquarters. Ney described Marmont's movement to the Elbe and especially Wittenberg as "essential so that I am free to operate there with all troops of IV and VII Corps to prevent the army of the crown prince of Sweden from debouching between the Saale and the Mulde."[24]

On 2 October, Marmont reported to the emperor that he could not comply with Ney's demands because he had received reports that an Allied corps of 20,000 men had indeed reached Altenburg. As soon as he received confirmation, Marmont planned to march there. In this case, he could only send one of his divisions to relieve Ney's troops at Delitzsch. He further noted that, "if I do not march on Altenburg and the enemy does not cross the Elbe, I will await further events by occupying Leipzig and its environs, Delitzsch, and Wurzen." From Ney came another complaint on the 2nd: "It is essential to combine a movement with the troops of the duc de Raguse [Marmont] and Dąbrowski to force the enemy to evacuate the region between the Saale and the Mulde, and to force him to cross to the right bank of the Elbe; this would have the great advantage of severing the enemy's communication with the Austrians and restoring our own with Magdeburg." Due to this impasse between Ney and Marmont, the former paid little heed to lifting the siege of Wittenberg. Moreover, Blücher's army would burst on the scene in the midst of this turmoil and change not merely Ney's situation, but that of the entire war.[25]

As for Blücher, he passed the night of 27/28 September at Königsbrück. There, he received a letter from Tauentzien conveying both positive and negative news. Writing after his meeting with Rühle at Elsterwerda, Tauentzien confirmed his countrymen's suspicions of Bernadotte: "The great commander operates on the right wing in such a manner that it must be God's will that the situation is still favorable." Tauentzien planned to maintain his position at Bad Liebenwerda, thirty miles northwest of Königsbrück, until he could operate "in unison" with Blücher. While Tauentzien again presented the prospect of IV Corps cooperating with the Silesian Army, news that Bernadotte had forced Borstell to disassemble the pontoon bridge at Elster frustrated the entire undertaking. "Borstell received orders to dismantle the pontoon bridge that was built with so much difficulty at

Elster," complained Tauentzien, "because a few enemy battalions have attempted to oppose the building of the bridgehead. As a result of the dismantling of the bridge at Elster, all offensive operations are now frustrated and the time used for building the bridge has been wasted."[26]

Blücher immediately wrote to Bernadotte. Uncertain of how to motivate the native Frenchman, the Prussians wanted to make him aware of the current opportunity and alleviate the fears that had prompted him to dismantle the bridge at Elster. At the same time, they could not resist employing a scare tactic. Thus, we see an interesting letter that seeks to both frighten and encourage the crown prince. In describing his operations, Blücher explained that he had learned from the local inhabitants that a courier from Dresden had reached Napoleon at Bischofswerda on the 25th. After reading the dispatches, the emperor immediately departed for Dresden – leaving behind a feast for forty – and ordered the troops to retreat. "There is no longer any doubt that he will quit the entire right bank of the Elbe today," Blücher assured Bernadotte, "but according to the news that I have received so far, it appears that the enemy army, perhaps seeing its communications threatened by the left of the Grand Army, has decided to descend the Elbe along its left bank and to move onto the plains of Leipzig to fight a decisive battle or proceed to Wittenberg to raise the siege and repulse you. Although this latter assumption appears less likely to me, I will skirt the right bank of the Elbe to be within range for all cases."[27]

Despite the setback at Elster, Tauentzien affirmed that the old bridgehead at Mühlberg could be utilized. However, the threat posed by the French pontoon bridge at Meißen, twenty-seven miles upstream of Mühlberg, first needed to be eliminated. Thus, for 28 September, Blücher ordered Sacken's vanguard "to drive the enemy across the Elbe and destroy the pontoon bridge at Meißen if the enemy has not already done so." General Jean-Pierre Doumerc's 3rd Heavy Cavalry Division of I Cavalry Corps held Meißen and its vicinity while one infantry brigade, one small cavalry detachment, and a few guns from VI Corps served as an advance post three miles to the northeast at Ockrilla. Vasilchikov attacked these troops early on the 28th, driving them to Meißen. The sole brigade of Sacken's 16th Division as well as the 8th and 39th Jäger Regiments assaulted the bridge.[28] Believing the Allies intended to cross the Elbe at Meißen, the French dismantled their pontoons and evacuated the town (see Map 4).[29]

Elsewhere on the 28th, Blücher met with Tauentzien at Elsterwerda, fifteen miles east of Mühlberg, to discuss the Elbe crossing and the ensuing operation, which the former decided would be a march on Leipzig. As the two commanders talked, Tauentzien's vanguard occupied Mühlberg while his main body remained at Bad Liebenwerda. Yorck led I Corps north from Radeburg to Elsterwerda, eight miles southeast of Bad Liebenwerda. Langeron's corps, including St.-Priest and Kaptsevich, moved to Ortrand, itself fourteen miles southeast of Elsterwerda; the rearguard reached Königs-brück. On the following day, Tauentzien personally inspected Mühlberg. He found that, despite the presence of French forces on the left bank, a bridge could be built due to the fair condition of the old bridgehead. Yet, unless Blücher acted quickly, the imperials would doubtlessly present greater obstacles.[30]

Tauentzien ultimately dropped a bombshell on his countrymen at Blü-cher's headquarters. Despite all his recent assurances, he revealed his plans to force-march IV Corps thirty miles northwest to Jeßen in compliance with Bernadotte's most recent order to move closer to the Army of North Germany for a general operation. As a result, he withdrew his van from Mühlberg. Blücher and Gneisenau tried to remain optimistic, hoping that this general operation would be Bernadotte's crossing of the Elbe. Thus, the Silesian Army continued its preparations to cross the Elbe at Mühlberg; the East Prussian Fusilier Battalion from Yorck's corps scrambled to take pos-session of the town.[31]

During the course of 29 September, the majority of the Silesian Army moved into positions to make a lunge for Mühlberg as soon as the Russians had completed the pontoon bridge. Yorck retraced his steps, marching a few miles south to Gröden, eighteen miles east of Mühlberg. Langeron moved into Yorck's former position at Elsterwerda while Sacken's main body remained at Großenhain (see Map 4). From Meißen, Sacken's vanguard commander, Vasilchikov, reported large enemy troop movements from there toward Torgau and Leipzig. On the 30th, one brigade from Souham's III Corps arrived and sharply attacked Vasilchikov, but Blücher allowed the army to rest in anticipation of the crossing at Mühlberg. At 6:00 P.M., Sacken forwarded several reports to Blücher, including one from a captured imperial commissar who had traveled down the right bank of the Elbe to Meißen. He stated that Dresden's garrison of 40,000 men could evacuate the city as early as that very day. Napoleon planned to move the army through Freiberg to Leipzig. Moreover, the prisoner attested to the demoralized state of the entire army, which viewed the war as a waste.[32]

News that the Russian bridge train could not reach Bad Liebenwerda until 1 October disrupted the timing of Blücher's operation. This setback, along with news from the tsar, Knesebeck, Bernadotte, and Rühle, forced Gneisenau to change plans. From Allied Headquarters, Tsar Alexander informed Bernadotte in a letter of 24 September that, rather than the Silesian Army, Bennigsen's Army of Poland would march to Bohemia. He urged the crown prince to cooperate with Blücher. On the next day, 25 September, Alexander wrote to Blücher, who received the letter on the 29th. According to the Russian monarch, Schwarzenberg would attempt another foray into Saxony but this time would make for Leipzig rather than Dresden. Alexander believed that Napoleon would either launch an offensive against the Bohemian Army at Freiberg or invade Bohemia to attack Bennigsen. In the latter case, Bennigsen would fall back to the Eger and unite with Bubna, coming from Leitmeritz. Blücher could assist by crossing the Elbe at Pirna or further downstream and fall on the rear of the Grande Armée. Even better, if the crown prince crossed the Elbe, Blücher could unite with him at Wurzen and advance on Leipzig. Above all, Alexander wanted Blücher to cross the Elbe as soon as Napoleon either advanced south toward Bohemia or moved west in the direction of Leipzig. If the Army of North Germany remained on the right bank of the Elbe, Alexander instructed Blücher to turn toward Dresden and fall on Napoleon's rear. Hinting at the dangers of crossing the Elbe, the tsar urged Blücher to wait until the Army of Poland had reached Pirna and then cross the Elbe there under its protection. "If you continue," he concluded, "as you have done so well up to now, not losing sight of the enemy for one moment and you combine your operations with those of the Bohemian Army, Napoleon will never have time to throw all his forces at any point."[33]

At this moment, when Allied Headquarters had again resolved to enter Napoleon's lair, the monarchs again looked to Blücher as the possible savior who could prevent another mauling of the Bohemian Army. Although their appreciation for Blücher had increased, they still underestimated him and Gneisenau. They had no idea that Blücher had already decided to take matters into his own hands and had no intention of waiting on the operations of Schwarzenberg or Bernadotte or even Napoleon to determine his next move.

On the night of the 28th, Gneisenau received a long letter from Knesebeck dated the 26th. "I have not written anything official for two days," explained the king's advisor, "because nothing has changed here. Our movement will probably not begin before the 29th. We still have not completely decided how and where we will advance, whether through Marienberg, or through Zwickau, or through Eger. In all cases, we need six to seven marches before we reach a point where we can seriously engage the enemy. Therefore, the enemy's main force probably will not distance itself from the Elbe before 4 or 5 October if it turns toward Chemnitz; and not before the 2nd or 3rd if it turns against Bennigsen." He cautioned Gneisenau that, if Blücher attempted to cross the Elbe any earlier, "the Silesian Army would expose itself to serious danger." He advised that Blücher be certain Napoleon was marching against the Bohemian Army before he led the Silesian Army across the Elbe.

At noon on 26 September, Knesebeck was in the midst of drafting this letter when he received Gneisenau's missive from the 25th that revealed Blücher's plans to hijack Bülow and Tauentzien for a crossing of the Elbe. According to Knesebeck, the king walked into the room before he could finish reading the long communiqué. "I could not prevent His Majesty from reading the whole letter, especially because I was in the king's room. The king had already agreed to the idea of the entire Silesian Army marching to the right and uniting with the crown prince, its place being taken by Bennigsen's army. You know from my earlier memo the reasons opposed to this idea that reigned here. Then we reached the part of the letter where you mention that, to avoid losing time, you wrote to Bülow and Tauentzien over this. I cannot conceal from you that this aroused the king's displeasure, because the crown prince is guaranteed Bülow's corps by treaty." Knesebeck warned Gneisenau to prepare himself "to receive a letter over this, for even if the king completely believes that the crown prince perhaps could have pursued his victory [at Dennewitz] with more intensity he nevertheless believes that the entire business has been conducted by him with much prudence. It is undeniable that his position, where he is threatened from the rear by Davout and has to fear Magdeburg in his right flank, Wittenberg in front, and a movement from Torgau in the left flank, is very difficult and requires great caution."[34]

Gneisenau responded on the 29th: "Because I now know His Majesty's displeasure, I will take no further steps to induce Bülow to unite with us but instead will strive to bring this about only by convincing the crown prince to operate in unison with us. This was my original intent, and only then, if our efforts failed, would we have induced Bülow to jointly operate with us." Referring to the letter from Alexander that Blücher had just received, Gneisenau expressed his relief "that the tsar has based the operations of the Bohemian Army on the principle that the crown prince of Sweden will cross the Elbe. Therefore, we can assume an agreement over this has been made with the crown prince. We are ready to simultaneously cross the river with him; therefore, I can assume he will pose few obstacles to doing this."

Despite this apparent good news, Blücher and Gneisenau wanted the events at Elster made known at Allied Headquarters. "When some enemy battalions appeared there," continued Gneisenau in his letter to Knesebeck, "the crown prince gave the order to quickly dismantle the bridge and for the troops to recross. We still do not know how this was carried out and if there were losses." Regarding Bernadotte himself, the staff chief assured Knesebeck that, "if you were as close to the complaints about the crown prince of Sweden as we are, your judgment of him would be more severe. Prussians and Russians talk about it. Everything good that has occurred in his army has been done against his will. Thus, based on my knowledge of this individual, can I judge him any differently than I have? It is my constant concern that he will cause mischief." In a postscript, Gneisenau added that Tauentzien had received a very firm order from the crown prince directing IV Corps to immediately unite with the Army of North Germany and undertake a great operation. "We can only hope that this operation is a crossing of the Elbe, which will facilitate our own," concluded the usually pessimistic staff chief.[35]

As for Rühle, after his meeting with Tauentzien on the 27th, he journeyed to Elster. There, he found that the bends of the Elbe met all of Gneisenau's prerequisites for the entrenched camp. The generally flat bank at Elster favored a strong camp of three redoubts with 100 twelve-pound guns. He estimated that 3,000 men could build the fortifications in thirty-six hours. Using the available boats and barges, some forty-eight hours would be required to span the 450 yards that separated the two banks of the Elbe; a bridgehead would take just as long to build according to his calculations. He found the neighboring villages, woods, dead arms, and ponds all conducive to Gneisenau's plan. Should Bülow likewise agree to cooperate with Blücher, he judged the locale to be so strong that the Silesian Army would not need a fortified camp on the right bank of the Elbe. From Elster, Rühle traveled to Bülow's headquarters near Wittenberg. During their meeting, Bülow stated his intentions to follow the Silesian Army across the Elbe. Like Tauentzien, Bülow expressed his commitment to cooperating with Blücher but advised the major to inform Bernadotte of Blücher's intentions. Although Bülow's disgust about the crown prince's conduct of the war exceeded Tauentzien's, he had more experience dealing with the recalcitrant native Frenchman. Bülow knew the crown prince would not respond well to a covert attempt to detach half his army. Thus, he urged his countrymen to discuss the situation with Bernadotte and arrange a joint crossing of both armies.

Regardless of Bülow's sage advice, Rühle lacked the authorization to negotiate with the crown prince. He solved this quandary by volunteering to deliver Bülow's report on his meeting with Rühle to Bernadotte's headquarters at Zerbst. After the crown prince read the contents of the letter, Rühle requested his thoughts. The Swedish prince royal answered that he would act in unison with Blücher. Moreover, although the monarchs had guaranteed that all Allied corps operating in his vicinity would be placed under his command, he and Blücher would fight next to each other as equals. He then asked Rühle how many troops Blücher intended to bring across the Elbe. According to the major, after answering that the entire Silesian Army would cross the river, the crown prince immediately resolved to likewise move the entire Army of North Germany across the Elbe. In addition, Bernadotte endorsed Elster as a favorable point for Blücher's crossing. He even promised to conduct serious demonstrations from Roßlau and Aken to distract the imperials. Should Napoleon launch an offensive against the Silesian Army, he pledged to come to Blücher's aid. Conversely, he expected the same from Blücher if the emperor directed his blow against the Army of North Germany. Again displaying his dexterity, Rühle somehow managed to persuade the prince to state in writing his promise to cross the Elbe in three to four days. If the Silesian Army crossed the Elbe at Elster, the Army of North Germany would do so at Aken and Roßlau within three or four days.

Rühle returned to Silesian Army Headquarters on 30 September with the crown prince's written vow to cooperate with Blücher as well as the favorable report concerning Elster. This news, combined with Napoleon's apparent intent to defend the Elbe, convinced Gneisenau to scrap the plans to cross the river at Mühlberg. Instead, Blücher informed the crown prince that the Silesian Army would cross the Elbe at Elster on 3 October and engage Ney's Army of Berlin at Kemberg on the 4th. Following Ney's defeat, the army would be ready to unite with the Army of North Germany at Bad Düben on the Mulde River. "Our business here has finally gained some good results," Gneisenau reported to Knesebeck. "Major Rühle returned from the headquarters of the crown prince of Sweden with a verbal and written declaration from him that he would cross the Elbe with us. All persons attached to his headquarters are stunned by his sudden change of mind." Gneisenau confessed that he believed Bernadotte's petty desire to prevent Blücher from beating him across the Elbe accounted for this change.[36]

Meanwhile, Knesebeck shared with Gneisenau the prevailing views at Allied Headquarters in a long communiqué written late on the afternoon of the 28th. One point he made clear was that the Allied leaders believed the Silesian Army should cross the Elbe at Elster rather than Mühlberg. "Here," he explained, "we believe that, if Napoleon remains at Dresden, a crossing at Mühlberg would be dangerous for the Silesian Army." He also explained that, strategically, the short distance between Dresden and Mühlberg would not suffice to force Napoleon to abandon Dresden, whereas a crossing at Elster would pose more of a threat. Yet, if Blücher's movement forced Napoleon to direct the Grande Armée to either the Zwickau–Chemnitz region or to Bohemia, "then indeed the crossing at Mühlberg is preferable because it would threaten the enemy's lifeline. For the same reason, we believe the position of Elster must be the real point of operation for the Silesian Army; we are convinced that the Bohemian Army would be in a better position at Zwickau rather than Chemnitz." Based on this assumption, Knesebeck explained that Schwarzenberg planned to post his main body at Zwickau, the vanguard at Chemnitz, the reserve at Komotau, and the Army of Poland at Teplitz. However, he did not think the main body could reach Zwickau before 10 October. He informed Gneisenau that Schwarzenberg planned to conduct short marches in part to be able to return to Bohemia should Napoleon invade the province and in part to prevent the axles of his transports and artillery from being completely ruined on the generally poor roads.

According to Knesebeck, Bernadotte had chastised Allied Headquarters by pointing out "the evil consequences of the current inactivity of the Allied armies, which will allow Napoleon to reorganize his forces." Never short of cheek, the crown prince insisted that his next step, especially in regard to taking Wittenberg and the bridgehead of Torgau, would be determined by the activity displayed by the other Allied armies. He offered two options. First, the Bohemian Army could undertake a great offensive to Franconia. Second, Schwarzenberg could fix the Grande Armée on the upper Elbe while the Silesian Army marched downstream, united with the North German Army, and both assumed the offensive. To comply with Bernadotte's call for action, Knesebeck related that Allied Headquarters had drafted two plans. The first involved a general operation against Leipzig, the second an offensive through Kassel, Hamburg, and Holland. "The latter suggestion will be rejected, as you will easily judge, in favor of working concentrically." Knesebeck reminded Gneisenau that the spirit of both the Reichenbach Plan and the *kleinen Krieg* remained strong at Allied Headquarters. "The main goal," he explained, "is to always retain the power to accept or avoid battle according to circumstances. Also, to continuously conduct the war directly against the enemy's food and ammunition supply in order to destroy his forces through these indirect yet certain means." As for intelligence, Knesebeck related that the Grande Armée again stood in the triangle formed by Dresden, Pirna, and Freiberg, with Napoleon at the last named location. "At Würzburg, Augereau's army [corps] daily receives reinforcements and in a few days will contain 100 cannon; some say it is expected at Bamberg on the 25th. Of Bavaria, there is great hope that it will soon declare for us."[37]

Frederick William ordered Knesebeck to write Gneisenau a second time on the 28th concerning the plan to hijack the two Prussian corps from Bernadotte's army. "Today, the king spoke to me about the point that you mentioned in your last memo; and said to me that I may inform you in a friendly manner to bear in mind the situation of the corps belonging to the crown prince, that disagreement already has started to tear apart this army, and that this could be so very disadvantageous for the general good. Moreover, the king was very pleased about the view that you provided concerning operations and was also in agreement that they will force the crown prince to display some activity. But, all the same, His Majesty suggests that you maintain and bring about friendly terms and harmony; you will encounter praiseworthy enthusiasm on one side and possibly great caution on the other." According to Knesebeck, the king concluded by stating that his admonitions should be viewed by Gneisenau as orders but winked his eye. "I acquit myself of this task," finished Knesebeck, "and free myself of it knowing that my last expressed concern over this circumstance is seen as final. Therefore, I request that you mention this no further."[38]

While at Elsterwerda on 1 October, Blücher received a long missive from Bernadotte, communicating reports of an enemy advance toward Wittenberg apparently to attack Bülow. He explained that this news – and not plans for a general crossing of the Elbe – had prompted him to order Tauentzien to force-march to Jeßen. His letter requested that Blücher cross the Elbe as quickly as possible at either Elster or Mühlberg. "If your disposition can conform to my wishes," concluded the crown prince, "together we would form a mass of 120,000 men which can quickly move on Leipzig and venture a battle against the majority of the emperor Napoleon's forces." Blücher responded that he would have 50,000 men at Jeßen by 2 October with another 20,000 following one march behind; he would cross the Elbe on the 3rd and fall on the enemy's flank. The crown prince pledged to push Wintzingerode's light cavalry across the Elbe and up the Mulde to Bitterfeld, Bad Düben, and Delitzsch. To cross the Elbe, he directed the Russians to Aken, the Swedes and Bülow's Prussians to Roßlau, and Tauentzien's corps to Coswig. He urgently requested a combined operation with the Silesian Army and expressed his satisfaction about Blücher's proximity. From Bülow's headquarters, Boyen urged Gneisenau to conduct a rapid drive. Demonstrating the frustration felt by the Prussians in the Army of North Germany, Boyen concluded: "Only your arrival makes us hope that we won't spend the winter inactive on the Elbe."[39]

In the meantime, Prussian Jäger from Borstell's 5th Brigade crossed the Elbe by boat and drove off the Württemberger cavalry post at Wartenburg; Prussian engineers started restoring the bridgehead in compliance with Bernadotte's orders. As noted, this news prompted Bertrand to dispatch one brigade of Franquemont's 38th Division to Wartenburg. Blücher and his staff attributed the movement of IV Corps to Wartenburg to Bernadotte's failure to make suitable demonstrations along his sector of the middle Elbe. "This not only rendered the crossing of the Silesian Army more dangerous," affirmed Müffling, "but also enabled the enemy on the 2nd to move a corps from the region of Wörlitz, opposite the crown prince, to Wartenburg, opposite Elster." Regardless, neither Napoleon nor Ney had any idea that Blücher's army had marched down the Elbe. Numerous factors account for this critical oversight. After the Silesian Army moved north, Shcherbatov and Bubna had taken positions at Schmiedefeld and Stolpen respectively (see Map 4). This proved crucial after deserters claimed that the 35th, 36th, and 39th Divisions of XI Corps as well as all of II Cavalry Corps would remain on the right bank of the Elbe. Thus, while Blücher's main body marched north, the movement west by light forces under Katzler, Vasilchikov, and Rudzevich combined with Shcherbatov and Bubna to create an impenetrable curtain that concealed the right wheel. In addition, Sacken's attack on Doumerc at Meißen along with Tauentzien's appearance at Mühlberg served to distract French attention from the actual point where Blücher intended to cross the Elbe.[40] Langeron explains:

> They [the French] initially directed their attention on Wartenburg when the prince royal of Sweden approached it to build a bridge of boats. However, after he abandoned this project and moved further downriver toward Aken,

Napoleon observed that point and Dessau, never believing that Blücher could execute such a bold movement as to turn and cross great rivers; he did not know it nor divine it and, even when we did cross the Elbe, he believed it was only a weak detachment of our army that was exposed as a diversion to fool him. After he finally noticed that our corps were no longer near Bautzen, he still could not convince himself that we had all crossed the Elbe. In the papers of Marshal Macdonald, we found a letter from Berthier telling him: "The emperor absolutely wishes to know what has become of Langeron, Sacken, and Yorck." We were then at Bad Düben, twenty miles from Leipzig, and Napoleon had no idea![41]

In the meantime, Franquemont's lead brigade reached Wartenburg that same evening (30 September) and assaulted the bridgehead on the left bank. Borstell's small post retreated across the Elbe but the French only partially destroyed the works. On 1 October, three Prussian companies recrossed the Elbe. Supported by artillery on the right bank, they repulsed the Württemberger outposts and started restoring the palisades and tambours. As a result, Franquemont moved the rest of his division to Wartenburg and Bertrand sent one brigade from Morand's 12th Division, which arrived on the afternoon of the 2nd. That evening, Bertrand – one of the best engineers of the Napoleonic period – arrived with the rest of 12th Division as well as Fontanelli's 15th Division. Morand's troops camped at Wartenburg, Franquemont's at Bleddin, and Fontanelli's at Globig (see Map 5).[42]

Elsewhere, Langeron's Russians and Yorck's Prussians marched twenty-three and twenty-eight miles respectively to reach Herzberg – itself twenty-two miles southeast of Elster – on 1 October.[43] Blücher and Army Headquarters likewise proceeded down the Black Elster to Herzberg. To deceive the imperials, Sacken's main body moved into Mühlberg. Despite orders to march north, it appears that Vasilchikov remained at Meißen with Sacken's vanguard. His presence there attracted attention: Souham's entire III Corps arrived. On 2 October, Langeron's and Yorck's corps trooped another sixteen miles northwest. Crossing the Black Elster, they bivouacked at Jeßen, less than seven miles southeast of the village of Elster. Sjöholm's detachment of three battalions and one battery each of horse and foot joined Borstell's battalions at Elster that evening to cover the bridge work. Yorck's corps was selected to cross first and, as Blücher's report to Frederick William states, "to make the attack so that the enemy, accustomed to fighting Prussian troops at this point of the Elbe, would not observe that he had to deal with the Silesian Army." Army Headquarters likewise moved to Jeßen while the Russian pontoon train reached Elster. Sacken's corps legged twenty miles, pushing north from Mühlberg to Herzberg.[44]

Reports that the bridge construction at Elster lacked sufficient wagons prompted Yorck to empty his baggage and forage carts so they could be used to haul the necessary materiel. Blücher blamed these shortages as well as any other inconvenience on the machinations of the crown prince. Despite Bernadotte's promises, the Prussian sensed that the prince royal wanted to complicate the crossing of the Silesian Army in any way possible.[45] Gneisenau, Müffling, and Rühle went to Elster during the afternoon of the 2nd to accelerate the construction. That night, one horse battery and some troopers from Bülow's Reserve Cavalry likewise arrived to support Sjöholm's detachment. Surprisingly, the imperials did nothing on the 1st. Finally, around 6:00 P.M. on the evening of the 2nd, a line of skirmishers followed by some support advanced toward the bridgehead but its small garrison as well as the artillery on the right bank of the Elbe quickly forced the Württembergers to retire. At nightfall, the Russians drove up their trestles and canvas pontoons. Starting at 9:00 P.M., the Russians went to work assembling one boat bridge and another consisting of seventy-two pontoons. Blücher credited the diligence of the Russian engineers, especially Majors Ivanov and Shishkin, for making possible the crossing on the following morning.[46]

Blücher hoped the two bridges would be ready by morning but knew very little concerning the strength and position of the imperial force at Wartenburg. Earlier in the day, Bülow had reported the noon departure of some 6,000 men (Fontanelli's division) from a position south of Wittenberg eastward in the direction of Wartenburg. Blücher's headquarters knew even less about the terrain on the opposite bank. Thick undergrowth concealed the details. His only map, the standard Petri map, did not suffice for a tactical operation. Statements from local peasants failed to provide a clear picture. Oddly, not one officer from Bülow's staff, which had spent one week preparing a crossing at Elster, fighting at Wartenburg during the process, made a report on the conditions on the left bank. Even stranger, none was present at Blücher's headquarters on 3 October.[47]

While the Elster–Wartenburg position contained all the key requirements to make a good crossing point – a considerable meander in the river, a domineering right bank, a firm river bed, solid banks, a suitable current for bridging preparations, and an unobstructed approach march on a good road – the impassable terrain on the left bank completely outweighed these advantages. Had Gneisenau received more details of the conditions on the left bank, he would not have chosen this point. During his journey to Zerbst, Rühle postponed a detailed inspection of the terrain on the left bank until his return trip. Unfortunately for the Prussians, while returning to Blücher's headquarters, the presence of imperial forces on the left bank prevented the major from surveying the ground. As Delbrück dramatizes, "This failure to reconnoiter would now be paid for with a river of blood." With hardly any knowledge of the terrain and the size of the enemy force on the opposite bank, the Silesian Army prepared to cross the Elbe. "It pleases me greatly," wrote Blücher to Knesebeck, "to see from the letter you wrote to Gneisenau

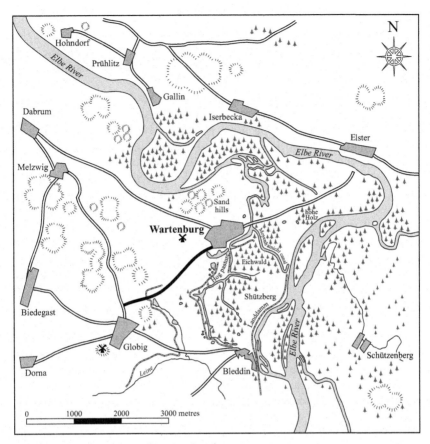

22. Engagement at Wartenburg, 3 October 1813

that [the monarchs] agree with our decision to cross at Elster. Even if I did not think the crossing at Mühlberg was dangerous, I still would have moved closer to Tauentzien, whom I have already spoken with. Once we are across, I will bring him forward and His Highness [Bernadotte] will have to come."[48]

Situated on the right bank less than one mile downstream of a sharp meander in the Elbe, the village of Elster indeed met all of Gneisenau's requirements. Just upstream of Elster, the generally northward-flowing Elbe cut sharply northeast taking in the discharge from the Black Elster River, then made a 180-degree rotation and continued northwest so that the land on the left bank resembled a peninsula. This U-shaped curve greatly facili-tated the movement of forces from the concave bank (northern and right) to the convex bank (southern and left). Artillery on the concave bank could easily protect bridge construction, especially because in this region of the Elbe the right bank dominated the left. Of equal importance, the area between the concave banks remained large enough for the crossing troops to deploy.

While the French could not prevent Blücher from crossing the Elbe at Elster, the terrain on the left bank presented almost insurmountable obstacles. Several dead arms of the Elbe crisscrossed the peninsula, granting only narrow access to both Bleddin and Wartenburg. Undergrowth and woods mixed with boggy meadows covered the majority of the peninsula. The old river bed stretched south to north from the village of Bleddin twisting and turning to sand dunes, which the lower portion of the bend in the Elbe washed. On the southernmost of these dunes rose the village and Schloß of Wartenburg, described by Langeron as a "veritable fortress." Heavy rains in August and September had rendered the already marshy ground around the village impassable as far as Bleddin. A long embankment, referred to as the Landdamm, formed a semi-circle extending from northeast of the village south to help protect Wartenburg from unwelcome flood waters, not to mention unwelcome guests.[49]

On 3 October, Blücher would have his hands full, not with crossing the Elbe, but with driving Bertrand from a position that appeared unassailable. To make matters worse, Bertrand knew well the advantages of his position after having inspected Wartenburg on 23 September. In his ensuing report to the emperor, the general expressed his confidence that the soaked and partially flooded ground would enable IV Corps to prevent the Allies from making any progress.[50] In his after-action report following the engagement on 3 October, he still noted that "Wartenburg is one of those good positions where a small army can fight with advantage against a larger army."[51] On returning to Wartenburg on the 2nd, Bertrand had no warning that soon he would face the entire Silesian Army. Instead, he believed that a detachment from the Army of North Germany was making a demonstration at Elster to mask an operation at Roßlau, Bernadotte's main point of passage. Inexplicably, the numerous Allied guns on the right bank that repulsed the Württembergers did not indicate to him that he had to contend with more than a detachment. Thus, for fortifications, he merely blocked the footpath along the levee leading to Elster, built gun emplacements behind the Landdamm, and cleared some trees to create fields of fire for the artillery.

Not only did Bertrand neglect to better fortify his position, his troop placement made no sense. In total, IV Corps consisted of 14,000 men and 32 guns. For his left wing, Bertrand posted the eleven battalions of Morand's 12th Division at Wartenburg and along the portion of the Landdamm that extended north of the village. Franquemont's 38th Division took a position two miles south of Wartenburg at Bleddin to form the right wing. Bertrand situated the fourteen battalions of Fontanelli's 15th Division west of Wartenburg on the road to Globig. General André Louis Briche's Württemberger light cavalry brigade filled the gap between the two wings. While the terrain made his left wing virtually unassailable, the more open ground between Bleddin and the bridgehead offered the enemy the means of out-flanking Wartenburg. For the defense of this vital stretch of his front, Bertrand assigned the 4 battalions and 6 guns – 1,500 men in all – of Franquemont's weak 38th Division. After reconnoitering the terrain, Franquemont purportedly expressed concern about being overwhelmed before support could arrive. Recognizing the vulnerability of his right flank, Bertrand nevertheless dismissed Franquemont's unease by claiming that Morand would not allow the enemy to pass Wartenburg in order to attack Bleddin. Unfortunately for the imperial cause, Bertrand failed to utilize the considerable defensive advantages offered by the terrain and critically weakened his position by the unnecessary extension of his line.

Sunday, 3 October, broke with foggy, cold, wet weather. Around 5:00 A.M., Yorck's corps marched northwest from Jeßen in two columns. At Elster, Gneisenau met the commander of the first column, Prince Karl, who arrived well ahead of his 2nd Brigade. The staff chief instructed Karl to lead Sjöholm's detachment across the Elbe as soon as the engineers finished the two bridges. On reaching the left bank, Karl would continue to Wartenburg. Gneisenau told the prince he should expect to encounter a small post but nothing significant. As soon as Karl reported that he had secured the village, the rest of I Corps would follow.

Around 7:00 A.M., the prince led the three battalions and a half-battery across the bridge. Advancing on the road to Wartenburg, he soon encountered imperial outposts. After a short firefight, the Württembergers withdrew into a thick wood east of Wartenburg called *das hohe Holz* (the High Wood).[52] The small-arms fire immediately alarmed the garrison at Wartenburg, prompting Bertrand to post his cavalry on the plain between Wartenburg and Bleddin and to summon Fontanelli's division from Globig.[53] Although they could not see the village, the Prussians could clearly hear the commands being shouted: it became obvious that they faced a far stronger enemy force than initially assumed. Karl quickly found that his battalions could not march through the swampy terrain and thick undergrowth. After dividing the battalions into squads to increase mobility, the prince realized that even these small groups would not get far in such terrain. He ordered a halt, reported the situation to Yorck, and requested reinforcements.

By the time Karl's adjutant reached the right bank, Yorck had arrived. After a short time, three battalions from the 2nd Brigade crossed the Elbe and moved up. One assumed the coverage of the right wing and so swung into the front line, while the other two remained in the second line. After

Karl signaled the advance to resume, the Prussians drove the enemy skir-mishers from the *hohe Holz* and took some prisoners. Emerging from the wood, the Prussians moved into a clearing about 1,500 yards east of Warten-burg. This opening separated the *hohe Holz* from a larger thicket, the *Eichwald* (Oak Forest), which stretched north–south between the concave banks of the meander. A brutal crossfire sent them scrambling back to the cover of the trees. For the moment, Karl could not consider a further advance. By now the fog had lifted, and from the *hohe Holz* the Prussians could finally survey the terrain and gain an overview. Realizing they could not reach Wartenburg on this road, Karl decided to envelop the village from the south. He ordered Sjöholm to employ four battalions to somehow fix the enemy's front without exposing the men to fire. With the half-battery and the remaining two battalions as well as the two that had just finished crossing the bridge, Karl planned to turn left (south) and envelop the right flank of the enemy position.

Again, the Prussians found the terrain so overgrown that they could not get through. After futile attempts to find a passage through the marsh, Karl sent back the artillery to Sjöholm. With locals serving as guides, he led his troops south along the eastern bank of the Moyenhainicht Canal to the Landdamm, a narrow pathway through the Eichwald between the beginning of the canal and the Elbe. Although Württemberger skirmishers were guarding this tiny "pass," the Prussians drove them back with ease. Around 9:00 A.M., Karl led his battalions through and out of the Eichwald. South of the wood, the terrain opened in an area called the Schützberg; the village of Bleddin could be seen in the distance. Two of Franquemont's battalions held the Schützberg clearing, while the remaining two occupied Bleddin. Lacking cavalry and artillery, Karl did not want to risk crossing this open field. Instead, he decided to turn north and attempt to move through Wartenburg's orchards to reach the village. Despite his guides' insistence on the futility of this plan, the prince of Mecklenburg left two battalions to hold the Land-damm and made for the orchards with the other two.

The difficult ground soon proved the accuracy of the admonitions of Karl's guides. Officers sent forward to reconnoiter found the terrain com-pletely impassable. Even worse, the imperials held unassailable positions behind large ponds. Karl did not have time to contemplate his next move. An intense crossfire from enemy guns at Wartenburg and Bleddin took a toll on his men. He then received a report that the Württembergers had advanced from Bleddin, repulsing the Prussian skirmishers deployed by the two battalions holding the Landdamm. With few sensible options available, the prince ordered his two battalions to turn around and return to the Landdamm to prevent the loss of this important conduit. On arriving, the battalions deployed their skirmishers, enabling the Prussians to again repulse the Württemberger marksmen. Karl scribbled a report to Yorck requesting more reinforcements. In the meantime, he dispatched scouts to find other suitable points of passage across the Moyenhainicht canal.

For his part, Sjöholm pushed west across the clearing toward Wartenburg. His skirmishers gradually pushed through the bushy meadows to get close to Wartenburg. Losses mounted as the Prussians received a high volume of fire in the front and right flank. Soon, Sjöholm's advance faltered. For support, Yorck moved up Steinmetz's 1st Brigade, which had crossed the Elbe in the meantime. Steinmetz concealed the majority of his battalions along the eastern edge of the Eichwald. From there, he had to reinforce the skirmisher line numerous times to replace the considerable losses sustained from enemy caseshot and salvo fire. With the imperials protected behind the high Landdamm, the Prussian foot could do little. Yorck and his staff soon came up and rode through the High Wood to get an overview of the combat and the terrain. Steinmetz's skirmishers pressed forward to the dead arm of the Elbe but suffered terribly from caseshot and musket fire. Yorck rode up to their line: a ball from canister fire struck one of his adjutants in the mouth; Lieutenant-Colonel Schmidt, the commander of Yorck's Reserve Artillery, had his horse shot out from under him while two soldiers from the staff guard fell from wounds. "One saw clearly," wrote one of Yorck's adjutants, "the sandy hills behind [north of] Wartenburg covered with artillery." Bertrand reported that Morand had repulsed these early attacks and inflicted "enormous losses" on the Prussians.[54]

Yorck remained calm and quickly grasped the situation: a frontal attack would achieve nothing; only the envelopment through Bleddin could gain Wartenburg. While the flanking force worked around the village, he wanted the enemy's front fixed and his artillery on the Sand Hills north of Wartenburg silenced. To their disbelief, the Prussians could not find suitable ground for artillery positions. Only from the high right bank of the Elbe could their counterbattery fire be effective against the enemy guns. Schmidt received orders "to silence the battery on the Sand Hills with one twelve-pound battery on the right bank of the Elbe and to shell the flank of the enemy position." The task of fixing the enemy's center and left wing fell to Steinmetz's 1st Brigade. With instructions to take Bleddin, Karl assembled his 2nd Brigade. "Prince Karl will quickly advance on the village of Bleddin," stated Yorck at 9:00 A.M., "eject the enemy, and through a right wheel seek to envelop him in his right flank." Horn's 7th Brigade took a concealed position along the east bank of the Moyenhainicht Canal to both support the prince and plug the gap between 1st and 2nd Brigades. "As soon as the 2nd Brigade takes Bleddin and envelops the enemy's right wing," continued Yorck, "the 1st and 7th Brigades will attack his front, storming Wartenburg with several battalions and enveloping it on both sides with their remaining troops." Hünerbein's 8th Brigade formed the Reserve and remained some 2,000 yards west of the bridges on the road to Wartenburg.[55]

16 General Yorck at Wartenburg, 3 October 1813

During this time, Yorck's remaining units crossed the bridges, forming columns on the left bank. Blücher reached the bridges as the last battalions of I Corps marched across. Looking through the treetops, he could see smoke rising from what he held to be breakfasts being cooked in Wartenburg. "Look, my children," shouted Blücher, "the cursed French are baking bread for breakfast; let's take it from them while it's still hot!" After the remaining infantry of I Corps crossed the river, the troopers of the Mecklenburg and Black Hussars led their horses across the bridge. Old Blücher shouted to them: "Hussars! If you are not victorious, you will drown in the Elbe; I am having the bridges burned down behind us." According to Nostitz, "this pronouncement offended the pride of the soldiers, who saw in it a threat made for the sake of assuring the loyal fulfillment of their duty, and opined that the utilization of such means was not merited since they had fought as worthy Prussians in the battles and engagements that had taken place up to now and had always earned Blücher's praise. The general was pleased by this sensitivity: 'You cannot take a joke,' he said to them smiling, and with this all was forgotten."[56]

Professor Steffens provides a romantic description of the Prussians crossing the Elbe:

> For many hours the infantry continuously crossed in close and rapid order along the floating-bridge, then the cavalry crossed, slower and more carefully. The arms glanced in the sunbeams, and old legends sprang up in my

memory, while first the reflection of their bright weapons, and then host after host, was seen coming from afar, till every hill blazed with glittering life. The enemy was hidden behind the great forest of oaks which borders the river; a few cannonballs reached the Elbe, and some that struck the surface of the water rebounded and sprang in wide arches upwards. The whole was a most lively spectacle: we feasted long on it, for Blücher and his staff did not cross the river until a considerable part of the army had reached the opposite shore. The enemy, divided from us as they were by the forest, had misdirected their fire, and as long as I stayed to witness the passage not a shot reached the bridge. As the troops landed, they disappeared again behind the wood. Our headquarters remained for some time in the wood but Blücher soon disappeared with some of his adjutants, and I and others were ordered to remain there and wait for him.[57]

Orderlies posted on the left bank recited Yorck's orders to the units as they completed the crossing. Soon, the brigades trooped west. Lobenthal with the battalions from 2nd Brigade that had yet to join Karl led the march; Yorck accompanied them. In addition, Yorck placed five guns from 7th Brigade at the prince's disposal. In total, Karl commanded six battalions, seven squadrons, and thirteen guns. Horn's brigade of eight battalions came next. Six took a position in the portion of the Eichwald east of the Moyenhainicht canal while two others pushed forward into the orchard before the portion of the Landdamm east of the hog pasture to secure Horn's right flank.

Langeron's Russians started crossing as soon as Yorck's last battalion reached the left bank. Blücher also spoke electrifying words of encouragement to the men: Goltz translated Blücher's German into French for the Russian commanders and they further transmitted Blücher's message in Russian to their men: "You old Muscovites, you have never turned your backs on the enemy. I will place myself at your head." Pointing toward Wartenburg, he shouted: "That is where you shall attack those dogs, the French. I know that on this day you will not show them your backs. Vamoose!" Although the Russians enthusiastically responded with a loud hurrah, the struggle ended before they could deploy.[58]

Meanwhile, Karl's troops managed to establish a crossing over the Moyenhainicht canal so their artillery could pass. At 1:00 P.M., the prince ordered the general advance southwest toward Bleddin. Two battalions formed the first echelon. The two battalions that had been holding the pass since 9:00 – reduced by constant skirmishing with the Württembergers to a few hundred men each – followed as the second echelon. Further rearward, two battalions and seven squadrons formed the third echelon. Nine guns unlimbered in the intervals of the echelons.

After Prussian skirmishers drove the Württemberger forward troops from the Landdamm, Franquemont recognized the danger. Tripling the size of his vanguard, he ordered his men to retake and hold the Landdamm.

With much tenacity and courage, a total of two and one-half Württemberger battalions hurled themselves against the advancing Prussian brigade. Seeing Prussian cavalry and artillery advance across terrain he considered impassable forced Franquemont to accept the futility of a prolonged resistance, despite the bravery of his soldiers. Further north, he observed Horn's infantry move into the gap between Bleddin and Wartenburg. In addition, he received Bertrand's negative response to his plea for support. Although the corps commander could not spare any reinforcements for the Württembergers, Fontanelli's division would advance. In light of this, Franquemont decided that his best option would be to withdraw on Bleddin. His troops executed the retreat in a slow and orderly fashion. His last battalion entered the combat, while his reserve of two weak companies occupied Bleddin and received their countrymen. This small rearguard managed to keep the Prussians out of Bleddin until Franquemont established a new position southwest of the village.

Meanwhile, during the time 2nd Brigade needed to deploy, Steinmetz's 1st Brigade took a beating while holding its ground in front of Wartenburg. Intense artillery fire from eighteen-pound guns that mainly fired shells mowed down the Prussians like a great scythe. Despite the gut-wrenching losses, Steinmetz could not order a retreat. If he fell back, the Wartenburg garrison would certainly attack 2nd Brigade's right flank as it advanced on Bleddin. In accordance with Yorck's order, Schmidt unlimbered a heavy battery on the right bank of the Elbe to take out the enemy artillery on the Sand Hills. However, the imperials had concealed their guns so well in the wooded terrain that they could not be seen from either bank. Moreover, the Prussian artillery chief had failed to locate a suitable position for his cannon. Unchallenged by counterbattery fire, the imperial artillery unleashed their fury on the Prussian skirmishers, who suffered horrific losses that had to be replaced immediately.

Several times Steinmetz fed reinforcements into the sausage grinder. "From 7:00 to 11:00," wrote Bertrand, "the enemy made the most vigorous attacks on Wartenburg; his columns, which were re-formed every half-hour, moved very close to our dikes; our troops lay in ambush, allowed them to approach, and opened fire while the artillery fired grapeshot; everywhere these columns were repulsed; the dead and injured were piled before the dikes; several times the enemy had to remove the dead to open a passage for his columns." "I have seen few infantry battles that were as ferocious as that near the Wartenburg dike," recalled Langeron, "which was defended for a long time: there were more than a thousand dead, laid out in rows, in the place where they had fought, at fifty paces from their adversaries, and no Prussian was seen on French terrain, and no Frenchmen on Prussian terrain." According to Yorck's after-action report, only sixty men led by one wounded lieutenant remained in the line of the 1st Battalion of the 2nd East

Prussian Regiment after six hours of combat dispersed as skirmishers. "With his typical cold-bloodedness," Steinmetz replaced this battalion with three Landwehr battalions. Likewise sustaining horrendous losses, the militia had to be both reinforced and resupplied with ammunition twice. After a short time, mounting casualties forced Steinmetz to commit the manpower of all three battalions as skirmishers. Regardless, the French killed or wounded almost all of them. "Morand's division fought for eight hours," boasted Bertrand, "with the greatest valor; the approaches to the dike were covered with the enemy's dead and wounded; we allowed his columns to march right up to the abatis, and there they received either grapeshot or a brisk fusillade, which destroyed everything. The 8th, 13th and 23rd Regiments competed with each other in courage."[59]

Finally, the lieutenant who commanded Steinmetz's battery directed his fire at the smoke rising from the French position; his first shot blew up a caisson. Yet his exposed position offered the imperials a fine target. Many gunners fell and could be replaced only by infantry rushing up from the nearby battalions. While one battalion after another melted under the murderous fire, Steinmetz waited anxiously for a sign of Karl's envelopment. Nothing could be seen. In fact, a momentary lull in the Prussian fire due to the rotation of the skirmishers resulted in an immediate counterattack. Although repulsed, this attempt reinforced Steinmetz's conviction that a retreat would allow the imperials to immediately seize the offensive. Some relief finally came when the chief of the heavy battery on the opposite bank of the Elbe managed to find a position for his guns near the village of Gallin, more than three miles downstream. From there, the Prussian guns shelled the battery on the Sand Hills as well as its escort. The imperials responded with effective counterbattery fire from their larger eighteen-pound pieces. Four guns opened direct fire on the Prussian battery, while six others shelled its flank. Shortly afterward, the Prussian battery withdrew, allowing the imperials to resume the mauling of 1st Brigade.

Around 2:00, the Prussians finally overwhelmed the brave defenders of Bleddin to win the village. Karl's skirmishers pursued the Württembergers southwest but his cavalry and artillery continued west, with the latter unlimbering by the windmill west of Bleddin. Franquemont decided to continue the retreat three miles further southwest to Trebitz but received the explicit order from Bertrand to unite with Morand's division at Wartenburg. To comply, he had to march west to Globig and then two and one-half miles northeast to Wartenburg. As the Württemberger infantry rushed toward Globig, the seven squadrons of Prussian Hussars spotted Briche's light cavalry brigade just east of this village. Four well-aimed shots by the Prussian guns on the windmill hill had already shaken the Württemberger troopers. After some movements, they halted approximately 100 yards from Globig and awaited the Prussian attack standing still. With a loud hurrah,

17 Combat at Wartenburg, 3 October 1813

the hussars charged; Briche's cavalry broke and attempted to flee. Most
could not escape the Prussian first wave, which cut down or captured the
majority.

Of the second wave, the 4th Squadron of the 2nd Leib Hussars received
the task of driving between the enemy cavalry and infantry to attack the
Württemberger artillery retreating from Bleddin. Confident that Briche's
cavalry would stand against the approaching Prussian troopers, the Württembergers halted near the Globig windmill. The artillery commander
ordered the crews to unlimber their guns to cover the infantry's passage of
the Leine rivulet. After the cavalry turned tail, the crews did not have time to
limber the guns before the Prussians charged their position. As a result, the
troopers of 4th Squadron captured five guns and four caissons. One officer
of the Black Hussars played a "trick," reported Gneisenau. "The regiment
captured an enemy battery including all the gunners and horses. The officer
demanded that the captured gunners fire on their own column. The gunners
refused, so he cut down two of them and the others promised to open fire. 'If
one of you refuses,' he shouted to them, 'all of you will be cut down,' and in
their fear the chaps fired on their own column with caseshot."[60]

Quickly re-forming, the hussars charged the battalion about to escort
Franquemont and his staff across the Leine. Before they could form a square,

the Württembergers found themselves surrounded. Rather than surrender, the battalion cut through the Prussian cavalry to escape across the Leine albeit with considerable losses. No longer concerned about uniting with Morand, Franquemont led his survivors southwest to Schnellin from where he marched sixteen miles through the night all the way to Bad Düben. The day cost the Württembergers 500 men, most of their cavalry, and all their artillery. "This division," reported Bertrand, "which I supported with General Beaumont's cavalry, was to withdraw to Wartenburg, but when I saw the enemy's guns beyond Globig, and when the cavalry and artillery which had passed through Bleddin placed itself on our flanks and our rear, I ordered the retreat that was conducted with great order." "The terrain between the crossing point and the village of Wartenburg was unfavorable for cavalry," reported Blücher, "and thus prevented me from moving up my cavalry, which stood at the bridge in readiness, in time to destroy the enemy corps as thoroughly as possible. The 2nd Leib Hussar and the Mecklenburg Hussar Regiments, the only cavalry that the prince of Mecklenburg had with him, did inflict considerable damage on the enemy."[61]

We left Horn's brigade in a position behind the Moyenhainicht Canal, with two battalions in the orchard east of the hog pasture. Just as 2nd Brigade's assault on Bleddin succeeded, both French and Italian reinforcements arrived and fiercely attacked these two battalions. Horn's skirmishers needed to be reinforced so many times that all the manpower of both battalions had to be dispersed. For support, the brigade commander moved up the 2nd Battalion of the Leib Regiment. In addition, the Russians completed their crossing. Blücher became concerned after no results of the attempt to envelop Bleddin could be observed. Aside from having no news concerning the enemy's strength, one of St.-Priest's spies had reported that Napoleon was approaching from Torgau with 20,000 men. It appeared urgently necessary to press forward with all available troops and force a decision. After a stout speech, Blücher ordered Langeron's vanguard to advance. St.-Priest's infantry corps moved between Yorck's 7th and 2nd Brigades, assuming the coverage of Karl's right and thus releasing 7th Brigade to participate in the engagement. Horn pushed his battalions through the orchards toward the formidable hog pasture.

With its east side enclosed by the Landdamm, the west side by a second embankment, and the north and south sides bordered by dead arms of the Elbe, the hog pasture served the Italians like a fortress. Concealed behind the embankment, the defenders could pour a murderous volume of small-arms fire and caseshot into the ranks of the attackers. Under this lethal hail, the attackers had to then cross a marshy canal that linked the two dead arms of the Elbe west of the Landdamm. Accompanying Horn's advance, Yorck immediately recognized the extreme difficulty of this attack. He originally wanted Hünerbein's 8th Brigade to support 2nd Brigade's envelopment but decided to have it move up behind Horn and support 7th Brigade's attack. As soon as 8th Brigade arrived, Horn's two right wing battalions would envelop Wartenburg from the south, while the rest of the brigade stormed the Landdamm. Pressing forward, the two wing battalions received withering small-arms fire and caseshot that halted the advance. According to Bertrand's after-action report, after "the superior forces that the enemy moved on Bleddin forced the Württemberger division to evacuate this village," he moved up General Étienne Hulot's 3rd Brigade from Morand's 12th Division as well as General Ange-Pierre Moroni's 3rd Brigade of Italians from Fontanelli's 15th Division to support the Germans. Bertrand asserted that "the enemy was thrown back in the swamp and fell back along the whole line, but the column that pursued the Württemberger division had already turned Bleddin. At the head of his division, General Fontanelli inflicted great damage on the enemy."[62]

To break the stalemate, Horn requested permission to storm the Landdamm before 8th Brigade arrived. After some thought, Yorck consented. The 2nd Leib Battalion led the advance followed by the Löwenberg Landwehr battalion and then the 1st Leib Battalion. Yorck instructed the officers to remain as much as possible on the left to avoid the deep water. Consequently, they marched through the orchard where many helped themselves to a plum or two. At the head of the 2nd Leib Battalion, Horn led the march on horseback until a ball struck his horse in the chest; it collapsed dead. After shouts went up that the general was dead, Horn responded with a fit of vexation. Those closest helped him wiggle out from under his horse. As soon as he was free, he grabbed the musket of a wounded soldier and bellowed: "*Ein Hundsfott, wer noch schießt* [Only a scoundrel shoots]!" Horn exhorted his soldiers to attack with the musket-butt and bayonet. He then led them on foot. Unable to fire as they waded through the marshy canal, the Prussians sustained considerable losses. Horn led his men out of the canal and onto the Landdamm, repulsing all that Fontanelli threw at them. With one Landwehr battalion and the Leib Regiment's 1st Battalion following, the 2nd Battalion executed an unstoppable charge through the hog pasture that drove the Italians over the western or rearward embankment. Purportedly, the Prussians ejected five battalions from the pasture. Fontanelli's division completely collapsed; Italian fugitives covered the terrain west of Wartenburg. In addition, the two right wing battalions waded through the canal and ascended the Landdamm. The lead battalion penetrated Wartenburg but Morand's Frenchmen repulsed the Prussians. Regardless, the loss of the Landdamm marked the beginning of the end of the defense of Wartenburg. After laboriously dragging some guns onto the embankment, Horn's gunners shelled the village. Around 3:30, the Prussians broke into Wartenburg. From the Sand Hills, the French artillery sought to halt the pursuing Prussians but withdrew after the loss of two guns.[63]

Meanwhile, Steinmetz's situation became increasingly difficult with each passing minute. Almost every tree concealed a wounded or dead soldier. Murderous fire prevented any forward movement; the need to buy time for 2nd Brigade made any retrograde movement impossible. After ordering Langeron's corps to move up, Blücher rode forward to the plain of the Schützberg. He arrived around the time of the attack on Briche's cavalry. Recognizing the need to exploit 2nd Brigade's breakthrough to reach a decision quickly, he instructed Karl "to attack the rear of the enemy's position at Wartenburg at any price because all frontal attacks are futile." With only two battalions readily available and nine guns, the prince immediately turned north toward Wartenburg. He sent orders for the cavalry to follow but the squadrons needed time to reorganize after some had pursued the retreating Württembergers, while others had escorted the prisoners and captured artillery to the rear.

Reaching the windmill some 800 yards west of Wartenburg, Karl noticed Fontanelli's battalions fleeing toward him. His artillery greeted them with caseshot, forcing the unfortunate Italians to turn back toward Wartenburg. Without cavalry, the prince could do little. His own brigade cavalry remained unavailable for reasons already noted; that of the 7th Brigade remained at the bridges, and Yorck's Reserve Cavalry had just started crossing the Elbe at this time. Likewise at this point, Bertrand received news of the collapse of his right wing and center. With no reserves to commit, he broke off the engagement and evacuated Wartenburg. Despite enduring almost eight hours of continuous combat, Steinmetz did not pass on the opportunity to participate in the final push. Observing the enemy withdraw his artillery, he gave his foremost battalion the order to advance. Clearing away the abatis blocking the Landdamm consumed so much time that 1st Brigade did not reach Wartenburg until after Morand's troops pulled out. Steinmetz pursued the French north for only a short while before his troops dropped from exhaustion.

After taking the second embankment, Horn reorganized his battalions, swung north, and advanced toward the Sand Hills north of Wartenburg. Under the protection of the batteries located on this high ground, Bertrand assembled Morand's troops and received the wreck of Fontanelli's division. Withdrawing west in two columns, the imperials soon received artillery fire from Yorck's batteries on the right bank of the Elbe. To make matters worse, Karl's brigade cavalry finally came up and attacked the Italian column. Lacking the manpower to rout the division, the Prussians did manage to capture some guns as well as a quantity of caissons and baggage wagons. Although the pursuit ended eight miles west of Wartenburg at Pratau just south of Wittenberg, Bertrand continued another eight miles to Gohrau. That night, I Corps camped south of Wartenburg on the other side of the hog pasture; Langeron's corps bivouacked between the Prussians and

Globig. Not reaching the Elster until midnight, Sacken's corps remained on
the right bank of the Elbe. Blücher dispatched Yorck's Reserve Cavalry nine
miles west toward Wittenberg. From Langeron's corps, Emmanuel led the
1st and 3rd Ukrainskii Cossack Regiments as well as two Donskoye Cossack
Regiments including one horse battery nine miles southwest to Kemberg
while Yuzefovich moved up the Elbe to Trebitz with the Kievskii and
Kharkovskii Dragoon Regiments, one regiment of Kalmyks, and two guns
from 2nd Donskoye Cossack Battery.[64]

Combat ended around 3:00 that afternoon. Yorck issued orders for the
troops to cook, and to bury their dead. That same night, Blücher held a
victory dinner at the Wartenburg Schloß, as Steffens explains: "With a
number of staff officers, we were brought into a great hall, where the walls
and floor were torn and damaged by the cannonballs; one ball had rico-
cheted off the floor and passed completely through the wall. Preparations
were made for a feast of rejoicing, and we all assembled. The day had been a
glorious one but as yet we could hardly reckon the results." Blücher gave a
stirring speech. Gneisenau, who did not like large festivities, retreated with
some friends to a small antechamber to dine. Suddenly, just as they finished,
Blücher knocked loudly at the door. Turning to all those present, he roared:
"Today, thank God, we have taken a good step for the liberation of the
Fatherland. I feel like a craftsman who has completed his task but here
everything was prepared so that we were all able to work together to achieve
success." He then summoned Lieutenant Scharnhorst to his side: "Your
father," he began, but overwhelmed by emotion, words escaped him. After
regaining his composure, Blücher continued: "Look down, radiant spirit of
our Scharnhorst, and see how we all pledge a solemn oath on your dear son,
to emulate you in word and deed until we free the German Fatherland from
the enemy and the oppressors, and have again covered the name of Prussia
with honor." "Our repast was truly joyous," continued Steffens; "but some
sad and solemn feelings clouded our happiness before we parted: thoughts
turned to the memory of Scharnhorst. Blücher spoke; and I never listened to
words as eloquent as those he used when he painted in glowing terms the
character and services of the hero. The almost involuntary rush of language
was the outpouring of poetry itself. At the conclusion, he called to him the
son of the great departed, who, although used to concealing his feelings
under a calm exterior, could scarcely hide his emotions as he stood before
the aged leader and orator."[65]

The merrymaking did not extend beyond the walls of the Wartenburg
Schloß, as Droysen reiterates the note in Schack's journal: "Sad scenes
among the wounded." "Our losses are considerable," wrote Blücher at
2:30. Yorck's casualties amounted to 67 officers and 1,548 killed and
wounded compared to fewer than 500 of Bertrand's soldiers. Overall, 1st
Brigade suffered the most casualties: 992 dead and wounded including

29 officers. "I do not believe I would be exaggerating if I estimated the enemy's losses to be between 5,000 and 6,000 men," noted Bertrand; "ours are not considerable because of the advantage that our infantry had, being situated behind a dike." Blücher claimed to have taken 1,000 prisoners, 50 caissons, and 11 guns. "General Bertrand commanded against me," he reported to the king. "Captured staff officers cited his strength at 23,000–25,000 men. According to the reports that have arrived, I will find no other enemy as far as the Mulde except the VII Corps." Although Blücher firmly believed he faced more than 20,000 men, Bertrand's corps numbered only 13,000 men and 32 guns against Yorck's 12,000.[66]

Not numerical superiority but the bravery of the Prussian troops combined with the prudence and calmness of the leadership produced the success of this day. "The exhausting marches, sickness, and desertion," explains Friederich, "had gradually removed all doubtful elements, all the physically and morally unfit from the ranks; what remained were worthy members of the army who competed with the veteran troops of Yorck's corps." Droysen echoes the sentiments of Yorck and his officers: "Infinitely more important was it that the Prussian corps alone with a loss of almost 2,000 dead and wounded had driven an enemy ... from such a position without any Russian assistance. Finally, Blücher's headquarters now had to honor the truth in the army report and not, as up until now, award the glory to the Russians for what the Prussians had achieved; finally, Herr von Müffling, who wrote the reports, now had to recognize what Prussian troops had achieved." After the battle, the troops marched past Yorck, who greeted each commander. When the 2nd Battalion of the Leib Regiment, which Horn led in the storming of the Landdamm, approached, Yorck asked: "Is this the 2nd Battalion of the Leib Regiment? The men shouted "*Ja!*" Yorck then removed his cap and his entire entourage followed the example until the battalion marched past." "This brave battalion," Yorck purportedly said to his staff, "has earned the respect of the entire world." The Landwehr also received praise for having fought like the grenadier battalions of Frederick's army. "Now the Silesian Landwehr has also passed the great test with honor," Yorck purportedly claimed. "The bravery of the troops carried them in the battle," Gneisenau explained to Hardenberg, "and after six hours of combat they finally stormed the village. The Landwehr played a superb role in this, namely the Sommerfeld Battalion from the Hirschberg District, which for the most part consists of linen-weavers. Thus the young now form the troops for war! 'See! There advances the battalion of the Leib Infantry Regiment against the enemy; they want to be better than you,' said General Horn to the Landwehr men. 'No! No! We are just as good as them,' they answered and at the same time advanced against the enemy." With an eye toward the shortage of cash, Gneisenau added: "It would break your heart if you could see how these brave, poor men lack the necessary clothing and succumb to sickness and despondency." Based on Gneisenau's after-action reports, Frederick William decided to reward the Landwehr regiments with their own standards.[67]

As for the leaders of I Corps, Blücher reported to Frederick William that Prince Karl had "executed his assignment with the decisiveness and energy of a distinguished officer and his movement, combined with the bravery of Horn's troops, who fought between Steinmetz's brigade and that of the prince of Mecklenburg, brought us a complete victory around 2:00 P.M. General Yorck supported me in a most satisfactory manner through the decisive execution of the general disposition. Cut off from Torgau and Leipzig, the enemy fled to Wittenberg." Droysen claims that Blücher once said: "That lady-killer Yorck is difficult to bring into the fire, but once I have done so, there is none better than he." Claiming that 1st Brigade needed to be looked after more than the other brigades, Yorck scolded Steinmetz for failing to advance with fortitude. Yet in his report to the king, the old curmudgeon expressed his admiration: "On this day, Colonel Steinmetz held the most difficult post which he maintained with his customary cold-bloodedness; his brigade stood opposite Wartenburg, which was unassailable due to a wall, marsh, and abatis. During eight hours of combat he defied the enemy here and only because of this was it possible to envelop the village from Bleddin while the enemy concentrated his forces against Colonel Steinmetz." During the Russian campaign, Macdonald had called Horn the Prussian Bayard because of his outstanding bravery. The nickname stuck. "Well sir, you are indeed a man! Compared to you, even Bayard is a dog," declared Yorck when he saw Horn the morning after the battle.[68]

"The courage and impetuosity of the Prussian troops," concludes Langeron, "and the good dispositions of General Yorck, who, by his energy and his talent, placed himself among the ranks of the best generals in this campaign, allowed my troops to arrive only as witnesses to the success of their glorious companions." "Nauseatingly friendly were the gallantries of Count Langeron toward Yorck," notes Droysen; "'my illustrious comrade,' is how he addressed him, whereupon Yorck only answered 'Your Excellency' with a slight bow. 'May the hangman fetch these Russian comrades' is what he said when he was alone with his Prussian comrades." Nor did the victory cause him to think any more favorably of Gneisenau. In private, "Yorck expressed that he had been led to the slaughterhouse." "Regardless," laments Delbrück, "his relationship with Gneisenau remained unchanged. Yorck used this opportunity to rage against him."[69]

Despite Yorck's personal feelings, the 3 October 1813 engagement at Wartenburg demonstrated the synergy that existed among Blücher, Gneisenau, and Yorck. The idea belonged to Gneisenau, the decision to Blücher, the deed itself to Yorck. A bold decision earned success based on the energy of its execution. On 2 October an entire French corps moved into an uncommonly strong position to hold the left bank opposite Elster. Bertrand even assured Napoleon that his corps would suffice to hold the position. Fortune smiled on the bold. Not only did the Prussian General Staff select an excellent point for the crossing, but the imperials failed to disrupt the bridge construction. Yet the tenacity, energy, and self-sacrificing spirit of Yorck's corps earned the victory. Frederick William later united this deed with the name of the man whose corps opened the road for the Silesian Army to march to Leipzig: Hans David von Yorck became Hans David Count Yorck von Wartenburg. Blücher played his part in the operation and the decisive order for the envelopment came from him.

Notwithstanding the bravery of Yorck's men, they would have failed had it not been for inexcusable French errors. By utilizing the majority of his infantry to hold Wartenburg and the segment of the Landdamm north of the village, Bertrand squandered his limited manpower on the strongest part of his position. Due to the terrain, Bleddin represented the only accessible point along his line. Yet he assigned only 1,500 Württembergers and 6 guns to defend this village even after acknowledging that it represented the weakest point of his entire position. In his center, the portion of the Landdamm before the hog pen remained unguarded, with Fontanelli's division standing one mile to the rear in reserve. During the battle, Bertrand should have committed some of Fontanelli's battalions to reinforce Franquemont, especially after he received several status reports from the Württemberger general. The timely arrival of the Italians at Bleddin could have changed the course of the battle.

Much of Bertrand's faulty disposition can be attributed to his belief that he faced only weak detachments from the Army of North Germany rather than the Army of Silesia. Based on Bertrand's arrangements, it appears that he intended to take the offensive with Fontanelli's division if the enemy managed a breakthrough at Bleddin. Such a strike at the moment the Allies debouched from Bleddin would have produced a favorable result had Bertrand faced only a weak Allied detachment. If Bertrand had known that he faced Blücher, a position east of Wartenburg would have been preferable. A successful defense could have been executed had he deployed Franquemont's weak division to hold the Elster–Wartenburg causeway while the rest of IV Corps took a position behind the Moyenhainicht Canal. In this case, the numerical superiority of the Silesian Army would not have played a role because the difficult terrain would have prevented Blücher from deploying both Yorck and Langeron.

Regarding Yorck's conduct, few excuses can justify leaving 1st Brigade in an exposed position for almost eight hours. Steinmetz could have accomplished his task just as well by withdrawing to a position that allowed him to merely fix the French division at Wartenburg. Yorck could have directed his three other brigades directly to Bleddin. His foremost brigade, Karl's 2nd, could have driven Franquemont from Bleddin while 7th and 8th Brigades crossed the Moyenhainicht Canal and turned north to attack Wartenburg. Yorck's Reserve Cavalry and Langeron's corps would have had to follow immediately to exploit the breakthrough and roll up Bertrand's line. Instead, Yorck kept his Reserve Cavalry and 8th Brigade in reserve. Perhaps out of mistrust of Langeron, Yorck acted as if he had to fight only with his own corps and could not risk committing all of his forces. Here we find the absence of the army's leadership. We do not know why Blücher and Gneisenau did not take a more active role in this engagement. They as well as Yorck knew the army could not remain at the bridges, meaning that open terrain had to be won. This emerges as all the more necessary considering the Allies did not know the size of the imperial force at Wartenburg. It could have been a detachment or the entire Army of Berlin. Thus, it is odd that neither Army Headquarters nor Yorck sought to achieve a decisive break- through from the start. Equally puzzling is the limited use of Langeron's corps. Unger claims that, had Blücher known beforehand that Bertrand's entire corps were defending Wartenburg, he would not have hesitated to commit the Russians – an unconvincing excuse for failing to take advantage of having mass at the point of attack.[70]

As for Langeron's cavalry, the French émigré recalled: "Had my cavalry arrived in time to charge the enemy fugitives, they would have taken a great number, but they were too late: General Korf had left to seek good quarters and no one could find him. Only Emmanuel arrived with two regiments, but he was too late." That the Russians did not have more cavalry on hand for the pursuit displeased Gneisenau: "Due to the uncommon ignorance of General Neydhardt, chief of staff of Langeron's corps, there was not suffi- cient cavalry available to exploit the victory. The few and weak squadrons of ours which engaged the enemy did wonders of bravery."[71]

Regardless, the Prussians basked in the success of their operation: 64,000 battle-hardened veterans supported by 332 guns now stood on the left bank of the Elbe. Blücher crossed the river with the intention of motivating Bernadotte to take the same step. "The consequences of this victory may be very important if His Royal Highness the Crown Prince of Sweden, as discussed, quickly crosses the Elbe," stated Gneisenau in Blü- cher's after-action report to the king. Before the guns fell silent, Blücher dispatched Bernadotte's liaison officer from Silesian Army Headquarters to that of the crown prince with a report on the victory. This courier had delivered a letter from Bernadotte to Blücher written earlier that day that stated: "I received the letter that you addressed to me yesterday. I thank you and I am happy to have you as a neighbor. I'll send an officer of my staff to you so you can tell me where you are; I can [then] make my arrangements." The short note concludes by informing Blücher that

Russian forces under Chernishev had taken Kassel, prompting the king of Westphalia, Jerome Bonaparte, to flee. Although doubting Bernadotte's resolve to accept battle on the left bank, Blücher requested that the Army of North Germany likewise cross the Elbe. During that same night, an encouraging letter arrived from Bülow's headquarters stating that the crown prince planned to cross the Elbe with his entire army on the 5th. In addition, Tauentzien reported that Bernadotte had ordered him to march twenty-two miles west from Seyda to Coswig, halfway between Wittenberg and Roßlau, presumably to cross the river.[72]

Through a combined operation with Bernadotte, Blücher hoped to entice Napoleon to turn north. By baiting the emperor, he wanted to buy time for the Bohemian Army to reach the plains of Saxony. This scheme sparked debate at Silesian Army Headquarters. Some argued that Blücher's numerical superiority would allow him to quickly drive the remnants of Ney's Army of Berlin west across the Mulde. Next, the vanguard of the Silesian Army could cross the forty miles to reach Leipzig by the 7th. A union at Leipzig with the Army of North Germany could occur as early as the 8th. Others, mainly Müffling, countered that such a rapid advance and premature arrival at Leipzig would needlessly expose the Silesian Army to a setback. They based their dissension on sound reasoning. Doubtless, Napoleon would learn on the 4th that the Silesian Army had crossed the Elbe at Wartenburg. He would cover the seventy miles that separated Leipzig from Dresden to arrive at the former with considerable forces no later than the 9th. Accepting a battle with the master meant accepting the possibility of defeat. Yet by waiting a few days for the Bohemian Army to reach Leipzig, the Allies would secure numerical superiority.

The next question to be addressed concerned escaping Napoleon's blow. On his approach, both Blücher and Bernadotte would be forced to fall back either across the Elbe or behind the Saale. As Napoleon most likely would give chase, the limited number of crossings over both rivers meant that high losses would be sustained in rearguard actions. Moreover, if Blücher and Bernadotte separated, Napoleon would receive the opportunity to isolate and defeat each in turn. Consequently, temporarily remaining at the Mulde and uniting with the Army of North Germany appeared prudent. Should Napoleon move north to the Mulde, Schwarzenberg would gain plenty of time for the Bohemian Army to enter Saxony. Moreover, if from Dresden the emperor turned directly against Schwarzenberg, the Prussians felt confident that they would learn of this movement early enough to rush through Leipzig and Altenburg to support the Bohemian Army.[73]

Never prone to councils of war, Blücher ended the debate. He stood by his decision: the Silesian Army would march southwest and cross the Mulde on 6 October. To his friend, Bonin, Blücher wrote: "The trophies are not as considerable as at the Katzbach but the consequences of the victory are much greater because now everything will cross the Elbe and the Bohemian Army can advance from Bohemia. The great man [Napoleon] will be at Leipzig and I will expect him in a few days." Little did Blücher know that the great man was already on the move.[74]

Notes

1 Müffling, *Aus meinem Leben*, 83–84; Pertz and Delbrück, *Gneisenau*, III:375–76; Bogdanovich, *Geschichte des Krieges*, IIb:36; Droysen, *Yorck*, II:178. Droysen could not find Yorck's thoughts on the plan.

2 Gneisenau to Boyen, Bautzen, 25 September 1813, in Boyen, *Erinnerungen*, ed. Nippold, III:647–50; Höpfner, "Darstellung," 1844:281; Unger, *Blücher*, II:95–96; Leggiere, *Napoleon and Berlin*, 226–28, 235–38.

3 Boyen to Gneisenau, Nudersdorf, 27 September 1813, GStA PK, VI HA Rep. 92 Nl. Gneisenau, Nr. 23.

4 General Vaudoncourt, in *Histoire de la guerre*, I:192, cites the incorrect French view that, when Bennigsen reached Leitmeritz on 26 September and thus made contact with the Bohemian Army, this was the signal for the Coalition to commence its general offensive. He points to Blücher's departure from Bautzen, which he claims occurred on 28 September, as the start of this offensive but as we have seen the operation had already commenced on the 26th. Moreover, Bennigsen reached Zittau, forty-six miles northeast of Leitmeritz, on the 26th.

5 Panchulidzev's cavalry consisted of 2 squadrons of the Tverskii Dragoon Regiment and 3 squadrons of the Chernigovskii Mounted Jäger as well as the 2nd Ukrainiskii Cossack Regiment and 250 warriors of the Donskoye Cossack Regiment.

6 Blücher's disposition for 26 September is in GStA PK, VI HA Rep. 92 Nl. Gneisenau, Nr. 18; Blücher to Bubna, Bautzen, 25 September 1813, ÖStA KA, FA 1533, 884b; the instructions for Kaptsevich and Bubna are in ÖStA KA, FA 1533, 884; Bubna to Schwarzenberg, Langburkersdorf, 26 September 1813, ÖStA KA, FA 1533, 844. Bubna provided Schwarzenberg with reports of varying detail on Blücher's operations starting on the 28th and continuing to 12 October: Bubna to Schwarzenberg, Stolpen, 9:30 P.M., 28 September 1813, ÖStA KA, FA 1533, 893, and Bubna to Schwarzenberg, Preschwitz an der Elbe, 12 October 1813, ÖStA KA, FA 1535, 277. See also Blücher to Alexander, Elsterwerda, 29 September 1813, RGVIA, f. VUA, op. 16, d. 3913, l. 268; Höpfner, "Darstellung," 1844:286–87; Bogdanovich, *Geschichte des Krieges*, IIb:36–37; Pertz and Delbrück, *Gneisenau*, III:376–77.

7 Gneisenau to Knesebeck, Bautzen, 7:00 A.M., 26 September 1813, in Pertz and Delbrück, *Gneisenau*, III:379–82.

8 "If the stretch between the two sides of the bend in the Elbe extends 6,000 to 7,000 paces," continued Gneisenau, "a great battery for fifty twelve-pounders will be constructed in the middle of this stretch, and between it and the Elbe on each side one of twenty-five twelve-pounders to provide it with a strong profile and good glacis. In this manner, crossfire of caseshot can be produced between these redoubts. Moreover, these batteries will be furnished with *epaulements*

[breastworks] to create maneuverable batteries, which will open the battle and distract the enemy's attention from the great battery, which will be employed in the actual attack on the troop masses and will support an offensive against the enemy's columns. For the infantry, nothing more is needed than a trench to protect them from the effects of the enemy's artillery": Gneisenau to Rühle, Bautzen, 24 September 1813, GStA, PK, VI HA Rep. 92 Nl. Gneisenau, Nr. 18.

9 Gneisenau to Rühle, Bautzen, 24 September 1813, GStA, PK, VI HA Rep. 92 Nl. Gneisenau, Nr. 18.

10 Blücher to Alexander, Elsterwerda, 29 September 1813, RGVIA, f. VUA, op. 16, d. 3913, l. 268; Höpfner, "Darstellung," 1844:286–87; Disposition for 27 September, Bautzen, 26 September 1813, ÖStA KA, FA 1533, 884d, and Add MSS, 20112, 144; Bubna to Schwarzenberg, Neustadt, 27 September 1813, 9:00 A.M., ÖStA KA, FA 1533, 884.

11 Blücher to Alexander, Elsterwerda, 29 September 1813, RGVIA, f. VUA, op. 16, d. 3913, l. 268; Bubna to Schwarzenberg, Stolpen, 28 September 1813, 9:00 A.M., ÖStA KA, FA 1533, 893; Langeron, *Mémoires*, 288; Höpfner, "Darstellung," 1844:287–88; Gneisenau to Knesebeck, 5:00 P.M., Königsbrück, 27 September 1813, in Pertz and Delbrück, *Gneisenau*, III:398.

12 SHAT, C¹⁷ 180: Berthier to Ney, 17 and 18 September 1813. As for XII Corps, Ney divided its artillery among VII and IV Corps and transferred the survivors of 14th Division to 13th Division, which he assigned to VII Corps. Oudinot's 29th Division, consisting of Bavarians, was dissolved, and the remaining four battalions went to Dresden along with the 2nd Brigade of the corps's light cavalry, also Bavarians. The remaining 1st Brigade of light cavalry – Hessians and Westphalians – was transferred to IV Corps. Moreover, Ney combined the remnants of VII Corps's two Saxon divisions, the 24th and 25th, so that only the former remained. See SHAT, C² 156: Ney to Berthier, 19 September 1813; Friederich, *Herbstfeldzug 1813*, II:195.

13 SHAT, C² 155: Ney to Berthier, 12 September 1813; SHAT, C² 156: Ney to Berthier, 23 September 1813.

14 SHAT, C¹⁷ 133: Order of the Day, 15 September 1813; Charles John to Tauentzien, 19 September 1813; SHAT, C¹⁷ 133: Charles John to Bülow, 13 September 1813; SHAT, C² 156: Ney to Berthier, 17 September 1813.

15 SHAT, C² 156: Ney to Berthier, 22 September 1813; Ney to Arrighi, 24 September 1813; SHAT, C¹⁷ 133: Charles John to Bülow, 22 September 1813. Bertrand's detailed after-action report, written to Ney from Trebitz at 6:00 P.M. on the 23rd, is in Fabry, *Étude sur les opérations de l'empereur*, III:22. See also Friederich, *Herbstfeldzug 1813*, II:196–97.

16 SHAT, C¹⁷ 180: Berthier to Ney, 22 September 1813; SHAT, C² 156: Ney to Berthier, 8:00 A.M., 23 September 1813; Fabry, *Étude sur les opérations de l'empereur*, III:20–21.

17 SHAT, C² 156: Ney to Marmont and Berthier, 25 September 1813; SHAT, C¹⁷ 180: Berthier to Ney, 27 September 1813.

18 SHAT, C¹⁷ 133: Charles John to Bülow, 24 September 1813; Leggiere, *Napoleon and Berlin*, 240–41, 247; Friederich, *Herbstfeldzug 1813*, II:198.

19 SHAT, C² 156: Ney to Berthier, 26 September 1813, 7:00 P.M. and 10:00 P.M. on 27 September 1813, and 8:00 A.M. on 28 September 1813.

20 SHAT, C¹⁷ 133: Charles John to Stedingk, 26 and 27 September 1813; Charles John to Bülow, 27 and 28 September 1813; SHAT, C² 156: Reynier to Ney, 30 September 1813, and Ney to Berthier, 28 and 29 September 1813. On the 29th, Reynier's 13th Division occupied Jonitz and Dessau, the latter serving as Reynier's headquarters; 32nd Division stood just south of the confluence of the Mulde in the Elbe, having one infantry regiment east of Wörlitz observing the point of passage across the Elbe at Coswig; and 24th Division and General François Fournier's 6th Light Cavalry Division held Pötnitz, the position of Ney's headquarters. As for IV Corps, Morand's 16th Division and Defrance's 4th Heavy Cavalry Division escorted Bertrand's headquarters to Wörlitz; Fontanelli's 15th proceeded to Schleesen; and Franquemont's 38th pushed one brigade each to Schleesen and Kemberg. Reynier reported losing 250 killed in the fighting around Roßlau–Dessau between 26 and 29 September. For the details of these operations, see Fabry, *Étude sur les opérations de l'empereur*, III:162–85, 183–84.

21 This figure included what Napoleon estimated to be the 30,000 infantry of IV and VII Corps, the 4th and 6th Divisions of III Cavalry Corps, 27th Division, and General Pierre Margaron's division of 6,000 infantry and 2,000 cavalry which would be formed at Leipzig on the 28th: C¹⁷ 180: Berthier to Ney, 26 September 1813.

22 Franquemont to Bertrand, 30 September 1813, in Fabry, *Étude sur les opérations de l'empereur*, III:187–88; Bertrand to Franquemont and Ney, 30 September 1813, *ibid.*, III:188.

23 According to Napoleon's letter to Marmont at 4:00 A.M. on the 27th, the emperor wanted VI Corps to immediately cross to the left bank of the Elbe with I Cavalry Corps. One infantry brigade would be left at Meißen to defend the bridgehead. Napoleon instructed Marmont to echelon his first two divisions and a portion of I Cavalry Corps along the road to Torgau so that the head of his column remained one good march from the fortress. "According to the news that we receive in the course of the day from Dessau and from the prince de la Moskova [Ney], you must be ready to execute a great march to come to his support." Five hours later, Napoleon issued Marmont new orders for the following day to move his first division to Eilenburg, his second as well as corps headquarters to Wurzen, and his third to Oschatz; I Cavalry Corps would move on Dahlen and Schildau. "From this position on the Eilenburg–Wurzen–Oschatz line, you will be able to move to join the prince de la Moskova to cover Leipzig and cut off the enemy from the Elbe or take the offensive on Wittenberg to destroy all the enemy's bridges or go back to Dresden, Chemnitz, or Altenburg to oppose the movements the enemy can make from Bohemia": *CN*, Nos. 20643 and 20644, XXVI:252–54. Two days later, Berthier informed Ney that "the emperor desires that he [Marmont] be employed in the operation that has the goal of raising the siege of Wittenberg": SHAT, C¹⁷ 180: Berthier to Ney, 29 September 1813.

24 *CN*, No. 20663, XXVI:267–68; SHAT, C² 157: Ney to Berthier, 1 October 1813; Ney to Marmont, 1 October 1813, in Fabry, *Étude sur les opérations de l'empereur*, III:207; Ney to Berthier, Pötnitz, 1 October 1813, *ibid.*, III:208.

25 Marmont to Napoleon, 2 October 1813, and Ney to Berthier, 2 October 1813, are in Fabry, *Étude sur les opérations de l'empereur*, III:233, 240–41.

26 Tauentzien to Blücher, Bad Liebenwerda, 8:00 A.M., 27 September 1813, in Höpfner, "Darstellung," 1844:288–89. Boyen also confirmed this news in Boyen to Gneisenau, Nudersdorf, 27 September 1813, GStA PK, VI HA Rep. 92 Nl. Gneisenau, Nr. 23.

27 Blücher to Charles John, Königsbrück, 27 September 1813, Add MSS, 20112, 55–56; Droysen, *Yorck*, II:177.

28 Numbering 1,202 combatants at the outset of the campaign, this single brigade – itself composed of the single battalions of the Kamchatskii and Ochakovskii Regiments – of Sacken's XI Corps demonstrates the thinness of some Russian units.

29 Blücher to Gneisenau, 27 September 1813, GStA PK, VI HA Rep. 92 Nl. Gneisenau, Nr. 18; Blücher to Sacken, Elsterwerda, 28 October 1813, RGVIA, f. VUA, op. 16, d. 3851, ll. 213–214. Blücher's short disposition for 28 September is in GStA PK, VI HA Rep. 92 Nl. Gneisenau, Nr. 18, and Add MSS, 20112, 145; Sacken to Barclay de Tolly, 1 October 1813, in Bogdanovich, *Geschichte des Krieges*, IIb:38; Höpfner, "Darstellung," 1844:290. General Vaudoncourt, in *Histoire de la guerre*, I:192, errs by claiming that VI Corps was also at Meißen. See CN, Nos. 20643 and 20644, XXVI:252–54.

30 Blücher to Alexander, Elsterwerda, 29 September 1813, RGVIA, f. VUA, op. 16, d. 3913, l. 268; Höpfner, "Darstellung," 1844:290; Friederich, *Herbstfeldzug 1813*, II:277.

31 SHAT, C[17] 133: Charles John to Tauentzien, 29 September 1813; Tauentzien to Blücher, Bad Liebenwerda, 3:00 P.M., 29 September 1813, in Höpfner, "Darstellung," 1844:290.

32 Blücher's disposition for 29 September is in GStA PK, VI HA Rep. 92 Nl. Gneisenau, Nr. 18, and Add MSS, 20112, 146; Blücher to Alexander, Elsterwerda, 29 September 1813, RGVIA, f. VUA, op. 16, d. 3913, l. 268; Bubna to Schwarzenberg, Stolpen, 1 October 1813, ÖStA KA, FA 1534, 20; Sacken to Blücher, Großenhain, 6:00 P.M., 30 September 1813, RA KrA, 25. On 1 October Bubna reported that both "the emperor Napoleon and the king of Saxony are at Dresden with the French and the Saxon Guard."

33 Alexander to Blücher, Teplitz, 25 September 1813, in Höpfner, "Darstellung," 1844:291; Pertz and Delbrück, *Gneisenau*, III:376.

34 Knesebeck to Gneisenau, Teplitz, 26 September 1813, GStA PK, VI HA Rep. 92 Nl. Gneisenau, Nr. 23. See Janson, *Friedrich Wilhelm*, 216–17.

35 Blücher to Alexander, Elsterwerda, 29 September 1813, RGVIA, f. VUA, op. 16, d. 3913, l. 268; Gneisenau to Knesebeck, Elsterwerda, 8:30 P.M., 29 September 1813, in Pertz and Delbrück, *Gneisenau*, III:399–400.

36 Charles John to Blücher, Zerbst, 29 September 1813, Add MSS, 20112, 57; Blücher to Charles John, 30 September 1813, GStA PK, VI HA Rep. 92 Nl. Gneisenau, Nr. 23; Gneisenau to Knesebeck, Elsterwerda, 8:00 P.M., 30 September 1813, in Pertz and Delbrück, *Gneisenau*, III:401–02; Bogdanovich, *Geschichte des Krieges*, IIb:39; Friederich, *Herbstfeldzug 1813*, II:278–79.

37 Knesebeck to Gneisenau, Teplitz, 4:00 P.M., 28 September 1813, GStA PK, VI
   HA Rep. 92 Nl. Gneisenau, Nr. 23.
38 Knesebeck to Gneisenau, Teplitz, 28 September 1813, GStA PK, VI HA Rep. 92
   Nl. Gneisenau, Nr. 23.
39 Charles John to Blücher, Zerbst, 30 September and 3 October 1813, Add MSS,
   20112, 58–60; Blücher to Charles John, Herzberg, 1 October 1813, GStA PK, VI
   HA Rep. 92 Nl. Gneisenau, Nr. 23; Pertz and Delbrück, *Gneisenau*, III:406.
40 Bubna to Blücher, Stolpen, 2 September 1813, ÖStA KA, FA 1534, 111b. Bubna
   reported that Macdonald had moved closer to the entrenchments east of
   Dresden's Neustadt, closely monitored by the forward posts of both Bubna (in
   the Hartha Forest) and Shcherbatov (at Weißig and Radeberg). Bubna also
   established communication with Bennigsen through Major Ferdinand Wilhelm
   Franz Bolstern von Boltenstern's detachment. See Bogdanovich, *Geschichte des
   Krieges*, IIb:41; Müffling, *Die Feldzüge*, 60.
41 Langeron, *Mémoires*, 289–90.
42 Bertrand's "Rapport sur le combat de Wartenburg" is in Fabry, *Étude sur les
   opérations de l'empereur*, III:266; Friederich, *Herbstfeldzug 1813*, II:281–83; see
   also Fabry, *Étude sur les opérations de l'empereur*, III:184–85, 200–01.
43 Blücher issued a two-day disposition on 30 September that covered 1 and 2
   October: "On 1 October, Langeron's corps will march to Herzberg, Yorck's to
   Herzberg, and Sacken's to Mühlberg giving the impression that it will cross
   there. Langeron's vanguard will march to Bad Liebenwerda, Yorck's to Koßdorf,
   and Sacken's to Streumen. Headquarters will go to Herzberg. On 2 October,
   Langeron's and Yorck's corps will cross the Black Elster and bivouac opposite
   Jeßen. Sacken's corps will go to Herzberg. Langeron's and Yorck's vanguards
   will go to Annaburg, Sacken's to Koßdorf. Headquarters will go to Jeßen. The
   pontoons (which should arrive at Bad Liebenwerda on 1 October) will travel at
   the head of Langeron's corps. On 2 October they will go to Elster." Blücher
   included a copy of this disposition with his letter to Bernadotte on the 30th:
   Disposition, Elsterwerda, 30 September 1813, Add MSS, 20112, 147.
44 Blücher to Frederick William, Wartenburg, 6:00 P.M., 3 October 1813, ÖStA KA,
   FA 1534, 74; Blücher to Bubna, Wartenburg, 3 October 1813, *ibid.*, 149c; Höpfner, "Darstellung," 1844:300–01.
45 To be fair to Bernadotte, he wrote Vorontsov on the 3rd claiming that he had just
   received news from Blücher that the Silesian Army would throw bridges across
   the Elbe at Elster to cross the river that same day. "One has heard cannon –
   probably General Blücher attacking the enemy on the road to Kemberg. Therefore, I ask that you send this same night Cossacks to Raghun and Bitterfeld to
   harass the communications of Bertrand's corps, which faces Blücher. To save time,
   I ask that you report directly to me and I will share your information with
   Wintzingerode. Tomorrow we cross the Elbe": SHAT, C¹⁷ 133: Charles John to
   Vorontsov, Zerbst, 3 October 1813.
46 Gneisenau to Clausewitz, Wartenburg, 3 October 1813, GStA PK, VI HA
   Rep. 92 Nl. Gneisenau, Nr. 21; Blücher to Frederick William, Wartenburg, 6:00
   P.M., 3 October 1813, ÖStA KA, FA 1534, 74; Müffling, *Die Feldzüge*, 59;
   Bogdanovich, *Geschichte des Krieges*, IIb:40. Droysen credits Lölhöffel von

Löwensprung: "Meanwhile, under Captain Lolhöffel's leadership, the bridge was zealously built. It progressed so far that on 2 October he reported that he could finish that same day if he did not run out of planks to cover the bridge and did not lack the necessary carts to transport the planks": Droysen, *Yorck*, II:180.

47 Blücher to Frederick William, Wartenburg, 6:00 P.M., 3 October 1813, ÖStA KA, FA 1534, 74.

48 Pertz and Delbrück, *Gneisenau*, III:407; Blücher to Knesebeck, Elsterwerda, 1 October 1813, *Blüchers Briefe*, ed. Unger, 184.

49 Langeron, *Mémoires*, 291.

50 SHAT, C² 156: Bertrand to Berthier, Wartenburg, 23 September 1813.

51 Bertrand's "Rapport sur le combat de Wartenburg" is in Fabry, *Étude sur les opérations de l'empereur*, III:266.

52 This wood no longer exists, the land having been cleared for cultivation.

53 Bertrand claims that his forward posts alerted him at 6:00 A.M. that a large quantity of enemy cavalry and infantry was crossing the bridge. Bertrand's "Rapport sur le combat de Wartenburg" is in Fabry, *Étude sur les opérations de l'empereur*, III:267.

54 Quoted in Droysen, *Yorck*, II:185; SHAT, C² 157: Bertrand to Ney, 8:00 P.M., Klitzschena, 3 October 1813.

55 Blücher to Frederick William, Wartenburg, 6:00 P.M., 3 October 1813, ÖStA KA, FA 1534, 74, quoted in Droysen, *Yorck*, II:186.

56 Quoted in Unger, *Blücher*, II:99–100; Nostitz, *Tagebuch*, 67.

57 Steffens, *Adventures*, 115.

58 Quoted in Bogdanovich, *Geschichte des Krieges*, IIb:47.

59 Langeron, *Mémoires*, 292; SHAT, C² 157: Bertrand to Ney, 3 October 1813.

60 Yorck was very angry about this event, calling such proceedings "un-soldierly," and "a brutal act." He rejected the officer's excuse that the enemy infantry would have retaken the cannon: Droysen, *Yorck*, II:195–96.

61 SHAT, C² 157: Bertrand to Ney, 3 October 1813; Blücher to Frederick William, Wartenburg, 6:00 P.M., 3 October 1813, ÖStA KA, FA 1534, 74.

62 SHAT, C² 157: Bertrand to Ney, 3 October 1813.

63 Blücher to Frederick William, Wartenburg, 6:00 P.M., 3 October 1813, ÖStA KA, FA 1534, 74.

64 The account of the battle of Wartenburg is based on Blücher to Frederick William, Wartenburg, 6:00 P.M., 3 October 1813, ÖStA KA, FA 1534, 74; Blücher to Charles John, between Wartenburg and Globig, 2:30 P.M., 3 October 1813, RA KrA, 25; SHAT, C² 157: Bertrand to Ney, 8:00 P.M., Klitzschena, 3 October 1813; Friederich, *Herbstfeldzug 1813*, II:281–98; Droysen, *Yorck*, II:181–98; Höpfner, "Darstellung," 1844:303–15; Plotho, *Der Krieg*, II:283; Wagner, *Plane der Schlachten*, II:64–65; Bogdanovich, *Geschichte des Krieges*, IIb:49; Petre, *Napoleon's Last Campaign*, 297–99; Unger, *Blücher*, II:98–99; Vaudoncourt, *Histoire de la guerre*, I:192.

65 Steffens, *Adventures*, 116; Unger, *Blücher*, II:101; Pertz and Delbrück, *Gneisenau*, III:416.

66 Droysen, *Yorck*, II:197; Blücher to Charles John, between Wartenburg and Globig, 2:30 P.M., 3 October 1813, RA KrA, 25; SHAT, C² 157: Bertrand to Ney,

3 October 1813; Blücher to Bubna, Wartenburg, 3 October 1813, ÖStA KA, FA 1534, 149c; Blücher to Frederick William, Wartenburg, 6:00 P.M., 3 October 1813, ÖStA KA, FA 1534, 74. In appendix 104 of the second volume of Plotho's *Der Krieg*, he cites Yorck's losses at 67 officers killed or wounded and 1,539 soldiers wounded with an additional 291 killed and 182 missing for a slightly higher total of 2,012 casualties among the enlisted personnel.

67 Friederich, *Herbstfeldzug 1813*, II:298; Droysen, *Yorck*, II:194; Pertz and Delbrück, *Gneisenau*, III:409, 416.

68 Quoted in Pertz and Delbrück, *Gneisenau*, III:416; Droysen, *Yorck*, II:195–96.

69 Langeron, *Mémoires*, 292; Droysen, *Yorck*, II:193–94, 196; Pertz and Delbrück, *Gneisenau*, III:416; Blücher to Frederick William, Wartenburg, 6:00 P.M., 3 October 1813, ÖStA KA, FA 1534, 74.

70 Unger, *Blücher*, II:100.

71 Quoted in Droysen, *Yorck*, II:196; Langeron, *Mémoires*, 292–93.

72 Blücher to Frederick William, Wartenburg, 6:00 P.M., 3 October 1813, ÖStA KA, FA 1534, 74; Charles John to Blücher, Zerbst, 3 October 1813, GStA PK, VI HA Rep. 92 Nl. Gneisenau, Nr. 23; Blücher to Charles John, between Wartenburg and Globig, 2:30 P.M., 3 October 1813, RA KrA, 25; Bogdanovich, *Geschichte des Krieges*, IIb:50. The letter, written on behalf of Boyen by Major August von Reiche of Bülow's staff, stated that the crown prince had decided to cross the Elbe on the 5th but would probably commence the operation on the 4th as soon as he learned of Blücher's crossing at Wartenburg. See Reiche to Gneisenau, Rudersdorf, 6:30 P.M., 3 October 1813, in Höpfner, "Darstellung," 1844:315.

73 Friederich, *Herbstfeldzug 1813*, II:303–04.

74 Blücher to Bonin, Wartenburg, 4 October 1813, *Blüchers Briefe*, ed. Unger, 185.

11

The Mulde

Bertrand's 8:00 P.M. report to Ney on 3 October stated that the Army of Silesia led by "Blücher, Yorck, and Prince Karl" had attacked him "vigorously" and "with numerous forces" that day, turning his right, and forcing him to retreat in the direction of Bad Düben. Based on this sketchy information, Ney planned to withdraw ten miles south from Pötnitz to Raguhn on the Mulde with VII Corps the next day. He requested that Marmont strongly occupy the point of passage across the Mulde at Bad Düben some twenty miles upstream of Raguhn. Noting that Bertrand had directed his retreat on Bad Düben, Ney emphasized to Marmont "that it is thus indispensable that you move all the forces that you have at your disposal to this point" and to notify him "the moment you commence your movement." In a postscript, he added that some units of Bertrand's corps had retreated south to Pretzsch on the Elbe and others southwest toward Bad Düben on the Mulde. On the morning of the 4th, Marmont marched from Leipzig to Eilenburg with one division of his corps and I Cavalry Corps; a second division of VI Corps that already stood at Eilenburg had moved eleven miles downstream to Bad Düben (see Map 5).[1]

By the morning of the 4th, Ney possessed accurate information regarding the events at Wartenburg. A captured Prussian sergeant of the Black Hussars confirmed that "the Silesian Army, commanded by Generals Blücher, Yorck, and the prince of Mecklenburg-Strelitz, composed of four corps, and 90,000-men strong, had moved from Silesia to Bautzen, from where it moved after a sojourn through Königsbrück on Wittenberg. On October 2, it passed the night one mile from the village of Elster. This army was followed by the Russian corps commanded by Generals St.-Priest and Langeron." The report goes on to state that the Allies had utilized the bridge that Bülow had built at Elster as well as a second that the Russians constructed a little further upstream. At daybreak on the 3rd, the Prussians

499

commenced the passage; Blücher himself crossed at 8:00 and the whole army by 10:00. Allied cavalry had captured several caissons retreating on the road to Gräfenhainichen.[2] Ney informed Marmont that, "after marching continuously for five days and five nights," the Silesian Army had bridged the Elbe at Elster and attacked Bertrand at Wartenburg. After fighting for twelve hours and inflicting considerable losses on the enemy, Bertrand withdrew eleven miles west to Klitzschena. Prisoners taken by his troops claimed to be from the corps of Langeron, Sacken, and Kleist. "The losses of IV Corps are not considerable because the troops were advantageously posted behind dikes and abatis; but the Württemberger division, which numbered 1,400 men and was defending the village of Bleddin, was completely destroyed."

Not known as a gifted strategist, Ney nevertheless recognized the implications of the operations unfolding around him: "As I find my right thus turned by very considerable forces and I can be attacked on both banks of the Mulde by the army of the prince of Sweden, it appears indispensable for me to retreat on Delitzsch. It is of the utmost importance for the emperor to immediately take decisive action because, by the 6th, the enemy will be able to direct more than 100,000 men on Leipzig." Consequently, Reynier's corps continued the retreat from Pötnitz through Raguhn toward Delitzsch, a march of twenty-four miles; the marshal himself passed the night of 4/5 October at Bitterfeld.[3] During the 4th, Bertrand's IV Corps crossed the Mulde thirteen miles north of Delitzsch at Raguhn and Jeßnitz; the rearguard burnt the bridges and followed the corps south. Bertrand united with VII Corps and III Cavalry Corps at Delitzsch – thirteen miles north of Leipzig – to provide Ney with a total of 30,000 men. Reports that a weak enemy detachment had reached Bad Düben sparked concerns at Blücher's headquarters that it represented the vanguard of an imperial army approaching from Leipzig.[4]

Despite these tidings, good news arrived from Bernadotte on the morning of the 4th in the form of a letter written the day before. After learning of Blücher's crossing of the Elbe, Bernadotte decided that his army would also start crossing on the 4th. He informed Blücher that Wintzingerode would push his light cavalry to Jeßnitz, Bitterfeld, Bad Düben, and Delitzsch. Wintzingerode would unite his main body at Aken while the Swedes would assemble at Roßlau. Leaving behind his 4th Brigade (6,000 men) to blockade Wittenberg on the right bank of the Elbe, Bülow would lead his other three to Roßlau on the morning of the 4th. Tauentzien received orders to assemble his corps at Coswig, march to Roßlau, and cross the Elbe on the 5th to form the army's reserve. "Do me the favor of providing me news of you during the day so we can march in concert and support each other," concluded Bernadotte's letter to Blücher. Silesian Army Headquarters also learned that Bülow's corps had marched at 9:00 A.M. from Nudersdorf – itself five miles north-northeast of Wittenberg – through Coswig to Roßlau and would commence the river crossing that same day. In fact, although the Swedish corps already stood at Roßlau, Bernadotte ordered III Corps to cross the river *before* them; these orders were later rescinded and the Swedes crossed on the 4th and the Prussians on the 5th.

The Swedes received orders to reconnoiter Dessau and send patrols on the road running east from there to Wörlitz. Bernadotte believed the imperials had evacuated Dessau, but wanted the Swedish corps commander, Stedingk, to proceed with caution and "not fall into a trap." If the imperials still held Dessau, Bernadotte wanted the Swedes to attack "without indecision." As it turned out, Wintzingerode's entire corps crossed on the 4th and pushed its vanguard to Köthen from where small detachments continued south-southeast to Radegast and Zörbig. Patrols raided deep into Ney's rear area by reaching Landsberg and Delitzsch. French reports state that an enemy force of 2,000 infantry and several guns reached Halle by the 5th. Meanwhile, Stedingk's Swedes crossed at Roßlau. While his vanguard proceeded to Raguhn, the main body marched to Dessau, where Bernadotte established his headquarters. Bülow's corps moved into Roßlau. General Karl Friedrich von Hirschfeld's brigade from Tauentzien's corps guarded the bridge and continued work on a bridgehead.[5]

With Ney retreating, Blücher's vanguards obtained little news concerning the location of his main body. In the hope that reports would clarify the situation, Gneisenau postponed cutting orders for the 4th.[6] The guns and caissons taken at Wartenburg as well as the prisoners and wounded went to Elster, from where they continued another sixty miles north to Berlin. Gneisenau, Rauch, Müffling, Rühle, and Oppen inspected Wartenburg and its environs after sunrise in search of a position for the army should it confront a numerically superior force led by Napoleon. They did not have to look very far: Wartenburg and Bleddin provided the optimum site for an entrenched camp. To build the field works, Blücher issued orders for each of his 3 corps to provide 4,000 infantry to labor for the pioneers and engineers in 3 detachments for 7 days and nights under the direction of General Rauch. The two and one-half miles between Wartenburg and Bleddin would be entrenched; works included three redoubts on the right wing, one battery for fifty guns to guard the western approaches to the village of Wartenburg, and a massive battery for a hundred guns between Wartenburg and Bleddin. Blücher wanted the camp to be a defensive bastion for 50,000 men. He instructed each corps to have small detachments comb the stretch between the Mulde and the Elbe to collect wagons, workers, entrenching tools, and especially wheelbarrows. With 10 October as the target date for completion, construction began on the 4th, but the shortage of tools delayed the work considerably.[7]

After reports failed to uncover the direction of Bertrand's retreat, Blücher and Gneisenau decided on a short march southwest. This movement aimed to find the imperials, establish communication with Bernadotte's army, and secure the crossing over the Mulde at Bad Düben.[8] Consequently, Yorck's soldiers broke camp at 1:00 P.M. on the 4th and trooped five miles to Rackith-Gaditz followed by Langeron's men; Sacken's corps proceeded five miles to Trebitz. The army's vanguards and patrols fanned west and south to Coswig, Oranienbaum, Gräfenhainichen, Bad Düben, Mockrehna, and Torgau. Blücher's headquarters moved to Kemberg (see Map 5). On Blücher's extreme left, Langeron's cavalry detachment under Yuzefovich – the Kievskii and Kharkovskii Dragoons, one Kalmyk regiment, and two guns from the 2nd Donskoye Cossack Battery – rode south from Pretzsch to Dommitzsch on the Wittenberg–Torgau highway that ran along the left bank of the Elbe. At Dommitzsch, less than nine miles north of Torgau and fifteen miles south of Wartenburg, it surprised a small detachment of one officer and forty-two men of the 5th Würzburg Battalion guarding a palisaded redoubt, which the Russians destroyed. It was one of fifteen redoubts and blockhouses the imperials had built between Dommitzsch and Meißen to observe the Elbe.[9] Yuzefovich and his main body remained at Dommitzsch, but four miles further south at Neiden his lead elements captured a blockhouse with a Würzburger garrison of similar size. His patrols reached the Meißen–Torgau road. Reconnoitering Torgau, they intercepted a French courier near the city en route from Dresden to Dessau, capturing his entire forty-man escort. From 3 to 5 October, the Silesian Army netted some 2,000 prisoners including several couriers.[10]

At 4:00 P.M., Katzler reported that both Ney and Bertrand had commenced the retreat to Leipzig, where they expected to meet Napoleon. Leipzig itself purportedly contained 10,000 men. Other reports placed Napoleon at Meißen en route from Dresden. Two hours later, one Prussian patrol sent to Wörlitz reported the crossing of Bernadotte's Swedish corps at Roßlau. For the first time in the war, Bernadotte established his headquarters south of the Elbe. Langeron's vanguard reached Bad Düben and its bridge over the Mulde but could not drive off the imperial post that guarded it. At 9:00, the French departed after completely burning the bridge.[11] Sacken's vanguard under Vasilchikov reached Bad Schmiedeberg, pushing patrols toward Eilenburg on the Mulde some eleven miles south of Bad Düben. A bridgehead guarded the eastern access to the crossing, and locals informed the Russians that Eilenburg served as headquarters of I Cavalry Corps and that considerable reinforcements had arrived from Leipzig on the 3rd to reinforce the garrison.

Blücher and his staff carefully considered the reports concerning Napoleon. While Allied Headquarters in Bohemia speculated that the emperor would fall back to Saxony's second city, the Prussians found the supporting evidence to be lacking. Instead, Katzler's report that only 10,000 imperial soldiers stood at Leipzig influenced their planning. Added to Ney's army, this meant merely 60,000–70,000 men would be at hand for the emperor. With such paltry numbers awaiting him, Napoleon certainly would arrive with numerous reinforcements. As the patrols found no sign of large-scale movements, Blücher dismissed the rumor that Napoleon would soon reach Leipzig. It helped that Bubna's 3 October report – confirming Napoleon's presence at Dresden as of the 3rd and that the main body of the French army stood between Freiberg and Nossen – reached Blücher on the 5th. Moreover, Blücher knew that Schwarzenberg's great "left wheel" northwest toward Chemnitz and Zwickau should have commenced already and that his movement through the Erzgebirge would probably attract Napoleon's attention. Blücher and Gneisenau decided that the best course of action for the Silesian Army would be to drive to the Mulde, throw back Ney, arrive at Leipzig on the 6th, and unite with the Army of North Germany on the 8th.[12] Momentarily delayed by the destruction of Bad Düben's bridge, Gneisenau decided late on the 4th that operations would resume on 5 October with the vanguards of all three corps reaching the Mulde. However, only the cavalry would cross to scour the region between Leipzig and Dessau. Late on the morning of the 5th, he ordered the army to move closer to the Mulde. Thus, Yorck proceeded toward Gräfenhainichen, Langeron to Bad Düben, and Sacken to Dahlenberg. Blücher insisted that his corps commanders ensure the safety of the inhabitants. In particular, he did not want the officers or soldiers stealing horses.[13]

Meanwhile, seven squadrons from Yorck's vanguard moved across the repaired bridge over the Mulde at Raguhn and advanced south on the road to Delitzsch. More than halfway to Delitzsch, Polish troops from Dąbrowski's 27th Division forced the Prussian horse to turn back. Polish troops likewise prevented Katzler from fording the Mulde at Mühlbeck with the bulk of Yorck's vanguard. Yorck's main body reached Gräfenhainichen, ten miles northeast of Mühlbeck that afternoon but remained too distant to support the van. Nevertheless, pressure from Bernadotte's Russian cavalry eventually forced Fournier's 6th Light Cavalry and Defrance's 4th Heavy Cavalry Divisions to retreat to Delitzsch; Dąbrowski likewise withdrew his 27th Division to Delitzsch after evacuating Bitterfeld. By nightfall on the 5th, Ney's forces held a short line extending ten miles east from Delitzsch to Naundorf.[14] Moreover, Marmont refused to comply with Ney's request to debouch eastward through Eilenburg. Instead, he withdrew and broke the bridge, earning a rebuke from Imperial Headquarters.[15] Regardless, the combined advance of the Silesian and North German Armies along with Marmont's intransigence broke Ney's resolution to hold the line of the Mulde. He planned to move closer to Leipzig.[16]

Elsewhere, Korf led all of Langeron's cavalry toward Bad Düben, encountering Ney's weak post there as well as imperial pickets along the left bank of the Mulde. Aided by the fire of horse artillery from the opposite bank, one Cossack regiment that swam across the river drove the French from the town and started rebuilding the bridge over the Mulde. Later in the day, the imperials – Marmont's division – returned to Bad Düben, ejected the Cossacks, and unlimbered cannon to prevent the Russians from continuing their work on the bridge. Bad Düben went up in flames during the ensuing artillery engagement. As Langeron's main body approached, the Russians managed to move up sufficient guns to silence the French artillery. By nightfall on the 5th, all of Langeron's corps reached Bad Düben, where Army Headquarters also passed the night amidst the smoldering remains of the town.[17]

East of Langeron, Sacken's vanguard pushed south to Weidenhain, sending patrols to Wurzen, Schildau, and the Dresden–Leipzig road; his main body reached Dahlenberg, eleven miles east of Bad Düben. On Blücher's extreme left flank, Langeron's cavalry detachment under Yuzefovich patrolled from Dommitzsch toward Torgau. At Süptitz, less than four miles east of Torgau, the Russians surprised another company of Würzburgers guarding a blockhouse; they captured a second small garrison holding a blockhouse further south. Reaching the Meißen–Torgau road, one of Yuzefovich's patrols intercepted a courier dispatched from Dresden on the night of 3/4 October with correspondence for Marshal Ney. The letters he bore offered little information but his verbal testimony placed Napoleon at Dresden at the time the courier had departed. This confirmed Bubna's report that Napoleon and the Old Guard stood at Dresden as of 3 October. Napoleon at Dresden meant the Grande Armée stood between the Mulde and the Elbe. Consequently, Blücher decided to drop his plan to force the passage of the former on the 6th. Instead, he would await the emperor's next move. For now, the Silesian Army would push further south toward Dresden to better observe Napoleon's movements. If he crossed the Mulde, Blücher planned to sacrifice his own line of communication by likewise crossing the Mulde and uniting with Bernadotte.[18]

Northwest of Blücher, Bernadotte intended to concentrate the 80,000 men of the Army of North Germany in the square formed by the towns of Aken, Köthen, Jeßnitz, and Dessau (see Map 5). On the 5th, Bülow's Prussians followed the Swedes across the Elbe but continued ten miles south of Dessau to Hinsdorf, with Borstell's brigade reaching Jeßnitz on the banks of the Mulde some eight miles east of the main body. Wintzingerode's Russians and Stedingk's Swedes received a day of rest. Tauentzien reached Dessau with one brigade while his second remained at Roßlau. Along the right bank of the Elbe, General Heinrich Ludwig von Thümen observed Wittenberg with Bülow's 4th Brigade while General Karl George von Wobeser's brigade from Tauentzien's corps monitored Torgau.[19] Cossacks continued to unsettle Ney's rear areas by prowling as far south as Delitzsch and Landsberg, where they encountered the 6th Light and 4th Heavy Cavalry Divisions of III Cavalry

Corps. The Russian warriors retreated for the moment, taking 120 prisoners with them, but their constant pressure unnerved the imperial horsemen and contributed to Ney's decision to retreat to Delitzsch.[20]

With Blücher's advance on Gräfenhainichen, Bad Düben, and Dahlenberg threatening to cut his communication with Dresden and thus the Grande Armée, Ney destroyed all of the bridges across the Mulde and planned to withdraw IV and VII Corps along with 27th Division fourteen miles east-southeast from Delitzsch to Eilenburg on the 6th. Before departing from Delitzsch, he informed Marmont of a critical shortage of ammunition. In fact, IV Corps had none after the vicious firefight at Wartenburg. He asked Marmont to provide Bertrand with enough munitions for six 12-pound guns, two 6-inch mortars, twelve 6-pound guns, and four 24-pound mortars as well as ten caissons of cartridges for the infantry. "We are certain that a considerable depot exists at Torgau and that it contains, among other things, more than one million rounds in reserve; you can resupply yourself from this city," wrote Ney.[21]

By transferring his headquarters to Eilenburg on 6 October, Ney actually moved closer to Blücher's command post eleven miles to his north at Bad Düben. Yet at Eilenburg, Ney increased his forces to 50,000 men by uniting with I and V Cavalry Corps. From his headquarters halfway between Bad Düben and Eilenburg, Marmont suggested defending the Mulde. "My dear marshal," responded Ney, "I received the letter you wrote me today from Hohenpriesnitz. It is not, I believe, [necessary] to concentrate at Eilenburg to hold this outlet but to unite as quickly as possible at Leipzig." He insinuated that the Allies would overrun his position at any moment and requested that Marmont withdraw VI Corps and I Cavalry Corps west to a central position at Luckowehna. With Blücher's back to the Mulde, Ney did not believe he would engage an imperial army consisting of three infantry and two cavalry corps. In this case, they could maintain their position for another day. "Should the enemy show only weak forces," Ney instructed the junior marshal, "we can offer resistance along the Delitzsch–Luckowehna front. In the opposite case, we can fall back in unison. Messages from the emperor will probably arrive by that time and hopefully His Majesty will play a great role. If you think it fit to unite at Luckowehna or Krostitz, I'll await the enemy tomorrow at Delitzsch. I await, my dear marshal, your response to my proposal before I make my final arrangements."[22]

Marmont received this letter during the night of 5/6 October. He disagreed, seeing no satisfactory reason to surrender the line of the Mulde to Blücher. To add to his disgruntlement, the emperor's orders arrived, which placed him under Ney's command, leaving him little choice but to bow to Ney's wishes. Nevertheless, he delayed evacuating his position throughout the daylight hours of the 6th. Writing to Ney at 4:00 that morning, Marmont explained that the Allies had managed to repair the bridge over the Mulde at

Bad Düben. Consequently, he could not withdraw from his position during the day because he did not want to see his rearguard mauled by the Allies.[23]

Meanwhile, Ney also received the emperor's orders and instructions that placed VI Corps and I Cavalry Corps as well as III Corps under his direction. At 6:00 on the morning of the 6th, he changed his mind about making a stand at Delitzsch and withdrawing south on Leipzig. Instead, the marshal wanted to move his army closer to the emperor. Thus, he proposed crossing the Mulde and streaking east toward Torgau to unite with III Corps. To allow enough time for Marmont's VI Corps to move across the Mulde at Eilenburg, Ney planned to maintain his positions until 4:00 P.M. on the 6th. At that hour, IV and VII Corps as well as the cavalry would troop seventeen miles southeast to cross the Mulde at Wurzen and then proceed another eleven miles northeast to Schildau. "After passing Eilenburg, take a position at Mockrehna and Langenreichenbach; we will then be situated to march against the enemy's flank," he instructed Marmont.[24]

Although Ney assured Marmont that he would remain at Wölkau until 4:00, he commenced the march to Wurzen at 1:00 P.M. on the 6th. Already aggravated by Ney's evacuation of the Mulde, Marmont became furious over his senior colleague's sprint to Wurzen, which uncovered the left flank of VI Corps. Exasperated, Marmont remained on the heights of Eilenburg. A miffed Ney complained to Berthier that Marmont "did not judge it appropriate to debouch through Eilenburg." Marmont received another order from Ney around nightfall instructing him to march south to Taucha to better cover Leipzig and guard a convoy coming from Naumburg. Ney also instructed him to conduct reconnaissance east of Eilenburg. "Marshal Ney," Marmont later wrote, "brave and intrepid soldier, man of the battlefield, understood nothing about combined movements. His mind was terrified of what he could not see. Calculations never dictated his actions." After receiving this dispatch, Marmont fired his own complaint to the emperor: "In the interest of the service, I will take the liberty to speak openly: it is indispensable that you come here. If you do not come, we will conduct the poorest business, which I fully believe to be the case based on the measures I see being taken. Had I complied with the first order that I received, I would have placed the army in the worst situation possible because it was given without any consideration of time or purpose. To avoid pestering you, I will not go any further into the details but will limit myself to repeating with certainty that nothing can be more counterproductive for your service in the poor situation that we are in than to see the leadership of the operation entrusted in the current hands." This letter earned a response via Berthier: "His Majesty has received the letter that you wrote to him. It is insignificant. Send all the information you have on the enemy."[25]

A furious Marmont led VI Corps and I Cavalry Corps to Taucha – a march of eight miles southwest from Eilenburg – that same night (see Map 5). He also ordered Souham to march west from Torgau to Eilenburg – an odd move considering Ney's plan to lead IV and VII Corps and III Cavalry Corps east from Wurzen to Torgau. One possible explanation is that Marmont believed Ney had exaggerated the threat posed by Blücher. As for Ney, despite starting his march three hours early, only III Cavalry Corps reached Wurzen; the rest of his army camped at various points along the left bank of the Mulde between Eilenburg and Wurzen. Ney himself reached Bennewitz, across the Mulde from Wurzen. Dąbrowski's division, which had remained at Delitzsch to cover Marmont's march, departed for Taucha at 1:00 A.M. on the 7th swarmed by Cossacks and Allied light cavalry. Twenty miles northeast of Wurzen, III Corps assembled at Torgau on the 6th. At 7:00 P.M. on the 6th, Ney reported to Berthier that the enemy appeared to have renounced his intentions to immediately march on Leipzig. Instead, Blücher seemed intent on defending the right bank of the Mulde and awaiting the fall of Wittenberg. One column of enemy cavalry and artillery marched up the Mulde while the Cossacks held Wurzen. Ney planned to send a strong detachment from Dahlen toward Torgau to establish contact with III Corps. He hoped to unite VII and IV Corps as well as the divisions under Dąbrowski and Fournier in the region of Bennewitz.[26]

To be prepared to counter Napoleon, Blücher wanted confirmation that Bernadotte would keep his word. In a letter dated 5 October, he reminded the crown prince that "your army and the Silesian [Army] have Leipzig as the objective of their operations" based on the tsar's instructions of 25 September. "Thus," he continued, "three suppositions must be taken into consideration: (1) the enemy undertakes offensive movements against both of our armies; (2) the enemy stands firm and awaits us on the plains of Leipzig; (3) the enemy withdraws his forces from Leipzig to attack the Bohemian Army. The first condition subdivides into three: (A) the enemy turns against your army; (B) the enemy turns against the Silesian Army; or (C) the enemy turns against both. It appears that we can assume the following principle: the army that is attacked by superior forces will fall back one march while the other maintains its position to fix the enemy or to attack him in the flank and rear." He informed Bernadotte of the entrenched camp under construction at Wartenburg, exaggerating its size by claiming that it could hold 150,000 men. If a superior enemy forced the Silesian Army to retreat into this camp, Blücher wanted Bernadotte to move his left wing toward Kemberg while taking the offensive with his right. In fairness, he conceded that Bernadotte would "have the honor of determining the movements that the Silesian Army would make as soon as the enemy turns against you."

Regarding the second supposition, Blücher flatly stated: "If we receive confirmed news from the Bohemian Army ... then it would be very advantageous to attack the enemy the same day this information arrives."

According to all reports, the imperials apparently posted separate armies at Leipzig, Altenburg, and Dresden. "The first two can unite very quickly to fight. Your *Streifkorps* that stand along the Saale and are disrupting enemy communication can provide news of the enemy's positions and intentions while those of the Silesian Army can advance toward Wurzen and Hubertusburg to hinder the enemy's march between Dresden and Leipzig. Thus, for the second supposition, we only have to ascertain the enemy's strength and position to determine the day and the point of attack."

Concerning the third supposition, Blücher insisted on maintaining contact with the imperials: "It appears that the vanguards of the Allied armies, each a strength of 20,000 men, with numerous cavalry and horse artillery, must always remain close to the enemy and fall on his rearguard while the armies themselves follow one strong march behind them. In this case, the direction of Merseburg and Weißenfels may offer the greatest advantage for your army; for the Silesian Army, [it will be] the direction between the Mulde and the (White) Elster."[27]

On the 6th, Bernadotte responded: "I received your letter from yesterday. The memo that it contains is in complete agreement with my ideas ... but due to the circumstances, which are so crucial, we cannot do enough to guard against [unforeseen] events. This consideration, as well as the longing to renew an old acquaintance with you, stirs in me the wish for us to meet if possible at Mühlbeck, where we can speak with each other and through a discussion we can cut short what takes so long to write." He notified Blücher of his intention to transfer his headquarters to Zehbitz, twenty-five miles west of Bad Düben, on the 7th. With Mühlbeck roughly in the middle of their respective command posts, the crown prince proposed a meeting on the evening of the 7th.[28]

As noted, Blücher halted operations on 6 October until reports clarified the overall situation. Moreover, he wanted the entrenched camp at Wartenburg completed before he commenced a general offensive. In his immediate vicinity, Blücher estimated that one division faced Langeron at Bad Düben and appeared to be awaiting his attack. Thirteen miles south of Bad Düben, a second imperial division held Eilenburg and its bridge over the Mulde, which the French secured through a bridgehead on the eastern bank. Both divisions belonged to VI Corps. Late on the 6th, the imperials evacuated Delitzsch and withdrew toward Eilenburg, thus enabling Emmanuel to strike the road to Leipzig with Langeron's vanguard cavalry. Blücher knew that the Army of North Germany had crossed the Elbe and that its outposts had reached the hills of Bitterfeld, thirteen miles west of Bad Düben. He also learned from Katzler that Bernadotte's advance had forced Dąbrowski's 27th Division to withdraw southwest from Mühlbeck toward Leipzig during the night of 5/6 October. Based on this news, Blücher believed his right wing to be "completely secure and all our attention must now be directed to our left flank." Regarding his left, one of Sacken's patrols captured a courier sent from the frantic governor of Torgau, General Louis Narbonne, to Marmont at Eilenburg with a letter stating that Blücher was marching on Torgau and that his vanguard had already reached Dommitzsch. Word had spread and soon Napoleon would know for certain that the Silesian Army had crossed the Elbe.[29]

Blücher received this intercepted dispatch along with a short note from Sacken on the morning of the 6th. Sacken communicated the news he had received from Colonel Madatov at Mühlbeck on the Elbe: his patrols had found endless troop columns along the left bank of the river stretching for forty miles from Dresden through Meißen to Strehla. Numerous bivouac fires – those of III Corps en route to Torgau – had dotted the environs of Strehla during the previous night (4/5 October). With admirable prudence and patience, Blücher decided to await further reports from Sacken before determining the army's next move. He responded by instructing Sacken to rest his main body but to push forward his "vanguard and partisans as far as possible in order to be correctly oriented over the troop masses that are in movement on the highway from Dresden to Leipzig. The most important point for us is to know whether the emperor Napoleon is leading a considerable mass against us in the stretch between the Elbe and the Mulde from Dresden, Freiberg, or Wurzen. In this case, a rapid concentration of all our corps will be necessary. But to be able to do this early enough, I must be informed in time by you of the enemy's movement and I am certain . . . that it will be impossible for us to be surprised from this direction." At the moment, Yuzefovich's detachment from Langeron's corps had the important task of observing Torgau and thus the army's left flank. After the breakout at Wartenburg, Sacken's corps moved to the left wing. As a result, Blücher directed Yuzefovich to Eilenburg and ordered Sacken to observe the Elbe from Torgau upstream.[30]

That same morning, 6 October, Blücher forwarded copies of several intelligence reports as well as Narbonne's intercepted dispatch to the crown prince of Sweden. Not only does his cover letter provide a snapshot of the prevailing views at Silesian Army Headquarters, but it is also interesting for what the communiqué leaves unsaid: "The enemy has taken a position vis-à-vis Bad Düben. Yesterday, he attempted to stop us from rebuilding the bridge. He must have received reinforcements from Leipzig because today he showed a lot of infantry who, during the night, dug a trench to defend the passage. Eilenburg as well as the entire left bank of the Mulde is occupied by the enemy's VI Corps. Yesterday, reinforcements from Leipzig arrived at Eilenburg." Regarding Napoleon, Blücher informed the prince royal that the captured courier who had departed from Dresden on the night of 3/4 October placed the emperor and his Guard at the Saxon capital as of the 3rd. "My posts before Dresden," continued Blücher, "inform me that everything there remains unchanged." To avoid spooking Bernadotte, he made no mention of the troop columns moving northwest from Dresden to Strehla. All Blücher revealed was that he had issued orders to drive further south between the Elbe and the Mulde "to determine whether the emperor is at Dresden or if he is marching to Freiberg or Leipzig." His cover letter concluded: "I believe the enemy will evacuate the Mulde as soon as he learns that your troops have reached Delitzsch. Then I will fall on him with my entire cavalry." That evening, he received the crown prince's response to his 5 October treatise in which Bernadotte requested a meeting at Mühlbeck on the evening of the 7th. "Gneisenau," explained Müffling, "who hated the crown prince with every fiber of his being, believed that more could be achieved with him by verbal intercourse than by written negotiations." Thus, Blücher accepted Bernadotte's invitation.[31]

On 6 October, Blücher and Gneisenau decided against a further advance. Per Müffling's cautious advice, Blücher chose to remain at the Mulde and to await the Bohemian Army's drive on Leipzig. "Alone and without the cooperation of the neighboring army," noted Müffling in his history of the Silesian Army, "the commanding general could proceed no further. His army consisted of approximately 60,000 men and his entrenchments at Wartenburg could not be completed until 12 October."[32] Yet the pursuit of Ney's army drew Blücher's vanguards across the Mulde. Rudzevich found an imperial division of approximately 6,000 infantry and 2 heavy cavalry regiments in battle order at Hohenprießnitz on the Mulde between Bad Düben and Eilenburg. Cossacks had purportedly forced the French to retreat two miles south along the left bank to Zschepplin. This allowed Emmanuel to lead the cavalry of the Russian vanguard across the Mulde at Hohenprießnitz and pursue to Zschepplin.[33] Fourteen miles downstream of Hohenprießnitz, the East Prussian National Cavalry Regiment led Katzler's vanguard across the Mulde at Mühlbeck in pursuit of Dąbrowski's division. The East Prussian commander, Major Karl Friedrich Ludwig von Lehndorff, reported that the enemy had retreated south toward Eilenburg and Taucha and that Delitzsch should be free. Vasilchikov added his belief that the French appeared to be retreating from Eilenburg to Wurzen (see Map 5).

A letter from Bennigsen dated 4 October indicated that 60,000 men of the Bohemian Army had commenced the advance toward Leipzig on that day and that Allied Headquarters would follow from Teplitz on the 5th. Bennigsen also planned "to make a movement on the left bank of the Elbe with a part of my army in order to at least support your bold operation strategically."[34] Despite this good news concerning Ney's forces and Schwarzenberg's advance, Langeron delivered pivotal tidings: "General Yuzefovich reported that based on the quantity of troops that are between Meißen and Torgau it is probable that the enemy will soon attack our left wing and thus it would be expedient to strongly reinforce the post at Dommitzsch."[35]

Based on these reports, the leadership of the Silesian Army reached a decision on 7 October. "A complete change in the judgment of the strategic situation appears to have taken place, which was probably due to Blücher himself. The prolonged standstill at the Mulde hardly corresponded to the character of the commander. His bold way of thinking obviously favored a continuation of the advance, making him master of Leipzig, and from there striving to unite with the Bohemian Army and delivering a decisive battle wherever Napoleon was found."[36] Thus wrote Major Friederich in 1904. In the century that has passed since the Historical Section of Germany's Great General Staff published its official history of the war, nothing of note has surfaced to counter the assertion of this erudite scholar. Not one soul at Blücher's headquarters knew exactly where Schwarzenberg's army stood on 7 October, but that mattered little. All assumed that the Austrian, Russian, and Prussian legions of the Allied Grand Army were beating the plains of Saxony.[37] To comply with basic strategy, the needs of coalition warfare, and the spirit of the Reichenbach Plan, not to mention honor itself, Blücher felt he had to do his utmost to immediately move his army closer to Schwarzenberg. Overcoming Müffling's caution proved easy enough, but would Blücher be able to convince the crown prince of Sweden to participate in this operation?

During the course of 6 September, Bülow's corps trooped southeast to Jeßnitz. His vanguard, Borstell's 5th Brigade, reached Bitterfeld, with forward troops coming within six miles of Delitzsch and linking with Yorck's cavalry to the east. The Swedes and Russians remained in their positions: the former at Dessau with their vanguard at Raguhn, the latter at Aken with their van at Köthen. In total, the combined outpost line of the Silesian and North German Armies extended forty-five miles east from Halle on the Saale to Dommitzsch on the Elbe.[38] That evening, Yorck dined with Bülow at Jeßnitz. Like Blücher, Yorck had bad history with Bülow. Nevertheless, the two corps commanders found common ground in their complaints about their respective commanders. An intense conversation took place at the table. "*Jawohl*," said Yorck, "the Old Hussar chased me across the Elbe and here we sit without any communication with the opposite bank; if Napoleon realizes this situation, he can drive us into the Elbe to such a degree that no one will escape. But this is the work of the clever gentlemen at headquarters, this Gneisenau, this Müffling: this is a mess that can no longer be tolerated." "At least yours will take the bait," responded Bülow, "my generalissimo always thinks of running away; we brought him to this point only with great difficulty but, should Napoleon turn against us, I believe he will immediately race across the Elbe and drag us with him."[39]

While Bülow and Yorck carped about their respective superiors, Blücher hoped to win over Bernadotte. Success appeared elusive after the old Prussian received a letter from him on the morning of the 7th that responded to the intelligence reports Blücher forwarded to his headquarters the previous day. Not surprisingly, the crown prince expressed a substantially different view of the situation. Bernadotte pointed to the report that placed Napoleon at Dresden on 3 October. Claiming that he had yet to receive any news that indicated the emperor had left the Saxon capital, Bernadotte attempted to turn the tables on Blücher and spook him. "His insistence on holding this city suggests that he may intend a desperate strike. Thus, we must stop at nothing to be informed of his decision at least twenty-four hours in advance. I believe we must hold ourselves fast and avoid giving him an opening." Bernadotte continued by sharing his intelligence. One recent report pinpointed the march of 8,000–10,000 men to Hamburg purportedly to replace a division that had departed for Magdeburg. He also claimed that General Pierre Lanusse's 6,000-man division from Magdeburg had concentrated at Calbe on the Saale with orders to immediately advance against the bridge at Aken as soon as the Army of North Germany moved south. Along with this attack on his right, he speculated – correctly – that Napoleon would target Blücher's left. "This operation, which was ordered by the emperor himself, makes me believe that he intends to attack your left wing. You are in a better position than me to ascertain his movements. With much desire I await the news that you have the goodness to communicate to me. In the meantime, I will attack the enemy by Aken and Bernburg tomorrow."[40]

Based on the march of Lanusse's 6,000 men to Calbe, Bernadotte informed his corps commanders that this signaled Napoleon's intention to attack Blücher's left. To prevent Lanusse from taking the bridge at Aken, the crown prince ordered Hirschfeld's brigade to arrive there by 7:00 A.M. on the 8th. He also instructed Lieutenant-Colonel Ludwig von der Marwitz to move his Prussian *Streifkorps* as close as possible to Magdeburg to prevent the French from reinforcing Lanusse. During the 7th, Tauentzien's IV Corps remained in the Roßlau–Dessau area while the Russians and Swedes marched to Radegast to come on line with Bülow's corps, which extended from Hinsdorf to Jeßnitz. Wintzingerode's vanguard, commanded by Vorontsov, stood closest to Leipzig. With his command post at Sylbitz, Vorontsov's pickets stretched along the Halle–Landsberg–Delitzsch line (see Map 5). Cavalry detachments and Cossacks patrolled from the suburbs of Leipzig to Halle. Skirmishing with French cavalry ensued throughout the day. That evening, the Cossacks repulsed French cavalry coming from Leipzig, pursuing them to the very gates of the city. Of particular note, Wintzingerode's Cossacks established communication with those of Schwarzenberg's army. The news soon reached Bernadotte and Blücher that the Bohemian Army had reached Chemnitz, fifty-three miles south of Leipzig, and would continue to Altenburg.[41]

On the morning of the 7th, Ney informed Marmont that to facilitate communication between them VII Corps would throw another bridge across the Mulde at Kollau, four miles upstream of Eilenburg. Ney added that IV Corps would continue toward Torgau with the goal of uniting with III Corps "if it is still close to this place." "Give orders so that all convoys between Leipzig and Erfurt arrive hastily at the former; recall all detachments and remain concentrated. As you have noted, gaining time is no longer an issue; the emperor, who is definitely moving, undoubtedly will soon change the face of the affair." After receiving Reynier's report that Marmont's division had completely evacuated Eilenburg and marched to Taucha the previous night, Ney ordered the general to detach 1,000 to 1,200 men to guard the bridge. He also gently admonished Marmont by explaining that the Eilenburg bridge would become "an important *débouché* at the moment the reinforcements arrive that the emperor is leading in person, thus announcing that we will resume the offensive." He also informed Berthier that, on the previous day, the Cossacks had delivered a proclamation to Wurzen announcing that Blücher would march on Leipzig with 60,000 men and that the French army had been destroyed.[42]

Ney's troops did not make much progress on 7 October. Reynier's VII Corps assembled at Püchau, less than two miles west of Bennewitz, and Dąbrowski's 27th took post near Wurzen. Ney's orders to Bertrand directed IV Corps through Wurzen to Schildau in the direction of Torgau to seek contact with III Corps but only 12th Division attained this objective. Bertrand's 15th and 38th Divisions trooped six miles east to Falkenhain because for several hours they had waited in vain for the emperor to arrive at Wurzen. Elsewhere, III Corps completed its march west by reaching Wurzen. Marmont's VI Corps remained at Taucha; and I Cavalry Corps bivouacked along the Leipzig–Wurzen road. Meanwhile, the reconnaissance by VI Corps that Ney requested to be conducted east of Eilenburg found nothing but enemy cavalry patrols. This led Ney to believe that "the enemy has his principal forces at Bad Düben and downstream from there."[43]

Although confirming that Ney had evacuated the left bank of the Mulde, the intelligence that reached Silesian Army Headquarters during the course of 7 October proved so contradictory that Blücher's staff could not determine the enemy's intentions. "The movements of the various enemy corps seemed to cause a great deal of surprise amongst our own and much indecision," recalled Langeron. Katzler confirmed the news that the French had evacuated Delitzsch during the night and that all imperial forces appeared to be withdrawing southwest to Taucha and Eilenburg, six and fourteen miles northeast of Leipzig respectively. The East Prussian National Cavalry Regiment as well as Borstell's 5th Brigade and Bülow's Cossacks were pursuing. At 10:30 on the morning of the 7th, Blücher received a report from Emmanuel at Zschepplin written at 9:30 A.M. stating that Lukovkin's Cossacks had followed the French after they evacuated that village and retreated through Eilenburg, which the Russians occupied. Lukovkin's patrols crossed the Mulde and likewise pursued the imperials; Emmanuel himself struck the road that ran from Bad Düben to Leipzig. Lukovkin confirmed the enemy's evacuation of Eilenburg and the destruction of its bridge over the Mulde. Other reports claimed that Marmont with 12,000 men and part of I Cavalry Corps had stood at Bad Düben before retreating to Zschepplin on 6 October and toward Eilenburg on the 7th. "I await confirmation of this," Blücher explained to the king; "I can offer no explanation of this movement . . . [but] a traveler arrived here from Leipzig without having encountered a single enemy soldier."[44]

Based on these reports as well as the knowledge that Schwarzenberg had commenced his offensive, the Prussians concluded that Napoleon would soon lead his masses from Dresden. Blücher and his staff assumed that he intended to unite his forces at Leipzig either to accept a battle there or lead his army from there against either Schwarzenberg or Blücher and Bernadotte. The march west of Souham's III Corps particularly baffled the Prussians. A message from Yuzefovich sent at 5:00 A.M. from Langenreichenbach and delivered to Blücher at noon reported the arrival of 35,000 imperials (III Corps and the 10th Hussar Regiment) at Torgau on the evening of 6 October. Although this development perplexed the Prussians, they bowed to caution and decided to reinforce the army's left wing. Langeron received instructions to move his IX and X Infantry Corps from Bad Düben ten miles northeast to Bad Schmiedeberg to support Sacken if necessary. Moreover, Blücher ordered Shcherbatov to quickly cross the Elbe "somewhere between Meißen and Torgau" as soon as the enemy evacuated the left bank. After crossing, Blücher wanted the Russian commander "to operate in the rear of the enemy columns and link with my left wing."[45]

Around 1:00 on the afternoon of the 7th, Blücher received news concerning the march of Souham's III Corps *from* Torgau southwest toward Schildau. Silesian Army Headquarters could not determine if III Corps had relieved Torgau's garrison, which had then commenced the march to Schildau, or if Souham had reinforced it and then continued to Schildau with the remaining units of his command.[46] Blücher recognized that the reinforcement of Torgau's garrison could be the preliminary step for an operation along the right bank of the Elbe against his bridge at Wartenburg–Elster, the latter standing only twenty-five miles downstream of Torgau. To alert Wobeser, whose brigade was observing Torgau from the right bank of the Elbe, Blücher wrote directly to him, bypassing both Bernadotte and Tauentzien, his immediate superiors. Should significant forces emerge from Torgau on the right bank, Blücher instructed Wobeser to withdraw to Jeßen "to cover our bridge over the Elbe at Elster, destroying all bridges over the Black Elster from its mouth to as far above Herzberg as it is in your ability to do."[47] Blücher instructed Sacken to double his attention on Torgau, reinforce his post at Dommitzsch, and "remain ready to fall on the enemy's throat" if he attempted to advance downstream along the left bank of the Elbe from Torgau toward Wartenburg. He also requested confirmation from Sacken regarding the report of Souham's march from Torgau toward Schildau.[48]

From 1:00 P.M. onward during 7 October, reports of imperial troop movements flooded Blücher's headquarters in rapid succession. Vasilchikov informed Blücher "that the enemy is moving from Belgern and Dahlen in great masses. All reports indicate that great enemy masses face our left flank." Sacken also detected large French camps on the left bank of the Mulde just west of Wurzen at Bennewitz. In addition, one of his patrols reported the arrival of large French forces at Schildau. Lastly, Sacken forwarded a message from the magistrate of Eilenburg stating that Marmont's VI Corps and Reynier's VII Corps – both of which had stood in and around Eilenburg – had retreated in the night. Where they had gone the Saxon civil official did not know, but French forces stood six miles west of Eilenburg at Liemehna on the road to Leipzig. Marshal Ney had likewise marched through Eilenburg to Wurzen. More importantly, the magistrate reported that Napoleon's baggage as well as Murat's had passed through Eilenburg during the night en route to Leipzig. Although quarters had been arranged for Napoleon at Eilenburg, they remained vacant. This led the magistrate to believe that Napoleon had passed the night at Eilenburg incognito. Finally, a second report from Vasilchikov written around 4:30 that afternoon stated that imperial forces occupied the villages of Langenreichenbach, Wildschütz, and Schöna. To the Russian general, the enemy appeared to be headed for Eilenburg to cover the advance from Torgau through Schildau to Wurzen. Locals confirmed the conclusions drawn by his patrols that the imperials planned to move considerable forces through Schildau to Wurzen, itself less than twenty miles up the Mulde from Blücher's headquarters at Bad Düben. Prisoners taken from the Torgau region confirmed the arrival and departure of Souham's III Corps but could not state where it had gone. Thus far, Vasilchikov's post at Mockrehna, halfway between Torgau and Eilenburg, had not been attacked. Thick forests shielded the imperials from roving Cossacks, which meant few prisoners were brought in for interrogation.[49]

Some of these reports had not yet reached Silesian Army Headquarters when Blücher and Prince William of Prussia commenced the eleven-mile ride west from Bad Düben to Mühlbeck for the rendezvous with Bernadotte, who had to travel fourteen miles east from Zehbitz. "General Blücher required an interpreter for this – a role that Gneisenau absolutely refused to play but to my great horror entrusted to me," recounted Müffling. Gneisenau declined to accompany Blücher, mainly because of his aversion to the native Frenchman. Of course, Gneisenau publicly stated that he could not distance himself from headquarters in the midst of such a tense situation. He drafted instructions for Müffling, which the latter terms "impracticable," concerning the proposals Blücher should present to the crown prince. Müffling claimed that Bernadotte, accompanied by Bülow and Carl Johan Adlerkreutz, met Blücher on his arrival that evening. Calling him *"mon cher frère d'armes* [my dear brother-in-arms]," Bernadotte embraced Blücher with the *bonhomie* of an old soldier.

While Müffling employed his French language skills to explain Gneisenau's proposals for the march on Leipzig, the crown prince sat "nodding all the time kindly" to Blücher. The Prussian expressed the need for an advance on Leipzig by both armies. By distracting and containing the emperor, they would facilitate Schwarzenberg's march through Saxony. Bernadotte countered that the most important service they could do for the Bohemian Army would be to entice Napoleon to the Mulde. "Then he began," continues Müffling, "and spoke at first with the finest phrases in the sense we desired; but he gradually deviated in essential parts so materially that our proposition was no longer at all the same. He concluded with the words: '*Ainsi nous sommes d'accord* [there, we agree].'"

Yet their two positions remained far apart. Blücher sought a battle to provide time for Schwarzenberg to advance. He believed they could strike the imperials before Napoleon could concentrate all his forces. Conversely, Bernadotte did not want a battle, either sooner or later. Although he attempted to give the impression that he did indeed seek a battle, his words betrayed him. Müffling pointed out the differences between their two positions but Bernadotte "contrived to gloss over all my arguments with the ease natural to a Frenchman, and always repeated, turning to the general, '*mais nous sommes d'accord* [but we agree].'" Mainly, the crown prince argued that a battle should be sought on the lower Mulde. In this way, they could entice imperial forces to march north from Dresden and Leipzig, thus opening the road to the latter for Schwarzenberg. Müffling countered that the exact opposite would occur. Instead of marching to confront the Silesian and North German Armies on the Mulde, Napoleon would concentrate the Grande Armée and pounce on Schwarzenberg south of Leipzig. From the lower Mulde, Blücher and Bernadotte would not be able to arrive in time to support Schwarzenberg.

With this last rebuttal, the crown prince changed tactics, assenting to all the movements the Prussians suggested. To claim that Bernadotte agreed with the Prussians is misleading. Blücher wanted a bold offensive and did not fear a battle with Napoleon. On the other hand, the crown prince wanted to position his army on the left bank of the Pleiße and the Elster to disrupt Napoleon's communications and avoid battle with him until Schwarzenberg arrived. For now, as both commanders believed Napoleon remained at Dresden, they assumed their armies could reach Leipzig before his. Thus, they agreed to begin the advance to Leipzig on the very next day, the 8th, to challenge only a small imperial force. As preparatory movements, Blücher agreed to push his forces southwest while the North German Army advanced on the road to Delitzsch, sending cavalry to Eilenburg to cover Blücher's left wing. Both armies would continue the march to Leipzig on 9 September. At the end of the meeting, Bernadotte turned to Blücher "with the greatest show of regard for his '*cher frère d'armes*.'" With a heartfelt hug, the crown prince took his leave. Climbing into the carriage, Müffling purportedly predicted to Blücher that the crown prince's excuses for not adhering to the agreement would arrive in the morning. Blücher thought Bernadotte expressed too much goodwill to mask such intentions but made no secret of how much he scorned "all such chaps who are only out for themselves."[50]

Despite the agreements made during their meeting, Bernadotte maintained his positions at Radegast and Jeßnitz on the 8th; only Tauentzien's IV Corps moved up from Dessau to Hinsdorf. From Hirschfeld's brigade, two battalions and six guns guarded the bridgehead at Roßlau, two battalions held the crossing over the Mulde at Dessau, while the rest – six battalions, two cavalry regiments, and two batteries – moved to Aken to secure the bridge against Lanusse's division. In addition, Bernadotte ordered Tauentzien's Kurmark Landwehr brigade commanded by General Friedrich Wilhelm von Putlitz to build a bridgehead on the right bank of the Elbe at Ferchland, thirty miles down the Elbe from Magdeburg, and to defend it to the extreme. Bernadotte's orders for 9 October – issued on the 8th – proved more promising. He instructed Bülow to slide southwest to Brehna, pushing his vanguard to Landsberg. Wintzingerode received orders to move his corps from Radegast to a position just southwest of Zörbig, with his van reaching Schkeuditz on the Elster, less than nine miles northwest of Leipzig. Vorontsov would lead one of Wintzingerode's divisions to Halle while Russian cavalry patrolled the Halle–Leipzig highway. Bernadotte directed his Swedes to Zörbig (see Map 5). Unfortunately for the Allied cause, the crown prince rescinded all of these orders at midnight on 8/9 October based on the intelligence he had received from Blücher.[51]

On returning to Bad Düben after his meeting with Bernadotte, Blücher assessed the new intelligence that had arrived during his absence. Korf reported that the imperials had driven off Yuzefovich's post between Klitzschen and Langenreichenbach. South of Langenreichenbach, a Russian patrol discovered a large column of enemy infantry marching from Torgau to Schildau. Finally, Yuzefovich's troopers had captured a captain from the staff of XI Corps. Although the dispatches he bore contained no information of use, he stated that the troops marching from Torgau to Schildau belonged to Souham's III Corps. Of greater importance, the captain claimed that up to this point Napoleon still had no news of the movements of the Silesian Army. In fact, on 5 October the emperor actually conducted extensive reconnaissance toward Stolpen in the hope of finding Langeron's corps.

Later interrogated at Blücher's headquarters, the prisoner stated that, when he had departed from Dresden on the 6th, Napoleon was still there but planned to make a great movement. To where the prisoner could not answer but his own corps commander, Macdonald, had received orders to go to Meißen. From Madatov at Mühlberg on the Elbe arrived news from the evening of the 6th concerning the march of a French army – infantry, cavalry, artillery, and baggage – from Dresden through Meißen and Strehla on the highway to Leipzig. More perplexing news arrived late on the 7th. After a detachment from Reynier's VII Corps unexpectedly evacuated Eilenburg on the 7th, the Russians moved in. However, the enemy returned in the evening, ejected the Russians, and reoccupied Eilenburg. Moreover, the French troops at Schildau who appeared to be headed southwest to Wurzen suddenly turned due west toward Eilenburg at sunset.[52]

Ultimately, these reports failed to clarify Napoleon's intentions. Obviously the Grande Armée would concentrate at Leipzig but what then? At this point, Blücher found no reason to renounce his drive across the Mulde and toward Leipzig. Gneisenau issued orders for the 8th "to seek the enemy in the region of Leipzig." With headquarters remaining at Bad Düben, Blücher directed Yorck's corps to Mühlbeck and his vanguard to Sausedlitz, nine miles west of Bad Düben. Langeron's corps would concentrate at Bad Düben, with his van proceeding five miles southwest of there to Brösen. Sacken's corps would move up to Mockrehna, pushing his vanguard ten miles further west to Eilenburg. Blücher wanted Sacken's engineers to quickly strike a bridge at Eilenburg suitable for artillery to cross. Two additional pontoon bridges would be thrown across the Mulde north and south of Bad Düben. One of Sacken's cavalry detachments would observe Torgau. Blücher sent a copy of the disposition for the 8th to the crown prince along with a cover letter. Admitting that his left flank was exposed, he requested that the Army of North Germany "conduct a great cavalry movement toward Eilenburg."[53]

Early on the 8th, the Silesian Army marched. Yorck's advance guard crossed the Mulde at Mühlbeck: the infantry on ferries, the cavalry forded the river. Its forward units rode far and wide; two of its squadrons joined Hellwig's *Streifkorps* from the Army of North Germany as well as Bülow's Cossacks in a clash with French cavalry four miles north of Leipzig at Wiederitzsch, driving the imperials into the city. Yorck's main body achieved its goal by reaching Mühlbeck. As for Blücher's Russians, Langeron's main body concentrated at Bad Düben on the right bank of the Mulde. From there, Rudzevich led the vanguard across the Mulde and southwest on the highway to Leipzig to Noitzsch, where he posted his infantry. The vanguard's cavalry continued to Krensitz, twelve miles northeast of Leipzig. His patrols observed a large imperial corps at Taucha. Sacken's vanguard could not move beyond Eilenburg on the 8th; his main body reached Mockrehna.

Katzler described Leipzig as being only weakly garrisoned and reported the sound of heavy artillery – ostensibly Schwarzenberg's – from the direction of Altenburg the day before. At noon, Sacken reported that the columns marching from Torgau through Schildau to Eilenburg on the previous day had turned around and were presently heading through Schildau toward Torgau. Prisoners claimed that the destruction of Eilenburg's bridge accounted for the retrograde march. Other reports indicated the concentration of large imperial forces at Wurzen. Of the troops that remained on the right bank of the Elbe, Major Falkenhausen's *Streifkorps* severed communication between Meißen and Dresden. Learning of the march of a French column between these two points, he commenced the hunt. His horsemen took many prisoners, horses, an empty supply train, and some boats. More importantly, his post opposite Meißen clearly recognized Napoleon, who struck the road to Leipzig preceded and followed by huge columns. His dispatch reporting Napoleon's appearance at Meißen reached Blücher at noon on the 8th.

One final report from Sacken, although confusing in itself, finally enabled Blücher and his staff to gain a clear picture of the situation. Writing from Mockrehna at 7:30 on the evening of the 8th, the Russian corps commander confirmed that the imperials had again occupied Eilenburg but "much infantry and two cannon" had moved east across the Mulde to occupy Eilenburg Ost. Thirteen miles due east of Eilenburg, French infantry and cavalry maintained their position at Schildau throughout the day, pushing outposts as far as Langenreichenbach, only five miles east of Sacken's position at Mockrehna. "Behind these forward posts, it appears that the enemy moves in force to Wurzen." Four miles north-northeast of Wurzen, the French occupied the village of Großzschepa. From the hills surrounding it, the Russians observed "great enemy columns" moving toward Wurzen on the Leipzig–Dresden highway and "infantry, cavalry, and artillery marching from Torgau to Schildau."[54]

Despite the confusing aspects of Sacken's brief, it became clear that Napoleon intended to concentrate huge masses at Wurzen, less than twenty miles south of Blücher's headquarters at Bad Düben. Moreover, it appeared that the Grande Armée would reach Leipzig before Schwarzenberg's arrival south of the city could impact Napoleon's operations. Regardless, some important questions still needed to be answered. Did Napoleon intend – just as Bernadotte warned – to launch an offensive against Blücher's left? Would the emperor first seek to gain Leipzig and then proceed either north against Bernadotte or south against Schwarzenberg? Or would he seek a decisive battle with Bernadotte and Blücher before turning against Schwarzenberg? Notwithstanding Napoleon's plans, if Blücher continued his advance on Leipzig, he risked an encounter with the emperor. Certainly the Prussian did not shirk from the thought of such a confrontation but the extenuating circumstances demanded prudence.

A major impediment to decisive action on Blücher's part remained the sobering realization that he had to defer the initiative to both Bernadotte and Napoleon and by extension Schwarzenberg. If the emperor turned against the Bohemian Army, then Blücher and Bernadotte had to follow and be in position to fall on his rear and flanks as soon as he engaged Schwarzenberg. As for Bernadotte, preexisting agreements with Blücher would dictate their responses to a French offensive. If Napoleon attacked the Silesian Army between the Mulde and the Elbe, Blücher would retreat to the entrenched camp at Wartenburg, sending the majority of his cavalry to unite with the Army of North Germany. Thus reinforced, Bernadotte would operate against Napoleon's flank and rear if he pursued Blücher to Wartenburg. On the other hand, if Napoleon commenced an offensive against Bernadotte between the Saale and the Elbe, the Army of North Germany would withdraw to the bridgehead at Roßlau while Blücher operated against the emperor's flank and rear.

Under the circumstances, an immediate retreat to Wartenburg, where work on the fortifications lagged behind schedule due to insufficient man-power, hardly appealed to Blücher. Occupying an incomplete entrenched camp, fighting with his back against the Elbe, and ceding his cavalry to Bernadotte, whom he did not trust, ran contrary to Blücher's nature. Yet he could not face Napoleon without Bernadotte's full support. Thus, the Silesian Army could remain in the theater only if the Army of North Germany held its ground. Blücher understood that he could not face Napoleon alone and that he needed the staunch support of at least Bülow's III Corps. This left him little choice but to unite his forces with Bernadotte's as quickly as possible. Only then would the combined Armies of Silesia and North Germany be strong enough to face the Grande Armée. Total agreement with Bernadotte over their next step remained paramount; Gneisenau dispatched Rühle to the crown prince's headquarters at Zehbitz on the afternoon of the 8th. He tasked the major with gaining the crown prince's assurance that the Army of North Germany would assume the role of the *Angriffsflügel* (attacking wing) in a battle at Wartenburg. To honor protocol, Gneisenau instructed the major to ask Bernadotte for his suggestion on the proper manner to proceed but to clearly state and insist on the views of Silesian Army Headquarters.[55]

Rühle reached Zehbitz late on the evening of the 8th. Although already in bed, Bernadotte received the Prussian major, who informed him of Napoleon's possible approach. According to Rühle's recollection of their conversation, the crown prince appeared more determined than before to avoid a battle with Napoleon. Bernadotte informed him that he, too, no longer planned to adhere to the original plan he had communicated to Blücher. Instead of withdrawing to the bridgehead at Roßlau to evade Napoleon's blow, the prince royal preferred to escape across the Elbe at Aken.

He spoke of the need to provide time for Schwarzenberg to advance by fixing Napoleon but insisted on retreating to the right bank of the Elbe, destroying the bridge behind him, and awaiting further developments. Bernadotte suggested that Blücher should likewise retreat across the Elbe. Rühle claimed to know for certain that Blücher would not withdraw to the right bank of the Elbe. Instead, he claimed that the Prussian commander preferred to move across the Saale, where he could operate against Napoleon's communications and cooperate with Schwarzenberg. Upon hearing this answer, the surprised crown prince asked how Rühle knew that Blücher would cross the Saale. "Based on the character of his general, he would certainly escape across the Saale," responded the Prussian major. This response further surprised Bernadotte but he accepted the idea and proposed that both armies cross the Saale. "Good ... if Napoleon follows, we will cross the Elbe at Ferchland," determined the crown prince. Rühle repeated his opinion that under no circumstance would Blücher cross the Elbe. Instead, he would march up the Saale and unite with the Bohemian Army. Bernadotte countered that such a movement violated all of the rules of war because Blücher would completely sacrifice his communications and cut off the army from its ammunition transports, supply convoys, and reinforcements. "And what shall become of Berlin," he purportedly asked. "As Moscow was burned, we can also sacrifice Berlin," answered Rühle. Bernadotte gradually became receptive to the idea of retreating across the Saale and uniting with the Bohemian Army. His conditional acceptance required Blücher to position the Silesian Army south of his own to cross the Saale at Wettin, where the crown prince promised to strike a bridge. He also conceded to Rühle's request for an officer to return with him to Bad Düben with a written confirmation of these negotiations. In Rühle's presence he dictated the following letter, which Count Alexis Noailles delivered to Blücher:

> Major Rühle has delivered your letter and informed me of the emperor Napoleon's march on Meißen and of his apparent intentions against your left flank. Because we have no other purpose than to fix the forces of this commander to provide the Bohemian Army with time to advance against his rear and flanks, I thus believe that you should not rush [forward], especially because a further advance on Leipzig will offer the emperor Napoleon the opportunity to move between you and your bridges. If the emperor Napoleon shows the intention to attack us from the side and from the front, I believe we must either withdraw to the right bank of the Elbe or cross to the left bank of the Saale. In the latter case, your bridges must be quickly dismantled and struck along with the one that I had built at Ferchland. For my part, I will dismantle the one at Roßlau, burning it if necessary, and leave only ten battalions at Aken to hold this point and guard the bridge. We will then be in a position to choose whether we want to cross the Saale or turn to cross the Elbe at Ferchland. In both cases, Napoleon will lose time. Once

more I say that this is necessary for the success of the Bohemian Army. As soon as a movement against you is recognized, not a moment can be lost in either withdrawing upon the right bank [of the Elbe] or to assume the line of the Saale.[56]

By convincing Bernadotte to remain on the left bank of the Elbe, Rühle achieved his purpose. Still, he failed to attain the crown prince's complete agreement with Blücher's plans. The Prussians regarded a movement across the Saale as a means by which to seek the union with the Bohemian Army, while Bernadotte viewed such a crossing as the prelude to a further retreat across the Elbe at Ferchland to preserve his communications.[57]

As noted, Bernadotte intended for the Army of North Germany to move closer to Leipzig on the 9th but canceled his orders at midnight on 8/9 October as a result of the information delivered by Rühle. He explained to his corps commanders that a report from Blücher stated that two imperial corps had reached Leipzig. Moreover, Blücher informed him of Napoleon's march down the Elbe with his Guard. "General Blücher has just indicated to me that the emperor Napoleon has made a reconnaissance in front of Eilenburg toward Bad Düben with a corps of 10,000 cavalry," Bernadotte wrote to Bülow. "As all of this announces the plan for an attack on General Blücher, I have advised him to cross to the left bank of the Mulde, and move between Jeßnitz, Zörbig, and Bitterfeld. If he can make that movement before being attacked, we will be in a retracted position with more than 110,000 men, and thenceforth we can have a nice affair." Until further news arrived, the crown prince did not want the orders for 9 October executed: "Thus, nobody will move until further notice and each army corps will maintain the position that it occupies at this moment."[58] On Bernadotte's extreme right, a cavalry detachment from Wintzingerode's corps occupied the Saale crossing at Bernburg on the 9th but failed to prevent Lanusse's troops from destroying the bridge four miles downstream at Nienburg. Thus, the Army of North Germany did little on either 8 or 9 October.

Rühle returned to Bad Düben on the morning of the 9th. Although recognizing he would be forced to sacrifice all rearward communications, Blücher consented to the retreat across the Saale. Emphasizing that this plan bore the stamp of the unorthodox, Gneisenau expressed his support. While the Silesian Army turned toward Napoleon's communications, it would expose its own to the enemy. "This was a very unique movement," explains Müffling, "through which the connection with the Army of Bohemia would be established on the most exposed point of the enemy's rear. Although by this movement the Silesian Army lost its line of communication, it was of the utmost importance to remove every reason that might induce the crown prince to retreat across the Elbe." As it turned out, the Silesian Army would not see its baggage, which remained on the other bank of the Elbe, until the trains caught up with it at the Rhine in mid November. Moreover, this movement would open the road to Berlin. Regardless, Blücher planned to move into the fertile region between the Saale and the Harz Mountains to spin a web around the enemy and establish communication with the Bohemian Army. "Convinced that at this moment," responded Blücher to the letter delivered by Count Noailles, "a movement to the right [west] in order to get us to the left bank of the Saale is preferable to any other, I will immediately order my army to march in this direction. My right column, namely Yorck's corps, will reach Jeßnitz this evening ... I will leave only a few companies in the entrenchments at Wartenburg. Demonstrations against Leipzig appear necessary to mask our movements. Thus, I will attack Eilenburg today."[59]

Returning to Napoleon, he did not pay heed to Blücher until 1 October. In a letter to Macdonald, the emperor called attention to Sacken rather than the entire Silesian Army, the bulk of which he placed between Stolpen and Bautzen. "General Sacken has moved vis-à-vis Meißen. He attacked the bridgehead [the day before] yesterday." Napoleon initially thought of marching from Dresden with 30,000 to 40,000 men but preferred to hold firm at the Saxon capital in anticipation of Schwarzenberg's advance: "All information confirms that the enemy has made a movement on Marienberg on the road from Komotau." His letter to Macdonald suggested that Napoleon viewed Sacken's movement as a demonstration: "No doubt the enemy does not consider attacking at this moment, yet the time may come when it suits him." Consequently, he left III Corps to contend with Sacken, and XI Corps to guard the roads from Meißen and Großenhain, with one division of II Cavalry Corps patrolling the plain between the two routes.[60]

On 2 October, Napoleon and Berthier ordered the reorganization of III, V, VII, XI, and XIV Corps so that all of the battalions of each regiment served in the same corps. The most notable changes occurred in XIV Corps, which sent ten battalions to III Corps, two to XI Corps, and one to VII Corps while receiving nine from III Corps, two from XI Corps, and one from V Corps.[61] All transfers took place on the 3rd, providing Allied spies much confusing information to report. It was on 2 October that Napoleon finally became aware of Blücher's disappearance: "It appears that the corps of Langeron, Sacken, and Blücher have all moved on Elsterwerda and Großenhain," he wrote Macdonald. Regarding the reason behind Blücher's movement, the emperor speculated that Dresden could be the target: "It is possible that this is to attack the entrenched camp on the side of the plain by way of the roads from Berlin and Meißen. Because they would thus avoid the forest, this is the point most assailable."[62]

By the end of the day, his attention switched back to Schwarzenberg thanks to Poniatowski's report that one regiment each of Allied infantry and cavalry had occupied Chemnitz on 1 October; the size of this purported force eventually grew to 20,000 men. Moreover, confirmed reports arrived that Matvei Platov, ataman of the Don Cossacks, had reached Altenburg with his warriors. Consequently, at 11:00 P.M. on the 2nd, Napoleon issued orders for Murat to go to Freiberg, halfway between Dresden and Chemnitz, that same night. There, the king of Naples would take command of II, V, and VIII Corps and IV and V Cavalry Corps as well as 1st Heavy Cavalry Division of I Cavalry Corps. "It appears to the emperor that Your Majesty's presence at Freiberg is needed to coordinate the movements of these various corps and to keep His Majesty informed of what is happening at Chemnitz," instructed Berthier. "Everything indicates that the enemy is moving and His Majesty thinks that we must know positively what the enemy is doing at Chemnitz."[63]

By 4:30 on the morning of the 3rd, Napoleon had received enough information to dispel the rumors of 20,000 Allied soldiers reaching Altenburg. Moreover, he referred to rumors of Bavaria's defection as unfounded. "The emperor tasked me with telling you that all rumors are false," Berthier explained to Ney, "that Bavaria has not changed its alliance; that the enemy has not yet debouched on the side of Chemnitz; that near Kassel [capital of Westphalia] he has only partisans; that in general, the enemy is spreading all kinds of rumors against which we must be on our guard, but it appears that the enemy is moving, and we are waiting on this movement to decide to act."[64]

Regardless of the emperor's attempts to control the bleeding, most of the rumors proved true. On 2 October, Schwarzenberg's lead units crossed the Erzgebirge to commence the offensive on Leipzig. By 3 October 70,000 Allied soldiers held a 33-mile line north of the Erzgebirge stretching from Eibenstock through Annaberg-Buchholz to Marienberg while another 80,000 men stood south of the mountains from Karlsbad (Karlovy Vary) to Komotau (see Map 4). Further northeast, the 50,000 men of Bennigsen's Army of Poland held Teplitz and Außig. On 4 October, the vanguard of Schwarzenberg's II Corps reached Chemnitz but could not hold it against Lauriston's V Corps. However, Lauriston withdrew thirteen miles north to Mittweida after being menaced by Platov's Cossack corps, the purported 20,000 men at Altenburg.

Also on 4 October, Napoleon received information from spies confirming the departure of the Silesian Army from the Bautzen area in the direction of Elsterwerda. To obtain news, he ordered Macdonald to reconnoiter all major roads. In addition, he ordered Souham to transfer his headquarters and one division of III Corps to Meißen. To guard the Elbe against Blücher, Napoleon instructed him to post one division each at Riesa and Strehla, seventeen and twenty-one miles downstream of Meißen respectively. The emperor demanded that Souham's troops "subject themselves to good discipline, monitor the banks of the Elbe, and camp in the countryside."[65]

Owing to Schwarzenberg's advance toward Chemnitz, Napoleon concluded that Blücher would either make for Dresden or drive on Leipzig. Belated reports from the commander of 3rd Light Division of I Cavalry Corps, General Louis-Pierre Chastel, concerning Blücher's activity at Meißen and Mühlberg unsettled the emperor but reinforced his presumption that the Prussian would attempt to pass the Elbe between the former and Torgau. Intelligence seemed to support this assumption. In his report of 3 October, Ney attributed the Allied activity at Elster and Wartenburg to Bülow's III Corps rather than the Army of Silesia.[66] During the course of 3 October, Napoleon clarified and emphasized his instructions for Souham to send a strong advance guard to obtain news of Blücher's army, particularly Sacken, whose vanguard had purportedly cleared Ockrilla and Meißen on 28 September. "Has he retired on Großenhain and Elsterwerda, or has he retired on the road from Torgau? One of your divisions must be at Strehla, and the other at Riesa. It is necessary, general, that the division at Strehla monitors the enemy's movements; if he attempts to throw a bridge between Strehla and Torgau, you will move quickly to prevent it."[67]

At 4:00 A.M. on 4 October, Napoleon sent his aide-de-camp, Lebrun, to Meißen to find Souham. After meeting with the corps commander, Napoleon wanted Lebrun to ride through Strehla and Riesa to Mühlberg, thirteen miles downstream from the latter. If he found that the enemy had indeed built a bridge there, then 3rd Light Cavalry Division, the two divisions of III Corps at Strehla and Riesa, and General François Bony's 2nd Brigade from Souham's 8th Division at Meißen – all supported by III Corps's Reserve Artillery – would "march on this point to drive the enemy to the opposite bank and destroy the bridge. If the enemy is in great force, you will write to the duc de Raguse [Marmont] at Leipzig, who has specific orders not to allow the enemy to establish a passage of the Elbe." Again the emperor's emphasis on the incessant exchange of accurate, verified information is conspicuous: "As soon as you arrive at Meißen and Strehla, you will write me all the news that you and General Souham have learned. Confirm with your own eyes that the enemy has thrown a bridge at Mühlberg; I don't think he has."

From Mühlberg, Lebrun would continue fifteen miles further downriver to Torgau "to see how things are going there. Write to me from Torgau. From Torgau, you will take the road through Wartenburg to Dessau to see how the river is guarded. You will be certain to write me from Wartenburg and Dessau. You will return via the same route along the river." Lebrun also delivered the emperor's letter to Souham, instructing the corps commander to prevent Blücher from crossing the Elbe between Torgau and Riesa, and reiterating the instructions for the operation at Mühlberg. That such detailed instructions were issued not only to a general, but to one of Napoleon's aides who had served him since 1800, underscores the emperor's ubiquitous demand for intelligence. "I am waiting for news all the time," he vented to Marmont. "Yesterday, we took 200 or 300 prisoners ... between Chemnitz and Freiberg. You send me officers who are children who know nothing and cannot provide me with any information verbally: send me men."[68]

Becoming more inclined to believe the rumors of Blücher's presence at Mühlberg, Napoleon issued instructions for Marmont to handle the affair. If the marshal learned that the enemy had indeed thrown a bridge at Mühlberg, he would immediately march from Leipzig with his entire corps and destroy it. Souham would support with his heavy artillery as well as 9th and 11th Divisions. Describing this operation as "very urgent," Berthier conveyed the master's desire to see the Allies driven across the Elbe and their bridge destroyed if one existed. Later in the day, Napoleon explained to Macdonald that "intelligence claims the enemy has a camp, probably Sacken's corps, at the village of Lindenau, about halfway from Meißen to Dresden ... Try to confirm this through reconnaissance." Still that same day, 4 October, he again wrote Macdonald with a hint of desperation: "I attach great import-ance to knowing exactly what became of Langeron, Sacken, and Yorck. Therefore, tomorrow, I want you to reconnoiter with 7,000 to 8,000 infan-try, cavalry and artillery toward Großenhain (Sacken was there); you will send patrols in other directions so that you know positively what has become of the enemy army from Silesia." Napoleon's anxiety is echoed in Berthier's 4:00 P.M. order to Souham to transfer the division at Strehla twelve miles downriver to Belgern, and replace it with the division at Riesa: "The emperor also commands, general, that tomorrow you conduct a strong reconnaissance on Großenhain to see clearly what infantry you have before you and to try to find out positively what has become of Sacken and what is happening on this side."[69]

Napoleon knew of the Allied bridge work at Wartenburg but still attrib-uted it to the Prussians of Bernadotte's army. To put an end to the nuisance caused by his former marshal, he authorized Marmont to assemble VI Corps and I Cavalry Corps at Bad Düben on the Mulde and "march against the enemy. Eliminate his bridges at Wartenburg, Dessau, and Aken; then he will have none." Napoleon urged Marmont to communicate to Ney the import-ance of destroying all the enemy's bridges. From Eilenburg on the 4th, Marmont wrote to the emperor at 11:00 A.M. of Bertrand's engagement at Wartenburg but could provide little information. His cursory report reached Imperial Headquarters at Dresden sometime before 3:00 A.M. on the 5th and long before the more detailed accounts provided by Ney and Bertrand. This caused the emperor to snap on 5 October: "I have heard about General Bertrand's affair only through your letter from yesterday. I wish you had provided a few details; give me all you have."

Although uncertain about who had attacked Bertrand, Napoleon's response to Marmont suggests that he did not think the Silesian Army had crossed the Elbe at Wartenburg. "It is of the highest importance that you restore the bridge at Bad Düben and that you march quickly to destroy the enemy's bridge. Your union with the prince de la Moskova [Ney] and Dąbrowski is also of utmost importance. I have ordered the duc de Castiglione [Augereau] to cover Leipzig with his corps. It is urgent that we drive the enemy across the river before he receives reinforcements." To unify command on the Mulde–Elbe front, Napoleon instructed Berthier early on 5 October to place III Corps, en route to Torgau that morning, under Marmont's command, which currently consisted of VI Corps and I Cavalry Corps. In the same letter to Berthier, he formally added all of Marmont's command to Ney's army, which consisted of IV and VII Corps and III Cavalry Corps as well as Dąbrowski's 27th Division. Napoleon then instructed Berthier to write Marmont and "alert him that, as the Marshal Prince de la Moskova is more senior, he and his army are under the command of that prince; it is necessary for them to immediately unite and quickly maneuver to drive the enemy across the river."[70]

Still suspecting Blücher to be in the Meißen–Mühlbeck region, Napoleon prepared to go to the former. He cut orders for Oudinot, now commanding a Young Guard corps of two divisions, to move one of them as well as his headquarters to Meißen along the left bank of the Elbe early on the 5th. To secure his rear, Napoleon emphasized to Murat the importance of holding Chemnitz. With II Corps in a good position between Chemnitz and Zschopau, and VIII Corps at Penig, the emperor assured Murat that he would master all of the enemy's communication. He mentioned sending Mortier to Freiberg but did not specify the number of Guard units that would accompany him. With Schwarzenberg's forward troops already at Schellenberg, ten miles east of Chemnitz, Napoleon stressed that "it is especially important to force the enemy to evacuate Schellenberg and retreat to his camp at Marienberg."[71]

Sometime before 3:00 A.M. on the 6th, the news arrived that Napoleon had been waiting for: the entire Silesian Army stood in the region of Wittenberg. Reports from Ney, Bertrand, and Lebrun allowed Napoleon to construct the events that had occurred between the Mulde and the Elbe. "At night, the vanguard of the Silesian Army threw a bridge across the Elbe at Wartenburg. Bertrand held the isthmus, behind the dikes and marshes. He fought for twelve hours; seven times the enemy assaulted but failed to dislodge him. Seeing this army grow stronger every moment, Bertrand retired in the night. Last night, the 5th, the prince de la Moskova, Bertrand, and Dąbrowski were at Raguhn, Bitterfeld, and Bad Düben, guarding the Mulde." He placed Marmont's VI Corps at Eilenburg, occupying the bridgehead and holding Wurzen. Napoleon calculated on all of III Corps reaching Torgau on this day, the 6th, with the Guard, XI Corps and II Cavalry Corps following.[72]

Napoleon saw an opportunity. Apparently, Blücher and Bernadotte would unite to drive on Leipzig from the north while Schwarzenberg rumbled toward the city from the south. The advance of the Allies in two large masses from opposite directions completely changed the situation by bringing the decisive battle within his reach. Although he had been on the verge of being strategically enveloped, the situation actually improved drastically for Napoleon. Facing two enemy armies instead of three meant he could focus his attention on just two directions, enhancing his personal command and control of his forces. His adversaries entered a region where he could fully exploit his central position and interior lines. They had ventured into the heart of his lair, where they would be unable to easily avoid his blows. Although Großbeeren, the Katzbach, Kulm, and Dennewitz had broken the confidence of his best subordinates and left gaping holes in his ranks, one decisive victory would wipe away the memory of those setbacks. He could wage the decisive battle that he had long sought but which the Allies had always evaded with great skill. Yet the key to victory in Germany became clear: he had to prevent the union of all Coalition forces. Should Blücher, Bernadotte, Schwarzenberg, and Bennigsen unite their forces, they would possess overwhelming numerical superiority. Thus, the emperor had to defeat the enemy armies individually and before they could unite.

For the Allies, a drive on Leipzig likewise offered the opportunity to end the war in Germany. From the start of the Fall Campaign, both the Trachenberg Protocol and the Reichenbach Plan identified Leipzig as the natural midpoint of the theater of war. Seven weeks after commencing hostilities, all Allied forces finally made the Saxon city the objective of their movements. This left Napoleon three unfavorable options. First, he could unite his army at Leipzig and accept battle in a well-prepared, defensive position. There, he would be forced to surrender the initiative and accept being strategically enveloped. Moreover, he would risk being tactically enveloped on the battlefield and surrounded. Facing such a numerical superiority, he would expose his army to a decisive defeat. Second, he could fall back on his line of communication and withdraw west of the Saale. With the resources of Germany slipping through his hands, he had to make a stand in Saxony. A retreat west would lead to the total collapse of the Confederation of the Rhine. In fact, despite Napoleon's insistence to the contrary, secret negotiations ensued between the Austrians and King Max Joseph I of Bavaria. On 8 October, the king signed his name to the Convention of Ried: Bavaria entered the War of the Sixth Coalition as Austria's ally. As a third option, Napoleon could mask one of his adversaries to provide time for him to seek and destroy the other Allied army. This option promised the most success because it aimed to exploit the concentration of Allied forces in two major masses. Equally important, it corresponded perfectly with the advantages offered by Napoleon's central position and interior lines. Manpower remained the only question: did the emperor still possess enough combat power to form two armies that could execute these tasks? Although his estimates notoriously exaggerated the size of imperial forces, in early October the Grande Armée still remained a formidable fighting force. Including Augereau's approaching reinforcements, the legions of the French Empire numbered more than 270,000 men and 851 guns.[73]

With these numbers, Napoleon could assemble an army of 180,000 men in three days to confront Schwarzenberg's 185,000. With the smaller army of 90,000 men, Ney would receive the task of masking Bernadotte and Blücher. Although outnumbered, Ney's forces would suffice to check their advance. On the other hand, should the emperor decide to direct his first blow against Bernadotte and Blücher, he could unite 200,000 men at Bad Düben in four days. This would leave 70,000 combatants to hold the ninety-mile Leipzig–Altenburg–Freiburg line against Schwarzenberg. Typical of Napoleon's operations, timing decided where he would direct his first blow. The Silesian and North German Armies stood within three marches of Leipzig while the bulk of the Bohemian Army had only commenced its movement across the Erzgebirge. As long as his tired soldiers rallied to his call, the furious pace of Napoleon's operations would allow him to confront Blücher and Bernadotte at the same time that Schwarzenberg's columns cleared the Erzgebirge and regrouped on the Saxon plain. Furthermore, the Bohemian Army could easily elude his attack by again escaping across the Erzgebirge and retreating behind the Eger. For Bernadotte and especially Blücher, such an escape would not be easy, with the Elbe at their backs and imperial garrisons holding Magdeburg, Wittenberg, and Torgau. With Blücher having the sole bridge at Wartenburg and Bernadotte the bridges at Aken and Roßlau, Napoleon could expect decisive results if he drove them against the Elbe. Based on such obvious advantages, the emperor decided to first turn against the Silesian and North German Armies while masking Schwarzenberg. After crushing Blücher and Bernadotte against the Elbe, he then planned to concentrate all his forces to destroy the Bohemian Army. A lesser commander would have collapsed under the weight of the approaching enemy masses but not Napoleon. This very simple plan evolved not from his genius but from his boldness and *sangfroid*. By crossing the Elbe, the Allies had crossed their Rubicon: they could only retrace their steps in defeat. They finally exposed themselves and offered the master a target he could hit. His plan should have worked. That it failed can be attributed to Blücher alone.

At 3:00 A.M. on 6 October, Napoleon instructed XI Corps to march along the right bank of the Elbe to Meißen, where it would cross to the left bank. At 7:30 A.M., Berthier reiterated the order for Macdonald to immediately place XI Corps on the road to Meißen joined by II Cavalry Corps, which again passed under the marshal's authority. The master demanded reports from Sébastiani's troopers: "Send scouts in the direction of Torgau and Wurzen for news of General Souham and the duc de Raguse [Marmont]. I'll be at Meißen early tonight. Your scouts will interrogate everyone they encounter and you will communicate to me all the news you obtain." Oudinot moved his young bearskins one league northwest of Meißen to the junction of the roads coming from Wurzen and Torgau. Orders went to Augereau to accelerate the march of IX Corps to Leipzig. On the plain south of Leipzig, Murat received instructions to mask Schwarzenberg's slow-moving army. "The passage of the enemy on the lower Elbe should in no way impact your operation," Napoleon explained to his brother-in-law.[74]

Throughout the 6th, not only did XI Corps and II Cavalry Corps march from Dresden to Meißen in two columns along both banks of the Elbe, but the army's Reserve Artillery and Park, the engineers and bridge train, and the ambulances and surgeons all followed. To conceal their departure, Macdonald fiercely attacked Bubna's Austrian 2nd Light Division at Stolpen with one brigade supported by cavalry. After considerable losses on both sides, the marshal broke off the engagement to proceed to Meißen.[75] Napoleon communicated his intentions to Marmont:

> I will reach Meißen this evening with 80,000 men; my vanguard will be at the intersection of the roads to Leipzig and Torgau. There, I will receive your report, from which I will decide which of the two roads I take. I intend to turn on Torgau and from there to advance on the right bank [of the Elbe] to cut off the enemy and to take all of his bridges without having to attack his bridgeheads. An advance on the left bank has the disadvantage of allowing the enemy to withdraw across the river and avoid a battle. In this case, we could certainly debouch through Wittenberg. Because the enemy has the initiative of movement, I will only be able to decide this evening when I know the situation.[76]

As for Dresden, St.-Cyr recommended an evacuation of the Saxon capital due to the region's exhaustion, which made the task of feeding man and horse in the city as well as the surrounding countryside increasingly difficult. Allied partisan activity had rendered the transportation of food supplies on the Elbe almost impossible. With Dresden's magazines empty, French agents descended on the poor inhabitants with requisitions that could not be filled. The hungry soldiers resorted to foraging, which soon degenerated into pillaging. Napoleon's instructions to St.-Cyr and Count Pierre-Antoine Daru, director of the Department of the Administration of the Army, suggest that Napoleon finally gave serious consideration to abandoning the city. He ordered St.-Cyr to post one division of I Corps as well as corps headquarters at Pirna while St.-Cyr transferred his headquarters to Dresden's southwest suburb, less than ten miles downstream the Elbe from Pirna.

Two divisions of XIV Corps would occupy Dresden and part of St.-Cyr's cavalry would guard the left bank of the Elbe from Dresden to Pirna. Engineers dismantled the pontoon and boat bridges at Pirna and Pillnitz.[77]

Daru received instructions to embark 1,500 sick and wounded from Dresden's hospitals on ten boats to be sailed to Torgau. As many as possible of the remaining patients, preferably officers and noncommissioned officers, would be evacuated by road through Nossen to Erfurt. Without drawing too much attention to his task, the emperor wanted Daru to find as many sick officers or generals as possible who had their own transportation and urge them to likewise go to Erfurt. Later in the day, Napoleon increased the number of sick to be evacuated to 6,000 on 40 boats. "Six thousand patients, 200 to 300 wagons, 30,000 to 40,000 artillery rounds were embarked at Dresden and will arrive at Torgau," Napoleon notified the commandant of Torgau, Narbonne. "This is an additional burden. Arrange it as best you can. I signed the order to send 300,000 to 400,000 francs to the paymaster of Torgau. From Wittenberg, I will send you powder and flour. From Leipzig, Count Daru will send to Torgau 10,000 hundredweights of flour. This should rectify everything. The wounded and sick will recover. You have clothing and supplies." A convoy of seventy boats, including those laden with wounded, would sail down the Elbe on the 7th bound for Torgau.[78]

Napoleon assessed the situation that confronted him at 1:00 A.M. on the night of 6/7 October. In an interesting document titled "Notes sur les mouvements des différents corps d'armée," the emperor drafted a plan to both evacuate Dresden and concentrate the Grande Armée at Wurzen. The document appears to have been generated as a reaction to Murat's report from 4:00 P.M. on the 6th. After failing to attack the vanguard of Schwarzenberg's army at Chemnitz that day, Murat expressed concern about the Bohemian Army's advance. According to his "Notes," Napoleon planned for "a great march toward Wurzen" on the 7th to unite with Ney's army. With II Cavalry Corps, the Guard Cavalry, and Oudinot's Guard corps, he calculated on coming within twelve miles of Wurzen on the 7th and then reaching Leipzig on the 8th "if it becomes absolutely necessary." By combining XI Corps, II Cavalry Corps, and the Guard with Ney's army, Napoleon calculated on having more than 160,000 men to crush Blücher and Bernadotte as they marched on Leipzig. After defeating and driving them across the Elbe, the master would return to Leipzig, unite with Murat, and attack the Bohemian Army (see Map 5).

Regarding Murat's situation along the southern front, Napoleon believed V and II Corps could unite with VIII Corps some twenty-four miles south of Leipzig at Frohburg on the 8th to contain the head of Schwarzenberg's army. As for St.-Cyr, he would withdraw I and XIV Corps to Dresden on the 7th and evacuate the city that same day. The emperor wanted him at Meißen on the 8th, from where he would lead I and XIV Corps to Wurzen.

If necessary, he should be ready to evacuate Dresden in the night of 8/9 October "after destroying the blockhouses, burning the artillery carriages, spiking the fortress guns, and destroying all ammunition and equipment that otherwise must be left behind. Only 5,000–6,000 sick that are too weak to transport can be left behind." "By the result of this movement," he concluded, "I shall be master to do what I want: from Wurzen I can move on Torgau and on the enemy debouching from Wittenberg, or move my whole army on Leipzig and have a general battle, or recross the Saale. On the 8th, the army under my personal command will be at Wurzen. On the 10th, the corps of Marshal St.-Cyr will be at Wurzen."[79]

Satisfied with this plan, Napoleon issued the necessary directives to Berthier. He then impressed on Murat that the king's "main goal must be to delay the enemy's march on Leipzig [and] not allow himself to be cut off from the Mulde, so that we can approach Leipzig at the same time, keeping the enemy away, or, if necessary, delivering a general battle." If the Allies managed to move between Murat and the Mulde, Napoleon would lose not only Leipzig, but also the advantages of mutual support, interior lines, and central position. Two hours later, at 3:00 A.M., the emperor issued orders for 1st and 2nd Divisions of Old Guard to commence the march to Meißen that morning at 5:00 and 6:00 respectively; Imperial Headquarters would follow at 10:00. He also cut orders for Oudinot's Young Guard corps and Bony's 2nd Brigade of III Corps's 8th Division to commence the forty-mile march northwest from Meißen to Wurzen on the Mulde at 6:00 A.M. followed by II Cavalry Corps, XI Corps, and the Old Guard Cavalry, as well as the artillery and engineer parks. Napoleon placed the brigade of III Corps that remained at Meißen under Oudinot's temporary command and it likewise departed with the Young Guard. He also ordered that the king and queen of Saxony be escorted to Meißen by Saxon and Polish troops. "They do not want to stay in Dresden during my absence," he explained. "The other princes of the family can remain."[80]

Indicative of the emperor's superior system of disseminating information to his subordinates, he again wrote Marmont at 4:00 A.M. on the 7th: "Based on the direction you have given to III Corps, in summoning it to the Mulde, I have given orders . . . for a forced march on Wurzen today, so that we can be at Leipzig tomorrow during the day if it becomes absolutely necessary. I myself will be at Wurzen tonight." In his last dispatch from the Saxon capital, Napoleon informed Murat of his imminent departure for Meißen. "The whole army from Silesia debouched through Wartenburg," he wrote, "and there is nobody from Dresden to Görlitz, or Dresden to Berlin. St.-Cyr remains at Dresden. Hold back the Austrians as much as possible so I can defeat Blücher and the Swedes before their union with Schwarzenberg's army."[81]

Departing Dresden around 6:00 A.M. on 7 October, Napoleon had much to contemplate as he rode to Meißen. His confidence about the prospects of defeating Blücher and Bernadotte must have increased during the four-hour ride. This optimism induced the emperor to change his mind about evacuating Dresden. The arrival of Ney's report written from Bennewitz on the evening of the 6th explaining that Blücher had stopped his drive on Leipzig and appeared to be holding the right bank of the Mulde, presumably to cover the siege of Wittenberg, considerably influenced Napoleon.[82] He wrote to St.-Cyr around 1:00 P.M. after arriving at Meißen:

> I have ordered the flour transports to continue on their way to Dresden. I hope to draw the enemy into a battle. Defend all of your positions south of Pirna throughout the 8th. My plan will be complete tomorrow and if I maneuver the enemy into a battle, my intention is to hold Dresden; all the more so because I will operate through Torgau and because my communications will be secure on both banks [of the Elbe]. Bake bread; work on an entrenched camp, and evacuate as many wounded as possible. Reassure the city, tell everyone you will not evacuate Dresden; that you have 50,000 men to defend it, and that you are certain you can be quickly rescued if necessary. Grand Headquarters is now at Meißen. I will transfer mine to Oschatz. From there, I will probably go to Torgau.[83]

This decision ultimately cost Napoleon the manpower of I and XIV Corps at the battle of Leipzig and provides a glaring example of Emperor Napoleon's political needs superseding General Bonaparte's military judgment.

Leaving Meißen on the afternoon of 7 October, Napoleon rode another fourteen miles northwest to the Schloß at Seerhausen. After issuing instructions for the 8th, he continued seven additional miles northwest to Oschatz, where he passed the night with his *petit quartier-général* (little headquarters). To feed the soldiers, imperial authorities forced the local villages to provide 100,000 rations of bread. All detachments from I and III Cavalry Corps along the Elbe between Meißen and Torgau received orders to assemble at the latter under Chastel's command. According to Napoleon's instructions, Oudinot's young bearskins would commence the thirty-mile march from Meißen to Dahlen at 6:00 on the following morning. From Dahlen, the army would have only a twelve-mile march due west to Wurzen. Napoleon expected Augereau's IX Corps to reach Leipzig on the 8th and to be ready to participate in the offensive by the 9th. Following to Seerhausen with Grand Headquarters and the king of Saxony in tow, Berthier disclosed to Ney the emperor's intentions. On reaching Dahlen on the 8th, Napoleon expected to find a report from Ney concerning the enemy. If he did not receive news from the marshal, he would continue to Wurzen. "His Majesty intends to immediately push the enemy against

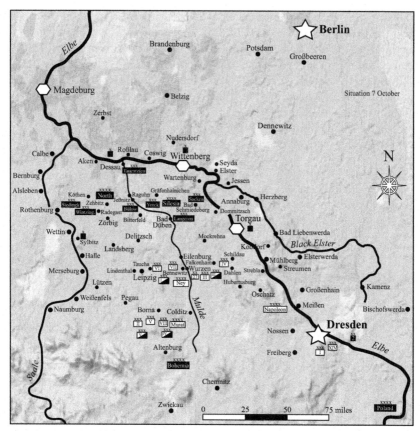

23 Situation, 8 October 1813

Wittenberg and drive him across the river to the right bank and to eliminate all of his bridges; it appears necessary that you unite all your forces." Moreover, "His Majesty hopes to receive tomorrow at Dahlen details concerning the enemy's situation as well as the positions of VI and III Corps and I Cavalry Corps."

Marmont's complaint about Ney seems to have had little impact on the emperor. In fact, not only is Berthier's annoyance with Marmont for failing to report his position obvious, but Imperial Headquarters also blamed the junior marshal for Ney's erratic orders. "His Majesty is surprised to see that after ordering this corps to Eilenburg, the duc de Raguse destroyed the bridge there, retired to Leipzig, and particularly compromised this corps; secure it as soon as possible." To Marmont, Berthier wrote: "The emperor learned with astonishment that after you ordered III Corps to move from Torgau to Eilenburg, an order that General Souham has executed ... you departed from Eilenburg after destroying the bridge that His Majesty ordered to be built. His Majesty will be at Dahlen early tomorrow, where he hopes to receive news on the current state of affairs to be able to give the orders for the movement of the 9th."[84]

At 9:00 on the morning of the 8th, Napoleon went to Wurzen escorted by 1st Old Guard Division and Oudinot's Young Guard. On departing from Oschatz, he had no news of Ney's position. He still hoped to receive intelligence from Ney to determine the orders for the 9th. For the time being, the rest of the army continued marching northwest to Dahlen. During the course of the day, Ney's report finally reached Napoleon: III Corps took a position on the right bank of the Mulde between Wurzen and Eilenburg while VII Corps stood at Püchau likewise between the two towns but on the left bank. Bertrand's IV Corps reached Schildau, eleven miles northeast of Wurzen. By nightfall on the 8th, the emperor's position appeared formidable. Some 150,000 men grouped in 22 infantry and 12 cavalry divisions held a front that stretched a mere 22 miles from Taucha to Schildau.[85]

In addition to finding Ney's army, the emperor learned enough about Blücher's whereabouts to issue an attack disposition for 9 October. With the Army of Silesia extended along the Mulde and purportedly isolated, he sought to engage Blücher around Bad Düben. Escorted by Oudinot's Young Guard, Napoleon planned to go to Bad Düben early on the 9th. Ney received instructions to have III, IV, and VII Corps and I Cavalry Corps likewise moving toward Bad Düben by 6:00 A.M. His initial march objectives called for VII Corps to cross the Mulde and reach Sprotta, ten miles south of Bad Düben. Napoleon directed IV Corps eight miles northwest from Schildau to Mockrehna, some thirteen miles southeast of Bad Düben. Ney himself would determine the movements of III Corps and I Cavalry Corps. The emperor promised to be right behind Ney, supporting him with the rest of the army. Yet Ney could not make a move unless he received instructions from the master. "I am waiting this night for the latest intelligence but I must give preparatory orders," Napoleon explained almost apologetically. Berthier alerted Macdonald to be ready to move XI Corps and II Cavalry Corps to Mockrehna to support Bertrand's IV Corps but not to commence the march until he received new orders. However, if he heard the sound of the guns coming from Mockrehna, "you can press your movement to support it and from that moment you will establish communication with that general. It is also suitable for you to summon the [units] belonging to Chastel's cavalry that are at Torgau." Lastly, Napoleon wanted Grand Headquarters, the Saxon king, the Old Guard, Mortier's Young Guard divisions, bridging equipment, and Reserve Artillery and Park to be on the road to Wurzen by 9:00 A.M. "I arrived today at Wurzen," stated Napoleon's last dispatch of 8 October, addressed to Murat. "There is nothing new. All is well here."[86]

The reports that reached Napoleon late on the 8th confirmed that little had changed in the dispositions of his adversaries. Aside from underestimating the size and proximity of the Army of North Germany, he had gained a fairly accurate picture of the Coalition forces that stood between him and the Elbe. "I am leaving for Wittenberg," he wrote Murat on the morning of the 9th, "which the enemy is besieging. I intend to attack Blücher at Bad Düben, where I am assured that the Army of Silesia is in position. Tomorrow, I hope to be at Wittenberg to lift the siege, cross to the right bank of the Elbe, and eliminate the enemy's two bridges [Roßlau and Wartenburg]. According to the information that I have, Blücher, with the Army of Silesia forming about 60,000 men, is at Bad Düben and the prince of Sweden, with 40,000 men, is at Dessau." The emperor instructed his brother-in-law "to prepare everything to debouch on the rear of the enemy if he moves on Dresden." He also warned Murat not to believe the news of Bavaria's defection, "or anything that benefits the enemy."[87]

A little past midnight on 9 October, Napoleon started issuing instructions to move the Grand Reserve to Eilenburg to form the anvil. He wanted 1st, 2nd, and 3rd Divisions of the Guard Cavalry united there as soon as possible. Souham's III Corps immediately marched followed by Oudinot's Young Guard. At daybreak, 2nd Old Guard Division would move up to Wurzen followed by the Guard Artillery Reserve with the light batteries at the head of the column. The bridge train and engineer park, the army's park, Grand Headquarters with Frederick August's suite, and 1st Old Guard Division all had to be at Wurzen by 2:00 that afternoon. The emperor himself with his "Little Headquarters" planned to depart from Wurzen at 9:00 A.M. and establish a command post near Eilenburg.[88]

To provide the hammer, Ney received orders to have his army marching by 6:00 that morning. With III Corps moving along the right bank of the Mulde to Eilenburg, VII Corps would proceed there from Püchau along the left bank. From Schildau, IV Corps followed by XI Corps would march eight miles northwest to Mockrehna. Napoleon did not place Macdonald's XI Corps under Ney's command. "You will depart today at 6:00 A.M. with your army corps and proceed to Mockrehna," Berthier explained to Macdonald, "if IV Corps is at Schilda, it will precede you. You will support it if circumstances require it. I inform you, marshal, the emperor will leave at 6:00 this morning for Eilenburg and go from there to Bad Düben. As soon as you arrive at Mockrehna, it will be necessary for you to move on Bad Düben so you can contribute to the attack on this point where they say Blücher is located." All of the cavalry – two brigades – that had united at Torgau was placed under Macdonald's command but Napoleon placed II Cavalry Corps under Ney's command, informing the marshal that at 6:00 A.M. Sébastiani would leave his bivouac just east of Wurzen and make for Eilenburg. Napoleon wanted Ney to accompany III Corps, with II Cavalry Corps forming the vanguard. Reynier would lead VII Corps across the Mulde at Eilenburg to serve as Ney's left wing as Bertrand pushed IV Corps to Mockrehna to form the right. To obtain intelligence and facilitate the march of IV Corps, the master instructed Ney to have III Corps between Eilenburg and Bad Düben as soon as possible. "Consequently, prince," noted Berthier, "you have under your command III, IV, and VII Corps, II Cavalry Corps, and Dąbrowski's division; the emperor himself will be there to support you with the Imperial Guard: cavalry, infantry, and artillery. The emperor attaches importance to being master of Bad Düben today and, if the enemy has no more than 30,000 men, His Majesty intends to attack tonight."[89]

For his Regular Reserve, Napoleon directed Marmont to have I Cavalry Corps depart from Taucha at 6:00 that morning to reach Eilenburg no later than 11:00 A.M. From there, the troopers would take the direct road to Bad Düben. Their patrols had to scour the countryside along the Leipzig–Eilenburg and Leipzig–Bad Düben roads. Behind the cavalry, Marmont would also have a large combined-arms vanguard from VI Corps on the Leipzig–Bad Düben road likewise at 6:00 A.M. The marshal would follow with the main body of VI Corps and 5th Light Cavalry Division from III Cavalry Corps, with a flying column reconnoitering along the Leipzig–Delitzsch road. "It is necessary for you to reach the height of Eilenburg before 11:00 A.M. today," Berthier instructed Marmont. "The emperor will be at Eilenburg at 8:00 this morning to march on Bad Düben, today, the 9th, with 120,000 men." With the Grand Reserve at Wurzen, Napoleon would have his famous *bataillon carré* of 120,000 men formed along a front ten miles wide and fifteen miles deep: success appeared guaranteed. He arranged for the Grande Armée to advance against Blücher's position at Bad Düben in three main columns along the shortest roads. "Today, I march on Bad Düben," he wrote to Narbonne at Torgau, "tomorrow on Wittenberg, where I will give battle to the enemy. With God's help, I hope to have complete success. At the least, I will force the enemy to raise the siege of Wittenberg and I will take possession of his two bridges at Wartenburg and Dessau; and, as he has huge baggage trains on the left bank, his retreat will be difficult."[90]

Napoleon entrusted Jean-Toussaint Arrighi, duc de Padua and commander of III Cavalry Corps, with the defense of Leipzig. "We occupy Colditz, Rochlitz, Penig, and Frohburg," noted the emperor, "Leipzig is well covered on all sides, except those of Halle and Dessau." Arrighi had at his disposal an ad hoc division of six infantry battalions and sixteen guns under General Pierre Margaron as well as the 2nd Brigade of 4th Heavy Cavalry Division of III Cavalry Corps and a march regiment of reinforcements belonging to V Corps. "These troops are sufficient to guard Leipzig and to protect it from the attack of cavalry or a vanguard," continued Napoleon.

In addition, he projected the arrival of Augereau's lead division under General Étienne-Nicolas Lefol consisting of 6,000 or 7,000 infantry, 3,000 cavalry, and 10 guns. He instructed Arrighi to post Lefol's regiments at the city's various gates and bridges as well as on the roads from Halle and Dessau, and to form from them "two strong vanguards of infantry, cavalry, and artillery that will occupy the villages that are one league from the city." "You have 1,800 Honor Guards there," added Berthier; "you will not do anything with them in battle but place them in reserve to intimidate the enemy."[91]

After issuing these orders at 1:00 A.M., Napoleon clarified his instructions merely sixty minutes later. So much depended on this battle; every aspect and every detail had to be clearly explained to his subordinates. "Start the march of Dąbrowski and the divisions of III Cavalry Corps early today," Berthier instructed Ney, "so they are across the river before 6:00 A.M." Breaking protocol, the emperor wrote directly to Reynier: "The prince de la Moskova [Ney] will order you to depart at 6:00 A.M. to march on Eilenburg. I myself will be there at 7:00 A.M. It is essential that the head of your corps arrives at 8:00, so that between 9:00 and 10:00 it will pass and be on the way to Bad Düben, where I want to attack the enemy today. You will depart at 6:00 A.M., sharp."[92]

Napoleon's legions commenced their movements early on the 9th in accordance with the master's orders. With 6th Light and 4th Heavy Divisions from III Cavalry Corps and Dąbrowski's cavalry leading, the infantry of the 27th Division and VII Corps crossed the Mulde at Eilenburg. Seven miles east of Eilenburg, the vanguard encountered Russian cavalry from Sacken's corps at Böhlitz. After driving the enemy troopers four miles north to Doberschütz, Ney received instructions to prepare the mainly Saxon VII Corps to be inspected by the emperor at Kültschau on the right bank of the Mulde facing Eilenburg. Odeleben recounts:

> Napoleon endeavored to reanimate the courage of his troops through a harangue. He told them "that he was aware of how many reverses the VII Corps had experienced; that he had come to repair those misfortunes by placing himself at their head to repulse the enemy beyond the Elbe; that the Prussians planned to seize Saxony but he would protect it in concert with the king, his faithful ally; that all who no longer felt inclined to further his cause were at liberty to quit the service, and that the commanding officers should express his sentiments to all who could not hear him." This discourse had no effect. It was longer than those that the soldiers had been accustomed to hearing on such occasions; he expressed himself in a drawling manner, correcting himself by repetitions ... To add to his misfortune, his speech was translated into worse German than ordinary by the grand equerry, Caulaincourt, to all the generals and officers standing at attention before their regiments.

After the review, a dejected Napoleon slumped into the corner of his carriage, "full of vexation and ill-humor," and took the road to Bad Düben.[93] With the cavalry leading, VII Corps turned north followed by III Corps; 1st and 3rd Guard Cavalry Divisions formed the rearguard. Napoleon's advance benefited from Russian inefficiency. Lanskoy stood between Eilenburg and Bad Düben with Sacken's advance guard, which replaced Langeron's vanguard on the right bank of the Mulde after it crossed the river. Without dispatching a report to Bad Düben, Lanskoy withdrew east to rejoin his main body at Mockrehna. Consequently, the imperials encountered only one Cossack regiment, which quickly scattered. Around 3:00 P.M. the heads of the French columns reached Bad Düben, completely surprising the Silesian Army. The great man had arrived.

Notes

1 SHAT, C² 157: Bertrand to Ney, 3 October 1813; Arrighi to Augereau, 4 October 1813; Ney to Marmont, 3 October 1813.
2 SHAT, C² 157: Report to Bertrand dated 3 October 1813.
3 Ney to Marmont, Bitterfeld, 2:00 P.M., 4 October 1813, in Marmont, *Mémoires*, V:344; Weil, *Campagne de 1813*, 202–03.
4 Gneisenau to Bubna, Wartenburg, 4 October 1813, ÖStA KA, FA 1534, ad121. This letter stated that Blücher had crossed the Elbe on the morning of the 3rd at Wartenburg. Gneisenau also stated that the main body of the Army of North Germany would cross the Elbe on the 4th near Roßlau. On receiving this report on 6 October, Bubna immediately forwarded it to Schwarzenberg, who received it on the 7th according to the entry noted on the letter itself: Bubna to Schwarzenberg, Stolpen, 6 October 1813, *ibid.*, 121; Plotho, *Der Krieg*, II:285; Bogdanovich, *Geschichte des Krieges*, IIb:51; Vaudoncourt, *Histoire de la guerre*, I:193; Friederich, *Herbstfeldzug 1813*, II:299–304.
5 SHAT, C¹⁷ 133: Charles John to Wintzingerode, Tauentzien, Bülow, and Stedingk, 3 October 1813; Charles John to Blücher, Zerbst, 3 October 1813, Add MSS, 20112, 60; Reiche to Gneisenau, Nudersdorf, 4 October 1813, in Höpfner, "Darstellung," 1845:318; SHAT, C² 157: Arrighi to Ney, 5 October 1813; Blücher to Frederick William, Kemberg, 5 October 1813, GStA PK, VI HA Rep. 92 Nl. Gneisenau, Nr. 16.
6 During the night of 3–4 October, Gneisenau ordered six of Sacken's Cossack regiments under General Gavriil Lukovkin to Kemberg, where they arrived at 6:00 A.M. on the 4th and found Korf's Cossacks from Langeron's corps. Lukovkin continued to Bad Düben; Korf's Cossacks rested until 11:00 A.M. at which time they received orders for the 4th: Höpfner, "Darstellung," 1844:319.
7 Blücher to Rauch, Wartenburg, 4 October 1813, in Höpfner, "Darstellung," 1844:316; Unger, *Blücher*, II:102–03; Müffling, *Die Feldzüge*, 62; Bogdanovich, *Geschichte des Krieges*, IIb:50. The Prussians provided 42 officers and 1,332 men, of which four Landwehr battalions accounted for 38 officers and 1,103 men while 1 officer and 51 troopers of the Lithuanian and West Prussian Dragoons and 3 officers

and 178 pioneers completed Yorck's contribution. The Russians provided 88 officers and 3,025 men of which 78 officers and 2,719 were infantry and 10 officers and 306 men were pioneers and pontooniers. Together, the Russians and Prussians amounted to 130 officers and 4,357 men. However, manpower needed for prisoner-escort duty and to transport the sick and wounded reduced this figure to some 3,000 men. This forced the Allies to requisition laborers from the surrounding villages, which contained very few hearty males. As a result, greybeards, children, and women reported for work. After subtracting the labor force for the entrenched camp at Wartenburg, approximately 60,000 men remained at Blücher's disposal for field service.

8 Blücher to Schwarzenberg, Wartenburg, 4 October 1813, ÖStA KA, FA 1534, 90; Disposition, Wartenburg, 4 October 1813, RA KrA, volym 25, and Add MSS, 20112, 148.

9 These blockhouses were part of Napoleon's system to defend the Elbe between Torgau and Meißen. On 27 September, he ordered Marmont to utilize VI Corps and I Cavalry Corps "to form 3 columns, each consisting of 300–400 cavalry, 1 battalion of infantry, and 6 pieces of horse artillery. You will send one to Mühlberg, one to Strehla, and one between Strehla and Meißen, where the ferries operate. These columns will patrol the length of the bank and prevent any crossing. They will build blockhouses between those that already exist, so that instead of having one every other league there will be one every league. These columns will show their artillery on the road along the river so they can be seen on the other side and so the enemy knows that their boats can be destroyed by cannon. You will form 2 columns, each of 500 cavalry, 500 infantry, and 2 pieces of cannon, and you will have intelligent officers command them. They will coordinate their movements with Prince Poniatowski, General Lefebvre-Desnoettes, the duc de Padua [Arrighi], and General [Jean-Thomas] Lorge [5th Light Cavalry Division, III Cavalry Corps] to drive off enemy partisans and ensure that none operate between the Elbe and Leipzig. Instruct all columns that none can pass the night where they see the sun go down. All these columns must be very active, communicate with each other, and purge the countryside of all enemy parties." On the 28th, the commander of V Cavalry Corps, Lhéritier, also received instructions to form two columns each of 400–500 cavalry and 2 guns. One column would monitor the Elbe downstream along the right bank on the twenty-mile stretch from Meißen to Riesa; the other would patrol upriver the fifteen miles that separated Meißen and Dresden: *CN*, Nos. 20644 and 20653, XXVI:253–54, 261.

10 Höpfner, "Darstellung," 1845:319–21; Langeron, *Mémoires*, 293–94; Blücher to Frederick William, Bad Düben, 7 October 1813, GStA PK, VI HA Rep. 92 Nl. Gneisenau, Nr. 16; SHAT, C² 157: Narbonne to Bertrand, 4 October 1813; Weil, *Campagne de 1813*, 202.

11 Blücher to Frederick William, Kemberg, 5 October 1813, ÖStA KA, FA 1534, ad108.

12 Blücher to Frederick William, Kemberg, 5 October 1813, ÖStA KA, FA 1534, ad108; Höpfner, "Darstellung," 1845:324.

13 Blücher to Frederick William, Bad Düben, 7 October 1813, GStA PK, VI HA Rep. 92 Nl. Gneisenau, Nr. 16; Disposition for 5 October, Kemberg, 4 October

1813, RA KrA, volym 25 and Add MSS 20112, 149; Disposition, Kemberg, 5 October 1813, Add MSS 20112, 150.

14 SHAT, C² 157: Ney to Berthier, 5 October 1813. As rearguard, 27th Division held Delitzsch. Eight miles east, VII Corps stood at Wölkau and IV Corps at Naundorf. The 6th Light Cavalry Division took a position at Lindenhayn, dispatching patrols through Reibnitz toward Bitterfeld, while the 4th Heavy Cavalry Division halted at Gollmenz.

15 "Monsieur le duc, the emperor learned with astonishment that, after having ordered III Corps to move from Torgau to Eilenburg, an order that General Souham has executed by departing at 4:00 A.M. this morning, you left Eilenburg after destroying the bridge that His Majesty had ordered to be built there." Ney's compensation stated: "It was with astonishment that His Majesty learned that after ordering III Corps to move to Eilenburg, the duc de Raguse [Marmont] cut the bridge, retired on Leipzig, and singularly compromised this corps": SHAT, C¹⁷ 180: Berthier to Marmont, 7 October 1813; Berthier to Ney, 7 October 1813.

16 SHAT, C² 157: Ney to Berthier, 6 October 1813.

17 Langeron, *Mémoires*, 294.

18 Blücher to Frederick William, Bad Düben, 7 October 1813, GStA PK, VI HA Rep. 92 Nl. Gneisenau, Nr. 16.

19 Tauentzien's brigades did not receive numerical designations because they were chiefly composed of Landwehr regiments.

20 The account of 5 October is based on Blücher to Frederick William, Kemberg, 5 October 1813, ÖStA KA, FA 1534, ad108; Müffling, *Die Feldzüge*, 62–63; Plotho, *Der Krieg*, II:285–86; Marmont, *Mémoires*, V:266–67; Langeron, *Mémoires*, 293–95; Höpfner, "Darstellung," 1845:322–24; Friederich, *Herbstfeldzug 1813*, II:305–07; Bogdanovich, *Geschichte des Krieges*, IIb:51–52; Vaudoncourt, *Histoire de la guerre*, 193.

21 Ney to Marmont, 5 October 1813, in Marmont, *Mémoires*, V:346–47.

22 SHAT, C² 157: Ney to Bertrand, 5 October 1813; Ney to Marmont, 5 October 1813, in Marmont, *Memoires*, V:347–48.

23 SHAT, C² 157: Marmont to Ney, 6 October 1813.

24 Ney to Marmont, 6 October 1813, in Marmont, *Memoires*, V:351–52.

25 Marmont, *Memoires*, V:266–67; SHAT, C² 157: Ney to Berthier, 6 October 1813; SHAT, C¹⁷ 180: Berthier to Marmont, 7 October 1813; Marmont to Napoleon, 6 October 1813, in Marmont, *Memoires*, V:354–55.

26 C² 157: Ney to Berthier, 6 October 1813; Ney to Marmont, 7 October 1813, in Marmont, *Memoires*, V:353–54; Friederich, *Herbstfeldzug 1813*, II:307–08.

27 Blücher to Charles John, Kemberg, 5 October 1813, GStA PK, VI HA Rep. 92 Nl. Gneisenau, Nr. 23. A copy of this memo was sent to the tsar and king: Blücher to Alexander, Kemberg, 5 October 1813, RGVIA, f. VUA, op. 16, d. 3913, ll. 424–424b, and ÖStA KA, FA 1534, 108; Blücher to Frederick William, Kemberg, 5 October 1813, ÖStA KA, FA 1534, ad108. "Attached I include a memo that I have just sent to the crown prince in order to learn his intentions and make further arrangements."

28 Charles John to Blücher, Dessau, 6 October 1813, Add MSS, 20112, 65; Blücher to Charles John, Bad Düben, 7 October 1813, RA KrA, volym 25; Blücher to

Frederick William, Bad Düben, 7 October 1813, GStA PK, VI HA Rep. 92 Nl. Gneisenau, Nr. 16.

29 Narbonne's intercepted report from midnight on 4 October confirmed this news: SHAT, C² 157: Narbonne to Bertrand, 4 October 1813; Müffling, *Die Feldzüge*, 62; Blücher to Frederick William, Bad Düben, 7 October 1813, GStA PK, VI HA Rep. 92 Nl. Gneisenau, Nr. 16; Plotho, *Der Krieg*, II:287; Höpfner, "Darstellung," 1845:322–25. Katzler also reported that Dąbrowski's "division" consisted of four regiments of infantry, two of cavalry, and two guns. The captured courier also revealed that Torgau's garrison consisted of 10,000 to 11,000 men but mostly from the depots of the army; approximately one-third were sick and the number of dead increased each day.

30 Blücher to Sacken, Bad Düben, 6 October 1813, in Höpfner, "Darstellung," 1845:325–26.

31 Blücher to Charles John, Bad Düben, 6 October 1813, Add MSS, 20112, 66; Müffling, *Aus meinem Leben*, 84.

32 Müffling, *Die Feldzüge*, 63.

33 The reports from Rudzevich and Emmanuel to Gneisenau are in Höpfner, "Darstellung," 1845:326.

34 Bennigsen to Blücher, Teplitz, 4 October 1813, in Höpfner, "Darstellung," 1845:327–28.

35 Quoted in Höpfner, "Darstellung," 1845:327.

36 Friederich, *Herbstfeldzug 1813*, II:313.

37 On 8 October, Schwarzenberg's headquarters reached Chemnitz, sixty-three miles south of Bad Düben.

38 Leggiere, *Napoleon and Berlin*, 258; Höpfner, "Darstellung," 1845:327.

39 Quoted in Pertz and Delbrück, *Gneisenau*, III:417.

40 Charles John to Blücher, Dessau, 7 October 1813, Add MSS, 20112, 67.

41 SHAT, C¹⁷ 133: Charles John to Tauentzien, Wintzingerode, Hirschfeld, and Putlitz, 7 October 1813; Blücher to Shcherbatov, Bad Düben, 7 October 1813, ÖStA KA, FA 1535, ad228; Plotho, *Der Krieg*, II:317–18; Friederich, *Herbstfeldzug 1813*, II:315–16.

42 Ney to Marmont, Bennewitz, 6:00 A.M. and 1:00 P.M., 7 October 1813, in Marmont, *Memoires*, V:352–54; SHAT, C² 157: Ney to Berthier, Bennewitz, 1:00 P.M., 7 October 1813.

43 Ney's report states "Eilenburg to Sprottau," but this must be a mistake as the latter stood 142 miles east of the former. At fifteen miles east of Eilenburg, the village of Schildau appears to be the endpoint of Marmont's reconnaissance: SHAT, C² 157: Ney to Berthier, 7 October 1813; Friederich, *Herbstfeldzug 1813*, II:313.

44 Langeron, *Mémoires*, 295; Blücher to Charles John, Bad Düben, 7 October 1813, RA KrA, volym 25; Blücher to Frederick William, Bad Düben, 11:00 A.M., 7 October 1813, GStA PK, VI HA Rep. 92 Nl. Gneisenau, Nr. 16; Höpfner, "Darstellung," 1845:330–32.

45 Blücher to Shcherbatov, Bad Düben, 7 October 1813, ÖStA KA, FA 1535, ad228. Shcherbatov received these orders on the evening of the 9th: Höpfner, "Darstellung," 1845:327, 330–31.

46 Blücher to Frederick William, Bad Düben, 11:00 A.M., 7 October 1813, GStA PK, VI HA Rep. 92 Nl. Gneisenau, Nr. 16.

47 Blücher to Wobeser, Bad Düben, 7 October 1813, in Höpfner, "Darstellung," 1845:331.

48 Blücher to Sacken, Bad Düben, 7 October 1813, in Höpfner, "Darstellung," 1845:331. Acting on Blücher's orders during the afternoon of the 6th, Yuzefovich turned over the post at Dommitzsch to Colonel Rakhmanov of Sacken's corps; he also turned over the posts he held facing Torgau to Vasilchikov. Yuzefovich then led his detachment to Langenreichenbach, reinforcing the post at Schildau, and detaching two dragoon squadrons and 200 Cossacks toward Mehderitzsch on the road that led from Meißen to Torgau.

49 The reports by Vasilchikov and Sacken are in Höpfner, "Darstellung," 1845:331–32.

50 Unger, *Blücher*, II:104–05; Müffling, *Die Feldzüge*, 63, and *Aus meinem Leben*, 85–86; Bogdanovich, *Geschichte des Krieges*, IIb:52; Schneidawind, *Prinz Wilhelm*, 85; Unger, *Blücher*, II:104.

51 SHAT, C^{17} 133: Charles John to Tauentzien, Wintzingerode and Hirschfeld, 7 October 1813; Charles John to Putlitz, Bülow, and Stedingk, 8 October 1813; Charles John to Stedingk, Bülow, and Wintzingerode, 9 October 1813.

52 Höpfner, "Darstellung," 1845:332–33.

53 Disposition, Bad Düben, 8 October 1813, Add MSS, 20112, 153; Blücher to Charles John, Bad Düben, 8 October 1813, GStA PK, VI HA Rep. 92 Nl. Gneisenau, Nr. 23; Vasilchikov's report is in Höpfner, "Darstellung," 1845:333.

54 Falkenhausen to Shcherbatov, Baslitz near Meißen, 11:00 A.M., 6 October 1813, ÖStA KA, FA 1534, 149a; Sacken to Blücher, Mockrehna, 7:30 P.M., 8 October 1813, in Höpfner, "Darstellung," 1845:338; Friederich, *Herbstfeldzug 1813*, II:316–18; Unger, *Blücher*, II:105.

55 Unger, *Blücher*, II:105.

56 Charles John to Blücher, Zehbitz, 8 October 1813, GStA PK, VI HA Rep. 92 Nl. Gneisenau, Nr. 23, and Add MSS, 20112, 153.

57 Two variations of the discussion between Bernadotte and Rühle exist. According to the first, which is based on Rühle's verbal report on his return to Blücher's headquarters, the crown prince proposed that both armies cross the Saale. Müffling's 1827 history of the Silesian Army supports this version: "The confidential officer [Rühle] sent by the commanding general . . . returned early on the 9th, delivering the news that the crown prince wished to remain behind [north of] the Elbe, and consented to remaining on the left bank only on the condition that General Blücher resolved to jointly cross the Saale with him to take a position behind that river." See Müffling, *Die Feldzüge*, 63–64. The second version, published in Höpfner, "Darstellung," 1845:332, is based on Rühle's oral testimony thirty years later and not surprisingly attributes the idea for the joint passage solely to Rühle. Yet in General Unger's biography of Blücher, written several years after Höpfner's account, Bernadotte receives sole credit for suggesting the joint passage: Unger, *Blücher*, II:106; Friederich, *Herbstfeldzug 1813*, II:319–22.

58 SHAT, C^{17} 133: Charles John to Bülow, Stedingk, and Wintzingerode, 9 October 1813.

59 Müffling, *Die Feldzüge*, 64; Blücher to Charles John, Bad Düben, 9 October
    1813, GStA PK, VI HA Rep. 92 Nl. Gneisenau, Nr. 23, and Add MSS, 20112, 70;
    Unger, *Blücher*, II:106.

60 *CN*, No. 20673, XXVI:275. At the end of September, Napoleon situated his I, III,
    V, XI, and XIV Corps as well as II and IV Cavalry Corps in the tight triangle
    formed by Dresden, Pirna, and Weißig. Victor's II Corps stood at Freiberg, while
    Poniatowski held Penig and Altenburg with VIII Corps. Marmont's VI Corps
    along with I and V Cavalry Corps moved to Leipzig, to where Augereau's IX
    Corps was marching from the Main River valley.

61 SHAT, C¹⁷ 181: Berthier to St.-Cyr, Souham, Macdonald, Lauriston, Arrighi, and
    Durosnel, 2 October 1813.

62 *CN*, Nos. 20678 and 20679, XXVI:280–81.

63 According to Berthier, II Corps stood between Freiberg and Öderan; V Corps
    held Mittweida; and VIII was marching from Frohburg to Altenburg: *CN*,
    No. 20677, XXVI:279–80; SHAT, C¹⁷ 181: Berthier to Murat, 2 October 1813.

64 SHAT, C¹⁷ 181: Berthier to Ney, Arrighi, Augereau, and Kellerman, 3
    October 1813.

65 SHAT, C² 157: Lauriston to Berthier, 3 October 1813; Poniatowski to Berthier,
    3 and 4 October 1813; SHAT, C¹⁷ 181: Berthier to Macdonald and Souham, 3
    October 1813.

66 SHAT, C² 157: Ney to Marmont, 3 October 1813.

67 SHAT, C¹⁷ 181: Berthier to Souham, 3 October 1813; Berthier to Chastel,
    4 October 1813. Chastel received a reprimand on the 4th: "The emperor charged
    me with communicating to you his displeasure over your conduct in quitting the
    banks of the Elbe, where the duc de Raguse placed you. Return immediately to
    the river. His Majesty has the right to expect more zeal for his service from a
    general of division. How could you neglect to immediately send an officer to
    headquarters and to General Souham to communicate the passage of the enemy?
    How could you push caution so far that you believed you were compromised
    when the enemy had not even built his bridge? The emperor is exasperated by
    such conduct and such negligence."

68 *CN*, Nos. 20690, 20691, and 20694, XXVI:288–90; SHAT, C¹⁷ 181: Berthier to
    Souham, Dresden, 3 October 1813.

69 SHAT, C¹⁷ 181: Berthier to Marmont and Souham, 4 October 1813; *CN*,
    Nos. 20692 and 20693, XXVI:290.

70 *CN*, Nos. 20694–20696, XXVI:290–92; SHAT, C¹⁷ 181: Berthier to Souham,
    Marmont, and Ney, 5 October 1813. One brigade from III Corps would remain
    at Meißen to guard the bridge.

71 *CN*, Nos. 20697 and 20698, XXVI:292–93; SHAT, C¹⁷ 181: Berthier to Drouot, 5
    October 1813.

72 *CN*, Nos. 20703 and 20704, XXVI:295.

73 In and around Dresden stood the 44,000 men and 202 guns of the Guard; the
    25,000 men and 68 guns of XI Corps; the 12,500 men and 47 guns of I Corps; the
    28,000 men and 60 guns of XIV Corps; and the 6,800 men and 12 guns of II
    Cavalry Corps, for a total of 116,300 men and 389 guns. Between the Elbe and
    Mulde were the 15,900 men and 61 guns of III Corps; the 15,500 men and 32 guns

of IV Corps; the 22,000 men and 48 guns of VII Corps; the 22,500 men and 82 guns of VI Corps; the 3,200 men and 8 guns of 27th Division; the 2,500 men and 6 guns of III Cavalry Corps; and the 6,000 men and 27 guns of I Cavalry Corps, for a total of 87,600 men and 264 guns. On the Leipzig–Altenburg–Freiberg front stood the 16,000 men and 55 guns of II Corps; the 14,200 men and 53 guns of V Corps; the 6,900 men and 30 guns of VIII Corps; the 3,000 men and 12 guns of IV Cavalry Corps; the 2,450 men and 6 guns of V Cavalry Corps; the 1,000 men of 1st Brigade of I Cavalry Corps; and the 7,200 men and 22 guns of the Observations Corps of Leipzig for a total of 50,750 men and 178 guns. Approximately 5,000 cavalry and 6 guns kept open communications across the Saale, while IX Corps marched on Leipzig with 12,700 men and 14 guns. See Friederich, *Herbstfeldzug 1813*, II:300–01.

74 *CN*, Nos. 20701–20703, 20706, and 20707, XXVI:294–97; SHAT, C^{17} 181: Berthier to Macdonald, Augereau, and Sébastiani, 6 October 1813.

75 SHAT, C^{17} 181: Berthier to Rognait, Sorbier, and Durrieu, 6 October 1813; Norvins, *Portefeuille de mil huit cent treize*, II:372; Plotho, *Der Krieg*, II:286–87; Friederich, *Herbstfeldzug 1813*, II:306–08.

76 *CN*, No. 20705, XXVI:296.

77 Bogdanovich, *Geschichte des Krieges*, IIb:57; St.-Cyr, *Mémoires*, IV:185–88; *CN*, No. 20699, XXVI:293; SHAT, C^{17} 181: Berthier to St.-Cyr, 6 October 1813.

78 *CN*, Nos. 20709 and 20733, XXVI:297–98, 312–13; SHAT, C^{17} 181: Berthier to Daru, Sorbier, and Durosnel, 6 October 1813.

79 *CN*, Nos. 20711 and 20714, XXVI:299–302.

80 *CN*, Nos. 20712, 20713, 20715, and 20716, XXVI:301–03; SHAT, C^{17} 181: Berthier to Macdonald and Drouot, 7 October 1813.

81 *CN*, Nos. 20717 and 20718, XXVI:303–04.

82 SHAT, C^2 157: Ney to Berthier, 6 October 1813. Writing in 1845, Höpfner of the Prussian General Staff asserted that this prompted Napoleon to abandon his initial plan to march to Wurzen and instead to march directly through Dahlen to Bad Düben in order to catch Blücher between the Mulde and the Elbe. Jean-Jacques Pelet, in *Des principales opérations de la campagne de 1813*, 153–54, claimed that Napoleon received this report on the evening of the 7th at Seerhausen while Höpfner, in "Darstellung," 1845:329, which Friederich, *Herbstfeldzug 1813*, II:312–13 follows verbatim, believes this report reached him at Meißen during the afternoon of the 7th. Based on Berthier's correspondence, it does not appear that Napoleon received this information until the 8th.

83 *CN*, No. 20719, XXVI:304; St.-Cyr, *Mémoires*, IV:433.

84 *CN*, No. 20720, XXVI:304–05; SHAT, C^{17} 181: Berthier to Marmont, Ney, Joinville, Drouot, Daru, Chastel, and Augereau, 7 October 1813.

85 On the left wing, Marmont's VI Corps and General Lorge's 5th Light Cavalry Division of III Cavalry Corps remained at Taucha, with forward posts extending northwest toward Delitzsch. In the center, on the left bank of the Mulde, two divisions each from I and III Cavalry Corps stood at Machern, and Reynier's VII Corps at Püchau and Eilenburg. On the right bank of the Mulde, Dąbrowski's 27th Division took post west of Eilenburg, Souham's III Corps at Großzschepa, 1st Old Guard Division and Oudinot's Young Guard corps at Wurzen. The right

wing comprised 2nd Old Guard Division and Mortier's two divisions of Young Guard echeloned between Wurzen and Oschatz, Bertrand's IV Corps at Schildau, Macdonald's XI Corps and the II Cavalry Corps at Dahlen, and Chastel's cavalry detachment at Torgau. See *CN*, No. 20723, XXVI:306–07; SHAT, C[17] 181: Berthier to Macdonald, 8 October 1813; Bogdanovich, *Geschichte des Krieges*, IIb:57–58; Vaudoncourt, *Histoire de la guerre*, 193–94; Friederich, *Herbstfeldzug 1813*, II:316–17; Bernhardi, *Toll*, III:366–67.

86 *CN*, No. 20723 and 20724, XXVI:306–07; SHAT, C[17] 181: Berthier to Souham, Latour-Maubourg, and Ney, 8 October 1813.

87 *CN*, No. 20735, XXVI:313–14.

88 *CN*, No. 20725, XXVI:307–08; SHAT, C[17] 181: Berthier to Drouot, and Arrighi, 9 October 1813. Lefebvre-Desnouettes's 2nd Guard Cavalry Division stood at Leipzig with VI Corps and I Cavalry Corps. For the movement on the 9th, the 2nd Guard Cavalry Division was temporarily placed under the orders of Latour-Maubourg, commander of I Cavalry Corps.

89 *CN*, No. 20727, XXVI:309; SHAT, C[17] 181: Berthier to Ney and Macdonald, 9 October 1813.

90 *CN*, Nos. 20728 and 20733, XXVI:310, 312; SHAT, C[17] 181: Berthier to Marmont, 9 October 1813.

91 *CN*, No. 20726, XXVI:308; SHAT, C[17] 181: Berthier to Arrighi, 9 October 1813.

92 *CN*, Nos. 20730 and 20731, XXVI:311; SHAT, C[17] 181: Berthier to Ney and Sébastiani, 9 October 1813.

93 The text of the speech to the Saxons can be found in Bogdanovich, *Geschichte des Krieges*, IIb:59; Odeleben, *A Circumstantial Narrative*, II:2–4. The French troops of VII Corps were also "solemnly harangued."

I2

Hide and seek

The preliminary reports that reached Blücher on 9 October indicated Leipzig as the objective of French movements. Unaware of the emperor's offensive down the Mulde that very day, Silesian Army Headquarters did not make haste. Gneisenau and Müffling rescinded the disposition for the march on Leipzig and drafted new orders, entitled the "Secret Disposition for 9 October," to evacuate the entire stretch between the Mulde and the Elbe. Rather than along the left bank of the Elbe, the Army's communication would run on the right bank through Roßlau and Aken starting on 11 October. Rauch received instructions to dismantle the pontoon bridge at Wartenburg and post one battalion and twenty troopers at Elster to defend the bridgehead. He would proceed through Wörlitz to Dessau with his remaining units and the bridge train. All three corps would slide west: Yorck's corps would move across the Mulde at Jeßnitz; he would post his advance guard five miles south of there at Bitterfeld. While Langeron's corps crossed five miles upstream of Jeßnitz at Mühlbeck, his vanguard would take a position eight miles further south at Sausedlitz. Sacken would move to Bad Düben, directing his vanguard to Pristäblich east of the Mulde with cavalry patrolling the Eilenburg–Torgau road. If Shcherbatov had yet to cross the Elbe, Blücher instructed him to force-march to Elster and there await further orders. At 11:30 A.M., Blücher reported these measures to Frederick William as well as the news that he and Bernadotte had agreed that the imperial columns at Wurzen had come from Torgau and would proceed to Leipzig. Thus, both commanders viewed a *Rechtsabmarsch* (march to the right) as suitable for all contingencies (see Map 5).[1]

Already on the left bank of the Mulde, Yorck's vanguard, commanded by the capable Katzler, patrolled toward Leipzig. After observing Marmont's columns debouch, he withdrew to Bitterfeld, where Bülow's 5th Brigade stood. Katzler's detachments continued to observe the roads to Delitzsch

547

and Bad Düben. Rudzevich stood even further south with Langeron's vanguard. With his command post at Pressen – only four miles west of Eilenburg – the Russian general found himself in the midst of the imperial columns. Throughout the day, his troopers sparred with Marmont's cavalry, which a captured cuirassier claimed to total three divisions. That evening, Rudzevich withdrew ten miles north to Sausedlitz. At that time, he finally reported the march of large columns from Leipzig to Eilenburg, as well as along the right bank of the Mulde toward Bad Düben. Two officers who had defected swore that Napoleon would be at Eilenburg, where the Guard and four army corps had already arrived.

Although Blücher did not receive Rudzevich's report until nighttime, news did reach him from Sacken around noon on the 9th of the enemy's march down both banks of the Mulde toward Bad Düben. Sacken stated that a report from Lukovkin dated 7:00 that morning warned of the movement of imperial infantry and artillery led by two cavalry regiments from Wurzen down the eastern bank of the Mulde toward Eilenburg. The Russians also spotted imperial forces moving down the western bank of the Mulde. Enemy forces remained at Großzschepa, Schildau, and Wurzen. Two hours later, Silesian Army Headquarters received a report from Katzler concerning the movement of large imperial forces northwest from Taucha. This report also stated that Napoleon's baggage escorted by three Guard Cavalry Regiments had rolled through Taucha the previous evening en route to Leipzig on the great highway from Dresden. Blücher wanted to wait for Sacken to arrive before he departed with Langeron's corps but the Russians never appeared; anxiety over their fate mounted. Finally, Blücher's posts reported the approach of a column marching down the right bank of the Mulde. Believing the column to be Sacken's corps, the commander delayed his departure even longer and ordered Langeron's rearguard to remain at Bad Düben.

Soon, columns could be seen marching down both banks of the Mulde but they did not belong to Sacken's corps. Realizing that the enemy was fast approaching, Blücher finally took the road to Pouch at 2:00 in the afternoon. Less than sixty minutes after he departed, French cavalry entered Bad Düben. Langeron's Reserve Artillery, escorted by Kaptsevich's X Infantry Corps, had just marched out. Among the last to leave, Gneisenau barely avoided capture. Thus, Rudzevich's negligence almost caused a disaster for Langeron's corps and Blücher's headquarters. "Langeron's Reserve Artillery marched in its usual place behind the columns," recalled Müffling, "and the enemy might have taken it had they known how to exploit the misunderstanding. Meanwhile, because he was so slow, we had time to send infantry and some cavalry against them." Three Jäger regiments and four guns from Kaptsevich's corps sufficed to confine the French vanguard at Bad Düben. Although Langeron's rearguard escaped, Napoleon succeeded in cutting off Sacken's corps at Mockrehna.

With the French IV and XI Corps approaching his position, Sacken planned to withdraw due north to Bad Schmiedeberg but first sought Blücher's permission. Hours passed as Sacken waited in vain for instructions. His anxiety increased after reports arrived of imperial columns estimated to be 40,000 to 50,000 men marching down the Elbe. Threatened in both the front and the right flank, Sacken decided to withdraw through Bad Schmiedeberg to Wartenburg. As he prepared to retreat, the Russian general finally received the "Secret Disposition" some three hours later than expected. According to Müffling, the "Secret Disposition" called for one officer from each corps staff to be sent to Army Headquarters so that he could "transmit safely all urgent orders either by day or night. On the morning of the 9th, when this orderly officer from Sacken's corps should have taken the disposition to General Sacken, he was nowhere to be found, having already returned to his corps." Another officer had to be sent. He apparently lost his way, thus delivering the orders three hours late.

With the imperials contesting his vanguard around Eilenburg, Sacken figured that the enemy already stood between him and Bad Düben. Correctly concluding that he could not contest 40,000 to 50,000 imperials for control of the village, Sacken also realized he could not execute the march to Wartenburg. As Blücher decided to cut all communication along the left bank of the Elbe, a march to Wartenburg would separate his corps from the rest of the army. Sacken and the Prussian liaison who served at his headquarters as de facto chief of staff, Major Wilhelm Ernst von Brockhausen, hatched a brilliant scheme to both escape the French and rejoin the army by immediately marching northwest, circumventing Bad Düben, and cutting through the large forest, the Düben moor, north of that town to reach Jeßnitz. Without encountering the imperials, his troops legged twenty miles that day, reaching Schköna, seven miles north of Bad Düben and eleven miles east of Jeßnitz, around midnight.[2] He planned to depart for the latter at 5:00 A.M. "The army could have suffered a disaster," concluded Müffling, "if the enemy had been more attentive and General Sacken less resolute."[3] Sacken's cavalry eventually rejoined the corps at the Mulde.

Meanwhile, Yorck had arrived at Jeßnitz earlier that day and found Bülow's corps on the opposite bank and the two bridges too weak to support cavalry and artillery. Such information should have been obtained long before the corps moved in this direction: yet again the negligence of subordinates hindered Blücher's operations. Ever cautious, Yorck decided to postpone the crossing until the following morning, when the infantry would pass the Mulde at Jeßnitz while the other arms crossed three miles downstream at Raguhn. After forwarding his lead units there, Yorck established a bivouac for his main body between Jeßnitz and Müldenstein. This did not bode well for Langeron, whose corps Blücher determined would cross at Jeßnitz in light of the French offensive. With his corps back to back on the right bank of the Mulde, Blücher grumbled over Yorck's measures after reaching Jeßnitz that evening. He ordered the crossing to be executed that night and a third, stronger bridge immediately built for Langeron's corps.

Consequently, I Corps crossed the Mulde at Jeßnitz around midnight and moved into a bivouac two miles further west at Bobbau, very close to Bülow's corps. Yorck's units that crossed at Raguhn rejoined his main body around 6:00 A.M. on the 10th. Langeron's troops marched through the night to Jeßnitz and crossed the Mulde on the morning of the 10th by way of the three bridges. In response to Sacken's report that he would march to Jeßnitz on the 10th, Blücher directed him to cross the Mulde at Raguhn. The bold maneuver completely succeeded. On the next morning, 10 October, Yorck dispatched Schack to Gneisenau with his report. In their meeting, the staff chief could not contain his joy over outwitting the master: "Yesterday, Napoleon struck in the air; he will do the same this morning because we will withdraw across the Saale; the Mark is sufficiently covered by Putlitz before Magdeburg, Hirschfeld at Aken, Tauentzien at Dessau, and Thümen before Wittenberg. Moreover, Prince Shcherbatov is force-marching from Dresden to reach the mouth of the Black Elster at Jeßen."[4]

After delivering the army from the brink of chaos, Blücher, Gneisenau, and Müffling drafted a detailed letter to Bernadotte describing the enemy's operation. They explained to the crown prince that the movement along the right bank of the Mulde appeared too serious to be a mere reconnaissance. Yet this concentration cost Napoleon one full day. Consequently, the Prussians judged that the Army of North Germany could march to Halle unmolested. Never happy with retreating, Blücher proposed making a stand: "I believe that if you want to take a position between Halle and Leipzig while you prepare your crossing over the Saale at Halle, and if I take a position in the region of Zörbig with crossings at Rothenburg or Bernburg, we will be in position to await the enemy and proceed according to circumstances." Müffling informed Blücher that Bruckdorf, on the road to Leipzig four miles southwest of Halle, offered a strong position. "The right wing of this position would lean on the Elster River, the front would be covered by a large pond and a small stream that flows through a swampy meadow, and the left wing of this position offers the cavalry a very advantageous field," concluded Blücher.[5]

With imperial forces moving east from Leipzig to the Mulde to join the large columns advancing north on Bad Düben, Blücher offered to shield the Army of North Germany, which did nothing on the 9th, while it slid southwest to a position between Halle and Leipzig. Meanwhile, Blücher would assess the situation from Zörbig, with crossings over the Saale available twenty-three miles northwest at Bernburg and eighteen miles due west at Rothenburg. The intent and genius of this plan should not be overlooked.

Blücher and his staff ultimately believed that both armies would be compelled to cross the Saale. Upon doing so, the Prussians wanted both armies to march south along its left bank to unite with the Bohemian Army. Yet they feared Bernadotte would attempt to slip across the Elbe and fall back into Brandenburg under the pretext of guarding Berlin. By offering to shield the Army of North Germany as it marched southwest to Bruckdorf or some other point between Halle and Leipzig, Blücher created the façade of sacrificing his army for Bernadotte's. Blinded by this magnanimous offer, Bernadotte would accept, thus placing the Army of Silesia between his army and its bridges to escape across the Elbe. Thus, with Blücher driving him from behind, Bernadotte would have no choice but to march south and seek the union with Schwarzenberg.

Although this was a cunning ploy, Bernadotte was no fool. He rejected Blücher's suggestion to cross the Saale at Halle and place the Army of North Germany south of the Silesian Army. To protect his army, he preferred that Blücher remain at Zörbig – halfway between the Mulde and the Saale – on the 10th while his army took a position north of the Silesian Army, bridging the lower Saale at Alsleben and Bernburg. The crown prince again appeared more concerned with securing his line of retreat to the Elbe bridges rather than cooperating with the approaching Bohemian Army. "As the emperor Napoleon has turned against you today, it is completely impossible to execute our movements to the left bank of the Saale without being intensely harassed and pressured by him," he informed Blücher. "To avoid a disadvantageous battle under the current circumstances, I believe there is nothing better to do than for you to quickly place your army between Jeßnitz, Zörbig, and Bitterfeld. In this way, we support our left wing on the Mulde and have no need – after the bridges are downed – for concern about this side. Our right wing can extend toward the Saale." Moreover, the crown prince pledged to bridge the Saale at Bernburg as well as eight miles further upstream at Alsleben.

While Bernadotte's proposal appeared to concur with Blücher's bid to make a stand between the Saale and the Mulde, the specific details proved too suspect for the Prussians. In his letter from the evening of the 9th, Blücher clearly explained Marmont's eastern movement from Leipzig to Eilenburg as well as Napoleon's northern drive down the Mulde. Thus, the threat clearly came from the east and not from Leipzig to the south. Yet Bernadotte's claim that the "left" of the army would be secured along the Mulde while the "right" extended to the Saale applied only to a situation where an enemy force moved north from Leipzig. However, it was no mistake that his notion of "left" and "right" did not conform to the actual disposition of the opposing armies. By recommending that Blücher take a position between Jeßnitz, Zörbig, and Bitterfeld to counter an enemy force moving west, the crown prince actually meant for the

Silesian Army to assume the first line while the North German Army safely remained west of it in the second line.

Equally important, Bernadotte made no mention of Blücher's suggestion for the Army of North Germany to slide southwest to a position between Halle and Leipzig. Instead, the crown prince expressed his intention to bridge the Saale far downstream at Alsleben and Bernburg, the latter being twenty-five miles north of Halle. Thus, his vague assertion that the right wing of the combined armies would "extend to the Saale" really meant due west to the Saale rather than sharply southwest as Blücher proposed. Bridging the Saale downstream of Halle at Alsleben and Bernburg indicated that Bernadotte did not intend to abandon the immediate vicinity of the Elbe and the bridges that could safely deliver his army to Brandenburg. The crown prince's penultimate statement appeared the most dubious of all. Assuming Blücher had dismantled his bridge at Wartenburg, Bernadotte advised him to "immediately transport the pontoons to Aken or Roßlau." Therefore, the Prussians believed he wanted to maintain the liberty to either take part in a great battle with Napoleon or fly across the Elbe. "This new demand was most annoying," explains Müffling. "If the crown prince found it inconvenient to quit the Elbe, how much more inconvenient was it for General Blücher, who had his base in Silesia, and had detached Shcherbatov to Dresden. At headquarters, it was considered proof that through this the crown prince wished to reserve for himself the option of participating in a general battle."[6]

In fact, Bernadotte proved much too clever to fall for Blücher's ruse. Despite the latter's *selfless* offer to shield the Army of North Germany as it marched southwest to Bruckdorf, Bernadotte refused to allow the Silesian Army to come between him and his bridges across the Elbe. This placed the Prussians in a difficult situation by jeopardizing the entire purpose of crossing the Elbe at Wartenburg. For the moment, the Prussians accepted this check in their chess match with Bernadotte. Rather than attempt another move, Blücher and Gneisenau wanted to convince the crown prince that the roads to the Saale remained open. They forwarded a 9 October report from Sacken stating that Napoleon had reached Eilenburg with the bulk of his forces. In addition, according to the statements of two defected Württemberger officers, the 16,000-man VI Corps had marched northeast from Taucha on the road to Bad Düben. Based on this news, the Prussians did not believe Napoleon could force a battle on the 10th. Consequently, Blücher planned to maintain his rearguard (Sacken) on the left bank of the Mulde: the bridges at Raguhn and Jeßnitz would be burned at the enemy's approach. While the Silesian Army marched to Zörbig, a bridge train would proceed sixteen miles further west to Wettin. "In this manner," concluded Blücher, "I believe I will fulfill your intentions, which can then lead to the crossing of the Saale. Because the enemy can move against Dessau to cut us off from the crossing at Roßlau, I hold it as dangerous to accept battle without a secure retreat."[7]

Blücher's disposition for 10 October called for Sacken's rearguard to hold the bridge at Raguhn; should the enemy arrive in strength Blücher wanted the Russians to torch the structure. Langeron's rearguard would do the same at Jeßnitz. All three corps should forward nonessential vehicles to Dessau for the immediate passage of the Elbe at Roßlau. In accordance with the disposition, Yorck's corps marched at 2:00 that afternoon in two columns from Bobbau to a camp on Zörbig's west side. Katzler moved the vanguard from Bitterfeld to Brehna, where it joined the outpost of Bülow's vanguard. Langeron's soldiers likewise retreated in two columns to a bivouac just southwest of Zörbig. Rudzevich posted the advance guard eight miles further southwest at Roitzsch and only three miles west of Katzler. After Korf's cavalry crossed the Mulde at Jeßnitz, Russian engineers dismantled the twenty pontoons that formed one of the bridges and sent the train on a forced march to Wettin. The Russians prepared the second bridge for burning; only one post from Langeron's corps remained east of the Mulde at Friedersdorf, a little more than four miles upriver from Jeßnitz. After Sacken's corps crossed the Mulde at Raguhn late on the morning of the 10th, the Russians made preparations to destroy that bridge as well. Likewise, only one post from Sacken's corps remained on the right bank to observe the imperials. Sacken's troops camped on the left bank of the Mulde at Jeßnitz and Raguhn to observe the enemy's march along the right bank of the Mulde. Lanskoy positioned the vanguard on the highway to Delitzsch not far from Bitterfeld. Cavalry patrols reported that the imperial forces on the right bank had moved in huge columns north through Bad Düben and into the Düben moor (see Map 5).[8]

Passing through Zehbitz on the road to Zörbig, Blücher and Gneisenau – already in a foul mood over Bernadotte – met with the prince royal. According to Müffling, who again served as interpreter, the conversation proved less friendly than their first meeting: "The crown prince was much more agitated and no longer so level-headed. The great decision was approaching; we gave up trying to accomplish something through reasoning. The fear of being compromised and for giving cause to complain to the Allied sovereigns – who had entrusted their troops to his leadership – was the only means of forcing him out of his passivity."[9] Bernadotte soured the meeting at the very start by informing Blücher that, rather than transferring his headquarters to join Blücher's at Zörbig, he would move to Radegast. The growing difference in their military objectives only exacerbated the situation. Countering Blücher's insistence that no significant imperial forces stood between Leipzig and the Saale, the crown prince shared the news of Augereau's march from Erfurt toward Leipzig with IX Corps. He correctly asserted that Napoleon planned to concentrate the Grande Armée to first defeat their two armies and then march against Schwarzenberg. To escape Napoleon's blow, Bernadotte suggested having both armies cross the Saale and concentrate at Bernburg, twenty-five miles downstream of Halle.

Not wanting to merely escape, Blücher proposed moving closer to the Bohemian Army by marching across the plains of Leipzig from Zörbig to Halle and up the right bank of the Saale. United, he believed they could accept a battle with Napoleon if necessary. In Blücher's opinion, moving closer to the Bohemian Army would force Napoleon to yield the Leipzig plain and withdraw across the upper Saale to the region of Erfurt. Returning to his earlier idea, he declared to Bernadotte that the movement to the Saale would be effective only if their two armies united at Halle. There, they could extend their right wing to Bruckdorf, where it would be covered by several lakes and ponds as well as the Elster. Meanwhile, their combined cavalry could hold the left wing, exploiting their numerical superiority on the Saxon plain. Between the two armies, five bridges could be thrown across the Saale between Halle and Schkopau in case of a retreat. Thus positioned, they could accept battle or evade it, shield the approaching Bohemian Army, and forestall Napoleon on the middle Saale.

Unmoved by Blücher's argument, the crown prince rejected the position at Halle, claiming that he had found it too risky in 1806 – a year the Prussians did not want to remember. Moreover, imperial forces at Leipzig concerned him.[10] Thus, he insisted that a march up the left bank of the Saale offered more security than a direct trek from Zörbig to Halle. Seeing that he could not win this showdown with the eloquent native Gascon, Blücher finally abandoned the idea of placing the Silesian Army on the left wing – between Bernadotte and his bridges across the Elbe – and driving the Army of North Germany toward Schwarzenberg. Instead, he consented to posting the Silesian Army on the right wing and crossing the Saale at Wettin, thus leaving Bernadotte a clear path to his bridges. According to the Prussians, the crown prince promised to immediately strike a bridge at Wettin and to extend his left wing only as far as Alsleben.[11] At this point, Blücher lost all faith in the crown prince. Nostitz explains the way the Prussians at Silesian Army Headquarters viewed their proceedings with Bernadotte:

As long as the crown prince of Sweden viewed our crossing of the Elbe as a mere feint, he willingly promised all support and cooperation; when it was reported to him on 2 October that the army would cross the bridge on the following day, he was very inclined to hold this as boasting. After the crossing actually occurred, the victory at Wartenburg had been fought, and he was involuntarily pulled one step forward with [the Silesian Army], the enemy moved a corps against this part of the Elbe, forcing the bridges at Aken and Roßlau; having made necessary the dismantling of our bridge at Elster, he then began to regret the steps taken and he exerted everything to make apparent the need for a retrograde movement for the Silesian Army as well. The general rejected this suggestion with contempt; from now on, the last glimmer of confidence died out which we had harbored up to that point in the talents and the goodwill of the crown prince. We concluded that we could count only on our own strength and not on the support of such an unreliable ally. "For the sake of keeping himself in the good graces of both Paris and Stockholm, the crown prince will not sacrifice any Swedes or do anything to make the French suffer," said Blücher. Meanwhile the day of the decision moved ever closer. Napoleon left Dresden and concentrated the army at Leipzig. Everything now depended on the outcome there. On our side, everything depended on uniting all of our forces on this great battlefield; the most urgent verbal and written proposals regarding this were sent to the crown prince. The commanding generals of the various corps of his own army recognized the necessity of these measures but he remained immovable, the cooperation, which he promised, was insignificant, and what he promised he never intended to provide.[12]

During the course of the 10th, Bülow's corps reached Zörbig while his vanguard extended three miles further south to Quetzdölsdorf, approximately five miles northwest of Yorck's vanguard at Brehna. Bernadotte instructed Bülow to cooperate with the Silesian Army by supporting it at Jeßnitz if necessary. On learning that the Prussian III Corps had arrived at Zörbig, Blücher sent Müffling to inform Bülow of the result of the meeting at Zehbitz. He tasked Müffling with convincing Bülow to unite his corps with the Silesian Army if Bernadotte refused to participate in a battle with Napoleon. Although he had little love for Blücher, Bülow not only promised to cooperate, but also expressed his conviction that Wintzingerode would proceed in the spirit of Tsar Alexander and do the same. Blücher's personal visit with Bülow later in the day sealed their secret agreement. For his part, Gneisenau contacted the Prussian, Russian, Austrian, and British envoys attached to Bernadotte's headquarters. Of this group, assistance from Charles Stewart proved invaluable. Stewart monitored Bernadotte's actions to determine if the prince royal had conformed to the stipulations of the subsidy agreement between Great Britain and Sweden. He also held the purse strings, having the authority to apportion the funds or refuse payment. Stewart did not fail to threaten Bernadotte that he would exercise his power should the crown prince proceed in a manner contrary to the general cause.[13]

As for the rest of the North German Army, Wintzingerode held Radegast with instructions to remain combat-ready and to assemble all his cavalry. Bernadotte also requested a status report on "the state of affairs at Bernburg, so we can send the infantry there if necessary" and "to hasten the construction of the bridge over the Saale."[14] Vorontsov moved Wintzingerode's vanguard from Sylbitz to Halle and his own lead elements to Bruckdorf with Cossacks at Schkeuditz and Merseburg. At the other end of the army, Tauentzien received lengthy directives from the prince royal to cover the rear. First, he would lead the Prussian IV Corps from Hinsdorf back to Dessau, "destroying all the bridges and burning all the pylons so the enemy cannot use them under any circumstances." If imperial forces crossed the Mulde and advanced against IV Corps, Tauentzien should withdraw into the bridgehead at Roßlau, defending it to the extreme. If the French drove Thümen from Wittenberg and then advanced along the right bank of the Elbe, the crown prince instructed Tauentzien to abandon Roßlau, send all bridging material to Aken, summon all Allied troops on the right bank of the Elbe (Thümen and Hirschfeld) to him, and proceed according to circumstances. However, if the imperials remained on the left bank of the Elbe and moved to the left bank of the Mulde without attacking him, he should threaten the enemy's right flank and defend the bridgeheads at Roßlau and Aken. Bernadotte cautioned his Prussian subordinate that he might find himself cut off from the rest of the army. To prevent Tauentzien from being surprised, the crown prince urged him to deploy his Cossacks on both banks of the Mulde until they found the enemy. The Swedes marched to Gröbzig, thirteen miles west of Zörbig, on 10 October. Stedingk received orders to forward an engineer officer fluent in German another twenty-two miles northwest to Alsleben, where work would ensue night and day until a bridge spanned the Saale. At Aken, Hirschfeld complied with the crown prince's command to send a dozen anchors each to Bernburg and Alsleben for the bridges.[15]

For the 11th, Bernadotte planned to have his army marching by 4:00 A.M. Wintzingerode would cross the Saale at Rothenburg while Vorontsov guarded Halle. If Stedingk's Swedes could not cross at Alsleben because the engineers had yet to complete their work, they would march downstream to Bernburg, cross the Saale, and proceed upstream to Alsleben. Bülow's III Corps would accompany the Silesian Army across the Saale at Wettin. To reiterate this last point, Bernadotte informed Bülow on the evening of the 10th that Vorontsov had reported that he would throw a bridge across the Saale near Wettin. However, the crown prince did not seem certain that this would be the case. "If it is finished," stated his next sentence to Bülow, "your corps can cross there. The prince desires that you send an officer there to press the construction." If the Russians failed to complete the bridge, he directed Bülow to cross either at Rothenburg with the Russians or at Alsleben. Like Stedingk, if Bülow found the Alsleben bridge incomplete, he would march to Bernburg. Apparently, Bernadotte believed that Blücher would strike his own bridge at Wettin per the latter's letter of 10 October. Thus, if Vorontsov built a bridge, it would be for Bülow's use. This likewise emerges from the prince royal's letter to Bülow: "But if the bridge that General Blücher builds suffices for the passage of his army and your corps, you can cross on this same bridge, and thus united with the Army of Silesia you will find yourself in a position to resist the attacks that the enemy may execute against you." After issuing his orders, Bernadotte informed Blücher that the Army of North Germany would cross the Saale at 4:00 A.M. on the next day in accordance with their agreement. Bülow's corps would accompany the Silesian Army across the Saale at Wettin.[16]

After meeting with Bernadotte on the 10th, Blücher, Gneisenau, and Müffling rejoined Silesian Army Headquarters at Zörbig. Katzler reported the movement of large imperial columns from Eilenburg northwest to Delitzsch. From the hills of Delitzsch, Major Klüx observed a French force of approximately 20,000 men approaching from Hohenrode on the road to Eilenburg around 11:00 A.M. Two miles east of Delitzsch at Beerendorf, the column split with half continuing to Delitzsch and the other half marching northeast through Sausedlitz toward Bad Düben. At Delitzsch, the first column halted for thirty minutes and then reversed course, returning to Hohenrode. At the same time, the Prussians observed the column headed toward Bad Düben return to Hohenrode. Klüx speculated that the movement constituted merely a reconnaissance. Korf's 3:00 P.M. report from Jeßnitz stated that all the imperial forces that had marched from Bad Düben to Tornau had returned to the former. The infantry camped south of Bad Düben while the cavalry continued southwest on the road to Leipzig. However, this report proved to be incorrect. Korf actually observed the Guard establishing a camp just south of Bad Düben. Rather than return to Bad Düben, the troops that marched north continued to Kemberg, as a 6:00 P.M. report from Sacken confirmed. Moreover, a second column from Bad Düben followed the course of the Mulde downstream to Mühlbeck. Yet Blücher and his staff had no way of knowing that Korf was mistaken. In addition to these puzzling reports, interesting news arrived from the direction of Leipzig. Borstell, the commander of Bülow's 5th Brigade, reported the arrival of 45,000 fresh imperial troops at Leipzig on the evening of the 9th. After analyzing the intelligence, Silesian Army Headquarters reached the conclusion that, after Napoleon failed to find the Allies in the angle formed by the Elbe and the Mulde, he had renounced his offensive northward and now planned to cross the Mulde and advance on Zörbig.[17]

Returning to Napoleon, such a promising start to the day of 9 October ultimately ended in failure for the master of war. All that the cavalry could show for his well-laid plans amounted to twenty wagons loaded with biscuit as well as twenty-six wounded Allied soldiers, all of which Blücher had been forced to leave behind at Bad Düben. Including foraging parties cut off and captured by imperial forces, the Allies lost 105 men on the 9th. On this occasion, blame could not be placed on a hapless subordinate, not even Ney. Blücher escaped because of quick thinking and cooperation with Bernadotte. While Ney established his quarters at Bad Düben, a dejected Napoleon passed the night of 9/10 October at Eilenburg, where he received enough intelligence to gain an accurate picture of Blücher's plans for the 9th – plans he had just foiled. "It appears," he explained to Ney at 4:00 A.M. on the 10th, "that the enemy intended for Sacken to take possession of the bridge at Eilenburg, Langeron the one at Bad Düben, and Yorck the one at Bitterfeld; each corps would then have its bridge and its direction to quickly advance to Leipzig." He also knew that Sacken had beaten a hasty retreat from Mockrehna through Weidenhain and that Langeron had evacuated Bad Düben. But where had Blücher gone? "We have to find where he has moved," continued his letter to Ney. "I believe that you arrived too late to know the direction he has taken."

For 10 October, Napoleon assumed that Langeron would withdraw through Mühlbeck toward Dessau and Sacken would retreat north toward Kemberg or east to Wartenburg. He planned to pursue the Russians with individual corps supported by additional cavalry to determine Blücher's intentions. At the least, he hoped to cut off Sacken's isolated corps. On his left, the horsemen of Lefebvre-Desnouettes's 2nd Guard Cavalry Division moved down the Mulde from Eilenburg along the left bank to Bad Düben, scouring the countryside between Eilenburg, Bad Düben, Delitzsch, and Dessau. The emperor instructed Lefebvre-Desnouettes to secure Marmont's left flank and confirm the withdrawal of the enemy rearguard from Delitzsch to Dessau. Marmont's VI Corps trooped seven miles northeast from Lindenhayn likewise to Bad Düben. Fournier's 6th Light Cavalry Division moved west across the Mulde at Bad Düben to rendezvous with Marmont and Lefebvre-Desnouettes. Fournier's patrols also sought news of the Allies at Bitterfeld and Delitzsch. The master entrusted Marmont with alerting him to any enemy movements toward Bitterfeld, Delitzsch, or Leipzig. Should the Army of North Germany march on Leipzig, the marshal would take a flanking position with his rear facing Bad Düben and Eilenburg. "It appears that our offensive movement was totally unexpected and that the enemy believed we were one hundred leagues away," he boasted to Marmont. "In this situation, it is essential that you observe carefully what occurs at Delitzsch and what kind of movement the enemy is making. Report several times during the day."[18]

In the center of the army, Dąbrowski's 27th Division formed the spearhead of the pursuing forces. Supported by VII Corps and Defrance's 4th Heavy Cavalry Division, the Poles marched north to Kemberg with orders to open communication with Wittenberg. With his light cavalry reconnoitering in the direction of Mühlbeck, Souham led III Corps halfway to Kemberg, halting at Schköna, some seven miles north of Bad Düben. Bertrand's IV Corps and Sébastiani's II Cavalry Corps marched to Pressel, five miles east of Bad Düben. To cut off Sacken, Napoleon's right wing – XI Corps, 3rd Light Division of I Cavalry Corps, and 2nd Light Division of II Cavalry Corps – advanced from Mockrehna toward Weidenhain, seeking signs of the Russians. Napoleon instructed Macdonald to pursue Sacken wherever he went: Dommitzsch, Pretzsch, or Kemberg. The parks, bridge train, and Grand Headquarters moved from Wurzen to Eilenburg.[19]

While the army marched, the emperor remained at Eilenburg. Uncertainty about the enemy's intentions caused him considerable concern. To his foreign minister, Maret, he addressed three letters starting at 10:00 in the morning. The first two ordered the minister, who quartered at Wurzen, to inform Paris "that we are on the eve of a great event that will have significant influence on the affair. Also, write in cipher to Lauriston and the king of Naples to request news from them. Write to Lauriston to establish communication with Nossen, where Marshal St.-Cyr has a brigade." Aggravated by Augereau's failure to communicate the whereabouts of IX Corps, Napoleon snapped. "I still don't know if the duc de Castiglione [Augereau] has arrived at Leipzig. I count on the arrival of this corps to send the king of Saxony there." Apparently, the emperor felt that Frederick Augustus deserved better than following with the imperial baggage. "If I learn that the duc de Castiglione has reached Leipzig, possibly tomorrow I will send the king of Saxony to that city." He also directed Maret to "write in duplicate and triplicate to St.-Cyr, have the former delivered by local agents and the latter by courier, and above all you must send me news of Leipzig three or four times a day. At this moment, all information is most important to me. I am in great haste to receive information from Leipzig on the movements of the enemy, and whether they are retreating or advancing; it appears that his greatest strength is between the Mulde and the Saale. It is between the Mulde and the Elbe that I prepare to maneuver until new information and events make me move all to the Elbe."

In the third letter, Napoleon informed Maret that a report from St.-Cyr dated 10:00 P.M. on the 9th had arrived. He tasked the foreign minister with conveying his response, which revealed his plans, in code: "Tell him that the head of my army will be at Wittenberg today; that a battle is possible tomorrow or the day after tomorrow; that, as soon as this occurs, I will return to him. Tell him that you have news of the king of Naples, who is at Altenburg, Frohburg, Penig, and Colditz." He expressed his desire that St.-Cyr hold Dresden but, if the marshal could not, he should retreat to Torgau along either bank of the Elbe. "If I fight and beat the enemy here," advised Napoleon, "the Austrians will return to their borders, and I will approach Torgau along the right bank, establish communication with him [St.-Cyr], and then visit Berlin." On the contrary, if he could not force Blücher and Bernadotte into a battle, "it is very possible that I will maneuver on the right bank of the Elbe because, as all of the enemy's plans have been based on my movements along the left bank, I would thus fall on their line of operation, and following the events of today and tomorrow [the effect of] this could be incalculable; I plan on firmness and prudence."[20]

Around noon, the emperor rode to the new headquarters prepared for him at the Bad Düben Schloß, where he finally received crucial information. The news was not good. He learned of the Bohemian Army's advance on Leipzig. The Austrians had debouched through Penig while Wittgenstein moved through Altenburg and Zeitz purportedly with 25,000 men. This meant that Murat would probably be forced to yield his positions at Frohburg, Borna, and Rochlitz, and withdraw on Leipzig. Further east, Bubna attacked St.-Cyr at Dresden. Despite this news, the emperor still sought a decisive battle with Blücher and Bernadotte. Unwilling to break off the chase and rush to Murat's aid, he made a momentous decision. Rather than worry about Leipzig and Dresden, he would withdraw all of his forces to the right bank of the Elbe.

At 3:00 on the afternoon of 10 October, a courier sped to Wurzen bearing a fourth letter addressed to Maret ordering the evacuation of all war materiel from Leipzig to Eilenburg, beginning that very night. Instead of going to the second city of his kingdom, Frederick August would be escorted to Eilenburg as well. "In case the king of Naples is forced to evacuate Leipzig, my intention is to cross the Elbe with my entire army; by doing this I will either drive the Armies of Silesia and Berlin [North Germany] onto the right bank of the Elbe and obtain time to destroy them or, if they prefer to sacrifice their bridges, I will leave them on the left bank and transfer my line of operations to the right bank of the Elbe, from Dresden to Magdeburg." If Schwarzenberg forced Murat to abandon Leipzig, Napoleon instructed his brother-in-law to withdraw toward Torgau and Wittenberg: "My plan is to cross over to the right bank of the Elbe."[21]

Thus, the emperor prepared to abandon Saxony and transfer the theater of war to North Germany. With Magdeburg as his new base of operations, he could maneuver on the right bank of the Elbe, slashing the communications of the North German and Silesian Armies, and debouching at will through Wittenberg, Torgau, Magdeburg, and Dresden to surprise the Allies, relieve the Oder garrisons, raise the Poles, and trap the Swedes on the continent. Communication with France would run along the Magdeburg–Wesel road. By transferring his army to the relatively untouched lands of North Germany, his headaches over supply would be alleviated. Conversely, the Allied armies would face starvation on the now-barren wastelands of Saxony until convoys could arrive from Silesia and Bohemia. Lastly, the master would be able to unite with his best lieutenant: the iron marshal, Davout.

Instructing Maret to also inform St.-Cyr of these arrangements, he insisted that the minister use the cipher: "it is better to write nothing than write without using the code; see to it that for three days this is the great secret of the army; if the enemy manages to get hold of these plans, it would cause me the greatest damage. You will send this news to Dresden by post and by locals. Also write in code to the foreign ministry at Paris so that no one is surprised by anything published by the enemy, and so they know that this is a combined movement on my part to bring the enemy to battle and produce something decisive." As for his erstwhile ally, Frederick August, Napoleon counseled Maret to keep him in the dark: "There is no need to entrust this secret to the king. You will tell him only that the affair goes well; that I have raised the siege of Wittenberg, but that the combined movements do not allow him to go to Leipzig at this moment; that it is better for him to go to Wittenberg or to Torgau."[22]

By 4:00, Napoleon's mind was set. He issued orders sending III Corps and 4th Heavy Cavalry Division to Gräfenhainichen, VII Corps to Kemberg, and 27th Division to Wittenberg. According to reports, Sacken appeared to be retreating eastward to Wartenburg. Consequently, Napoleon directed IV Corps and II Cavalry Corps to Trebitz on the road to Wartenburg, with XI Corps following. Indicative of the emperor's demand for speed, he wrote directly to Reynier and Bertrand. "It is essential that you arrive promptly" at Kemberg, he urged the former, while to the latter he emphasized that "it is indispensable that you march rapidly on Wartenburg." Napoleon wanted the Young Guard posted in a "military position" north of the Bad Düben windmill while the Old Guard moved into Bad Düben with VI Corps to form the reserve. All marches needed to be completed that night and all materiel coming from Leipzig would continue to Wittenberg.[23]

No sooner did Napoleon finish dictating the letter to Bertrand than a new report arrived: instead of marching east, Sacken's corps had escaped westward by crossing the Mulde at Raguhn. In a postscript, Napoleon modified Bertrand's orders. As soon as he received confirmation that the enemy no longer possessed a bridge at Wartenburg, Bertrand would lead IV Corps to Wittenberg. Despite the emperor's admonishment, Bertrand could get his men to go no farther than Bad Schmiedeberg, where they halted after midnight; XI Corps bivouacked at Falkenberg and Weidenhain. Already exhausted from the day's march, most of the troops failed to achieve their objectives. Only III Corps and 4th Heavy Cavalry Division (Gräfen-hainichen and Gröbern), VII Corps (Kemberg), and the Guard (Bad Düben) met the emperor's expectations. Dąbrowski forwarded only a small detachment to Wittenberg while Marmont's VI Corps remained on the left bank of the Mulde opposite Bad Düben (see Map 5).[24]

The news that Napoleon received from several sources confirmed Blücher's retreat to Dessau, where Sacken had also arrived. With Blücher on the run, he considered his next step, the relief of Wittenberg, to be indispensable. "For tomorrow," he explained to Reynier, "it is essential to overwhelm the corps that is in front of Wittenberg [and] seize the right bank, where it is possible I will cross with my whole army because I ordered all military materiel transferred from Leipzig to Wittenberg." Reports also placed the Army of North Germany at the Saale, a move that the emperor believed to be in concert with Schwarzenberg's advance. "To wreck these plans, I will go to the Elbe where I will have the advantage because I possess Hamburg, Magdeburg, Wittenberg, Torgau, and Dresden." He still hoped to have a battle on the next day, the 11th, with at least Blücher. "The Army of Silesia is retreating on all sides," he informed St.-Cyr. "We have taken several hundred prisoners; tomorrow I will oblige it to accept battle or surrender its bridges at Dessau and Wartenburg. Then, I may decide to cross to the right bank with my whole army; it is along the right bank that I will move on Dresden."[25]

Napoleon felt certain Blücher could be maneuvered into a battle in the Dessau–Roßlau region. If the Prussian evaded a confrontation, Napoleon would cross the Elbe at Wittenberg, destroying the bridges at Roßlau, Aken, and Wartenburg from the right bank. He hoped that, if he threatened these bridges, both Blücher and Bernadotte would accept battle to protect their points of passage. He figured that the defeat of these two adversaries would prompt Schwarzenberg to fly across the Erzgebirge without risking battle. If Schwarzenberg held his ground, Napoleon would return to Dresden and commence an operation to drive the Bohemian Army out of Saxony. As soon as the Allies evacuated Saxony, he would return to his pet project of taking Berlin.[26]

With the likelihood of battle increasing, Napoleon's confidence returned and he shook himself free of the despondency and uncertainty that had purportedly seized him for much of the 10th. "If you have nothing else facing you besides Wittgenstein and you do not experience any mishaps," he encouraged Murat, "you will be equal in number to him after you are reinforced by the duc de Castiglione and the garrison of Leipzig. If it means detaching a corps of 20,000 men to facilitate your defense of Leipzig, I could send it to you in a few hours. The Austrians, having a considerable corps this side of Dresden, could be very strong compared to you. Finally, my general instructions that I have issued and my intentions ... will remedy all." To Arrighi at Leipzig, he explained his plans with some exaggeration: "I have relieved Wittenberg and the Silesian Army is in complete retreat to Dessau and its bridges. Tomorrow I will either force it to accept battle or take its bridges. I assume that the king of Naples, united with you and Augereau, can hold Leipzig. If this is not the case, the retreat should proceed to the bridges over the Mulde at Eilenburg and Bad Düben, and if necessary to the Elbe through Wittenberg and Torgau." If he did not have time to defeat Blücher and Bernadotte before Schwarzenberg reached Leipzig, he intended "to thoroughly confuse the enemy by abandoning the entire left bank to obtain time to destroy this army, having at my disposal the magazines and crossings at Dresden, Torgau, Wittenberg, and Magdeburg. This requires the utmost secrecy; write only in code."[27]

At 5:00 P.M., he again wrote to reassure Murat: "During tomorrow, the day of the 11th, I will have either swept away the enemy or destroyed his bridges and driven him across the river. Having expelled the Army of Silesia, I will then be at Leipzig with my whole army on the day of the 13th." He estimated Murat's strength to be 49,000 infantry and 12,700 cavalry, repeating that he could easily send 20,000 reinforcements, "which would give you more than 80,000 men." Moreover, the master assumed that, if only Wittgenstein and Kleist confronted Murat, they could field no more than 50,000 men. Yet if Schwarzenberg added a single Austrian corps to the mix, the Allies could easily advance with 80,000 men. Consequently, he warned Murat to take a very good position and accurately estimate the size of the force facing him. "I have already noted," stated Napoleon's last sentence, almost in the form of a plea to encourage his brother-in-law, "that the whole army can be at Leipzig on the 13th."[28]

Shortly before 1:00 A.M. on the 11th, Napoleon received confirmation that Sacken's corps had reached Dessau. Based on this verification, he concluded that the rest of the Silesian Army as well as the North German Army would concentrate there as well. Napoleon initially reacted by ordering Macdonald to march on Wittenberg at dawn so XI Corps could cross the Elbe that same day. He tasked Bertrand's IV Corps with confirming the removal of the bridge at Wartenburg, leaving a post there, and then likewise proceeding to Wittenberg. After two hours of thought, Napoleon issued a more comprehensive plan for operations at 3:00 A.M. on the 11th. He informed Berthier that "all of the enemy's army appears concentrated at Dessau." Thus, he intended to cross the Elbe and proceed along the right bank to Roßlau. To achieve mass on the right bank, he demanded that VII Corps and 27th Division reach Wittenberg very early on the 11th and immediately cross the river followed by II Cavalry Corps. Souham's III Corps would remain at Gräfenhainichen, monitoring the roads to Dessau, Raguhn, Jeßnitz, and Mühlbeck. Marmont received orders for VI Corps to cross the Mulde and occupy Bad Düben as soon as the Guard and I Cavalry Corps departed for Kemberg at 6:00 A.M. Instead of following his main body, the marshal himself would depart one hour before dawn with his own cavalry brigade as well as the 5th Light Cavalry Division from III Cavalry Corps and enough infantry to form a combined-arms column of 4,000 to 5,000 men to clear the enemy from Bitterfeld and reconnoiter toward Jeßnitz, Delitzsch, and Leipzig. Napoleon simply reiterated his assignments for Bertrand and Macdonald. Lefebvre-Desnouettes's 2nd Guard Cavalry Division would form the rearguard and maintain communication with Leipzig throughout the day. After issuing this flurry of orders, all Napoleon could do was wait and wonder if he could catch Blücher.[29]

Around 5:00 on the morning of 11 October, the Silesian Army commenced its march to Wettin. Blücher's disposition for the 11th called for

Yorck's corps to march sixteen miles west from Zörbig to Wettin. Blücher informed Yorck that his corps would cross the Saale over Bernadotte's pontoon bridge, which would be built slightly downstream of Wettin. On different roads than those used by Yorck, Langeron's corps would march seventeen miles from Zörbig to Wettin, where it would cross the Saale by way of the Silesian Army's pontoon bridge slightly upstream of the town. Sacken would recall all posts that still stood east of the Mulde, dismantle the bridges at Raguhn and Jeßnitz, and then march through Radegast to Wettin. Yorck's and Langeron's vanguards would serve as rearguards by maintaining the positions they moved into on the 10th, while Sacken's would follow its main body. Blücher informed his corps commanders that 5,000 Allied soldiers had already occupied Halle and that the Army of North Germany would likewise cross the Saale: Bülow at Wettin, Wintzingerode at Rothenburg, and the Swedes at Alsleben.[30]

Difficulties plagued this operation from the start. On 10 October, Gneisenau sent a Lieutenant Ösfeld to the position upstream of Wettin between the villages of Pfützthal and Salzmünde to report on the construction of Blücher's pontoon bridge, which Headquarters expected to have already reached Jeßnitz, some twenty-seven miles to the northwest. As of Ösfeld's 10:00 P.M. report on 10 October, the Russian pontoons had yet to arrive. This report reached Blücher during the predawn hours of the 11th. Nevertheless, the movements commenced. As the columns of Yorck and Langeron approached Petersberg, some eight miles east of Wettin, Blücher learned that the pontoon train would not reach Wettin until evening. This meant that the Silesian Army would be limited to the sole bridge that the Prussians *believed* Bernadotte would have ready at Wettin at daybreak. About four miles northeast of Wettin, Lieutenant Scharnhorst, who had been sent forward to check on the progress of the crown prince's bridge, returned with the discouraging news that no bridge existed at Wettin and no preparations were underway to build one. Naturally, Blücher interpreted this as Bernadotte's insidious attempt to force the Silesian Army to remain with him on the lower Saale. To be sure the crown prince learned a lesson, he ordered the army to immediately swing south, strike the highway that ran from Magdeburg to Halle, and cross the Saale at the latter. Describing the result of this apparent breach of faith, Müffling relates: "Here, the commanding general appears to have resolved to no longer proceed in concert with the crown prince, to rely only on his own forces, to make decisions in the future without consulting the crown prince, and to communicate to him only his decision."[31]

Several times the Russian and Prussian columns became entangled, making an extraordinarily long and exhausting march of twenty-three miles much worse. Langeron's corps reached Halle first, crossed the Saale, and bivouacked north of the town. Yorck's corps arrived shortly after but had to wait several hours for the Russians to finish parading through the city and crossing its sole bridge; the Prussian troops did not step foot on the left bank until 2:00 A.M. on the 12th. Despite the hour, the inhabitants purportedly rejoiced throughout "the good old Prussian city." "The town," recalled Steffens, who had earlier worked as a professor at the University of Halle, "had suffered much and was in great excitement. It was known that the Bohemian Army had advanced and was concentrating; that the enemy had drawn all his forces toward Leipzig; and that a great battle could be expected. Gneisenau occupied my old dwelling, and it seemed strange to see him in that former retreat of household joys and cares." The Prussian troops bivouacked in and around Halle, with the Reserve Cavalry remaining on the right bank. As a result of miscommunication, Langeron's cavalry never received orders to march to Halle but instead went to Wettin. On arriving, it received instructions to continue to Halle, where it arrived at 12:00 A.M. on the night of the 11th/12th. The Russian cavalry crossed the Saale later in the day and bivouacked a few miles upstream of Halle. Blücher's cavalry posts extended as far east as Bitterfeld; detachments from Vorontsov's vanguard patrolled southeast from Halle toward Leipzig.

Around 5:00 A.M. on 11 October, Sacken's corps marched southwest from the left bank of the Mulde. Sacken himself remained at Raguhn awaiting reports from patrols on the right bank. At 9:30 he dispatched a summary of their findings to Blücher. The Russians encountered French bivouacs at Gräfenhainichen and Gröbern. No imperial forces had appeared at Raguhn by the time Sacken departed. After a march of twenty-five miles, his corps reached Wettin shortly before midnight and bivouacked on the right bank of the Saale.

Northeast of the Silesian Army, the Army of North Germany marched west to the Saale early on the morning of the 11th. The Swedes crossed at Alsleben and the Russians at Rothenburg. After learning of Blücher's march to Halle, Bülow led his corps to Rothenburg as well. Yet Wintzingerode's troops took so long to cross the river that Bülow's men passed the night on the right bank. Tauentzien's IV Corps remained at Dessau astride both banks of the Mulde with forward troops pushed to Wörlitz and Oranienbaum.[32]

That evening, Blücher reported his progress to Tsar Alexander: "The enemy continued his march. Our patrols found his bivouac on the night of the 10th at Gräfenhainichen. Therefore, it appears that the enemy thinks I took the road to Dessau, where Tauentzien's corps stands. Tomorrow I will occupy Merseburg with St.-Priest's corps. After this secures communication with the Bohemian Army, I will await your orders. The three armies now stand so close to each other that a simultaneous attack can occur on any point where the enemy concentrates his forces." To Bernadotte he wrote: "On arriving at Wettin, I found that the bridges still had not been built; I thus decided to march to Halle and concentrate the army there. According to the reports that the courier will give you, I assume that you will push your corps toward Leipzig to be able to attack the enemy in unison with the Bohemian Army. I request that you give me your decision over this."[33]

"I heard you encountered many obstacles in striking a bridge at Wettin and so decided to go to Halle," responded the crown prince. "The position you have taken at Halle implicitly places you in the front line." According to Bernadotte, the latest intelligence indicated that Napoleon had united all of his troops at Leipzig apparently to proceed south to Altenburg. Moreover, Augereau stood somewhere between Naumburg and Weißenfels. If Blücher intended to maintain his position astride the Saale at Halle on the 12th, the crown prince offered to leave Bülow's corps on the right bank as well. North of III Corps, the Swedes and Russians would remain ready to march. "Positioned in this manner," continued Bernadotte, "we will be able to march to Leipzig if the emperor Napoleon moves on Altenburg. If he comes toward us, we will be able to decide to fight or withdraw to the left bank of the Saale." Moreover, the crown prince would direct Tauentzien to Zörbig "so that we can always maintain communication with Aken and thus with Dessau. I request that you inform me of your plans because it is extremely necessary that we act together to cause the emperor Napoleon as much damage as we can in his critical situation. When our troops are united, we will, you and I, be in the position to deliver a battle or to avoid it if we mutually agree on our plan of operations." While he did not reject the idea of accepting battle, the crown prince offered no response to Blücher's request for him to move closer to Halle – classic Bernadotte.[34]

For 12 October, Blücher issued specific orders to his corps commanders. To form the army's vanguard, St.-Priest's corps would occupy Merseburg, nine miles south of Halle and seventeen miles west of Leipzig. Korf likewise would lead Langeron's Reserve Cavalry to Merseburg while Rudzevich remained at Petersberg with the Langeron's vanguard to shield the army. If the French pursued in force, Rudzevich would withdraw across the Saale via the Russian pontoon bridge that Blücher still expected to be built at Wettin, unlimber his artillery on the left bank, and cover the dismantling of the bridge. Yorck received instructions to remain at Halle with his Reserve Cavalry on the right bank. Katzler and the Prussian vanguard, likewise at Petersberg, would cooperate with Rudzevich. For Sacken, Blücher's disposition called for the Russian corps to cross the Saale at Wettin and march twelve miles south.[35]

During the 12th, St.-Priest moved his 12,000 men into Merseburg and established communication with the Bohemian Army's forward cavalry detachments. Sacken's corps crossed the Saale at Wettin and proceeded south along the only available road, which left much to be desired. Due to its poor condition, the Russians reached only Teutschenthal, eight miles west of Halle, by nightfall. Little about the imperials could be gleaned from the confusing reports that reached Blücher's headquarters. Near Bad Düben, prowling Cossacks captured an army surgeon attached to the Young Guard. He claimed that Napoleon had first intended to go from Dresden to Leipzig but then turned north to Bad Düben from where he planned to continue to Wittenberg. Katzler reported that his patrols encountered only weak enemy posts on the highway from Delitzsch to Eilenburg. Moreover, only two infantry regiments purportedly held Leipzig. General Joseph O'Rourke, a native Russian of Irish descent who patrolled the Halle–Leipzig road with a detachment of Wintzingerode's cavalry, informed Blücher that the imperials had moved west across the Mulde to occupy Bitterfeld but had evacuated the town in the evening. At Leipzig, O'Rourke's patrols encountered French posts along the length of the Parthe River but found no signs of the enemy on the roads running from Leipzig to Merseburg and Lützen. His troopers reported hearing heavy artillery fire from the direction of Borna. On the roads leading south from Zwenkau and Pegau, the Russians found Murat's army awaiting the arrival of Schwarzenberg's legions.[36]

Blücher and his staff viewed the prospect of Napoleon's continuing his offensive to Wittenberg with skepticism, thinking any movement in that direction to be a demonstration intended to mislead the Allies. Nevertheless, to determine if the emperor intended to continue north toward Wittenberg or turn south against the Bohemian Army, Blücher ordered a general reconnaissance toward Leipzig for the 13th. The disposition called for Yorck's and Langeron's vanguards to depart at daybreak from Petersberg with Katzler's infantry marching to Bruckdorf and Rudzevich's to Reideburg. Katzler's cavalry and horse artillery would make for Brehna while Rudzevich's would proceed to Kölsa on the Landsberg–Leipzig road. "The cavalry of both vanguards will reconnoiter toward Leipzig and seek the enemy. It is very important to send reports of his movements. At the same time, the cavalry of the crown prince of Sweden will reconnoiter toward Bitterfeld and Delitzsch." At dawn, Blücher wanted the Russian pontoon bridge at Wettin disassembled and rebuilt at Giebichenstein, less than two miles north of Halle. If the French launched an offensive, Rudzevich would retreat across the Saale at Giebichenstein while Katzler did so at Halle. Blücher requested that Bernadotte conduct reconnaissance toward Bitterfeld and Delitzsch with 5,000 to 6,000 troopers supported by the appropriate horse artillery.[37]

News from Tsar Alexander's headquarters at Altenburg reached Blücher during the afternoon of the 12th. According to a Russian officer from Alexander's entourage, General Mikhail Vlodek, Schwarzenberg had reached Chemnitz on 8 October. To his east, the vanguard of the Austrian I Corps reached Zehista, less than two miles south of Pirna. That same day, Bubna took the bridgehead on the right bank of the Elbe opposite Pirna. The combined offensive forced the imperials to break their bridge at Pirna and retreat to Dresden. After reconnoitering Dresden, Bennigsen left 20,000 men under Osterman-Tolstoy to observe St.-Cyr's XIV and I Corps while he marched toward Leipzig via Colditz on the 10th with 30,000 men. In front of Schwarzenberg, Murat retreated north on the 10th after the Austrians had taken Penig the day before. On the 11th, Wittgenstein, Kleist, and General Johann von Klenau's Austrian IV Corps reached Borna, less than twenty miles south of Leipzig while Schwarzenberg moved to Altenburg, twenty-seven miles south of Leipzig.

According to Vlodek, patrols from General Ignác Gyulay's Austrian III Corps reached Lützen, less than thirteen miles southwest of Leipzig, the previous day. Twenty miles southeast of Gyulay, Kleist and Wittgenstein reached Borna. Further south, Allied Headquarters and the monarchs halted at Altenburg. Moreover, after posting Osterman-Tolstoy's corps to blockade Dresden, Bennigsen led the right wing of the Bohemian Army toward Leipzig as well. In light of this news, Blücher decided to have Yorck make an attempt to seize Leipzig. Yorck received instructions to advance early on the 13th and storm the city if he deemed it to be weakly guarded. In the opposite case, I Corps would remain before the city and await the support of the Bohemian Army. St.-Priest would facilitate the operation by sending forward a combined-arms detachment of 2,000 men to secure Yorck's left.[38]

Like the Silesian Army, the Army of North Germany maintained its positions on the 12th. Around 2:00 that afternoon, Bernadotte learned that a French force had crossed the Elbe at Wittenberg: its size and intentions could not be determined. In addition, imperial forces moved down the left bank of the Elbe toward Oranienbaum. Later in the day, the crown prince received word that the imperials had overrun Dessau and destroyed the bridge over the Elbe at Roßlau. Believing the corps that crossed at Wittenberg formed an advance guard, Bernadotte correctly assumed Napoleon intended to move his army from the left bank of the Elbe to the right, thus transferring the theater of war from Saxony to Brandenburg. He informed his corps commanders that 100,000 imperials stood between the Elbe and the Mulde. As a result, the crown prince ordered his army to unite at Köthen, twenty miles due north of Halle on the 13th.[39]

"I have just learned that the enemy is moving through Wittenberg and has repulsed Thümen," the crown prince informed Blücher. "Tauentzien has been forced to withdraw to the right bank of the Elbe in order to support Thümen. At the same time, I received news that the enemy has taken Dessau. All reports that arrived yesterday claim that the emperor Napoleon was at Eilenburg and intends to go to Bad Düben; a report from today claims that 25,000–30,000 men are between the latter and Wittenberg." We know from the crown prince's orders to his subordinates that he actually estimated this number to be 100,000 men. Bernadotte impressed on Blücher that "it would be imprudent to leave this corps to our rear if we march on

Leipzig. Because it is important to determine its actual strength, I have ordered Bülow and Wintzingerode to Köthen and from there to advance and attack it." While no mention of attacking this corps is made in his order of the day, he did instruct Bülow and Wintzingerode to push cavalry detachments eastward to Dessau, Jeßnitz, Bitterfeld, Landsberg, and Brehna. In his letter to Blücher, he repeated the claim that only a small force held Leipzig. Yet he attributed this to the rumor that the Bohemian Army had fought a battle at Altenburg on the 11th. "According to one report, only 2,000 men remain at Leipzig and the rest have moved to Altenburg, from where many wagons laden with wounded arrived in Leipzig. On Saturday [9 October], 7,000 cavalry arrived there from France and went to Altenburg on Sunday."[40]

Based on this news, the leadership of the Silesian Army concluded that, instead of attempting to mislead the Allies, Napoleon did indeed intend to move the Grande Armée across the Elbe, perhaps to retreat through Magdeburg. Should this be the case, Murat would be compelled to abandon Leipzig and withdraw across the Mulde to Wittenberg. Hoping to trap Murat, Blücher added a postscript to his letter to Yorck: "From the crown prince of Sweden I have just received the news that the enemy has repulsed Thümen from Wittenberg. Through your movement, you will probably be able to determine with certainty whether this is a demonstration or a retreat on Magdeburg."[41] Gneisenau wrote a few lines to his wife at Hirschberg in Silesia that conveyed the optimism that permeated Blücher's headquarters on the eve of the great confrontation at Leipzig:

> Since the 3rd of this month, on which day I last wrote you and gave you news of the combat of that day, our operations again have taken on the character of the unorthodox. To the rear of the enemy, we have crossed the Mulde and the Saale and since yesterday we have been here at Halle. Through this movement we have severed the enemy's communication with France but must expect that the enemy will throw himself on our communications and you will not have any news from us for a period. The situation is excellent. If great mistakes are not made ... victory for the good cause is completely guaranteed. Our Silesian Army under General Blücher earned great merit through the speed and boldness of its marches, through its exertions, and through the bravery with which it has fought.[42]

We left Napoleon at Bad Düben on 11 October. On this day, he expected VII, IV, and XI Corps, Dąbrowski's 27th Division, and I and II Cavalry Corps to cross the Elbe at Wittenberg, drive off the Prussian troops blockading the fortress, and then move downstream along the right bank to Bernadotte's bridge at Roßlau. This westward movement would be covered from the left bank by Ney with III Corps at Gräfenhainichen and Marmont with VI Corps at Bad Düben. The cavalry of both corps would observe all roads from Dessau to Delitzsch and maintain the emperor's communication with Leipzig. At Kemberg, the Guard would remain ready to engage in any direction. By the end of the day's toils on the 11th, the situation of the Grande Armée hardly corresponded to these plans. Of all the troops ordered to cross the Elbe, only 27th Division and VII Corps as well as 2nd Light Cavalry Division of II Cavalry Corps and 3rd Light Cavalry Division of I Cavalry Corps reached Wittenberg but considerably later than the emperor expected. Dąbrowski's and Reynier's troops deployed that evening along the right bank of the Elbe, facing the Prussian trenches. Thümen, who observed the large columns entering Wittenberg, withdrew west to the suburb of Piesteritz before departing in the night for Coswig. A heavy rain, the onset of darkness, and sheer exhaustion prevented the Saxons, Poles, and French from pursuing.[43]

While his army moved north, Napoleon had no idea that Blücher and Bernadotte had already escaped to the west. Uncertainty over Allied intentions and positions fouled the emperor's mood throughout the 11th. "The enemy had lots of people at Jeßnitz," he declared to Ney, "but this morning, no one. Some information suggests that the enemy will remove his bridges and remain on the left bank, vis-à-vis Roßlau. If so, where do we march to attack him, do we seize Dessau and block its bridgehead?" Although his orders indicated that he would proceed to Kemberg with the Young Guard, Napoleon remained at Bad Düben, where news could reach him more easily. "Maybe in the night I will go to Kemberg," he wrote Ney. "Have you any news from the detachments you sent to Dessau and other points along the Elbe?"

After cavalry sweeps found few enemy troops at Bitterfeld and Jeßnitz, Napoleon ordered Ney to move III Corps to Oranienbaum to cover the Wittenberg–Dessau road. He instructed the marshal to have Reynier send patrols west and northeast "to obtain clues about the enemy's intentions." As soon as the general drove off "the five or six battalions" observing Wittenberg, Napoleon wanted VII Corps and I Cavalry Corps to cross the Elbe and debouch on the northern side of the fortress. The news from Wittenberg itself did not appear very encouraging: "It appears we have few resources at Wittenberg," continued Napoleon in his letter to Ney. "There are many grains indeed but little flour and few means to grind." "I assume that the division blockading Wittenberg has now departed," Napoleon later wrote Reynier. "Drive it off as far as possible so flour can be delivered there along both banks."

Further reports indicated that the two Allied armies no longer stood at Dessau, but where they had gone could not be ascertained. Rumors claimed that the North German Army had withdrawn across the Elbe while the Silesian Army turned toward Halle. "Latour-Maubourg will soon arrive," Napoleon informed Reynier; "have him cross the bridge. With

Latour-Maubourg and the Saxon and Polish cavalry, you can patrol far and gain some indication of the enemy's intentions at Dessau. Does he intend to withdraw upon the right bank and deliver a battle, or does he intend to break the bridge and remain on the left bank? If you can reach Coswig, you will be able to obtain plenty of news. As soon as you have obtained intelligence on the situation, take a position north of the fortress [Wittenberg] so there is room for all the corps that will cross this night and tomorrow. The Guard will be close to Wittenberg tonight."[44]

Around 3:00 on the afternoon of 11 October, Napoleon again received news that no Allied forces remained at Raguhn and only a post held Dessau. "The enemy appears to be retreating on Köthen and Radegast," he wrote Ney. "Send strong reconnaissance parties toward Raguhn and Dessau to confirm this news." Marmont's patrols indicated that the Allied armies remained south of the Elbe. Ney's troops encountered enemy cavalry while patrolling toward Raguhn and Oranienbaum but failed to provide substantial news of the whereabouts of the Allied armies. Therefore, the reports that reached Napoleon during the night of 11/12 October offered little clarification: "All the information that I've been able to obtain states that, during the day of the 10th, Blücher went to Halle, the enemy's headquarters was near Radegast, and a lot of baggage remained at Köthen." Yet good news from the south helped ease his mind. Murat reported that he had repulsed Wittgenstein at Borna on the 10th. "Wittgenstein engaged the king of Naples at Borna," Napoleon wrote to Ney at 3:00 A.M. on 12 October. "Wittgenstein was beaten. At 11:00 A.M. on the 11th, Wittgenstein and the Austrian prince Schwarzenberg retreated on Frohburg."[45]

Thus, some reports claimed large Allied forces had retreated from Raguhn, Jeßnitz, and Bitterfeld in the direction of Halle while others indicated movements to Dessau–Roßlau – the opposite direction. This led Napoleon to assume that Blücher and Bernadotte had separated. Influenced by the presence of Tauentzien's corps in the Dessau–Roßlau region, the emperor hoped to find all or at least a significant portion of Bernadotte's army at Dessau. He concluded that Blücher must have gone to Halle. Consequently, Napoleon ordered VII Corps, Dąbrowski's 27th Division, and II Cavalry Corps to rapidly drive along the right bank of the Elbe to Roßlau. He figured XI Corps would complete the seven-mile march north from Rackith to reach Wittenberg later that morning. If the Allies offered resistance at Roßlau, XI Corps and I Cavalry Corps would cross the Elbe to support Reynier. If nothing opposed Reynier, these units would remain on the left bank. With III Corps and all the cavalry at his immediate disposal, Napoleon believed Ney could take Dessau and its bridgehead. As soon as Reynier secured Roßlau and made its bridgehead untenable, he wanted Ney to raze the bridgehead at Dessau, occupy the town in force, and build two bridges. "If your cavalry can debouch onto the plain of Dessau," speculated Napoleon, "I think it will do much harm to the enemy, who seems completely preoccupied with his offensive operations." Should VII Corps not need support on the right bank, IV Corps would join Ney at Dessau. Oudinot's Young Guard corps would take the place of III Corps at Gräfenhainichen, occupying both Raguhn and Jeßnitz with a vanguard. To observe Halle and Leipzig, Napoleon directed VI Corps to backtrack to Delitzsch. Mortier's Young Guard corps as well as the Old Guard received a day of rest on the 12th "because I think that if the enemy continues to disseminate I will need to march on him with my Guard and the duc de Raguse [Marmont]."[46]

Over the next sixty minutes, Napoleon's conviction that his adversaries had separated increased. "From this side, it appears fairly consistent that the majority of the Allied army is marching in the direction of Halle and the lower Saale," he notified Maret. Based on this belief, Napoleon formalized and expanded the ideas he had first expressed to Ney. His orders suggest that the master wanted to dictate where his adversary would go next. By taking the bridges at Dessau–Roßlau, he hoped to entice the Allies into accepting a battle to save their line of retreat. Between 4:00 and 4:30 A.M., he wrote direct to Reynier, Oudinot, and Marmont while Berthier addressed instructions to Ney and General Antoine Drouot. Only Reynier received a detailed explanation of the emperor's intentions: "All of the enemy's dispositions lead me to believe that Roßlau is not guarded in force and if you march with your corps and Dąbrowski, you will take possession of the enemy's bridges and a lot of baggage. Spread disorder everywhere and capture baggage. The enemy may well have counted on the incursion of some parties coming from Wittenberg but he did not foresee a serious operation." Oudinot's instructions called for his Young Guard to forward a combined-arms detachment to Raguhn and restore its bridge while 1st Guard Cavalry Division dispatched large patrols to Jeßnitz. Napoleon demanded that Oudinot remain in close communication with Ney and keep his bearskins ready to march wherever the situation demanded. Marmont received a challenging task. Not only did the emperor direct him to take a position at Delitzsch to cover Bad Düben, Jeßnitz, and Leipzig, but he also had to be prepared to attack any enemy forces marching from Halle to Leipzig. Thus, the orders issued early on the 12th sought to attack the Allied forces suspected to be at Dessau, to take Dessau and Roßlau, and to observe the enemy at Halle, keeping him in check should he advance on Leipzig.[47]

At Bad Düben, Napoleon waited impatiently for information that would clarify the situation. Late on the morning of 12 October he received news, but not the sort he wanted. Around 9:00 arrived Murat's report from the 11th, stating that, rather than retreating, Schwarzenberg had launched another offensive. Murat had already fallen back to the outer suburbs of Leipzig; his further retreat to the Mulde appeared likely. The impact of this report cannot be overstated. In an instant, Napoleon dropped his plans to transfer his army to the right bank of the Elbe. Instead, he considered concentrating the entire army for a showdown with the Allies at Taucha, six miles northeast of Leipzig.

Thirty minutes later he fired a dispatch to Berthier, instructing the staff chief to order Ney "to immediately, on receipt of this order, move all his troops to Bad Düben, cross the river there, and march to Taucha, where he must arrive on the 14th because it is my intention to reunite all of my forces and deliver a battle there." Instructions for Macdonald specified that the marshal should "move as fast as possible to Bad Düben, where it is indispensable that he arrive on the morning of the 14th." Reynier and Dąbrowski should "return to Bad Düben, where they must arrive on the 13th in order to be at Taucha on the 14th, where I intend to deliver a battle. Order Generals Bertrand, Sébastiani, and Latour-Maubourg to move immediately to Bad Düben." Napoleon planned for the Grande Armée to cross the Mulde at Bad Düben and converge on Leipzig on the 14th. By that evening, he wanted the forces under his command echeloned north of Leipzig from Taucha through Bad Düben to Kemberg.[48]

Thirty minutes after dictating these instructions to Berthier, the emperor committed his thoughts to paper in a note titled "Concerning the Concentration of the Various Army Corps at Taucha." Again, timing played the crucial role in Napoleon's calculations. "I have sent orders to Ney to proceed to Bad Düben. Ney cannot receive this order before 2:00 P.M. [on the 12th]; his troops will commence their march at 3:00; they cannot cross the bridge at Bad Düben until tomorrow the 13th (the Guard will have crossed already); they can reach Taucha by the evening of the 13th without difficulty." Regarding Latour-Maubourg's I Cavalry Corps, Napoleon assumed that, because it stood at Kemberg, it would have no difficulty likewise reaching Taucha by the 14th. Mortier, Oudinot, and the Reserve of the Guard would cross the Mulde at Bad Düben that day, 12 October, and reach Taucha early on the 13th. South of Leipzig, Murat's 50,000 men had reached the vicinity of Cröbern on the 12th, less than ten miles south of Leipzig, from where they would fall back to Taucha on the 13th. Napoleon planned to be at Taucha on the 13th with the 40,000 men of the Old and Young Guard as well as VI Corps. Together with Murat's 50,000, the emperor would have 90,000 men available for battle on the 13th. Moreover, "these 90,000 men will be reinforced during the course of the day by Ney, Bertrand, and Latour-Maubourg" (see Map 6).

As for the rest of the Grande Armée, Napoleon calculated that Macdonald would not receive the summons to Bad Düben until 3:00 that afternoon. If XI Corps had already crossed the Elbe, Napoleon figured it would need the entire night to recross the river. This meant XI Corps would reach Bad Düben on the 13th and commence the march to Taucha on the 14th. Reynier, en route to Roßlau with 27th Division, VII Corps, and II Cavalry Corps, could only reach Wittenberg by the evening of the 12th, meaning that he could not arrive at Taucha via Eilenburg until 15 October. Based on these calculations, the emperor concluded that "our entire army will be concentrated on the 15th." The forty-eight hours needed to concentrate the army did not trouble him. Figuring that Schwarzenberg's lead elements would reach Cröbern on the 13th, he assumed they would learn of the concentration at Taucha and respond by massing their troops throughout the 14th. "Therefore, I have the 13th and 14th to concentrate mine. Furthermore, even if my whole army were at Bad Düben it could not arrive any earlier unless it had at least five or six crossings" over the Mulde. As for numbers, Napoleon believed that by the 14th he would have 120,000 men in his first line and 70,000 men in the second.[49]

Napoleon completely changed his plans from an offensive to destroy Bernadotte in the Dessau–Roßlau region to a decisive battle with Schwarzenberg around Taucha. While criticism of Napoleon's supposed irresolution between 10 and 12 October is overly harsh, Blücher again seemed to have become an afterthought in Napoleon's planning.[50] "Tell me what you know of the Silesian Army from your side," he wrote to Marmont, "and the positions that could be taken against this army and against the army coming from Halle and or through Dessau."[51] Such carelessness combined with Blücher's determination to cooperate with Schwarzenberg ultimately ruined Napoleon's chances for a decisive victory over the Bohemian Army.

With only Tauentzien's Landwehr standing in his way, Ney smashed through the Prussian positions at Oranienbaum and Wörlitz early on the 12th; 1st Brigade of 8th Division took Wörlitz, destroying Figner's Russian *Streifkorps* consisting of Italian and German deserters. At noon, Delmas's 9th Division secured Dessau and its bridge. Thanks to the bridgehead, Tauentzien's troops managed to escape across the Mulde and then the Elbe via Roßlau but panic completely disordered the Landwehr. Reports that immense baggage trains and parks could be seen on the right bank of the Elbe north of Roßlau persuaded Napoleon that Bernadotte's army had fled across the Elbe at Aken. "The enemy appeared to be in great terror," he informed Marmont. Ney reported that his advance had netted more than 1,500 Allied prisoners, which Napoleon inflated to 2,500 men including 50 officers. Meanwhile, Reynier and Dąbrowski marched west from Wittenberg along the right bank toward Coswig. Six miles west of the fortress, Thümen decided to make a stand at the village of Griebo. As his brigade deployed in two waves, the Prussian general observed the approach of overwhelming numbers, threatening both his front and his flank. Seeing no need to sacrifice his men, Thümen commenced an orderly retreat to Roßlau around 4:00 P.M. Although exhausted stragglers fell into French hands, the brigade reached Roßlau intact around 9:00 that night.

Darkness ended Reynier's pursuit, which brought in 400 prisoners. Aside from this action, all other French units reached their objectives per Napoleon's orders but had relatively little to report.[52]

Although faulty intelligence placed the Army of North Germany on the right bank of the Elbe, Napoleon did not second-guess his decision to deliver a battle near Leipzig. In fact, the thought that he would have 40,000 to 50,000 fewer Allied soldiers to face in the upcoming battle pleased him. Throughout the 12th, he proceeded with preparations for the epic clash that he planned to deliver on 15 October. These included the distribution of 31,000 pairs of shoes from the depot at Leipzig. Nevertheless, anxiety set in. Around 4:00 on the afternoon of the 12th, Napoleon sent an officer to Leipzig to confirm that Murat had held his position at Cröbern and faced at least 60,000 Allied soldiers. To Maret he confided that, if Murat could hold his position throughout the 13th, Napoleon would continue with his plan to go to Leipzig and deliver a battle near Taucha. As soon as the officer confirmed that Murat held his position at Cröbern throughout the 12th, Napoleon would "depart with my Guard, so tomorrow during the day I will have 80,000 men at Taucha, and the rest of the army will arrive during the 14th." Should Murat fail to maintain his position, Napoleon would concentrate the army on the Mulde with Murat's units forming the left wing at Grimma and Wurzen. "I will then maneuver to give battle to the enemy."[53]

The officer Napoleon dispatched bore the emperor's letter to Murat asking hard questions but offering encouragement in the former's classic style. "During the course of the 13th," explained Napoleon, "I will be at Taucha with 70,000 men and during the course of the 15th all my army will be united there; I will not be in a position to give battle to save Leipzig until the 15th." He then bluntly asked: "Can you maintain both your position and Leipzig throughout the day of the 13th without compromising yourself?" Napoleon assured Murat that he would receive reinforcements throughout the day and especially during the night of 13/14 October. He instructed him to take a position with his left supported by Connewitz and his right extended toward Wurzen. "You will be increased by 80,000 men, whom I will bring to you; the rest of the army will arrive on the 14th. We will have 200,000 men by the morning of the 15th. If you cannot hold your position, direct your movements on Taucha and Wurzen."[54]

During the evening of the 12th, Napoleon's confidence increased. He learned of Ney's success at Dessau and eagerly awaited similar news from Reynier at Roßlau. He also received word that Augereau had reached Leipzig with enough reinforcements to reconstitute General Claude Pierre Pajol's V Cavalry Corps and boost Murat's troop strength to 60,000 men. According to reports from Dresden, Bennigsen had blockaded the city "with a bunch of poorly trained recruits who up to now have been considerably abused by our people." Again Blücher appeared to be an afterthought. "Apparently Blücher's corps was near Zörbig," he told Murat. "Some claim that it is marching toward Rothenburg near Könnern but this seems very apocryphal. It is to impose on him that I purposefully sent Marmont, as head of the column, in this direction. One report claims that Schkeuditz is a good position to take against an army coming from Halle. Reconnoiter the terrain." Based on this positive news, Napoleon briefly reconsidered going to Taucha and postponing his operation against Schwarzenberg. Although he did not reveal an alternative plan, the emperor informed Murat that, "if I do not go there to take part myself, I will send enough men to give you between 85,000 and 90,000; with them you need to win a few days. A good ruse is to fire salvos announcing a victory over another army. You should hold a review as if I was there and make the men shout: "*Vive l'Empereur!*" Do not forget the fact that it is very important to hold Leipzig. At around 1:00 in the morning I will receive reports from all sides and I will decide what my part will be."[55]

Four hours later, at 12:00 A.M. on the 13th, Napoleon revealed his alternative plan in a letter to Marmont, whom he now placed under Murat's command. "If Reynier has not seized Roßlau today, this will give me time to take it tomorrow, to defeat the army from Berlin, and finish all of the business there." Again, it would appear that charges of uncertainty and indecision can be leveled at the emperor. Instead, we see Napoleon's personality flaws influencing his judgment. Rather than censuring Napoleon for irresolution and torpor, we can consider him to be guilty of spite, stubbornness, pride, arrogance, and wishful thinking. Detesting Bernadotte, he had wanted to humiliate him since the Fall Campaign commenced. He harbored no respect for the Army of North Germany, derisively referring to it as a cloud of Cossacks and pack of bad Landwehr. Although two of his marshals had suffered reversals at its hands, the emperor would make short work of it to impress his mastery on them. Finally, the destruction of the Army of North Germany would partially fulfill his master plan centered on the Berlin offensive and perhaps initiate the further advantages he espoused in this scheme. Demonstrating his contempt for enemy troops, he believed Reynier and Ney could easily catch Bernadotte's retreating army and destroy it under the emperor's direction. Lastly, Napoleon surely wanted to have something to show for all his labors since leaving Dresden. Instead of irresolution and uncertainty, Napoleon is guilty of being fixated on destroying his former marshal. He desperately needed a victory; crushing Bernadotte's army would serve many purposes and fulfill many needs. Even with Schwarzenberg's army lumbering across the Saxon plain, he could not take his eyes off of the crown prince of Sweden. The vengeance of Emperor Napoleon appeared to master General Bonaparte.[56]

Yet by no means did Napoleon consider turning his back on the Bohemian Army. Although Murat had failed to stop Schwarzenberg's advance throughout the month of October, Napoleon had apparently convinced himself that his brother-in-law would finally halt the Coalition's main army. After destroying Bernadotte, the master would return to Leipzig and concentrate 200,000 men against Schwarzenberg. In the same letter to Marmont, he informed the marshal that "the decisive moment appears to have arrived. March in such a manner that you can help maintain Leipzig and send a request to the king for orders to join the battle; there is no longer a question that we will fight. If you hear the sound of the guns from the direction of Leipzig, accelerate your march and take part in the affair." Here again we see the conflict between Emperor Napoleon and General Bonaparte. Thirty minutes later, he informed Maret that "there is no longer any doubt that the army from Berlin has recrossed to the right bank" of the Elbe. Having reinforced Murat with Augereau and Marmont to a total of 90,000 men, Napoleon expressed his belief that he would "have the time to finish tomorrow the operations against the army that has crossed to the right bank." As for Blücher, he speculated to Marmont with a hint of indifference: "I suppose that the reconnaissance parties you sent in the direction of Halle have already reported back to you; conduct strong reconnaissance in this direction."[57]

As promised, Napoleon wrote to Murat at 1:00 A.M. on the 13th with a summary of the evening reports. He again confirmed that the Army of North Germany had withdrawn to the right bank of the Elbe. However, Ney reported hearing a cannonade from Reynier's vicinity between Coswig and Roßlau. "We do not yet know the outcome," wrote Napoleon, meaning he had yet to decide whether he would pursue Bernadotte or unite with Murat. Three hours later, he returned to the idea of concentrating the army for a decisive battle near Leipzig. Writers such as Petre and Yorck von Wartenburg have attributed this decision to Napoleon's discovery that Bernadotte's army had remained south of the Elbe. However, the emperor's correspondence suggests that he did not know of Bernadotte's whereabouts at the time he made this decision.[58] Instead, at 4:00 A.M. on the 13th, he informed Maret that Reynier took Roßlau along with 600 prisoners but the enemy had dismantled the bridge; Reynier would now march to Aken. At the same time, he issued orders to Berthier to instruct I Cavalry Corps as well as the Guard units under Oudinot, Mortier, Frédéric-Henri Walther, and Ornano to move to Bad Düben without delay. One hour later, Napoleon summoned IV and III Corps to Bad Düben as well.[59] According to Yorck von Wartenburg's assessment:

> It cannot be open to any doubt, that, as matters stood on 12 October, the emperor no longer had any choice but to depart for Leipzig; this was the punishment for his irresolution. To have now carried out that bold operation

beyond the Elbe would have meant only a blind sally into air; there were no longer any forces there, and Murat, left to face thrice his numbers unsupported, would have been lost. But the departure for Leipzig was, in itself, only a maneuver dictated by despair; were the whole French army there, it would face greatly superior forces, for nothing could now prevent the enemy from advancing thither with all their forces, and the tactical position there, as Marmont said very appositely, "at the bottom of a funnel," would lead to annihilation should the battle be lost. Strategically the emperor was already lost. Blücher and Schwarzenberg stood ominously near his only lines of communication with their main forces, and had already effected communication with each other to his rear. If we take the most unfavorable positions in modern warfare – Ulm, Jena, Sedan – we shall find none worse than this.[60]

Rather than irresolution and despair, Napoleon's decision arose from a practical reassessment of the situation. Schwarzenberg's army stood right under his nose. Although assembling his forces, he kept an open mind, cautioning Ney that "we should not concentrate too hastily." Moreover, he did not renounce completely his pet project of smashing Bernadotte: "If the crown prince of Sweden has moved to the right bank with his army from Berlin, that means we will face 40,000 fewer men in battle; if, on the contrary, the crown prince of Sweden is still on the left bank, then he will have all the more reason to withdraw." Clinging to the hope of inflicting some damage on any units of the Army of North Germany that remained south of the Elbe, Napoleon charged Ney with collecting as much information as possible concerning the enemy troops that had passed through Dessau, "division by division, regiment by regiment." In light of this, Napoleon planned to have Reynier continue his march to Aken on the 14th. To support VII Corps, he instructed Ney to make a diversion on the left bank of the Elbe near Aken. Regardless, as soon as Reynier destroyed the bridge at Aken, the emperor wanted Ney to move to Bad Düben "because undoubtedly there will be a great battle at Leipzig."[61]

Between 5:00 and 6:00 on the morning of the 13th, Napoleon learned that Bernadotte's headquarters had been at Bernburg on the Saale – some forty-five miles west of Bad Düben – on 11 October. His resolve to deliver an epic battle at Leipzig hardened as his interest in Bernadotte's whereabouts ebbed. He figured that Reynier would be master of Roßlau by daybreak. From there, VII Corps would obtain news of the situation at Aken. Believing the operation on the right bank of the Elbe no longer required XI Corps and II Cavalry Corps, he summoned them to Bad Düben. "After completing his operation," Napoleon explained to Macdonald, "General Reynier will return to Wittenberg to likewise move to Leipzig, where I think we will have a general battle. He should be able to cross the bridge at Bad Düben tomorrow before dark. If you know of Bertrand's whereabouts, let him

know he has been summoned to march today, the 13th, to Bad Düben."
Napoleon explained that 90,000 men under Murat held Leipzig against
the "Austrian army." He correctly placed Blücher's army at Halle. "We
are at a very important moment. I think the battle will take place on the
15th or 16th. If the entire army from Berlin has crossed to the right bank,
as is asserted, we would be rid of 40,000 men." With this, the emperor finally
shook himself free of his obsession with Bernadotte and turned to the
business at hand.[62]

By 10:00 on the morning of the 13th, thoughts of the situation around
Leipzig consumed Napoleon. By reinforcing Murat to 90,000 men, he
figured the king could hold Schwarzenberg south of Leipzig. In light of
this, Napoleon decided to deliver the battle at Leipzig rather than Taucha.
He issued orders for the rear echelons of the Guard to immediately
commence the march to Bad Düben. He calculated on the Young Guard
divisions (two each) under Mortier and Oudinot clearing Bad Düben during
the course of the day and reaching Hohenleina and Lindenhayn respectively,
the halfway points to Leipzig. Napoleon contemplated going to Hohenleina
that night; he expected the rest of the army to arrive there during the course
of the 14th. As they arrived, he planned to place them around Leipzig,
keeping the Guard in the center as his reserve.[63]

Between 8 and 13 October, Napoleon missed a great opportunity to
defeat Blücher's Army of Silesia and probably the Army of North Germany
as well. Instead of crushing these two armies against the Elbe River, the
French emperor found that his prey had escaped west and across the
Saale River. Although the Allied retreat across the Saale opened the road
to Berlin and North Germany, the time for Napoleon to execute a *coup de
théâtre* had passed. Moving north and across the Elbe would have saved him
the garrisons at Torgau, Wittenberg, Magdeburg, and Stettin as well as
Davout's XIII Corps at Hamburg. Moreover, by exchanging places with
the Allies, Napoleon could have stranded the Bohemian, Silesian, and North
German Armies in the depleted Saxon countryside and held the right bank
of the Elbe against them from Hamburg to Dresden. His forces south of
Leipzig could probably have escaped eastward to Torgau before the Allies
caught them. Yet the time for running was over. No maneuver, flank march,
or surprise attack could truly alter the course of the war unless it led to
the destruction of one or more of the Allied armies. At this late stage of the
campaign, Napoleon knew that it mattered little if he reached Hamburg or
Danzig; he still needed to destroy the enemy's ability to wage war. Mounting
war-weariness in France meant that a decision soon had to be reached.
Instead of wasting his scant resources by evacuating the theater, he decided
to draw the Allies to Leipzig for an epic struggle. He hoped to unite 200,000
men at Leipzig by 14 October to wage a decisive conclusion to the campaign: the Battle of Nations.

Notes

1 "Secret Disposition for 9 October," Bad Düben, 8:00 A.M., 9 October 1813, ÖStA KA, FA 1535, 277b, and Add MSS, 12,112, 154; Blücher to Shcherbatov, Bad Düben, 8:00 A.M., 9 October 1813, ÖStA KA, FA 1535, 277a; Blücher to Frederick William, Bad Düben, 9 October 1813, GStA PK, VI HA Rep. 92 Nl. Gneisenau, Nr. 16.
2 Sacken's march proceeded through Wildenhain, Pressel, Authausen, Durchwehna, and Söllichau to Schköna.
3 Müffling, *Die Feldzüge*, 64–66.
4 Quoted in Droysen, *Yorck*, II:203. The account of 9 October is based on Plotho, *Der Krieg*, II:293–95; Beitzke, *Geschichte der deutschen Freiheitskriege*, II:485–86; Höpfner, "Darstellung," 1845:343–46; Bogdanovich, *Geschichte des Krieges*, IIb:59–60; Unger, *Blücher*, II:106; Yorck, *Droysen*, 202–03; Friederich, *Herbstfeldzug 1813*, II:325–26.
5 Blücher to Charles John, Jeßnitz, 9 October 1813, GStA PK, VI HA Rep. 92 Nl. Gneisenau, Nr. 23, and Add MSS, 20112, 71–72.
6 Charles John to Blücher, Zehbitz, 9 October 1813, Add MSS, 20112, 69; Müffling, *Die Feldzüge*, 66–67; Unger, *Blücher*, II:106.
7 Blücher to Charles John, Jeßnitz, 10 October 1813, Add MSS, 20112, 74.
8 Disposition, Jeßnitz, 10 October 1813, Add MSS, 20012, 155; Höpfner, "Darstellung," 1845:351, 354.
9 Müffling, *Aus meinem Leben*, 86; Unger, *Blücher*, II:106.
10 SHAT, C¹⁷ 133: Charles John to Wintzingerode, 9 October 1813.
11 Müffling, *Die Feldzüge*, 68.
12 Nostitz, *Tagebuch*, 67–68.
13 SHAT, C¹⁷ 133: Charles John to Bülow, 9 October 1813; Müffling, *Die Feldzüge*, 68–69, and *Aus meinem Leben*, 87; Höpfner, "Darstellung," 1845:352.
14 SHAT, C¹⁷ 133: Charles John to Wintzingerode, 9 and 10 October 1813.
15 SHAT, C¹⁷ 133: Charles John to Tauentzien, Hirschfeld, and Stedingk, 10 October 1813.
16 SHAT, C¹⁷ 133: Order of the Day, 10 October 1813; Charles John to Bülow, 10 October 1813; Charles John to Blücher, Großweißandt, 10 October 1813, Add MSS, 20112, 73.
17 The reports from Klüx, Korf, and Sacken are in Höpfner, "Darstellung," 1845:353–54.
18 *CN*, Nos. 20740 and 20741, XXVI:316–17; Odeleben, *A Circumstantial Narrative*, II:4; Friederich, *Herbstfeldzug 1813*, II:324–25.
19 *CN*, Nos. 20736–20739, XXVI:314–15; SHAT, C¹⁷ 181: Berthier to Lefebvre-Desnouettes, Marmont, Macdonald, Ney, Latour-Maubourg, Bertrand, Sébastiani, Sorbier, Rogniat, and Lassaux, 10 October 1813.
20 *CN*, Nos. 20743–20745, XXVI:318–20.
21 *CN*, No. 20746, XXVI:320–21.
22 *CN*, No. 20746, XXVI:320–21.
23 *CN*, Nos. 20747, 20750, and 20751, XXVI:321–22, 324–25; SHAT, C¹⁷ 181: Berthier to Ney and Druout, 10 October 1813.

24 Friederich, *Herbstfeldzug 1813*, II:332–33.

25 SHAT, C¹⁷ 181: Berthier to Sébastiani, 10 October 1813; *CN*, Nos. 20750 and 20752, XXVI:324–25.

26 SHAT, C¹⁷ 181: Berthier to Marmont, 10 October 1813; Friederich, *Herbstfeldzug 1813*, II:331.

27 *CN*, Nos. 20748 and 20749, XXVI:322–23. For Napoleon's despondency, see Petre, *Napoleon's Last Campaign*, 309–10.

28 *CN*, No. 20754, XXVI:325–26. Napoleon based these figures on the following calculations, which he had no doubt inflated: VIII Corps: 5,000 infantry and 3,000 cavalry; V Corps: 12,000 infantry and 500 cavalry; II Corps: 16,000 infantry and 1,200 cavalry; IX Corps: 8,000 infantry; V Cavalry Corps: 2,000 sabers; Arrighi's Leipzig garrison: 8,000 infantry and 3,000 cavalry.

29 *CN*, Nos. 20757–20760, XXVI:327–29; SHAT, C¹⁷ 181: Berthier to Marmont, Latour-Maubourg, Macdonald, Bertrand, Sébastiani, Ney, Curial, and Lefebvre-Desnouettes, 11 October 1813.

30 Disposition, 10 October 1813, Add MSS, 20112, 156.

31 In his 1827 work, Müffling definitively states that the crown prince promised to have a bridge available at Wettin. Yet the extremely pro-Prussian Stewart simply comments that "General Blücher was not enabled – the bridge being incomplete – to traverse the Saale at Wettin": Stewart, *Narrative*, 149. Unbiased reporting by the Prussian General Staff must be acknowledged in this case. In the official history of the Silesian Army written by the Prussian General Staff between 1843 and 1845, Höpfner points to a letter from Bernadotte's chief of staff, Adlerkreutz, to Bülow written on 10 October. According to this document, Vorontsov informed Bernadotte that he planned to build a bridge at Wettin. Thus, Adlerkreutz informed Bülow that, should it be completed, III Corps would cross the Saale there. "The prince desires that you send an officer there to direct the construction," state the orders to Bülow. "If the bridge is not ready and too much time would be needed to complete it, the prince wants you to immediately effect your crossing at Rothenburg with Wintzingerode or at Alsleben if the bridge there is finished, or you may do so at Bernburg. However, if the bridge that General Blücher builds is suitable for the crossing of his army and your corps, then you should cross at that point": SHAT, C¹⁷ 133: Charles John to Bülow, Großweißandt, 10 October 1813. Höpfner concludes: "According to this, it appears that, based on a report from Vorontsov, the crown prince himself believed that a bridge would be built at Wettin." However, later that same day, Adlerkreutz informed Wintzingerode that, "having learned that the bridge at Wettin is not in a state to service the passage of Bülow's corps with those of General Blücher, the prince royal has ordered Bülow to cross at Rothenburg": SHAT, C¹⁷ 133: Charles John to Wintzingerode, Radegast, 10 October 1813. This led Höpfner to question how the crown prince knew that the bridge was not ready to support the passage of the Silesian Army as well as Bülow's corps when absolutely no steps had been taken by Vorontsov to build a bridge: Höpfner, "Darstellung," 1845:360. Friederich's unbiased reporting also must be acknowledged: "Omitting to build the bridge at Wettin has been portrayed as a deliberate attempt to deceive Blücher in order to deny him a point of passage and thus force him 'to follow the North German Army and go in the direction that the crown prince had

previously failed to persuade him to take.' If we examine the existing service letters with unprejudiced eyes, the crown prince appears to be completely innocent of this omission. Obviously, misunderstandings existed that emerged from a report from Vorontsov indicating the construction of a bridge at Wettin. It is not worth investigating the matter further as it is just typical to always give the worst possible interpretation to the efforts, actions, and omissions of the crown prince": Friederich, *Herbstfeldzug 1813*, II:340. As for the historian of the Russian General Staff, Modest Bogdanovich, he follows earlier German historians in stating that Bernadotte had promised to build a bridge at Wettin. See also Bogdanovich, *Geschichte des Krieges*, IIb:61. Müffling, *Die Feldzüge*, 68–70; Höpfner, "Darstellung," 1845:357; Droysen, *Yorck*, II:204.

32 Charles John to Blücher, Rothenburg, 11 October 1813, Add MSS, 20112, 75–76; Steffens, *Adventures*, 116; Höpfner, "Darstellung," 1845:357; Bogdanovich, *Geschichte des Krieges*, IIb:62; Droysen, *Yorck*, II:204; Friederich, *Herbstfeldzug 1813*, II:340–41.

33 Blücher to Alexander, Halle, 11 October 1813, in Höpfner, "Darstellung," 1845:358; Blücher to Charles John, Halle, 11 October 1813, Add MSS, 20112, 77.

34 Charles John to Blücher, Rothenburg, 11 October 1813, Add MSS, 20112, 75–76.

35 Blücher to Langeron, Yorck, and Sacken, Halle, 11 October 1813, Add MSS, 20112, 157–59.

36 Höpfner, "Darstellung," 1845:363.

37 Disposition for 13 October 1813, Halle, 12 October 1813, Add MSS, 20112, 160; Blücher to Charles John, Halle, 12 October 1813, GStA PK, VI HA Rep. 92 Nl. Gneisenau, Nr. 23.

38 Blücher to Yorck, Halle, 6:00 P.M., 12 October 1813, GStA PK, VI HA Rep. 92 Nl. Gneisenau, Nr. 18; Petre, *Napoleon's Last Campaign*, 316–17.

39 SHAT, C^{17} 133: Order of the Day, 12 October 1813.

40 Charles John to Blücher, Rothenburg, 12 October 1813, Add MSS, 20112, 78.

41 Blücher to Yorck, Halle, 6:00 P.M., 12 October 1813, GStA PK, VI HA Rep. 92 Nl. Gneisenau, Nr. 18.

42 Gneisenau to Caroline, Halle, 12 October 1813, GStA PK, VI HA Rep. 92 Nl. Gneisenau, Nr. 21.

43 Although ordered to march at 6:00 A.M., Reynier's troops did not depart for Wittenberg until 11:00 A.M. Making a long halt at Pratau to observe the Prussian positions on the right bank, VII Corps finally crossed the Elbe in the evening. Dąbrowski's division, which Napoleon had expected to be at Wittenberg the day before, moved from Kemberg to the fortress. Sébastiani's II Cavalry Corps reached the vicinity of Wittenberg. Bertrand's IV Corps marched around 7:00 A.M. through Schmiedeberg to Trebitz, where it halted. In the evening, the general pushed his 38th Division to Wartenburg. The lead elements of XI Corps reached Rackith; its cavalry appears to have reached Wittenberg. Latour-Maubourg's I Cavalry Corps halted at Kemberg; the Young Guard stood between Kemberg and Gräfenhainichen; III Corps at Gräfenhainichen; VI Corps at Bad Düben; the Old Guard at Bad Düben and Eilenburg. Friederich attributes this tardiness to the total exhaustion of the starving troops. Endless straggling required long halts for the tired soldiers to catch up. See Friederich, *Herbstfeldzug 1813*, II:337–38, 339–40.

44 *CN*, Nos. 20761 and 20763, XXVI:329–31.
45 *CN*, Nos. 20764 and 20765, XXVI:332.
46 *CN*, Nos. 20763 and 20765, XXVI:331–33.
47 *CN*, Nos. 20766 and 20768–20770, XXVI:333–36; SHAT, C¹⁷ 181: Berthier to Ney and Drouot, 12 October 1813. On 13 October, Tauentzien sent the unescorted baggage of the North German and Silesian Armies through Brandenburg and behind the Havel River.
48 *CN*, No. 20771, XXVI:336.
49 *CN*, No. 20772, XXVI:336–38.
50 For "proof of the irresolution and uncertainty" that allegedly mastered Napoleon at Bad Düben, see Petre, *Napoleon's Last Campaign*, 313–14. Petre fails to recognize that this campaign was unlike Napoleon's earlier wars because he no longer faced Frederician armies commanded by Frederician generals, although Schwarzenberg comes close to fitting this description. As Napoleon himself admitted, the animals had learned something and in this case they demonstrated a suitable understanding of the art of operational warfare and distributed maneuver. As always, Napoleon required detailed information to plan his operations with exactitude. He waited for his enemy to make a mistake. As the information arrived, he adjusted his plans accordingly. Yorck von Wartenburg, in *Napoleon as a General*, II:340–41, likewise is critical of Napoleon for his indecision at Bad Düben. Undoubtedly, stress had taken its toll, but to criticize him for waiting for reports to arrive rather than riding ten leagues per day to "superintend everything and conduct everything" is unfair. Where Petre at least objects to Odeleben's pathetic description of Napoleon confining himself to his bedroom, Yorck von Wartenburg accepts this portrayal. See Odeleben, *A Circumstantial Narrative*, II:5–6.
51 *CN*, Nos. 20771 and 20775, XXVI:336, 339.
52 *CN*, Nos. 20780, 20782, and 20785, XXVI:342, 344, 346; Friederich, *Herbstfeldzug 1813*, II:343–44.
53 *CN*, Nos. 20774–20776 and 20779, XXVI:338–40, 342.
54 *CN*, No. 20779, XXVI:341–42.
55 *CN*, No. 20781, XXVI:342–43.
56 Yorck von Wartenburg's declaration that as late as the 11th Napoleon could have changed "the fortune of the war" had he quickly united with Murat and pounced on Schwarzenberg or effected a *coup de théâtre* by throwing all his forces onto the right bank of the Elbe fails to take into consideration that the objective of his operation was to destroy either Blücher or Bernadotte or both on the left bank. As of the 10th, this goal still appeared to be well within Napoleon's reach. Instead, the Prussian General Staff historian faults Napoleon for adopting "no general resolution but, acting as Mack and Brunswick had done in the past and as MacMahon was to do in the future, he pushed individual corps forward, intending to arrive at a decision if he should be able by this means to obtain definite news of the enemy." Yet was not this the means that he had won his great victories in 1805, 1806, 1807, and 1809 – by pushing forward individual corps to find the enemy and then concentrate the army for the decisive battle? See Yorck von Wartenburg, *Napoleon as a General*, 344–45.
57 *CN*, Nos. 20782 and 20783, XXVI:344–45.

58 See Petre, *Napoleon's Last Campaign*, 314–15; Yorck von Wartenburg, *Napoleon as a General*, II:344–45.

59 *CN*, Nos. 20785–20788, XXVI:346–48.

60 Yorck von Wartenburg, *Napoleon as a General*, II:344.

61 *CN*, No. 20789, XXVI:348.

62 *CN*, No. 20790, XXVI:349. Yorck von Wartenburg's assessment continues: "Formerly, he always had advanced rapidly against the enemy's most vulnerable point, sure that the latter would then be forced to meet him with his main body; now, while he hesitated to act and always sought full information first, Bernadotte disappeared and Blücher evaded him despite the corps he pushed forward as far as and even beyond the Elbe; despite staying for four days at Bad Düben, the emperor was entirely mistaken regarding Bernadotte and lost time that could not be regained at the most decisive moment of the campaign." Again, the Prussian staff officer fails to acknowledge that Napoleon's entire operation had been directed at the "enemy's most vulnerable point." His offensive to the Mulde and then the Elbe had forced Blücher and Bernadotte to react in a totally unorthodox fashion: sacrificing their lines of communication. After attacking the bridges across the Mulde and the Elbe, Napoleon sought his opponents in the same manner he always had practiced. That they resorted to the unexpected to escape cannot be blamed on him. Thus, Napoleon does not deserve censure, but instead Blücher and Bernadotte should be praised for embracing the unorthodox. As for Napoleon wasting time and the most decisive moment of the campaign, the time became decisive only because the emperor willed it. Had he not ordered the concentration at Leipzig, a battle would not have taken place. See Yorck von Wartenburg, *Napoleon as a General*, II:345.

63 *CN*, Nos. 20792, 20794, and 20795, XXVI:352–53. Napoleon's orders to Drouot, "aide-major" of the Guard, sent Mortier's first division to Hohenleina, his second one league north of it at Hohenroda; Oudinot's first division to Gollmenz, the second to Lindenhayn along with the Guard Artillery. Napoleon's cousin and future marshal of the Second Empire, Ornano, was to move the 1st Guard Cavalry Division likewise to Hohenleina with Walther's 3rd Guard Cavalry Division behind him. General Philibert Jean-Baptiste Curial's 2nd Division of Old Guard at Eilenburg and General Louis Friant's 1st Division of Old Guard at Bad Düben would commence their march at 4:00 A.M. on 14 October; the former would escort the king of Saxony to Leipzig should the monarch desire to be so near the battle. In addition, Napoleon directed Latour-Maubourg's I Cavalry Corps "to the right" of Gollmenz, observing Delitzsch and assumed IV Corps "would be in position at Bad Düben's windmill." The parks, pontoon train, and Grand Headquarters would go to Eilenburg.

13

Opening round

At Silesian Army Headquarters, confusing information reached Blücher during the night of 12/13 October. Katzler reported that, according to deserters, the rumors circulating through the French army claimed that Napoleon planned to march on Berlin. Moreover, Rudzevich's patrols reported the advance of considerable imperial forces from Bad Düben to Delitzsch, and therefore toward Halle. News from St.-Priest that Augereau's IX Corps had moved from Naumburg through Weißenfels to Lützen, and probably would continue to Leipzig, did little to clarify the situation. A report from one of Katzler's patrols, which the colonel forwarded to Blücher around 10:00 P.M., stated that a merchant coming from Leipzig estimated its garrison to be 4,000 men. Murat's army stood one hour south of the city at Connewitz. Napoleon's army, some 120,000 men, straddled the Mulde from Wurzen to Eilenburg to Bitterfeld; a burgher from Leipzig had spotted the emperor at Eilenburg on the 10th. Rumors circulated through Leipzig of a battle with the Bohemian Army at Borna on the 11th. Fugitives without arms drifted into the city throughout the night of the 11th and all day during the 12th. With Augereau's corps very close to Leipzig, another imperial corps at Delitzsch, and the expectation that Murat would move across the Mulde and follow Napoleon to Wittenberg, Blücher wanted the Silesian Army ready to react. As a result, he rescinded the orders for Yorck's operation against Leipzig on the 13th. Nevertheless, both Yorck's and Langeron's vanguards would conduct the general reconnaissance. At Halle, the Silesian Army remained concentrated and ready to turn toward either Leipzig or Magdeburg according to the enemy's movements (see Map 6).

Early on the 13th, the infantry of Yorck's vanguard marched to Bruckdorf while Langeron's proceeded to Reideburg. Emmanuel led the Russian cavalry twelve miles west from Merseburg to Rückmarsdorf; Katzler's troopers rode fifteen miles south from Brehna to Schkeuditz on the Halle–Leipzig highway. Six miles southeast of Schkeuditz, the Prussians encountered one French battalion supported by one cavalry regiment at Möckern. With three guns and the majority of his cavalry, Katzler charged the right flank of the enemy cavalry. The imperials retreated to Gohlis while the infantry withdrew from Möckern along the Elster. Katzler shelled the retreating enemy with a half-battery of horse artillery. He broke off the pursuit at dusk and returned to Schkeuditz after receiving word from Emmanuel that the Russians had run into Marmont's entire corps. After leaving a considerable number of his troopers to guard the road coming from Delitzsch, Emmanuel reached Wiederitzsch, some three miles northeast of Katzler's position at Möckern, in the evening. There, the Russians found French infantry, cavalry, and artillery from Marmont's corps, itself in the process of retreating from Delitzsch through Taucha. Prisoners claimed that Murat and Marmont had reached the city while the latter's corps had marched from the Mulde to Leipzig. Others stated that the corps approaching under Augereau numbered 30,000 men and consisted mainly of troops recalled from Spain, including a large, veteran cavalry unit. Elsewhere on the 13th, Rudzevich's patrols described a large imperial force at Delitzsch (Marmont's VI Corps) that later withdrew. To the north, two of his detachments found Dessau occupied by French forces; Cossacks reported hearing a cannonade along the Elbe on the 12th. While returning to Allied Headquarters at Altenburg, General Vlodek, a member of the tsar's staff, passed through Halle and shared the news with Blücher that Austria and Bavaria had concluded a treaty. As a result, a combined force of 10,000 Austrians and 20,000 Bavarians under General Karl Philipp von Wrede would soon march on Würzburg to cut Napoleon's line of communication with France.[1]

In the midst of processing this information, Blücher received a shrill letter from Bernadotte, demonstrating the impact of Napoleon's maneuver. "Tauentzien has informed me that four army corps are marching on Wittenberg and he believes that the emperor himself is leading them," warned the crown prince. Calling this movement "unusual," he claimed to have no other option but to withdraw his army to the right bank of the Elbe. After the approaching imperials had prompted Tauentzien to burn the bridge at Roßlau, only the bridge at Aken remained at Bernadotte's disposal. He requested that Blücher proceed "according to the information that you have on the enemy's movements and that you send all your cavalry against the enemy's rear. I have not a moment to lose. I must accelerate the march of my troops to execute my crossing, if possible, without incident. If you can, accompany my movement." Saving his best for last, Bernadotte attempted to play his trump card: "Tsar Alexander has informed me that you will carry out my orders if I find that it is necessary. I thus request that you consider this letter as an invitation for you to unite the majority of your troops with me. As soon as we are united, we will have nothing to fear and we can go anywhere circumstances require." Just as Blücher had pulled the Army of North Germany to the left bank of the Elbe, Bernadotte sought to pull the Army of Silesia back to the right bank.[2]

Charles Stewart himself delivered this letter to Blücher at Halle. He explained to the Prussians that "the most discordant opinions" existed at the crown prince's headquarters. "One party thought Napoleon would march to Magdeburg, another that he would join Davout in Mecklenburg, a third assumed Berlin to be his objective, a fourth, Stralsund to get revenge on Sweden. Others went still further; they foresaw reinforcements reaching the Oder fortresses and Napoleon sparking a revolution in the heart of Poland – none of which required communication with France."[3] A second letter arrived later on 12 October. "My dear General Blücher," continued the crown prince, "thirty minutes after I mailed you my morning letter a secret agent arrived and informed me that the emperor's Guard stands at Dessau. You see that the moment is critical and there is not a moment to lose for us to unite. I direct my march on Köthen: I do not know if I will have time to complete it. In all cases, you must advance on the shortest road against the enemy's rear; but I would prefer if you would unite with me and that your cavalry follow close on his heels."[4]

Despite Bernadotte's politeness of employing requests and stating preferences rather than issuing direct orders, the Prussians read between the lines of his eloquent prose. Mentioning Tsar Alexander's mandate raised the specter of an international crisis at such a crucial phase of the war. What if Bernadotte demanded control of the Silesian Army? What if he attempted to have Blücher arrested, as he had threatened to have Bülow arrested after a previous disagreement? What if he switched his allegiance back to Napoleon? Although Blücher had never received any notification that Bernadotte could pull rank on him, Knesebeck had warned of just such a scenario in his 13 September letter to Gneisenau. After rebuffing the tsar and Schwarzenberg throughout September, could Blücher afford to ignore the crown prince's orders – especially if his reports proved true? Gneisenau informed Müffling that "General Vlodek just saw me and explained to me that the crown prince had complained about us; that we had carried him away in the current movements: that this cannot continue, that he must have our army under his command, that we should take our position with our left wing leaning on Delitzsch and more such foolishness."[5]

To make this monumental decision that would have irreversible consequences, Blücher carefully weighed the evidence. According to all reports that reached Silesian Army Headquarters, Napoleon remained at Bad Düben, the midpoint of the Wittenberg–Leipzig line. Yet assuming the accuracy of Bernadotte's reports of Napoleon personally leading an offensive through Wittenberg with four army corps while Ney remained on the left bank with considerable forces, the Prussians continued their attempt to divine the emperor's intentions. One scenario pictured Napoleon assembling his army on the right bank of the Elbe for the march to Magdeburg. Second, he could move his main force to the right bank of the Elbe to strike Berlin in unison with Davout coming from Hamburg. Third, he could send part of his forces across the Elbe to the right bank to threaten both Berlin and the rearward communications of the North German and Silesian Armies. In this way, Napoleon could influence both armies to return to the right bank and leave Schwarzenberg on his own. Then, he could quickly reunite his forces and turn against the Bohemian Army.

Although solid arguments could be made in support of each case, common sense separated fact from fiction. If Napoleon pursued either the first or the second scenario, he would need the troops he left south of the Elbe. Moreover, the Prussians did not believe Murat's army, despite being reinforced by Marmont and Augereau, could stand against the numerical superiority the Coalition could throw at Leipzig. Consequently, leaving behind such a considerable part of his army in and around Leipzig could mean only that the master intended to return shortly, per the third scenario. Thus, Murat's actions would reveal Napoleon's intentions. Without a doubt, Murat would follow the emperor across the Mulde and the Elbe in cases one and two, but he would seek to hold his current position at Leipzig in the third case. Blücher could only hope that the reconnaissance conducted toward Leipzig would clarify the situation. Augereau's arrival and the news of Marmont's march from Delitzsch to Taucha and Eilenburg seemed to indicate that the imperials would hold Leipzig. If this proved true, Napoleon's movement through Wittenberg and along the right bank would be a mere demonstration.[6]

No sentimental consideration for Berlin mastered Blücher's headquarters. "Napoleon moved with a part of his army as if he intended to threaten Berlin," explained Professor Steffens, "believing that he would be able to wreck our plans and compel us to separate from our concentrated position. Had he carried out this view, Berlin would have been surrendered to him. But the strong mind of Germany, which now ruled in our army, was too bold and wise to be deceived. We foresaw that if our combined forces stood firm, he must abandon his design; he could not spare a portion of his army from the coming struggle, on which his future – his very existence – could be staked. The great day that would seal the fate of Germany thus approached."[7]

Needing to buy time for the final reports from the forward cavalry to arrive, Blücher delayed acting on Bernadotte's "orders." After alerting the army to remain ready to march north should the imperials evacuate Leipzig and move across the Mulde toward Wittenberg, Blücher responded to the crown prince:

> Please allow me to remind Your Royal Highness that it was you who suggested the crossing of the Saale and that by executing it I have corresponded to your wishes. I canceled my plans to conform to those of Your

Royal Highness. According to the order of battle, your army should have occupied the place upon which I now stand; when I saw that you placed value on remaining close to the Elbe, I wasted no time in contenting myself with the position that Your Royal Highness had not taken but needed to be filled to establish communication with the Bohemian Army by securing the crossings at Merseburg and Halle, and becoming master of the line of the Saale.

Your Royal Highness told Major von Rühle "that you would burn the bridge at Roßlau; that you would post ten battalions at Aken; that, if necessary, you would sacrifice the bridge at Aken and move onto the left bank of the Saale." Thus, when I saw Your Royal Highness so firmly resolved, I accepted without hesitation the proposal to march to the left bank of the Saale. Your Royal Highness now informs me that you will cross the Elbe at Aken. Through this movement, I will be cut off from the Elbe. There remains nothing else for me to do than to unite with the Bohemian Army. It is still not clear to me how Your Royal Majesty intends to execute your crossing of the Elbe and how you will proceed after the crossing if you are concentrated between the enemy, the Elbe, Magdeburg, and the Havel.

The reconnaissance that I am conducting today toward Leipzig and Delitzsch will clarify the enemy's position. I will send my First Adjutant to His Majesty Tsar Alexander to inform him of the situation of our armies and the position of the enemy and I must await the orders that His Imperial Majesty will give me. An officer returning to Grand Allied Headquarters informed me that the treaty between Austria and Bavaria was signed on 4 October according to which 10,000 Austrians and 20,000 Bavarians are marching on Würzburg.[8]

Gneisenau's deft quill is clearly discernible in this brilliant letter. If Napoleon really were to lead an offensive along the right bank of the Elbe, the thought of crossing the river and finding himself hemmed in by it and the Havel with Napoleon in front of him and Davout behind him must have truly terrified Bernadotte. Moreover, the Prussians ignored the whole issue of Bernadotte taking command of the Silesian Army. Blücher had never heard a word about this and doubted that Tsar Alexander had actually granted such a concession. Although furious and giving "loud expression to his anger," Blücher simply but firmly reiterated the stand he had taken in September: he would obey only orders issued by the monarchs. This missive gained him the time he needed to allow further reports to arrive and be evaluated. Gneisenau wrote to his opposite at Bernadotte's headquarters, Adlerkreutz, asking him to use his influence to convince the crown prince to remain in the theater. Blücher also decided to send his First Adjutant, Count Goltz, to Alexander's headquarters with a report on Bernadotte's proceedings and to ask if Schwarzenberg would support an attack on the enemy forces around Leipzig.[9]

The situation at Bernadotte's headquarters became frantic. The Prussian envoy to the Army of North Germany, General Krusemarck, informed

Blücher "that the news of the march of a strong French corps on Wittenberg and the enemy's capture of Dessau has unnerved the crown prince ... he ardently wishes that your army can come to his aid through a movement toward Bitterfeld. It would be very meritorious work to lift the drooping spirits of this merciful lord because he already believes all is lost. I ask you earnestly to give him more hopeful advice." After transferring his headquarters to Köthen, Bernadotte issued orders for the army to commence the march toward the Elbe. Learning that Rauch had reached Aken with the pontoons of Blücher's army, the crown prince instructed the Prussian officer to remain there and build a second bridge with a bridgehead on the right bank. Writing before he received Blücher's evasive response, the prince royal seemed confident that Blücher would obey his orders. "General Blücher is moving to Aken in forced marches to unite with me," Bernadotte told Rauch. "United, we will deliver a battle if the enemy comes back to the left bank; we will cross the Elbe with all of our forces if he remains on the right bank. In order to cover you in your responsibility, I inform you that I have received a letter from Tsar Alexander authorizing me to give General Blücher the necessary orders. Therefore, you can see that the success of the operations of the Allied armies depends on your execution of this order."[10]

En route to reunite with the Silesian Army, Rauch reached Steutz, opposite Aken, on 12 October. Owing to Reynier's advance, he quickly crossed the river and proceeded south through Köthen. While marching through Köthen on the 13th, he received Bernadotte's orders. Having received a letter from Blücher earlier in the day summoning him to Halle as soon as possible, Rauch found himself in an unenviable predicament. While weighing his options, he learned that Reynier had assaulted Aken and forced Hirschfeld to dismantle the bridge. With the bridge out of service, neither army could cross. Under these circumstances, Rauch believed that he had no choice but to turn around and lead his trains back to Aken.[11]

On the following morning, 14 October, Blücher received Rauch's report on the affair. To provide a general reason to disobey the crown prince, Blücher and Gneisenau drafted a persuasive letter:

> From the moment you left Wartenburg, your detachment served as an escort for the reserve ammunition, the baggage, and the pontoon train, all of which are quite indispensable to the army. You were never detached from it and you should have told the crown prince that you are not in a position to start a campaign for his army. His Royal Highness was very wrong to interfere with executing the instructions you received from me and you should have followed your orders. As you know well, I have no ammunition with me other than that which belongs to the batteries and I will be in the greatest quandary if I have to deliver a two-day battle and I am separated from the

ammunition that you now escort. The news that His Majesty Tsar Alexander has placed me under the command of His Royal Highness is just as unknown to me as the news that I am marching to Aken.

Despite this free pass, only Rauch himself reached Halle, prompting Blücher to give the younger general a tongue-lashing. Rauch tried to explain that he had been forced to follow the orders of the crown prince. Blücher answered him: "If I run out of powder in the next battle, I will have you court-martialed." Fortunately for Rauch, supplies captured at Leipzig would replenish the ordnance expended during the ensuing battle.[12]

In the end, the intelligence that arrived during the evening and night of the 13th confirmed the Prussians' appraisal of the situation. All signs indicated that Napoleon had directed the Grande Armée to march with haste through Bad Düben to Leipzig, where the emperor himself would arrive. Some 15,000–20,000 men (VI Corps) were marching toward Halle apparently to mask his concentration at Leipzig. One of Rudzevich's patrols netted a French lieutenant-colonel attached to the imperial suite who confirmed that Napoleon remained at Bad Düben. According to the prisoner, Napoleon had sent him from Bad Düben to Marmont around 6:00 A.M. with orders to position his corps three leagues from Leipzig and to await further orders from Murat. Moreover, the statements of a captured Prussian officer from Tauentzien's corps led Napoleon to believe the Prussian army had retreated across the Elbe and that only a small portion of it remained south of the river. The Frenchman also revealed that III Corps had taken Dessau and probably remained there; that the Guard still stood at Bad Düben as of that morning; and that the king of Naples had reached the region of Leipzig with the troops that faced Schwarzenberg's army. He also claimed that great shortages, especially of bread and fodder, reigned in the army; that the way Napoleon had conducted the war was strikingly different from that of earlier times; that his former energy had abandoned him; that he showed a great need for comfort, especially sleep; and that he was as surly as ever.

Around 5:00 on the morning of the 14th, Blücher received the final critical piece of the puzzle. A report from Rudzevich written one hour earlier from Reideburg revealed the movements of massive imperial forces from Bad Düben toward Leipzig since the 13th. "Already since yesterday great numbers of fires can be seen from Leipzig to Taucha. It now appears that the whole riddle of the enemy's movement has been solved and that he is concentrating his entire strength at Leipzig." This information convinced Blücher that Napoleon had absolutely no intention of transferring the theater of war to the right bank of the Elbe. Instead, the emperor wanted to mislead the Silesian and North German Armies so they would retreat across the Elbe, thus allowing him to make a rapid movement against Schwarzenberg.[13]

Blücher and his staff went to work. They completed the report to Tsar Alexander that Goltz would deliver. Blücher not only relayed the information provided by the French lieutenant-colonel captured near Bad Düben, but sent the officer as well for further interrogating. "As for the emperor Napoleon," wrote Blücher, "he was still at Bad Düben as of 6:00 A.M. yesterday with the forces of the French army; it is probable that he does not intend to cross the Elbe with considerable forces, but that he wants to induce the Armies of North Germany and Silesia to recross the Elbe so that he can engage the Grand Army without being threatened in his right flank. As the captured officer claims, they are convinced at the emperor's headquarters that the Army of North Germany and that of Silesia have recrossed the Elbe so that there is nothing between the Mulde, the Saale, and the Elbe except partisans or small corps. I assume that the French army will march toward Leipzig and Wurzen where it will effect its concentration." Blücher also forwarded the news from Bernadotte that the bridge at Roßlau had been burned and the bridge at Aken dismantled. "Thankfully, the prince royal cannot recross the Elbe, which is of great importance based on today's news. At this moment, General Rudzevich informed me that his patrols have observed a great movement by the enemy that took place throughout the night of 13–14 October. The direction of this march has been from Bad Düben to Leipzig or toward Taucha. And the Grand Army should expect an attack. I will immediately give all of this information to the prince royal and I will get him to commit to driving toward the Mulde, Bitterfeld, and Delitzsch."[14]

Just as Blücher and Gneisenau finished this brief, the former received a flattering missive from Schwarzenberg that expressed his joy over Blücher's proximity and explained his plans. A note from the tsar to Blücher written on 13 October accompanied Schwarzenberg's packet. According to Alexander, "Prince Schwarzenberg is sending you the plan that he intends to follow. I have approved it, but I must add news, that I cannot confirm, of Napoleon's march through Bad Düben on Wittenberg, apparently from there to threaten your bridges and your communication, perhaps to clear a passage along the right bank of the Elbe from Wittenberg to Magdeburg, although this would be very risky. I hope the parties and detachments on your left will notify you in time of any movement such as this and that you take your countermeasures in concert with the prince royal of Sweden. I only ask you to inform us as soon as possible of each new circumstance that occurs on your side."[15] What an opportunity for Blücher: not only could he expose Bernadotte's poor leadership to Allied Headquarters, but he could also provide the crucial news of the French concentration at Leipzig.

As for Schwarzenberg's letter, the Allied commander in chief wrote: "With true enjoyment I received news from my forward posts that they are in communication with your army between Weißenfels and Naumburg.

This is extraordinarily pleasing to me and I recognize it as an honor to have such a revered commander nearby at such an important moment, which is so crucial for the entire world. I hurry herewith to send you in the enclosed the plan of operations, which has been approved by His Majesty the Tsar of Russia, as well as the arrangements that I have made for the Bohemian Army for tomorrow. Through this you will obtain complete information on the situation of the Bohemian Army and I will personally hurry to inform you of any changes that may arise. I request that you likewise communicate everything that occurs on your side, the position of your army, and what you can learn regarding the intentions of the enemy."

Schwarzenberg's cover letter for the 14 October disposition stated: "All news that we have received of the enemy confirms that he has concentrated his entire force between Leipzig, Grimma, Wurzen, and Eilenburg. Our ultimate purpose must be to surround the enemy in this position and to proceed against him with all of our combined forces. After obtaining his subsistence on the Elbe went from being difficult to being impossible, he abandoned this river and concentrated in a region that allows us to tighten the noose daily. The advantages of our current position allow us to view as possible the destruction of the enemy army. Any rashness deserves to be punished and we must thus proceed with caution. For this purpose, the following general disposition has been suggested and will be executed by the Grand Army tomorrow."

According to the disposition, reconnaissance conducted on the 13th by Wittgenstein would confirm the enemy's strength and position. For the 14th, Schwarzenberg ordered Bernadotte "to extend his right wing to Merseburg. General Blücher has united with him on the Saale. The terrain of this region grants to both an advantageous position between Merseburg and Halle. Their outposts can proceed to Schkeuditz and jointly occupy Lützen with our outposts." Ten miles southwest of Lützen, the vanguard of Gyulay's Austrian III Corps would take a position at Weißenfels while the main body occupied Naumburg. Schwarzenberg instructed the left wing of the Bohemian Army, namely General Maximilien-Friedrich von Merveldt's Austrian II Corps, General Prince Frederick Joseph of Hessen-Homburg's Austrian Reserve, and Grand Duke Constantine's Russo-Prussian Guard, to move to Zeitz. The Bohemian Army's right wing, namely Wittgenstein's Russian army corps, Kleist's Prussian II Corps, and Klenau's Austrian IV Corps, would slide west. Wittgenstein and Kleist would lead their corps to Pegau. Klenau would march to Borna and forward light troops toward Colditz and Grimma. Schwarzenberg ordered the Russian III Grenadier Corps and 3rd Cuirassier Division to temporarily remain at Altenburg. South of Schwarzenberg's main body, General Hieronymous von Colloredo's Austrian I Corps received instructions to occupy Chemnitz and Penig (see Map 5).

Regarding the Army of Poland, Schwarzenberg wrote: "Bennigsen will seek as much as possible to master the roads from Nossen and Meißen and from there to win as much ground as possible but cautiously. In this position, we can and must await the arrival of General Bennigsen if the enemy allows us the time and then with the greatest certainty and the fullest cooperation all armies will daily seek to win more ground." This last statement does much to explain the mindset behind the pitiful generalship that had characterized Schwarzenberg's operation since it commenced on 27 September. In terms of strategy, Schwarzenberg concluded that Wrede's Bavarian corps would "move in forced marches on Bamberg and do everything possible to make itself master of Würzburg, hold the line of the Main, and march against Marshal Kellermann, in case he does not encounter him sooner, at Frankfurt-am-Main. The emperor Napoleon will have no choice other than to cut a way through our armies; we, on the other hand, have no disposition to follow other than to march together against the point where he attacks and which must be defended for as long as possible. This will be facilitated all the more by the true cooperation of the armies with each other, which will gradually tighten the circle that we have built around him."[16]

From these letters, Blücher learned that Allied Headquarters sought to surround the French army at Leipzig. While Schwarzenberg's plan stressed slow, cautious conduct and counted on the enemy running out of supplies, at least the Allied commander in chief no longer spoke of retreating. The key words "the destruction of the enemy army" won over the Prussians. Reinvigorated by these letters, Blücher assured the tsar that he would execute all of the prescribed instructions "with exactitude."[17] He also forwarded the intelligence summaries as well as Schwarzenberg's disposition to Bernadotte: "My advance posts have just informed me that the French army marched through the night from Bad Düben toward Leipzig and Taucha." He explained to Bernadotte that, based on Schwarzenberg's disposition, he "must beg the crown prince to attack without delay any enemy forces still found on the left bank of the Mulde and to advance from Bitterfeld toward Leipzig."[18] To impress the sense of urgency on Bernadotte, Gneisenau dispatched Lieutenant Gerlach to Köthen with a letter for Charles Stewart that described the situation. Gneisenau urgently sought the British envoy's assistance in convincing Bernadotte to unite with Blücher and march to Leipzig the following day. As for the Army of Silesia, its main body received a day of rest on 14 October.[19]

Meanwhile, the role that Blücher could play increased Napoleon's anxiety. He expressed his thoughts, as if thinking aloud, to Marmont at 10:00 on the morning of the 13th: "I think it is necessary that you enter the line on the left bank of the Parthe only if the king [Murat] is attacked; yet it would be a great mistake for you to move into the line on the left bank of the Parthe because of the fear that Blücher could debouch from Halle or some other point. If you are placed in line on the left bank of the Parthe and something comes against you from Blücher's side, it will disrupt the entire line and have the worst effect. It is important that the Army of Silesia does not come within two leagues of Leipzig. With the good troops that compose your three divisions, they can be spaced apart widely." Based on this concern, the emperor ultimately instructed Marmont to reconnoiter Breitenfeld and the line of the Parthe as far as Taucha. He recommended posting vanguards at Schkeuditz and on the road to Landsberg. "By these means," he wrote, "you will be able to deploy quickly, your left on the Elster and your right on the Parthe, to receive anything that comes down these roads. Acquaint yourself well with this position. You have three bridges over the Parthe to debouch quickly to the left bank if need be, but keep your cavalry facing Halle and Landsberg; patrol the roads to Delitzsch and Bad Düben to keep all communication completely open."[20]

Napoleon reiterated these points to Murat, adding a lesson in the art of war: "The duc de Raguse [Marmont] ... arrived at Hohenleina at 8:00 this morning. It is very important that you do not have this marshal enter the line on the left bank of the Parthe because if you have him enter the line here and Blücher debouches from Halle you will have to weaken your line at an important moment. It is this type of movement that loses every battle; battles are won by reinforcing the line at the critical moment." He informed the king that he wanted Marmont posted at Breitenfeld, "where I have been told that a good position can be found," with his right anchored on the Parthe and his left on the Elster (see Map 25). "He will hold the roads from Halle and Landsberg; all his cavalry will be placed in the forefront on these 2 roads, 500 to 600 men each, with 2 battalions and 6 pieces of cannon, so that these roads are observed well." Napoleon advised Murat to monitor the left bank of the Parthe as far as Taucha with cavalry and artillery posts. "On the Parthe are several bridges: three shall be reserved for the case that the enemy at Halle makes no movement but the Austrians attack and you need VI Corps; it can debouch by these three bridges and cross the Parthe. But be careful not to employ VI Corps until the last extremity because it is likely that the Army of Silesia will advance from Halle. I think Marmont must immediately build some redoubts in the position he chooses at Breitenfeld. I think you should immediately build a tambour at Connewitz and at Leipzig's various bridges and especially at Lindenau."[21]

To the north, Reynier reached Roßlau on the right bank of the Elbe around 11:00 A.M. on the 13th but found the town evacuated and the bridge dismantled. Although he had directed Sébastiani's cavalry to Aken, the French troopers did not arrive in time to prevent Hirschfeld from detaching the bridge from the left bank. Reynier arrived, unlimbered three guns, and fired on the Prussians along the left bank. He ended the shelling at 4:00 in the afternoon after it proved futile. After receiving the emperor's orders, he commenced the march to Wittenberg. On the left bank, Ney's troops likewise found the bridge at Roßlau dismantled. To support Reynier, one cavalry division and one infantry brigade continued toward Aken. The detachment's commander, Brayer, attempted to storm the part of the town situated on the left bank of the Elbe after midnight and long after Reynier had quit his position on the right bank. Ensconced in a ring of palisades, Aken served as a bastion for Hirschfeld's Landwehr. Realizing the pointlessness of this operation, Brayer broke off the engagement around 4:00 on the morning of the 14th.[22]

Rather than join the Young Guard at Hohenleina on the night of 13/14 October, Napoleon decided to remain at Bad Düben and postpone the battle until the 16th to provide more time to prepare.[23] He issued orders for Maret to impress on the Saxon government at Leipzig the need to prepare rations of bread and brandy for 300,000 men. Specifically, the master ordered "100,000 rations of bread, 500 quintals of rice, and 300,000 rations of brandy per day. This large amount of rice will be distributed at 6 ounces per man, so that 100,000 rations of bread, which is only one-third of the necessary rations, will suffice. Make them understand the importance of the measures they need to take to achieve this." He also continued to obsess over Marmont's sector of the line. "The position of Eutritzsch on the road to Halle," he mused to Murat, "anchors its left on the Elster and its right on the Parthe, can be occupied by 12,000 men, who would be protected from being forced from their position; order the duc de Raguse to reconnoiter it; the duc de Raguse must have arrived by now."[24]

Yet the news that reached the emperor on the evening of 13 October increased his confidence. Bertrand's IV Corps had reached Bad Düben and he expected Macdonald's XI Corps to arrive at 1:00 on the afternoon of the 14th; he hoped Reynier would arrive sometime in the evening. "We destroyed the bridges of Wartenburg, Dessau and Aken," he boasted to Maret. "In these various affairs we took 3,000 prisoners, 20 guns, 200 to 300 wagons, spread the alarm all the way to Berlin, and my whole army will be assembled at Leipzig on the 16th to deliver a battle. The news is that the headquarters of the prince of Sweden was at Bernburg on the 12th. Tauentzien's corps and part of Bülow's corps were repulsed on the right bank with baggage, a large proportion of the park, and are now separated from their army. Communicate these results to Dresden and Leipzig, but increase the numbers."[25]

At 3:00 on the morning of the 14th, Napoleon announced his intention to depart for Leipzig in four hours. He issued orders to Maret for Frederick Augustus to be escorted from Eilenburg to Taucha by Curial's 2nd Division of Old Guard and Lefebvre-Desnoettes's 1st Guard Cavalry Division. At Taucha, the Guard would take post while the Saxon king continued to his second city with the small battalion of Saxon grenadiers he had brought with him from Dresden and a detachment of the Guard Cavalry. "I leave at seven in the morning to go to Leipzig," Napoleon informed Maret. "Thus, I will be on the direct road from Bad Düben to Leipzig. The town of Eilenburg will be guarded by General [Antoine-Simon] Durrieu, who arrived yesterday with Grand Headquarters and the parks. Six hundred Cossacks who had escaped the business at Dessau attempted to swim across the Elbe but as the wind was too strong they all drowned." With his mind set, Napoleon made the final calculations to concentrate the army at Leipzig.[26]

Indicative of the emotional highs and lows associated with the over-whelming weight on his shoulders, Napoleon's anxiety increased as the morning lengthened and he received confirmed reports of Blücher's location. "I hope you will arrive here early today," he wrote to Macdonald at 7:00 while still at Bad Düben. "You must cross the river immediately. There is no doubt that we will be attacked tomorrow, the 15th, by the Army of Bohemia and the Army of Silesia. So march in haste, and if you hear the sound of the guns turn toward it. The Silesian Army debouches through Halle and Zörbig." Around the same time, Ney's report from Pötnitz at 5:00 P.M. on the 13th reached Napoleon. According to the marshal, Bernadotte had marched south from Bernburg on the 12th. "The news you have of the prince royal should cause you to accelerate your march," responded the emperor; "if he left Bernburg on the 12th, he may reach Leipzig today, the 14th, and be able to attack us tomorrow: so march with all dispatch on Leipzig. It is likely that we will be attacked tomorrow at Leipzig. If you hear the sound of the guns tomorrow, double your march."[27]

Shortly after addressing instructions to Berthier around 7:00 A.M. on the 14th, the emperor departed. Traveling twenty-two miles south-southwest from Bad Düben to Leipzig, he covered the distance by noon. En route, Napoleon heard "a fairly brisk cannonade." Instead of halting in the city, he continued to the open fields south of the Leipzig–Wurzen road and estab-lished his command post. From there he could see forty pieces of Murat's artillery engaging an equal number of guns belonging to the Bohemian Army. Reports arrived around 4:00 stating that his troops had thus far captured 300 Russians, Prussians, and Austrians. "The enemy greatly extends his right," Berthier informed Macdonald. "We saw many columns arrive; it looks like the day before or the day of a battle." After following the course of the combat, Napoleon rode in the evening to the village of Reudnitz, some one and one-half miles southeast of Leipzig on the right bank of the Parthe at the intersection of the Leipzig–Taucha and Leipzig–Wurzen roads. From his headquarters at the village inn, the emperor informed Marmont that "the enemy was repulsed. We occupy Liebertwolk-witz, the right leaning on the Elster; the enemy is extended on his left, that is to say, on our right."[28]

The engagement at Liebertwolkwitz, described by Napoleon as a "vanguard affair," proved to be both the greatest cavalry clash of the war and the opening round of the epic battle of Leipzig. Murat's 32,400 infantry, 9,800 cavalry, and 156 guns held a 5-mile line extending east from Markkleeberg (VIII Corps and IV Cavalry Corps) through Wachau (II Corps) to Liebertwolkwitz (V Cavalry Corps and 1st Heavy Division of I Cavalry Corps). Less than three miles due north of Wachau, V Corps stood in reserve. Early on the 14th, Wittgenstein's vanguard of 2,800 Russian and Prussian cavalry under Pahlen III supported by 20 guns advanced north from Cröbern toward the French positions. By pushing forward, the Allies hoped to see what stood between Murat and Leipzig and determine if the king of Naples intended to hold his position (see Map 6). After observing Murat's masses south of Markkleeberg and Wachau, Pahlen halted. Kleist moved up twenty squadrons and fourteen guns from his Reserve Cavalry. As soon as the Prussians started to arrive, Pahlen resumed the advance and Murat committed his cavalry to a back-and-forth struggle that ended slightly in favor of the Allies. On Murat's left, Klenau's Austrian IV Corps attacked Liebertwolkwitz around 2:00 that afternoon. The village fell to the Allies except the churchyard, which the imperials defended like a fortress. Although Klenau repulsed all French counterattacks during an afternoon of hard fighting, he withdrew in the evening.

Easily identifiable by his outlandish costume and tiger-skin saddle pad, Murat narrowly escaped capture on more than one occasion during the many cavalry clashes. Allowing himself to become embroiled in a needless battle, the renowned cavalry commander proved unfit for the task at hand. Rather than use his infantry and artillery to stop the Allies as they approached the heights extending between Markkleeberg and Liebertwolkwitz, Murat charged forward with the emperor's precious cavalry. He kept his troopers so tightly packed that command and control broke down as soon as one regiment became disordered. Fortunately for the French, the Allies attacked piecemeal and did not have the numbers available to gain a decisive victory. Yet they managed to obtain their goals of looking behind Murat's position; his resistance indicated that the imperials meant to hold their ground. The Allies lost some 2,200 killed, wounded, and missing; French losses are estimated to have been slightly higher.[29]

While Murat's troops fought the lead elements of the Bohemian Army, Napoleon pushed the troops coming from the Mulde further south. As for Marmont, the emperor suggested that "it would be appropriate for you to move some dirt. Make some abatis and place some palisades where they could be useful. I send you an account of the battle of Gustavus Adolphus, which concerns the positions that you now occupy."[30] According to Marmont's version of the story, he received orders during the night of

13/14 October to find a position north of Leipzig that could cover the city from the direction of Halle and Landsberg:

> I have traveled the country enough times to know that this position existed one and one-half leagues from Leipzig, at Lindenthal and Breitenfeld, on the same ground where Gustavus Adolphus fought, then 142 years earlier, and won a signal victory.[31] I occupied it; after reconnoitering the battlefield with care and detail, I assured him [Napoleon] that it was too big for my corps, but with some works that could be easily built and 30,000 men, I could hold in check the Armies of North Germany and Silesia for twenty-four hours. I reported this to Napoleon, who ordered me to perform the work without delay and told me that, when the time came, I would have III Corps at my disposal, bringing my strength to the number of men I desired. I went to work and neglected nothing to fulfill my task. I built many abatis in the wood west of Lindenthal and east of Radefeld. Then I occupied them strongly. This wood was like a fortress.[32]

Meanwhile, XI Corps started crossing the Bad Düben bridge at 2:00 on the afternoon of the 14th. At 4:30, Berthier wrote to Macdonald imploring him to accelerate his march on the 15th. Napoleon hoped Reynier and Dąbrowski would soon follow but as of 6:00 on the evening of the 14th he remained uncertain of their whereabouts. At 8:30, Berthier issued orders summoning the ambulances and petite headquarters to join the emperor at Reudnitz. He directed all other baggage to Mockau. Despite the preparations, many questions remained unanswered. "It is 8:00 in the morning," Napoleon wrote to Macdonald on 15 October. "None of our patrols have encountered anything. Has the enemy taken a defensive position to receive battle or has he retired, seeing that we are able to crush him? We will know the answer to this question in a few hours." The overall situation simply did not make sense to Napoleon. Once again we find him obsessing over his former marshal, who he believed commanded Blücher's army as well. "All the information agrees that, by way of a maneuver that I cannot comprehend, the prince of Sweden has crossed the Saale and moves on Merseburg in such a manner that the duc de Raguse [Marmont] has nothing before him except cavalry. If this march is intended to take us in the flank, I see further evidence of the madness that has seized the prince of Sweden at this moment because in the meantime he leaves the Austrians and Wittgenstein's army to their own devices. Send a copy of this letter to the prince de la Moskova [Ney]." In any case, Napoleon directed Macdonald to Taucha. Already thinking of making short work of Schwarzenberg by turning his right, the emperor did not want Macdonald to cross the Parthe at Taucha "because I may send you to Naunhof." By way of the copy of this letter that Macdonald would forward – an odd method of disseminating orders given Napoleon's penchant for constant communication – the emperor instructed

Ney to continue his march in the current direction. Orders likewise went to Reynier to unite his corps on the left bank of the Mulde at Bad Düben and await further orders.[33]

If, as Napoleon expected, a battle occurred on the 16th, he would have 190,000 men and 690 guns at his disposal; only the 14,000 men of VII Corps would not be available. Of the Allies, Blücher and Schwarzenberg combined could commit 205,000 men and 1,026 guns.[34] Bernadotte, Bennigsen, and Schwarzenberg's I Corps – altogether 125,000 men – would remain too distant to participate. In this sense, Napoleon had succeeded in concentrating his forces at Leipzig faster than Schwarzenberg, who appeared more intent on establishing communication with Blücher and Bernadotte than fighting the French. Moreover, Napoleon needed to win the battle on 16 October. With the difference in numbers on 16 October being 15,000 men as opposed to 140,000, he would stand the best chance of success as long as he deployed his legions in the most effective manner. To do so, he needed accurate news of the enemy.[35]

After a long conversation with Murat, Napoleon mounted his horse around 10:00 on the morning of the 15th and the two rode to the heights between Wachau and Liebertwolkwitz. He remained there for several hours conversing with Murat and Berthier, making adjustments to the positions of his corps. During the course of the 15th, the Grande Armée continued to move into positions around Leipzig. North of the city on Napoleon's right, VI Corps occupied the Lindenthal sector facing Halle to the west and having IV Corps behind it and to the east at Eutritzsch. Slightly east of IV Corps, two divisions from III Corps reached Mockau with the third still en route from Bad Düben. South and east of Leipzig, Napoleon's left curved southwest to northeast for seven miles with VIII Corps holding Markkleeberg and Dölitz; IV Cavalry Corps was at Dösen; II Corps at Wachau; V Corps at Liebertwolkwitz; IX Corps at Zuckelhausen; V Cavalry Corps at Holzhausen; I Cavalry Corps at Ober- and Unternaundorf; and all of the Guard remained around Reudnitz as the Grand Reserve. On the far left wing, XI Corps reached Taucha that evening with II Cavalry Corps en route from Bad Düben, where VII Corps arrived. To close the gap on his left wing and hopefully deliver the *coup de grâce* for Schwarzenberg, Napoleon summoned Macdonald to depart from Taucha at daybreak and march six miles south-southwest to Holzhausen. From there, the marshal would move three miles east to Seifertshain "where he will receive orders to turn the enemy's right" by way of Naunhof (see Map 6).[36]

Napoleon also received reports placing Bernadotte at Merseburg. Numerous campfires observed seven miles west-southwest of Leipzig around Markranstädt led him to incorrectly believe that Bernadotte's main force, which included Blücher, stood on the southwest-to-northeast-running Weißenfels–Leipzig road rather than the northwest-to-southeast-running

Halle–Leipzig highway. From Markranstädt, he assumed Bernadotte would link with Schwarzenberg's left through Zwenkau or Pegau. The emperor could not have been more wrong. Rather than the Armies of North Germany and Silesia, the fires observed at Markranstädt belonged to the left wing of the Bohemian Army. Moreover, Blücher's army had already advanced from Halle to Schkeuditz, eight miles northwest of Leipzig. Bernadotte still loitered far to the north in the Wettin–Zörbig region.

Responding to Marmont's report that the marshal had failed to push his patrols to Schkeuditz, Napoleon merely expressed his regret for the oversight.[37] Despite this negligence, the marshal insisted that he had provided Napoleon with plenty of intelligence concerning the approach of Blücher's army. One officer and two sappers, captured by Allied forces two days earlier near Delitzsch and taken to Blücher's headquarters at Halle, managed to escape and reach French lines on the 15th.[38] They informed Marmont that both the Silesian and North German Armies would reach his position at Lindenthal by the morning of the 16th. Moreover, the marshal reported that Prussian cavalry and artillery supported by infantry had forced him to pull back his outposts and abandon Hänichen. That night, the marshal ascended the church steeple at Lindenthal. He claimed that from the belfry "I could see with my own eyes all of the enemy's campfires. The horizon was ablaze. I hastened to report this to the emperor and to remind him that my position demanded 30,000 men. I asked him not to lose a moment in putting III Corps at my disposal per his promise." In his memoirs, Marmont noted that he climbed Lindenthal's tower at 10:00 P.M. but that he reported all this information – the statements of the escaped sappers, the appearance of Prussian infantry before his posts that prompted him to withdraw them, and the view from Lindenthal's belfry – to Napoleon at 9:00 P.M. The marshal maintains that he was looking "forward to the results of my reports and the effects they would have, when, on the 16th at 8:00 A.M., I received a letter from Napoleon ... criticizing all of my reports and their conclusions. He claimed that I was totally mistaken. He said I had nobody in front of me. Accordingly, he ordered me to withdraw immediately to Leipzig, cross through this city, and form the army's reserve."[39]

This episode again provides proof of Napoleon's tendency to see the situation only as he wished it to be. Not until 3:00 A.M. on the 16th did the master write the response that Marmont received at 8:00 A.M. acknowledging the emperor's receipt of a report from him penned at 9:00 P.M. on the 15th. In between, Marmont received a communiqué from Berthier drafted at Reudnitz at 11:00 P.M. on the 15th. It expressed Napoleon's unpleasant surprise that Marmont had yet to establish communication with Bertrand, who had been at Eutritzsch since the 14th. In addition, Berthier relayed the news that Napoleon planned to engage the Austrians "on the height of Liebertwolkwitz, where the emperor's headquarters will be tomorrow, the 16th, at 7:00 A.M. If you have only a few cavalry or infantry before you, drive them off and prepare to join the emperor. General Bertrand will suffice to maintain the position on this side as long as the entire Army of Silesia does not debouch there. In the opposite case, the prince de la Moskova's corps is at Mockau, and if the enemy debouches before you in great strength, your corps, that of General Bertrand, and that of the prince de la Moskova are intended to be used against him."[40]

Marmont commented that this arrangement would have been "perfectly wise and in accordance with logic had I not received the report of the sappers who escaped from Halle, which informed me of the [enemy] army's resolute march; had not the report of 9:00 P.M. on the 15th made known that Prussian infantry was facing the outposts, and that the sight of the campfires proved that the whole enemy army was present; and had not the order been given on the morning of the 16th for IV Corps to march on Lindenau, and for III Corps to go to the Grande Armée."[41] In all likelihood, Berthier had yet to read Marmont's report from 9:00 P.M. when he issued his dispatch at 11:00 P.M. on the 15th. Nevertheless, both he and Napoleon had read its contents when the latter responded at 3:00 A.M. on the 16th:

> I received your letter dated 9:00 P.M. on 15 October. I am not certain that a battalion of infantry forced your battalion to retreat from Hänichen. On the contrary, it appears that it only faced cavalry. It would have been appropriate for you to support the battalion at Hänichen in order to take some prisoners. Regulations do not permit an enemy reconnaissance that is not supported by an army to approach and reconnoiter our army. The instructions that you gave to this battalion to retreat if it encountered an enemy army corps were misapplied because your troops withdrew without the enemy presenting a *corps de bataille*. With this manner of making war, it is impossible to learn anything. Over the last two days, you should have sent spies to Halle and Merseburg, and do what is customary in war, ordering the mayor to give you a peasant whose wife would be held hostage and sending with this peasant a soldier disguised as a servant who would conduct this mission.

In his memoirs, Marmont responds to this last point: "The French sappers who escaped and arrived on the 15th provided better information than any peasant would have been able to give." Napoleon continues: "Although this succeeds all the time you do not employ any of the precautions that are used in war. How, with 30,000 men, have you not captured any prisoners for two days?" Again Marmont responds: "How can you take prisoners when 4,000 to 5,000 cavalry surround you and you have fewer than 1,000 to 1,200 horses?" Napoleon concludes: "The fact is that your corps is one of the finest in the army, that it is in battle against nothing, and that you maneuver as if you have an enemy army a league and a half from you while it is clear that the day before yesterday and yesterday you did not see anyone."[42] Four hours later, at 7:00 A.M. on the 16th, Napoleon again wrote directly to Marmont:

> It appears to me that there is nothing to indicate that the enemy wants to debouch through Halle, and that there is only one cavalry corps there. It seems doubtful that some infantry battalions were observed yesterday, as one report claims. This will be completely verified when the reconnaissance returns this morning. As I am going to attack the Austrians, I think it is appropriate that you cross the Parthe by way of the bridge in the suburbs and that you come and place yourself in reserve, half a league from the city, between Leipzig and Liebertwolkwitz, with your divisions in echelons. From there you move on Lindenau if the enemy makes a serious attack on this side, which to me seems absurd. I will summon you to battle as soon as I see the strength of the enemy and I am sure that he is committed. Finally, you can move to support Bertrand, who has placed posts on your position, if an enemy army appears on the road from Halle, *which is unlikely to happen.*[43]

A second dispatch from Berthier, penned at Reudnitz at 8:00 A.M. on the 16th, made clear that Ney commanded all forces north of the Parthe: VI, IV, and III Corps as well as three cavalry divisions. "In consequence," stressed Berthier, "follow the orders of the prince de la Moskova. If this morning we have no glimpse of an army debouching by Halle, as there is every indication that we have not seen anything, you will cross the Leipzig bridge and place yourself in battle order between Leipzig and Liebertwolkwitz, your three divisions in echelons, and you will remain at Liebertwolkwitz half a league on the main road from Leipzig in a house where you will establish your headquarters. To execute this disposition, you will await the orders of the prince de la Moskova."[44] Taken together, these four letters from Imperial Headquarters probably baffled Marmont.

As for Bernadotte, he remained determined to fly across the Elbe on 14 October. Tauentzien's report that Napoleon had crossed the Elbe at Wittenberg with four corps placed him in a state of panic. During the night of 13/14 October, he learned of Ney's advance on Aken along the left bank of the Elbe as well as Reynier's operation on the opposite bank. He interpreted these movements to be the prelude of a great French offensive in North Germany, which he believed would completely change the complexion of the war. Yet a report that cited the presence of strong French forces at the Mulde cast doubt on Napoleon's intention to cross the Elbe with his main body. Regardless, Blücher's 13 October letter made it clear that the Silesian Army would not follow the Army of North Germany across the Elbe. Thus, Bernadotte would find his army isolated on the right bank if he proceeded with his plan. Blücher's decision angered him, prompting the native Frenchman to express his irritation with much emotion. He remained firm in his decision to return to the right bank of the Elbe to pursue

Napoleon, who he expected would take the road to Berlin. Yet he needed Blücher's cooperation to confront the master. What a predicament for the Swedish prince royal![45]

During the night of 13/14 October, the crown prince wrestled with this issue. Early on the 14th, he sent Bülow's 3rd Brigade to support Hirschfeld at Aken but remained uncertain about his next move. Rather than follow 3rd Brigade with the rest of the army, he issued orders for it to maintain its current position but remain ready to march. Whether Blücher's refusal to obey his orders prompted him to change his mind cannot be determined. The reports that arrived during the night probably caused him to question his view of the situation. Around 5:00 A.M. on the 14th, Adlerkreutz repeated the order for Rauch to remain at Aken (rather than depart to rejoin the Silesian Army) until a bridge across the Elbe was struck. However, the penultimate sentence of the letter states: "as soon as the bridge is finished, His Royal Highness plans to march to Halle."[46] A second letter written to Rauch sometime between 5:00 A.M. and 12:00 P.M. on the 14th claims that a change in circumstances no longer required him to remain at Aken. The crown prince thanked Rauch for his services and wished him a speedy journey "to his first destination, conforming to the orders that you have received from General Blücher." Also, a letter to Blücher, written before noon on the 14th, concludes with the statement: "The army marches early tomorrow morning and I will unite with you tomorrow evening." A letter from Stewart to Gneisenau at 11:00 A.M. likewise communicates the decision to march to Halle. Finally, Bernadotte's headquarters issued the orders for the army to march to Halle on the 15th before noon on the 14th. Thus, based on the documentary record, Bernadotte reversed his decision about retreating across the Elbe sometime around sunrise on 14 October.[47]

Bernadotte's disposition for 15 October called for the entire Army of North Germany to advance in two columns with the Prussians and Russians forming one, the Swedes and Hirschfeld's brigade the other. Bülow received orders to depart from his current position near Köthen around 3:00 A.M. and proceed twenty-three miles south to Halle. Wintzingerode's Russian corps would commence its march at 8:00 A.M. and follow the Prussians. The Swedes would also march at 3:00, trooping thirty-three miles from Köthen to Halle. Bernadotte's headquarters would follow the Swedish corps while Hirschfeld's brigade brought up the rear of the column. The crown prince instructed each corps commander to send one "intelligent" officer and four troopers to the domineering Peters height by the village of Petersberg some nine miles due north of Halle "to observe the enemy's movement as far as the eye can see." Should the enemy approach, a great fire would be lit on the Peters to signal the main bodies of the respective corps to halt and for their rearguards to rejoin them.[48]

These measures somewhat complied with the expectations of Allied Headquarters, where Schwarzenberg hoped the Army of North Germany could be extended between Halle and Merseburg by the 14th. Schwarzenberg's disposition for the 14th required Bernadotte to "extend his right wing to Merseburg. General Blücher has established communication with him on the Saale. The terrain of this region grants to both an advantageous position between Merseburg and Halle. Their outposts can proceed to Schkeuditz and jointly occupy Lützen with our outposts." Merseburg, however, stood an additional nine miles south of Halle. As noted, to reach Halle, Bernadotte's right column faced a march of twenty-three miles while his left trudged thirty-three miles. Another twenty-two miles separated Halle from Leipzig. Although the Allies anticipated a clash somewhere between the two cities rather than at Leipzig itself, little chance remained for the Army of North Germany to arrive in time to participate. At most, Bülow's corps could reach the vicinity of the probable battlefield in the course of the afternoon and receive the Allies should they suffer a setback. However, if the crown prince intended to prevent his troops from participating in the anticipated battle, as Stewart claimed, but wanted to avoid the appearance of subterfuge, then positioning his army at Halle and behind Blücher would serve this purpose perfectly.[49] Such speculation becomes moot in view of Bernadotte's next move, which astonished contemporaries, outraged allies, and continues to baffle historians.

In his 14 October letter to Blücher, Bernadotte explained that he had "held back General Rauch with the pontoons because I urgently needed them for the Elbe crossing. But after I learned through a report from a secret agent that the emperor Napoleon stood between Wittenberg and Eilenburg with six corps and his Guard, and that 50,000 men [had] already crossed to the right bank, I dropped that plan, especially because I knew that the duc de Raguse had taken the direction from Delitzsch to Leipzig, and Marshal Augereau had left Lützen to likewise move to Leipzig." As noted, Bernadotte pledged that his "army marches early tomorrow morning and I will unite with you tomorrow evening." Although pleased by the news that the North German Army would unite with them, Blücher and his staff remained suspicious of the crown prince. In particular, his decision to march to Halle drew their ire. Perhaps asking too much of Bernadotte, the Prussians wanted him to hold the Mulde. They interpreted his march to Halle as a means to position the Army of North Germany in the second line, thus maintaining his freedom to participate or not in the imminent contest. Blücher immediately responded: "I request that you attack the enemy at Dessau and anywhere he can cross the Mulde, and that you send detachments through Bitterfeld, etc. Only then will we be able to see if Your Royal Highness can execute these movements. I also request that you forgo your march to Halle. This will give the enemy the opportunity to advance toward

Bernburg. I am convinced that the Elbe crossing was nothing more than a demonstration to deceive us into taking incorrect measures."[50]

Bernadotte replied at 7:00 on the evening of the 14th: "I have received your letter from this afternoon. You will see from mine that, from the moment I was informed that the enemy was going from Wittenberg and Bad Düben to Leipzig, I made the decision to move to the region of Halle. The more we are united on the day of battle, the greater are the chances of success. If the Grand Army is successful, no one will be happier than me. But if it manages to only provide balance, we will thus decide the battle." The crown prince went on to assure Blücher that he had sent the majority of his cavalry toward Eilenburg; Wintzingerode's vanguard moved to Brehna, patrols found Delitzsch free of the enemy, and one of his detachments occupied Bitterfeld (see Map 6). Thus, the native Frenchman had apparently abandoned his plan to withdraw north across the Elbe. Instead, he decided to transfer his headquarters to Halle on the 15th and unite with the Silesian Army for the decisive battle that Schwarzenberg expected on 16 October. Informing his corps commanders that a large battle would probably occur in the vicinity of Leipzig on the 16th, the prince royal exhorted them to prepare their corps to support the Bohemian and Silesian Armies at a moment's notice.[51]

Following the great cavalry clash at Liebertwolkwitz on 14 October, the Allied monarchs demanded that Schwarzenberg direct all his troops against the French forces at Leipzig and to provide Bernadotte and Blücher with specific points to attack. Schwarzenberg still remained uncertain of both French strength and intentions. Reports stated that Napoleon himself had entered Leipzig on the 14th with his Guard. Numerous reports confirmed his presence at Leipzig on the 15th; around noon, the Allies clearly heard the shout of "*Vive l'Empereur!*" coming from thousands of voices on the hills north of Wachau. Around 5:00 P.M. on the 15th, Schwarzenberg received the report that the French had reinforced Liebertwolkwitz and that the position of Napoleon's left wing clearly indicated his intention to attack the next day. Based on all of this news, the Allies ultimately concluded that Napoleon would not withdraw from Leipzig.

In response, Schwarzenberg and his staff prepared detailed orders to attack the imperial forces in the Leipzig area no later than 16 October. The key feature of the disposition drafted during the night of 14/15 October is Schwarzenberg's complete uncertainty over Napoleon's intentions. The disposition itself is mainly attributed to General Karl Friedrich von Langenau, a former Saxon staff officer. After serving as the chief of staff of Reynier's VII Corps during the invasion of Russia, Langenau joined the Austrian General Staff. Claiming to possess detailed knowledge of the region around Leipzig, Langenau demanded and received the task of formulating the directives that would produce victory on the 16th. Schwarzenberg

placed complete trust in Langenau's judgment while his own chief of
staff, Radetzky, exerted little influence on the decisions made during the
night of 14/15 October. This proved to be a mistake. As Toll's biographer,
Theodor von Bernhardi, has noted, Langenau's disposition "is of such
a peculiar nature that it requires only a very superficial knowledge of the
region – indeed, even a glance at the map – to become convinced of the
uselessness of his proposals."[52]

Schwarzenberg meticulously described the Allied offensive as consisting
of two parts: "Preparation," to occur on the 15th and "Execution" on the
16th. "To the former" states his cover letter, "belongs a secure and reliable
communication between the respective armies, which will be achieved
tomorrow, the 15th, through the following disposition." His instructions
for 15 October called for Blücher's main body to march through Merseburg,
pushing its vanguard nine miles east to the hills of Günthersdorf on the
Merseburg–Leipzig road. A detachment would also move into Schkeuditz,
six miles northeast of Günthersdorf. Both objectives stood nine miles from
Leipzig. Unclear about Napoleon's intentions, Schwarzenberg described
Blücher's movement as "absolutely necessary." Fearing that the emperor
could be marching to Leipzig with his main force, Schwarzenberg
wanted Blücher's army to prevent Napoleon from enveloping the Army of
Bohemia's left wing while Murat fixed its center. Referring to Gyulay, he
added that "a single column marching from Schkeuditz on Leipzig could
be easily crushed by him [Napoleon]." South of Blücher, Gyulay's vanguard
would advance on Lützen. Schwarzenberg chose Markranstädt as the point
for Blücher's troops to link with Gyulay's Austrians.

Fifteen miles south of Günthersdorf, Schwarzenberg planned to unite
52,000 men of the Austrian II Corps, Austrian Reserve, and Russo-Prussian
Guard at Pegau to form the left wing of his army. Thirteen miles east
of Pegau, the Russian III Grenadier Corps and 3rd Cuirassier Division
would unite with Wittgenstein and Kleist at Espenhain. Seven miles further
east, Klenau's Austrian IV Corps would remain in its position at Pomßen
to observe the roads coming from Grimma. Although Barclay's name is
conspicuously absent from the disposition, he would command this army
group, which formed the right wing of the Bohemian Army. The two wings
of the army would be linked by General Moritz Joseph von und zu Liechtenstein's 1st Light Division, which along with two *Streifkorps* (Thielmann's
and Colonel Count Emanuel von Mensdorff-Pouilly) would advance to
Zwenkau. South of both wings, the Austrian I Corps received orders to
march from Chemnitz northwest to Penig.

For the "Execution" phase on the 16th, Schwarzenberg instructed all
units of the Bohemian Army to be marching toward Leipzig at precisely
7:00 A.M. He ordered the Silesian Army to be concentrated at Günthersdorf
by dawn and to likewise commence the march to Leipzig at 7:00. Blücher's

detachment at Schkeuditz would seek to gain the bridge over the Parthe, taking precautions to secure its line of retreat to Halle. Ceding command of Gyulay's corps and Liechtenstein's light division to Blücher, Schwarzenberg instructed them to unite at Markranstädt at dawn and likewise commence their march to Leipzig at the appointed hour; Blücher would provide further orders based on the situation.

The left wing of the Bohemian Army that reached Pegau on the 15th would assemble six miles to the northeast at Zwenkau early enough on the 16th to be able to start the march at 7:00. It would then drive through Connewitz and between Leipzig and Murat's position to attack Napoleon's right and rear. For the right wing, Schwarzenberg stipulated that Wittgenstein's army group supported by Klenau should attack the enemy forces facing them at 7:00 and drive on Leipzig. Finally, Schwarzenberg wanted the Austrian I Corps to cover the nineteen miles from Penig to Borna by 10:00 A.M. Thus, Schwarzenberg's left, 28,000 Austrians and 24,000 Russo-Prussian Guards – some 52,000 men – would advance north through the marshy and densely overgrown region between the Pleiße and the Elster. His right, 72,000 Russians, Prussians, Austrians, and the elite grenadiers and cuirassiers of the Russian Reserve, would advance north and attack Napoleon's left and center. On Blücher's front, 19,000 Austrians along with his own 54,500 men would push east and attack along the Elster to close the Lindenau defile through which ran the main highway from Leipzig to the west.

If the Allies took Leipzig, Schwarzenberg directed Blücher to position the Silesian Army north of the city to observe the roads coming from Bad Düben and Zörbig. The left wing of the Bohemian Army including Gyulay's III Corps would halt northeast of Leipzig on the roads running to Eilenburg and Wurzen while the right wing placed itself on the road to Grimma. Should the Allies suffer a reverse, Schwarzenberg instructed Blücher to retreat to Merseburg; Gyulay and Liechtenstein to Weißenfels and Naumburg respectively; the left wing of the Bohemian Army through Pegau to Zeitz; the right wing to Altenburg; and the Austrian IV and I Corps to Penig. Finally, "should the unbelievable yet still possible case arise that the enemy is hastening to the Elbe and is covering Leipzig and its area with one corps, then the Bohemian Army will emphatically execute the above attack on the 16th, exploiting the advantages according to circumstances while General Blücher simultaneously marches north and the Bohemian Army quickly follows his movements."

Many at Allied Headquarters bemoaned Schwarzenberg's disposition. Radetzky, Toll, Volkonsky, Barclay, Diebitsch, and Jomini immediately recognized the blueprint's shortcomings. They argued that Langenau based the entire plan on the supposition that the Allies could force Napoleon to retreat to the Elbe. Toll pointed to the difficult nature of the terrain, which made any movement between the Elster and the Pleiße impossible. Jomini accused Schwarzenberg's disposition of being so poor that Napoleon himself must have drafted it to guarantee French success. Mainly, the 52,000 men (28,000 Austrians and 24,000 men of the Russo-Prussian Guard) that formed Schwarzenberg's left would be separated from the 72,000 men on the right by the marshy valley of the Elster and the Pleiße. Although Schwarzenberg held a long meeting with Langenau to discuss the complaints, the Russian generals failed to convince the former sufficiently to correct the latter's mistakes. Schwarzenberg deserves some censure as well. Although he personally reconnoitered the flats between the Elster and the Pleiße, the Allied commander in chief failed to appreciate the difficulty of the terrain. Bernhardi refers to the disposition "as a mere *Lieblingsgedanke* [pet idea] from which they [Schwarzenberg and Langenau] could not easily break free. If we consider the marches of the previous days, we see that the use of the main force between the two rivers was decided earlier and strategically introduced."[53]

After Toll's reasoning failed to move Schwarzenberg and Langenau, he requested that, at the least, the Austrians delay issuing the disposition until he could speak with Alexander. Toll immediately went to the tsar and quickly convinced him of the problems with the disposition. Alexander also summoned Diebitsch and Jomini for their thoughts on the issue. The general agreement over the inadequacies of Schwarzenberg's disposition purportedly shocked Alexander, who immediately summoned the Allied commander in chief. During a long meeting, the tsar employed all his powers of persuasion in a vain effort to convince Schwarzenberg to change the disposition. In the end, the Russian monarch lost patience. "Now, my good field-marshal, you can do whatever you like with the Austrian army; but concerning the Russian troops of Grand Duke Constantine and Barclay, they will cross to the right bank of the Pleiße where they will remain and nowhere else!" Consequently, Schwarzenberg had no choice but to accept the reduction of his left wing from 52,000 men to 28,000 Austrians and the increase of his right from 72,000 men to 96,000 through the addition of the 24,000 men of the Russo-Prussian Guard.[54]

Early on the morning of 15 October, an Austrian officer arrived at Blücher's headquarters in Halle bearing a small note written in minute handwriting. Explaining that his orders required him to swallow the dispatch should he be captured, he delivered Schwarzenberg's disposition. The cover letter opens with the statement: "General Blücher stands at Halle; it is determined that he will join the movements of the Grand [Bohemian] Army and participate in a combined attack on the enemy toward Leipzig." Yet the very next line stated that Blücher's operation would be determined by the actions of the Army of North Germany. If Bernadotte had already retreated north across the Elbe, then the Silesian Army would advance along the left bank of the Elster on the Merseburg–Leipzig road toward the latter in unison with Gyulay's Austrian III Corps. However, if the crown prince remained south of the Elbe, Schwarzenberg wanted the Silesian Army to advance as far as possible toward Leipzig along the right bank of the Elster in the direction of Schkeuditz on the 15th, attacking the enemy wherever Blücher found him on the 16th. In this case, the Army of North Germany would seek to achieve two objectives on the 16th. First, the crown prince would march toward the Mulde at dawn on the 16th "to attract the enemy's attention in this direction through demonstrations." Second, Bernadotte would "powerfully support General Blücher's left wing."[55]

All reports that reached Blücher's headquarters early on 15 October placed the Army of North Germany on the march to Halle. Consequently, Blücher issued a disposition to have the Army of Silesia marching by 11:00 A.M. on the 15th based on Schwarzenberg's directions to advance along the right bank of the Elster toward Schkeuditz on the road to Leipzig. Yorck received orders to proceed ten miles southeast through Bruckdorf and Großkugel to Schkeuditz, pushing his vanguard toward Leipzig. North of Yorck's corps, Langeron would march along a parallel road through Reideburg to Kursdorf on the hills north of Schkeuditz; Blücher wanted the Russian vanguard to reach Lindenthal, five miles north-northwest of Leipzig. Blücher instructed Sacken to escort Army Headquarters through Halle to Großkugel, where his corps would remain in reserve. He directed St.-Priest east from Merseburg to Günthersdorf with his vanguard continuing four miles further east to Rückmarsdorf (see Map 6). Blücher informed his corps commanders of the positions to be taken by Gyulay and Liechtenstein. "On 16 October the enemy at Leipzig will be attacked on all sides and St.-Priest will concentrate with Gyulay," he explained. "General Rauch, who will arrive today at Halle with the detachment from Wartenburg, will remain on the left bank of the Saale with the pontoons and all superfluous baggage and throw at least two bridges across the Saale." If possible, the troops should receive a supply of rations to last three days.[56]

At Silesian Army Headquarters, Blücher learned during the course of the morning of 15 October that his patrols had found strong columns marching from Bad Düben to Leipzig. At the head of an Ukrainian Cossack brigade, General Witte reported that the Imperial Guard as well as a huge artillery train had reached Leipzig on the 14th; prisoners attested to the preparations for battle being made by the French army. Rudzevich's compelling report at 8:45 on the morning of the 15th stated: "According to the movements the enemy has made from Bad Düben toward Leipzig since 6:00 on the evening of the 13th, I believe the enemy concentrated all his forces yesterday between Leipzig and Taucha and, if the enemy does not place himself in a defensive position, we should, according to my opinion based on his current position, expect him to attack Merseburg or even Halle."[57]

Meanwhile, around 10:00 on the morning of the 15th, large swarms of imperial skirmishers from Marmont's VI Corps pressed westward on the Halle–Leipzig highway. Taking advantage of cover provided by villages and undergrowth, the French drove back Yorck's cavalry posts. Combined-arms columns followed the French skirmishers. The Brandenburg Hussars supported by the Brandenburg Uhlans took a flanking position, observing the enemy cavalry and horse artillery that surged forward. Although the imperials made a forceful showing, the Prussians concluded that their adversaries simply sought to conduct reconnaissance. Content to leave the imperials to their business, Katzler ordered a retreat to Großkugel. Before this could be executed, he received Blücher's disposition, which ordered Yorck's vanguard to drive on Leipzig. Instead of withdrawing, the Prussians turned around to engage the French skirmishers. After marching ten miles east from Bruckdorf, Hiller reached Schkeuditz with the vanguard's infantry around 4:00. Katzler directed him to continue on the Halle–Leipzig highway toward the French-occupied village of Hänichen, some two miles southeast of Schkeuditz. With the Elster to their right and the Prussian cavalry advancing on the open plain to their left, Hiller's men proceeded. After clearing Schkeuditz, three Jäger companies and one battalion each of Line and Landwehr left the road with instructions to hug the Elster and move through Modelwitz in an attempt to flank Hänichen. Although Katzler's squadrons took the French cavalry in the right flank and caused it to seek cover east of Hänichen, by the time the Prussian foot arrived the imperials had withdrawn from the village. Halting behind a dam, the French surprised the pursuing Prussian skirmishers with a volley. A bayonet charge drove the French from this position but the onset of darkness forced the Prussians to halt their pursuit at Lützschena on the Halle–Leipzig road some three miles east of Hänichen, where Katzler's main body camped for the night. Behind the van, I Corps bivouacked in and around Schkeuditz. The outposts at Lützschena stood very close to those of the enemy, with the right extending to the Elster and the left toward Lindenthal. Through Lindenthal, which the French occupied, ran the road closest to the Halle–Leipzig highway: the Landsberg–Leipzig road. Possession of Lindenthal meant the imperials could threaten the flank of the Silesian Army as it marched to Leipzig. Only Bernadotte's Army of North Germany could prevent this.[58]

As for the rest of the Silesian Army, around noon on the 15th it marched from Halle in two columns to the region of Schkeuditz; only St.-Priest advanced from Merseburg south of the Elster in the direction of Leipzig. Emmanuel led the cavalry of Rudzevich's vanguard toward the villages of Freiroda and Radefeld: both stood four miles north of Hänichen and both were held by Marmont's troops. Two miles north of Schkeuditz, Rudzevich himself reached Kursdorf with the infantry of Langeron's vanguard while the main body of the Russian corps arrived at Werlitzsch, two miles west of Kursdorf and approximately thirty minutes from Schkeuditz. Sacken's corps encountered numerous delays marching through Halle due to clogged roads and so did not reach its bivouac between Gröbers and Großkugel until midnight. Instructed to spread the rumor that the entire Silesian Army would advance on Lindenau, St.-Priest's corps trooped eight miles east from Merseburg to Günthersdorf, approximately five miles southwest of Schkeuditz. Thus, the Silesian Army held an eleven-mile line extending southwest to northeast from Günthersdorf to Radefeld. Schkeuditz, which formed the center of Blücher's position, stood less than nine miles northwest of Leipzig (see Map 6).[59]

Although they were committed to complying with Schwarzenberg's disposition, the situation did not please the leadership of the Silesian Army. In the first place, Blücher and Gneisenau rejected the idea that Schwarzenberg – being so far away and having so little knowledge of Napoleon's intentions – should presume to issue detailed orders for the Silesian Army. Instead, they felt that the Allied commander in chief should have communicated his plans for the Bohemian Army, provided a status report on the imperials, and identified the general objectives according to which Blücher could determine his own operation. Second, they found themselves at the mercy of Bernadotte, whose conduct would dictate the movements of the Silesian Army. Based on Bernadotte's 7:00 P.M. letter on the 14th as well as the incoming reports, Blücher assumed that the Army of North Germany would march to Halle. Thus, Blücher and his staff issued orders for the Silesian Army to proceed in accordance with Schwarzenberg's instructions for this case. However, the further advance from Schkeuditz toward Leipzig on the 16th would require great caution. Even if Bernadotte complied with Schwarzenberg's disposition, the Silesian Army would still risk being attacked in the left flank and rear by imperial columns marching from Bad Düben to Leipzig. For this reason, the Prussians hardly thought it possible to execute Schwarzenberg's orders exactly according to his disposition. Instead, the movements of the Silesian Army most certainly would need to be modified based on those of the enemy as well as Bernadotte's operations.

More importantly, neither Blücher nor Gneisenau felt they could depend on Bernadotte's cooperation in a battle near Leipzig. Consequently, they did not think the Silesian Army could spare the manpower of St.-Priest's corps to unite with Gyulay and operate against Lindenau. Schwarzenberg's decision to confine Blücher's army of 54,500 men within the angle formed by the Elster and the Pleiße to prevent the few enemy forces that appeared to be operating there from participating in the struggle on the right bank of the latter hardly seemed sensible to the Prussians. A simple glance at the map revealed how the Pleiße would separate Schwarzenberg's left from the Silesian Army, meaning that either could be attacked and easily crushed by the entire weight of Napoleon's army before the other could arrive in support. Lastly, Schwarzenberg directed Blücher's entire army of 54,500 men along with Gyulay's 19,000 men against the highly defensible Lindenau defile. If they failed to storm it, which seemed likely, they would have no impact on the battle.

To Blücher and his staff, Schwarzenberg's disposition appeared to be a half-measure indicative of indecision. Apparently, Allied Headquarters could not totally abandon the original idea of advancing northwest to place the Coalition's main force on Napoleon's line of communication. Now, Schwarzenberg decided to operate on the right bank of the Pleiße while small forces situated between the Pleiße and the Elster and between the Elster and the Saale seemed sufficient to maintain the communication between the Silesian and Bohemian Armies and attract considerable imperial forces. These concerns prompted Blücher to dispatch Rühle to Allied Headquarters with a list of protests and counterproposals. Again, Rühle was the right man for the job. He possessed intimate knowledge of Leipzig and its environs thanks to the thorough reconnaissance of the region he had conducted for the late Scharnhorst prior to the 2 May battle of Lützen. He departed from Halle with instructions to explain to the tsar and Schwarzenberg the reasons why the disposition needed to be changed. Moreover, he had to persuade them that Bernadotte's cooperation could not be counted on with certainty.[60]

Alexander's power play also persuaded Schwarzenberg to issue a revised disposition. With regard to the Silesian Army, the first line of the new orders states: "As a result of agreement, General Blücher's army will depart from Schkeuditz precisely at 7:00 and march to Leipzig." Schwarzenberg not only changed his plans for Gyulay, so that Austrian III Corps would not operate under Blücher's orders on the 16th, but he also spared the Silesian Army from having to take the Lindenau defile. Instead, Blücher could advance directly to Leipzig on the main highway from Halle; Gyulay's III Corps along with Liechtenstein's 1st Light Division and St.-Priest's infantry would march from Markranstädt toward Leipzig, attacking the enemy forces facing him and maintaining communication between the Bohemian and Silesian Armies. After taking Lindenau, Schwarzenberg wanted Gyulay to push south to facilitate the advance of Schwarzenberg's left wing, mainly his Austrian II Corps. Consequently, Rühle, who reached the tsar's headquarters at Rötha around midnight on 15/16 October, had little work to do.[61] Alexander received him and agreed with Blücher's proposals. Schwarzenberg also offered no opposition to Blücher's suggestions and noted that the second disposition had already eliminated some of his concerns. Moreover, he made St.-Priest's union with Gyulay optional.[62]

Based on the reports that arrived during the course of the 15th, Blücher and his staff knew that the entire French army probably stood in the vicinity of Leipzig. Nevertheless, the Prussians still did not know the details of the enemy's position, particularly regarding the size of the forces that faced the front and left flank of the Silesian Army. Moreover, they still did not know if further French forces remained en route to Leipzig from Bad Düben. Should Blücher proceed to Leipzig on the 16th, any French forces approaching from Bad Düben would pose a threat to his left. Thus, around 9:00 on the night of 15 October, Blücher issued orders for patrols to reconnoiter toward the Mulde throughout the night. For the morning, he instructed the Reserve Cavalry and the adjoining horse artillery of all three army corps to move out by 6:00. As soon as the Reserve caught up with the vanguard's cavalry, the latter would lead the former toward Leipzig. With Blücher at their head, Yorck's troopers would continue along the Halle–Leipzig highway while Langeron's would take the road running from Radefeld through Lindenthal. Besides escorting Army Headquarters, Sacken's cavalry would follow Yorck's through Schkeuditz toward Leipzig. If the French did not hold a position west of the Parthe, Blücher wanted Yorck's Reserve Cavalry to move between Möckern and Gohlis while Langeron's pushed southeast of the Wiederitzsch villages (see Map 6). In this case, "the cavalry of both vanguards will advance in order to find the enemy and tell me if his position is behind the Parthe or on the road to Bad Düben." Blücher wanted all infantry to cook early enough so that they could march by 10:00 A.M. on 16 October.[63]

The Prussians assumed that the news of Schwarzenberg's intended attack on the 16th as well as the advance of the Silesian Army had reached Bernadotte some time before noon on the 15th. By sending a copy of Blücher's orders for the 16th to Charles Stewart, Gneisenau hoped the British envoy could influence the crown prince to accept the Prussian request to cooperate in the attack. Blücher likewise sent a copy of his disposition to Bernadotte along with a humble, almost pitiful entreaty: "I ask that you tell me your dispositions so I can continue my movements. My left flank is exposed. Your Royal Highness had the grace to tell me that you wanted to make a great cavalry movement toward Eilenburg. I dare to ask if you have given the necessary orders for the execution of this movement." Unfortunately for the soldiers of Yorck's I Corps, Blücher did not receive a satisfactory response. Thus, on 16 October, the Prussian commander would commence an operation against Leipzig believing Napoleon's main force stood northeast of the city on a plateau across which ran the roads from Delitzsch, Bad Düben, Eilenburg, and Wurzen. Although Blücher and his staff would overcome this error in judgment, Yorck's men would pay dearly for this mistake.[64]

Shortly after issuing these orders, Blücher received a letter from Volkonsky, the tsar's chief of staff, written at 10:00 on the morning of the 15th. Schwarzenberg requested that he inform Blücher that the Bohemian Army's reserves would be concentrated at Pegau and Borna by the end of the day;

Bennigsen and Bubna would reach Colditz on the 16th and Colloredo would pass the night at Borna. It also acknowledged Alexander's receipt of Blücher's 14 October report from Halle and provided news regarding the successful cavalry clash on the 14th. According to Volkonsky, Wittgenstein's left stood at Crostewitz and his right at Liebertwolkwitz. After the engagement on the 14th, Murat retreated toward Leipzig, leaving posts at Wachau. "You will see by the disposition of our armies," wrote the Russian staff chief, "that the concentration of our forces is the principal goal of our movements, so that if the circumstances require we are in position to accept a battle or to make a general attack on all points as soon as we learn what is occurring on your side."[65]

Believing that the imperials had completely evacuated the right bank of the Elbe, Bernadotte issued orders early on the 15th for Tauentzien to rebuild the bridge at Roßlau and reoccupy the fortifications at Dessau. Apparently committed to marching to Halle, the crown prince made no attempt to delay his army from commencing its march in two columns early on the 15th. However, while en route, he received Schwarzenberg's first disposition for a general attack on Leipzig. From these instructions, the crown prince clearly saw that his own actions would determine Blücher's movements.[66] As noted, Schwarzenberg's instructions for the 16th called for Bernadotte to attract the enemy's attention through demonstrations on the Mulde and to strongly support Blücher's left wing. Yet the crown prince perceived an insurmountable contradiction in these assignments. With Halle being some thirty miles from the Mulde, he did not think his army could march to the former and still conduct demonstrations on the latter. Moreover, he refrained from adjusting his march so that his right wing could support Blücher's left while his own left demonstrated toward the Mulde. In addition, Boyen asserts that Bernadotte received confirmed reports concerning the continued withdrawal of French forces from Leipzig as a result of Schwarzenberg's approach. This news rendered the further advance of the North German Army superfluous.

Moreover, the head of intelligence at Bernadotte's headquarters, Lieutenant-Colonel Ludwig Ernst Heinrich von Kalckreuth, a Prussian, signed his name to a detailed report at 7:00 P.M. on 15 October at Halle. Written in French, the intelligence brief states that "30,000 enemy troops that had marched toward the Elbe retraced their steps on the 13th and were directed toward Eutritzsch in front [northeast] of Leipzig, where they were still found on the 14th of this month. Marshal Augereau's corps, some 8,000 men, reached Lützen on the afternoon of the 13th, passed through the city of Leipzig, and arrived in the environs of Taucha. This corps did not possess any cannon but had around 1,500 cavalry. The king of Naples and Prince Poniatowski were at Leipzig on the evening of the 13th. The enemy corps that had been detached toward Wittenberg and Dessau returned on the

14th through Bad Düben and reached Radefeld on the Dessau–Leipzig road, where it remained until 3:00 P.M., at which time it again marched on the road to Bad Düben. In the meantime it has been impossible for the secret agents to ascertain whether this corps went to Bad Düben or Taucha. All day throughout the 14th, one heard a strong cannonade from the direction of Altenburg. The duc de Padua [Arrighi] is at Leipzig with a garrison of 10,000 men. The prince de la Moskova [Ney] has command of the corps detached toward the Elbe. The emperor Napoleon himself commands the army assembled near Leipzig, which is estimated to be around 180,000 men. One report makes it certain that the emperor Napoleon will march on Halle. The king of Saxony is near the emperor Napoleon. On the evening of the 14th a corps of 6,000 men pushed [west] toward Freiroda and Lützschena on the Leipzig–Halle road. As of yesterday morning, the emperor Napoleon was still at Leipzig." This unclear and exaggerated report concerning the movement of large imperial columns between Bad Düben, Dessau, and Leipzig as well as strong speculation that Napoleon would advance on Halle caused Bernadotte to fear being outflanked. Under these circumstances, explains Boyen, the crown prince "amended" the march to Halle. Instead of continuing his march to Halle, the crown prince ordered a general halt.[67]

From Sylbitz, seven miles north of Halle, Bernadotte issued new instructions to his corps commanders for execution on 16 October.[68] Wintzingerode received the place of honor, being ordered to position his corps in the front line at Oppin, five miles northeast of Halle and seventeen miles northwest of Blücher's left at Schkeuditz. The Russians would occupy Zörbig and observe the entire 25-mile stretch between Dessau and Delitzsch. Bernadotte instructed Bülow to remain a few miles north of Wintzingerode, with his right leaning on the Peters hill and his left extending east toward Radegast. The cavalry of his vanguard would proceed to Brehna, some fourteen miles north of Schkeuditz, with patrols moving through Schkeuditz and as close as possible to Leipzig. West of Bülow, the Swedes would remain between Wettin and the Peters hill (see Map 6). Except for 100 troopers whom Stedingk would send around 3:00 A.M. on the 16th through Schkeuditz toward Leipzig, the entire Swedish cavalry would take a position behind the army.

General instructions called for each corps to send detachments toward the Elbe around 3:00 on the morning of the 16th: the Russians to Dessau, the Prussians to Aken, and the Swedes to Bernburg. "Each army corps has to move into its camp so that one brigade will remain 1,000 paces behind the main bivouac with its front facing the Elbe; the remaining part of the infantry will camp in two waves. Because it is possible that there will be a battle tomorrow in the vicinity of Leipzig, the army must be combat-ready either to support the Bohemian Army or, if it is victorious, to inflict great damage on the enemy. Wintzingerode must initiate the concentration and readiness of as many Cossack regiments as possible. The army will be under arms tomorrow at 7:00 A.M. and remain ready to march, for which reason the soldiers should cook in the night. General Hirschfeld and Colonel [Woldemar Hermann von] Löwenstern must defend their posts with extreme stubbornness, namely the former at Aken, the latter at Bernburg."

Thus, to the great surprise of not only his own army, but also the leadership of the Silesian Army, Bernadotte halted five miles from Halle on the 15th. This decision placed his army in a position to be unable in any way, not even indirectly as a reserve, to participate in the decisive struggle that all expected to occur on the following day. His apparent unwillingness to take part in the battle and the accompanying duplicity he displayed toward his allies justifiably aroused the suspicion of both contemporaries and posterity. In a letter to Alexander, the crown prince stated that he had halted his march on the 15th because of troop fatigue. After they had rested on the 14th and marched only ten to twelve miles on the 15th, this excuse hardly seems justifiable. Instead, his orders to halt, to post one brigade from each corps with its front facing the Elbe, to send patrols north to Dessau, Aken, and Bernburg, and for Hirschfeld and Löwenstern to defend the bridges at Aken and Bernburg *à outrance* (to the extreme) can be traced to Bernadotte's unforgivable, self-serving caution. Later on the 15th, he ordered Stedingk to send two Swedish battalions with two guns to Bernburg; Bülow received orders to send one Prussian battalion there as well. Fixated on the situation north and east of him, the crown prince refused to place his army in position to support Blücher and Schwarzenberg. Evidently, he assumed Napoleon would either win the battle at Leipzig or order a general retreat in the direction of Bad Düben and Bitterfeld.[69]

Bernadotte's halt troubled the military envoys attached to his headquarters. Consequently, Thornton suggested that Stewart, Krusemarck, Karl von Vincent, Pozzo di Borgo, and himself, all of whom had gone to Halle in expectation of his arrival, draft a very pointed letter to the prince royal that same day, 15 October. To avoid offending Bernadotte by lending the air of military advice to the letter, they employed the hand of the career British diplomat Thornton to produce the final draft. Thornton requested that Wetterstedt, who observed these proceedings, inform the crown prince that the letter should be viewed only in regard to diplomacy. The final draft stated:

> We went to Halle where Your Royal Majesty had determined to move your headquarters. General Stewart has informed us that you have changed your mind and that you have decided to halt at Sylbitz. We know the resolution of the Grand Army [of Bohemia] is to make a general attack against the enemy who is concentrated between Leipzig and Taucha; for this General Blücher has moved his headquarters to Großkugel. Your Royal Majesty has been informed by him of his movements and plans. We come together to beg you

to put yourself in a position from where you can take part in an event that must decide the fate of Europe. Your eminent talents as well as the Allied forces entrusted to your disposition can effectively influence success. We wish to see your name forever associated with this great result."[70]

As Bernadotte did not change his mind and move the army to within supporting distance of Blücher, it appears that this letter had no influence on him. On 21 October, he frankly informed Thornton "that if he had not been actuated by *égards* for the persons and for the sovereigns whom they represented, he should have done right to send back the letter unopened, and that, on a second occasion of the kind, he would do so."[71]

Regardless of Bernadotte's actions, the board was set and the pawns would soon close the distance between their respective lines. "Minute to minute," Schack wrote in his journal, "the knot becomes tighter and more dangerously tied. Napoleon, who should have concentrated his troops at Leipzig, led them to Bad Düben; a captured lieutenant-colonel depicts him to be odd: he sleeps long, cannot be woken, and refuses to listen to the complaints of the troops about shortages. It must soon bend or break. We lived in the greatest joy at Halle." Officers and soldiers alike found the three days of rest at Halle quite enjoyable. The old university town rejoiced over being liberated from the Kingdom of Westphalia and Jerome Bonaparte's foreign rule. Army Headquarters as well as Yorck's headquarters and Hünerbein's brigade quartered in the town. Yorck's other brigades camped in the nearby villages on the opposite bank of the Saale. Received by the locals with gratitude and friendship, the Prussians enjoyed several hearty meals. Many in Yorck's corps – officers, volunteers, and Landwehr – had studied at the University of Halle. Utilizing their free time, they renewed acquaintances and visited old haunts. Many of their professors still lived in Halle; Professor Steffens met with several old colleagues. In the evenings, many of the men could be found in the *Ratskeller* carousing with the locals and students. "The educated and uneducated," noted Droysen, "staff officer and Landwehr man, all next to each other, in the spirit of this Prussian army, of this German war."[72] For many of these soldiers, the merriment they briefly enjoyed at Halle would be their last.

Notes

1 Blücher to Charles John, Halle, 13 October 1813, Add MSS, 20112, 82–83.
2 Charles John to Blücher, Rothenburg, 13 October 1813, Add MSS, 20112, 80.
3 Stewart himself makes no mention of one or more journeys to Blücher's headquarters at Halle in his *Narrative*. On the 13th, Gneisenau informed Boyen that Bernadotte had sent Stewart to Halle on the 12th "with complaints about the danger of his situation." Stewart returned to Halle on the morning of the 13th with this letter. Gneisenau wrote: "In the morning, Stewart came again with a

letter from the crown prince, who asked us to go back across the Elbe with him!!!": Gneisenau to Boyen, Halle, 13 October 1813, GStA PK, VI HA Rep. 92 Nl. Gneisenau, Nr. 23.

4 Charles John to Blücher, Rothenburg, 12 October 1813, Add MSS, 20112, 79.

5 Gneisenau to Müffling, Halle, 4:00 A.M., 13 October 1813, GStA PK, VI HA Rep. 92 Nl. Gneisenau, Nr. 23.

6 Müffling, *Die Feldzüge*, 72.

7 Steffens, *Adventures*, 117.

8 Blücher to Charles John, Halle, 13 October 1813, Add MSS, 20112, 82–83.

9 Müffling, *Die Feldzüge*, 74; Unger, *Blücher*, II:107; Höpfner, "Darstellung," 1845:373–74.

10 Krusemarck to Blücher, Rothenburg, 13 October 1813, in Höpfner, "Darstellung," 1845:373; SHAT, C¹⁷ 133: Charles John to Rauch, 13 October 1813. For the situation at Bernadotte's headquarters, see Stewart, *Narrative*, 151–52.

11 Rauch to Charles John, Köthen, 14 October 1813, RA KrA, volym 25; Müffling, *Die Feldzüge*, 74. Müffling believes that the attack on Aken's bridge "did Napoleon bad service, for, had it not been for this, the Army of North Germany would have crossed the Elbe on the 13th, and either followed the same route as Tauentzien, who was force-marching on side roads to reach Berlin before the enemy, or in any case would not have been present at the battle of Leipzig."

12 Rauch to Blücher, 13 October 1813, in Höpfner, "Darstellung," 1845:374–75; Blücher to Rauch, 14 October 1813, *ibid.*, 378–79; Unger, *Blücher*, II:108.

13 Katzler's and Rudzevich's reports are in Höpfner, "Darstellung," 1845:375, 379; Müffling, *Die Feldzüge*, 73.

14 Blücher to Alexander, Halle, 14 October 1813, in Höpfner, "Darstellung," 1845:379–80.

15 Alexander to Blücher, Altenburg, 13 October 1813, in Höpfner, "Darstellung," 1845:381.

16 Schwarzenberg to Blücher, Altenburg, 13 October 1813, ÖStA KA, FA 1535, 338, and Add MSS, 20112, 16–18.

17 Blücher to Alexander, Halle, 14 October 1813, in Höpfner, "Darstellung," 1845:379–80.

18 Blücher to Charles John, Halle, 14 October 1813, Add MSS, 20112, 89.

19 Friederich, *Herbstfeldzug 1813*, II:363.

20 As a point of interest, Napoleon instructed Marmont to discard the traditional three-deep line: "Place your troops in two rows instead of three; the third rank is useless in a firefight; it is even less useful with the bayonet. When we are in close columns, three divisions will form six ranks and three rows of closed lines. You will see the advantages of this; your fire will be better; your strength will be increased by one-third; the enemy, accustomed to seeing us in three ranks, will believe our battalions are one-third stronger. Give the most precise orders for the enforcement of this provision." He extended this order to the rest of the army that same day: *CN*, Nos. 20791 and 20793, XXVI:349–50, 352.

21 *CN*, No. 20792, XXVI:350–51.

22 Höpfner, "Darstellung," 1845:378.

23 "I will not be able to attack the enemy until the 16th," he wrote to Murat at 7:00 P.M. on the 13th: *CN*, No. 20797, XXVI:355. In *Herbstfeldzug 1813*, III:23, Friederich claims that as of the 14th Napoleon still hoped to have the majority of his army concentrated at Leipzig by that evening so that he could attack Schwarzenberg on the 15th. Based on this letter to Murat, Napoleon had already given up hopes of fighting on 15 October.

24 *CN*, Nos. 20796 and 20797, XXVI:353–55.

25 *CN*, No. 20796, XXVI:354; Petre, *Napoleon's Last Campaign*, 317.

26 *CN*, Nos. 20797–20800, XXVI:356–57; SHAT, C¹⁷ 180: Berthier to Ney, Macdonald, Reynier, Sébastiani, Latour-Maubourg, Drouot, Bertrand, and Durrieu, 14 October 1813.

27 *CN*, Nos. 20801 and 20802, XXVI:358.

28 *CN*, No. 20805, XXVI:360; SHAT, C¹⁷ 181: Berthier to Macdonald, 14 October 1813; Yorck von Wartenburg, *Napoleon as a General*, II:346.

29 See http://greatestbattles.iblogger.org/GB/Liebertwolkwitz/Liebertwolkwitz-PartIII-ByHofschroer.htm. See also Bogdanovich, *Geschichte des Krieges*, IIb:82–88.

30 *CN*, No. 20805, XXVI:359–60.

31 King Gustavus Adolphus of Sweden had defeated Johann Tserclaes, Count of Tilly, at Breitenfeld on 17 September 1731 in the Protestants' first major victory of the Thirty Years War. The victory ensured that the German states would not be forcibly reconverted to Roman Catholicism and induced many Protestant German states to ally with Sweden against the German Catholic League, which was led by Maximilian I, Elector of Bavaria, and Holy Roman Emperor Ferdinand II of Austria.

32 Marmont, *Mémoires*, V:278–79.

33 SHAT, C¹⁷ 181: Berthier to Macdonald, Dąbrowski, Reynier, and Terrier, 14 October 1813; *CN*, No. 20807, XXVI:360–61.

34 Numbers are based on Friederich, *Herbstfeldzug 1813*, III:22–23, 27–28.

35 Napoleon's "mistake" of leaving St.-Cyr at Dresden with XIV and I Corps – some 30,000 men – has been well documented as a politically motivated error of judgment. However, St.-Cyr managed to tie down some 65,000 Russians and Austrians monitoring Dresden so that these troops were not available for battle on the 16th. True, Napoleon could have used the additional 30,000 men on 16 October but a further 65,000 Allied soldiers would have followed St.-Cyr as soon as his forces departed from the Saxon capital and probably would have been available to Schwarzenberg on the 16th. Using the 30,000 men of XIV and I Corps to tie down 20,000 Russians under Osterman-Tolstoy admittedly does not offer an expedient example of economy of force but in the end their presence at Dresden made the odds of victory on the 16th much more favorable for Napoleon. In the realm of pure speculation, we can only wonder how Schwarzenberg would have reacted had St.-Cyr escaped from Dresden and marched due west across the Saxon plain to sever his communications with Bohemia. See the discussions in Yorck von Wartenburg, *Napoleon as a General*, II:346–48; Petre, *Napoleon's Last Campaign*, 319–22.

36 *CN*, No. 20811, XXVI:362.

37 *CN*, No. 20812, XXVI:362.

38 Höpfner, "Darstellung," 1847:90.

39 Marmont, *Mémoires*, V:279–80.

40 SHAT, C¹⁷ 181: Berthier to Marmont, Reudnitz, 11:00 P.M., 15 October 1813.

41 Marmont, *Mémoires*, V:374.

42 Napoleon to Marmont, Reudnitz, 3:00 A.M., 16 October 1813, Marmont, *Mémoires*, V:376–77. Incidentally, this letter is not included in the nineteenth-century publication of Napoleon's *Correspondence* but can be found in Marmont's memoirs. Moreover, Napoleon's headquarters at Reudnitz was six miles southeast of Marmont's command post at Lindenthal. It is curious that the imperial courier, identified by Marmont as being the orderly officer Lavesaut, took five hours to cross six miles.

43 *CN*, No. 20814, XXVI:364–65, emphasis added.

44 SHAT, C¹⁷ 181: Berthier to Marmont, 16 October 1813.

45 Müffling, *Die Feldzüge*, 72; Friederich, *Herbstfeldzug 1813*, II:364–65.

46 Adlerkreutz to Rauch, Köthen, 14 October 1813, in Höpfner, "Darstellung," 1845:376.

47 SHAT, C¹⁷ 133: Charles John to Rauch, Köthen, 14 October 1813; Charles John to Blücher, Köthen, 14 October 1813, Add MSS, 20112, 85; Stewart to Gneisenau, Köthen, 11:00 A.M., 14 October 1813, GStA PK, VI HA Rep. 92 Nl. Gneisenau, Nr. 28. The existence of several accounts of the proceedings at Bernadotte's headquarters during 13 and 14 October render a precise retelling extremely difficult. Friederich's unbiased reporting again must be recognized: "When we compare these various reports that have come to us with unprejudiced eyes we see immediately that we have to deal with a colorful mixture of truth and falsehood that has apparently driven the legend to its most luxuriant blooms. When we peel out of this jumble of conflicting accounts the historically established and probable corresponding core, we obtain the following picture: as all vacillating characters tend to do in such a situation, he [Bernadotte] summoned a council of war, during which he presented the pros and cons of crossing the Elbe, apparently favoring it. Because all who were present declared in favor of uniting with the Silesian Army, the crown prince thus approved this decision." See Friederich, *Herbstfeldzug 1813*, II:368.

48 SHAT, C¹⁷ 133: Order of the Day, Köthen, 14 October 1813.

49 Schwarzenberg to Blücher, Altenburg, 13 October 1813, ÖStA KA, FA 1535, 338, and Add MSS, 20112, 17; Friederich, *Herbstfeldzug 1813*, II:362.

50 Charles John to Blücher, Köthen, 14 October 1813, Add MSS, 20112, 85; Blücher to Charles John, Halle, 12:00 P.M., 14 October 1813, GStA PK, VI HA Rep. 92 Nl. Gneisenau, Nr. 23; Friederich, *Herbstfeldzug 1813*, II:364.

51 Charles John to Blücher, Köthen, 7:00 P.M., 14 October 1813, Add MSS, 20112, 84; Leggiere, *Napoleon and Berlin*, 264.

52 Bogdanovich, *Geschichte des Krieges*, IIb:88; Bernhardi, *Toll*, III:420.

53 Bernhardi, *Toll*, III:422–23. Lieven, in *Russia Against Napoleon*, 439 and 441, concludes: "Prince Schwarzenberg's operational plan for the battle seemed guaranteed, however, to ensure that Napoleon need not worry about defeat." Lieven correctly argues that Schwarzenberg liked the plan because he never intended to deliver a decisive battle at Leipzig. Instead, his plan for the month of October was

to block Napoleon's retreat to the west. "Though not totally implausible as a strategic concept, his efforts to translate this idea into tactical deployments around Leipzig were a disaster. There was in any case a very basic problem with the Austrian plan. Napoleon had not concentrated his forces in Leipzig in order to retreat westwards. He was intending to smash the Army of Bohemia and win the campaign." Maude wrote: "Viewed by the light of subsequent events, Schwarzenberg's conduct appears almost imbecil[ic]." See Maude, *Leipzig Campaign*, 253–54.

54 Jomini, *Précis politique et militaire*, II:155–56; Friederich, *Herbstfeldzug 1813*, III:10–14; Bogdanovich, *Geschichte des Krieges*, IIb:108–11.

55 Schwarzenberg to Blücher, Altenburg, 14 October 1813, in Höpfner, "Darstellung," 1845:385–86. Although this disposition can be found in numerous secondary sources, it is not in either the Austrian archives or the British manuscript collection.

56 Disposition, Halle, 15 October 1813, Add MSS, 20112, 161.

57 Friederich, *Herbstfeldzug 1813*, III:15–16; The reports by Witt and Rudzevich are in Höpfner, "Darstellung," 1845:387–88.

58 Höpfner, "Darstellung," 1845:388–89; Droysen, *Yorck*, II:211–12; Aster, *Leipzig*, I:333.

59 Müffling, *Die Feldzüge*, 77; Aster, *Leipzig*, I:334; "Die Mitwirkung des k.k. dritten, von dem Feldzeugmeister Grafen Ignaz Gyulay befehligten Armeekorps während der Schlacht von Leipzig, bis zur Überschreitung der Saale; vom 13 bis 21 Oktober 1813," *Österreichische militärische Zeitschrift* (1836), III:121. Mistrust of Bernadotte made St.-Priest's return to the Silesian Army all the more urgent. On the evening of the 15th, Blücher instructed him to cross the Elster at Günthersdorf and march to Schkeuditz to unite with Langeron's corps. He directed St.-Priest's vanguard through Rückmarsdorf. To inform Gyulay of this change, the Austrian military envoy assigned to Blücher's headquarters, Captain Baron Wenzel Philipp Leopold von Marschall von Biberstein, rode to Lützen. He delivered Blücher's letter informing Gyulay that St.-Priest would not be able to support him at Lindenau on the 16th. Blücher also explained the considerable terrain difficulties that Gyulay's troops would encounter on the road from Lützen to Leipzig – difficulties which the Prussian opined would only be increased by having St.-Priest's corps likewise operating in the area. For this reason, Blücher instructed St.-Priest to advance on the right bank of the Elster rather than its left.

60 Höpfner, "Darstellung," 1845:387; Friederich, *Herbstfeldzug 1813*, III:9–10, 14–15.

61 The tsar quartered at Rötha, eleven miles south of Leipzig and nine miles east of Schwarzenberg's headquarters at Pegau.

62 Disposition for the Attack on 16 October, Pegau, 15 October 1813, Add MSS, 20112, 163–66.

63 Disposition for 16 October, Schkeuditz, 15 October 1813, Add MSS, 20112, 162; Aster, *Leipzig*, I:336.

64 Blücher to Charles John, Schkeuditz, 15 October 1813, Add MSS, 20112, 86; Pertz and Delbrück, *Gneisenau*, III:455; Müffling, *Die Feldzüge*, 77; Droysen, *Yorck*, II:212.

65 Volkonsky to Blücher, Altenburg, 10:00 A.M., 15 October 1813, in Höpfner, "Darstellung," 1845:389.

66 As Schwarzenberg's second disposition makes no mention of the Army of North Germany, the Allied commander in chief may have elected not to forward a copy to Bernadotte.

67 "News from the Secret Agents," Halle, 7:00 P.M., 15 October 1813, RA KrA, volym 25. It is not known if a copy of this brief was sent to Blücher; German and Swedish sources make no mention of it, which is surprising because its contents strengthen Swedish historian Georg Swederus's defense of Bernadotte's actions. Because the brief is written in French, we can assume it was sent to Bernadotte. See also Boyen, *Erinnerungen*, ed. Schmidt, II:678–79; SHAT, C¹⁷ 133: Charles John to Tauentzien, 15 October 1813.

68 On the 14th, Bernadotte had issued his orders of the day for the 15th from Köthen. He issued these orders from Sylbitz, some fourteen miles south of Köthen.

69 SHAT, C¹⁷ 133: Order of the Day and Charles John to Stedingk and Bülow, 15 October 1813; Aster, *Leipzig*, I:334; Stewart, *Narrative*, 161–62; Höpfner, "Darstellung," 1845:391; Friederich, *Herbstfeldzug 1813*, II:372–73. "I must here observe," noted Stewart, "that the orders intentionally (for they could not be ignorantly) issued on this day by the Prince Royal were for the different corps to have brigades formed towards the Elbe, evidently to give the impression that the enemy were to be looked for in that quarter." In the Prussian General Staff's official account of the Silesian Army, Höpfner simply states that "determining the reason for this unexpected halt must be left to the reader." Bernadotte never offered an explanation for this bizarre behavior. Once again, Friederich of the German General Staff demonstrates his objectivity: "When we consider the total political situation of the crown prince and his dependence on the Allied great powers, we consider that it was absolutely necessary for his political existence that Napoleon be defeated in the decisive battle expected at Leipzig, and that the Army of North Germany not be spared in obtaining a decisive victory, we can only reach the conclusion that it is impossible for bad faith to have caused him to halt behind the Peterswege, that apparently there must have been rather serious reasons that prompted him to make this decision. In the absence of any evidence we are dependent only on conjecture." For a weak defense of Bernadotte's actions, see Swederus, *Schwedens Politik und Kriege*, II:304–12.

70 Reproduced in Höpfner, "Darstellung," 1845:392.

71 Thornton to Castlereagh, Leipzig, 22 October 1813, CVC, IX:67–68.

72 Droysen, *Yorck*, II:208–09.

1 4

"A battle of the most obstinate and sanguinary class"

The wide lowland through which the Elster and the Pleiße Rivers flowed in a northern direction gradually curved westward from the walls of Leipzig toward the valley of the Saale. Between both rivers sprawled a wooded marsh that formed an eastward projecting salient in front of which stood Leipzig. North of the city, the course of the Parthe ran northeast while the Elster flowed northwest, giving the terrain sector between these two water courses the appearance of a broad funnel into which the great highways from Halle, Magdeburg, Dessau, Wittenberg, and Torgau merged. These arteries ran through gentle inclines and over shallow hills, which at most rose no more than twenty to thirty yards above the lowlands of the Elster and the meadows of the Parthe. Steady rains in August and September had rendered the clay soil very soft; low-lying farmlands and meadows hindered the movement of close-ordered troop units. Due to the wet summer and autumn, the marshes of the Elster, Parthe, and Pleiße could be crossed only by way of the existing roads; the rivers themselves formed obstacles because of their depth and could not be crossed without preparation.[1]

From every direction roads converged on Leipzig like the radii of a circle. The Allies controlled the two running west to Naumburg and Merseburg on the Saale; Napoleon commanded all the opposite roads leading east and northeast to Wurzen, Eilenburg, and Bad Düben on the Mulde as well as the roads to Torgau and Wittenberg on the Elbe. In between lay three roads that ran north and three that ran south; the ensuing battle would determine which side controlled these six avenues. With the possession of Leipzig, Napoleon held the hub of all the roads. Simultaneously, he flanked the Bohemian Army by the road to Wurzen and the Silesian Army by the highway to Bad Düben; his forces separated the two Allied armies like a wedge between them. For the 16th, Allied Headquarters wanted to drive through this wedge and take Leipzig.[2]

Napoleon did not intend to fight a defensive battle. Instead, he wanted to destroy the Army of Bohemia south of Leipzig. With II, V, and VIII Corps as well as IV Cavalry Corps, all under Murat, the emperor planned to hold Schwarzenberg's army along the six-mile line extending from Connewitz to Liebertwolkwitz. While Murat fixed Schwarzenberg, IX and XI Corps along with I, II, and V Cavalry Corps would pivot on Liebertwolkwitz and envelop his right. Once the Allies weakened their center to support their right, Napoleon planned to unleash his Regular Reserve – IV, VI, and III Corps and III Cavalry Corps – and ultimately his Grand Reserve – the whole of the Imperial Guard – against their center. He calculated on having 160,000 men at his disposal to face the 96,000 Allied soldiers in that sector – great odds for the emperor. Napoleon positioned 120,000 south of Leipzig by the morning of the 16th. Including Leipzig's garrison, another 60,000 men remained north of the city.[3]

French positions on the morning of the 16th from left (west) to right (east) indicate that Napoleon planned to let nature protect his right flank. Defending the Pleiße from its eastern bank allowed the emperor to mass superior forces against Schwarzenberg's center. On his right, the Poles of VIII Corps and IV Cavalry Corps as well as a 2,000-man French division of march units under General Étienne-Nicolas Lefol held the Pleiße's eastern bank by occupying the northeast-to-southwest-running line of Connewitz, Lößnig, Dölitz, Markkleeberg, and Dösen. From Markkleeberg, the French line extended east with II Corps behind and on both sides of Wachau; V Corps between Wachau and Liebertwolkwitz supported by the Young Guard and 2nd Old Guard Division; IX Corps at Zuckelhausen northeast of Liebertwolkwitz; XI Corps and II Cavalry Corps en route from Taucha to Holzhausen. Around Probstheida stood I and V Cavalry Corps as well as the Grand Reserve: 1st Old Guard Division and the Guard Cavalry. As for the situation north of Leipzig, Napoleon firmly believed the Silesian Army still stood at Merseburg with elements (St.-Priest) approaching Markran- städt. Marmont had guaranteed him that he could hold the Silesian and North German Armies for one day. For this, Napoleon promised him a stronger force than he could actually provide: Souham's III Corps. More- over, early on the 16th, both Ney and Marmont received the master's summons for VI Corps to march south through Leipzig to Liebertwolkwitz where it would form the emperor's Regular Reserve for the struggle with Schwarzenberg. Napoleon assured Marmont that only cavalry faced VI Corps, and that Blücher's army stood on the opposite bank of the Elster.

Ultimately, confusion hampered French operations north of Leipzig, leading to the complete collapse of Napoleon's entire plan. Reaching Eutritzsch around 9:00 A.M., Ney realized that III Corps had yet to arrive. Adjusting to the situation, he ordered Bertrand's IV Corps and Defrance's 4th Heavy Cavalry Division to move four miles northwest from Eutritzsch to relieve Marmont at Lindenthal and thus enable VI Corps to march to Liebertwolkwitz and form the emperor's Regular Reserve. Yet around the same time, Marmont learned that approximately 1,500 Allied soldiers faced his front. Although this seemed an insignificant number, the bivouacs behind them indicated the presence of much larger forces. At 10:00, Ney decided to comply with the emperor's order by sending Bertrand's IV Corps to Liebertwolkwitz while Marmont determined the intent of the Allied forces opposite his position. Before IV Corps could march, Ney received word from a panicked Arrighi at Leipzig. Charged with defending the city, he informed Ney of the advance of an Austrian corps toward Lindenau and the sole road to the west that still remained open to the Grande Armée. Ney felt he had no choice but to redirect Bertrand to Lindenau.[4] Consequently, IV Corps turned west and spent the day locked in combat with Gyulay's Austrian III Corps. Moreover, Bertrand's detour meant that Ney still had not complied with Napoleon's orders to send his Regular Reserve to Liebertwolkwitz. "Sire," he reported at 10:30, "I just sent IV Corps to Lindenau to support the duc de Padua [Arrighi], who has only four battalions there, and who has informed me that he will be attacked by a large column coming from Lützen. The VI Corps has one division at Schönefeld to protect the parks and baggage there. Its other two divisions will be relieved by III Corps; immediately after this occurs, it will be echeloned on Liebertwolkwitz. If the enemy does not come in great force from the direction of Halle, III Corps, except for one division that will remain at Eutritzsch, will follow the movement of VI Corps."[5] Yet VI Corps never reached Liebertwolkwitz, being pinned and defeated in a bloody struggle with Blücher's army north of Leipzig at Möckern.

As for III Corps, much uncertainty exists over its exact whereabouts on 16 October. According to the journal of the corps, the commander of 11th Division, General Ricard, reached Mockau at 11:30 A.M. After hearing a strong cannonade south of Leipzig, he received orders to move his 1st Brigade to Lindenau to support Arrighi and his 2nd to a position south of Leipzig. Brayer's 8th Division "marched to support the divisions of Fournier and Defrance at Eutritzsch that were covering the roads from Halle and Delitzsch. At 1:00 P.M., 8th Division quit this position and marched through Schönefeld to take a position to the left of one division of Old Guard between the villages of Dölitz and Markkleeberg, where it arrived around 5:00 P.M. The 11th Division followed the movement of the 8th." The journal affirms that poor roads slowed the march of both divisions and neither reached their destination with artillery. Despite this confusion, it is apparent that the 12,000 men of Souham's 8th and 11th Divisions did not relieve VI Corps so it could march to Liebertwolkwitz per Ney's 10:30 A.M. report to the emperor.[6] Napoleon later viewed the nonappearance of III Corps as the greatest calamity of the day.[7]

Including Cossacks, Allied forces totaled approximately 205,000 men supported by 1,026 guns for battle on 16 October. How much of the artillery actually saw action remains unclear as 108 guns of the Austrian Reserve Artillery en route from Zeitz never reached the battlefield. On Schwarzenberg's extreme left, Gyulay's III Corps, Liechtenstein's 1st Light Division, and the two *Streifkorps* under Thielmann and Mensdorff attacked Lindenau and became embroiled with Bertrand's IV Corps for the entire day. Schwarzenberg's left wing – Merveldt's Austrian II Corps supported by the Austrian Reserve – received the task of advancing on Leipzig between the Elster and the Pleiße. Swampy terrain prevented Merveldt from moving up his artillery, and he failed to get across the Pleiße. By 11:00 his attacks had failed, and he reverted to the defensive for several hours.

Although Barclay de Tolly commanded the right wing of the Bohemian Army, he vested Wittgenstein with executive authority for the battle. Wittgenstein decided to advance against the French positions along the Markkleeberg–Wachau–Liebertwolkwitz line in five widely separated columns that extended west to the Pleiße along the Cröbern–Güldengoßa–Großpösna line. From left (west) to right (east), the five Allied assault columns consisted of Kleist's 12th Brigade, one battalion from his 9th Brigade, and the Russian 14th Division from General Andrey Gorchakov's Russian I Infantry Corps. This column received the task of advancing from Cröbern against Markkleeberg and supporting the attack on Wachau. From Güldengoßa, Wittgenstein's second column – Prince Eugen of Württemberg's Russian II Infantry Corps and 9th Brigade of Kleist's II Corps (11,000 men and 31 guns) – would assault Wachau from the southeast. Gorchakov would lead the third column consisting of his 5th Division as well as Kleist's 10th Brigade, altogether some 9,000 men and 20 guns, north from Störmthal to assault Liebertwolkwitz from the south. Fourth, some 5,400 Russian and Prussian cavalry (one division each of Russian hussars and uhlans as well as Kleist's Reserve Cavalry) and 24 guns under the command of Pahlen III would proceed from Güldengoßa to the hills between Wachau and Liebertwolkwitz to fill the gap between Wittgenstein's third and fifth columns. Fifth, the 33,000 men and 80 guns of Klenau's Austrian IV Corps and Kleist's 11th Brigade would advance from the Großpösna–Fuchshain sector to attack Liebertwolkwitz from the east. As a reserve, the 10,500 men and 34 guns of the Russian Grenadier Corps and Cuirassier Brigade stood south of Gruhna while the 24,000 men and 243 guns of the Russo-Prussian Guard and Reserve Cavalry were en route to Rötha, less than 8 miles south of Güldengoßa.[8]

North of Leipzig, Blücher commanded 54,500 men with 310 guns and 3,516 Cossacks. Yorck's corps, which again would shoulder the burden of the fighting, mustered 20,831 men.[9] Langeron's corps totaled some 15,000 men[10] and Sacken a total of 14,000 men.[11] Still uncertain about the position

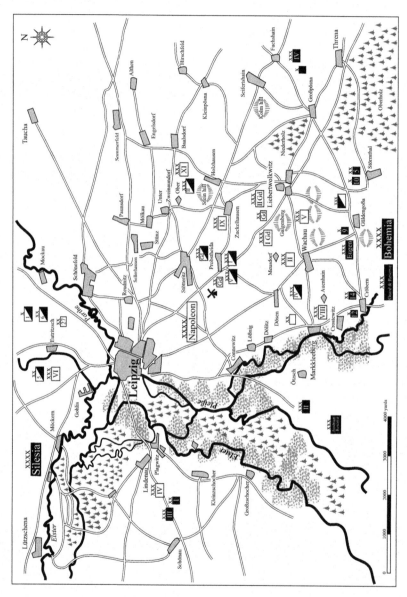

24. Battle of Leipzig, southern front, 16 October 1813

of the Grande Armée, Blücher and his staff placed it on the highways leading to Leipzig from Bad Düben and Delitzsch.[12] Before departing from his headquarters at Großkugel early on the 16th, Blücher received a dispatch from Rudzevich's command post at Kuhrsdorf. The Russian confirmed the presence of imperial forces at Radefeld and Freiroda. Based on the campfires he had observed during the night, Rudzevich outlined a French position between those two villages and Lindenthal. Ten miles north-northeast, one of his patrols found Delitzsch free of enemy forces but a second patrol spotted an imperial camp at Krostitz, halfway to Leipzig on the road from Bad Düben (see Map 6). As of the previous evening, French forces still held Bad Düben but Rudzevich awaited the latest report. Closer at hand, Hiller reconnoitered from Hänichen along the Halle–Leipzig road with a small detachment of Yorck's vanguard just after first light on the cold, foggy autumn morning of 16 October. He found a weak enemy force holding Stahmeln, imperial cavalry on the hills north of the village, and what appeared to be a large bivouac further east near Möckern.

At 6:00 A.M., the Reserve Cavalry of Blücher's three corps moved out to unite with the vanguard cavalry detachments on what Steffens described as a "bright and mild" day that followed a cold windy night that had seen gusts uproot trees and damage roofs.[13] On Blücher's left, Langeron's Reserve Cavalry under Korf rode through Kursdorf toward Freiroda and united with Emmanuel's vanguard cavalry but could go no further due to the French garrison at Radefeld. On the army's right, Yorck's cavalry rode three miles east from its bivouac to Schkeuditz. Then, with Blücher leading, the Prussian horse advanced southeast on the Halle–Leipzig road. According to Colonel Hudson Lowe, whom Charles Stewart had ordered to accompany Blücher's staff during the battle of Leipzig, "The infantry he left at its bivouac in front of Großkugel with orders to hold itself in readiness to march at an instant's notice. On coming within view of the village of Freiroda, it was ascertained that the enemy held possession of it, and different parties of the enemy's infantry, cavalry, and artillery were observed to occupy the ground lying between it and the villages of Radefeld and Lindenthal." From the rear of the army, Sacken's cavalry advanced from its bivouac between Gröbers and Großkugel, following Yorck's troopers through Schkeuditz.[14]

Blücher halted west of Stahmeln, itself two miles east of Schkeuditz. Over the next two hours he received reports from his forward patrols, indicating that enemy infantry held the villages immediately opposite the Silesian Army: Stahmeln, Wahren, Radefeld, and Freiroda. The French position appeared to extend south from Radefeld–Freiroda to Lindenthal and from there to Stahmeln–Wahren. Further afield, large imperial forces still occupied Bad Düben and camped at Krostitz on the Bad Düben–Leipzig road but Delitzsch, thirteen miles north-northeast of

Schkeuditz, remained free of the enemy. The ridge of hills between Radefeld and Lindenthal formed the dominant watershed in the region, extending eastward through Hohenossig to a plateau on which ran the roads from Delitzsch, Bad Düben, Eilenburg, and Wurzen. Blücher and his staff surmised that Napoleon held this plateau and would accept battle on it or eight miles north of Leipzig in the Podelwitz–Hohenossig region on the Bad Düben–Leipzig road (see Map 6). Reports that imperial forces remained in the Bad Düben area during the night of 15/16 October appeared to confirm this assumption. Thus, the Prussians believed that French forces occupied Radefeld and Lindenthal to guard the ascent to this plateau.[15]

Around 8:00 A.M., Blücher rode to the hills of Lützschena, where he received the cavalry's reports. Yorck's troopers found a small imperial post just east of Lützschena at Stahmeln. Further east, they could see that the enemy also held Wahren, which apparently anchored the French left. From Wahren, the French line extended one mile north to Lindenthal while the French right wing curved three miles northwest from Lindenthal toward Radefeld along the Leipzig–Landsberg road. Imperial cavalry, estimated by the Prussians to number 1,200 troopers, stood west of the pine grove that separated Lindenthal and Radefeld; infantry occupied the woods. French cavalry could also be seen on the hills between Stahmeln and Wahren. Major Hiller of Yorck's vanguard observed a large infantry camp further east and beyond Möckern on the Halle–Leipzig highway. Strong combined-arms units occupied Lindenthal, Radefeld, and the woods between the two villages. An accurate estimate of French strength could not be obtained because the pine grove north of Lindenthal prevented the Russians and Prussians from gaining an overview.

This information did little to shake the Prussians free of the thought that the French intended to accept battle either on the Breitenfeld plateau between Lindenthal and Radefeld or further northeast in the Podelwitz–Hohenossig region. In either position, they could be reinforced by the troops coming from Bad Düben or, if defeated, they could withdraw through Hohenossig to Bad Düben. This left Blücher two options: he could either drive to Leipzig, ignoring the enemy forces facing his left flank, or he could attack them. He could not expose his flank unless Bernadotte complied with Schwarzenberg's disposition and advanced on the road from Delitzsch toward Leipzig. Already the artillery of the Bohemian Army could be heard engaging the French south of Leipzig. Thinking the crown prince would comply with Schwarzenberg's disposition, Blücher felt himself drawn to the sound of the guns. He started preparing for the advance to Leipzig but had to abandon this plan after Stewart, "much chagrined at the Prince Royal's resolutions," arrived at Lützschena. The British general delivered the news that the Army of North Germany would not be in position to support the Silesian Army that day.[16] Stewart explained that all he "had been able to accomplish by dint of persuasion was to get the Russians to Zörbig; and General Blücher fairly and naturally sympathized with my painful sensations on this result." Yet, should the enemy attack Blücher on the 17th, Bernadotte would be able to support him by sending 8,000 to 10,000 cavalry and light artillery through Delitzsch to Eilenburg.[17] Langeron thus recalled the feeling shared by the leaders of the Silesian Army: "The prince royal of Sweden, who had 70,000 men under arms, marched quietly (as we have seen) between Halle, Dessau, and Bad Düben; it was, he said, in the conviction that Napoleon was moving against Berlin or Magdeburg; finally, persuaded of the futility of his promenades, and no longer being able to reasonably explain why he would not join us, he approached us ... but he could arrive only on the evening of the 17th."[18]

After Stewart divulged his news, a dispatch arrived from Langeron communicating the latest news from Rudzevich: a Cossack regiment now occupied Delitzsch; the report of a large imperial camp at Krostitz was confirmed; French forces still held Bad Düben. In a postscript, Langeron added that the imperials had just evacuated Radefeld but still held Freiroda. Müffling asserts that Blücher, unable to count on Bernadotte to shield his left flank, had no choice but to confront the enemy facing him "in the supposition that they would retreat on the causeway from Radefeld to Hohenossig." According to Lowe: "Though General Blücher felt himself deprived, by the change in the disposition of the Prince Royal's army, of the aid of that army, a change which withdrew from his immediate and direct support a force of no less than 60,000 men, he nevertheless decided without an instant's hesitation on the part he himself was to take." Blücher could take comfort in the thought that, while he could not march to the decisive struggle south of Leipzig, neither could his immediate adversary.[19]

As the wind scattered the mist and clouds, the Prussians recognized that the French forces facing the Silesian Army intended to accept battle on the Radefeld ridgeline; earthworks could be discerned on the summits and behind them long rows of cannon. For his first objective, Blücher wanted to gain the ridge so he could obtain an overview of the situation from which he could base his subsequent actions. His staff cut orders for the infantry to march immediately. Followed by St.-Priest, whose troops would cross the Elster at Schkeuditz, Langeron would attack Freiroda and Radefeld. Yorck would continue his march southeast from Schkeuditz on the Halle–Leipzig road but turn his main body east at Lützschena and attack Lindenthal from the west. With the infantry of the vanguard, Hiller would remain at Lützschena monitoring the road from Leipzig. Sacken would follow the Prussians as their reserve.[20]

Müffling explains that, through this preliminary movement, Blücher hoped "to discover the position and intentions of the enemy." Planning to establish his command post on the hills between Lützschena and Radefeld,

Blücher rode north to join Langeron's corps. As he passed the lines of Yorck's cavalry accompanied by the king's brother, Prince William, the old general exhorted the troopers in his coarse manner. "Children, today you will attack in the old Prussian style," he shouted to the East Prussian National Cavalry Regiment; to others he said: "Whoever is not either dead or enraptured this evening must have fought like a dishonorable dog." Blücher planned to observe the battle from the Lindenthal windmill hill on the road that ran to Landsberg. Neither he nor Gneisenau could conceal their satisfaction that finally they would engage Napoleon in a general battle. Gneisenau beamed with joy, reported his adjutant, Stosch.[21]

As Blücher and his staff drafted the attack disposition, Stewart penned a firm note to Bernadotte. He explained to the crown prince that, because the French no longer held Delitzsch, Blücher considered it crucial for the Army of North Germany to move east to a position just behind Delitzsch, some thirteen miles north-northeast of Schkeuditz. Stewart noted that the marshes and defiles east of Delitzsch would shield the army from any danger. Attempting to play on Bernadotte's vanity, the British envoy added that from this position the crown prince would be able to take part in the battle, "which would be much more decisive with your army and your military talents. Because all the enemy's forces are around the city of Leipzig, permit me to point out that moments are precious." Changing tactics, he became more forceful: "The English nation is watching; it is my duty to speak frankly. England will never believe that you are indifferent, as long as the enemy is beaten, if you take part or not. I beg you, if you remain in second line, to send Captain [Richard] Bogue with his rocket brigade, to operate with General Blücher's cavalry." After Stewart sent his adjutant to deliver this letter to Bernadotte, Blücher strongly urged him "to hasten to the prince royal in person [so] that the object of this letter might be insured." En route, he met one of Bernadotte's adjutants on the road bearing a letter from Adlerkreutz informing him that the crown prince had decided that only his vanguard – Wintzingerode's Russian corps – would march to Landsberg, fifteen miles north of Schkeuditz. Bülow's Prussian corps remained one march behind the Russians, and the Swedes one march behind the Prussians. Stewart rode on, hoping he could persuade Bernadotte in a personal meeting. A few hours later, Gneisenau sent Professor Steffens to Bernadotte's headquarters with another request for support.[22]

As noted, Napoleon believed the Silesian Army still stood at Merseburg. Should Blücher and perhaps Bernadotte as well approach Marmont, the emperor had the marshal's assurance that VI Corps could hold the Allies for one day as long as Souham's III Corps arrived; Napoleon agreed. Regardless, early on the 16th, Marmont received orders to move VI Corps to Liebertwolkwitz and form Napoleon's Regular Reserve. Although the emperor assured Marmont that only cavalry faced VI Corps, the marshal's patrols informed him of eight enemy battalions approaching on the road from Halle and three on the road from Landsberg. Reporting from Lindenthal at 10:30 A.M., he informed Napoleon that these forces would reach his position in less than three hours. Nevertheless, because he could hear the sound of the guns south of Leipzig, Marmont guaranteed Napoleon that he would commence his movement to Liebertwolkwitz. He sent his equipment and ordered the infantry to follow, thus evacuating the Wahren–Lindenthal–Breitenfeld position. "Due to the good organization of my troops," wrote the marshal, "their training and discipline, one half-hour after the order was received they were formed in six parallel columns and were marching to get to Leipzig. But hardly had the movement began when the enemy debouched on us."[23]

The bulk of Marmont's vanguard, consisting of General Louis-Jacques Coëhorn's 1st Brigade of 22nd Division, occupied Radefeld. Around 12:30 P.M., the Württemberger general Karl Friedrich von Normann, who commanded Marmont's 25th Light Cavalry Brigade, recognized the enemy's superior numbers and commenced the retreat along with the rest of the vanguard. "A strong vanguard occupied the village of Radefeld," recalled Marmont. "It was commanded by a general of great value and great ability, a man of an illustrious military name, General Coëhorn. It was forced to withdraw, but it did so slowly and in good order." As noted, Marmont did not intend to remain north of Leipzig but had already made plans to march through the city to form the Grande Armée's reserve in compliance with Napoleon's orders. In his after-action report, the marshal attempted to explain the situation he found himself in: "His Majesty having the intention to attack the enemy and, as no considerable corps had yet to appear before me, I received on the morning of the 16th the order to move close to Leipzig so that while still covering everything I could take part, where appropriate, in the battle that was to be fought on the other side of the city. I started the march of my equipment and soon after my corps moved out." To cover the march of VI Corps to Leipzig, Coëhorn's vanguard became Marmont's rearguard.[24]

In his report to the emperor, Marmont explained his thought process: "It was too late, and I was too weak to hold the position of Lindenthal. Therefore, I continued my march to Leipzig, supporting my movement with a brisk cannonade. The enemy followed with activity, but in so doing showed that his forces were not too superior to mine. I had two courses to take: either to continue my march and pass through the defile of Leipzig, under the fire and the efforts of the enemy, with all the disadvantages that the terrain has, or face the enemy." Years later, when crafting his memoirs to defend his reputation, he took a swipe at the emperor: "Napoleon's opinion was no longer relevant. The enemy was there; we were face to face with him. It was the entire Army of Silesia which was present and with which we had to contend. We could not move to the battlefield south of Leipzig. Entering Leipzig and forming behind the Parthe would have been perilous for us. Passing through a defile like the one we had before us, a defile subjected to the action on the heights that immediately dominated it, could produce great confusion and cause a disaster."[25]

Like Blücher, Marmont faced a decision: he could either continue the march to Leipzig per the emperor's instructions, which would be a difficult maneuver in the presence of Blücher, or he could accept battle on the hills between Eutritzsch and Möckern. To confront the Silesian Army, Marmont looked for support from the neighboring corps but nothing remained within reach north of Leipzig. He explained in his memoirs that "General Bertrand, having received the order to clear the enemy in the rear of the army and open the defile of Lindenau, had started his march to execute it immediately. But III Corps could still be at Leipzig and *à portée* to support me. I reconnoitered a position that was not as good as that of Lindenthal but narrower and closer to the city [Leipzig], where the right is at Eutritzsch and the left at Möckern. I sent an officer to Marshal Ney, who was at Leipzig and to whom the emperor had given command, to see if III Corps was still there. He gave me an affirmative answer and said that I could count on it to be at my disposal. I did not hesitate to order a halt, take a position, and deliver a battle. I stopped my columns on the plateau and formed my line of battle." In his report to Napoleon, Marmont emphasized that he had based his decision on Ney's response: "I was all the more determined after I received several assurances from the prince de la Moskova [Ney] that the disposition ordered by His Majesty for III Corps to support me would be executed and that he would march to my support. I turned to face the enemy; I held the position that has the creek of Eutritzsch to its right and the Elster to its left, at the village of Möckern, and I prepared to fight, supported by nearly 100 pieces of cannon."[26]

Marmont held a strong position: all of VI Corps and Lorge's 5th Light Cavalry Division defended a line of 3,000 yards. Anchored by Möckern, his left leaned on the Elster while his right extended to the marsh of the Rietschke stream, which flowed southeast from Lindenthal passing by the western edges of Kleinwiederitzsch, Großwiederitzsch, and Eutritzsch before emptying into the Pleiße at Gohlis some 2,000 yards before Leipzig's northern gate. The Rietschke stream and the Elster marsh enclosed a terrain sector that the road from Lindenthal cut through almost in the middle and which gently rose as it extended south between Möckern and Eutritzsch. Two miles north of Eutritzsch, the 3,700 men and 14 guns of Dąbrowski's 27th Division, Fournier's 6th Light Cavalry Division, and General Jacques-Philippe Avice's 1st Brigade from Defrance's 4th Heavy Cavalry Division reached Groß- and Kleinwiederitzsch, both of which stood on the right bank of the Rietschke. With only four weak battalions

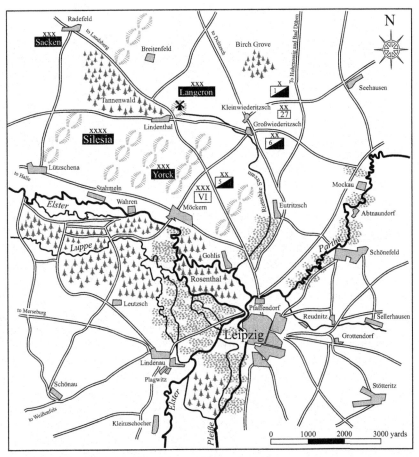

25. Battle of Leipzig, northern front, 16 October 1813

at his disposal, Dąbrowski placed one each in Groß- and Kleinwiederitzsch with one in reserve east of each village. A total of fourteen French and Polish squadrons stood between Großwiederitzsch and Seehausen. From these positions, Dąbrowski and Fournier could fall on Blücher's left flank if he attempted to attack the Möckern–Eutritzsch line.[27]

The villages of this northern portion of the Leipzig battlefield stood mostly in the low areas so that their roofs and orchards hardly hindered vision. Except for the Tannenwald north of Lindenthal, insignificant thickets crowned the hills. Tree lines accompanied the roads only in the vicinity of Leipzig yet thick bushes and woods bordered the water courses. With winter fast approaching, the bare, harvested fields granted a wide overview. From the hills at Lindenthal, the Allies could clearly see between Leipzig's spires and further southeast they could discern the shallow hills on the other side of the Pleiße and even further to the somewhat higher hills of Probstheida, Wachau, and Liebertwolkwitz. Looking northwest from the hills between Möckern and Lindenthal, Marmont could clearly view the approach of the Silesian Army. Despite the previous reports he had made predicting an attack from this direction, the marshal seemed surprised. "The enemy army rapidly marched against me," he wrote in his after-action report; "its forces appeared to rise up out of the earth; on closer examination it continued to increase: it was the entire Silesian Army."[28]

After Marmont positioned his three divisions between Möckern and Eutritzsch, only the cavalry remained in reserve: Normann's brigade stood in second line behind (southeast of) the left wing while Lorge's division stood further rearward. Had Marmont commanded the 30,000 men that Napoleon had promised, his position would have been impregnable. An experienced artillery officer, he counted on his guns to hold the enemy until III Corps arrived. Marmont positioned his artillery with particular care, acknowledging the importance of Möckern. "The enemy's attack could only come from our left," he recounted. "Our right was rearward, supported and covered by a small Polish division commanded by General Dąbrowski, and placed on the other side of the marsh and creek that flows to Eutritzsch, was in a good position to take the enemy's left in the rear. So I had to conclude that it would be on my left and on Möckern that the enemy would move. All my artillery was placed on the highest point of the line occupied by my corps. My eighty-four guns were disposed to stop the enemy. Twelve pieces of twelve, among others, were pushed forward on the flank to the right of the village of Möckern." With orders to hold it for as long as possible, the 2nd Marine Regiment that formed the extent of the 2nd Brigade of Lagrange's 21st Division occupied Möckern. A small detachment moved across the Elster to take positions in the thick undergrowth along the southern bank. As Marmont explained, a large battery of twelve-pound guns took position on the hill right next to Möckern north of the Halle–Leipzig road. Including Lorge's 5th Light Cavalry Division, Marmont commanded around 17,000 men. Unlike most of the corps of the Grande Armée by this point in the campaign, VI Corps had a spotless record, having never suffered a defeat.[29]

After a cold rainy night, thick mist hung over the southern portion of the battlefield, forcing Wittgenstein to delay his attack until the wind could clear away the fog and smoke. At 8:00, the Allied columns commenced their advance. One hour later, just as Wittgenstein's troops made contact with the French, Alexander reached his command post on a hill southwest of Güldengoßa. Although no Napoleon, the Russian monarch had seen enough war to have a decent eye for the proper positioning of forces. He immediately recognized that Wittgenstein's widely spread columns had little chance to support each other and thus risked being defeated piecemeal. To provide some support, the tsar summoned the Russian Grenadier Corps and Cuirassier Brigade to the sheep farm of Auenhain, a little more than one mile west-northwest of Güldengoßa. Moreover, he ordered the Russo-Prussian Guard and Reserve Cavalry to continue through Rötha to Cröbern and Güldengoßa. Lastly, he requested that Schwarzenberg send the Austrian Guard and Reserve across the Pleiße to support Wittgenstein. The Allied commander in chief reluctantly complied around noon but it would take hours before either the Russo-Prussian or Austrian Guards arrived.

Napoleon himself reached Liebertwolkwitz around 9:00 and established his command post on the *Galgenberg* (gallows hill) immediately west of that village.[30] He met with Murat, who had passed the night at the Wachau Schloß. Around the same time, Wittgenstein launched his assault before all of Napoleon's units had reached their appointed positions. Powerful and unexpected, the Allied advance forced the emperor to retire almost two miles north from the Galgenberg to the sheep farm of Meusdorf. His line began to buckle with the mainly Polish defenders of Markkleeberg losing that village to Kleist's column and II Corps being pushed out of Wachau by Prince Eugen of Württemberg's Russians by 9:30.

Although Wittgenstein's first and second columns achieved initial success, the others floundered. Lauriston's V Corps managed to hold the smoldering remains of Liebertwolkwitz thanks to Gorchakov's impatience and Klenau's poor timing. Without waiting for Klenau's column to attack from the east, Gorchakov commenced his assault. Devastating French artillery smashed the approaching Russian columns and sent them scurrying for cover in the Niederholz Forest between Liebertwolkwitz and Großpösna. This widened the gap between Gorchakov and Eugen, which the latter plugged with the Prussian 9th Brigade from his second line. The cavalry of Pahlen's fourth column likewise could not withstand the French artillery. Klenau's column commenced its advance from Großpösna at 10:00: two hours later than Wittgenstein's other columns. After securing the Kolm hill east-southeast of Liebertwolkwitz with two battalions and twelve guns, Klenau finally sent five battalions, four squadrons, and fourteen guns against Liebertwolkwitz. However, he observed large French columns approaching Holzhausen: Macdonald's flank corps. Klenau requested support from Pahlen, who dispatched fourteen of his forty-six squadrons. By this point, Klenau's column became divided in two with his left assaulting Liebertwolkwitz while his right – the troops on the Kolm hill supported by one Austrian brigade and Pahlen's cavalry – monitored the enemy forces at Holzhausen. Another Austrian brigade and the Prussian 11th Brigade remained in reserve between Großpösna and Fuchshain.

Despite the uneven success of Wittgenstein's first attack, the damage to Napoleon's plan and timetable proved irreversible. To prevent the Allies from overrunning his line, he directed General Louis-Michel Letort's brigade of Guard Cavalry as well as IX Corps from his left wing to support the Poles on his right after Kleist took Markkleeberg. He moved up Oudinot's I Young Guard Corps to prevent Eugen's Russians from breaking out of Wachau. The 1st Old Guard Division marched a little over a mile southeast from Probstheida to the sheep farm of Meusdorf where it could support either the Poles against Kleist or the I Young Guard Corps against Eugen. To meet Klenau's late attack on Liebertwolkwitz, Mortier's II Young Guard Corps and the 2nd Old Guard Division bolstered V Corps. Napoleon returned to the Galgenberg but he had few units remaining at his disposal as VI and III Corps still had not arrived from north of Leipzig to form his Regular Reserve.

Meanwhile, Macdonald reached Holzhausen with XI Corps and II Cavalry Corps around 11:00. After storming the Kolm hill and almost capturing Klenau, he continued to Seifertshain and Kleinpösna to envelop Wittgenstein's right. Observing Macdonald's progress, Napoleon ordered a general advance around 1:00. With the Grand Reserve already engaged and no sign of VI Corps, Napoleon assembled I Cavalry Corps and the Guard Cavalry at Meusdorf to exploit any breakthrough. Mortier led II Young Guard Corps south between the Kolm hill and Liebertwolkwitz toward the Niederholz Forest. Lauriston's V Corps drove the Austrians out of Liebertwolkwitz and all the way to Großpösna. Klenau's collapse caught the attention of Gorchakov and Pahlen, who retired to the Güldengoßa–Oberholz Forest line; the wood stood between Güldengoßa and Großpösna. At Wachau, Victor's II Corps supported by Oudinot's I Young Guard Corps drove Eugen's badly battered force one mile south to the sheep farm of Auenhain. On the French right, Augereau with IX and VIII Corps pushed southeast to retake Markkleeberg. After leaving a detachment to hold that village, Kleist slowly retreated toward Cröbern, launching a counterattack after observing the approach of the Russian III Grenadier Corps. Regardless, the French and Poles proved too strong and he continued his retreat to Cröbern. The lead elements of General Johann Nepomuk von Nostitz's Cuirassier Corps, part of the Austrian Guard and Reserve, crossed the Pleiße just as Letort's Guard Cavalry brigade and ten squadrons from I Cavalry Corps's 1st Light Division prepared to pursue Kleist. Although the Austrian horse drove back the French troopers, thick musket fire from enemy squares as well as the arrival of more French cavalry forced Nostitz to sound the recall to Cröbern. By 2:00, all five of Wittgenstein's columns stood where they had started the battle.

Returning to Blücher, Langeron's troops, advancing southeast on the road from Landsberg, found Freiroda and Radefeld abandoned. Langeron recalled that, "with the cavalry of my vanguard, Emmanuel turned the villages of Freiroda and Radefeld, from which the enemy retired precipitously; there was a small advance guard of 2,000 to 3,000 men and a few cannon that exchanged some shots with my horse artillery. Rudzevich followed Emmanuel with the infantry of the vanguard, and the corps of Kaptsevich and Olsufiyev followed the vanguard." Attempting to emerge from Radefeld, the Russian infantry received artillery fire from a French battery posted north of the Tannenwald. Müffling noted that "the position of this battery was in the direction that Blücher expected the enemy to retreat." Around 12:30 Russian guns unlimbered; effective counterbattery fire soon drove off the French, "but the enemy unexpectedly turned on Lindenthal."[31]

To the surprise of Blücher and his staff, Marmont's vanguard withdrew south toward Lindenthal rather than northeast along the road to Hohenossig. Blücher directed Langeron's infantry to follow the French while his vanguard's cavalry under Emmanuel reconnoitered toward Hohenossig to ascertain if the enemy's main force stood on that plateau or could be seen approaching from Bad Düben. For reasons unknown, Emmanuel's cavalry did not comply with this directive but instead followed the vanguard's infantry. Blücher ordered Langeron to advance almost due south against both the Tannenwald and Lindenthal.[32] After clearing the wood, the Russians would look for enemy forces marching toward Leipzig on the roads from Bad Düben and Delitzsch. Should they encounter imperial columns, Blücher wanted the Russians to prevent them from reaching Leipzig "and if possible crush them by a sudden onslaught." Sacken's infantry would remain in reserve at Radefeld until Emmanuel confirmed that Blücher had nothing to fear from the direction of Hohenossig; once again, Emmanuel's cavalry remained with Rudzevich.

At Schkeuditz, Yorck received his orders. "As he always cared for us," wrote an officer of his entourage, "he had called us together for a warm breakfast with him; the horses stood saddled before the door. Count Brandenburg arrived with Blücher's orders. Yorck stood up, his glass in his hand, and recited his favorite prayer: 'May beginning, middle, and end turn out for the best,' emptying the glass and setting it down. We did the same. In a solemn, serious mood we went to battle. We all felt that upon these so often blood-soaked fields we were about to wage the decisive struggle over our Prussian, our German Fatherland."[33] To execute Blücher's disposition, Yorck decided that, as soon as the head of the column – Hünerbein's 8th Brigade – reached Lützschena, it would slide left of the road and form to attack Lindenthal. Horn's 7th Brigade would follow the 8th en echelon while Steinmetz's 1st Brigade formed further to the rear. As Prince Karl's 2nd Brigade contained mainly Line troops, it would provide the reserve. Yorck's disposition states that "all will form battalion columns and place themselves *en échiquier* [checkerboard formation] so that the brigades form two lines." Until he received further orders, Hiller would remain between Lützschena and Stahmeln with the vanguard's infantry. With the vanguard's cavalry, Katzler covered the deployment of the brigades. Yorck attached the Reserve Artillery's two twelve-pound batteries to 8th Brigade; their four ten-pound howitzers led the heavy guns forward.[34]

"Initially," recalled Henckel von Donnersmarck, "everything remained quiet on the morning of the 16th until suddenly the vanguard was summoned to advance and take Lindenthal. The brigades were all next to each other marching in battalion columns, the Reserve Cavalry behind them."[35] After moving southeast along the Halle–Leipzig highway for three miles from Schkeuditz to Lützschena, 8th Brigade turned east around 12:30. Hünerbein's men trooped along a field-path from Lützschena toward Lindenthal, dragging both twelve-pound batteries with them to the foot of the Radefeld–Lindenthal hills facing the left wing of Marmont's vanguard. Observing that the French held the Tannenwald between Lindenthal and Radefeld, Yorck moved up Horn's 7th Brigade to form his right rather than have it follow 8th Brigade en echelon. At 1:00, he ordered Hünerbein to clear the imperials from the Tannenwald while Horn assaulted Lindenthal. As second echelon on the oblique right, 1st and 2nd Brigades would follow Horn's 7th. Jürgaß's Reserve Cavalry formed in two waves and moved up to form the third echelon.

Normann's eight squadrons halted west of the Tannenwald to take in the troops retreating from Radefeld; one horse battery and numerous skirmishers stood at the edge of the wood opposite Lindenthal. Acting on orders from Yorck, Katzler instructed the East Prussian National Cavalry Regiment supported by two squadrons of the Leib Hussars and the Brandenburg Uhlans to attack Normann's cavalry. The Württembergers allowed the Prussians to approach and at the last minute pivoted and retreated. This uncovered the front of an infantry square that the Württemberger cavalry had concealed from sight. Supported by skirmishers in the woods and the battery at the edge of the Tannenwald, the infantry fired on the approaching East Prussian troopers from the western edge of the pine grove. Led by its 1st and Jäger Squadrons, the East Prussians could do little against the sustained musketry of the imperials, described by one eyewitness as "the most galling." After losing eleven prisoners and sustaining several casualties, the East Prussians withdrew in order.[36]

The French battery shelled the Prussians as they withdrew and opened fire on the Russians as they approached the Tannenwald. Finally, blasts of canister from Katzler's Nr. 2 Horse Battery induced the French to evacuate their position along the western edge of the Tannenwald. More importantly for the Allies, Marmont's decision to march to Liebertwolkwitz caused the imperials to completely abandon Lindenthal. The retreating enemy troops did not go far before they joined Coëhorn's main body in a strong position on the hills between Wahren and Lindenthal. In and next to one of the three redoubts that Marmont had hastily built along the 2,500 yards separating these two villages stood a battery of sixteen guns that poured murderous fire into the ranks of the advancing Prussians. Yorck directed his two heavy batteries against the French artillery. Behind the Prussian guns, his brigades advanced with Hünerbein's 8th closing on Lindenthal. An intense artillery duel ensued between the French and the Prussians during which time Langeron's troops reached Breitenfeld.[37]

After one hour, Coëhorn took the next step in his calculated withdrawal. Under the protection of Normann's Chasseurs, Coëhorn withdrew east to unite with Marmont's main body on the hills between Möckern and Großwiederitzsch. "The 2nd [21st] Division, commanded by General Lagrange, stayed behind to support the rearguard and take it in," noted Marmont. "When all was in order and properly disposed of, the movement to Leipzig continued, every moment exchanging cannon shots with the enemy. One brigade of Württemberger light cavalry, a part of my corps and attached to the vanguard, also acted with valor and courage. It was the last move of honor and loyalty by General Normann and his soldiers. A few hours later, they would be fatal to us rather than helpful."[38]

Yorck ordered the infantry to pursue while Katzler led his cavalry onto the plain north of the road to Möckern to cover the march of the infantry. As the skirmishers of the 3rd Battalion of the 14th Silesian Landwehr plunged into the Tannenwald, some of Hünerbein's battalions marched through Lindenthal while others passed its southern side; all made for the main French position. Yorck's other brigades followed as fast as they could. Not wanting to offer his flank to the imperials, Yorck decided to refuse it, execute a right wheel, and turn his corps southeast to face the enemy's front. Without awaiting new orders, he pivoted his corps southeast to align it with the Möckern–Eutritzsch line. Horn's 7th Brigade formed the pivot and now faced southeast with the village of Lindenthal behind its right wing. This movement forced Hünerbein's 8th Brigade to swing far to the east to establish contact with Langeron's corps, which momentarily continued east in the direction stipulated by Blücher's original intention to meet the enemy's masses supposedly on the plateau by Hohenossig. Consequently, large gaps opened between the two corps as well as between 8th and 7th Brigades. The situation only became worse when an even larger gap opened between Horn's brigade and Hiller's vanguard on the Halle–Leipzig highway. Yorck ordered this gap temporarily filled by Jürgaß's Reserve Cavalry. Yet no quick fix could be found to fill the hole between Hünerbein and Langeron even after Blücher turned the Russians southeast. Initially, 8th Brigade's cavalry – 3rd and 4th Squadrons of the Brandenburg Hussars – moved into the gap but Blücher himself redirected them to a different sector of the field. For the time being, Hünerbein's left was completely in the air.

On Blücher's left, Langeron's Russians advanced through Breitenfeld and slowly moved toward Groß- and Kleinwiederitzsch. Reaching the Radefeld ridge, Blücher found a large enemy force holding a strong position along a three-mile line extending east from Möckern to Eutritzsch. Moreover, Russian reports indicated that considerable imperial forces also held both Wiederitzsch villages, which stood at almost a 90 degree angle to the Möckern–Eutritzsch line. Thus, it appeared that Marmont held the sector north of Leipzig between the Elster and the Parthe. Although seeing the extent of Marmont's position, the leadership of the Silesian Army could not free itself from the fear of superior enemy forces advancing through Hohenossig. To engage Marmont, the army would have to slide to the southeast, increasing the danger posed to the left wing by the enemy columns Blücher expected to be approaching from the Mulde. Yet across the horizon, on the hills at Liebertwolkwitz and Wachau, on the edge of the Pleiße valley and further west at Lindenau, the battle between Schwarzenberg and presumably Murat raged with incomparable intensity. Despite the incorrect perceived threat to his left, Blücher knew that he had to allow himself to be fixed by attacking Marmont. Rather than continue northeast to Hohenossig or south to Leipzig, Blücher decided that Langeron and Yorck would continue the advance southeast. Around 2:00, he signed orders for Langeron to march along the Delitzsch–Leipzig road to take Groß- and Kleinwiederitzsch. After the Russians had secured these two villages, Yorck would attack the Möckern–Eutritzsch line. Gneisenau sent Langeron's Reserve Cavalry under Korf toward Podelwitz to secure the left flank. To fill the gap between Hünerbein and Langeron, the staff chief wanted Sacken's cavalry to move up. However, due to a misunderstanding, Sacken's troopers followed Korf. A sole Russian Hussar Regiment that arrived by chance was all that Gneisenau could find to plug the gap; it took a position east of Lindenthal. Blücher established his command post on the Lindenthal windmill hill near the road to Landsberg.[39]

From Lützschena on Blücher's extreme right, Hiller observed the progress of Yorck and Langeron. He also saw Katzler's cavalry receive flanking fire from the direction of Stahmeln and Wahren as it moved toward the Radefeld–Lindenthal hills to cover Yorck's artillery. Without waiting for orders, Hiller ordered Major Klüx to advance along the Elster and drive the imperials from Stahmeln. To take Stahmeln, Klüx assembled three platoons of Jäger, the skirmishers of two infantry companies, and one company from the Fusilier Battalion of the 2nd East Prussian Regiment; the rest of the Fusilier Battalion would follow in support. Three Jäger companies and the 4th Battalion of the 15th Silesian Landwehr would march three hundred paces behind this group. As he prepared his columns, a platoon from the Austrian 2nd Jäger Battalion sent by Gyulay to link with the Silesian Army arrived on the opposite bank of the Elster. Greeted by the Prussians with shouts of joy, the Austrians also marched on Stahmeln. The imperials evacuated the village without resistance and withdrew less than one mile southeast to Wahren. At that moment, orders arrived from Blücher to advance on Leipzig and pressure the enemy. Before Klüx could launch his attack, some 100 French soldiers withdrew from Wahren to Möckern as that small village did not favor a defense. "From the hill of Wahren," stated Hiller in his after-action report, "I observed that the enemy moved into Möckern, strongly occupied this village, and positioned much artillery and infantry masses on the hill of Möckern, and that the left wing of I Army Corps as well as the corps under Count Langeron advanced fighting through Radefeld and Lindenthal. I thus ordered the troops assigned to me to take up arms, formed them for the attack, and advanced." Klüx followed, halting east of the village and sending a small detachment to reconnoiter toward Möckern. Meanwhile, Hiller's main body moved up in battalion columns on both sides of the Halle–Leipzig road. The pursuit then continued to Möckern, only one mile from Wahren.[40]

After obtaining an overview of Marmont's position, Yorck likewise recognized the importance of the village of Möckern. The large enemy forces in his flank at Groß- and Kleinwiederitzsch ruled out a general advance of I Corps against the Möckern–Eutritzsch line. For this reason, he instructed Hünerbein and Horn to halt until Langeron's corps came on line with them. But the Prussians already stood too close to the French position and were suffering from the enemy's artillery on the hills north of Möckern; to hold their ground would have been tantamount to suicide. Thus, Yorck decided to pull back his left and occupy Marmont's right with fifty guns that gradually unlimbered on both sides of the Lindenthal–Großwiederitzsch road.[41] Meanwhile, Yorck's own right would attack Möckern, the anchor point of Marmont's left. "So in this way," explains Friederich, "an echelon attack from the right wing took place while without doubt it would have been more appropriate to persist in its original form by beginning the echelon attack from the left wing and in this way envelop the strongest point of the enemy position, the village of Möckern."[42]

Returning to the struggle south of Leipzig, as Macdonald moved on Seifertshain, Napoleon ordered an assault against the Allied center, still thinking VI and III Corps would arrive to deliver the death blow. To soften the enemy, he instructed Drouot to form a battery of eighty-four guns on the ridge between Wachau and Liebertwolkwitz. Arranged in battalion columns, II and V Corps advanced from Wachau and Liebertwolkwitz respectively. Oudinot's I Young Guard Corps moved into the line between II and V Corps while II Young Guard Corps followed V Corps and 1st Old Guard Division marched to Wachau. After clearing Liebertwolkwitz, V Corps moved southwest to assault Güldengoßa; Mortier's II Young Guard Corps moved against the Oberholz Forest. A Russian battery of ninety-four guns inflicted horrendous casualties on the approaching French infantry yet the human waves steadily closed on their targets. Around 2:30, II Corps and I Young Guard Corps successfully stormed Auenhain but V Corps could not take Güldengoßa. To break the enemy's resistance, the 2,500 cuirassiers of General Étienne Bordessoulle's 1st Heavy Division of I Cavalry Corps charged from the right (west) side of the great French battery. Bordessoulle assigned four Saxon squadrons the unenviable task of attacking the enemy battery.[43] The fatigued Russian and Prussian troops of Eugen's column melted before this onslaught. Bordessoulle's sabers reached the ponds in front of the Allied command post on the hill southwest of Güldengoßa where Alexander and Frederick William stood. As the spent imperial troopers tried in vain to get through the morass, the tsar's Cossack escort attacked their front while thirteen squadrons of Russian cuirassiers charged their left flank. The combined attack sapped their remaining strength, and they whipped their tired horses to make for the safety of Drouot's guns. By 3:30, the last of Bordessoulle's cavalry had reached the French artillery, whose withering fire promptly ended the Russian pursuit. In all, the imperials managed to spike twenty-six Russian guns.

Although the French cavalry returned to their lines, the infantry continued to press the Allies. On the right, II and IX Corps closed on Cröbern while V Corps struggled to wrest Güldengoßa from Eugen's battered Russians and Prussians. The Allies dug in, wisely taking cover in the villages, woods, and coppices. Thus protected, they sustained the continued artillery bombardment with minimal losses. Moreover, reinforcements started to arrive. At 4:00, General Vincenzo Federico Bianchi reached Cröbern with 2nd Infantry Division of the Austrian Reserve. Behind Eugen, General Nikolay Rayevsky's Russian III Grenadier Corps prepared to move into the line; the Prussian Guard likewise reached Güldengoßa. Lauriston's 16th Division broke into Güldengoßa but the fresh Allied troops countered with such ferocity that the division broke. Mortier's Young Guard failed to clear the Oberholz Forest of Allied forces. On Napoleon's right, Augereau's IX Corps at Cröbern fell back before Bianchi's Austrians and the survivors of Kleist's column. Augereau's retreat impacted II Corps to his left (east), which had gained Auenhain but could not dislodge the Russians from its Schloß. With IX Corps retiring, Victor had little choice but to order II Corps to withdraw from Auenhain. The arrival of General Nicolaus von Weißenwolf's 1st Infantry Division of the Austrian Reserve enabled Bianchi to take Markkleeberg and advance toward Dölitz. In addition, Merveldt's Austrian II Corps finally crossed the Pleiße and took Dölitz by 5:30. On the verge of turning Napoleon's right, the mainly Austrian drive soon came to a halt with the arrival of 2nd Old Guard Division and 11th Division of III Corps. Thus reinforced, the imperials stopped Bianchi, retook Dölitz, and drove Merveldt's troops back across the Pleiße, capturing the Austrian corps commander in the process.

Shortly after 2:00, Yorck's artillery opened the struggle with counter-battery fire against the twenty-four French guns the Prussians could see. Behind the artillery, I Corps formed to assault Möckern. The village stood on the reverse slope of the Möckern hill which descended toward wooded, bushy lowlands through which the Elster meandered. At Möckern, the river itself formed the edge of this lowland so that the village stood on its steep right bank. One bridge approximately halfway through the long, narrow village spanned the Elster on Möckern's southern side. The northern side of the village bordered the Halle–Leipzig highway so that it ran between houses and walled gardens. The western side of the rectangular-shaped village was only 300 yards wide.

Hiller received orders for the vanguard infantry reinforced by the Leib Grenadier Battalion to lead the attack. Prince Karl's 2nd Brigade would follow obliquely to his left, supporting if necessary but seeking contact with Horn's 7th Brigade south of Lindenthal. As the reserve, Steinmetz's 1st Brigade would follow behind 2nd Brigade. During the advance, 7th and 8th Brigades would slide further right (southeast) to close the gap between them and the portion of the corps attacking Möckern. Behind the infantry followed the Reserve Cavalry and Katzler's vanguard cavalry. After receiving Blücher's orders for I Corps to delay its main attack until Langeron took Groß- and Kleinwiederitzsch, Yorck held back his brigades but allowed Hiller to proceed with the attack on Möckern, thus playing right into Marmont's hands. With the Prussian left appearing very far from the battlefield and moving forward only slowly, the marshal reinforced the artillery on his right wing but moved more infantry to his left.

With the artillery still blazing, Major Klüx surged forward with Hiller's first wave: two platoons of Jäger and the skirmishers of the Fusilier Battalion of the 2nd East Prussian Infantry Regiment supported by the rest of the battalion. Some 300 yards behind this first wave followed three Jäger companies, the 4th Battalion of the 15th Silesian Landwehr Regiment, and the Austrian Jäger, all supported by the Leib Grenadiers; five battalions remained in reserve at Wahren.[44] Opposite Möckern, Hiller's Nr. 12 Battery of six-pound guns unlimbered on both sides of the defile through which the Halle–Leipzig road ran. The half-battery on the right of the road supported the assault on Möckern while that on the left offered counterbattery fire to the French guns on the northern side of the village. Klüx's small first wave penetrated the village but they lost their foothold after a brutal counterattack.

A second attack ended with the same result. Klüx's skirmishers came flying back, closely pursued by the French and enfiladed from the opposite bank of the Elster. Such fear gripped them that they disordered the heads of the Jäger companies that moved up in the second wave. Hiller stated in his report that "now it appeared as a matter of honor to take the village." His men claimed that the French had barricaded all the houses and barns in the village, knocking out loopholes to make each structure a miniature fortress. After restoring order, Hiller launched a third attack with the forces of both waves. While one Jäger company countered the fire of French skirmishers posted in the undergrowth on the southern bank of the Elster, two Jäger companies and the fusiliers sought to penetrate Möckern in small detachments wherever they could find an opening. Meanwhile, the 4th Battalion of the 15th Silesian Landwehr, whose commander, Count Gottlob Wilhelm von Wedel, a former government official (*Kammerpräsident*) with no prior military experience, requested the honor of being the first unit to storm the village, assaulted the massive manor house that stood to the right (north) of the short side of the village that faced Wahren. Lastly, the Leib Grenadier Battalion attempted to envelop the village from the northern bank of the Elster.

Hiller's troops executed the attack with determination and appeared to achieve success despite receiving devastating fire. The Jäger and fusiliers penetrated the village at various places while the Landwehr stormed the manor house with bayonets. Yet after the Prussians gained footholds on the outskirts of Möckern, the French refused to allow them to advance deeper into the village. Hiller reported that French grenadiers "strongly occupied and fiercely defended each house and every wall," barricading doors and windows, and pouring murderous fire into the Prussians from every direction.[45] French artillery on the hills north of Möckern enfiladed Hiller's men with canister. Advancing from the manor house, the 4th Battalion of the 15th Silesian Landwehr managed to reach the crossroad that led from the Halle–Leipzig road to the bridge over the Elster. There, they encountered fresh battalion columns; Marmont moved the 37th Light Infantry Regiment into Möckern to support the 4th Marine Regiment. "The enemy furiously attacked the village of Möckern," noted Marmont, "and supported the attack through the fire of numerous cannon that he deployed opposite my front. But for a long time all his efforts were in vain. After repeated attacks on the village, part of it was evacuated, but soon retaken by the same regiment that defended it and that was charged with retaking it. Overthrown again, the 4th Marine and 37th Light successively moved on Möckern, where the whole battle seemed to be."[46] In murderous hand-to-hand combat, the French gradually drove the Prussian militia out of the village. Fortunately for the Landwehr, the Leib Grenadier Battalion, which had failed to gain entry into the village along the steep bank of the Elster, returned in time to take them in.

As is often the case in such engagements, the Prussians turned the tables on the pursuing French. After repulsing the imperials, Hiller's troops – fusiliers, Jäger, grenadiers, and Landwehr – all drove into the village with little order. Again reaching the crossroads, the Prussians received a severe blast of canister in their front as well as heavy small-arms fire in the rear and on both sides. Again the French fed fresh battalions into Möckern, overwhelming the Prussians and driving them from the village. "Because I not only encountered new enemy columns," wrote Hiller, "but also received the heaviest artillery fire in the front and musket fire in the rear, I saw myself forced to again surrender the village after considerable losses in killed and wounded." Not content with ejecting the Prussians, the French closely pursued and reached the Prussian half-battery on the northern side of the defile. In vain, the half-battery on the southern side tried to cover the retreat with caseshot. Just as one Prussian howitzer fell into French hands, four battalions from Hiller's reserve arrived. Under heavy fire, Hiller reorganized the troops, who escaped the burning village while the skirmishers of the West Prussian Grenadier Battalion worked around the northern side of Möckern.

After directing the 1st Battalion of the Brandenburg Infantry Regiment to advance on the northern side of the defile toward the French twelve-pound battery, Hiller led the other three – the 3rd Battalion of the 13th Silesian Landwehr, the 2nd Battalion of the 14th Silesian Landwehr, and the 2nd Battalion of the 12th Reserve Regiment – as well as the survivors of the earlier attacks back to Möckern. With drums beating, Hiller ordered the men to fix bayonets. Shouting "Long live the king," he led the charge against the two French columns that emerged from Möckern. The fresh Prussian units managed to drive back the enemy, retake the howitzer, and enter the village at the same time as the retreating French. In what was tantamount to a suicide mission, the 1st Brandenburg Battalion advanced toward the French battery but caseshot shattered its front while a marine battalion attacked its left flank. In just a matter of minutes the Prussians sustained such grisly losses that the survivors broke and fled down (south) the slope toward Möckern. There they joined Hiller's battalions that had penetrated the burning village. While some companies pursued the French to the opposite exit of the village, others battled with the enemy soldiers holed up in the houses. Although practically destroying the 2nd Marine Regiment which stood in reserve in the streets of Möckern, the Prussians could not venture beyond the village. A few companies that attempted to advance in the open received deadly blasts of canister from numerous guns and quickly fell back. According to Hiller: "I was received by such heavy canister fire from several batteries that I not only had to give up the pursuit but also had to again reassemble and reorder several retreating battalions."[47]

Unsupported, Hiller's spent battalions could not hold Möckern against Lagrange's 1st Brigade, consisting of the three battalions of the 4th Marine Regiment and the four battalions of the 37th Light Infantry. "The enemy first directed his attack on the village of Möckern," Marmont noted in his report. "This village was attacked with vigor, and the enemy received all the fire of my artillery. It was defended well by the troops of the 2nd [21st]

Division under the command of General Lagrange. The 2nd Marine Artillery, which was responsible for this position, fought with vigor and tenacity, held this village for a long time, and lost and regained it several times. The 37th Light and 4th Marine Regiment were successively brought to the village; they regained and defended it with all the courage we could expect from fine troops."[48] After again being ejected from Möckern, Hiller informed Yorck that he could not take and hold the village without support. Observing that the combat around Möckern had taken an unfavorable turn, Yorck decided to deviate from the disposition and no longer wait for the Russians to take the Wiederitzsch villages per Blücher's orders. Yorck replied to Hiller that the closest brigade, Prince Karl's 2nd, would support his next attack. Karl received orders to rush to Möckern with Steinmetz's 1st Brigade following. Based on Yorck's answer, Hiller summoned his last remaining fresh battalion – the West Prussian Grenadiers – and launched his seventh assault on Möckern.

Facilitated by the advance of 2nd Brigade, Hiller's troops again penetrated the burning village, driving the French out of the opposite end. Again fresh French forces threw them back but this time the Prussians managed to hold the outlying houses. Again the attack proved costly: Hiller left the field with a serious wound; the commander of the 2nd Battalion of the 14th Silesian Landwehr, Major Thiele, fell wounded, while the commander of the 3rd Battalion of the 13th Silesian Landwehr, Major Rekovski, numbered among the dead. With his last breath, Count Wedel purportedly shouted to his men: "Children, save the Fatherland! Help us God!"[49] Hiller explained his thoughts in the after-action report:

> Everyone was burning with desire to get close to the enemy, and on my shout that today must decide Germany's fate, the battalions did not hesitate to again charge across the corpses of their brothers and engage the enemy with cries of hurrah. Notwithstanding the courage and fury of the troops, which had increased to the extreme, it was still impossible to silence the fire of the enemy battalions posted in the houses. Nevertheless I thoroughly enjoyed the satisfaction of watching the courage and perseverance of the brave troops, especially the Landwehr battalions, turn back the enemy grenadiers and Guardsmen who had moved up as reinforcement. As I saw them running away, I also saw the other brigades of the Army Corps advancing. At that moment I was wounded. I sank to the ground in unconsciousness with the blessed feeling that we would be victorious.[50]

Establishing a firm foothold in Möckern proved impossible. French infantry strongly occupied the dominant points but also gallantly defended every house, cellar, stable, shed, barn, roof, and wall; fresh reinforcements constantly moved into the village. Finally acknowledging the grim lesson that the French had unmercifully taught them, the Prussians realized that they would have to drive the enemy from each individual structure to secure Möckern. Forced to admit the pointlessness of advancing in tight attack columns that offered perfect targets to the barricaded imperials, the Prussians resolved to take the village house by house. At each structure, the surrounding wall would be stormed, the doors smashed, and floor by floor the enemy would be cleared. Calm contemplation would have led the Prussians to a far less costly conclusion: let the fires that blazed in Möckern do the bloody work for them. But consumed by the heat of battle and thirsting to avenge their fallen comrades, the Prussians descended like locusts on individual houses in groups of thirty to forty. All order collapsed as Jäger, fusilier, grenadier, musketeer, and Landwehr – all mixed together – savagely fought with unity of purpose and will. A gruesome struggle ensued where neither side granted quarter; all were cut down without mercy. Although Klüx fell along with one-third of his men, the Prussians slowly made progress, even taking the Elster bridge.

To support the attack on Möckern, Yorck directed 2nd Brigade against the French artillery position on the hill north of the village and instructed Steinmetz to follow with 1st Brigade. For massive firepower, Yorck combined the Nr. 2 Horse Battery, Nr. 12 six-pound battery, and the batteries of 2nd and 1st Brigades. Behind the artillery, the cavalry of the vanguard formed: two squadrons of Leib Hussars, three squadrons of Brandenburg Hussars, the Brandenburg Uhlan Regiment, and the National Cavalry Regiment. Yorck established his command post in the midst of the cavalry. Balls fell all about the Prussians; one crashed through the midst of Yorck's staff. With a stern glance, the man of Tauroggen quelled any thoughts of panic. Reaching into his pocket, he pulled out his box of snuff, took a pinch between his fingers, and closed the box. Still looking around, he noted that his six-pound batteries could achieve nothing against Marmont's twelve-pound pieces. Aggravated, Yorck threw down the snuff, shouting: "Let's give those chaps a surprise." He then ordered an adjutant to move the twelve-pound batteries closer to the enemy line. In fact, the entire artillery line of 88 pieces followed by the cavalry moved to within 1,100 yards of Marmont's position. To minimize the losses to his cavalry, Yorck ordered it to form in a single long line. Under the protection of its intense fire, Prince Karl led 2nd Brigade forward. At the same time Hiller commenced his seventh assault on Möckern with bayonets fixed and drums beating. Horn and Hünerbein also advanced with orders to close the gap between themselves and 2nd Brigade by sliding right (southeast). By this time Blücher and his staff had corrected the mistake made by Sacken's cavalry, which Nostitz brought back and posted close to Lindenthal, thus closing the gap between Yorck and Langeron.

Observing the advance of a fresh Prussian brigade toward Möckern, Marmont ordered his entire corps to execute a 45 degree turn to the left to better support the struggle on the left wing. "The enemy redoubled his efforts and sent powerful support to take this position. So I made an oblique change of front by brigade, which immediately formed six lines by echelon so that all were equally well disposed to support this village, where the entire battle seemed to hinge."[51] He also moved up his reserve artillery to reinforce the left wing and ordered Compans's 20th Division to be ready to support Lagrange's division in and next to Möckern. Forming his troops in six echelons, one behind the other, the marshal did not wait for Karl's Prussians to attack. According to Yorck's chief of staff, Zielinsky, Marmont clearly saw the Prussian deployment. After observing "that the left wing of the army – Langeron's corps – was advancing very slowly and still remained very far from the battlefield, he concentrated his main strength through a march to the left close to Möckern, assembled around ninety cannon, and began his very superior attack on our left wing."[52] Protected by his twelve-pound battery, Marmont personally led a few battalion columns between the intervals of the guns to engage the Prussians.

With drums beating, 2nd Brigade's five battalions advanced: the Fusilier Battalion of the 1st East Prussian Regiment and 2nd Battalion of the 2nd East Prussian Regiment formed the first wave. Behind in second line followed the 1st and 2nd Battalions of the 1st East Prussian Regiment. Major Fischer's entire 2nd Battalion of the 6th Silesian Landwehr Regiment dispersed as skirmishers. As murderous caseshot from the twelve-pound battery smashed its front and the small-arms fire from Möckern enfiladed its flank, 2nd Brigade ascended the hill. At fifty paces, a marine battalion of the Guard opened fire and then charged the Fusilier Battalion of the 1st East Prussian Regiment. After some brief hand-to-hand fighting that claimed the life of their commander, Major Pentzig, a small group of survivors from the Prussian battalion could do nothing more than flee south to join Hiller's seventh attack on Möckern. From the second line, Lobenthal, the commander of the 1st East Prussian Infantry Regiment, moved up Major Schleuse's 1st Battalion. Ferociously attacking the French marines, the battalion steadily pushed forward despite stubborn resistance. After overwhelming the marines, 1st Battalion closed on the twelve-pound battery with bayonets fixed. In the meantime, the commander of the 2nd East Prussian Infantry Regiment, Sjöholm, led Karl's other first-line battalion, Major Dessauniers's 2nd Battalion, close to the French battery, reaching a small hollow that protected the men from the vicious artillery fire. In this position, the battalion deployed into line and opened a sustained fire on the French gunners that prompted some of the crews to abandon their guns. With the rate of French fire considerably slowed, Schleuse's battalion made a dash for the guns. Just before it could reach the artillery line, fresh French battalions poured through the intervals to protect the guns. Instinctively, the Prussians slowed their advance. As Prince Karl rushed toward the battalion encouraging his men to advance, his horse collapsed under him. While climbing into the saddle of another mount, the prince too sank to the ground with a serious wound; Lobenthal assumed command.

Close-range volley fire from Dessauniers's 2nd Battalion, still well positioned in the hollow, momentarily froze the French infantry. In addition, four French caissons with the ammunition for one of Marmont's twelve-pound batteries suddenly exploded thanks to a well-aimed shot by Yorck's artillery commander, Lieutenant-Colonel Schmidt. "At the time of a new attack by the enemy," wrote Marmont, "the battery of twelve-pound guns, whose effect had been so favorable and so powerful, was suddenly taken out of service, a shell having blown up four caissons. These caissons also contained shells. The shells exploded just as the enemy made a decisive charge. This accident had disastrous consequences."[53] The French guns fell completely silent and the imperial infantry yielded. This enabled Schleuse's 1st Battalion to capture two guns and their crews. Lobenthal then directed Major Kurnatowsky's 2nd Battalion of the 1st East Prussian Regiment to advance and take possession of the remaining guns.[54]

Before the Prussians could secure their prizes, Marmont launched a counterattack with the 20th and 25th Provisional Regiments of Compans's 20th Division. Charging in column, one battalion slammed into the flank of Schleuse's 1st Battalion, putting it to flight; three other French battalions closed on Kurnatowsky's 2nd Battalion. Lobenthal ordered Kurnatowsky to charge the closest enemy battalion, which did not expect to be attacked and so fell back. The two others initially followed but blinding smoke from the artillery still hung thick in the air, preventing Lobethal from seeing them execute a left wheel. Suddenly, the two French battalions emerged in the right flank of Kurnatowsky's 2nd Battalion. Lobenthal ordered a retreat and then fell from his horse wounded; Sjöholm assumed command. The imperials hotly pursued, forcing most of Yorck's batteries to fall back but two held their ground: Foot Battery Nr. 1 (six-pound cannon) and Heavy Battery Nr. 2 (twelve-pound cannon). Their caseshot along with a charge by the Mecklenburg Hussars halted the French advance and allowed the wreck of 2nd Brigade to reorganize by a partially destroyed brick barn that provided good cover on the side of Möckern. According to Marmont:

> I decided to engage the troops of the 1st [20th] Division, who in echelon formed the center, and directed these to assist those already engaged against the enemy, who was moving against our center. The battle assumed a new character, and in an instant our infantry masses found themselves less than thirty paces from the enemy. No action was more intense. The 20th and 25th Provisional Regiments, commanded by Colonels [Jean-Pierre] Maury and [Jean] Druot, covered themselves with glory in this situation. They advanced against the enemy and forced him to yield but, overwhelmed by numbers,

these regiments were forced to halt, yet they managed to hold their position. The 32nd Light also worked wonders.[55]

After losing more than 1,500 men – 419 from Schleuse's battalion alone – almost half of its manpower, and almost all of its officers, 2nd Brigade could do little more on 16 October. Prince Karl and his chief of staff, Major Schütz, as well as Lobenthal, Kurnatowsky, Dessauniers, and Fischer, numbered among the wounded; Schleuse and Pentzig were dead. "The wounded came back in such masses," recalled Henckel von Donnersmarck, "that at first we were inclined to believe that entire battalions had been destroyed."[56] Steinmetz's 1st Brigade now arrived to take its turn on the killing fields.

Meanwhile, Langeron's corps marched through Breitenfeld and prepared to assault Kleinwiederitzsch. On Langeron's right, Kaptsevich's X Infantry Corps deployed against the latter village. With the eight battalions of Langeron's vanguard, Rudzevich formed the left wing by moving north and around Kleinwiederitzsch to a position between it and a birch grove situated further to the northeast. Emmanuel's vanguard cavalry covered the left wing while, as noted, Korf's Reserve Cavalry rode north toward Podelwitz. Behind X Infantry Corps, the 9th Division of Olsufiyev's IX Infantry Corps moved up in reserve.[57] Kaptsevich attacked Kleinwiederitzsch at the same time as Hiller launched his first assault on Möckern. Despite their slight number, Dąbrowski's Poles greeted their Russian foes with stubborn resistance. As at Möckern, the struggle went back and forth before superior Russian numbers overcame the Poles. After evacuating the village, the imperials also abandoned Großwiederitzsch and fled south in an attempt to reach Eutritzsch. According to Langeron, "Kaptsevich attacked and carried the two villages of Wiederitzsch with the courage and resolution that distinguished him as well as the brave corps that he commanded. The enemy was routed and fled toward Leipzig and the Parthe." Reinforced by the Derptskii and Liflyandskii Mounted Jäger from the Reserve Cavalry, Emmanuel charged eight Polish squadrons and Fournier's Light Horse close to Großwiederitzsch with the Kharkovskii, Novorossiiskii and Kievskii Dragoon Regiments. Supported by the attack of the 1st and 3rd Ukrainskii Cossack Regiments against Fournier's right flank, the Russians drove the imperials toward Eutritzsch in disarray, taking 7 guns, several caissons, and some 500 prisoners.[58]

"But all of a sudden," continues Langeron, "at 2:00 in the afternoon, I saw these runaways stop and re-form, and I saw strong columns arriving from the Parthe and Leipzig. They attacked the Wiederitzsch villages with great vigor and despite the resistance of X Infantry Corps, these villages were momentarily lost. Lieutenant-Colonel Voyevodsky of the Staroskolskii Infantry Regiment was killed, Major Yuzefovich, gravely wounded; the fight was very lively, my losses bad enough." Contrary to Langeron's statements, French reinforcements did not arrive from the Parthe and Leipzig.[59] Instead, Dąbrowski managed to reorganize his men and launch a bloody counterattack that regained Groß- and Kleinwiederitzsch. After sustaining tremendous losses, both Kaptsevich and Rudzevich fell back in complete disorder. The imperial counterattack delivered a blow that sent the Russians reeling. First, the cavalry and artillery of Rudzevich's vanguard fled west toward the Rietschke stream. Behind them followed the infantry of the vanguard. Confusion and disorder reigned on the left bank of the Rietschke as the Russians panicked at the crossing. In his published memoirs, Langeron described the scene:

> The cavalry of my vanguard was forced to recross the Rietschke brook; the fire of the enemy columns and the grapeshot caused them to suffer considerable losses. The infantry of this same vanguard was also momentarily forced to retreat; the fire was terrible, but this was not the moment to spare the troops: we had to win. This moment was critical; my columns, forced into a precipitated retreat by the masses that were moving on them, by the fire of grapeshot, and by a cloud of skirmishers, moved [west] quickly (but not in a disorderly fashion) toward the swampy brook, which was very difficult to cross, and on the left bank my cavalry and artillery were bunched, both of which had had a great deal of trouble crossing it; if the infantry had also arrived, closely followed by the enemy, the confusion there would have been general, and I would have suffered great losses: we had to stop the infantry.[60]

From both villages, the Poles advanced toward the Rietschke. Imperial artillery mowed down the Russians, claiming numerous officers and men. Despite the shelling, Langeron, Rudzevich, and the other generals restored order and turned the Russian vanguard infantry east to face the villages. Langeron described the action from his perspective:

> I had Russians under my orders; I knew their precise obedience and courage; I passed the Shlisselburgskii Regiment and without amusing myself with witty phrases or haranguing them, without talking to their officers or soldiers, I commanded in a loud voice: 'Halt, half-turn to the left, forward; fix bayonets, march, march!' The regiment stopped, as if at an exercise, turned and marched forward, the other regiments stopped as well and moved forward. Shocked by this movement, the enemy stopped and seemed to hesitate, believing that numerous forces had come to my aid. This hesitation saved me; my cavalry and my artillery crossed the brook and formed on the right bank. My infantry also arrived and took up positions. The enemy then stopped all of a sudden and this small setback which I had just suffered, the result of which would have been so dangerous for other soldiers, was immediately repaired by the intrepidity of the infantry of my vanguard and those of

Kaptsevich's X Corps, which had found themselves in the same situation as me and pulled themselves out in the same way.[61]

At this point, the Russians spotted a French column approaching on the Bad Düben–Leipzig road almost in the rear of their position; its depth indicated a considerable force. After the main body halted between Podelwitz and Göbschelwitz, its vanguard deployed against the Russian left wing. Although the column consisted of III Corps's trains, baggage, and Reserve Artillery escorted by Delmas's 9th Division – 10 battalions and 14 guns totaling 4,800 men – its size convinced Langeron that it represented an entire army corps.[62] Langeron noted:

> At the same time, Ney's corps, commanded by Souham, and 7,000 to 8,000 men strong, appeared on the road from Bad Düben, on my left flank, which was in the air, and which I could not anchor anywhere. This moment was extremely critical; I was obliged to extend this flank using Olsufiyev's IX Infantry Corps, and ending with General Korf's cavalry, in a way that left me with a single immense line, without reserves. Therefore, my line was extremely extended and weak everywhere; without the steadfastness of my generals, their firm dispositions, the intrepidity of my troops, I ran the risk of seeing the enemy pierce my line again and being obliged to retreat on Breitenfeld. The recapture of the Wiederitzsch villages, which stood near the center of my line, was indispensable for assuring the success of the day.[63]

While Olsufiyev's 9th Division deployed against Delmas, Kaptsevich arranged another attack on the Wiederitzsch villages with his 22nd and 8th Divisions. Again the Russians overwhelmed Dąbrowski's warriors, regaining both villages with the bayonet and ejecting the Poles in disorder. As that assault proceeded, Langeron and Rudzevich turned the villages to the north with the vanguard infantry followed by Emmanuel's cavalry. We hear one last time from Langeron:

> General Kaptsevich, although wounded with a bad bruise caused by a ball that killed his horse, never quit the battlefield; he once again attacked the villages with the greatest decisiveness. Perfectly seconded by Generals Turchaninov and Prince Urusov, commanders of the 22nd and 8th Divisions [respectively], Vasilchikov, commander of the Vyatskii Regiment, who particularly distinguished himself and Colonel Magdenko of the artillery, who although wounded never left his post, and by all the regimental commanders of this brave corps, he took the two villages while Rudzevich and myself once again drove the infantry of the vanguard to attack the enemy troops moving up to support those who were defending the villages. The enemy was again overthrown and withdrew in disorder, leaving many dead, wounded, and prisoners.[64]

Around this same time, Olsufiyev instructed General Udom to occupy the birch grove northeast of Kleinwiederitzsch with the 10th and 38th Jäger Regiments (one battalion each) and the skirmishers of the Nasheburgskii, Apsheronskii, and Yakutskii Regiments. Olsufiyev also moved up the twelve guns of Light Battery Nr. 29 from the reserve. Fortunately for the Allies, Delmas had not been informed of the events in this sector. For about one hour he debated whether to directly support Dąbrowski or continue to Schönefeld per his orders. Instead of being decisive, Delmas settled on a half-measure. To cover his march to Schönefeld, he pushed a detachment west to attack the birch grove. A "very obstinate engagement" ensued amidst the beautiful white bark. To support Udom, Olsufiyev sent the Ryazhskii and Kolyvanskii Regiments (three battalions total) into the wood. During bitter hand-to-hand combat, the Ryazhskii Regiment took the flag of the 125th Line and forced the French to evacuate the wood, "leaving the ground covered with his dead and wounded."[65] Due to the Russian break-through, Delmas withdrew through Seehausen and crossed the Parthe at Plösen and Neutzsch.[66] Korf's cavalry pursued Delmas, with the Mitavskii Dragoon Regiment alone bringing back 400 prisoners. General Lukovkin's four regiments of Don Cossacks on loan from Sacken's corps rode northeast on the highway to Bad Düben. They found 6 guns and around 100 wagons abandoned by the French because the exhausted horses could pull them no further.

Meanwhile, after Dąbrowski had again reorganized his troops, he attempted to cross the Rietschke between Großwiederitzsch and Eutritzsch to exploit the large gap between Yorck and Langeron. To stop the Poles, Langeron sent Vasilchikov with the Vyatskii and Arkhangelogorodskii Regiments as well as Heavy Battery Nr. 34 across the stream above Kleinwiederitzsch. He also requested that St.-Priest, whose lead units had just cleared Lindenthal, support him with the three battalions of Bistrom's Jäger brigade. In danger of being cut off by Vasilchikov and seeing the approach of St.-Priest's fresh units, Dąbrowski withdrew to Eutritzsch. Two of St.-Priest's batteries escorted by the 3rd and 4th Squadrons of the Brandenburg Hussars moved into the gap between Yorck's left and Langeron's right. The onset of darkness ended the fight on this part of the battlefield.

Thus far, Blücher had spent the entire day with Langeron's corps on the highway forward of Lindenthal, in part because he feared large enemy forces would arrive from Bad Düben via Hohenossig, in part because he trusted Yorck to handle the situation on the right wing. At 4:00, Charles Stewart returned to Blücher's headquarters. Disagreement exists over the nature of the news that Stewart delivered. According to Lowe, Stewart communicated "the Prince Royal's acquiescence in all that General Blücher had desired, and his intention of marching his army that night."[67] However, Stewart claims that, after Bernadotte had refused to meet with him, he settled on explaining to Adlerkreutz "how imperiously necessary it was for the Russian cavalry and light artillery to advance immediately [southeast] in the direction of Taucha." Adlerkreutz responded that, if Stewart could convince Wintzingerode to take such a step, "he would answer for the concurrence of the prince." Stewart then hurried to find the Russian commander, "who stated that his orders were positive from the Emperor of Russia not to act but by the express commands of the crown prince; that he dared not move in person."[68] Thus, the consequences of Blücher's earlier attempt to hijack Bernadotte's two Prussian corps. Nevertheless, Wintzingerode pledged to send 3,000 Cossacks to be followed in the morning by 8,000 cavalry if Stewart "could procure such [an] order. I returned to General Blücher greatly disappointed; but was happy to learn, in sequel, that 3,000 horses were actually pushed forward that evening, on [account of] General Adlerkreutz seeing the Prince."[69] In fact, Bernadotte issued orders for the 5,000 troopers of Wintzingerode's Reserve Cavalry to continue another six miles further south from Landsberg to Kölsa, itself ten miles northwest of Möckern.[70]

This did Blücher little good regarding the situation at hand. Yet finally, around 5:00, he received the report that he had so impatiently awaited: Russian patrols had found no more enemy forces on the road from Bad Düben. He immediately ordered Sacken to commence the one-hour march from Radefeld to support Yorck at Möckern – an order that the Russian troops purportedly received with joy. Although the corps advanced on the most direct route toward the burning village, it did not arrive until nightfall, which came at 6:00, and thus did not see action. According to Nostitz:

> After the struggle became general and the decision became doubtful, Blücher sent Sacken the order to reinforce the attack of the Prussian corps with one brigade; this order was repeated by a second officer and yet the help they so desperately needed approached only slowly. Then Blücher tasked me with accelerating the march of the [Russian] troops. When General Sacken saw me approaching, he rode toward me with a serious face and said: "What have I done to the general to deserve being placed in reserve?" "Your Excellency knows," I answered, "that one always places in reserve the general and the troops in which one has the most trust, and considering this point, it certainly appears that you have the highest honor." General Sacken extended his hand to me in a friendly manner, placed himself at the head of the foremost marching Jäger regiment, and had it proceed at the double-quick; nevertheless it arrived on the battlefield too late in order to be able to take part in the glory of the day.[71]

St.-Priest also received orders to advance along an arm of the Rietschke that flowed from Lindenthal directly to Eutritzsch, post his three twelve-pound batteries, and attack Marmont's right wing. Yet his march proceeded so slowly that Blücher had to repeat the order several times. Aside from two batteries, St.-Priest's corps likewise did not arrive in time to participate in the battle.

While the struggle around Möckern raged, Horn and Hünerbein slowly advanced on Yorck's left, sliding southeast until they finally crossed the Lindenthal–Leipzig road. Although neither brigade had engaged the imperials, both had already suffered tremendous losses from the enemy's murderous artillery fire. Thus, only the eight battalions of Steinmetz's 1st Brigade – Yorck's last reserve – still remained intact. Considerable firing still could be heard in Möckern, meaning that the Prussians had yet to secure the village. The 5:00 hour struck and Yorck knew what needed to be done. Although it was extremely risky, he could not delay in committing 1st Brigade to finally drive Marmont from Möckern and the surrounding hills. Yet, if Steinmetz failed, Yorck would have spent his last reserve and no support could be expected from Langeron, while nothing could be seen of Sacken and St.-Priest. At this point, Yorck finally sent one of his adjutants, the count of Brandenburg, with orders for Horn and Hünerbein to attack.

To drive back the French, Yorck reinserted Heavy Battery Nr. 1 in the artillery line next to Foot Battery Nr. 1 and Heavy Battery Nr. 2. The batteries on the left that had fallen back after 2nd Brigade broke likewise returned to the line. Their fire as well as Steinmetz's advance prompted Marmont's infantry columns to retreat to the hills, where they prepared to meet the new Prussian attack. "The combat was maintained with the same fury for three hours," reported Marmont, "the enemy had suffered huge losses because of the advantageous position of our artillery, which allowed us to crush his masses. But new forces were arriving constantly and renewed the attacks." "We had arranged ourselves in battalion masses," explained Gneisenau. "The enemy artillery raged among them. Our Landwehr battalions acted splendidly. When an enemy ball mowed down ten to fifteen men, they shouted: 'Long live the king' and closed the gaps by coming together over the dead." From their high vantage point on the hills, the French could clearly see the Prussians approaching; they could also see that nothing stood behind Steinmetz. Marmont realized he had a golden opportunity before him. If he could break though Yorck's corps, he stood the chance of rolling up Blücher's left.[72]

Yorck's artillery skillfully exploited the enemy's retrograde movement by advancing 700 yards. While the Prussians poured caseshot into the French ranks, Steinmetz steadily advanced with the 1st, 2nd, and 4th Battalions of the 13th Silesian Landwehr Regiment supported by the Silesian Grenadier Battalion in the first wave, and the 1st, 3rd, and 4th Battalions of the 5th Silesian Landwehr Regiment supported by the 1st East Prussian Grenadier Battalion in the second. The survivors of 2nd Brigade formed the third wave followed by the cavalry of 1st Brigade: the Black Hussars. Steinmetz instructed his two right wing battalions (2nd Battalion of the 13th Silesian Landwehr and 3rd Battalion of the 5th Silesian Landwehr) as well as the Silesian Grenadiers to advance through Möckern while his center and left assaulted the hills north of the village. Thus, the three battalions of Steinmetz's right wing advanced eastward along the Halle–Leipzig highway close to the northern edge of the village before turning south where the village's outlying structures reached the highway. With the 2nd Battalion leading, the Silesian Landwehr penetrated the burning village despite receiving heavy fire from the houses on their left. Reaching the crossroads in the middle of the village, the Prussians turned left (east) and charged toward the opposite end of Möckern. On reaching their goal, the Silesian militia received such a devastating blast of caseshot that they broke, throwing themselves on the grenadiers who followed. Led by Major Friedrich August von Burghoff, the grenadiers pushed through the demoralized militia and fixed their bayonets. Behind them the officers of the Landwehr reorganized the battalions and followed. Running the gauntlet between the fortified houses from where the French poured fire into their ranks, the Prussians managed to emerge on the eastern side of Möckern and storm the enemy's barricades. Again the Prussians sustained horrendous losses; if relief did not come from outside Möckern the advantages that had just been won could not be held.

Meanwhile, the five battalions of Steinmetz's center and left attacked the wall of artillery estimated to number forty guns that lined the hills north of Möckern. Led by the commander of the 13th Silesian Landwehr Regiment, Major Gädicke, the 1st and 4th Battalions of that regiment led the advance "*im Sturmschritt* [at the double-quick]" with bayonets fixed, according to Yorck's after-action report. Like 2nd Brigade earlier, they received horrendous fire in the front and in the right flank from Möckern. According to Prussian after-action reports, the French infantry stood in squares. Advancing in attack columns, Steinmetz's first wave managed to come within 110 yards of the French but could not break through the wall of lead that greeted them. Gädicke's two Landwehr battalions received such intense fire that within a few minutes all mounted officers were either dead or wounded. Two balls mortally wounded Gädicke but the battalion commanders, Larisch (1st) and Martitz (4th), remained unscathed. For a few moments the shaken Prussians staggered forward before the survivors broke rank and started firing. Steinmetz rushed forward to stop this ineffective fire. In the process he too fell and command passed to Colonel Michael Heinrich von Losthin.[73] Along with Larisch and Martitz, Losthin managed to get the columns to continue the advance. Regardless, steady French volley fire broke the Landwehr, which retreated in disorder. According to Marmont, he ordered the Württemberger cavalry brigade to attack the broken

Prussians, but General Normann did not obey. Only after the marshal repeated the order did the cavalry advance, yet the favorable moment had passed: "We had fought hard for more than four hours. The enemy had suffered huge losses from the superior fire of our artillery and its devastating effect on the masses, when he executed a new attack. It failed like the previous ones and produced a great disorder among his troops. I gave orders for the Württemberger cavalry brigade, commanded by General Normann, to charge this infantry with the goal of creating the greatest confusion. He initially refused to execute my orders, and the time passed so that there was nothing useful that could be undertaken. However, after receiving a second order, it moved off; but it threw itself on a battalion of the 1st Marine Regiment, overthrew it instead of charging the enemy, who recovered and resumed his offensive."[74]

As the first wave fled back to the Prussian lines, the three battalions of the second line – Yorck's last battalions – advanced at the double-quick. They rushed past the remnant of the first wave on their left heedless of their own losses. Like Gädicke, Major Malzahn, the commander of the 5th Silesian Landwehr Regiment, led his 1st and 4th Battalions, commanded by Majors Mumm and Kossecki respectively, up the hill through the hail of lead followed by Major Leslie's 1st East Prussian Grenadier Battalion. Again French musketry claimed the majority of Prussian officers: Malzahn and Kossecki fell dead while Losthin, Mumm, Leslie, and numerous others collapsed with serious wounds. Despite the devastating losses, the columns of the second wave continued uphill, driving over the corpses of their comrades. Behind them the first wave reorganized and followed. "The fate of this day hung on a silk thread," wrote Schack.

Yorck's situation became worse as his artillery started to go silent due to counterbattery fire, lack of ammunition, and having its field of fire obstructed by Steinmetz's troops. Conversely, Marmont's guns reached their greatest intensity. Yorck watched as Steinmetz's second wave faltered. With nothing left but his cavalry, Yorck issued orders for the troopers to charge. Committing the cavalry changed the entire situation and produced the result. According to one eyewitness: "The struggle grew more intense with each moment until its severity in and beside Möckern reached such a height that all at once hundreds of wounded from the ranks of the engaged battalions came streaming back creating such a crisis that it appeared the approaching climax of the bloody drama would be to our disadvantage. In this important moment, when everything was at stake, Major Sohr charged the enemy."[75] It appears that Katzler's vanguard cavalry stood behind the left wing (7th and 8th Brigades) and the Reserve Cavalry behind the center (1st and 2nd Brigades) but further rearward than Katzler while the brigade cavalry had remained close to their individual brigades. Although Sohr with his 1st and 2nd Brandenburg Hussar Squadrons and the Jäger detachment of that regiment served with Katzler's vanguard that day, he had been tasked with supporting Hiller's effort to take Möckern. Therefore, his troopers stood in squadron columns on the Halle–Leipzig highway only a few hundred yards west of Möckern; 2nd Brigade's cavalry – the Mecklenburg Hussars – remained a few hundred paces behind them. During the attack of Steinmetz's first wave, Sohr moved his three squadrons close behind the second with Möckern to their right (south). Sometime after the attack of the second wave bogged down, Yorck himself galloped madly toward them and shouted: "Major Sohr attack!"[76] Sohr complied, ordering his men to take no prisoners.[77]

Yorck sent the same order to all troops: infantry and cavalry. As the closest echelon, Sohr's hussars, with the Brandenburg Uhlans and 5th Silesian Landwehr Cavalry Regiment led by Katzler in second echelon on their left (north), led the desperate assault. Behind them followed the remaining regiments of vanguard cavalry, then the Reserve Cavalry and brigade cavalry, and finally the reorganized infantry of 1st Brigade with the remnant of the 2nd. On Yorck's left wing, 7th and 8th Brigades finally hurried to close the distance between them and Marmont's position. Thick smoke from the fires that were devouring Möckern prevented Sohr's troopers from seeing the French; only the numerous flashes from the enemy's muskets informed them that the French had accelerated their counterattack. Fortunately for the Prussians, the smoke also concealed their approach. Perhaps ten minutes passed before Sohr gave the order for the bugler to sound the trot. After moving through the intervals of the Prussian infantry, they completely surprised Marmont's approaching columns. The charging Prussian Hussars – light cavalry – managed to break two battalion columns. With the hussars pursuing hard on their heels, the fleeing infantry sought the safety of Marmont's great battery. Sohr's troopers plunged into the artillery line, taking six guns. To save the infantry and artillery, Normann's Württemberger cavalry slammed into Sohr's left flank with "great determination," according to the Prussian major. A musket ball pierced Sohr's right arm as he led his hussars toward the Württembergers; he switched his saber to his left hand. A few minutes later, the second echelon of Prussian cavalry arrived – the Brandenburg Uhlans and 5th Silesian Landwehr Cavalry Regiment – on Sohr's left and in the flank of the Württembergers.

Seeing Sohr threatened in the flank by Normann's cavalry, Yorck placed himself at the head of three Black Hussar squadrons. With saber in hand, he shouted "March, march, long live the king!" and reiterated his orders for a general advance.[78] On the French side, one brigade from Lorge's 5th Light Cavalry Division rushed up to support the Württembergers but the imperials could not stem the Prussian tide. From the Reserve Cavalry, Jürgaß arrived with the 1st West Prussian Dragoons. Behind them in the second wave galloped the Lithuanian Dragoons led by Yorck himself; the 1st

Neumark Landwehr Cavalry and 10th Silesian Landwehr Cavalry followed the Lithuanians. Not only did the Prussians sweep away the imperial cavalry but they also delivered the decisive blow to Marmont's lines. "This was the situation," reported Marmont, "and III Corps, whose arrival would have been so decisive, had not appeared when the enemy threw 6,000 horses against our masses, which were already grappling at a short distance with the enemy infantry. In general, our infantry showed composure and courage. But several battalions of the 1st and 3rd Marine Regiments, which held an important position, broke, forcing our masses to move closer for better support."[79] As Marmont's center caved, the survivors of Lagrange's division evacuated Möckern. The remains of Yorck's right wing emerged from the village to take part in the general attack. Marmont judged that his left wing could no longer hold; he now strove to use his still seemingly unbroken right wing to cover the retreat southeast toward Gohlis.

After Count Brandenburg delivered Yorck's orders to advance, 7th and 8th Brigades proceeded toward Marmont's right wing in two waves of battalion columns with drums beating and bugles blaring. Horn's first echelon consisted of the 1st Battalion of the 15th Silesian Landwehr, the two remaining battalions of the 4th Silesian Landwehr Regiment, and the Thuringian Battalion from Weimar. The three battalions of Lieutenant-Colonel Konstantin Gottlieb von Zepelin's Leib Regiment and the 2nd Battalion of the 15th Silesian Landwehr formed the second wave. To the left of Horn, Hünerbein's 8th Brigade, reduced to five battalions after having supplied Yorck's vanguard with three, marched with the Fusilier and 2nd Battalions of the Brandenburg Infantry Regiment and the 3rd Battalion of the 12th Reserve Regiment in the first wave; the 1st Battalion of the 12th Reserve and the remaining battalion of the 14th Silesian Landwehr Regiment, the 3rd, provided the second wave.[80]

As 7th Brigade approached Marmont's center and right wing, the French artillery bit deeply into the Prussian ranks. This caused the first wave to slow but the second wave to accelerate. As a result, the battalions of the second wave pushed their way up to the first wave without orders although only the commander of the 15th Silesian Landwehr Infantry Regiment, Colonel Wollzogen, fell wounded in the assault. At the head of 1st Battalion of the Leib Regiment, Horn found himself swept away. According to Count Brandenburg's after-action report, Horn's men advanced steadily but did not fire a shot; the thicker the enemy caseshot became, the louder the troops shouted "Hurrah! Long live the king! Forward, forward! We must have victory!"[81] Now that Horn's two waves had melded into one, the far right wing battalion (3rd Battalion of the 14th Landwehr) charged the batteries of Marmont's center, which managed to escape after losing only one gun. After clearing the French artillery line, the Prussians moved toward the thick battalion columns of Friederichs's 22nd Division, purportedly storming the French infantry as they would a redoubt and repulsing a French cavalry attack. Suddenly, a strong blast of artillery raked the left flank of the Leib Regiment – Russian guns from St.-Priest's infantry corps had mistakenly opened fire on the Prussians and continued to blast them until the error could be corrected. Regardless, Horn's brigade cavalry moved up. Along with the infantry, they captured an entire battalion, bringing back some 400 prisoners, 1 flag, and 1 howitzer. Around this time, the Prussian cavalry slammed into the portion of the marshal's center that stood close to Möckern. The combined effect of Horn's attack and the cavalry charge broke the French center; the effects rippled across the French line. Simultaneously, Horn's left and Hünerbein's five battalions smashed into Marmont's right, which likewise started to buckle and retreat.

Hünerbein's men had advanced with the same resolution as their comrades in 7th Brigade but several officers fell to devastating enemy artillery fire including the commander of the 12th Reserve Regiment, Major Götze, who numbered among the killed while the commander of the Brandenburg Infantry Regiment, Lieutenant-Colonel von Borcke, the commander of the 2nd Battalion of the Brandenburg Regiment, Major Othegraven, and the commander of the 3rd Battalion of the 12th Reserve Regiment, Major Laurens, received wounds. In his report, Hünerbein explained that the brigade endured a "hail of caseshot," "the blood-lust of the heavy balls," and "the bone-shattering crack of bursting grenades." Finally reaching the French line, the Fusilier Battalion of the Brandenburg Infantry Regiment charged an enemy square with bayonets fixed. Struck by a musket ball and pierced by a French bayonet, the battalion commander, Major Heinrich Krosigk, fell out of his saddle. With his last breath, he purportedly pointed his sword toward the French and ordered his men to continue fighting. Friederichs's fresh troops fought savagely, making the Prussians pay dearly for each yard gained. "What poetry tells us of Spartan courage, what the artist's brush has painted for us of Roman boldness, was infinitely surpassed by what took place in this battle," continued Hünerbein.[82] After redirecting St.-Priest's two batteries, the Russian guns provided much-needed artillery support for the Prussians. Still the French fought tenaciously until Friederichs received Marmont's order to retreat.

Marmont ordered a general withdrawal during which his left fell back one mile southeast to Gohlis and his right went a little further to Eutritzsch. Unfortunately for the French, all of Yorck's cavalry had reached the field and engaged. The Brandenburg Hussars and the Brandenburg Uhlans together brought back twenty-eight guns and five caissons. After cutting down 200 men, the Black Hussars captured 7 guns and 400 prisoners. The East Prussian National Cavalry Regiment brought back four guns. Numerous French columns and squares collapsed under the weight of the Prussian attacks. According to Commandant Weil, Major Stößel, with two squadrons of Black Hussars, broke a square, was then repulsed by French cavalry, rallied, and overwhelmed the French troopers. In another example, three squadrons of Mecklenburg Hussars attacked the rear of a French battalion while Horn's infantry assaulted its front. In total, the regiment's four squadrons brought back 700 prisoners and 1 Eagle or as the hussars called it, a "*Vogel* [bird]."[83] Leading the 1st West Prussian Dragoon Regiment, Jürgaß drove off Normann's cavalry, captured four guns, and pursued the French all the way to Gohlis. Yorck's other regiments enjoyed similar success.

Yet the thrill of victory eroded Prussian command and control, which provided the French with some breathing room.[84] The retreat of Marmont's right toward Eutritzsch necessitated a left wheel by 7th and 8th Brigades. Already during the approach march and assault, the battalions of Horn's right and Hünerbein's left had collided. Now, the left wheel disordered all of the latter's battalions because of the lack of space on the field. Seeking to exploit this confusion, Friederichs counterattacked and managed to drive back 8th Brigade. "On our left side toward our rear appeared enemy masses," noted the journal of the Lithuanian Dragoons. Led by Henckel von Donnersmarck, the second wave of the Reserve Cavalry – Lithuanian Dragoons and 10th Silesian Landwehr Cavalry – came back from the pursuit, turned toward the threatened wing, and engaged numerous marine battalions while Hünerbein and his surviving officers worked to restore order. Forming two large squares, the French awaited the Prussian attack. The 10th Silesian Landwehr, commanded by Sohr's brother, scattered the closest square but heavy fire from the adjacent square sent the mounted militia reeling. At that moment, Yorck rode up to the Lithuanians and shouted: "Go, go, old Lithuanians, cut them down. Do this and everything is ours." Despite facing rows of blood-thirsty bayonets, the Lithuanians immediately charged. According to the journal of the Lithuanian Dragoons:

> The square was broken on the first attempt. We had driven deep into the enemy's ranks when the Marine Guard opposed us. All who had already received pardon immediately seized discarded weapons, and now danger was before us and behind us and a dreadful carnage was the result. On our right wing, other cavalry joined us; Colonel Welzien came to our support with a detachment of Silesian Landwehr. Now our Lithuanians abandoned all caution, because the overpowered [enemy] shot and stabbed like mad everything around them. But the Guard succumbed. The scene was gruesome. We penetrated deeper and deeper into the mass that by this time had become very confused; those who did not fall to the weapon were trampled under the horses' hooves; heaps of twenty to thirty of these unfortunates lay jumbled together; through this some found protection from the fury of our people; and certainly nothing of this column (1,200 strong) would have escaped had not an unexpected heated artillery fire from our left side disturbed us from completing our work.[85]

The shelling came from Eutritzsch, where the French right wing had conducted an orderly retreat aided by nightfall and Prussian exhaustion. With his left and center broken, Marmont sought to reorganize his troops as much as possible and position them on the left bank of the Rietschke stream between Gohlis and Eutritzsch. On his orders, 300 Württembergers secured the crossing over the Rietschke stream at Gohlis. Marmont squarely blamed Ney for his defeat: "Thus, the troops of VI Corps resisted a force quadruple its strength for five hours and victory would have been the fruit of our efforts, despite the disproportion of forces, if the orders given by His Majesty to support me had been executed."[86] Despite voting for Ney's death in 1815, Marmont later absolved the bravest of the brave of any wrongdoing: "I had to rely on III Corps but Marshal Ney had been disposed of by the order of the emperor, and had marched to join the Grande Armée. Informed of my engagement, Napoleon sent him the order to march back, but he was already beside him. However, he did set in motion to return without being able to arrive in time to help us, and during this decisive day, having marched from one army to another, he was not useful anywhere." Of course this did not prevent Marmont from blaming the defeat on the failure of III Corps to arrive: "I felt a great impatience for the arrival of III Corps based on what Marshal Ney had told me. If it had been available to me, as I was authorized to believe, it would have debouched on my right, and an offensive movement against the enemy's left would have ensured the success of the battle, that is to say the maintenance of our position throughout the day." Marmont likewise held Normann accountable: "If the Württembergers had done their duty, a complete success would have been the fruit of our efforts. Aside from maintaining the entire battlefield, we would have taken numerous prisoners."[87]

After observing the final struggle at Möckern, Blücher rode to Lindenthal. "He had his cooking wagons bring back the wounded from the battlefield, gave shirts and bed sheets for dressings, used the houses or villages for the wounded," recalled his surgeon, Dr. Carl Ludwig Bieske, "and remained in the field near the watch fires until finally a half-dilapidated empty smithy was found for him to get a few hours of rest in. His staff camped in the open field despite the raw weather."[88] The question of how the Bohemian Army had fared and what the next morning would bring occupied everyone's mind. Yorck had no idea of the extent of his losses but expected them to be extremely numerous. Nevertheless, spirits at Blücher's headquarters remained high due in part to Gneisenau's declaration that this victory meant the liberation of Germany. That night, Captain August von Hedemann departed for Bernadotte's headquarters to deliver news of the victory as well as Blücher's request for support on the 17th.[89] Captain Knakfuß sped off through Schkeuditz to Schwarzenberg's command post. In the darkness, he missed the road through the difficult Elster valley.

Thus, Knakfuß did not arrive until the following morning around the same time as Colonel Goltz, Blücher's first adjutant, who delivered the captured Eagle.[90]

During the night, Marmont continued his retreat and crossed the Parthe, leaving behind Delmas's division as well as Lorge's and Fournier's cavalry between the Parthe and the Rietschke with strong posts holding Gohlis and Eutritzsch. Gneisenau moved Sacken and St.-Priest into the front line; the former east of Möckern, the latter facing Eutritzsch. Rudzevich's vanguard bivouacked to the northeast at Mockau. In second line, Langeron's corps passed the night at Groß- and Kleinwiederitzsch while Yorck's vanguard, 1st, and 2nd Brigades camped east of Möckern, the 7th and 8th west of St.-Priest, and outposts along the Rietschke stream. Yorck's cavalry camped in a bivouac west of Möckern. Flames from that village and several others licked the heavens on the cold, damp night. One participant noted in his journal that "the corps bivouacked on the battlefield, exhausted from the bloody work of this day. As once before at Leuthen, there sounded a solemn chorus of the hymn of thanksgiving: '*Nun danket alle Gott* [Now all thank God].'" In the silence of the night, fires sprang up here and there. Each of us counted friends and acquaintances among the fallen of this day but the lamenting was mixed with joy because their blood had not been shed in vain and we had won."[91]

Yorck's troops had defeated an imperial corps that was well led, equal in number, and defending an advantageous position.[92] His Prussians had broken and routed Marmont's center and left, capturing 2,000 men, 40 guns, 2 flags, 1 Eagle, and enough caissons to replenish the ammunition expended that day. Langeron noted:

> There were few enemy forces facing me; they were assembled between Möckern and Gohlis. The first of these villages was occupied by a great number of infantry. Yorck attacked it; this intrepid general and the brave troops under his orders were covered in glory in all the affairs of this immortal campaign, but, if it is permissible to say so, they once again surpassed themselves in this memorable battle: one cannot carry heroism further. Each general, each officer, [and] each soldier in this brave corps merited on this day the eternal recognition of his country and the admiration of posterity. The village of Möckern was carried; thirty pieces of cannon [and] one Eagle of the marines of the French Guard were taken at the point of the bayonet by the infantry or carried off by the cavalry despite the enemy's ferocious resistance. The fighting lasted all day and was equally fierce on both sides but Prussian valor triumphed over all. This fight may be regarded as one of the most brilliant but bloodiest of the campaign.[93]

In particular, the Prussian cavalry earned praise for delivering the decisive blow and deciding the battle. According to Commandant Weil, "It was universally recognized that the victory at Möckern was due to the cavalry, and the first to render this arm the justice it deserved was General Yorck. He spoke to Major Sohr, who after the battle and although seriously wounded went riding in front of him: 'To you alone I owe the victory that we have just won; I will never forget what you and your brave regiment did today.'"[94]

The honor of winning "a battle of the most obstinate and sanguinary class" certainly belonged to the Prussians.[95] Yet success came at a heavy price. Of the 20,831 men who mustered on the morning of 16 October, only 13,150 men remained fit for service on the following day. Of 16,120 infantry, no more than 9,000 men answered roll call.[96] The 172 dead and wounded officers included Steinmetz and Prince Karl in the latter category as well as 4 brigade, 3 regimental, and 12 battalion commanders from the infantry.[97] Although only one member of Yorck's staff was wounded, Karl's chief of staff along with two of Horn's adjutants had received wounds. Among the dead were Steinmetz's chief of staff as well as two regimental and six battalion commanders. "What could easily have been won in the battle at Möckern by the combined forces of the Silesian and North German Armies," recounted Nostitz, "was laboriously gained by the heroics and the perseverance of Yorck's corps. There, the trophies were dearly bought by one-third of these brave warriors who were killed or wounded."[98] Langeron continues: "The Prussians paid dearly for the immortal glory with which they covered themselves. Yorck's corps, already greatly weakened by the losses it had previously suffered, lost nearly 7,000 men in this terrible affair. Almost all of the generals, brigade, and battalion commanders were killed or wounded. Young Prince Karl of Mecklenburg, Colonels Katzler, Steinmetz, and Lieutenant-Colonel Hiller; a multitude of other brave officers were gravely wounded and some regiments were nearly destroyed."[99] "The battlefield is uncommonly covered with dead and maimed," wrote Gneisenau on the morning of the 18th. "Praise God, there are more French than ours. Yet our losses are likewise great. Yorck's corps alone lost 6,000 men without counting Russian losses. We have taken forty-one cannon and just as many caissons, which we can use to replenish what we expended in the battle."[100]

Langeron estimated Russian losses to be 1,500 men. His trophies included 1 flag, 13 guns, numerous baggage wagons, and a few hundred prisoners. "The Army of Silesia had never fought with more courage or success," noted the French émigré; "the indebtedness that I had that day to the generals and troops under my command attracted Blücher's attention; he informed them of his satisfaction and gave an account to the tsar and the king of Prussia of the success of the day, in adding that he was indebted to me for a great part of his glory."[101]

In his memoirs, Marmont claims to have lost 6,000 to 7,000 men and 27 guns but these figures are probably too low.[102] In his report to Berthier, the marshal made special mention of Lagrange, "who fought a lot at the beginning of the action" and the commander of Friederichs's 1st Brigade, Coëhorn, "who supported all the efforts [to stop] the enemy at the end of the day." French wounded included Marmont himself, Compans, and Friederichs. "We have suffered great losses," reported Marmont, "but those of the enemy are huge." In his after-action report, the marshal claimed that VI Corps had taken 10,000 prisoners but this figure appears highly excessive and is not repeated in his memoirs. There he noted:

> In this battle, the whole of Yorck's corps, 22,000 men strong, was engaged, and almost all general or senior officers were killed or wounded as they had to pay in person to hold their troops together and to maintain their positions against the fury of our attacks or the energy of our defense. Langeron's corps was only partially engaged. Our battlefield was the bloodiest on this memorable day, the place where the action was the strongest. I have heard from various Prussian officers, among them, Goltz, adjutant-general sent by the king of Prussia to serve with Blücher ... that after the evacuation of Leipzig the Allied sovereigns, visiting all the battlefields, were struck by the appearance of it, the number of dead, and especially the proximity of the dead of the two armies.[103]

Although a victory, Möckern does not rank among the shining moments of the Silesian Army's leadership.[104] Certainly Bernadotte's participation could have magnified the results of the day but Blücher's restraint also contributed to prolonging the struggle and the suffering of Yorck's men.[105] Rather than the boldness that characterized his operations up to that point of the campaign, he and his staff demonstrated indecision and even paralysis. Blücher's lackluster role in the battle becomes even more puzzling due to the lack of contemporary and historical commentary. With few exceptions, neither the men who participated nor their great biographers discuss his underperformance, let alone pass judgment.[106]

For most of the engagement, Blücher (and apparently his staff as well) feared a flank attack by large imperial forces debouching from the plateau of Hohenossig. Like Schwarzenberg during the night of 14/15 October, Blücher possessed no clear idea where Napoleon stood. Unlike Schwarzenberg, Blücher did not have the benefit of hearing thousands of throats proclaim Napoleon's arrival at Leipzig on the 15th with wild shouts of "*Vive l'Empereur!*" As noted, Blücher learned on the morning of 15 October that his patrols had found strong columns marching from Bad Düben to Leipzig. Witte reported that the Imperial Guard as well as a huge artillery train had reached Leipzig on the 14th; prisoners stated that the French army expected to deliver a great battle. Rudzevich's 8:45 A.M. report on the 15th stated his belief that Napoleon's entire army had concentrated between Leipzig and

Taucha on the 14th. He speculated that, unless Napoleon planned to take the defensive, Blücher should expect the French emperor to attack toward Merseburg or even Halle on the 16th. On the morning of the 16th, Rudzevich reported that, as of the previous night, imperial forces still occupied Bad Düben and that his patrols had found a camp at Krostitz on the Bad Düben–Leipzig road.

Blücher, the hussar general, had 15,000 cavalry troopers at his disposal on the 16th. Although Yorck's horse delivered the *coup de grâce* at the end of the battle, neither they nor the Russian cavalry did much at the beginning of the struggle. Blücher hardly sought to exploit the numerical superiority this arm enjoyed over Marmont. Instead of attempting to envelop the enemy's right, which in turn would have provided a view of what if anything stood behind Marmont, he allowed it to remain inactive before the imperial position at Lindenthal. Because Emmanuel's cavalry remained with Rudzevich, Blücher did not receive Korf's precise report that no French forces could be found on the road to Bad Düben until 5:00. Thus, only at this time, when they could no longer influence the battle, did Blücher commit Sacken and St.-Priest.

Blücher obviously thought that the fighting south of Leipzig marked Schwarzenberg's assault on Murat's army and that Napoleon still remained somewhere between Bad Düben and Leipzig with the Grande Armée.[107] Despite the threat presumably posed by Napoleon, the measures taken by Blücher to secure his left wing are baffling. To defend his left against French forces supposedly approaching from the Mulde, he sacrificed his reserve by holding back Sacken's corps some four miles west of the battlefield rather than moving it northeast. Moreover, he also halted St.-Priest's infantry, which in turn retarded the deployment of Langeron's corps. Merely stopping St.-Priest and Sacken in their tracks did little to defend Blücher's left. Not until 2:00 did he send a sizeable cavalry force – Langeron's Reserve Cavalry under Korf – to Podelwitz.

More critically, the retreat of Marmont's van southeast to Lindenthal rather than northeast toward Hohenossig revealed Blücher's faulty assumption. Recognition of Marmont's position on the Eutritzsch–Möckern line and the sustained intensity of the guns in the Wachau sector both provided strong proof that Napoleon's main force stood south of Leipzig. Based on this evidence, Blücher should have concluded that only small detachments remained on the Bad Düben–Leipzig highway. If further concern over his left flank still troubled him, he could have echeloned Sacken and St.-Priest behind Langeron's left wing, sending Sacken's entire cavalry toward Hohenossig for security. This would have allowed the Silesian Army to wage a uniform battle. With his left thus secured, Langeron could have concentrated his superior numbers against Dąbrowski. After driving the Poles across the Parthe, he could have left their pursuit to his cavalry while his infantry wheeled south to attack Marmont's right flank. Instead of holding back Horn and Hünerbein until the Wiederitzsch villages had fallen, Yorck could have advanced in echelon from the left wing. Langeron's attack combined with the advance of Yorck's left would have driven Marmont against the Elster unless he quickly withdrew across the Rietschke stream. Had Sacken's cavalry been sent toward Hohenossig, it could have reported the approach of Delmas's division as well as the news that no further enemy troops could be found on the road from Bad Düben. In view of the task that Delmas had taken on – protecting III Corps's trains – Sacken's cavalry alone would have sufficed to either halt his advance or force him to retreat across the Parthe. Blücher could have then pushed the infantry belonging to Sacken and St.-Priest into the angle between the Parthe and Rietschke in case Marmont attempted to make a stand between Gohlis, Eutritzsch, and Schönefeld.

By simply halting Sacken, Yorck and Langeron became mired in two widely separated and generally mutually exclusive engagements. Unable to influence the course of the other's combat, both fought without support, which required the Prussians to sustain horrendous losses to attain their objective. In this case, the fixation of the army's leadership on Hohenossig rather than the situation at hand again led to an oversight that contributed to the slaughter of Yorck's men. Instead of wheeling southeast after taking Lindenthal and directing his attack on the strongest point of Marmont's position, Yorck should have advanced in unison with Langeron's corps to ensure mutual support and a uniform battle. By fixing Marmont's left at Möckern with Hiller's brigade-size vanguard, Yorck could have punched through Marmont's center and right while Langeron – with Sacken and St.-Priest echeloned behind his left wing – crushed the Poles. Success would have forced the French to evacuate Möckern without a struggle to avoid being cut off from Leipzig or driven into the Elster. Blücher and his staff should have provided Yorck with instructions, because the corps commander did not have the necessary overview of the battle to make such a decision. Rather than requesting orders, the man of Tauroggen decided to take the bull by the horns. While blame for the lack of coordination between the two corps should be placed on the army's leadership, Yorck can be faulted for his execution of the battle. In holding back his left wing per Blücher's order, he also should have delayed Hiller's attack on Möckern. By refusing his left and attacking with his right, Yorck allowed Marmont to achieve mass on his own left wing. Yorck then fed his men into the sausage grinder. Bogdanovich is very critical of Yorck for not following Blücher's plan: "The weakest point of this [Marmont's] position was without doubt its right wing, on which Blücher personally led the attack; Yorck should have supported Langeron's corps."[108]

French success on Napoleon's right and center counterbalanced Allied gains on his left, mainly Blücher's victory over Marmont at Möckern. Around 4:00, Macdonald started to roll up Wittgenstein's right: II Cavalry Corps and 35th Division took Kleinpösna; 31st Division prepared to attack Seifertshain; and 36th Division turned west against the Niederholz. By 5:00, the French held Seifertshain and had driven the Austrians from the Niederholz. Yet, as darkness fell, the imperials ran out of steam. After failing to eject the Prussians from Großpösna, Macdonald's 36th Division returned to the Niederholz; 35th Division withdrew from Kleinpösna to Fuchshain; and 31st Division receded to the Kolm hill. By nightfall, the French again held the Connewitz–Wachau–Liebertwolkwitz line from where they started the battle.[109]

Ultimately, Napoleon lost the battle of Leipzig on 16 October. His own miscalculation coupled with Blücher's commitment to battle and Gyulay's appearance at Lindenau cost the emperor dearly. David Chandler asserts that the arrival of either VI, IV, or III Corps "would almost certainly have led to victory" in the Wachau sector.[110] Napoleon's instructions to Ney on the morning of the 16th strongly indicate that he did not believe the Silesian Army would advance on Leipzig from the direction of Halle. Ney's orders, arriving via Berthier's office, stem from Napoleon's directives to the major-general: a letter that was not included in the nineteenth-century publication of Napoleon's correspondence. According to Berthier's dispatch, Ney, having under his command VI, IV, and III Corps as well as the three divisions of III Cavalry Corps, should remain close to Leipzig throughout the 16th. "*If this morning we have no glimpse of an army debouching from Halle, as there is ample evidence that no one has seen anything*, the duc de Raguse [Marmont] will cross the Leipzig bridge and be ready to enter the battle between Leipzig and Liebertwolkwitz with his three divisions in echelons," explained Napoleon. General Jean-Thomas Lorge's 5th Light Cavalry Division would conduct reconnaissance toward Halle on the high-way from Leipzig. The cavalry divisions of Defrance and Fournier would "patrol all roads." Napoleon also instructed Ney to send German-speaking soldiers disguised as peasants toward Halle to collect intelligence. "If one sees the enemy infantry in the direction of Halle and Landsberg, he must attack strongly and try to take prisoners in order to obtain news. The prince de la Moskova [Ney] will send patrols to Taucha and to Eilenburg."[111]

Some historians attribute the emperor's mistake to the rumor spread by St.-Priest concerning the march of the entire Silesian Army to Lindenau.[112] In fact, Napoleon's certainty that Blücher actually stood on the *western* (left) bank of the Saale is reiterated in Ney's orders to Marmont, Bertrand, and Souham: "All reports claim that the enemy is in position on the left bank of the Saale between Halle and Merseburg." Consequently, Ney, who had reached imperial headquarters at Reudnitz early that morning, sent instructions directing VI Corps to Liebertwolkwitz while Souham's III Corps assumed Marmont's former position between Lindenthal and Breitenfeld. Yet Ney incorrectly assumed that III Corps had already arrived from Bad Düben.[113] With the exception of Delmas's 9th Division, III Corps marched only ten miles southwest from Bad Düben to Hohenroda on 15 October. Reaching Hohenroda at 12:00 A.M. on 16 October, Souham granted his men three hours of rest. Meanwhile, 9th Division bivouacked at Bad Düben during the night of 15/16 October. At 3:00 A.M. on the 16th, III Corps continued its march with 11th Division leading followed by the artillery and 8th Division; cavalry covered the corps's right flank by scouring the region between the Leipzig–Bad Düben and Leipzig–Delitzsch roads. Having to first march ten miles meant that the head of 11th Division could reach the outskirts of Mockau sometime after 11:30 A.M.[114] It would then have to cross the Parthe and march eight additional miles to reach Liebertwolkwitz. Thus denied his Regular Reserve and forced by Wittgenstein's attack to bolster the line with his Grand Reserve, Napoleon experienced the same difficulties as did many of the marshals who failed him at independent command: insufficient reserves. Having a Regular Reserve would have allowed him to support weak sectors along his own line while making diversions to weaken points along his enemy's front, which in turn would have provided the opportunity for the Grand Reserve to punch through and shatter Allied cohesion. This simple formula, which had brought Napoleon so much success in the past, broke down thanks to Prussian impetuosity.

Notes

1 Unger, *Blücher*, II:109. For an excellent description of the terrain around Leipzig, see Petre, *Napoleon's Last Campaign*, 324–26.

2 Droysen, *Yorck*, II:211.

3 This figure includes Marmont's VI Corps (20,000 men) and Lorge's 5th Light Cavalry Division (1,500 men) of III Cavalry Corps between Breitenfeld and Radefeld; Bertrand's IV Corps (14,000 men) at Eutritzsch with Ney's headquarters as well as at Groß- and Kleinwiederitzsch and Seehausen; Souham with 8th and 11th Divisions (12,000 men) of III Corps and Defrance's 4th Heavy Cavalry Division (1,500 men) of III Cavalry Corps at Mockau; Dąbrowski's 27th Division (3,000 men) and Fournier's 6th Light Cavalry Division (1,200 men) of III Cavalry Corps along the Parthe close to Mockau. Leipzig's garrison and depot consisted of 3,500 and 2,250 men respectively. The 4,000 men of 9th Division of III Corps were en route from Bad Düben. See Pelet, *Des principales opérations de la campagne de 1813*, 231.

4 Later in the day, Napoleon endorsed Ney's decision by ordering Bertrand to hold the Lindenau sector to the last man.

5 SHAT, C² 157: Ney to Berthier, 17 October 1813; Pelet, *Des principales opérations de la campagne de 1813*, 235, 238, 242; Höpfner, "Darstellung," 1847:94; Ney to Napoleon, Eutritzsch, 10:30 A.M., 16 October 1813, in Pelet, *Des principales opérations de la campagne de 1813*, 238.

6 Fabry, ed., *Journal des opérations du IIIe Corps*, 83–84. General Pelet claims that "long after, when the battle against Blücher was engaged, Marshal Ney made Souham's [Brayer's] and Ricard's divisions of III Corps march. But instead of directing them to Liebertwolkwitz, he moved them to Schönefeld where they remained at his disposal and covered the parks. They passed part of the afternoon near the mill, sometimes summoned by the emperor, other times called by the marshal, whom Blücher strongly pressed. Thus, they found themselves almost completely detached from the events of the day": Pelet, *Des principales opérations de la campagne de 1813*, 242. In *Histoire de la guerre*, I:209, Vaudoncourt claims that "this movement was most unfortunate in that these divisions wasted the day in marches and countermarches." Although Aster's chronology is wrong regarding the time of departure of the two divisions of III Corps, he makes an interesting point: "Because a significant number of troops (apparently) had remained inactive, the actions of these two divisions [8th and 11th of III Corps] on the 16th have been blamed on various factors. But to what extent this complaint is justified can be difficult to determine. Also, their actions were not absolutely caused by Marshal Ney ... Ney was not the commander who led the troops on a useless march when they were necessary for winning a battle. Instead, it is important to observe here that Napoleon, standing in the background, was in a bad situation and even needed reinforcements, and so gave the orders. The escort of the large parks at Schönefeld required troops; thus these two divisions initially were directed there before Delmas's division from III Corps arrived, whereupon the first two, after they had taken Groß- and Kleinwiederitzsch, departed for Liebertwolkwitz and Dösen and therefore had to put a five-hour march behind them. That all such changes of troop masses are not so quick and easy to perform as that of an individual and that they require more time are obvious; therefore, the criticism expressed over this is unjust. Considering how Napoleon left Vandamme to his fate at Kulm, it is quite possible that here he acted the same and withdrew the troop masses he had earlier promised Marmont": Aster, *Leipzig*, I:504–05. Yorck von Wartenburg affirms that Ney sent these two divisions through Schönefeld to Napoleon but after receiving "more accurate information regarding the danger that threatened Marmont," the emperor returned both divisions to this marshal "but they did not arrive in time to take their part in the fighting": Yorck von Wartenburg, *Napoleon as a General*, II:349.

7 Fain, *1813*, II:404.

8 Friederich, *Herbstfeldzug 1813*, III:18–20. Maude explains that Wittgenstein distributed Russian divisions and Prussian brigades, even regiments, with "no system at all": Maude, *Leipzig Campaign*, 254–55.

9 This number breaks down to 16,120 infantry, 3,101 cavalry, and 1,610 gunners arranged in 34.75 battalions, 43 squadrons, and 104 cannon in 13 batteries. In the heat of battle, Yorck failed to utilize all his artillery. Of his 104 guns, only 88 came into action and 2 entire batteries remained in reserve until the end of the battle. From the 88 guns that came into action, the Prussians fired 2,477 cannonballs, 546 canisters, and 316 shells. See Höpfner, "Darstellung," 1847:108.

10 Langeron's units consisted of 33 battalions, 24 squadrons, 2 Cossack regiments, and 110 guns. Shcherbatov's VI Infantry Corps from Langeron's army corps still had not rejoined the army.

11 Sacken's corps contained 8,931 infantry and gunners, 2,986 regular cavalry, and some 2,000 Cossacks: Höpfner, "Darstellung," 1847:95.

12 In *Die Feldzüge*, 77, Müffling states that Blücher *believed* all French forces had already reached Leipzig from Bad Düben but could not be certain.

13 Lieven, *Russia Against Napoleon*, 442.

14 Rudzevich to Blücher is in Höpfner, "Darstellung," 1847:92; Friederich, *Herbstfeldzug 1813*, III:82; Steffens, *Adventures*, 118; "Operations of the Army of Silesia in the Battles Before Leipzig," Lowe, 20 October 1813, Add MSS, 20111, 163.

15 Friederich, *Herbstfeldzug 1813*, III:82, 111. Friederich maintains that these reports warranted Blücher's caution: "And, indeed, had Reynier not in the last moment decided to take the detour through Eilenburg, not merely the 4,000 men of Delmas's division but instead a total of 17,000 men could have appeared in the left flank of the Silesian Army. Under these circumstances a prudent view of the situation appears completely understandable, even justifiable, in the early hours of the 16th."

16 Lowe explained that on the 16th, "simultaneously" with "Blücher's discovery of the enemy's position, information arrived that the Prince Royal had changed the disposition adopted for his army on the preceding day, having given directions for its proceeding [southwest] by the way of Gröbzig and Wettin to Halle instead of directing its march [southeast] in a straight line by Zörbig toward Leipzig. At the same time a continued fire of artillery with clouds of smoke, to the right and on the opposite side of the town of Leipzig, announced that the engagement had already commenced between the Allied Armies and the enemy in that direction": "Operations of the Army of Silesia in the Battles Before Leipzig," Lowe, 20 October 1813, Add MSS, 20111, 163. Lowe added in his report to Bunbury that, had Bernadotte "moved on Zörbig during the 15th," the Army of North Germany "would have been at hand to support the Army of Silesia": Lowe to Bunbury, Leipzig, 20 October 1813, Add MSS, 20111, 177.

17 Stewart comments on this situation twice in his *Narrative*. First, he notes that "hopes were entertained, which proved fallacious, that the cavalry and flying artillery of the Prince Royal's army would be in line." "A direct march on … Radefeld, would, without question, have brought the Army of North Germany into action on the 16th, which would have rendered the victory much more decisive." Second, he claimed that "the Prince Royal, however, assured me that in case General Blücher should make an attack the following day, I might give the General his word that he would be on the ground in the direction of Delitzsch and Eilenburg with 8,000 or 10,000 cavalry and light artillery to support him, even if his infantry could not arrive. This pledge I stated *totidem verbis* to General Blücher when I joined him": Stewart, *Narrative*, 155–56, 162.

18 Stewart, *Narrative*, 162; Friederich, *Herbstfeldzug 1813*, III:82–83; Quistorp, *Geschichte der Nord-Armee*, II:210; "Journal de Langeron," Add MSS, 20112, 273.

19 "Operations of the Army of Silesia in the Battles Before Leipzig," Lowe, 20 October 1813, Add MSS, 20111, 164; Langeron to Blücher is in Höpfner, "Darstellung," 1847:93; Müffling, *Die Feldzüge*, 78–79.

20 Blücher's disposition is in Höpfner, "Darstellung," 1847:93. See also Lowe to Bunbury, Leipzig, 20 October 1813, Add MSS, 20111, 178.

21 Quoted in Blasendorff, *Blücher*, 229; Unger, *Blücher*, II:113; Müffling, *Die Feldzüge*, 80.

22 "Operations of the Army of Silesia in the Battles Before Leipzig," Lowe, 20 October 1813, Add MSS, 20111, 164; Stewart to Charles John, 9:15 A.M., 16 October 1813, in Stewart, *Narrative*, 162–63. In his defense of Bernadotte, Swederus attempts to discredit Stewart. "One finds nothing but contradictions in the behavior of the subordinate Allies toward the commander of the North German Army. Stewart says that he had delivered the prince's promise that cavalry and light artillery would come to Blücher's aid, even if the infantry could not arrive as quickly. Now, in Blücher's name, Stewart asked in writing if the prince would have the North German Army 'go to Delitzsch on the left wing' so that the prince would have the opportunity to participate in the fighting, which through this would be decisive. This supposedly occurred by 9:45 on the morning of the 16th. Now the prince, if he had received Stewart's letter while on the march from the area of Sylbitz, and had he deemed it appropriate, could have complied with Blücher's wishes but under no circumstances could he have reached Delitzsch with the troops before evening and then nothing more could be done. So it was not surprising that (according to Stewart's own report) the prince replied: 'One would be a fool to follow his words.'" Moreover, Swederus incorrectly claims that in his letter Stewart guaranteed the security of Bernadotte's march to Delitzsch by assuring the crown prince that all the bridges over the Mulde were down. On the contrary, Stewart makes no mention of bridges in his letter. Swederus also questions the feasibility of the demands made on the crown prince: "Why should Blücher write letters to him [the crown prince] or have to send Stewart to verbally persuade him to do what he had promised? Also, the fulfillment of the promise could not be accomplished before the 17th." In the end, Swederus resorts to character assassination: "on every occasion, Stewart showed himself to be unreliable in the highest degree; also he certainly would not mention here that others would not rely on him." See Swederus, *Schwedens Politik und Kriege*, II:314–15.

23 SHAT, C² 157: Marmont to Berthier, 19 October 1813; Pelet, *Des principales opérations de la campagne de 1813*, 238; Weil, *Campagne de 1813*, 239; Höpfner, "Darstellung," 1847:89; Marmont, *Mémoires*, V:281–82.

24 Marmont, *Mémoires*, V:282; SHAT, C² 157: Marmont to Berthier, 19 October 1813. Weil laments that, "although the day before he had reported the march and approach of the Silesian Army to headquarters, Marmont nevertheless received on the morning of the 16th the order to cross through Leipzig and arrive to serve as the reserve to the Grande Armée": Weil, *Campagne de 1813*, 239. Yet Pelet is critical of Marmont, suggesting that with quicker action and economy of force on his part, VI Corps still could have supported Napoleon in the Wachau sector: "But it seems that the retreat of VI Corps could have started before 9:00; if it had, VI Corps could have been near Liebertwolkwitz before noon; and if it had operated with a rearguard masking Blücher, he would not have been able to reach Gohlis before 3:00 P.M." According to this line of thought, Napoleon already

would have secured his victory over Schwarzenberg and Blücher's presence north of the city would have meant little: Pelet, *Des principales opérations de la campagne de 1813*, 239.

25 SHAT, C² 157: Marmont to Berthier, 19 October 1813; Marmont, *Mémoires*, V:282–83.

26 Marmont, *Mémoires*, V:283; SHAT, C² 157: Marmont to Berthier, 19 October 1813. Commandant Weil adds that Marmont's position between Möckern and Eutritzsch was "more favorable and stronger" than the one he had quit at Lindenthal and that the marshal could hope to maintain it as long as he received support from III Corps. "It was, in fact, impossible for him to expect that only one of the divisions of the corps (Delmas) would be able to take part in the battle": Weil, *Campagne de 1813*, 239. On the other hand, Pelet claims that Marmont had the "disastrous idea to accept battle on the bare plain that extends from Wiederitzsch to Möckern instead of retiring behind the valley of the Rietschke": Pelet, *Des principales opérations de la campagne de 1813*, 238.

27 Altogether, Dąbrowski's division of 4 battalions, 8 squadrons, and 8 guns totaled 2,500 men. Combined, Fournier's division and Avice's brigade at most provided 1,200 troopers.

28 SHAT, C² 157: Marmont to Berthier, 19 October 1813; Unger, *Blücher*, II:110.

29 Marmont, *Mémoires*, V:283–84. Marmont's VI Corps consisted of many recently formed units that did not see much action during the Fall Campaign. Jean-Dominique Compans's 20th Division contained two Marine Regiments (1st and 3rd), 32nd Light Infantry Regiment (two battalions), and two provisional Line regiments (20th and 25th). The 20th Provisional Line consisted only of the 5th Battalion of the 66th Line and the 3rd Battalion of the 122nd Line while the 25th consisted of the 3rd Battalions of the 47th and 86th Line Regiments. Joseph Lagrange's 21st Division comprised the four battalions of the 37th Light Infantry Regiment, the sole battalion of the Spanish Joseph Napoleon Regiment, three battalions of the 4th Marine Regiment, and the six battalions of the 2nd Marine Regiment. Jean-Parfait Friederichs's 22nd Division contained the two battalions (4th Battalion of the 1st Line and 2nd Battalion of the 62nd Line) of the 11th Provisional Line Regiment, the two battalions (3rd Battalion of the 14th Line and 4th Battalion of the 16th Line) of the 13th Provisional Line, two battalions of the 23rd Light Infantry Regiment, two battalions of the 15th Line, the two battalions (6th Battalion of the 26th Line and 6th Battalion of the 82nd Line) of the 16th Provisional Line, two battalions of the 121st Line, and two battalions of the 70th Line. Marmont's cavalry consisted of Normann's 2nd and 4th Regiments of Württemberger light cavalry each containing four squadrons.

30 For an excellent description of the advantages the Liebertwolkwitz ridge afforded Napoleon, see Lieven, *Russia Against Napoleon*, 438.

31 "Journal de Langeron," Add MSS, 20112, 269; Müffling, *Die Feldzüge*, 80; Höpfner, "Darstellung," 1847:95.

32 Blücher ordered Langeron to send troops both through and around Lindenthal but this did not occur. It is likely that Blücher observed Yorck's advance on Lindenthal and redirected Langeron to Breitenfeld.

33 Quoted in Droysen, *Yorck*, II:213. The Count of Brandenburg (1792–1850) was the illegitimate son of King Frederick William II of Prussia and Countess Sophia Dönhoff, his morganatic second wife.

34 Höpfner, "Darstellung," 1847:95. On the day of Möckern, Yorck's vanguard contained eight squadrons, eight and three-quarters battalions, and one battery each of foot and horse artillery. Katzler's cavalry included the 2nd Leib Hussar Regiment (two squadrons), the Brandenburg Hussar Regiment (three squadrons), the Brandenburg Uhlan Regiment (four squadrons), the 5th Silesian Landwehr Cavalry Regiment (four squadrons) and Horse Battery Nr. 2. Hiller's infantry consisted of eight and three-quarters battalions: two companies of East Prussian Jäger, one company of Guard Jäger, the Leib Grenadier Battalion, the West Prussian Grenadier Battalion, the 1st Battalion of the Brandenburg Infantry Regiment, the 1st Battalion of the 12th Reserve Infantry Regiment, the Fusilier Battalion of the 2nd East Prussian Infantry Regiment, the 4th Battalion of the 15th Silesian Landwehr Regiment, the 3rd Battalion of the 13th Silesian Landwehr Regiment, the 2nd Battalion of the 14th Silesian Landwehr Regiment and the Nr. 12 Foot Battery. Incidentally, this large allotment for the vanguard considerably weakened Yorck's 2nd and 8th Brigades, leaving Karl and Hünerbein with five battalions each: Wagner, *Plane der Schlachten*, II:96.

35 Henckel von Donnersmarck, *Erinnerungen*, 227.

36 Stewart, *Narrative*, 156; Marmont, *Mémoires*, V:282.

37 As noted, Langeron rerouted his troops to march southeast from Radefeld to Breitenfeld rather than south from Radefeld to Lindenthal per Blücher's orders: Bogdanovich, *Geschichte des Krieges*, IIb:150.

38 Marmont, *Mémoires*, V:282.

39 Gneisenau issued verbal orders for Langeron's cavalry to move to the left wing and for Sacken's to fill the gap between Langeron and Yorck. The adjutant who delivered the orders incorrectly stated to Sacken that *all* cavalry should move to the left wing.

40 Quoted in Droysen, *Yorck*, II:214.

41 At the beginning of the battle, Yorck's Heavy Battery Nr. 1, the mortars assigned to both heavy batteries, and 7th Brigade's Nr. 3 Battery of six-pound guns, all protected by four squadrons from the 1st Neumark and 10th Silesian Landwehr Regiments, opened fire on what appeared to be an enemy rearguard on the hills north of Möckern. Shortly after, Heavy Battery Nr. 2 unlimbered to the right of its sister battery, next to it stood 1st Brigade's Nr. 2 Battery of six-pound guns. After the Nr. 3 Battery rejoined 7th Brigade, the Nr. 1 and 3 Horse Batteries unlimbered to the left of Heavy Battery Nr. 1 with 8th Brigade's Nr. 15 Battery anchoring the left of the artillery line. Most of the smaller mortars were left in the rear: Wagner, *Plane der Schlachten*, II:84.

42 Friederich, *Herbstfeldzug 1813*, III:87.

43 Bordessoulle's 1st Heavy Division contained three brigades, the third being all Saxons including the cuirassiers of the Royal Guard.

44 It is not known why Yorck did not send a small detachment with some artillery across the bridge at Wahren to operate on the left bank of the Elster against the flank of the French skirmishers and artillery posted in and around Möckern.

45 Quoted in Droysen, *Yorck*, II:216–17.

46 Marmont, *Mémoires*, V:284.

47 Quoted in Droysen, *Yorck*, II:217–18.

48 SHAT, C² 157: Marmont to Berthier, 19 October 1813.

49 Quoted in Blasendorff, *Blücher*, 230.

50 Quoted in Droysen, *Yorck*, II:218.

51 SHAT, C² 157: Marmont to Berthier, 19 October 1813.

52 Quoted in Droysen, *Yorck*, II:219.

53 Marmont, *Mémoires*, V:286.

54 Some accounts claim that Marmont was wounded by the blast. In his after-action report, he states that "I was wounded and my uniform riddled; everyone around me was killed or struck down": SHAT, C² 157: Marmont to Berthier, 19 October 1813. However, in his memoirs he states that "wounded in the left hand by a ball while leading the 20th and 25th Regiments to the charge, I finally left the battlefield. I was not bandaged until 10:00 P.M.": Marmont, *Mémoires*, V:287. Weil also implies that Marmont was indeed wounded by the blast: Weil, *Campagne de 1813*, 241.

55 SHAT, C² 157: Marmont to Berthier, 19 October 1813.

56 Henckel von Donnersmarck, *Erinnerungen*, 228.

57 Olsufiyev's other division, the 15th, provided the infantry for Rudzevich's vanguard.

58 "Journal de Langeron," Add MSS, 20112, 270–71.

59 Lowe, Stewart, and Langeron incorrectly attribute this turn to the arrival of considerable reinforcements from Leipzig led by Napoleon himself. Lowe notes that "another corps had moved forward on his [Langeron's] right and regained possession of the village of Großwiederitzsch. And after the victory had declared in his favor on all sides, General Blücher had the gratification to learn that Napoleon, alarmed at the rapid strides which the Silesian Army was making toward Leipzig, had himself come to the ground in front of Langeron's line of attack and arrived just in time to witness the defeat of his troops and capture of his artillery." In his report to Bunbury, Lowe puts Napoleon's arrival at 5:00 P.M. According to Stewart, "Sacken's corps, which supported General Langeron, very much distinguished itself in the presence of Napoleon, who, it seems (according to the information of prisoners), had arrived from the other wing of his army at 5:00 in the evening." Langeron's journal states: "according to reports from prisoners, the emperor Napoleon himself had come to direct the attacks." He corrects this in his published memoirs: "The quantity of troops that advanced on me at that moment, in enormous, tightly packed columns, at first made me believe that it was Napoleon, and that he had disengaged from the Grand Army [of Bohemia] to fall on us but we later learned that he had remained to the right [southeast] of Leipzig, and had detached some corps against us which would have been necessary for him to use to follow up the success he initially had against the Grand Army [of Bohemia], to whom our brilliant and audacious maneuver was most helpful." Napoleon did not appear in this sector of the battlefield and it is very doubtful that reinforcements had arrived from Leipzig because no French troops were available to come to Dąbrowski's aid. In addition, Marmont makes

no mention of the arrival of reinforcements. More likely, Emmanuel had faced only a detachment of Dąbrowski's cavalry at Großwiederitzsch while the main body of this cavalry as well as possibly also Avize's brigade still stood at Eutritzsch or had just arrived. See "Operations of the Army of Silesia in the Battles Before Leipzig," Lowe, 20 October 1813, Add MSS, 20111, 165–66; Lowe to Bunbury, Leipzig, 20 October 1813, *ibid.*, 180; "Journal de Langeron," Add MSS, 20112, 271; Langeron, *Mémoires*, 314; Stewart, *Narrative*, 157; Friederich, *Herbstfeldzug 1813*, III:63.

60 Langeron, *Mémoires*, 314–15.

61 Langeron, *Mémoires*, 315–16.

62 The 9th Division departed from Bad Düben at 4:00 A.M. to unite with the rest of III Corps. Although the park and reserve were ahead of it, bad roads slowed their progress along with fear that the ordinary escort did not suffice to protect the convoy from prowling Cossacks. As a result, 9th Division caught up with the trains and Delmas decided to escort the convoy. See Fabry, ed., *Journal des opérations du IIIe Corps*, 85.

63 "Journal de Langeron," Add MSS, 20112, 271–72. "It is completely inexplicable," judges Friederich, "how the Russians, with the superiority in numbers that they enjoyed, fought such a seesaw and prolonged battle and how it was even possible for the Russians to have been thrown back on the defensive for a while. Most accounts seek to explain this wonderful fact by claiming that a division from Souham's corps had arrived to help, an explanation whose incorrectness has been proven with certainty. No doubt, the error that the long wagon train of the III Corps caused Langeron to make contributed much to his uncertain behavior; a mistake that would have been easily avoided with proper use of his numerous cavalry": Friederich, *Herbstfeldzug 1813*, III:114. Indeed, some accounts such as Wagner, *Plane der Schlachten*, II:92–93, incorrectly state that a second division from III Corps – Souham's 8th – supported Delmas, but this mistake can also be traced to the errors in reporting by Lowe and Langeron. Lowe wrote: "General Count Langeron still pursued his advantages and even made preparation for crossing the stream of the Parthe when a strong body of the enemy's infantry consisting of about 8,000 or 10,000 men was observed approaching on his left flank, commanded as it was afterwards appeared by Marshal Ney and coming from the direction of Eilenburg." See "Operations of the Army of Silesia in the Battles Before Leipzig," Lowe, 20 October 1813, Add MSS, 20111, 165. Neither Vaudoncourt nor Weil makes this mistake. Bogdanovich's account has a slight twist. The Russian General Staff historian states that at 3:00 Dąbrowski and Delmas, whose division escorted the trains on the road from Bad Düben, attacked the Russians, took both Wiederitzsch villages, and drove Langeron's men across the Rietschke. "At the same time, there appeared on the road from Bad Düben, near Hohenossig, a large column. The enemy column observed on the road from Bad Düben consisted of the parks and trains of the French III Corps, which was moving with a small escort to unite with the army. Langeron did not know this and believed he had to reinforce his wing; thus he could not assist Yorck, and Kaptsevich became separated from St.-Priest": Bogdanovich, *Geschichte des Krieges*, IIb:158.

64 Langeron cites the twelve battalions of the 7th, 12th, 22nd, 30th, and 48th Jäger Regiments as well as the Olonetskii and Shlisselburgskii Infantry Regiments supported by Emmanuel's cavalry as participating in the advance that he and Rudzevich led. The 30th and 48th Jäger formed a brigade belonging to the 17th Division of St.-Priest's infantry corps. Langeron does not explain how this brigade came to fight alongside his corps on this day: "Journal de Langeron," Add MSS, 20112, 272.

65 "Operations of the Army of Silesia in the Battles Before Leipzig," Lowe, 20 October 1813, Add MSS, 20111, 165.

66 Unfortunately, the journal of III Corps contains few accurate facts about these events: Fabry, ed., *Journal des opérations du IIIe Corps*, 85.

67 Lowe to Bunbury, Leipzig, 20 October 1813, Add MSS, 20111, 180.

68 According to Swederus, "Stewart did not find the prince at Sylbitz. The head-quarters of the North German Army was moved four times that day; first it was at Sylbitz, then Marschwitz, later at Hohenthurm, and finally at Rensdorf by Landsberg, thus the four locations where the prince had signed and dated letters. In deep resentment, Stewart attacked Adlerkreutz with his wishes; to be rid of him, Adlerkreutz referred him to Wintzingerode, who replied that his emperor had made it his duty to strictly obey the crown prince – a response which proves that the disaffected Stewart had made the attempt to persuade Wintzingerode to do the same as the Prussian generals and give himself orders and execute them": Swederus, *Schwedens Politik und Kriege*, 316.

69 Stewart, *Narrative*, 163–65. Stewart concludes this episode by stating: "I think I have said enough to show that, if the Prince had exerted all his faculties, and the mental and physical energy he possessed, the corps of Marmont ... would have been more completely overthrown, and the serious losses of Yorck's corps of Prussians spared, by the timely arrival of the Prince Royal's army." Swederus counters Stewart's portrayal of these events: "Now, had Stewart's journey from Radefeld to Sylbitz (four [twenty-one] miles) at 9:45 A.M. produced a resolution, which, executed for the (incorrectly predicted) struggle of the day, which in reality did not take place, could it have brought about some benefit? Stewart could not have reached Sylbitz before 11:00. If the army had marched according to the desire of the ignorant strategists, it could not cover these four or five miles until very late in the evening and especially considering how bad and rain soaked the roads were at that time." While true to a degree, Swederus's apology fails to take into consideration the crown prince's decisions on the 15th. Moreover, as Schwarzenberg had ordered a general attack on the 16th, how can Swederus claim that the struggle was "incorrectly predicted"? See Swederus, *Schwedens Politik und Kriege*, 316.

70 SHAT, C^{17} 133: Charles John to Wintzingerode, Rensdorf, 16 October 1813. Even in this move, retired Prussian Generalleutnant Barthold von Quistorp, a veteran of the nineteenth-century Prussian wars against Denmark, Austria, and France, found disingenuous activity by Bernadotte. Quistorp states that "relying comfortably" on Wintzingerode's obedience, the crown prince decided to have him personally accompany the cavalry rather than Wintzingerode's "very active" vanguard commander, Vorontsov. It should be noted that, unlike many

nineteenth-century historians, General Quistorp meticulously footnoted his work. His three volumes contain 1,117 endnotes.

71 Nostitz, *Tagebuch*, 68.

72 SHAT, C² 157: Marmont to Berthier, 19 October 1813; Gneisenau to Caroline, Kleinwiederitzsch, 18 October 1813, GStA PK, VI HA Rep. 92 Nl. Gneisenau, Nr. 21.

73 In the order of battle for Yorck's corps, the 5th and 13th Silesian Landwehr Infantry Regiments formed a Landwehr Brigade commanded by Losthin and attached to 1st Brigade. A battalion commander at Jena in 1806, Losthin retreated to Silesia after the defeat to defend the fortress of Glatz. At the head of a newly formed Grenadier Battalion, he fought with distinction and received the *Pour le Mérite* for his actions, albeit three years later. As a lieutenant-colonel in 1809, he received command of the 2nd Silesian Infantry Regiment. Losthin's promotion to colonel came in 1811. In the spring of 1813, he was one of many officers charged with making the Landwehr capable of field service. In the Waterloo Campaign, Losthin commanded the 15th Brigade of Bülow's IV Corps, which consisted mainly of Landwehr. That the Prussian army performed as well as it did in the wars of 1813–1815 was due to officers such as Losthin who labored to make the Landwehr combat-ready. Without the 100,000 men of the Landwehr who participated in the campaigns during these years, Prussia could not have played such a decisive role in Napoleon's defeat.

74 Marmont, *Mémoires*, V:285. It should be noted that Marmont does not mention this incident in his after-action report: SHAT, C² 157: Marmont to Berthier, 19 October 1813.

75 Quoted in Droysen, *Yorck*, II:224.

76 Quoted in Blasendorff, *Blücher*, 231; and in Henckel von Donnersmarck, in *Erinnerungen*, 228.

77 Sohr gave this order to maintain the cohesion of his squadrons and prevent the weakening of their combat power by detaching for prisoner escort. His hussars brought back only one colonel and a few officers as prisoners: Höpfner, "Darstellung," 1847:102.

78 Quoted in Blasendorff, *Blücher*, 231.

79 SHAT, C² 157: Marmont to Berthier, 19 October 1813.

80 In the order of battle for I Corps, the 4th and 15th Silesian Landwehr Infantry Regiments formed a Landwehr Brigade commanded by Colonel Heinrich Wilhelm von Welzien and attached to 7th Brigade. In September, attrition prompted the Prussians to combine the 2nd and 4th Battalions of the 4th Regiment into one. Moreover, the 1st Battalion of the 4th along with the 3rd Battalion of the 15th formed part of the garrison at Wartenburg, meaning the 4th Regiment contained only two battalions on 16 October and, because Wedel's 4th Battalion served with the vanguard at Möckern, the 15th Regiment likewise consisted of two battalions. From the 14th Silesian Landwehr, the 1st and 4th Battalions formed part of the garrison at Wartenburg while Thiele's 2nd Battalion served with the vanguard at Möckern. The 1st Battalion of the Brandenburg Infantry Regiment likewise served with the vanguard on the day of Möckern.

81 Quoted in Blasendorff, *Blücher*, 231.

82 Blasendorff, *Blücher*, 231.

83 Lowe to Bunbury, Leipzig, 20 October 1813, Add MSS, 20111, 179.

84 According to the Journal of the Lithuanian Dragoons: "Our regiment maintained its order while the others had scattered after eight charges." The *Tagebuch des Königlichen Preußischen Ersten Dragoneregiment (Litthauischen) aus den Kriegsjahren 1813 und 1814* is reproduced in an appendix in Henckel von Donnersmarck, *Erinnerungen*, 448.

85 Henckel von Donnersmarck, *Erinnerungen*, 448–49.

86 SHAT, C² 157: Marmont to Berthier, 19 October 1813.

87 Marmont, *Mémoires*, V:285, 287–88.

88 Quoted in Unger, *Blücher*, II:114.

89 "The conduct of the prince (as he was a prince) was constantly very fishy, as I will have occasion to mention again; on the evening of the 16th Blücher wrote him a very strong letter; I addressed him another one, with a bit of irony, that informed him of our success that morning and the desire that he join us to share in what was coming": Langeron, *Mémoires*, 320.

90 Sources for the battle of Möckern: "Operations of the Army of Silesia in the Battles Before Leipzig," Lowe, 20 October 1813, Add MSS, 20111, 163–67; "Journal de Langeron," Add MSS, 20112, 273–74; Müffling, *Die Feldzüge*, 77–85; Höpfner, "Darstellung," 1847:89–111; Bogdanovich, *Geschichte des Krieges*, IIb:147–62; Friederich, *Herbstfeldzug 1813*, III:81–116; Blasendorff, *Blücher*, 228–32; Pflugk, *Das Preußische Landwehrbuch*, 83–91; Varchmin, *Die Völkerschlacht bei Leipzig*, 66–73; Vaudoncourt, *Histoire de la guerre*, I:209–10; Anon., *Précis militaire de la campagne de 1813*, 206, 210–12; Wagner, *Plane*, II:85–92; Droysen, *Yorck*, II:212–19; Weil, *Campagne de 1813*, 239–41; Henckel von Donnersmarck, *Erinnerungen*, 228; Unger, *Blücher*, II:111–14; Pertz and Delbrück, *Gneisenau*, III:455.

91 Quoted in Friederich, *Herbstfeldzug 1813*, III:100.

92 Much like his fellow officers in the Historical Section of the Great German General Staff, Generalmajor Wolfgang von Unger, in *Blücher*, II:114, considered critical evaluation to be more important than nationalistic reporting. He cautions that "naturally one overestimated the results considerably. The 'best French corps,' as Gneisenau put it, which in this campaign up until now had fought only victoriously and consisted of mainly veteran, proven troops, was decisively defeated by some equally strong forces including Landwehr. Moreover, [the Prussians] believed that the Silesian Army had faced two enemy corps, a portion of the French Guard, and one Polish corps. With enthusiasm one celebrated the deeds of the Prussian corps." Yet German historians are not alone in claiming that Marmont commanded some of the best troops in the army at that time. Pelet refers to VI Corps as "elite troops": Pelet, *Des principales opérations de la campagne de 1813*, 231.

93 "Journal de Langeron," Add MSS, 20112, 269–70. "The conduct of the troops, whether it was infantry, cavalry, or artillery, whether it was Line or Landwehr, was beyond praise; the conduct of the officers, from old Yorck down to the most junior lieutenant, will serve as a model for all times of heroic self-sacrifice and devotion to duty": Friederich, *Herbstfeldzug 1813*, III:110.

94 Weil, *Campagne de 1813*, 241–43. Weil also points out that Marmont attributed his defeat to the explosion of the caissons that robbed his heavy guns of precious ammunition as well as the charges of Yorck's cavalry.

95 "Operations of the Army of Silesia in the Battles Before Leipzig," Lowe, 20 October 1813, Add MSS, 20111, 165.

96 Friederich, *Herbstfeldzug 1813*, III:101. In all, Yorck lost 34 officers, 1,009 men, and 161 horses killed; 138 officers, 3,765 men, and 158 horses wounded; and 1 officer, 658 men, and 3 horses missing for a total loss of 173 officers, 5,432 men, and 322 horses. Among the three arms, Yorck lost 139 officers and 5,127 men from the infantry, which equated to 1/3 its manpower; 21 officers and 332 men from the cavalry, or 1/9 its strength; and 2 officers and 73 men from the artillery, or 1/22 of its total. Hiller's vanguard infantry lost 38 officers and 1,146 men while 2nd Brigade sustained the loss of 38 officers and 1,493 men, close to one-half of its effectives. Schleuse's 1st Battalion of the 1st East Prussian Regiment from 2nd Brigade, which King Frederick William commended for its valor at Möckern, lost 1 officer and 128 men killed and 8 officers and 291 men wounded. Four battalions from 8th Brigade each lost over 200 men. See Höpfner, "Darstellung," 1847:107–08.

97 "The loss of one-third of the force employed in this attack attests in a remarkable degree to the high valor and noble patriotism of the Prussian army. Almost the whole of the officers in command ... were wounded. On the side of the Russian army several severe losses were experienced. The total loss of the Allied Russian and Prussian force is stated at between 6,000 and 7,000 men killed and wounded, but the wounds of several being of musketry alone give fair hope of recovery": "Operations of the Army of Silesia in the Battles Before Leipzig," Lowe, 20 October 1813, Add MSS, 20111, 165–66. In his report to Bunbury, Lowe cited Prussian casualties at "perhaps 5,000 men" and Russian losses at "2,000 killed and wounded": Lowe to Bunbury, Leipzig, 20 October 1813, *ibid.*, 179.

98 Nostitz, *Tagebuch*, 68.

99 "Journal de Langeron," Add MSS, 20112, 270.

100 Gneisenau to Caroline, Kleinwiederitzsch, 18 October 1813, GStA PK, VI HA Rep. 92 Nl. Gneisenau, Nr. 21.

101 Langeron, *Mémoires*, 319.

102 Marmont, *Mémoires*, V:287, 289. In *Histoire de la guerre*, I:210, Vaudoncourt claims that VI Corps lost 2,000 men killed, wounded, and captured as well as 10 guns lost. Lowe commented that "the loss of the enemy cannot be rated at less than 10,000 in prisoners, killed, and wounded, the greater part of the latter of whom remained in possession of the Allied army. Their loss in artillery [is] thirty-four pieces and ammunition sufficient to replace all that the Allied troops had expended": "Operations of the Army of Silesia in the Battles Before Leipzig," Lowe, 20 October 1813, Add MSS, 20111, 166.

103 SHAT, C² 157: Marmont to Berthier, 19 October 1813; Marmont, *Mémoires*, V:287–88.

104 Friederich concedes that the victory at Möckern "could have been even greater, even more decisive, even more momentous had not manifold reasons led the leadership of the Silesian Army to a view that we are not accustomed to seeing it have. Regarding the motives for Blücher's conduct, we have no direct reports but instead only poor third-person accounts. The critic of the army's leadership thus encounters great difficulties": Friederich, *Herbstfeldzug 1813*, III:110.

105 "If he [Bernadotte] had been able to join us on the 16th, the results of the battle of this day would have been, perhaps, the same as those on the day of the 18th": Langeron, *Mémoires*, 320. Swederus counters by arguing that blame for the slaughter of Yorck's men rested squarely on Blücher's shoulders. The Swedish historian maintains that because Blücher did not know precisely where the main enemy force stood but speculated that a French retreat would be directed through Hohenossig and toward the Elbe, he should not have overextended his army by pushing it eastward. While Swederus errs in stating that Blücher believed a French retreat would go via Hohenossig to the Elbe when in fact on the 16th he thought the attack would come from Hohenossig, the Swedish historian does make a point worthy of a rebuttal. He asserts that because Blücher feared the arrival of large forces east of the Parthe he should have held his position on the 16th, awaited the great battle, and made the enemy attack him on the 17th. Swederus speculates that one more day would have allowed Blücher to better concentrate his army and "with his 60,000 men he would have been able to quickly drive Marmont back to Leipzig without significant losses." Here Swederus obviously misses completely the important role Blücher played – not to mention the fact the Allied Headquarters ordered a general attack on the 16th. Had Blücher waited twenty-four hours, his attack would have mattered little, for Napoleon would have defeated Schwarzenberg the day before. See Swederus, *Schwedens Politik und Kriege*, 315.

106 Generalmajor Unger is an exception: "Certainly the results could have been greater had Blücher committed his reserves earlier. Had Yorck developed his attack more uniformly he would not have had to commit as many troops to the struggle around the village. Also, the combat by Langeron probably would have proceeded faster. The threat to the left flank by the enemy expected from Bad Düben and by the enemy corps approaching from Eilenburg had kept Sacken and St.-Priest as well as the majority of the cavalry away from the battle for too long. The absence of the Army of North Germany caused understandable caution. A particular desire by Blücher's headquarters to save strong reserves was caused by the thought that Napoleon would break off combat with the Bohemian Army and throw himself on Blücher as soon as he saw his only line of communication through Leipzig to the west seriously threatened. Above all, however, one held it as probable that Napoleon, if he did quit the battle, would take the road to the Elbe where he would unite with strong forces from the fortresses, sever Allied communications, and then go west. We know that Napoleon had initially planned such an undertaking when Blücher and Bernadotte withdrew before him across the Saale." See Unger, *Blücher*, II:115.

107 As noted, the head of intelligence at Bernadotte's headquarters, Kalckreuth, signed his name to a detailed report at 7:00 P.M. on 15 October at Halle stating that spies are "certain that the emperor Napoleon will march on Halle": "News from the Secret Agents," Halle, 7:00 P.M., 15 October 1813, RA KrA, volym 25. Current Swedish archivists maintain that this letter was sent to Blücher but no mention of it is made in the literature.

108 Friederich, *Herbstfeldzug 1813*, III:112–16; Bogdanovich, *Geschichte des Krieges*, IIb:160–61.

109 Yorck von Wartenburg, *Napoleon as a General*, II:350–52.

110 Chandler, *Campaigns of Napoleon*, 932–33.

111 SHAT, C[17] 181: Berthier to Ney, 16 October 1813, emphasis added. Napoleon's letter to Berthier which, per his habit, the latter reiterates almost verbatim in his instructions to Ney, is in Pelet, *Des principales opérations de la campagne de 1813*, 228–29.

112 Höpfner, "Darstellung," 1847:91; Weil, *Campagne de 1813*, 239. Weil asserts that it is likely Napoleon had been misled by false news spread by St.-Priest per Blücher's orders during his march to Günthersdorf that the Army of Silesia stood on the Leipzig–Merseburg road. Bogdanovich, in *Geschichte des Krieges*, IIb:147, also tells this story.

113 Ney ordered Souham to place one brigade west of Stahmeln facing Schkeuditz and Halle and the other brigade "of this division" north of Möckern. "The two other divisions will deploy by brigade at a distance of 100 paces; the artillery on the wings on the line of Lindenthal and Breitenfeld. The light cavalry of III Corps will occupy Radefeld." As for IV Corps, Ney ordered Bertrand to remain in position at Eutritzsch. Regarding the cavalry, Ney wanted Fournier to place his division at Podelwitz on the road to Delitzsch but Defrance's would remain at Mockau, reconnoitering all the bridges over the Parthe from Schönefeld to Taucha. No mention is made of Dąbrowski's division. Ney's orders, dictated to Colonel Louis-Samuel Béchet de Léocourt at Reudnitz, are in Pelet, *Des principales opérations de la campagne de 1813*, 229–30.

114 Fabry, ed., *Journal des opérations du IIIe Corps*, 83.

15

Leipzig

French losses for the 16th neared 25,000 while the Allies lost 30,000: an ominous ratio because Napoleon's reinforcements would increase the Grande Armée only to 200,000 men and 900 guns while the Allies would reach 300,000 men and 1,500 guns with the arrival of the North German and Polish Armies.[1] Although the emperor considered the 16th a victory, he could not predict what the Allies would do next. Would they retreat as they had done after less decisive battles such as Lützen, Bautzen, and Dresden? If they did retreat, should Napoleon pursue or move closer to Dresden or to France? If they concentrated their armies north and south of Leipzig, should he retreat? If they attacked, Gyulay's position at Lindenau could jeopardize his retreat. Alone in his tent with maps spread before him, Napoleon awaited news of the enemy, considering all the movements he could execute the following day, including a retreat to the Rhine. Odeleben tells us that he "passed a very uneasy night. [General Étienne-Marie-Antoine] Nansouty and other generals were called to his bedside."[2]

According to Jean-Jacques Pelet,[3] "in the middle of the night he [Napoleon] learned the true state of affairs and the misfortunes that had befallen his lieutenants who were engaged away from him." From Schönefeld at 1:00 A.M. on the 17th, Ney announced that VI Corps had fought the combined armies of Blücher and Bernadotte supported by one Austrian division and lost over half of its effectives and more than thirty guns. He also informed the master that Bertrand had been attacked by at least 20,000 men and had suffered large losses. Ney added that, if such disproportionate forces attacked his army group on the 17th, it would be forced to fall back on Liebertwolkwitz. Marmont added that he could not determine his losses until the corps could be reorganized on the 17th but that the more than 60,000 infantry and 12,000 cavalry facing him had increased visibly. From Holzhausen, Macdonald reported that the enemy opposite him numbered between 40,000 and 50,000 men. He predicted the Allies would attack him on the 17th with even more forces. Bertrand expressed the same concerns; he and Poniatowski claimed to be out of ammunition.

At this time, Napoleon's aide-de-camp, Colonel Gaspard Gourgaud, returned from a tour of the bivouacs. He found the ranks quite thinned, especially those of II Corps. Fatigue weighed heavily on everyone and all had been impressed by the immensity of the enemy's forces. Zeal lagged but confidence remained steady. The artillery had expended an enormous quantity of ordnance. Despite the arrival of the army's main park from Eilenburg, many feared that ammunition supplies would not suffice for a second battle. Moreover, prisoners claimed that the Allies would launch their main attack as soon as Bennigsen and Bernadotte arrived with the Armies of Poland and North Germany. Lack of news regarding the whereabouts of Reynier's VII Corps and Grand Headquarters increased the emperor's anxiety. At daybreak on 17 October, reports indicated that the enemy remained concentrated in his positions both north and south of Leipzig. All his measures looked defensive in nature and reinforcements appeared to have arrived. Further discouraging news of Wrede's Austro-Bavarian force-marching from the Inn River against Napoleon's line of communication with France made a retreat inevitable. "From that moment," concludes Pelet, "Napoleon was fully decided to retreat; but it could not begin before the arrival of VII Corps and Grand Headquarters, before the union of the army and the parks around Leipzig. It must necessarily proceed from this city to Erfurt, an intermediate position with our frontiers, from where we could reach France in fourteen days. Would it stop at this position, facing the mountains of Thuringia? It could not; because ... reports from captured officers left no doubt over the movement of the Austro-Bavarian army. The Allied sovereigns would join it by Ilmenau and Schweinfurt. Wrede would form their vanguard and soon reach the Rhine." This news meant that Napoleon would ultimately seek a position between the Main and the Lahn, in front of Koblenz and Mainz.[4] Nevertheless, Napoleon postponed the retreat until the 18th.

During the course of the 16th, the Army of North Germany marched toward Landsberg, some sixteen miles northwest of Möckern. Wintzingerode's Russians bivouacked at Landsberg itself, the Swedes seven miles to the west at Zöberitz, and Bülow's corps four miles northwest of Landsberg. Bernadotte himself went to Halle. That evening, Hedemann arrived from Silesian Army Headquarters to deliver news of the victory at Möckern as well as Blücher's request for Bernadotte to support him on the 17th. Bernadotte purportedly reacted to the report with marked indifference – a reaction that became known at Silesian Army Headquarters.[5] That evening, the crown prince issued his dispositions for the 17th. Inconceivably, the Army of North Germany would remain at Landsberg rather than advance toward Leipzig. Somewhat later arrived an urgent plea from Stewart: "I have come from General Blücher's battlefield and have the honor to send you a report of this battle. I dare to request that you depart and go to Taucha at the moment you receive this letter. There is not a moment to lose. You have promised me this. This was spoken as a friend. I speak now as a soldier and you will only regret it if you do not begin your march now." Although this letter befouled the prince royal's mood, Stewart had apparently strummed the right chords. Some, such as Müffling, maintain that the veiled threat of withholding London's subsidy installment motivated the crown prince. Around 12:00 A.M. on the 17th, Bernadotte finally issued orders for the Army of North Germany to march, adding that "yesterday the Grand Army as well as the Army of Silesia had very sharp engagements around Leipzig; the Allies had success, but it is time to support the Army of Silesia, which in all probability will be attacked at daybreak by a corps coming from Bad Düben. The Prince counts on the bravery of the troops and on the talents and experience of the generals. The fate of Europe can be decided today. The Allied cause is just, and God will bless our arms."[6]

Returning to the Silesian Army, shortly after dawn on Sunday, 17 October, Yorck held a solemn open-air religious service. With few officers and tattered flags, his soldiers marched up to attend. The staggering losses from the previous day forced Yorck to reorganize his corps after the service. For the rest of the war, I Corps would consist of two weak divisions.[7] Despite the incredible loss of life, Blücher resolved to continue the struggle, expecting Schwarzenberg to do the same. He ordered the troops to cook early and prepare to march. "According to the agreement made with the Bohemian Army," claimed Nostitz, "a general attack on the French position should take place on the 17th. All arrangements were made and with impatience; but nevertheless the general waited in vain for the arranged signal." Just after dawn, which at that time of year came at 6:30, Blücher and his staff rode to the outposts. There they observed imperial forces at Eutritzsch and Gohlis with pickets along the Rietschke; skirmishing had already commenced. "General Blücher surveyed several lines of enemy infantry between the Parthe and the road to Landsberg," recalled Langeron, "and we could assume that Napoleon was making a move against our armies." Although Schwarzenberg's signal never came and Blücher still did not know what had become of the Bohemian Army on the 16th, he decided to drive all imperial forces from the terrain north of Leipzig so his army could link with Schwarzenberg's right. He planned to fix the imperials with Sacken's corps while Langeron enveloped their right from the Wiederitzsch villages. Yorck's battered corps would remain in reserve but could do little until the troops received ammunition by way of the caissons taken from Marmont. The few units that remained fairly well organized received the task of escorting the captured prisoners and guns to Halle. While Yorck's corps probably would not be able to contribute much, the 5,000 Russian troopers from Wintzingerode's corps had arrived to support the Silesian Army. Wintzingerode himself joined Blücher early on the 17th and willingly executed a request to take possession of the bridge over the Parthe at Taucha and establish communication with the Bohemian Army. His troopers reached Taucha in the afternoon, having an inconsequential skirmish with elements of Reynier's VII Corps en route to Leipzig from Eilenburg.[9]

Around 9:30 A.M. on the 17th, Sacken advanced southeast from Möckern toward Gohlis while Sacken's cavalry under Vasilchikov followed by St.-Priest and Langeron likewise moved southeast from Groß- and Kleinwiederitzsch toward Eutritzsch. Marmont had already recrossed the Parthe to reorganize VI Corps but Ney arrived to take command.[10] He ordered Dąbrowski's division to relieve the Württembergers at Gohlis. Ney also pulled back Delmas's division southeast from Eutritzsch to a position on the rolling hills between Gohlis and Schönefeld so that the French stood to the right (east) of the Poles. While Sacken's fresh units made little progress against the Poles at Gohlis, Vasilchikov led his cavalry toward Eutritzsch. Behind him Langeron unlimbered twenty-four twelve-pound guns supported by X Infantry Corps. After finding Eutritzsch abandoned, Vasilchikov's cavalry continued southeast toward Shönefeld per orders from Blücher.[11]

After Marmont's artillery on the opposite bank of the Parthe shelled Vasilchikov's troopers, Blücher moved up two batteries to challenge the French guns. He observed Delmas's infantry as well as 5th and 6th Light Cavalry Divisions of III Cavalry Corps posted on its right wing. Nostitz overheard Blücher say to Vasilchikov, who stood close by him, "If I was still at the head of my old hussar regiment, I would attack this infantry in the front, envelop its flank, and take that battery." "If Your Excellency permits, I will attempt this with my hussars," answered the Russian.[12] Vasilchikov assigned the task to Lanskoy, who formed the two brigades of his 2nd Hussar Division into two waves of columns.[13] After the foremost put to flight a few squadrons that had moved up to ward off "the large body of Cossacks" that accompanied the Hussars, it turned against the mass of the French cavalry.[14] Neither French division awaited this attack but instead fled in complete disorder: some went toward the Gerber Gate of Leipzig's Halle suburb, others across the Parthe to Schönefeld, while still others fled further northeast, smashing through Reynier's columns as they arrived at the Heitererblick manor.[15] Two of the Russian regiments pursued the groups that had made for Leipzig, passing the battalions of Delmas's division, which formed squares and opened a furious fire. Lanskoy's troopers pressed through the suburb all the way to the Halle Gate that led to Leipzig's inner city, taking 5 guns and 200 prisoners and "sabering everything that presented itself" before withdrawing.[16] "The attack was executed with much determination and to the great joy of the general," continued Nostitz, "who closely oversaw the combat; the cannon were captured."[17] Meanwhile, the two other regiments made little progress against Delmas's infantry, which staunchly held its ground in the middle of the field because no Allied infantry or artillery arrived to oppose it. Delmas managed to withdraw to the Halle suburb before Langeron's infantry reached the vicinity of Eutritzsch.[18]

During this time, Sacken's combat with Dąbrowski's division at Gohlis became intense. As on the previous day, the Poles defended themselves with typical stubbornness and repulsed several attacks, prompting Blücher to move up a portion of Yorck's infantry. However, after Delmas's division retreated to the Halle suburb, thus exposing Dąbrowski's right, the Poles finally evacuated Gohlis. Although they withdrew in good order, one portion moved directly south into the Rosenthal (Valley of Roses) north of Leipzig between the Elster and the Pleiße, while the other marched southeast to the Pfaffendorf manor and its surrounding farm. With the exception of a few houses and entrenchments near the Gerber Gate, the Silesian Army cleared the right bank of the Parthe of French forces by 10:00 A.M. Should strong forces attempt to emerge from Leipzig and attack Blücher, he now would have plenty of time to make the necessary arrangements. Yet to continue the push and prevent Napoleon from concentrating all his forces against Schwarzenberg, Blücher needed to cross the Parthe. Marshy banks on both sides of the river as well as the close proximity of French forces in Leipzig rendered a crossing near the city imprudent. Moving six miles upstream to cross at Taucha would eliminate these difficulties.

Blücher decided that Langeron's corps along with the majority of Wintzingerode's cavalry would cross the Parthe further upstream while Sacken and Yorck – some 20,000 men combined – remained on the defensive between the Pleiße and the Parthe north of Leipzig.[19] Attacking Leipzig – the central point of Napoleon's might – on the left bank of the Parthe with the 25,000 men of his left wing while his right wing remained separated by the Parthe smacks of both audacity and imprudence. Any French forces en route from Bad Düben could easily smash into the rear of the Silesian Army. Around noon, the cavalry of Reynier's VII Corps reached Schönefeld to increase the French forces defending the Parthe but its infantry would not reach Paunsdorf until 4:00.[20]

We will never know what the results of this operation would have been. Just as Blücher commenced his movement, news arrived that Schwarzenberg had postponed his attack until the 18th to give Bennigsen's army time to arrive. Schwarzenberg also congratulated Blücher for his success at

Möckern and informed him that the Bohemian Army would resume its attack on the morning of the 18th to coincide with the arrival of Bennigsen's army. Schwarzenberg's messenger informed the Prussians that the Bohemian Army had gained no appreciable results on the 16th and that Gyulay had failed to take Lindenau. Shortly afterward, Blücher received word that the Army of North Germany had commenced its approach march and would link with the Silesian Army that evening. According to Müffling, both accounts taken together pleased Blücher immensely because decisive results could now be expected on the 18th. Consequently, he canceled the operation and ordered the army to make camp. Sacken's corps bivouacked east of Gohlis, Yorck's west of Möckern, and Langeron's between Eutritzsch and Seehausen. Blücher went to his headquarters at Großwiederitzsch and little else occurred on his front that day. In the afternoon, word reached him that the Army of North Germany had arrived on his left while the Army of Poland filled the gap between the Armies of Silesia and Bohemia.[21]

Regarding the situation south of the city, Hudson Lowe reported that "on the side of the Grand Combined Army and the French Grande Armée, this morning, was silence. Both armies rested closely opposite to each other; their batteries established within almost musket shot of each other without any fire being exchanged. On the part of the enemy, there was no inducement to commence." Langeron noted that "this delay could have hurt us if Napoleon had known how to use it, but he made no movement." The Grande Armée did nothing on 17 October, "which was wise, as Napoleon fulfilled our expectations by doing nothing." Around 10:00 A.M., the sound of artillery could be heard north of Leipzig. News of Blücher's victory at Möckern had already arrived, leading Schwarzenberg to believe that Napoleon had turned against the Silesian Army. To take some of the pressure off Blücher, Schwarzenberg arranged an attack in four columns to commence at 2:00 P.M. From the west, the Austrian II and III Corps would advance while from the south a left wing column would march down the right bank of the Pleiße, a middle column assaulted Liebertwolkwitz, and the right wing column attacked both Liebertwolkwitz and Holzhausen. Just as the advance commenced at 2:00, Schwarzenberg convened a council of war with his subordinates on the hill south of Güldengoßa to discuss the attack disposition. By this time, the firing north of Leipzig had ceased. Reports stated that Bennigsen reached Fuchshain, some three miles east of Liebertwolkwitz, with the Army of Poland's van. However, the main body would not be within supporting distance until evening. Colloredo's Austrian I Corps had arrived but its troops needed rest. No word came from Bernadotte, meaning Allied Headquarters could not depend on the intervention of the Army of North Germany on 17 October. Based on these circumstances as well as the stormy weather, Schwarzenberg suggested that the attack be postponed until the following day. All members of Allied Headquarters accepted this suggestion and Tsar Alexander approved as well.[22]

Bernadotte's army bivouacked on the hills of Breitenfeld late on the afternoon of the 17th after having commenced its march before daybreak.[23] At Breitenfeld itself, the Russians formed the army's right wing, Bülow's corps stood to their left (northeast) at Kleinpodelwitz, and the Swedes behind the Russians at Freiroda and Radefeld.[24] Cavalry patrolled toward Taucha while Cossacks destroyed the bridges at Eilenburg, Taucha, and Wurzen. Should French forces appear at Taucha en route northeast to Eilenburg, Bernadotte instructed General Nikolay Vuich – Wintzingerode's vanguard commander – to close on the former with all his cavalry and attack the enemy.[25] From Breitenfeld, Bernadotte wrote Blücher a vague letter which the latter received in the afternoon:

> I send you my sincere congratulations for your success yesterday and earlier today. They are the forerunners of those that you can expect in the course of the morrow. My movement on Leipzig has no purpose other than to support you and to facilitate the operations of the Grand Army. I most fervently wish that we can emerge from the awkward condition in which we find ourselves. In order to achieve great results, I believe it is beneficial to attack the enemy tomorrow. To provide you with the necessary details, I have sent Chamberlain [Peter Heinrich] von Podewils to deliver this dispatch as well as the request that you send me one of your General Staff officers who enjoys your trust and knows your plans in order to consult with me. General Gneisenau has assured Podewils that after you awaken one of your officers will come. Time slips away and the evening advances. Tsar Alexander has requested that you and I agree over what appears to be most useful for the success of the common cause.
>
> You must feel, my dear general, that it is most essential not to lose a moment. The troops are exhausted from the bivouacs and the misery they have suffered. I do not doubt for a moment that we will be successful if we have unity of action in our movements. I have already informed you of my wish that each will take his appointed place in the order of battle. My interests in Sweden, the number of cavalry that I have detached to Westphalia [Aleksandr Chernishev], an army and detached corps on the right bank of the Elbe [Tauentzien and Thümen], the bridge at Aken, and a thousand other military considerations and interests make me hope that you encounter no inconveniences.[26]

Müffling is adamant that Blücher and his staff interpreted this letter as an attempt by Bernadotte to shield his army from Napoleon by placing it behind Blücher's right wing, just as it had been during the retreat from the Mulde to the Saale.[27] Despite the ambiguity of this letter, reason for Bernadotte's desire to hide behind Blücher could be found in his orders to Wintzingerode, which indicated his expectation that Napoleon would

withdraw to the Mulde and from there across the Elbe. Blücher and his
staff opposed any suggestion that smacked of a time-consuming realign-
ment of the two armies. "It would have been completely useless,"
explained Müffling, "to move a strong army into a defensive position that
30,000 men could defend. Therefore, the commander in chief refused this
demand."[28] Instead, the Prussians insisted on crossing the Parthe in
strength, meaning both armies. Knowing that Gyulay's 20,000 Austrians
at Lindenau blocked Napoleon's only escape route to the west, Blücher
and his staff concluded that the French emperor would seek to escape the
Allied net before it could close. To do this, he would have to utilize the
only remaining open road that ran northeast from Leipzig through Taucha
to Eilenburg.[29] From there, Napoleon could direct his army to Magdeburg,
Wittenberg, Torgau, or even Dresden. Thus, believing Napoleon would
evacuate Leipzig rather than allow himself to be surrounded, Blücher made
the bold decision to cross the Parthe and drive into the heart of the enemy's
might.[30]

Bernadotte also requested a personal meeting with Blücher, which the
Prussian refused. Blücher purportedly told the Swedish officer who
delivered Bernadotte's letter that the crown prince could do as he pleased
with the Swedes as long as he released the Russian and Prussian troops under
his command.[31] To counter Bernadotte's scheming, Blücher dispatched a
"confidential officer" to Bülow's headquarters with Prince William of Prussia's request that he join Blücher's advance across the Parthe on the 18th
regardless of the crown prince. He also invited Bülow to discuss the situation with Wintzingerode. Bülow responded that same night: he would not
fail when the welfare of the Fatherland and Europe was at stake.[32] Moreover,
Wintzingerode would proceed in the same manner.[33]

During the night of 17/18 October, Blücher received a second request for
a meeting with the crown prince. This time, Bernadotte wanted to discuss
the details for the combined attack by their two armies on the 18th.[34]
Believing he could not refuse, Blücher departed for Breitenfeld long before
dawn. Again, due to his aversion to Bernadotte, Gneisenau refused to attend
this "battle of wits."[35] Instead, Blücher asked Prince William to accompany
him and Nostitz. With a prince of the blood in attendance, Blücher hoped to
have the upper hand in convincing Bernadotte "to do what all of Europe
expected on this day from the Army of North Germany."[36] Nostitz maintains that Blücher took William with him so that the Hohenzollern prince
could personally secure Bülow's promise "to join the Silesian Army with at
least his corps, in case on this so decisive day the cooperation of all the forces
of the North German Army should be denied."[37]

According to notes taken by Rühle, who served as the interpreter, only
Adlerkreutz and Bernadotte initially met with the Prussians.[38] In addition,
the Hungarian captain Count István Széchenyi de Sárvár-Felsővidék, who

had just arrived from Schwarzenberg's headquarters, likewise participated.[39] Széchenyi delivered a communiqué stating "that Their Majesties Tsar Alexander, the Kaiser of Austria, and the King of Prussia intend to attack the enemy and that they wish for the North German and Silesian Armies to cooperate in this great undertaking."[40] Later, the entire entourage of foreign envoys joined the group: Pozzo di Borgo, Krusemarck, Vincent, and Stewart. Despite their presence, the Prussians failed to convince the prince royal to immediately cross the Parthe with the Silesian Army and attack the left wing of the French position. "Also on this occasion the crown prince remained true to the system that he always followed," noted Nostitz; "for each task that he should tackle, he found the means at his disposal too weak and thus he criticized every disposition slated for him."[41] Bernadotte, whose "strength lay in bringing forward astonishing counterproposals, simply did not agree with the Prussian response to the situation."[42] Knowing that in addition to his own army, Bennigsen and Colloredo would also arrive for the battle on the 18th, he too dismissed the idea that Napoleon would remain at Leipzig and allow himself to be surrounded by vastly superior forces. Like Blücher, the crown prince assumed Gyulay's presence at Lindenau would close the French emperor's escape route to the west. Again like Blücher, the prince royal concluded that Napoleon would seek to escape the Allied net via the Leipzig–Taucha–Eilenburg road.

At this point, however, the similarities between Bernadotte and Blücher came to a screeching halt. Bernadotte could not reconcile himself with Blücher's demand that the North German Army join the Silesian Army in crossing the Parthe and placing themselves on the very road they believed Napoleon would utilize to break out of Leipzig. Nothing terrified Bernadotte more than risking his reputation in a battle with his former master. Ever mistrustful of his allies, the crown prince also doubted that Schwarzenberg's masses would arrive in time to support himself and Blücher. His imagination only allowed him to envision the 200,000 men of the Grande Armée led by the emperor himself desperately fighting to escape Leipzig. Outnumbered two to one, Bernadotte would be forced to use every available resource including his Swedes, whom he had carefully spared from battle over the previous two months. Thus, rather than absorbing the brunt of Napoleon's assault frontally, the former French marshal preferred to attack the flank of the French march columns he anticipated would be retreating northeast through Taucha to Eilenburg.[43] Despite the inherent advantages of a flank attack, such a maneuver did not guarantee success, as Wittgenstein had discovered at Lützen on 2 May 1813.

For this reason, Blücher held his ground, determined to throw his weaker army into the last remaining gap and completely close the iron cage around Napoleon.[44] During the verbal contest, Prince William declared that as the king's brother he would take command of Bülow's corps and lead it to battle unless Bernadotte agreed with Blücher.[45] Even this threat did not break the crown prince's determination. After Blücher utterly rejected his request to place the North German Army on the right wing of the Silesian Army, the crown prince demanded that it follow as second echelon behind the army's left wing. He reasoned that this position would allow the Army of North Germany to immediately launch a flank attack to counter any attempt by Napoleon to break out via the Leipzig–Taucha–Eilenburg road. Blücher continued to insist that both armies cross the Parthe as quickly as possible. With the Allied envoys present, it became clear to Bernadotte that his refusal to accept the Prussian proposal would jeopardize his standing in the Coalition. At last, he agreed to cross the Parthe and advance through Taucha but on one condition. Arguing that detaching Tauentzien's corps and Thümen's brigade from Bülow's corps had considerably weakened his army to merely 65,000 men, the crown prince of Sweden demanded that Blücher place 20,000 men at his disposal to execute this risky operation. Gradually this requirement escalated to 25,000 and ultimately 30,000 men.[46]

Blücher struggled with himself, weighing the pros and cons of submitting to such a demand.[47] He knew that, on its own, the Silesian Army could do little to prevent Napoleon from breaking out and taking the road to the Elbe. In the end, the paramount importance of getting the Army of North Germany onto the battlefield persuaded him to agree. Thus, Blücher placed the needs of the Coalition in front of his own desire to influence the great struggle against Napoleon.[48] Despite having the assurance that Bülow and Wintzingerode would cooperate with him regardless of any interference from Bernadotte, Blücher could not be certain. Moreover, Langeron's past behavior did not offer him any guarantees that the French émigré would fight despite any orders to the contrary he received from Bernadotte. Thus, Blücher resolved to remain at Langeron's side for the course of the battle.[49] Ready for combat and in a malicious tone Blücher answered: "On my honor, Your Royal Highness can personally lead Langeron's corps."[50] The council of war ended at 7:00 on the morning of the 18th. Leaving Rühle behind to work out a convention with the crown prince and Nostitz to remain at Bernadotte's headquarters, Blücher and William rushed back to Silesian Army Headquarters.[51] "The mistrust that one placed in the fulfillment of such promises was already so great," noted Nostitz, "that the general ordered me to remain by the person of the crown prince and to determine for myself whether or not the arrangements that were taken conformed to the agreement; in the latter case he [Blücher] had decided to recall the detached corps and to proceed according to circumstances. The crown prince was troubled by the presence of one of General Blücher's adjutants, and he attempted many times in vain to rid himself of me by sending instructions to the general."[52]

After Blücher and William departed, Bernadotte dictated the following protocol to Rühle:

According to Field-Marshal Prince Schwarzenberg's communiqué ... Their Majesties Tsar Alexander, the Emperor of Austria, and the King of Prussia intend to attack the enemy and they wish that the North German and Silesian Armies cooperate in this great undertaking. After a meeting between General Blücher and the crown prince it was agreed that:

(1) General Blücher will provide the crown prince of Sweden with 30,000 men from his army including infantry, cavalry, and artillery, and that these troops will unite with the North German Army and under the command of the crown prince attack the army of the emperor Napoleon through Taucha; General Blücher with his troops will maintain the position before Leipzig and as soon as the general struggle has commenced will seek to take the city itself with all means.

(2) Should the emperor Napoleon turn with all of his forces against the Silesian and North German Armies, it is agreed that the two armies will fight jointly until the Bohemian Army comes to their aid. In this case, the crown prince and General Blücher will act in accord, and each commander will discuss their operations with the other.[53]

Meanwhile, few at Silesian Army Headquarters had failed to grasp the importance of this day, as Steffens noted:

I would convey a false sense of the scene in Blücher's vicinity to suggest that anything like haste or confusion was to be perceived there. Although such a great battle was certain to be fought – although all felt that it would decide the fate of the whole war – there was no sign of any such important crisis near the great commander. Every officer rose and dressed himself leisurely [sic] and carefully; the few grooming tools on hand were taken to the wells, and when used by some were instantly claimed by the servants of others to be replenished. The windows were opened and laid back on the walls. Coffee was brought in; some drank from the cups and some from the saucers. Any little difficulty or accident was seized on to give a cheerful turn to the remarks but these were never extended to the great event that was impending; they spoke on indifferent subjects, even of gay recollections, and a joke was seized on and passed around with thankful eagerness; to a superficial observer they might have seemed like men who were preparing to pursue a journey and were amusing themselves with the minor inconveniences of an uncomfortable night's lodging.[54]

With Blücher at Breitenfeld, Gneisenau took the opportunity to pen his thoughts to his wife:

I write you on the morning of a battle the likes of which have never been fought in the history of the world. We have the French emperor completely surrounded. This battle will decide the fate of Europe. Already the day before yesterday Blücher's army again fought a glorious victory. God be with you! A half-million men now stand pressed together in a narrow space, ready to destroy themselves. If great mistakes are not made, we will be the victors. Through the steps that our army has made, through its bold movements, through the battles and combats that it has won, and through the advice that our headquarters has given, so much has been done for the advantageous turn of the war. The victories of the other armies remained without results and only ours have altered the course of events. One day the secret history of this war will be told, and posterity will be astonished.[55]

Blücher rode four miles from Breitenfeld to the hills of Eutritzsch; the struggle between Napoleon and Schwarzenberg had already commenced. Soon after, Rühle returned with the crown prince's protocol. Gneisenau did not like the news. "It was now our responsibility to once again make the first attack while the crown prince placed himself in the fourth line," he later wrote.[56] A few minutes later, one of Bernadotte's adjutants delivered orders for Langeron to examine all points of passage across the Parthe upstream of Taucha, repair any bridges, and cross the river while Wintzingerode's corps moved across downstream of Taucha. Stedingk's Swedes would cross somewhere between the two Russian corps. Should the imperials attack either the Silesian or North German Armies before they crossed the Parthe, the latter would await the French on the hills of Plaußig, two miles west-northwest of Taucha and six miles northeast of the heart of Leipzig. Despite his earlier resolution to remain at Langeron's side, Blücher accompanied his subordinate as far as the Gips windmill hill at Mockau, where the army commander halted and remained on the right bank of the Parthe for the rest of the battle.[57]

Returning to Napoleon, the 17th passed with much stress. Murat spent the early morning with him; both looked "very serious and pensive ... Napoleon appeared constantly much absorbed; he again shut himself up in his tent." During the course of the day, Napoleon learned that his Grand Headquarters and the rest of the parks could not rejoin the army because they had been directed to Wurzen. In the evening, the 1st Old Guard Division escorted the emperor to the Little Headquarters at the village of Stötteritz, less than three miles southeast of Leipzig. "The rain was pouring down upon the wretches who were encamped; a gloomy silence reigned around the emperor's bivouac. The other persons about Bonaparte were visibly in consternation." Knowing that his dwindling supplies meant that he could not expend the same amount of ammunition on the 18th as he had on the 16th, the emperor resigned himself to preparing for the retreat.[58]

At 7:00 P.M., Napoleon issued orders for Bertrand's IV Corps, reinforced by Reynier's 13th Division, one battery of heavy artillery, and one dragoon brigade from Defrance's 4th Division of III Cavalry Corps, to secure the bridges over the Saale and Unstrut at Merseburg, Freiburg, Weißenfels, and Bad Kösen. To reach his rearward base at Erfurt, some seventy miles southwest of Leipzig, two roads remained open to Napoleon. The first, which ran through Merseburg, Freiburg, and Buttelstedt, would bring the Grande Armée within the range of Blücher and Bernadotte at the Saale crossing. The second, running through Weißenfels, Bad Kösen, and Weimar, served as the most direct route but would bring the army dangerously close to the Bohemian Army, which could either march on parallel roads to reach Weißenfels first or take perpendicular routes to attack Napoleon's left flank.[59] Beyond Weißenfels, this route would also force the French to cross the Unstrut and gain Buttelstedt by bad roads. A third route leading through Zeitz, Jena, and Coburg could bring the army to Schweinfurt, some eighty miles south of Erfurt, if it could get past the Army of Bohemia. A retreat to either Erfurt or Schweinfurt required the Grande Armée to debouch through Leipzig's western exit, cross the bridge over the Elster, and utilize the causeway to cross the marsh to Lindenau.[60] Despite the risks entailed, Napoleon chose the direct route through Weißenfels.

Around 2:00 on the morning of Monday 18 October, Napoleon contracted his southern front by a few miles in preparation for the retreat. Although the great captain accepted that he could not win the battle, he resolved to fight one more day. In streaming rain, the imperial troops marched from their bivouacs to a new line that extended from the Connewitz–Dölitz position along the Pleiße east to Probstheida, Zuckelhausen, and Holzhausen to Ober- and Unternaundorf, from where it turned north to Paunsdorf and continued to Schönefeld on the Parthe, crossed this river, and ended at Göhlis, the Halle suburb, and the Pfaffendorf estate. To deceive the Allies, the forward posts kept their campfires blazing. The emperor himself climbed into his open carriage and "calmly but with a serious countenance" made for Probstheida.[61]

Murat assumed command of Napoleon's right, an L-shape that stretched from the Pleiße to Probstheida. Augereau's 52nd Division and Lefol's division defended both banks of the Pleiße at Connewitz while the Poles of VIII Corps and IV Cavalry Corps held the terrain along the Pleiße between Connewitz and Lößnig. South of the Poles, the rest of IX Corps occupied Dölitz to anchor Murat's right; weak forward posts extended further south through Dösen. To their east, Victor positioned II Corps between IX Corps and Probstheida supported by V Cavalry Corps. North of Probstheida between Stötteritz and the Thon hill stood the Old Guard and I Cavalry Corps in reserve.

Macdonald commanded Napoleon's center, extending east from Probstheida to the Naundorf villages with XI Corps holding positions at Zuckelhausen, Holzhausen, and north of the Stein hill. Part of Lauriston's V Corps occupied the Naundorfs and Mölkau while the other stood between Stötteritz and Probstheida as support for XI Corps. To support XI and V Corps, 3rd Guard Cavalry Division took post north of Zuckelhausen with II Cavalry Corps to its left (east) between Holzhausen and the Naundorfs. The emperor allocated the city's garrison,[62] Dąbrowski's and Lorge's divisions, and Mortier's 2nd Young Guard Corps to defend Leipzig itself as well as the Halle suburb along the Pleiße to Gohlis. Should Bertrand's IV Corps depart for Weißenfels, Mortier's Young Guard would move into its position at Lindenau.

Napoleon entrusted his left wing, which ran from Paunsdorf to Schönefeld on the Parthe, to Ney, who posted most of his troops to confront the threat posed by Blücher north-northeast of Leipzig. The emperor allocated the only reinforcements to arrive – VII Corps – to Ney's sector. Reynier's sole Saxon division stood in and around Paunsdorf supported by Avice's 1st Brigade of Dragoons from Defrance's 4th Heavy Cavalry Division. Reynier's 32nd Division of all French troops held the ground left or north of Paunsdorf, which in turn linked with the right wing of Marmont's VI Corps, which Ney tasked with the defense of Schönefeld. To support Marmont, Fournier's 6th Light Cavalry Division took post behind (west of) Schönefeld and next to III Corps, which Ney kept in reserve between Schönefeld and Volkmarsdorf. Shortly after the battle commenced in this sector, Ney abandoned his position along the Parthe due to the simultaneous threats posed by the Armies of Poland, Silesia, and North Germany. His new line faced north and extended three miles west to east between the villages of Schönefeld and Paunsdorf. Two light cavalry brigades and their accompanying horse batteries – all German troops – guarded the plain before Ney's front that extended from the Heiterblick estate to Taucha. This cavalry consisted of Normann's 25th Light Cavalry Brigade (Württemberger) attached to VI Corps and Major Friedrich Joseph von Fabrice's 26th Light Cavalry Brigade (Saxon) that belonged to VII Corps. One mile southwest of the Heiterblick, Lagrange's 21st Division and Fournier's 6th Light Cavalry Division held Schönefeld on Ney's extreme left. To their right (southeast) extended Marmont's 22nd and 20th Divisions respectively. The 32nd Division of VII Corps faced Paunsdorf and a gap existed between it and Compans's 20th Division. Ney anchored his right wing with Reynier's all Saxon 24th Division, which stood between Paunsdorf and Stünz, the latter being the position of Avice's 1st Brigade from 4th Heavy Cavalry Division. One mile southeast of Schönefeld, Souham's III Corps served as the reserve at Volkmarsdorf.

As darkness prevented Napoleon from reconnoitering the terrain around Probstheida, he repaired to Ney's headquarters at Reudnitz, where he found the marshal fast asleep. After awakening the bravest of the brave, Napoleon conversed at length with his subordinate. At 5:00 in the morning, the emperor's carriage rode through Leipzig to Lindenau. Accompanied by Bertrand, Napoleon observed the terrain on both sides of the highway that led west to Weißenfels as much as the grey, foggy morning allowed. Although he instructed Bertrand on his task of securing that town's crossing over the Saale, the general could not commence the march to Weißenfels until orders arrived to do so. After dismissing Bertrand, Napoleon returned to his headquarters at Stötteritz, which he reached at 8:00. Per his tradition, he then rode across the front to inspire his troops before settling at his command post at the tobacco mill owned by the wealthy Quandt family near Probstheida. Despite the losses on the 16th and the posting of Bertrand's IV Corps at Lindenau in readiness to march to Weißenfels, Napoleon still commanded a considerable force: 160,000 men and 630 guns. Yet this number did not suffice to hold the eighteen-mile line that shielded the southern, eastern, and northern approaches to Leipzig. The three-mile gap that existed between the Naundorfs and Paunsdorf could be exploited if the Allies managed to move their forces into position in time to take advantage of this weak point.

Schwarzenberg issued orders to have the troops ready to attack at 9:00 on the morning of 18 October. His disposition for the 18th has been lost but apparently he and his staff simply followed the blueprint that had been drafted for the 17th. Including the Armies of Silesia and North Germany, the Austrian staff planned six massive attacks along the entire front. Counterclockwise from west of Leipzig, Schwarzenberg's first army group, Gyulay's III Corps, Moritz von Liechtenstein's 1st Light Division and the two *Streifkorps* commanded by Thielmann and Mensdorff – together some 18,000 men – would make another attempt to take Lindenau from Kleinzschocher. Commanded by Prince Frederick of Hessen-Homburg, Schwarzenberg's all-Austrian second group (I, II, and Reserve Corps) of 43,600 men would drive north from Markkleeberg toward Connewitz along both banks of the Pleiße. The 4,000 men of General Ignaz Ludwig von Lederer's 1st Division of II Corps would operate between the Elster and the Pleiße to attempt to envelop Murat's right and to maintain communication between Gyulay and Hessen-Homburg. Barclay de Tolly would lead the third group – Kleist, Wittgenstein, Pahlen's cavalry, and the Russo-Prussian Guard and Reserve, some 32,600 Russians, and 14,500 Prussians totaling 47,100 men – against the Wachau–Liebertwolkwitz sector southeast of Leipzig. After securing these villages, Barclay would target the linchpin of Napoleon's entire position: Probstheida. Consisting of the 28,000 men of the Army of Poland, the 23,500 Austrians of Klenau's IV Corps and Bubna's 2nd

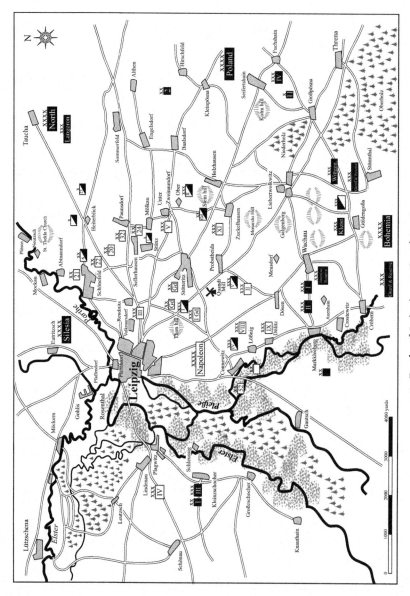

26. Battle of Leipzig, 18 October 1813

Light Division, the 5,000 men of Ziethen's Prussian 11th Brigade, and Platov's 3,000 Cossacks, the 59,500 soldiers of this group – Schwarzenberg's fourth – commanded by Bennigsen, would envelop Napoleon's left flank by advancing on Leipzig from the east. From Fuchshain and Seifertshain, Bennigsen would first seek to secure Zuckelhausen and Holzhausen. The fifth group, the 83,000 men of Langeron's corps and the Army of North Germany, would cross the Parthe at Taucha, attack Leipzig from the northeast, and establish contact with Bennigsen's forces. Finally, the forces that remained at Blücher's disposal, around 25,000 men, would assault the city between the Elster and the Parthe. Altogether, some 295,000 Coalition soldiers supported by 1,466 cannon would assault the imperial lines around Leipzig. Strategically and tactically confined to the defensive, Napoleon stood in the middle of a position that catered solely to the circumstances by allowing him to quickly bolster weak spots. Schwarzenberg would facilitate the French defense by attacking concentrically along the entire front rather than concentrating superior combat power against one point. Allied numerical superiority should have managed at least one breach in the French line.[63]

During the night, heavy downpours fell as if the heavens wept over man's barbarity. Cloud and fog hung thick over the killing fields of Leipzig following a cold night. Before daybreak, Schwarzenberg's army groups formed for the approach march. At 5:30 A.M., Alexander and Frederick William mounted their horses and proceeded to the assembly point of Barclay's columns. Reports from the outposts already indicated that the French had evacuated Wachau and Liebertwolkwitz; cavalry patrols confirmed this news. Around 7:00, Schwarzenberg issued orders for the advance to commence and soon the artillery of both sides opened the struggle. Shortly after 8:00 the sun started to break through. One hour later, a bright autumn light illuminated the giant battlefield. After almost one week of continuous rain, the beautiful weather raised the spirits of the troops on both sides.

By 9:00, Napoleon had seen enough of Schwarzenberg's movements to divine the Austrian's intent. As soon as he learned of the advance of enemy columns toward the three-mile gap between the Naundorfs and Paunsdorf, he sent orders to Bertrand to commence the march to Weißenfels: the emperor knew he was fighting a battle he could not win. Starting at 11:00, all that could not be utilized on the battlefield commenced the retreat: the diplomatic corps, the wounded that could be transported, and the army's baggage.[64]

From left to right, Gyulay's command, which formed Schwarzenberg's first group, camped south of Lindenau at Klein- and Großzschocher. Most of his cavalry and a few battalions observed the Lindenau defile from a marsh between Kleinzschocher and Leutzsch. Still exhausted from the marches of the previous days, the majority of Gyulay's infantry bivouacked south of Großzschocher. His 1st Division, commanded by the French émigré Louis Charles Folliot de Crenneville, had yet to arrive from Cröbern. Lacking these troops as well as elements from Murray's 2nd Division that were holding Weißenfels and Naumburg, Gyulay had seventeen battalions and twenty-five squadrons at his disposal. Early on 18 October, the forward posts reported the march of imperial columns from Lindenau. Gyulay responded by calling his troops to arms and taking a position on the ridge between Kleinzschocher and Schönau. Soon the Austrians viewed the heads of two columns: one consisting of all arms, the other only of infantry. Both overran Gyulay's weak posts and marched west but the former struck the road to Markranstädt while the latter took the highway to Merseburg. Through the thick fog that blanketed the area, the Austrians discerned three battalions from the French 13th Line Regiment deploy against Kleinzschocher while imperial horse made for Gyulay's left at Schönau. Deceived by the fog into thinking that he faced vastly superior numbers, Gyulay ordered his artillery park to retreat across the Elster. He also informed Schwarzenberg and Blücher of the "offensive" and notified his posts at Weißenfels and Naumburg to be on their guard. Bertrand attacked Kleinzschocher so quickly that the Austrian 1st Jäger Battalion fled. Pursued to the bridge over the Elster near Schleußig, the hapless Austrians found it destroyed and themselves surrounded. Some 12 officers and 404 men – more than half the battalion – surrendered to the French. One battalion from the Kottulinskii Infantry Regiment that Gyulay had moved up in support reached Kleinzschocher too late to save the Jäger but attempted to retake the village. Despite hard fighting, it could not dislodge the French; this failure cost the Austrians more than 400 casualties and 298 prisoners.

After securing Kleinzschocher, Bertrand ordered the advance to continue to Großzschocher while his combined-arms column continued toward Markranstädt. Gyulay responded by moving his left wing toward Großzschocher protected by the cavalry of Thielmann and Mensdorff. His right wing, the three battalions of General Markus von Csollich's 1st Brigade of 3rd Division, managed to halt the French push on that side of the Austrian line. Around this time, Gyulay received orders from Schwarzenberg to march the entire Austrian III Corps ten miles southeast from Lindenau to Cröbern, crossing the Pleiße to join the main army. After Gyulay learned that the 4,000 men of Crenneville's 1st Division, en route to Kleinzschocher, had already halted at Gautsch to comply with these instructions, he made arrangements for the rest of the corps to likewise march to Gautsch. Leaving behind Liechtenstein's 1st Light Division as well as the two *Streifkorps* under Thielmann and Mensdorff on the left bank of the Elster to observe Bertrand's march, III Corps departed. At Knauthain, less than halfway between Kleinzschocher and Cröbern, Gyulay received instructions to halt and remain on standby as the situation on the right bank of the Pleiße had taken a turn for the better. Regardless, the Austrians failed to close Napoleon's escape route to the west. Protected by 3rd Heavy Cavalry Brigade from 4th Division of III Cavalry Corps, 12th, 14th, and 38th Divisions followed by Bertrand's artillery and parks marched to Markranstädt; his rearguard consisted of two squadrons: all that remained of a Württemberger cavalry brigade.

Schwarzenberg's second army group – the Austrian I, II, and Reserve Corps – stood closest to the imperials. After leading the troops to Markkleeberg, Hessen-Homburg halted in compliance with Schwarzenberg's verbal orders to wait for Barclay and Bennigsen to come on line with him. On receiving confirmation that the imperials had evacuated Wachau, he disregarded these orders and commenced the march toward Leipzig. His vanguard, General Ignaz von Hardegg's light division (two Grenzer battalions and nine squadrons) of Colloredo's I Corps, struck the road from Wachau to Dösen while the rest of the column followed in two waves. Poniatowski's cavalry as well as some French battalions that held the road stopped the Austrian van in its tracks. Stubborn combat ensued until the imperials observed the approach of Hessen-Homburg's first wave, the size of which threatened to envelop them on both sides. Leaving Hardegg's infantry behind, the Austrian cavalry pursued the French and Poles to Dösen. The weak French post before Dösen broke under the weight of the Austrian cavalry, which pursued the imperials through to Dösen toward Murat's main line. After Hessen-Homburg's right cleared Wachau and took positions to its north and east, he decided to wait for the neighboring columns to come on line while his artillery commenced the shelling of Murat's position. Aside from the cannon, the situation remained quiet except for a French combined-arms counterattack on the forward Austrian position at the Meusdorf sheep farm. Meanwhile, General Friedrich von Bianchi led Hessen-Homburg's left along the Borna–Leipzig road toward Dölitz. After driving back Augereau's forward post, the Austrians cleared Dölitz with the bayonet and penetrated the outskirts of Lößnig but could go no farther due to fierce French resistance. Yet the success generated by Hardegg and Bianchi motivated Hessen-Homburg's center to advance into the groves northeast of Dösen. Murderous French artillery and musket fire did little to help the Austrians navigate through the tall trees and difficult terrain. After sustaining considerable losses, they managed to reach the northern edge of the wood but could go no further.

Napoleon quickly perceived the serious threat posed to his right by Hessen-Homburg's success. Should the Austrians push Murat east and away from the Pleiße, the army's line of retreat would be compromised. To drive the enemy from Lößnig, Dölitz, and Dösen, the emperor dispatched

Oudinot with the twelve battalions of General Pierre Decouz's 3rd Division of I Young Guard Corps. Oudinot's approach gave the appearance of a general offensive after the Young Guard linked with Poniatowski's troops to their left and Augereau's to the right. The sight of the advancing imperials prompted Hessen-Homburg's entire line to fall back, surrendering Dölitz and exposing Dösen. After Hessen-Homburg fell seriously wounded, Colloredo assumed command but could do nothing to stem the approaching French tide. He summoned the second wave of his left wing, namely Weißenwolf's 1st Grenadier Division of the Austrian Reserve, which still stood at Markkleeberg. Meanwhile, Schwarzenberg, who had arrived just before the French retook Dölitz, summoned reinforcements from Rayevsky's Russian Grenadier Corps as well as General Ilya Duka's 3rd Cuirassier Division from the Russian Reserve Cavalry. As noted, he also sent the orders for Gyulay to march III Corps from the Lindenau sector to Cröbern. Until these reinforcements arrived, Colloredo had to make do with Weißenwolf's grenadiers. The lead battalion of these crack troops fixed bayonets and smashed through Dölitz in two columns, driving the imperials to the opposite end of the village. As the Prussians had experienced at Möckern two days earlier, the French tide returned just as fast as it had receded. As the Austrians fell back to the midpoint of Dölitz, a second Grenadier battalion arrived to help eject the imperials. The French doubled their efforts to retake the village and a third Austrian Grenadier battalion had to be committed. This seesaw battle continued for some time until the Austrians finally managed to secure Dölitz by 2:00.

Meanwhile, Oudinot's young bearskins made excellent progress against Colloredo's right thanks to the Guard Artillery's ability to silence the Austrian cannon. The French then overran Dösen, sending Hardegg to the rear with a serious wound. To prevent the Austrian right from collapsing, one brigade from Colloredo's 3rd Division moved up from the second wave. With Dösen on its right, the brigade advanced north, collecting the re-formed units of Bianchi's 2nd Division and Hardegg's light division to gradually push back the French to the hill chain that ran from the old brickworks to Dölitz. From noon onward, the artillery of both sides mainly continued the struggle as exhaustion prevented either from executing attacks on a large scale. Gyulay arrived around noon but did not receive orders to move into the battle line. Moreover, Rayevsky's grenadiers and Duka's cuirassiers received orders sometime after the noon hour to return to their former position. Due to the difficulty of the terrain, the two Austrian divisions[65] that had advanced along the right bank of the Pleiße could do little except offer artillery support for the action on the opposite bank. Hessen-Homburg's decision to wait for Barclay and Bennigsen to come on line with him prevented him from exploiting his initial success and achieving decisive results in the first half of battle on 18 October.

Around 7:00 A.M., I and II Infantry Corps of Wittgenstein's Russian army corps formed one large column between Güldengoßa and the Oberholz Forest. Left (west) of Wittgenstein, the Prussians of Kleist's II Corps likewise moved into a huge column. One hour later, Barclay ordered both columns to commence the advance. Kleist's three brigades formed the head of the left column while Wittgenstein's corps led Barclay's right. The majority of the artillery belonging to both corps preceded the two columns. Behind Kleist followed the 2nd Russian Grenadier Division, 3rd Cuirassier Division, and Russian Light Guard Cavalry. Wittgenstein's support consisted of Pahlen III's cavalry corps, the 2nd Cuirassier Division, and 1st Grenadier Division. Marching from its camp between Güldengoßa and Störmthal, the Russian and Prussian Guard Infantry split the middle of the two columns and followed as Barclay's third wave. The 1st Cuirassier Division and the Prussian Guard Cavalry brought up the rear.

As noted, Schwarzenberg tasked Barclay with taking Wachau and Liebertwolkwitz and then directing his efforts against Probstheida. Kleist led his column close to Güldengoßa on the road to Wachau as Wittgenstein's I Infantry Corps, commanded by General Andrey Gorchakov, made for Liebertwolkwitz. Behind Gorchakov, Prince Eugen of Württemberg's II Infantry Corps moved northwest into the gap between the Russians and Prussians. On Kleist's left, General Klüx's 9th Brigade linked with the Austrians of Hessen-Homburg's right near Wachau. Klüx halted on the hill north of that village to wait for Kleist's 10th and 12th Brigades, representing the Prussian center and right respectively, to come up on his right and close the gap between him and Gorchakov's lead elements. After clearing small French posts from Liebertwolkwitz, Gorchakov came on line with Klüx and both columns continued the advance. As Kleist's column came within cannon range of Probstheida, Gorchakov's passed the left (western) side of Zuckelhausen. Around 10:00, both columns halted until Hessen-Homburg and Bennigsen reached positions that would allow them to support a general attack against Napoleon's center. Pahlen III's light cavalry and the Guard Cavalry's 2nd Cuirassier Division established the link between Barclay and Bennigsen.

Barclay moved his second and third echelons forward. On the Monarchenhügel (Monarchs' Hill), Alexander and Frederick William established their command post; Kaiser Francis joined them in the afternoon. South of the hill stood the Russo-Prussian Guard and Reserve. By 2:00, Kleist and Wittgenstein succeeded in driving all French forward troops in their sector into Probstheida. Intense skirmishing ensued between the Allies and Victor's II Corps as the Russo-Prussian guns shelled Probstheida's numerous stone structures. Barclay only awaited Bennigsen's group to come on line with his to give the signal for the Russians and Prussians to storm the French stronghold. To soften the enemy, one battery each of heavy Russian,

Prussian, and Austrian guns lambasted Probstheida while the Russo-Prussian skirmishers blunted Victor's numerous counterattacks. Confining Victor to Probstheida proved relatively easy compared to the daunting task that awaited Barclay's men.

As for Bennigsen, he received instructions to envelop what the Allies believed to be Napoleon's left between Probstheida and the Naundorf villages. Moreover, he had to establish communication with Blücher and Bernadotte as well as close the gap between their armies and the Bohemian. These responsibilities meant that Bennigsen's army group had the farthest to march on the 18th. To find the end of Napoleon's line, he dispatched Platov's Cossacks at 3:00 A.M. north through Hirschfeld, Althen, and Engelsdorf to the Leipzig–Wurzen highway. From Sommerfeld, the Cossacks followed the highway west to Paunsdorf to link with the Silesian and North German Armies. The sudden appearance of Platov's warriors emerging in the grey morning caused panic among Macdonald's unsuspecting train columns as they stood between Sommerfeld, Engelsdorf, and Mölkau. Despite the attractive booty, Platov maintained discipline and led his men to the Heiterblick manor where they linked with Korf's troopers to establish communication with Blücher.

Thirteen miles east of Leipzig, the 6,500 men of Bubna's 2nd Light Division marched from Machern at 3:00 A.M. on the morning of the 18th. Turning southwest, the Austrians trooped through Brandis toward Beucha to cross the Parthe (see Map 6). Three hours later at 6:00, Bennigsen united his group four miles southwest of Beucha at Fuchshain to provide time for Bubna to cross the Parthe. Unfortunately for the Austrians, the river's rain-swollen waters had swallowed Beucha's bridge. Fording the river with infantry and artillery presented numerous obstacles, none greater than the loss of time. With the exception of his caissons, which took a long detour through Althen to stay dry, Bubna's troops completed the crossing around 8:00 A.M. and commenced their advance west toward Kleinpösna. As Bennigsen's right wing, Bubna turned north-northwest from Kleinpösna to advance through Engelsdorf and Sommerfeld seeking to win the Leipzig–Wurzen highway and attract the enemy's attention to himself.

Based on the reports he had received about the French positions opposite him, Bennigsen arranged his troops in four columns that would advance as soon as he received word of Bubna's approach. From left to right, Zieten's 11th Brigade from Kleist's Prussian II Corps received the task of clearing the French from the Niederholz Forest and establishing the link with Barclay's group at Liebertwolkwitz. To its right, Bennigsen's second column, Klenau's Austrian IV Corps, would assault the Kolm hill from the south and east while his third column, consisting of General Fyodor Lindfors's Russian 13th Infantry Division and elements of General Yefim Chaplits's cavalry division, both part of Dokhturov's army corps, attacked the northern side of the hill. Stroganov's vanguard, Dokhturov's 12th and 26th Infantry Div-isions, and the remainder of Chaplits's troopers – thus the majority of Bennigsen's Army of Poland – formed the fourth column. Accompanied by Bennigsen himself, Dokhturov would lead this group southwest from Hirschfeld to attack what the Russians believed to be the French left wing at Kleinpösna.

Shortly after commencing his advance, Bennigsen learned with relief that the situation had changed overnight. The French had already evacuated both the Niederholz and Kolm hill and now withdrew from Kleinpösna and Baalsdorf after offering only token resistance. Regardless, Bennigsen did not change his original disposition; rather than concentrate his dispersed columns he continued their extensive movements in order to establish communication with Bernadotte as soon as possible. By 10:00 that morning, Zieten's brigade had reached Zuckelhausen; Klenau sent Prince Ludwig von Hohenlohe-Bartenstein's division in pursuit of the French through Seifert-shain to Holzhausen while turning General Josef von Mayer's division toward Liebertwolkwitz, which the French evacuated around this time, to shield Zieten's right and rear. Bennigsen's third column – Lindfors's 13th Division supported by Chaplits's cavalry – continued to march west from Kleinpösna toward a position next to the Austrian troops facing Holzhau-sen. Meanwhile, Dokhturov's column stood at Baalsdorf with Bubna's division to its right between Engelsdorf and Sommerfeld.

Although achieving his first objectives with relative ease thanks to the enemy, Bennigsen remained cautious. A steady wind blew the heavy smoke clouds caused by Bennigsen's artillery west toward the Pleiße. From the north, he could hear Blücher's guns. Yet he could neither hear nor see, in the gap between his army and Blücher's, any sign indicating that Bernadotte's army would soon fill the space between the Armies of Silesia and Poland. Concerned that Napoleon would exploit this hole in the Allied line to break out of Leipzig, the Russian commander wanted to extend his army north-east. To prevent exposing Barclay's right, Bennigsen had no choice but to continue the forward momentum of his left wing, meaning that Zieten and Klenau would have to take Zuckelhausen and Holzhausen before he could move his right wing columns outside supporting distance to fill the gap to his right.

Unfortunately for the Allies, Zuckelhausen and Holzhausen represented the teeth of Macdonald's position. Marchand's 39th Division of Hessians and Badenese held the former while Charpentier's 36th Div-ision defended the latter; a strong line of skirmishers filled the gap between the two villages. Artillery mastered the southern approaches to both while north of the villages artillery crowned the Stein hill, behind which stood Gérard's 35th Division in reserve. Klenau answered the French cannon by moving up 24-pound guns from his reserve escorted by the Alois

Liechtenstein Infantry Regiment, the Hohenzollern Light Cavalry, and the Kaiser Cuirassier Regiment. After a long bombardment of both villages, General Adalbert Johann de Best's 2nd Brigade of Mayer's 3rd Division attacked Holzhausen while General Franz Abele von und zu Lilienberg's 1st Brigade of that division moved against Zuckelhausen. Part of Zieten's brigade also assaulted Zuckelhausen from the west as the other half contended with Badenese troops posted west of the village. Brutal French resistance at Holzhausen took its toll on the sole Austrian battalion that first penetrated the village only to be driven out by a counterattack. General Ignatius Rossi's 1st Brigade of Lindfors's 13th Division then arrived from Kleinpösna to support the Austrians. Moreover, Dokhturov's column had cleared Baalsdorf two miles northeast of Holzhausen and could launch a flanking attack against the village. Dokhturov sent additional support in the form of General Nikolay Khovansky's 12th Division led by the Narvskii Infantry Regiment and the twelve guns of the 45th Battery Company. Linfors's 2nd Brigade under General Ivan Ivanov also arrived as well as the 47th and 53rd Light Battery Companies. Around 1:00, four Austrian divisions attacked Holzhausen from the south while the Russian 12th and 13th Divisions attacked from the east. Overwhelmed by Allied numerical superiority, Charpentier's 36th Division conducted a disorderly withdrawal, losing three guns and several caissons to pursuing Austrian cavalry.

At Zuckelhausen, the Hessians and Badenese prevented Hohenlohe's two battalions from entering the village. Not until Zieten's brigade attacked from the south and the west did the imperials withdraw to Stötteritz, protected by the guns on the Stein hill. With Zuckelhausen and Holzhausen secure, Bennigsen decided to assault the Stein hill and its outcrops, which Gérard's 35th Division now deployed across. To provide counter-battery fire, the Allies moved up their artillery to establish a powerful line while three columns of Russian infantry formed. On the left, Lindfors's 13th Division received orders to advance through Holzhausen as Khovansky's 12th and General Ivan Paskevich's 26th Divisions marched to its right (east) to form the center and right columns respectively. West of Holzhausen, Klenau re-formed his infantry and likewise marched toward the hill. Bennigsen's plan broke down quickly due to the flames that engulfed Holzhausen. Unable to get through the village, Lindfors slid his 13th Division east, somewhat disordering his men and falling behind Dokhturov's other columns. This left a large gap between Dokhturov and Klenau, which Sébastiani's II Cavalry Corps and General Frédéric-Henri Walther's 3rd Guard Cavalry Division exploited to charge the lead brigade of Khovansky's 12th Division. Composed of the Smolenskii and Narvskii Regiments, the Russian brigade blunted the attack and then watched as ten squadrons of hussars and uhlans from Stroganov's van turned the tables on the French. After the French troopers retreated, the Russian foot soldiers resumed the march toward the Stein hill.

Horrific artillery fire rained down on the Russians; one ball ripped off Lindfors's right leg, putting an end to the general's life two days later. Finally, the Austrian assault columns came on line with the Russians. Not expecting to be attacked from two directions, Gérard's 35th Division retreated in some disorder to Probstheida. To cut it off, Pahlen received orders to lead his cavalry from Barclay's group. Receiving deadly fire from the French guns at Sötteritz and Probstheida, the Russian cavalry rode toward the latter but failed to catch Gérard's men. The Austrians ascended the Stein hill and establish a strong artillery line to pound Macdonald's position between Probstheida and the Naundorfs. At this point, Bennigsen issued orders for Stroganov and Dokhturov to extend northeast until they faced Mölkau. On his left, Zieten likewise slid west to maintain contact with Barclay's group yet moved his artillery into position to shell Probstheida. As for the key French positions north of his line, Bennigsen refused to risk an assault on Ober- or Unternaundorf, Mölkau, or Paunsdorf – which, as we will see, Bubna failed to secure – until Bernadotte filled the gap between the Armies of Poland and Silesia.

Meanwhile, on Bennigsen's extreme right, Bubna had his hands full at Paunsdorf facing Reynier's VII Corps.[66] Moving northwest between Engelsdorf and Sommerfeld, around 10:00 the Austrians made contact with the handful of Saxon and French companies posted in the village. Two Saxon batteries totaling ten guns shelled the Austrians from the windmill hill west of Paunsdorf. To draw their fire away from his infantry, Bubna brought up the twelve pieces of his two horse batteries. After a two-hour artillery duel, the Austrian gunners mastered their Saxon opposites and Bubna ordered his infantry to advance. Despite incredible resistance, General Theophil Joseph von Zechmeister's 6th Jäger Battalion drove into Paunsdorf only to be repulsed by a Franco-Saxon counterattack. Bubna committed one battalion from the Peterwardeiner Grenzer Regiment to support the Jäger. Together, the two Austrian battalions managed to take and hold Paunsdorf, in part because Reynier ordered the 2nd Brigade of his all-Saxon 24th Division to withdraw on to its 1st Brigade at Sellershausen. Around noon, Platov warned Bubna that Reynier appeared to be preparing to envelop the Austrian's right with General Pierre-François Durutte's 32nd Division. To counter, Bubna committed Neipperg's 3rd Brigade. The smallest of his three, 3rd Brigade consisted of Jäger Battalion Nr. 5 (846 men), the six squadrons of the Kaiser Hussar Regiment (838 troopers), and six six-pound horse guns. Unable to hold his ground against Durutte, Neipperg requested reinforcements. As the engagement intensified, Bubna gradually committed his entire light division. Not only did the Austrians lose Paunsdorf in the process, but

Reynier also gained the upper hand. Only the arrival of Bülow's corps saved Bubna's division from being routed.

North of Leipzig, Langeron went to Bernadotte's command post. According to the French émigré, "Blücher informed me ... that on this memorable day I was destined to be under the orders of the Prince Royal of Sweden. I immediately went to Breitenfeld. When I arrived at his head-quarters, I found him dictating in French, or rather in Gascon (as he did not know a word of Swedish), the dispositions to his generals; they seemed to me to be very good, but somewhat too detailed; he even designated the place of the junior officers in the columns; this exactitude proved to me that appearance is now the general malady of all sovereigns and of those destined to be one." Bernadotte then gave Langeron instructions, which proved very different from those that his adjutant delivered to Blücher. According to these verbal orders, Langeron would temporarily remain on the left bank of the Parthe at Mockau and Plösen to cover the approach of the North German Army. As soon as it engaged the imperials on the right bank Langeron could commence his crossing.[67]

According to Bernadotte's orders, Bülow's III Corps rather than Wint-zingerode's Russian corps would lead the march of the North German Army to the Parthe.[68] Bülow received instructions to cross the Parthe at Taucha and send detachments east toward Wurzen to make contact with Bennigsen's army. Wintzingerode's Russians would follow Bülow, dispatching cavalry to Wurzen and northeast to Eilenburg to shield Bernadotte's left. As noted, the Swedes would cross somewhere between Langeron and Wintzingerode.[69] Bülow informed Blücher that he planned to cross the Parthe on the shortest line in conjunction with Langeron's corps and thus requested that Langeron accelerate his crossing to support the movement. Learning that Bülow still remained a considerable distance from Taucha, Blücher became impatient and loudly complained about Bernadotte's lethargy as the thunder of the guns south of Leipzig intensified.[70] Fearing that the prince royal would waste too much time marching through Taucha and thus give Napoleon an opportunity to throw superior forces against Schwarzenberg, Blücher ordered Langeron's vanguard to immediately cross the Parthe at Mockau. He informed Bernadotte that Langeron's corps would await his further orders on the other side of the Parthe at Abtnaundorf. According to Müffling, "Blücher resolved not to wait for Bülow but to force the Parthe at Mockau. He was persuaded to make this decision mainly because we saw very few troops on the opposite bank of the Parthe; but with good tele-scopes, he observed a column moving from Leipzig toward the Stötteritz windmill. Therefore, the commander in chief feared that the majority of the French army would turn against the Grand Army in order to bring the battle to a decision before the North German and Silesian Armies could move up."[71]

"The enemy had strong lines of infantry and cavalry along the left bank of the Parthe on the immense open plain that encircled Leipzig on the side of Bad Düben, Torgau, and Dresden," noted Langeron. "The Parthe is marshy, enclosed, and full of trees and thorny underbrush that rendered passage of the river very difficult when it was defended."[72] His forward troops made contact with the French around 9:00; a heated skirmish occurred along the Parthe between Rudzevich's vanguard and Marmont's troops. French artillery, sharing a dominant hill with the St. Thekla Church, tore apart the Russians as they attempted to move across the river. To counter Marmont's guns, the Russians divided three heavy batteries, of twelve guns each, among two hills so that eighteen unlimbered on the elevation northwest of Neutzsch and eighteen took position on the height northeast of Plösen. From these advantageous points on the right bank of the Parthe, the Russians managed to silence Marmont's artillery by 10:00.

After the French guns went silent, the Russians observed the imperials withdraw from the left bank of the river. Rudzevich's infantry and Emmanuel's cavalry wasted little time in crossing the Parthe by Mockau. The infantry either waded across the waist-deep water or hitched a ride on the back of a Cossack's horse. Langeron explains the situation:

> All of a sudden, the enemy, either from the fear of being outflanked by the Prince Royal of Sweden and Bennigsen, whom they could see marching, or by the need to employ greater forces against the Grand Army, which was attacking them with great vigor toward Connewitz and Probstheida while Bennigsen and Bubna moved on Sommerfeld, commenced to distance himself from the banks of the Parthe. Observing the enemy's retrograde movement, Rudzevich and Emmanuel instantly forced the passage of the river; they crossed it at a ford near Mockau: this decision earned them a great deal of honor but in no way was their action surprising. They made it without waiting for my orders and against the dispositions given by the Prince Royal of Sweden but they acted as they should have; there was no time to lose and these two generals knew it. Nevertheless, the French still had some troops and sixteen cannon on the heights; despite the presence of these sixteen pieces and that of their skirmishers, the 7th, 12th, 22nd, 30th and 48th Jäger, [and] the Shlisselburgskii and Olonetskii Regiments forced the crossing with great bravery and the enemy withdrew toward Schönefeld. Coming from Breitenfeld, I reached my vanguard at this moment; I admired Rudzevich's movement and made him aware of my satisfaction.[73]

The Russians drove back Marmont's skirmishers and artillery from the St. Thekla Church and pursued the imperials south to Schönefeld. Langeron's main body crossed the Parthe at Plösen by way of a ford and a hastily thrown footbridge made of barn doors and gates. From the windmill hill at Mockau on the right bank of the Parthe, Blücher tasked Rühle with delivering an order to Langeron instructing the corps commander to attack; if the Russian commander failed to engage the enemy with zeal, Rühle had the authority to forcefully reiterate Blücher's orders to do so. In general, however, Blücher and his staff remained little more than spectators on 18 October.

By 11:00 A.M., Langeron's corps stood between Mockau and the St. Thekla Church to cover the approach of the North German Army. Emmanuel with the vanguard cavalry held a forward position at the Heiterblick estate while Korf's cavalry controlled the Leipzig–Taucha road. Langeron's Cossacks took possession of the plain between the Parthe, Taucha, and Paunsdorf, establishing contact with Platov.

Two hours later, Bernadotte informed Langeron that, as soon as the head of Bülow's corps reached Paunsdorf, the Russians should storm Schönefeld and take the village at all costs. Kaptsevich prepared to assault the village with seven battalions (1,800 men) from his X Infantry Corps. Behind X Infantry Corps followed VIII and IX with Korf's cavalry bringing up the rear; Emmanuel's regiments stood at Heiterblick. Bernadotte visited Langeron's command post shortly after dispatching the order and both French émigrés predicted that the Russians would encounter considerable resistance at Schönefeld, the key to Napoleon's position north of Leipzig. Situated on the left bank of the Parthe, Schönefeld's defenses benefited from the extension of the river's marsh which prevented an attacking force from flanking the village from the north. Although not completely enclosed by a wall, Schönefeld had few points of entry, and these the French had strongly barricaded. As in many of Leipzig's suburbs, thick hedges and a thick wall with freshly made loopholes presented the first obstacle an attacking force would encounter. Large farm buildings often stood outside the walls, providing the defenders flank protection. Well-constructed two-story stone houses each with a garden lined Schönefeld's streets. French artillery dominated all approaches to the village, which faced northeast. A walled cemetery in the southern part of the village served as a fortress for its defenders. Marmont personally commanded, and doubtless he looked to punish the Allies as he had done Yorck's corps two days prior.[74]

After receiving intense fire from Lagrange's 21st Division, Kaptsevich's Staroskolskii, 29th, 38th, and 45th Jäger Regiments forced their way into Schönefeld.[75] His troops took the eastern half of the village before Marmont unleashed a counterattack by Lagrange supported by fresh elements from Friederichs's 22nd Division. Inflicting great losses on the Russians, the French drove them back to Schönefeld's outlying houses and farm buildings. During the combat, the French nearly destroyed the Staroskolskii Regiment in a bayonet attack. Cut off in the courtyard of Schönefeld's manor house and leaderless after their commander was killed, some 200 survivors surrendered. Despite the French success, the Russians managed to retain control of the entrance to the village. Around this time, the British Rocket Battery and Bülow's artillery chased Durutte's 32nd Division from Paunsdorf to Sellerhausen. This provided an opportunity to pour flanking fire into Schönefeld from the French right (south) and attack the village from the northeast and south. A wounded Kaptsevich managed to reorganize his shaken men. From the 1st Brigade of Turchaninov's 22nd Division, he moved the Vyatskii and Olonetskii Regiments into the first line. For his part, Langeron pushed his artillery line closer to the enemy position, moved up Olsufiyev's IX Infantry Corps, and slid St.-Priest's VIII Infantry Corps and Rudzevich's vanguard to his left (south).

As these forces advanced, Kaptsevich's corps attacked Schönefeld from the northeast while the eight battalions of St.-Priest's 17th Division followed by two from the 11th assaulted the village from the south and east. In all, these Russian forces probably equaled the strength of Marmont's 21st and 22nd Divisions. Colonel Vasilchikov led the Vyatskii Regiment into the village at the head of the Russian storm columns. After a fierce struggle with bayonets and musket-butts, the French repulsed the Russians from Schönefeld a second time. Langeron reacted by committing Olsufiyev's IX Infantry Corps. From it, the Nasheburgskii and Irkutskii Regiments joined the Staroingermanlandskii from Kaptsevich's 8th Division to lead the third Russian assault. Shortly afterward, the Ryazhskii, Vilmanstrandskii, Belozerskii, and Brestskii Regiments from the 17th Division of St.-Priest's VIII Infantry Corps likewise stormed Schönefeld from the south. Although flames began devouring the village, French resistance again forced the Russians to retreat. The wounded of both sides that could not be retrieved from Schönefeld perished in the flames. Langeron's subordinates prepared for a fourth attack.

Meanwhile, the Saxons of Fabrice's 26th Light Cavalry Brigade had already repulsed the first Cossack charge at Heiterblick. Just as Olsufiyev's men prepared for the third attack on Schönefeld, the Saxons observed the approach of Emmanuel's cavalry, formed for a second attack, and charged. On reaching the vicinity of the Russians, they sheathed their sabers and summoned their adversary with a loud hurrah. Emmanuel rode toward them and met with Fabrice who informed him of their decision to defect to the Allies. Langeron describes this dramatic episode:

Kaptsevich's corps as well as those of St.-Priest and Olsufiyev and my Reserve Cavalry followed my vanguard and I moved in mass on the left bank of the Parthe between the monastery of St. Thekla and the village of Abt-naundorf. Two beautiful regiments of Saxons, one each of hussars and uhlans, then moved, at a grand trot, toward Emmanuel; my Cossacks prepared to charge them with the Kievskii Regiment; the Saxons stopped, cried "Hurrah!" and the officers advanced out of the ranks; Emmanuel went to talk to them; they announced the desire to join us and cross into our ranks. Emmanuel informed me of this; I hurried there and arranged an interview with the officers of the two regiments.[76]

Korf provides another eyewitness account:

On 18 October, when the entire army was crossing the river in order to attack the enemy, General Emmanuel, with four Cossack regiments, was first to move across the river, followed by other cavalry regiments that comprise his detachment. Once across the river, he deployed his cavalry [in battle formation] and ordered it to advance, but just as our *flanquers* caught up with the enemy skirmishers, they saw two cavalry regiments advancing straight at them. They sent out a trumpeter to convey their desire to surrender, so General Emmanuel immediately halted his regiments. The commander of these Saxon forces soon arrived and assured Emmanuel that these two regiments (one hussar and another uhlan) desired to defect to our side and serve with us against our common enemy.[77]

While the horse battery belonging to the cavalry brigade returned to the main French position at Paunsdorf, one Saxon battalion posted in the Parthe meadows near Seegeritz likewise defected. Although the Saxons expressed their desire to fight against the French, Blücher ordered them to be sent to a reserve position and they took no part in the engagements of the day. As for the Württembergers, Norman decided against waiting for a general retreat to execute his king's orders. Followed by some 556 troopers, he left the French line to join Platov. Unlike the Saxons, Norman declared that neither he nor his men could take up arms against the French without their sovereign's express permission.

Just as Langeron's troops made contact with the French around 9:00, Blücher ordered Sacken to attack both the Halle suburb, its Gerber Gate and bridge over the Parthe, and the Rosenthal; only in the extreme case should the Russian request support from Yorck. From Gohlis, Sacken's fresh troops advanced while Yorck's two divisions moved into position between Gohlis and Eutritzsch. The battle-hardened veterans of Neverovsky's 27th Division attacked Pfaffendorf while Colonel Rakhmanov advanced toward the Rosenthal with the Kamchatskii and Okhotskii Regiments. General Jacob Guine moved twenty-four guns to within pistol range of the wall that enclosed the Rosenthal. Arrighi's forward cavalry quickly fell back but Dąbrowski's Poles supported by 1st Brigade of Brayer's 8th Division from III Corps offered ferocious resistance on the Pfaffendorf estate. Guine and Neverovsky received mortal wounds; Rakhmanov as well as the commander of the Kamchatskii Regiment, Major Salmanov, were killed in the fighting.[78]

Gourgaud arrived and observed that Dąbrowski's division, hardly 1,500 men, and the reserve assigned to it, the 2,600 bayonets of General Jean-Louis Fournier's 1st Brigade from 8th Division of III Corps, would not hold for long against Sacken's superior numbers. At this point of the battle, only the highway running northeast through Taucha remained open to the Grande Armée. With Sacken now threatening to close it, Gourgaud sped off to warn Napoleon. The colonel induced him to send General Michel-Marie Pacthod's 1st Young Guard Division of 6,000 men and 24 guns as reinforcements. After a forced march, the bearskins reached the Halle suburb shortly after 11:00 to restore the balance of forces in this sector. As a result, Sacken not only failed to gain any ground, but an imperial counterattack drove the Russians back to Gohlis. By 1:00 P.M., Sacken found himself forced to request support from Yorck to prevent the French from taking Gohlis. Horn dispatched the Fusilier Battalions of the Leib and East Prussian Regiments, which helped the Russians hold back the imperial tide.

Thus, the situation at 2:00 on the afternoon of the 18th reflected a mixed bag that favored Napoleon, who spent much of the day at his command post by the windmill south of Thon hill and close to the Quandt family's tobacco mill. Nearby, the Old Guard stood watch as the emperor rested on the bare ground for a few minutes. Generals and orderlies came and went; Murat arrived and held a longer conversation with the emperor. Around 12:00, they mounted their horses and, joined by Berthier, rode to the line of Guard Artillery batteries on the hills at Probstheida. Roundshot filled the air as several balls whistled past Napoleon's head. Observing Allied preparations to attack Probstheida, he summoned the 2nd Old Guard Division to form in columns behind (north of) the village and sent the Saxon and Westphalian Guard battalions to reinforce Poniatowski. After a short while at Probstheida, Napoleon returned to his command post. Although his troops had lost their forward positions at Dölitz, Dösen, Zuckelhausen, Holzhausen, and Baalsdorf, they retained control of Lößnig, Probstheida, Mölkau, the Naundorfs, Paunsdorf, and Schönefeld. They repulsed Sacken's attack on the northern side of Leipzig and checked Gyulay at Lindenau. Napoleon's main position remained untouched, and Bertrand had opened the line of retreat to Weißenfels. Bernadotte's late arrival paralyzed the Allies at the most vulnerable point of the French line. If 18 October was to be the day the Allies triumphed over Napoleon, the afternoon would have to provide decisive results.

Once again, we will survey the course of the battle counterclockwise. During the fighting at Kleinzschocher, Gyulay reported to Schwarzenberg that he could not determine with certainty that Bertrand's attack signaled the start of Napoleon's retreat. From the hill at Probstheida, Schwarzenberg responded at 2:00 by emphasizing that the importance of Gyulay's position on the left bank of the Elster did not require him to defeat Bertrand but to determine positively which road the French had taken: the one leading to Merseburg, the one to Weißenfels, or both. The Allied commander in chief wanted Gyulay's detachment approaching from Naumburg to reverse its march and return there and his cavalry patrols to observe the Saale and report French movements. Consequently, Allied Headquarters became aware of the likelihood that Napoleon would retreat: for what other reason would he send an entire corps marching away from Leipzig?

Gyulay tasked Mensdorff and Thielmann with following the French columns as closely as possible. Around 5:00, the French cleared Lützen and headed for Weißenfels, where Murray promptly destroyed the bridge over the Saale. Believing his forces to be insufficient to defend Weißenfels, Murray commenced his retreat to Zeitz, where stood the Bohemian Army's trains. Late on the evening of the 18th, Gyulay received news from Schwarzenberg that the French would probably attempt to retreat on Naumburg. Gyulay should do his best to beat them there and occupy Bad Kösen. Schwarzenberg wanted Gyulay's cavalry as well as the Austrian II Corps at Pegau by 7:00 A.M. on the 19th to take the road to Naumburg. Yet should the French threaten to overwhelm Gyulay, Schwarzenberg advised him to retreat to Zeitz, sending the trains to Altenburg. Should Napoleon press Gyulay at Zeitz, Schwarzenberg instructed his corps commander to do everything possible to harass the retreating French army but not allow his own troops to suffer *"einen Echec."* As soon as the French cleared the Austrians to open a road for the further retreat, Schwarzenberg wanted Gyulay to follow "only with strong cavalry."[79] Around 2:00 A.M. on the 19th, Gyulay's III Corps and Liechtenstein's 1st Light Division commenced the thirteen-mile march south-southwest to Pegau.

Returning to Colloredo's front, after losing Dösen and Dölitz, Murat withdrew all his forces to the main French position around Lößnig's ponds. The two sides exchanged brutal artillery fire. Colloredo recognized that he could not attempt to force Murat's position until Barclay's group took Probstheida. Shortly after 2:00, Murat launched a counterattack with fresh forces to regain Dölitz and Dösen. At the former, the imperials mauled the 1st Brigade of Bianchi's 2nd Division from the Austrian Reserve Corps, requiring Colloredo to transfer three battalions (one from the Reserve Corps's 1st Division, two from 1st Division of II Corps) from the left bank of the Pleiße to the right to maintain control of the village. On the Austrian right, the French drove them from the ridge that stretched between Dölitz and the small wood northeast of Dösen. The Austrians managed to stay the French advance at Dösen and the wood. From the 2nd Division of the Austrian Reserve Corps, the Hessen-Homburg Infantry Regiment bravely defended the wood but soon its position again appeared to be in jeopardy after the French penetrated the grove. General Alois Gonzaga Joseph von und zu Liechtenstein, commander of 2nd Division of the Austrian II Corps, committed the two battalions (1,651 men) of his Reuß-Greiz Infantry Regiment to drive the imperials from the wood. Gradually the Austrians pushed back the French from Dösen and the wood to their former position behind

Lößnig's ponds. The Austrians resumed their line along the ridge and the artillery duel recommenced.

Shortly afterward, the Austrians made a general advance. Bianchi's 1st Brigade, which re-formed south of Dölitz, marched on Lößnig. This brigade, commanded by General August von Beck, penetrated Lößnig several times only to be repulsed by Poniatowski's Poles and Decouz's bearskins. Despite the bravery of the Poles, Bianchi's division managed to gain ground along the Pleiße. Observing these developments, Colloredo personally led two regiments from the 3rd Division of his own I Corps in the successful storming of Lößnig. Although the Austrians maintained the village, all attempts to take Connewitz, particularly the village cemetery, shattered on the heroic resistance directed by Poniatowski. A timely counterattack ordered by Napoleon and led by General Henri Rottembourg's small, non-French 2nd Brigade[80] of the 2nd Old Guard Division turned the tables on Colloredo. Switching to the defensive, the Austrians repulsed every French attempt to regain Lößnig. Fatigue on both sides brought the fighting in this sector to a sustained firefight that gradually weakened and finally ended with the last light of day. On the western bank of the Pleiße, General Lederer's 1st Division of II Corps gained no success enveloping Murat's right, despite being reinforced by two battalions from Bianchi's division.

Meanwhile, the morning operation had ended with Barclay's army group facing Probstheida, which Napoleon recognized as the key to his position. To defend it, numerous French batteries unlimbered on either side of the village while large columns of infantry and cavalry could be seen north of it; Napoleon expected them to defend Probstheida to the extreme. A man-high, one-foot-thick wall with loopholes completely surrounded the rectangle-shaped village, which contained stone structures, making it a solid position for its defenders. Flanked by batteries, Probstheida's wall presented an almost insurmountable obstacle. Penetrating the village on its eastern and western sides presented problems as well because only one narrow point of entry existed at each. Barclay clearly observed the strength of the position. Not wanting to sacrifice his men, he decided to wait until Colloredo and Bennigsen had advanced far enough to envelop Probstheida. Conversely, both of these commanders were waiting for Barclay to take Probstheida before they launched attacks on either side of him against Lößnig and Stötteritz respectively.[81] Tsar Alexander broke this stalemate around 2:00 by ordering Barclay to storm Probstheida, most likely to relieve pressure on Bennigsen at Stötteritz. Kleist's 10th and 12th Brigades supported by the 1,800 men of Prince Eugen's Russian II Infantry Corps received instructions to storm the village.

Unfortunately for the Prussians leading the charge, Barclay launched the attack before the Allied artillery could soften the French position. In particular, the Allied guns failed to demolish the wall. Instead, the balls passed through smoothly without causing significant breaches.[82] Under devastating fire from French cannon, the Prussians advanced toward Probstheida at the double-quick. Commanding 10th Brigade, General Georg Dubislav von Pirch I led his men against the portion of the wall southwest of the village while the 2nd Silesian and 11th Reserve Regiments of Prince August of Prussia's 12th Brigade attacked from the east. Preceding Pirch's first wave, the skirmishers of the Fusilier Battalion of the 2nd West Prussian Infantry Regiment dodged musket and cannonballs to reach the man-high wall, behind which stood the enemy's forward infantry. After the Prussians managed to hop the wall, the imperials withdrew fifty paces to a second garden wall. Despite the hail of musket fire, the Prussians also cleared this second obstacle. As the skirmishers moved into the streets of Probstheida, the Fusilier Battalion and the only remaining battalion, the 2nd, of the 9th Landwehr Regiment gradually cleared the two walls to likewise penetrate the village. In this way, Pirch managed to assemble enough fire-power to drive the French reserves from Probstheida. Napoleon arrived to personally lead reinforcements from Victor's II Corps to retake the position. Prussian fatigue as well as the breakdown of command and control due to the chaotic storming of the village meant that Pirch did not have long to enjoy his success. After some brief but deadly hand-to-hand combat, the Prussians withdrew from Probstheida under the protection of their skirmishers.

On the eastern side of Probstheida, Prince August's 12th Brigade encountered numerous terrain obstacles that impeded its march. Followed by a detachment of Russian hussars, the skirmishers of its lead battalion braved the storm of lead to reach the outer wall. At the gate, the Prussians took two abandoned guns whose draft horses had been killed; the Russian troopers carried the prizes back to Allied lines. Yet the delays that August encountered en route meant that his skirmishers entered the eastern side of Probstheida just as Victor launched his counterattack. With the first wave of 12th Brigade just reaching the outer wall, the skirmishers also had to retreat in the face of the French onslaught. August reacted by assembling his first wave in a column at Probstheida's eastern entrance. His foremost battalions had just pushed into the village when suddenly a concealed French battery of fifteen guns lambasted the column's right flank with canister and a large column of cavalry bore down on it. Forming squares to defend against the cavalry took precedence over the attack on Probstheida. Thanks to the Russian hussars who engaged the French in hand-to-hand combat, the Prussians retreated in good order.

Undaunted, Prince August re-formed his columns and placed himself at the head of his two foremost battalions.[83] The nephew of Frederick the Great[84] led his men through the hail of grape from the fifteen-gun battery that greeted them as they approached Probstheida's eastern entrance. With bayonets fixed, the Prussian prince led his men into the village, driving Victor's warriors from building to building. On reaching the village square, the Prussians received brutal flanking fire from a French battery northwest of Probstheida. Simultaneously, Rochambeau led troops from his 19th Division of Lauriston's V Corps to retake the village. Although Rochambeau and many of his officers fell with mortal wounds, the French smashed through the village. August received reinforcements in the form of two battalions from the 19th Reserve Regiment, one battalion of Silesian fusiliers, and one company of marksmen from Zieten's 11th Brigade, which had just taken Zuckelhausen. Despite this support, August could not hold his ground. Just as the Prussians came flying out of Probstheida hotly pursued by the French, Eugen's Russians arrived to enable August to organize an orderly retreat. Eugen's men, who had been shredded in the brutal fighting on the 16th, then took their turn in the cauldron of Probstheida. Prince Ivan Shakhovsky led Eugen's 3rd Division north and bravely stormed the village only to be repulsed by French counterattacks. Eugen lost 600 men or one-third of his effectives during the struggle at Probstheida. Russian grape prevented the French from exploiting Eugen's setback through a deadly pursuit.

As noted, the carnage around Probstheida had attracted Napoleon's attention. Rushing over to this crucial point of his line, he quickly observed the exhaustion of Victor's corps, which included a 75 percent casualty rate for General Honoré Vial's 6th Division. This prompted the emperor to commit the rest of Lauriston's V Corps to the defense of Probstheida. To encourage his warriors, Napoleon entered the firing line, exposing himself to tremendous danger. He responded to a report that the artillery would soon expend its ammunition by ordering the gunners to slow their rate of fire. No longer thinking of victory, the French ferociously fought to survive. Instead of breaking French resolve, the defection of the Saxons and Württembergers seemed to strengthen their determination. Vial's 2nd, 4th, and 18th Line Regiments ferociously resisted the Allied attacks.[85] At 5:00, just as the concussion of a cannonball that flew past Vial killed him, Napoleon summoned elements of his last reserve: the fusiliers of General Louis Friant's 1st Old Guard Division. Together with a few hundred dragoons, these fresh forces helped Lauriston's men and Victor's survivors seal the French victory at Probstheida.

Despite this setback, the Allies found much hope in Gyulay's report that the French had started the retreat to the Saale. With the aid of a glass, French wagon trains could be seen rolling out of Leipzig and across the Lindenau defile. This signaled to the Allies that the French quite possibly would abandon Probstheida. Based on this thought, Barclay pulled his men out of range of French caseshot, sent Kleist's Reserve Cavalry to his left to establish the link with Colloredo, and reinforced his artillery line to prevent the French from breaking out of Probstheida. Both sides exchanged artillery blasts until darkness silenced the guns. Although Friederich unfairly criticizes Barclay for not committing the idle Russo-Prussian Guard units standing south of Meusdorf to storm Probstheida and force a decision on the 18th, the fact remains that Barclay's group achieved no decisive results during the course of the afternoon.[86]

Returning to Bennigsen's group, his troops faced the Naundorf–Mölkau–Paunsdorf line with numerous batteries opposite the French defenders of the first two. Yet, by pushing Bubna to Paunsdorf, Bennigsen overextended himself, creating large gaps between his columns that prevented mutual support. Conscious of this factor, he delayed attacking the Naundorfs and Mölkau until Bernadotte's army arrived. Finally around 2:30, the lead brigade of Bülow's III Corps – Hessen-Homburg's 3rd – appeared. Bennigsen immediately dispatched his adjutant to Bernadotte's headquarters with a status report; a little later Bennigsen himself arrived to discuss a combined operation. Together, they decided that Bennigsen would not attempt to extend his right wing through Paunsdorf but instead the Army of North Germany would fill the gap between the Parthe and that village by pushing Bülow's 3rd Brigade to a position facing Paunsdorf. This in turn allowed Bubna to slide south so Bennigsen could concentrate his forces for the assault on the Naundorf villages and Mölkau. Regardless, the overly cautious Bennigsen refused to authorize the advance until all of Bernadotte's army had arrived. In the meantime, both sides exchanged vicious artillery fire. The French seized the initiative through a bold cavalry attack by Nansouty's Guard Cavalry – which Napoleon himself had ordered – but Allied steadfastness turned back these elite mounted warriors. Following this failed attack, the French cavalry supported by twenty pieces of horse artillery made for the gap between Stünz and Mölkau which separated Bubna from Bennigsen's main body. To counter them, Dokhturov assembled three batteries whose effective caseshot along with intense small-arms fire from Bubna's 6th Jäger Battalion slowed the French long enough for Chaplits's cavalry to arrive and repulse the attack.

By this time, the 5:00 hour had struck and Bennigsen finally felt that enough of the Army of North Germany had arrived so that he could order a general advance. Bubna received orders to attack Mölkau; Stroganov followed by Dokhturov marched against Unternaundorf; and Klenau's IV Austrian Corps assaulted Obernaundorf. Bubna's troops quickly carried Mölkau as did Klenau's at Obernaundorf but the Russians encountered determined French resistance at Unternaundorf. After Dokhturov reinforced Stroganov with General Ivan Paskevich's 26th Division, the Russians took the village. A French counterattack drove them out again but after a second attempt the Russians managed to take and hold

Unternaundorf. Russian Jäger from the 6th and 11th Regiments moved into the thickets to the right (north) of the Naundorfs. To contain the Russians in Unternaundorf, Sébastiani led his II Cavalry Corps supported by Walther's 3rd Division of Guard Cavalry toward the village. Backed by a powerful battery of twenty-four guns west of Unternaundorf, the French engaged the approaching Russian cavalry. The melee produced no clear results until Stroganov's 6th Jäger Regiment moved close enough to the French battery to spook the gunners into withdrawing. After losing their artillery support, the French cavalry retreated to Stötteritz, bringing back a severely wounded Sébastiani. Paskevich's 26th Division moved west from Unternaundorf, taking the windmill hill behind the village.

From Obernaundorf, Klenau directed his troops slightly southwest toward Stötteritz. Like the Prussians at Probstheida, the Austrians found that the features of Stötteritz – a clay wall, hedges, and trenches protecting the village's south and east sides – favored the defender. A large French force of infantry and artillery guarded Stötteritz. Knowing that possession of Stötteritz would facilitate the capture of Probstheida – the key to Napoleon's line – Klenau did not allow these obstacles to intimidate him. Personally leading 1st Brigade of Hohenlohe-Bartenstein's 2nd Division, Klenau marched toward Stötteritz. Before he could cross the one and one-half miles that separated the Stötteritz and Obernaundorf, his Zach and Colloredo Infantry Regiments received withering blasts of grape in the front and flank, forcing him to retreat. Not content with setting Obernaundorf ablaze with their shells, the French launched a counterattack but failed to drive the Austrians from the village. As in the other sectors of the line, an artillery duel ensued until dark. Despite losing the forward positions of the Naundorfs, Mölkau, and Paunsdorf, the French maintained the critical point of Stötteritz, thus denying Bennigsen decisive results.

As for Bernadotte's army, Langeron's artillery commenced the shelling of Schönefeld from Abtnaundorf around 1:00 P.M. Delays and blocked roads slowed Bernadotte's detour through Taucha, meaning that his vanguard – Bülow's corps – did not appear on Langeron's left until 2:00; the rest of the North German Army followed even later. Consequently, the gap between the Armies of Poland and Silesia would not close until around 4:00. In the meantime, Prince Louis William of Hessen-Homburg led Bülow's 3rd Brigade toward Paunsdorf shortly after 2:30 P.M. Bülow's other brigades as well as Wintzingerode's Russians and Stedingk's Swedes had yet to reach the battlefield. Opposite the Army of North Germany, the main body of Durutte's 32nd Division stood behind (west of) Paunsdorf while one of its battalions along with two Saxon companies held the village itself. West of Paunsdorf, Reynier sought to position his 1st Saxon Brigade on the windmill hill at Stünz and his 2nd Brigade north of it at Sellerhausen. As soon as 3rd Brigade reached Paunsdorf, Bülow rolled up four batteries and the British

Congreve Rocket Brigade to engage Durutte's artillery and shell Marmont's right wing. Just as Bülow's guns opened fire, he received orders from Bernadotte to take Paunsdorf with Hessen-Homburg's three left wing battalions. Linking with Bubna's 6th Jäger Battalion, the Austro-Prussian force broke into the village, forcing the French and Saxons to withdraw on their main position. Prussian infantry along with Austrian Jäger and Grenzer pursued as Bülow's batteries moved up. Coming within caseshot range of Durutte's division, the Prussian guns pelted the French. As Durutte's division stood on the brink of collapse, the rocket battery opened fire. This proved to be too much for the French, who fled to Sellerhausen in complete chaos.

Some of Durutte's fugitives crossed the path of Reynier's two Saxon brigades. Disgusted by what they had seen and believing that this served as the last opportunity they would have to defect, some 3,000 Saxons with 19 guns, including 1 battery of 12-pound pieces, prepared to march toward Unternaundorf. After Reynier sent orders for the heavy battery to withdraw to Sellerhausen, the gunners led their teams toward the Allied line followed by the infantry of the Saxon 1st Brigade and then the 2nd. Assuming the Saxons were marching to attack the Allies, the troopers of General Vincent Axamitowsky's 1st Brigade of Defrance's 4th Heavy Cavalry Division accompanied them with shouts of "*Vive l'Empereur!*" Believing that his men had misunderstood Reynier's orders, the division's general, Heinrich von Zeschau, hurried over to the commander of his 2nd Brigade, General Xavier Reinhold von Ryssel, who informed him of their intention to defect.[87] Zeschau refused to condone such dishonorable conduct and pleaded for his officers and men to turn around. Zeschau managed to convince only two battalions (24 officers and 593 men) to return to their positions but concerns over their loyalty prompted the French to send them to Leipzig. At Unternaundorf, the Saxons encountered Stroganov's cavalry and defected to the Allies. In all, only 710 Saxons remained loyal to the French.[88] Bennigsen honored Ryssel's request that his men be spared from further combat until Frederick Augustus could openly declare for the German cause. While the Saxon infantry retired to a bivouac south of Engelsdorf, the Allies impressed four guns each from the two Saxon horse batteries. The complete battery joined Stroganov's artillery.[89]

Returning to Durutte, the Allied artillery and rocket battery pursued his fugitives. Taking a position between Paunsdorf and Sellerhausen, the Allies shelled the latter. As flames engulfed Sellerhausen, the two battalions of Bülow's 4th Reserve Regiment moved up and dispersed the forward French skirmishers. Entering Sellerhausen the same time as the retreating skirmishers, the Prussians and Bubna's Peterwardeiner Grenzer secured the village after a short fight but could advance no further due to Ney's strong reserves. Meanwhile, Durutte's flight from Paunsdorf had exposed Marmont's right along the Schönefeld–Paunsdorf line. This prompted Marmont to bend his right westward so that his corps ultimately held a line extending from Schönefeld to Sellerhausen. With the Prussians in control of Sellerhausen, Marmont again found his right in danger of being flanked. Ney recognized that Sellerhausen needed to be retaken to prevent the collapse of his sector. From his reserves at Volkmarsdorf, he assigned the task to Delmas's 9th Division of III Corps as well as Durutte's reorganized division. No match for two French divisions, Bülow's two battalions and the Austrian Grenzer attempted to hold Sellerhausen but eventually fled to Paunsdorf in complete disorder, sweeping the Allied artillery with them. Both the guns and the rocket battery suffered such considerable losses that they could no longer take part in the battle. Durutte's division occupied Sellerhausen and Stünz while Delmas's men filled the gap between Durutte and Marmont's right wing. Allied canister turned back two French cavalry regiments that attempted to exploit the situation.

Around 3:00, Langeron received orders from both Blücher and Bernadotte to again storm Schönefeld. Blücher reinforced Langeron's artillery by moving additional batteries to the right bank of the Parthe. After softening the enemy position, St.-Priest's VIII Infantry Corps attacked the village. Marmont claims that the two divisions of his VI Corps at Schönefeld had never fought as heroically as they did to defend the village. According to Bogdanovich's account, "Amid the cries of the soldiers, the thunder of the artillery, the crackling of musket fire, the bursting of shells, the church steeple suddenly collapsed in flames; smoke and dust obscured the light of day and for a few minutes this night interrupted the efforts of the combatants."[90] Olsufiyev moved up Rudzevich's and Udom's divisions from his IX Infantry Corps to support St.-Priest. Also at this time, Langeron's artillery gained the upper hand in its duel with Marmont's guns, which proceeded to withdraw after losing numerous pieces to Russian counterbattery fire. The retreat of Marmont's artillery meant the end of his infantry's resistance; the marshal withdrew the remains of his two divisions almost three miles south-southwest to Reudnitz around 4:30.

Despite Marmont's capitulation, Ney decided to throw his last reserves – Ricard's 11th Division and 2nd Brigade from Brayer's 8th, some 7,000 men and 40 guns – against the Russians at Schönefeld. He tasked Souham with regaining the village. While reconnoitering to determine the best point to attack, both Ney and Souham received wounds that put them out of action. Command devolved to Ricard, who received a break when Langeron's guns sped off due to a lack of ammunition and the grape from his own forty guns drove off St.-Priest's troops from the southern side of Schönefeld. Despite being reinforced by six fresh battalions, Kaptsevich's men in the village could not prevent Ricard's assault columns from penetrating Schönefeld. Success proved fleeting after Bernadotte directed sixty guns from

Wintzingerode's corps and twenty from Stedingk's to replace Langeron's. Protected by these eighty guns, Langeron formed his entire army corps for a final assault on Schönefeld. Olsufiyev personally led six battalions of his 9th Division southwest along the Parthe while Kaptsevich, St.-Priest, and Rudzevich attacked Schönefeld from the south and east. Ricard could not hold his position in the face of such overwhelming numbers. Severely wounded in the process, Brayer brought up his 2nd Brigade to reinforce Ricard but nothing could stop the repeated Russian attacks, which numbered eight altogether. After a brief hand-to-hand skirmish around 6:00, Ricard's troops broke in disorder, fleeing toward Reudnitz after losing 117 officers and 5,009 men as well as 459 prisoners. Wintzingerode's cavalry gave chase, taking four guns from the fugitives. French forces rallied on the windmill hill between Schönefeld and Reudnitz, which they defended until the Allies drove them into Reudnitz around 9:00 P.M. Russian loses in the struggle for Schönefeld surpassed 4,000 men; the French lost more in addition to several officers being wounded, including Friederichs, Compans, Coëhorn, and most of Marmont's staff.[91]

During this action, the rest of Bülow's 3rd Brigade reached Paunsdorf, taking a position with its right leaning on the village and its left extending south and linking with Bubna's right. Behind 3rd Brigade, the rest of the North German Army gradually arrived on the field to close the circle around Leipzig toward 4:00 on the afternoon of 18 October. To form Bülow's right wing, Borstell's 5th Brigade halted between Paunsdorf and the northeast-running Leipzig–Taucha road. As a reserve, Bülow posted Karl August von Krafft's 6th Brigade east of Paunsdorf with his Reserve Cavalry behind it. Bülow's artillery unlimbered along a line extending between Paunsdorf and the Leipzig–Taucha road. Langeron's corps faced Schönefeld with its right leaning on the Parthe. Wintzingerode's Russian corps filled the gap between Bülow's right and Langeron's left. Behind (east of) Wintzingerode stood the Swedish corps as the army's reserve. Strong French batteries formed on a line between Schönefeld and Stünz. Bülow responded with seventy-six Prussian pieces, mauling Nansouty's cavalry in crossfire with Bennigsen's guns.

Just as Ricard launched his counterattack on Schönefeld, Bülow's artillery engaged the batteries of the French 21st, 22nd, and 32nd Divisions. To their credit, the French gunners did not waver in the face of Prussian numerical superiority. Yet this advantage enabled the Prussian guns to move very close to Sellerhausen. More than one hour later, thus around 5:30, as Bennigsen commenced the movements of his columns to assault Mölkau and Unternaundorf, and Langeron's corps gained uncontested possession of Schönefeld, Bernadotte ordered Bülow to take Stünz and Sellerhausen. Following a bombardment by 150 Russo-Prussian guns of the North German Army, two battalions from the 3rd East Prussian Regiment of

Bülow's 3rd Brigade advanced against Stünz while skirmisher detachments from two others swarmed Sellerhausen. After Mölkau to the left (south) of Bülow's corps fell to the Austrians, the Prussians stormed and secured Stünz in unison with one of Bubna's Jäger detachments. However, Bülow underestimated the number of defenders at Sellerhausen. There, a prolonged struggle ensued until the main bodies of the battalions whose skirmishers initially sought to take the village moved up along with four battalions from Bülow's 6th Brigade. This show of force prompted Delmas's 9th and Durutte's 32nd Divisions to evacuate Sellerhausen but not until well after nightfall. In view of the late hour, the Allies did not advance beyond the Schönfeld–Sellerhausen–Stünz line. Delmas lost his life in the combat.

Due to his agreement to cede Langeron's corps to the North German Army, Blücher did little on 18 October other than observe Sacken's attempts to take the Pfaffendorf manor and the Rosenthal. Sacken's first effort had failed thanks to the timely arrival of the twelve battalions of Pacthod's 1st Young Guard Division as well as three Guard batteries. Around 3:00, Sacken resumed the attack. Each time Sacken's troops managed to wrest the stone buildings of the Pfaffendorf estate from the Poles, brutal French artillery fire from the Rosenthal forced the Russians to evacuate the structure. As flames devoured the manor house, many Polish and Russian wounded who could not escape suffered a cruel death. In the evening, Sacken's troops crossed the Pleiße and took the Rosenthal but failed to hold it and retreated to Gohlis. The struggle ensued until dark without either side gaining an advantage. At the least, Sacken tied down imperial forces, including Guard units that could have been used to defend Schönefeld. "With Sacken's very weak corps," explained Gneisenau, "we attacked the suburb of Leipzig, which was defended by Marmont; it was taken, lost, and retaken. The bloody battle lasted into the night; we could hold only a part of the suburb. Yorck's corps, which had been reduced from 19,000 men on the 16th to 12,700, needed rest and took only a small part in the struggle on this day."[92]

News that the Saxons had defected brought Napoleon to Ney's command post, where the two engaged in a lengthy discussion. Keeping the traitorous behavior of the Saxons and Württembergers a secret so that his army would not panic became the emperor's main concern. Around 4:00 that afternoon, he issued orders for I Cavalry Corps, followed by III and V Cavalry Corps, to commence the army's retreat by withdrawing into a position at Schönau *west* of Lindenau before nightfall. The entire artillery park would follow after resupplying the troops and burning the empty caissons. Napoleon finally accepted that he could no longer maintain his position. Only darkness prevented the Allies from completing their success on the 18th and critically threatening his line of retreat. Each side suffered between 20,000–25,000 casualties on this day, meaning the advantage went to

18 Schwarzenberg's victory report to the three Allied monarchs, Leipzig,
18 October 1813

the Allies, who had much more manpower to spare. Only a miracle could
prevent the Allies from delivering the final blow on the 19th.

At 5:00 P.M. on 18 October, an exhausted Napoleon returned to his
command post south of Thon hill. Surrounded by generals, adjutants, and
orderlies, Napoleon slumped down by a campfire he ordered lit near the
tobacco mill, providing a scene that Friederich terms "indescribably tragic."
The 2nd Brigade of 1st Old Guard Division soon arrived from Stötteritz.
After dozing for fifteen minutes on a wooden stool, he awoke after a shell hit
the campfire. He then calmly dictated further instructions for the retreat on
the 19th. These instructions have been lost but according to French sources
the artillery and parks would retire from the field followed before daybreak
by the Old Guard, Oudinot's Young Guard Corps, IV Cavalry Corps, IX
and II Corps, with II Cavalry Corps forming the rear. The remaining corps
(III, V, VI, VII, VIII, and XI) received the task of defending Leipzig and
covering the retreat.[93]

Around 6:30, the emperor called for his tent to be established. Learning
that it had already departed with the imperial baggage, he decided to pass the
night in Leipzig itself. Accompanied by Murat, Napoleon left the battlefield.
By now the jam of wagons and men in Leipzig so clogged the roads that

Napoleon had to utilize detours to reach his quarters at the Hôtel de Prusse, around 9:00 P.M. Certainly the irony of the inn's name was not lost on him.

Napoleon, Berthier, and Maret spent the night finalizing the measures for the Grande Armée's retreat. With every minute becoming more precious than the last, no time could be lost. Orderlies rushed to the various corps commanders to deliver the master's commands to accelerate their movements. To cover the retreat, Poniatowski, Macdonald, and Marmont received command of the right, center, and left respectively. Poniatowski's VIII Corps anchored the French line south of Leipzig with its right at Connewitz on the Pleiße. From there, XI, V, and III Corps extended to the Grimma Gate on the city's eastern side. From the Grimma Gate to the Parthe, Marmont's VI Corps would defend the line while the only remaining division of VII Corps – Durutte's 32nd – reinforced by the Leipzig garrison held the Halle suburb. As soon as circumstances allowed, III, V, and VI Corps would follow the army while Macdonald sought to hold the city for at least twenty-four hours with the 30,000 men of VII, VIII, and XI Corps. After this rearguard evacuated Leipzig, the Hohenbrücken (high bridge) over the Elster's main arm and leading to the Lindenau causeway would be blown by the charges placed on a boat anchored under its western end. As soon as the rearguard reached Lindenau, the Rat-Forsthaus-Brücke (Forestry Council Bridge), which was the bridge closest to Lindenau, would also be blown. After the engineer in chief of the Grande Armée, General Joseph Rogniat, departed for Weißenfels, the execution of this task fell to his assistant, chief of staff of the engineers of the Grande Armée, Colonel Joseph de Montfort. Only the commander of the rearguard – presumably Macdonald – could give the order to detonate the charges. Unfortunately for the French, Montfort never received clear instructions regarding which units would cover the retreat, which troop units would be the last to cross, and who would give him the signal to detonate the bridge. This lack of clarification would lead to disaster.[94]

After making these arrangements, Napoleon dictated instructions for Bertrand at Weißenfels to extend IV Corps between Merseburg and Bad Kösen while observing the passages of the Saale and occupying Freiburg, and to ensure that victuals were prepared along the line of retreat at Erfurt, Fulda, and other points. The same courier would then continue to Mainz to deliver the emperor's instructions to Marshal François Christophe de Kellermann regarding the recall to Frankfurt-am-Main of all march units en route to join the army.[95] Ominously, Napoleon's orders to Kellermann included directives for the summoning of the French National Guard and measures to defend France against the imminent Allied invasion. The commandants of Erfurt and Würzburg received notification to provision those cities as quickly as possible. To St.-Cyr at Dresden went a short summary of the events of 16 and 18 October as well as the permission to escape as best he could and negotiate the surrender of Torgau and Wittenberg. The letter-writing lasted long into the night; Napoleon finally took a short nap at dawn.[96]

Meanwhile, Bertrand reached Weißenfels at 7:00 P.M. on 18 October with the main body of IV Corps after leaving one division at Lützen to maintain communication with the rest of the army. Early on the following morning he repaired the Saale bridge and started construction on a second further downstream. After forwarding a detachment to secure the crossing over the Unstrut at Freyburg, Bertrand reconnoitered all the way to Naumburg, thirty miles southwest of Leipzig. At Naumburg, an Austrian garrison of five companies and one squadron launched a bold sortie, which caused him to grossly overestimate the Allied force. He withdrew to Weißenfels, where V Cavalry Corps arrived that evening. Rather than clear the Allies from Naumburg, Bertrand decided to turn off the great highway and lead the army on a detour through Freyburg. Napoleon spent the night at Markranstädt with the majority of the Guard while the main body of the French army camped at Lützen; two Young Guard divisions under Oudinot remained at Lindenau as rearguard.

Back at Leipzig, chaos ensued in the dark, unlit city streets as imperial troops poured into the inner city from three gates, all making for the single western exit: the Ranstädt Gate. Order broke down, roads became clogged with jettisoned equipment, dead horses, broken wagons, and overturned caissons, columns collided, cavalry and artillery rode through the infantry, wagons and horses trampled the wounded that lay scattered throughout the streets. "After the shadows of night covered Leipzig, the suburbs, and the defile, an orderly retreat became all the more necessary," recalled Pelet. "Not only should there have been multiple routes instead of one, but the streets should have been illuminated and officers posted to give directions and maintain the columns without interruption. Unfortunately, of those who by duty and by order were responsible for this service, not a one occupied a point. One encountered difficulties finding the road to the bridge. A column of 4,000 to 5,000 prisoners, which set out too late and marched very slowly, steadily increased the confusion." In the cold hour before dawn the moon's sinking rays provided some light to guide the last of the infantry – II and IX Corps followed by V Corps – to the Ranstädt Gate. The complete lack of food compounded this awful situation. So bare was Leipzig that the emperor's servants had trouble finding bread for him and his immediate entourage. As dawn broke, thousands of hungry and exhausted stragglers emerged from Leipzig's houses where they had sought refuge to join the disorderly masses moving west through the city. Also numbering in the thousands were men who had fought for their emperor and now, incapacitated from wounds, were left behind without care or food to die a painful death, such was the master's gratitude.[97]

At 8:00 P.M., Maret had sent a message to Frederick Augustus. Per Napoleon's instructions, the French foreign minister assured the Saxon king that the battle was won and that the Allies would inevitably retreat in the night. Pelet claims that Maret actually went to see Frederick Augustus to personally convince him to withdraw from the French alliance. Other accounts state that Maret made his way through the throngs to the residence of the Saxon king to deliver the promise that, if Frederick Augustus joined the emperor on the journey to Erfurt, Napoleon would guarantee his security. If any individual had more to fear about the future than Napoleon, it was certainly Frederick Augustus. Knowing that leaving his kingdom could cost him his crown, he decided to await the Allied monarchs and so politely declined the proposal.[98]

That night, the armies camped where they had ended the day's events: Colloredo's group along the Lößnig–Dölitz–Dösen line; Barclay's opposite Probstheida from Dösen to Zuckelhausen; Bennigsen's along the Zuckelhausen–Naundorf–Mölkau line; Bernadotte's in several waves from Stünz–Sellerhausen to Paunsdorf–Abtnaundorf; Langeron's corps at Schö-nefeld; Sacken's corps between Gohlis and the Parthe, close to Leipzig. Napoleon's line extended from Connewitz to Probstheida and then cut sharply north to Stötteritz, where the reserves bivouacked, and ran through Crottendorf and Reudnitz to the Halle suburb and Gohlis. The outposts of the two sides stood so close that each side could clearly hear the other talking.

To defend Leipzig itself, the French withdrew into the city's immediate suburbs or outer city at 2:00 A.M. Like Schönefeld and Probstheida, their large stone buildings, brick and clay garden walls, hedges, and wooden fences would have greatly facilitated the defense had time been available for the French to prepare. According to Pelet and Napoleon's secretary, Baron Fain, some of the emperor's entourage insisted that the suburbs of Leipzig's outer city be burned to open fields of fire. They predicted that 6,000 men with 60 guns could defend the inner city and that "our retreat would be secure: the army could tranquilly regain the Saale. But the emperor could not bring himself to expose one of the capitals of Germany to such a harsh fate. He preferred to lose a few hundred wagons than to lower the French army to sustain the war of barbarians. It would suffice to leverage the means of resistance that the gates of the suburbs and the inner city wall offer us to delay the progress of the enemy." Pelet simply notes that "it was useful to retain before the suburbs the four armies that the emperor had drawn there, and which could significantly disturb our retreat."[99]

As apocryphal as Fain's statements appear, darkness prevented the imperials from evaluating the means at their disposal while clogged roads obstructed the movement and positioning of the resources needed for a proper defense. Napoleon's selection of the corps that stood closest to the enemy for the defense of the city left them little time to ready their new positions before the Allies attacked. Yet this did not mean that the imperials did nothing. In general, they closed and fortified points of access, made loopholes in walls, transformed larger buildings into bastions, palisaded fences and hedges, situated batteries, and placed reserves. Because of the haphazard nature of these preparations, some important points were neglected while others received too much attention.[100]

Eleven outer gates provided entry through Leipzig's outer city wall, which consisted of mostly brick and thin boards.[101] Suburbs and gardens formed Leipzig's outer city. Between the inner and outer cities extended large open areas cut by finely manicured esplanades and avenues. Four inner gates – the Peters, Grimma, Halle, and Ranstädt – provided access through the old, fairly weak wall that ringed Leipzig's inner city. Despite the uneven preparations, Leipzig's 30,000 defenders occupied a perimeter of 6,500 paces, which equated to four or five men per pace – a slightly better ratio than that of the 18th, when 160,000 men had defended a perimeter of 38,000 paces. After the departure of V Corps, Durutte's 32nd Division reinforced by the battalions that formerly garrisoned the city defended the Gerber Gate and Halle suburb supported by 8th and 9th Divisions of Souham's III Corps. East of Durutte and facing northeast, Souham's 11th Division supported by 22nd Division of Marmont's VI Corps occupied the Taucha suburb and extended to Leipzig's Hinter Gate. South of 11th Division, Marmont's 20th and 21st Divisions in the Grimma suburb faced due east, holding the walled gardens between the Blinden and outer Grimma Gates. From the Grimma Gate to the Windmill Gate, thus facing southeast, Macdonald's 31st and 35th Divisions supported by his 36th Division took position to defend the Bose Gardens and the Johannis suburb. From his 39th Division, Macdonald posted its 1st Brigade of Badeners in the Bose Gardens and the 2nd Brigade of Hessians at the inner Grimma Gate. Finally, from the Windmill Gate to the Münz Gate in the Pegau suburb, Poniatowski positioned his own VIII Corps and the two remaining battalions of Rottembourg's non-French Old Guard brigade with Dąbrowski's 27th Division in the Richter Garden as reserve. Behind these forces in Leipzig's inner city stood two Badenese and one Italian battalion under the command of Prince William Louis Augustus, the 21-year-old second son of Grand Duke Karl Frederick of Baden, who had replaced Arrighi as commandant of Leipzig.[102] The Badeners garrisoned the four inner gates of the city with fifty men each while one company supported Durutte's division at the Gerber Gate. Some 1,200 Saxons stood guard on the marketplace in front of their king's residence.[103]

Returning to Blücher, believing that he had fulfilled his commitment to Bernadotte, he ordered Langeron to return to the right bank of the Parthe that same night and take a position to support Sacken's corps if necessary.

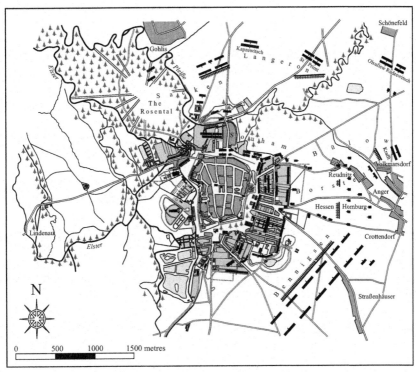

27. Battle of Leipzig, 19 October 1813

The exhaustion of Langeron's troops made it impossible for the native Frenchman to comply with Blücher's demand. In the evening, Blücher received word from Schwarzenberg's headquarters that the enemy appeared to be retreating to Merseburg and Weißenfels. Consequently, the Allied commander in chief instructed Blücher to make an attempt to reach the Saale before the French. Shortly after 7:00 P.M. on the 18th, Blücher ordered Yorck to secure the bridges over the Saale at Halle and Merseburg, which the French would likely utilize during their retreat from Leipzig.[104] Blücher also instructed Yorck to cause as much damage as possible to the retreating enemy forces. For this purpose, the cantankerous man of Tauroggen obtained a degree of independent command with the freedom "to operate according to his own view of the circumstances."[105]

Reinforced by two of Sacken's Cossack regiments, the Saxon cavalry brigade that had defected, and half of an Austrian Jäger company, Yorck's corps commenced its march to Schkeuditz around 8:00 P.M. and marched through the night, reaching Halle at 7:00 the following morning with the

Reserve Cavalry and Horn's division; Hünerbein's division and the Reserve Artillery halted at Bruckdorf and Burgliebenau. Although the march to the Saale signaled an attempt to exploit a victory, Yorck's soldiers thought differently. After they had sustained horrendous casualties at Möckern, their retrograde movement appeared very similar to the march that had taken place after the supposed Allied "victory" at Lützen on 2 May 1813. A black night did not help the situation. The darkness, haste, jam of wagons, entanglement of units, and general confusion usually associated with hated night marches typically lowered morale, but in this case served to reinforce the appearance of a retreat after a lost battle. Yorck, too, succumbed to despair. Observing portions of the fighting on the 18th from the hills of Eutritzsch north of Leipzig, he noted the stalemate south of the city, where Schwarzenberg's army fought over the same ground for the entire day. North of Leipzig, he could discern the lack of coordination between Langeron's Russians and Bernadotte's army. Likewise, he watched Bernadotte withhold his Swedish corps and Wintzingerode's Russians while Bülow's Prussians bore the brunt of the fighting. With no details on the status of the Allied and French armies, a disgusted Yorck viewed his current march to the Saale as a retreat. Even if Napoleon was retreating, Yorck did not want to disperse his weak corps of 14,000 men across the wide plain between Halle and Merseburg in the path of the approaching French army. For this reason he directed his corps to the northernmost of its objectives, Halle, from where it would proceed according to circumstances.

Around 6:00 P.M. on the 18th, Schwarzenberg convened a council of war on the Monarchs' Hill with the corps commanders in the vicinity. With Alexander's endorsement, the Allied commander in chief gave very short and simple verbal instructions for the attack on the 19th. There would be no day of rest as on the 17th. At first light, Schwarzenberg wanted all army groups in battle order and ready to resume the struggle. Should the enemy retreat, the army groups would remain the same as on the 18th, concentrically attack Leipzig, and storm the city's gates. Schwarzenberg explained that only the capture of Leipzig would make the victory decisive. His orders assigned each army group a specific gate to attack. Colloredo would advance along the Borna road and attack the Peters Gate; Barclay on the Colditz highway to attack the Windmill and Sand Gates; Bennigsen through Stötteritz to attack the Hospital Gate. He tasked the North German Army with taking the Grimma and Hinter Gates while the Silesian Army assaulted the Gerber Gate.

To hinder the French retreat, Schwarzenberg directed Gyulay's group to Pegau while Blücher sent Yorck's I Corps to Halle and Merseburg. Some accounts claim that Alexander expressed the desire to have the Russo-Prussian Guard and Russian Grenadier Corps march fourteen miles southwest to Pegau and cross the Elster that very evening so that these fresh troops would be in a position to fall on the French during their retreat. In view of the exhaustion of the army and the lack of food, Schwarzenberg and his staff disapproved. No documentary evidence exists to support this tale, and if Alexander had desired to send the Guard and Grenadiers to Pegau Schwarzenberg would not have been able to stop him.[106] Instead, Platov received orders to lead his Cossacks across the Pleiße at Dölitz and the Elster at Zwenkau that night so they could harass the French on the 19th. Although "all reports convincingly indicate that after today's defeat the enemy will retreat to Merseburg," the Allies did not do more to block the roads west due to their expectation of having to fight a third major battle at Leipzig on the 19th.[107] During the course of the night, Schwarzenberg issued further orders for an additional 40,000 Austrians (II Corps and General Nostitz's Cuirassier Corps of the Austrian Reserve) to reach Pegau by 7:00 A.M. on the 19th where they would unite with Liechtenstein's 1st Light Division. Moreover, Bubna should likewise lead his 2nd Light Division to Pegau as soon as his men had rested. These orders did not reach Bubna until 8:00 A.M. on the 19th.[108]

Late on the evening of the 18th, Schwarzenberg changed his mind concerning the pursuit. Sometime after midnight on the 19th, he recalled II Corps and Nostitz's Cuirassier Corps, citing as the reason that the enemy's actual movements did not confirm a retreat. In view of Allied numerical superiority, the dispatching of only Platov and Bubna prompted Russian historian Bogdanovich to ask "how could one expect decisive results with such measures?" Of course German historians found no military reasons to account for this change and thus attribute it to Metternich's political scheming. Even objective scholars such as Friederich could find no cause – military or political – for Schwarzenberg's waffling. True, it was not until 2:00 A.M. that the French began to evacuate Connewitz, Probstheida, and Stötteritz and fall back on Leipzig. A dark, misty night coupled with expert outpost service by the French to prevent the Allies from confirming the withdrawal to Leipzig until 5:00 A.M. on the 19th.[109]

During the night of 18/19 October, several reports confirming a great commotion in the French camp reached Allied Headquarters. Opinion remained divided over whether these movements signaled the beginning of a general retreat or marked French preparations for the defense of the city. As the beautiful autumn day of Tuesday, 19 October, dawned and allowed an overview, the Allies discovered that in all sectors the imperials had evacuated their forward positions and retreated into Leipzig's suburbs. Schwarzenberg and his staff appeared on the battlefield very early on 19 October followed by Alexander and Frederick William. The growing light of day left no doubt over the retreat of the French army but the Allied leaders made no effort to block its retreat on the other side of the Elster. For the present, they focused on what they believed would be heavy rearguard action and remained content with the arrangements Schwarzenberg had made during the previous night for the pursuit.[110]

Between 7:00 and 8:00 on the morning of 19 October, the Allied columns commenced their march on Leipzig. As noted, Schwarzenberg tasked Colloredo with proceeding along the Borna–Leipzig road to the Peters Gate. Colloredo's I Corps led the march on the Pegau–Leipzig road with General Franz von Mumb's 1st Brigade of 3rd Division at the head of the column followed by Hardegg's 1st Division and Maximilian Alexander von Wimpffen's 2nd. Hardegg and Wimpffen halted just west of Probstheida to await further orders while Mumb's brigade marched to the Borna–Leipzig road in two attack waves; four batteries covered by Austrian cavalry sped in front toward the Peters Gate. The Poles fell back fighting, seeking to protect their departing artillery from the approaching Austrian cavalry through intense skirmisher fire.

East of Colloredo, Wittgenstein's corps from Barclay's group advanced at daybreak on the Colditz–Leipzig highway to a position west of the Straßenhäuser. At 9:00, the Russian artillery commenced its duel with the French guns that defended the Windmill and Sand Gates; a long pause ensued while the guns battled. Kleist used this time to move into the charred remains of Probstheida and retrieve the dead of both sides, many of whom had sought refuge in the village after being wounded but could not escape being burned alive. The Prussians also found numerous French stragglers as well as several full caissons. After Bennigsen returned Ziethen's 11th Brigade, Kleist led his entire corps to Napoleon's former command post by Quandt's mill.

Next to Barclay's group, Bennigsen's troops, who stood furthest from Leipzig's outer city, started advancing northwest at first light. Minus Bubna's 2nd Light Division, which had already departed for Pegau, Bennigsen's army group moved toward Leipzig's east-facing Hospital Gate. Observing a strong line of French guns, Bennigsen ordered the 60 pieces of General Dmitry Rezvyi's Reserve Artillery to unlimber 300 paces from Leipzig's outer wall. Meanwhile, the infantry took a position between the Straßenhäuser and Crottendorf just beyond the reach of the French guns. Klenau's Austrian IV Corps marched from Zuckelhausen to Stötteritz, pushing one brigade to the Straßenhäuser. By the time Bennigsen's Reserve Artillery unlimbered opposite Leipzig's eastern Johannis suburb and its neighboring Bose Gardens, Bülow's skirmishers had reached the wall of the latter. After the Prussians withdrew to open a field of fire, Bennigsen's Russian guns pounded the walls of the Bose Gardens in an attempt to reduce them to rubble. As Barclay's gunners had experienced at Probstheida the day before, the balls passed through the walls smoothly without causing significant damage. During the bombardment, Bennigsen moved up his infantry in two waves of attack columns with his 26th Division on the left, 13th forming the center, and 12th holding the right.

Turning to the Army of North Germany, at dawn Bülow's cavalry patrols reported the French retreat but found that imperial forces still held the villages of Crottendorf, Volkmarsdorf, Anger, and Reudnitz east of Leipzig. From its bivouac at Paunsdorf, Bülow arranged his corps in two waves behind the line of Prussian outposts that guarded the short gap between Stünz and Sellerhausen. Hessen-Homburg's 3rd Brigade formed on the left while Borstell's 5th stood on the right. Bülow's 6th Brigade and Reserve Cavalry stood in second line. Not expecting to encounter significant resistance, Bernadotte interfered and ordered Hessen-Homburg supported by Borstell to take the villages opposite Bülow's corps. He directed Bülow's Reserve Cavalry to Stötteritz, where French cavalry had been spotted. Moreover, he inexplicably ordered Krafft's 6th Brigade to join the Swedes as rearguard. Bülow could do little but comply at 7:00 A.M. With seven battalions, four squadrons, and twenty-four guns of his brigade, Hessen-Homburg attacked Volkmarsdorf and Reudnitz while a left flank column of three battalions advanced on Anger. After token resistance, the imperials evacuated Volkmarsdorf and Anger. However, as soon as Hessen-Homburg's lead battalions cleared the villages, they received devastating artillery fire from a ten-gun battery posted at the outer Grimma Gate. For counterbattery fire, one and one-half Prussian batteries unlimbered at Anger while one of the Russian heavy batteries attached to Bülow's corps opened fire from Volkmarsdorf. Supported by one of Bennigsen's batteries at the Straßenhäuser, this crossfire soon silenced the French guns. During the artillery exchange, the majority of Bülow's corps moved west through the villages of Crottendorf, Volkmarsdorf, Anger, and Reudnitz with Hessen-Homburg's flank column linking with Bennigsen's right. East of the villages, ten Prussian battalions stood in reserve.

North of Leipzig, French movements had not gone unnoticed by the Silesian Army's outposts. Based on the loud creaking of wagon wheels coming from the city throughout the night, Blücher and his staff correctly concluded that the French army was retreating. Unlike the other sectors of the battlefield, first light revealed that the imperials had not evacuated their forward positions. At 8:00, Blücher ordered Langeron to support Bülow's attack on Reudnitz, with one heavy battery. Blücher had intended to send Langeron's corps to follow Yorck after the Russians had recrossed the Parthe. However, the need to support Sacken at the Halle suburb prevented this. Now, he had to await the arrival of Langeron's corps before he could launch his own attack. Moving exceptionally slowly, its lead units did not cross the Parthe until 8:00, meaning that the corps would not be ready to attack until 10:30. Realizing that cavalry would be of little use in storming a city, Blücher sent the cavalry of both Russian corps after Yorck; at 11:00, they crossed the Elster at Schkeuditz.

Shortly before 10:00 A.M., a delegation from the city's magistrate reached Alexander and Frederick William, whose command post had replaced that of

Napoleon's near the Quandt tobacco mill. In a plot hatched by Napoleon earlier that morning to gain time for his army to escape, the deputies came to negotiate with Schwarzenberg over Leipzig's surrender based on the free exit of the French garrison. Shortly after their arrival, the Saxon colonel Anton Friedrich von Ryssel appeared with a plea from Frederick Augustus to the Allied sovereigns to spare the city – again orchestrated by Napoleon. Willing to negotiate with the city leaders but not the Saxon king "because all earlier proposals by the Allies had been rejected," Alexander ordered a thirty-minute ceasefire to sound out the proposals. The Russian and Prussian monarchs decided to send Toll and the king's adjutant, Lieutenant-Colonel Oldwig von Natzmer, to Frederick Augustus. They gained access to the inner city because earlier Napoleon had ordered the commanders of his rearguard to allow the enemy's envoys to pass. Yet the negotiations amounted to nothing as the French marshals took orders only from Napoleon.[111]

Starting with Bennigsen's group, the commander of the Army of Poland used the thirty-minute pause in the fighting to swing his right wing division – Khovansky's 12th – in a wide arc west-southwest around the city's eastern side so that it faced the Peters gate on Leipzig's southern side and now formed Bennigsen's left wing. Paskevich's 26th Division slid southwest opposite Leipzig's Windmill Gate. Bennigsen ordered his 13th Division to attack the Sand Gate leading to the Johannis suburb. After these shifts, only Bennigsen's Reserve Artillery faced the wall of Bose Gardens. After the artillery failed to make a breach, sappers from 13th Division blew a hole in the wall and penetrated the gardens while the main body broke through the Sand Gate. Meeting no resistance, 13th Division pushed its way through both the gate and the gardens while Bennigsen personally led six battalions and two guns from 26th Division through the Windmill Gate. There, the Russians encountered fierce resistance that prompted Bennigsen to take a side road that led him to the open Roßplatz around 11:30 A.M., at which time he linked with a Prussian column from Bülow's corps. Meanwhile, Khovansky's 12th Division on Bennigsen's left overpowered Poniatowski's Poles in the lumber yard facing the Münz Gate, itself on the Floßgraben west of the outer Peters Gate. From there, Khovansky's men drove through the gate and along the Peters Causeway toward the Esplanade. Arriving at this point around 12:30, the Russians accepted the surrender of more than 300 Poles with at least 47 guns and 27 caissons.[112]

Bennigsen's westward shift remains unexplained as no documentary evidence of the orders for it exists, yet the move effectively blocked both Colloredo's and Barclay's army groups from advancing further. We can only speculate that Allied Headquarters considered dispatching these two army groups to Pegau as they stood closest to Napoleon's line of retreat. Another possible reason was to spare these troops as both army groups had sustained considerable losses on the 16th and 18th. Regardless of who issued the orders and why, Wittgenstein and Kleist bivouacked their troops opposite the outer Peters Gate around 2:00 P.M. while Colloredo's group commenced the march to Pegau one hour later.

On Bennigsen's other side, Bernadotte utilized the thirty-minute pause to commence the movement of Wintzingerode's corps around Bülow's Prussians to a position between them and Bennigsen's army group. Shortly after 10:00, all of Bülow's corps stood west of Reudnitz, Anger, and Crottendorf. Convinced that the imperials would offer no significant resistance, Bernadotte ordered Stedingk to prepare the Swedish corps to parade into Leipzig. Noticing the advance of Bennigsen's 13th Division toward the Bose Gardens, the crown prince ordered Borstell's first wave to attack. Skirmishers from the Fusilier Battalions of the 2nd Reserve Regiment and 1st Pomeranian Infantry Regiment and the 1st Battalion of 6th Brigade's Kolberg Infantry Regiment led the way as their parent battalions followed in columns. The Kolberg battalion's skirmishers made for the walled St. Johannis church compound while to their right (north) the 2nd Reserve Regiment's Fusilier Battalion advanced toward the outer Grimma Gate and the Pomeranians sprinted toward the edge of a garden situated to the right of the gate. Brutal fire from Marmont's troops behind the city wall greeted the tightly packed Pomeranian Fusilier Battalion as it drew closer. Despite considerable losses, the Pomeranians reached the wall and managed to open a narrow, barricaded portal. Gradually, the battalion penetrated the garden. Although engaging in murderous hand-to-hand combat with Marmont's troops, the Prussians managed to hold their ground.

Meanwhile, when the fusiliers of the 2nd Reserve Regiment, accompanied by Bernadotte himself, came within 100 paces of the outer Grimma Gate, they received withering fire from the three-story St. Johannis hospital to the left (south) of the gate that was part of the walled St. Johannis church compound, which included a cemetery as well as a large building nine windows wide. Caught in the hail of fire coming from the compound, Bernadotte shouted in French to the battalion's commander to advance in column. Closing their ranks, the Prussians ran this gauntlet to reach the gate, which consisted of two large brick pillars with portals on the right and left for pedestrian traffic; barricades made of wagons, beams, planks, and posts closed all three entrances. Despite devastating flanking fire from the church compound, the Prussians managed to pry open one of the side portals enough so that individual soldiers could squeeze through. Although the battalion gradually assembled, the men could not open the main entrance. On the other side of the gate, the Prussians lacked the manpower to make any headway. After sustaining numerous casualties in a firefight with French defenders holed up in the buildings surrounding the gate, the Prussians withdrew north into the garden secured by the Pomeranians.

Realizing he needed more manpower, Bernadotte ordered Hessen-Homburg's flank detachment of three battalions to storm the gate. As soon as they broke in, the lead unit – Major Karl Friedrich Friccius's 3rd Battalion of the 3rd East Prussian Landwehr – would turn left (south) on the first available road while the second battalion turned right (north) and the third continued straight ahead (west). Despite the fire from the church compound, Hessen-Homburg led Friccius's Landwehr battalion toward the still closed Grimma Gate. The bottleneck there caused by the fusiliers of the 2nd Reserve Regiment prevented him from reaching the gate. However, a Landwehr officer found what he believed to be a weak point in the wall to the right of the gate. He directed his men to pound the wall with the butts of their muskets. In this way, the Prussians opened a narrow breach through which the battalion gradually flowed. To partially comply with Hessen-Homburg's orders, Friccius gathered a sufficient number of men and led them down the first street he could find to turn left – the aptly named Todtengasse (Death's Lane) – while a second group worked with the fusiliers of the 2nd Reserve Regiment to open the main gate. A third group of Friccius's battalion moved through the breach to storm the two houses that flanked both sides of the gate. At last, the Prussians managed to force open the main gate. This allowed the second battalion of Hessen-Homburg's flank detachment – the 2nd of the 3rd East Prussian Regiment – to enter. The column's third battalion, the fusiliers of the 3rd East Prussian Regiment, moved through a portal in the gardens just north of the gate to enter the Wendler estate. At this moment, Hessen-Homburg fell gravely wounded. Bülow placed 3rd Brigade under Borstell's oversight.

From the Grimma Gate, the Grimma Causeway ran west to the inner city. The gradual penetration of Hessen-Homburg's three battalions coincided with several counterattacks by the French reserves. Prussian aggression broke on French tenacity as individual battalions from Charpentier's 36th Division moved east along the causeway. Their push along with pressure from the garrison at the St. Johannis church compound forced Friccius to fall back to the wide Johannisplatz just inside the Grimma Gate. As more French reinforcements arrived, bloody fighting at close quarters ensued involving the majority of Friccius's Landwehr battalion, the fusiliers of the 2nd Reserve Regiment, and the 2nd Battalion of the 3rd East Prussian. After much back-and-forth fighting that after-action reports fail to clarify, the Prussians started to waver. The approach of Swedish reinforcements reinvigorated the Prussians, some of whom had started to flee through the Grimma Gate. On arriving, a Swedish Jäger battalion received such heavy fire in the front and flank that the men broke after their commander fell dead. However, grape from two Swedish guns that had unlimbered just inside the gate managed to clear the French and Hessians from the Johannisplatz. Their fire and the arrival of two additional Swedish Jäger battalions made any

19 Pursuing the French into Leipzig's inner city, 19 October 1813

further counterattacks along the Grimma Causeway impossible, thus allowing the Allies to finally secure the outer Grimma Gate. Pursuing the enemy along the causeway, the Prussians attacked but failed to break the stout French and Hessian resistance. After the two Swedish guns joined by two Russian pieces moved up, the French and Hessians had no choice but to withdraw into the inner city.

In the gardens north of the Grimma Gate, the 2nd Battalion of the 3rd East Prussian Regiment – the third and last battalion of Hessen-Homburg's flank column – linked with the fusiliers of the 1st Pomeranian Infantry Regiment to resist a fierce counterattack by superior numbers from Marmont's corps. Although suffering large losses, the Prussians held their position in the gardens until a final French push drove them out of the gardens and all the way back to the Purzelgraben. In response, Borstell himself led four battalions from his reserve: one penetrated the Blinden Gate, the other three entered the gardens through various openings. After a hard fight, the Prussians threw back Marmont's troops onto their reserves standing on the Quer Lane. In the courtyards of the buildings and in the houses that stood along the Quer Lane bloody hand-to-hand fighting resumed. There, the Prussians again triumphed, driving the French toward the inner city. Before reaching it, the Hessian brigade of Marchand's 39th Division arrived led by the Guard Fusilier Battalion followed by the 1st Battalion of the Leib Guard Regiment. Together with Marmont's rejuvenated battalions, the Hessians drove the Prussians back to the Quer Lane. Success proved fleeting for the French and their Hessian allies. After regrouping, the four Prussian battalions gradually managed to push the French toward the inner city. The fighting in the garden coincided with the taking of the Milchinsel and the Hinter Gate at a considerable cost by other battalions from Borstell's 5th Brigade. By this time, the Swedish and Russian artillery had secured the Grimma Gate so that the Prussians controlled the two thoroughfares in their sector that led to the inner city: the Grimma Causeway and the Hinter Lane.

Around 11:30, just as Bennigsen's 13th and 26th Divisions arrived on the open Roßplatz, the Prussians reached the inner city wall that faced east. Before any further attacks could be launched, Prussian officers needed to reorganize their units after the brutal street fighting.

While fighting the French and Hessians, Borstell had sent a request to Bülow for an attack to the left (south) of the Grimma Gate to draw off some of the troops facing the Prussians. Bülow complied by sending his last fresh battalion, the Pomeranian Grenadiers, to attack the Hospital Gate. Just as this unit reached the gate, the five battalions of Wintzingerode's van arrived there based on orders from Bernadotte. Along with the two battalions of Wintzingerode's 14th Jäger Regiment, the Pomeranians entered the undefended Hospital Gate while the three remaining Russian battalions moved into the Bose Gardens. The imperials had so clogged the open space on the other side of the gate with overturned wagons and even several abandoned artillery pieces that the Allies first had to clear a path so that their own guns could follow. After this occurred, Wintzingerode placed himself at the head of a small cavalry escort and led the 14th Jäger to the inner Grimma Gate. En route, the Russians came under attack by a squadron of French cuirassiers and a half-squadron of Polish lancers. Behind the imperial cavalry followed the 2nd Battalion of the 3rd Badenese Infantry Regiment in tight columns with bayonets fixed. After a brief clash, Wintzingerode's cavalry escort broke and fled through the Jäger, disordering their ranks and causing a mass flight back to the Hospital Gate pursued by the imperials. At the gate, the Pomeranian Grenadiers just barely managed to avoid being swept away by the Russians. Fortunately for the Allies, the Badeners broke as a result of receiving heavy friendly fire. This enabled the Prussians to drive them off. After the Russian Jäger re-formed, the Allies again pushed to the wall of the inner city.[113]

Thus, the Army of North Germany secured the eastern portion of Leipzig's outer city just as the Army of Poland mastered the southern sector. In the northern zone, Blücher had no easy task before him as the French placed special emphasis on defending the Halle suburb and Pfaffendorf because those two points stood closest to their line of retreat. To reach Leipzig, Blücher could take one of two roads. The first ran across the Gerber Bridge over the Parthe to the Gerber Gate while the other crossed the Pleiße bridge to the Rosenthal. On the French side, a fleche defended by Badenese troops and armed with three guns guarded the Gerber Bridge and one battery on the left bank of the Parthe flanked the access to it. Durutte's 32nd Division at the Pfaffendorf manor secured the Pleiße bridge with numerous guns posted in a flanking position on the left bank of the Pleiße. A strong line of skirmishers held the left banks of both rivers. All the advantages belonged to the defenders. Blücher decided to direct the main attack against the Gerber Bridge because that road provided the most direct

20 Allied forces storming Leipzig, 19 October 1813

route to the French line of retreat. Yet, to distract the imperials, he also planned to assault the Pfaffendorf manor. Langeron's corps received the task of storming the Gerber Bridge while Sacken's corps attacked the Pleiße bridge.

Around 11:00, Blücher heard the sound of musket fire in the eastern suburbs, indicating that Bülow had commenced his attack. Some of Langeron's units had yet to arrive but Blücher ordered Sacken to commence the assault on Pfaffendorf. Following an ineffective bombardment, the four battalions of Sacken's first wave managed to penetrate the burned-out manor but could not hold it. Fighting with desperation, Durutte's warriors repulsed repeated charges by the Russian infantry until they heard musket fire behind them. This prompted Durutte to evacuate the manor and withdraw to the left bank of the Parthe. Sacken then turned against the stone Gerber Bridge, which the French and Badeners defended with extreme bravery, repulsing the Russians.

After Kaptsevich's and St.-Priest's infantry corps arrived, Blücher sent four battalions from the former's X Infantry Corps to attack the bridge while St.-Priest made a futile attempt to cross the Parthe above the bridge and thus envelop the defenders. Kaptsevich's efforts to take the fleche and bridge by storm failed as bravery could not counter the murderous artillery and musket fire directed against the attackers from the houses and gardens on the opposite bank. St.-Priest attacked with the three battalions of the Yekater-inburgskii and Rylskii Regiments, and still the Russians could not gain ground. After inflicting 1,000 casualties on the Russians, Durutte finally found himself forced to gradually withdraw his troops from the right to the left bank of the Parthe due to the westward push of Bülow's troops coming from the Milchinsel and Hinter Gate directly to his rear. As soon as the enemy fire weakened around 1:00, the Russians attacked both the fleche and the Gerber Bridge with what Friederich describes as "death-defying courage."[114] With the Arkhangelogorodskii and Staroingermanlandskii Regiments formed in storm columns, Blücher accompanied the attack. As his promotion to field-marshal had been made known to the troops that morning, Blücher's constant shouts of "forward, forward," during the advance earned him the Russian nickname of "Marshal Forwards." Not allowing the advantage to slip away, the Russians drove at the same time with the retreating French through the Gerber Gate and into the Gerber Alley that led to the Halle Gate. After savage street- and house-fighting that particularly took a toll on the Arkhangelogorodskii Regiment, the Russians pushed the enemy through the Gerber Alley. They reached the protracted promenade before the Halle Gate around 12:30 P.M., taking many prisoners along with fifty guns.[115]

Although losing the suburbs of the outer city, the imperials conducted a fairly orderly retreat to the inner city. From that point, the French and their German allies thought only of escaping to Lindenau. Order collapsed as the columns exiting the city collided with those retreating from the outer city. In many places, the artillery took up the entire width of the city's narrow lanes. Thanks to the confusion, unit cohesion disintegrated, thus adding to the chaos. At many points, stoppages along the main line of retreat led to involuntary resistance against the advancing Allies while at other places a deliberate defense continued the unprecedented bloodletting.

On Bülow's right, Borstell's battalions that drove from the Milchinsel and the Hinter Gate raced toward the Halle Gate. Their advance prompted Durutte to evacuate the right bank of the Parthe. This allowed Langeron's troops to storm the Gerber Bridge over the Parthe and move through the Gerber Gate. At the timber market opposite the Halle Gate, two French guns put an end to the advance of Borstell's battalions until Langeron's Russians arrived from the Gerber Alley. Attacked from two sides, the French suffered horrendous losses. After several minutes of slaughter, some surrendered while others fled toward the Ranstädt Gate pursued by the Russians and Prussians.

On Bülow's left, the struggle before the locked and barricaded inner Grimma Gate proved bloodier than that which took place at the Halle Gate. Charpentier and Marchand rallied their divisions outside the former, where Bülow's soldiers attacked from three sides. With nowhere to run, the French and Hessians found themselves backed against the inner Grimma Gate, which the Badeners refused to open per their instructions. Despite their predicament, the French and Hessians fought like lions. Prince Emil of Hessen-Darmstadt saved his men by ordering them to cut their way through to the Leipzig canal that flowed in front of the inner city wall, follow it to the Georg Portal at the northeastern corner of the wall, and enter the inner city. Protected by a rearguard, the majority of the Hessian brigade escaped in this manner. However, the Prussians slowly pushed the rearguard and the French against the roundabout in front of the inner Grimma Gate, where a slaughter ensued led by two battalions of Borstell's 2nd Reserve Regiment. Horrible screams, cursing, and ranting filled the air in front of the locked gates. After another desperate push, the gate finally gave way and the masses streamed into the inner city. With much trouble the Badeners managed to reclose and barricade the gate before the Prussians could enter. As more Prussians arrived they too pressed against the gate, in part seeking cover from the fire coming from the inner city wall. After finally managing to pry open the gate, the 2nd Battalion of the 2nd Reserve Regiment entered the inner city followed by four more battalions and numerous detachments from other regiments.

The successful breaching of the inner Grimma Gate marked the end of serious fighting in Bülow's sector as the French fled west along Grimma Lane, before some broke to the north erroneously thinking they could escape through the Halle Gate, while the others made for the Peters Gate with the same intentions. Instead of pursuing, the Prussians turn right (north) and proceeded to the St. Nicolai Church, where they encountered Prince Emil's Hessian brigade. Although the prince had restored order, the Hessians, as well as numerous French soldiers who accompanied them, surrendered. From the church, the Prussians again moved west through the city to the central marketplace. There, they found Prince Louis with one Badenese battalion as well as the 1,200 Saxons guarding their king's residence; both groups surrendered to the Prussians. It was now a little after 12:00 and three Prussian battalions went in pursuit of the French who had fled to the inner Peters Gate while the 2nd Battalion of the 2nd Reserve Regiment set out for the Halle Gate. At 12:30, Paskevich's 26th Division from Bennigsen's army reached the inner city via the inner Grimma Gate.

In Leipzig's southern sector, Macdonald sent the Badenese brigade of Marchand's 39th Division to support Augereau's troops at the inner Peters Gate around 11:00. In the process of marching to that gate, the Badenese commander, General Karl von Stockhorn received counterorders from Marchand to immediately send his 3rd Infantry Regiment to the outer Grimma Gate. Stockhorn responded by dispatching the 1st Battalion of that regiment on the shortest route to the outer Grimma Gate while the 2nd Battalion took a side road, eventually breaking Wintzingerode's column

21 Fighting before Leipzig's Peters Gate, 19 October 1813

before being turned back by the Pomeranian Grenadiers, as noted. After the Russians and Prussians mastered the eastern portion of the outer city, both battalions of the Badenese 3rd Infantry Regiment slowly withdrew toward the inner Peters Gate to reunite with the brigade's 1st Infantry Regiment. One battalion from that regiment had moved inside the city to garrison the Pleißenburg demilune while Prince Louis had summoned the other to the central marketplace, where it surrendered. Shortly before the Badenese 3rd Regiment reached the inner Peters Gate, French troops with Macdonald in tow raced *out* of the gate. After fleeing from the inner Grimma Gate, these troops from XI Corps had retreated through the central marketplace, pursued by a battalion of Pomeranians. Soon, various imperial columns converged on the inner Peters Gate: the Badenese 3rd Regiment from the east and another part of XI Corps and the rest of VIII Corps from the south. None thought of resistance and all pushed west to get to the single access lane that led to the Pleiße. They suffered considerably at the hands of the sole battalion of Pomeranians. At the Pleiße, Poniatowski managed to organize some of his troops and unlimber three guns at the waterworks to finally stop the pursuing Prussians, whose attack had been taken up by Khovansky's 12th Division coming from the Esplanade.[116]

Meanwhile, one of Sacken's detachments penetrated the Rosenthal from Gohlis, pushing the weak French posts there southwest to the right bank of the Elster where they finally surrendered. As a bitter struggle erupted at the waterworks and while Bülow's battalions pushed westward through the inner city and Blücher led Langeron's troops south through the Halle Gate, one of Sacken's small Jäger detachments found an intact footbridge over the Elster near Jakobs Hospital. A few hundred paces south of this footbridge ran the Ranstädt Causeway, across which marched the thick columns of the retreating Grande Armée to Lindenau. After crossing the rain-swollen Elster, the Russians immediately opened fire. As noted, Montfort had never received clear instructions on the measures of the retreat. For clarification, he decided to seek Berthier at Lindenau and so crossed the causeway. Before leaving, he instructed a Corporal Lafontaine to blow the bridge should the enemy appear to prevent its capture. Montfort reached Lindenau but his attempt to ride east and return to his post east proved impossible because of the thick masses marching west on the causeway.

Back at the bridge, Sacken's Jäger opened fire. As no friendly troops appeared to resist this flank attack, Lafontaine and the three sappers with him believed the time had come to blow the bridge regardless of the troops marching across the structure. He lit the fuse and a deafening explosion rose above the din of battle. While the blast still echoed throughout the city, a ghastly shower of body parts – both human and equine – along with red-hot stones and flaming beams, planks, and wagons fell in the neighboring gardens and streets. The throng of soldiers still on the right bank of the Elster stopped short. Those closest to the bridge suffered the horror of having ripped limbs, torsos, and heads fall upon them. The soldiers further away could see nothing for a few minutes as a thick cloud of smoke and steam blocked visibility. Still they pressed forward only to find that their sole way out of the city was gone. Some surrendered while others threw off their gear, discarded their weapons, and attempted to swim to safety; many drowned.[117]

After the destruction of the bridge, the units of XI and VIII Corps between the Thomas Portal on Leipzig's western side and the waterworks found themselves cut off. Turning north, they followed the only lane to the Pleiße. Only via the footbridges over the Pleiße that led to the Reichel and Rudolph Gardens on the western edge of the city could they hope to reach the Elster. Across the footbridges and through these gardens now streamed the French and Poles like herds of wild animals hotly pursued by the Allies who shot or bayoneted the stragglers. In the gardens, several waterways including the Elstermühlgraben, a millrace fed by both the Elster and the Pleiße, made the going tough. Like several others on this side of Leipzig, the swampy canal served the double purpose of marking the borders of property and deterring burglary, thus their colloquial name of *Diebsgräben* (thief trenches). Poniatowski's horse plunged into the millrace but could not work its way through the muddy bottom, forcing the Polish commander to leap into the water. Just barely able to keep his head above water, Poniatowski won the opposite bank thanks to the help of his staff. Exhausted, he mounted another horse and hastened to the opposite end of the Reichel

Garden to swim the Elster. Still closely pursued by Allied skirmishers, he spurred his horse and leaped into the swollen Elster. Before he could reach the opposite bank, a musket ball pierced one side of his torso and exited the other. Just like downstream at the blown bridge, the French and Poles faced a difficult choice. Among those who attempted to swim across the Elster, Macdonald reached the opposite bank but many drowned, including Poniatowski, who had received his marshal's baton the previous day. Thousands of others accepted their fate and surrendered.[118]

While these events were unfolding, Leipzig's meat market north of the Thomas Portal provided the stage for a bloody struggle. From there north to the point of entry to the Ranstädt causeway, all the troops fleeing from the Halle Gate and the inner city jammed together, immediately pursued by Blücher's and Bülow's troops. Attempting to move west from the inner Halle Gate, Blücher's troops encountered so many roadblocks in the form of abandoned guns and wagons that he halted Langeron's and Sacken's troops at the timber market. Only two Jäger Regiments from Kaptsevich's corps slowly pressed forward and united at the meat market with Bülow's troops as they emerged from several streets. Remnants of various French corps pressed together in thick masses and, forced by Allied fire, they desperately raced across the Pleiße via footbridges to reach the Richter Gardens on Leipzig's northwest side. In a matter of minutes, French and Poles of all arms poured into the meadows west of the Reichel and Richter Gardens. Pressed by the Allies, they savagely fought a bitter bayonet struggle to reach the Elster. Many jumped into the river and attempted to swim despite their great fatigue. Soon the river filled with bodies of drowned horses and men, whose heads, arms, and feet jutted out of the water in hideous groups. In places the corpses became so thick and bunched together that they provided footbridges over which their countrymen could pass to reach the safety of the opposite bank. Many escaped this way and by swimming but the majority surrendered around 1:00. Firing continued for hours because Marmont wisely posted skirmishers and artillery on the left bank of the Elster to prevent the Allies from getting across the river.

Around 1:00, Alexander and Frederick William accompanied by Schwarzenberg rode through the Hospital Gate into the city and along Grimma Lane to the central marketplace. There, they met Bennigsen and Bernadotte, a little later Blücher and Gneisenau arrived from the Ranstädt Gate. Countless generals from all four Allied armies gathered around the two monarchs, who showered them with praise and recognition. From the central marketplace, the monarchs passed the king of Saxony's residence en route to the Ranstädt Gate. Frederick Augustus waited in vain for an invitation to join them. The victorious procession ended quickly due in part to the shells the French lobbed into the city from Lindenau – one of which exploded close to the tsar – as well as the inability to move along roads clogged with troops, discarded arms, and wagons, not to mention the dead and wounded. Thus, the monarchs turned around and made for the Grimma Gate to meet Kaiser Francis, who arrived at that time from Rötha. From there, Alexander and Frederick William went to Reudnitz to review the Swedish corps at Bernadotte's invitation. The onset of darkness finally ended the continuous French musket and artillery fire into the city from Lindenau.[119]

Allied losses in the four-day struggle amounted to 1,792 officers and 51,982 men or around 54,000 men. Friederich also provides losses based on nationality:

(I) Russians: 865 officers and 21,740 men thus divided:

Bohemian Army: 512 officers and 11,411 men
Silesian Army: 250 officers and 6,897 men
North German Army: 33 officers and 432 men
Polish Army: 70 officers and 3,000 men

(II) Prussians: 498 officers and 15,535 men thus divided:
Yorck's Corps: 176 officers and 5,467 men
Kleist's Corps: 244 officers and 7,882 men
Bülow's corps: 78 officers and 2,186 men

(III) Austrians: 420 officers and 14,538 men thus divided

General Staff: 10 officers

1st Light Division: 25 officers and 525 men
2nd Light Division: 11 officers and 227 men
I Army Corps: 53 officers and 1,441 men
II Army Corps: 53 officers and 1,885 men
III Army Corps: 39 officers and 1,486 men
IV Army Corps: 99 officers and 3,900 men
Reserve Corps: 130 officers and 5,074 men

(IV) Swedes: 9 officers and 169 men

French losses in dead and wounded amounted to some 38,000 men. An additional 15,000 men became prisoners of war due to the premature blowing of the Elster bridge as did the 21,000 sick and wounded in Leipzig's hospitals. A further 5,000 either deserted or defected. The Allies captured 28 flags and Eagles, 325 guns, 900 caissons, 720,000 kg of powder, and some 40,000 muskets, numbers which understandably only increased during the pursuit. Thirty-six French generals including Lauriston, Reynier, Charpentier, Prince Emil of Hessen-Darmstädt, and Prince William of Baden were among the prisoners. Marshals Ney, Macdonald, and Marmont were wounded, along with the corps commanders Reynier, Lauriston,

Souham, Latour-Maubourg, Pajol, and Sébastiani, and divisional commanders Maison and Compans.[120]

Darkness not only brought an end to the epic Battle of Nations, but it
also marked the conclusion of the German Campaign and the struggle for
European mastery. Napoleon's hope that tactical maneuvering would crush
the Allies on the 16th and that some stroke of good fortune would allow him
to triumph on the 18th had eluded him. Just as in Russia exactly one year
earlier, no other option remained open but retreat. He probably reproached
himself for not having retreated on the 17th. "The retreat," observes Yorck
von Wartenburg, "which the monarch had refused to begin voluntarily on
the 17th, the defeated general would be compelled to begin on the 19th."
"Now the retreat as far as the frontier was certain," observes Pelet; "but it
depended on the progress of the Austro-Bavarian army. The retreat could be
strong and slow, and made by increments to the Saale, to the Gera, and to the
Werra. We could gain time to prepare the defense of the Rhine and the more
remote parts of France." Thus, the magnitude of the Allied victory and the
pace of Napoleon's retreat as well as his ability to mobilize France depended
on how much damage the Allies could inflict on the French army during its
retreat to France.[121]

Notes

1 In *Mémoires de chirurgie militaire*, IV:441, the chief surgeon of the Grande Armée,
  Dr. Dominique-Jean Larrey, calculates the number of wounded to be 6,500 on the
  16th. Under normal circumstances, this would mean the number killed approached
  2,000.
2 Odeleben, *A Circumstantial Narrative*, II:23.
3 Pelet was commander of 2nd Brigade of 3rd Division of Oudinot's I Corps of
  Young Guard.
4 Pelet, *Des principales opérations de la campagne de 1813*, 275–77.
5 Müffling, *Die Feldzüge*, 92.
6 Stewart to Charles John, Halle, 9:00 P.M., 16 October 1813, reproduced in Stewart,
  Narrative, 164. As for Stewart's authorization to withhold payment, a letter to him
  from Cathcart on 6 October states that "you are alone and supreme in the military
  administration of the forces in the north of Germany in British pay and their
  supplies": Cathcart to Stewart, Kommotau, 6 October 1813, Add MSS, 20111, 157.
  For Bernadotte's reaction, see Stewart, *Narrative*, 177. As for Stewart's effectiveness, Müffling, in *Aus meinem Leben*, 86–87, states that "Lord Stewart did not
  hesitate to avow, on some new instance of intractability in the crown prince, that,
  according to his instructions, there might be occasions in which he would be
  obliged to refuse the order for the payment of the subsidy. On the refusal of the
  crown prince, which was repeated daily, to advance to the battle of Leipzig, Lord
  Stewart at last took occasion to fulfill his threat, undeterred by the prince's
  irritability, or his flattering offers of reconciliation. To this circumstance the plains

of Breitenfeld are indebted for the honor of being trodden by a successor of the great king of Sweden. The general in chief of the Silesian Army would never have succeeded in moving him to take part in the battle of Leipzig." In *Geschichte der Nord Armee*, II:211, Quistorp adds: "The offensive tone of this letter did not fail to achieve its purpose with the highly sensitive crown prince, and the threat it contained would be incomprehensible if it had not been supported by a realistic background. Stewart had dropped the hint that under certain circumstances the conventional English subsidy payments could be adjusted. With one stroke the view changed: the commander of the Army of North Germany decided to enter the line." Thornton wrote to Castlereagh on 22 October 1813: "I must beg to inform your lordship that I have spoken both with Adlerkreutz and Wetterstedt on the subject of Sir Charles Stewart's conversations with the Prince Royal ... and both of them expressed the warmest ... gratitude, for his conduct, ascribing much, if not most of all, the good that has happened to it alone, and particularly with regard to the reputation of the Prince Royal himself and of the Swedes, who (Adlerkreutz observed to me) were dishonored by the line of conduct which [Bernadotte] was pursuing, and who were furious at the manner in which they were treated": *CVC*, IX:68; see also SHAT, C^{17} 133: Order of the Day, Hohenthurm, 12:00 A.M., 17 October 1813.

7 Both contained 20.75 battalions – only 8 of which were Landwehr – totaling 10,066 men commanded by Horn and Hünerbein. The 2nd and 7th Brigades formed Horn's 1st Division, while 1st and 8th Brigades made up Hünerbein's 2nd. Most regiments consisted of only two battalions. A mere 3,200 Landwehr infantry remained. See Höpfner, "Darstellung," 1847:108.

8 Unger, *Blücher*, II:114–15.

9 Müffling, *Die Feldzüge*, 87–88; "Journal de Langeron," Add MSS, 20112, 276; Nostitz, *Tagebuch*, 68–69; Swederus, *Schwedens Politik und Kriege*, II:349.

10 SHAT, C^2 158: Marmont to Berthier, 19 October 1813. "Throughout the day of the 17th," recalled Marmont, "the Army of Silesia followed by the Army of North Germany defiled before our very eyes and ascended the right bank of the Parthe. I occupied the various bridges on the upper part of the river, and for observation I placed my light cavalry on the left bank. My infantry was encamped perpendicular to the Parthe, facing Taucha, the left at the village of Schönefeld, the right in the direction of the village of Paunsdorf": Marmont, *Mémoires*, V:290–91.

11 Langeron, *Mémoires*, 322.

12 Nostitz, *Tagebuch*, 69.

13 Langeron, *Mémoires*, 322–23. The division's 1st Brigade, commanded by Vasilchikov's younger brother, Colonel Dmitry Vasilchikov, contained the Belorusskii (five squadrons) and Akhtyrskii (seven squadrons) Regiments. The 2nd Brigade, led by the native Hungarian general Anastasy Yurkovsky, consisted of the Aleksandriiskii (five squadrons) and Mariupolskii (six squadrons) Regiments.

14 "Operations of the Army of Silesia in the Battles Before Leipzig," Lowe, 20 October 1813, Add MSS, 20111, 168.

15 Friederich, *Herbstfeldzug 1813*, III:134–35. Reynier's VII Corps had left Eilenburg early on the 17th and reached Taucha in the afternoon. After an insignificant

combat with Wintzingerode's cavalry followed by several hours of rest, the Franco-Saxon corps continued its march to the Heiterblick manor. Arrighi's fleeing cavalry forced Reynier to take a position facing Schönefeld (west). After Blücher halted his advance, Reynier's Saxon division marched to a bivouac at Paunsdorf; his 32nd Division remained between Paunsdorf and Schönefeld; the Saxon cavalry took a position at the Heiterblick manor; and the 14th Division marched to Lindenau in accordance with Napoleon's orders.

16 "Operations of the Army of Silesia in the Battles Before Leipzig," Lowe, 20 October 1813, Add MSS, 20111, 168.

17 Nostitz, *Tagebuch*, 69.

18 Müffling, *Die Feldzüge*, 89–90.

19 According to Müffling, Blücher ordered Langeron's right wing to lean on the Parthe while his left wing and Wintzingerode's cavalry crossed the Parthe at Taucha, moved down the river, and cleared the left bank of imperial forces. Langeron's right wing would then cross the Parthe and the entire corps would assume the offensive.

20 Pelet, *Des principales opérations de la campagne de 1813*, 281.

21 Schwarzenberg to Blücher, Güldengoßa, 3:00 P.M., 17 October 1813, Add MSS, 20112, 167; Müffling, *Die Feldzüge*, 90–92.

22 "Journal de Langeron," Add MSS, 20112, 275–76; "Operations of the Army of Silesia in the Battles Before Leipzig," Lowe, 20 October 1813, Add MSS, 20111, 167–68. "The Prince Marshal Schwarzenberg had strong motives for not engaging until the subsequent day," continues Lowe, "when the junction of the Prince Royal of Sweden and of the Army of Reserve [Poland] under General Bennigsen would ensure complete success. The Army of Silesia, however, did not admit the same motives for inaction. This day was also productive of its show of glory." See also Petre, *Napoleon's Last Campaign*, 355.

23 Langeron met with Bernadotte at Breitenfeld: "It was there that I saw him for the first time; we went together to see the battlefield of the previous day; he made a few remarks in the style of his region of birth, and I was forced to make myself a Gascon to reply; when I left him, he saw me off with an *adiousias* which was certainly of the style of the Garonne." See Langeron, *Mémoires*, 323.

24 Quistorp, *Geschichte der Nord Armee*, II:211–12.

25 SHAT, C^{17} 133: Order of the Day, Breitenfeld, 17 October 1813.

26 Charles John to Blücher, Breitenfeld, 17 October 1813, GStA PK, VI HA Rep. 92 Nl. Gneisenau, Nr. 18, and Add MSS, 20112, 87–88.

27 According to Müffling: "All prepared for the battle on the 18th. The crown prince of Sweden appeared determined to participate. He treated the battle of Möckern as a small engagement, and Blücher was willing to let this pass provided the Army of North Germany moved into the line on the 18th. It still had not arrived when the crown prince made a new and unexpected demand. He wanted the old order of battle immediately restored, that is to say: to move on the right wing of the Silesian Army." See Müffling, *Die Feldzüge*, 92. Although Bernadotte made no such suggestion in the letter, Quistorp follows Müffling, maintaining that "the acceptance of this suggestion would have led to the still intact Army of North Germany taking a defensive position between the Pleiße and the Parthe,

which could have been held by 30,000 men and – because the enemy troops had already been driven into Leipzig's suburbs – engaging in no serious combat": Quistorp, *Geschichte der Nord Armee*, II:212. Twenty years later, even the usually objective Friederich wrote: "This somewhat unclear letter only can be interpreted as meaning that the crown prince again wished to assume his former position on the right wing of the Silesian Army probably in the belief that Napoleon would start the retreat to the Elbe on the 18th, in which case the Army of North Germany would have to endure the main blow while in the terrain between the Parthe and the Reitschke it would not experience a serious engagement." See Friederich, *Herbstfeldzug 1813*, III:135. Unger stated the case in similar terms: "From the unclear phrases, one believed to be reading the crown prince's earlier demands to push himself to the right of Blücher in order to avoid any danger if Napoleon made an attempt to drive to the Elbe." See Unger, *Blücher*, II:117.

28 Müffling, *Die Feldzüge*, 92–93.

29 Langeron's testimony supports Bernadotte's logic. In describing Napoleon's inaction on the 17th, Langeron noted that it "seemed more extraordinary than any of his other faults in this campaign; he could no longer ignore Bennigsen's march nor the return of the Prince Royal of Sweden and, if he was not informed, it was even more inexcusable that he was so poorly served by his spies in the country of which the sovereign was an ally. He saw that our forces would be seriously augmented; he had 160,000 to 170,000 men under arms, we had more than 300,000; it was the first time since his first campaign in Italy that he had to fight a battle with inferior numbers. His position was detestable, he was almost encircled and obliged to face all sides. *His only open road was the Eilenburg road, where he could cross the Mulde and move rapidly on Wittenberg, which we thought he would do*": "Journal de Langeron," Add MSS, 20112, 275, emphasis added.

30 Unger, *Blücher*, II:116.

31 Quistorp, *Geschichte der Nord Armee*, II:212.

32 Throughout the 16th, Bülow had to listen to the sound of Yorck's guns at Möckern without being able to assist his countrymen. In the southern sector, Kleist's 2nd Corps also fought. As his corps stood idle while the other Prussian corps commanders led theirs to battle, Bülow vainly attempted to convince Bernadotte to support Blücher. Bülow would never forget the shame he felt while he and his men stood and listened to the combat at Möckern. See Boyen, *Erinnerungen*, ed. Schmidt, II:679; Leggiere, *Napoleon and Berlin*, 266.

33 Unger, *Blücher*, II:117; Müffling, *Die Feldzüge*, 93.

34 Swederus, *Schwedens Politik und Kriege*, II:348.

35 Unger, *Blücher*, II:118.

36 Müffling, *Die Feldzüge*, 94; Schneidawind, *Prinz Wilhelm*, 93.

37 Nostitz, *Tagebuch*, 69. Schneidawind also supports this assertion.

38 Delbrück and Friederich disagree over who was the interpreter. The former maintains that "Prince William served as the interpreter and of course in a superb manner": Pertz and Delbrück, *Gneisenau*, III:467.

39 Schneidawind, *Prinz Wilhelm*, 93.

40 Quoted in Pertz and Delbrück, *Gneisenau*, III:468.

41 Nostitz, *Tagebuch*, 69.

42 Henderson, *Blücher*, 176.

43 Swederus, *Schwedens Politik und Kriege*, II:347–48.

44 Friederich again must be complimented for unbiased reporting: "The historical critic sees in the conduct of the crown prince and in his demands the renewed manifestation of the effort continued by him right up until the last decisive moment to deprive the Alliance of the commitments that he had entered into and to leave the armed forces of the Allies entrusted to him unused in favor of Napoleon. That this view overshoots the mark hardly needs detailed proof." Despite being objective, he still judges Bernadotte harshly: "Here again we have to deal with that manifestation of [Bernadotte's] generalship, which was prone to the utmost caution, with that lack of boldness, which extends through the entire political and military life of this man. At no moment of the campaign can the difference between the characteristics and the mindset of the crown prince and Blücher be seen so sharply: before making a decision, the one calculates most carefully every chance of success and is willing to be satisfied with lesser results while the other aspires to the highest attainable, to the complete destruction of the enemy and does not hesitate to gamble on his own existence." See Friederich, *Herbstfeldzug 1813*, III:137–39. Delbrück merely states: "What was said there to the crown prince and of course in strong statements had the desired effect, and the crown prince marched. Blücher's noble self-abnegation overcame the arrogance and the stubborn obstinacy of the crown prince." See Pertz and Delbrück, *Gneisenau*, III:467.

45 Schneidawind, *Prinz Wilhelm*, 94.

46 According to Langeron, "Bernadotte had made it known that he would not attack unless he had 100,000 men under his orders; he had only 70,000 in his own army; I was taken from Blücher and given to the prince: he was told that I had 30,000 men; I had only 21,000": Langeron, *Mémoires*, 323.

47 Quistorp, *Geschichte der Nord Armee*, II:213.

48 As Henderson notes in *Blücher*, 175, "The next development in the affair with Bernadotte is as creditable to Blücher as anything that ever happened in his whole career. One notes an utter absence of every selfish consideration, a burning desire to do only what was best for the cause." In *Napoleon's Last Campaign*, 357, Petre adds that "it is difficult to condemn too strongly Bernadotte's conduct in the whole of this campaign or to praise too highly Blücher's honesty and devotion to the general cause."

49 Müffling, *Die Feldzüge*, 94.

50 Quoted in Unger, *Blücher*, II:117.

51 The events of this meeting are reiterated almost verbatim by many contemporaries and historians, particularly Schneidawind, *Prinz Wilhelm*, 93–95; Quistorp, *Geschichte der Nord Armee*, II:212–14; Friederich, *Herbstfeldzug 1813*, III:136–39; and Unger, *Blücher*, II:117. One point of disagreement concerns whether the meeting ended at 7:00 or 8:00. Swederus objects to the way the event has been described. Writing in 1865, he complains that "the council has been described as stormy, and on the Prussian side one has portrayed the scenes as if Blücher, Stewart, and the rest forced the crown prince to participate. Images

about it flow even now in the *deutschen Volkskalendar* [German People's Calendar] and this poetry certainly perpetuates the old wives' tales, while the history speaks an entirely different language." To defend Bernadotte, Swederus cites numerous examples of various Allied leaders who thought it probable that Napoleon would seek to break out of Leipzig through Taucha to the Elbe. He makes no mention of Prince William's presence nor the threat he purportedly made to detach Bülow's corps from the Army of North Germany. See Swederus, *Schwedens Politik und Kriege*, II:348–53.

52 Nostitz, *Tagebuch*, 69.
53 Breitenfeld, 8:00 A.M., 18 October 1813, reproduced in Pertz and Delbrück, *Gneisenau*, III:467–68.
54 Steffens, *Adventures*, 121–22.
55 Gneisenau to Caroline, Kleinwiederitzsch, 18 October 1813, GStA PK, VI HA Rep. 92 Nl. Gneisenau, Nr. 21.
56 Quoted in Pertz and Delbrück, *Gneisenau*, III:468.
57 Unger, *Blücher*, II:119.
58 Odeleben, *A Circumstantial Narrative*, II:25–26; Pelet, *Des principales opérations de la campagne de 1813*, 281. In *Campaigns of Napoleon*, 936, Chandler maintains that on the 19th French artillery ammunition reserves were down to 20,000 rounds after they had expended 200,000 rounds from 16 to 18 October.
59 The first leg of the Weißenfels–Bad Kösen–Weimar road ran from Leipzig to Markranstädt and Lützen. This route was parallel to the Leipzig–Zwenkau–Lützen and Leipzig–Pegau–Weißenfels roads. On either, Schwarzenberg could block the Grande Armée or attack its left flank as it sought to reach Weißenfels.
60 Pelet, *Des principales opérations de la campagne de 1813*, 277–78; Petre, *Napoleon's Last Campaign*, 354; Yorck von Wartenburg, *Napoleon as a General*, II:354.
61 Odeleben, *A Circumstantial Narrative*, II:27.
62 The garrison consisted of Margaron's ad hoc division of 4,320 men (1 French and 1 Badenese brigade and 2 French provisional cavalry regiments).
63 Friederich, *Herbstfeldzug 1813*, III:124–26, 139–43. Friederich bases his figure of 295,000 Allied soldiers supported by 1,466 guns on the following totals: Army of Bohemia including Colloredo and Bubna: 141,500 men and 784 guns; Army of Poland: 30,000 men and 134 guns; Army of Silesia: 42,000 men and 310 guns; Army of North Germany: 65,000 men and 226 guns; and Cossacks: 16,500 men and 12 guns. Bogdanovich, in *Geschichte des Krieges*, IIb:178, places Allied strength at 280,200 men. Part of the discrepancy is caused by the Russian historian's estimate of the North German Army to be 58,000 men and the Army of Poland to be 28,000; the number of Cossacks cited by Friederich probably accounts for the rest.
64 Friederich, *Herbstfeldzug 1813*, III:143; Unger, *Blücher*, II:118.
65 Both divisions were from II Corps: Ignaz Ludwig von Lederer's 1st and Alois Liechtenstein's 2nd.
66 Reynier's VII Corps reached the northern sector of the Leipzig battlefield on the 17th after cutting its way through Wintzingerode's Cossacks at Taucha. After taking a position at the Heiterblick estate, Reynier received orders from

Napoleon to hold Paunsdorf against Bennigsen. Napoleon sent Reynier's 13th Division to reinforce IV Corps at Lindenau. See SHAT, C² 157: Reynier to Berthier, 19 October 1813; Sauzey, *Les Allemands*, III:222–23; Finley, "Reynier," 417.

67 Langeron, *Mémoires*, 323; Friederich, *Herbstfeldzug 1813*, III:157. This is one of the few instances where Müffling's account is incorrect. He claims that Bernadotte instructed Langeron to cross the Parthe at Taucha along with the entire Army of North Germany. "This disposition," comments Müffling, "would have obliged this corps to march back for two hours and then again forward to reach the enemy's vicinity, where it already stood." He adds that, if they had utilized only the crossing at Taucha, Langeron's corps as well as the Army of North Germany "would have caused unnecessary pressure on the bridge ... and the whole day would probably be lost in the useless march": Müffling, *Die Feldzüge*, 94.

68 In terms of distance, Wintzingerode needed to cover 7.8 miles from his bivouac at Breitenfeld to Taucha; Bülow's troops likewise had to cross 7.8 miles from their camp at Kleinpodelwitz to Taucha. It is not known for certain why Bernadotte changed his order of battle but as the Prussians of his army always received the toughest assignments it is reasonable to assume that he preferred to throw Bülow's troops into the sausage grinder first rather than those of his benefactor, Alexander, and certainly before his Swedes. His attitude is adequately surmised by a statement he purportedly made: "Provided the French are beaten, it is of no difference to me whether I or my army take part, and of the two, I had much rather we did not." See Scott, *Bernadotte*, 114.

69 SHAT, C¹⁷ 133: Order of the Day, Breitenfeld, 18 October 1813.

70 Petre notes that "for days past he [Bernadotte] had been hanging back; even on the 18th he might easily have been up three or four hours before he was. Then there would have been an overwhelming force against Napoleon's left on the Parthe. Even when he did arrive, Bernadotte acted very feebly. His Swedes did practically nothing": Petre, *Napoleon's Last Campaign*, 370.

71 Müffling, *Die Feldzüge*, 94.

72 Langeron, *Mémoires*, 324. The Parthe, a right tributary of the White Elster thirty-seven miles in length, originates southeast of Leipzig between Colditz and Bad Lausick in the Leipzig lowlands. It flows northwest before turning west and discharging into the White Elster in the northwestern part of Leipzig.

73 Langeron, *Mémoires*, 324–25.

74 Lieven, *Russia Against Napoleon*, 455.

75 Kaptsevich's X Infantry Corps consisted of Urusov's 8th Division and Turchaninov's 22nd Division. The 29th and 45th Jäger Regiments formed the 2nd Brigade of 22nd Division while the Staroskolskii Regiment belonged to its 1st Brigade. The 38th Jäger was one of the three regiments that formed the 2nd Brigade of 8th Division.

76 Langeron, *Mémoires*, 325. "I must admit that I was momentarily embarrassed by that which I did to them," continues Langeron; "under the circumstances it was possible that this was an enemy ruse and that these so-called émigrés were destined, whilst they were mixed with my cavalry, to charge it in the rear or

flanks, at the moment of the attack; I wished to send them to my Reserve Cavalry but they begged to be sent forward with the cavalry of the vanguard; I did not relent and have never repented."

77 RGVIA, f. VUA, d. 3889, ll. 165–165b.

78 Bogdanovich, *Geschichte des Krieges*, IIb:191–92.

79 Friederich, *Herbstfeldzug 1813*, III:178.

80 Rottembourg's brigade consisted of one battalion each of Saxon, Polish, and Westphalian Guard.

81 Moreover, Bennigsen was waiting for Bernadotte's army to arrive and so could not launch his attack that could possibly have outflanked Probstheida and thus forced the French to abandon the key to Napoleon's position: Lieven, *Russia Against Napoleon*, 454.

82 Allied counterbattery fire proved far more effective. After taking Probstheida on the 19th, Kleist's men found thirty demolished French cannon: Friederich, *Herbstfeldzug 1813*, III:166.

83 The Fusilier Battalion of 2nd Silesian Infantry Regiment and 3rd Battalion of 11th Reserve Regiment.

84 August (1779–1843) was the youngest son of Prince August Ferdinand of Prussia (1730–1813), who himself was the youngest brother of Frederick the Great (1712–1786). August's more famous sibling, Prince Louis Ferdinand (1772–1806), was killed by the French at Saalfeld. Both Louis Ferdinand and August are often mistakenly referred to as brothers of King Frederick William III (1770–1840) when in fact they were second cousins, their first cousin being Frederick William's father, Frederick William II (1744–1797), who himself was the son of the oldest of Frederick the Great's younger brothers, August William of Prussia (1722–1758).

85 Vaudoncourt, *Histoire de la guerre*, II:214–15.

86 Friederich, *Herbstfeldzug 1813*, III:166.

87 Thinking the Saxons had misunderstood his orders, Reynier sent his chief of staff, François-Joseph Gressot, "to stop the Saxons and calm their ardor in an attack Reynier had not ordered." The Saxons received Gressot with shouts of "get back, general, this is not your place." See Sauzey, *Les Allemands*, III:225–26; Finley, "Reynier," 419.

88 The high-ranking Saxon officers had decided on this step earlier that morning. They communicated their intentions to the division's commander, Zeschau, and requested that he send an adjutant to Frederick Augustus in Leipzig to communicate the news that 26th Light Cavalry Brigade had already defected and to request instructions for the rest of the division. Around 2:00 that afternoon Zeschau received a response from his king: "Herr General von Zeschau! I have always placed trust in my troops and I do so in the current moment more than ever. Loyalty to my person can be proven to me only through the fulfillment of their duty and I am certain that you will do everything in your power to assure this. I pray to God that he takes you in his holy protection." Deeming this reply to be ambiguous, the Saxon officers assumed that their king could not speak his mind openly because of the French entourage that surrounded him. Moreover, they considered Frederick Augustus to be Napoleon's prisoner. If he was a free

man, they did not doubt that he would shed his pro-French politics. Viewing the battle and the war as lost, they believed that they could best aid their king by joining the Allies in the least to save what was left of the Saxon army from the disaster that awaited Napoleon. See Friederich, *Herbstfeldzug 1813*, III:168–69.

89 Napoleon later blamed the Saxons for his defeat at Leipzig but the 4,000 Saxons and Württembergers who defected would have hardly tipped the scales in his favor.

90 Bogdanovich, *Geschichte des Krieges*, IIb:202.

91 Marmont, *Mémoires*, V:183–85.

92 Quoted in Pertz and Delbrück, *Gneisenau*, III:468; Bogdanovich, *Geschichte des Krieges*, IIb:201; Lieven, *Russia Against Napoleon*, 455.

93 Friederich, *Herbstfeldzug 1813*, III:180.

94 Hofmann, *Leipzig*, 61; Pelet, *Des principales opérations de la campagne de 1813*, 309, 320. Aster, in *Leipzig*, II:266 and 270, claims that the French also planned on burning the Ranstädt suburb as soon as the rearguard had evacuated the city. Although nothing came of this, the city's authorities were told to provide thirty-six hundredweights of tar.

95 According to Pelet, *Des principales opérations de la campagne de 1813*, 312, a column of 5,000 men was en route to Kassel to chase the Cossacks from the city, the capital of Jerome Bonaparte's Westphalia. Kellermann had also sent the 54th March Column (3,000 men) from Fulda to Kassel. The 55th March Column – 4,000 men and 14 guns – was approaching Erfurt while the 3,000 men and 16 guns of the 56th March Column had departed from Mainz. Several other battalions were echeloned on the roads to Fulda and Würzburg.

96 French contemporaries such as Fain and Pelet claim that Napoleon issued orders for the building of three bridges over the Pleiße to facilitate the retreat but neither he nor Berthier insured that these orders were carried out. According to Pelet, "only one of these auxiliary bridges was built near the Richter Gardens, and so badly that it soon collapsed." As for blame, Pelet blasts Berthier: "As much as possible, we concealed anything that looked like a retreat. Unfortunately, the major-general, while confidently obliging the designs of the great captain, thought that some of the demonstrations were superfluous and neglected the most necessary precautions. The negligence in the construction of the bridges must be attributed to him as well as the refusal to drive off the reserve batteries and parks ... At Leipzig, Weißenfels, and Freyburg, the prince de Neufchâtel admonished those who were attempting to carry out the orders they had been given, saying that the emperor thought only of resuming the offensive." Petre and Yorck von Wartenburg claim that no such orders were issued while Chandler maintains that orders were issued for additional bridges to be built at Lindenau but that this was no longer feasible. Yorck von Wartenburg further maintains that the "complete want of bridges" indicates "how far the general's carelessness as to all the necessary details had gone." See Pelet, *Des principales opérations de la campagne de 1813*, 284, 311, 314; Fain, *1813*, II:442; Aster, *Leipzig*, II:198; Yorck von Wartenburg, *Napoleon as a General*, II:354; Petre, *Napoleon's Last Campaign*, 353–54; Chandler, *Campaigns of Napoleon*, 933.

97 Pelet, *Des principales opérations de la campagne de 1813*, 313–14; Aster, *Leipzig*, II:225–26, 230–32; Bogdanovich, *Geschichte des Krieges*, IIb:211, 215.

98 Bogdanovich, *Geschichte des Krieges*, IIb:211; Friederich, *Herbstfeldzug 1813*, III:196; Aster, *Leipzig*, II:228.

99 Pelet, *Des principales opérations de la campagne de 1813*, 315; Fain, *1813*, II:434–36.

100 Bogdanovich, *Geschichte des Krieges*, IIb:209–10; Aster, *Leipzig*, II:200–03.

101 Counterclockwise from left to right, these included the Münz, outer Peters, Windmill, Sand, Hospital, outer Grimma, Blinden, Hinter, Gerber, Floß, and Ranstädt.

102 In the accounts of the Napoleonic Wars, William is often referred to as the count of Hochberg.

103 Pelet, *Des principales opérations de la campagne de 1813*, 314–15; Bogdanovich, *Geschichte des Krieges*, IIb:214; Vaudoncourt, *Histoire de la guerre*, II:220.

104 Halle and Merseburg are twenty-one and seventeen miles from Leipzig respectively.

105 Müffling, *Die Feldzüge*, 97; Gneisenau to Clausewitz, 19 October 1813, GStA PK, VI HA Rep. 92, Nl. Gneisenau, Nr. 21.

106 In *Geschichte des Krieges*, IIb:207, Bogdanovich perpetuates this story, which he based on Plotho, *Der Krieg*, II:414.

107 Schwarzenberg to Bubna, 18 October 1813, in Friederich, *Herbstfeldzug 1813*, III:192.

108 Bernhardi, *Toll*, III:460.

109 Bogdanovich, *Geschichte des Krieges*, IIb:208; Aster, *Leipzig*, II:178–79.

110 Beitzke, *Geschichte der deutschen Freheitskriege*, II:636; Bogdanovich, *Geschichte des Krieges*, IIb:213–14.

111 Quoted in Bernhardi, *Toll*, III:464–69; Fain, *1813*, II:433; Bogdanovich, *Geschichte des Krieges*, IIb:216–19.

112 Aster, *Leipzig*, II:275; Bogdanovich, *Geschichte des Krieges*, IIb:219–20.

113 Plotho, *Der Krieg*, 2419–20; Beitzke, *Geschichte der deutschen Freheitskriege*, II:644–46; Aster, *Leipzig*, II:283–92.

114 Friederich, *Herbstfeldzug 1813*, III:206.

115 By the end of the fighting on the 19th, the Arkhangelogorodskii Regiment mustered only 30 officers and 180 men of the 550 men who had started the battle on the 16th: Bogdanovich, *Geschichte des Krieges*, IIb:223; Plotho, *Der Krieg*, II:420; Aster, *Leipzig*, II:292–94.

116 Bogdanovich, *Geschichte des Krieges*, IIb:224. Vaudoncourt, in *Histoire de la guerre*, II:221, and Norvins, in *Portefeuille de mil huit cent treize*, II:420, incorrectly claim that at the Peters Gate the Badeners defected to the Allies. In *Des principales opérations de la campagne de 1813*, 319–20, Pelet makes a similar accusation: "The defense of Leipzig's wall was entrusted to the Saxons and Badeners. But the former ... again betrayed the interests of their sovereign. The latter, holding the Peters Gate, delivered it to the Allies." Pelet also makes a vague reference concerning "the Germans of III Corps" during the struggle at the Hinter Gate: "Our soldiers threw themselves into the houses and the side streets; they defended each step. But a new defection by the Germans of III

Corps forced our troops to give ground." According to Hudson Lowe, one of the first accounts of Leipzig published by the French-controlled press at Frankfurt-am-Main stated that the defection of Napoleon's allies "and particularly that of Bavaria is assigned as the primary cause of all his disasters": Lowe to Stewart, Gießen, 3 November 1813, Add MSS, 20111, 204.

117 In *Des principales opérations de la campagne de 1813*, 320–21, Pelet insists that Montfort instructed Lafontaine to blow the bridge only on the express order of a general officer. Pelet reproduced a 20 October report made by a Captain Blay of the Engineers of the Guard to Berthier which confirmed that Montfort had ordered the corporal not to blow the bridge unless the enemy was about to seize the structure. Both Montfort and Lafontaine, the latter criticized in *La Moniteur* as a man of no intelligence, were arrested and scheduled to stand before courtsmartial. Montfort was incarcerated at Mainz but reinstated during the Allied siege to command the city's engineers until Napoleon's First Abdication. He went on to serve Louis XVIII, rallied to Napoleon during the Hundred Days, and afterward again served in the royal army. In 1834 he became a Grand Officer of the Legion of Honor.

118 Aster, *Leipzig*, II:317–18; Bogdanovich, *Geschichte des Krieges*, IIb:228–29. Poniatowski had sustained wounds on the 14th and 16th as well earlier on the 19th. Found by fishermen on the 24th, his body was laid out in the St. Johannis Church by the Grimma Gate, embalmed and initially buried with full military honors in the crypt at the St. Johannis cemetery. After the transfer of his remains to Poland in 1814, he was buried on 10 September with the consent of Tsar Alexander in the vault of the Holy Cross Church in the center of Warsaw but later transferred to Krakow and buried on 22 July 1817 in the Wawel Cathedral.

119 Bogdanovich, *Geschichte des Krieges*, IIb:225–26.

120 Friederich, *Herbstfeldzug 1813*, III:225–27; some of Hofmann's casualty figures in *Leipzig*, 62, are lower. For the Allies, killed and wounded amounted to 1,790 officers and 40,850 men. In terms of nationality, Hofmann reckons that the Russians lost 800 officers and 20,000 men; the Prussians: 620 officers and 13,550 men; the Austrians: 360 officers and 7,000 men; and the Swedes: 10 officers and 300 men. For the French, Hofmann cites 38,000 killed and wounded and 30,000 prisoners.

121 Yorck von Wartenburg, *Napoleon as a General*, II:354; Pelet, *Des principales opérations de la campagne de 1813*, 310. This account is based primarily on Friederich, *Herbstfeldzug 1813*, III:117–234; Aster, *Leipzig*, II:1–330; Bogdanovich, *Geschichte des Krieges*, IIb:175–231; Pelet, *Des principales opérations de la campagne de 1813*, 275–322.

16

Race to the Rhine

At Leipzig, Blücher and his staff recognized the extent of the costly but momentous victory. On 19 October, Gneisenau wrote to his wife that "our assault on Leipzig was very bloody. After many hours of work our troops stormed the city. General Blücher and I were the first to enter. We found a mass of prisoners, 20,000 wounded, even more sick. The dead lay everywhere. Destroyed houses, overturned baggage wagons, troops of all nations; it is a mess without equal. Every step has been taken to pursue the enemy briskly. We will destroy the remainder of his army."[1] Blücher also boasted to his wife that on the 16th he had engaged the French at Möckern, taking 4,000 prisoners, 45 guns, 1 Eagle, and various other standards. He described the events on the 18th and 19th as "the greatest battle the earth has ever seen; 600,000 men fought with each other; around 2:00 P.M. I took Leipzig by storm, the king of Saxony and many generals were captured, the Polish prince Poniatowski drowned; 170 cannon were taken and around 40,000 men are now prisoners. Napoleon escaped, but he is not safe. At this moment my cavalry has brought in another 2,000 prisoners; the entire [French] army is lost." Yet not all observers wrote such gleeful accounts. Commenting on the barbarity of war, the British ambassador to Austria, George Hamilton Gordon, Lord Aberdeen, noted: "For three or four miles the ground is covered with bodies of men and horses, many not dead. Wounded wretches unable to crawl, crying for water amidst heaps of putrefying bodies. Their screams are heard at an immense distance, and still ring in my ears."[2]

Blücher and Gneisenau started planning to exploit the victory even before the fighting around Leipzig ended. After Yorck's corps departed for Halle on the night of 18 October, Blücher instructed Langeron and Sacken to unite their corps between the Parthe and Pleiße Rivers to follow Yorck. According to Müffling, the fatigue of the Russian infantry and the dark night "prevented the immediate execution of this order. The corps did not reach Eutritzsch until 11:00 the next morning." With the bridges over the Elster down, the nearest point of passage could be found only at Schkeuditz, approximately twelve miles northwest of Leipzig and ten miles southeast of Halle. This meant that the two Russian corps of the Silesian Army first had to make a circuitous march to be able to directly pursue the imperials.[3]

Blücher received confirmation of the French retreat at 8:00 A.M. on the 19th, but the situation did not allow him to pursue. By this time, Langeron's men had only recrossed the Parthe. Moreover, Sacken became engaged in a heated combat with French forces in his sector and requested support. At noon on the 19th, Blücher instructed Vasilchikov to lead Sacken's cavalry across the Elster at Schkeuditz and turn south to strike the Leipzig–Merseburg road. That evening, Vasilchikov's advance guard reached Priesteblich on the road to Merseburg. There the Russians made contact with a French post and drove it further west to Großdölzig.[4]

Discussions about the next move occurred both before the storming of Leipzig and afterward, when the monarchs met with Blücher, Schwarzenberg, and Bernadotte on Leipzig's marketplace. Preliminary arrangements called for the Silesian Army to move north of Leipzig and then turn west to harry Napoleon's right flank. Schwarzenberg's Army of Bohemia would move southwest from Leipzig in two columns: the first through Naumburg and the second through Zeitz. The two columns would unite at Erfurt. Bernadotte's Army of North Germany and Bennigsen's Army of Poland would follow Blücher and then slide between the Silesian and Bohemian Armies. In this way, the French would be driven toward Wrede's Austro-Bavarian Army. Thus caught between the Allied forces, the remnant of Napoleon's army would be destroyed before it could reach the Rhine. Yet during the talks on Leipzig's marketplace, Bernadotte, purportedly dressed "like an opera-master," refused to endorse this plan. He intended to lead his army north to take Norway from the Danes but agreed to allow Tauentzien's corps to continue besieging Magdeburg, Wittenberg, and Torgau. His allies remained silent; Bennigsen's army would have to suffice.[5]

Although Blücher left the much-heralded meeting on Leipzig's marketplace elated, Gneisenau felt slighted. That night he complained in a letter to Clausewitz that the king had said "a few cold, but somewhat friendly words of satisfaction with our army. To me he said nothing. I have still received no word of satisfaction about our crossing of the Elbe and the subsequent events of the war." On the other hand, the tsar, the kaiser, and Schwarzenberg showered him with praise. "But," Gneisenau continues, "you see the king's deeply rooted antipathy against all those who do not share his political views. As soon as this holy war is over, I will leave his army. I would rather eat the bread of misery than serve as an unwelcome guest in the army of this unfriendly despot." Gneisenau would later admit that he had misinterpreted the king's silence, yet the same scene would be repeated more than once during the 1814 campaign in France.[6]

Gneisenau's overreaction to Frederick William's reserved demeanor certainly reflects the psychological and emotional exhaustion of the man who for two months had served as chief of staff of the Silesian Army and Chief of the General Staff of the Prussian Army. As he observed the carnage around Leipzig, he could only be grateful that his men had not died in vain. His adjutant, Stosch, recalls that on the 19th Gneisenau and his staff "rode over the battlefield of Möckern, where the corpses of the soldiers who had fallen on the 16th, mainly from the Silesian Landwehr, lay so close to one another that the horses could only get through in single file. I watched Gneisenau's solemn face, and he said to me: 'Victory was bought with German blood at great cost, at very great cost.' A tear was in his eye, the only time I ever saw him weep." When a grim Gneisenau met with Stein at Leipzig on the 20th, both agreed that, despite the great success, the war could end only with an invasion of France and Napoleon's downfall. This formed the basis of Gneisenau's operational doctrine for the next five months.[7]

By dawn on the 19th, Yorck's main body had covered fifteen miles from Leipzig to Großkugel, six miles southeast of Halle, where it rested for several hours. During the course of the day, various reports on the outcome of the battle filtered through Yorck's headquarters. "The first official and appeasing report of the [Allied] victory," as Schack noted in his journal, arrived at dawn. Yorck's staff quickly disseminated this news to restore morale and the march continued at 10:00 A.M. Later in the day, Blücher informed Yorck that the Allies had stormed and taken Leipzig; Sacken's and Langeron's corps would join the pursuit as soon as the Russian troops had rested. Blücher also stated that the two Russian corps would march southwest to Lützen, indicating that a union of the Silesian Army would not be possible for some time.[8]

Amid the cheers of its inhabitants, Yorck's main body entered Halle at 7:00 on the evening of 19 October. Horn's 2nd Division camped in and around Halle; Hünerbein's 1st Division marched through Halle and bivouacked a few miles east at Bruckdorf after detachments secured the bridges over the Elster at Burgliebenau and Beesen. Riding without rest, the Reserve Cavalry continued through Halle to Passendorf and Delitz am Berg. Despite the fatigue of man and horse, Jürgaß dispatched numerous patrols.[9]

Throughout 19 October, Schwarzenberg maneuvered the masses of the Bohemian Army away from the ruins of Leipzig; by that evening his forces stood between Zeitz and Naumburg. The Armies of Poland and North Germany remained in and around Leipzig. Of the Silesian Army, Sacken and Langeron reached Schkeuditz while Yorck's corps moved into positions in and around Halle.

Around 9:00 on the morning of 19 October, Napoleon accompanied by Murat rode to the king of Saxony's residence to bid him farewell. During the thirty-minute meeting, Napoleon assured Frederick Augustus that he would return to Leipzig in two days, much to the chagrin of the king, who had already asked for the tsar's terms. From the central marketplace, the emperor and his staff rode to the Ranstädt Gate. Napoleon could do little to get through the bottleneck that had formed at the narrow gate and along the Lindenau Causeway. He resolved himself to being carried along with the throng. Sometime before 11:30 that morning he reached Lindenau itself. After issuing further orders for Leipzig's defense, he fell fast asleep at the windmill. The roar caused by the exploding bridge woke him shortly before 1:00.[10]

Assuming the Allies would hold Naumburg and defend the Saale crossing at Bad Kösen, Napoleon chose to cross the river at Weißenfels. From there, his army would utilize a rain-drenched country road to reach the bridge over the Unstrut at Freyburg. Bertrand's patrol found Freyburg's bridge burned by the same Austrian unit that held Naumburg but the French used the available materials to build a new bridge. Upstream, Bertrand's men also repaired the slightly damaged crossing at the Zettenbach Mill; the French thus had two bridges operational in just a few hours.

At Halle, Yorck had not received any news of the other Allied units. He particularly hoped to hear something of the Austrian III Corps, which he believed would engage the French on the road to either Weißenfels or Merseburg. Virtually on his own, the Prussian commander could only guess the direction Napoleon would take. A movement due west to Merseburg offered the French emperor the most direct escape route across the Saale and would spare his exhausted army a long march on the open plain. On the other hand, crossing the Saale at Merseburg would then force the French to plod through the deep valley of the Unstrut to reach the bridges at Freyburg and Laucha. Yorck had few options other than to dispatch patrols and occupy the river crossings Napoleon's army needed to continue the retreat. He ordered his tired cavalry to turn south; part of the Reserve Cavalry would take post at Merseburg, while the light cavalry proceeded to Großkayna and Roßbach, a few miles north of Weißenfels. The Cossacks and one Brandenburg Hussar squadron raced toward Freyburg and Laucha on the Unstrut. Yorck granted the infantry some rest after the difficult night march, mainly because he could do nothing further until his cavalry found the French army.

While Yorck enjoyed a victory celebration in Halle, courtesy of the city magistrate, further details arrived regarding the storming of Leipzig and the collapse of the French army. Unfortunately, this encouraging news failed to mention the direction Napoleon had taken. The critical news that Napoleon intended to cross the Saale at Weißenfels finally arrived when the reports of

22 Napoleon after the battle of Leipzig

Yorck's cavalry reached Halle during the night of 19/20 October. To reach Weißenfels, I Corps would have to march almost twenty miles. Yorck believed his cavalry could reach the crossing before the imperials but had little hope his infantry would arrive in time.[11]

On the following day, 20 October, Bertrand secured Freyburg and forwarded a detachment across the hastily built bridge to reconnoiter the opposite bank of the Unstrut. To the east, Napoleon had spent the night of 19/20 October at Markranstädt, departing for Weißenfels at 11:00 A.M. There he learned that the Austrian III Corps had reached Naumburg, thus blocking his path on the direct highway that ran southwest to Jena, where it then angled due west to Erfurt. Not knowing the size of the Allied force around Naumburg, the emperor decided to leave the highway and follow Bertrand through Freyburg. After personally reconnoitering the area, he moved to Markröhlitz to observe the army's march. The main body reached Weißenfels and crossed to the left bank of the Saale under Napoleon's supervision. Marmont covered the crossing by taking a position facing Merseburg with III, VI, and VII Corps. Oudinot's rearguard evacuated Lindenau before daybreak, united with the I Cavalry Corps at Lützen, and proceeded to Weißenfels under the constant pressure of Sacken's cavalry.

As the hunted moved across the Saale early on the 20th, the hunters gave chase. Yorck's Reserve Cavalry saddled and departed around 3:00 A.M. with orders to move through Bad Lauchstädt to Weißenfels. Horn's 2nd Division followed at 5:00 A.M. while Hünerbein's 1st Division received orders to occupy Merseburg. Two twelve-pound and two six-pound batteries remained at Halle because the depleted corps did not have enough crews to man the guns. Yorck accompanied the main body of Jürgaß's Reserve Cavalry to Merseburg but ordered the cavalry to continue west. At the village of Markröhlitz, Jürgaß's regiments clashed with Polish lancers and French skirmishers. The Prussian cavalry observed French infantry at Weißenfels and Reichardtswerben. French skirmishers extended from Reichardtswerben along the Freyburg road; behind the hills stood several cavalry regiments. According to the statements of prisoners, the French force consisted of at least two cavalry divisions including the horse of the Young Guard; Napoleon was rumored to be at Weißenfels. Behind this screen, the French army retreated west on the road to Freyburg.

Reports of the enemy's march through Weißenfels gradually reached Yorck during the morning of 20 October. Around 9:00 A.M., news arrived of a large French column on the Weißenfels–Freyburg road. Yorck rode forward to personally confirm the report and observed the French army moving through Markröhlitz toward Freyburg. Strong French cavalry units belonging to Sebastiani's II Cavalry Corps could be seen advancing to Reichardtswerben to cover the column's right flank. Although his infantry still remained in the rear, Yorck ordered Jürgaß to attack. As soon as the Prussian cavalry appeared, the French adroitly deployed their infantry. The French cavalry and infantry that stood between the Prussians and the defiling columns had such considerable force that any attack would have been suicide. Even after the disaster at Leipzig, Napoleon's army remained more than a match for Yorck's Reserve Cavalry. In view of the sheer numbers that opposed him, Yorck called off the attack. Instead, he instructed Jürgaß to maintain contact with the French and harass their columns with his horse guns. Both sides exchanged artillery fire with little effect for several hours until Yorck's cavalry withdrew to Roßbach. Horn's division only reached Frankleben, while Hünerbein marched west to Bad Lauchstädt as the result of a misunderstanding.[12]

Closer to Leipzig, Sacken's cavalry pursued the French rearguard on the direct road that ran southwest from the city to Weißenfels. Vasilchikov's Cossacks reached Markranstädt by 6:00 A.M. on the 20th, attacking some 2,000 stragglers on the road and then harassing Oudinot's Guard divisions as far as Lützen. Steffens explains:

> The road to Weißenfels lies over a wide plain; we saw the last of the French troops before us; though in hasty flight, they kept tolerably good order; it was rather a misty morning and there was nothing to be seen between us and the retreating enemy; suddenly we noticed Cossacks in every direction, singly, or by twos or threes: in an instant they formed a troop, in another

they fell on the enemy: these consisted of the tired and weary who were not able to keep up with the rest; the Cossacks swarmed in between them and the main body, and they were instantaneously surrounded and cut off from it. The Cossacks and their prisoners then disappeared, as if by magic.[13]

Not far from where King Gustav Adolph of Sweden had fallen during the Thirty Years' War, the French I Cavalry Corps turned and ended the Cossack menace for the moment; the Russian horsemen withdrew to await the arrival of Vasilchikov's main body. After the commander came up with the bulk of his cavalry, the pursuit continued around 10:00 A.M. At Rippach, the French again deployed for combat. Following an insignificant cannonade, the French rearguard withdrew to Weißenfels in the evening. Vasilchikov's cavalry bivouacked by Rippach while his patrols pressed on to the Saale. Behind the Russian cavalry, Blücher led Langeron's and Sacken's infantry across the Elster at Schkeuditz, turned south, and struck the road to Weißenfels. He pushed his men as far as Lützen, where he established his headquarters.[14]

Napoleon issued a series of orders late on the 20th that reflected his growing concern over reaching the Unstrut ahead of the accelerated Allied pursuit. By pushing Gyulay's III Corps to Naumburg, Schwarzenberg had closed the direct highway that ran southwest from Leipzig through Lützen and Weißenfels. Because Napoleon had to take the detour through Freyburg, he needed to close the passes to the Thuringian plain before his pursuers reached them. This made possession of the bridge at Bad Kösen vital. "It is important," Napoleon emphasized to Berthier, "that no one advances across that bridge against us." Should the Allies take Bad Kösen, they could cross to the left or northern bank of the Saale and proceed to Freyburg, thus enveloping Napoleon's army and stranding it on the opposite bank of the Unstrut. This would provide time for Blücher, Bennigsen, and Schwarzenberg to converge on Freyburg and either drive Napoleon's army into the Unstrut or force a decisive battle. Consequently, Bertrand and the vanguard of the army received the task of securing Bad Kösen and the northern bank of the Saale. His three divisions and V Cavalry Corps would continue the march; a fourth division, which had remained at Weißenfels, would rejoin the corps.[15]

To keep the main body of his army on the move, the emperor instructed several units to continue the march to Freyburg early on 21 October. With III, VI, and VII Corps, Marmont commenced the march from Weißenfels to Freyburg at 2:00 A.M. Victor followed one hour later with II Corps, and then Augereau with one division of IX Corps at 4:00 A.M. Around 5:00 A.M. the Old Guard marched; two hours later XI and V Corps followed after regrouping as much as possible. From their positions facing Merseburg, II and III Cavalry Corps also started toward Freyburg around 4:00 A.M.

In the meantime, Mortier led his two Young Guard divisions and the Light Guard Cavalry division to Freyburg. Lefebvre-Desnouettes received orders to likewise direct his V Cavalry Corps to Freyburg early on the 21st. After uniting with Mortier's Light Guard Cavalry, Napoleon estimated Lefebvre-Desnouettes would have a cavalry force of between 5,000 and 6,000 men to secure Freyburg's bridge over the Unstrut and to collect news of the enemy. To avoid a bottleneck on the road, the French proceeded to Freyburg in two columns: the right wing through Zeuchfeld, the left through Markröhlitz. To the rear of the army, Oudinot dispatched I Cavalry Corps in the direction of Merseburg to fill the void left by II and III Cavalry Corps; he remained at Weißenfels with the two Young Guard divisions that served as the rearguard. Around noon, I Cavalry Corps returned and Oudinot led the Guard to Freyburg.[16]

On 21 October, the two Allied wings finally converged on the French army. From the left, an Austrian detachment from Gyulay's III Corps took possession of the bridge over the Saale at Bad Kösen. As Gyulay led his main body due west from Naumburg to Bad Kösen early on the 21st, reports arrived of strong French columns approaching Bad Kösen from the northeast direction of Freyburg. He accelerated the march but could not arrive before Bertrand's men utilized a thick fog to surprise the Austrian post and drive it across the bridge to Neu-Kösen. A struggle for control of the bridge ensued until 10:00 P.M., when Bertrand withdrew. The French lost 649 prisoners and each side suffered 1,000 casualties but Gyulay secured his objective by preventing Bertrand from destroying the bridge over the Saale. While the Austrian III Corps fought at Bad Kösen, Schwarzenberg's right column reached Naumburg and his left camped at Eisenberg.

On the Allied right wing, Yorck sought to prevent his adversary from crossing the Unstrut, yet the reports still did not make clear whether the French would cross the river at both Freyburg and Laucha, or Freyburg alone. To observe both crossings and to inflict maximum damage on the retreating enemy, I Corps needed to be reorganized. On the evening of 20 October, Henckel assumed command of a new advance guard in place of Katzler, who had been wounded at Leipzig on the 18th. Early on 21 October, Henckel advanced to Laucha with orders to either harass the French army as it crossed the Unstrut or make for Freyburg. As Henckel's column bore down on the French from the north, Yorck's main body and Reserve Cavalry moved west in an attempt to strike the French rear at Freyburg. For this purpose, Horn and Hünerbein received instructions to unite at Petzkendorf around 7:00 A.M.; Jürgaß assembled the Reserve Cavalry at Braunsbedra around the same time.[17]

Henckel delayed his march for two hours while his battalions and cavalry regiments made their way from their bivouacs. Finally, at 7:00 A.M. on 21 October, the colonel ordered the advance. Marching through

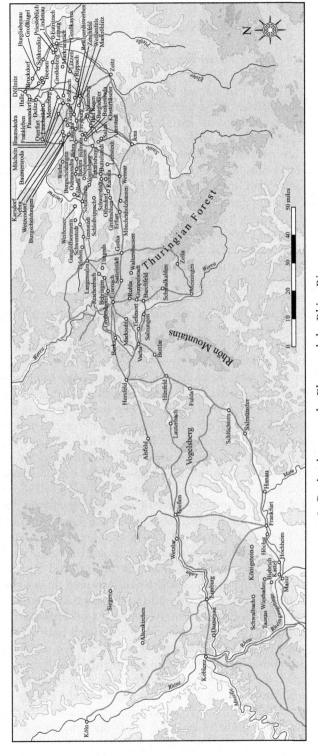

28. Region between the Elster and the Rhine Rivers

Baumersroda, he found the remains of a large bivouac. The village magistrate informed him that it was a pity he had not arrived earlier because a large number of prisoners had passed the night there guarded by two Polish battalions. Reconnaissance and further statements from the inhabitants confirmed that a large column of mainly Austrian prisoners of war, perhaps 4,000 men, had marched northwest. Henckel instructed the most senior officer after him, Major Burghoff, to continue the march to Laucha with the other troops while he pursued this column in the direction of Nebra with the Black Hussars and the Saxon Uhlan Regiment.

The two cavalry regiments pressed on for what seemed like an eternity until the large column finally came into view. Individual guards on both sides of the column escorted the prisoners while the two Polish battalions formed the head and the rear. Henckel ordered the four Prussian squadrons to pass the length of the column in order to attack it from the front while he and the Saxons followed behind the column. Near the village of Gleina, the Black Hussars overtook the column and trotted past; the prisoners broke rank and easily subdued the guards that marched to the left and right. Soon the field was covered with liberated prisoners running in all directions, similar to the effect of disturbing a mound of ants. Although the two escorting Polish battalions held their ground, the men of the foremost battalion cast aside their muskets and surrendered as soon as the Black Hussars formed for an attack. However, Henckel did not have the same luck. He ordered the Saxons to charge the rear battalion, which by now had formed a square. As the colonel bore down on the Poles, he noticed that he, his adjutants, the Saxon commander, Major Trotha, and the staff bugler charged the enemy square alone – the regiment refused to follow. Consequently, the few hundred Poles escaped into an adjacent forest and Henckel could not pursue.[18] On questioning the Saxons, Henckel and Trotha learned that many of the officers and men were on good terms with the Poles of that unit from their days of serving together in the Grande Armée. In his memoirs, Henckel admits that he "had not thought of this circumstance before, otherwise I certainly would have taken another regiment with me."[19]

Henckel's men liberated more than 100 officers and 4,000 men. The majority consisted of Austrians and Russians captured during the battle of Dresden in August or more recently during the combats around Leipzig on the 16th. Among the former prisoners were eighteen Prussian officers and the entire Austrian 1st Jäger Battalion. Those captured at Dresden had already marched as far as Thüringen but were returned to Leipzig out of fear that Allied raiding parties might liberate them. Now, for a second time, they had started the march to France. The Allies captured Colonel Marc Antoine Puton, baron de They, the commander of the escort, along with several officers and 400 men. Henckel decided to have a detachment of Saxon troops lead Putot, his men, and the liberated prisoners to

Merseburg. For some of Putot's men the transition from guard to prisoner was accompanied by acts of retribution for the suffering of the Allied soldiers. In addition, Henckel recalls that "it went very bad for one camp follower; in a few minutes she was stripped completely naked and I had to give her a coat."

Henckel himself was the hero of the day and it seemed that each of the 4,000 prisoners wanted to personally thank him. In trying to kiss his hand they almost pulled the colonel from his horse. He proudly notes that "never in my life have I been kissed more than on this day." As he reveled in his moment of glory, Captain Lützow of Yorck's staff arrived to express the commanding general's discontent with Henckel for leaving the vanguard. Henckel instructed the officer to immediately return and report the rescue; Lützow complied. Henckel intended to follow but at the moment had to establish order among the celebrating Austrians and Russians.

Meanwhile, Yorck learned that the French army had not taken the road to Laucha. Therefore, the Prussian commander wanted to concentrate his corps to attack the enemy at Freyburg. He sent orders for Henckel to unite with the rest of the corps at Münchroda, from where it would descend on Freyburg. Yorck himself caught up with Burghoff and the vanguard shortly after Henckel departed to follow the column of prisoners. Not finding the colonel with his troops infuriated Yorck. Ever the stern disciplinarian, he sent Lützow to find Henckel and relay a sharp reprimand. This transgression so aggravated Yorck that he turned and impatiently galloped after Henckel. A few minutes passed and he met Lützow riding back to him; the captain reported Henckel's success. "I allowed my cavalry to follow after some rest," relates Henckel in his memoirs, "but I now moved quickly to reach my other troops. On the way I came across Yorck with his entire entourage; in his impatience he had ridden after me, but was now completely satisfied since Lützow already reported to him. [The general] removed his cap and said: 'Gentlemen, three cheers for Count Henckel!' This statement, coming from this man, at this moment, I cannot deny, meant more to me than when I had received the *Pour le Mérite* with oak leaves for the day of Möckern."[20]

Aside from Henckel's exploits, Yorck's main body, which had departed from Petzkendorf around 7:00 A.M. with orders to march through Zeuchfeld to Freyburg, was on a collision course with Napoleon's army. As the Prussians moved southwest from Merseburg to Freyburg, the French struck the westward road from Weißenfels. Napoleon's weary men trudged along the muddy roads that twisted through the rain-drenched hills between the Saale and the Unstrut. "As we pursued them from Weißenfels to Freyburg, we witnessed fearful traces of the general consternation," noted Steffens. "I shall never forget the sight: weapons thrown away to lighten their load and increase their speed; guns, ammunition wagons, carriages of all kinds, even some handsome traveling equipages; all clearly abandoned because the tired horses could no longer pull them ... not only on the road but in the fields as far as the eye could reach in the direction of the flight. The way was often quite impassable, and we had to make considerable detours to continue."[21]

Reaching Freyburg brought no relief to the toil of man and horse. The town lay deep in the Unstrut valley, surrounded by a high, precipitous ridge. Access to Freyburg on the predominantly east–west road that ran from Weißenfels to Laucha required a steep descent along badly rutted tracks on either side of the town. Vineyards, gardens, and houses crowded the road, which narrowed to such an extent that infantry could barely march four abreast and wagons could hardly move. On reaching Freyburg, the washed-out approach route to the hastily built bridge over the rain-swollen Unstrut did little to raise morale. After crossing the bridges at either Freyburg or the Zscheiplitz estate, the imperial soldiers would face a taxing ascent from the deep valley up the high Eckartsberg Mountains.[22]

Napoleon took appropriate measures to shield his army at the time of its greatest vulnerability. French infantry occupied the town and Schloß of Freyburg as well as the Zscheiplitz estate. Both cavalry and infantry took positions among the hills and woods that stretched along the foot of the ridge that protected Zscheiplitz and Freyburg from the north. A chain of skirmishers occupied the thickets and vineyards between Weischütz and Freyburg – a front of almost three miles. Protected by these positions, the French raced across the bridges in disorderly masses. As Napoleon's exhausted men made this arduous journey, the sound of artillery rose above the rumble of the churning Unstrut. Although this signaled the combat between Bertrand and Gyulay at Bad Kösen to the west, the dejected French troops panicked. Believing the enemy had caught their rearguard to the east, they stampeded down the slope in a desperate attempt to reach the bridge. Odeleben observed that "all military discipline ceased; each wanted to save his own life. Only the appearance of the emperor restored order to the chaos and regulated the flood." Lieutenant Christian von Martens, a Württember-ger whose regiment had already crossed the Unstrut and taken a position on the opposite bank to cover the bridge, observed the collapse of the French units: "We now had before our eyes a miniature of the Berezina crossing. Here also one of the bridges over the Unstrut was designated for cavalry, artillery, and wagons of all kinds, the other for infantry. Both were in very bad condition, especially the one downstream, which was very crowded with numerous wagons; the crush and disorder were so great that the bridge soon collapsed."[23]

Yorck's main body moved southwest through Zeuchfeld to Freyburg. He believed this better, yet somewhat longer road offered an opportunity to make contact with the enemy sooner and possibly drive the French rear-guard toward Schwarzenberg's forces at Naumburg. From Zeuchfeld, Yorck steered his corps due west to Schleberoda and began the difficult march to Freyburg. Captured Westphalian officers claimed that the Guard occupied the city and Schloß of Freyburg, as well as the Zscheiplitz manor and the surrounding forest. Once again, caution mastered Yorck; he did not think his 9,000 men sufficed for an attack on the French position. Instead, he decided to continue west another three miles from Schleberoda through the Neue Gohle Forest to Münchroda. There he planned to unite with the advance guard and march on the second crossing over the Unstrut at the Zettenbach Mill on the Zscheiplitz estate. He planned to simultaneously attack Freyburg and Zscheiplitz but figured on only being able to take the latter. Yet, by taking this position, Yorck would limit the French army to the single bridge at Freyburg. By slowing Napoleon's retreat, he hoped to provide time for the rest of the Silesian Army to arrive.

After leaving the Mecklenburg Hussar Regiment at Zeuchfeld to maintain communication with the Reserve Cavalry, which stood in combat at Markröhlitz, I Corps plunged into the Neue Gohle Forest. Horn's and Hünerbein's divisions united with Henckel's vanguard at Münchroda around 2:00 and prepared for combat. The Prussians observed that the majority of imperial units had already crossed the Unstrut and had started to climb the likewise poor and steep roads on the opposite bank. Yorck ordered the assault to commence in thirty minutes. Henckel's infantry formed the right wing and advanced from Münchroda to attack the French-occupied village and Zscheiplitz Schloß. On the left wing, Horn's division received the task of driving the French from the thickets and vineyards at the foot of the ridge line. Hünerbein's division formed the reserve.

Henckel's Nr. 2 Horse Battery unlimbered on the plateau between Münchroda and Zscheiplitz to shell the French infantry positioned by the latter village as well as the columns defiling on the opposite bank of the Unstrut. To the extreme right of the artillery, the Austrian Jäger battalion descended into the Unstrut valley west of Zscheiplitz to drive the French from the town. Henckel's right wing, consisting of the 1st Battalion of the Leib Regiment and the Fourth Company of the Guard Jäger, also deployed to the right of the artillery with the task of storming the Schloß. On the left wing, the Thüringian Battalion and two companies of East Prussian Jäger received orders to clear the enemy skirmishers from the outlying thickets south of the Neue Gohle Forest in conjunction with three of Horn's battalions. Henckel's Silesian Grenadier Battalion occupied Münchroda while two Landwehr battalions, half of the Nr. 2 Foot Battery, and his cavalry remained in reserve slightly northwest of the village.

As for the rest of Horn's 2nd Division, half of the Nr. 3 Horse Battery took a position on the hills south of the Neue Gohle Forest to shell the French posts situated along the opposite lying hills of Freyburg. The Fusilier Battalion of the Leib Infantry Regiment stood at the foot of the hills to protect the battery. Horn placed his remaining troops – two Landwehr battalions, the East Prussian National Cavalry Regiment, and the other four guns of the Nr. 2 Foot Battery – in reserve east of Münchroda along the southern edge of the Neue Gohle Forest and astride the road to Freyburg. Hünerbein's division remained about two and one-half miles northeast of Freyburg in a concealed position on the eastern edge of the forest.

A strong line of French skirmishers faced the Prussians. Behind this screen, French infantry concentrated in the center, just north and northeast of the Zettenbach Mill. With the French appearing comparatively weak on either wing, Yorck ordered the attack to begin. Much to his chagrin, Henckel's right wing soon became bogged down. A French cavalry charge prevented the Austrian Jäger from reaching Zscheiplitz. Equally unsuccessful proved to be the attempt to storm the Schloß. Standing on a hill that dominated the surrounding region, the Schloß offered an excellent position for French artillery. Not far from the walled manor, caseshot halted the Prussian battalion. The defenders of the Zscheiplitz village and Schloß proved much stronger than the Prussians had initially believed. "Zscheiplitz was too strongly occupied," noted Henckel in his after-action report, "and also very strong due to the nature of its position; it could be supported at any moment since the enemy had a bridge close behind it. He used everything to hold this place because if we had mastered it, we would have been able to shell his two bridges and the town [at close range]." Aborting the operation, Yorck ordered Henckel to maintain a standing skirmish with the French, who did not attempt to counterattack. Combat ended on this wing around 9:00 P.M.

Before Henckel's right wing had made contact with the French, heavy fighting ensued in the woods northeast of Zscheiplitz on his left wing. Deployed in open order against the French skirmishers, the East Prussian Jäger companies and the Thuringian Battalion met stubborn resistance, but managed to push back the French just enough to allow Henckel to move his half-battery of six-pound guns into line next to the horse artillery. Nevertheless, the French skirmishers fought tenaciously. They not only defended bush and thicket, but actually drove back the Prussians. On two occasions Henckel had to withdraw his artillery to save the guns from falling into enemy hands. He shifted the 4th Company of Guard Jäger from his right wing to bolster the skirmishing line on his left. Horn's half-battery of horse artillery also unlimbered on a hill near the western edge of the wood. Shortly afterward, his battalions arrived to assist Henckel's hard-pressed men. After a long contest, the Prussians drove the French skirmishers from the woods. A constant stream of shells from Henckel's twelve guns forced the French to halt the crossing of the Unstrut until they could redirect their column further south on the ridge line.

Horn's half-battery of horse artillery then turned its guns on Freyburg itself, likewise spreading terror among the imperials. "Enemy shells, which were already flying over Freyburg," recalled the Württemberger, Martens, "intensified confusion to the extreme. A portion of the cavalry attempted to withdraw across the river and in the process many horses became stuck in the mud. The sick and wounded were trampled on the narrow bridge or pushed into the water. Most of the baggage wagons were lost along with eighteen guns. As had happened at Jüterbog [Dennewitz], we had an opportunity to observe that, despite all of their courage in battle, the French lose all self-control in misfortune, and in these circumstances order cannot easily be restored among them."[24]

Napoleon remained at Freyburg with Murat and Berthier watching his troops cross the Unstrut. Although he did not direct the combat with Yorck's corps, he could not allow the situation to continue. He issued orders for his battalions to regroup and attack Yorck's center. On a hill between Zscheiplitz and Freyburg, sixteen guns unlimbered to counter Horn's artillery and protect the northern approaches to Freyburg from Zeuchfeld, Schleberoda, and the Neue Gohle Forest. Several battalions drove the Prussians back across the plain to the thickets south of the forest. A couple of French squadrons attacked the Thuringian Battalion. Henckel considered the battalion as good as lost but its commander, a Major Lincker, ordered his men to fix bayonets and charge the cavalry; the surprised French stopped short, turned around, and received a volley in the rear. For his bravery, Lincker received the Iron Cross and the battalion received special recognition in the after-action report.

Both Horn and Henckel committed their infantry reserves – a total of five battalions – to muscle the French from the southern edges of the Neue Gohle Forest. The combat then spilled onto the small plain that separated the hills from which the artillery of both sides fired. "I had to call up two [Landwehr] battalions as well as the Silesian Grenadier Battalion from the village [Münchroda] to maintain communication with my two wings, and so the entire line was engaged in skirmishing," recalled Henckel. Yorck's men gradually pushed the French across the plain to the Lisiere stream on the opposite side. The French managed to stabilize their line so that the firefight continued until Yorck ordered Horn and Hünerbein to withdraw northwest to Gleina around 9:00 P.M. After eight hours of combat, Henckel's vanguard remained at Münchroda and skirmished throughout the night with the French.

Rather than follow the corps through the ravaged terrain to Freyburg, Yorck ordered his Reserve Cavalry to proceed through Roßbach in the direction of Markröhlitz. The usually dependable Jürgaß did not reach Markröhlitz until noon. Not only did he arrive late – the reason remains unknown – but strategic consumption had already claimed many of his units.[25] Consequently, Jürgaß did not have a substantial cavalry force when he encountered the French rearguard outside Markröhlitz. Oudinot's cavalry had already reached Markröhlitz; behind it marched the infantry and artillery on the road from Weißenfels. Jürgaß unlimbered Horse Battery Nr. 1 on an advantageous hill and shelled the French cavalry as his Lithuanian Dragoon Regiment attacked the French flank. Oudinot posted his infantry and artillery – which arrived only gradually – in a wood near the junction of the roads to Freyburg and Naumburg. An indeterminate cavalry skirmish ensued for two hours until the French cavalry withdrew to the hills just west of the woods where Oudinot's infantry and artillery stood. Jürgaß gave the Saxon hussars the honor of leading the pursuit. According to his after-action report, the unit performed admirably and, unlike Henckel's uhlans, this Saxon unit had no reservations about attacking their former allies. Jürgaß even claims that a single squad of 20 hussars captured 176 prisoners.

The 1st West Prussian Dragoon Regiment likewise attacked and drove the French cavalry from the hills, thus prompting Oudinot to abandon the road. The French marshal watched the Prussians gradually overwhelm his cavalry but did little to support his troopers. Late in the afternoon, the Prussian cavalry made one final charge. Supported by artillery, they forced Oudinot's riders to seek shelter in the wood. Skirmishing continued until dusk. Both Jürgaß and Oudinot claimed victory, yet the French rearguard did maintain its position until continuing the retreat to Freyburg. Jürgaß took 3 cannon including 1 twelve-pound gun, "many" caissons, and approximately 400 prisoners before moving to Zeuchfeld that evening.[26]

As for the rest of Blücher's army, the cliché "too little, too late" applies to its effort to catch Napoleon before his army escaped across the Unstrut. At noon on 21 October Sacken and Langeron reached Weißenfels and the right bank of the Saale. At this time, Oudinot's two Guard divisions still lined the hills along the opposite bank. Two battalions held the bridge, which was loaded with flammable material. To allow as many stragglers as possible to cross, the marshal delayed giving the order to ignite. In the meantime, two Russian Jäger regiments occupied the Schloß of Weißenfels while a battery of twenty-four guns unlimbered. Situated on the bank of the river, the old castle provided an overview of Oudinot's encamped rearguard of approximately 12,000 men. Russian Jäger launched a successful surprise attack on the bridge, yet the startled French managed to ignite it as they fell back. The Russians could do nothing to save the wooden structure from the flames: Blücher's pursuit stalled.[27]

When the Russian battery opened fire, the French blew their caissons and departed. As the French cleared the opposite bank, Blücher learned, presumably from prisoners, why Napoleon had crossed the Saale at Weißenfels to march crosscountry rather than continue on the highway through Naumburg to the bridge over the Saale at Bad Kösen. Apparently, the emperor had discovered that Schwarzenberg's army had reached

Naumburg and elements of Gyulay's III Corps had entered Bad Kösen. Blücher now had two options: take advantage of the highway, proceed through Naumburg to Bad Kösen and envelop the left wing of the French army, or repair the bridges at Weißenfels and resume the direct pursuit. The march to Bad Kösen would have caused a logistical nightmare if Blücher's columns became entangled with those of Schwarzenberg's army. Furthermore, a march in this direction would have isolated Yorck from the rest of the Silesian Army. However, Yorck's last report, dated the 19th, informed Blücher that I Corps reached Halle but not Merseburg. Blücher could only speculate where I Corps would be on the 21st. According to Müffling, Blücher "could depend on Yorck seeking the enemy and finding him, for the march to Freyburg would provide him with that opportunity." Based on the nature of the terrain around Freyburg, Blücher's headquarters believed that, if Yorck surprised the French there and the rest of the Silesian Army could catch up, considerable results could be expected.[28]

Thus, Blücher chose to continue the direct pursuit. He ordered the Russian pioneers to construct a bridge across the Saale from boats, rafts, planks, and whatever else they could find. The Russians conveniently found an ample supply of planks and rafts in the river, while staff officers scoured Weißenfels for carpenters. The officers found an old master-carpenter, who claimed to have been an apprentice in 1757 when Frederick the Great had ordered a bridge to be built at Weißenfels so he could confront the French at Roßbach. The greybeard promised not only to build Blücher's bridge in the exact place where Frederick's bridge had been fifty-six years earlier, but to have it ready in a few hours. Apparently, the old man kept his word. That evening, Russian light cavalry crossed the Saale and advanced in the direction of Freyburg while the cavalry of Langeron's vanguard made contact with Yorck's Reserve Cavalry at Markröhlitz. Although both corps moved across the Saale that same evening, it was too late: Napoleon's army had already escaped across the Unstrut.[29]

Convinced that the retreat over the Unstrut was secure, the emperor rode through Klosterhäseler on the road to Eckartsberga on the evening of the 21st. After Yorck withdrew that same night, the French continued their retreat unmolested. Sometime between 4:00 and 6:00 A.M., the last French units completed the breakout and destroyed the bridges behind them. As the sky began to grey, Henckel led a patrol to Freyburg and found that the French had just evacuated the town. The Silesian Grenadier Battalion took possession of Freyburg but Yorck's men could go no further. Reports vary regarding the prizes Yorck's corps took both during the combat and after occupying Freyburg. Most claim the Prussians captured 18 guns and 1,200 prisoners during the fighting on the 21st while an additional 11 guns and perhaps as many as 400 caissons were found at Freyburg. According to

Delbrück, Freyburg "was covered with abandoned guns, discarded packs, and ammunition wagons for a quarter-mile to the bank of the Unstrut." Regardless of the tally, such modest losses only enhanced Napoleon's accomplishment. In just two days he had put the Saale and the Unstrut between him and the Silesian Army. Oudinot had halted Blücher at Weißenfels while Bertrand's action at Bad Kösen stopped Gyulay. Nothing now stood between the French army and Erfurt's massive supply depot.[30]

Yorck's corps lost 17 officers and 827 men in the combat on 21 October. Criticism of Yorck's operation has been based on the general's after-action report, which states that I Corps had "attained great results in the combat and that it *could have* taken Zscheiplitz if it had attacked in earnest." Yorck explained that the French undoubtedly would have committed everything to retake Zscheiplitz and he would not have been able to hold the position. "With great sacrifice," wrote Yorck, "it might have been possible for me to take the Zscheiplitz Schloß and village, which lie upon a hill and were strongly occupied by enemy infantry and artillery since it was key to [the enemy's] position, before the onset of darkness. Meanwhile, in all likelihood I would have been dislodged from this position from the enemy batteries behind it."[31]

Yorck believed the losses incurred would not have been worth the results obtained. "How far this reasoning is valid," states Friederich, "is impossible to say." Or is it? The surviving after-action reports and published eyewitness accounts suggest that Yorck's corps was hard pressed just to hold its position south of Münchroda. Henckel's statements are clear: "it was impossible to detach more troops there [to Zscheiplitz], because all were already in combat." According to the colonel, he received support from both Horn and Hünerbein during the course of the eight-hour combat. Although Napoleon's army shrank almost hourly from desertion, disease, and despair, the emperor still had 100,000 men at his disposal with at least 80,000 under his personal supervision – more than enough to minimize Yorck's threat.[32]

Despite Napoleon's escape, the mood at Blücher's headquarters remained confident. During the march from Lützen to Weißenfels on the 21st, Prince William of Prussia rejoined the Silesian Army. The younger brother of King Frederick William III came from Leipzig after being named commander of Yorck's 2nd Brigade in place of the wounded Prince Karl of Mecklenburg. Of greater importance, he delivered the cabinet order that promoted Blücher to field-marshal. "By repeated victories," stated the cover letter drafted by the king himself, "you continue your services to the state more quickly than I can follow them with proof of my gratitude. Accept the promotion to field-marshal as new proof of my gratitude, and long may you grace this position to the joy of the Fatherland and as a model to the army, which you have so often led to fame and victory." Blücher's soldiers fully understood that this promotion reflected their bravery and sacrifices. The

Russians, with whom Blücher enjoyed an exceptional relationship, affectionately referred to him as "the Prussian Suvarov." A rumor spread among the Cossacks that Blücher actually had been born on the Don River.[33]

While still at Weißenfels, the leadership of the Silesian Army expected to catch at least a portion of the French army at Freyburg on the following day. "Right now, General Yorck is engaged with the enemy between the Unstrut and the Saale," Gneisenau wrote to Münster. "We hope to be able to take the majority of the enemy's guns at the bottleneck of the Unstrut. If everything goes as planned, the enemy will cross the Rhine with many fewer. Although we have taken more than 500 pieces of cannon from him in the various battles, he still has about 200 with him." Accompanied by the field-marshal and his staff, Langeron's corps marched through Markröhlitz toward Freyburg at 5:00 A.M. Sacken proceeded a few miles upstream to Laucha to rebuild the bridge over the Unstrut. Blücher reached Freyburg around noon on 22 October only to find Yorck's corps resting rather than bridging the Unstrut. One reason for Yorck's inactivity: the arrival of a transport containing new boots, which were as good as gold to his men. For Blücher and Gneisenau, the situation finally became clear: Yorck's small corps had failed to hold Napoleon and the Russians had not reached Freyburg in time. They quickly devised another plan to envelop Napoleon's army by force-marching the Silesian Army to Eisenach, some thirty miles west of Erfurt on the main highway to the Rhine. Silesian Army Headquarters issued new orders to be executed that same day; Blücher demanded speed. Yorck placed his Reserve Cavalry and horse artillery under Jürgaß to form the extreme right wing of the army. After crossing the Unstrut at Nebra, Jürgaß would proceed through Wiehe toward Weißensee. Yorck's main body received the task of rebuilding the Zettenbach Mill bridge. After crossing the Unstrut, I Corps would march west to Sömmerda while Langeron's corps crossed the river at Freyburg and trooped to Klosterhäseler. In accordance with Blücher's original orders, Sacken's corps would pass the Unstrut at Laucha and march to Bad Bibra. For the 23rd, Blücher planned a big push to get all three corps in line at Leubingen, Sömmerda, and Schloßvippach.[34]

Although Blücher berated his own corps commanders for not doing enough in the pursuit and complained about Schwarzenberg's laxity, the private correspondence issued from Silesian Army Headquarters painted a picture of confidence. "I just do not know what to do with all of these decorations," joked Blücher in a postscript to his wife; "I'm covered with them like an old coach-horse, but my greatest reward is the thought that I was the one who humbled the arrogant tyrant." "Since Leipzig, we, the Silesian Army, have pursued the enemy," boasted Gneisenau in a letter to Clausewitz's wife, Marie, "taking from him about 4,000 prisoners, setting free 3,000–4,000 captured Russians and Austrians. All roads are covered with partially destroyed caissons. There is no uplifting emotion as gratifying as national revenge. We now stride irresistibly to the Rhine in order to liberate this river of the Fatherland from its chains." To Clausewitz himself he wrote: "The enemy makes his way to Erfurt. I still hope to catch him at Eisenach. The Silesian Army is once again at the forefront and is closest to the enemy."[35]

Despite this enthusiasm, the difficulty of restoring the bridges cost the Silesian Army an entire day. Finding the bridge at Laucha likewise destroyed, Sacken dispatched Vasilchikov's cavalry northward around a wide bend in the Unstrut to cross the river at Burgscheidungen. Yorck's men actually gave up on trying to restore the Zettenbach Mill bridge due to the Unstrut's swift current. The colorful Henckel led the advance guard to Laucha, "which was occupied by skirmishers, who crossed the river in canoes." "The commanding general [Yorck]," continued Henckel, "went with all the brigadiers and me to the town in order to communicate the march order. I had the misfortune of falling into the river from which the pioneers pulled me out." That same night, Henckel led his column across the Unstrut after the Russians finished the bridge. Yorck instructed him to continue in the direction of Sömmerda on a night that Henckel claims "was so dark that one could not see one's hand in front of one's face." Meanwhile, Horn's 2nd Division marched to the Dorndorf estate one mile north of Laucha, and Hünerbein led his 1st Division to Burgscheidungen, where some of his units followed Sacken's men across the Unstrut. After experiencing similar problems with repairing the Freyburg bridge, Langeron's Russians eventually bivouacked since the pioneers could not finish their work until midnight. The difficulty of crossing the Unstrut wrecked Gneisenau's timetable, making it impossible for the corps to reach Leubingen, Sömmerda, and Schloßvippach by 23 October.[36]

Although the 22nd proved fruitless for the Silesian Army, the other Allied armies finally moved away from Leipzig. Bennigsen's vanguard crossed the Elster at Weißenfels and camped on the evening of the 21st at Reichardtswerben; the main body marched to Lützen. On the following day, the advance guard reached Freyburg. The Army of North Germany also started its march from Leipzig on the 22nd. While the Bohemian, Polish, and Silesian Armies made their way toward Erfurt, Bernadotte planned to lead his army northwest to Göttingen to contend with Marshal Davout at Hamburg. As for Schwarzenberg, the tsar was not pleased with his progress, particularly Gyulay's five-mile march on the 22nd. Alexander ordered the formation of a Russo-Prussian vanguard that would take the lead from Gyulay. Regardless, Schwarzenberg remained cautious and wanted to concentrate his army at Weimar, believing Napoleon would accept battle at Erfurt.[37]

After clearing Freyburg, the imperials made for the crossroads at Eckartsberga on 22 October. There, the east–west road from Naumburg to

Eisenach intersected the north–south road that ran between Eisleben and Weimar; at Weimar this road crossed Napoleon's main east–west line of communication from the Rhine to Erfurt. As French patrols had already reported the presence of Cossacks at Weimar, Napoleon chose to follow the east–west road for a short distance and then cut crosscountry to Buttelstedt, from where he would proceed southwest to Erfurt. To avoid being cut off at Bad Kösen, Bertrand marched through Auerstedt to Leibstedt. By nightfall on the 23rd, the rear echelon of Napoleon's main body camped at Buttelstedt while the advance guard had reached Ollendorf, some ten miles northwest of Erfurt; Oudinot's harried rearguard took a position at Eckartsberga. On the army's left flank, French cavalry patrolling toward Weimar made contact with Schwarzenberg's Cossacks.

On 24 October, Napoleon's tired infantry reached the safety of Erfurt; Sébastiani continued on the highway toward Gotha with the majority of the cavalry. Although the main body had reached a safe haven, the lead elements of the Bohemian Army closed on Bertrand and Oudinot. The latter evacuated Eckartsberga and halted slightly westward between Ramsla and Schwerstedt to link with Bertrand, who was approaching from Leibstedt. Wittgenstein's cavalry finally caught Bertrand's rear at Buttelstedt. The Russian horsemen easily dispatched the French cavalry but could do little against the infantry. Bertrand withdrew after losing a few hundred prisoners. Both he and Oudinot continued the retreat to Erfurt under the increasing pressure of Allied cavalry.

At Silesian Army Headquarters, the realities of the situation did not fail to influence Blücher and Gneisenau. The delay at the Unstrut allowed Napoleon to regain his lead. Moreover, the intended forced march had to be delayed until the bridges could be restored. To salvage his plans, Blücher wanted the vanguards of his three corps to reach the points designated in the march table issued the previous day. The forced marches required Yorck's vanguard to proceed twenty-five miles from Laucha to Sömmerda, Sacken's twenty-two miles from Laucha to Leubingen, and Langeron's twenty-five miles from Freyburg to Schloßvippach.[38]

The nightmarish march wound through the washed-out roads of the Thuringian plain. "Only on the morning of the 23rd did Yorck's brigades cross," explains Droysen, "and now began a hellish march on the most abominable roads, with frequent [river] crossings, with dreadfully exhausted troops, with confusion at every corner." Henckel led the vanguard across the Unstrut at Laucha around midnight on the 23rd after Sacken's corps had cleared the bridge. After marching west to Bibra, Henckel learned that his next road to Rastenberg was impassable. This forced him to follow the Russians. His infantry fell far behind but the cavalry and horse artillery passed Sacken's men and reached Sömmerda by 7:00 P.M.; his infantry began to arrive around 4:15 A.M. on the 24th. Jürgaß's Reserve Cavalry crossed the

Unstrut at Burgscheidungen early on the 23rd and also outdistanced Sacken to reach Ostramondra, about nine miles northeast of Sömmerda. Behind the Reserve Cavalry, Hünerbein's 1st Division moved from Burgscheidungen to Billroda. Horn led his 2nd Division across the Unstrut at Laucha around 6:00 A.M. on the 23rd and proceeded to Neuhausen, slightly closer to Sömmerda than Jürgaß. Apparently, Henckel did not share his intelligence regarding the road through Rastenberg, because Yorck's Reserve Artillery stumbled into a virtual quagmire. Sacken's advance guard camped just east of Jürgaß at Bachra but Langeron's vanguard failed to reach Schloßvippach.

Because of the tsar's demand for speed, the Bohemian Army steadily approached Blücher's left flank. Commanding one of Schwarzenberg's two columns, Barclay pursued the French on the main highway from Naumburg toward Erfurt. On the night of the 23rd his advance guard camped between Auerstedt and Eckartsberga; the main body extended between the latter and Naumburg. From there, he established communication with the Silesian Army to seek Blücher's opinion on the next step. He specifically requested a copy of the instructions that Blücher issued to his vanguards so that he could direct his own accordingly. To continue the pursuit of Oudinot, he directed Gyulay and Wittgenstein to Buttelstedt, with his headquarters and the Russo-Prussian Guard following.

Meanwhile, the Allied commander in chief made arrangements to confront Napoleon at Erfurt. Schwarzenberg's headquarters believed the stores there would allow Napoleon to refurbish his army and accept battle. Knowing that the emperor himself had reached the fortress, Schwarzenberg ordered the two wings of his army to concentrate between Erfurt and Weimar. He also instructed Blücher to proceed west on the direct road from Sömmerda to Langensalza. Should Napoleon accept battle, Blücher would be in a perfect position to envelop the imperials at Erfurt. If Napoleon refused, Blücher still would be able to attack the rear and flank of the French army. On 24 October, Gyulay's III Corps proceeded from Buttelstedt to Ollendorf, with his advance units at Großmölsen, less than ten miles from Erfurt. Bubna's 2nd Light Division reached Mönchenholzhausen on the highway between Erfurt and Weimar. Behind Bubna and echeloned eastward to Weimar stood the Russo-Prussian Guard, Kleist's Prussians, and Wintzingerode's Russians; the Austrian I, II, and Reserve Corps held the rear at Weimar. Cossack patrols scoured the region between Erfurt and Gotha.[39]

Although Blücher allowed his men to rest on the morning of the 24th, he continued to drive his army with a fury. At noon his unbelievable orders reached the various corps. The disposition called for Sacken to march eighteen miles to Tennstedt, Yorck twenty miles to Gangloffsömmern, and Langeron eighteen miles to Schwerstedt. Once again, Silesian Army Headquarters underestimated the paralyzing effect of the rain-drenched Thuringian clay. Neither man nor beast could escape its clutches; guns and wagons slithered through mud up to their axles. "The fatigue is excessive," attests I Corps's 24 October journal entry, "only a few days of exertions and [Blücher] will grant the exhausted corps some rest." The groundless, unpaved roads prevented Blücher's three corps from reaching their march objectives; only the vanguards arrived at Tennstedt, Gangloffsömmern, and Schwerstedt.[40]

While conducting reconnaissance on the morning of the 25th, Schwarzenberg's lead elements discovered that the French army had already left Erfurt. The Allied commander in chief quickly relayed this news to Blücher. According to the reports, Napoleon had divided his army into three columns: the first had reached Eisenach on the previous day, the second was en route, and the rearguard would follow from Erfurt on the 26th. Blücher decided to herd his army as fast as possible toward Langensalza; the cavalry and horse artillery of all three corps received instructions to reach the Langensalza–Eisenach road.

During the night of 24/25 October Yorck again reorganized his corps. Henckel dissolved his advance guard and returned the infantry units to their respective brigades. His 2nd Leib Hussar and Saxon Uhlan Regiments as well as the horse artillery rejoined Jürgaß's Reserve Cavalry, which now formed Yorck's vanguard. Henckel, who had originally commanded a brigade of two regiments in the Reserve Cavalry, resumed his former place under Jürgaß's command. Furthermore, Prince William officially assumed command of Yorck's 2nd Brigade. Yorck ended the divisional organization of Horn's command; Horn simply resumed his former position as brigadier of 7th Brigade. However, 1st and 8th Brigades remained merged in Hünerbein's 1st Division. Confusion over Blücher's orders added to the growing discontent at Yorck's headquarters caused by the apparent disregard for the suffering of the men. Schack's journal entry on 25 October depicts the vexation. "An extremely inadequate march disposition arrived; three corps were directed on the most abysmal roads through three defiles ... all three corps should depart at daybreak, Yorck and Sacken to the right on the road to Langensalza, Langeron to the left, no village was designated ... inconceivable indifference of the army's commanders toward the troops, who have been extremely fatigued due to negligence."[41]

Similar to the situation in August, the corps commanders wanted an explanation for the apparently useless marches. The amount of detail contained in Blücher's orders almost never provided a satisfactory overview of the general situation. One of the goals of the infant Prussian General Staff was to eliminate the tedious and time-consuming practice of issuing voluminous orders. However, it appears that officers reared in this tradition perceived brief dispatches to be disrespectful and a dangerous lack of communication. One of the major sources of friction between Yorck and Gneisenau was the latter's failure to provide sufficient information. The same would hold true in 1815, when Bülow misinterpreted Gneisenau's orders prior to the battle of Ligny on 16 June because they failed to provide details regarding the overall situation. Ostensibly, an order from the Chief of the General Staff of the Prussian Army – and in the case of Yorck in 1814 and Bülow in 1815, from the chief of staff of the army in which their corps was attached – was to be obeyed, and these extremely competent officers understood this basic military protocol. Arguments regarding their seniority to Gneisenau and the polite wording of his orders miss the point. These men demanded to be informed of the general situation. Short, concise orders instructing them to move from one point on the map to the next – which was usually the extent of the orders issued from Blücher's headquarters – caused frustration, misinterpretation, and, in some cases, outright insubordination.

On the French side, Napoleon harbored no illusions over the condition of his army. Weakened physically, mentally, and materially, it could not confront the Allies in the field: the retreat had to continue to the Rhine. The army's forced marches across the Unstrut and the Thuringian plain eroded the good order that had first characterized the retreat. Daily desertions added to the attrition that diminished Napoleon's forces; at most the emperor commanded 70,000–80,000 men. "The rapidity of their flight had completely exhausted the greater part of the army," recalls Professor Steffens, "at first we saw single Frenchmen lying among the bushes; as we proceeded the number of the exhausted, dying sufferers increased, and we found large groups of dead and dying; it was painful for me to observe that they viewed it as a great evil to be discovered by us; although we offered them assistance, they preferred to be left to perish from hunger and exhaustion among the undergrowth. I confess, I wished myself away from the horrid scene, it was more terrible to me than the violence of the fiercest battle."[42]

With Schwarzenberg and Blücher approaching Erfurt, Napoleon only thought of resting, reorganizing, and feeding his starving army. Considering his next move, he had already ordered the evacuation of all hospitals from the right to the left bank of the Rhine as well as the garrisoning, equipping, and provisioning of the Rhine fortresses, notably Mainz and Wesel. The emperor also expressed his intention to form one army at Mainz, a second at Wesel, and perhaps even a third at Strasbourg. On the 24th, the advance guard consisting of XI and II Corps and II Cavalry Corps marched on the highway to Eisenach, reaching Gotha the next day. At Erfurt, Napoleon left behind a garrison of 6,000 men and supplies for eight months. The emperor directed his main body to Gotha, covered on the right by the Guard's light cavalry and V Cavalry Corps; and on the left by Bertrand's troops. Mortier commanded the new rearguard – two divisions of Young Guard and I Cavalry Corps – which followed through Erfurt.

Furiously driven westward by Blücher's sheer will, the Russian and Prussian soldiers of the Silesian Army endured another horrible day in the

Thuringian plain on 25 October. Schack's journal entry on the 25th again provides testimony of the reigning sentiment at Yorck's headquarters: "confusion and embarrassment; unsurpassed indolence ... great misery among the troops, distribution of a few loaves among the poor soldiers. Count Henckel made a touching but true report regarding the condition of the troops: 'one Landwehr officer, unconscious from hunger and exhaustion, spent the night in a ditch.'" On the night of the 25th, after another grueling march, Sacken's corps reached Reichenbach, halfway along the road between Langensalza and Eisenach; his cavalry moved into Behringen, even closer to Eisenach. Arriving at Tüngeda, Yorck's cavalry came on line with Sacken's main body; Yorck's corps camped at Langensalza and Ufhofen. Langeron's corps stood just south of Langensalza with his advance guard likewise at Tüngeda. For its part, the Bohemian Army moved into positions around Erfurt.[43]

"Today," wrote Gneisenau to a friend on the morning of the 26th, "I hope to cut to pieces a part of the French army on the Hörselberg." This simple statement says much regarding the continued optimism and incessant drive of Blücher's headquarters. The Hörselberg ridge extended from Sattelstädt toward Eisenach. A small stream, the Hörsel, flowed northward through the Thuringian Forest and then westward to join the Werra River just west of Eisenach. The plateau on the Hörselberg offered the Allies an advantageous position from which to shell the highway. "The *chaussée* on which the enemy was proceeding runs through a valley," explains Charles Stewart, "bound on one side by the great chain of the Thuringian mountains, and on the other by a range of minor heights, called the Hurthberg, Hörselberg, and Kahlenberg." Gneisenau planned to converge on the French between the Hörsel and the Hörselberg but timing became the crucial factor in this operation. Moreover, "the ground was not, in consequence, favorable for the operation of cavalry or for bringing artillery speedily up to the attack," adds Stewart, "and the enemy had occupied all the ravines and lower eminences bordering on the road with his tirailleurs."[44]

Silesian Army Headquarters issued very detailed orders for the 26th. Blücher instructed the cavalry and horse artillery of all three corps to move to the Hörselberg at daybreak. Jürgaß received the task of arriving first to take possession of the ridge before the French could occupy the advantageous high ground. If Jürgaß secured this objective without being detected, he was to remain hidden, but forward small patrols toward the Gotha–Eisenach road to observe the enemy's march. Sacken's cavalry and horse artillery would join the Prussians in this concealed position while Langeron's units moved into a position north of the hills. If the opportunity arose, Blücher gave permission for the cavalry to attack the French before the corps reached their respective positions. As for the infantry, Sacken and Yorck received orders to advance to Großenlupnitz, a march of eight and fourteen miles respectively. Langeron's corps would reconnoiter the side roads that ran from Gotha to the Langensalza–Eisenach road and advance toward the two other corps at daybreak.[45]

On the cold morning of 26 October Yorck's men began their march in the face of a bitter wind. Jürgaß reached Hastrungsfeld at the northern foot of the Hörselberg around 8:00 A.M. Instead of taking a concealed position and forwarding small patrols to the highway, he ascended the hills. The Prussians rode to the southwest edge of the Hörselberg to discover they had arrived too late – below them trooped the French along the highway from Gotha. "The Hörselberg marches right up along the highway," explains Henckel, "and it was quite a view to see the enemy defiling below us." Skirmishers from Jean-Jacques Pelet's Guard brigade occupied the thickets on the Hörselberg itself to cover the pass at Sattelstädt. A volley of small-arms fire surprised the approaching Prussian cavalry. Jürgaß unlimbered his half-battery of horse artillery; caseshot soon drove the French skirmishers down the Hörselberg. Pursuing to the edge of the plateau, the Prussians observed the bivouac of Oudinot's Guard divisions on the other side of the Hörsel stream by Sattelstädt. According to Jürgaß, "the enemy had barely observed our arrival when he occupied the gorges and steep ravine of the mountains with skirmishers, to whose support two or three battalions were advancing and, at the overhang of the mountain, the cavalry was favorably positioned to repulse an attack."[46]

Jürgaß moved up his artillery. After several Prussian shells reached their camp, the French hastily resumed their march along the Hörselberg's western spur to Eichrodt. Oudinot's skirmishers bought time by attacking the Prussians. Ascending the steep slope, the French deftly utilized every shrub and crevice to move closer to the Prussians. Man and horse were soon exposed to their deadly fire; the artillery had to be pulled back to Hastrungsfeld after the gunners sustained numerous casualties. Jürgaß could do nothing to counter: his cavalry could not descend the steep paths that led to the Hörselberg valley. In order to pursue the French column, Jürgaß moved east along a muddy path to Sattelstädt, where he arrived in the afternoon.[47] By this time his exhausted cavalry could go no further; only the 2nd Leib Hussar Regiment continued the pursuit and captured some hundred transport personnel. That evening Jürgaß led his cavalry to a bivouac at Kälberfeld, about one mile west of Sattelstädt on the main highway between Gotha and Eisenach. Sacken's and Langeron's cavalry followed the Prussians but did not participate in the combat.

Slightly northwest of the Hörselberg, Sacken's and Yorck's infantry reached Großenlupnitz around noon. A few hours later Blücher received Jürgaß's report of the French retreat from Sattelstädt to Eichrodt. The field-marshal ordered Hünerbein's division to continue its march to Eichrodt, while Yorck's 2nd and 7th Brigades remained in reserve with Sacken's

Russians at Großenlupnitz. The troops did not greet this order – coming after a march of several hours and considering the muddy condition of the road – with joy. Hünerbein's 1st Division moved toward the defile at the village of Eichrodt, two and one-half miles northeast of Eisenach. After making slow progress along the awful road, his men reached a cleft in the western spur of the Hörselberg north of Eichrodt. They observed French cavalry trotting westward on the highway to Eisenach. Southeast of Eichrodt, the Prussians also noticed a French bivouac; this was Mortier with his two divisions of Young Guard: the very last units of the French rearguard. Hünerbein's half-battery of six-pound foot artillery unlimbered and lobbed a salvo into the French camp. Mortier followed standard French procedure and unleashed a mass of skirmishers to silence the enemy artillery. "His [Mortier's] position," states Yorck's report, "allowed him a stubborn defense, and the combat became extremely serious and bloody." In a short time the battery sustained so many casualties that Hünerbein pulled it out of the line. On several occasions his infantry had to fix bayonets to repulse the French skirmishers; combat continued late into the night until Hünerbein finally withdrew. French losses are not known, but both the civilian scholar Droysen and the General Staff historian Friederich agree that the results were hardly worth Hünerbein's loss of 300–335 killed and wounded. The French army again escaped Blücher; only Langeron's corps could boast of success. With two Russian divisions, Rudzevich attacked Mortier's rearguard at Gotha and took 2,000 prisoners.[48]

Both contemporaries and historians maintain that the Silesian Army should have achieved more results on this day. "Col. Hudson Lowe," notes Sir Charles Stewart, "being at this time attached by me to Marshal Blücher ... conceived that the 26th might have been a most fatal day for Bonaparte, had the Silesian Army put itself in movement at an earlier hour, or had there been officers of greater activity and combination at the head of the Russian cavalry. A prompt march upon Eisenach, which lies in the very center of defiles, would have rendered all further retreat on that line impossible." Such expectations far surpassed the physical capabilities of Blücher's men, who had just endured four days of strenuous marching. Friederich quotes the journal of the Leib Grenadier Battalion: "The march, in part on very bad mountain paths and in part over muddy, washed-out clay roads, was conducted with indescribable misery and was extremely harmful to the condition of the troops. So it came to pass that, despite the best will and the greatest devotion, the bivouac was only reached by the smallest portion of the soldiers, who, without seeking nourishment, sank to the ground dead tired. The 26th of October was the last, but also the worst of these terrible days." "The troops," Schack wrote in his journal, "suffered very much in the bivouac this night; three people froze to death." "To all of these hardships was added another, and by no means a small one, because it disturbed everyone's rest," wrote Dr. Wenzel Krimer; "all of us, from general to drummer, swarmed with lice. There was no question of keeping clean or of changing our linen. Many, including myself, had nose, ears, hands, and feet frostbitten, and in many cases these extremities had turned gangrenous and rotted away. No wonder so many became sick and a virulent form of typhus quickly spread. Eventually the hunger became so serious that the poor soldiers could scarcely perform their duties. Pigeons, sparrows, jack-daws, and ravens, which so far had served as food, were no longer available for shooting; we were already devouring cabbage stalks, vines, and winter corn as vegetables."[49]

The Silesian Army passed the night in the positions outlined in Blücher's orders: Langeron's corps at Behringen; Sacken at Großenlupnitz with Yorck's 2nd and 7th Brigades; Hünerbein's division outside Eichrodt; and Jürgaß at Kälberfeld. During the course of the 26th, Schwarzenberg's army proceeded westward in three columns. After detaching a siege corps at Erfurt consisting of one Russian division and two of Kleist's brigades as well as his Reserve Cavalry, the right wing – which stood closest to Blücher – reached positions between Erfurt and Gotha at dusk. Also on this day, Bennigsen dissolved his Army of Poland. After making short marches from Freyburg to Rastenberg on the 24th and 25th, Bennigsen received orders to forward 12,000 men to Wintzingerode and to march to the Elbe with his remaining 14,000.[50]

Napoleon himself entered Eisenach at 4:00 A.M. on the 26th; he continued the retreat that same night. Early on 27 October the rearguard left Eichrodt and cleared Eisenach by 8:00 A.M. Sacken's troops entered the city later that morning after a skirmish with Mortier's rearguard. From Eisenach, Gneisenau wrote to Hardenberg to assure the Prussian chancellor that the Silesian Army would not "fall back on our laurels. Everything has been done so that nothing more of the enemy army will exist. Blücher's army pursues hard on the heels of the enemy." He also complained of the conduct of the corps commanders: "We, the Silesian Army, have done much, but not every-thing that has been done has been executed with determination. The generals and their entourages scream curses on a large scale against us here in head-quarters; but we respond with nothing against them. When we have destroyed everything of the French that still remains on this side of the Rhine, then we will crown the work of our diminished army, and lead it to new deeds."[51]

The continued confidence and determination to destroy Napoleon that are apparent in this letter reflected Gneisenau's actual mood on the 27th. Having recently received the Commander's Cross of the Austrian Order of Maria Theresa with a flattering letter from Metternich himself, Gneisenau decided to celebrate. According to Stosch:

He arranged to have champagne with lunch and we all drank merrily. When four bottles had been emptied, Gneisenau ordered more, whereupon his secretary of financial matters, König, announced that according to the number of guests four bottles was plenty. "Get us more," shouted Gneisenau. "Today is my birthday and it is truly the happiest that I have had thus far." We now drank heartily to his health; General Kleist, who had just arrived, took part. The report of the birthday party spread throughout the Schloß and soon Blücher, Rauch, Müffling, and several others came to the party, which lasted until the evening.[52]

As Gneisenau's letter states, the pursuit of the French army continued, despite the festivities at headquarters. On 27 October, Napoleon led his army southwest toward Fulda, where the advance guard arrived that evening. Behind the emperor, Mortier and Oudinot struggled to follow. Both reached the crossing over the Werra at Vacha. Bertrand's IV Corps took country roads to reach Tiefenort. Captured French officers informed the Prussians that Bertrand had plunged into the foothills south of Eisenach in an attempt to make his escape via Ruhla. To envelop Bertrand, Yorck received orders to advance with all possible speed to the bridge over the Werra at Barchfeld; Langeron's corps would pursue through Marksuhl to Vacha.

After entering Eisenach, Sacken's infantry pursued the French in two directions: west to Berka and southwest to Vacha. A few miles southwest of Eisenach, the Russian detachment caught the French on the road to Vacha. Sacken's men captured three guns; the French blew fifteen caissons to cover their flight. Although the detachment made contact with the retreating enemy, Sacken recalled it, believing Langeron's corps would assume the pursuit to Vacha. Much to the chagrin of Yorck's headquarters, which grumbled that Langeron received a solid road for his march disposition while I Corps continued its trek on a horrible country path, the Russians failed to catch their prey. Langeron's main body never cleared Eisenach but his light cavalry reached Marksuhl. "Two hours from Eisenach," claims Droysen, "where the road steeply rises, the Russians caught up with the enemy rearguard; their ardor waned; only Cossacks still pursued the enemy." Although it is an unfair assessment of the situation, Droysen, whose research mostly depended on eyewitness testimony, accurately gauges the sentiment at Yorck's headquarters regarding the Russians. Following the combat on the Hörselberg, Schack commented in his journal that Sacken's men did not have to bivouac. Regarding Sacken himself, the journal states: "the illustrious comrade is not very intent on the enemy." Despite Blücher's outstanding relationship with his Russian subordinates, the Prussian and Russian corps commanders felt little love for each other.

Yorck proceeded to Barchfeld on the 27th with the task of catching Bertrand at the Werra. Although Blücher and Gneisenau had correctly guessed Bertrand's march direction, Yorck did not think he could stop the French general before he reached the road that led from Salzungen to Fulda. Moreover, the acute fatigue of his men convinced Yorck that they could go no further without some rest. He started the march late and then allowed the men to cook at Eisenach: their first hot meal since the battle of Möckern eleven days earlier. After a minor skirmish with Bertrand's rearguard, Jürgaß's advance guard camped at Gumpelstadt that evening with the corps echeloned behind it on the Barchfeld–Eisenach road. In addition to permitting his men to cook, Yorck also quartered the soldiers in the surrounding villages to spare them the hardships of the bivouac.

Squadrons from the Brandenburg Uhlan Regiment patrolled along the Werra and south on the road to Meiningen. They returned with several prisoners as well as the news that Bertrand had escaped. A critical Gneisenau groused over Yorck's dilatory march: "We, the Silesian Army, had finally cut off Bertrand's corps by Eisenach. He had to escape through the Thuringian Forest. Yorck's corps received the order to cut it off from the Werra. Disgruntled about the continuous marches, Yorck wasted time in curses and allegations against us at Blücher's headquarters instead of starting his movement. Meanwhile, Bertrand marched diagonally over the road that Yorck should have been marching on and thus escaped." The 2,000 prisoners brought in by the Cossacks provided little compensation.[53]

The distance between the opposing forces increased on the next day, 28 October, as Blücher's operations slowed. Silesian Army Headquarters remained at Eisenach; Sacken likewise held his position at Berka. Yorck's corps made a short march to Barchfeld and Salzungen while Langeron's main body moved to Marksuhl and his vanguard to Vacha. Schwarzenberg ordered Kleist to besiege Erfurt as Wittgenstein led the Bohemian Army's advance guard through Hersfeld to Alsfeld. Directly east of the Silesian Army, the columns of Schwarzenberg's army reached a line extending between Zella and Schmalkalden. Meanwhile, the French army stretched almost fifty miles southwest from the Werra through Fulda on the highway to Frankfurt. Napoleon with the Guard and III Cavalry Corps reached Schlüchtern; Macdonald led the advance guard further west to Salmünster, Oudinot arrived at Fulda, Mortier proceeded to Buttlar, and Bertrand crossed the Werra.[54]

"The number of dead bodies on the road had been considerably augmented," observed Charles Stewart, "from a resolution that had been taken to carry off all the sick and wounded ... several of these men were found abandoned on the road in the last gasp of hunger and disease: the dead and dying were frequently mixed together, lying in groups of six to eight by half-extinguished fires on the road-side. Several of these men must have been compelled to move on foot, as their bodies were found on the road with the sticks with which they had endeavored to support their march lying by their sides. The dead might have been counted by hundreds; and in the space from Eisenach to Fulda could certainly not have amounted to much less than a thousand."⁵⁵

On 29 and 30 October the Silesian Army continued its march to Fulda. Langeron's Cossacks entered the city on the evening of the 29th; the vanguard followed the next day. "I drive the emperor Napoleon before me every day," Blücher boasted to his wife. "Serious combat will no longer occur on this side of the Rhine. In seven days' time I will be in Frankfurt or Koblenz according to which way the enemy turns." Conversely, Yorck's headquarters cursed the misfortune of once again receiving a march disposition that required the corps to move west along poor country paths through the Rhön Mountains instead of on the highway assigned to the Russians. At Hünfeld, the Prussian corps finally struck the great north–south highway and turned left toward Fulda. Henckel provides a grim description of the suffering of the French army: "On all of these marches the deplorable situation of the retreating French army became all too clear. Everywhere lay dead people and horses, broken guns, muskets, wagons of all kinds, and discarded ammunition. We encountered large numbers of half-starved soldiers as well as men who had become sick with typhus due to the bitter weather. The enthusiasm of our soldiers prevailed, yet they gave these poor people who roamed about the fields like madmen bread and brandy. It was not worth taking them as prisoners. On the other side of Fulda, where the curve of the highway ascended the mountain, lay many half-burned corpses in a bivouac fire." "Nothing could be more unpleasant and disgusting," recalls Müffling, "than to follow in the wake of the French army. The whole way along the road lay corpses or dying men. The prisoners we took had death stamped on their faces. In short, it was impossible to contemplate sleeping on the same spot, perhaps even on the same straw, as this fever-ridden army, which had infected the local inhabitants along the route as well as consuming all the provisions." A sergeant-major of the Black Hussars adds:

Everywhere in the enemy's abandoned camps, which we usually reached in the early morning after he had left them, sick, dying, and dead soldiers lay in huge numbers around a smoldering fire. Those who were still alive lay there in torn, half-burnt coats and looked starved like skeletons. The dead had been pushed away from the fire to make room for the living to warm themselves. They often made use of other corpses as pillows. Whatever we had in the way of food we threw to them, as far as it went, and each evening we took care to save something for "the poor foreign devil who can't march any further." Often we dismounted in order to comfort a dying man with a schnapps as an extreme unction. We were always glad to get away from the places of misery, which remained the same all the way to the Rhine. The enemy may well have lost as many troops as a result of this retreat as he had lost in battle.[56]

On 29 October, Wittgenstein moved to Eisenach while Schwarzenberg's main body camped in the region around Meiningen. To the north, St.-Priest's vanguard reached Kassel and learned that King Jerome, Napoleon's youngest brother, had fled his capital the previous day; a 6,000-man French division had also withdrawn to the Netherlands. Cheering crowds greeted St.-Priest when he entered Kassel on the 30th.

Meanwhile, Napoleon won his last victory on German soil by smashing through Wrede's small Austro-Bavarian army at Hanau, a few miles east of Frankfurt, on 30 October. Unfortunately for Wrede, the French emperor outsmarted Schwarzenberg. The Allied commander in chief believed Napoleon would seek to avoid Wrede by turning off the main highway that ran southwest from Fulda through Frankfurt to Mainz and instead proceed crosscountry due west through Wetzlar to cross the Rhine at Koblenz. Napoleon made no such adjustment. Wrede learned of a French column on the march to Frankfurt. According to Schwarzenberg's estimates, this could be nothing more than a flank column of perhaps 20,000 men to cover Napoleon's left as he crossed the Rhine at Koblenz. Without waiting to be joined by 23,000 Austrians, Wrede planned to pounce on the French column at Hanau with 43,000 men. Wrede's failure cost him 9,000 men, and prompted Napoleon to comment that, although he had made Wrede a count, he had failed to make him a general.

Although the battle cost Napoleon significantly fewer men than Wrede, the disorganization of the French army had reached deplorable levels. Between 28 and 31 October the Allies captured as many as 10,000 stragglers. "Troops as disorganized as those we commanded," recalled Marmont, "as harassed and exhausted by marching and fighting as by reverses and privations, soon surrendered to indiscipline. The impossibility of providing enough regular distributions of rations provoked and justified their actions. Each man's prime concern was finding food; as all military discipline collapsed, an indescribable depression and disgust took its place." The marshal estimates that, of the 60,000 soldiers who still remained, "20,000 formed themselves into bands of eight or ten, scouring the countryside and marching on the flanks. The army gave these soldiers a nickname, which has become historic and recalls their sole occupation: the search for the means to stay alive. They were called *fricoteurs* [marauders]." On 2 November 1813, the main body of the French army arrived at Frankfurt, less than twenty miles from Mainz and the safety of the Rhine. Five days later, the French army crossed the historic river.[57]

On the day of Hanau, 30 October, the Silesian Army, some fifty miles northeast of Wrede, came on line around Hünfeld north of Fulda on the main north–south highway. Because Schwarzenberg expected Napoleon to turn northwest to avoid Wrede, he ordered Blücher to move on a parallel route through the Vogelsberg to Gießen. Blücher agreed with Schwarzenberg's supposition and so ordered his two Russian corps to march toward Gießen and Wetzlar; Yorck would pursue the French along the highway to Frankfurt. According to Gneisenau, "the supposition was an unfortunate one. Had Blücher followed up his march, Napoleon's total defeat and capture at Hanau could not, according to all human calculations, have been avoided. But the Silesian Army changed its line of operations." A few days later, Blücher reconsidered the course of events and complained to a friend about Schwarzenberg's orders: "I pursued the French emperor continuously on the highway and arrived daily in the quarters which he had abandoned. Had [Schwarzenberg] allowed me to continue on this road, I would have reached the enemy and attacked him in the rear as he was engaged with Wrede. But, and only God knows why, I actually received the order to take my direction from Philippstal upon Gießen; the Bohemian Army would pursue the enemy with its vanguard. But this vanguard was two marches behind me and arrived too late to support Wrede, and so the emperor escaped this trap."[58]

The news that Schwarzenberg planned to slow his march on the main highway to Frankfurt as the Silesian Army struggled through the Vogelsberg did not please Gneisenau. Already irritable from a painful case of gout, he berated the messenger, Langenau, of the Austrian General Staff. After venting his anger, Gneisenau turned his attention to improving the material status of the Silesian Army by writing to Frederick William and Hardenberg. In this correspondence, Gneisenau displayed a concern for the welfare of the troops that would have been difficult for Yorck's headquarters to believe. "The uniforms of the I Army Corps, especially its Landwehr, are very bad, in fact pitiful," Gneisenau explained, "some still do not have uniforms . . . I have noticed that the caps of the Landwehr are very poor; they do not completely cover the head. I have noticed many serious head wounds in the battalions, which were inflicted by cavalry. It is thus very important to give the Landwehr shakos. Although their tunics are comfortable, they nevertheless have one disadvantage: they are not held together by a string or belt, so they expose the abdomen to the cold air and thus cause illness." He also informed the king and Hardenberg that he would need additional equipment and uniforms for the manpower he planned to conscript in Prussia's former provinces between the Elbe and the Weser. Gneisenau had recently received a letter from Charles Stewart informing him that arms and uniforms for 40,000–50,000 men had reached Stralsund. According to Stewart, Gneisenau simply had to send an officer to Stralsund to take possession of the material. In his report to

Hardenberg, staff chief added Stewart's pledge: "You will have everything that is needed, I promise you, from England."[59]

Meanwhile, Blücher's headquarters and the two Russian corps reached Gießen on 3 November. As for Yorck, he continued southwest on the highway toward Frankfurt. After Blücher learned that Schwarzenberg would march on Frankfurt, he ordered Yorck to reach Gießen by 3 November. This change, which reached Yorck on the night of 31 October, caused more outrage at Yorck's headquarters. To reach Gießen in three days, the corps would have to march forty-two miles on side roads through the Vogelsberg. It did not help matters that Blücher assigned the paved road through Lauterbach to the Russians.[60] Such apparently inconsiderate treatment infuriated Yorck. "Strange assignment for the corps, which appears to be the plaything of the strategic whims and vanities of Blücher's General Staff," states one journal. "What sacrifices have been the cost of the indecision, idleness, and clumsiness of the generals! How much dear blood they could have spared! What is glory, and how insignificant are decorations!" Although not particularly fair to the men who were attempting to end the war with one final blow, such statements reflect the negative image of Blücher's headquarters.[61]

The march through the Vogelsberg, described by Henckel as "terrifying," took a toll on I Corps, which did not reach Gießen until 4 November.[62] "Very many cannon and wagons broke down on the awful roads and remained where they were left;" states one journal; "of the Reserve Cavalry's two horse batteries, only nine guns [of sixteen] remain." During the march to Gießen the corps reported its lowest musters: 9,993 men remained of the 37,800 who had opened the campaign in August. Fortunately for both the Prussians and the Russians of Blücher's army, the field-marshal allowed the men to rest until 7 November. Confirmed reports that Napoleon had continued his retreat through Frankfurt to Mainz convinced Blücher to grant this reprieve; the army as a whole had not received a day of rest since 14 October and the strain could be seen. "The successes of this Army have not been gained without considerable losses," wrote Lowe on 31 October. "The Battles of Leipzig and the forced marches subsequently have occasioned a diminution of nearly one-third of its force. Many of the men will of course be recovered, but so far as I can presume to form an opinion on the matter, it appears exceedingly desirable that this army should not only be kept up to its former force, but considerably augmented."[63]

Yorck's corps took quarters in the beautiful and fruitful villages of the Wetterau as far as the left bank of the Lahn, with Langeron on the right bank, and Sacken at Wetzlar. "I have marched for fourteen days without rest on this most abominable road," wrote Blücher. "Today is the first day of rest; our people particularly lack shoes and trousers but their goodwill, among both Prussians and Russians, is steadfast. When I go among them in the morning they greet me with joy." Blücher's men would need the rest, for the Prussian commanders of the Silesian Army did not plan on remaining idle for long.[64]

The reports that Blücher received at Gießen on 3 November indicated that the French had evacuated Frankfurt and would soon cross the Rhine. A local provided Blücher with a letter he had received from Frankfurt dated 2 November. It stated that Napoleon had established his headquarters at Frankfurt on 1 November. The marauders that preceded him had pillaged several houses but Napoleon's gendarmes had established order. The emperor departed at 3:00 P.M. that same day with the army taking a position at the Nidda River.[65] Platov's Cossacks entered Frankfurt around 10:00 that night and pursued the retreating French. On 5 November Blücher received news that despite the victory at Hanau, the French army – which at most numbered 60,000 men – teetered on the brink of collapse. "On the road, we passed 270 dead horses and 170 human bodies," noted Wilson, "and many half-dead men were not included in this 170. I did not see one wounded carcass – the whole had perished from disease and famine. Here we found a scene of general desolation and exterminating poverty." Such news made the immediate invasion of France appear more urgent than ever. Blücher sought permission to cross the Rhine. None of the reports he received indicated the concentration of French reserves at the frontier. Spies and sympathizers claimed that the French had failed to arm, provision, and adequately garrison the fortresses on the left bank of the Rhine. Reports also indicated that the crown prince of Sweden had reached Hanover, which led Blücher to incorrectly conclude that Bernadotte would soon invade Holland.[66]

Blücher refused to allow these favorable conditions to be wasted. He and his staff devised a bold plan to move across the middle Rhine and advance through Aachen and Liège toward Brussels. According to the Prussian scheme, Schwarzenberg would cross the Rhine between Mannheim and Mainz. Paris would be the general goal of all operations. "If we quickly set out for Holland and cross the Rhine with double strength," predicted Müffling on 3 November, "the conquest of Holland will be completed in two months and a lasting peace concluded. If we remain on this side and allow ourselves to be held up by negotiations, I thus predict a bloody campaign in 1814. Napoleon is in the most awful situation ... I am most eager to see how his genius will pull him out." Colonel Lowe urged London to support the Silesian Army. "General Gneisenau," he wrote to Stewart on 31 October, "has acquainted me that this army is likely to move in a northwest direction. If so I hope to cooperate with that of the Prince Royal toward the only object which it now seems to me can merit the appropriation of a large force in that quarter viz. the liberation of Holland and the Scheldt. Even Great Britain alone when Napoleon was engaged with Austria dared to menace Antwerp. With how much more hope of success could the

Allied Powers now detach part of their immense force on that point and thus at one blow cut off Holland from the French."[67]

Blücher believed he could cross the Rhine on 15 November and estimated reaching Brussels ten days later. "You ask what I will do now that I am on the Rhine," responded Blücher to a friend's query. "And I say to you, we will cross it, we will conquer Holland and Brabant, and we will rout him [Napoleon] so that he must make peace. The discontent of the nation is active and Napoleon's reign will end. This is my belief." On 7 November, an optimistic Gneisenau left for Frankfurt to seek approval for the plan at Allied Headquarters. That same day, Blücher led his army northwest toward Cologne without authorization to cross the Rhine. Yorck and Sacken moved upstream along the Lahn to strike the great Frankfurt–Cologne highway at Limburg; Langeron marched on the road that ran through Siegen, where St.-Priest's corps would reunite with him.[68]

Yorck and his staff did not share the enthusiasm of their Prussian comrades at Silesian Army Headquarters over the plan to immediately cross the Rhine. "If one considers the condition of I Corps," noted Schack in his journal, "one will not doubt that this corps cannot immediately cross the Rhine and commence the new campaign. The crossing itself would not be difficult due to the terrible condition of the enemy, but it is obvious that the corps would be destroyed in a short time through the increasing resistance it would encounter by further advancing as well as by the fatigue caused by this harsh time of year."[69] On 5 November, Yorck's chief of staff, Zielinsky, complained to Thile:

> The survivors of the corps are in such a weakened condition because of the extremely strenuous marches on the poorest roads that they arouse compassion. All of my requests, all of my suggestions to conserve as much as possible the precious remainder of this brave corps have gone unheeded; what has not been struck down by enemy balls will be overcome by fatigue if it remains under the leadership of these ingenious people, who take no consideration of the material needs of an army and move around all of the corps as if they are knights on a chessboard. We have seldom if ever maintained our order of battle: first we stand on the right wing, then on the left, now in the middle; that the extreme fatigue of the troops is directly connected to these brilliant moves is clear to see. If I were to provide more details I would have to write a book, and the most reasonable complaints would have no end.[70]

"Pathetic" and "absolutely pitiful" are some of the terms that have been used to describe the state of the uniforms of I Corps. Some of Yorck's veteran units from the Russian Campaign still wore the uniforms they had been issued in 1811. As testament to the impoverishment of the Prussian state, the trousers of the Silesian Landwehr had been made with the cheapest and thinnest cloth that could be found. This material shrank so much that the trousers had become too short and too tight. Overcoats remained in short supply, which forced some soldiers to clothe themselves with coats taken from prisoners of war. The doctrine of "ten patches on one hole" provided longer life for those lucky enough to have an overcoat. Moreover, none of Yorck's men had been issued warmer woolen breeches for the winter. Providing uniforms for new effectives posed difficulties since the convalescents arrived in civilian clothing and the replacements lacked shoes. Gneisenau complained to his wife that the army "suffers the most acute shortages of clothing. Many of our valiant soldiers had to wade through the groundless roads barefooted and in linen trousers. By Eisenach we encountered such cold weather that many of our people froze to death." Despite the attempts of Yorck's officers to commandeer used and new shoes from almost every city and village between the Saale and the Rhine, the shortage of shoes and boots persisted. In a stroke of luck, Yorck's staff finally managed to secure a double supply of shoes for the infantry: a prize worth its weight in gold because the shoes issued by the Prussian army were notoriously wretched.[71]

Manpower, however, provided Yorck's strongest argument. Currently, the Silesian Army numbered only 36,000 men. Yorck's I Corps ended the German Campaign of 1813 with 11,515 men. In three months of campaigning, it had lost 26,432 men, including 2,217 killed, 10,127 wounded, and 4,143 missing or captured. The majority of the other 9,945 men remained behind in the hospitals: sick and exhausted from malnourishment and overexertion. Losses among Yorck's Landwehr units greatly surpassed those of the Line. On 14 August, I Corps mustered twenty-four Landwehr battalions; by 17 October, the day after the bloody fighting at Möckern, only seven weak militia battalions remained. Of the 13,369 soldiers of the Landwehr infantry attached to Yorck's corps in August, only 2,164 reached the Rhine. Grueling marches, inadequate supply, and the harshness of bivouacking accounted for the high rate of attrition among the militia. As neither replacements nor convalescents would be able to catch up with the army if it continued to advance, strategic consumption, battlefield casualties, and illness would further reduce Blücher's combat power. Yorck did not believe Blücher could or should begin a winter campaign in the midst of French-controlled fortresses with an army that badly needed extensive refurbishing and rest. One day after Blücher commenced his march to the Rhine, Yorck wrote to Knesebeck, recounting the terrible state of the corps and advising against an invasion of France; Yorck's protest did not fall on deaf ears.[72]

Not only did Yorck vehemently disagree with Blücher and Gneisenau about continuing the advance, but during these days another affair surfaced to widen the rift between the Prussians. Yorck's headquarters complained about the account of the battle of Möckern published in the Ninth Bulletin of the Silesian Army. The emphasis on the role of Langeron's Russian corps appeared to minimize the Prussian achievement, causing Yorck's officers to view the report as a "malicious" distortion of the facts. Moreover, the Prussians claimed that the portrayal of Vasilchikov's cavalry attack on the morning of the 17th as "the most beautiful and boldest of the entire war" completely eclipsed the events at Möckern. To make matters worse, Professor Steffens made a speech at the University of Gießen before a large audience. With some of Yorck's officers in attendance, Steffens repeated the same version of the battle of Möckern published in the bulletin. "One knew well," explains Droysen, "that in these things Blücher was blameless; instead, one believed Gneisenau and Müffling and their aversion for Yorck had to be at fault. That Yorck's suggestions for promotions and decorations were usually ignored was attributed to their influence."[73]

After the Berlin newspapers refused to publish an anonymous account of Möckern submitted by Schack, Zielinsky sought to set the record straight. Although it is not known if Yorck authorized him to do so, Zielinsky complained to Thile. Zielinsky's letter of 5 November criticized the Ninth Army Bulletin for diminishing the role of I Corps and leading the public to believe that Langeron's Russians had done everything or at least as much as Yorck's men. Zielinsky adamantly stated that the officers who survived the battle, the general, and the entire corps felt deeply sickened "that not once has someone told our countrymen, for whose welfare so many fell and so many had spilled their blood, what the troops had achieved, and that one attributed to the Army of Silesia what Yorck's corps had accomplished alone without the cooperation of any other man or any other unit." Zielinsky expressed his hope that the world would soon learn the truth. "Since the army report was issued in the name of His Majesty the King," he concluded, "General Yorck himself cannot dispute it without having to issue a formal complaint against the field-marshal, which he will never do. However, since I know that Colonel Müffling is the author of this report, I request on behalf of the entire I Army Corps that you report this injustice suffered by General Yorck and his army corps, to His Majesty the King."[74] Although Thile's response is not known, the real importance of this episode is that the distrust and resentment between Blücher's and Yorck's headquarters continued and would contribute to some of the darkest days for the Silesian Army during the campaign in France.

Returning to Schwarzenberg, after receiving reports that Napoleon had not changed course to reach Koblenz, but instead remained on the direct road through Frankfurt and Mainz to the Rhine, he ordered the Bohemian Army to take the same road. However, cold weather and supply shortages further slowed the march of Schwarzenberg's usually torpid army. On 6 November, Bubna's advance guard relieved the forward troops of Wrede's Austro-Bavarian Army and made contact with

Bertrand's corps, which stood at Hochheim, just east of Mainz. Schwarzenberg ordered Gyulay's corps to attack the French position on the 9th. A spirited assault forced Bertrand to withdraw from Hochheim after losing 30 officers, 1,500 men, 4 guns, and 1 Eagle. In the aftermath, Napoleon's last units crossed the Rhine and only maintained positions on the right bank at Wesel and the bridgeheads at Kastel and Kehl, facing Mainz and Strasbourg respectively.

While Bubna's division blockaded Kastel, the Bohemian Army moved into extensive cantonments. Schwarzenberg's headquarters also issued new instructions for the distribution of the various Allied armies: the Bohemian Army moved into cantonments on the upper and middle Rhine, the Silesian Army on the middle Rhine from the Main to the Lahn, and the Army of North Germany on the lower Rhine. Austrian troops occupied the Grand Duchy of Baden and a part of Württemberg; the Russians were assigned the Grand Duchies of Frankfurt and Hesse-Darmstadt as well as the remaining districts of Württemberg.[75]

While en route to the lower Rhine, Blücher received explicit orders from Tsar Alexander to turn around and besiege Mainz. These instructions reached the field-marshal on 11 November at Altenkirchen, thirty-five miles southeast of Cologne. Gneisenau's mission had failed. On the following day the Silesian Army reversed its march. On 14 November 1813, Yorck's corps marched through the Rheingaugebirge to Wiesbaden in the Duchy of Nassau. From a height on the Taunus Mountains, the Prussians caught a glimpse of the flashing Rhine and greeted it with a loud cheer. A sergeant-major of the Black Hussars whose Jäger squadron had orders to reconnoiter the river bank, left this account: "We rode at full speed crosscountry, down wooded slopes, through vineyards, and greeted the German – or soon to be freed from foreign yoke – Rhine with repeated cheers. We dismounted and with our hands scooped up the holy water or else lay full length and drank it."[76] The Prussians had reached the Rhine, but they would have to wait another six weeks before crossing the historic river.

By early November, the question that divided the Coalition and caused a rift among the volatile Prussians themselves was whether the Allies should cross the Rhine and pursue Napoleon's weak army. The exhausted state of Yorck's corps offered compelling evidence that proved the Allies needed to halt at the Rhine. For this reason, Yorck became a persistent opponent of his countrymen's plan to cross the river without delay. Yorck protested against the immediate continuation of the pursuit out of concern for his troops. Although this was justifiable, Blücher and Gneisenau, as the leadership of the army, had to overlook the considerations of a corps commander. Müffling's prediction that delay would result in a bloody campaign in 1814 adequately summarizes the thought process behind Blücher's and Gneisenau's planning. By immediately resuming the campaign, they were prepared to accept further losses and to impose further hardships on their men. The reason was not callous indifference, as Yorck implied, nor blood-thirsty revenge as the Austrians suggested, but the simple belief that by exploiting Napoleon's current weakness the war would end sooner and with less loss than if they allowed the master of war to reorganize.

The operations of the Silesian and Bohemian Armies halted in November for both practical and political reasons. Allied physical and material exhaustion required reorganization and rest. Revitalizing on the march in the midst of winter did not promise success. Nevertheless, Blücher's plan to march to Belgium in early November could probably have succeeded without much detriment to his men. French forces were in no condition to resist, and the march route of the Silesian Army would have avoided the departments of "Old France," where trouble with the local population posed a threat to rear-area security. On reaching Belgium, Blücher would have facilitated Bülow's invasion of Holland and enabled the Prussian III Corps to unite with the Silesian Army by the end of 1813. Wintzingerode as well might have been spirited across the Rhine. Without having to detach Langeron's corps at Mainz and with Bülow and possibly Wintzingerode, Blücher could have launched an invasion of Old France from Belgium with an army of 125,000 men. Even considering strategic consumption, this figure still would have been triple the size of the Silesian Army that reached the Aube River in late January. Moreover, such an operation would have occurred one full month before the Silesian Army actually crossed the middle Rhine. The distance between Mainz and Paris was double the stretch that separated the French capital from Belgium's southern border. With the Silesian Army much closer to Paris and with the mobilization of the French army still in its infant stages, Blücher may well have reached Paris in January. Like Napoleon, Blücher and Gneisenau still measured victory in terms of military success alone. For this reason they wanted to lead the Silesian Army across the Rhine at the first opportunity and make for the heart of France. Instead of pursuing Napoleon's defeated army, the Allies lost precious time in long deliberations and councils of war in Frankfurt. Rather than achieving a quick, decisive end to the conflict in 1813, the war was prolonged, another campaign was fought, and tens of thousands of lives were lost in 1814.

Notes

1 Gneisenau to Caroline, 19 October 1813, GStA PK, VI HA Rep. 92 Nl. Gneisenau, Nr. 21.

2 Quoted in Balfour, *The Life of George*, I:125; Blücher to Amalie, 20 October 1813, *Blüchers Briefe*, ed. Unger, 188. Gneisenau's own estimates of the spoils vary. On the 19th, his letter to Clausewitz states that "more than 50 guns and 500 caissons fell into our hands." That same day, he placed the number of guns at 60 in a letter

to the military governor of Berlin, General Anton Wilhelm von L'Estocq. Two days later he informed his wife that more than 200 guns, 800 caissons, and 30,000 muskets were captured. Finally, in a letter to Clausewitz's wife on the 24th, he amended his totals to more than 200 guns, 600–700 caissons, and as many as 60,000 muskets. Gneisenau's letters to the above are in GStA PK, VI HA Rep. 92 Nl. Gneisenau, Nrs. 20b and 21.

3 Müffling, *Die Feldzüge*, 97–98.

4 Steffens, *Adventures*, 125.

5 Wilson, *Private Diary*, II:186; Friederich, *Herbstfeldzug 1813*, III:240; Pertz and Delbrück, *Gneisenau*, III:493.

6 Gneisenau to Clausewitz, 19 October 1813, GStA PK, VI HA Rep. 92 Nl. Gneisenau, Nr. 21.

7 Quoted in Pertz and Delbrück, *Gneisenau*, III:479.

8 Blücher to Yorck, 19 October 1813, GStA PK, VI HA Rep. 92 Nl. Gneisenau, Nr. 18; Droysen, *Yorck*, II:234; Friederich, *Herbstfeldzug 1813*, III:237.

9 "Journal of the Reserve Cavalry of I Corps" and "Report of the Battles and Combats of the Reserve Cavalry of I Corps," 26 November 1813, in Henckel von Donnersmarck, *Erinnerungen*, 517, 532; Friederich, *Herbstfeldzug 1813*, III:237. The Reserve Cavalry now consisted of 1st West Prussian and Lithuanian Dragoon Regiments, the East Prussian National Cavalry Regiment, the Saxon Uhlan Regiment, the Saxon Hussar Regiment, and Horse Battery Nr. 1.

10 Petre, *Napoleon's Last Campaign*, 378, 380.

11 Friederich, *Herbstfeldzug 1813*, III:239; Henckel von Donnersmarck, *Erinnerungen*, 231; Droysen, *Yorck*, II:234–35.

12 "Journal of 1st West Prussian Dragoon Regiment," "Journal of the Reserve Cavalry of I Corps," and "Report of the Battles and Combats of the Reserve Cavalry of I Corps," 26 November 1813, in Henckel von Donnersmarck, *Erinnerungen*, 500, 517, 533; Droysen, *Yorck*, II:235; Friederich, *Herbstfeldzug 1813*, III:242–43.

13 Steffens, *Adventures*, 125.

14 Friederich, *Herbstfeldzug 1813*, III:241–42; Pertz and Delbrück, *Gneisenau*, III:493.

15 *CN*, No. 20819, XXVI:369.

16 *CN*, Nos. 20820 and 20821, XXVI:370–71.

17 The new advance guard consisted of four Line and two Landwehr battalions; three Jäger companies; the Austrian 2nd Jäger Battalion; eight squadrons of Prussian hussars, four squadrons of Saxon uhlans; and one battery each of horse and foot artillery. See Henckel von Donnersmarck, *Erinnerungen*, 232; "Journal of the Advance Guard Formed After the Battle of Leipzig and Commanded by Col. Count Henckel," in Henckel von Donnersmarck, *Erinnerungen*, 547–48; Pertz and Delbrück, *Gneisenau*, III:493; Droysen, *Yorck*, II:236; Friederich, *Herbstfeldzug 1813*, III:248.

18 Henckel to Yorck, "Report of the Advance Guard on 21 October and Its Combats," in Henckel von Donnersmarck, *Erinnerungen*, 549.

19 Henckel von Donnersmarck, *Erinnerungen*, 233; Pertz and Delbrück, *Gneisenau*, III:493–94; Droysen, *Yorck*, II:236. No mention is made in any of these accounts of disciplinary action against the Saxon regiment.

20 Friederich, *Herbstfeldzug 1813*, III:248–49; Henckel von Donnersmarck, *Erinnerungen*, 234; Droysen, *Yorck*, II:236.

21 Steffens, *Adventures*, 126.

22 Brett-James, *Europe Against Napoleon*, 258–60; Friederich, *Herbstfeldzug 1813*, III:247–48. Two miles west of Freyburg, Zscheiplitz was a large agricultural estate with a village that contained the Zettenbach Mill, where the second bridge over the Unstrut stood.

23 The account of the French retreat through Freyburg on 21 October was taken from the testimony of three eyewitnesses reproduced in Brett-James, *Europe Against Napoleon*, 258–61.

24 Brett-James, *Europe Against Napoleon*, 259.

25 On the previous evening, Yorck had transferred the Silesian Uhlan Regiment to Henckel's vanguard and attached the East Prussian National Cavalry Regiment to Horn's division. En route to Markröhlitz, Jürgaß left posts facing Reichardtswerben, with the Brandenburg Uhlan Regiment in Roßbach for their support. Patrols also observed the Weißenfels–Freyburg road.

26 Accounts of the combat of Freyburg and the operations of Yorck's corps on 21 October were drawn from Henckel, *Erinnerungen*, 236–37, as well as the following documents that are reproduced in full in Henckel's memoirs: "Journal of the Lithuanian Dragoon Regiment," 451; "Report of the Battles and Combats of the Reserve Cavalry of I Corps," 26 November 1813, 534; "Journal of 1st West Prussian Dragoon Regiment," 500; and "Report of the Advance Guard on 21 October and Its Combats," 550–51; Friederich, *Herbstfeldzug 1813*, III:248–52.

27 Late on the day of 21 October, Blücher issued a three-day disposition covering 21, 22, and 23 October: Disposition, Weißenfels, 3:30 P.M., 21 October 1813, RA KrA, volym 25; Müffling, *Die Feldzüge*, 103; Gneisenau to Caroline, Weißenfels, 21 October 1813, GStA PK, VI HA Rep. 92 Nl. Gneisenau. Gneisenau claims that the French "had about 6,000 cavalry facing us and just as much infantry."

28 Müffling, *Die Feldzüge*, 104; Gneisenau to Münster, Weißenfels, 21 October 1813, GStA PK, VI HA Rep. 92 Nl. Gneisenau, Nr. 20b.

29 Disposition for 22 October, Add MSS, 20112, 171; Müffling, *Die Feldzüge*, 104–05.

30 Pertz and Delbrück, *Gneisenau*, III:494–95.

31 Quoted in Droysen, *Yorck*, II:237.

32 Friederich, *Herbstfeldzug 1813*, III:252; "Report of the Advance Guard on 21 October and Its Combats," in Henckel von Donnersmarck, *Erinnerungen*, 551.

33 Quoted in Henderson, *Blücher*, 189. According to Blücher's Nachlaß, the promotion was dated 16 October 1813: GStA PK, VI HA Rep. 92 Nl. Blücher von Wahlstatt; Müffling, *Die Feldzüge*, 103.

34 Gneisenau to Münster, Weißenfels, 21 October 1813, GStA PK, VI HA Rep. 92 Nl. Gneisenau, Nr. 20b; Friederich, *Herbstfeldzug 1813*, III:255.

35 Blücher to Amalie, 25 October 1813, *Blüchers Briefe*, ed. Unger, 189; Gneisenau to Marie von Clausewitz, 24 October 1813, and to Clausewitz, 22 October 1813, GStA PK, VI HA Rep. 92 Nl. Gneisenau, Nr. 21.

36 Henckel von Donnersmarck, *Erinnerungen*, 236.

37 Schwarzenberg to Blücher, Naumburg, 22 October 1813, Add MSS, 20112, 168.

38 Friederich, *Herbstfeldzug 1813*, III:257.

39 Droysen, *Yorck*, II:238; Pertz and Delbrück, *Gneisenau*, III:497–98; Friederich, *Herbstfeldzug 1813*, III:257–58.

40 Quoted in Pertz and Delbrück, *Gneisenau*, III:497; Henckel von Donnersmarck, *Erinnerungen*, 236; Disposition for 24 October, Add MSS, 20112, 172.

41 Quoted in Droysen, *Yorck*, II:238–39; Friederich, *Herbstfeldzug 1813*, III:258–61; Henckel von Donnersmarck, *Erinnerungen*, 236–37.

42 Steffens, *Adventures*, 123.

43 Quoted in Droysen, *Yorck*, II:239; Disposition for 25 October, Add MSS, 20112, 173; Friederich, *Herbstfeldzug 1813*, III:261–62.

44 Gneisenau to Siegling, 26 October 1813, quoted in Pertz and Delbrück, *Gneisenau*, III:498; Stewart, *Narrative*, 193.

45 Disposition for 26 October, Add MSS, 20112, 176; Henckel von Donnersmarck, *Erinnerungen*, 236–37; Fane (Lord Burghersh), *Memoir*, 35; Friederich, *Herbstfeldzug 1813*, III:263.

46 Henckel von Donnersmarck, *Erinnerungen*, 237; "Report of the Battles and Combats of the Reserve Cavalry of I Corps," *ibid.*, 535.

47 "The ground had become so muddy because of the weather," states Jürgaß's report, "that it was hardly possible to execute a rapid movement": "Report of the Battles and Combats of the Reserve Cavalry of I Corps," Henckel von Donnersmarck, *Erinnerungen*, 535.

48 Sources for 26 October: Blücher to Schwarzenberg, Gangloffsömmern, 25 October 1813, ÖStA KA, FA 1537, 114; "Journal of 1st West Prussian Dragoon Regiment," Henckel von Donnersmarck, *Erinnerungen*, 501; Friederich, *Herbstfeldzug 1813*, III:264–65; Stewart, *Narrative*, 193; Yorck's report is quoted in Droysen, *Yorck*, II:240–41.

49 Stewart, *Narrative*, 186–87; Friederich, *Herbstfeldzug 1813*, III:265–66; Schack's journal entry is quoted in Droysen, *Yorck*, II:241; Krimer's passage is in Brett-James, *Europe Against Napoleon*, 278–79.

50 Blücher to Schwarzenberg, Eisenach, 8:00 A.M., 27 October 1813, ÖStA KA, FA 1537, 636, and Add MSS, 20112, 174–75.

51 Gneisenau to Hardenberg, 28 October 1813, GStA PK, VI HA Rep. 92 Nl. Gneisenau, Nr. 20b.

52 Pertz and Delbrück, *Gneisenau*, III:502–03.

53 Sources for 27 October: Disposition for 27 October, Add MSS, 20112, 177; Gneisenau to Münster, 3 November 1813, GStA PK, VI HA Rep. 92 Nl. Gneisenau, Nr. 20b; Blücher to Schwarzenberg, Eisenach, 27 October 1813, ÖStA KA, FA 1537, 636; Friederich, *Herbstfeldzug 1813*, III:266–67; Droysen, *Yorck*, II:241–42; Pertz and Delbrück, *Gneisenau*, III:501–02; Müffling, *Die Feldzüge*, 107–08. "Journal of the Lithuanian Dragoon Regiment," "Journal of the Reserve Cavalry of I Corps," and "Report of the Battles and Combats of the Reserve

Cavalry of I Corps," 26 November 1813, in Henckel von Donnersmarck, *Erinnerungen*, 452, 518, 535.

54 Blücher to Schwarzenberg, Philipsthal, 7:00 P.M., 29 October 1813, ÖStA KA, FA 1537, 696, and RA KrA, volym 25.

55 Stewart, *Narrative*, 190.

56 Sources for 29 and 30 October: Disposition for 29 October, Add MSS, 20112, 178; Blücher to Schwarzenberg, Philipsthal, 7:00 P.M., 29 October 1813, ÖStA KA, FA 1537, 696 and RA KrA, volym 25; Blücher to Amalie, 30 October 1813, *Blüchers Briefe*, ed. Unger, 189; Henckel von Donnersmarck, *Erinnerungen*, 238; Müffling, *Die Feldzüge*, 109; the hussar's report is in Brett-James, *Europe Against Napoleon*, 277–78.

57 Marmont, *Mémoires*, V:302–03; Chandler, *Campaigns of Napoleon*, 938.

58 Blücher to Schwarzenberg, Hünfeld, 6:00 P.M., 30 October 1813, and from Fulda, 31 October 1813, ÖStA KA, FA 1537, 716, 732; Blücher to Amalie, 3 November 1813, *Blüchers Briefe*, ed. Unger, 190; Gneisenau, *Blücher*, 271. In his published account of Blücher's operations, Gneisenau makes no mention of Schwarzenberg but instead holds Blücher responsible for the army's change in direction: "The Bavarian army, under General Count Wrede was known to be on the march to Hanau to intercept the French army; Marshal Blücher drew a very natural conclusion that in all probability Napoleon would direct the course of his columns to cross the Rhine at Koblenz rather than throw himself, weak as he was, into Wrede's arms." Blücher himself simply wrote that, "had not a great mistake been made, he [Napoleon] and all of his army would have been captured": Blücher to Bonin, 3 November 1813, *Blüchers Briefe*, ed. Unger, 191.

59 Schwarzenberg to Blücher, Hünfeld, 7:00 A.M., 1 November 1813, Add MSS, 20112, 21–22; Gneisenau to Hardenberg, 31 October 1813, GStA PK, VI HA Rep. 92 Nl. Gneisenau, Nr. 20b; Gneisenau to Frederick William, 31 October 1813, GStA PK, VI HA Rep. 92 Nl. Gneisenau, Nr. 16.

60 Despite the belief held by Yorck's headquarters, Langeron's march was not easy and the Russians lost 400 horses on the mountain tracks.

61 Disposition for 31 October, 1, 2, and 3 November, Fulda, 31 October 1813, Add MSS, 20112, 181–83; Blücher to Yorck, 31 October 1813, Add MSS, 20112, 179; the journal is quoted in Droysen, *Yorck*, II:242.

62 Henckel von Donnersmarck, *Erinnerungen*, 239. According to the regimental journals reprinted in this work, the actual change in the march direction did not come until 2 November for the vanguard, which proceeded on the same highway to Frankfurt on 1 November, reaching Salmünster.

63 Lowe to Stewart, Fulda, 31 October 1813, Add MSS, 20111, 198.

64 Henckel von Donnersmarck, *Erinnerungen*, 243; GStA PK, IV Rep. 15 A Nr. 274; Blücher to Bonin, 4 November 1813, *Blüchers Briefe*, ed. Unger, 191–92.

65 The Nidda is a right tributary of the Main River that springs from the Vogelsberg on the Taufstein mountain range and joins the Main near Frankfurt.

66 Lowe to Stewart, Gießen, 3 November 1813, Add MSS, 20111, 204; Wilson, *Private Diary*, II:212. According to Thiers in *History of the Consulate and the Empire*, IX:294, "places indispensable to our home protection, Huningue, Strasbourg, Landau, Mainz, Metz, Mézières, Valenciennes, Lille, were left utterly

defenseless. The guns were not mounted; there was a lack of tools, of wood for blinds, of bridges of communication between the works, of horses for transport, of smiths and carpenters. The artillery and engineer officers who had remained in the interior of the country were nearly all old men, unfit to support the fatigues of a siege. Provisions had not yet begun to arrive, and money, which can supply so many wants, was not forthcoming, and it was doubtful whether it could be sent in time and in sufficient quantities."

67 Blücher to Frederick William, 3 November 1813, GStA PK, VI HA Rep. 92 Nl. Gneisenau, Nr. 16; Müffling, *Die Feldzüge*, 111; Müffling is quoted in Droysen, *Yorck*, II:246, emphasis added; Lowe to Stewart, Erfurt, 31 October 1813, Add MSS, 20111, 198–99.

68 Blücher to Bonin, 4 November 1813, *Blüchers Briefe*, ed. Unger, 192.

69 Quoted in Droysen, *Yorck*, II:248–49.

70 Zielinsky to Thile, 5 November 1813, quoted in Droysen, *Yorck*, II:245.

71 Gneisenau to Caroline, 11 November 1813, GStA PK, VI HA Rep. 92 Nl. Gneisenau, Nr. 21.

72 Janson, *Feldzuges 1814*, I:15; Damitz, *Geschichte des Feldzuges von 1814*, I:22; Craig, "Problems of Coalition Warfare," 33.

73 Droysen, *Yorck*, II:243.

74 Quoted in Droysen, *Yorck*, II:245.

75 Friederich, *Herbstfeldzug 1813*, III:310–12; Pertz and Delbrück, *Gneisenau*, III:524.

76 Quoted in Brett-James, *Europe Against Napoleon*, 292–93.

Assessment

Austria's declaration against France, on 12 August 1813, changed the dynamics of the war by transferring the Coalition's center of gravity from Russia to Austria. Aside from liberating the garrisons of the Vistula fortresses and perhaps rallying the Poles, the appearance of an imperial army and even Napoleon himself on the banks of the Vistula would not have had the same impact on the Allies in the Fall Campaign as during the Spring Campaign. Russian lines of communication could be rerouted through Austria. The provinces of the Prussian heartland would have been lost but the bulk of the Prussian regular army – I and II Corps and the Guard – would not have been affected. In fact, the main challenge for the Allies would not have been Napoleon's presence at the Vistula, but navigating the shock waves caused by the loss of the Army of North Germany, which had to be eliminated or driven into the Oder fortresses before any French force could reach the Vistula. Napoleon recognized that Austria's accession to the Coalition rendered unconditional victory through eccentric maneuvering unlikely. Instead, he had to defeat the Austrians, which meant decisively crushing the Bohemian Army. To accomplish this task, he planned to utilize his central position and operate from his base at Dresden.

Austria had certainly come a long way since the French emperor's 1809 proclamation that "the House of Lorraine has ceased to exist," in large part thanks to Napoleon's intransigence. Metternich's usurpation of the Coalition's diplomatic and military leadership provided by far the most decisive development of the armistice. In the former category, Metternich seized the reins of the Coalition. While a worthy adversary in his own right, Tsar Alexander simply could not outmaneuver Metternich in the ensuing diplomatic chess match for control of the Coalition. Determined to conduct a cabinet war for the equilibrium of Europe rather than a people's war of liberation, Metternich resolved to direct the struggle so that any peace would serve Austrian national security objectives. Emerging as the Coalition's prime minister, he aimed to wage war to restore Habsburg preponderance over Central Europe while limiting Prussian and Russian gains. Napoleon's fate became a secondary concern; Metternich did not aspire to remove Bonaparte from the French throne, believing that only a strong Napoleonic France could counter Russia.

A coalition consisting of Austria, Russia, Prussia, Great Britain, and Sweden bound together by a single treaty of alliance pledging each member to fight for specific objectives for European peace did not exist.[1] In fact, much of the War of the Sixth Coalition would be fought despite the absence of such a declaration, which did not come into existence until March 1814. Instead, the decisive Fall Campaign of 1813 began with the Allies held together by flimsy bilateral pacts and subsidy agreements. Only the ominous realization that the present moment offered the best opportunity to break French hegemony in Central Europe bound them. Another failure at the hands of Napoleon could not be fathomed, for it would truly usher in the unknown. Dominic Lieven maintains that, had Napoleon won the initial battles of the Fall Campaign, "it is possible that the rifts would have reopened between the Allies, and Austria would have resumed negotiations with Napoleon. That the Allies won these initial battles at Großbeeren, the Katzbach, and Dennewitz can be attributed only to Prussian leadership."[2]

Prussia's contribution exceeded all expectations. Numbering approximately 75,000 men at the end of the Spring Campaign, the Prussian field army increased to 193,000 men during the armistice. In total, the Prussians placed over 235,000 men under arms, quite an accomplishment for the state's five million inhabitants. By comparison, the Russians fielded 175,000 men and the Austrian army operating from Bohemia numbered around 150,000 soldiers. In terms of combat power, Prussia had risen from the position of Russia's auxiliary to an independent power in its own right. Anxious to exert this power, the Prussian generals would discover to their great disappointment that 250,000 men under arms did little to change Prussia's junior status in the Coalition.[3]

When Schwarzenberg remained outside the range in which Napoleon could strike the Bohemian Army and still guard Dresden, the emperor turned against the closest Allied force: the Silesian Army. Blücher, Gneisenau, and their staff certainly made mistakes in the Fall Campaign but we should bear in mind that, unlike the French, the Prussians had not waged war since 1807. Moreover, Blücher, the hussar general, had never commanded an army, nor had Gneisenau ever managed a large field force, nor had Müffling reached the mastery of drafting orders that later distinguished his work. Inadequate information, incorrect reports, and the countless contingencies of war made mistakes unavoidable. Despite the deficiencies associated with human nature, the leadership of this army laid the groundwork for the guiding principles that fundamentally helped destroy Napoleon's empire: the ruthless application of all force to a single objective, the interplay of the individual arms, the strategic utilization of the cavalry, the exploitation of the victory through pursuit. According to Friederich:

> These principles led our armies to victory in the later wars of the nineteenth century and are recognizable in our contemporary service regulations. If still greater results were not achieved, the cause was that the hands of the commanders of the Silesian Army many times were tied by the organization of the army, the spirit of the contemporary regulations, the education of the senior and junior officers, and the lack of combat experience of the troops. The spirit of linear tactics, in which all senior officers of the Prussian and Russian armies were trained, still wrestled with that of the new warfare of the French, and this spiritual struggle took place in many areas; for example, in the use of the cavalry, this even led to obvious regressions to Frederician times. Yet, the development of a new way of war is not difficult to recognize, a way of war, which at a given moment knows to deviate from the confines of the traditional system and which places the substance of the matter above the form. The birthplace of this new warfare lies in the struggles of the Silesian Army, whose thorough study will thus prove useful for all times.[4]

After moving across the neutral zone prior to the expiration of the summer armistice, Blücher's Silesian Army remained in constant contact with the imperials throughout August. Almost every day some part of his army engaged the enemy. Blücher's four army corps each consisted of a vanguard, main body, and rearguard, all of which received orders from the corps commander and usually reported to him. As we have seen, on occasion Blücher and Gneisenau engaged in direct communication with units and detachments, but the flow of communication usually followed the chain of command that ran through corps headquarters. Although the moments of interference by Blücher's staff probably irked Yorck and Langeron, the system operated suitably, especially when the army closed on a fixed point. Yet rarely between 15 and 26 August did the Silesian Army make for a fixed point. Instead, Blücher did his best to maintain contact with a large enemy army that operated on three main arteries along a broad front. To comply with the assignment he had accepted at Reichenbach on the eve of the war's continuation, he had to maintain contact with the enemy at all times. Consequently, the breadth of the front required him to keep his entire army within one march of his adversary to be able to execute optimal maneuvers with the greatest force possible. Complying with this unique task created problems. Blücher had to quickly change from one objective to the complete opposite: a decided attack had to be transformed into an immediate retreat based on his adversary's conduct. This imposed tremendous hardships and strains on the entire army in the form of marches and countermarches.

Whether Langeron served as a Russian mole in the Silesian Army purportedly to keep Blücher in check will never be known for sure. Certainly, Blücher did not enjoy the full support of all influential persons at Russo-Prussian Headquarters. His refusal on multiple occasions to comply with directives from Allied Headquarters indicates that the Sixth Coalition suffered from some of the same problems that had led to the destruction of the five previous anti-French alliances. Yet Alexander and Frederick William had thought enough of Blücher to place a fairly substantial army under his command albeit within strict operating parameters. Even in this, we have to question their judgment, for Blücher's reputation should not have led any to think that he would ape the warfare of Quintus Fabius Maximus. But, to the surprise of all, he did just that, retreating before Napoleon's onslaught on no fewer than four occasions. Each retreat can be completely justified as Napoleon – the master of central position, interior lines, mass, and speed – outnumbered Blücher on every occasion. Moreover, rather than merely conceding the field to Napoleon, the first two retreats required rapid withdrawals under extremely adverse conditions that lasted for days. In the third retreat, a veritable *coup de théâtre*, Blücher led his Army of Silesia 120 miles down the Elbe to cross the river and link with the Army of North Germany in early October. With both the Silesian and North German Armies on the left bank of the Elbe, the emperor launched a secret offensive against Blücher. Just barely escaping Napoleon's trap, Blücher retreated a fourth time, dragging the Army of North Germany with him across the Saale River. The significance of this maneuver – bearing the stamp of the unorthodox – cannot be overstated: while the combined Allied armies advanced toward Napoleon's communications, they exposed their own and opened the roads to Brandenburg and Silesia. More importantly, the maneuver on the Saale – a retreat forward – created the conditions that encouraged Schwarzenberg to seek a decisive battle with Napoleon at Leipzig. Had Blücher followed Bernadotte's demand to retreat across the Elbe, Schwarzenberg would have been forced to confront Napoleon on the plains of Saxony or return to Bohemia.

After the victory at the Katzbach, Blücher's constant pressure prevented Macdonald from rallying his army at the Bober, the Queis, or the Neiße Rivers. By driving the marshal to Bautzen, Blücher completely disrupted Napoleon's timetable and planning, costing the emperor an entire week of indecision. From 31 August to 3 September, Napoleon sat at Dresden uncertain if he should personally lead the Berlin offensive or secure Macdonald in the face of Blücher's constant pressure. Forced to stop the Army of the Bober from retreating across the Spree, Napoleon transferred his VI Corps and I Cavalry Corps from the Bohemian front to Bautzen, to where he proceeded with his Guard on 4 September 1813. Hoping to quickly engage Blücher and destroy his army, Napoleon lunged but missed. Again proving that going backward could be just as beneficial as going forward, Blücher retreated across the Neiße to the Queis. Owing to Blücher's pressure, Macdonald's retreat prevented Napoleon from taking personal command of the Berlin offensive from 31 August to 3 September. Then, Napoleon's pursuit of the Silesian Army cost the emperor another three days and culminated with his returning to Dresden rather than marching on Berlin. Thus, Napoleon squandered an entire week contending with the difficulties caused by Blücher.

Blücher's army paid for its success in Silesia with the loss of some 22,000 men. Including St.-Priest's corps, the Silesian Army numbered 81,000 men on 1 September. Since the end of the armistice on 10 August, Langeron's corps had lost more than 6,000 men while Sacken's losses amounted to a manageable 2,000.[5] On the other hand, eighteen days of campaigning had reduced Yorck's corps from 39,243 combatants on 11 August to 24,517 men on 31 August, with the Landwehr suffering out of proportion compared to the Line.[6] At the start of the campaign, Yorck's militia contained 13,370 men. After the loss of 7,092 men, only 6,278 mustered on 1 September. Conversely, his Line units lost 4,040 soldiers, dropping from 16,747 men to 12,707 combatants. Army Headquarters viewed desertion as the major cause of attrition. This induced the king to issue a cabinet order on 31 August to implement the Articles of War in Upper Silesia because this province "distinguishes itself so poorly through deficiency of devotion to the Fatherland."[7] One week later, Blücher's headquarters issued orders on 7 September authorizing physical punishment, mainly for the militia. An entry in Schack's journal captures the disgust in Yorck's headquarters over this measure that called for "tired Landwehr men to be refreshed with thirty lashes." According to Droysen, Blücher supposedly enacted "other, more abusive measures." By mining the official journal of I Corps, Droysen reached the conclusion that the "discipline" of the Landwehr improved substantially "after one had clothed their nakedness and satisfied their hunger." In fact, he claims that the journal itself stated that "the continued forced marches and the poor food must be recognized as valid, main causes for the weakness of the men." As they had not received reinforcements, the fact that Yorck's Landwehr rolls increased from 6,278 men to 8,540 by 14 September indicates that more than 2,000 men returned after recuperating in their nearby homes.[8]

Leaving Silesia behind him, Blücher executed the most crucial and consequential operation of the entire Fall Campaign. By marching down the Elbe and crossing the river at Wartenburg, he set the stage for the monumental struggle at Leipzig less than two weeks later. As Hudson Lowe concluded:

> The bold and decisive movement of the Army of Silesia, which had fought its way from the remotest corners of that province and by a series of the most

splendid victories had driven the enemy back under the walls of Dresden, and which now crossed the Elbe and abandoned the bridge that had served for its passage, infused fresh vigour into the councils of the Allied generals, disconcerted all the schemes and projects of the enemy, and rendered a series of active operations on both sides immediately necessary. The degree to which the enemy was disconcerted may be best inferred from his own relation, which states the departure of Napoleon from Dresden on 7 October, immediately after the Army of Silesia had crossed the Elbe, and the series of vague, perplexed, and uncertain movements which followed between that day and the 15th.

Stewart makes similar remarks in his *Narrative*: "The bold and offensive system now so gallantly commenced by General Blücher, gave a new tone to the operations of the Allies. The glorious career of the Silesian Army, daily engaged in action since the opening of the campaign, and hourly covering itself with laurels, merits the historian's loftiest eulogy: it stood preeminent in the advance [to] the next foe, with its venerable and gallant leader eagerly availing himself of every opportunity to augment his heroic reputation, rescue his country, and avenge her sufferings."[9]

Well planned and conducted, Blücher's bold campaign represents one of the best examples of operational planning to that point in military history. Army Headquarters kept its intentions so secret that the orders for the army to implement the plan came as a complete surprise. A mass of *Streifkorps* masked the army's departure from the Bautzen area. Napoleon himself did not become aware of Blücher's disappearance until 4 October.[10] Initially, Shcherbatov's corps covered the left flank against an attack from Dresden. Later during the operation, Sacken's corps guarded against a strike through Meißen. Sacken's demonstrations at Mühlberg also distracted the imperials. Had Ney's attention not been attracted to Wartenburg by the Army of North Germany, the Silesian Army could have executed the crossing without losing one man.[11]

For his part, Schwarzenberg decided to advance on Leipzig rather than attempt another offensive against Dresden: the Army of Bohemia began the march north on 1 October. By no means did he make haste after his army reached the Saxon plain. Despite the encouraging reports of Napoleon's absence and the retreat of Murat's small army, the Army of Bohemia advanced very cautiously, almost timidly. Robert Wilson attributed Schwarzenberg's inertia to an intercepted letter from Murat to his wife, Napoleon's sister Caroline, dated the 8th. "The Allies appear to have abandoned their strong position in Bohemia and have moved onto the plain," wrote the king of Naples; "this is what Napoleon has long wished for."[12] Apparently, the fear of walking into a well-laid trap froze Schwarzenberg and Alexander until news arrived on 13 October that completely changed the situation. On that day, Blücher's adjutant delivered the general's

11 October letter stating that the Silesian Army had not retreated across the Elbe, as Allied Headquarters had secretly feared, but instead stood at Halle with the Army of North Germany not far behind. Moreover, Blücher explained that Napoleon faced both Allied armies with his main force. The concluding sentence of his report – that "the three armies are now so close that a simultaneous attack against the point where the enemy has concentrated his forces can take place" – changed not just the situation, but the course of the war by making the battle of Leipzig possible.

Lieven maintains that, "however great Blücher's victories were, in the end the fate of the campaign would rest above all on the performance of the main Allied army, in other words Schwarzenberg's Army of Bohemia. It contained many more troops than the armies of Bernadotte and Blücher combined. Only the Army of Bohemia could hope to confront and defeat Napoleon himself." The numerical strength of the Bohemian Army certainly validates this assertion but the Coalition's leaders doubted whether it could oppose Napoleon without the support of the other Allied armies, as proven by the attempts made to bring the Silesian Army or at least part of it to Bohemia following the battle of Dresden. Wilson echoes the sentiment of Allied Headquarters in a 5 October letter during the opening phase of Schwarzenberg's offensive:

> It is not yet certain whether we shall advance or retreat. There will be movements made to ascertain whether Blücher and the crown prince have passed the Elbe or not, and what causes may have influenced any change of intention. You must remember that we have made an offensive demonstration to assist Blücher and the crown prince. Without that aiding movement, this army is not strong enough to give battle in Saxony against the enemy's whole force; therefore our progress must be regulated by the proceedings of those [Napoleon] for whose service we threaten and with whose cooperation [Blücher and Bernadotte] we can only act. Prince Schwarzenberg's view appears to me most correct, and he has embraced every possible movement that can be made by the enemy or ourselves on the *calcul* and *raisonnement* which I have had the good fortune to hear from himself this day.[13]

"Very strange and dangerous position of the enemy," wrote Schack in his journal on 13 October. "One expects a *coup d'éclat*. A very interesting, critical point in time."[14] Napoleon's desire to escape from the net steadily closing on him probably made sense to the generals and statesmen who labored to defeat him but still harbored a deep respect for his martial abilities. Indeed, his surprise movement through Wittenberg to the right bank of the Elbe must have seemed the prelude of the expected *coup d'éclat*. As the Allies pondered the reasons that would prompt Napoleon to cross the Elbe, numerous factors made such a move quite plausible. Bavaria's defection now threatened his main line of communication to the Rhine.

Thus, it would make perfect sense for him to transfer his communications to the secondary line that ran through North Germany. A *coup de théâtre* would enable the master not only to rally the troops at Magdeburg, but also to unite with the Franco-Danish forces at Hamburg. As the reasons for Napoleon to cross the Elbe grew increasingly advantageous for him, the Prussians came to the realization that this bold maneuver could unravel two months of hard campaigning. Little about Schwarzenberg's record up to that point led the Prussians to believe they could expect a rapid advance into a new and distant theater of war by the Army of Bohemia. Nor did they expect Bernadotte to set aside his personal ambition in favor of the Allied cause if Napoleon suddenly appeared on the lower Elbe. At both Blücher's and Yorck's headquarters, the Prussians appreciated Napoleon's bold turn as a strategic and psychological master stroke.[15]

Friederich describes the operations of the Bohemian Army from 27 September to 14 October as "purely negative." The early twentieth-century German General Staff historian goes on to criticize Schwarzenberg for marching "in the slowest tempo from Teplitz to Marienberg, from Marienberg to Chemnitz, and from Chemnitz to Altenburg." Moreover, he accuses Schwarzenberg of avoiding "any possible clash with the enemy; he did not act, but instead only threatened to act; for the most part, he fought useless and purposeless engagements because of the habit of always committing insufficient forces; despite numerical superiority, he failed to tear asunder the thin veil that Napoleon had pushed forward to mask his movements against the two other Allied armies; he did not do the slightest to prevent a defeat of the North German and Silesian Armies, and even less for the union of all forces for a decisive battle to thus bring about the end of the war."[16]

Criticism is not confined to Friederich's pen. Little evidence can defend Schwarzenberg against General Rudolph von Caemmerer's accusation that the Allied generalissimo's actions were "diametrically opposed to any reasonable interpretation of the agreements made at Reichenbach." Murat and by extension Napoleon greatly benefited from what Caemmerer terms the "most highly defective generalship" displayed by Schwarzenberg during his campaign in western Saxony. With only Murat's 45,000 men facing him, the Allied commander in chief spent seventeen days starting on 27 September maneuvering his 160,000 men a mere eighty miles from the southern feet of the Erzgebirge to within one march of Leipzig by 13 October. In this textbook example of economy of force, Murat succeeded brilliantly in masking Schwarzenberg. Despite several engagements, Schwarzenberg failed to overcome his adversary for the simple reason that he made little effort to do so. Caemmerer criticizes Schwarzenberg for failing to use his cavalry – as Napoleon had taught – to properly reconnoiter the enemy. Had he done so, insists Caemmerer, Schwarzenberg would have immediately recognized the weakness of Murat's army.

More damning is Schwarzenberg's indifference to the fate of the Silesian Army in October, which foreshadowed the Allied commander in chief's apathy that led to the near-destruction of Blücher's army in France in February 1814. On 9 October, Schwarzenberg knew that Napoleon had marched north from Dresden and could not support Murat. Conversely, he knew for certain thanks to communication with Bubna that Napoleon's offensive gravely endangered Blücher, whose army stood on the Mulde. Caemmerer contends that, to end the "crisis" that both Blücher and Bernadotte faced and to "correctly respond" to Napoleon's offensive, Schwarzenberg should have crushed Murat at Borna on 10 October. A victory at Borna, according to Caemmerer, would have forced Napoleon to terminate his offensive and move south to take in the remains of Murat's army. Surprisingly, the German critic does not view Napoleon doing this at Leipzig but instead contends that the city would have fallen to Schwarzenberg on the 11th, thus preventing the arrival of Augereau's IX Corps While this is pure speculation, we can accept Caemmerer's point that a victory over Murat would have enabled Schwarzenberg to achieve the union with Blücher sooner and the two Allied armies could have attacked Napoleon under more favorable conditions with double his numbers earlier than the 16th. "But what was omitted on 10 October," concludes Caemmerer, "still could have been executed with the same advantages on 11, 12, and 13 October and thus should have been done. Indeed, even on 14 October, when a large cavalry engagement took place at Liebertwolkwitz [six miles southeast of Leipzig], it still was not too late for this. The failure to deliver a battle against the king of Naples south of Leipzig is a serious reproach against the commander of the Allies, for which he must bear full responsibility."[17]

Despite attempts by Gunther Rothenburg and Allan Sked to exonerate the Austrians, it is difficult to take issue with this assessment. That Blücher and Bernadotte escaped a crushing defeat cannot be attributed to Schwarzenberg's advance on Leipzig. Instead, a series of fortunate circumstances as well as their own prudence saved them. Conversely, Blücher's bold and adamant determination to remain at Halle and not fly across the Elbe as Bernadotte demanded most likely saved Schwarzenberg from another drubbing at the hands of Napoleon. Had the North German and Silesian Armies taken the bait and moved across the Elbe to defend Berlin, Napoleon could have quickly enveloped Schwarzenberg's right, cutting him off from Bohemia and driving him against the upper Saale and Thuringian Forest. Lastly, Blücher and Gneisenau deserve sole credit for making possible a general attack on the 16th. Even with this development, Schwarzenberg did not seek to thoroughly exploit the favorable situation by delivering a blow that would end the war. Instead of envisioning a bold concentric offensive against Leipzig, the continuation of the army's shift to the left was decided. Surprisingly, Friederich ultimately exonerates Schwarzenberg:

"Any other Allied general, perhaps with the exception of the venerable commander of the Silesian Army, presumably would have acted the same way in Schwarzenberg's place. One believed an attempt had to be made to drive Napoleon from Germany without a decisive battle. Despite all of his weaknesses, Schwarzenberg was the most appropriate general to whom the Allies could give the responsibility for the main army."[18]

On 15 October, numerous reports confirmed Napoleon's presence at Leipzig. In the afternoon, the shout of *"Vive l'Empereur!"* coming from thousands of voices on the hills north of Wachau could be clearly heard along Schwarzenberg's front as Napoleon inspected the line. Around 5:00 P.M. on the 15th, Schwarzenberg received the report that the French had reinforced Liebertwolkwitz and that the position of Napoleon's left wing clearly indicated his intention to attack the next day. Based on all of this news, the Allies ultimately concluded that Napoleon did not have any intentions of withdrawing from Leipzig. Thus, Schwarzenberg finally made the decision to attack the enemy on the 16th after wasting much precious time and failing to exploit the opportunity to crush Murat's isolated forces.[19]

For the Allied commander in chief, the circumstances on 16 October would prove much less favorable than those of 14 and 15 October, when most of Napoleon's forces remained en route to Leipzig. Although postponing his attack on the 14th and 15th to secure Blücher's participation, Schwarzenberg should have delayed on the 16th as well, based on the near-parity in forces that Napoleon's concentration had achieved. Although we cannot fault Schwarzenberg for not being able to divine Napoleon's numbers, common sense and the emperor's way of war taught that he would not accept battle unless he possessed overwhelming mass. Schwarzenberg would have been better served by awaiting the arrival of his remaining corps as well as the entire Army of Poland, all of which were still thirty-seven miles south of Leipzig in the Waldheim–Penig region. Yet numerous concerns over both Napoleon's intentions and the strength of the French forces assembled at Leipzig convinced Schwarzenberg of the need to commence his main attack by the 16th. Some of Schwarzenberg's advisors speculated that the emperor would accept battle only on the northern side of Leipzig. Others assumed he would not accept battle at all but instead would withdraw to the Elbe and utilize all of his forces against the North German and Silesian Armies. Still others counseled that Napoleon would shed no further blood to maintain his position at Leipzig, although this idea held little sway by the evening of the 15th.

Unconfirmed reports correctly stated that Napoleon entered Leipzig on the 14th with his Guard. Except for a few detachments still en route to Leipzig, he managed to concentrate his masses. Yet the Allies had not. Moreover, their available forces were somewhat fragmented rather than concentrated. With all of its corps assembled, Schwarzenberg's Army of

Bohemia could face Napoleon's army alone. However, on 16 October, Schwarzenberg divided the Army of Bohemia into three parts incapable of mutual support due to the impassable waters of the Pleiße and the Elster. On Schwarzenberg's right, 96,000 soldiers attacked Napoleon's left and center on the Pleiße; in the Allied center, 28,000 Austrians advanced in the marshy and densely overgrown region between the Pleiße and the Elster to attack Napoleon's right and rear. On the left, Gyulay's 19,000 Austrians along with Blücher's army attacked between the upper and lower Elster to close the Lindenau defile through which ran the main highway from Leipzig to the west.

Planning for the opportunity that had eluded him since his victory at Dresden six weeks earlier, Napoleon no longer worried about keeping the Allied armies apart and welcomed the chance to decide the issue with one great battle. He had no clear idea how far south Bernadotte and Blücher had advanced but Schwarzenberg's mammoth army stood within striking distance. Unfortunately for Napoleon, the disjointed Allied assault that opened the battle in the Wachau sector commenced before his troops could move up, especially Macdonald's XI Corps, which had yet to reach its position for the flanking movement.[20] This forced the emperor to plug holes in his line with Guard units at the beginning of the battle rather than save the Grande Reserve for the *coup de grâce*. Although the French repulsed Wittgenstein's initial attack, Napoleon could not regain his balance and coordination for the rest of the struggle on the 16th. Moreover, his Regular Reserve never arrived. Northwest of Leipzig, Blücher's advance through Schkeuditz fixed Marmont's VI Corps; Gyulay's attack forced Ney to redirect Bertrand's IV Corps to Lindenau; and III Corps reached the emperor too late.[21] Thus, Napoleon's last opportunity to achieve a decisive victory on German soil failed. Had Napoleon enveloped Schwarzenberg on 16 October, he would have destroyed the Sixth Coalition that very day.[22]

Blücher's arrival denied Napoleon the forces he planned to use to destroy the Bohemian Army. Committed to the battle at the correct place and time, the 25,000 men of VI and III Corps would have obtained victory for him. Wittgenstein's early start, the late arrival of the French corps, Tsar Alexander's battlefield leadership, and the grit of the Allied soldiers did the rest.[23] Nevertheless, Blücher deserves much credit for preventing Napoleon from concentrating all his forces along the decisive front of the extended battlefield. Lieven compares Blücher's "achievement at Leipzig ... to his impact on the battle of Waterloo. By arriving on the battlefield much earlier than expected, he diverted a key part of the strategic reserve on which the emperor was counting to decide the battle on its main front." Although the French label the battle of Wachau as one of the emperor's victories, at best it ended in a draw. Considering Napoleon's dire need for a decisive victory on 16 October, it is not an exaggeration to label

Wachau a strategic defeat. Fighting the Allies to a draw meant that the emperor would be forced to wage a defensive struggle against enemy forces that would increase exponentially compared to the reinforcements he could expect to receive. Thus, Blücher's victory at Möckern proved monumental. Marmont maintains that "this battle on the 16th decided the fate of Germany" and that "the great question was answered on the 16th." Friederich goes as far as to say that "the salvation of the Bohemian Army must be attributed solely to Blücher's timely intervention: his victory at Möckern countered the success Napoleon had achieved at Wachau. Although the French are justified in labeling the battle of Wachau as one of the emperor's victories, this day actually produced the decision for the entire struggle and broke Napoleon's mastery over Germany."[24]

In summarizing the struggle on the 18th, we see that imperial forces defeated every Allied attack against Napoleon's right wing along the Connewitz–Probstheida line. Despite being outnumbered, Murat's men bravely defended Connewitz: a position vital to Napoleon's line of retreat. Thus, the loss of Dösen, Dölitz, and Lößnig mattered little as long as Murat held Connewitz. Along Napoleon's center and left wing, the Allies took his forward positions of Zuckelhausen, Holzhausen, the Naundorfs, Mölkau, Paunsdorf, Stünz, Sellerhausen, and Schönefeld, driving Macdonald and Ney into the main position of Stötteritz–Crottendorf–Reudnitz. Without Langeron's corps, Blücher made no progress against Napoleon's extreme left wing north of Leipzig. In the rear of the Grande Armée at Lindenau, Bertrand redeemed himself for Wartenburg by defeating Gyulay and opening the road to the Saale; his vanguard reached Weißenfels while his main body halted at Lützen.

Despite the overwhelming numerical superiority at Bernadotte's disposal, his army achieved little during the "Battle of the Nations." Bernadotte's late arrival on the field – along with Allied concerns that Napoleon would attempt to escape to the Elbe – shaped the battle on the 18th. Because the North German Army took so long to reach its position, Bennigsen could not concentrate his forces in the Probstheida–Naundorf sector but instead extended them north to close the gap between himself and Blücher: the gap created by Bernadotte's tardiness. Here we see a situation where Bennigsen's better judgment caused him to commit an error. Concerned that Napoleon would exploit the gap between his army and Blücher's, Bennigsen increasingly pushed his right north and into this gap rather than continue his offensive movement. This mistake, which arose from the ignorance of the situation at Lindenau and the misunderstanding of Napoleon's intentions, would have been avoided had Bernadotte's army reached its position by 11:00 A.M. rather than 4:00 P.M. After arriving, Bernadotte remained content with driving back the enemy some thousand yards and taking the villages of Schönefeld, Sellerhausen, and Stünz. His forces could have achieved much more had he committed them with determination and energy. Instead, only a part of Bülow's corps saw action, and of Wintzingerode's Russians and Stedingk's Swedes only the artillery played a role. The usually objective Friederich notes that "the blame for this weak leadership must alone be attributed to the person of the crown prince who, of course, on this day of numerous examples of outstanding bravery, could not put aside the excess of caution that he had displayed in his leadership throughout the entire campaign."[25]

Bernadotte's extreme prudence alone does not account for Schwarzenberg's failure to exploit his numerical superiority and deliver a crushing blow. Instead, the Allied commander in chief – with the approval of Alexander and Frederick William – relied on tactical maneuvers to grind up Napoleon's army, in turn doing the same to his own. If ever there was a time for "the Coalition's man" to rise to the occasion, 18 October was the day. The resources at Schwarzenberg's disposal had never before been seen on a European battlefield. Gneisenau thus described the situation on the 18th: "Yesterday, the vast masses struggled against each other. It was a spectacle that has not been seen for thousands of years. From a hill I could oversee the opposing armies. Much blood has been spilled. The dead and mutilated lay along a stretch that is miles long. We finally drove the French army thickly together in a narrow space close to Leipzig."[26] Allied forces outnumbered Napoleon's by 135,000 men; they possessed double the number of artillery and could oppose Napoleon's 30,000 cavalry with at least 60,000 sabers. In view of these numbers, it is difficult to exonerate Allied High Command for the day's paltry results. The shortcomings of the Allied attack plan become even more egregious when we bear in mind that circumstances clearly limited Napoleon to a defensive. While German historians such as Bernhardi and Friederich oversimplify by referring to 18 October as nothing more than a great rearguard engagement, securing the Grande Armée's line of retreat to Erfurt remained Napoleon's primary objective.[27]

As late as 17 October, Napoleon still could have directed his army to numerous points on the Elbe by marching north or east. Moreover, he could have salvaged the situation on 17 October by turning against Blücher. Unger maintains that "without doubt, had he found his old energy on the evening of 16 October, instead of negotiating on the 17th, he could have overrun Blücher. Without question, Bernadotte would have retreated before such a blow."[28] We can only imagine the reaction by Allied Headquarters to the news that Blücher had been crushed and Bernadotte was in full retreat. With Napoleon "on the loose," it is difficult to believe that Schwarzenberg would have maintained his position before Leipzig. The memory of having his flanks crushed at Dresden by Napoleon's superior operational skills would have proven too much for the Allies and a retreat from Leipzig would have ensued. Langeron offers another option for Napoleon on the 17th: "He still could have ... moved back with all of his forces, by the Lützen road, and opened a passage by attacking Gyulay's corps, which was not strong enough to resist an attack by the entire enemy force, and it would have been impossible for us [the Silesian Army] to have been able to help him in time, as between him and us was the Elster, the Lippe, and a marshy area that was slow and difficult to cross but easy to defend. Therefore, we would not have been able to make a strong enough diversion to save Gyulay if Napoleon had detached enough men to block us. Without us, without Bennigsen, or the prince of Sweden, the Grand Army was not strong enough to face him alone. Nevertheless, he had already lost too much time; either of the options that remained to him offered many dangers but they were still preferable to the one he chose, to wait for us at Leipzig and there to risk a battle that he could not hope to win and the loss of which could destroy his entire army."[29]

On the 18th, Bernadotte's army plugged the hole that provided the escape route to the Elbe, thus confining Napoleon to the only direction that remained open: west to the Saale. To complicate his situation, he had at his disposal only one road – the long Lindenau defile – across which the army could withdraw. Guarding that vital lifeline to the west required Napoleon to spread the army along a fourteen-mile semicircle around Leipzig. Naturally, his central position provided him with the advantage of being able to quickly shift reserves to bolster weak points, but the army's extension prevented him from maintaining any offensive action. Because only one escape route remained open, an Allied breakthrough *anywhere* along the line would jeopardize the entire army. Thus, his vaunted Imperial Guard received the defensive task of preventing the Allies from breaching the perimeter.

Conversely, the principal objective of the Allied attack plan should have been to direct overwhelming force at one point along the enemy line – a point where a breakthrough would have been especially detrimental to a French retreat. Meanwhile, economy of force diversions would be executed along other points of the French line to pin the enemy and prevent Napoleon from transferring reinforcements to counter the main threat. Either these points escaped the attention of the Coalition's military leaders such as the tsar, or the Austrians did not want to see French power destroyed on 18 October. Both reasons probably played a role at Allied Headquarters as did the lack of unity of command and the reluctance to place too much responsibility on the other Allied armies. Had Schwarzenberg truly served as the actual Allied commander in chief orchestrating the operations of four armies toward the goal of destroying French military power in Germany, his battle plan for the 18th would have been very different.

Although the fighting on the 16th ended in a relative stalemate south of Leipzig, Blücher's victory at Möckern had brought his army to the Halle suburb and the very gates of the city. This meant that the Army of Silesia stood closest to Napoleon's line of retreat when fighting resumed on the 18th. However, Schwarzenberg's attack plan on the 18th solely concentrated on the French position south of Leipzig while the same plan failed to provide Allied forces north of the city with a specific objective. Here we see the consequences of previous failed attempts by both Schwarzenberg *and* Alexander to coordinate the operations of the Silesian and North German Armies. During the Fall Campaign, both Blücher and Bernadotte refused to comply with directives from Allied Headquarters, whether signed by Schwarzenberg or the tsar. Thus, despite the exalted title of "Allied commander in chief," Schwarzenberg in practice thus far had enjoyed little of his theoretical authority. As for Alexander, as much as he fancied himself the generalissimo of the Allied armies, doubt remained whether he could hold Bernadotte or Blücher to his will.

Intertwined with this uncertainty was the concern of placing too much responsibility on an army other than the Bohemian. Tasking Blücher or Bernadotte with delivering the decisive blow would have required the risk of depending on the latter to take the most direct road across the Parthe as early as possible on the 18th and then conduct an energetic attack. Friederich maintains that, had the North German Army marched from Breitenfeld around 4:00 A.M. rather than at 9:00 and had it crossed the Parthe at Mockau instead of Taucha, Bernadotte could have engaged Ney's 36,000 men by 11:00 with some 80,000 men including Langeron. This numerical superiority would soon have forced Napoleon to send all his reserves to the Parthe, thus greatly facilitating Schwarzenberg's attacks along the Lößnig–Probstheida–Holzhausen line, regardless of Bernadotte's success.[30] Yet it is difficult to imagine any Allied leader having confidence in Bernadotte's willingness to comply based on his past actions. As we have seen, the crown prince effectively prevented Blücher from playing this role by stripping him of Langeron's corps. In the end, it is difficult to censure Bernadotte enough for his performance at Leipzig.[31]

As the criticism of Schwarzenberg benefits from hindsight, we must question whether it is fair to hold the Austrian commander as well as the rest of the Coalition's leaders accountable for failing to devise a more imaginative battle plan that sought a decisive victory. Napoleon's skill at maneuvering warranted the concern that he might attempt to reach Wittenberg or Torgau. Moreover, despite the disaster in Russia the previous year, his reputation as a genius on the battlefield largely remained intact. Memories of countless defeats at the hands of Napoleon going back to 1796 had been burned in the collective memory of the Austrian military establishment. Consequently, a cautious approach that left little room for errors that could benefit Napoleon appeared to be the wisest course of action. As Alexander stamped his approval on the attack disposition and, unlike the plan of attack for the 16th, did not make any modifications, we can assume that the will of Allied Headquarters strongly favored a conservative approach that provided no opportunities for the master to exploit.

Despite opting for prudence and its associated disadvantages, by the evening of 18 October the Allies had decisively defeated Napoleon's left wing, driving it back to the immediate vicinity of Leipzig. Only extreme efforts enabled Murat and Macdonald to maintain the right wing and center respectively. In a sense, the Allies fell just short of a total victory, which in view of Napoleon's situation could have been his Sedan. Almost 100,000 Allied soldiers and more than 100 guns had yet to be committed when darkness largely put an end to the fighting. At most, Napoleon had 10,000–12,000 fresh troops at his disposal. Had the Allies employed their additional 100,000 men in the right place and at the right time, French forces would have been driven into Leipzig on the 18th and their retreat on the 19th would have been seriously jeopardized. Fault for allowing this opportunity to slip away lies with Bernadotte, Schwarzenberg, and Alexander.

Older French works claim that Napoleon repulsed every Allied attack but that the shortage of ammunition ultimately forced him to retreat. This excuse proves to be as empty as Napoleon's own statements that the defection of the Saxons cost him the battle.[32] Even without these setbacks, the astounding numerical superiority of the Allies would have led to the destruction or surrender of his forces on the 19th. With the exception of a few brigades of Old Guard, all of Napoleon's troops saw action on the 18th while Allied reserves, including the majority of Bernadotte's army, remained relatively fresh. Thus, had Napoleon decided to make a stand at Leipzig, he would have suffered a military defeat that quite conceivably could have expanded to a political disaster like Waterloo. Exiting Leipzig enabled Napoleon to return to the open field, where he could hope to use his operational mastery to exploit Allied mistakes. By retreating, Napoleon secured the opportunity to extricate the majority of his 140,000-man army. Although it proved to be impossible for him to do this, his return to France with an army of 60,000 men at least provided him with the possibility of rallying his subjects. At this time, French forces still retained control of Italy and the Low Countries. The chance always existed that the Allies would stop at the Rhine or that Francis would not wish to see his son-in-law humbled any further. By sacrificing Germany, Emperor Napoleon gave General Bonaparte a chance in 1814. Considering the extent of Allied discord *after* the victory at Leipzig, this turned out to be a wise move. Thus, the question should not be why Napoleon retreated from Leipzig, but why did he not retreat as soon as the Allies foiled his plan for 16 October?

Napoleon postponed the retreat until the 18th for numerous reasons. First, he hoped the Allies might blunder. Second, he attempted to divide the Allies by offering to negotiate an armistice with his father-in-law, Kaiser Francis. After the fighting on the 16th, Napoleon resorted to his usual tactic of providing misinformation to intimidate his opponent. During a long conversation with the captured corps commander, Merveldt, Napoleon told the Austrian that he possessed 200,000 infantry and a huge force of cavalry. In the same breath, he expressed his earnest desire for peace. Napoleon paroled Merveldt, tasking him with the delivery of an offer for an armistice that included the French evacuation of Danzig, Modlin, Stettin, Küstrin, Glogau, Dresden, Torgau, and if necessary Wittenberg. Moreover, the Grande Armée would withdraw west of the Saale. As for peace terms, Napoleon declared himself ready to return Hanover to Great Britain; Hamburg and Lübeck would become neutral; the Netherlands would receive its independence; and the French and Italian crowns would be separated. Although Merveldt reported to the Allied sovereigns that Napoleon looked jaded, ill, and depressed, and would probably retreat all the way to the Rhine, "this insidious proposal, however, was of course rejected."[33] Not only did the peace initiative fail, but it also served to strengthen Allied resolve by convincing Napoleon's foes that he was spent.

Two contemporaries offer opposing views of Napoleon during the battle of Leipzig that reflected their personal feelings. First, the Saxon staff officer and member of Napoleon's suite, Odeleben, who did little to hide his contempt for the emperor, maintains that "all the dispositions and preparations at headquarters indicated the emperor's intentions to retreat." Nevertheless, Napoleon could not bring himself to retreat on the 17th after touting the struggle on the 16th as a French victory. "But he had caused his pretended triumph to be celebrated by the ringing of bells, and all possible demonstrations of joy. Therefore, greater results appeared justly to be expected." Conversely, if he retreated on the 17th, "everyone would have said he was beaten ... Thus, on Sunday, 17 October, he obstinately determined not to quit his position, lest he should appear to have been defeated. To justify a retreat in the eyes of his nation and army, he had to remain master of the field of battle for an entire day." In this way, a scapegoat could be found.[34]

Pelet, who commanded a brigade in Oudinot's I Corps of Young Guard and later became a historian of the French General Staff, claims that Allied positions and the very nature of the retreat provided Napoleon with solid reasons to postpone the retreat for twenty-four hours. Reports indicated that Liechtenstein's 1st Light Division still held Markranstädt but Napoleon did not know that Gyulay had withdrawn from Lindenau and recrossed the Elster. Yet he acknowledged that Austrian troops from General Murray's 2nd Division of Gyulay's III Corps held the easily defended defile of Bad Kösen. Moreover, the chance that Murray would receive support from the corps echeloned in the rear of the Bohemian Army or that they could be sent to the banks of the Elster concerned the emperor. Enemy detachments could also occupy the defile of the Rippach at Poserna and that of the Saale at

Weißenfels as well as various positions on the Saale as far as Bad Kösen. It would be difficult to force these defiles and dangerous to attack them when the possibility existed to be attacked from behind by a pursuing Allied army. Moreover, the unruly French national character likewise presented challenges. Pelet asserts that "the problem consisted of moving an army followed by 20,000 horses dragging 600 pieces of cannon, parks, and crews beyond Leipzig and on the long, narrow, and winding Lindenau defile ... a weakened army, shaken in its physical and moral organization ... A retreat performed in the presence of powerful [enemy] forces is the most difficult operation with French troops; we openly affirm this."

According to Pelet's polemic, Napoleon responded to these considerations by first concealing from the army "for as long as possible" his decision to retreat and then completely deceiving the Allies. Had the emperor commenced the retreat early on the 17th, Pelet argues that Gyulay, Colloredo, and Bernadotte could have moved toward Weißenfels and fixed the Grande Armée until Blücher and the rest of Schwarzenberg's army arrived. "On the 18th," Pelet declares, "the emperor would have found the enemy armies arranged against him between the upper and lower Elster." To avoid this scenario, Pelet argues, Napoleon implemented a two-step plan. Leaving Ney to make his arrangements north of the city and Bertrand to increase the defensive measures on Leipzig's western side, he ordered the corps that fought south of Leipzig to maintain the ground taken from the Allies on the 16th. "This offensive attitude intimidated them; and their fears are seen in their precautions," asserts Pelet. Second, he contracted his southern front at 2:00 A.M. on 18 October but still had Ney hold the Parthe north of Leipzig. "In this position," argues Pelet, "the French army maintained space to fight and maneuver in front of the city. On the 18th, it was able to withstand four armies that surrounded it." In contracting his southern front, Napoleon assumed that the Bohemian and Polish Armies would not reach the new position to engage his army until late on the morning of the 18th. Pelet states that Napoleon figured that, in the north, Ney would hold the Silesian and North German Armies at the Parthe. If either sought to take the detour through Taucha, it would not be able to come on line until the afternoon. Ney could then hold the narrow space between Schönefeld and Stünz, where he could easily stop Blücher and Bernadotte. All of this would buy time for IV Corps and Mortier's Young Guard to secure the road to Weißenfels, for the parks to cross the defile, and for the army to prepare to follow during the night of 18/19 October. "With such arrangements," concludes Pelet, "it was likely that the Allies would not try to attack, or they would have to delay it until the 19th in order to fully unite their armies."[35]

We will never be certain of Napoleon's exact thoughts in the period between the end of the fighting on the 16th and the issuing of his orders to

Bertrand to commence the retreat on the 18th. Admittedly it is hard to accept Pelet's eloquent explanation that Napoleon "feared" being caught by the perpetually slow moving Austrians or even Bernadotte and so used Leipzig as bait to lure all four Allied armies, fix them there, and make good his escape on the 19th. While this is certainly how the battle played out, Pelet may have employed too much hindsight to excuse his idol's mistakes. Much more likely appear the explanations provided by military historians. The heavy fighting on the 16th – particularly the events at Möckern – should have convinced Napoleon of the Coalition's resolve but, as Petre notes, "Emperor Napoleon was now, to a great extent, the master of General Bonaparte, and the Emperor could not bear to yield what practically meant his dominion in Germany, though the General saw that to do this was the only hope." Making the decision to retreat was not easy, as Yorck von Wartenburg comments: "only a very decisive victory on this day [the 16th], when the relative numbers were still fairly equal, could have saved him. Such a victory he had failed to gain, and in a military sense there was now only one thing to be done, namely, to retreat at once. But in that case Napoleon as a monarch was lost, and the interests of the sovereign had precedence over, though they were at variance with, those of General Napoleon."[36]

Schwarzenberg's failure to move more Allied cavalry and artillery followed by the reserves to Zwenkau and Pegau during the night of 18/19 October to harass Napoleon's retreat on the following morning remains unexplained. For more decisive results, this vanguard could have fixed the French army in a position that would have allowed the Bohemian Army to reach it after taking Leipzig. As the battle on the 19th unfolded, the Bohemian Army did little after Bennigsen shifted his forces to the west. Had Schwarzenberg acted on the initial reports that the French had evacuated the battlefield, he would have had plenty of time to move at least the reserves of the Bohemian Army west and order the entire Silesian Army to follow Yorck's corps. This would still have left the North German and Polish Armies to fix Napoleon's rearguard at Leipzig. Some German historians attribute this omission to Austrian diplomacy, claiming that Metternich wanted to leave the road to the Rhine open for Napoleon. No evidence exists to support this view but, if it was indeed the case, then Schwarzenberg would have received such instructions from Kaiser Francis and thus cannot be held accountable. Friederich maintains that an explanation for the omissions of the 18th and 19th can be found in "the general conditions of the coalition, but especially the personality of the commander in chief and from the motives and views that he and his entourage brought into this war."[37]

For the pursuit after Leipzig, we once again return to Blücher. "That the rejoicing over the hard-fought victory, the joy over the final union of the three Allied armies, the mutual salutations, the concern for the wounded, dead, and captured, the assembly and reorganization of the troops, and finally the general relaxation of the nerves that took such a claim on the leading personalities on the 19th led them to forget about the pursuit of the defeated enemy is humanly understandable, but inexcusable from a military point of view. Blücher was the only exception."[38] After reaching the timber market, he recognized that the blowing of the Elster bridge had cut off the French in the city. Rather than move more of his own troops into the city, he and Gneisenau issued orders to halt, reassemble, and march as fast as possible to Schkeuditz. He wanted his Russian infantry to reach Schkeuditz that evening so the advance to Lützen could begin on the morning of the 20th. As for the other armies, only Bülow sent forward his entire cavalry through Leipzig to the immediate pursuit of the French around 2:30. Nevertheless, the Prussians could not extend beyond the Halle Gate because of the backlog at the blown Elster bridge. In the evening, Bennigsen ordered the majority of his cavalry to swim across the Elster followed somewhat later by Paskevich's 26th Division, which crossed the river via footbridges that had been built with much difficulty.

As for the attempts to inflict damage on the Grande Armée after Leipzig, Yorck can be faulted for not renewing his attack before dawn on 22 October; he could have rested his men and then stormed Freyburg as the French army's baggage crossed the Unstrut. While capturing the enemy's train certainly would have provided a symbolic victory, it would not have brought the Allies any closer to preventing Napoleon's breakout at Freyburg. Due to the crushing superiority of Allied forces around Leipzig, the results of the pursuit should have been very different. In evaluating Yorck's operations between 18 and 22 October, it is difficult to imagine that his exhausted men could have done more. It is unlikely that I Corps could have moved any faster to Weißenfels and Freyburg after first being dispatched north to Halle. The reasons for the Allied failure lie in the nature of the French retreat and the Allied pursuit in general, rather than Yorck's specific actions. First, the retreat itself had started late on the 18th, when Napoleon ordered the baggage and part of his Reserve Cavalry to evacuate Leipzig over the Lindenau causeway and across the Elster River. At 2:00 A.M. on the 19th, the Reserve Artillery followed by the Imperial Guard, IV Cavalry Corps, X and II Corps, and II Cavalry Corps withdrew from Leipzig. As a result, the majority of French troops that escaped Leipzig had left the city long before the panic and horror at the Elster bridge. This circumstance allowed the retreat to the Saale to proceed in fairly good order, although discipline started to unravel almost as soon as the French army reached the river.

Second, the 19th slipped away while Allied High Command celebrated the great victory and debated the next step. This allowed Napoleon's main body to reach Lützen unmolested. Lacking bridges over the Pleiße and

Elster Rivers, the Allies could not launch an immediate pursuit. In addition, Oudinot's successful rearguard action at Lindenau stymied Allied attempts to directly pursue the emperor on the solid highway that ran southwest through Lützen, Weißenfels, and Naumburg to Erfurt and ultimately Mainz. The French army thus won a headstart of approximately eighteen hours. Schwarzenberg did much to close the gap by reaching Naumburg and forcing Napoleon to take the detour through Freyburg. This at least allowed the two wings of the Allied armies – Yorck and Gyulay – to establish contact with the enemy. However, Yorck did not possess the combat power to make much of a difference. Although Gyulay displayed the speed needed in a decisive pursuit by actually getting in front of Napoleon's army, he too commanded fewer than 15,000 men.

The reason for the Allied failure to catch the French army at two river crossings is simple: the favorable point in time to launch the pursuit had already been lost. This was the evening of 18 October, when Yorck's battered survivors of Möckern were ordered north to Halle. Stronger forces should have been dispatched to threaten the retreat, but the Allied sovereigns and monarchs did not want to weaken the armies around Leipzig. Instead of creating a trap that would close tightly, the Allies prepared a mighty blow that would once and for all smash the French army.[39]

An analysis of the Allied pursuit to the Rhine River following the epic four-day struggle at Leipzig must take into consideration the general situation rather than unrealistic expectations and overly critical evaluations. Blücher's army took the lead in the pursuit, but his battered forces hardly sufficed for the task. Müffling's remark that "the two corps of Sacken and Yorck were so thinned that they might be considered as only advance guards" cannot be viewed as an exaggeration.[40] It is difficult to find any real advantages that favored the men of the Silesian Army other than the simple fact that the French had lost at Leipzig and they had won. After clearing Freyburg, the French army struck a solid highway. Napoleon refused to allow the Silesian Army to close the gap.[41] Instead, his army marched continuously because the declining moral and physical health of his men would not permit the emperor to accept battle; if necessary, the rearguard would be sacrificed so that the army could reach the Rhine.[42] Hilly, sometimes mountainous, and barely passable terrain stretched on either side of his road from the Saale to the Rhine. This meant that little could be expected from flank maneuvers. Although human elements such as Yorck's defiance and Russian lethargy played a role, it was hardly possible for the Silesian Army to make up the ground between it and Napoleon, despite Blücher's forced marches. Numerous eyewitness testimonies attest not only to the deterioration of the French army, but also to the privations suffered by the pursuing Allied forces. Even Blücher admitted that he lost many people to exhaustion.[43] Müffling, however, offers the simplest explanation:

> There are days or seasons in an army, when all the operations, from the moment they are prepared, are well understood and executed by the troops. There are other times and other days when nothing will go right, when stoppages and difficulties, which no one has calculated, arise in the simplest matters. Such a time had now set in with the Silesian Army, but there was no accounting for the why or wherefore. Perhaps it was the thought that the enemy had to cross the Rhine and would march so fast that it would be impossible to overtake him, and thus it would be of little consequence to reach the Rhine a day or two later.[44]

In the final assessment, it is difficult to disagree with Gneisenau's view of the Silesian Army's operations: "Through the steps that our army has made, through its bold movements, through the battles and combats that it has won, and through the advice which our headquarters has given, it has done so much for the advantageous turn of the war. The victories of the other armies remained without results and only ours have altered the course of events."[45] Although extremely pro-Prussian, the frank and dour British officer Colonel Lowe argued in his 31 October letter to Charles Stewart that the Silesian Army should be considerably reinforced because "the Army of Silesia has been the principal *operating* army since the opening of the campaign, arising probably from the simple cause: its having one only leading military object in view, to find out the enemy and attack him where it could. Other armies have been more liable to be influenced by political considerations ... which lead sometimes into deviations that do not bear the test of military reasoning and as this Army has been and is still likely to be the principal operating weapon without any suspicion that political or other motives whatever can occasion it to deviate from the direction in which it can strike hardest, the more force with which it can give the blows the better."[46]

Turning to Napoleon, similar to the Russian Campaign one year earlier, his "Second Saxon Campaign" ended in failure: Germany was lost for good. Following Leipzig, the remnants of the Grande Armée of 1813 retreated to the Rhine River to defend France's natural frontiers as Napoleon's empire crumbled. The liberation of Germany, which started on the fields of Großbeeren, quickly accelerated after Leipzig as one by one Napoleon's satellites withdrew from the Confederation of the Rhine. However, the war did not end with Napoleon's defeat at Leipzig. Following the battle, the remnants of the Grande Armée of 1813 retreated across the Rhine at Mainz. Fewer than 60,000 soldiers returned to France in early November 1813. Although the emperor continued on to Paris, he left his shattered army on the left bank of the historic Rhine in the hands of his equally shattered marshals, who received the impossible task of defending the eastern frontier from Switzerland to the North Sea. Another bloody campaign ensued until the Allies captured Paris on 31 March 1814 and Napoleon abdicated on 6 April.

The Coalition's decisive victory in Germany raises the question: had Napoleon's skills deteriorated over time? The answer is inextricably connected to the quality of the Grande Armée, which peaked in the years 1805–1807 following the intense training it had received in the years prior to the War of the Third Coalition. After sustaining irreplaceable losses in 1807, Napoleon then committed many of the survivors to Iberia, from where they would never return. After exhausting this invaluable, highly trained force, he became increasingly dependent on German, Italian, and Polish manpower that had not received training on par with the original Grande Armée. The imperial forces that waged Napoleon's wars from 1809 onward simply could not rival the performance of the Grande Armée that had won the Wars of the Third and Fourth Coalitions. Coinciding with this qualitative decline is a marked change in Napoleon's tactics. Instead of continuing the progression of his tactical innovations for battlefield problem-solving, Napoleon became increasingly dependent on the weight of massed batteries, huge formations, and unimaginative frontal assaults as illustrated by the battles of Aspern-Essling, Wagram, Borodino, and Waterloo.

Defeat in 1813 in part can be attributed to the marshals whom Napoleon selected to conduct independent operations. While Davout, perhaps the greatest of Napoleon's lieutenants, languished in Hamburg in 1813, Marshals Ney, Oudinot, and Macdonald received independent commands at the army level. In particular, the emperor's failure to appoint officers capable of independent army command symbolizes the lapse in judgment that plagued his last campaigns. Particularly after the defection of his chief of staff, Jomini, Ney simply could not coordinate independent operations. Yet is it fair to condemn Napoleon's brave and loyal lieutenants? It should be noted that Oudinot, Macdonald, and Ney never possessed the same resources as did Napoleon. Wherever Napoleon went so did his Imperial Guard. Not only did the Guard serve as the epitome of the period's most elite fighting force, but it provided Napoleon with the ultimate trump card. As we have seen, Napoleon favored having both a Regular Reserve and a Grande Reserve – the Guard, infantry, cavalry, and artillery. In numerous battles, he committed the Guard to deliver the *coup de grâce* after expending his regular reserve. None of the marshals who commanded independently in 1813 enjoyed the luxury of being able to commit the bearskins. Moreover, as the Army of Berlin and the Army of the Bober each consisted of three army corps and one cavalry corps, their commanders would have been hard pressed to mimic the master's practice of assigning the role of Regular

Reserve to an entire army corps, or to one-third of the combined-arms forces. Admittedly, although the Guard probably would not have helped Macdonald all that much at the Katzbach, Oudinot and Ney certainly would have benefited from the use of these crack troops.

Napoleon's thoughts on his subordinates' failures are best seen in a long conversation he had on the evening of 8 September while dining with Murat and St.-Cyr. During the course of the dinner, Napoleon's aide-de-camp, General Anne-Charles Lebrun, arrived with a detailed account of Ney's defeat at Dennewitz. With "unshakable composure," the emperor listened to every detail and then asked a few questions. On finishing, Napoleon clearly and correctly explained to Murat and St.-Cyr the reasons for Ney's failure but showed not the slightest dissatisfaction with Ney or his subordinates. In Napoleon's view, the cause lay in the difficulty of the art of war, which had not yet been brought to light. "If," he concluded "time will allow me, I will produce a book in which I will develop all the rules of war with such clarity that it will be accessible to all military men like any other science." Then the discussion turned to the question of how far practice influenced a commander's skill in the art of war. Napoleon opined that only Louis XIV's general, Henri de La Tour d'Auvergne, Vicomte de Turenne, had succeeded in perfecting his own innate talent through experience. In his opinion, only Turenne had obtained what he hoped to explain in his future teachings on the art of war.[47] The fact that the marshals consistently failed to meet their master's expectations underscores Napoleon's failure to grasp the importance of an adequate general staff system. Moreover, his fatal tendency to underestimate the numbers of his adversaries and overestimate his own did little to help his lieutenants.

After losing the Grande Armée of 1812 in Russia, Napoleon commenced the War of the Sixth Coalition with young conscripts – both French and foreign – who lacked all but rudimentary training. With the exception of Bautzen, he rarely sought to achieve victory through operational maneuver. In itself, the absence of a progression on the operational level reflects three important considerations concerning Napoleon's generalship during the last years of the empire. First, he understood that the qualitative decline of his army placed limitations on his operations and tactics. Second, he increasingly viewed his adversaries with utter contempt. Lacking respect for his enemy's capabilities, Napoleon waged war with a false sense of infallibility that stifled his novel approach to battlefield problem-solving. Third, Emperor Napoleon increasingly placed emphasis on securing geographic objectives such as Berlin and Dresden as opposed to General Bonaparte's maxim of annihilating the enemy army and destroying his ability to resist. Compounding these developments, the aging marshalate and incompetent divisional generals often rendered "outside-the-box" thinking impractical. Odeleben offers an insightful explanation on this issue:

Napoleon, as it has been remarked, appeared to consider attacking his enemy not according to any particular plan, or in accordance with tactical principles, but rather according to a self-confidence in his own ability to overcome the enemy by taking advantage of his errors. He was uncertain where to expect the principal attack. He appeared to wait at Zittau and Görlitz, to ascertain on which side he had most to apprehend. Formerly accustomed to taking the offensive and deceiving his enemies by maneuvers that astonished them, he now changed his character and was obliged to wait in order to discover where he himself was to receive the most serious blow, ready at the same time to parry it, and on whatever point it might fall to assure himself of the victory. Therefore, he could not reckon on pursuing a well-grounded and invariable plan of operation because the offensive attitude of his enemies would determine all the measures he would take in response.[48]

In operations, Napoleon suffered no rival; the Coalition's commanders, including the duke of Wellington, could not match him. In strategy, however, the Reichenbach Plan exhausted both the emperor and his army, keeping him off balance and robbing him of one of his greatest maxims – initiative. Just as important as the Reichenbach Plan was the "community of interest" that solidified the Sixth Coalition in 1813. Political unity had not been a characteristic of the previous coalitions that France had faced. However, in 1813 Napoleon confronted a coalition marked by an unprecedented degree of unity. Lastly, the adoption of many French innovations, especially the corps system, which allowed for distributed maneuver on the operational level, enabled the Allies to meet Napoleon head on. As his own army declined in quality, Napoleon faced much improved adversaries. After the loss of the Grande Armée of 1813 in Germany, not even Napoleon's mastery of operations could offset the Coalition's vast numerical superiority in 1814.

Notes

1 As Schroeder concludes: "A coalition with a good chance of defeating Napoleon had finally come together; an alliance to forge a durable peace had not yet emerged." See Schroeder, *European Politics*, 476.
2 Lieven, *Russia Against Napoleon*, 356.
3 Unger, *Blücher*, II:53.
4 Friederich, *Herbstfeldzug 1813*, I:346.
5 Bogdanovich, *Geschichte des Krieges*, IIa:82.
6 GStA PK, VI HA Rep. 92 Nl. Gneisenau, Nr. 108. On 11 August, Yorck's corps totaled 1,022 officers and 38,221 men. This figure had dropped to 749 officers and 23,768 men by the 31st.
7 GStA PK, VI HA Rep. 92 Nl. Gneisenau, Nr. 16.
8 Droysen, *Yorck*, II:158.
9 "Battles of Leipzig," Lowe, Add MSS, 20111, 161–62; Stewart, *Narrative*, 149.

10 *CN*, No. 20693, XXVI:290.

11 Friederich, *Herbstfeldzug 1813*, II:281–98; Bogdanovich, *Geschichte des Krieges*, IIb:43–49; Droysen, *Yorck*, II:180–93.

12 Quoted in Wilson to Aberdeen, Penig, 10 October 1813, in Wilson, *Private Diary*, II:439.

13 Friederich, *Herbstfeldzug 1813*, III:431; Lieven, *Russia Against Napoleon*, 388; Wilson to Aberdeen, Marienburg, 5 October 1813, in Wilson, *Private Diary*, II:431.

14 Quoted in Droysen, *Yorck*, II:206.

15 Droysen, *Yorck*, II:206–07.

16 Friederich, *Herbstfeldzug 1813*, III:431–32.

17 Caemmerer, *Befreiungskrieg*, 72–73.

18 Friederich, *Herbstfeldzug 1813*, III:431–32, 468–47.

19 To Schwarzenberg's list of failures Friederich adds: "and to take advantage of the beautiful position of Wachau–Liebertwolkwitz." See Friederich, *Herbstfeldzug 1813*, III:10, 16.

20 Petre maintains that without the Regular Reserve (III and VI Corps and III Cavalry Corps) Macdonald's flanking maneuver would have failed even had the marshal been in position on time: Petre, *Napoleon's Last Campaign*, 349.

21 "This battle was very useful to the Grand Army [of Bohemia] because it forced Napoleon to divide his forces; but what seemed truly inconceivable was that he had so little expected an attack from Blücher that he had sent orders to the troops that were fighting us to join his left so he could reunite all his forces against the Grand Army": "Journal de Langeron," Add MSS, 20112, 274.

22 In *Russia Against Napoleon*, 441, Lieven explains that "Napoleon took it for granted that the bulk of the enemy army would be deployed in the only sensible place, in other words east of the rivers Elster and Pleiße. His plan was to turn the Allies' right flank east of Liebertwolkwitz, smash through their center, and drive Schwarzenberg's army into the Pleiße. Even without Bernadotte and Bennigsen the Allies had 205,000 troops available on 16 October against Napoleon's 190,000. But Schwarzenberg's plan, even after modifications to appease Alexander, meant that on the key southern front 138,000 French troops would face 100,000 Allies, of which Constantine's 24,000 reserves could not arrive on the battlefield for a number of hours. Of course the Allies would outnumber Napoleon in other sectors but the terrain would make it impossible to use this superiority. *On the first day at Leipzig Schwarzenberg therefore gave Napoleon a completely unnecessary chance to snatch victory against the odds and against the previous flow of the autumn campaign*" (emphasis added). Maude notes: "Thus failed one of the greatest, if not the greatest strategic conception in history; for had it succeeded Napoleon's success must have been final and irrevocable. Nothing the Silesian Army could have achieved on the other extremity of the battlefield could have altered the final result, and the Austrian center columns between the Pleiße and Elster could not conceivably have extricated themselves from their hopeless predicament." See Maude, *Leipzig Campaign*, 257.

23 Much credit must also be given to Alexander and his advisors Toll and Jomini for forcing the modification of Schwarzenberg's original plan of attack. In *Napoleon's*

Last Campaign, 348, Petre discusses how the battle on the 16th could have progressed had the Allies launched their attack based on Schwarzenberg's original disposition. Even with III, IV, and VI Corps unavailable, Napoleon could still have won a tactical victory in the Wachau sector. That this did not occur is largely due to Alexander's decision to move up the reserves early in the battle to support the attack of Wittgenstein's five columns.

24 Lieven, *Russia Against Napoleon*, 441–42; Marmont, *Mémoires*, V:289–90; Friederich, *Herbstfeldzug 1813*, III:116.

25 Friederich, *Herbstfeldzug 1813*, III:176.

26 Gneisenau to Caroline, Leipzig, 19 October 1813, GStA PK, VI HA Rep. 92 Nl. Gneisenau, Nr. 21.

27 Bernhardi, *Toll*, III:449; Friederich, *Herbstfeldzug 1813*, III:182; Neubauer, *Preußens Fall und Erhebung*, 475.

28 Unger, *Blücher*, II:115.

29 "Journal de Langeron," Add MSS, 20112, 275–76.

30 Friederich argues that the gap between Bennigsen and Bernadotte could have been filled by Bubna and Platov and, while the latter were too weak to prevent Napoleon from escaping north or east to the Rhine, they could have reported a French breakout early enough to enable Blücher and Bernadotte to advance against his left flank while Bennigsen closed on his right. Even with 160,000 men, Napoleon could hardly hope to reach the Elbe without suffering considerable losses. See Friederich, *Herbstfeldzug 1813*, III:184.

31 "[Charles] Stewart decidedly says that he [Bernadotte] not only did nothing, but willfully avoided doing anything," notes Robert Wilson in his journal, "although he might, by cooperating with Blücher, have crushed a great portion of the enemy's forces; and yet for such a fellow we are to pay £100,000 per month, and sacrifice our best interests and another nation [Denmark] whose enmity will be eternal": Wilson, *Private Diary*, II:186.

32 Vaudoncourt, *Histoire de la guerre*, 218–19; Fain, *1813*, II:430–32; Norvins, *Portefeuille de mil huit cent treize*, II:414.

33 Lowe to Bunbury, Leipzig, 20 October 1813, Add MSS, 20111, 180; Stewart, *Narrative*, 175–76.

34 Odeleben, *A Circumstantial Narrative*, II:24–25.

35 Pelet, *Des principales opérations de la campagne de 1813*, 278–80.

36 Petre, *Napoleon's Last Campaign*, 353; Yorck von Wartenburg, *Napoleon as a General*, II:352.

37 Friederich, *Herbstfeldzug 1813*, III:230–31.

38 Friederich, *Herbstfeldzug 1813*, III:224–25.

39 Müffling, *Aus meinem Leben*, 88; Droysen, *Yorck*, II:237; Friederich, *Herbstfeldzug 1813*, III:269–71.

40 Müffling, *Die Feldzüge*, 107.

41 "Hitherto he [Napoleon] has marched with such expedition that the most advanced of Blücher's advance guard is twelve hours behind him": Wilson to Aberdeen, Hünfeld, 31 October 1813, in Wilson, *Private Diary*, II:474.

42 Yorck von Wartenburg, *Napoleon as a General*, II:366.

43 Blücher to Bonin, 4 November 1813, *Blüchers Briefe*, ed. Unger, 192.

44 Müffling, *Die Feldzüge*, 108.
45 Gneisenau to Caroline, Kleinwiederitzsch, 18 October 1813, GStA PK, VI HA Rep. 92 Nl. Gneisenau, Nr. 21.
46 Lowe to Stewart, Erfurt, 31 October 1813, Add MSS, 20111, 198.
47 St.-Cyr, *Mémoires*, IV:148–50.
48 Odeleben, *A Circumstantial Narrative*, I:262.

Bibliography

ARCHIVES

Baden-Baden, Germany

Ehemals Mitteilungen aus dem Gräflichen Bülow Familien-Archiv zu Grünhoff. Friedrich Wilhelm Graf Bülow von Dennewitz. Dokumentation in Briefen-Befehlen-Berichten. Gesammelt Übertragen und mit Anmerkungen Versehen von Joachim-Albrecht Graf Bülow von Dennewitz

Berlin, Germany

Geheimes Staatsarchiv Preußischer Kulturbesitz zu Berlin

London, United Kingdom

British Manuscript Collection

Moscow, Russia

Rossiiskii Gosudarstvennyi Voenno-Istoricheskii Arkhiv

Paris, France

Service Historique de l'Armée de Terre

PUBLISHED PRIMARY SOURCES

Baillet de Latour, Theodor Franz von. *Erinnerungen an den k. k. Feldzeugmeister und Kriegsminister Theodor Grafen Baillet von Latour.* Gratz, 1849.
Bailleu, Paul, ed. *Briefwechsel König Friedrich Wilhelms III und der Königin Luise mit Kaiser Alexander I nebst ergänzenden fürstlichen Korrespondenzen.* Publicationen aus den königlichen preußischen Archiven, *vol. 75.* Leipzig, 1900.

Bantysh-Kamenskii, Dmitrii. *Slovar dostopamyatnykh lyudei russkoi zemli.* St. Petersburg, 1847.

Berthezène, Pierre. *Souvenirs militaires de la république et de l'empire.* Paris, 1855.

Bieske, Carl Ludwig. *Der Feldmarschall Fürst Gebhard Leberecht Blücher von Wahlstatt.* Berlin, 1862.

Blaise, Jean François and Édouard Lapène. *Campagnes de 1813 et de 1814; sur l'Èbre, les Pyrénées et la Garonne, précédées de considérations sur la dernière guerre d'Espagne.* Paris, 1823.

Blücher, Gebhard Leberecht von. "Aus Blüchers Korrespondenz." Edited by Herman Granier. *Forschungen zur brandenburgischen-preußischen Geschichte* 26 (1913): 149–78.

Blücher in Briefen aus den Feldzügen, 1813–1815. Edited by Wilhelm Günter Enno von Colomb. Stuttgart, 1876.

Blüchers Briefe. Edited by Wilhelm Capelle. Leipzig, 1915.

Blüchers Briefe: Vervollständigte Sammlung des Generals E. v. Colomb. Edited by Wolfgang von Unger. Stuttgart, 1912.

"Zwölf Blücherbriefe." Edited by Herman Granier. *Forschungen zur brandenburgischen-preußischen Geschichte* 12 (1900): 479–96.

Boyen, Hermann von. *Erinnerungen aus dem Leben des General-Feldmarschalls Hermann von Boyen.* Edited by Friedrich Nippold. 3 vols. Leipzig, 1889–90.

Erinnerungen aus dem Leben des General-Feldmarschalls Hermann von Boyen. Edited by Dorothea Schmidt. 2 vols. Berlin, 1990.

Brett-James, Antony. *Europe Against Napoleon: The Leipzig Campaign, 1813, from Eyewitness Accounts.* London, 1970.

Bunbury, Henry. *Memoir and Literary Remains of Lieutenant-General Sir Henry Edward Bunbury, bart.* London, 1868.

Burckhardt, Wilhelm. *Gebhard Leberecht von Blücher preußischer Feldmarschall und Fürst von Wahlstatt: nach Leben, Reden und Thaten geschildert.* Stuttgart, 1835.

Castlereagh, Viscount, Robert Stewart. *The Correspondence, Dispatches and Other Papers of Viscount Castlereagh.* Edited by Charles William Vane. 12 vols. London, 1848–53.

Cathcart, George. *Commentaries on the War in Russia and Germany in 1812 and 1813.* London, 1850.

Chotterel, François Frédéric. *Précis historique de la vie et du procès du maréchal Ney, duc d'Elchingen, prince de la Moskowa, ex-pair de France: avec des notes et particularités curieuses sur sa carrière politique, militaire, ses derniers momens, et les campagnes de Portugal et de Russie.* Paris, 1816.

Clausewitz, C. *La campagne de 1813 et la campagne de 1814.* Paris, 1900.

Der Feldzug 1812 in Rußland und die Befreiungskriege von 1812–1815. Berlin, 1906.

Hinterlassene Werke des Generals Carl von Clausewitz über Krieg und Kriegführung. 10 vols. Berlin, 1832–37.

Historical and Political Writings. Translated and edited by P. Paret and D. Moran. Princeton, NJ, 1992.

Damitz, Karl von. *Geschichte des Feldzuges von 1814 in dem östlichen und nördlichen Frankreich bis zur Einnahme von Paris: als Beitrag zur neueren Kriegsgeschichte.* 3 vols. Berlin, 1842–43.

Ermolov, A. P. *The Czar's General: The Memoirs of a Russian General in the Napoleonic Wars.* Welwyn Garden City, UK, 2005.

Fain, Agathon Jean. *Manuscrit de l'an 1813, contenant le précis des évènements de cette année pour servir à l'histoire de l'empereur Napoléon.* Paris, 1824.

Fane, J. (Lord Burghersh). *Memoir of the Operations of the Allied Armies, Under Prince Schwarzenberg, and Marshal Blücher, During the Latter End of 1813, and the Year 1814.* London, 1822; reprint edn., London, 1996.

Fezansac, Raymond. *Souvenirs militaires de 1804 à 1814.* Paris, 1870.

Gneisenau, August von. *Briefe August Neidhardts von Gneisenau: eine Auswahl.* Edited by Koehler & Amelang Verlagsgesellschaft mbH München. Munich, 2000.

Briefe des Generals Neidhardt von Gneisenau: 1809–1815. Edited by Julius von Pflugk-Harttung. Gotha, 1913.

Gneisenau: ein Leben in Briefen. Edited by Karl Griewank. Leipzig, 1939.

The Life and Campaigns of Field Marshal Prince Blücher. London, 1815.

Neithardt von Gneisenau: Schriften von und über Gneisenau. Edited by Fritz Lange. Berlin, 1954.

Hellwald, F. J. H. and Karl Schönhals. *Der k.k. österreichische Feldmarschall Graf Radetzky: eine biographische Skizze nach den eigenen Dictaten und der Correspondenz des Feldmarschalls von einem österreichischen Veteranen.* Stuttgart, 1858.

Henckel von Donnersmarck, W. L. von. *Erinnerungen aus meinem Leben.* Leipzig, 1846.

Hofmann, Georg Wilhelm von. *Die Schlacht bei Leipzig.* Poznan, 1835.

Höpfner, Eduard von. "Darstellung der Ereignisse bei der Schlesischen Armee." *Militair-Wochenblatt,* 1843–47.

Hüser, Heinrich von. *Denkwürdigkeiten aus dem Leben des Generals der Infanterie von Hüser.* Berlin, 1877.

Jaguin, Louis Ozé. *Historique du 137e régiment d'infanterie.* Fontenay-le-Comte, 1890.

Jomini, Antoine Henri de. *Lettre du général Jomini à M. Capefigue sur son histoire d'Europe pendant le Consulat et l'Empire.* Paris, 1841.

Précis politique et militaire des campagnes de 1812 à 1814. 2 vols. Lausanne, 1886.

Vie politique et militaire de Napoléon. 4 vols. Paris, 1827.

Kankrin, Yegor von. *Uber die Militairökonomie im Frieden und Krieg, und ihr Wechselverhältniss zu den Operationen.* St. Petersburg, 1820.

Koch, Frédéric. *Mémoires pour servir à l'histoire de la campagne de 1814.* Paris, 1819.

Körner, Theodor. *Leyer und Schwert.* Berlin, 1814.

Langeron, Alexandre Louis Andrault. *Mémoires de Langeron, général d'infanterie dans l'armée russe: campagnes de 1812, 1813, 1814.* Paris, 1902.

Larrey, Dominique Jean. *Mémoires de chirurgie militaire et campagnes,* vol. II, *1812–1840: campagnes de Russie, de Saxe et de France, relation médicale de campagnes et voyages, annexes.* 2 vols. Paris, 1817.

Macdonald, Étienne-Jacques-Joseph-Alexandre, duc de Tarente, and Camille Rousset. *Souvenirs du Maréchal Macdonald, duc de Tarente.* Paris, 1892.

Marbot, J. B. A. M. *Mémoires du général bon de Marbot.* 3 vols. Paris, 1891.

Marmont, A. de. *Mémoires du duc de Raguse.* 9 vols. Paris, 1857.

Martens, F. F. *Recueil des traités et conventions, conclus par la Russie avec les puissances étrangères*. 15 vols. St. Petersburg, 1874–1909.

Martens, G. F. *Recueil des traités d'alliance, de paix, de trêve, de neutralité, de commerce, de limites, déchange, etc., et plusieurs autres actes servant à la connoissance des relations étrangères des puissances et états de l'Europe depuis 1761 jusqu'à présent*. 16 vols. Göttingen, 1817–42.

Metternich, C. L. W. *Memoirs of Prince Metternich, 1773–1815*. 5 vols. Edited by R. Metternich. Translated by A. Napier. New York, 1970.

Mikhailovsky-Danilevsky, Aleksandr Ivanovich. *Denkwürdigkeiten aus dem Kriege von 1813*. Translated by Karl Goldhammer. Dorpat, 1837.

Opisanie voiny 1813 goda. 2 vols. St. Petersburg, 1840.

Müffling, Friedrich Karl Ferdinand von. *Aus meinem Leben*. Berlin, 1851.

Betrachtungen über die großen Operationen und Schlachten der Feldzüge von 1813 und 1814. Berlin, 1825.

Passages from My Life; Together with Memoirs of the Campaign of 1813 and 1814. Translated and edited by Philip Yorke. London, 1853.

Zur Kriegsgeschichte der Jahre 1813 und 1814: die Feldzüge der schlesischen Armee unter dem Feldmarschall Blücher von der Beendigung des Waffenstillstandes bis zur Eroberung von Paris. Berlin, 1827.

Napoléon I, Emperor of the French. *Correspondance de Napoléon Ier: publiée par ordre de l'empereur Napoléon III*. 32 vols. Paris, 1858–69.

Natzmer, Gneomar Ernst von. *Aus dem Leben des Generals Oldwig von Natzmer: ein Beitrag zur preußischen Geschichte*. Berlin, 1876.

Norvins, Jacques Marquet de. *Portefeuille de mil huit cent treize, ou tableau politique et militaire renfermant: avec le récit des événemens de cette epoque, un choix de la correspondance inéd. de l'empereur Napoléon*. 2 vols. Paris, 1825.

Nostitz, August Ludwig Ferdinand von. *Das Tagebuch des Generals der Kavallerie, Grafen von Nostitz*. 2 vols. Pt. 1 of *Kriegsgeschichtliche Einzelschriften*, 6 vols. Berlin, 1885.

Odeleben, E. O. von. *A Circumstantial Narrative of the Campaign in Saxony, in the Year 1813*. London, 1820.

Napoleons Feldzug im Sachsen im Jahre 1813. Dresden, 1816.

Osten-Sacken und Rhein, Ottomar von. *Militärisch-politische Geschichte des Befreiungskrieges im Jahre 1813*. 2 vols. Berlin, 1813.

Pelet, Jean-Jacques. *Des principales opérations de la campagne de 1813*. Paris, 1826.

Plotho, Carl von. *Der Krieg in Deutschland und Frankreich in den Jahren 1813 und 1814*. 3 vols. Berlin, 1817.

Prittwitz, Karl Heinrich. *Beiträge zur Geschichte des Jahres 1813: von einem höheren Offizier der Preußischen Armee*. 2 vols. Potsdam, 1843.

Radetzky von Radetz, J. J. W. A. F. K. *Denkschriften militärisch-politischen Inhalts aus dem handschriftlichen Nachlaß des k.k. österreichischen Feldmarschalls Grafen Radetzky*. Stuttgart and Augsburg, 1858.

Rahden, Wilhelm. *Wanderungen eines alten Soldaten*. 3 vols. Berlin, 1846–59.

Reiche, Ludwig von. *Memoiren des königlichen preußischen Generals der Infanterie Ludwig von Reiche*. Edited by Louis von Weltzien. Leipzig, 1857.

Rochechouart, Louis Victor Léon. *Souvenirs sur la révolution, l'empire et la restauration*. Paris, 1933.

Schack, Friedrich Wilhelm von. "Der Verluste der Armeen in den neueren Kriegen," *Militär-Wochenblatt* (1841):143–82, 192–208.

Scherbening, R. K. von and K. W. Willisen, eds. *Die Reorganisation der Preußischen Armee nach dem Tilsiter Frieden.* 2 vols. Berlin, 1862–66.

Schwarzenberg, K. zu. *Briefe des Feldmarschalls Fürsten Schwarzenberg an seine Frau, 1799–1816.* Leipzig, 1913.

Seidel, Friedrich von. "Die Mitwirkung des k.k. dritten, von dem Feldzeugmeister Grafen Ignaz Gyulay befehligten Armeekorps während der Schlacht von Leipzig, bis zur Überschreitung der Saale: vom 13 bis 21 Oktober 1813," *Österriechische militärische Zeitschrift* (1836), 3:115–63.

Seydlitz, August von. *Tagebuch des Königlich Preußischen Armee Korps unter Befehl des General-Lieutenants von Yorck im Feldzuge von 1812.* 2 vols. Berlin, 1812.

Steffens, H. *Adventures on the Road to Paris, During the Campaigns of 1813–1814.* London, 1848.

Stewart, Lieutenant General Sir Charles William Vane, Lord Londonderry. *Narrative of the War in Germany and France in 1813 and 1814.* London, 1830.

St.-Cyr, Laurent de Gouvion. *Mémoires sur les campagnes des armées du Rhin et de Rhin-et-Moselle. Atlas des cartes et plans relatifs aux campagnes du Maréchal Gouvion St. Cyr aux armées du Rhin et de Rhin et Moselle pendant les années 1792, 1793, 1794, 1795, 1796 et 1797.* 4 vols. Paris, 1828.

Valentini, Georg von. *Der grosse Krieg.* 2 vols. Berlin, 1833.

Lehre vom Kriege. 2 vols. Berlin, 1835.

Varnhagen von Ense, Karl August. *Das Leben der Generals Gräfen Bülow von Dennewitz.* Berlin, 1853.

Leben des Fürsten Blücher von Wahlstatt. Berlin, 1933.

Vaudoncourt, Guillaume. *Histoire de la guerre soutenue par le Français en Allemagne en 1813.* Paris, 1819.

Histoire des campagnes de 1814 et 1815 en France. 5 vols. Paris, 1826.

Venturini, Carl. *Rußlands und Deutschlands Befreiungskriege von der Franzosen-Herrschaft unter Napoleon Buonaparte in den Jahren 1812–1815.* 4 vols. Altenburg, 1816–18.

Wagner, C. A. von. *Plane der Schlachten und Treffen welche von der preussischen Armee in den Feldzügen der Jahre 1813, 14, und 15 geliefert worden.* 4 vols. Berlin, 1821–25.

Wilson, Robert. *General Wilson's Journal, 1812–1814.* Edited by Antony Brett-James. London, 1964.

Private Diary of Travels, Personal Services, and Public Events: During the Mission Employed with the European Armies in the Campaigns of 1812, 1813, 1814. London, 1861.

SECONDARY SOURCES

Anon. *Précis militaire de la campagne de 1813 en Allemagne.* Leipzig, 1881.

Aster, Heinrich. *Die Gefechte und Schlachten bei Leipzig im October 1813 Grossentheils nach neuem, bisher unbenutzten archivarischen Quellen dargestellt.* 2 vols. Dresden, 1852–53.

Atkinson, C. T. *A History of Germany, 1715–1815*. London, 1908.

Atteridge, A. Hilliard. *The Bravest of the Brave, Michel Ney, Marshal of France, Duke of Elchingen, Prince of the Moskowa 1769–1815*. London, 1912.

Bach, Theodor. *Theodor Gottlieb von Hippel, der Verfasser des Aufrufs: "An mein Volk." Ein Gedenkblatt zur fünfzigjährigen Feier der Erhebung Preussens*. Breslau, 1863.

Balfour, Francis. *The Life of George, Fourth Earl of Aberdeen, KG, KT*. 2 vols. London, 1922.

Barton, D. Plunket. *Bernadotte: Prince and King, 1810–1844*. London, 1925.

Beitzke, Heinrich. *Geschichte der deutschen Freiheitskriege in den Jahren 1813 und 1814*. 3 vols. Berlin, 1854–55.

Bernhardi, T. *Denkwürdigkeiten aus dem Leben des Kaiserlich Russischen Generals von der Infanterie Carl Friedrich Grafen von Toll*. 4 vols. Leipzig, 1856–66.

Blasendorff, Carl. *Gebhard Leberecht von Blücher: mit Bild und Nachbild eines eigenhändigen Briefes*. Berlin, 1887.

Bleck, Otto. *Marschall Blücher: ein Lebensbild*. Berlin, 1939.

Bogdanovich, Modest Ivanovich. *Geschichte des Krieges 1814 in Frankreich und des Sturzes Napoleon's I: nach den zuverläßigsten Quellen*. Translated by G. Baumgarten. Leipzig, 1866.

Geschichte des Krieges im Jahre 1813 für Deutschlands Unabhängigkeit: nach den zuverläßigsten Quellen. 2 vols. St. Petersburg, 1863–68.

Bowden, Scott. *Napoleon's Grande Armée of 1813*. Chicago, 1990.

Brett-James, Anthony. *Europe Against Napoleon: The Leipzig Campaign, 1813, from Eyewitness Accounts*. London, 1970.

Caemmerer, Rudolf von. *Die Befreiungskrieg, 1813–1815: ein Strategischer Überblick*. Berlin, 1907.

Chandler, David G. *The Campaigns of Napoleon*. New York, 1966.

Charras, Jean Baptiste Adolphe. *Histoire de la guerre de 1813 en Allemagne: derniers jours de la retraite, insurrection de l'Allemagne, armements, diplomatie, entrée en campagne*. 2nd edn. Paris, 1870.

Clark, Christopher. *Iron Kingdom: The Rise and Downfall of Prussia, 1600–1947*. Cambridge, MA, 2006.

Clercq, Jules de, and Alexandre J. H. de Clercq. *Recueil des traités de la France*. 23 vols. Paris, 1864–1917.

Conrady, Emil von. *Leben und Wirken des Generals Carl von Grolman*. 3 vols. Berlin, 1933.

Craig, Gordon A. *The Politics of the Prussian Army: 1640–1945*. Oxford, 1956.

"Problems of Coalition Warfare: The Military Alliance Against Napoleon, 1813–1814." In *War, Politics, and Diplomacy: Selected Essays by Gordon Craig*. London, 1966, 22–45.

Droysen, Johann. *Das Leben des Feldmarschalls Grafen Yorck von Wartenburg*. 2 vols. Leipzig, 1851.

Duncker, Max. *Aus der Zeit Friedrichs des Großen und Friedrich Wilhelms III*. Leipzig, 1876.

D'Ussel, Jean. *Études sur l'année 1813: la défection de la Prusse, décembre 1812–mars 1813*. Paris, 1907.

Elting, John and Vincent Esposito. *A Military History and Atlas of the Napoleonic Wars*. New York, 1964.

Fabry, Gabriel Joseph. *Étude sur les opérations de l'empereur, 5 septembre au 21 septembre 1813*. Paris, 1910.

Étude sur les opérations du maréchal Macdonald du 22 aou^t au 4 septembre 1813: La Katzbach. Paris, 1910.

Étude sur les opérations du maréchal Oudinot du 15 août au 4 septembre: Groß Beeren. Paris, 1910.

ed. *Journal des opérations des IIIe et Ve corps en 1813 par Capitaine Koch*. Paris, 1902.

Finley, Milton. "The Career of Count Jean Reynier, 1792–1814." Ph.D. dissertation, Florida State University, 1972.

Fisher, H. A. L. *Napoleonic Statesmanship in Germany*. Oxford, 1903.

Ford, G. S. *Hanover and Prussia: A Study in Neutrality, 1795–1803*. New York, 1903.

Stein and the Era of Reform in Prussia, 1807–1815. Princeton, 1922. Reprint, Gloucester, 1965.

Foucart, P. J. *Bautzen: 20–21 mai 1813*. 2 vols. Paris, 1897.

Freytag-Loringhoven, Hugo Friedrich Philipp Johann von. *Aufklärung und Armeeführung dargestellt an den Ereignissen bei der Schlesischen Armee im Herbst 1813: eine Studie*. Berlin, 1900.

Kriegslehren nach Clausewitz aus den Feldzügen 1813 und 1814. Berlin, 1908.

Friederich, Rudolf. "Die Aufassung der strategischen Lage seitens der Verbündeten am Schlusse des Waffenstillstandes von Poischwitz 1813." *Militair-Wochenblatt* (1902):1–36.

Die Befreiungskriege, 1813–1815. 4 vols. Berlin, 1911–13.

Geschichte des Herbstfeldzuges 1813. 3 vols. Berlin, 1903–06. In *Geschichte der Befreiungskriege, 1813–1815*. 9 vols. Berlin, 1903–09.

"Die strategische Lage Napoleons am Schlusse des Waffenstillstandes von Poischwitz." *Militair-Wochenblatt* (1901):1–36.

Gallaher, John. *The Iron Marshal: A Biography of Louis N. Davout*. Carbondale, IL, 1976.

Gérôme, Auguste Clementé. *Campagne de 1813*. Paris, 1904.

Görlitz, Walter. *Fürst Blücher von Wahlstatt*. Rostock, 1940.

History of the German General Staff, 1657–1945. Translated by Brian Battershaw. New York, 1954.

Griewank, Karl. *Hohenzollernbriefe aus den Freiheitskriegen 1813–1815*. Leipzig, 1913.

Grunwald, Constantin de. *The Life of Baron Stein: Napoleon's Nemesis*. Translated by C. F. Atkinson. New York, 1936.

Henderson, Ernest F. *Blücher and the Uprising of Prussia Against Napoleon, 1806–1815*. London, 1911.

Hochedlinger, Michael. *Austria's Wars of Emergence: War, State, and Society in the Habsburg Monarchy, 1683–1797*. Harlow, 2003.

Hofschröer, Peter. http://greatestbattles.iblogger.org/GB/Liebertwolkwitz/LiebertwolkwitzPartIII-ByHofschroer.htm.

Holleben, A. von, and R. von Caemmerer. *Geschichte des Frühjahrsfeldzuges 1813 und seine Vorgeschichte.* 2 vols. Berlin, 1904–09. In *Geschichte der Befreiungskriege, 1813–1815.* 9 vols. Berlin, 1903–09.

Holzhausen, Paul. *Davout in Hamburg.* Mülheim, 1892.

Hourtoulle, François Guy. *Ney, le braves.* Paris, 1981.

Janson, August von. *Geschichte des Feldzuges 1814 in Frankreich.* 2 vols. Berlin, 1903–05.

   König Friedrich Wilhelm III in der Schlacht. Berlin, 1907.

   "Die Unternehmungen des Yorckschen Korps gegen die nordfranzösischen Festungen." *Militär-Wochenblatt* 1903:1–66.

Jany, Curt. *Geschichte der königlichen preußischen Armee.* 4 vols. Berlin, 1929.

Josselson, Michael, and Diana Josselson. *The Commander: A Life of Barclay de Tolly.* Oxford, 1980.

Kaemmerer, M. *Ortsnamenverzeichnis der Ortschaften jenseits von Oder und Neiße.* Leer, 1988.

Kähler, Otto August Johannes. *Einhundert und fünfzig Jahre des königlich preussischen Litthauischen Dragoner-Regiments Nr. 1 (Prinz Albrecht von Preussen): seit seiner Errichtung am 1. Mai 1717 bis zur Gegenwart: nach urkundliche Quellen.* Berlin, 1867.

Kissinger, Henry. *A World Restored: Metternich, Castlereagh, and the Problems of Peace, 1812–1822.* Boston, 1990.

Kitchen, Martin. *A Military History of Germany.* London, 1954.

Klippel, Georg Heinrich. *Das Leben des Generals von Scharnhorst: nach grösstentheils bisher unbenutzten Quellen.* Leipzig, 1869–71.

Koch, H. W. *A History of Prussia.* New York, 1987.

Kraehe, Enno. *Metternich's German Policy.* 2 vols. Princeton, 1963.

Lanrezac, Charles Louis Marie. *La manoeuvre de Lützen 1813.* Paris, 1904.

Leggiere, Michael V. *Blücher: Scourge of Napoleon.* Norman, OK, 2014.

   The Fall of Napoleon. Vol. I, *The Allied Invasion of France.* Cambridge, 2007.

   Napoleon and Berlin: The Franco-Prussian War in North Germany, 1813. Norman, OK, 2002.

Lehmann, Max. *Freiherr vom Stein.* 3 vols. Leipzig, 1902–05.

   Scharnhorst. 2 vols. Leipzig, 1886–87.

Lieven, Dominic. *Russia Against Napoleon: The True Story of the Campaigns of War and Peace.* New York, 2010.

Lindemann, Mary. *Patriots and Paupers: Hamburg, 1712–1830.* New York, 1990.

Maude, F. N. *The Leipzig Campaign, 1813.* London, 1908.

Meinecke, Friedrich. *Das Leben des Generalfeldmarschalls Hermann von Boyen.* 2 vols. Stuttgart, 1896–99.

Mikaberidze, Alexander. *The Battle of Borodino: Napoleon Against Kutuzov.* Barnsley, UK, 2010.

   The Russian Officer Corps in the Revolutionary and Napoleonic Wars, 1792–1815. New York, 2005.

Muir, Rory. *Britain and the Defeat of Napoleon, 1807–1815.* London, 1996.

Nafziger, George. *Imperial Bayonets: Tactics of the Napoleonic Battery, Battalion and Brigade as Found in Contemporary Regulations.* London, 1996.

Lutzen and Bautzen: Napoleon's Spring Campaign of 1813. Chicago, 1992.

Neubauer, Friedrich. *Preußens Fall und Erhebung 1806–1815*. Berlin, 1908.

Nicolson, Harold. *The Congress of Vienna: A Study in Allied Unity*. New York, 1946.

Nipperdey, Thomas. *Germany from Napoleon to Bismarck, 1800–1866*. Translated by Daniel Nolan. Princeton, NJ, 1996.

Ollech, Karl Rudolf von. *Karl Friedrich Wilhelm von Reyher General der Kavallerie und Chef des Generalstabes der Armee: ein Beitrag zur Geschichte der Armee mit Bezug auf die Befreiungskriege von 1813, 1814, und 1815*. Berlin, 1874.

Oncken, Wilhelm. *Österreich und Preußen im Befreiungskrieg: urkundliche Aufschlüsse über die politische Geschichte des Jahres 1813*. 2 vols. Berlin, 1876–79.

Pajol, Charles Pierre Victor. *Pajol, général en chef*. Paris, 1874.

Paret, Peter. *Clausewitz and the State*. Oxford, 1976.

Yorck and the Era of Prussian Reform, 1807–1815. Princeton, NJ, 1966.

Parkinson, Roger. *The Hussar General: The Life of Blücher, Man of Waterloo*. London, 1975.

Pertz, G. H. *Das Leben des Ministers Freiherrn vom Stein*. 6 vols. Berlin, 1849–55.

Pertz, G. H. and Hans Delbrück. *Das Leben des Feldmarschalls Grafen Neithardt von Gneisenau*. 5 vols. Berlin, 1864–80.

Petre, F. L. *Napoleon's Last Campaign in Germany, 1813*. London, 1912. Reprint, London, 1992.

Pflugk, Ferdinand. *Das Preußische Landwehrbuch: Geschichte und Großthaten der Landwehr Preußens während der Befreiungskriege*. Berlin, 1863.

Pflugk-Harttung, Julius von, ed. *Das Befreiungsjahr 1813: aus den Akten des Geheimen Staatsarchivs*. Berlin, 1913.

Quintin, D. and B. Quintin. *Dictionnaire des colonels de Napoléon*. Paris, 1996.

Quistorp, Barthold von. *Geschichte der Nord-Armee im Jahre 1813*. Berlin, 1894.

Ranke, Leopold von. *Denkwürdigkeiten des Staatskanzlers Fürsten von Hardenberg*. 5 vols. Leipzig, 1877.

Richie, Alexandra. *Faust's Metropolis: A History of Berlin*. New York, 1998.

Ritter, Gerhard. *The Sword and the Scepter: The Problem of Militarism in Germany*. Translated by Heinz Norden. Coral Gables, Fl., 1969.

Rivollet, Georges. *Général de bataille Charles Antoine Louis Morand, comte d'Empire, 1771–1835: généraux Friant et Gudin du 3e corps de la Grande Armée*. Paris, 1963.

Rosenberg, Hans. *Bureaucracy, Aristocracy, and Autocracy: The Prussian Experience, 1660–1815*. Cambridge, 1958.

Ross, S. *European Diplomatic History, 1789–1815: France Against Europe*. New York, 1969.

Sauzey, Jean-Camille-Abel-Fleuri. *Les Allemands sous les aigles françaises; essai sur les troupes de la Confédération du Rhin, 1806–1814*. 6 vols. Paris, 1902.

Scherr, Johannes. *Blücher: seine Zeit und sein Leben*. 3 vols. Leipzig, 1887.

Schneidawind, F. J. A. *Prinz Wilhelm von Preußen in den Kriegen seiner Zeit: auch ein Lebensbild aus den Befreiungskriegen; mit dem Bildnisse und Faksimile des Prinzen*. Berlin, 1856.

Schroeder, Paul. *The Transformation of European Politics, 1763–1848.* Oxford, 1994.

Schwartz, Karl. *Leben des Generals Carl von Clausewitz und der Frau Marie von Clausewitz geb. Gräfin von Brühl.* Berlin, 1878.

Scott, Franklin D. *Bernadotte and the Fall of Napoleon.* Cambridge, 1934.

Seeley, J. R. *Life and Times of Stein or Germany and Prussia in the Napoleonic Age.* 3 vols. New York, 1969.

Shanahan, William. *Prussian Military Reforms, 1786–1813.* New York, 1945.

Sherwig, John. *Guineas and Gunpowder: British Foreign Aid in the Wars with France, 1793–1815.* Cambridge, 1969.

Showalter, Dennis E. "Hubertusberg to Auerstädt: The Prussian Army in Decline?" *German History* 12 (1994): 308–33.

"The Prussian Landwehr and Its Critics, 1813–1819." *Central European History* 4 (1971): 3–33.

Simon, Walter. *The Failure of the Prussian Reform Movement, 1807–1819.* Ithaca, 1955.

Six, Georges. *Dictionnaire biographique des généraux et amiraux français de la révolution et de l'empire.* 2 vols. Paris, 1934.

Sked, Alan. *Radetzky: Imperial Victor and Military Genius.* London, 2010.

Stamm-Kuhlmann, Thomas. *König in Preußens grosser Zeit: Friedrich Wilhelm III, der Melancholiker auf dem Thron.* Berlin, 1992.

Stern-Gwiazdowski, C. L. von. *Das Gefecht bei Goldberg-Niederau am 23. August 1813: zur fünfzigjährigen Jubelfeier desselben: nebst zwei Plänen.* Berlin, 1864.

Swederus, Georg. *Schwedens Politik und Kriege in den Jahren 1808 bis 1814: vorzüglich unter Leitung des Kronprinzen Carl Johan.* Leipzig, 1866.

Telp, Claus. *The Evolution of Operational Art, 1740–1813: From Frederick the Great to Napoleon.* New York, 2005.

Thiers, Adolphe. *Histoire du Consulat et de l'Empire: faisant suite à l'Histoire de la Révolution française.* 20 vols. Paris, 1845–62. Published in English as *History of the Consulate and the Empire of France under Napoleon.* 12 vols. London, 1893–94.

Tranié, J. and Juan Carlos Carmigniani. *Napoléon: 1813, la campagne d'Allemagne.* Paris, 1987.

Unger, Wolfgang von. *Blücher.* 2 vols. Berlin, 1907–08.

Varchmin, Friedrich Wilhelm von. *Die Völkerschlacht bei Leipzig, oder, Was uns gerettet und was uns noch retten kann: nebst einer Biographie des Fürsten Carl zu Schwarzenburg; eine Jubelschrift auf das Jahr 1863, ein Wort an Deutschlands Fürsten und Völker.* Brunswick, Germany, 1862.

Vaupel, Rudolf, ed. *Die Reorganisation des Preußischen Staates unter Stein und Hardenberg,* part 2, *Das Preußische Heer vom Tilsiter Frieden bis zur Befreiung: 1807–1814.* Publicationen aus den königlischen preußischen Archiven, vol. 94. Leipzig, 1938.

Webster, Charles. *The Foreign Policy of Castlereagh.* 2 vols. London, 1931–34.

Weil, Maurice-Henri. *Campagne de 1813: la cavalerie des armées alliées.* Paris, 1886.

White, Charles E. *The Enlightened Soldier: Scharnhorst and the Militärische Gesellschaft in Berlin, 1801–1805.* Westport, CT, 1989.

Wigger, Friedrich. *Feldmarschall Fürst Blücher von Wahlstatt.* Schwerin, 1878.

Woynar, Karl. *Österrikes förhållande till Sverige och Danmark under åren 1813–1814 hufvudsakligen dess politik vid Norges förening med Sverige.* Stockholm, 1892.

Yorck von Wartenburg, Hans Ludwig David Maximilian Graf. *Napoleon as a General.* 2 vols. Edited by Walter H. James. London, 1897–98.

Zychlinski, Franz von. *Geschichte des 24sten Infanterie-Regiments.* 2 vols. Berlin, 1854–57.

Index

Index

CPSIA information can be obtained
at www.ICGtesting.com
Printed in the USA
LVOW13*0309281117
557752LV00012B/491/P